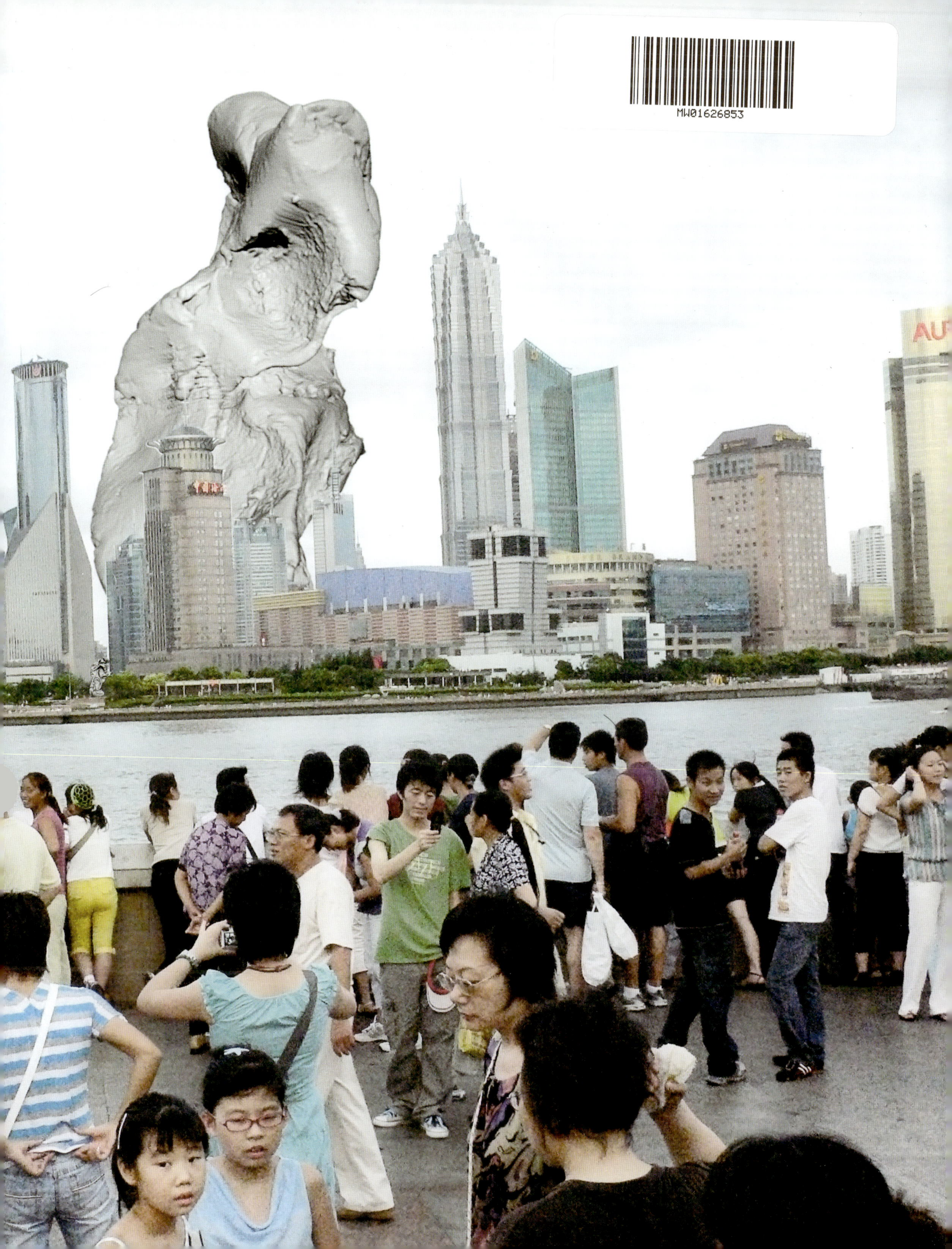

URS FISCHER

Untitled (Hole), 2007

Cast aluminum

212 ½ x 133 ⅞ x 106 ¼ inches (540 x 340 x 270 cm)

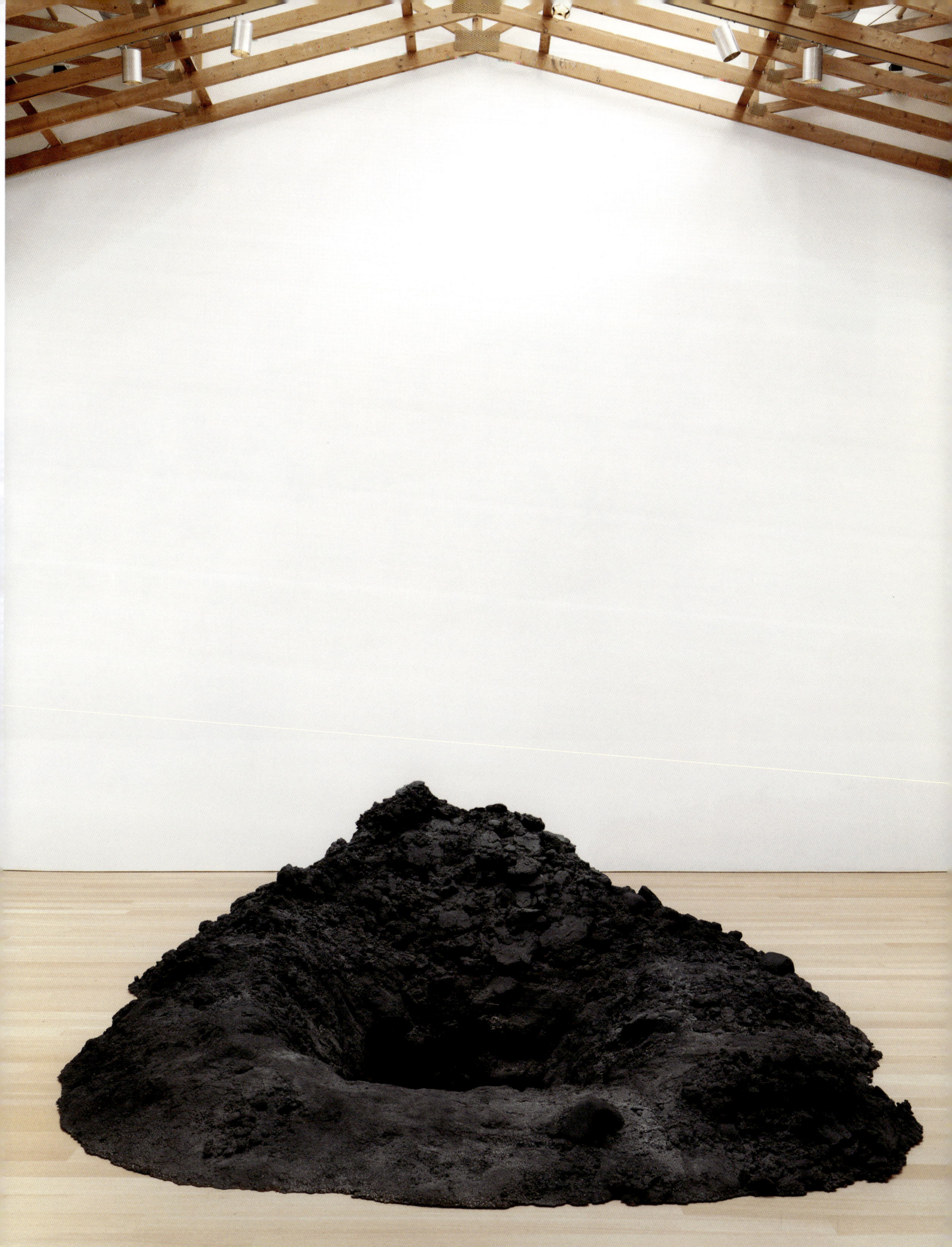

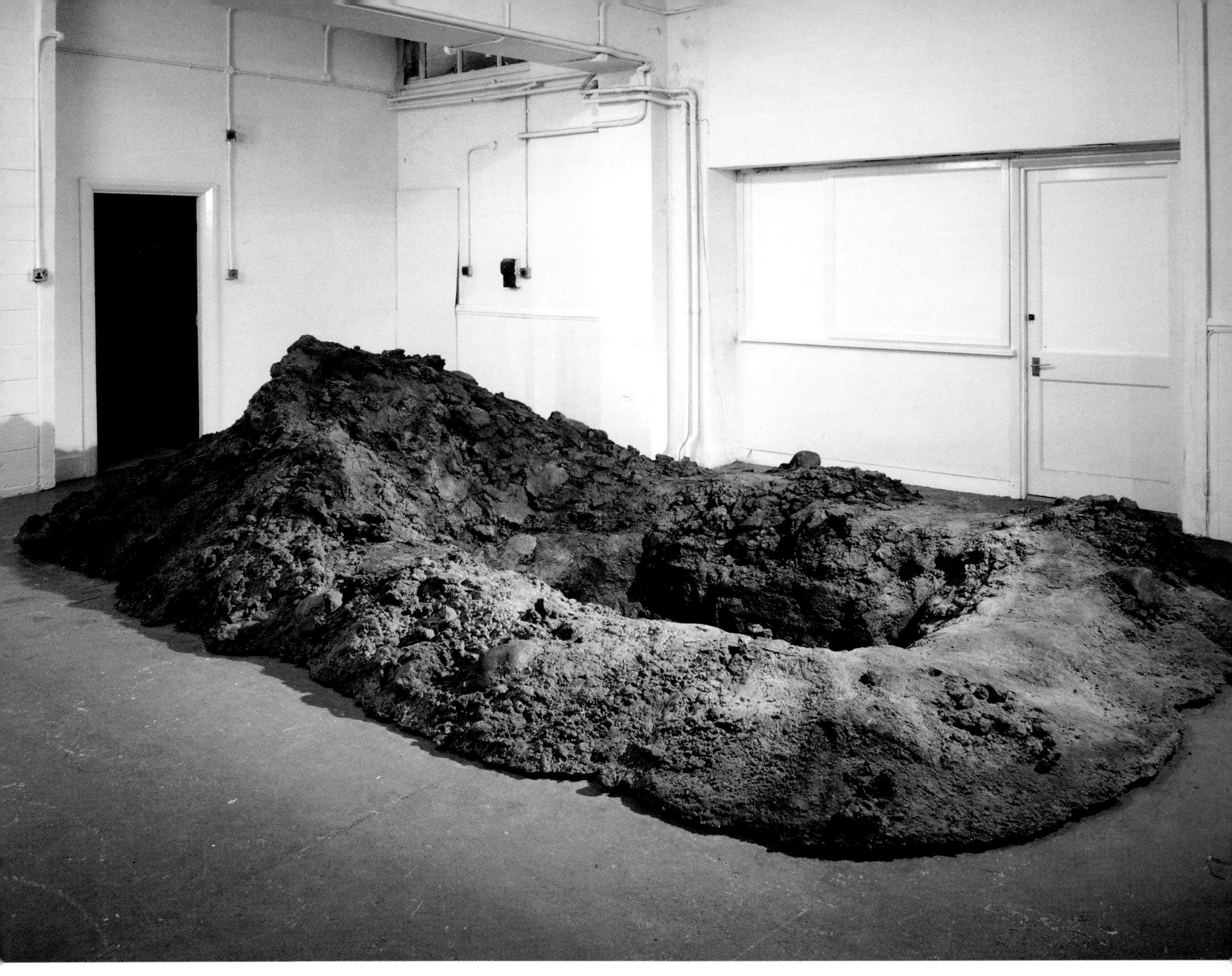

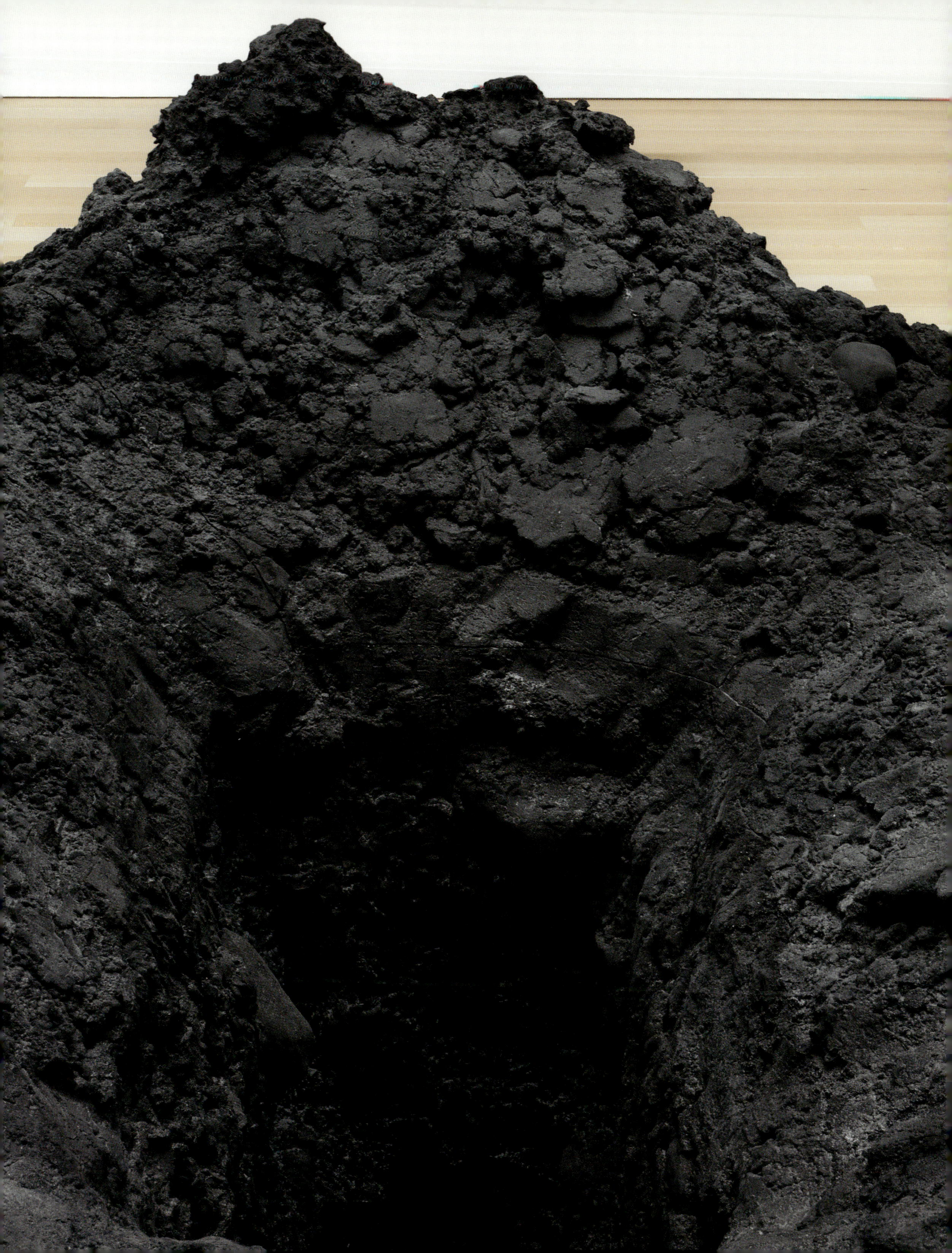

Installation view, "Oscar the Grouch," The Brant Foundation Art Study Center,
Greenwich, Connecticut, 2010
Untitled (Hole), 2007
Untitled (Standing), 2010; On wall: *Abstract Slavery*, 2008

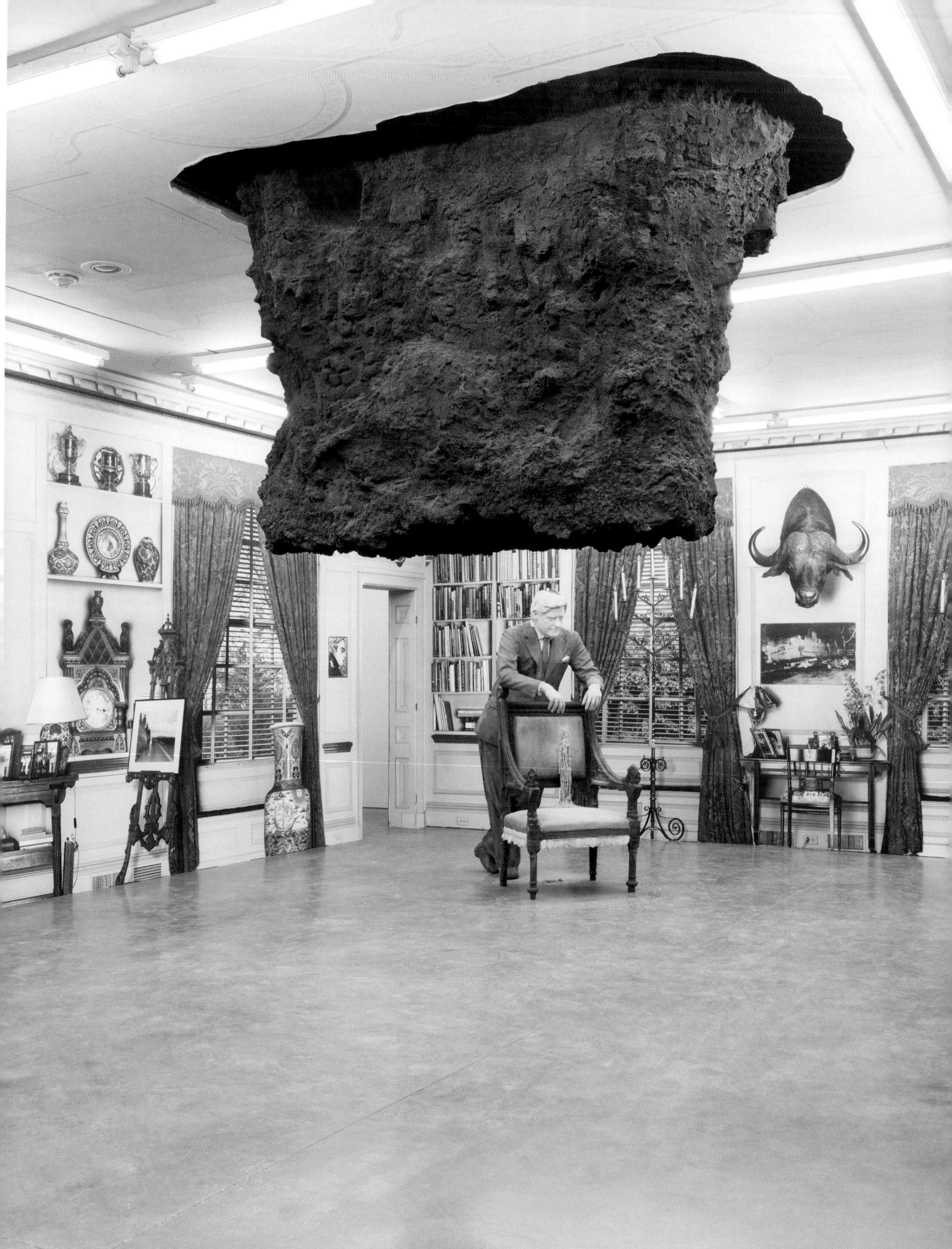

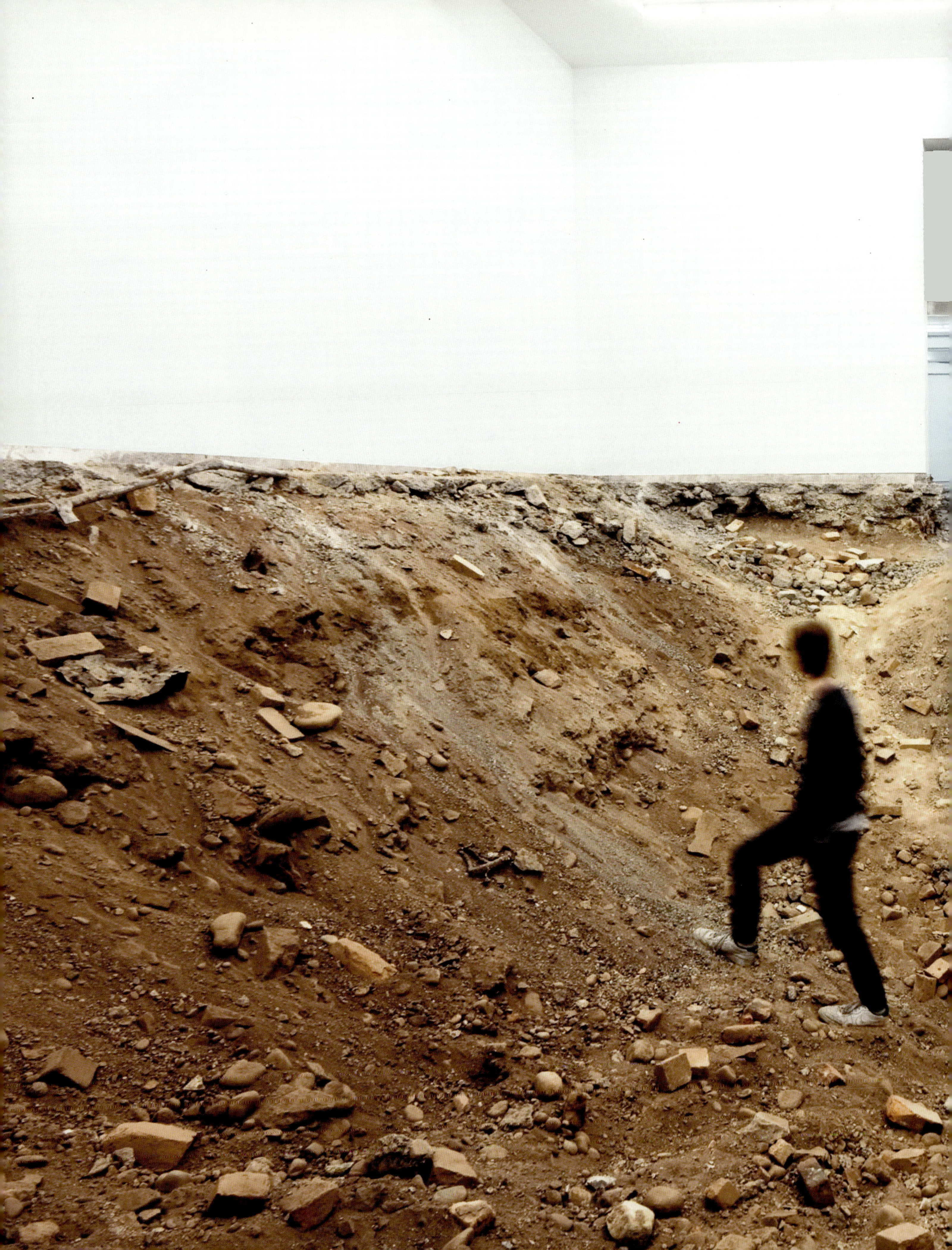

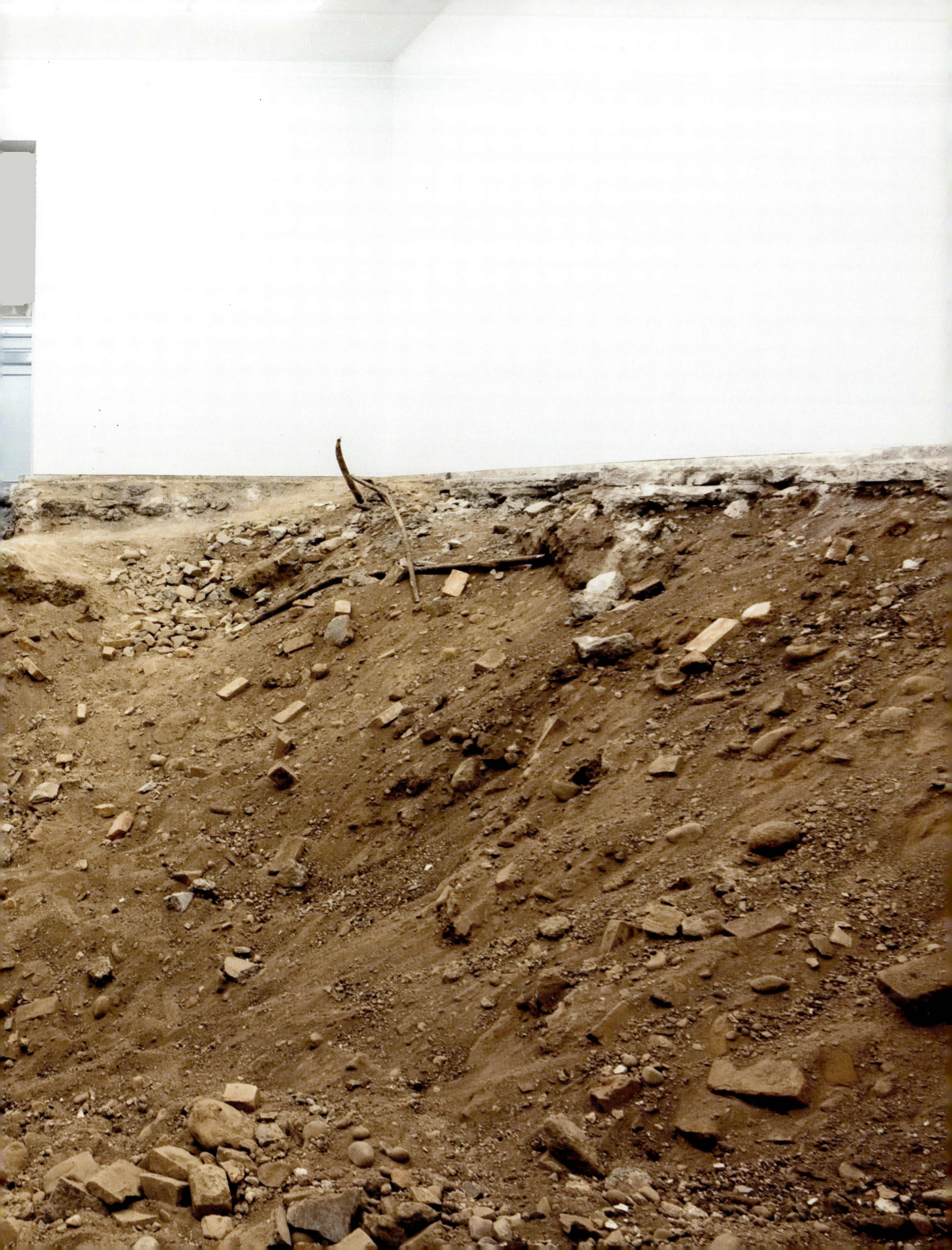

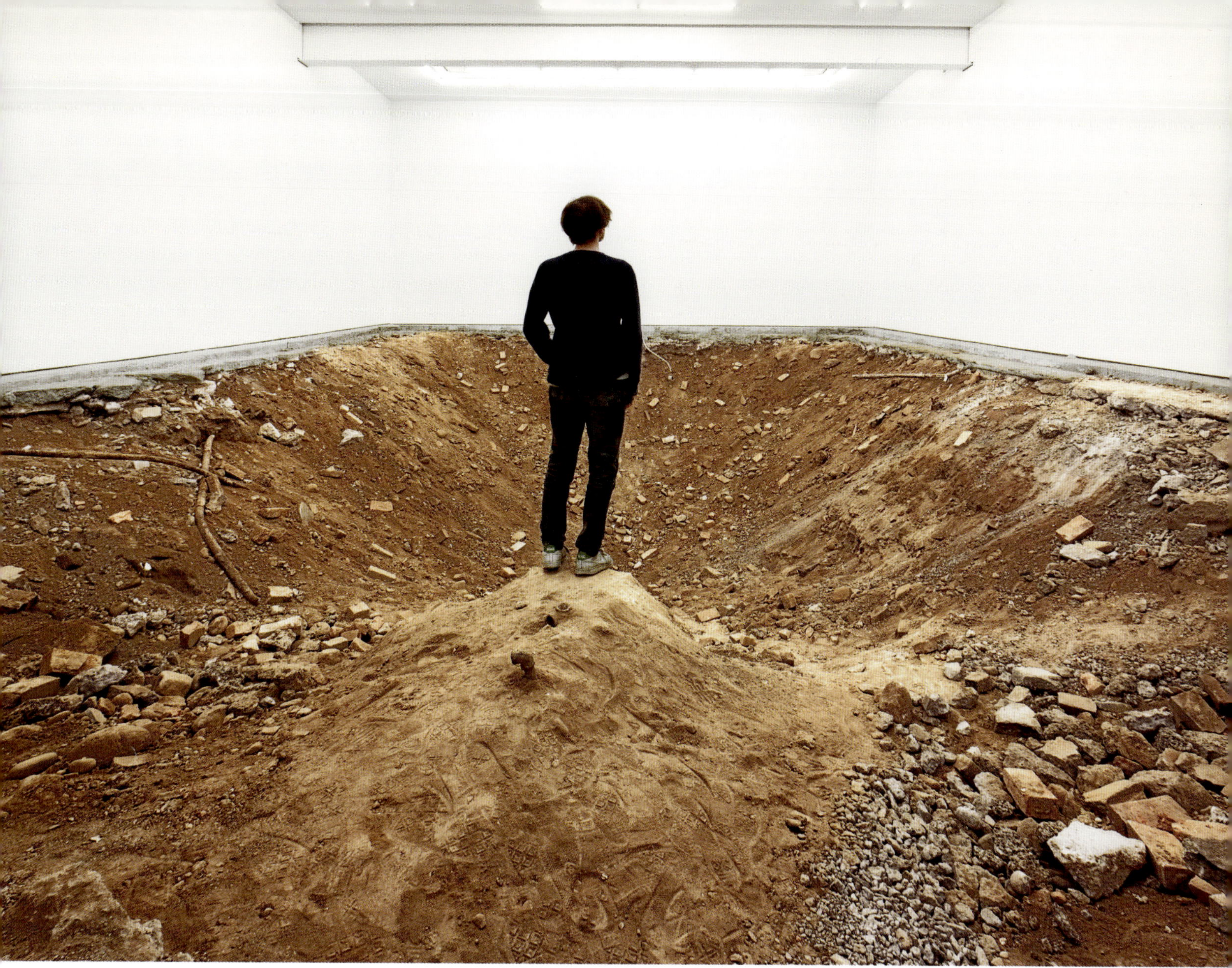

Previous spread and following pages:

You, 2007

Excavation, gallery space, 1:3 scale replica of main gallery space

Dimensions variable

Installation view, "you," Gavin Brown's enterprise, New York, 2007

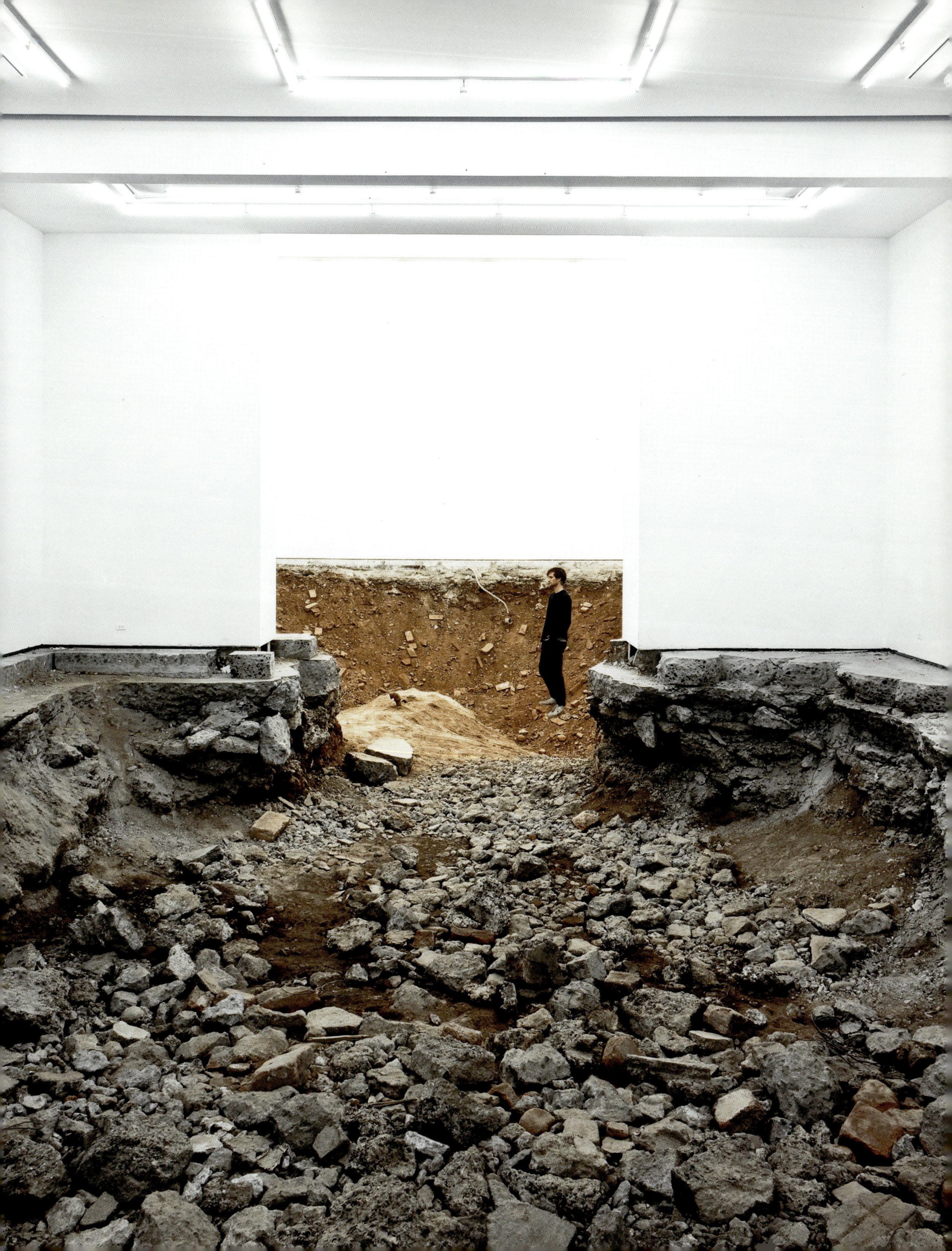

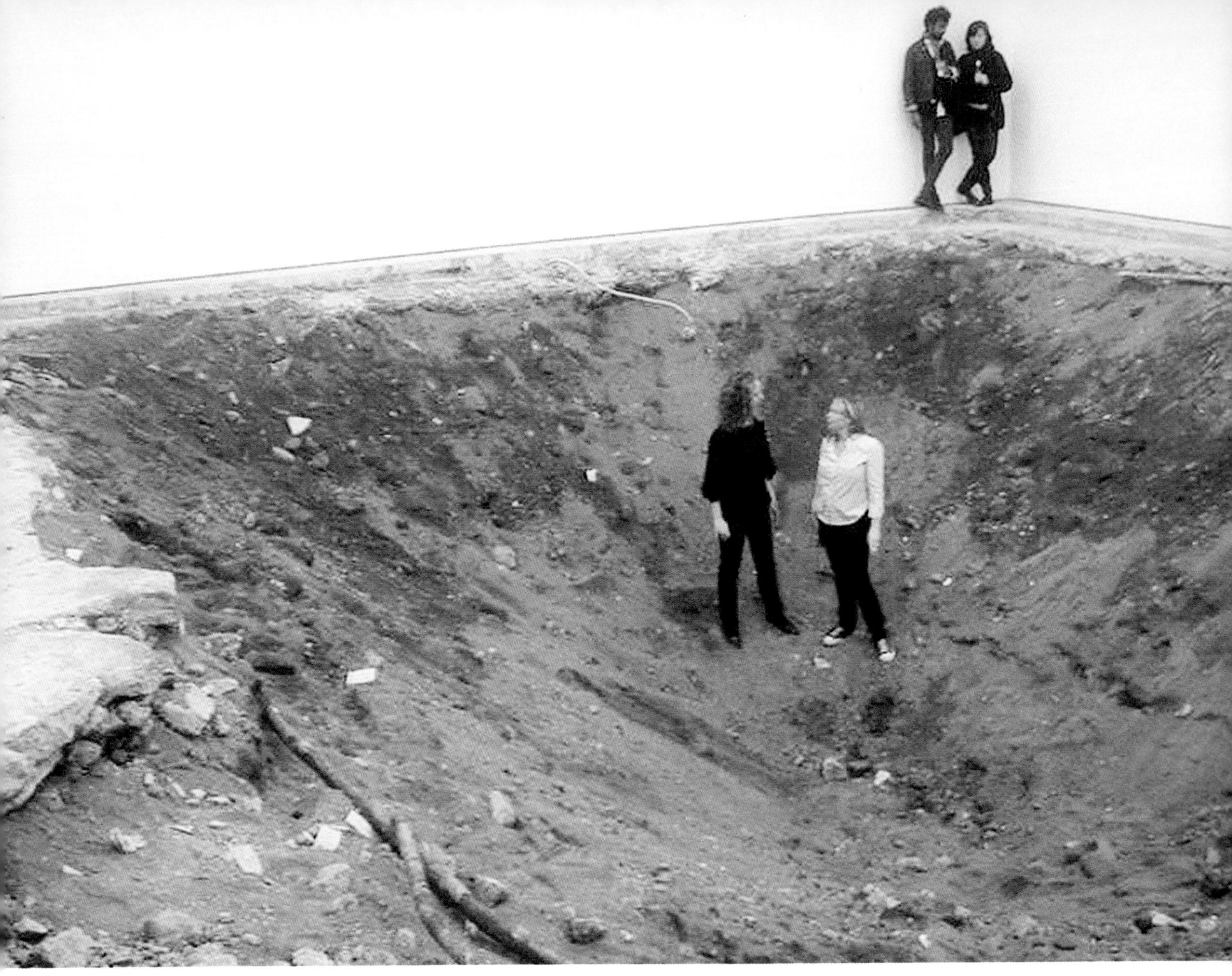

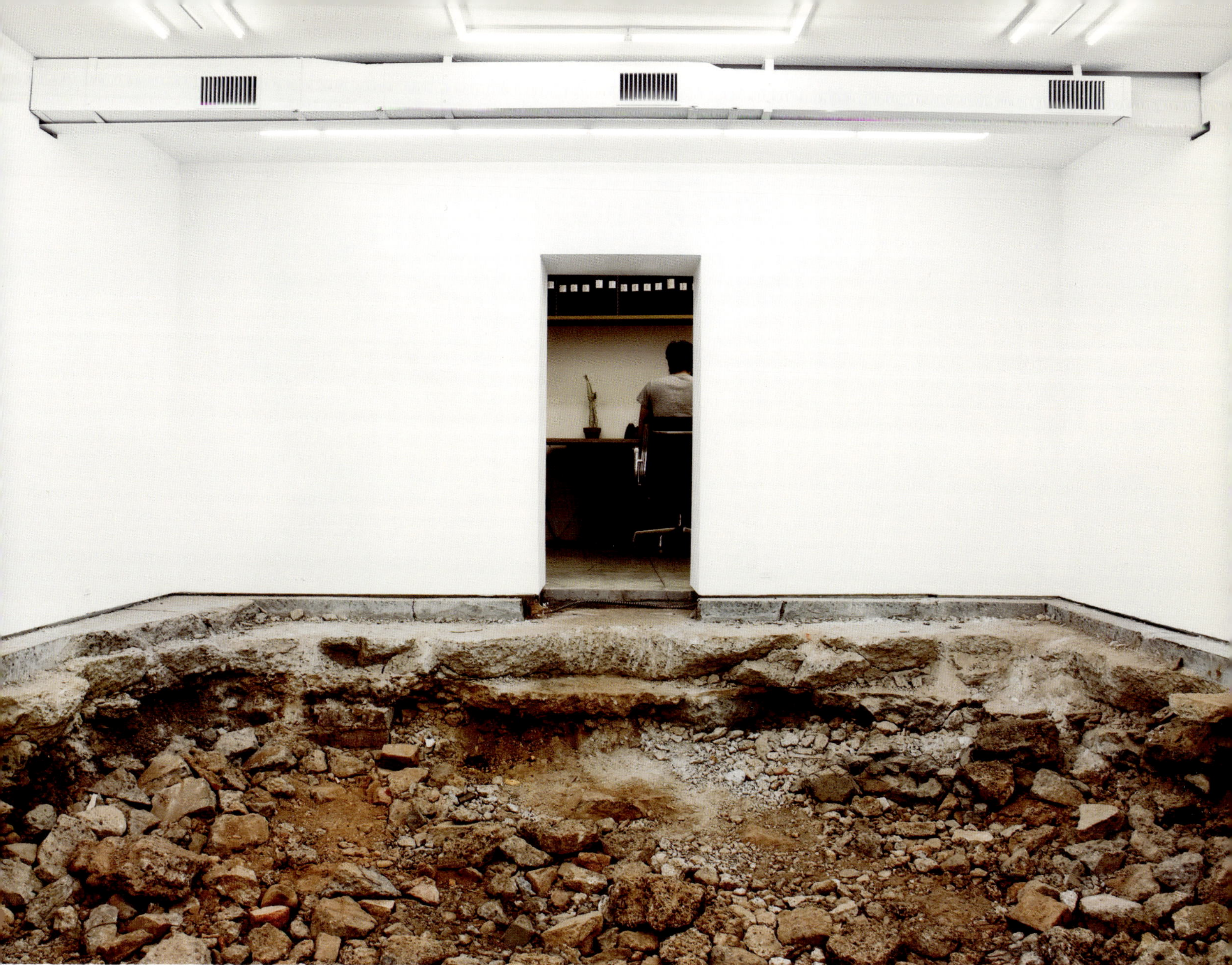

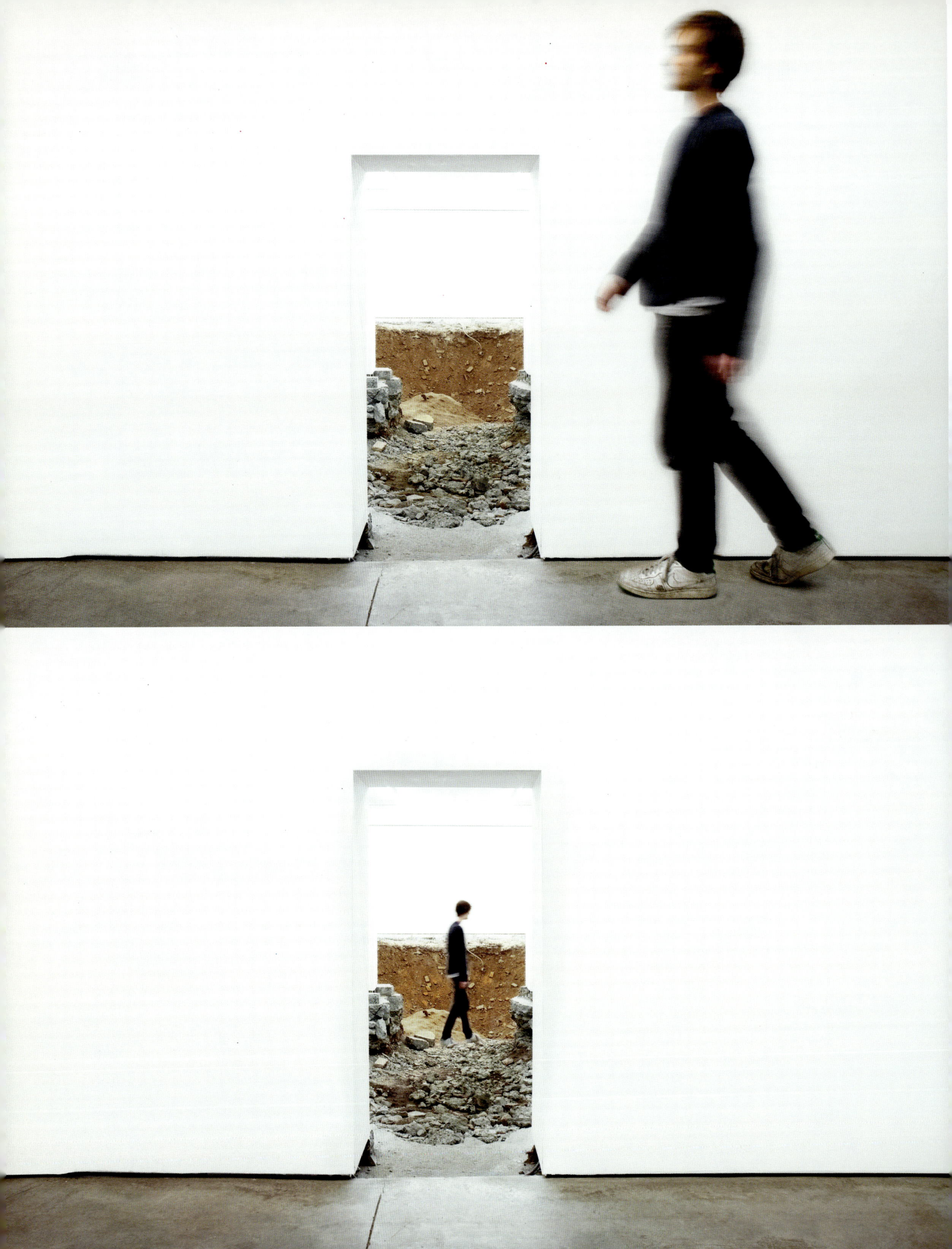

Installation view, "Oscar the Grouch," The Brant Foundation Art Study Center,
Greenwich, Connecticut, 2010–2011
You, 2007

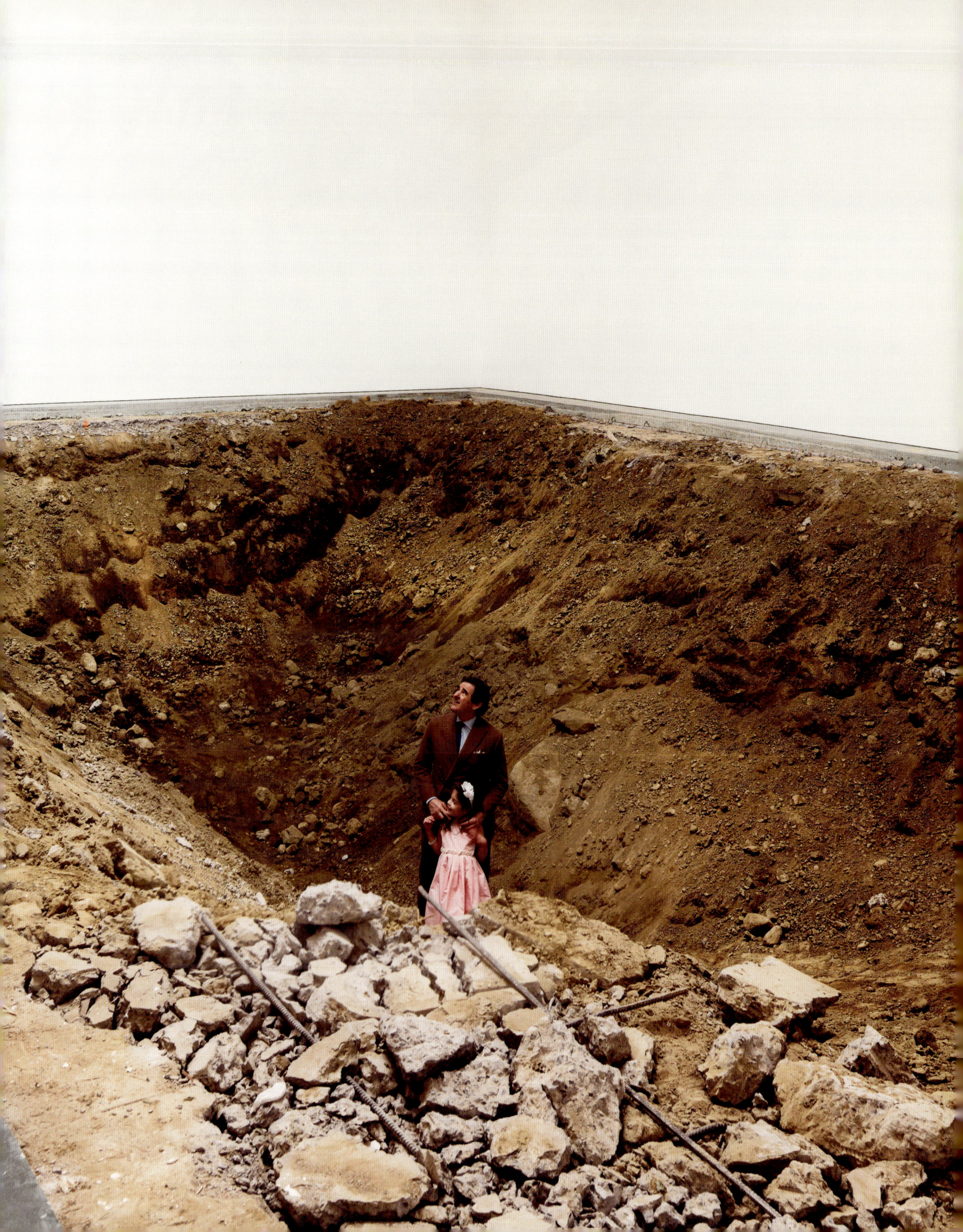

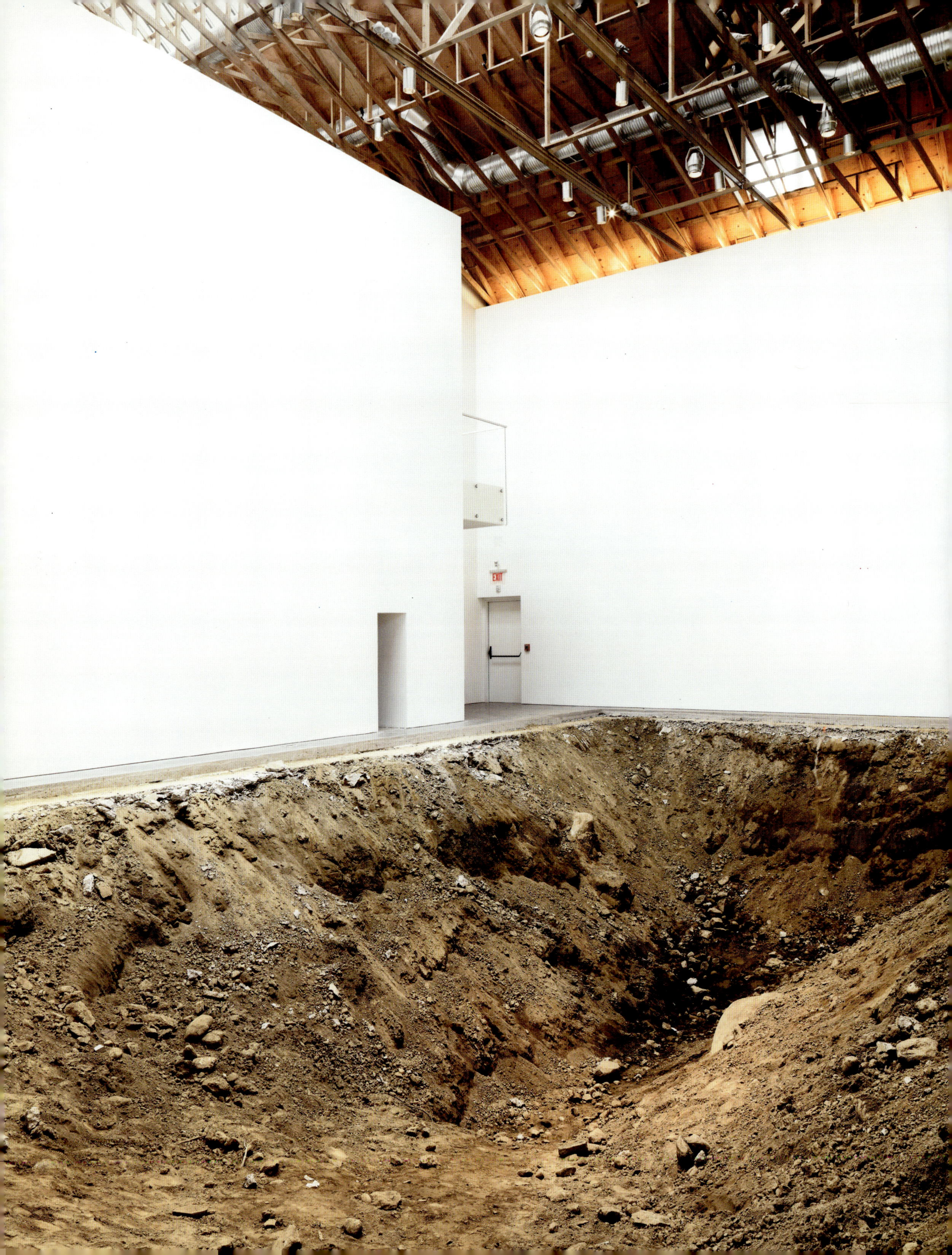
EXIT

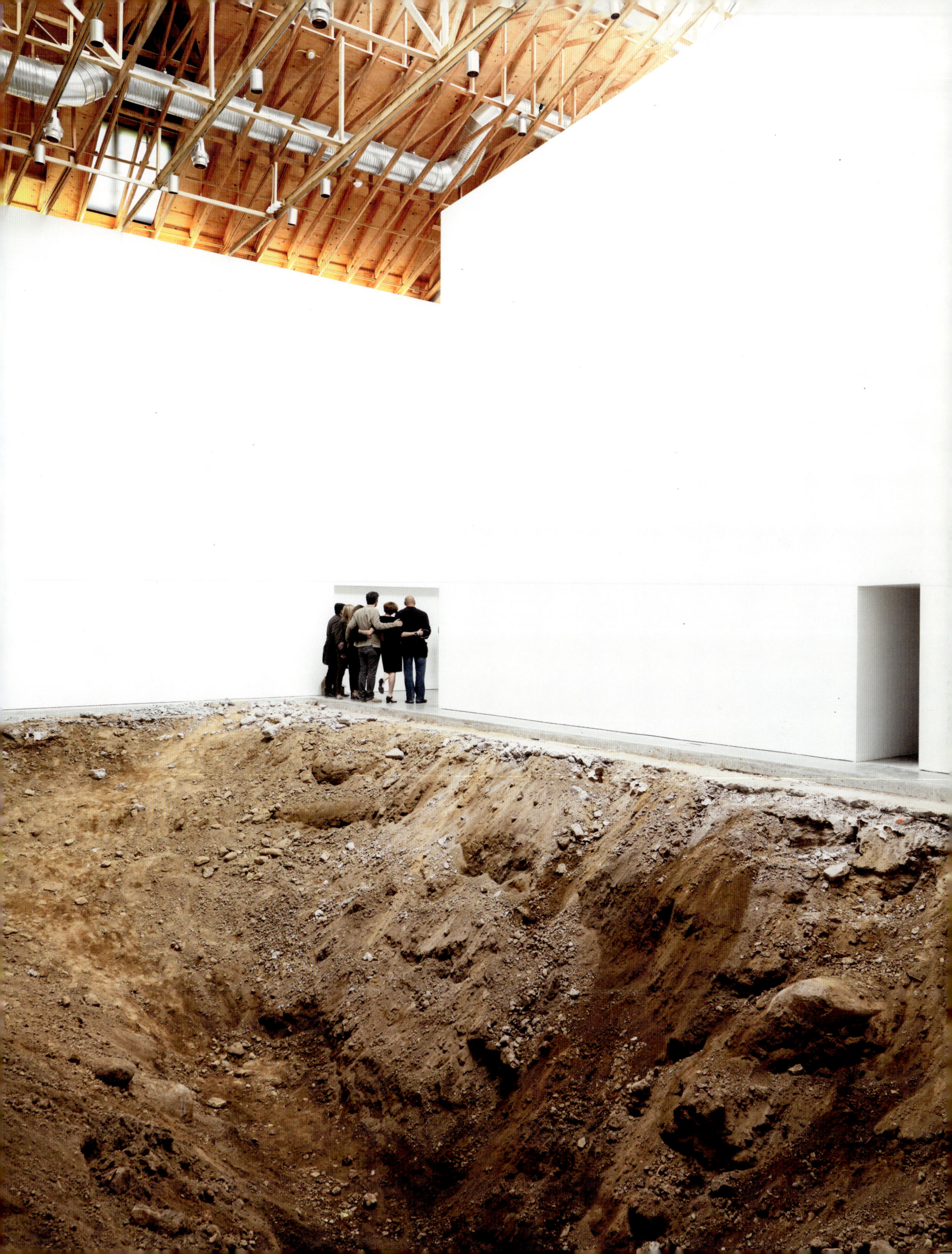

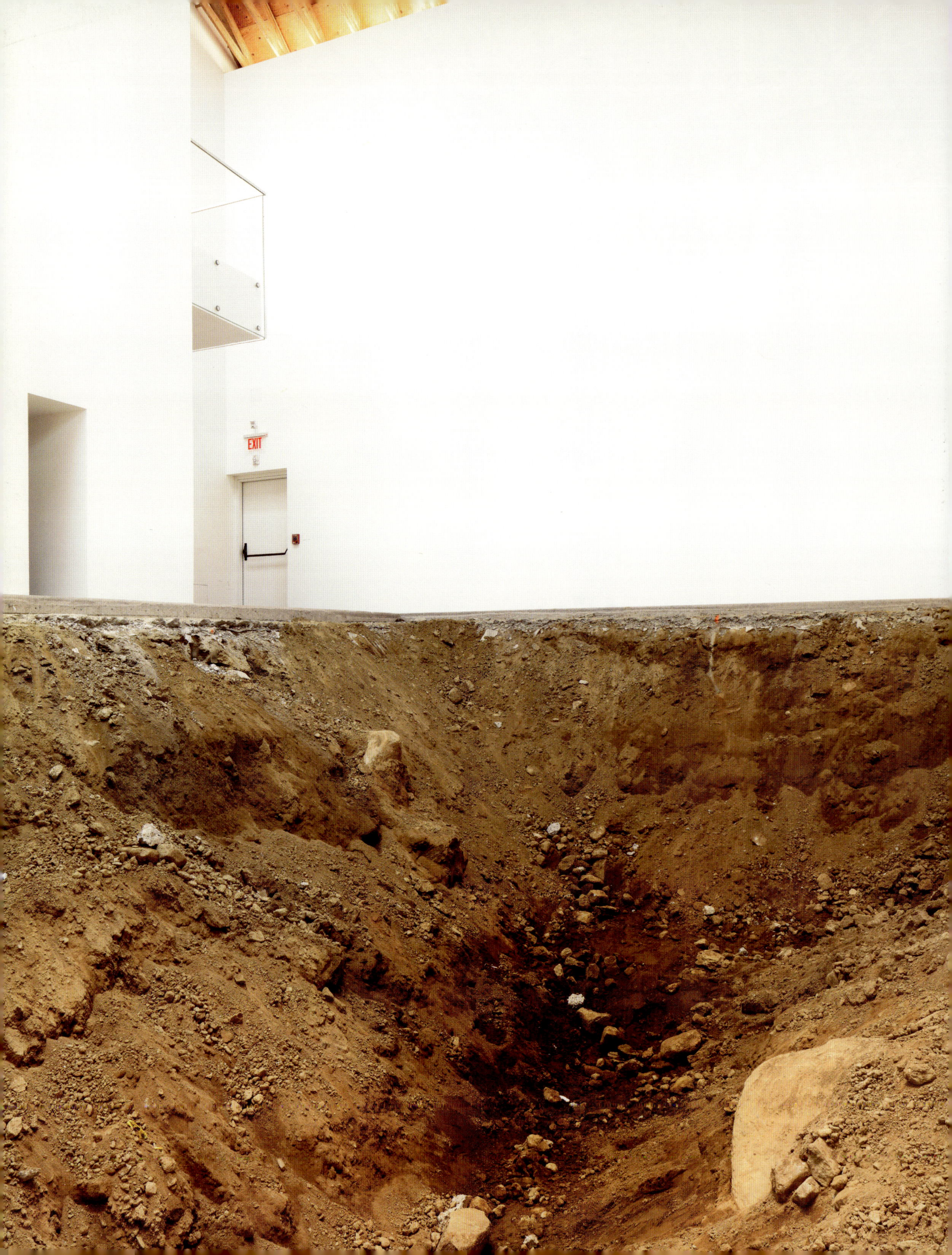
EXIT

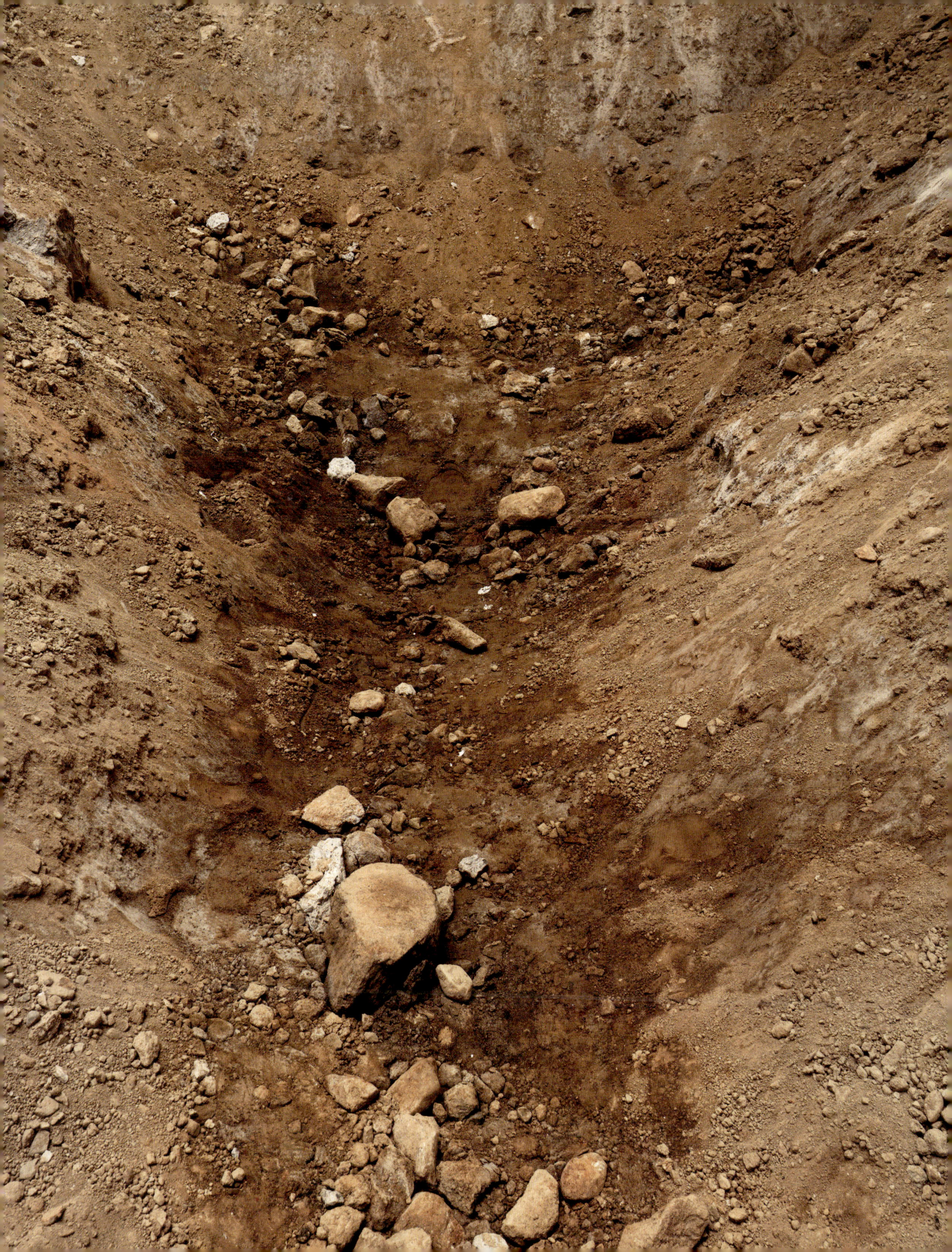

Page 26 and following pages:

Footnote to "You," 2010

Cedar, FXP, plywood, ultralight MDF, oak veneer edge banding, coffee, wood bleach, wood putty, wood stain, two-component polyester resin, spray enamel, steel, stainless steel, aluminum, glass, Plexiglas, Marmorino Veneziano plaster, ABS plastic, LED components, computer components, electrical components, latex paint, acrylic silkscreen medium, acrylic paint, polyurethane varnish, screws, nails, bolts, turnbuckles, washers, staples, Masonite, double-sided tape, spray adhesive, two-component acrylic adhesive, two-component epoxy glue, wood glue, acrylic adhesive
317 x 216 x 125 inches (805.2 x 548.6 x 317.5 cm)
Installation view, "Oscar the Grouch," The Brant Foundation Art Study Center, Greenwich, Connecticut, 2010–2011

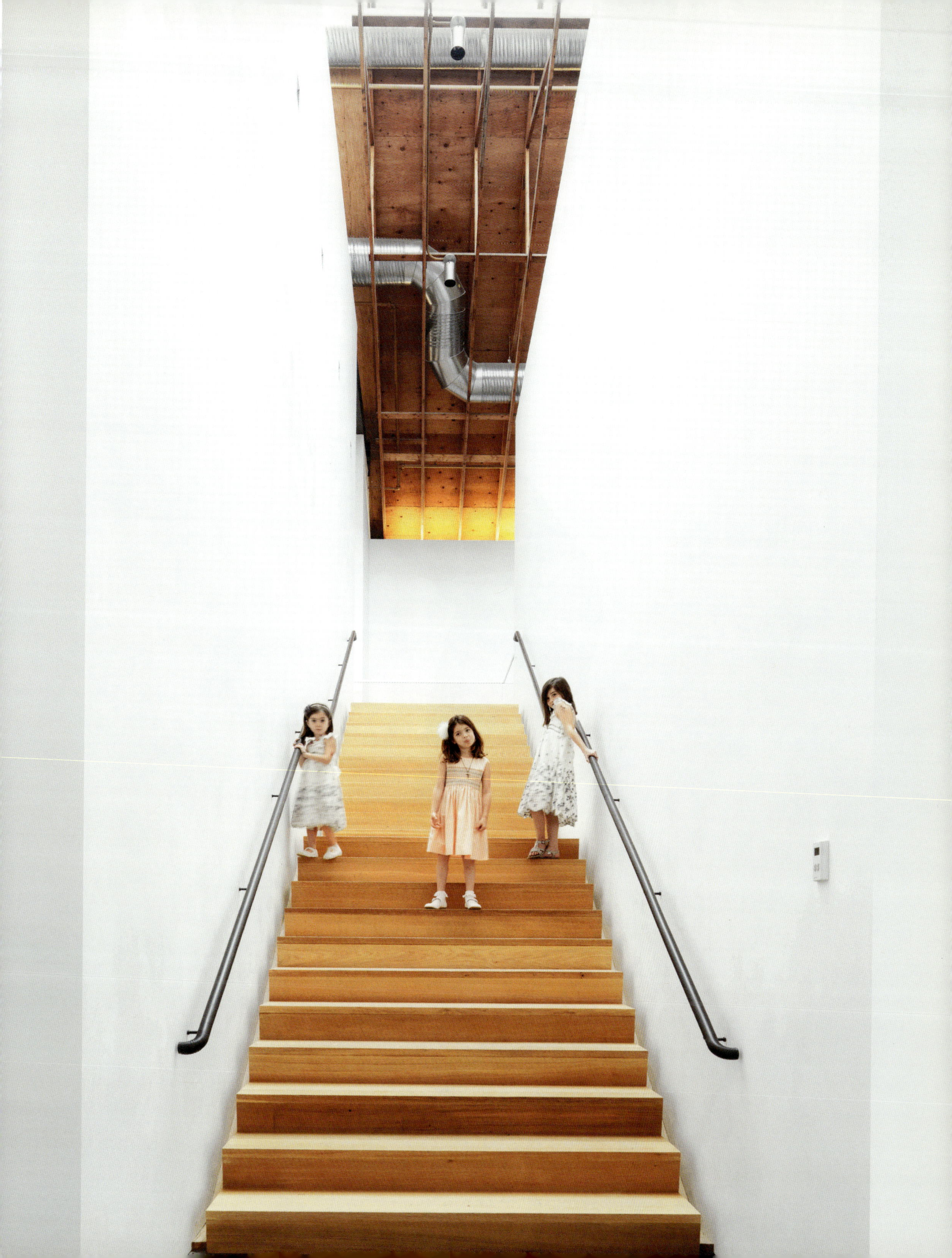

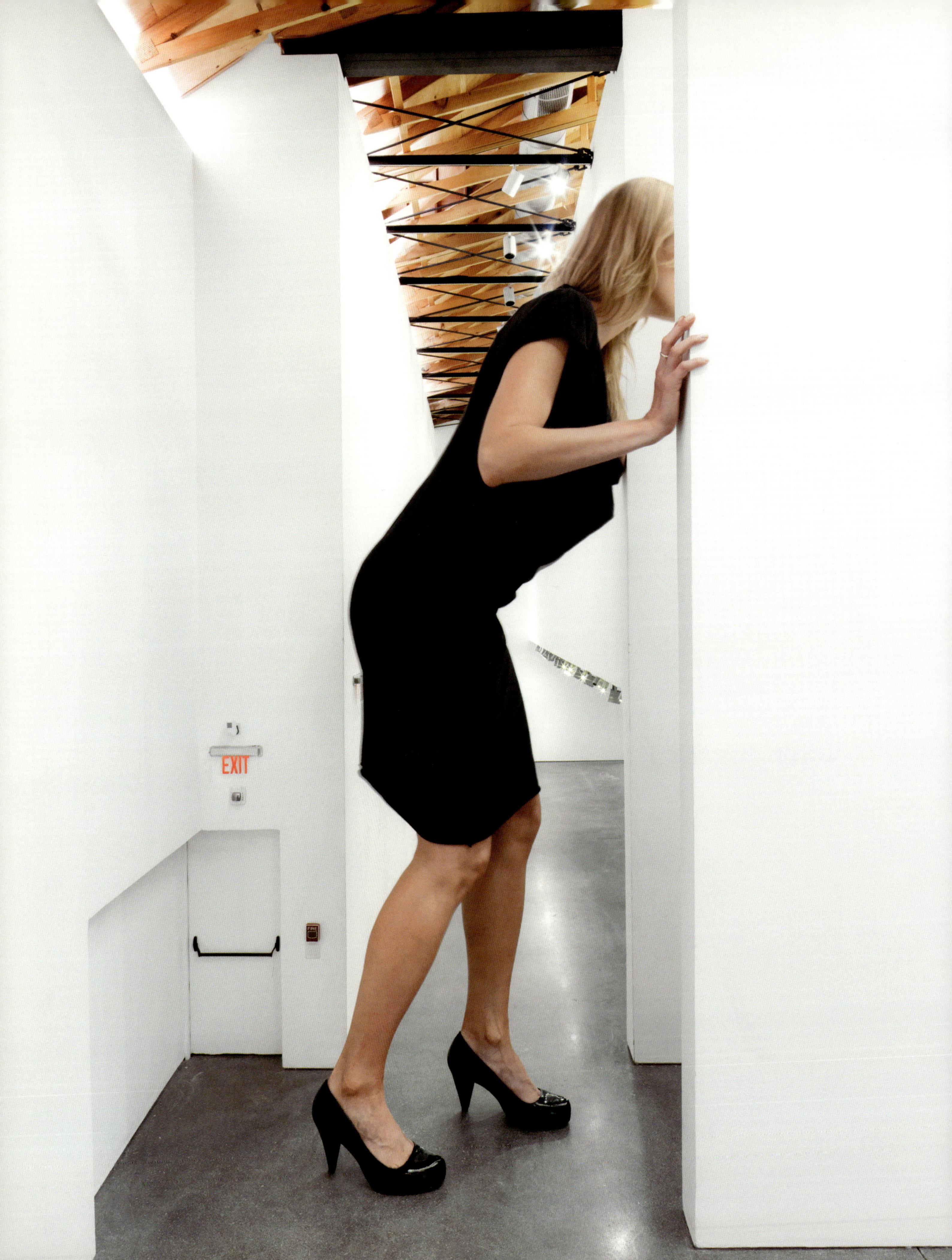
EXIT

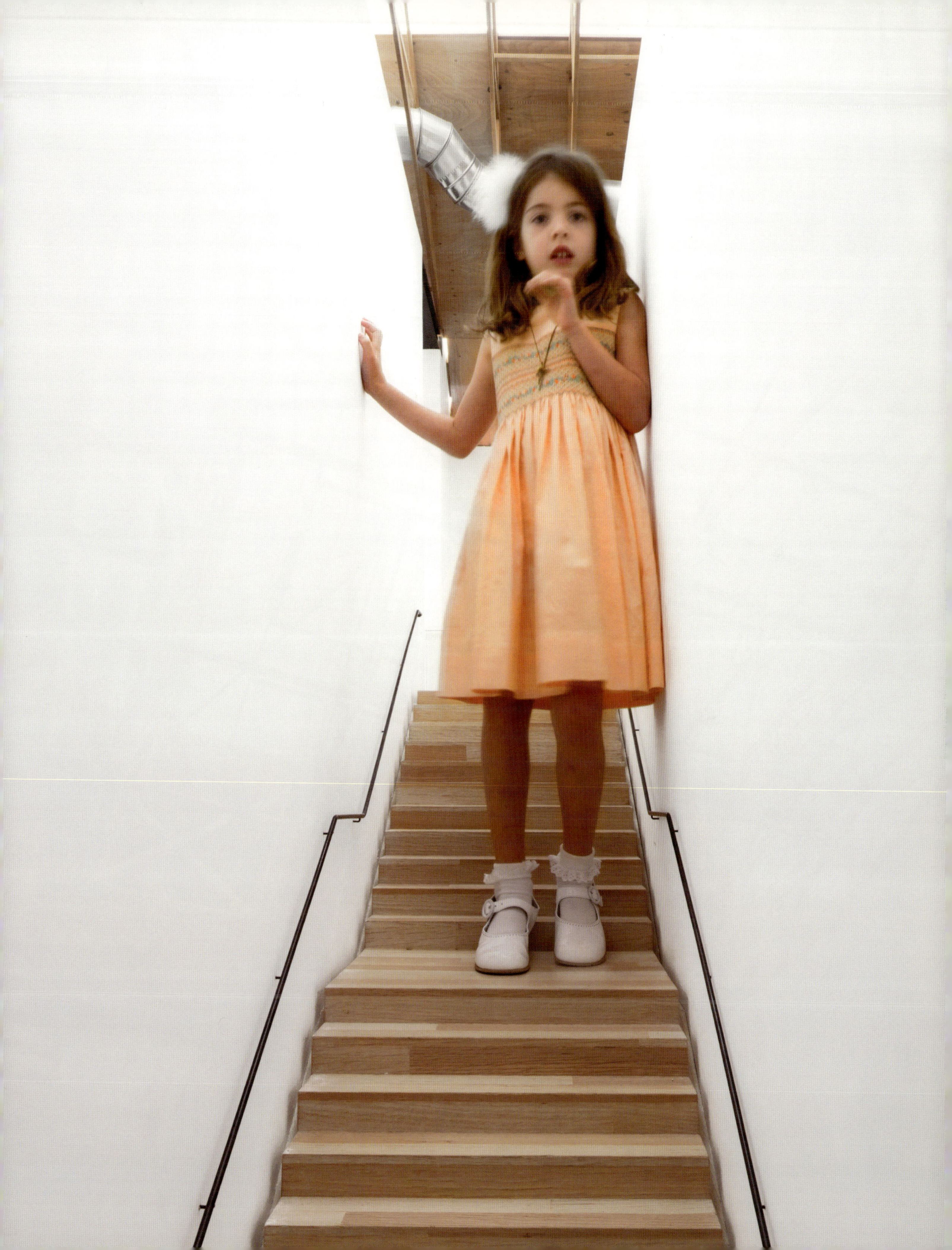

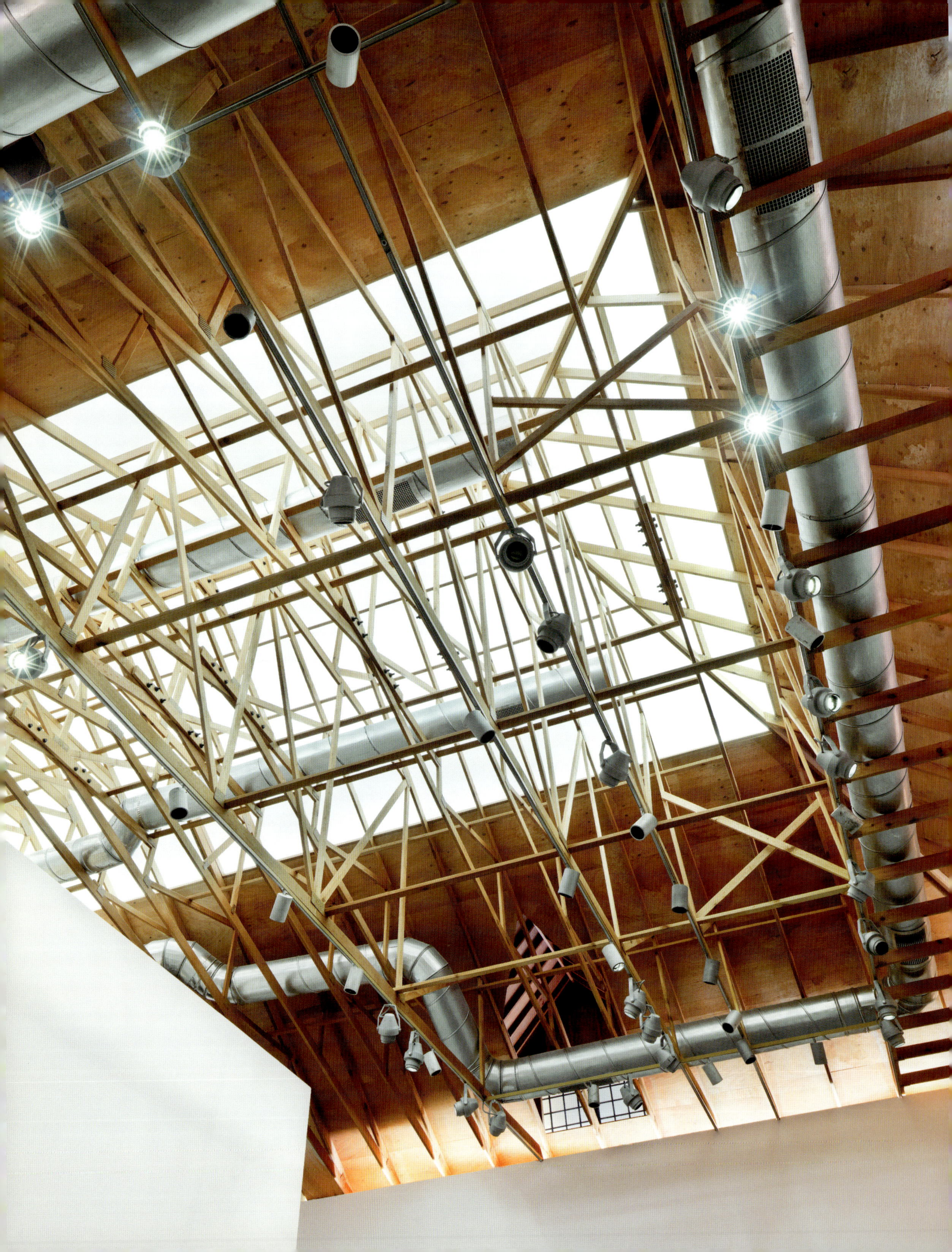

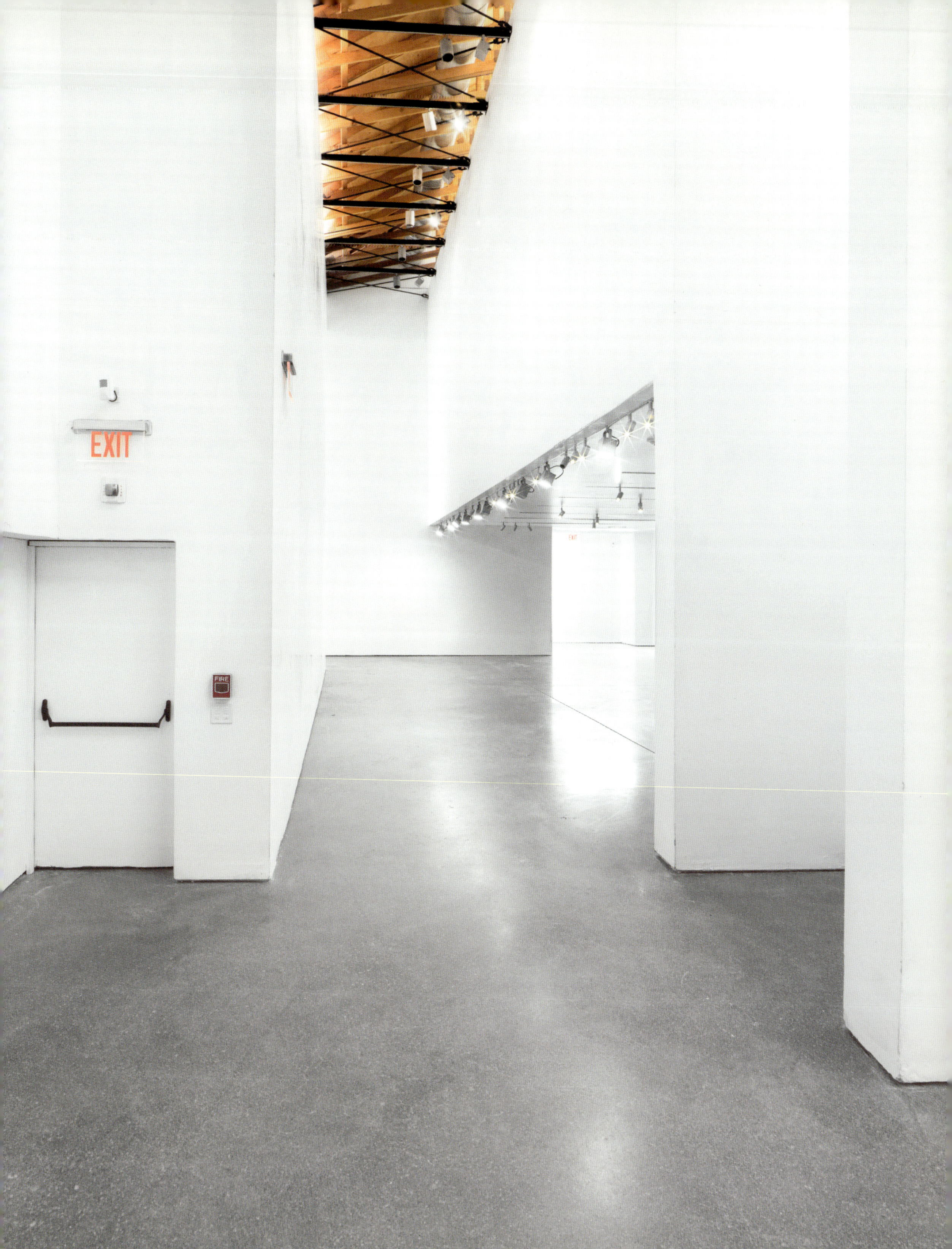
EXIT
FIRE

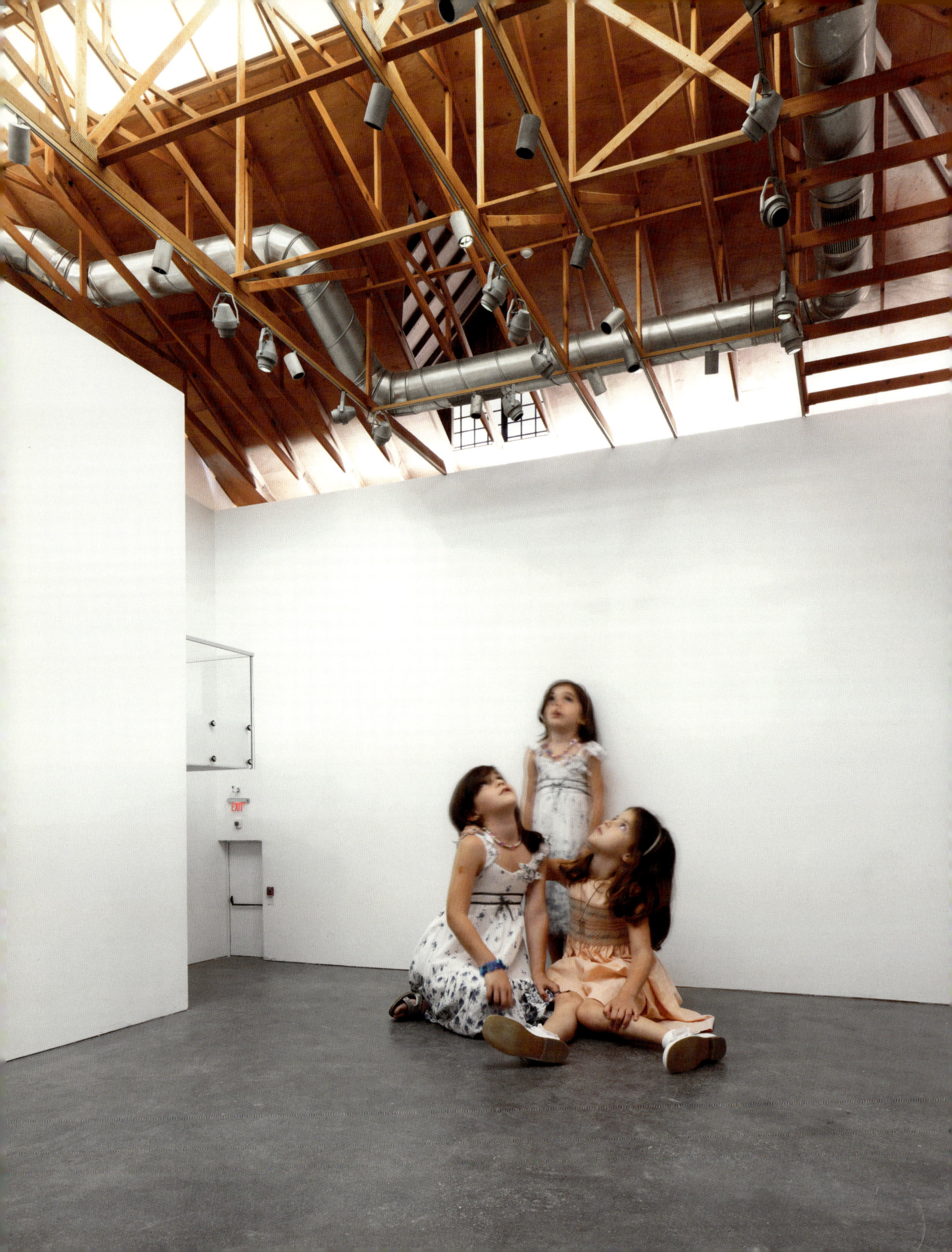
EXIT

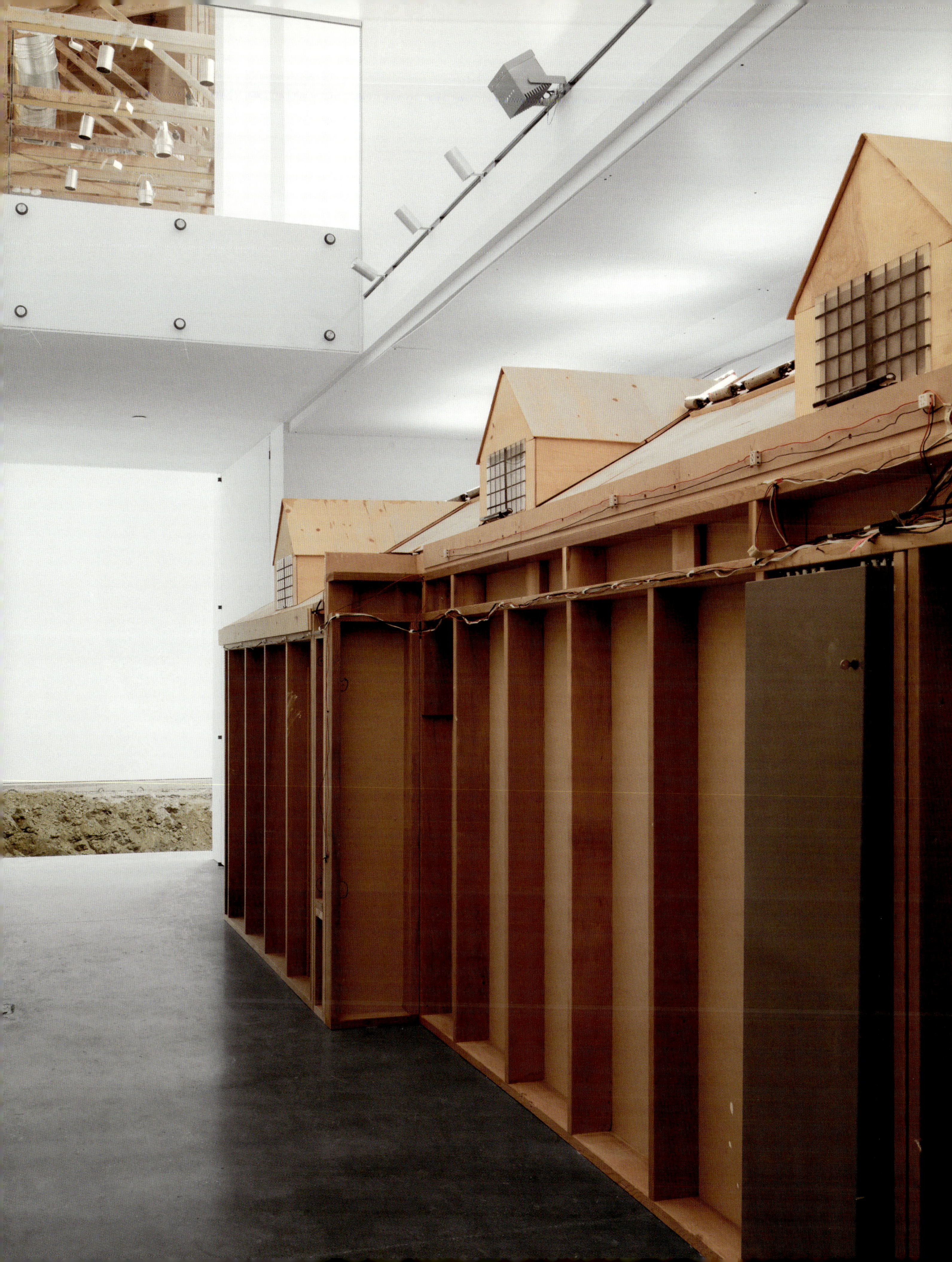

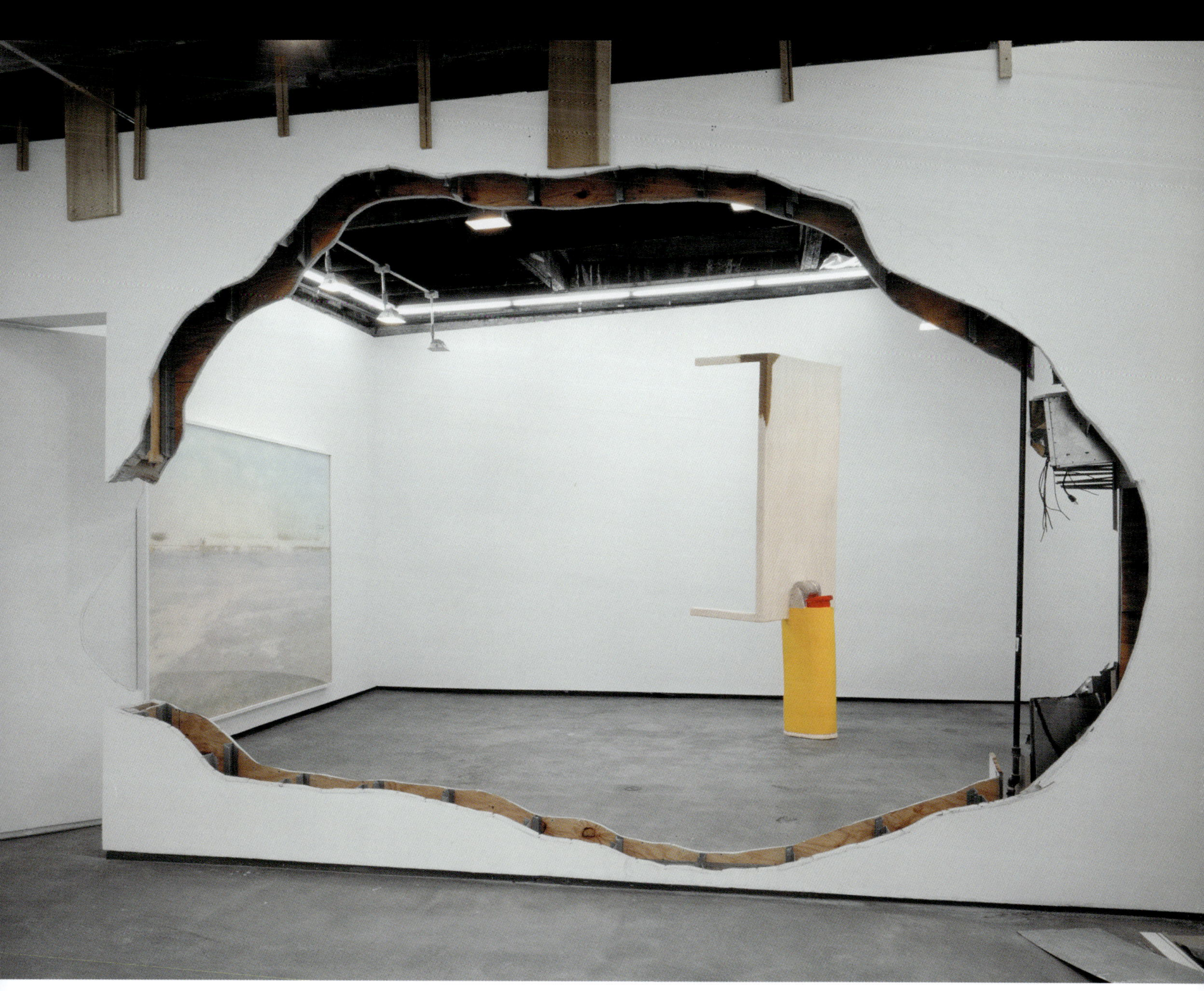

Portrait of a Single Raindrop, 2003
Cuts in wall with relocated cutouts
Dimensions variable
Installation view, "Portrait of a Single Raindrop,"
Gavin Brown's enterprise, New York, 2003
You Can Only Lose, 2003; On wall: *Make a Duck Out of a Cow*, 2003
Following spread: Installation view, "Portrait of a Single Raindrop,"
Gavin Brown's enterprise, New York, 2003
You Can Not Win, 2003; *You Can Only Lose*, 2003

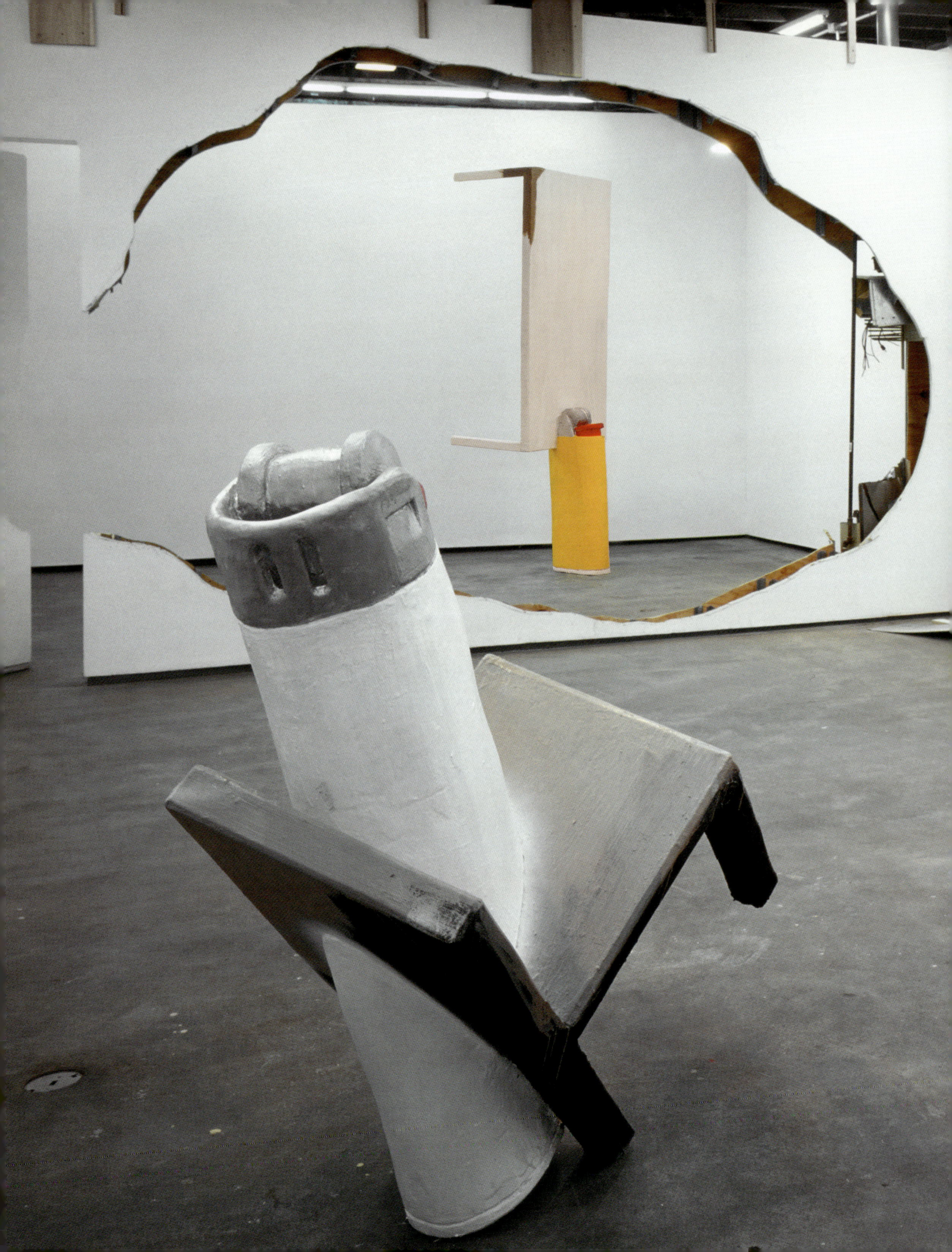

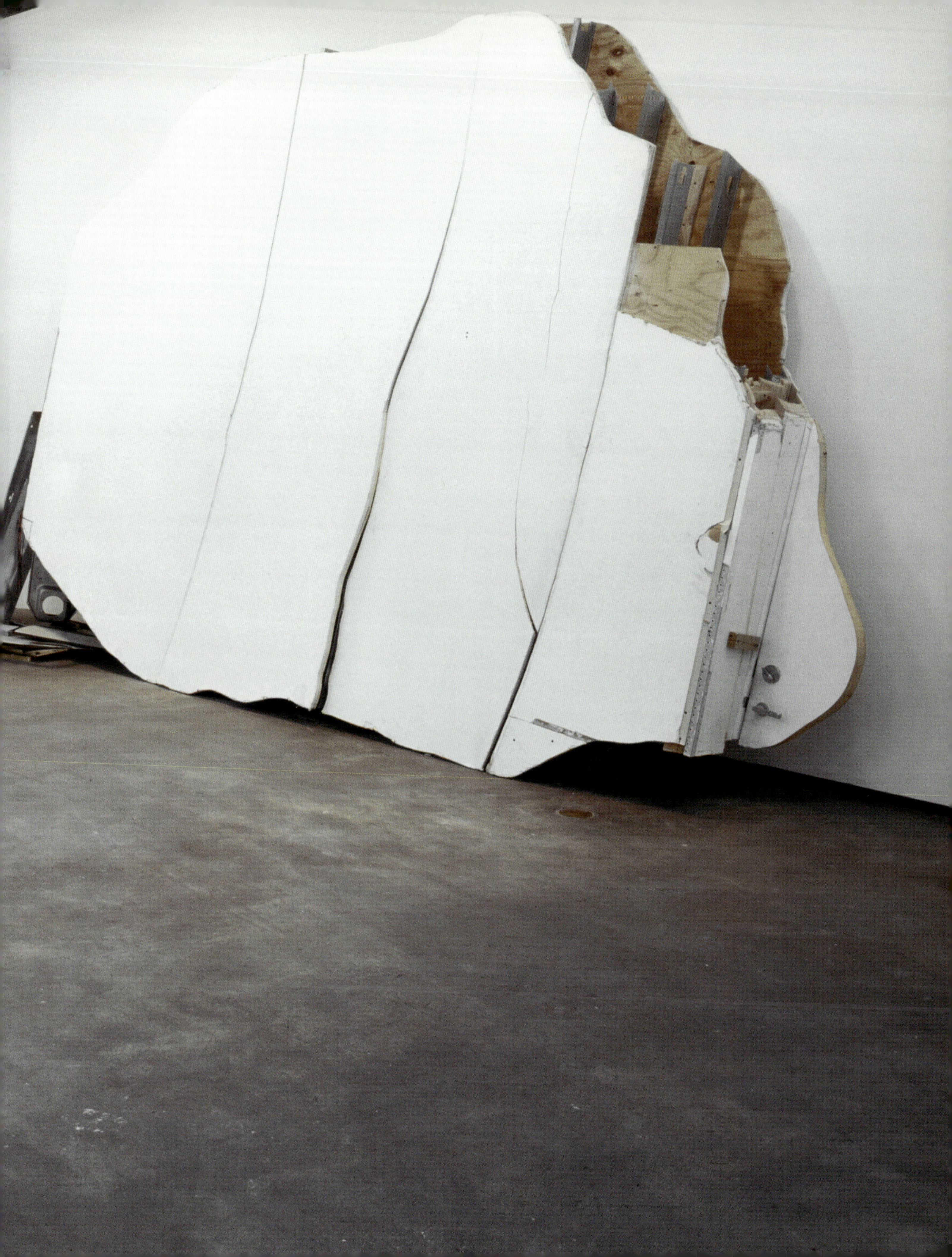

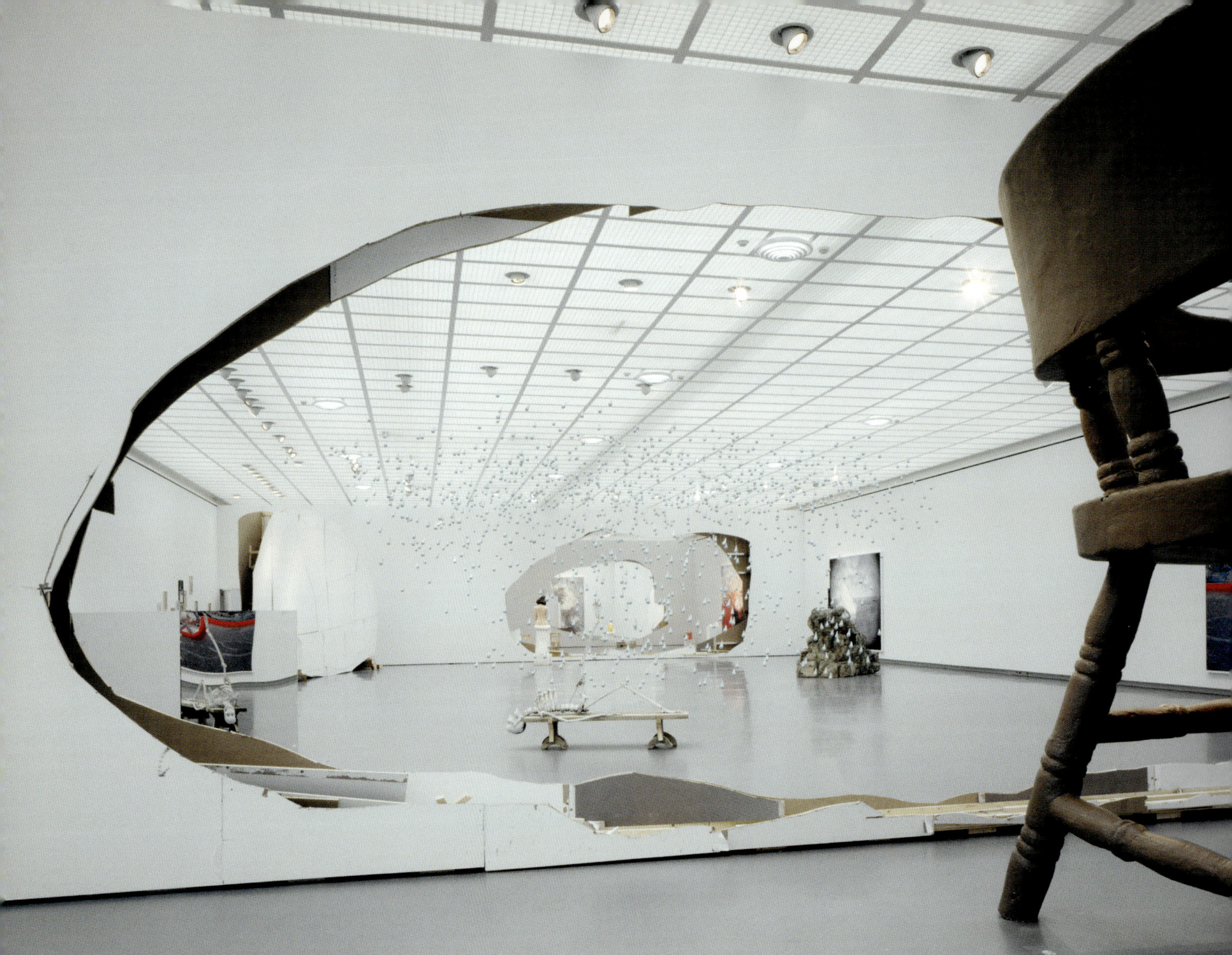

Middleclass Heroes, 2004
Cuts in wall with relocated cutouts
Dimensions variable
Installation view, "Kir Royal," Kunsthaus Zürich, 2004
Above: *Sodbrennen*, 2000–2004; *Kuckuck Backwards*, 2004; *Horses Dream of Horses*, 2004; *What if the Phone Rings*, 2003; *Untitled*, 2004; Prototype of *Bad Timing, Lamb Chop!*, 2004; On wall: *Stalagmites of Love*, 2004
Opposite page: *Erdnüsse im Vergleich*, 2004; *Your Deaths Your Births*, 2004; *What if the Phone Rings*, 2004

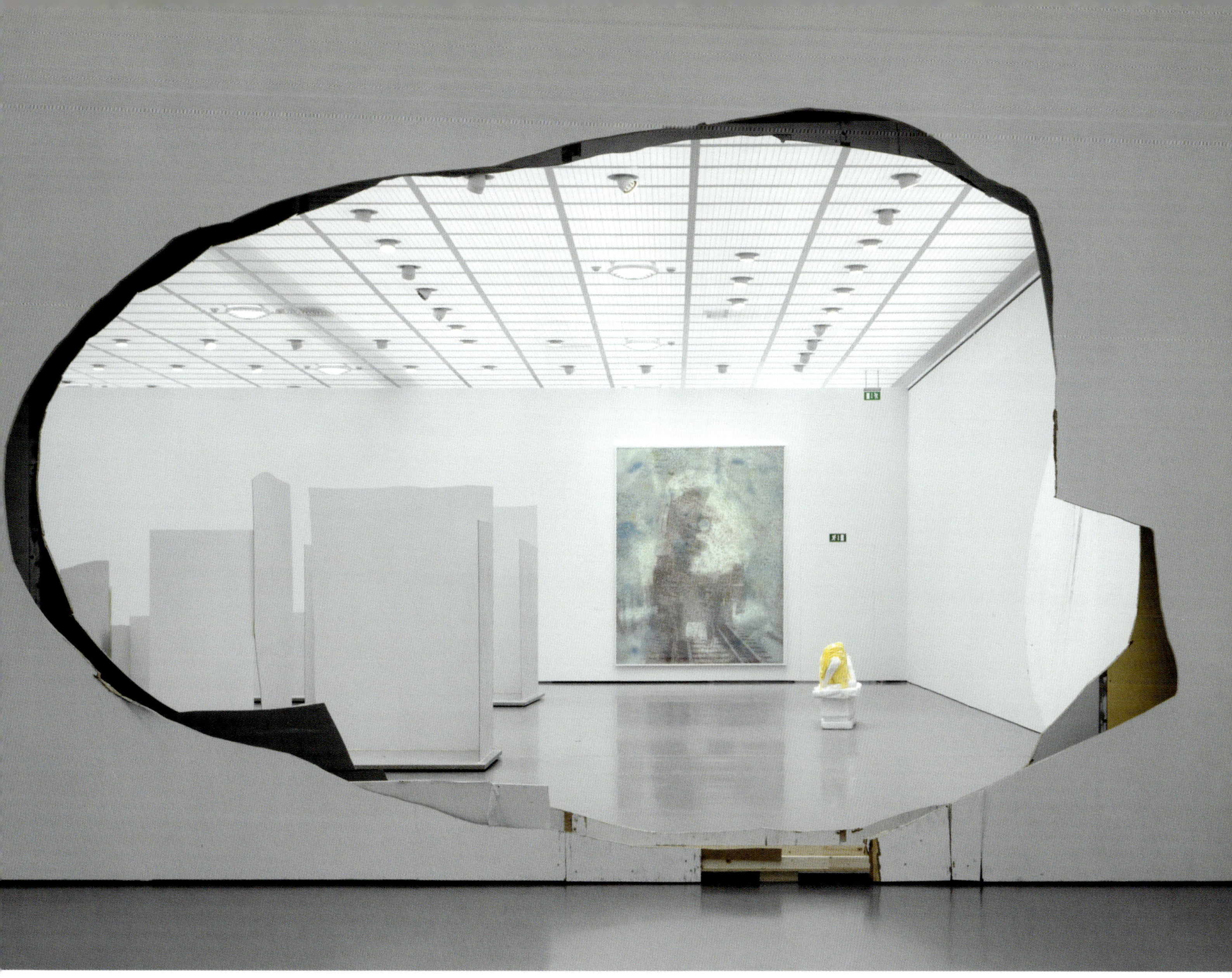

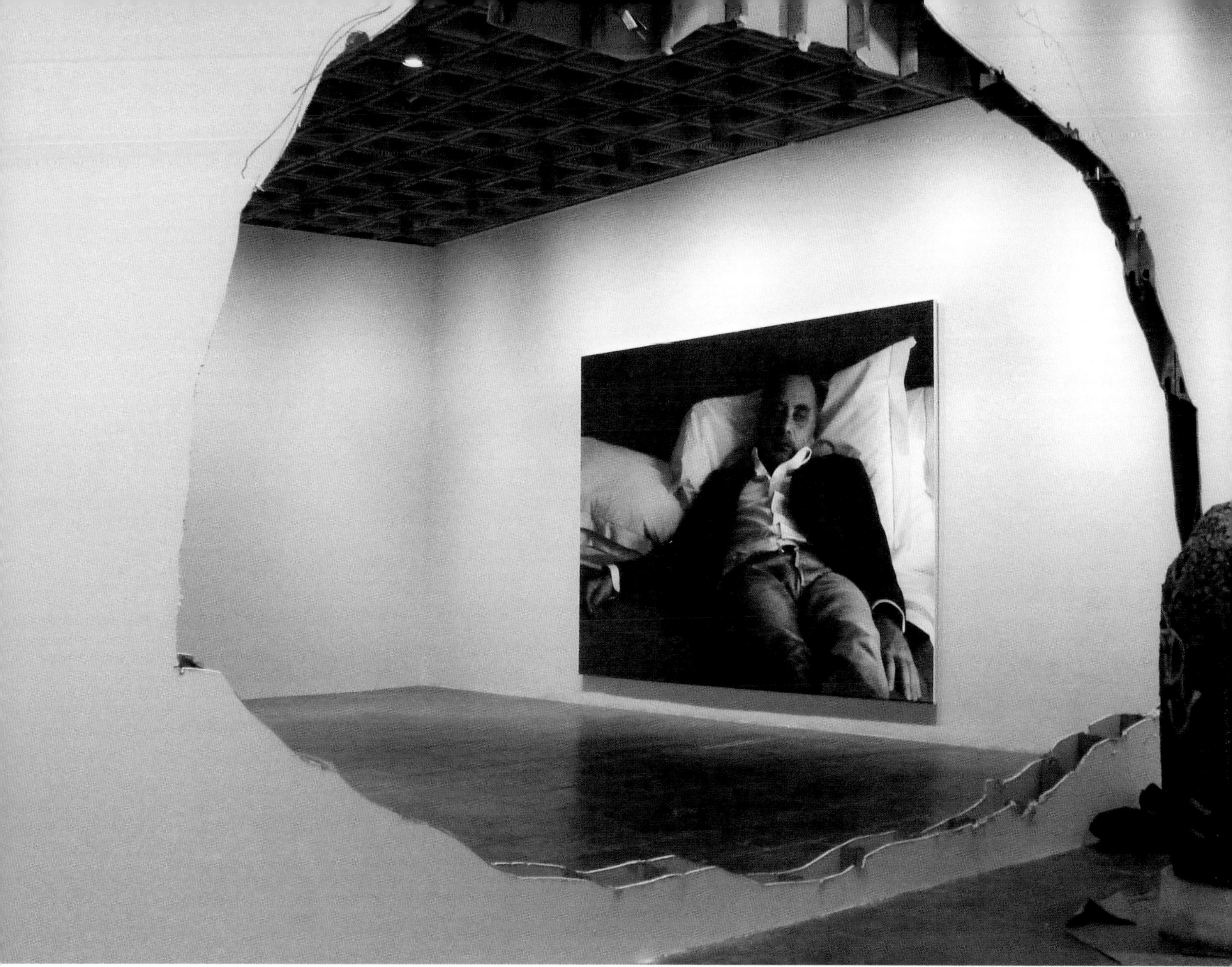

The Intelligence of Flowers, 2005
Cuts in wall with relocated cutouts
Dimensions variable
Installation view, "Day for Night," Whitney Biennial,
Whitney Museum of American Art, New York, 2006
Dan Colen, *Untitled (Zippideedoodah)*, 2006;
On wall: Rudolf Stingel, *Untitled (After Sam)*, 2005–2006

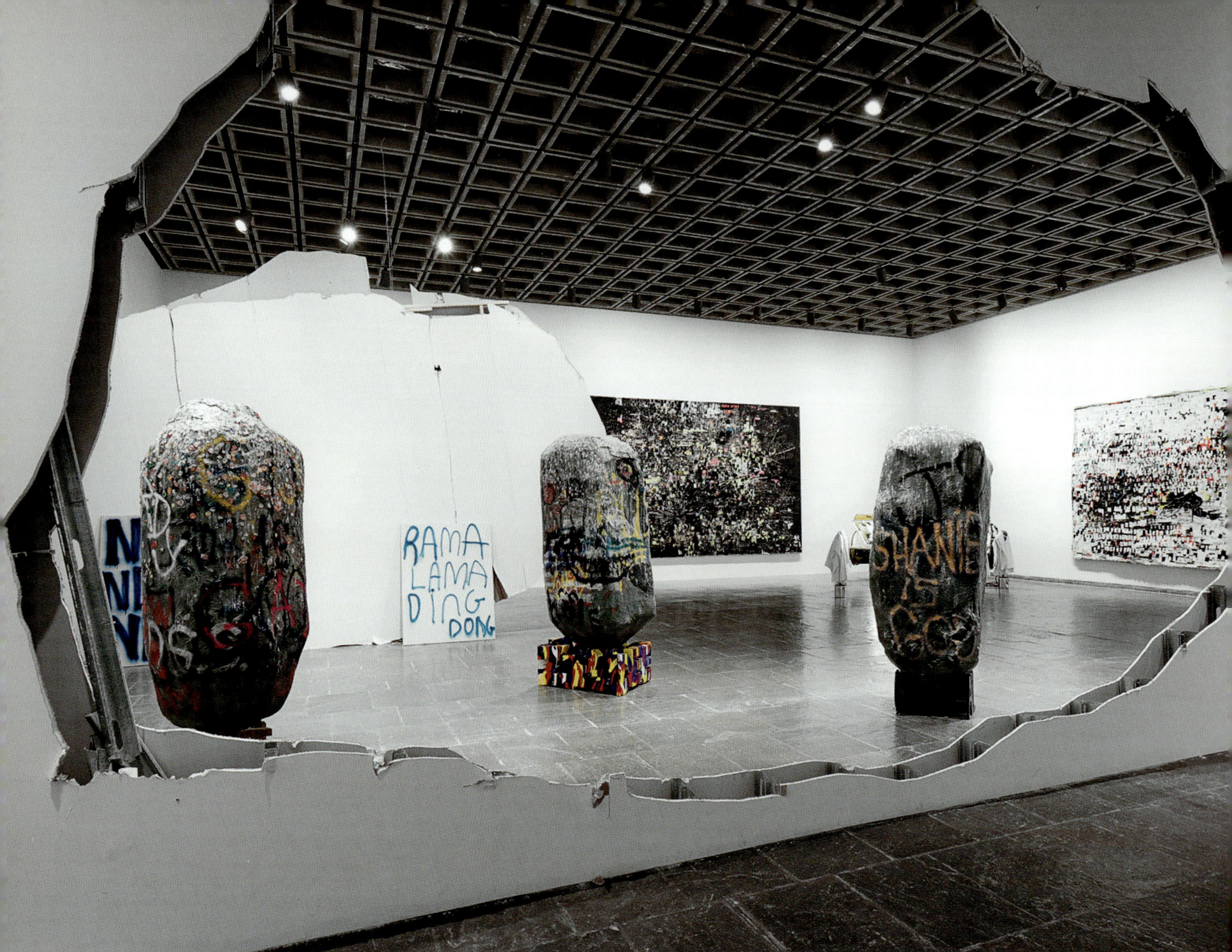

Installation view, "Day for Night," Whitney Biennial, Whitney Museum of American Art, New York, 2006
Above: *The Intelligence of Flowers*, 2005
Dan Colen, *Untitled (Zippideedoodah)*, 2006;
Dan Colen, *Rama Lama Ding Dong*, 2006;
On wall: Mark Bradford, *Los Moscos*, 2004;
Mark Bradford, *Untitled*, 2005–2006
Opposite page: *The Intelligence of Flowers*, 2005;
Untitled (Branches), 2005; On wall: Rudolf Stingel,
Untitled (After Sam), 2005–2006

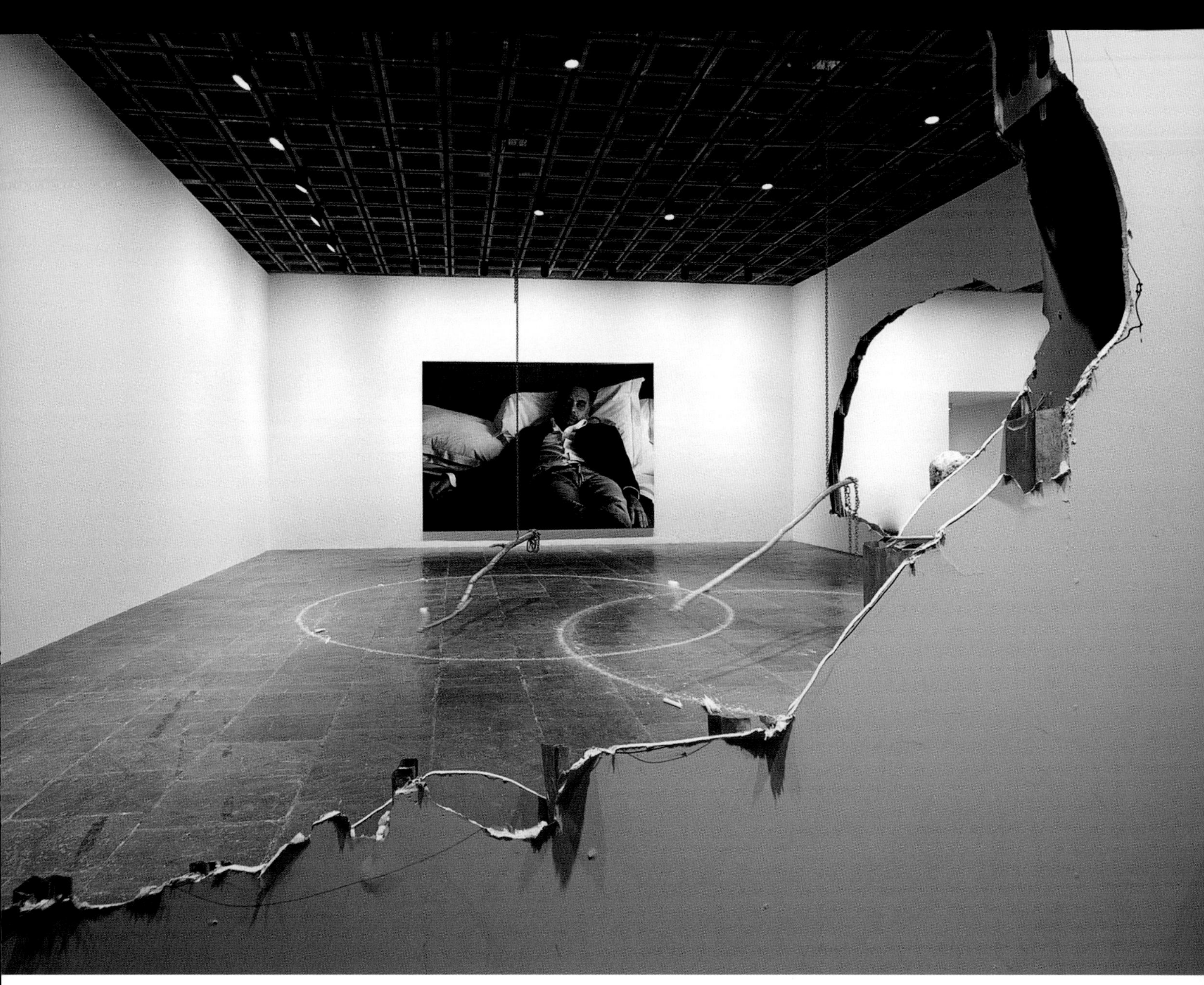

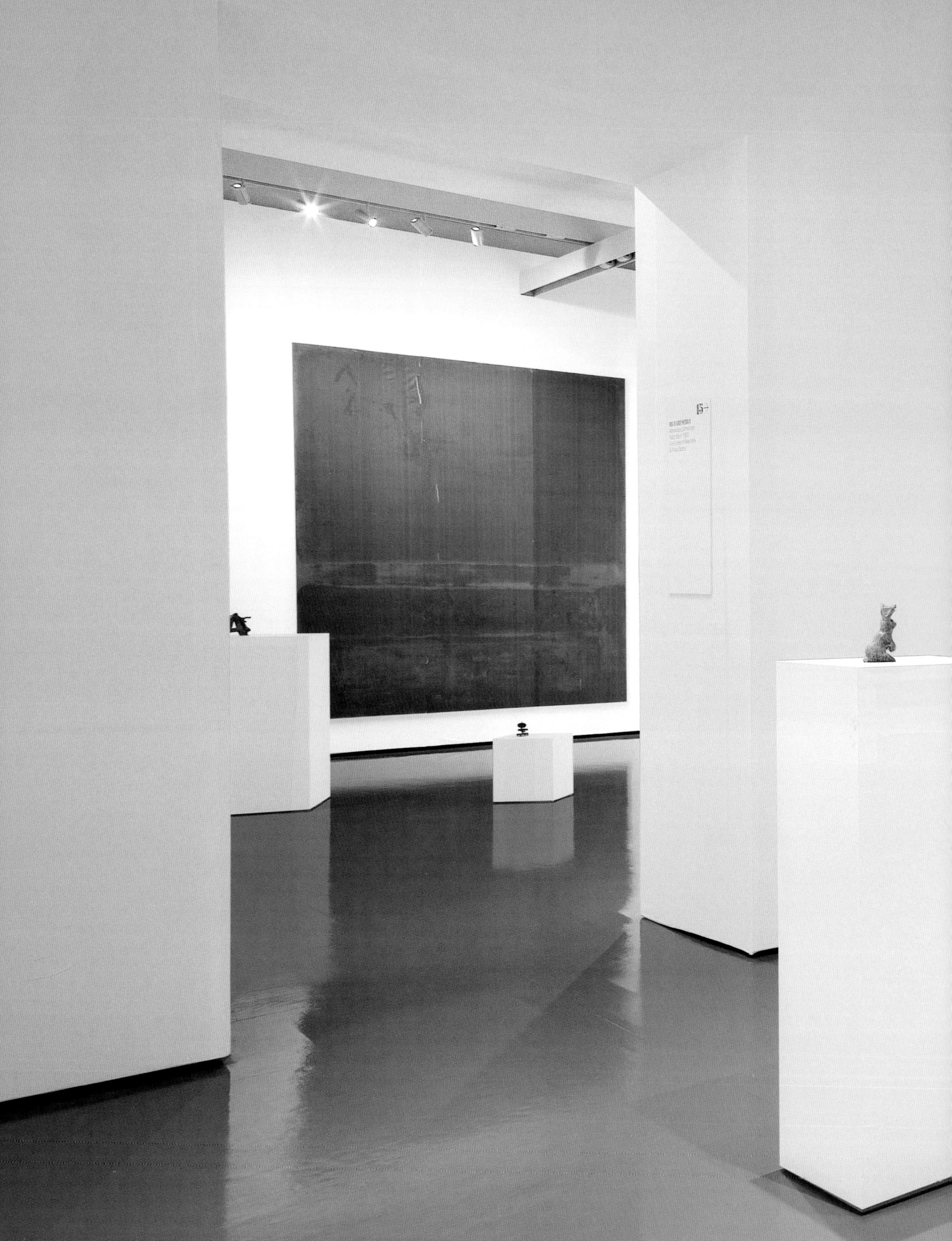
15→

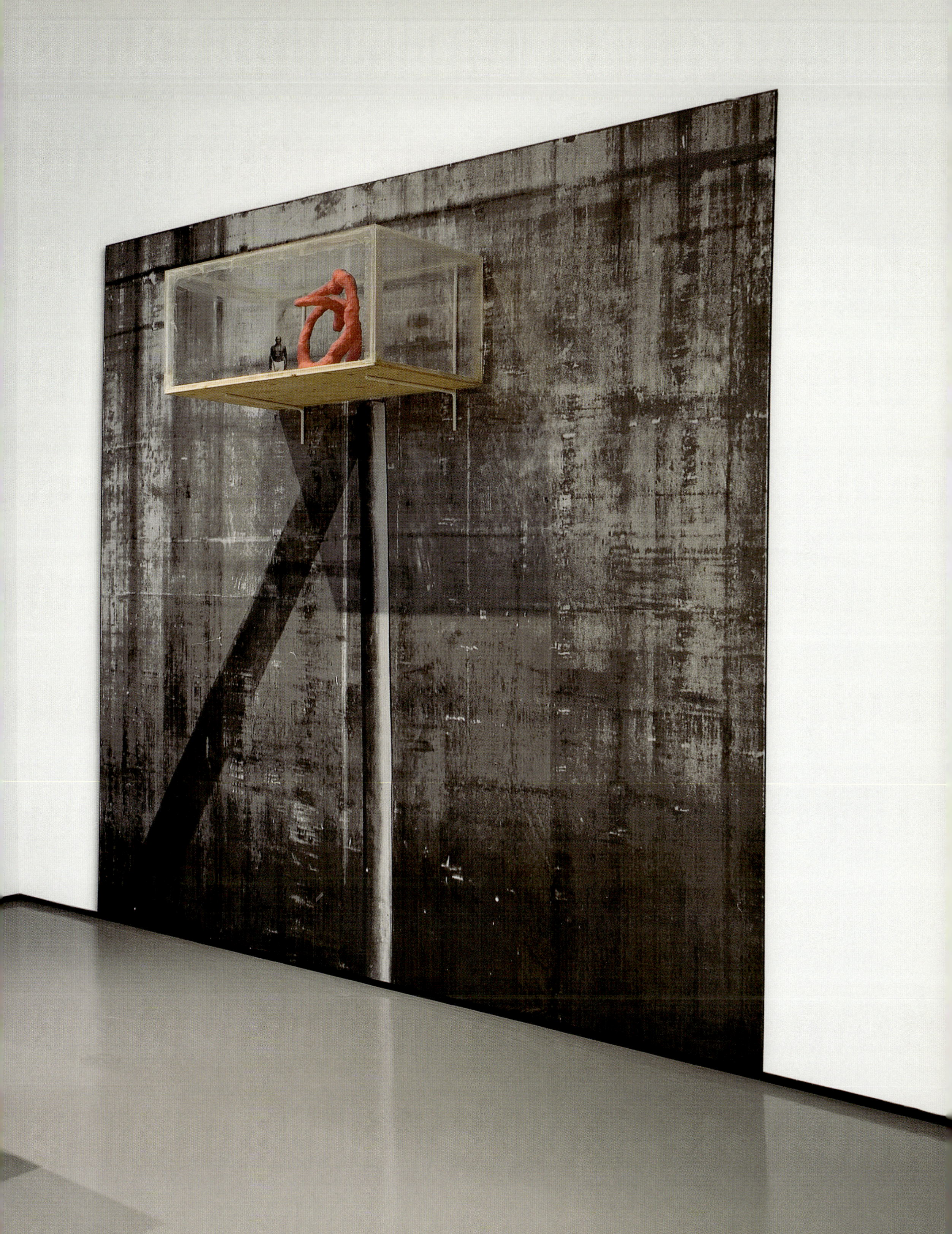

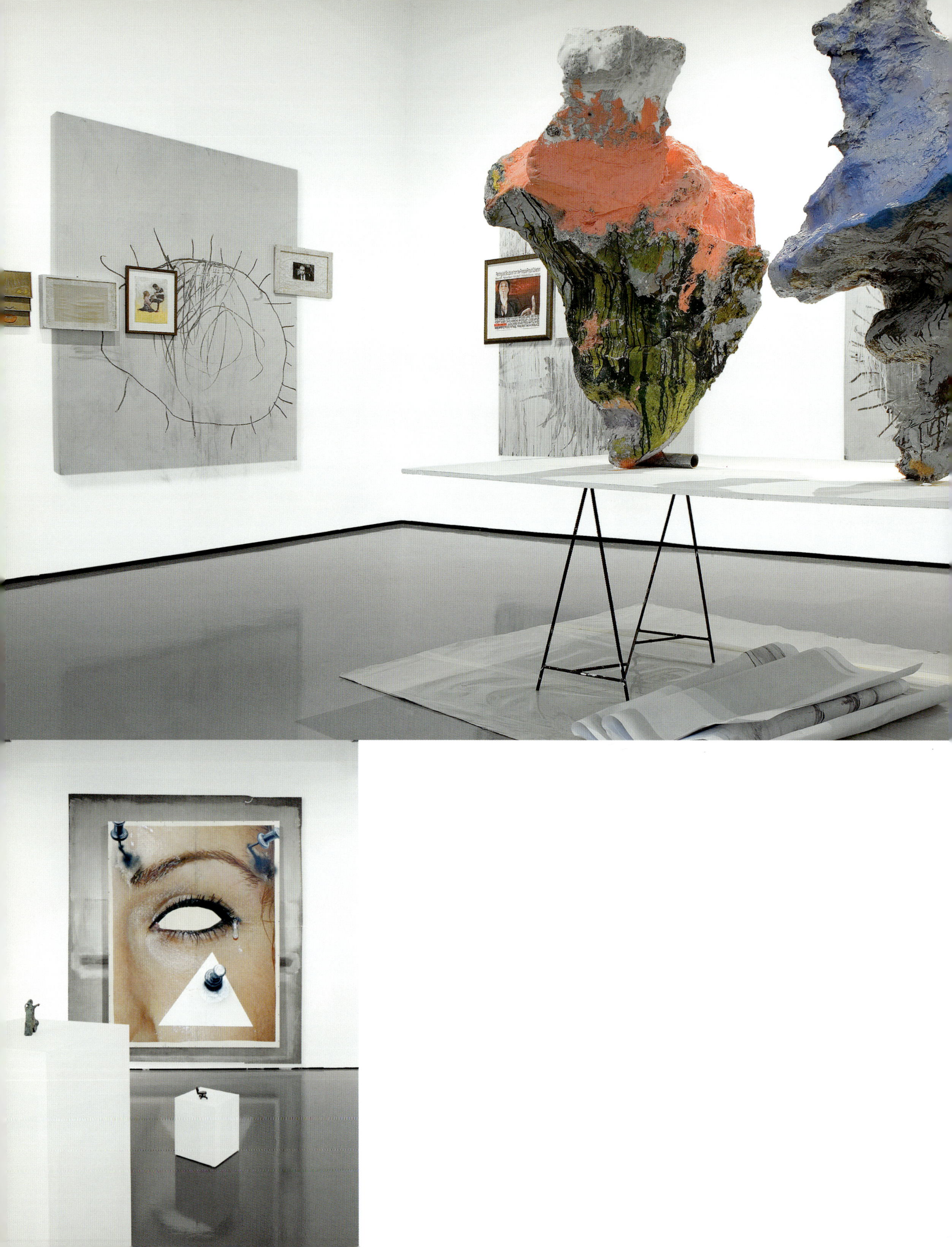

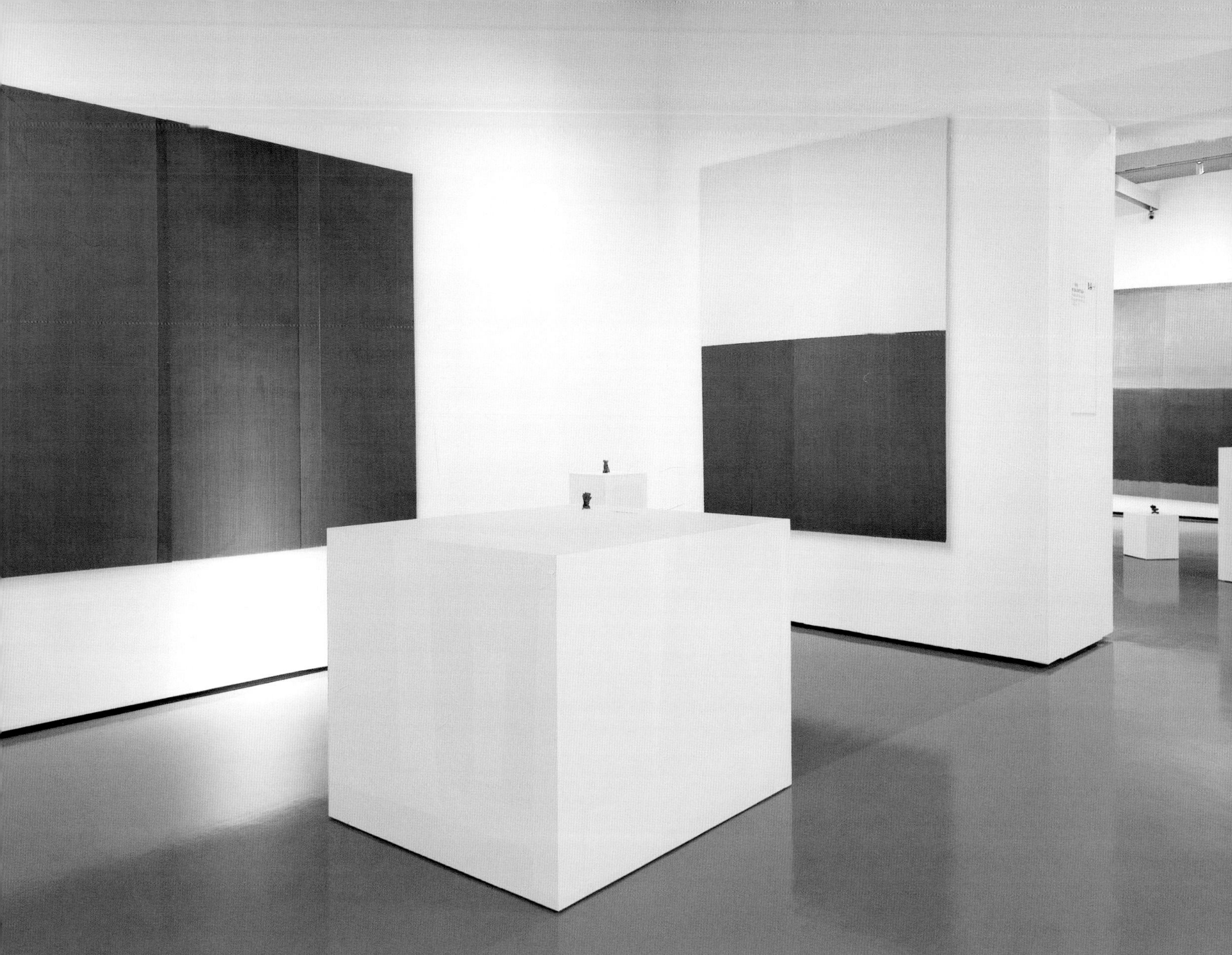

Verbal Asceticism, 2007
Wallpaper prints of photographic reproductions of interior spaces—content, scale, and lighting determined on a site-specific basis (1:1 scale black-and-white photographic reproduction of the gallery space during the previous exhibition, "Where Are We Going?")
Dimensions variable
Installation view, "Sequence 1: Painting and Sculpture in the François Pinault Collection," Palazzo Grassi, Venice, 2007
Previous spread: *Pop the Glock*, 2006; On wall: Franz West, *Flora (Model)*, 2006; vitrine by Rudolf Polanszky
Above: *Untitled*, 2007; *Untitled*, 2007
Opposite page, top: Franz West, *Worktable and Workbench*, 2006;
On wall: Franz West, *Collecting Wall*, 2007
Opposite page, bottom: *Untitled*, 2007; *Untitled*, 2007;
On wall: *office theme / addiction / mmmh camera*, 2006

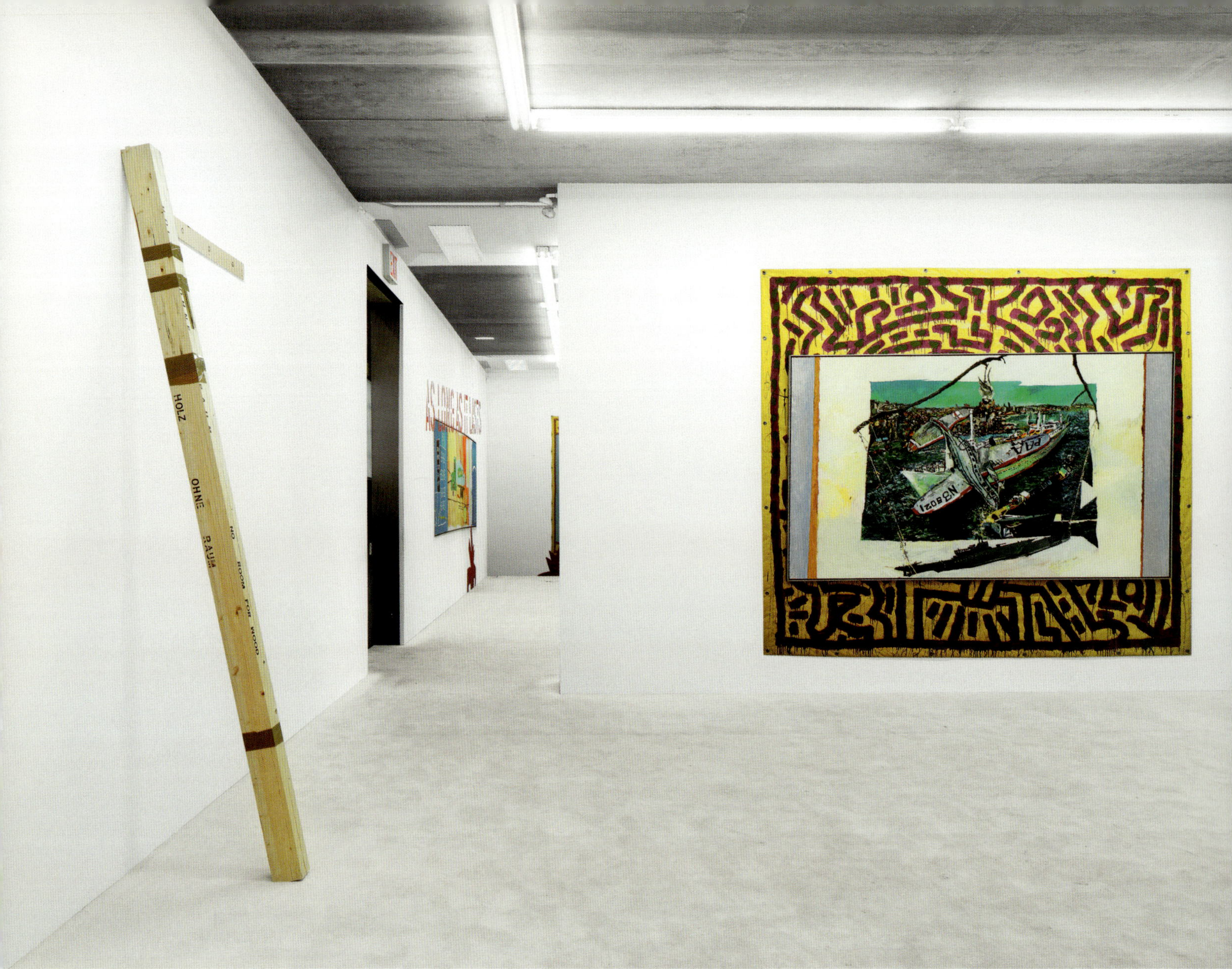

Abstract Slavery, 2008

Wallpaper prints of photographic reproductions of interior spaces—content, scale, and lighting determined on a site-specific basis (1:1 scale color photographic reproduction of the gallery space during the previous exhibition, "Four Friends")

Dimensions variable

Installation view, "Who's Afraid of Jasper Johns?," Tony Shafrazi Gallery, New York, 2008

Above: Georg Herold, *Holz Ohne Raum (No Room for Wood)*, 1988;
Malcolm Morley, *Age of Catastrophe*, 1976

Opposite page: Francis Picabia, *Portrait Einer Schauspielerin, Suzanne Romain*, 1943;
Georg Herold, *Eimer Neben Sockel*, 1987; Lily van der Stokker, *Pink Blubber*, 2008;
Francis Bacon, *Untitled (Head)*, 1949

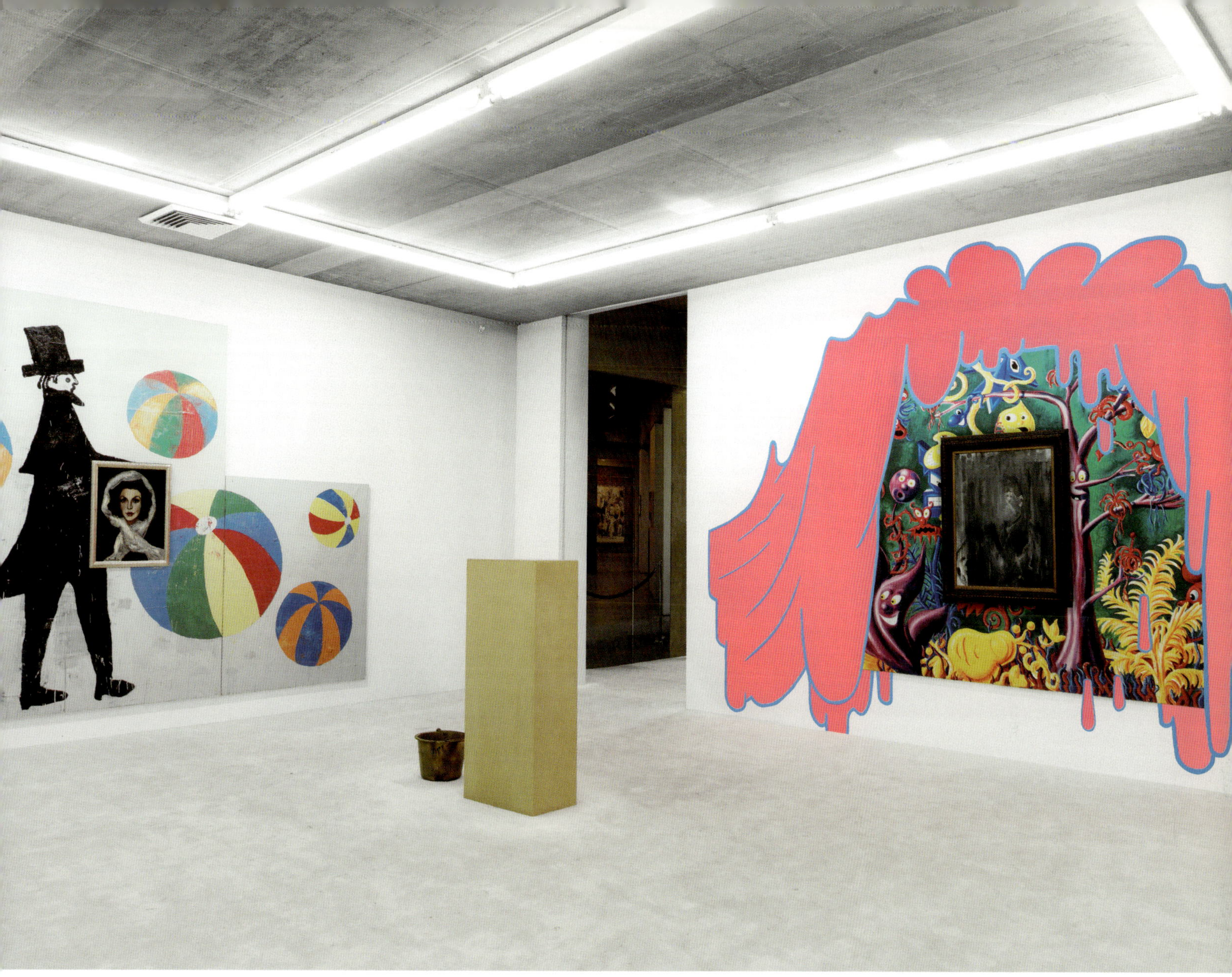

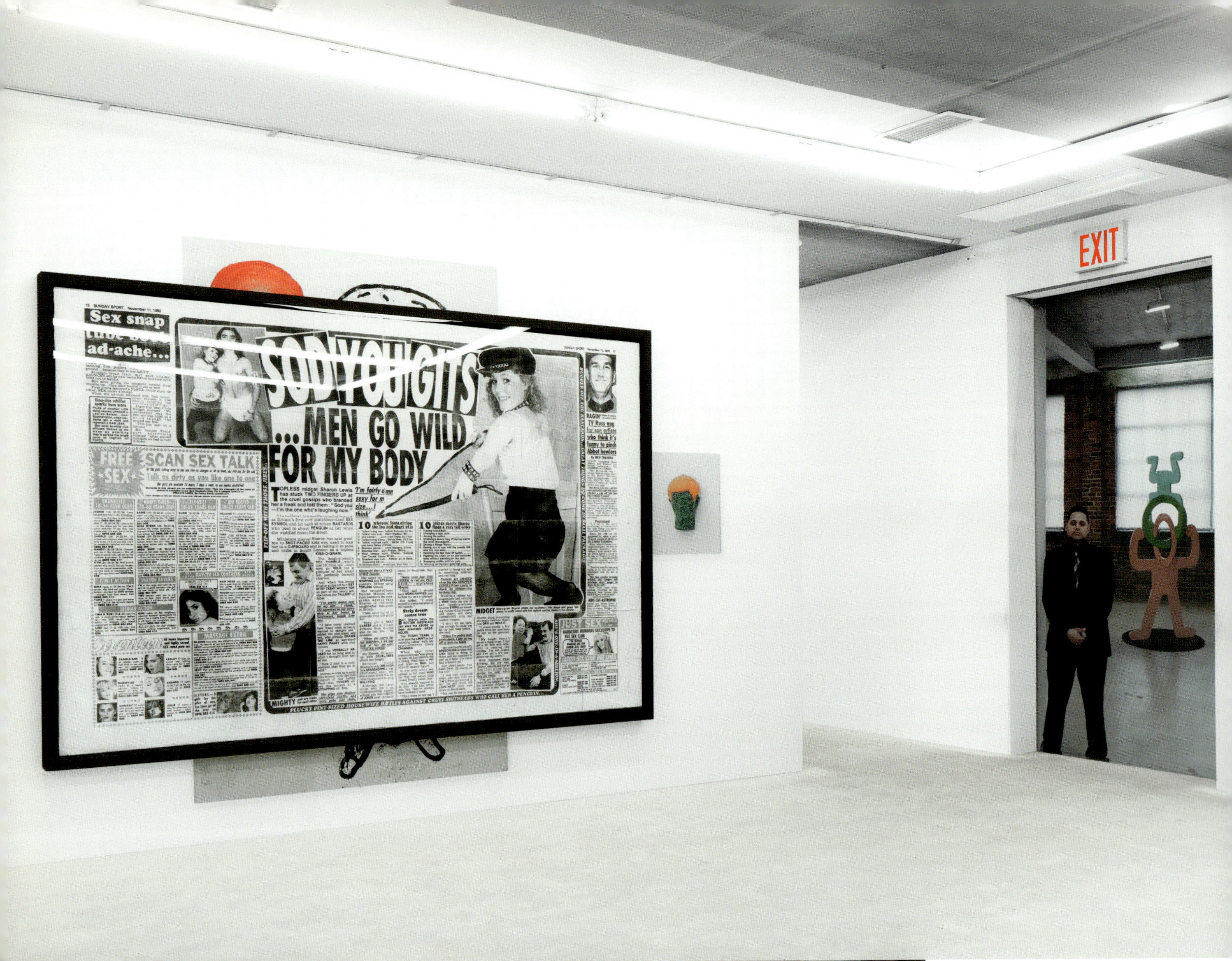

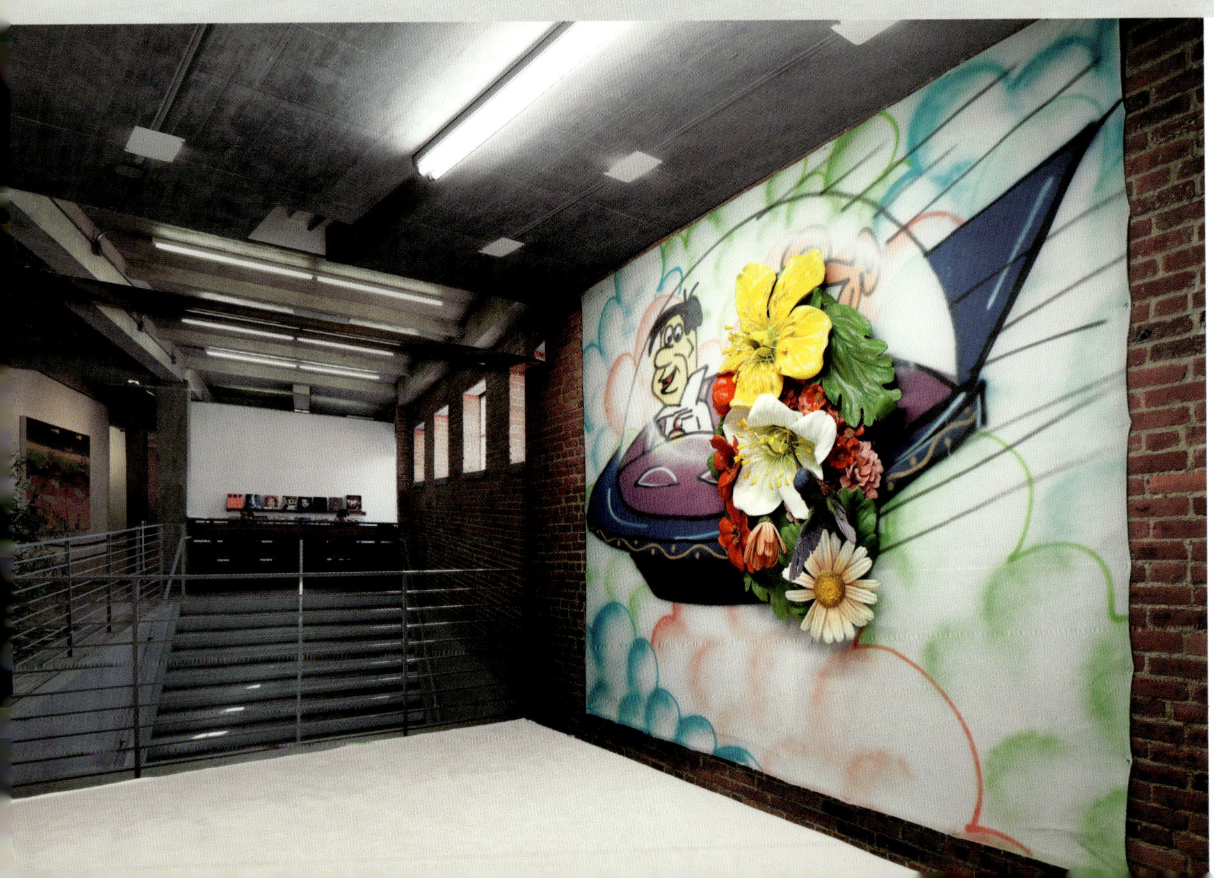

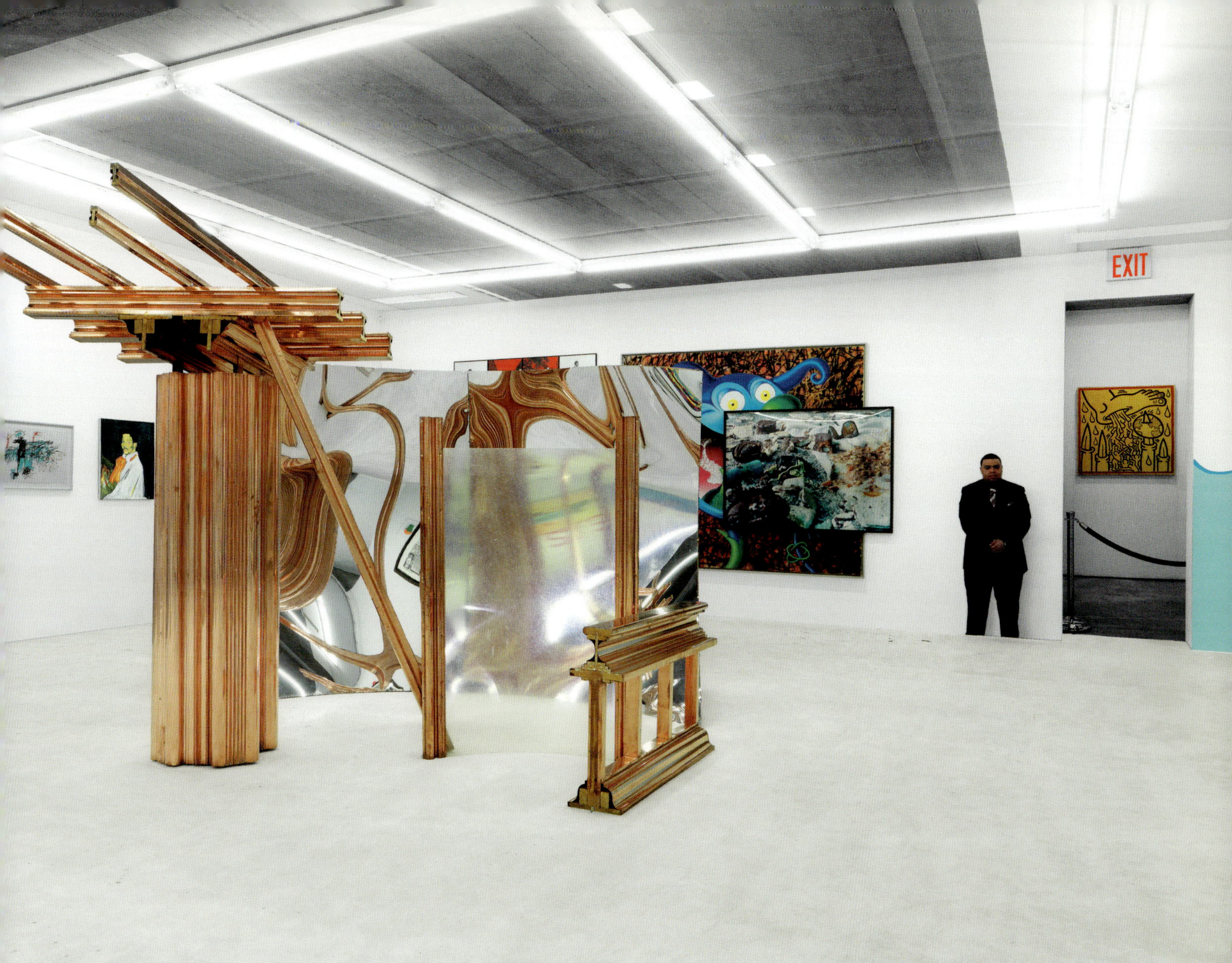

Installation view, "Who's Afraid of Jasper Johns?," Tony Shafrazi Gallery, New York, 2008
On wall: *Abstract Slavery*, 2008
Above: Mike Bidlo, *Not Picasso (Self-Portrait: Yo Picasso, 1901)*, 1986;
Robert Morris, *Untitled*, 1978; Cindy Sherman, *Untitled #175*, 1987
Opposite page, top: Sarah Lucas, *Sod You Gits*, 1990
Opposite page, bottom: Jeff Koons, *Wall Relief with Bird*, 1991

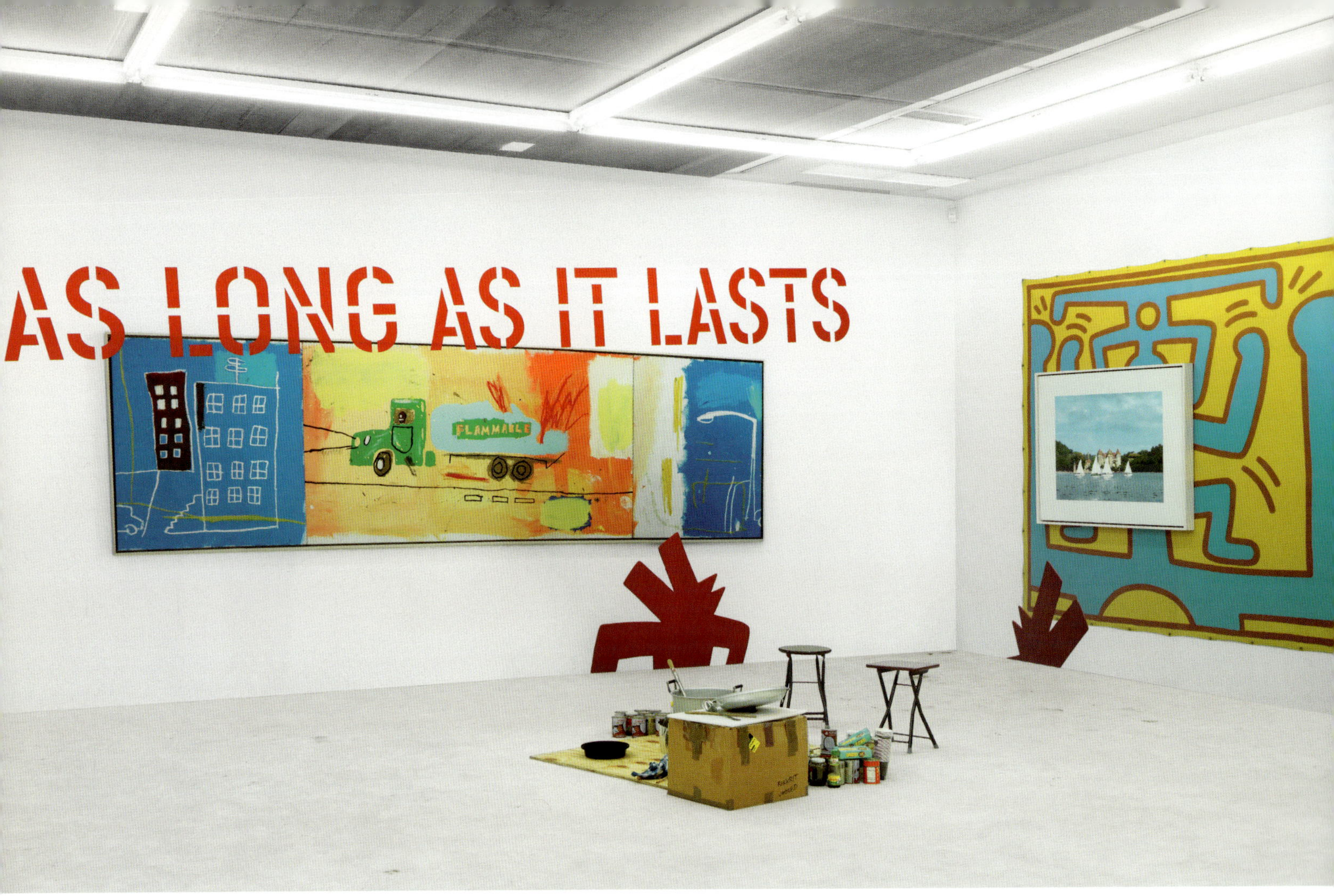

Installation view, "Who's Afraid of Jasper Johns?," Tony Shafrazi Gallery, New York, 2008
On wall: *Abstract Slavery*, 2008
Above: Lawrence Weiner, *AS LONG AS IT LASTS*, 1992;
Rirkrit Tiravanija, *Untitled (tom ka soup)*, 1991; Malcolm Morley, *Castle with Sailboats*, 1969
Opposite page, top: Gilbert & George, *MENTAL NO. 4*, 1976;
Cindy Sherman, *Untitled #175*, 1987
Opposite page, bottom: Rob Pruitt, *Eternal Bic*, 1999; Keith Haring, *Untitled*, 1984

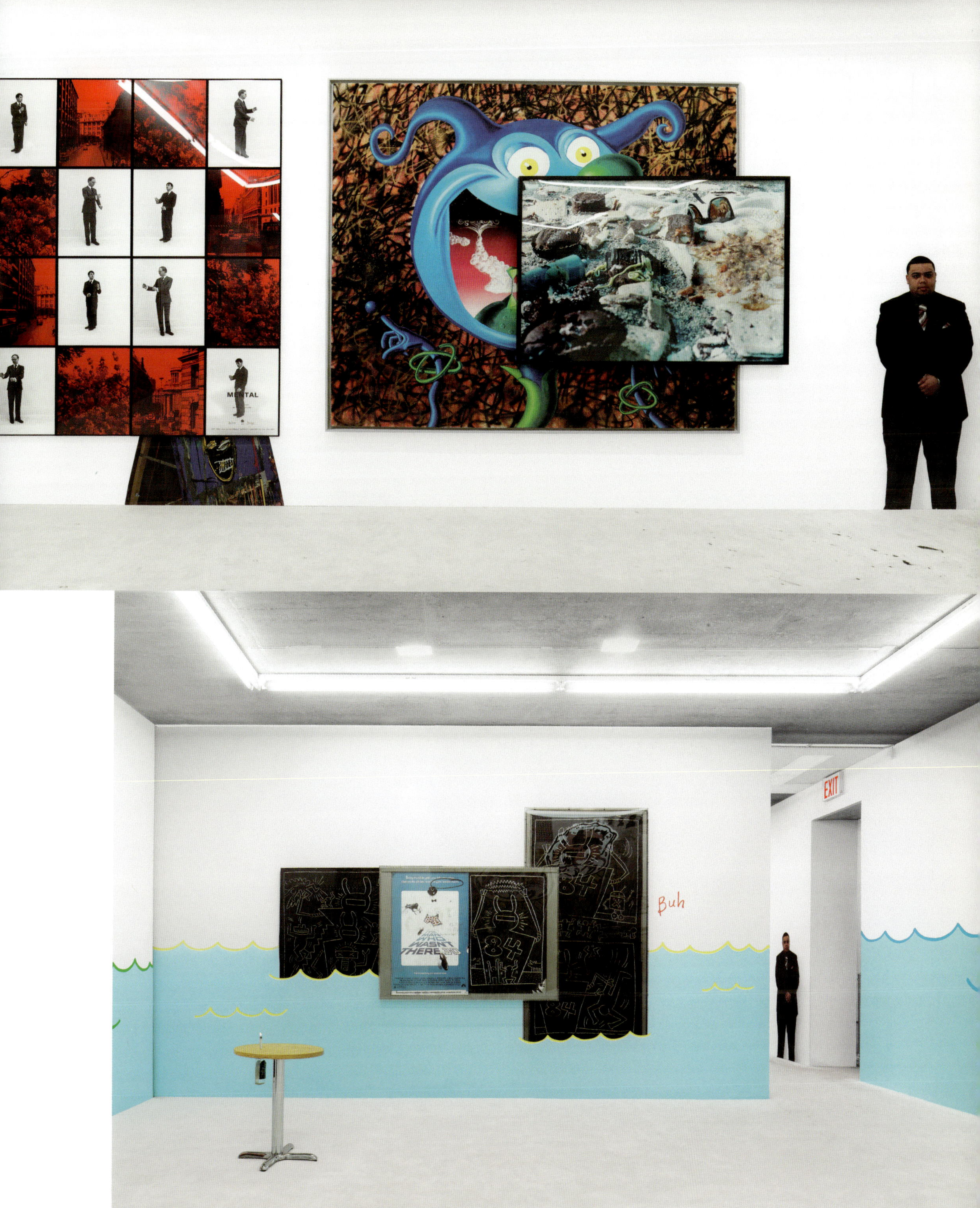
MENTAL
THE MAN WHO WASN'T THERE 3D
84
Buh
EXIT

Last Call, Lascaux, 2007

Wallpaper prints of photographic reproductions of interior spaces—content, scale, and lighting determined on a site-specific basis (1:1 scale color photographic reproduction of the empty gallery space illuminated by fluorescent light)
Dimensions variable
Installation view, "Urs Fischer: Marguerite de Ponty," New Museum, New York, 2009–2010

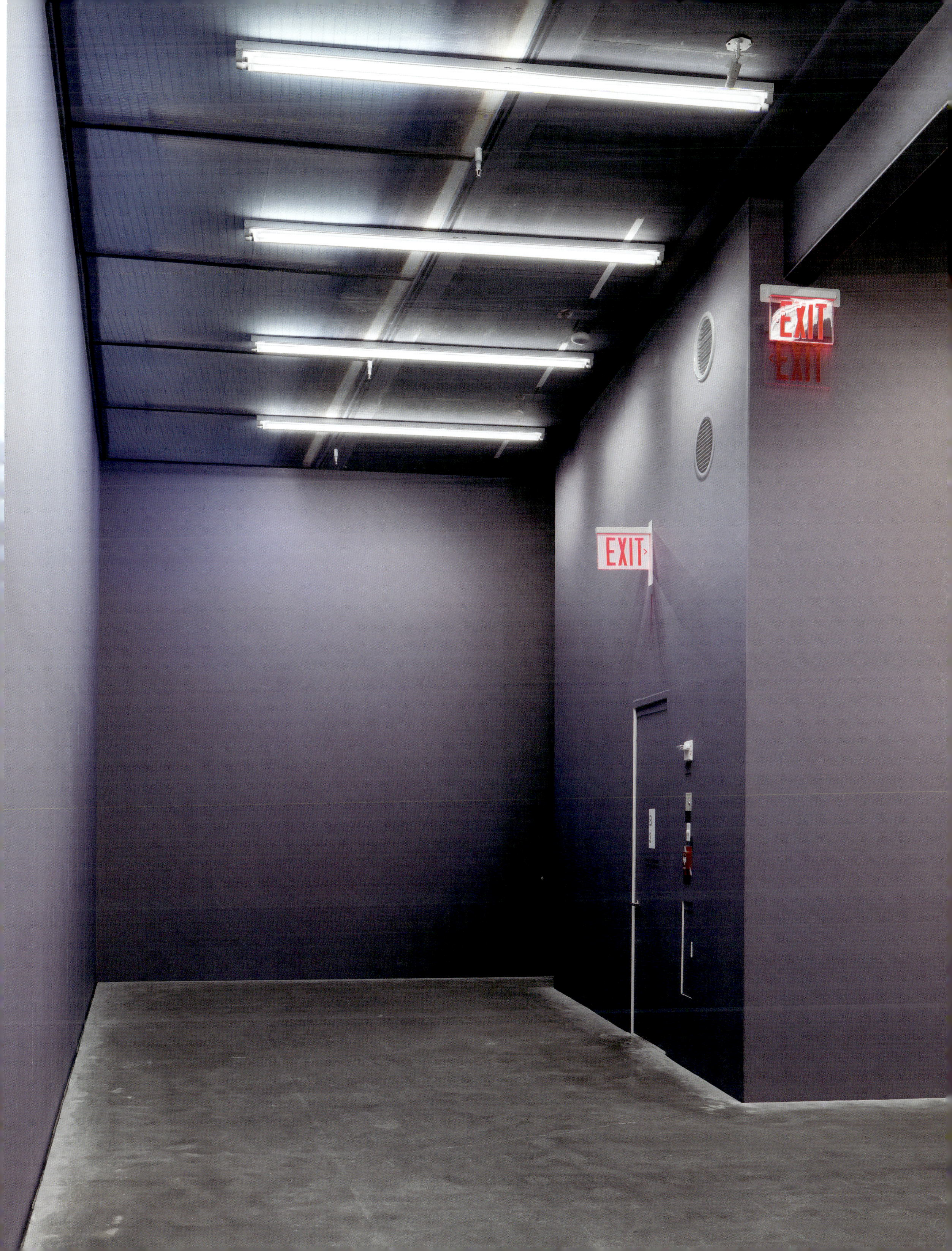
EXIT
EXIT

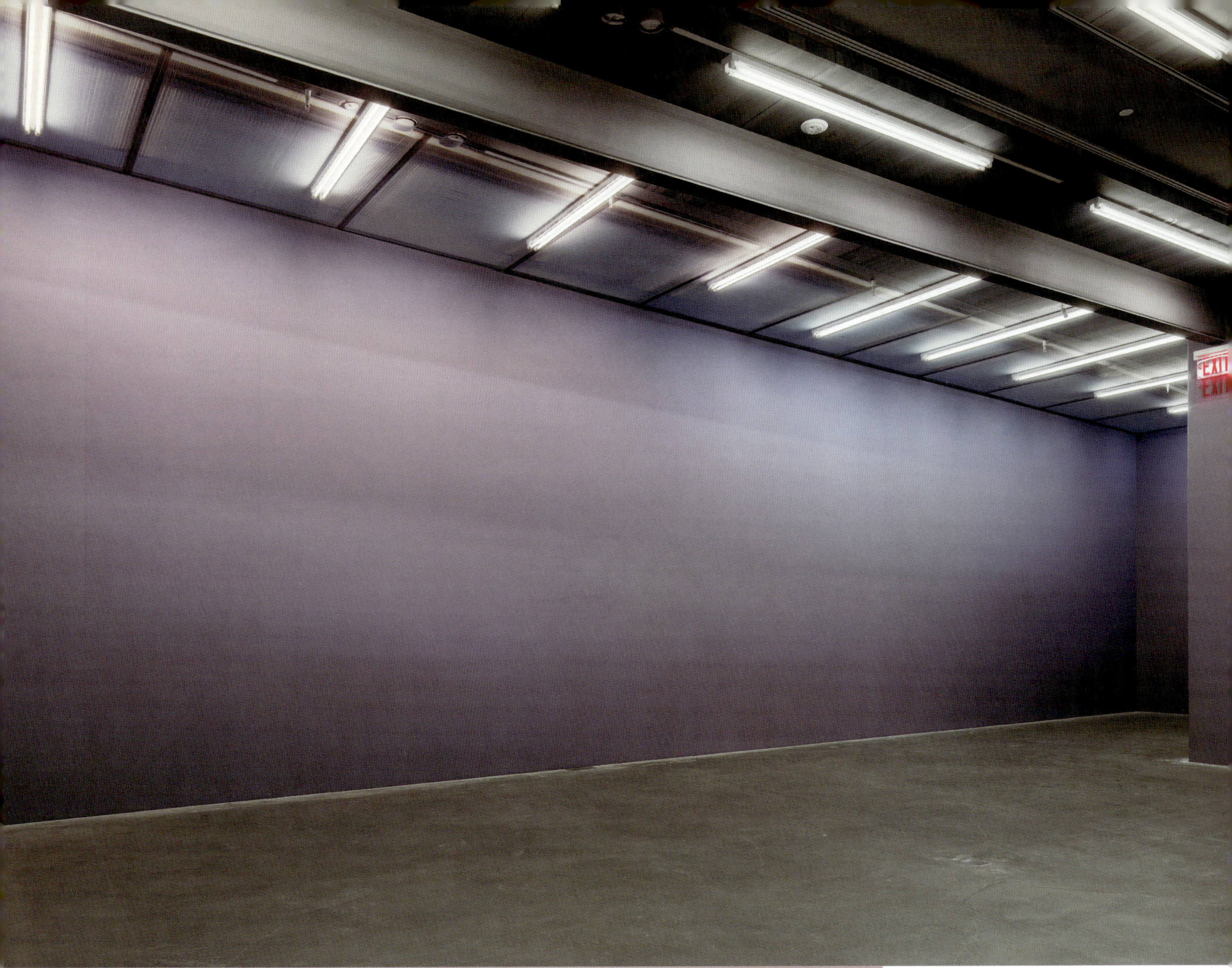

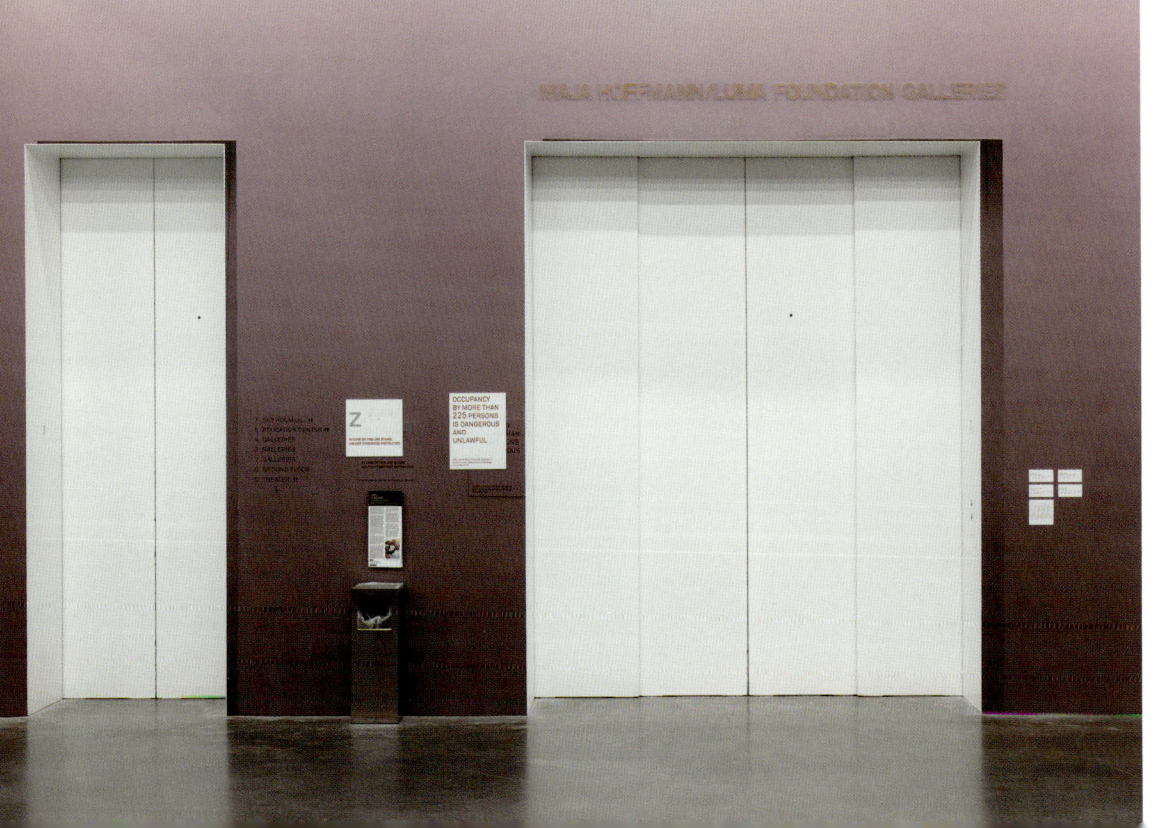
MAJA HOFFMANN/LUMA FOUNDATION GALLERIES
OCCUPANCY BY MORE THAN 225 PERSONS IS DANGEROUS AND UNLAWFUL

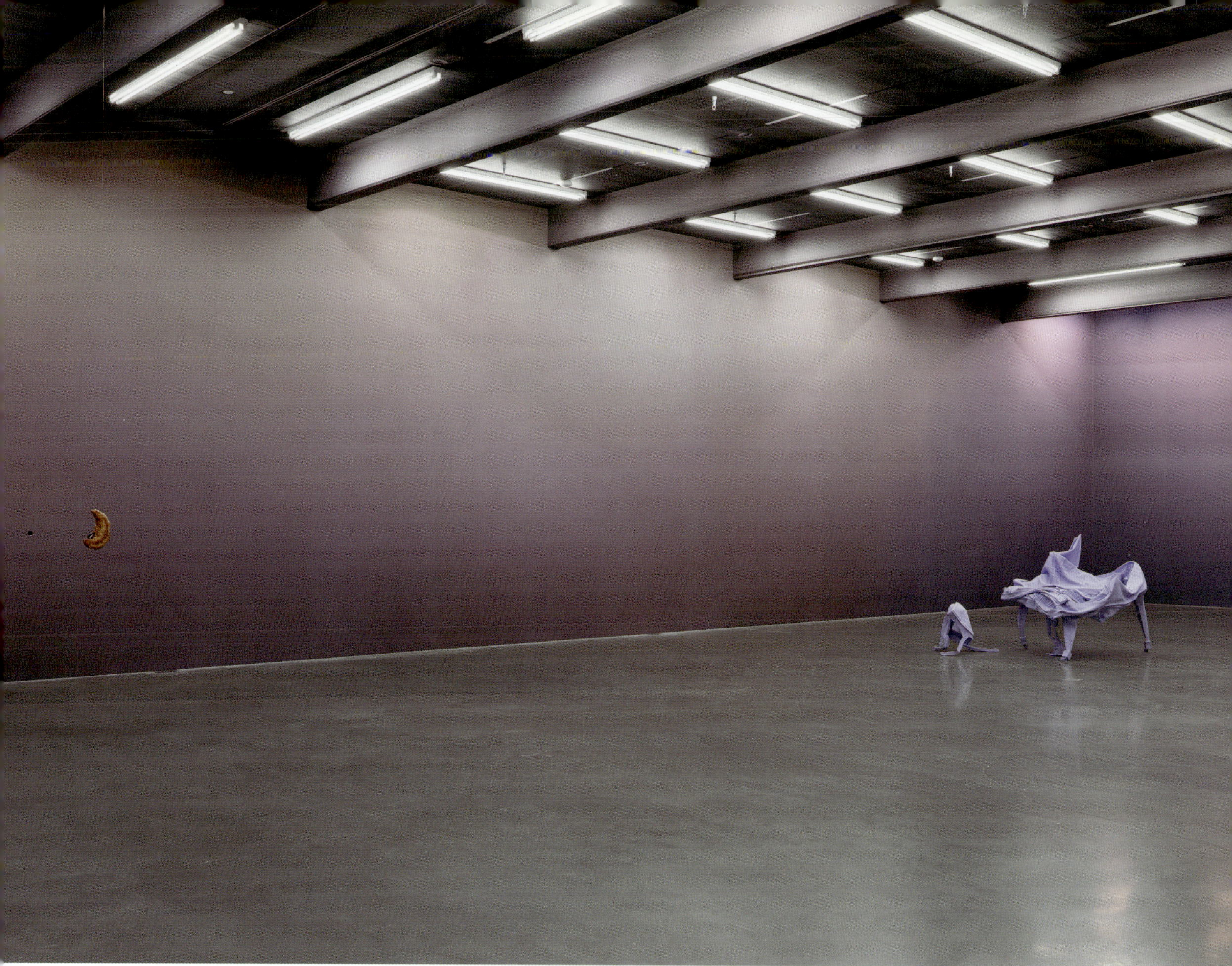

Installation view, "Urs Fischer: Marguerite de Ponty," New Museum, New York, 2009–2010
On wall: *Last Call, Lascaux*, 2009
Above: *Cumpadre*, 2009; *Untitled*, 2009; In wall: *Noisette*, 2009
Page 57: In wall: *Noisette*, 2009

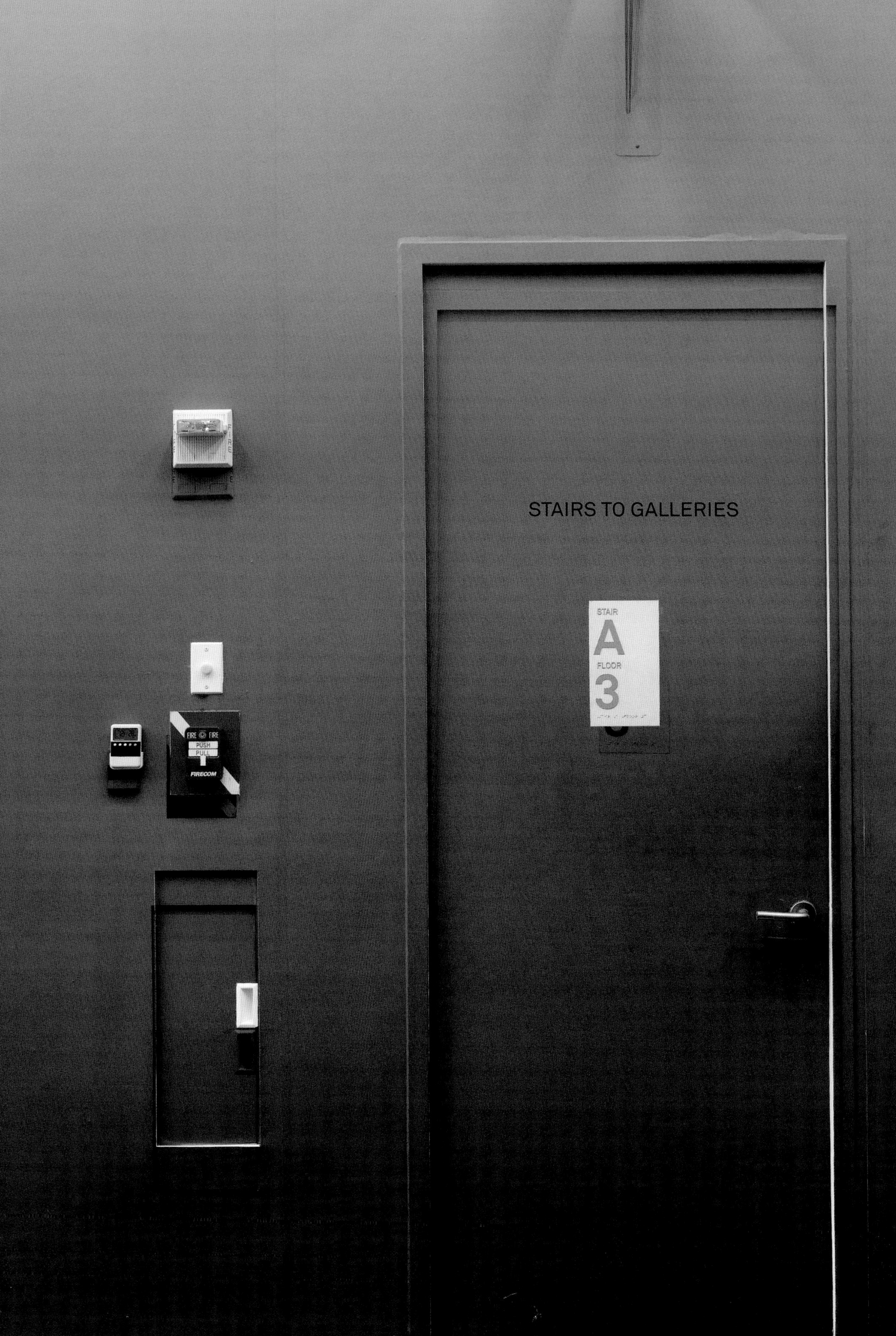
STAIRS TO GALLERIES
STAIR
A
FLOOR
3
FIRE
PUSH
PULL
FIRECOM

Abstract Slavery, 2008

Wallpaper prints of photographic reproductions of interior spaces—content, scale, and lighting determined on a site-specific basis (9:10 scale color photographic reproduction of the Brant family's living room and library)
Installation view, "Oscar the Grouch,"
The Brant Foundation Art Study Center, Greenwich, Connecticut, 2010–2011

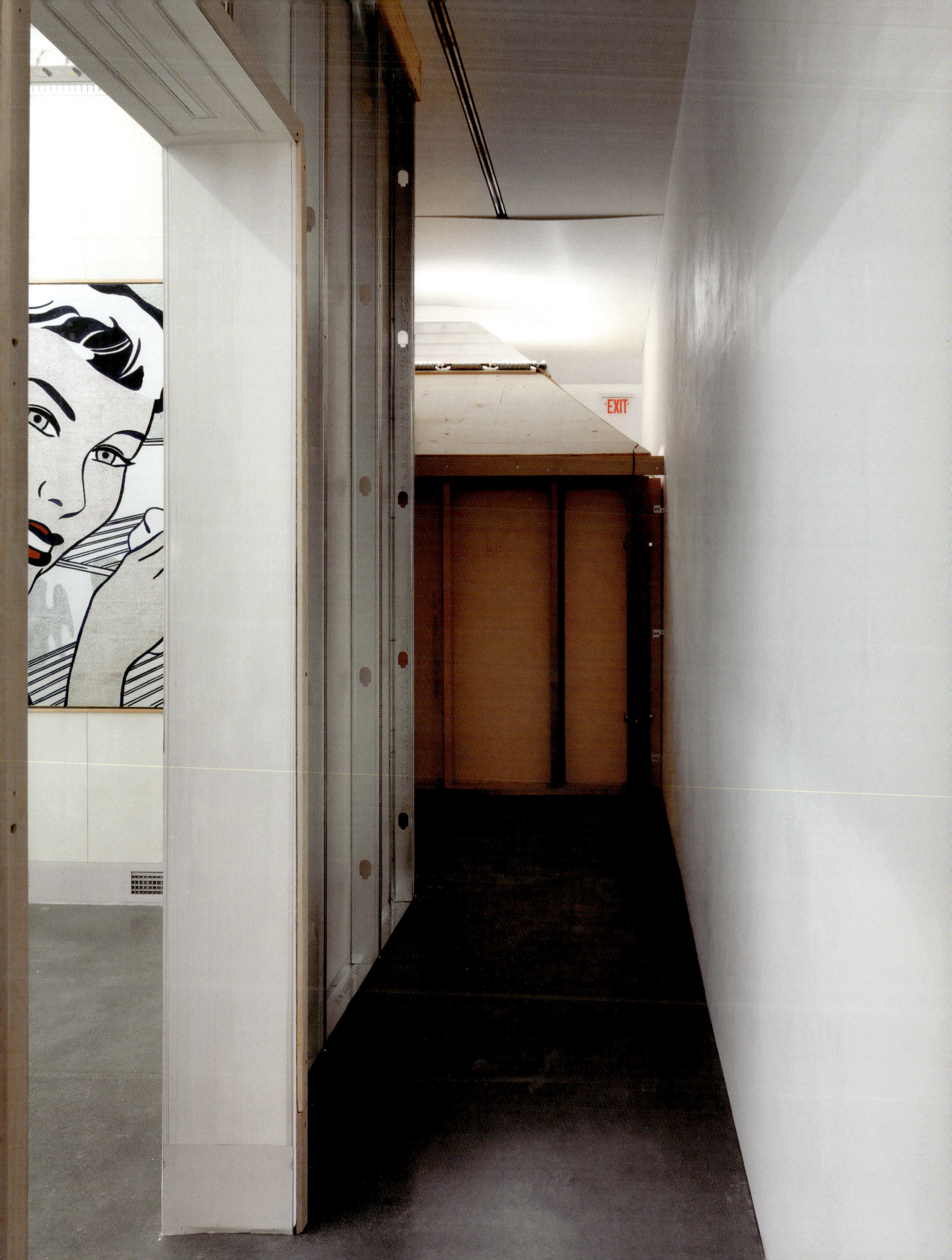
EXIT

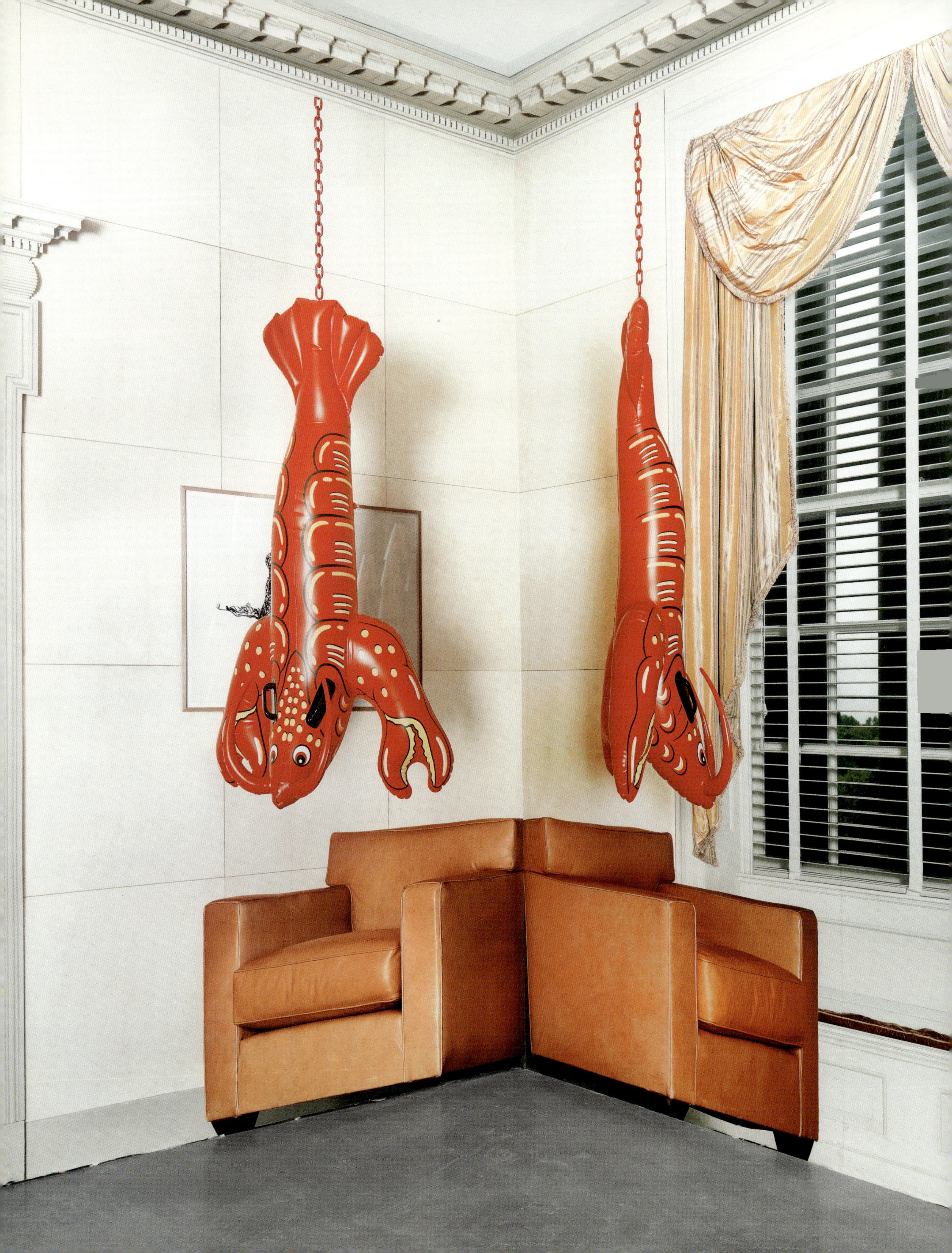

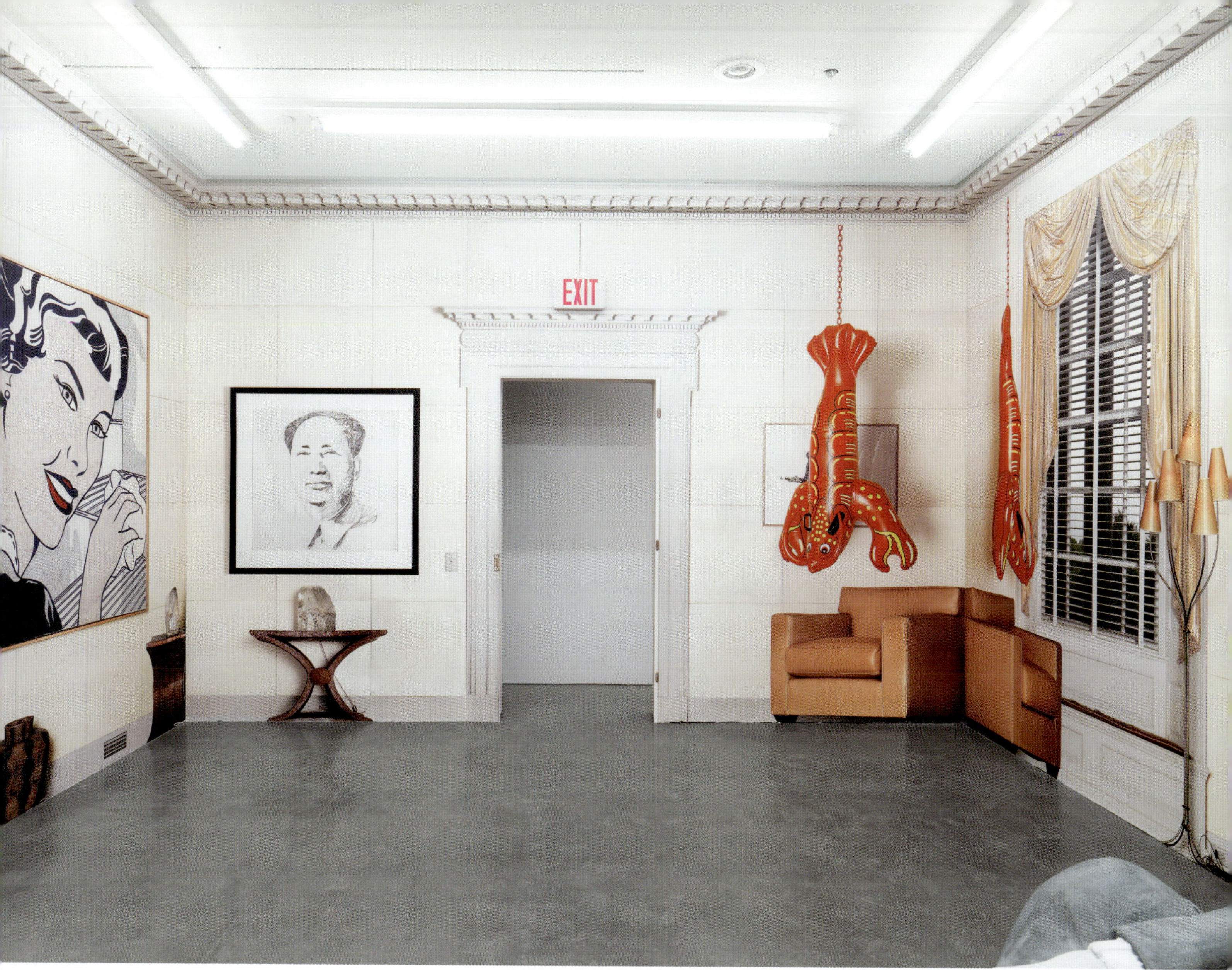
EXIT

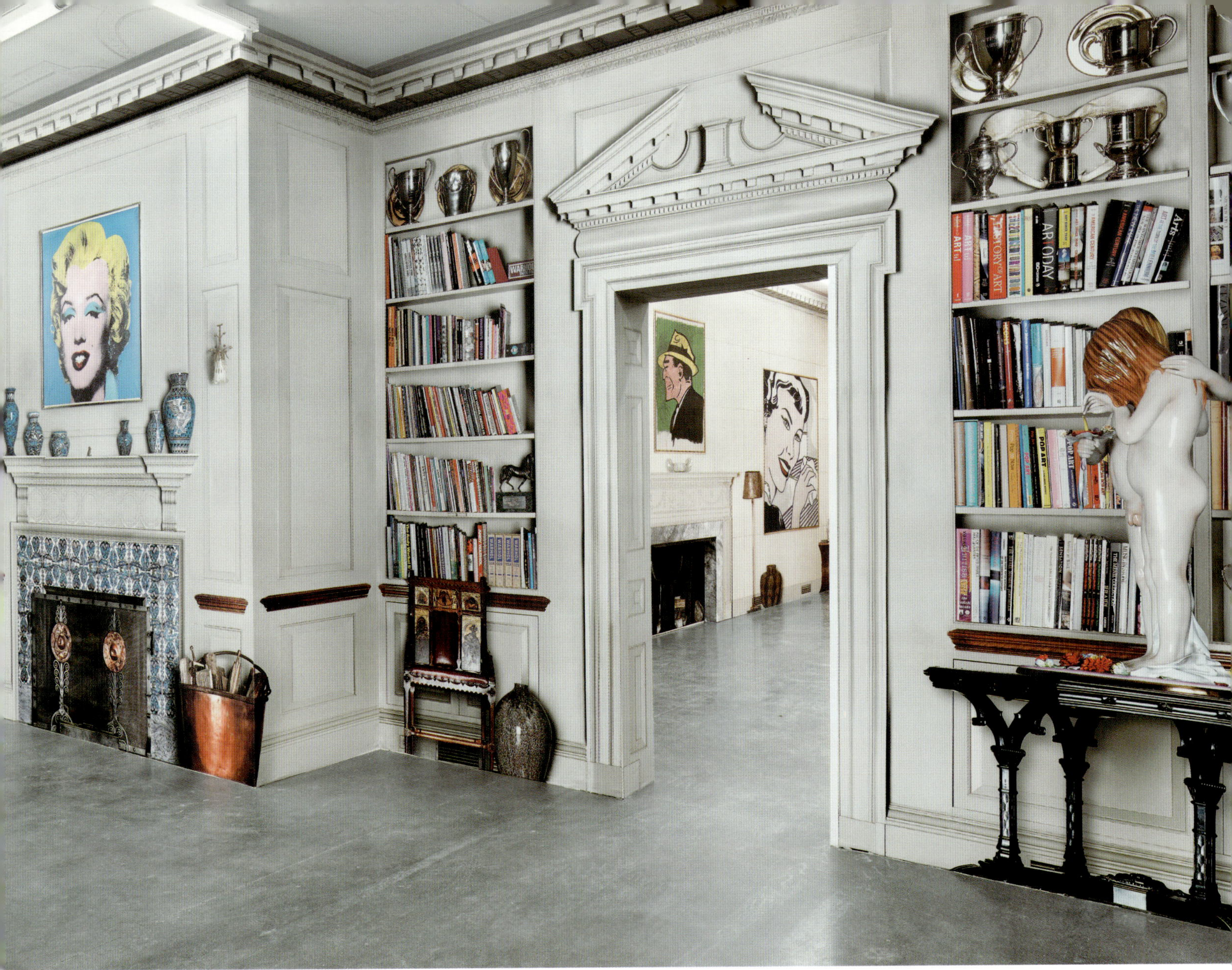

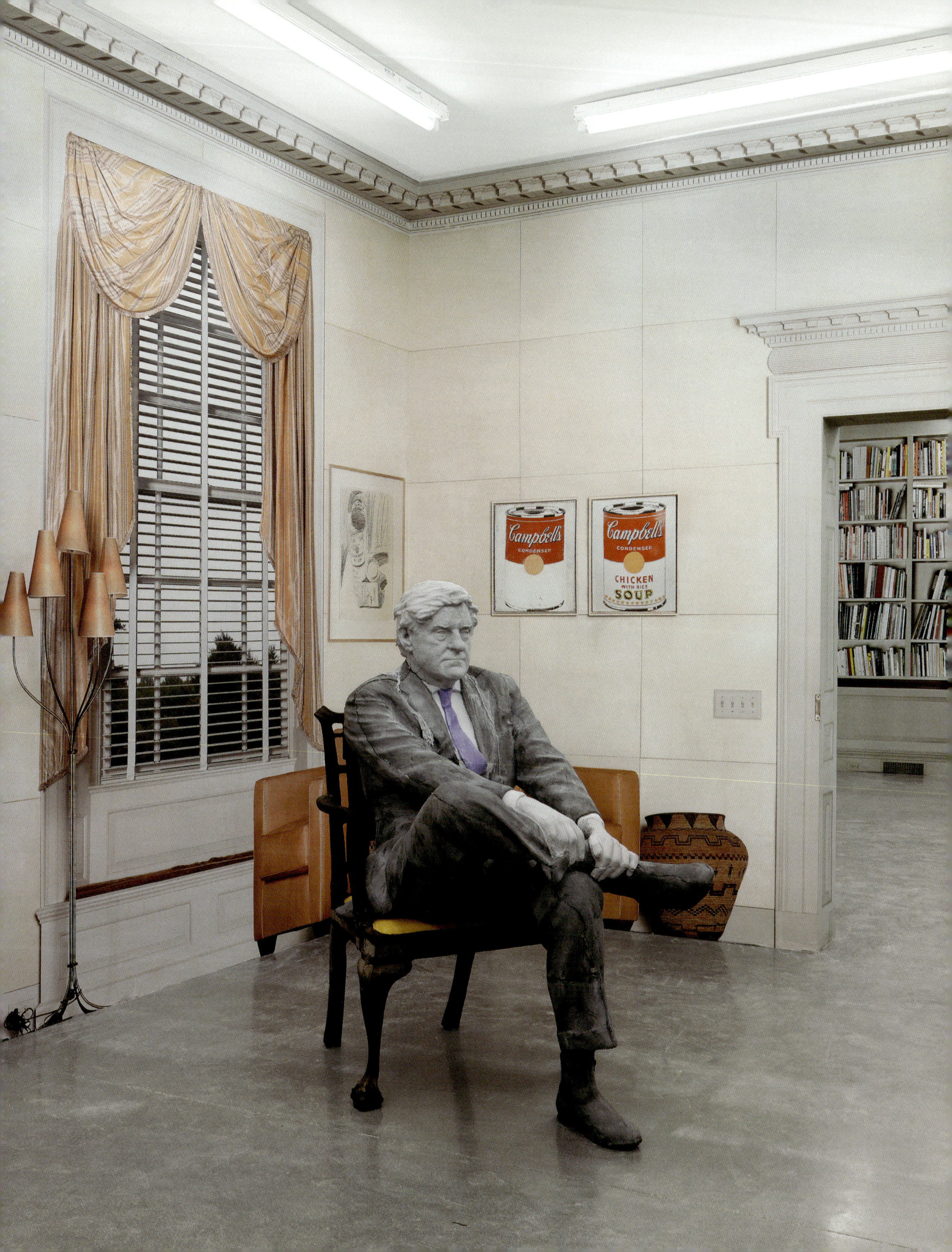
Campbell's
CONDENSED
Campbell's
CONDENSED
CHICKEN
WITH RICE
SOUP

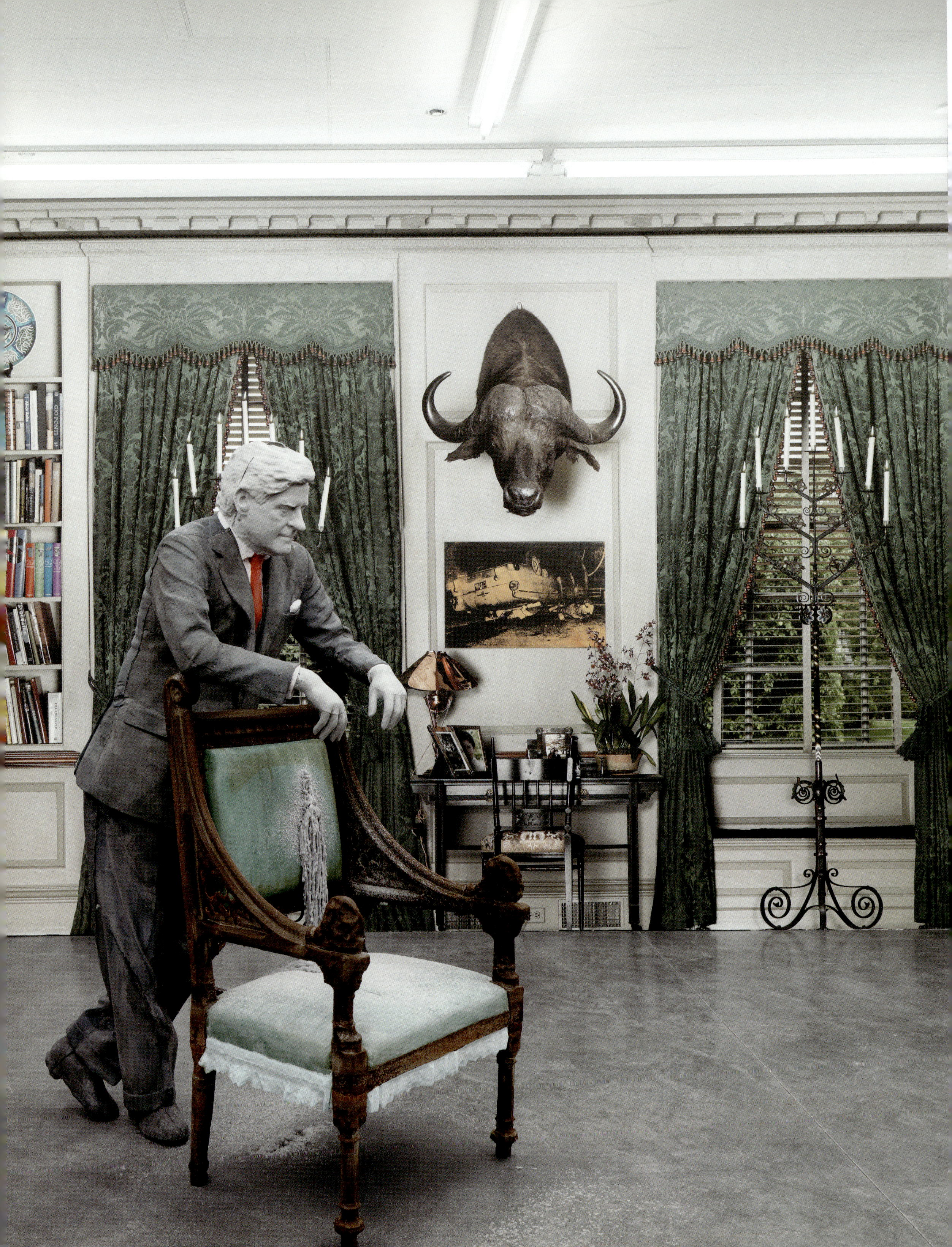

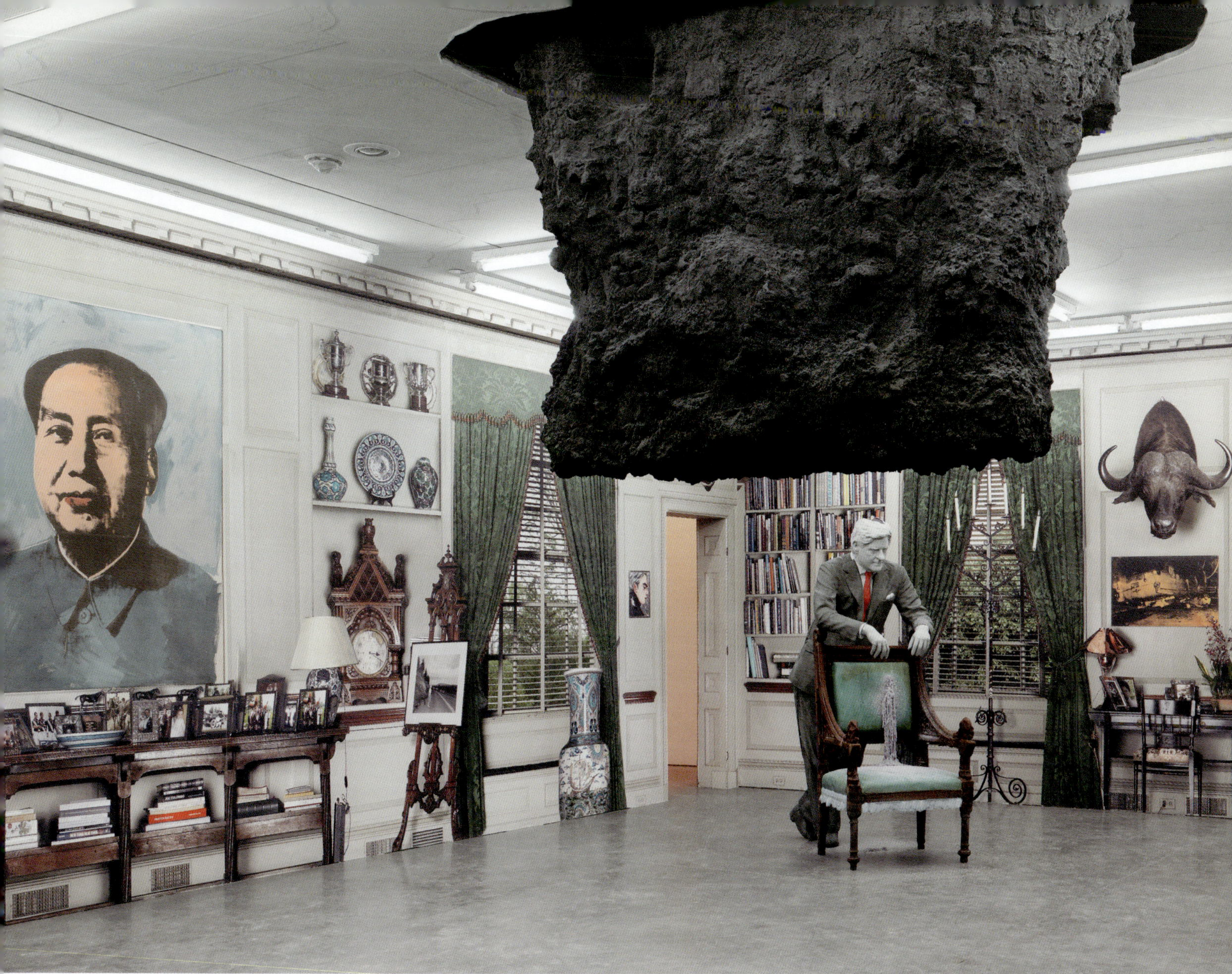

Installation view, "Oscar the Grouch," The Brant Foundation Art Study Center, Greenwich, Connecticut, 2010–2011
On wall: *Abstract Slavery*, 2008
Above: *Untitled (Hole)*, 2007; *Untitled (Standing)*, 2010
Opposite page: *Untitled (Standing)*, 2010
Page 63: *Untitled (Seated)*, 2010

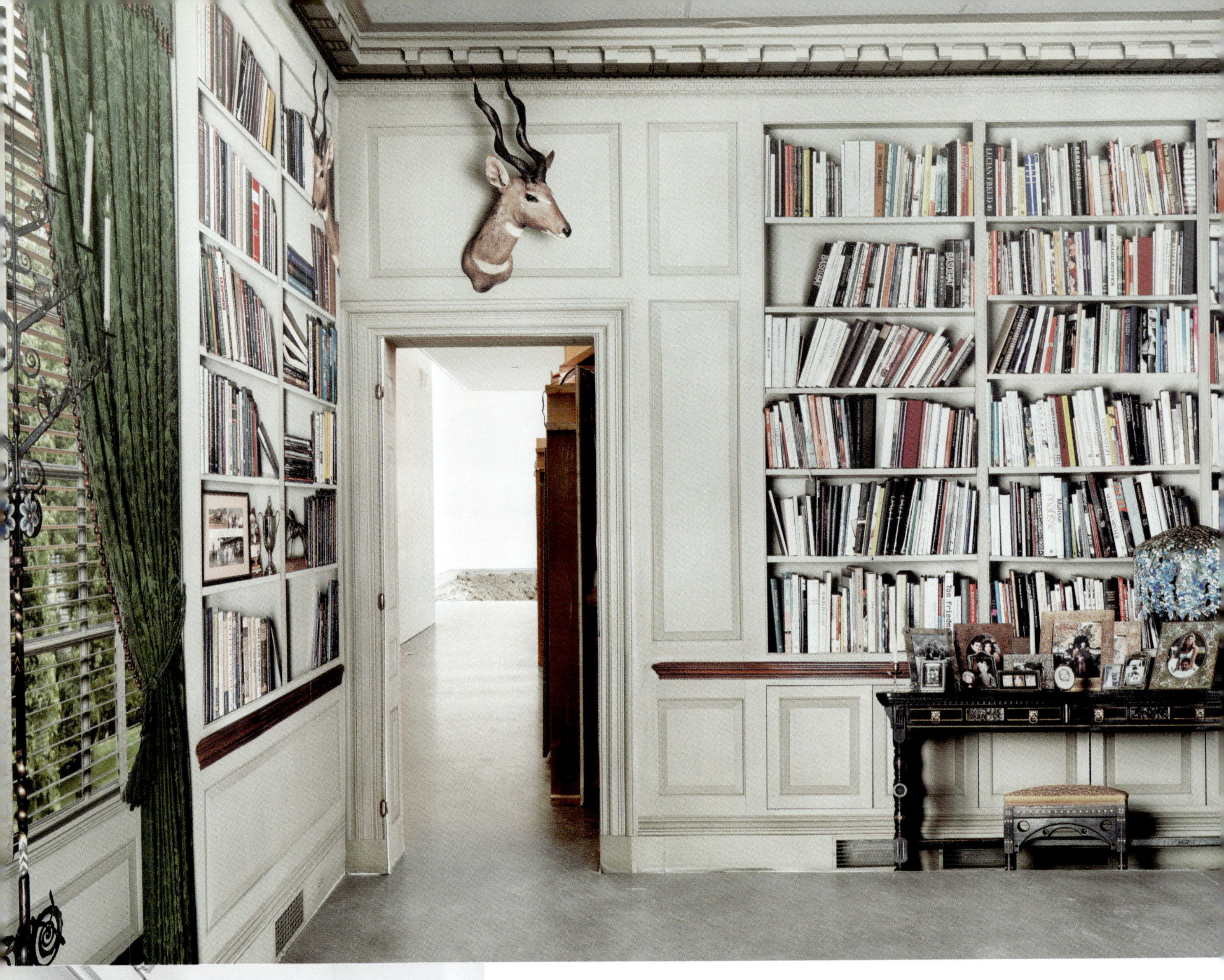

Installation view, "Oscar the Grouch," The Brant Foundation Art Study Center, Greenwich, Connecticut, 2010–2011
On wall: *Abstract Slavery*, 2008
Left: *Footnote to "You,"* 2010; *Untitled (Standing)*, 2010

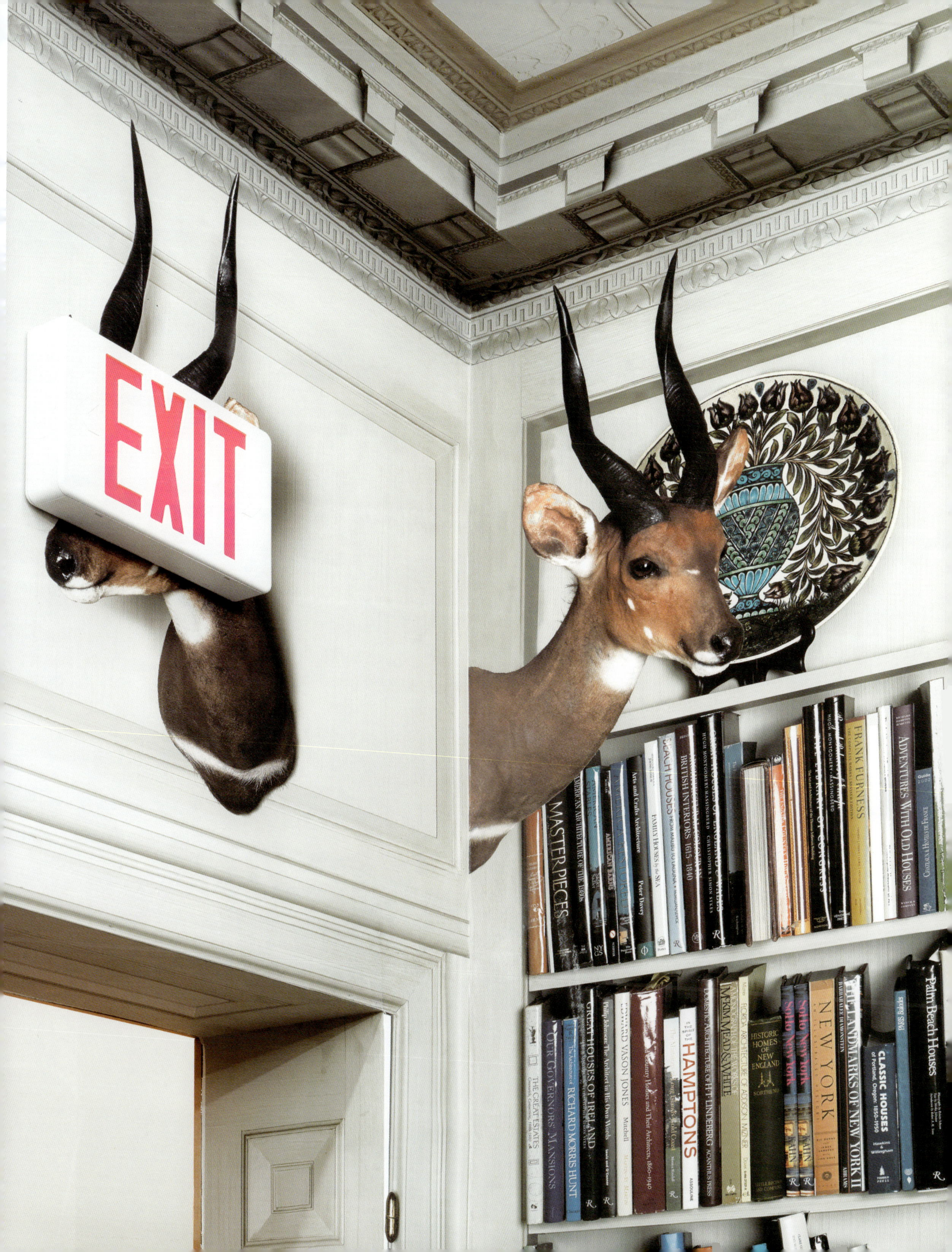
EXIT
MASTERPIECES
Arts and Crafts Architecture
Peter Davey
BEACH HOUSES
FAMILY HOUSES by the SEA
BRITISH INTERIORS 1615 1840
LIBRARY OF CONGRESS
FRANK FURNESS
ADVENTURES WITH OLD HOUSES
OUR GOVERNORS' MANSIONS
THE GREAT ESTATES
RICHARD MORRIS HUNT
GREAT HOUSES OF IRELAND
EDWARD VASON JONES
HAMPTONS
McKIM MEAD & WHITE
ADDISON MIZNER
HISTORIC HOMES OF NEW ENGLAND
NEW YORK
LANDMARKS OF NEW YORK II
CLASSIC HOUSES
Palm Beach Houses

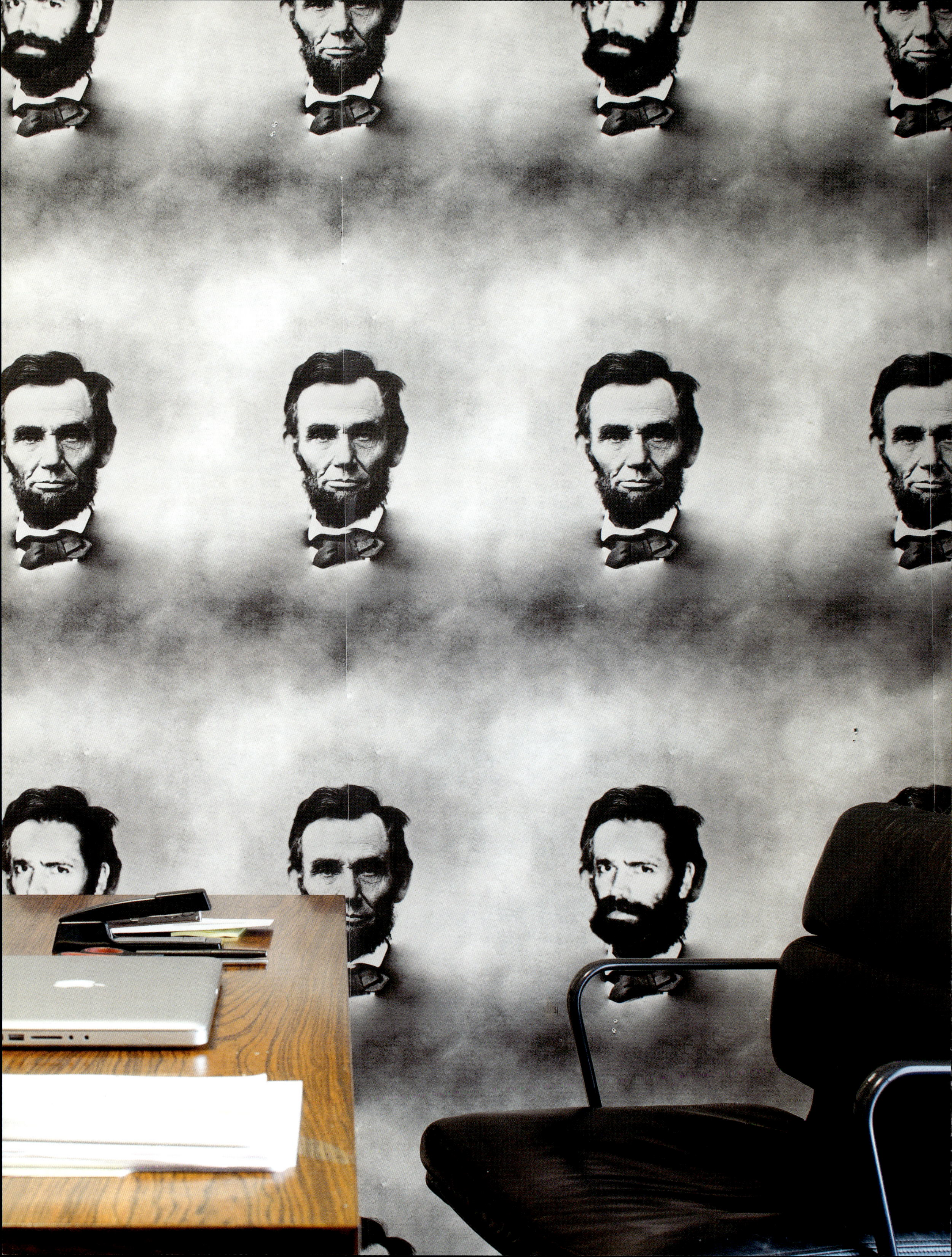

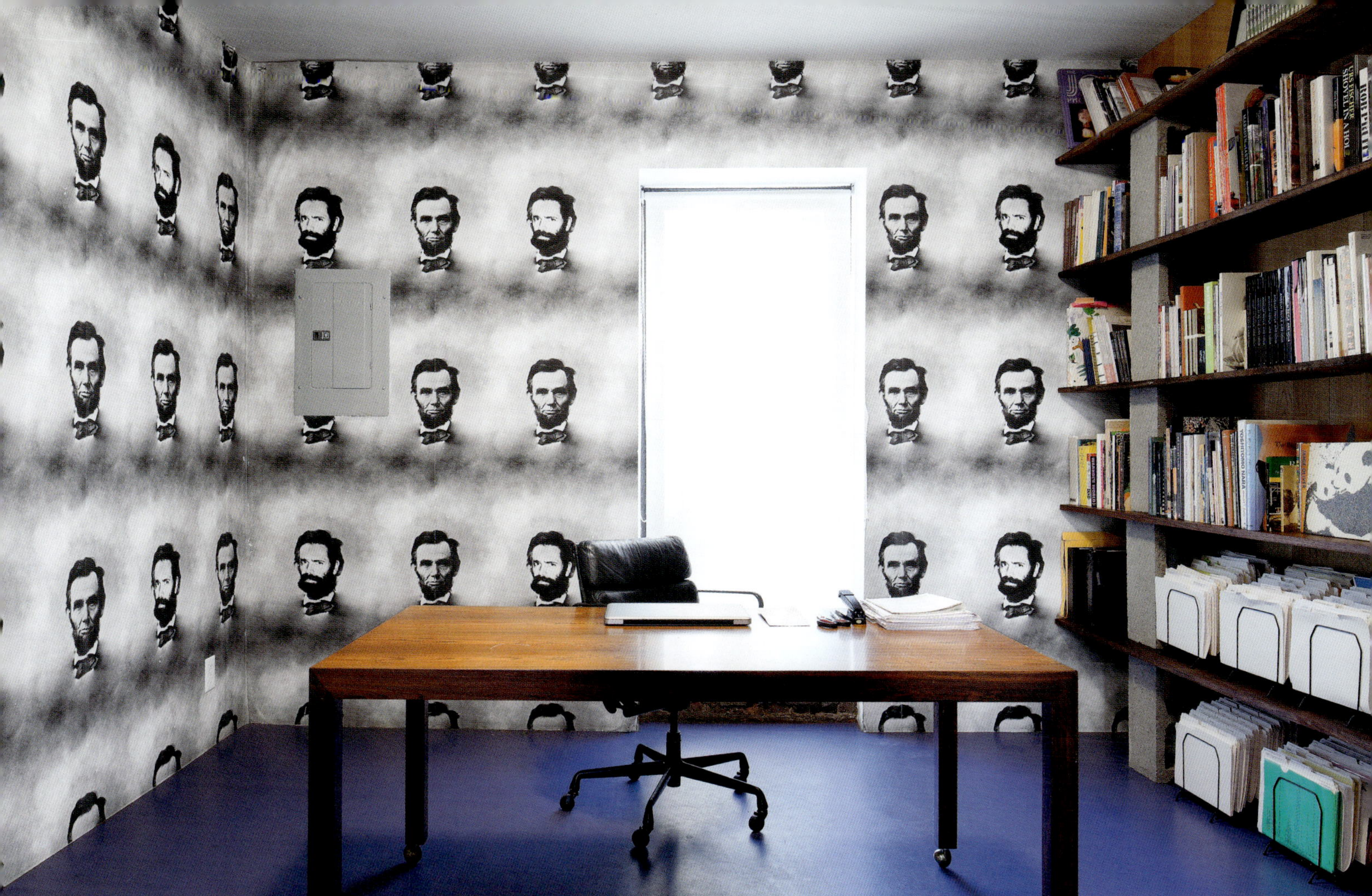

Daphne Brown, 2008
Inkjet wallpaper prints on nylon reinforced paper
Dimensions variable
Installation view, Office, Gavin Brown's enterprise, New York

Untitled (Floor Piece), 2006

Black adhesive vinyl, latex paint

Dimensions variable

Installation view, "Mary Poppins," Blaffer Gallery,
The Art Museum of the University of Houston, Texas, 2006

Nach Jugendstiel kam Roccoko, 2006; *Addict*, 2006

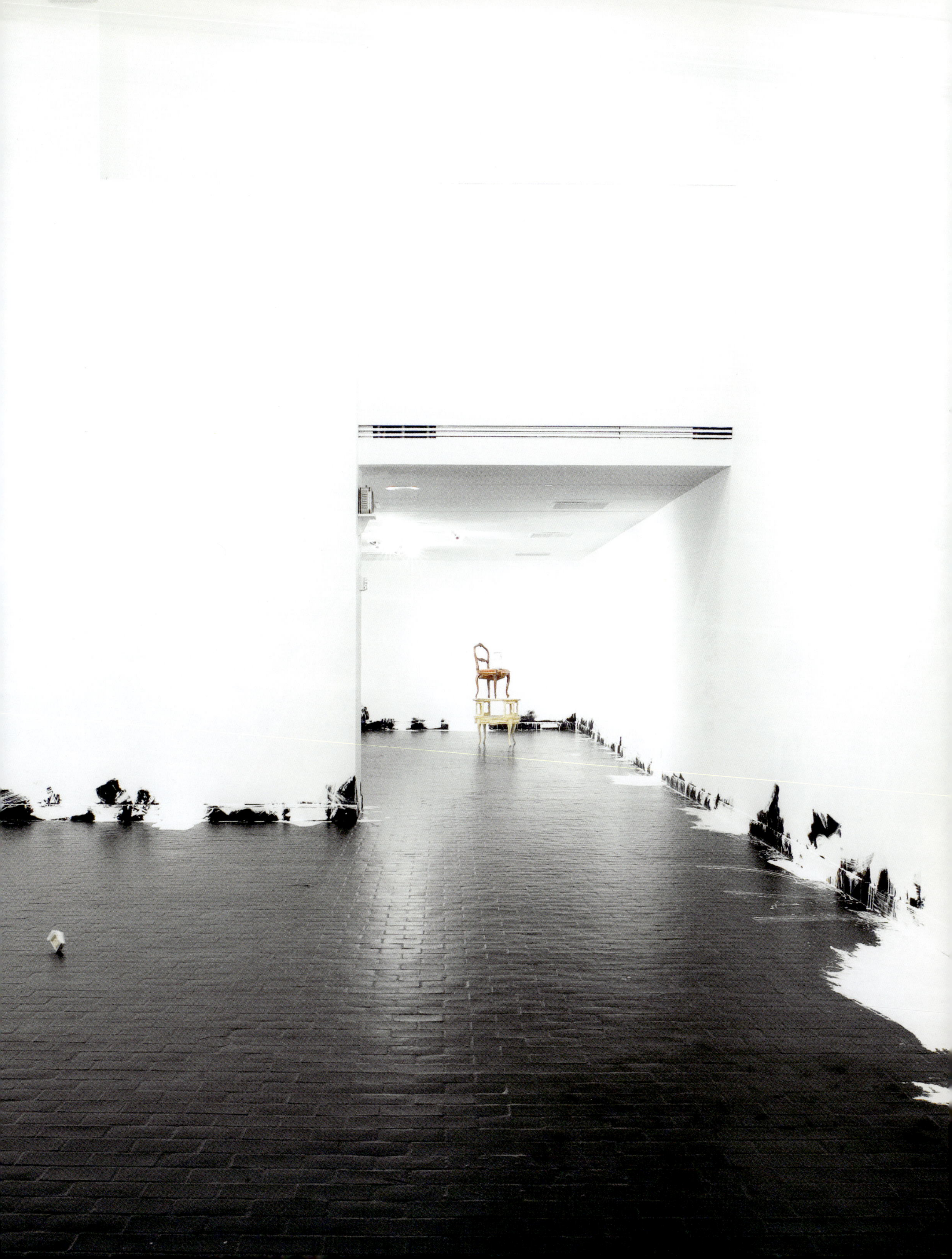

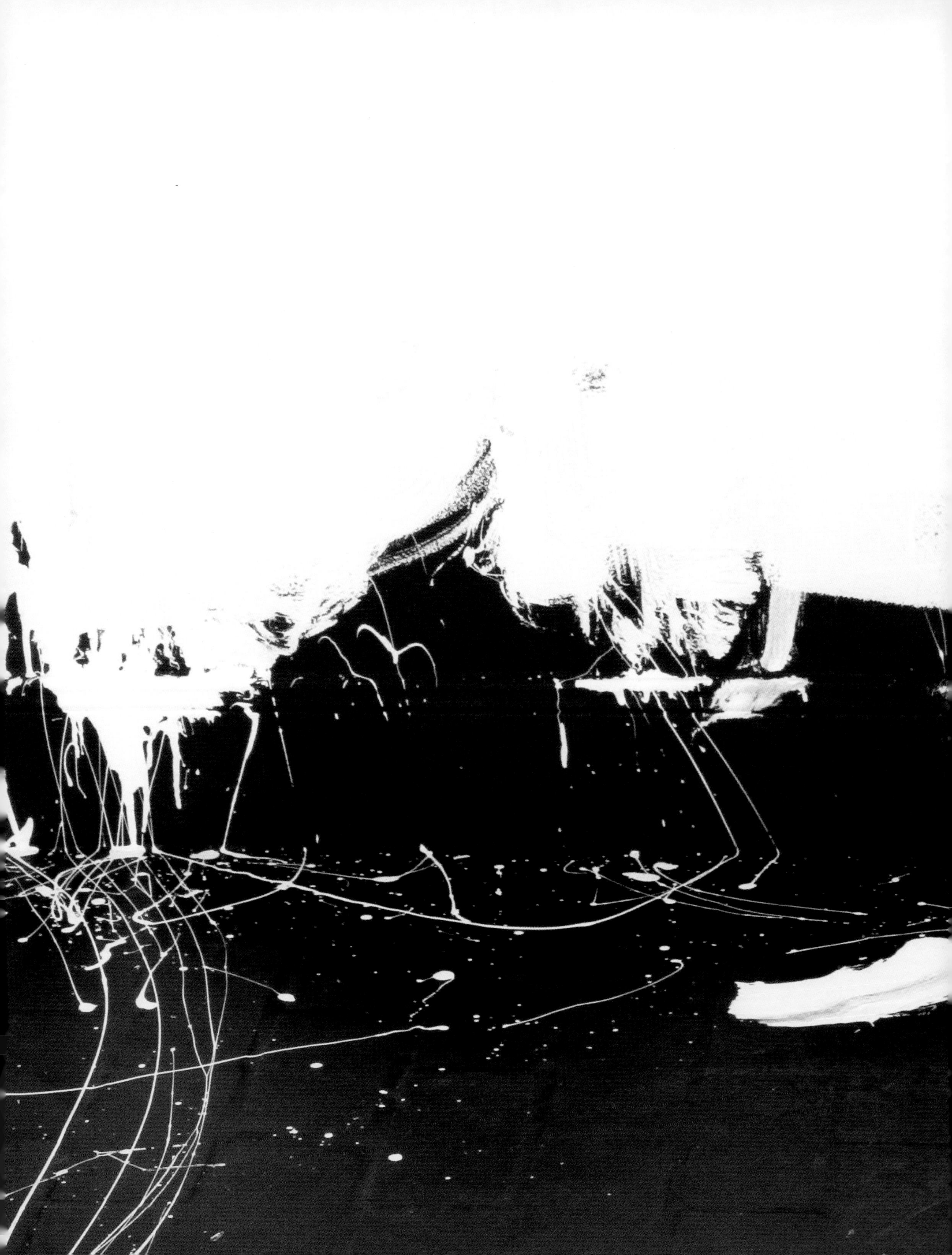

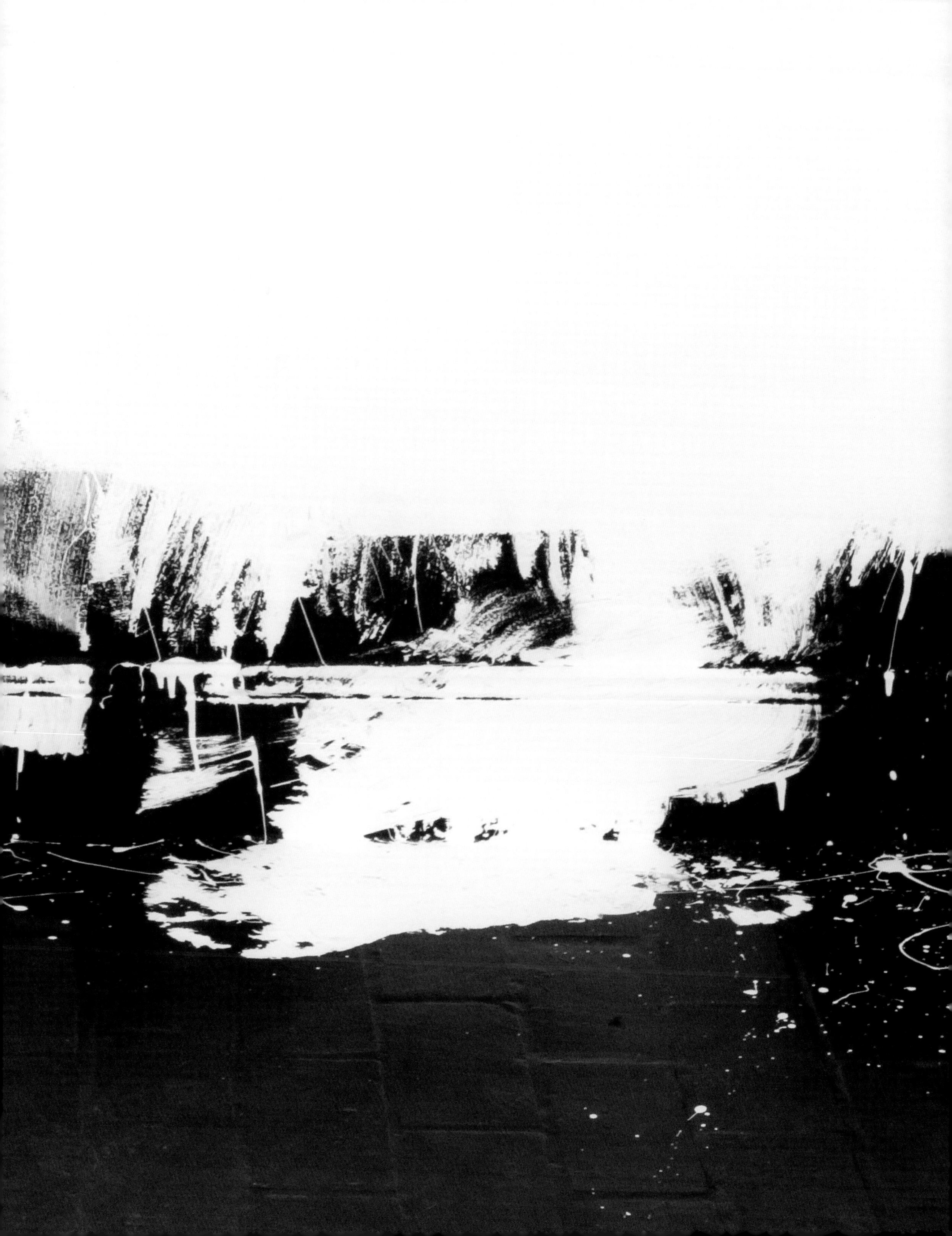

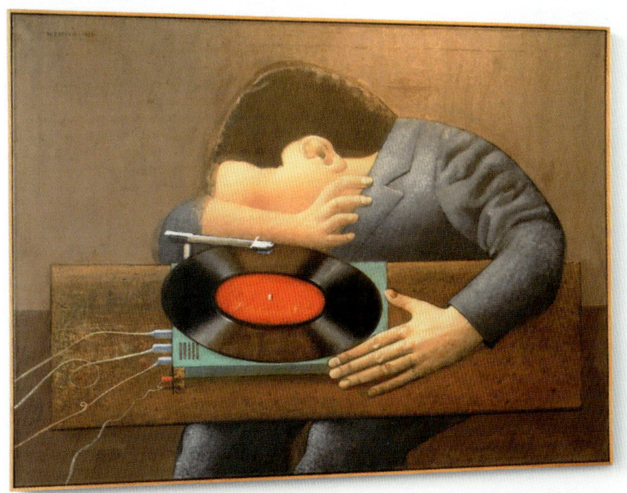

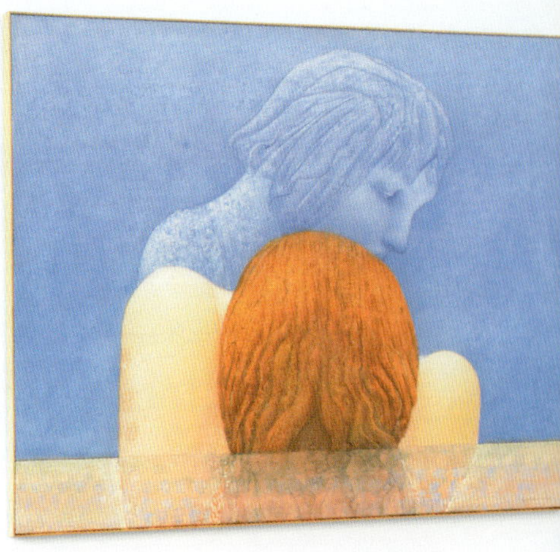

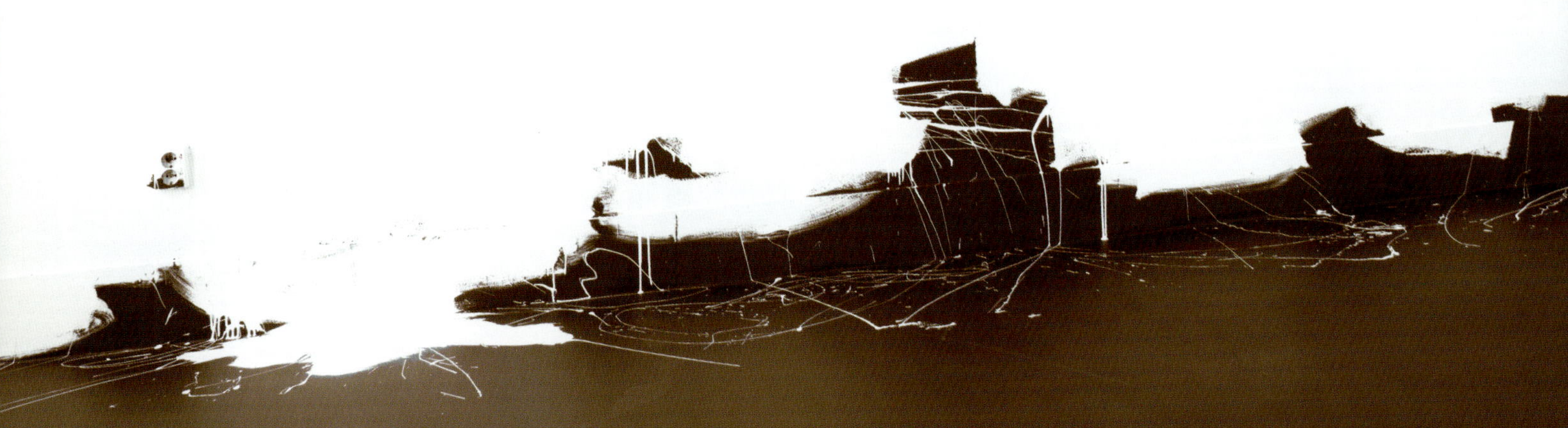

Barfuss mit Erich Muehsam, 2006
Brown adhesive vinyl, acrylic paint
Dimensions variable
Installation view, "Collection 1," Museum Boijmans Van Beuningen, Rotterdam, 2006–2008
Above: Co Westerik, *Gramophone-player*, 1971; Co Westerik, *Girl with hair in the water*, 1982
Opposite page: James Rosenquist, *Discs*, 1965; Christo, *Package on luggage rack*, 1962

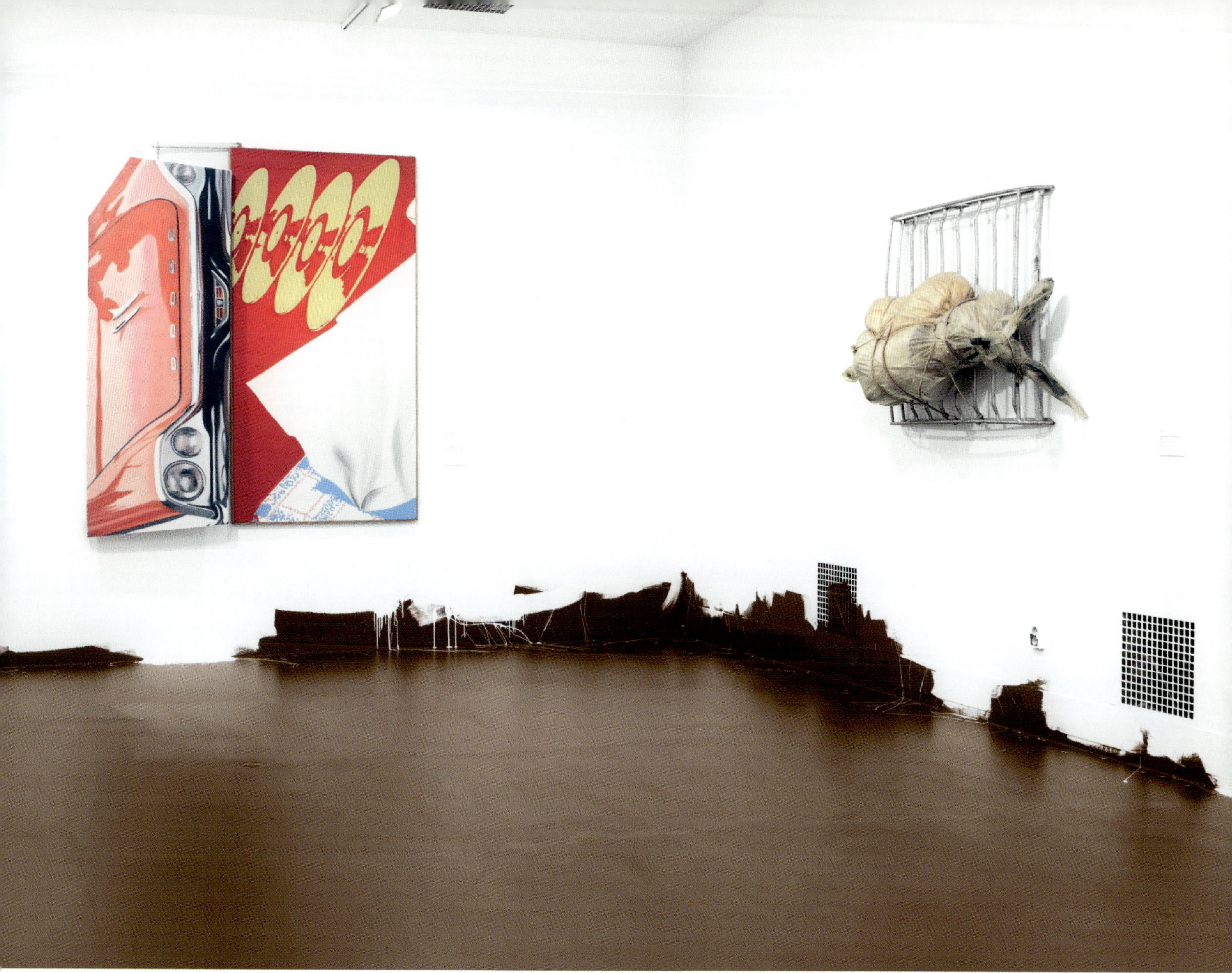

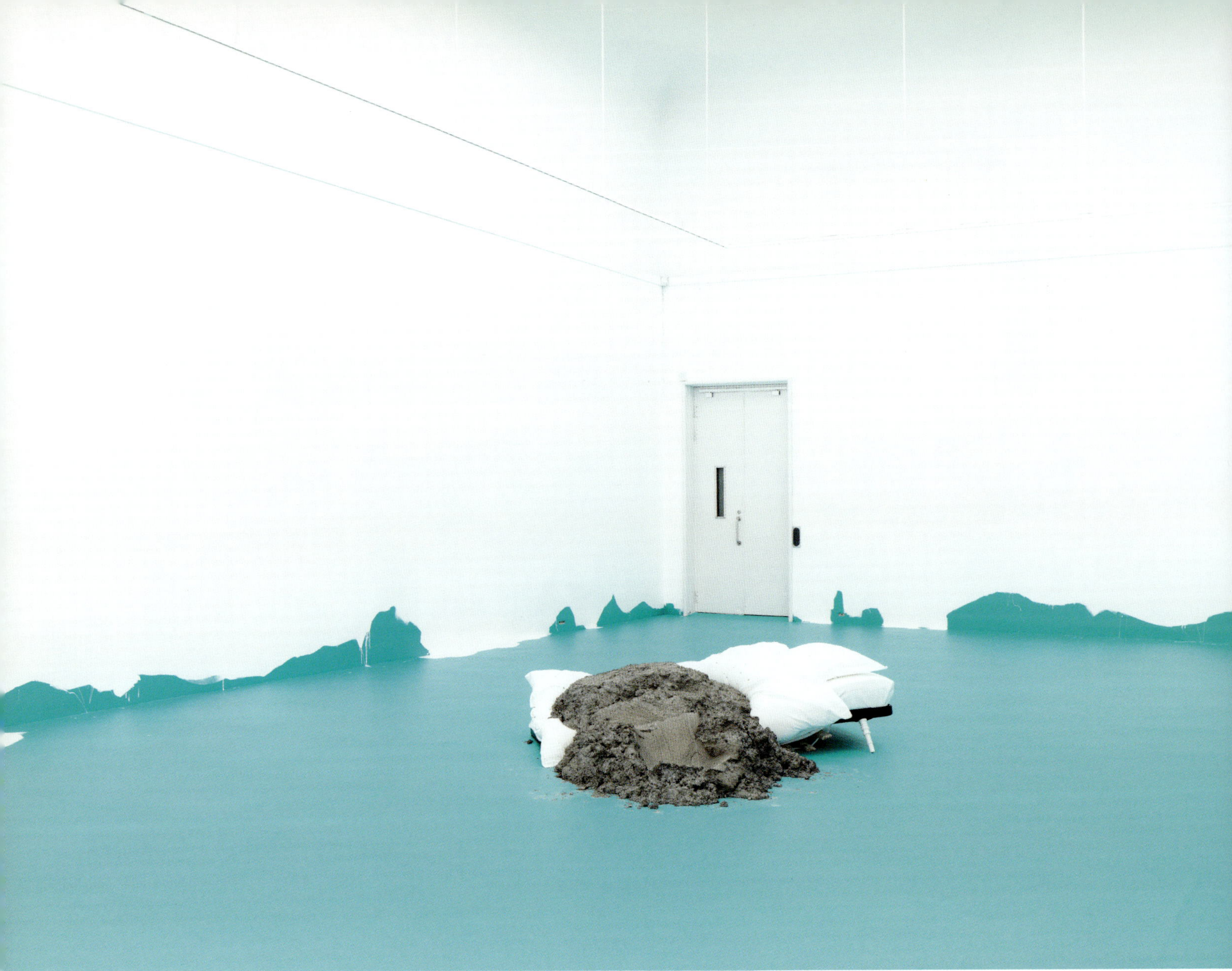

Barfood with Erich Muehsam / Langweile mit Richard Wagner, 2006–2009
Colored adhesive vinyl, latex paint
Dimensions variable
Installation view, "Dear ________! We _____ on ________, hysterically. It has to be _____ that _____.
No? It is now ______ and the whole ______ has changed ______. all the _____, ______"
(with Mark Handforth and Georg Herold), Kunstnernes Hus, Oslo, 2009
Above: *Kratz*, 2009
Opposite page: Georg Herold, *Event*, 2009; *Untitled*, 2009
Page 79: *Untitled*, 2009; On ceiling: Georg Herold, *Poetry Electrique*, 2009

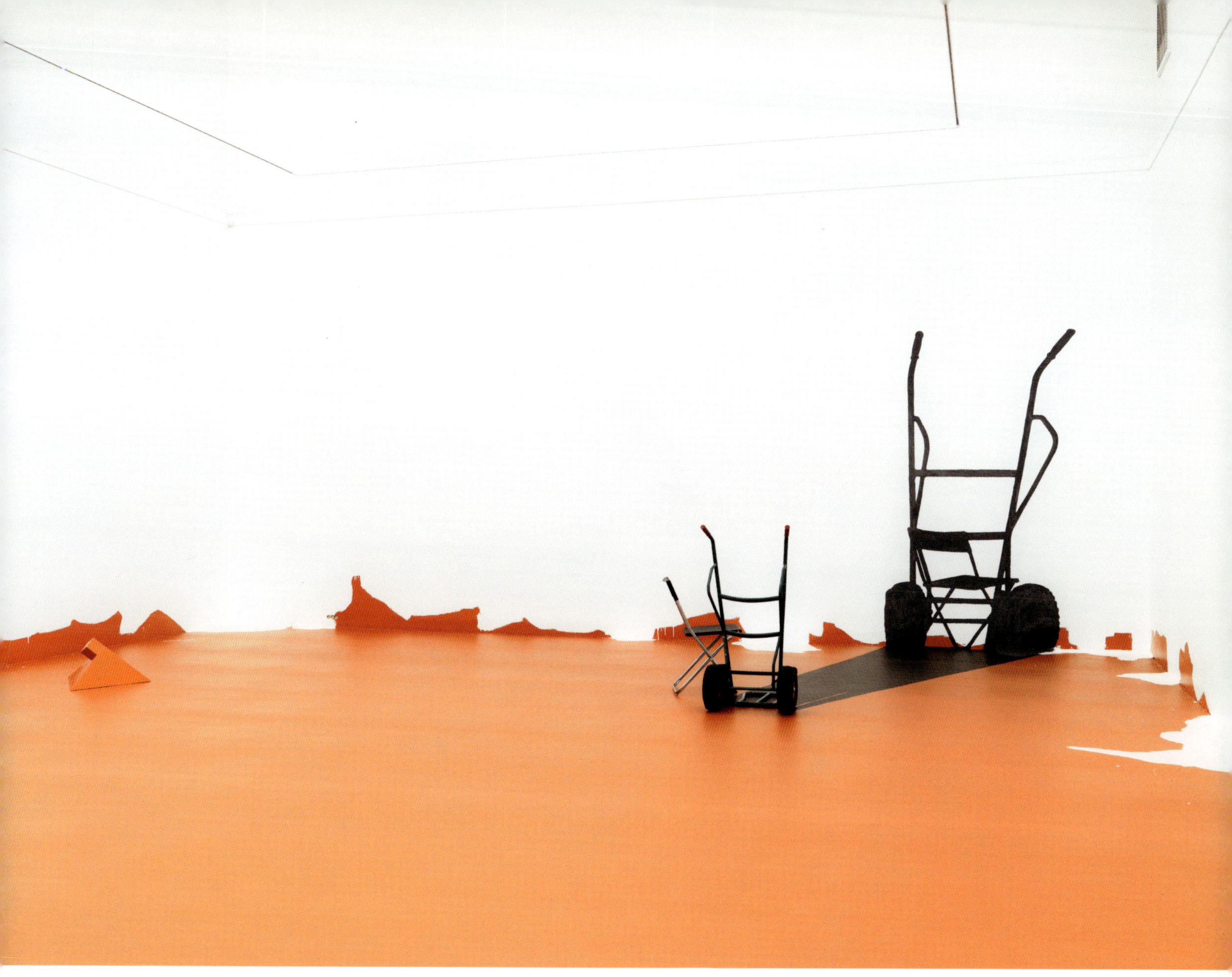

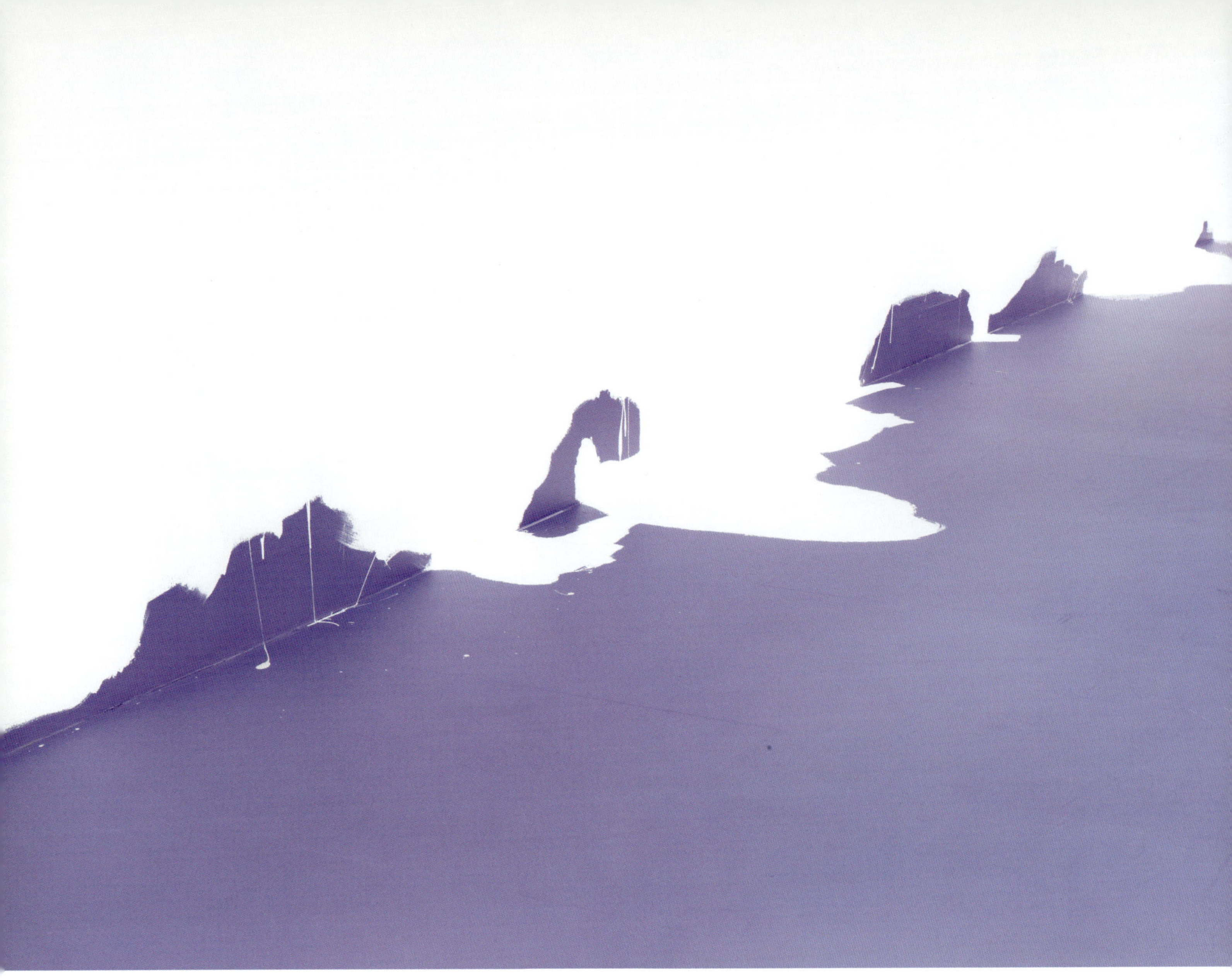

Studio view, Wallisellen, Switzerland, 1999

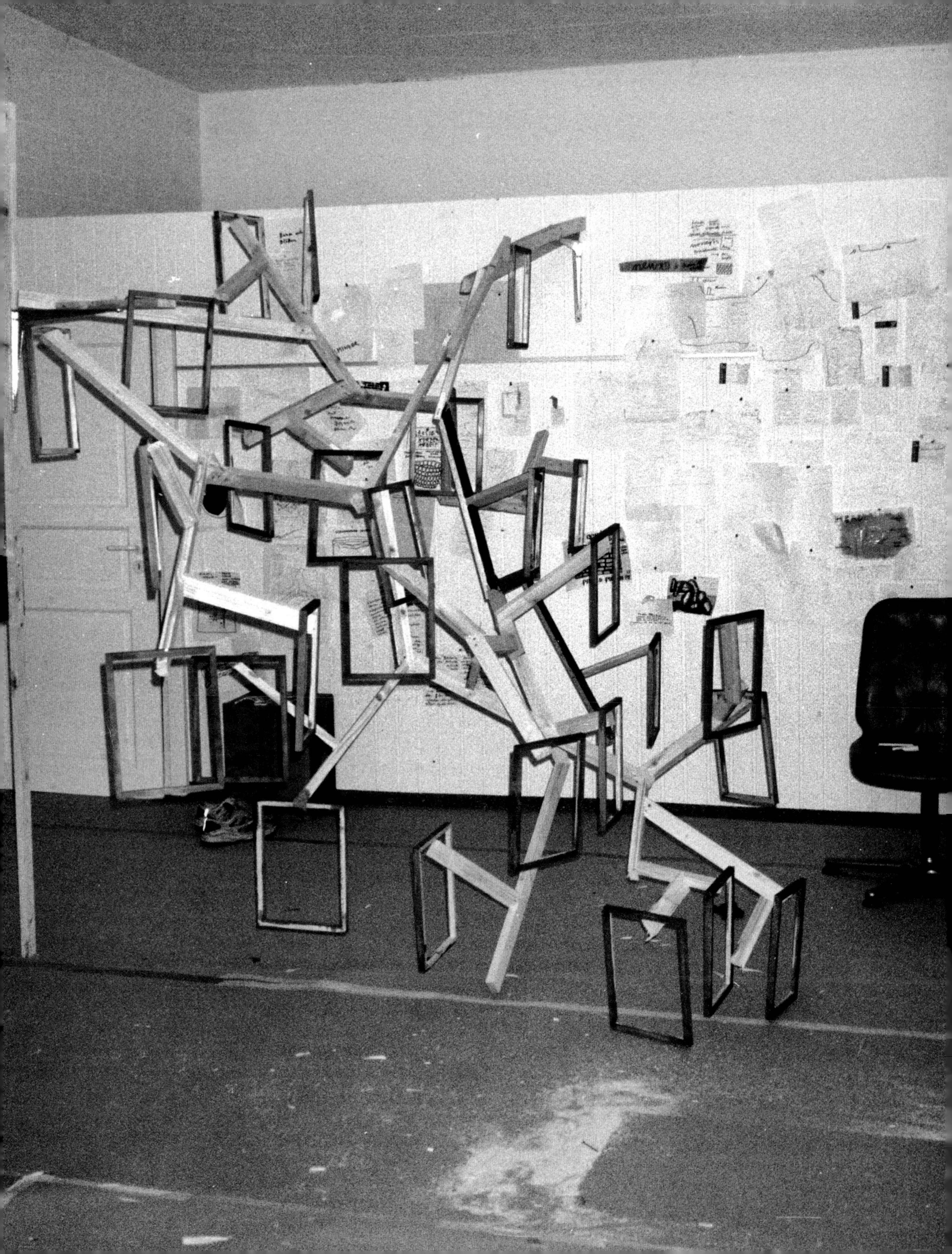

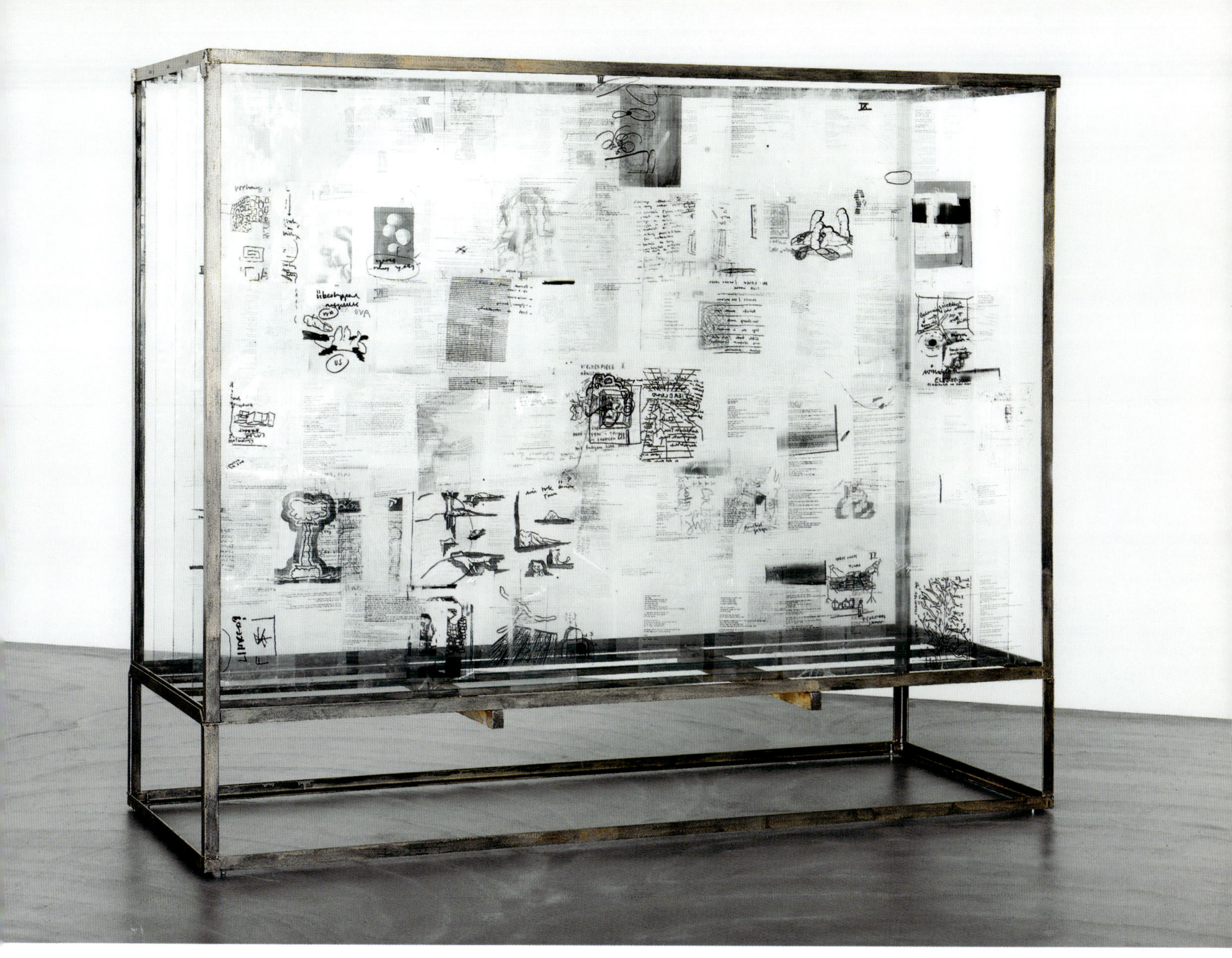

A Man and His Head Like a Hand with a Bread Unfiltered Summer / Autumn 99 Poetry and Brain Waste, 1999
Iron, glass, zinc phosphate paint, photocopies on polyester film, adhesive tape
92 ⅛ x 107 ½ x 39 ¾ inches (400 x 280 x 260 cm)

Jet Set Lady, 2000

Color copies, wooden frames, wood, iron base, acrylic glass, wood stain, acrylic lacquer, wood glue, screws
177 ⅛ x 177 ⅛ x 165 ⅜ inches (450 x 450 x 420 cm)
Prototype
Installation view, "Tagessuppen / Soups of the Days," and "6 ½ Domestic Pairs Project" (with Keith Tyson), Kunsthaus Glarus, Switzerland, 2000

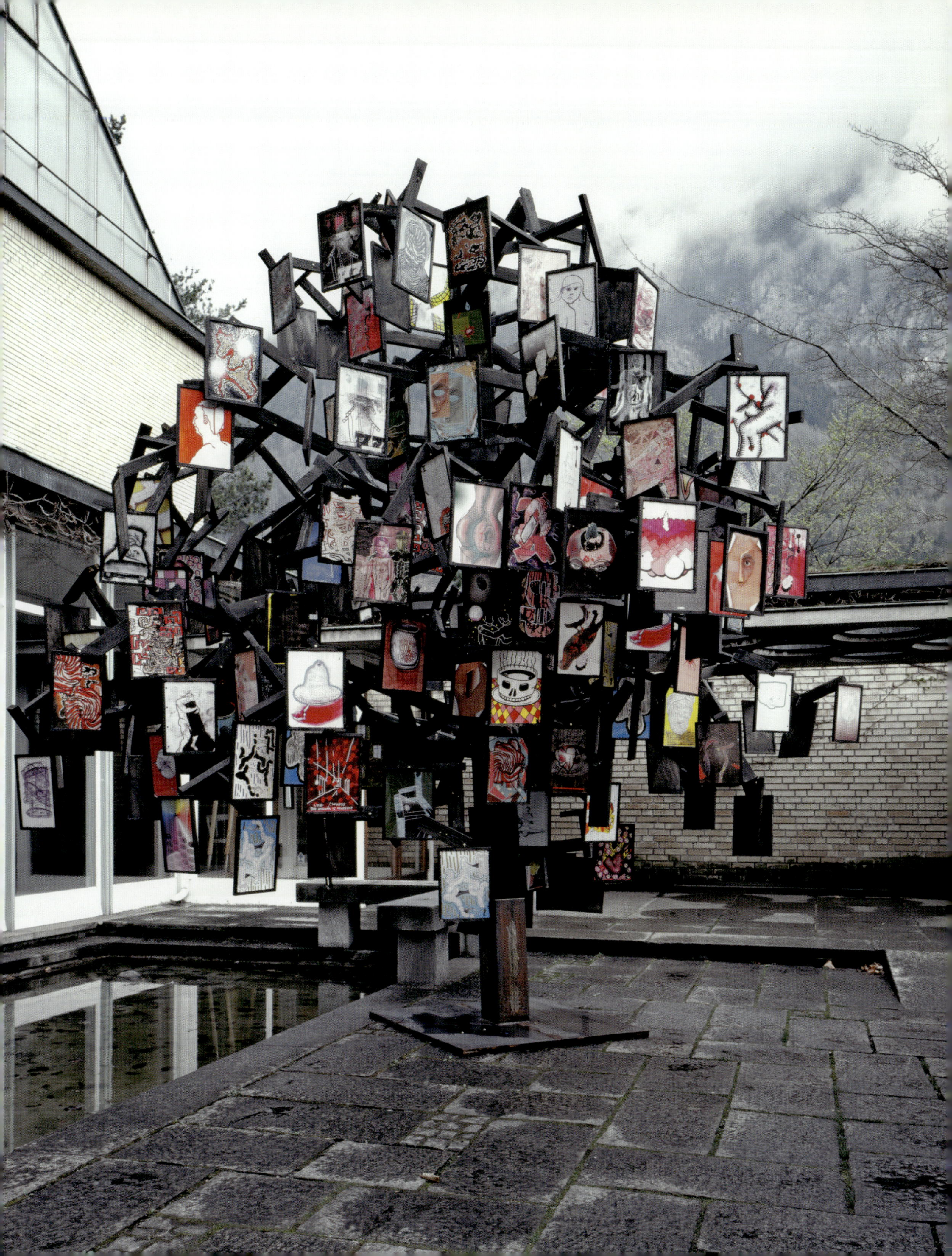

Jet Set Lady, 2000–2005
2,000 framed color prints of drawings, 24 fluorescent tubes,
wooden frames, iron, metal primer, UV-protective lacquer
354 ⅜ x 275 ⅝ x 275 ⅝ inches (900 x 700 x 700 cm)
Installation view, "Jet Set Lady," Fondazione Nicola Trussardi,
Istituto dei Ciechi, Milan, 2005

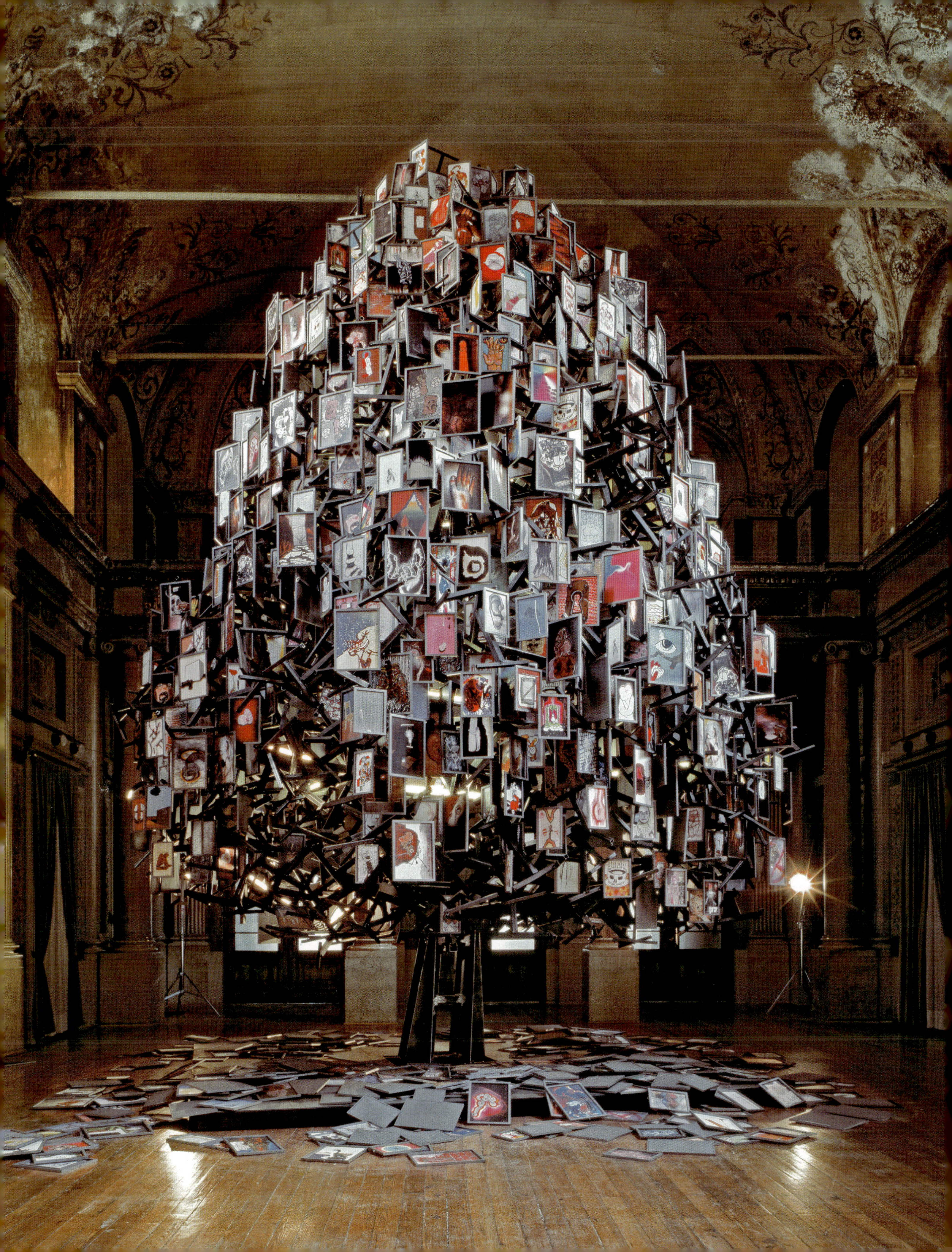

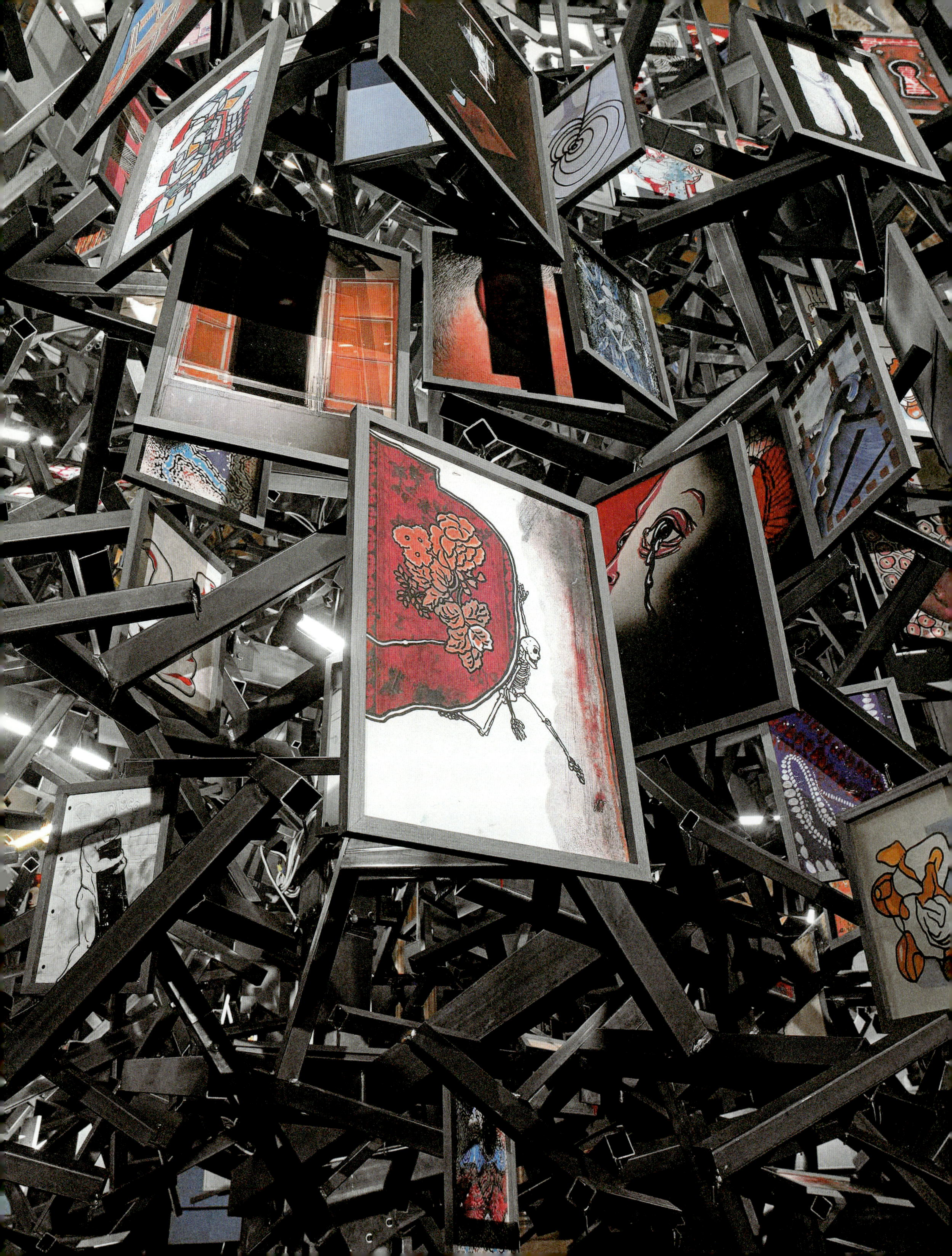

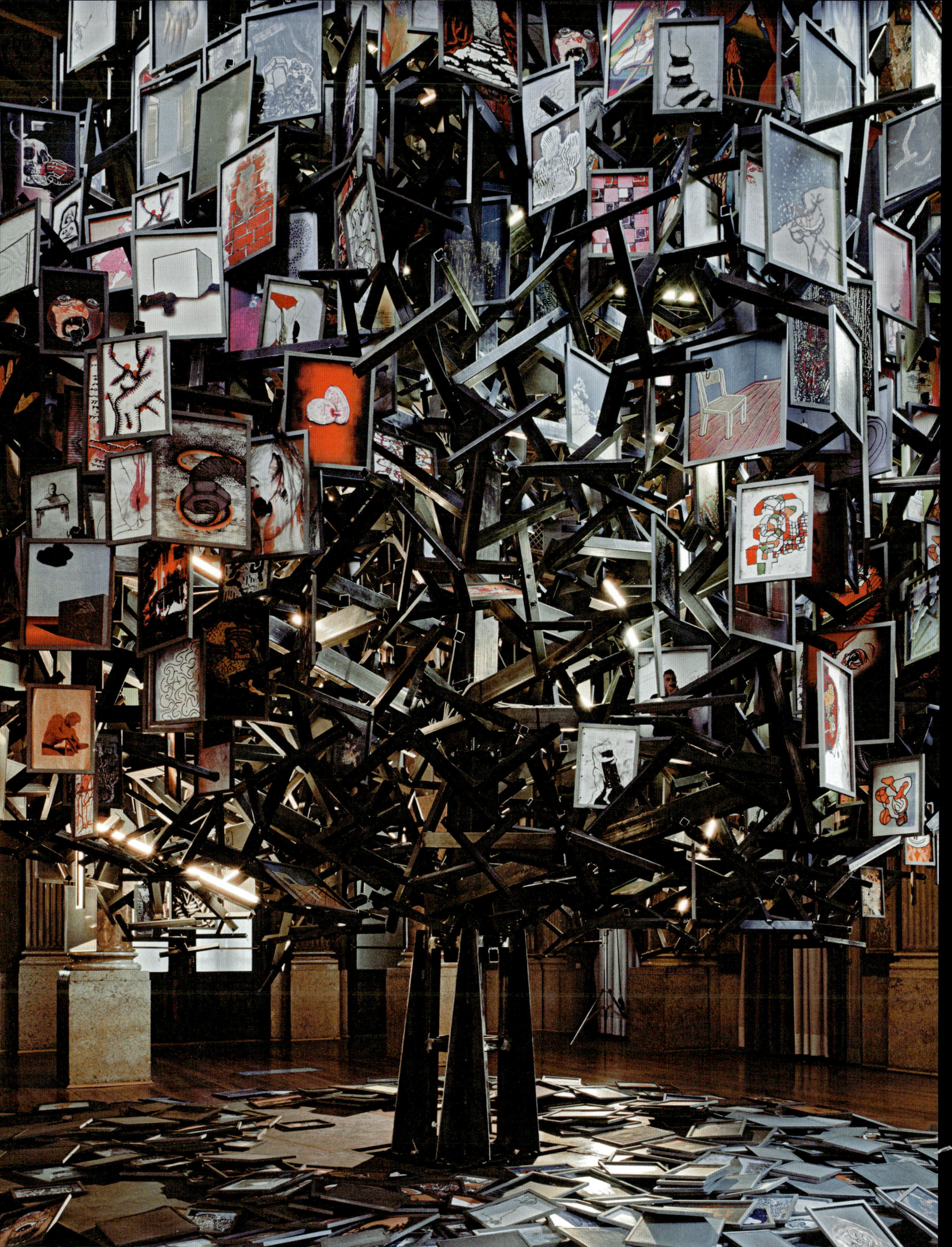

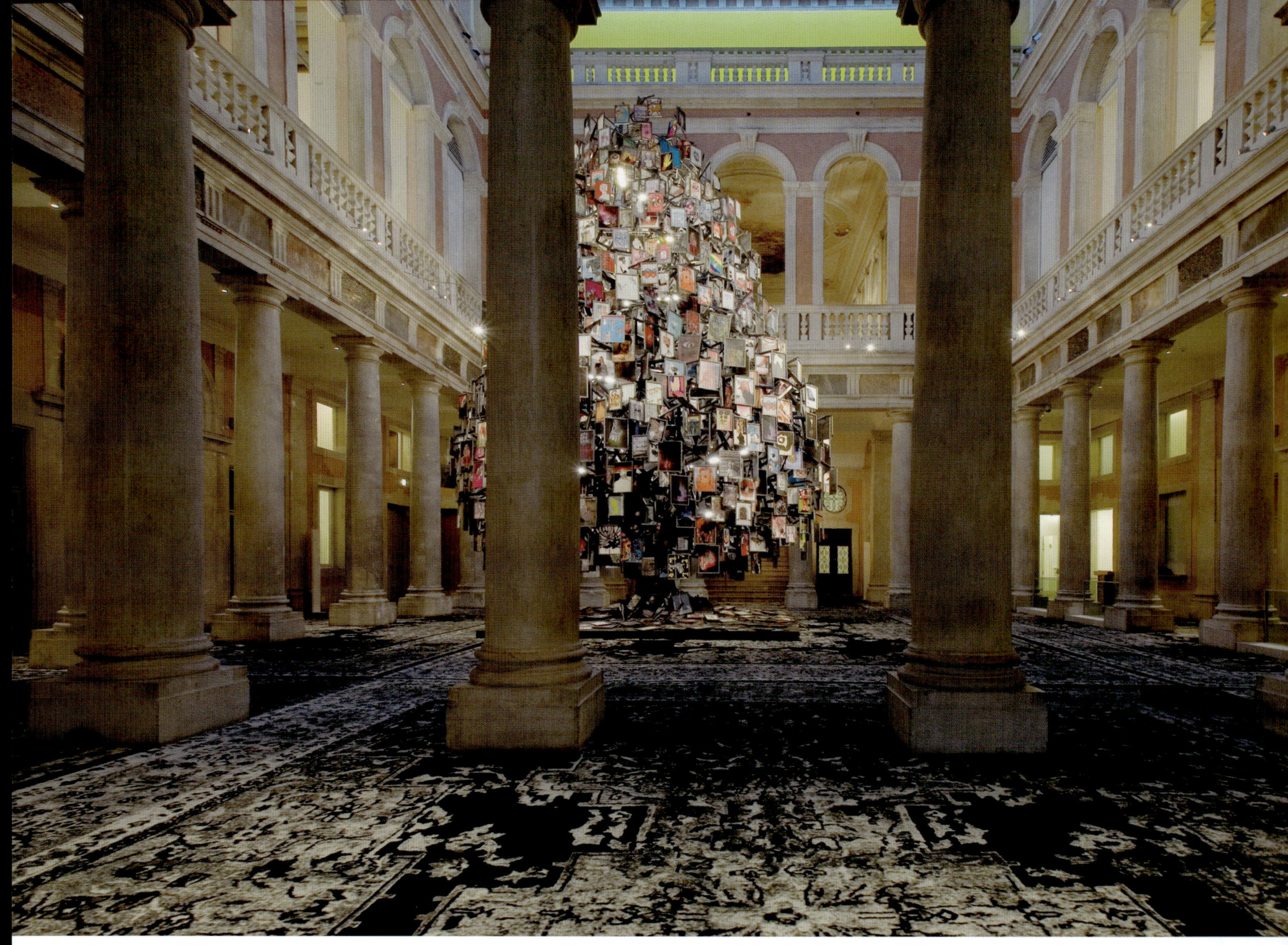

Installation view, "Sequence 1: Painting and Sculpture in the François Pinault Collection,"
Palazzo Grassi, Venice, 2007
Jet Set Lady, 2000–2005
On floor: Rudolf Stingel, *Untitled (Sarouk)*, 2006

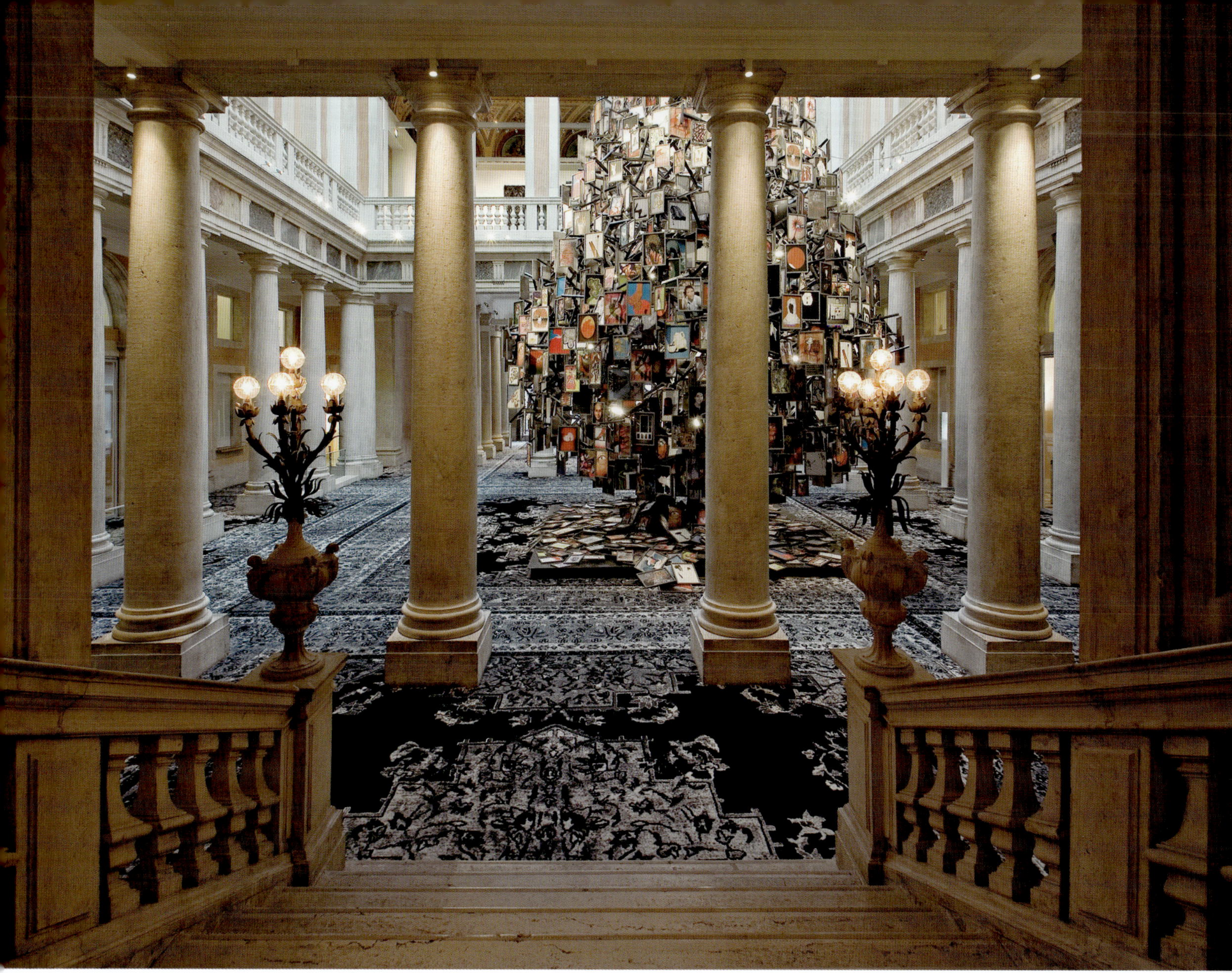

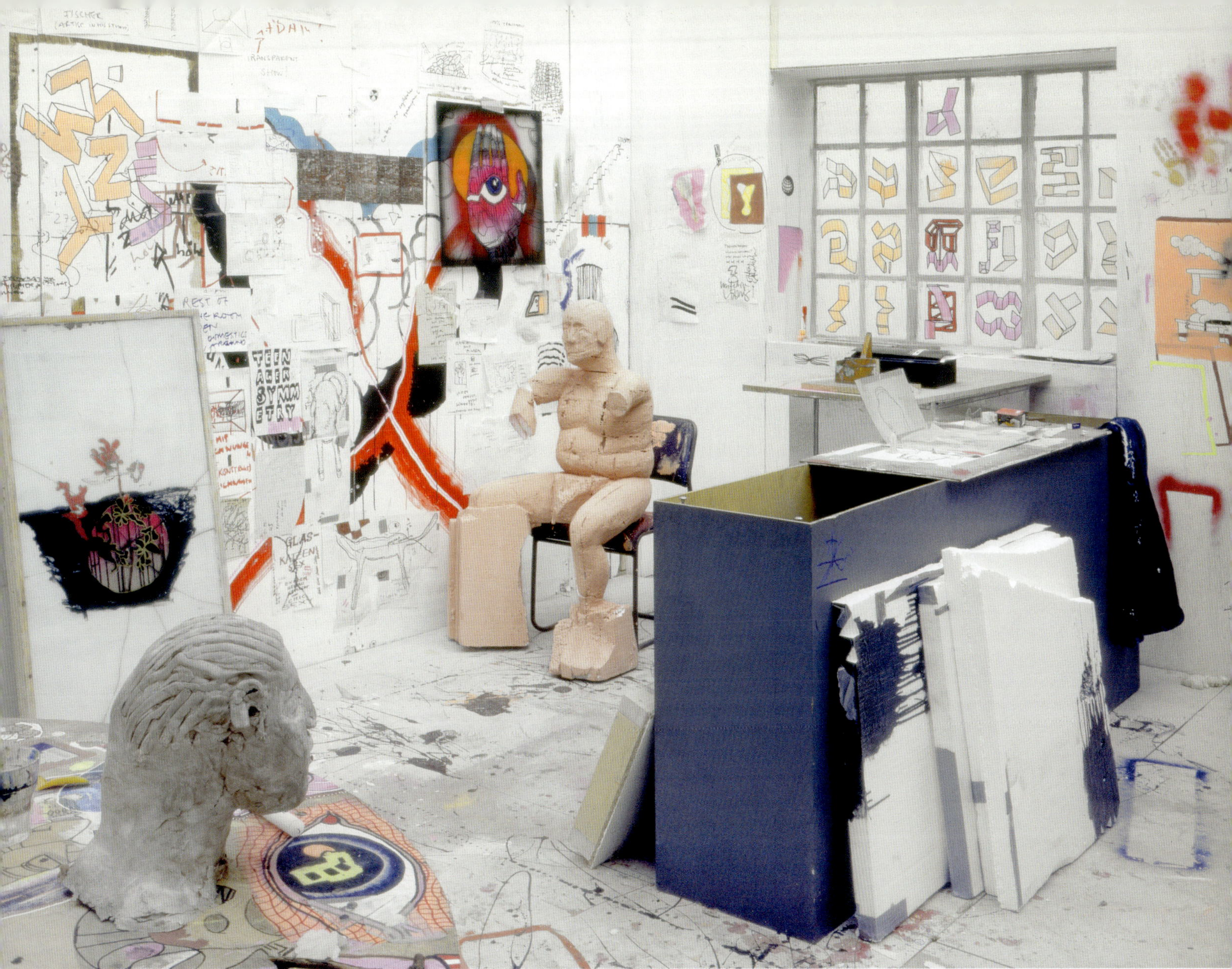

Madame Fisscher, 1999–2000
Mixed media
Dimensions variable

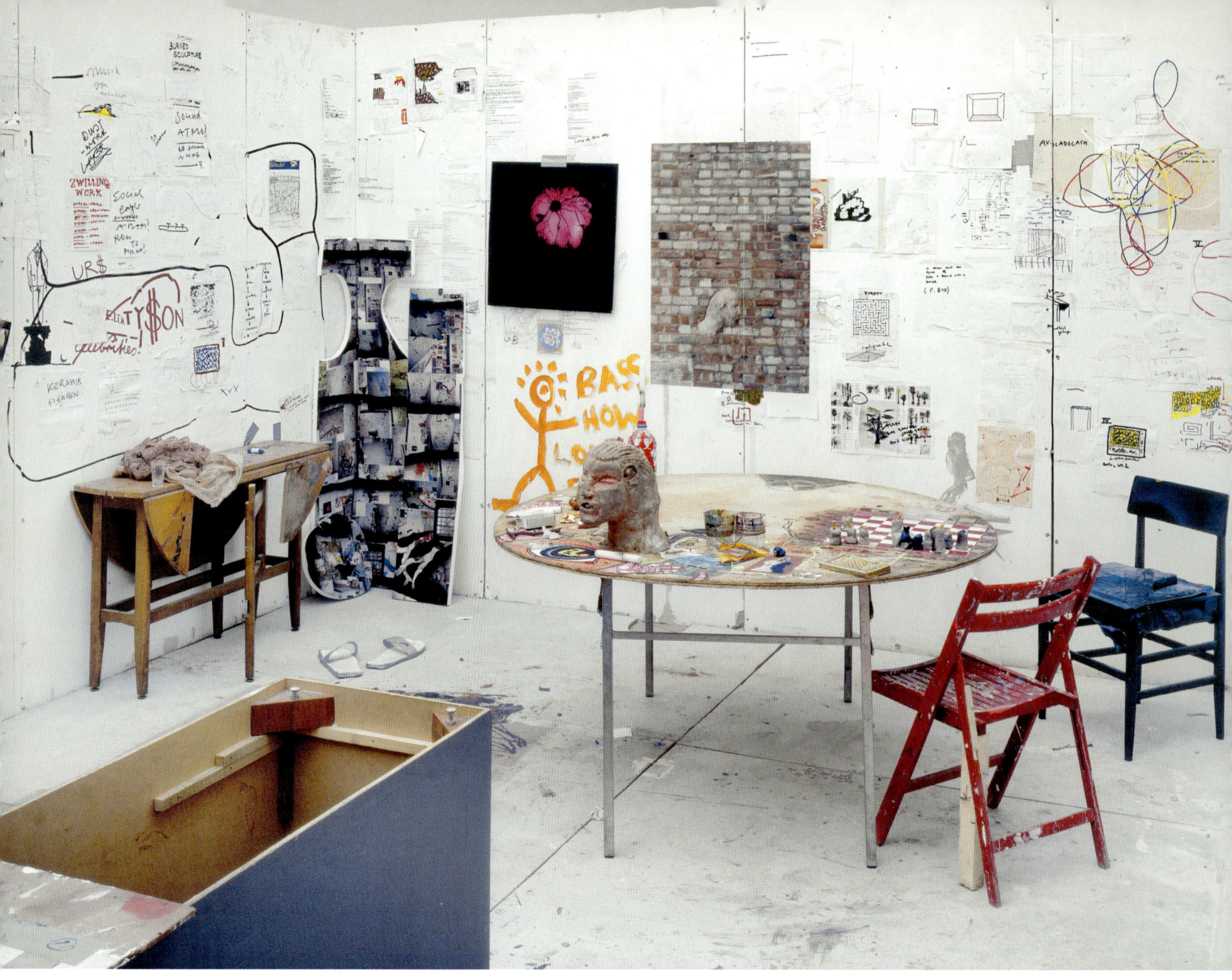

ZWILLING WORK
UR$
KERAMIK FIGUREN

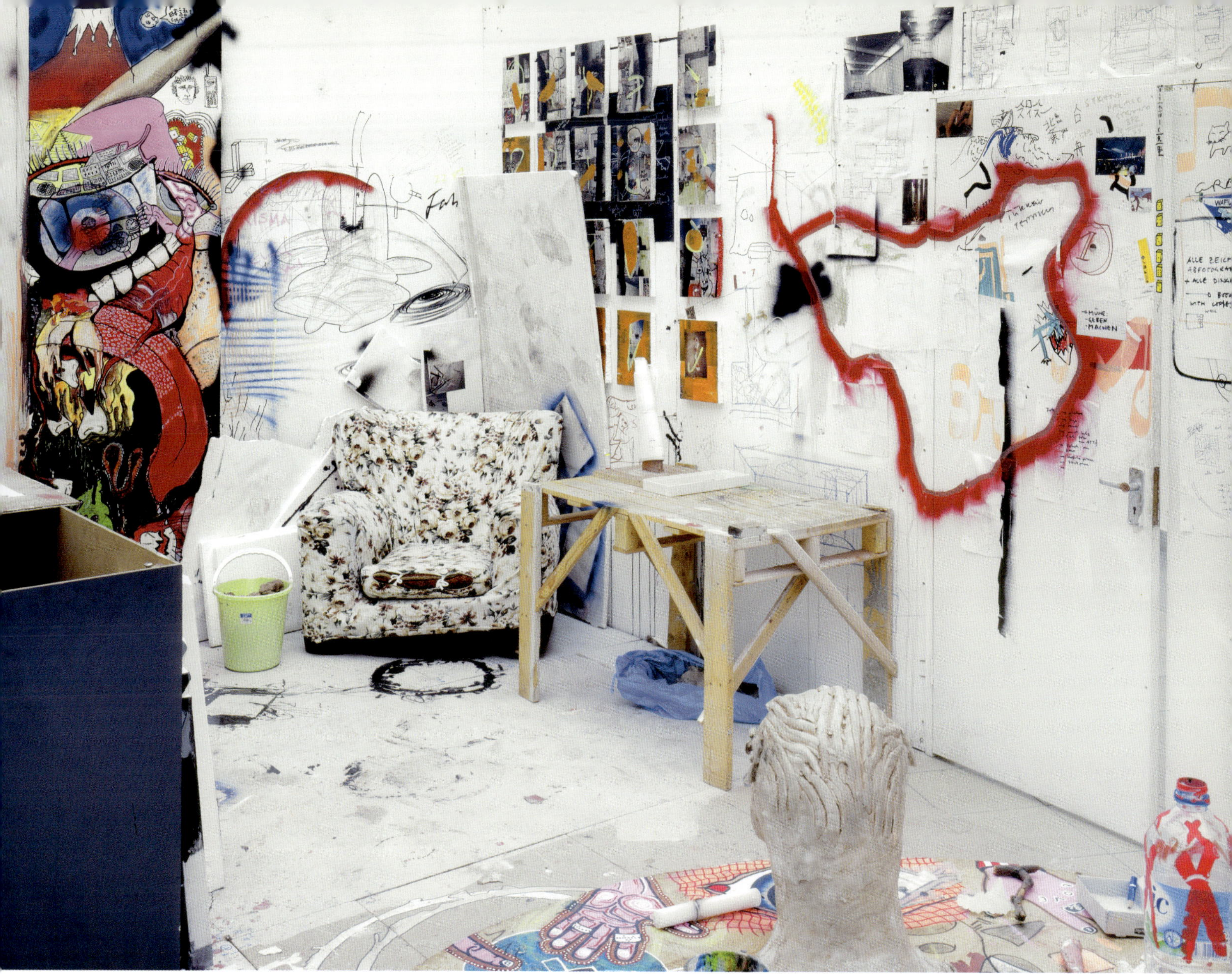

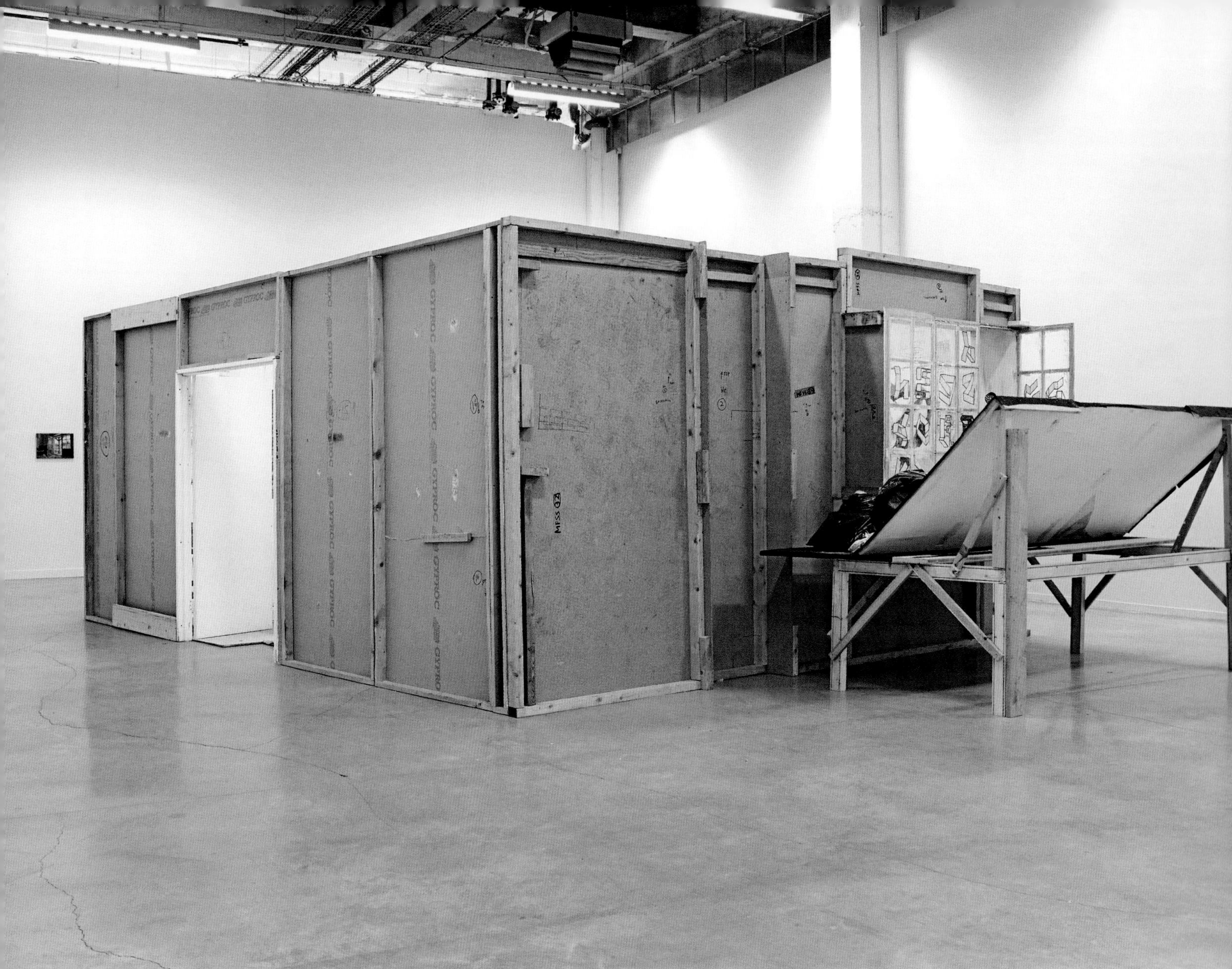

Above: Installation view: "Château de Tokyo / Palais de Fontainebleau," Château de Fontainebleau, Fontainebleau, France, 2008
Opposite and following page: Installation view, "Madame Fisscher," Palazzo Grassi, Venice, 2012
Madame Fisscher, 1999–2000
Following page: Jeff Koons, *Balloon Dog (Magenta)*, 1994–2006

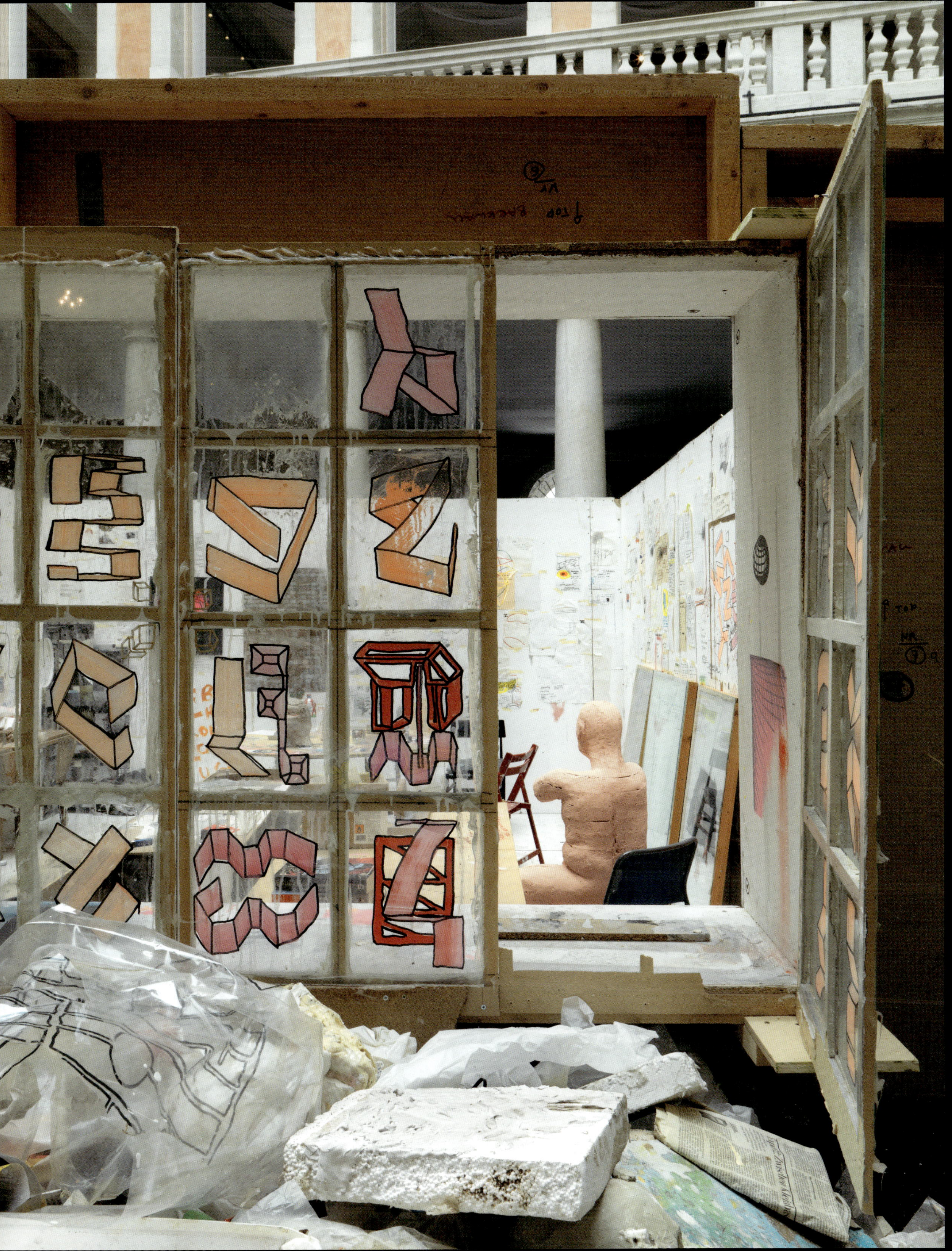

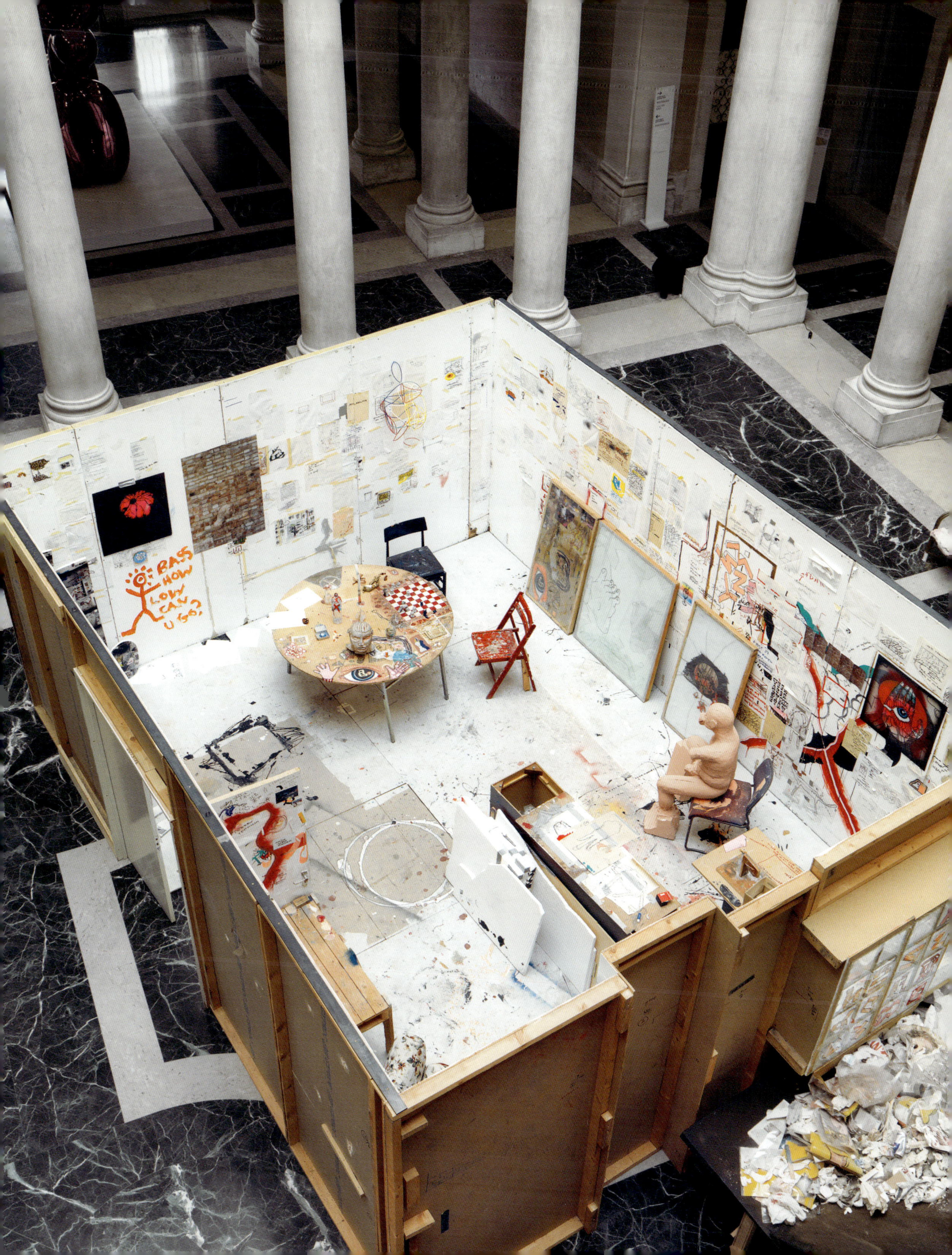
BASS
HOW
LOW
CAN
U GO?

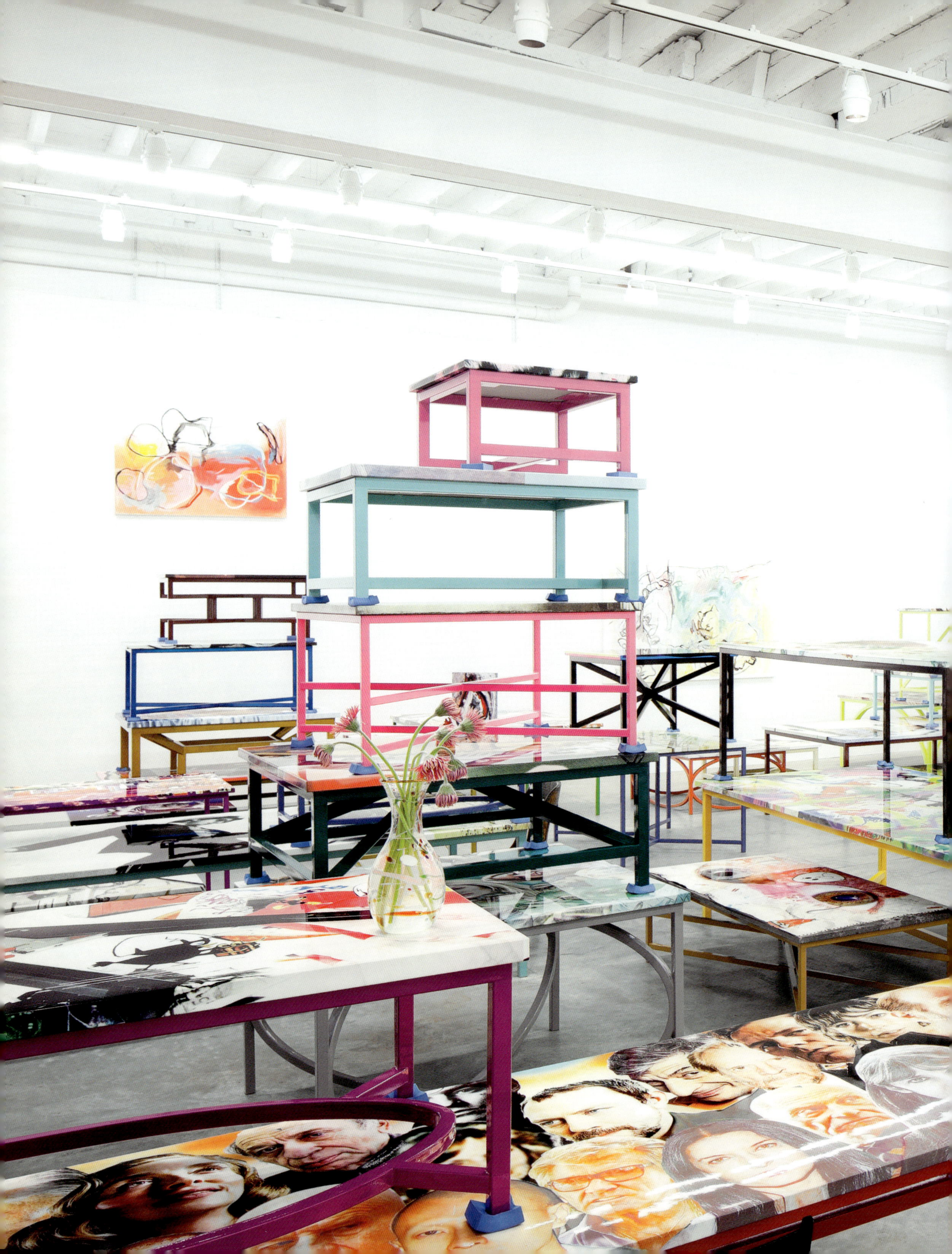

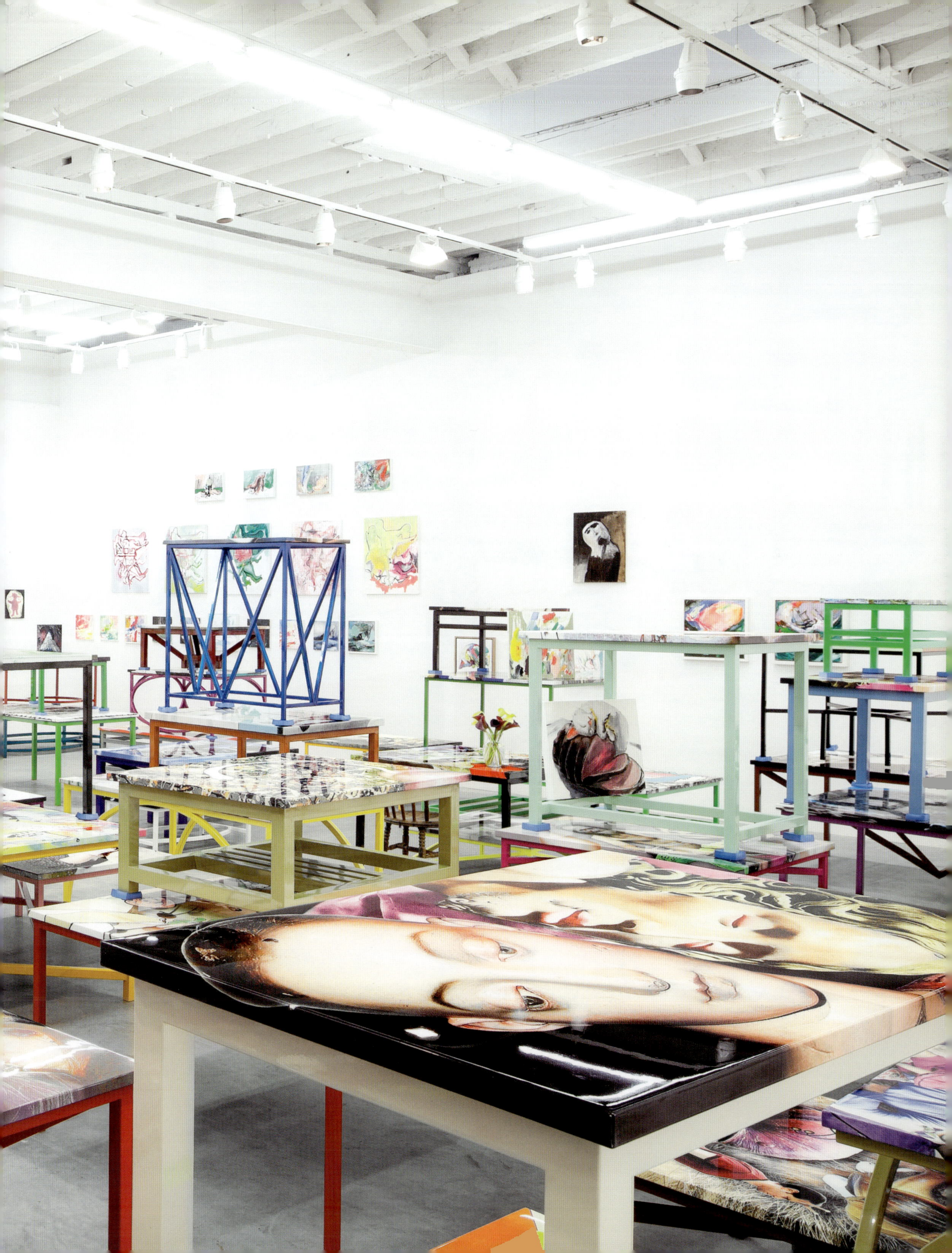

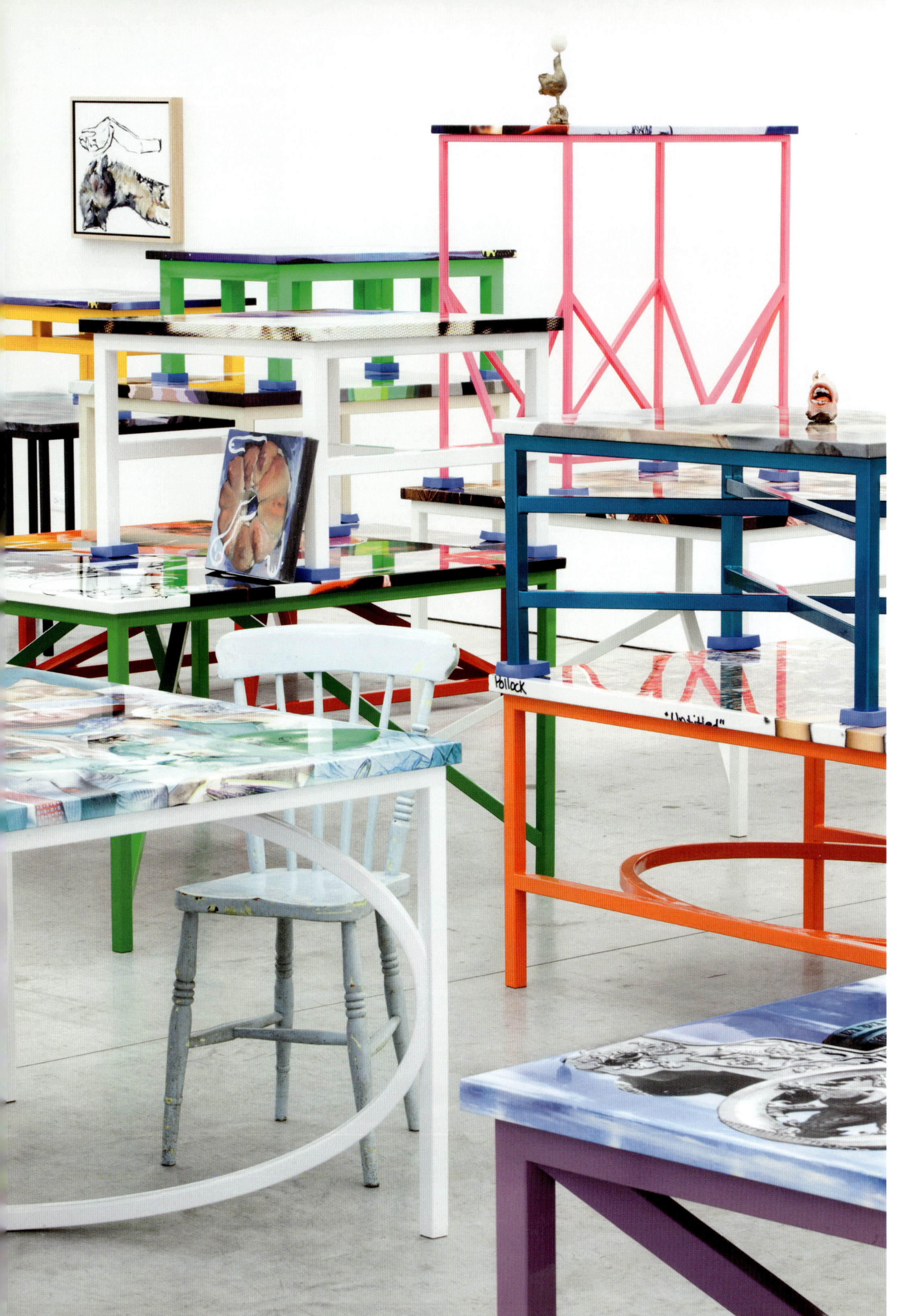
Pollock
"Untitled"

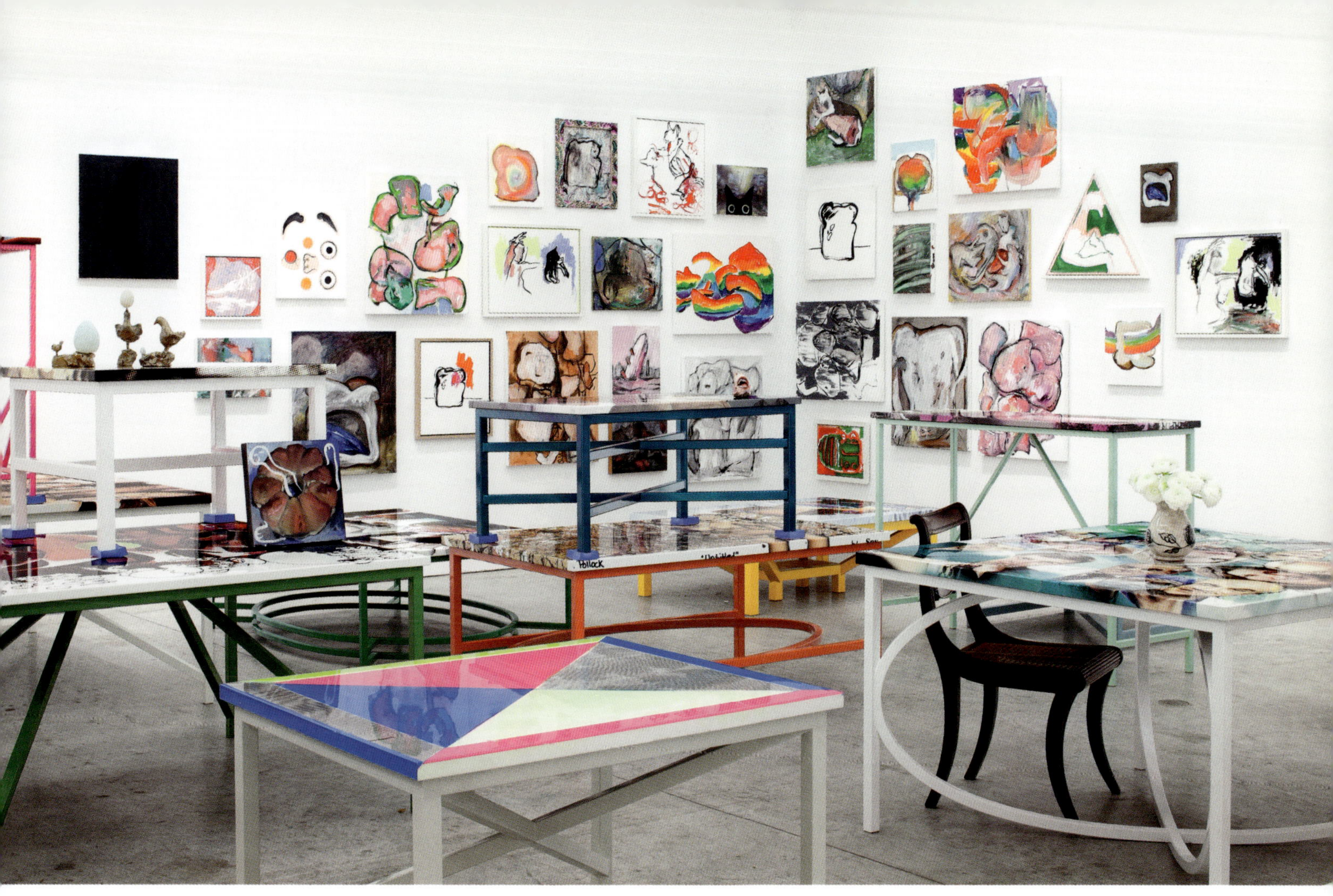

Previous spread and following pages:
Installation view, Urs Fischer and Cassandra MacLeod,
"dngszjkdufiy bgxfjkglijkhtr kydjkhgdghjkd,"
Gavin Brown's enterprise, New York, 2011
On wall: Paintings by Cassandra MacLeod

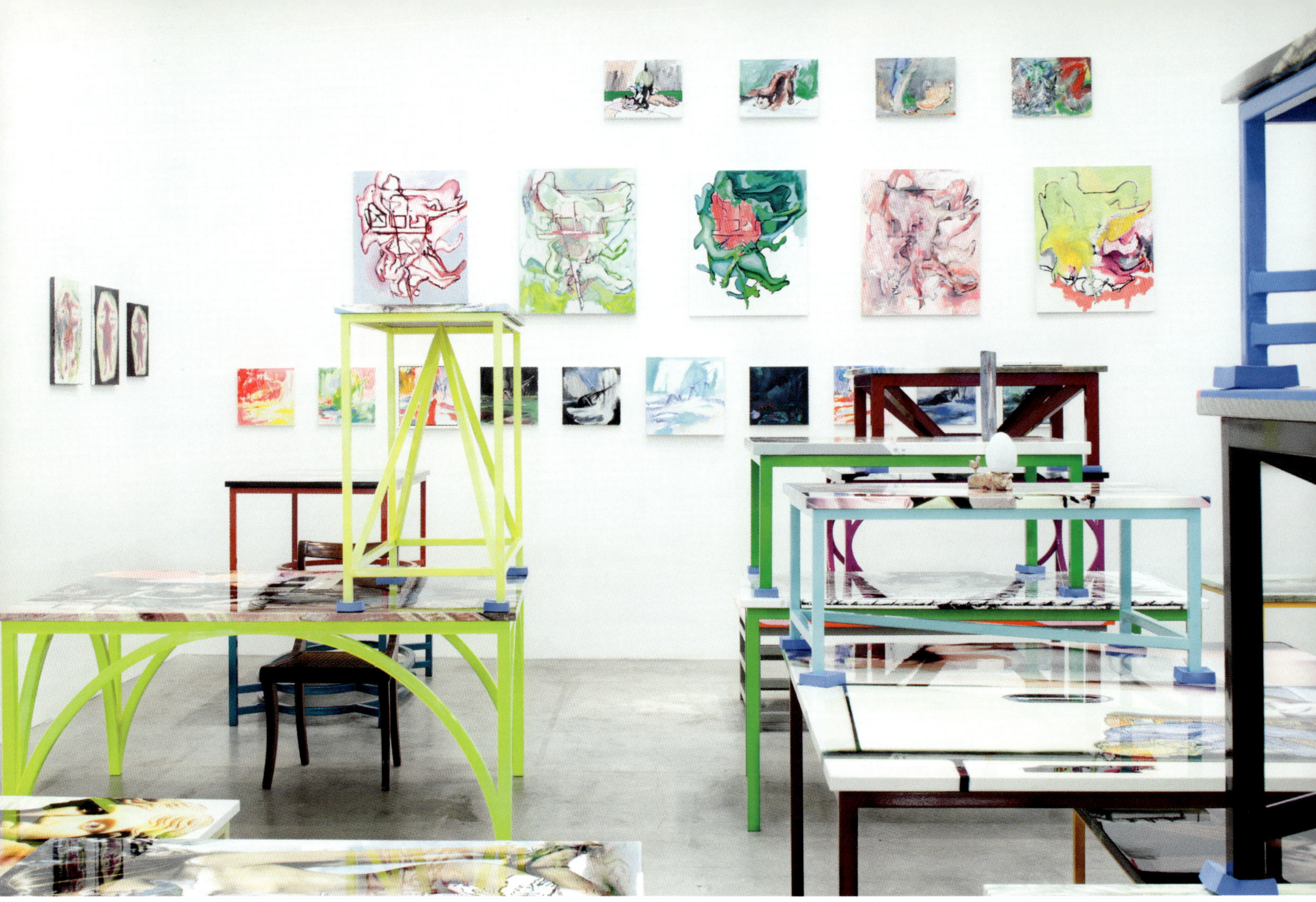

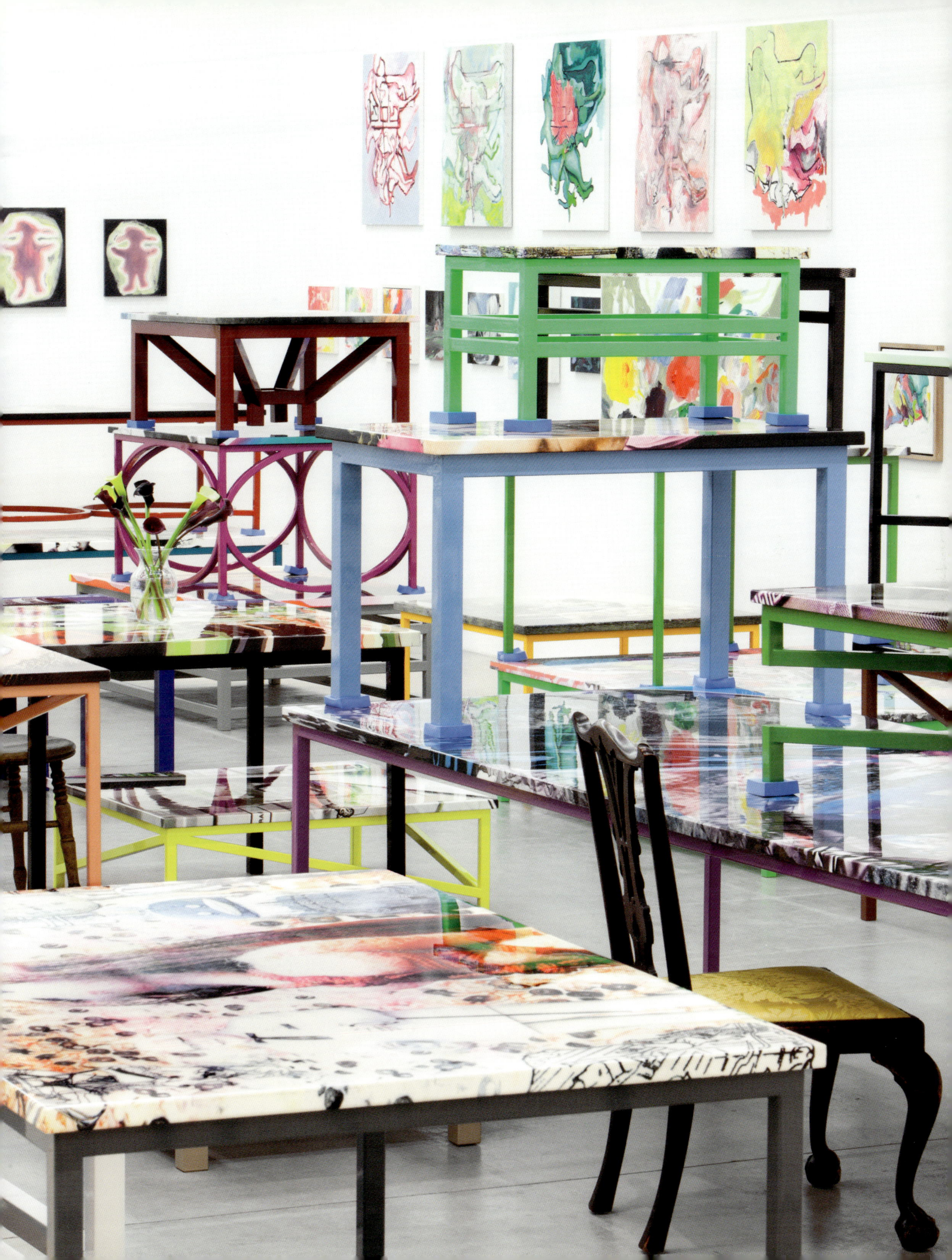

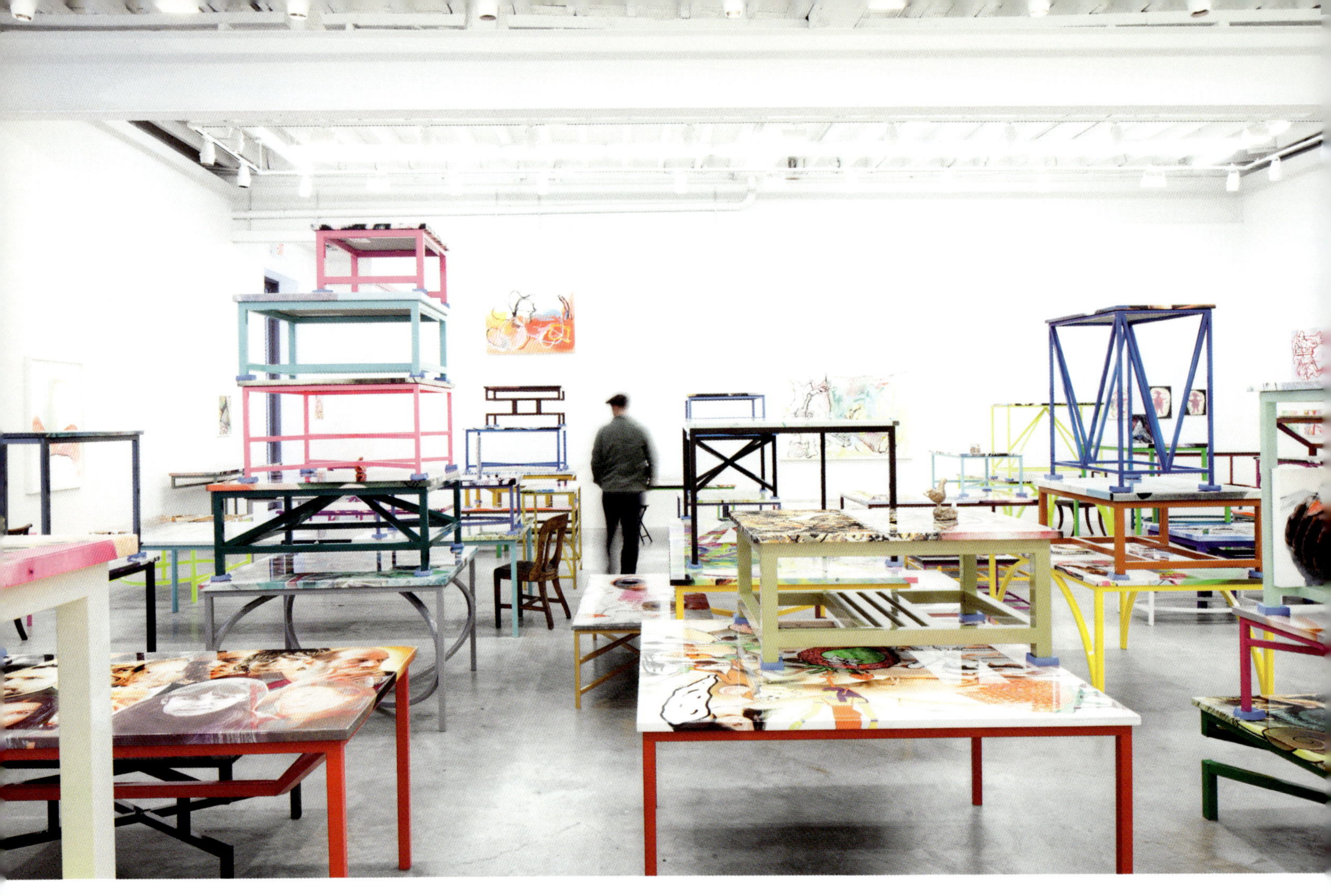

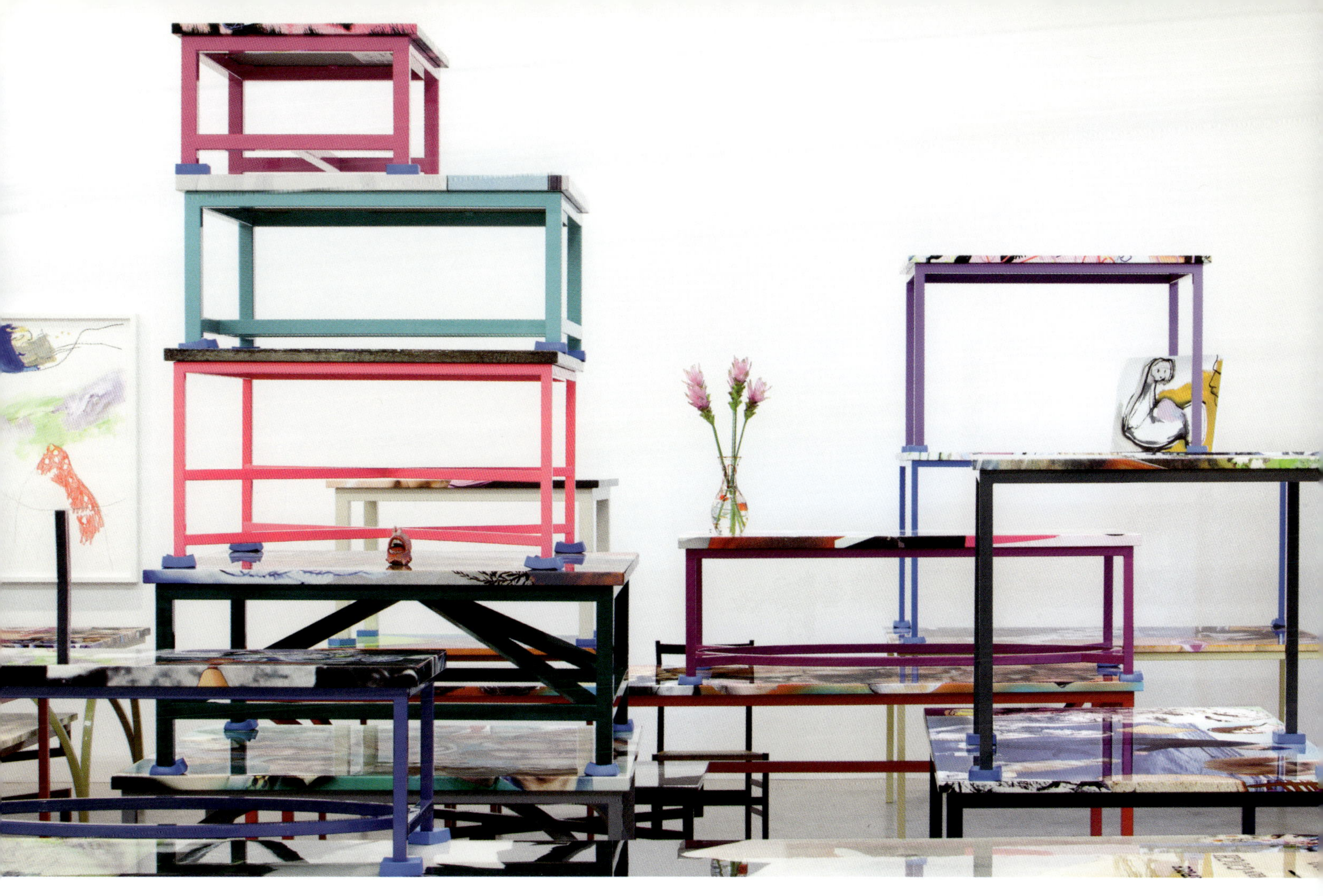

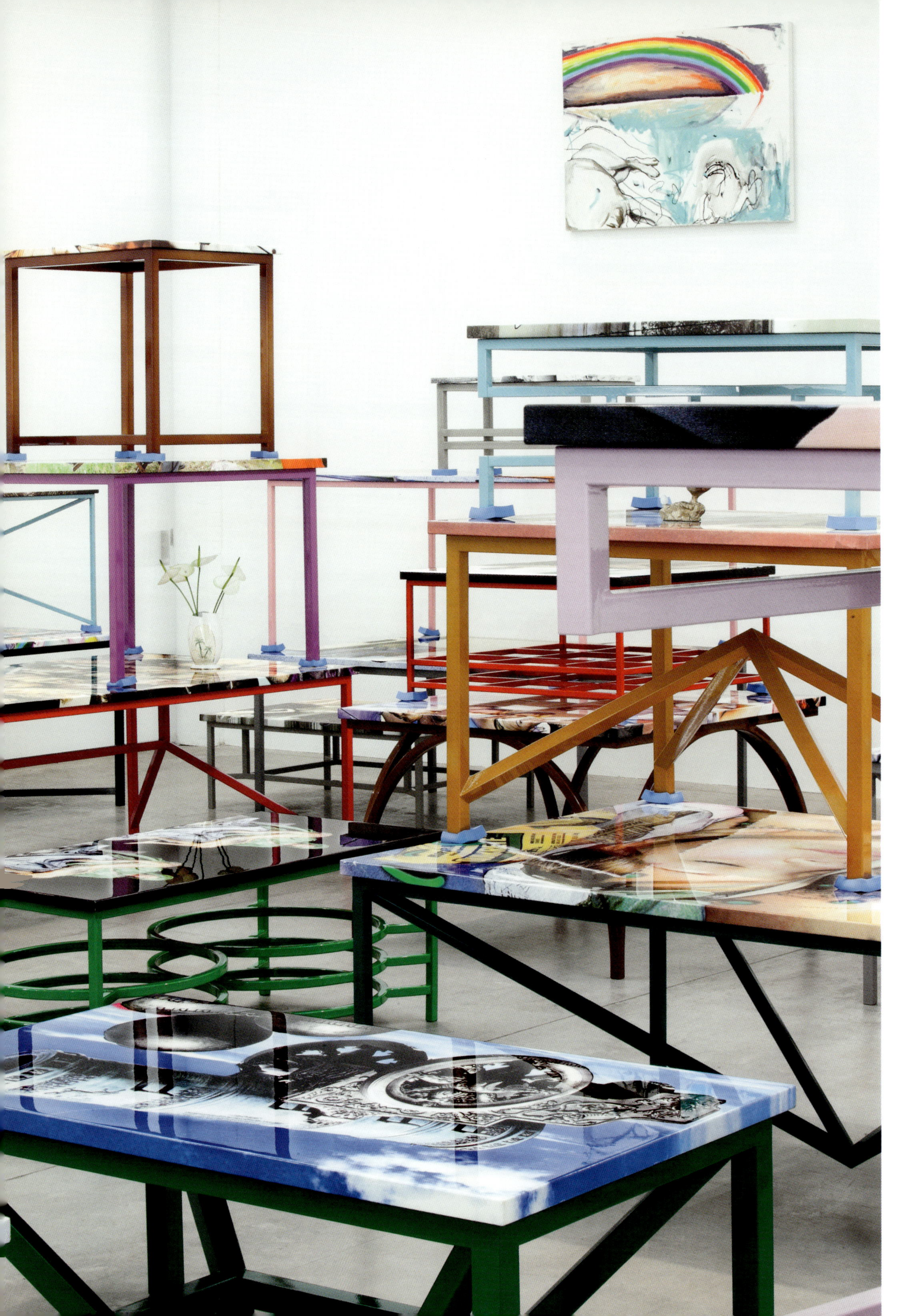

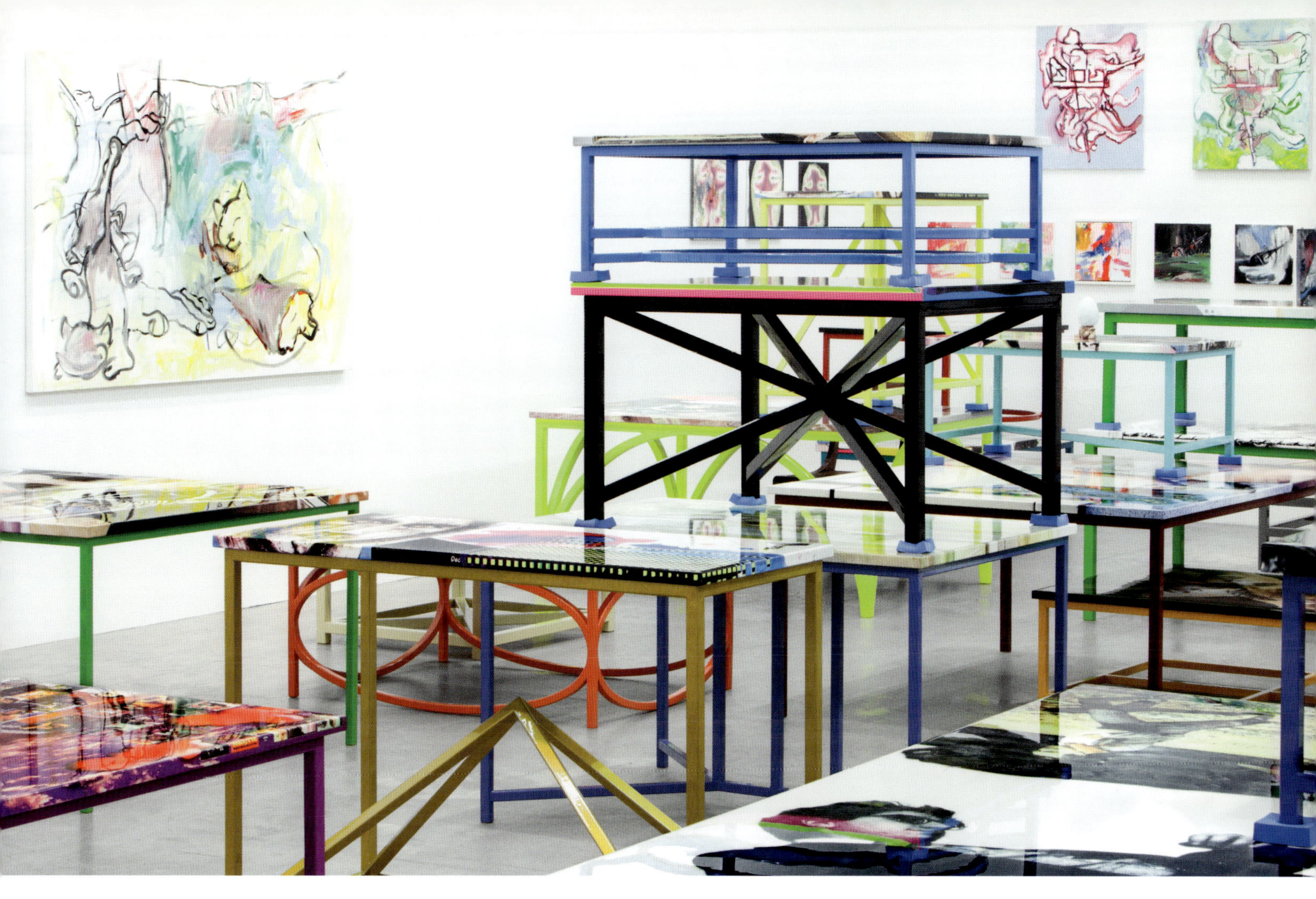

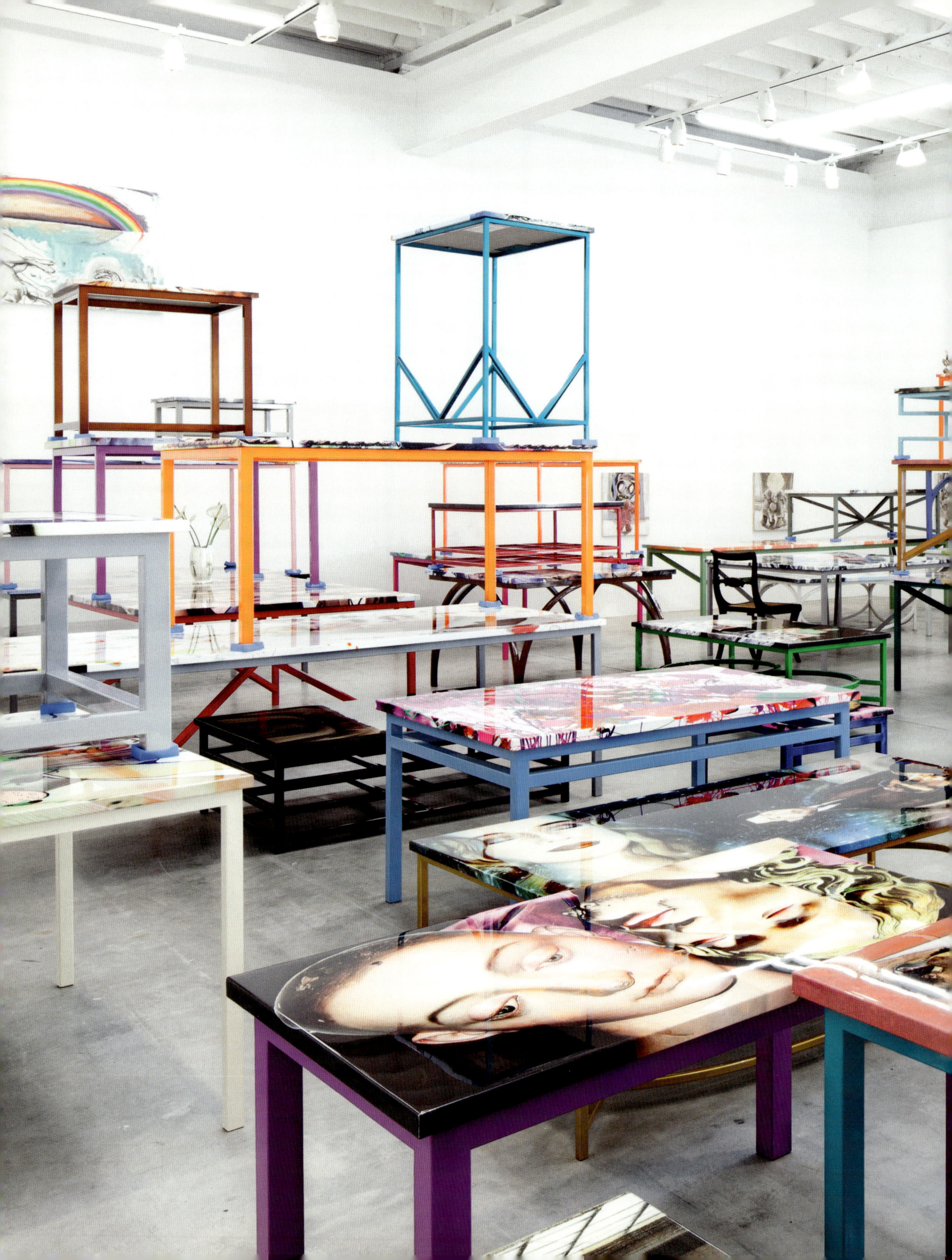

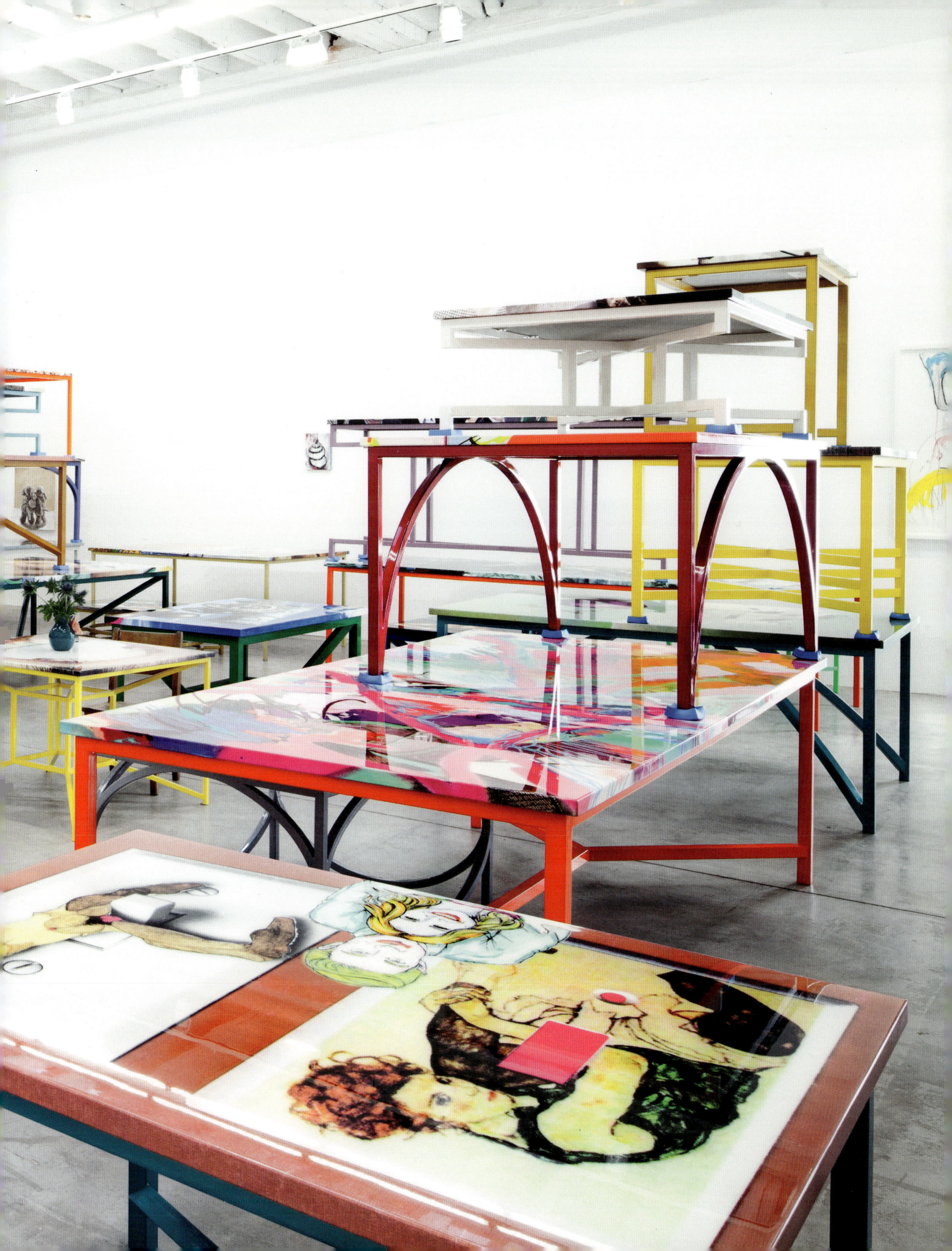

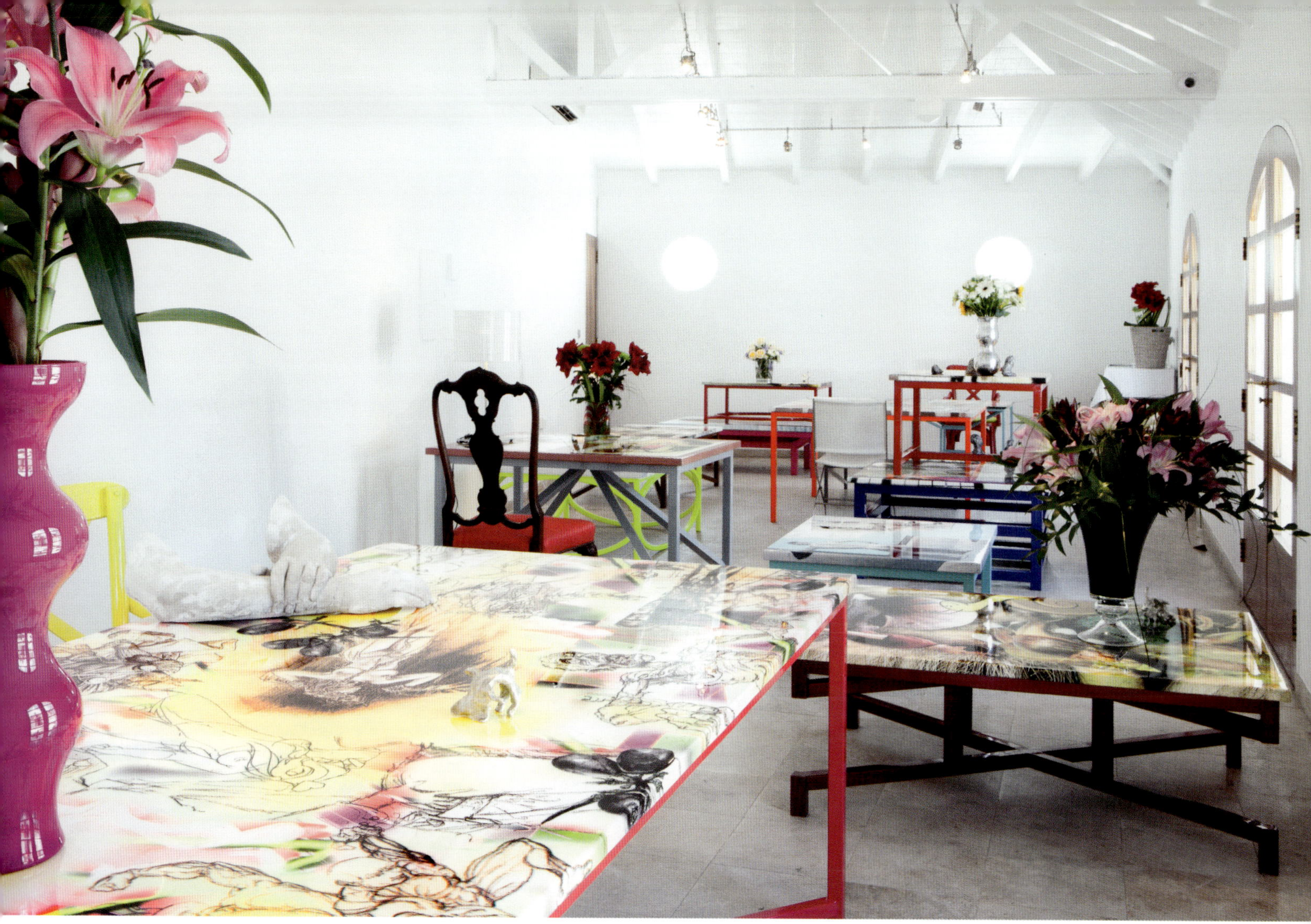

Installation view, "Tables, Heads, and Arms,"
Gagosian Gallery at Eden Rock Gallery, St. Barths, 2012–2013

Following spread:
Installation at "A Halloween Celebration," Performa11, Santos Party House,
New York, 28 October 2011

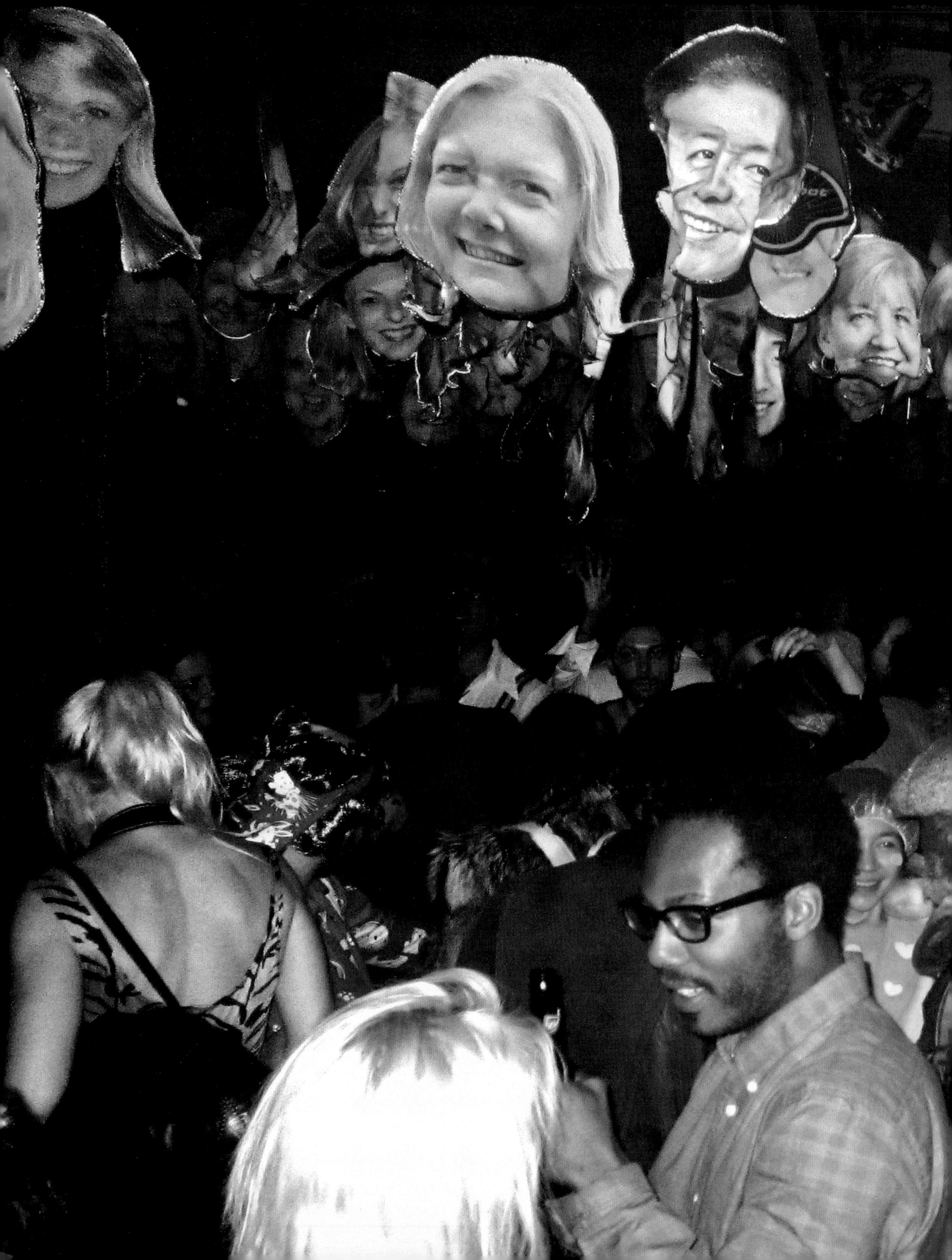

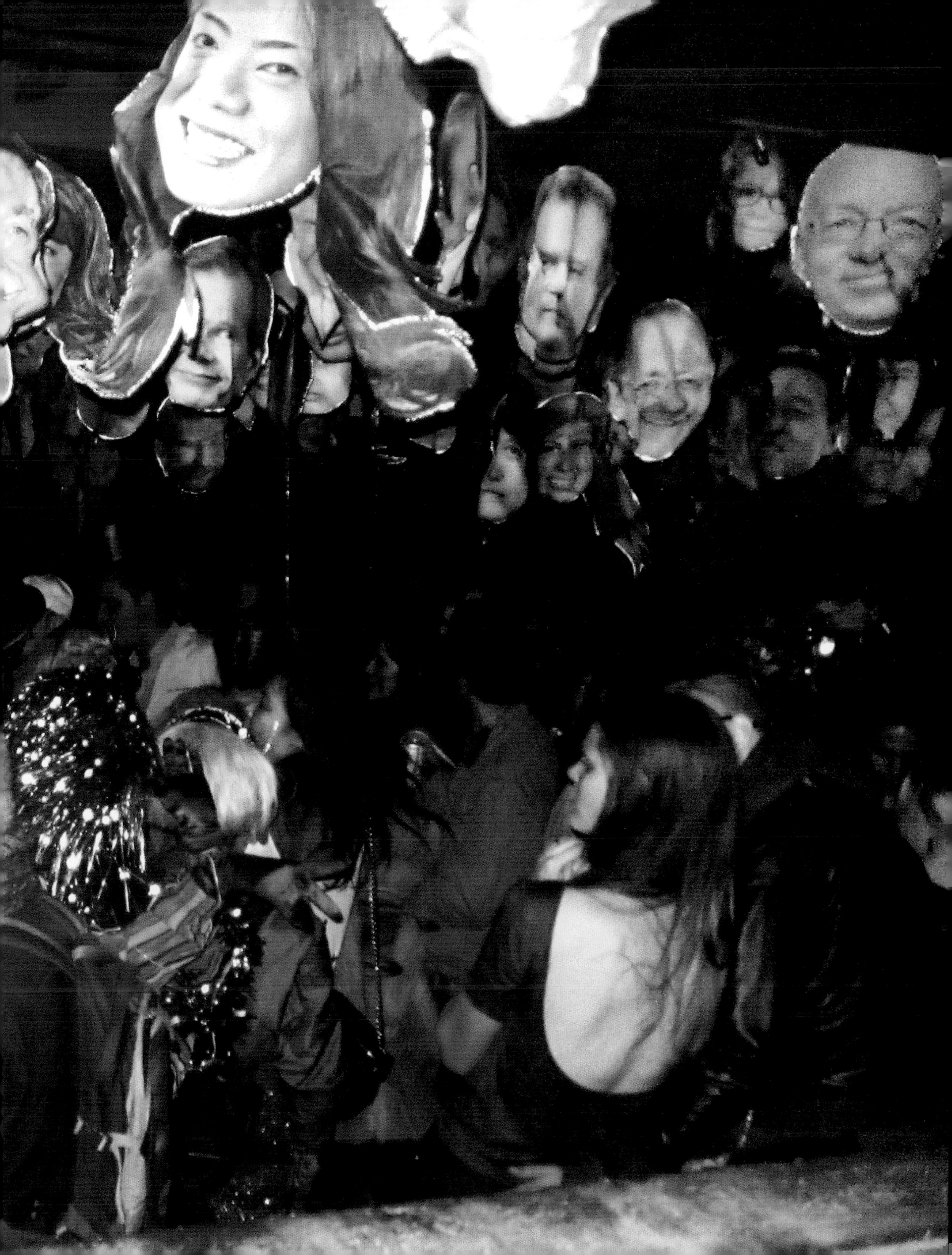

Sodbrennen, 2000–2004
Mirrors, aluminum, steel frame, silicone, orange juice, coffee, cigarettes
61 x 61 x 61 inches (155 x 155 x 155 cm)

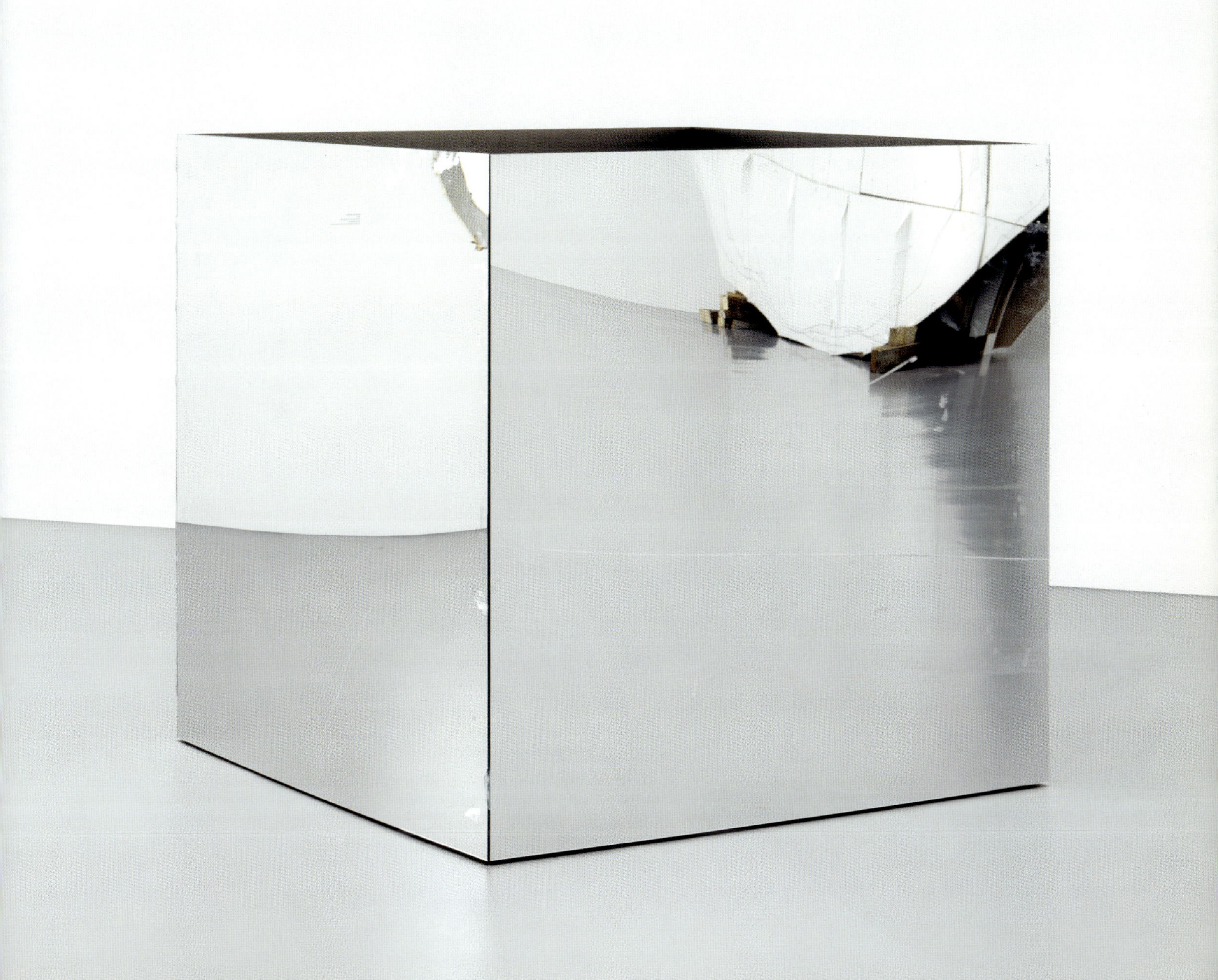

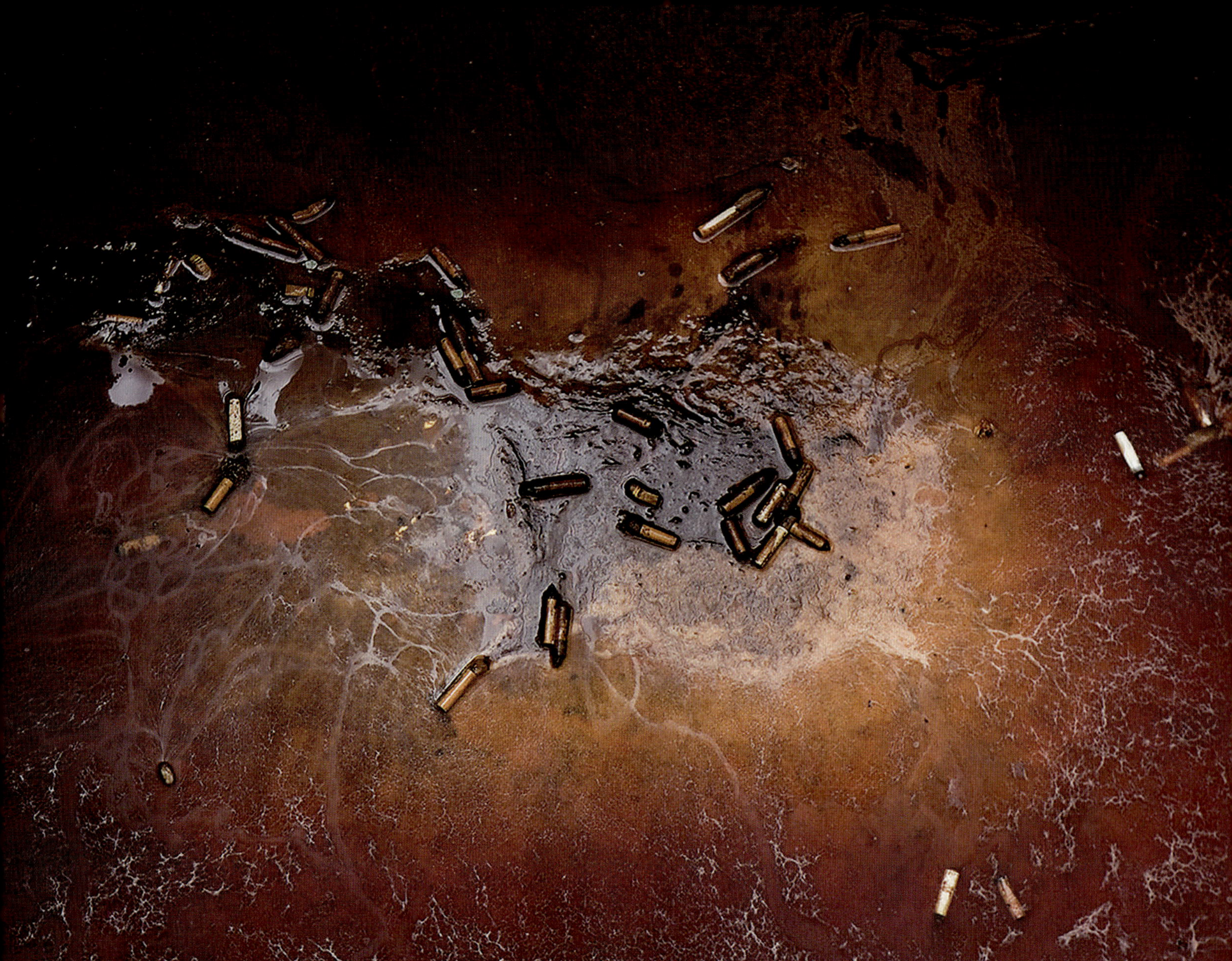

Above: Inside detail of *Sodbrennen*, 2000–2004

Left:

The Thing, 2003

Film, paint marker, acrylic paint, varnish, two-component polyurethane
18 x 15 x 1 inches (45.7 x 38 x 2.5 cm)

Opposite page:

Broom, 2007

Polished stainless steel, gesso, inkjet print, polyurethane foam, glue
54 x 26 ¾ x 3 ½ inches (137 x 68 x 9 cm)

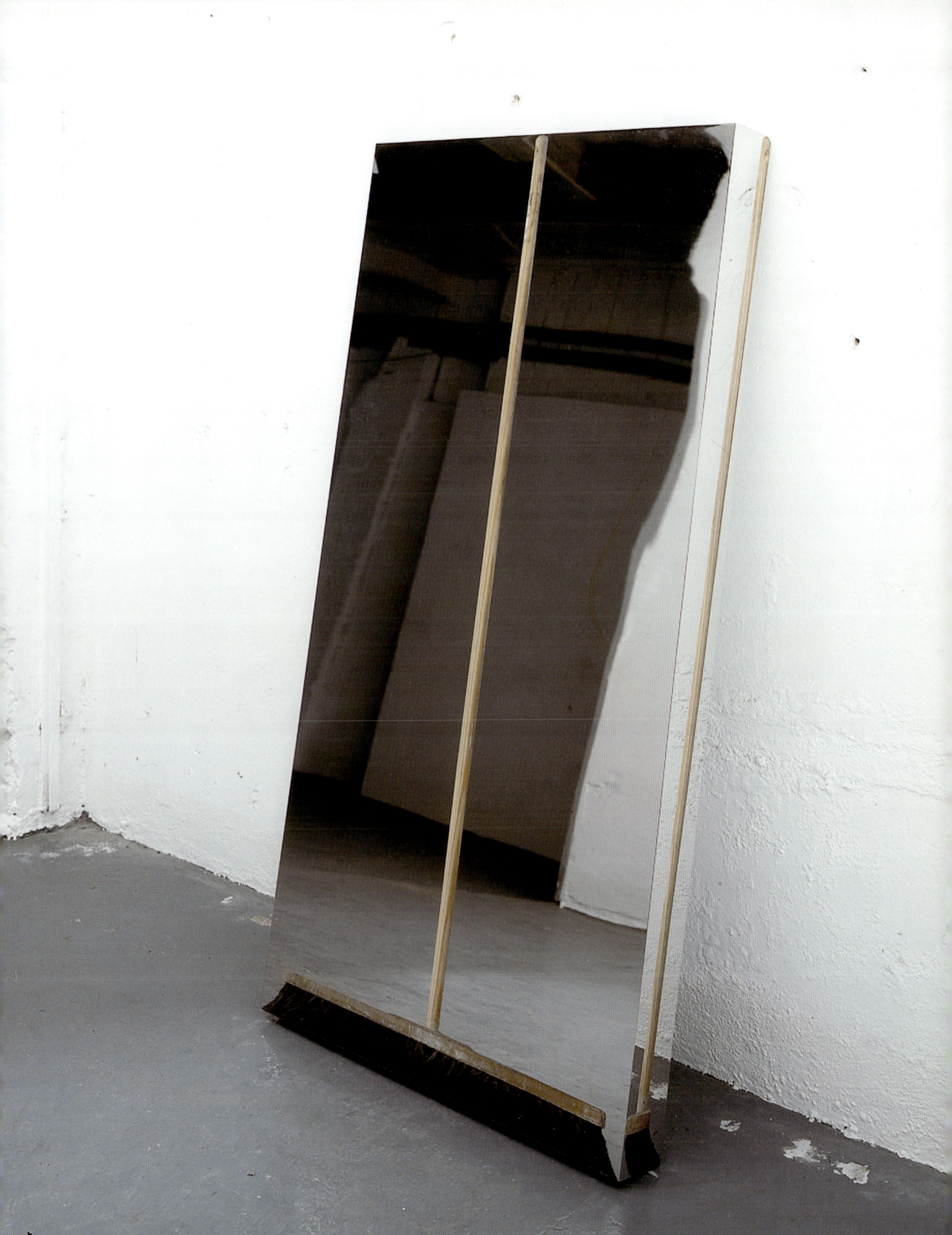

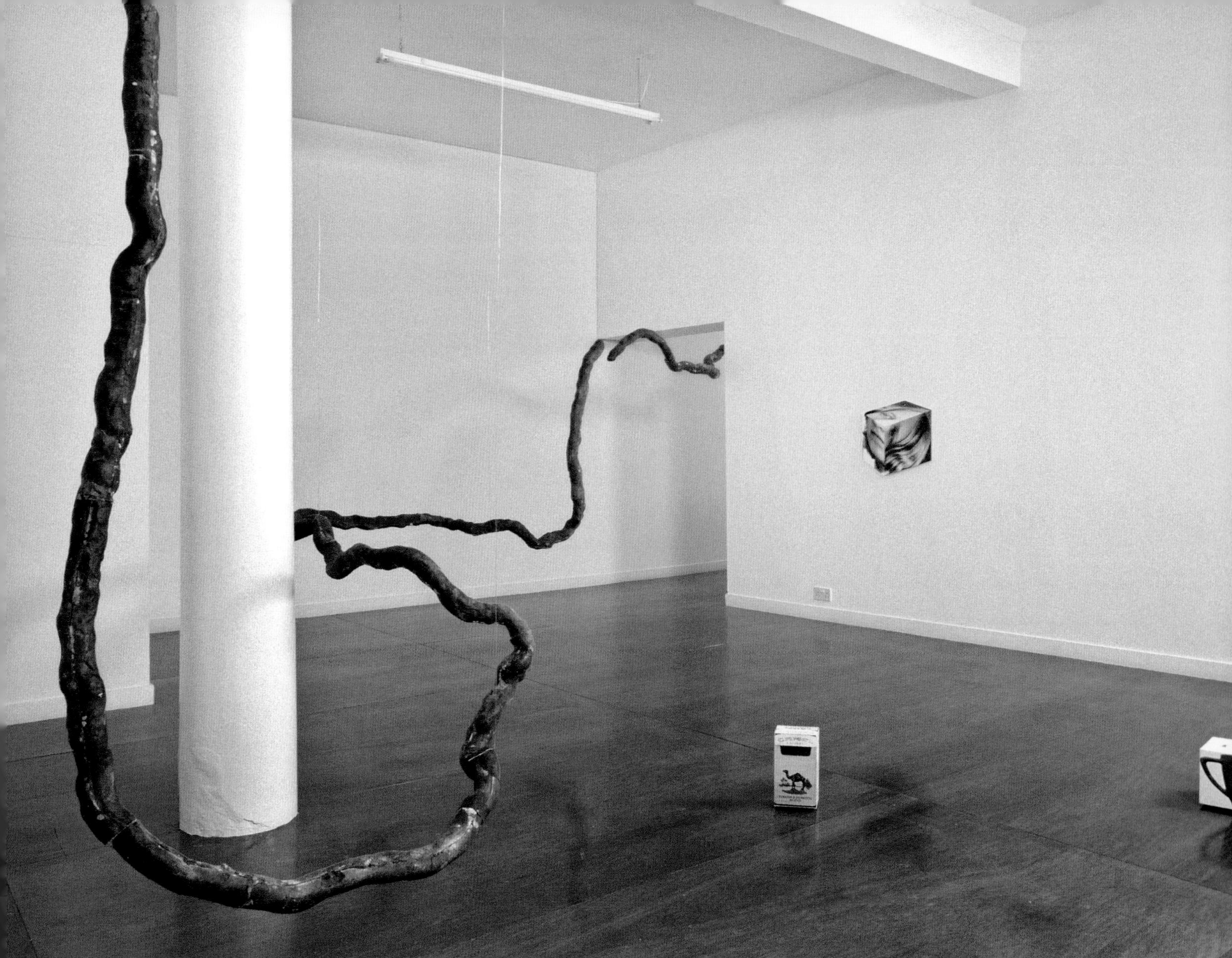

Cup / Cigarettes / Skid, 2006
Wood, polyurethane glue, acrylic paint, nails
Coffee cup: 7 ½ x 9 ⅝ x 7 ⅛ inches (19 x 24.3 x 18 cm)
Cigarettes: 10 ¼ x 5 ⅜ x 3 ½ inches (26 x 13.8 x 8.9 cm)
Pallet: 31 ⅞ x 26 ¾ x 3 ½ inches (81.1 x 67.8 x 8.9 cm)
Installation view, "Oh. Sad. I see.," The Modern Institute, Glasgow, 2006
Mackintosh Staccato, 2006; On wall: *Oh, Sad, I See*, 2006

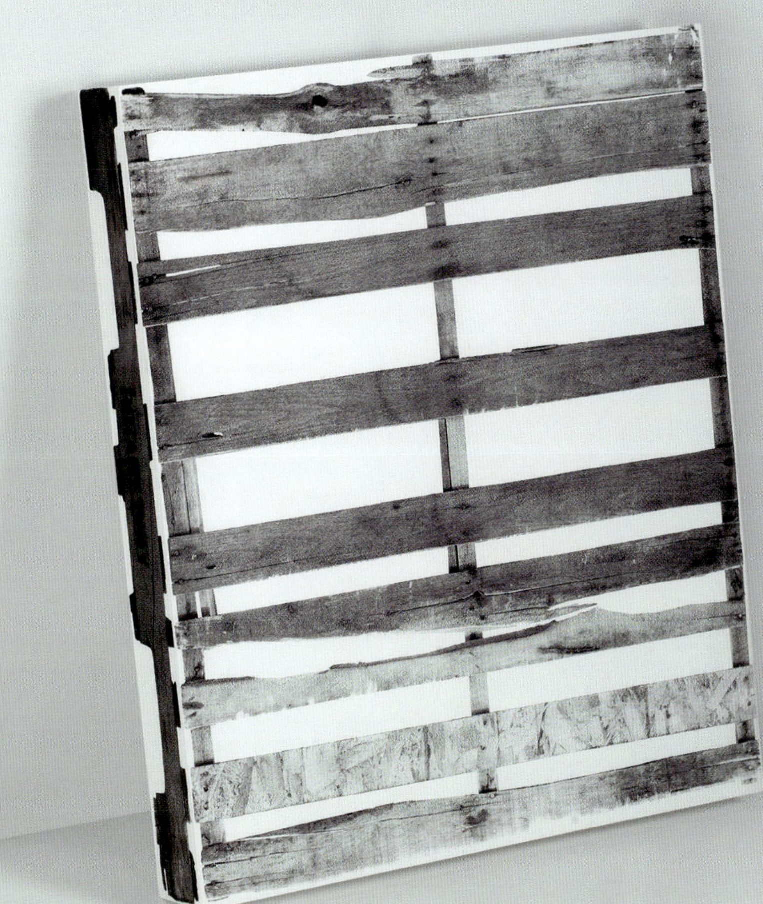

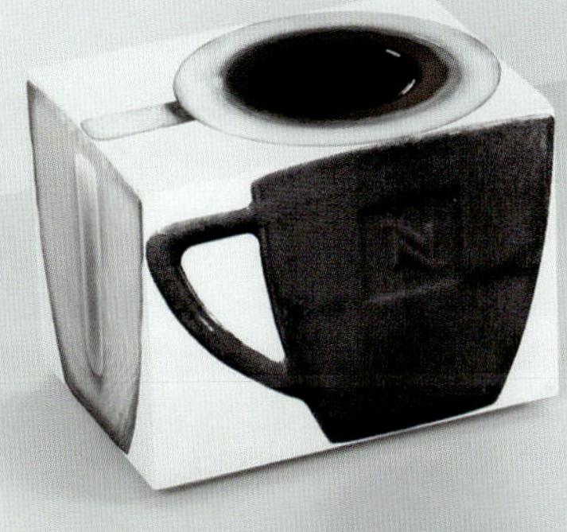

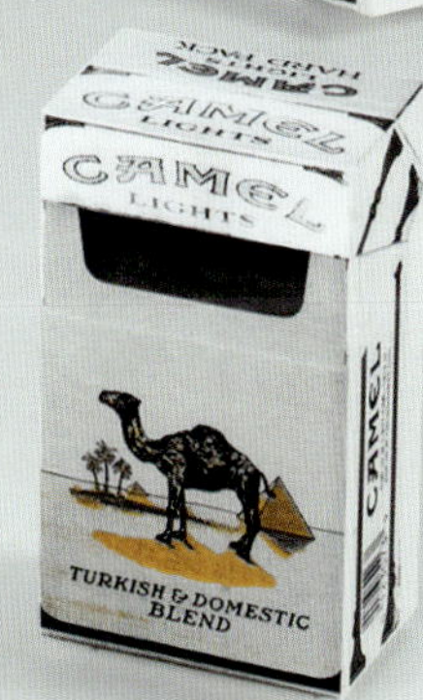
CAMEL
LIGHTS
TURKISH & DOMESTIC
BLEND

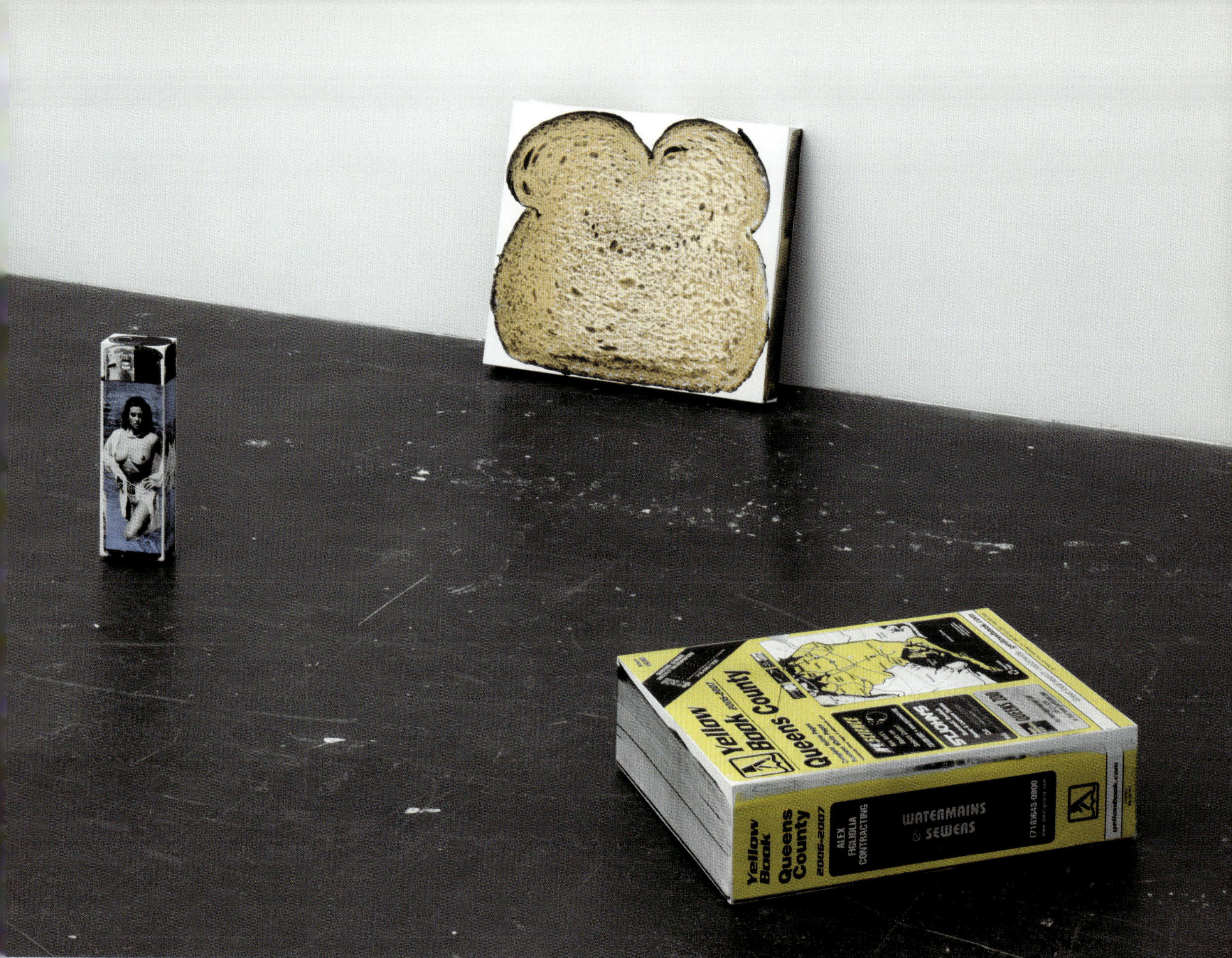

Untitled, 2006
MDF, gesso acrylic paint, wood, wood glue, screws
Lighter: 14 ⅜ x 4 ⅜ x 2 inches (36.6 x 11 x 5.2 cm)
Book: 6 ¼ x 21 ⅝ x 16 ⅜ inches (15.8 x 55 x 41.5 cm)
Toast: 21 ¼ x 23 ⅛ x 3 ⅛ inches (54 x 58.8 x 7.8 cm)

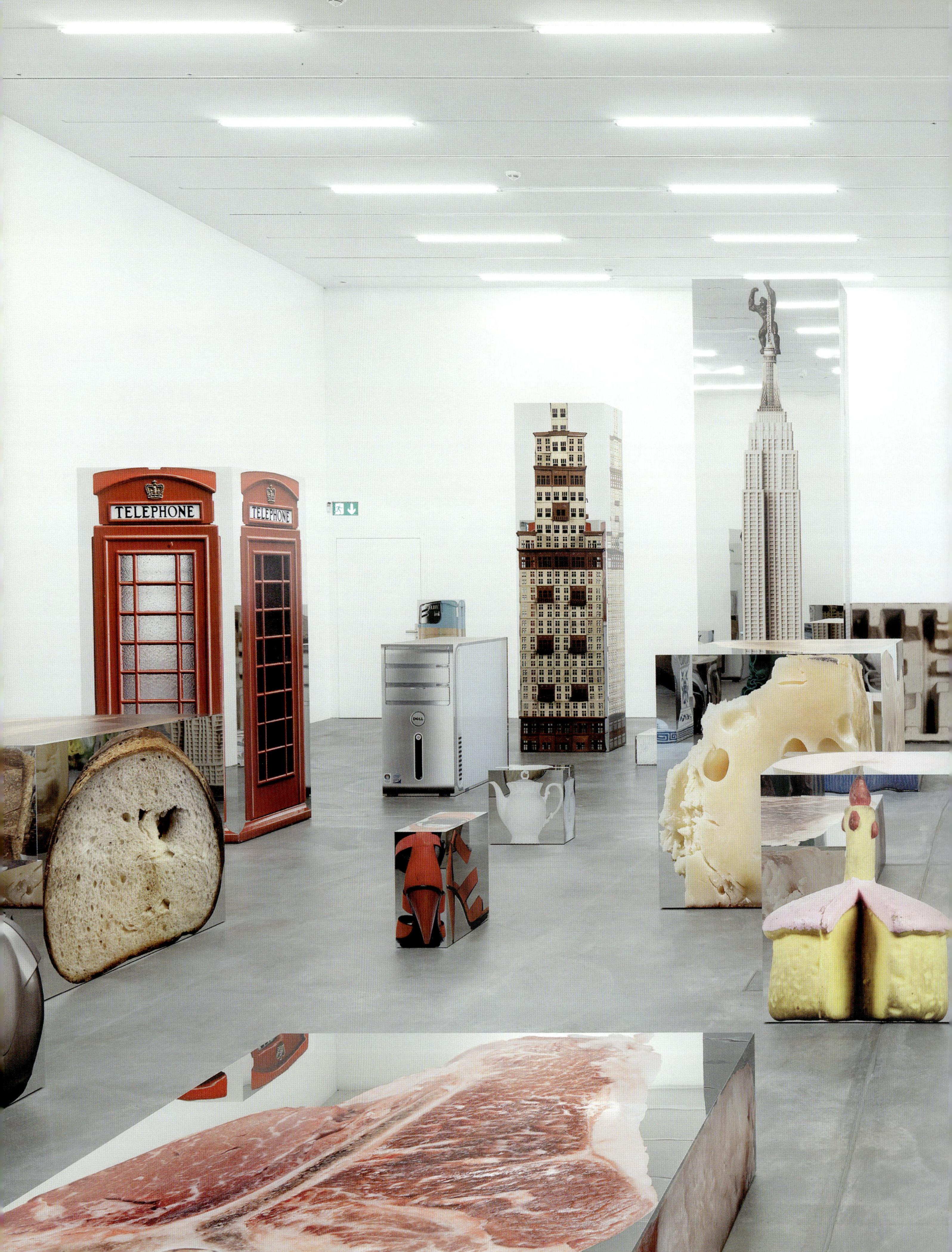
TELEPHONE
TELEPHONE

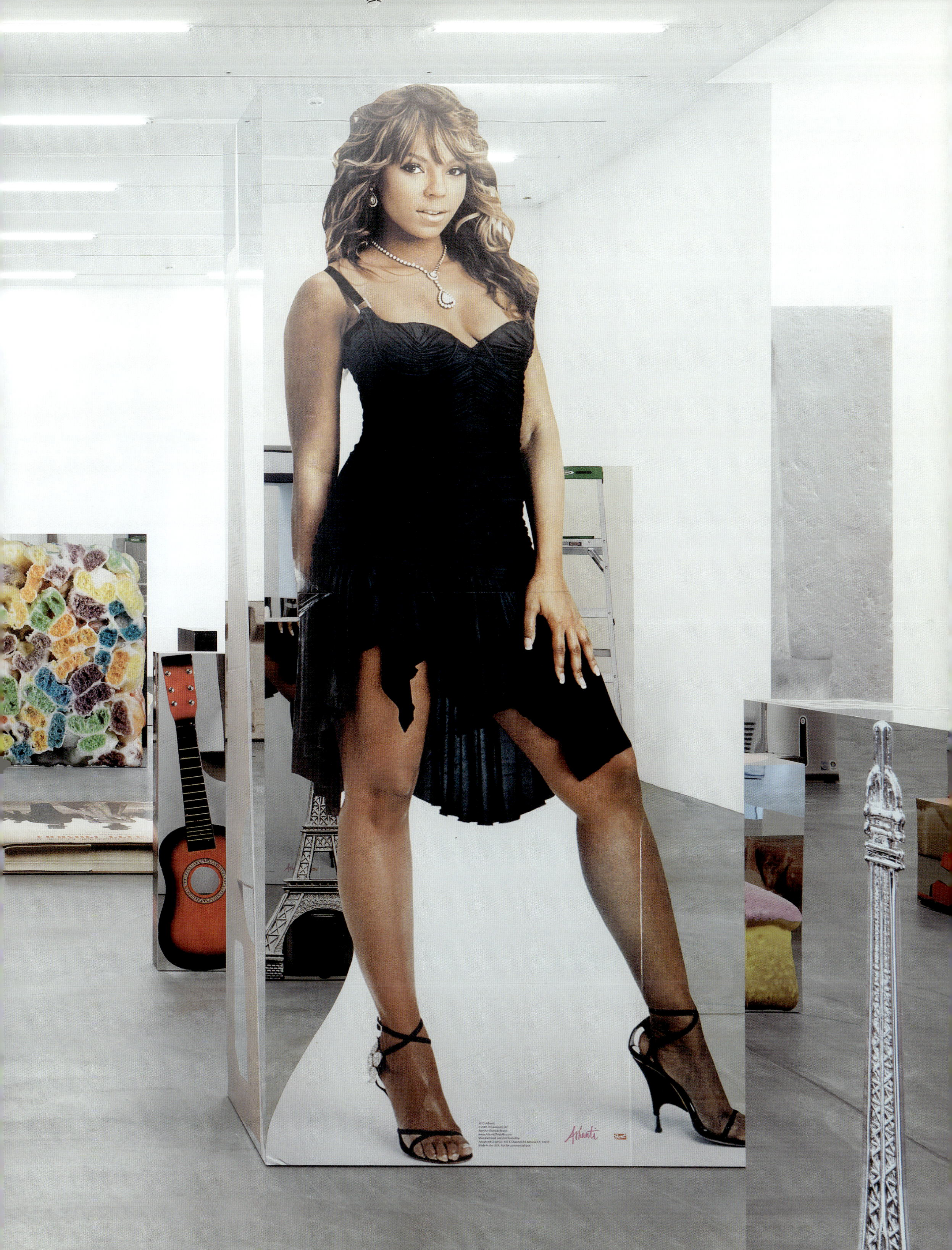
Ashanti

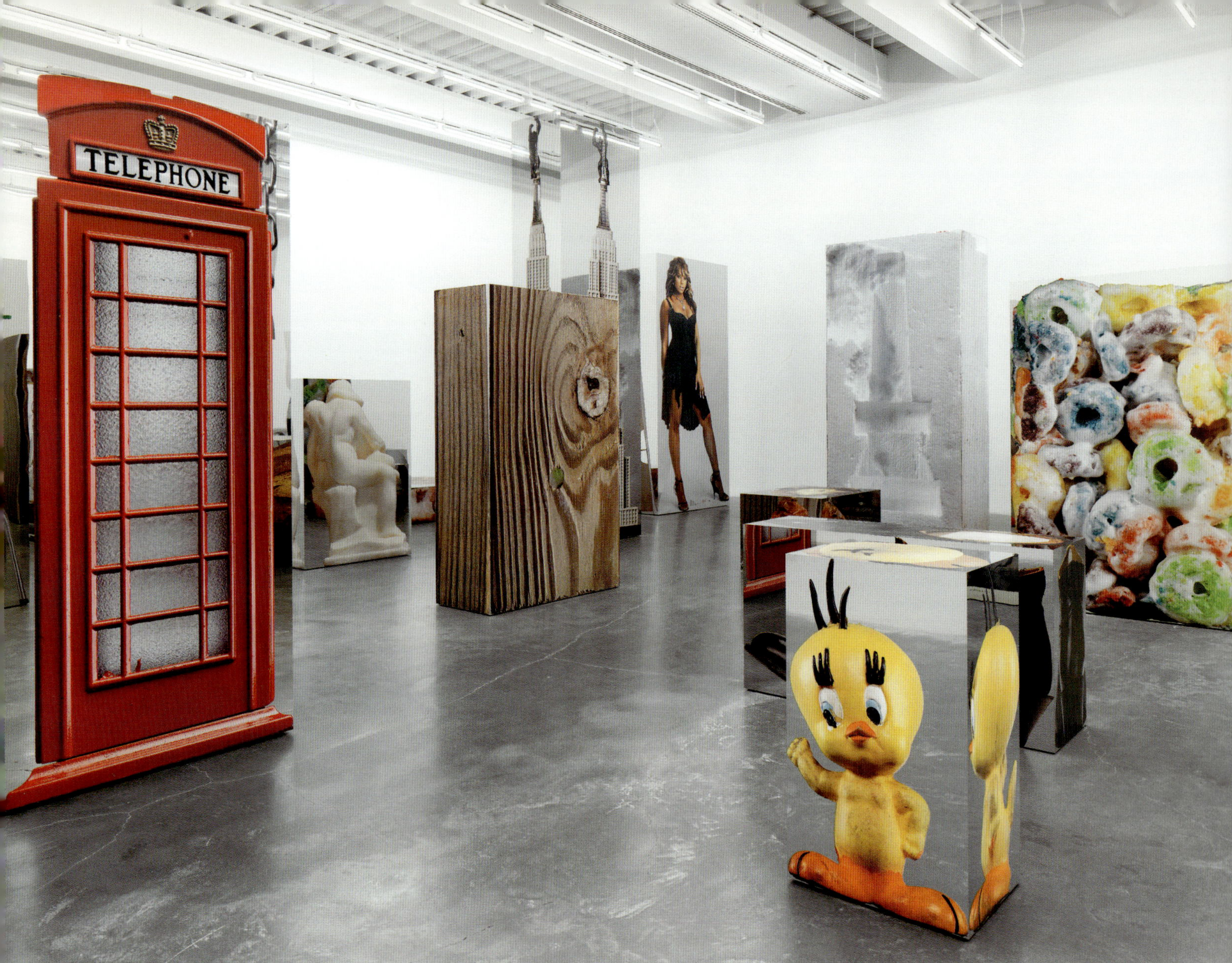

Previous spread and following pages:

Service à la francaise, 2009

Silkscreen print on mirror-polished stainless-steel sheets, polyurethane foam sheets, two-component polyurethane adhesive, stainless-steel beams, aluminum L sections, screws; in 52 parts

Installation dimensions variable

Installation view, "Marguerite de Ponty," New Museum, New York, 2009–2010

Above: Drug Dealer, Bookie, Court Jester, Dental Hygienist, Landlord, Taxi Driver, Professor, Unemployed

Opposite page: Factotum, Drug Dealer, News Anchor, Actor, Thief, Attorney, Dental Hygienist, Au Pair, Hairdresser, Branch Manager, Professor

Previous spread: Stripper, Undertaker, Drug Dealer, Thief, Actor, News Anchor, Factotum, Hairdresser, Au Pair, Dental Hygienist, Attorney, Professor, Branch Manager, Congressman, Landlord, Referee

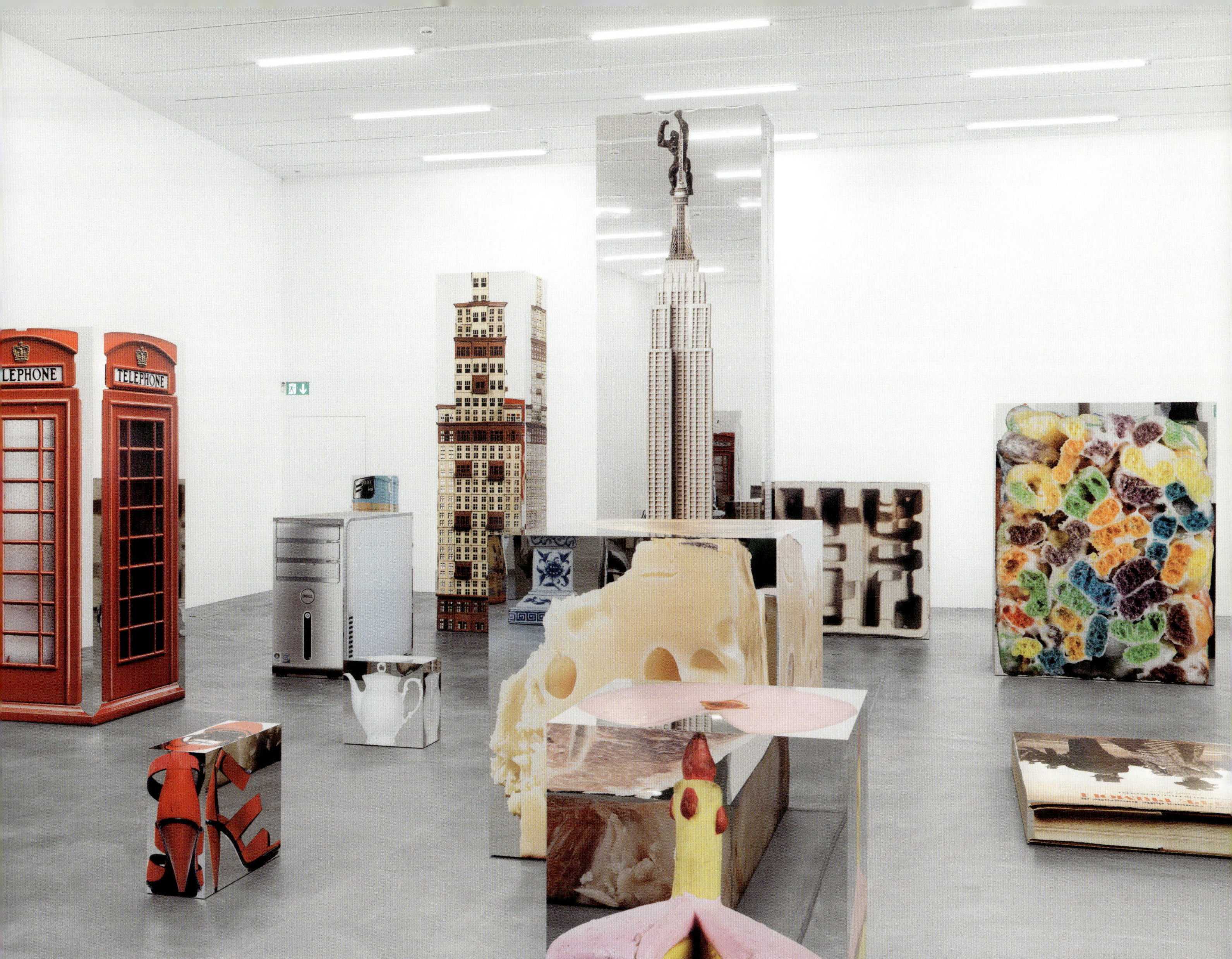
LEPHONE
TELEPHONE

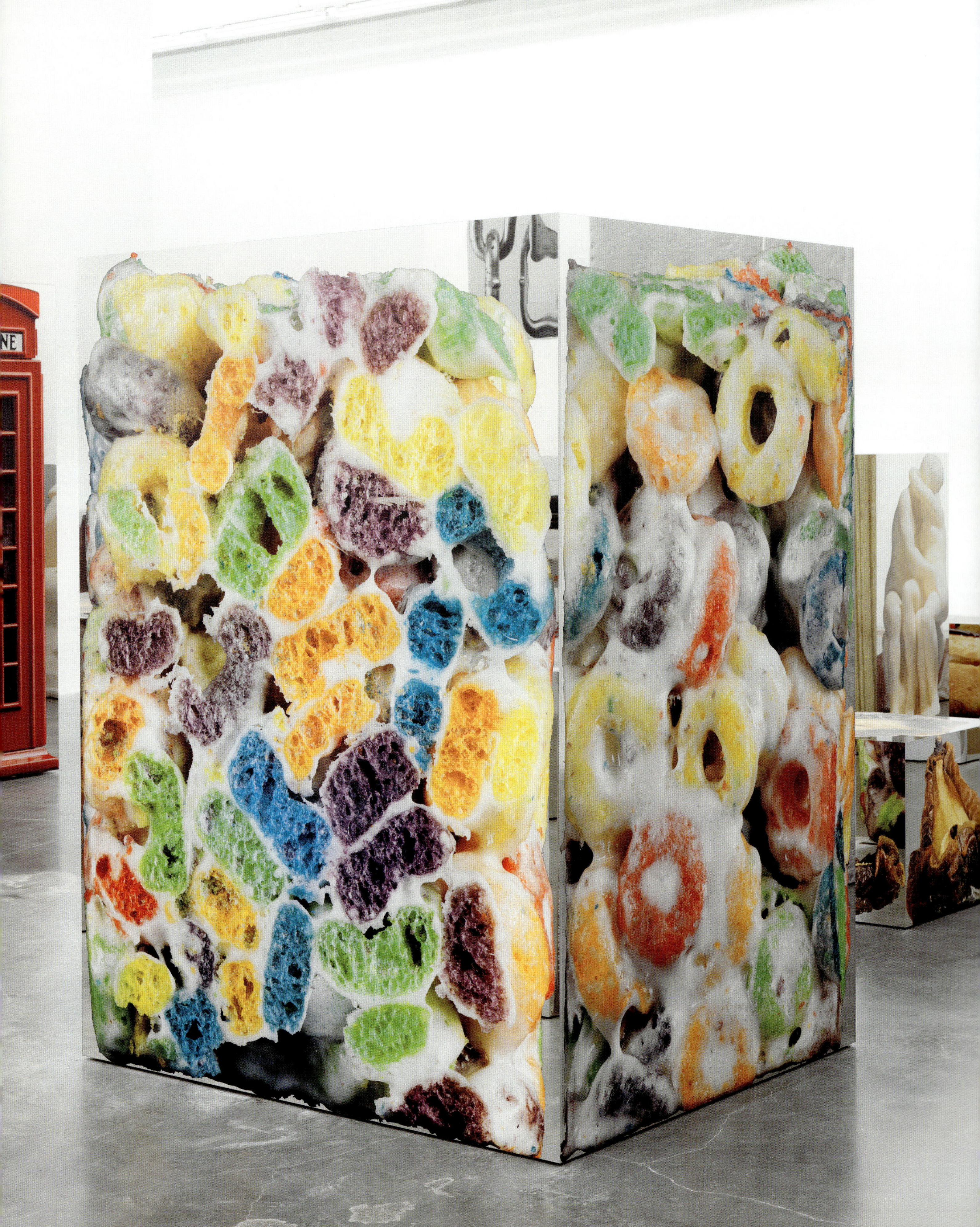

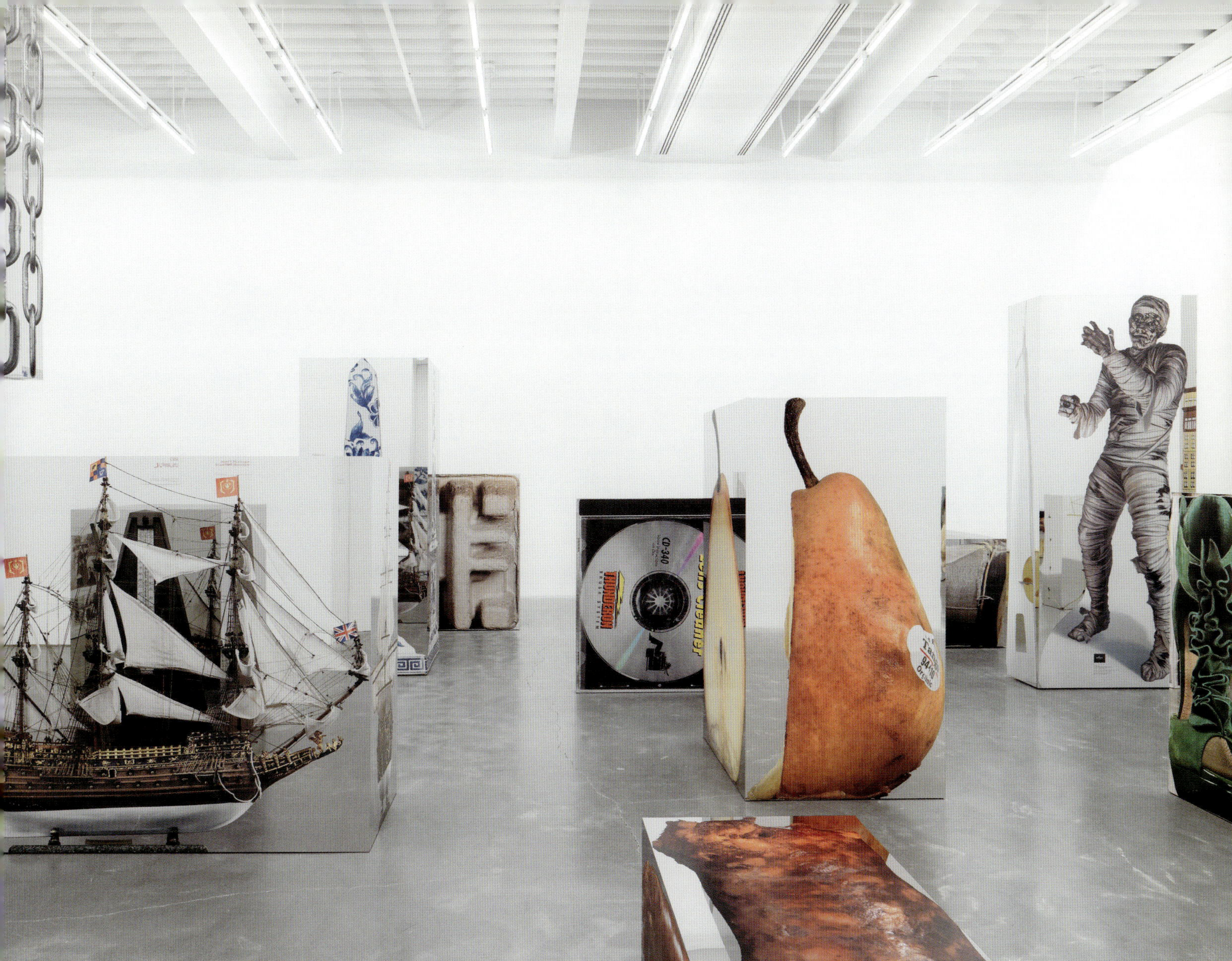

Above: Migrant Worker, Dentist, Cowboy, Attorney, Flight Attendant,
Tour Guide, Florist, Sheriff, Locksmith
Opposite page: Professor

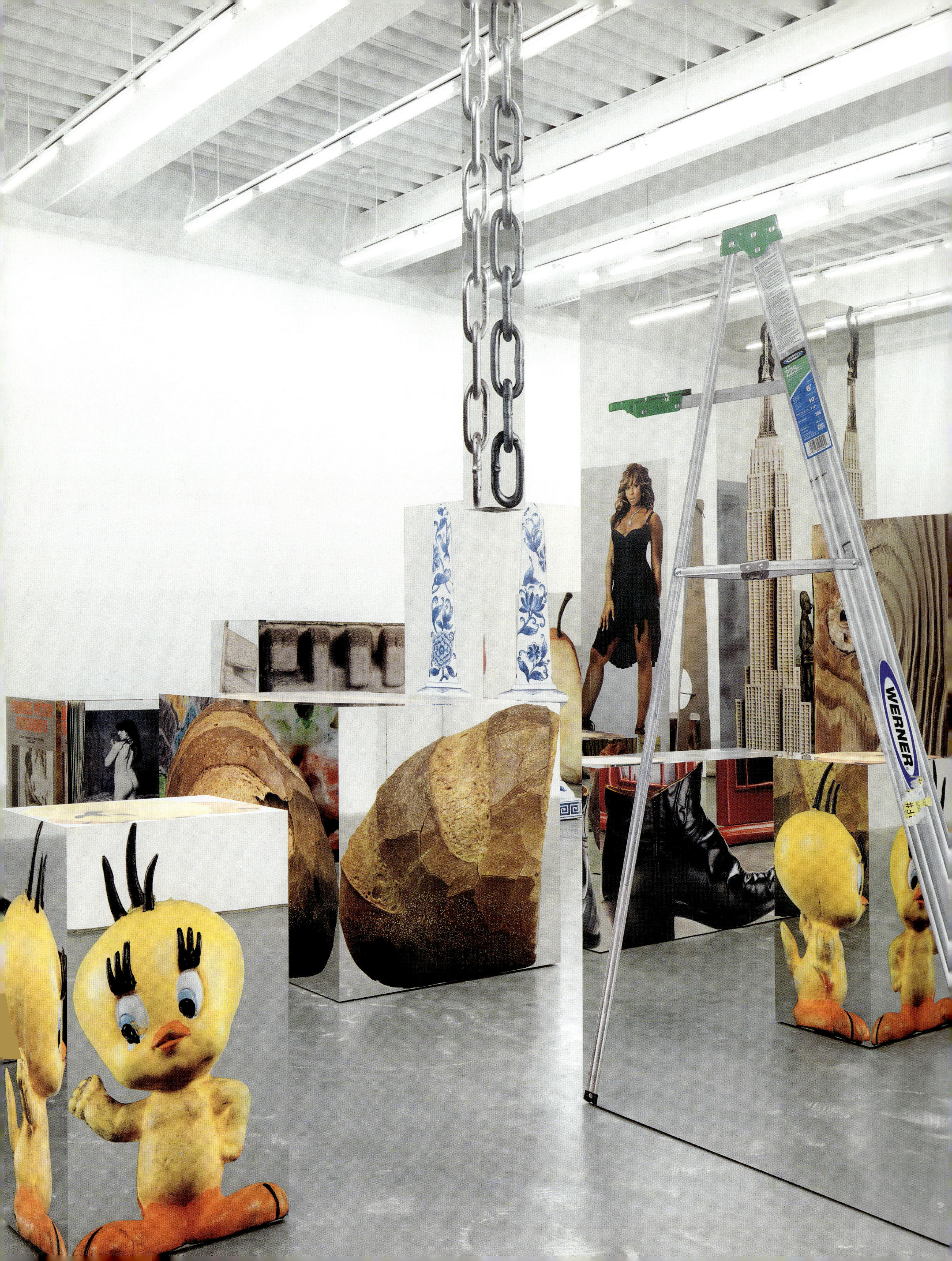
WERNER

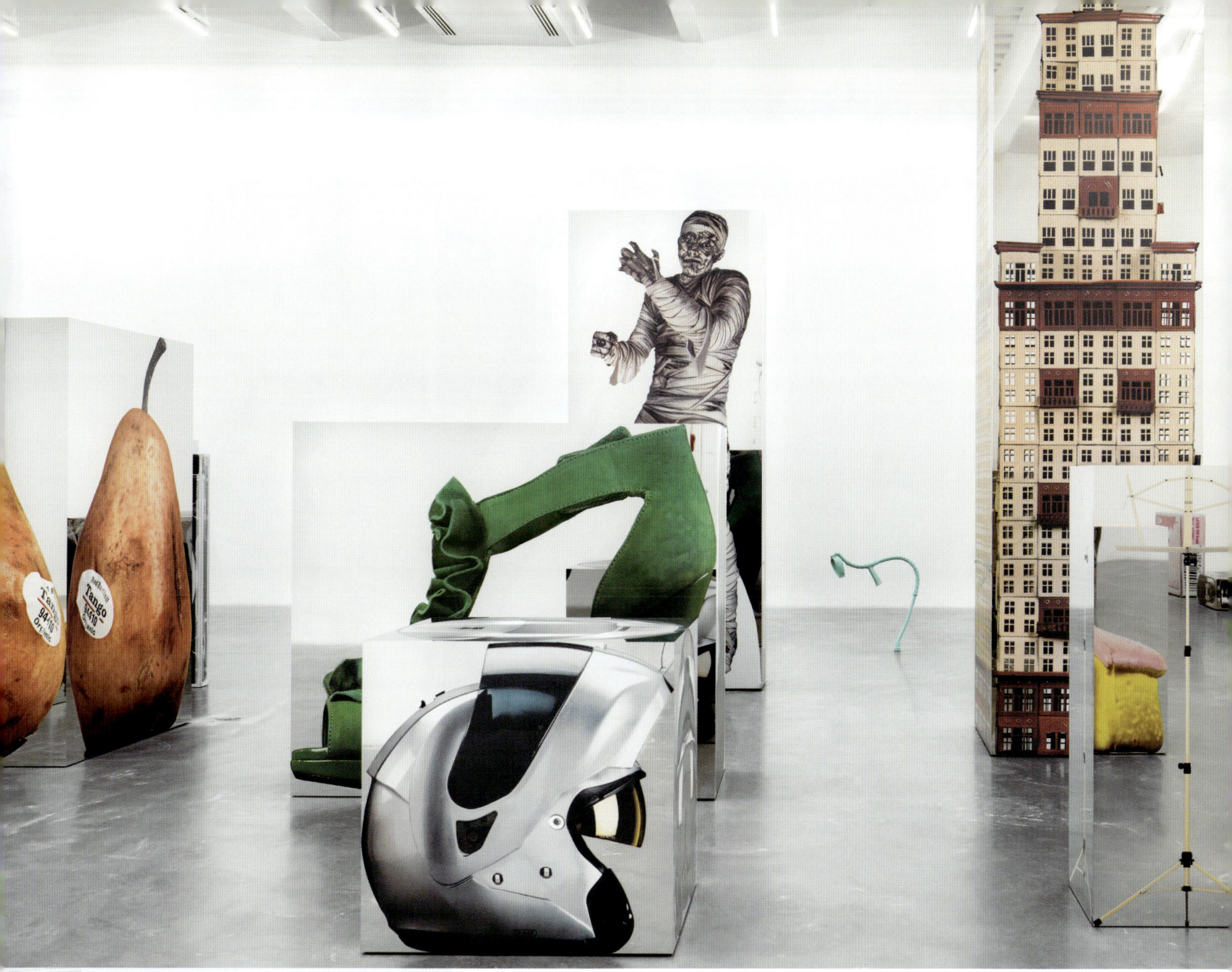

Above: Tour Guide, Teacher, Sheriff, Locksmith, Thief, Taxman; *4:15pm & 4:15pm*, 2009
Left: Congressman
Opposite page: Unemployed, Undertaker, Vice President, Attorney, Cowboy, Migrant Worker, Secretary

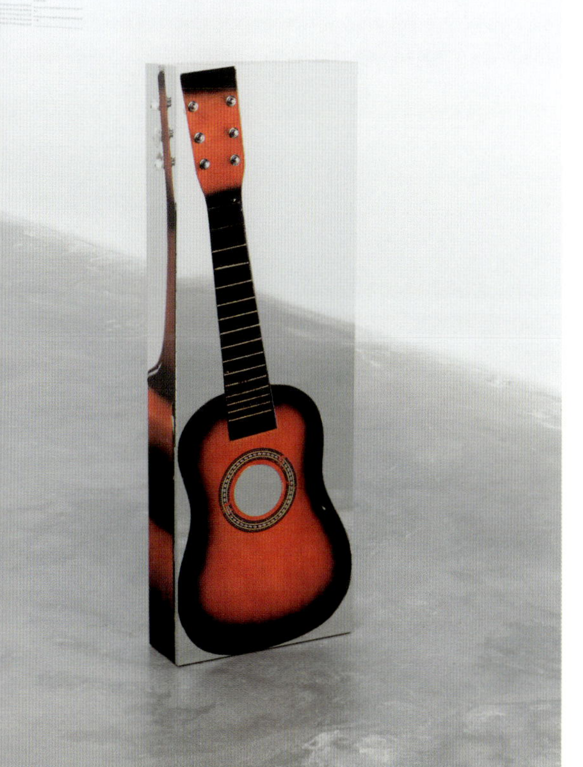

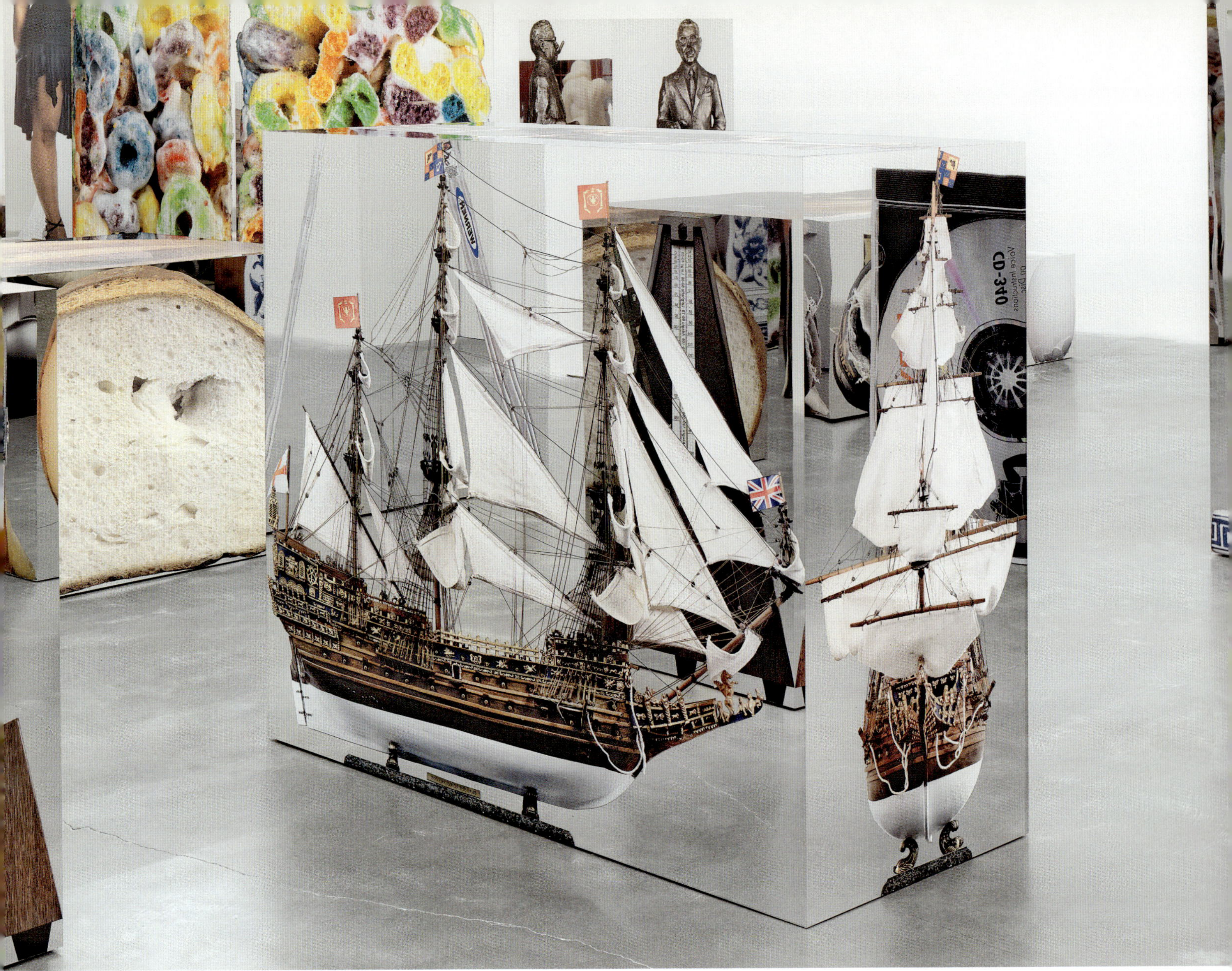

Above: Dentist, Undertaker, Professor, Cleaning Woman, Cowboy
Opposite page: Tour Guide, Migrant Worker, Undertaker, Court Jester, Dental Hygienist, Professor, Vice President, Cowboy, Flight Attendant

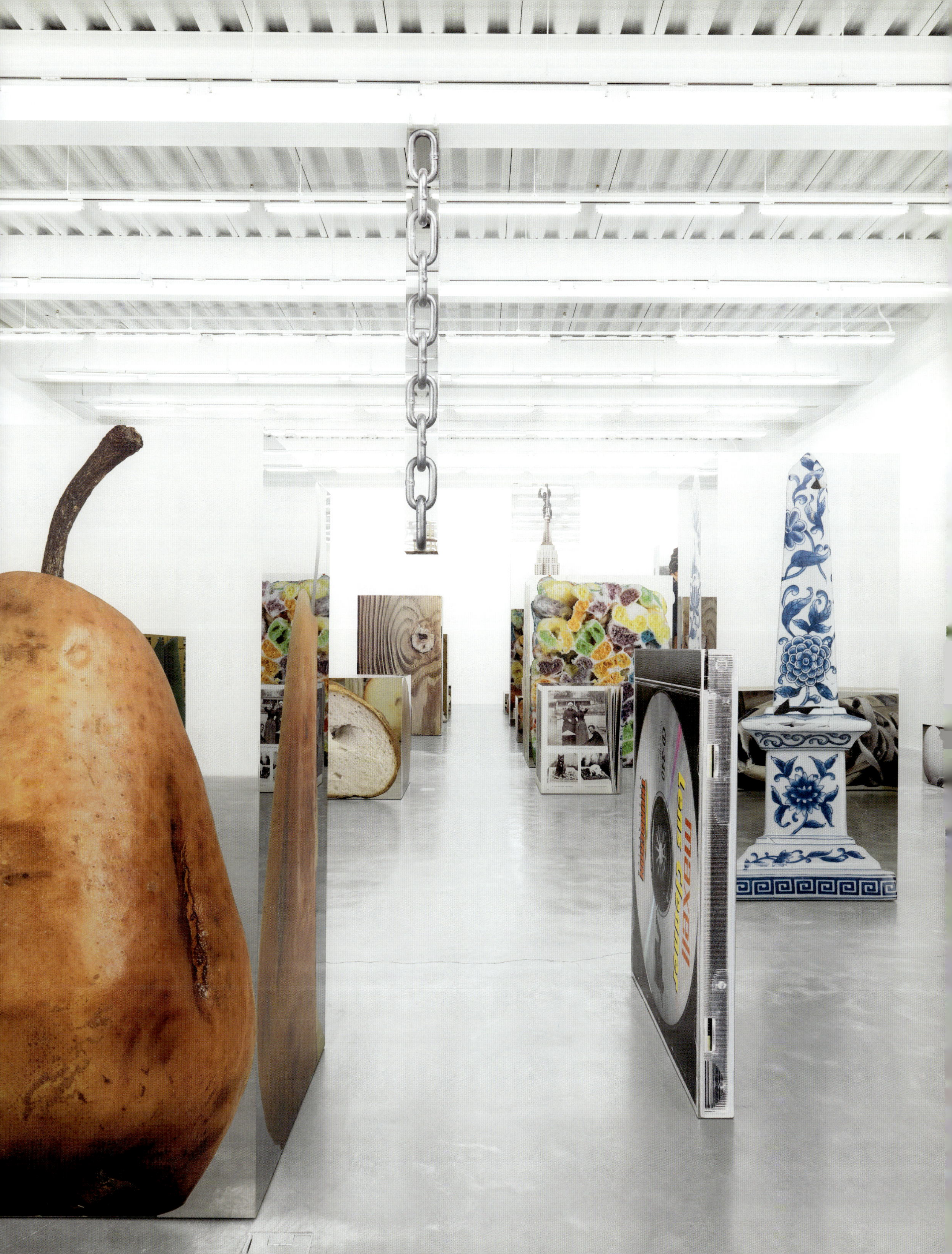
maxell
Lens Cleaner
CD-340

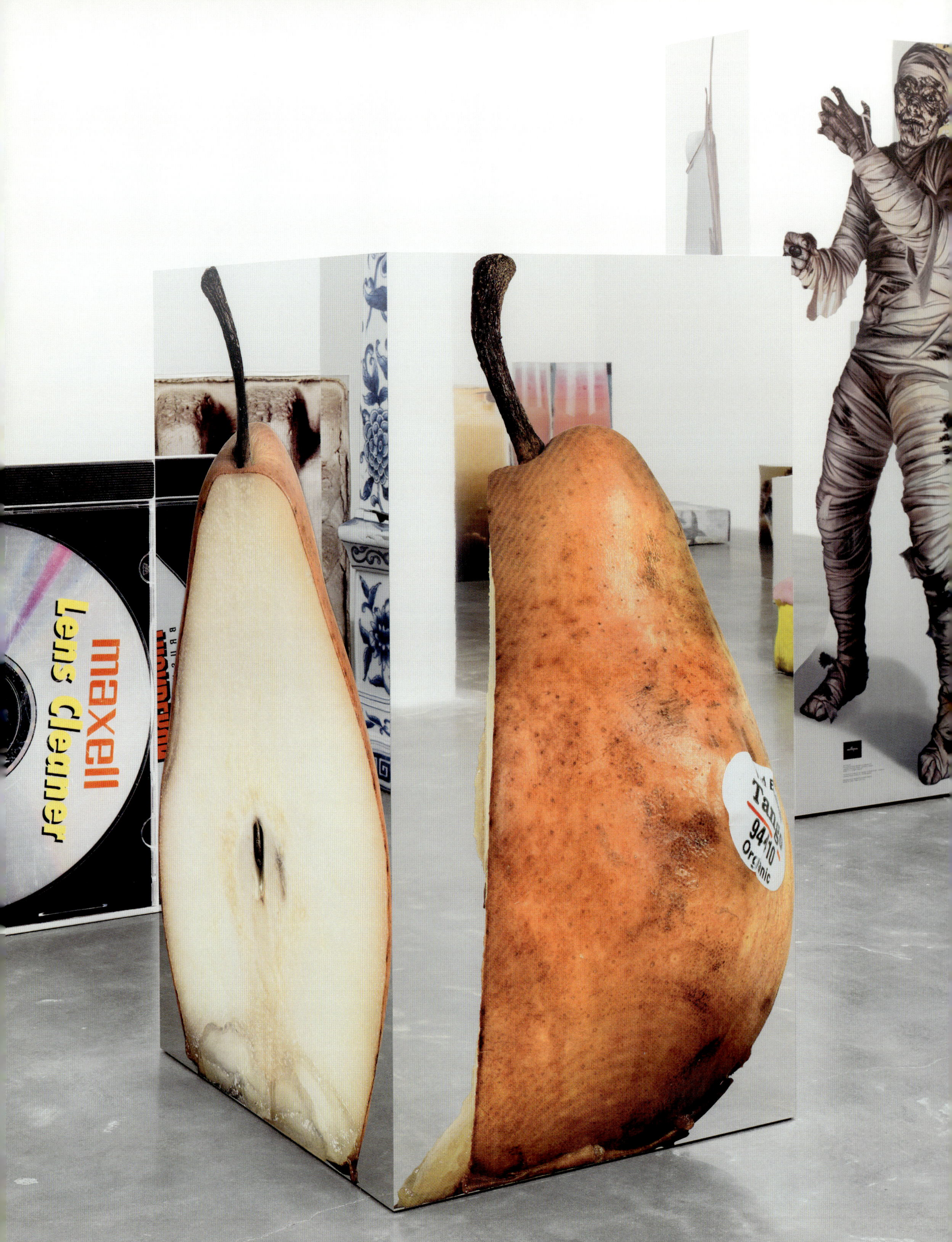
maxell
Lens Cleaner
Tango
94410
Organic

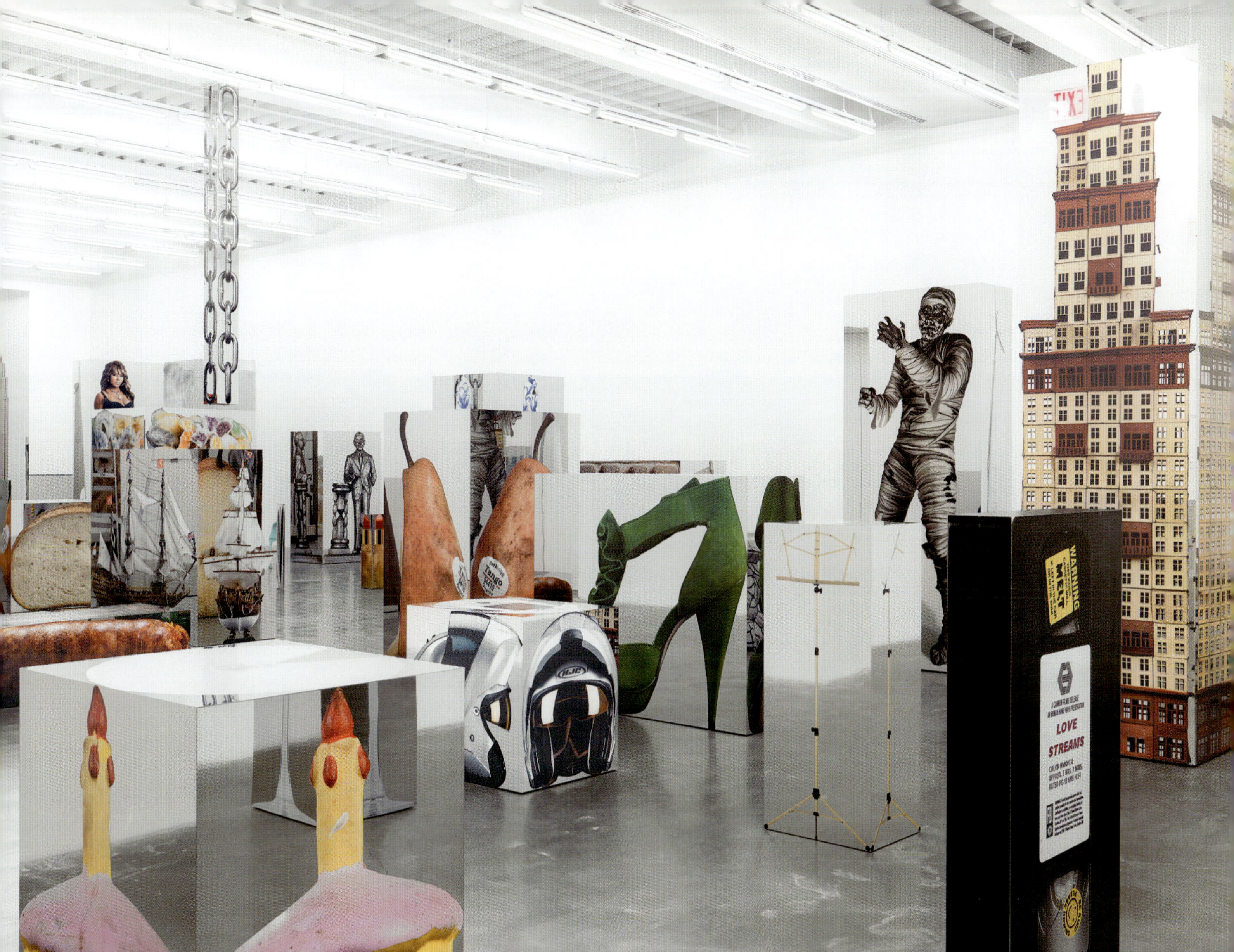

Above: Hairdresser, Florist, Dentist, Undertaker, Professor, Dental Hygienist, Landlord, Migrant Worker, Cleaning Woman, Cowboy, Tour Guide, Sheriff, Teacher, Chef, Taxman, Thief, Locksmith
Opposite page: Tour Guide, Flight Attendant, Locksmith
Next page: Actor
Page 137, top: Figure Skater; bottom: Stripper

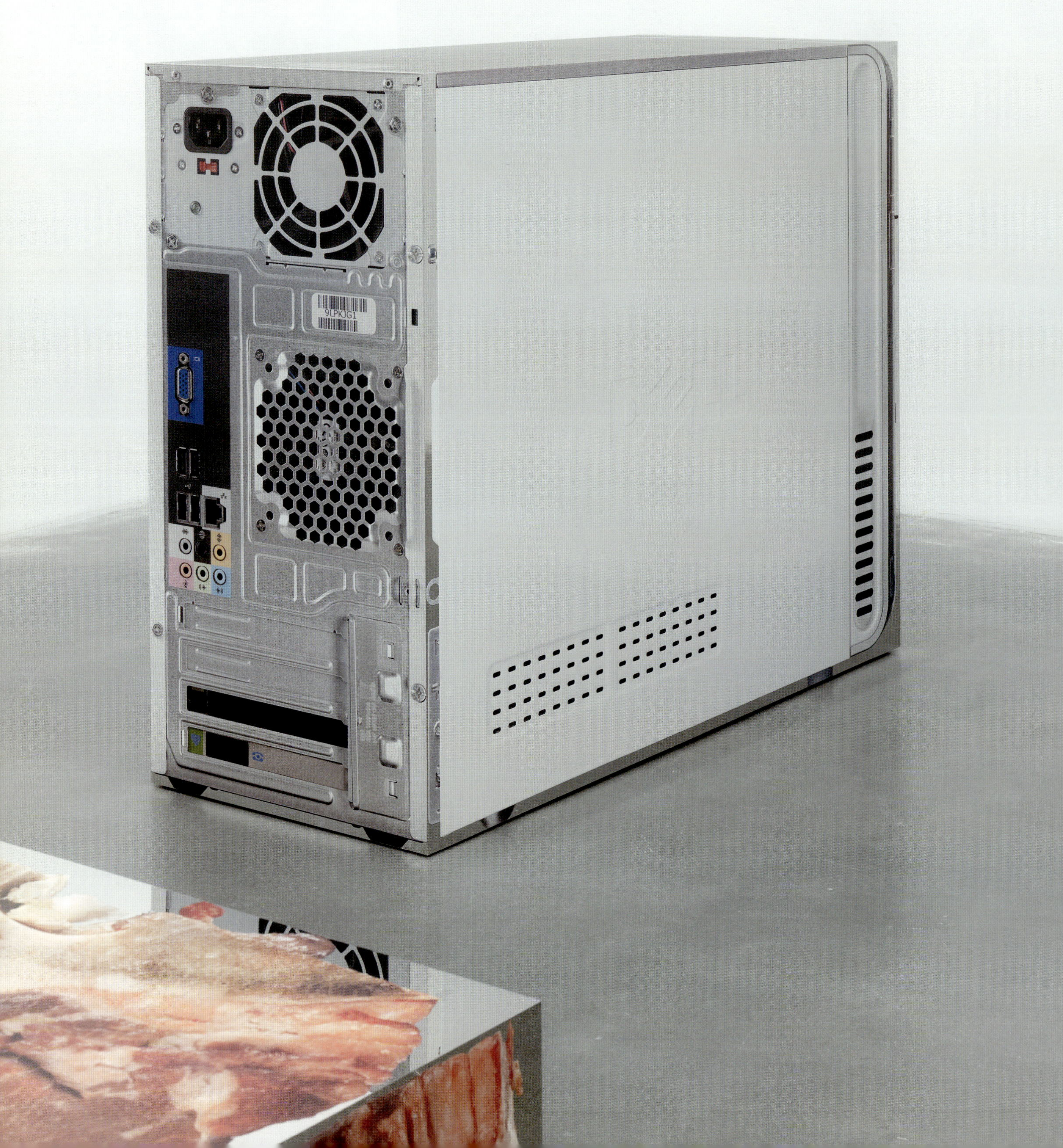
9LPKJG1

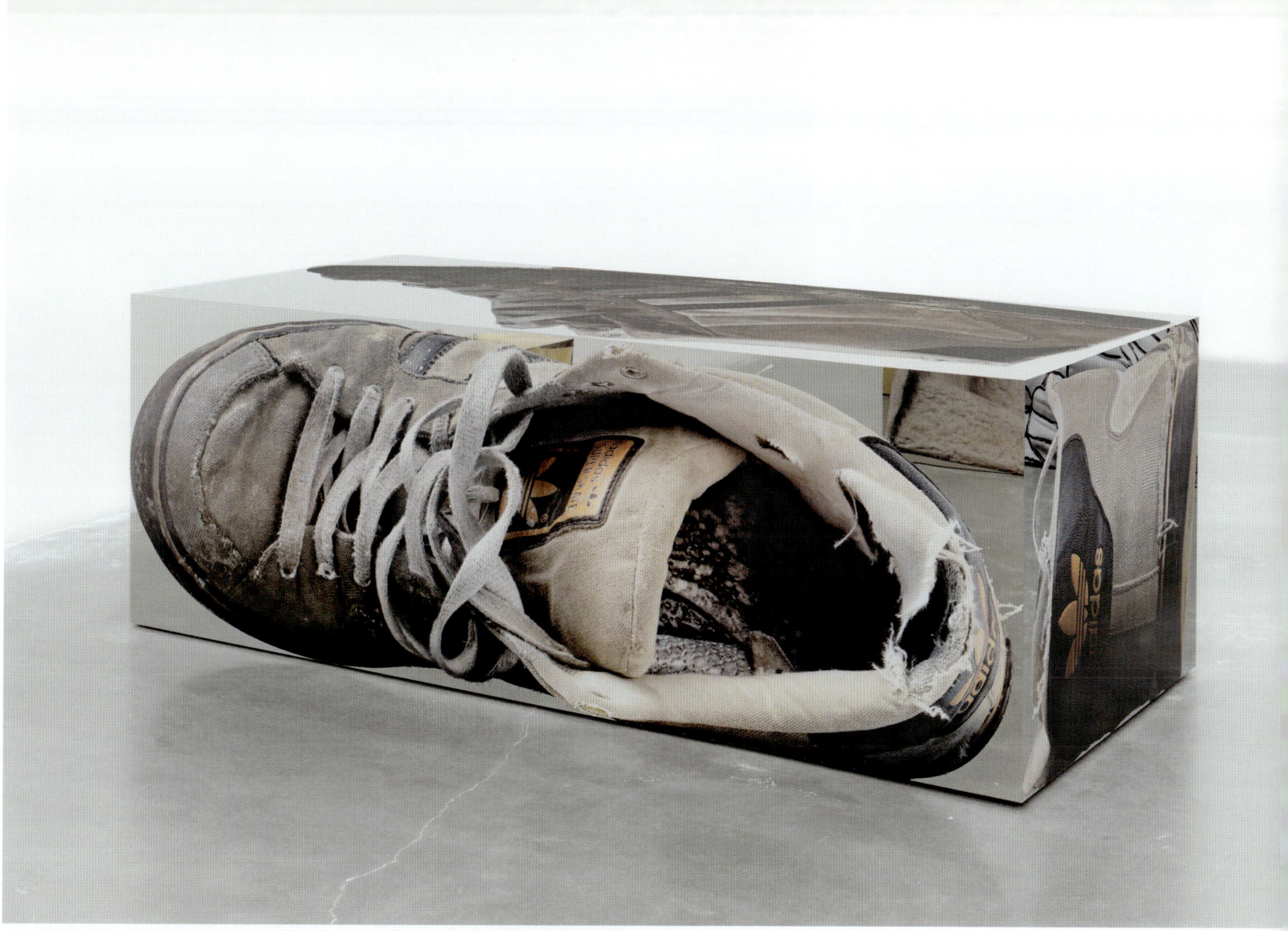

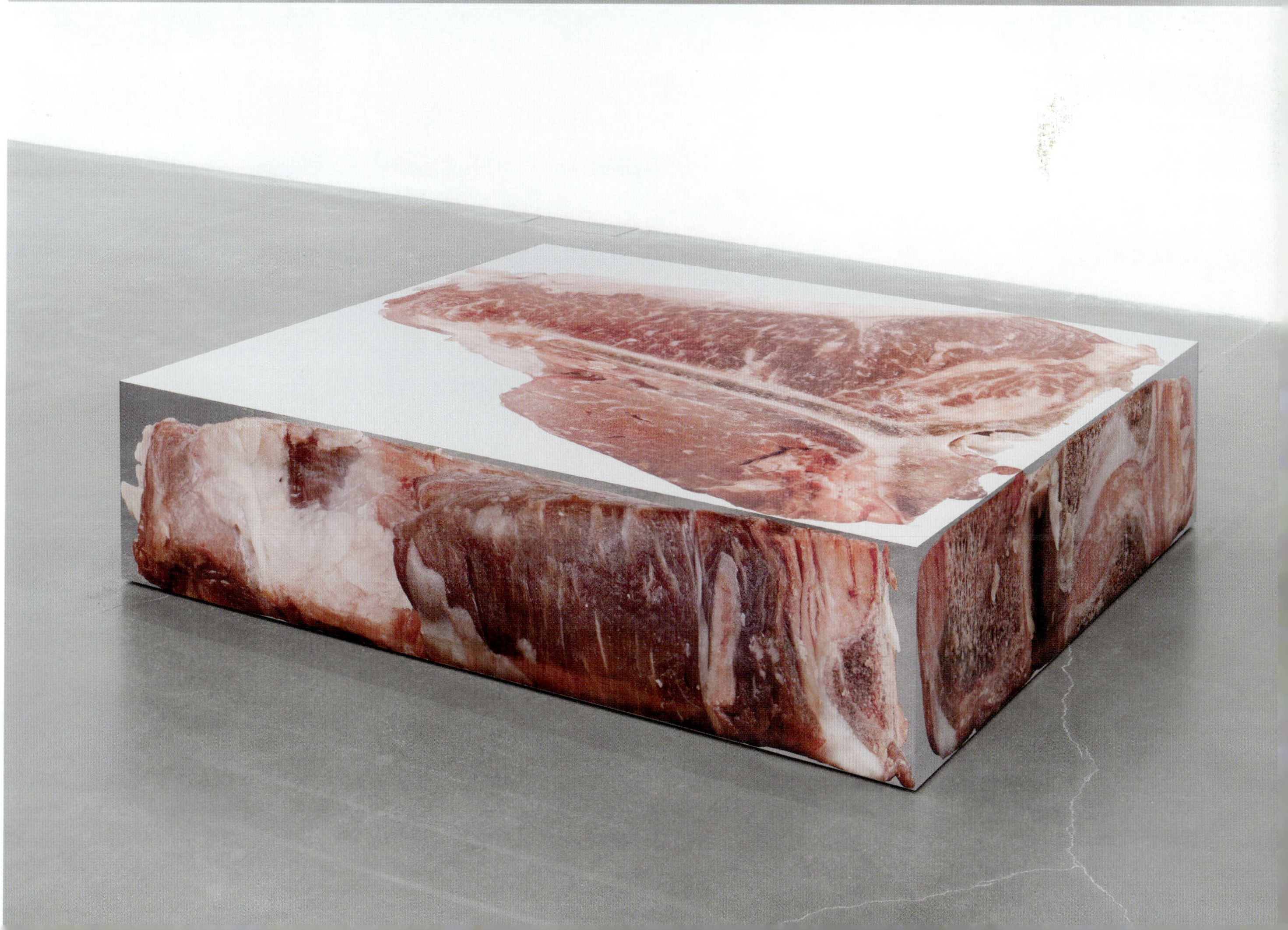

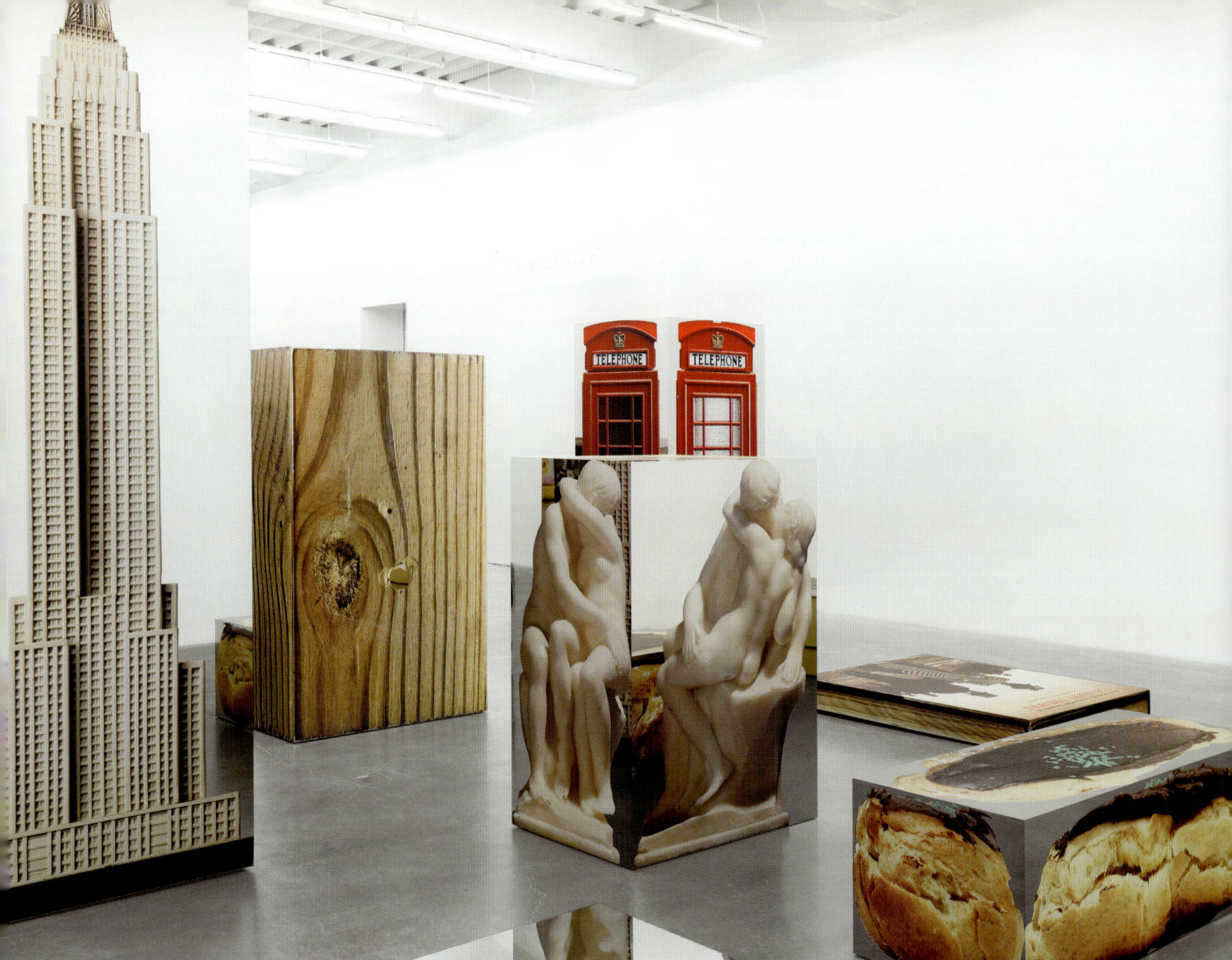

Above: Dental Hygienist, Court Jester,
Drug Dealer, Bookie, Bodyguard, Branch Manager
Opposite page: Bookie, Dental Hygienist,
Taxi Driver, Cleaning Woman, Court Jester

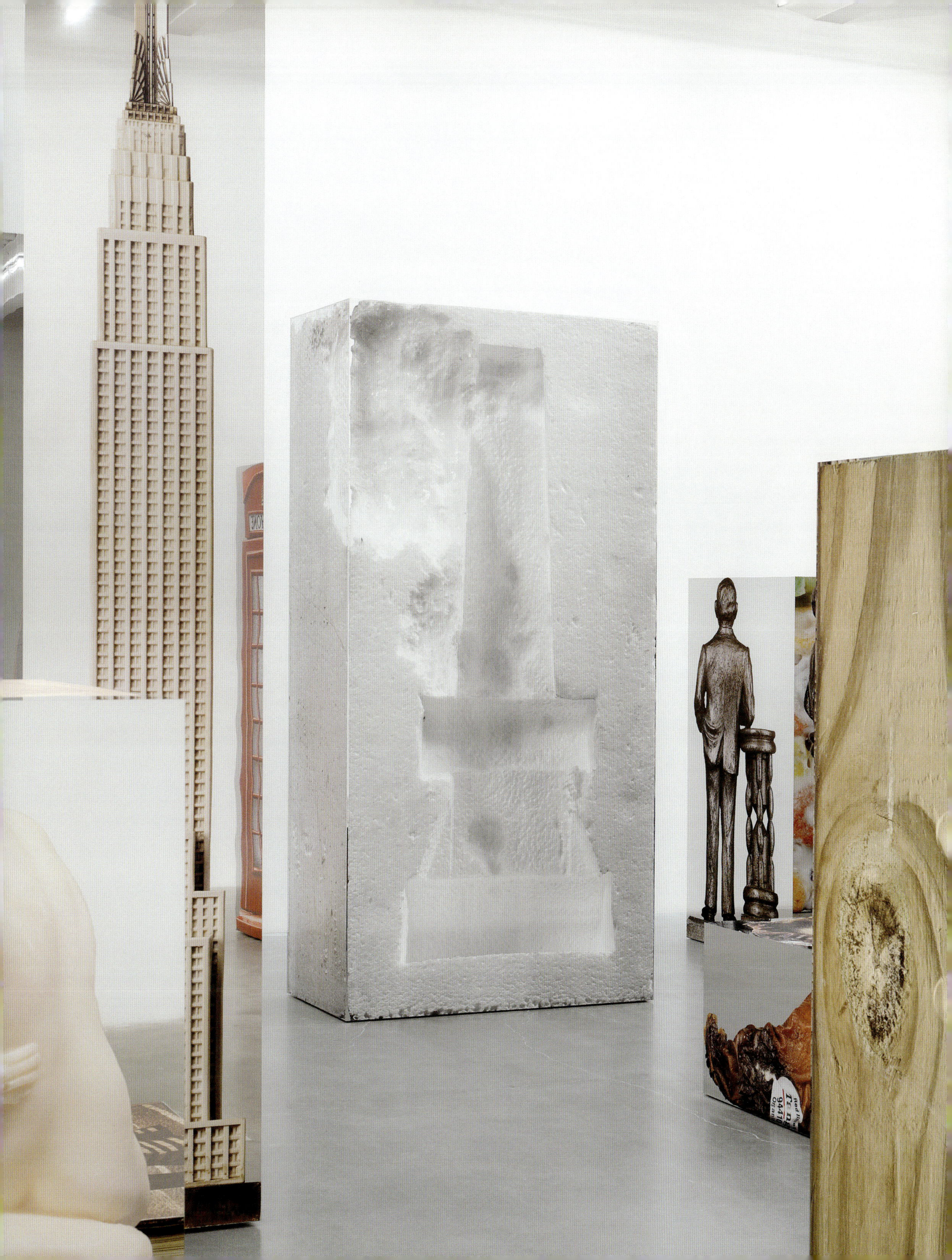

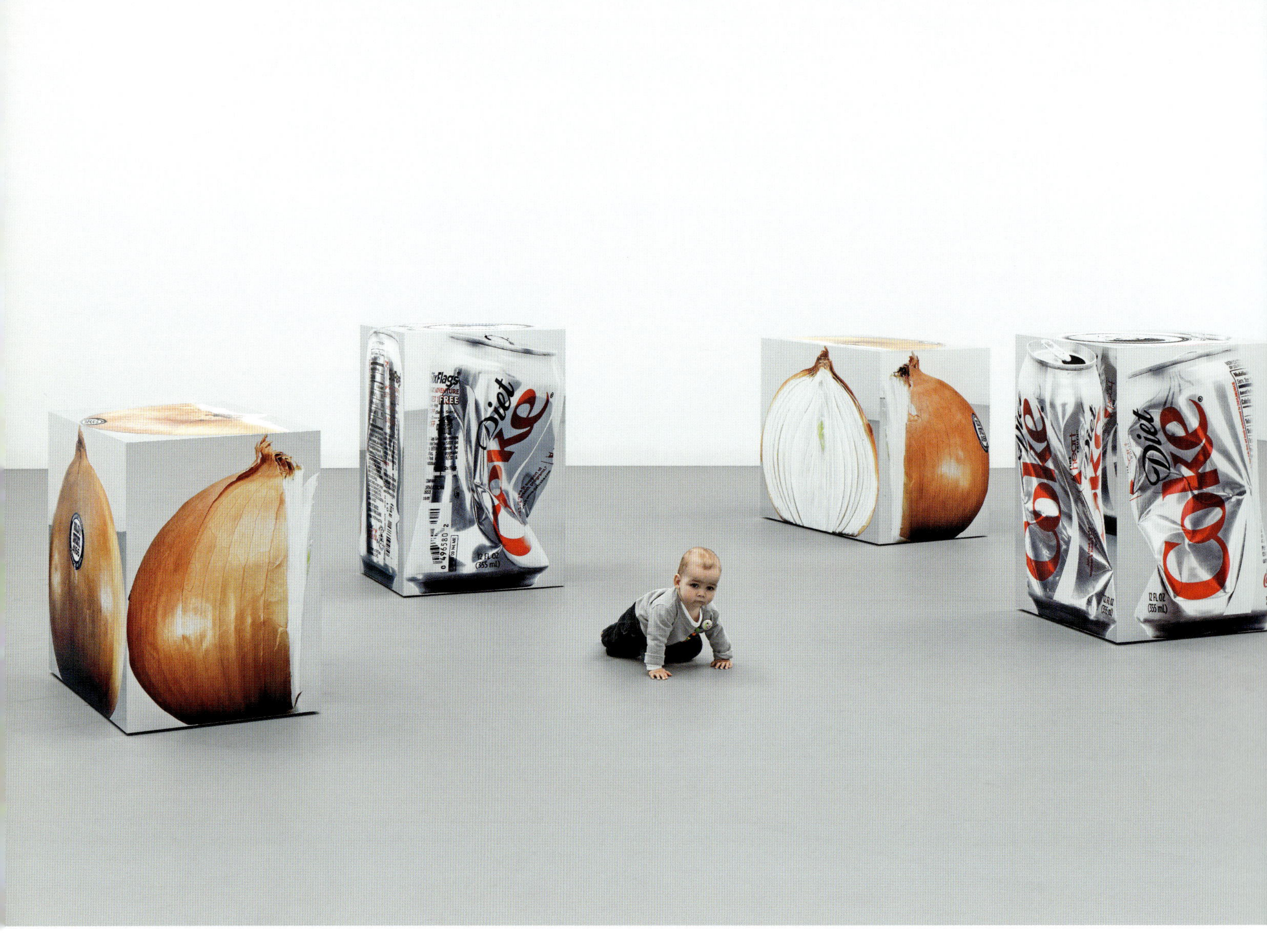

Lassie / Pizza, 2010
Silkscreen print on mirror-polished stainless-steel sheets, polyurethane foam sheets, two-component polyurethane adhesive, stainless-steel beams, aluminum L sections, screws; in 4 parts
Diet Coke can, each: 37 ¾ x 23 ½ x 24 ¾ inches (95.9 x 59.7 x 62.9 cm)
Onion, each: 32 x 35 ¾ x 21 ¼ inches (81.3 x 90.8 x 54 cm)
Opposite page: Installation view, "Oscar the Grouch,"
The Brant Foundation Art Study Center, Greenwich, Connecticut, 2010–2011
On wall: *Sliced*, 2010–2011

Following pages:
Paranoia / Squirrel, 2010
Silkscreen print on mirror-polished stainless-steel sheets, polyurethane foam sheets, two-component polyurethane adhesive, stainless-steel beams, aluminum L sections, screws; in 2 parts
Nut/bolt: 40 ½ x 17 ⅜ x 19 ¼ inches (103 x 44.2 x 49 cm)
Queen: 19 ¼ x 6 ¾ x 26 inches (49 x 17 x 66 cm)

Online / Parrot
Silkscreen print on mirror-polished stainless-steel sheets, polyurethane foam sheets, two-component polyurethane adhesive, stainless-steel beams, aluminum L sections, screws; in 4 parts
Brown boot, each: 57 ⅛ x 20 ½ x 58 ¼ inches (145 x 52 x 148 cm)
Dollhouse, each: 50 ⅜ x 38 ¼ x 52 ¾ inches (128 x 97.2 x 134 cm)

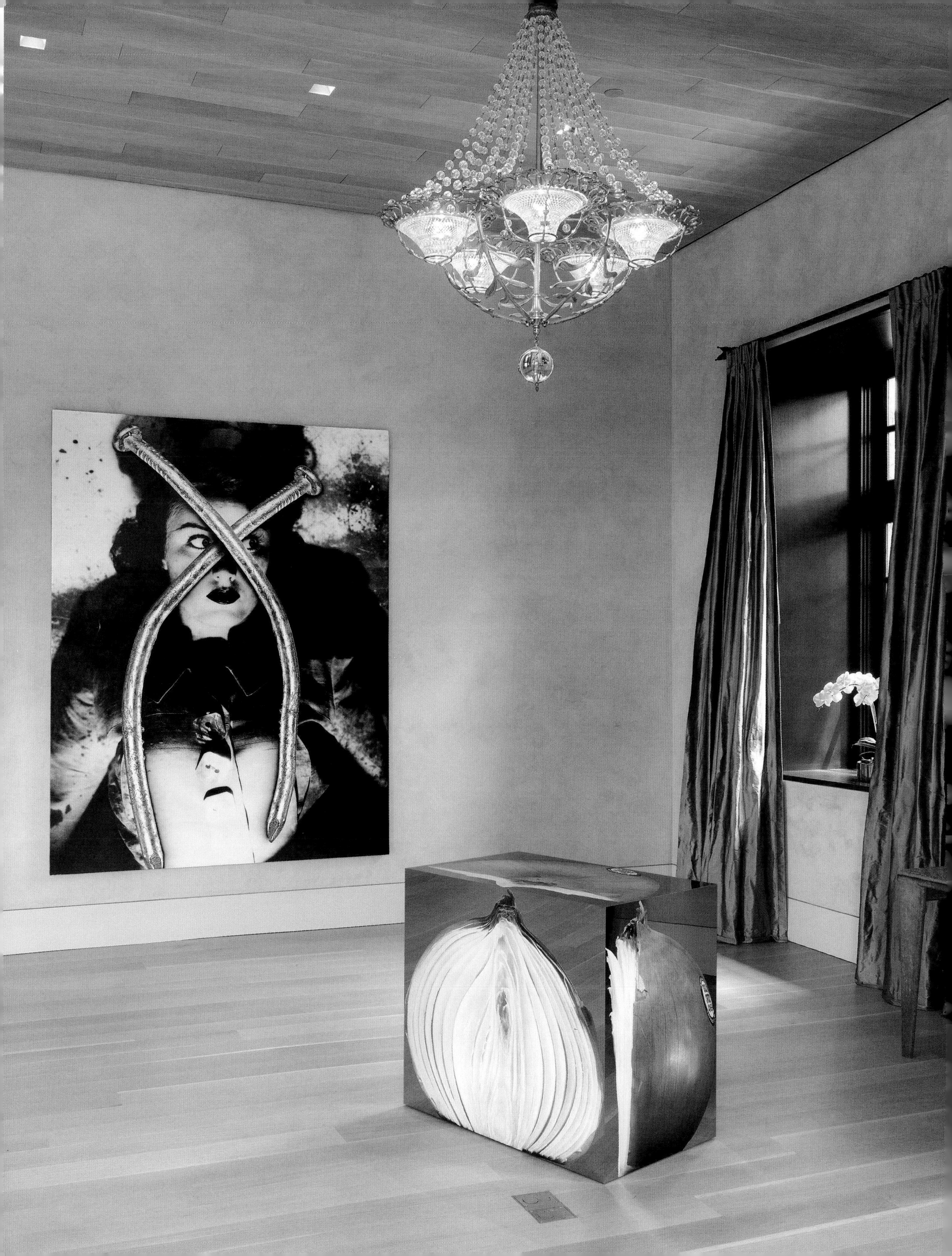

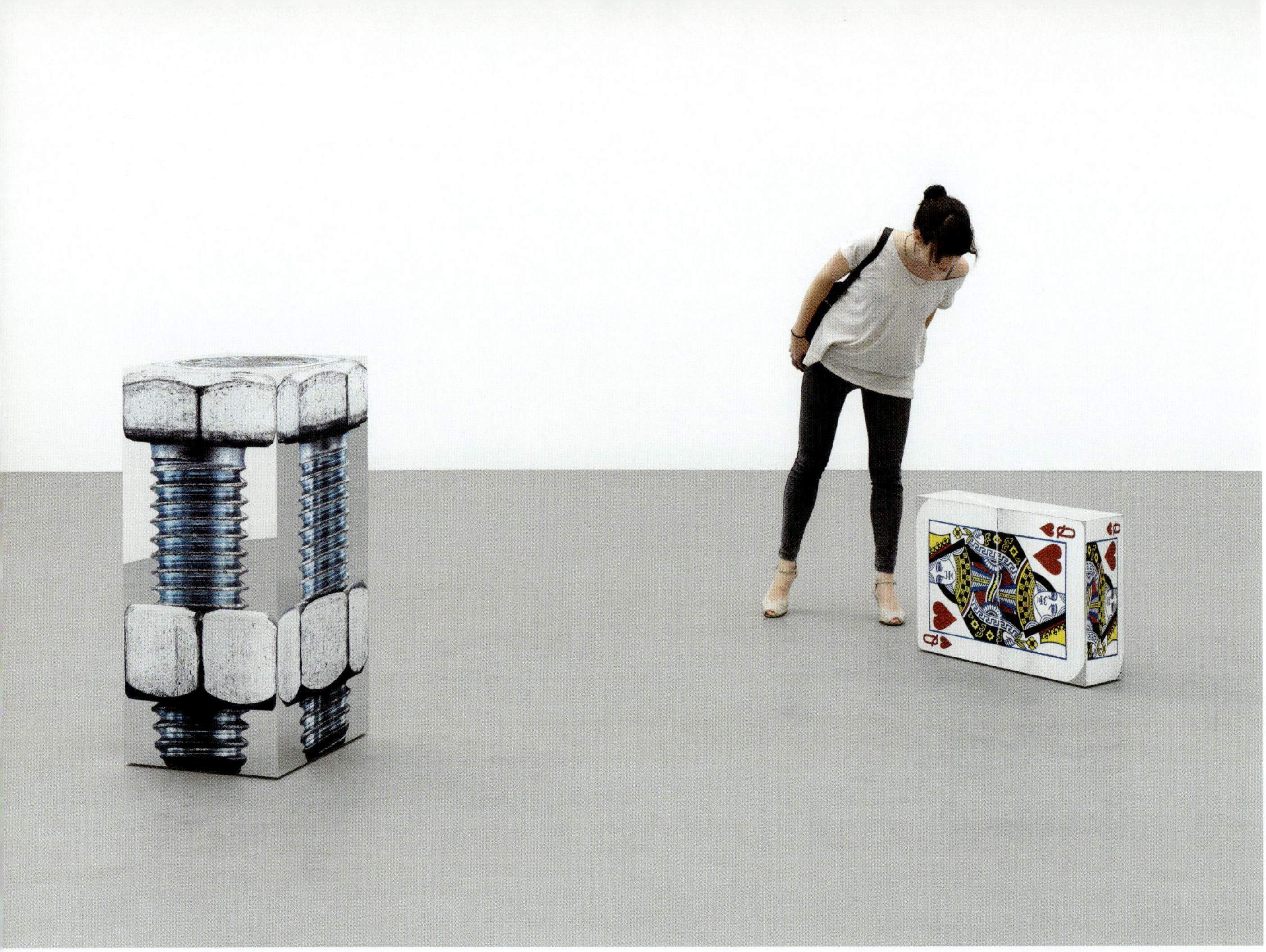

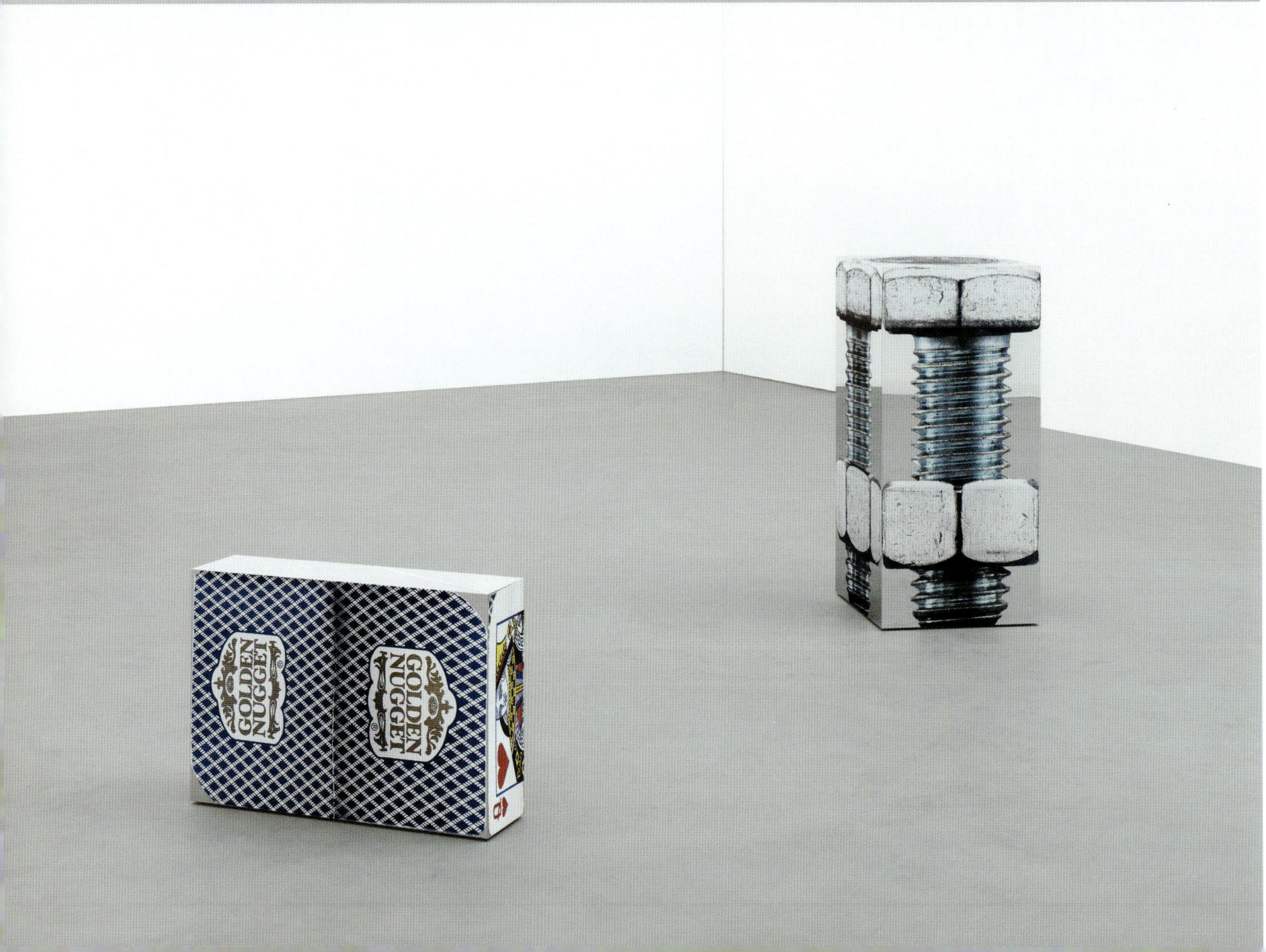

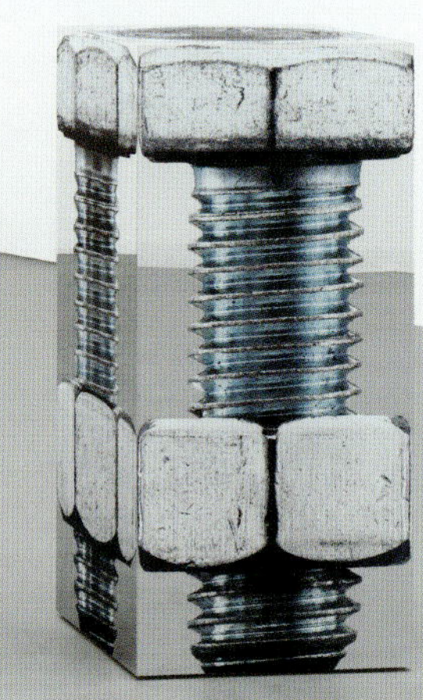

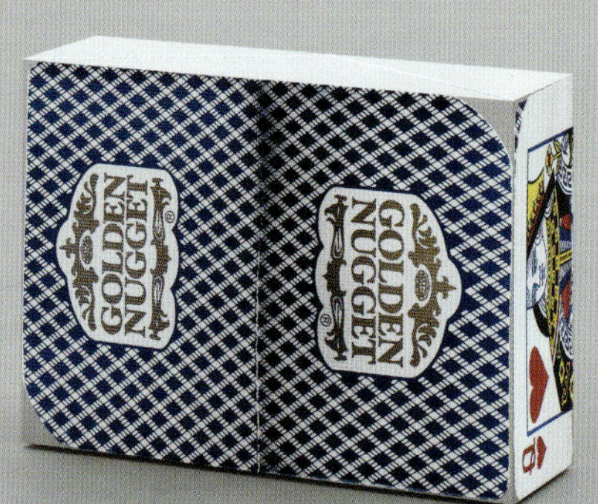
GOLDEN NUGGET
GOLDEN NUGGET

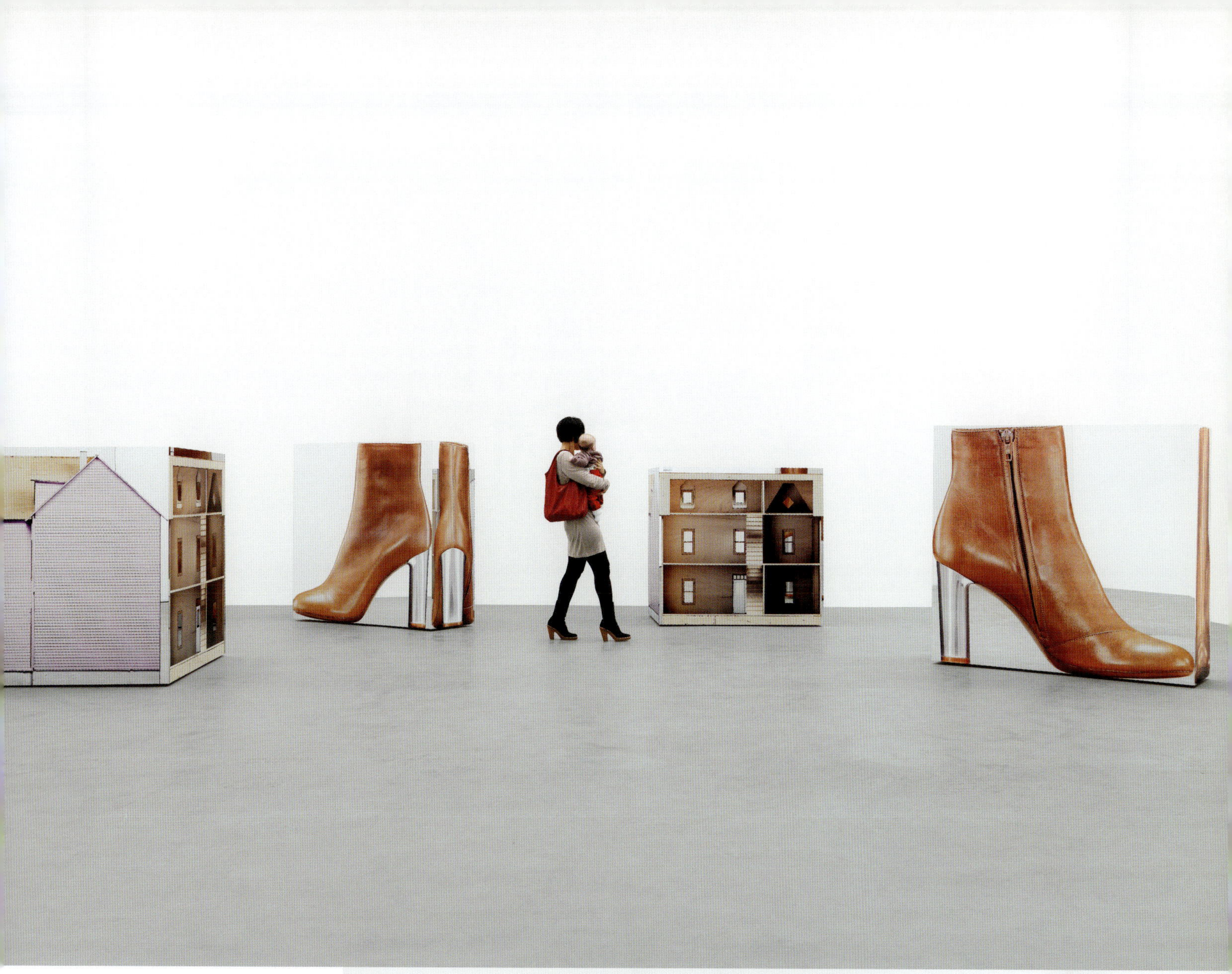

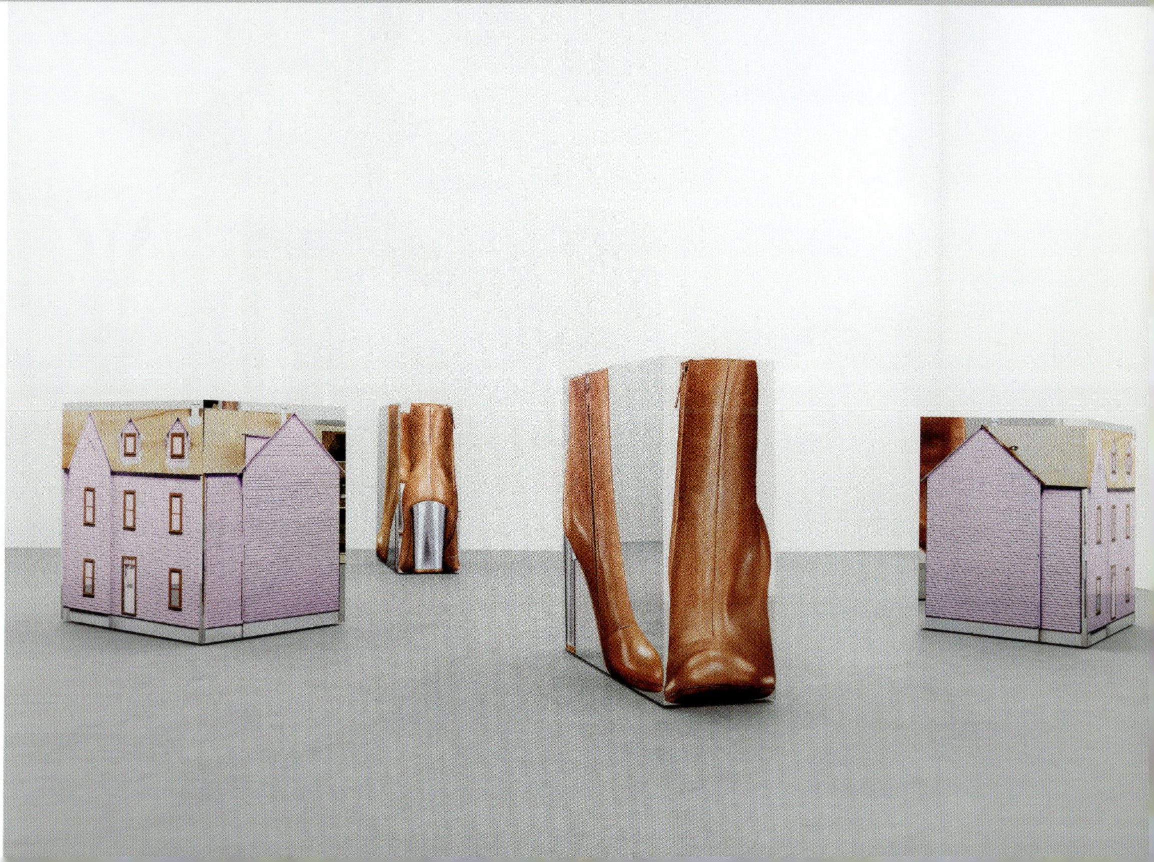

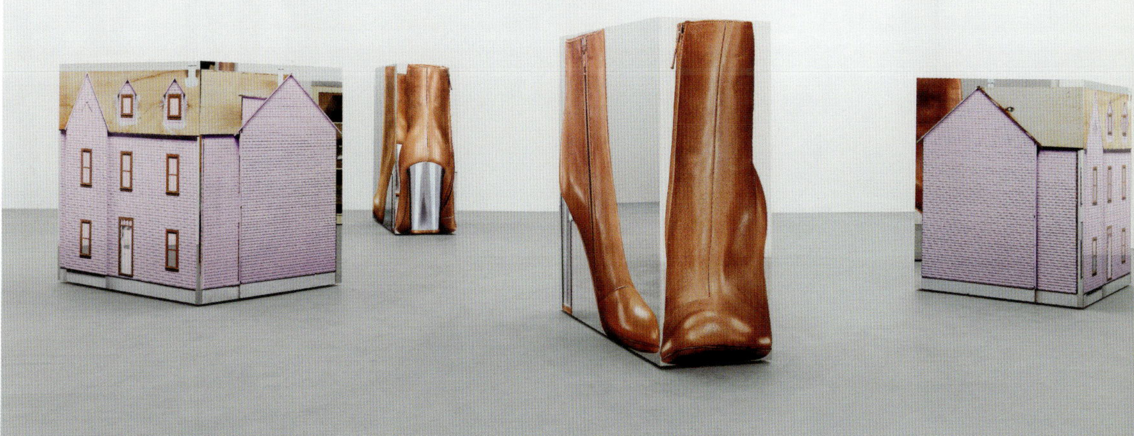

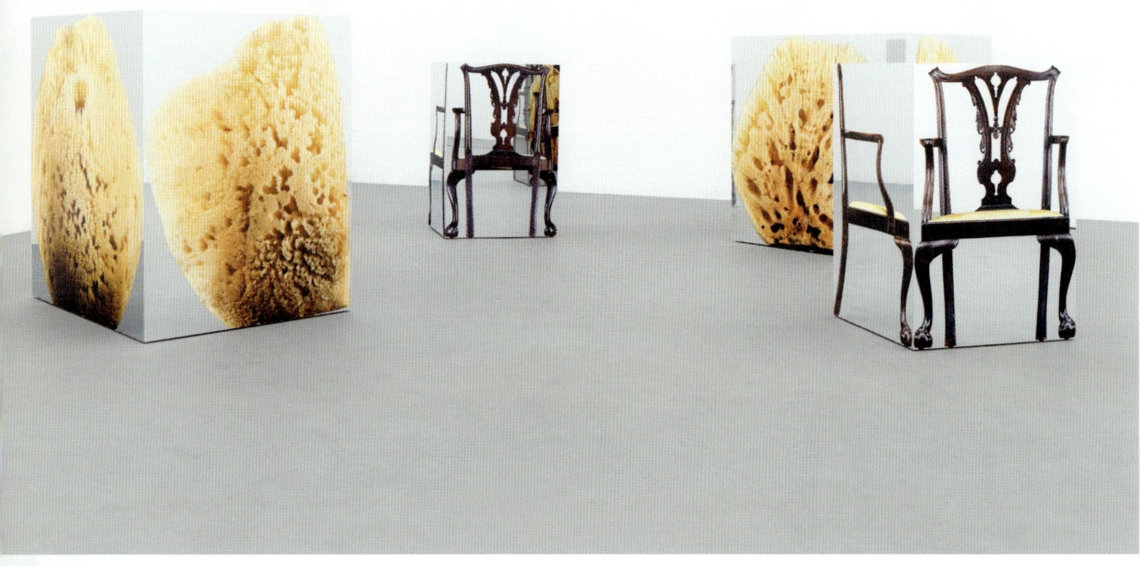

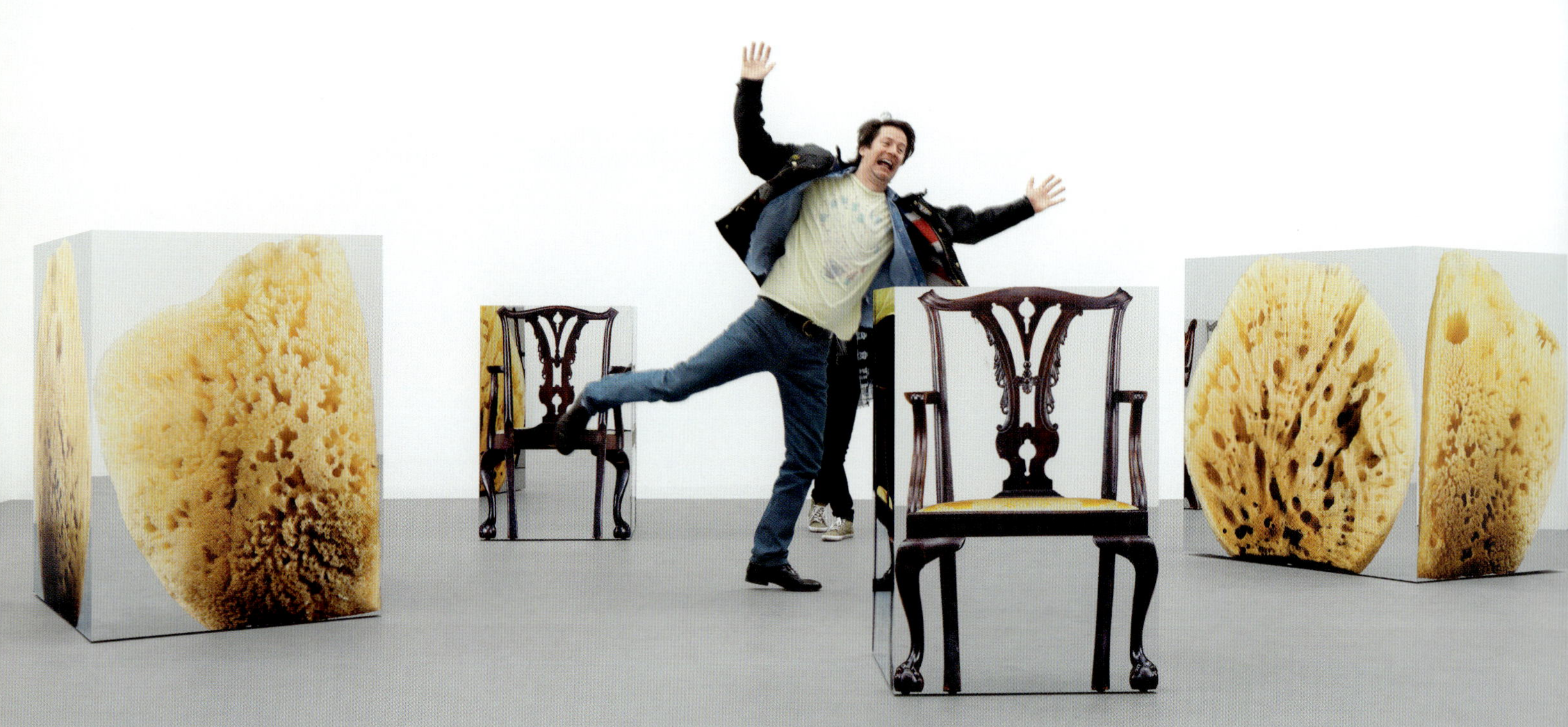

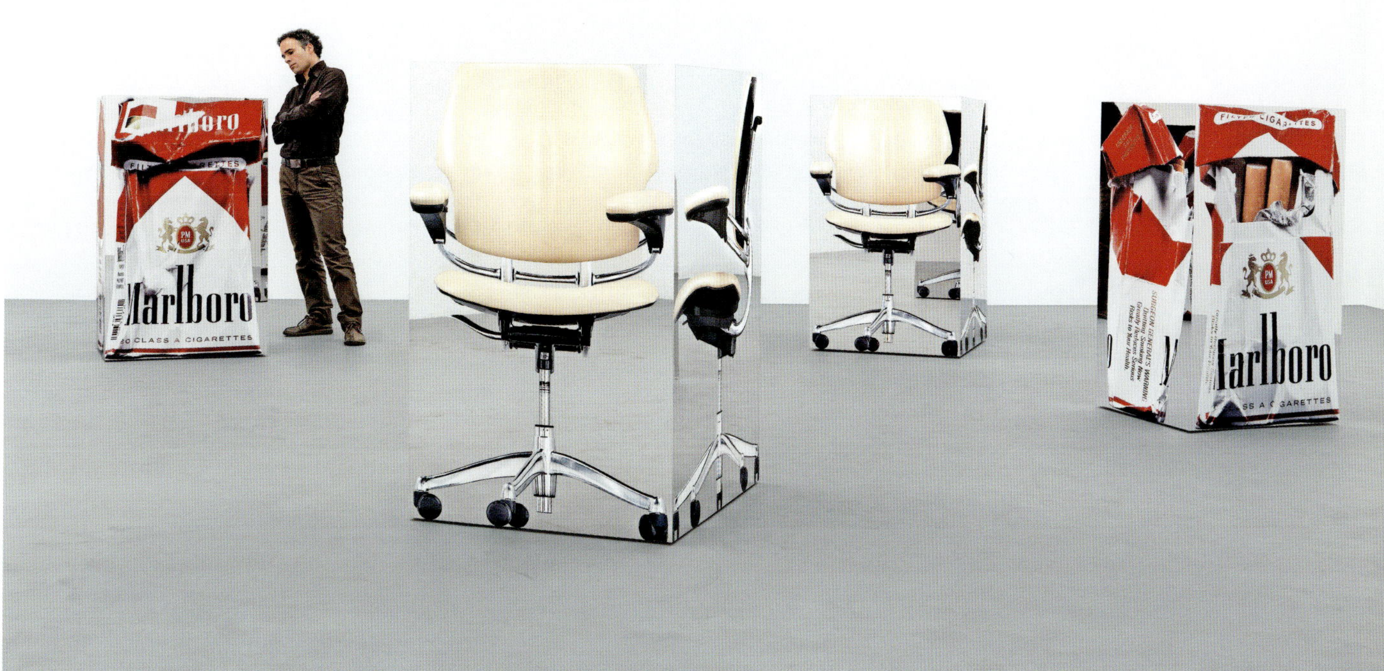
Marlboro
CLASS A CIGARETTES
Marlboro
FILTER CIGARETTES

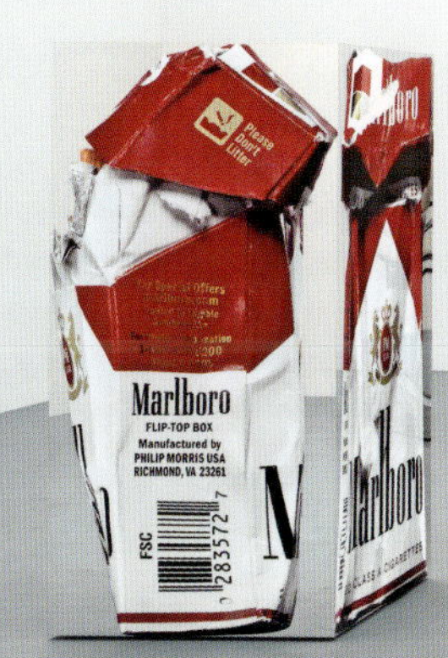
Marlboro
FLIP-TOP BOX
Manufactured by
PHILIP MORRIS USA
RICHMOND, VA 23261
FSC

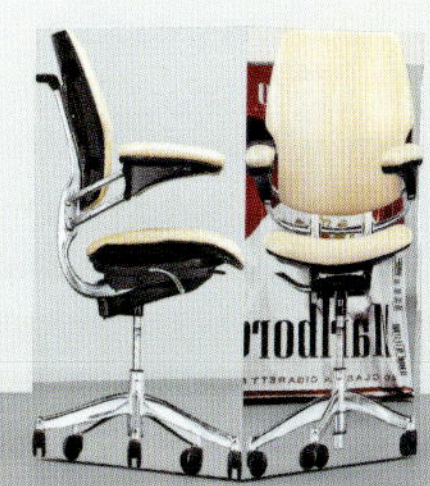

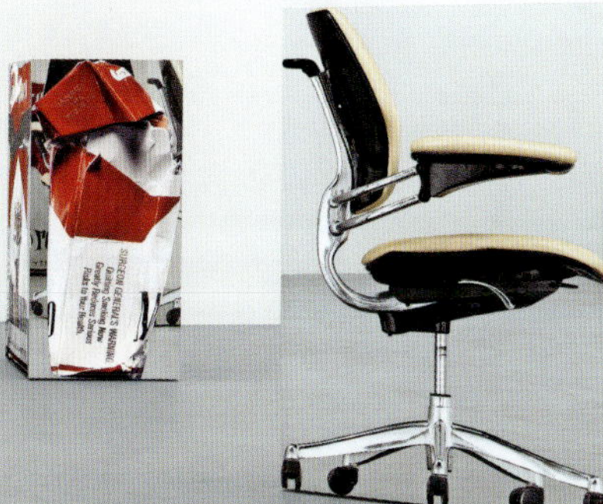

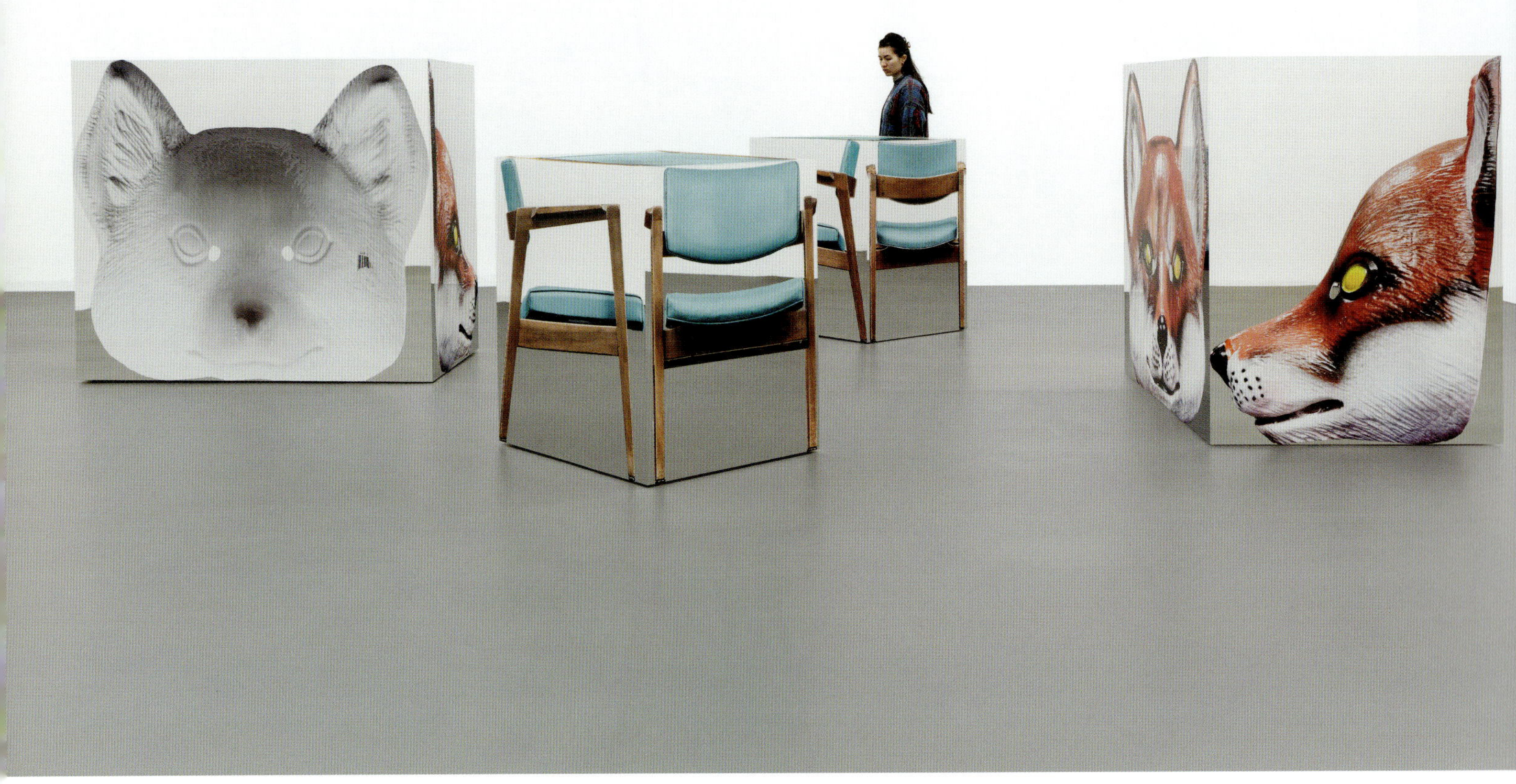

Salt / Sandra, 2010
Silkscreen print on mirror-polished stainless-steel sheets, polyurethane foam sheets, two-component polyurethane adhesive, stainless-steel beams, aluminum L sections, screws; in 4 parts
Fox mask, each: 57 ½ x 42 ½ x 64 ⅛ inches (146 x 108 x 163 cm)
Green chair, each: 42 ⅛ x 32 ¼ x 35 ⅜ inches (107 x 82 x 90 cm)

Opposite and next pages:
Fantasy / Extrusion, 2010
Silkscreen print on mirror-polished stainless-steel sheets, polyurethane foam sheets, two-component polyurethane adhesive, stainless-steel beams, aluminum L sections, screws; in 4 parts
Sphinx, each: 55 ½ x 14 ⅞ x 53 inches (141 x 37.9 x 134.5 cm)
Clementine, each: 37 ⅝ x 29 ⅜ x 47 ⅛ inches (95.5 x 74.5 x 119.6 cm)

Previous pages:
Pineapple / Melon, 2010
Silkscreen print on mirror-polished stainless-steel sheets, polyurethane foam sheets, two-component polyurethane adhesive, stainless-steel beams, aluminum L sections, screws; in 4 parts
Sponge, each: 55 ⅛ x 39 ⅝ x 52 inches (140 x 100.6 x 132 cm)
Chair, each: 46 ⅞ x 26 ⅜ x 52 inches (119 x 67 x 132 cm)

Horse / Fraud, 2010
Silkscreen print on mirror-polished stainless-steel sheets, polyurethane foam sheets, two-component polyurethane adhesive, stainless-steel beams, aluminum L sections, screws; in 4 parts
Marlboro, each: 50 ¼ x 23 ¾ x 29 ½ inches (127.5 x 60.4 x 75 cm)
Office chair, each: 53 ⅛ x 37 ⅞ x 34 ⅝ inches (135 x 81 x 88 cm)

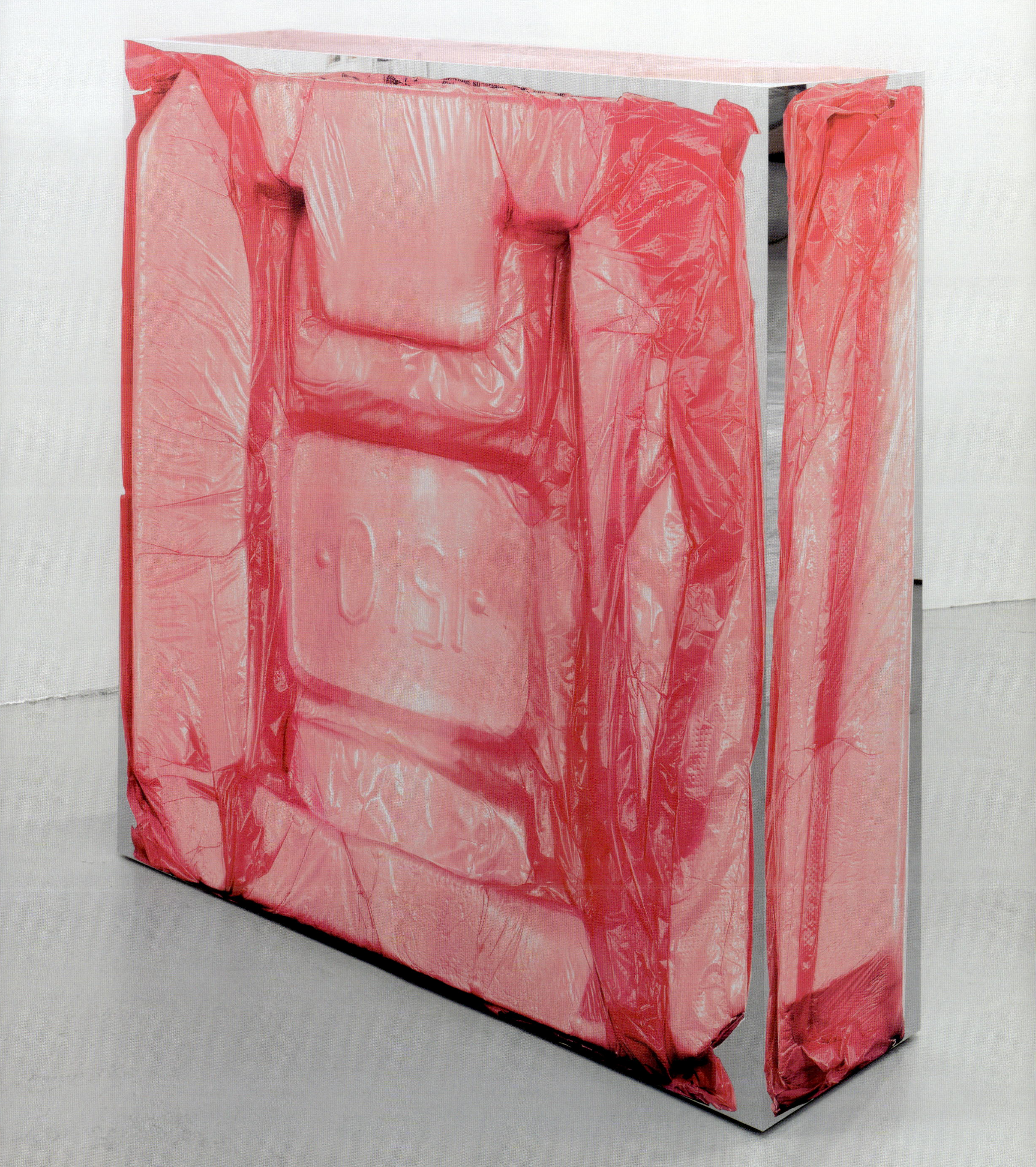

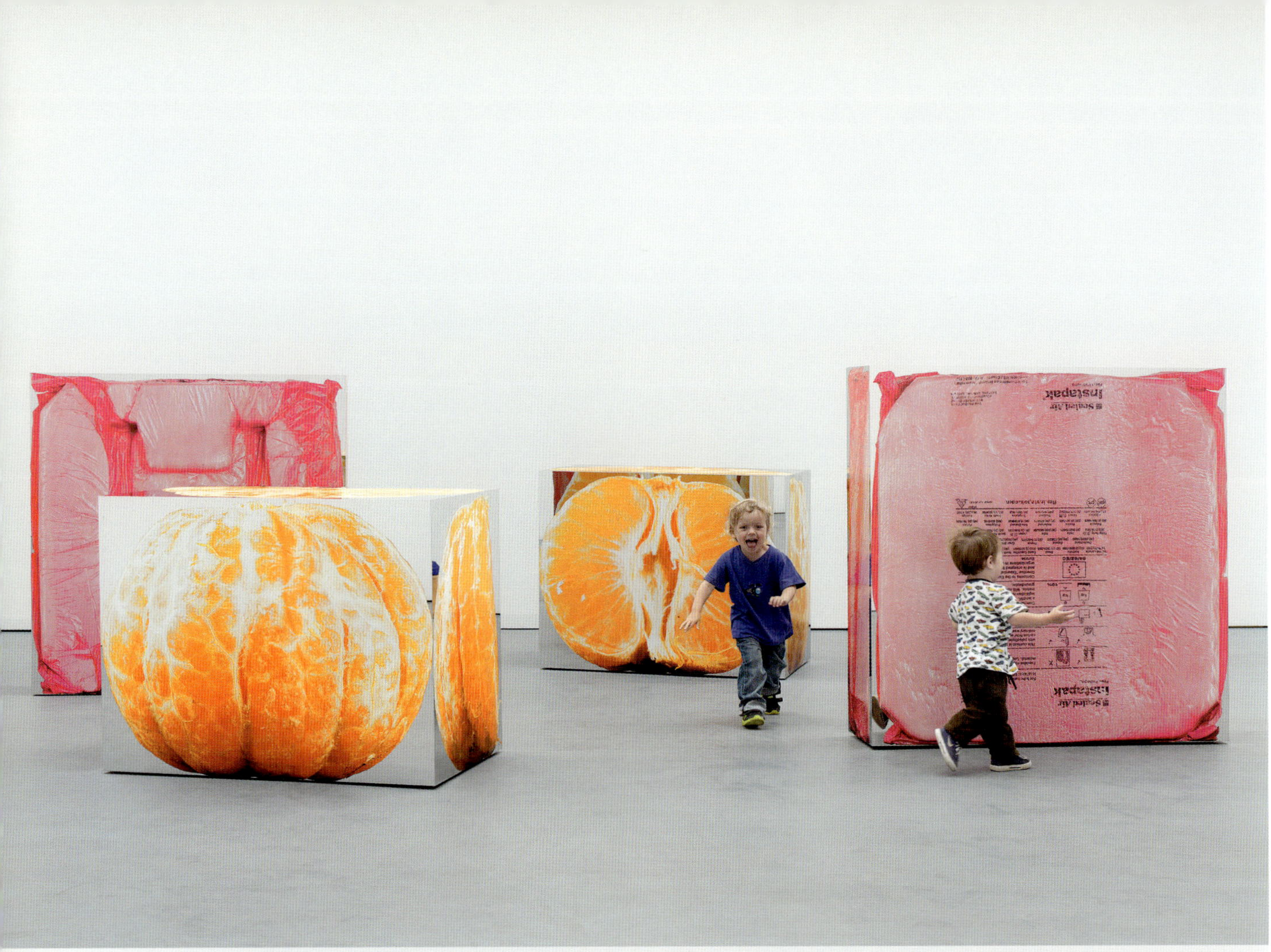

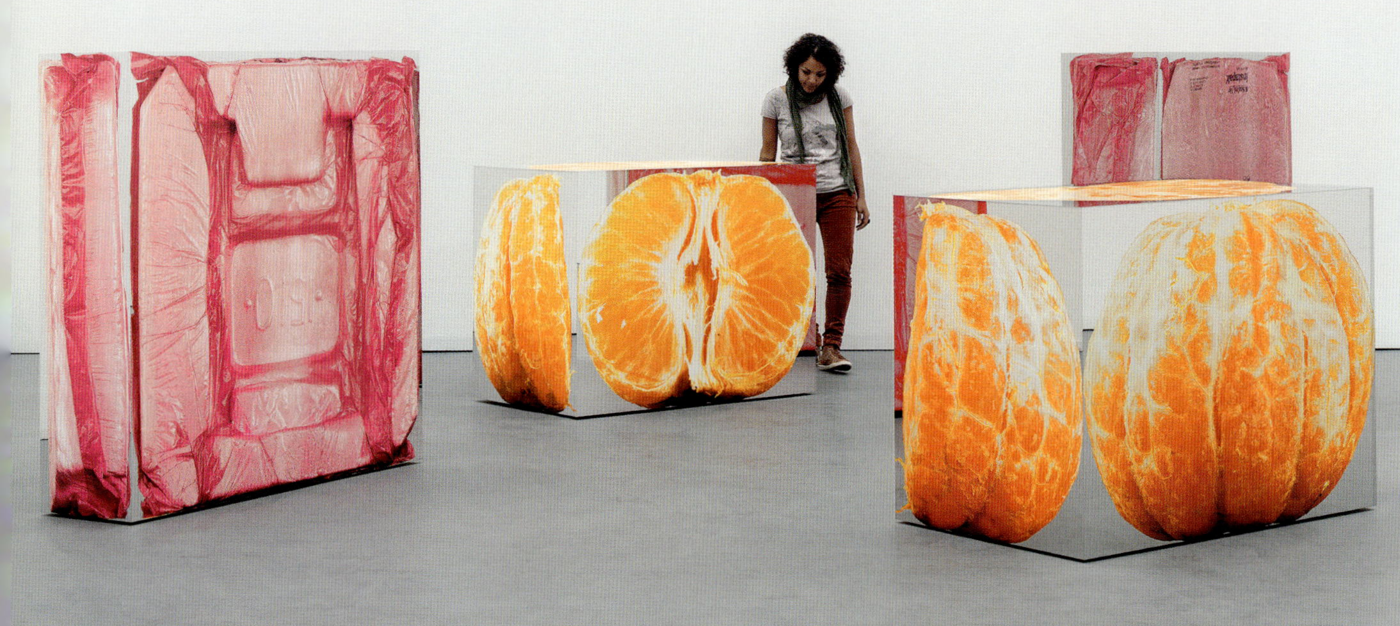

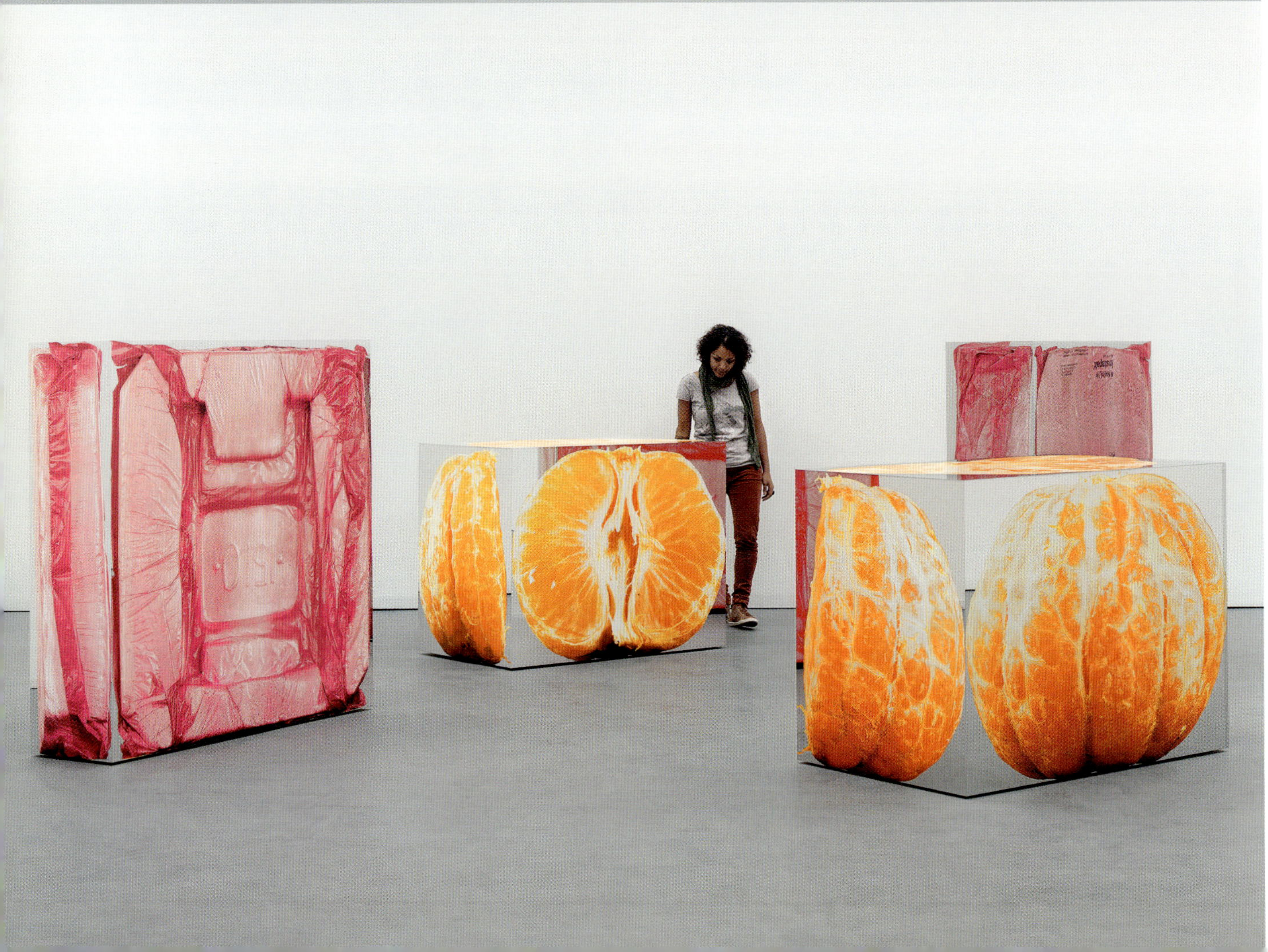

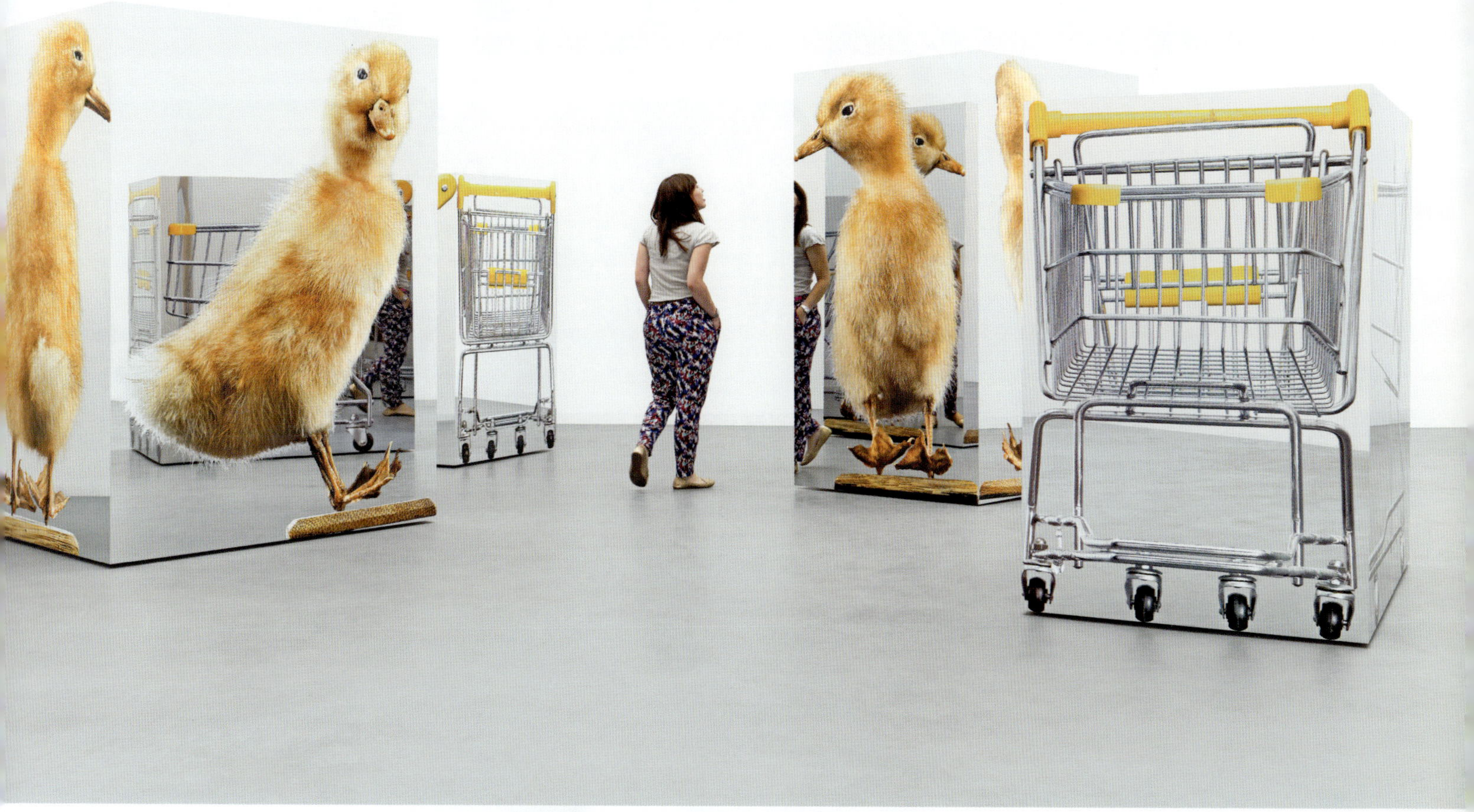

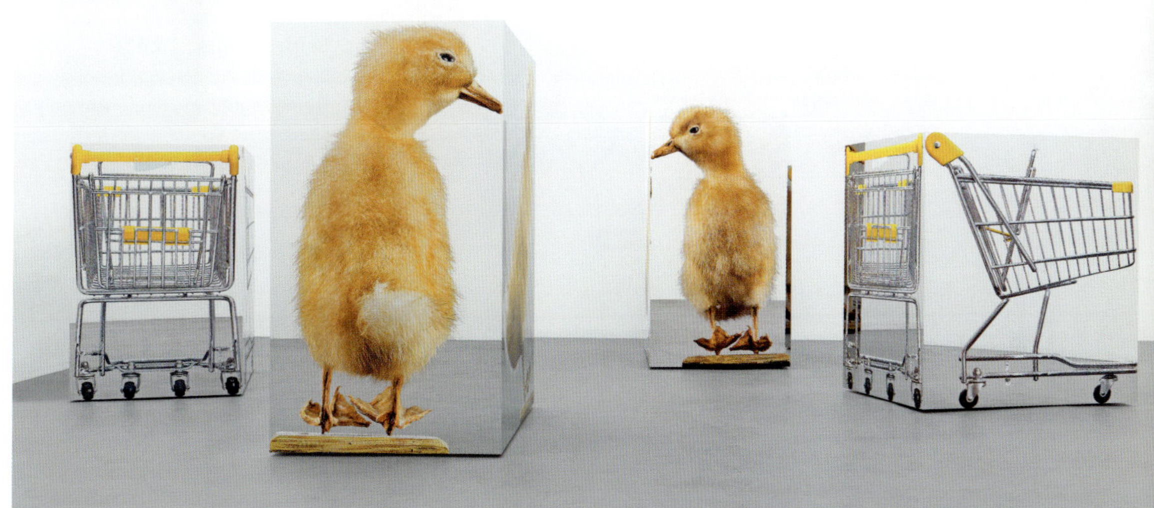

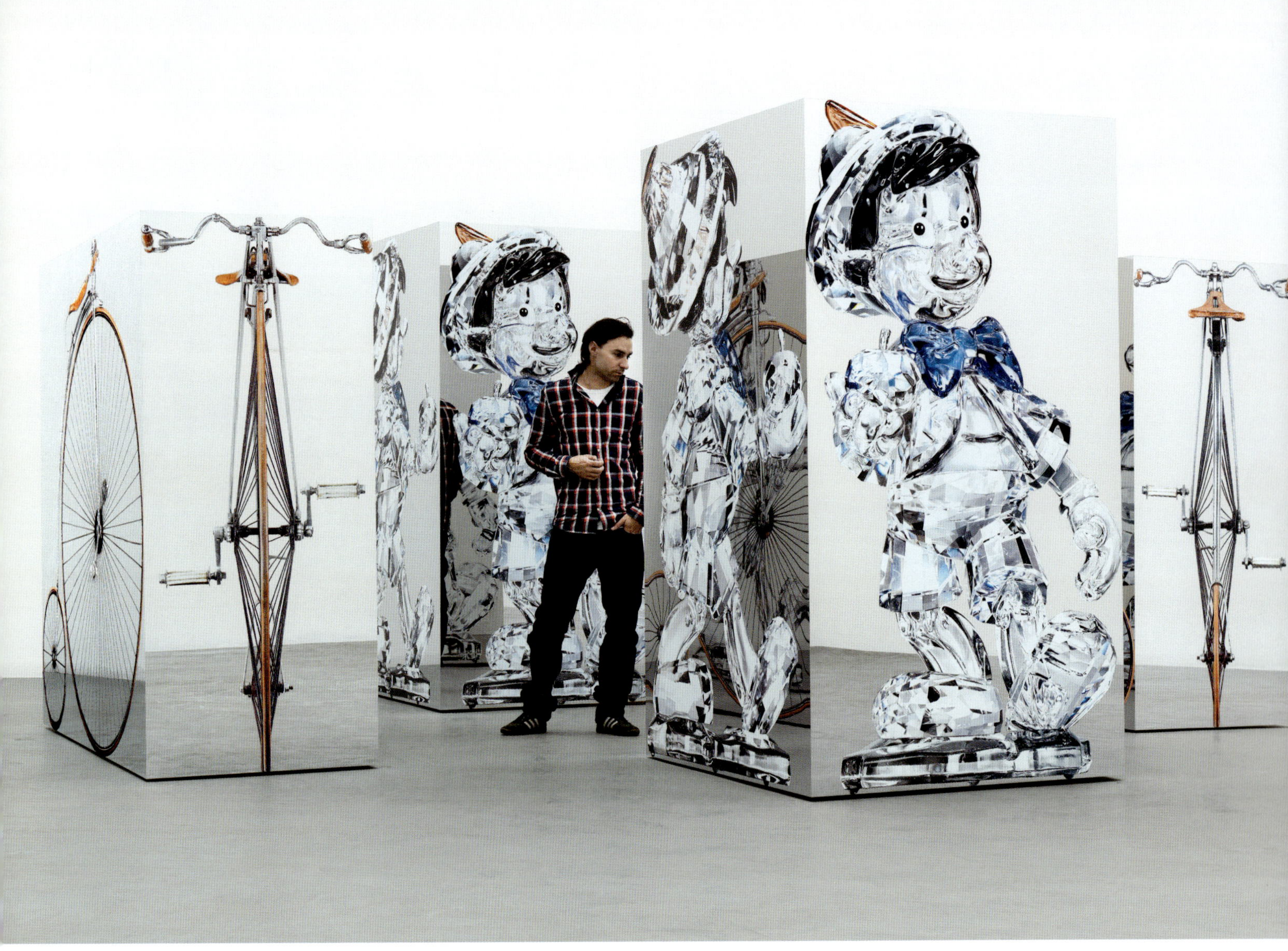

Concert / Cornichon, 2011
Silkscreen print on mirror-polished stainless-steel sheets, polyurethane foam sheets, two-component polyurethane adhesive, stainless-steel beams, aluminum L sections, screws; in 4 parts
Pinocchio, each: 51 x 88 ½ x 46 ¾ inches (129.29 x 225 x 118.8 cm)
Penny-farthing bicycle, each: 32 ½ x 85 ½ x 77 inches (82.5 x 217.4 x 196 cm)

Previous page:
Fritz Lang / Shorty, 2010
Silkscreen print on mirror-polished stainless-steel sheets, polyurethane foam sheets, two-component polyurethane adhesive, stainless-steel beams, aluminum L sections, screws; in 4 parts
Shopping cart, each: 64 ¾ x 40 ½ x 57 ½ inches (164.5 x 103 x 146 cm)
Ducky, each: 82 ⅝ x 57 ½ x 43 ¼ inches (210 x 146 x 110 cm)

Following spread:
Dark Darkness, 2010
Silkscreen print on mirror-polished stainless-steel sheets, polyurethane foam sheets, two-component polyurethane adhesive, stainless-steel beams, aluminum L sections, screws
47 ¼ x 37 ¼ x 44 ⅝ inches (120 x 94.5 x 113.2 cm)

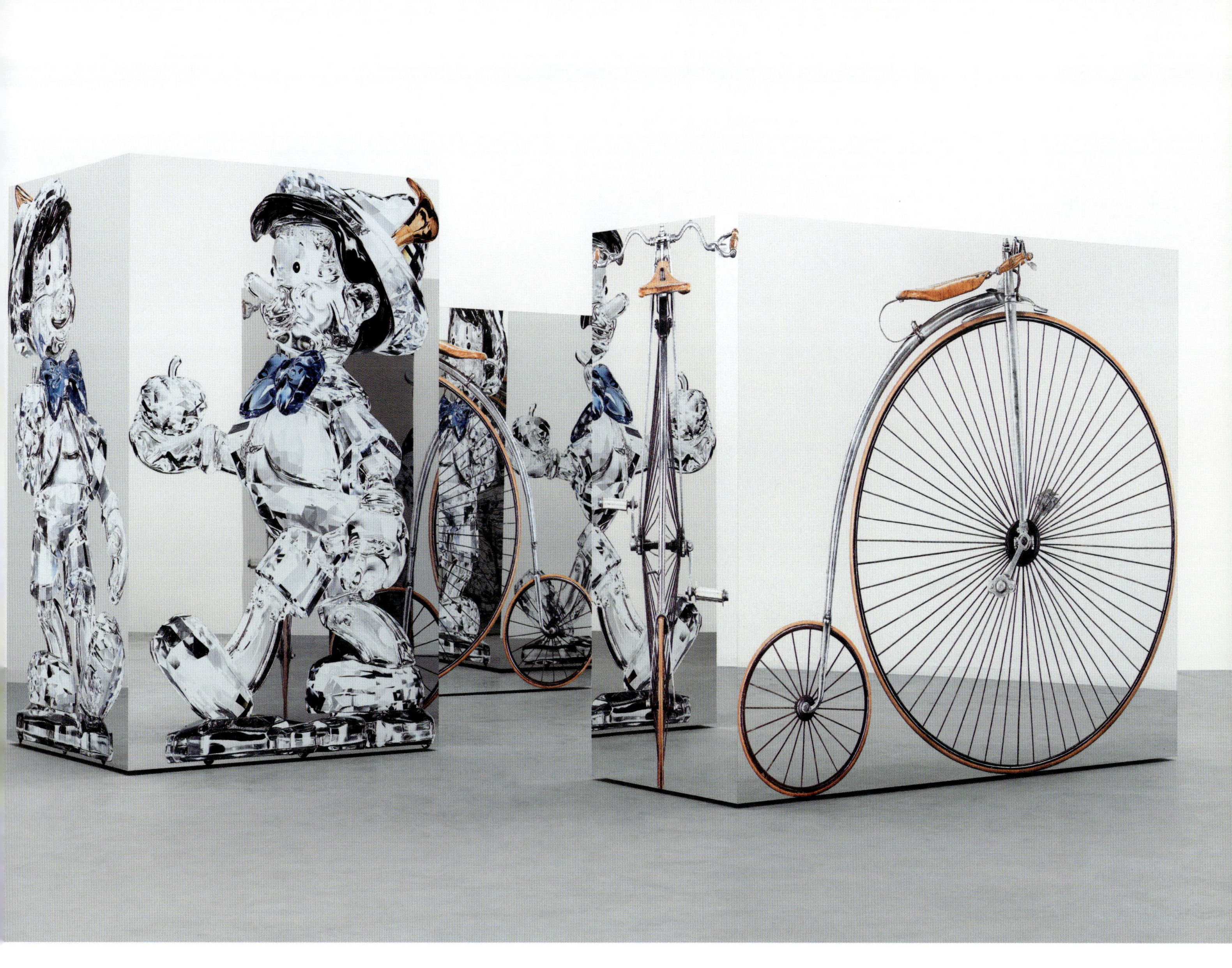

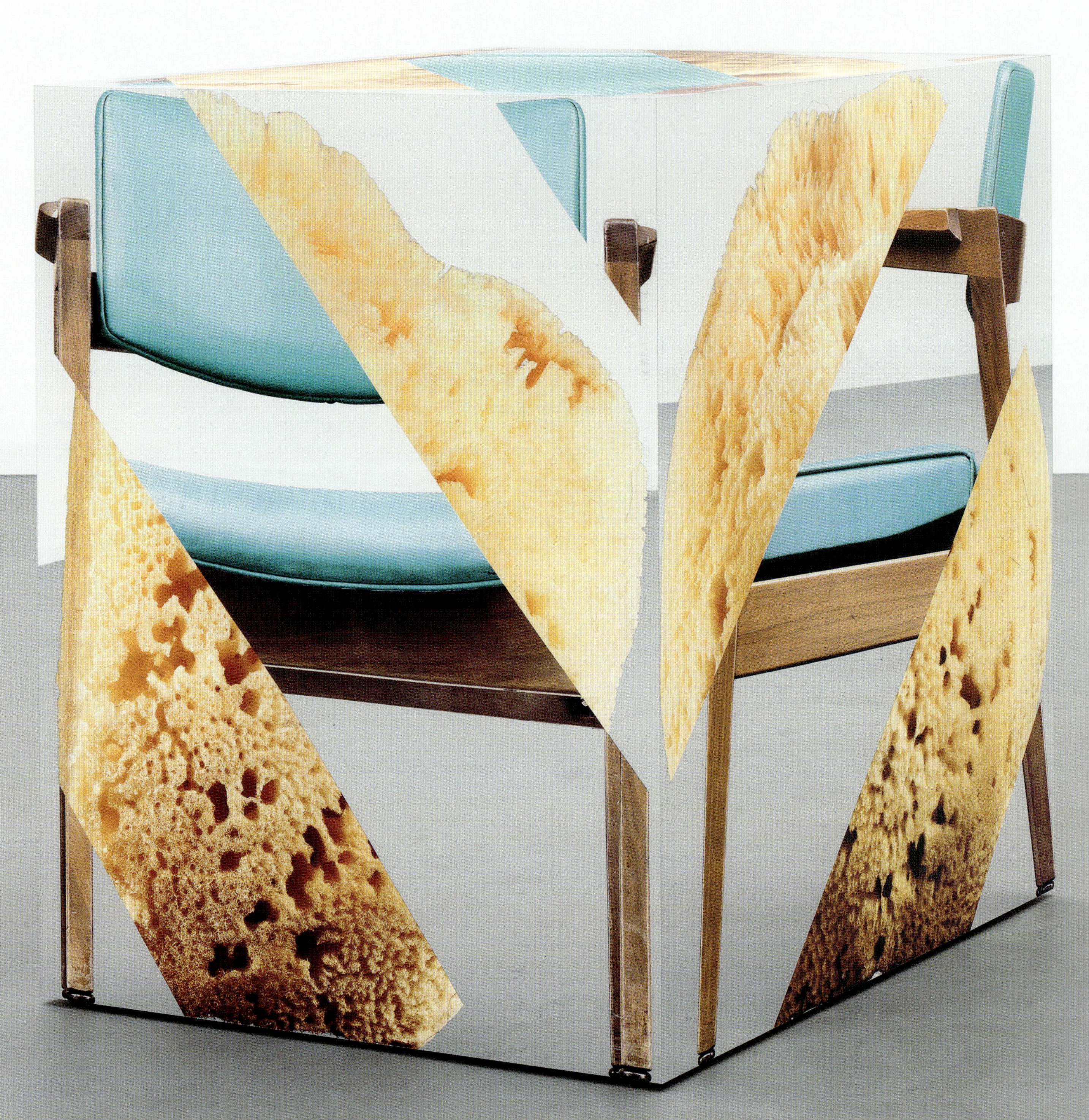

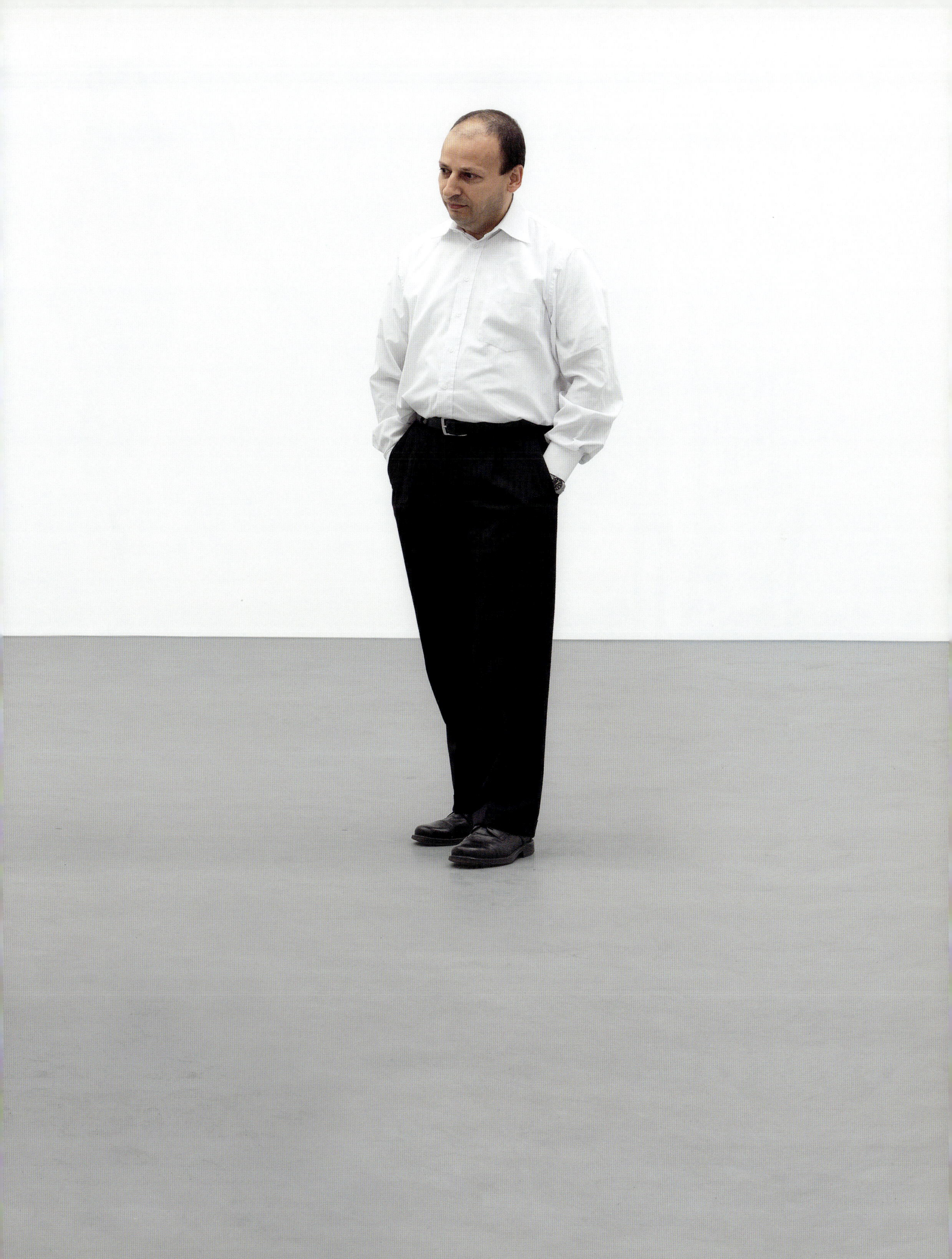

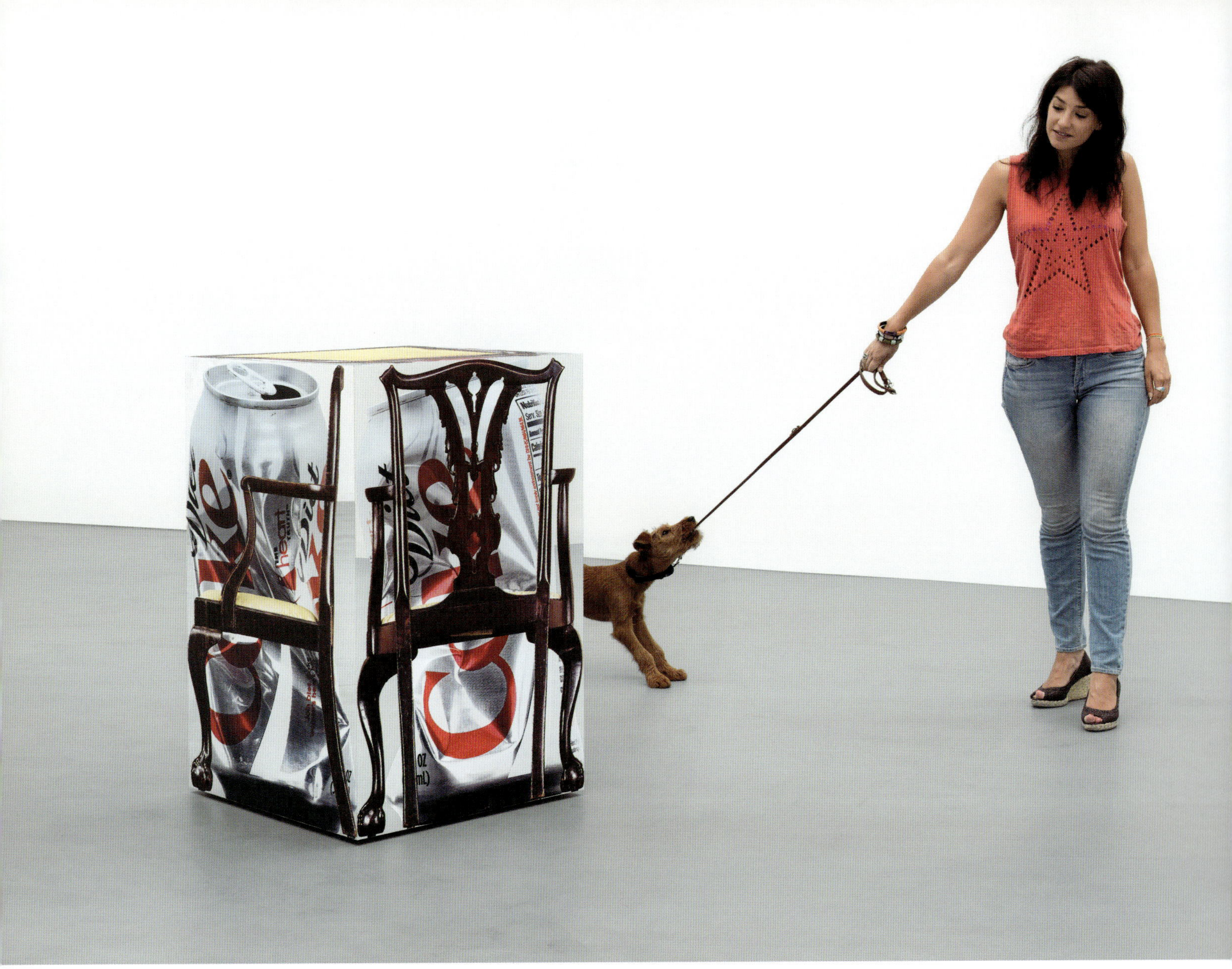

Merciless Mercy, 2010

Silkscreen print on mirror-polished stainless-steel sheets, polyurethane foam sheets, two-component polyurethane adhesive, stainless-steel beams, aluminum L sections, screws
40 ¾ x 25 ⅝ x 26 ⅞ inches (103.5 x 65 x 68.4 cm)

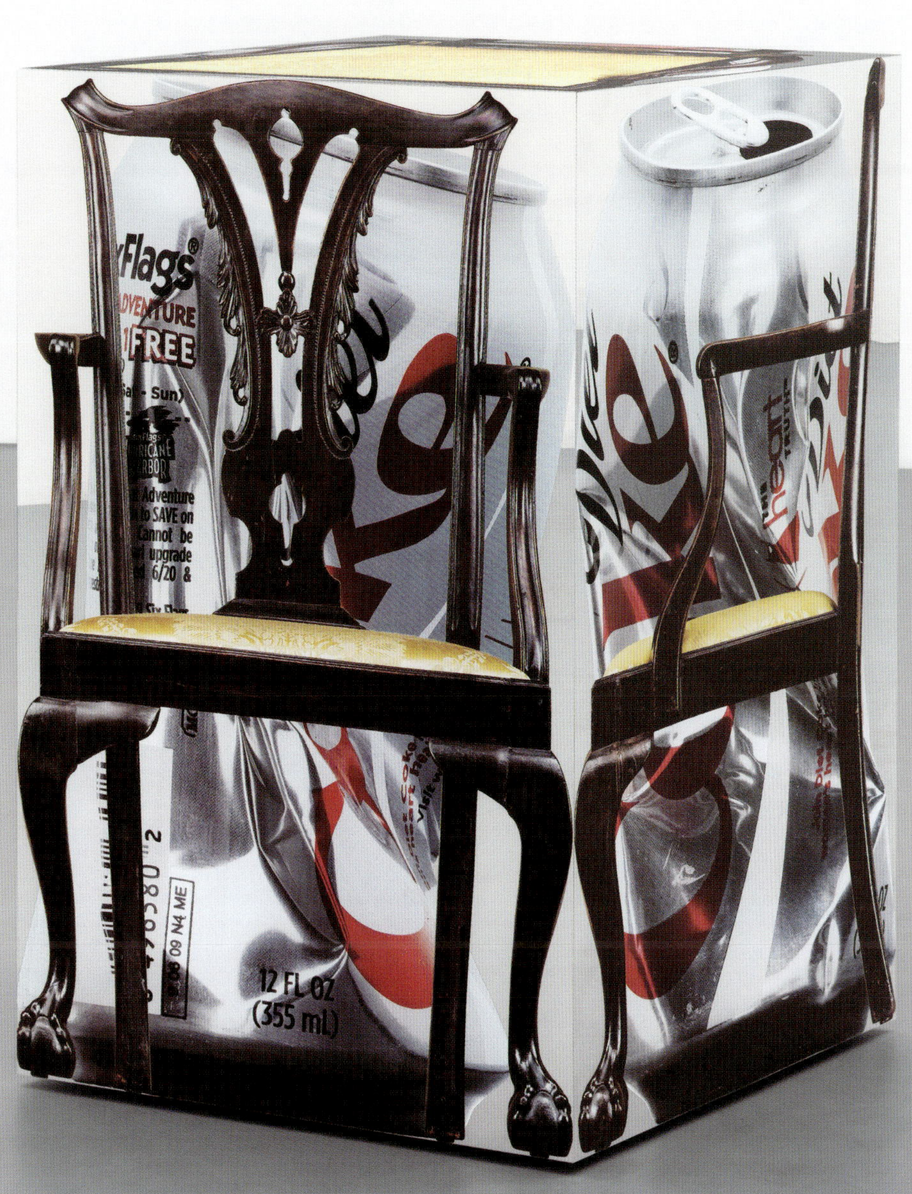
ADVENTURE
FREE
12 FL OZ
(355 mL)

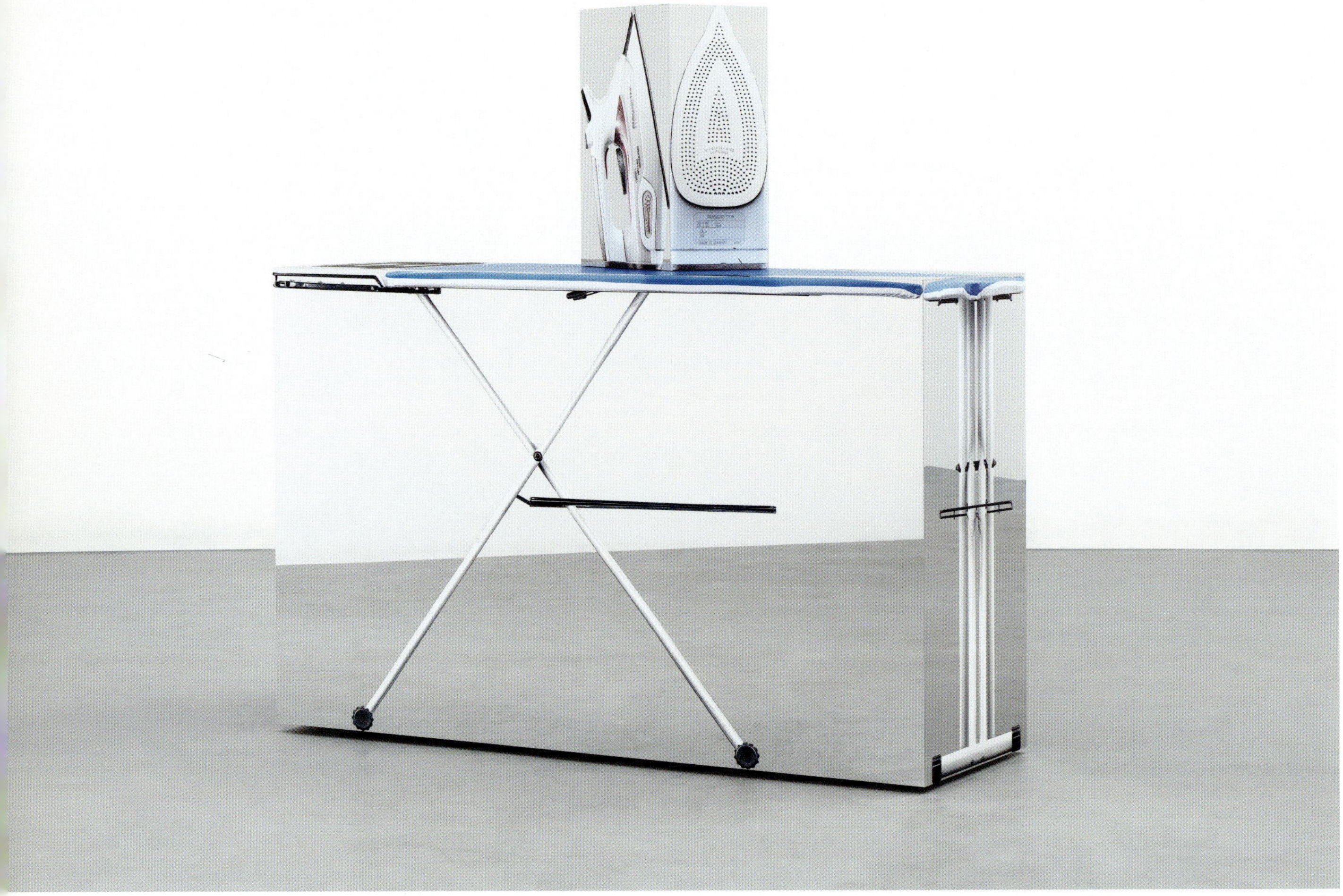

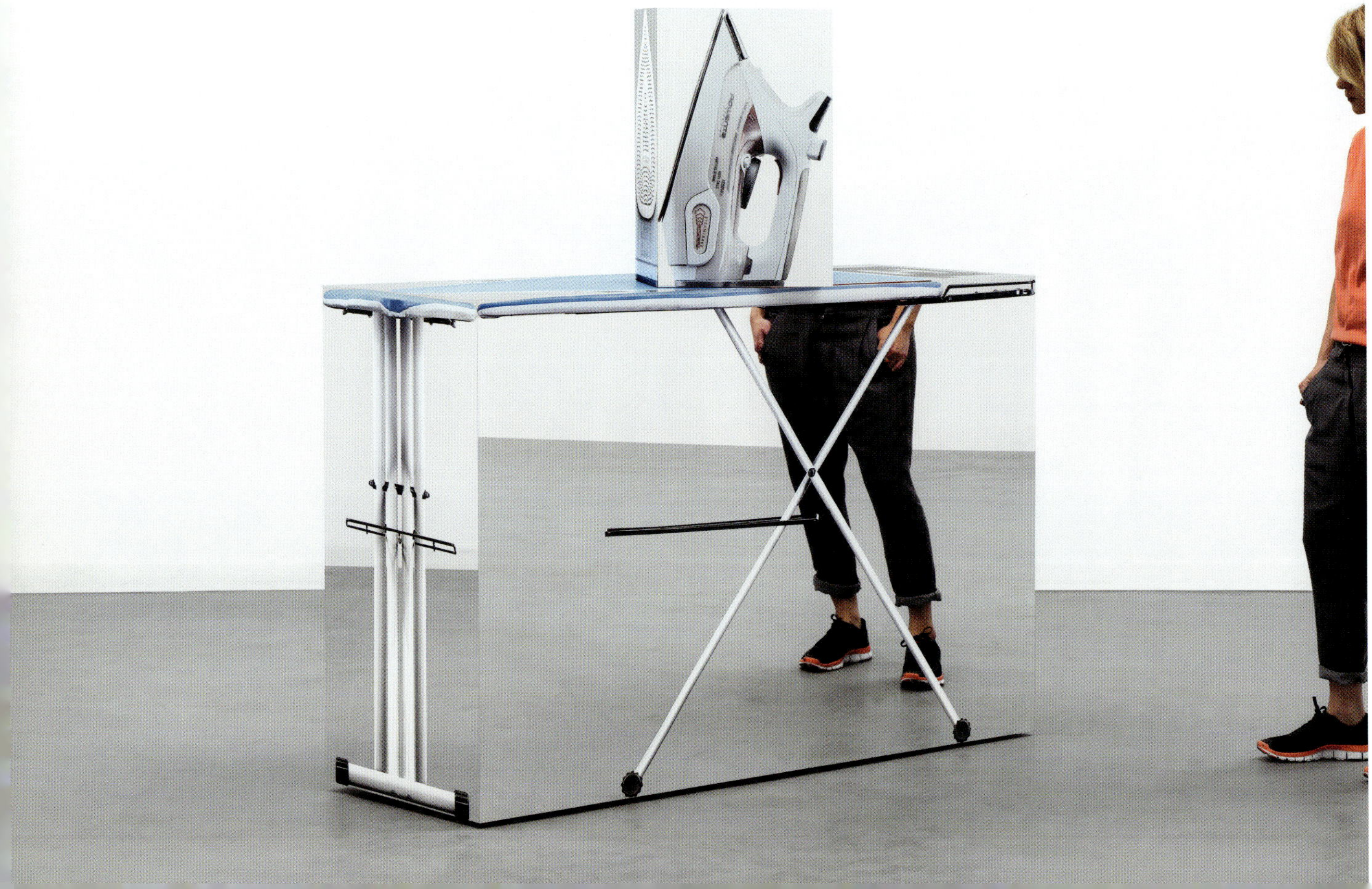

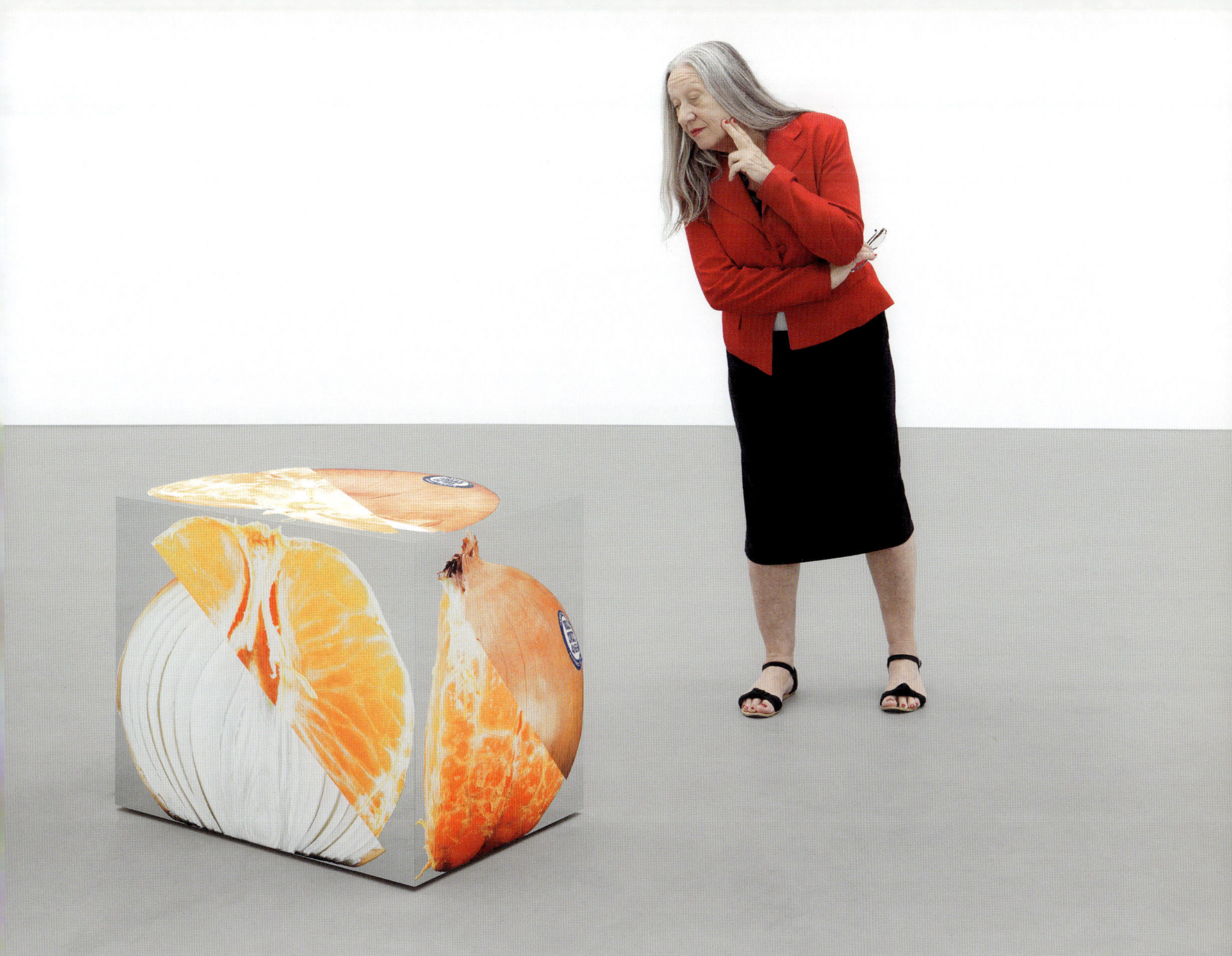

Shameless Shame
Silkscreen print on mirror-polished stainless-steel sheets, polyurethane foam sheets, two-component polyurethane adhesive, stainless-steel beams, aluminum L sections, screws
25 ⅝ x 19 ⅞ x 31 ⅞ inches (65 x 50.5 x 81 cm)

Opposite page:
Mr. E & Spotzy, 2011
Silkscreen print on mirror-polished stainless-steel sheets, polyurethane foam sheets, two-component polyurethane adhesive, stainless-steel beams, aluminum L sections, screws; in 2 parts
Iron: 22 ½ x 14 ½ x 9 ⅞ inches (57.1 x 37 x 25.1 cm)
Board: 48 x 76 ⅛ x 24 ⅝ inches (121.9 x 193.4 x 62.6 cm)

SMITH
JOHNSON
WILLIAM
JONES, 2012

Silkscreen print on mirror-glass, UV-adhesive, aluminum, glass, polyacetal, screws; in 4 parts
Asparagus: 25 ⅝ x 2 ⅞ x 2 ½ inches (65.1 x 7.3 x 6.3 cm)
Calculator: 18 ⅜ x 24 ¾ x 7 inches (46.7 x 62.9 x 17.8 cm)
Ping-Pong paddle: 25 x 14 ⅞ x 2 ¾ inches (63.5 x 37.8 x 7 cm)
Staple gun: 17 ½ x 20 ⅝ x 3 ⅞ inches (44.5 x 52.4 x 9.8 cm)

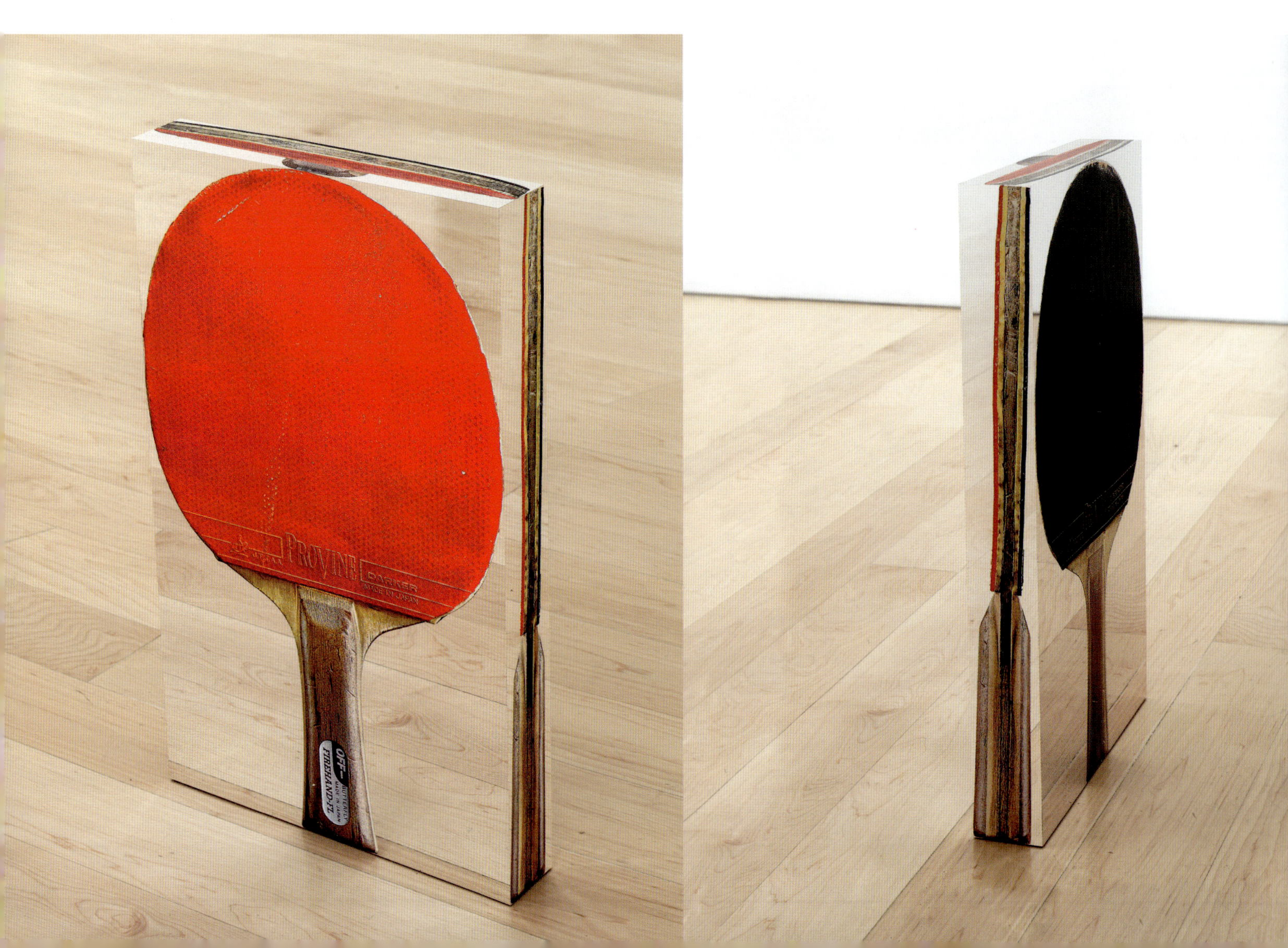

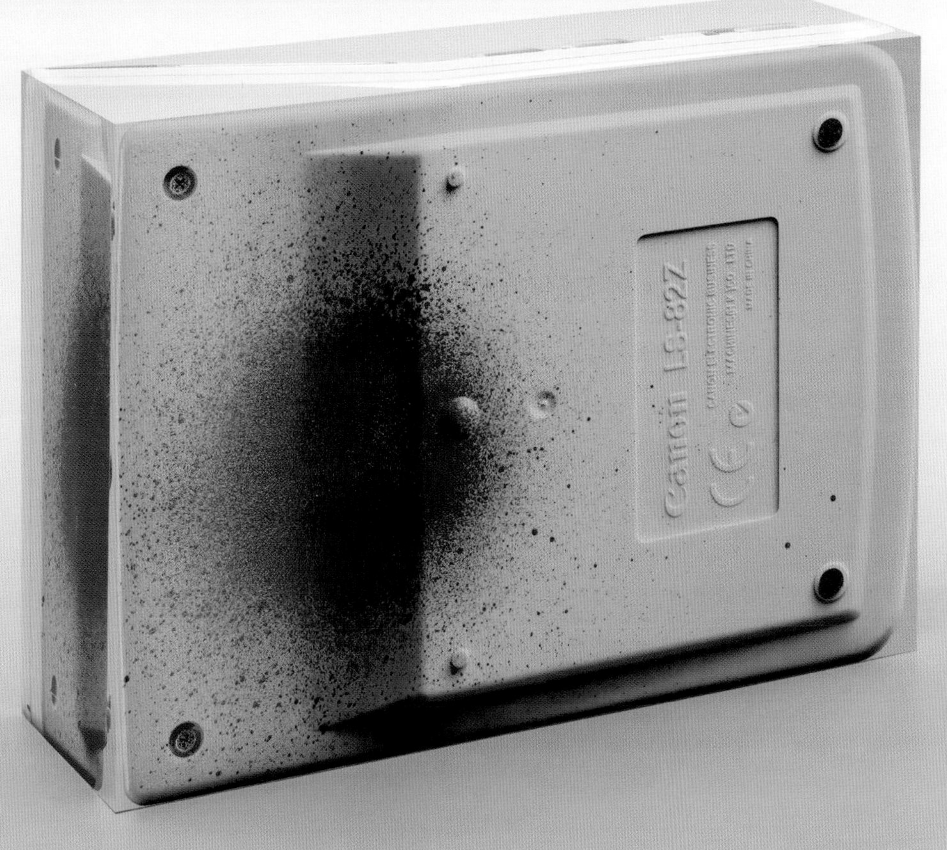
Canon LS-82Z

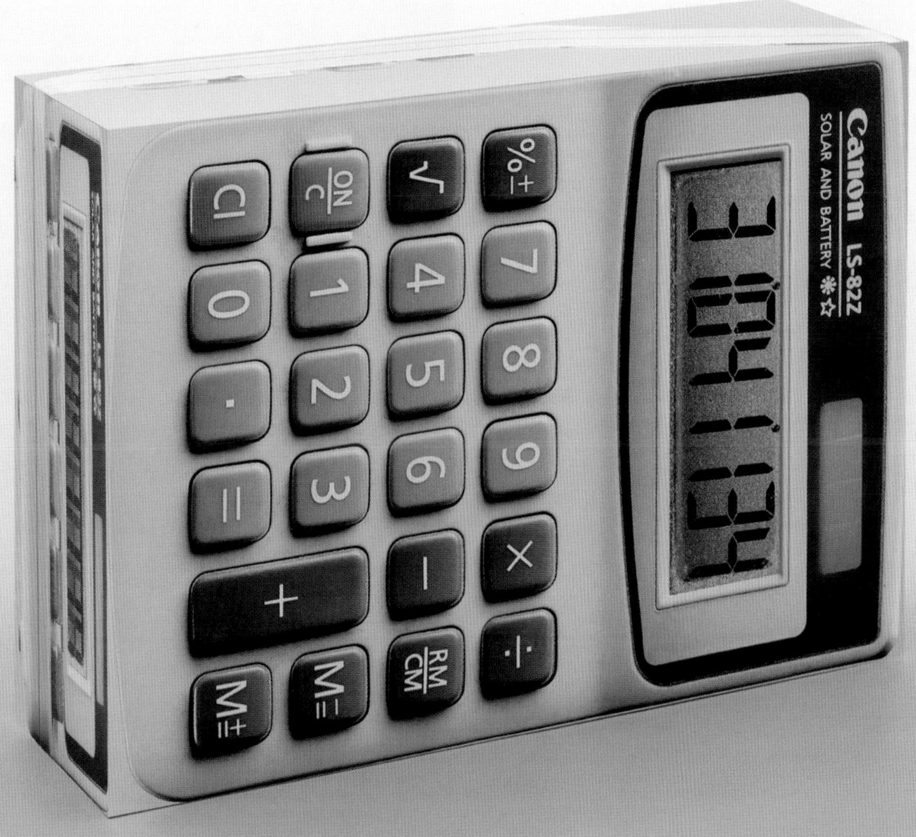
Canon LS-82Z
SOLAR AND BATTERY

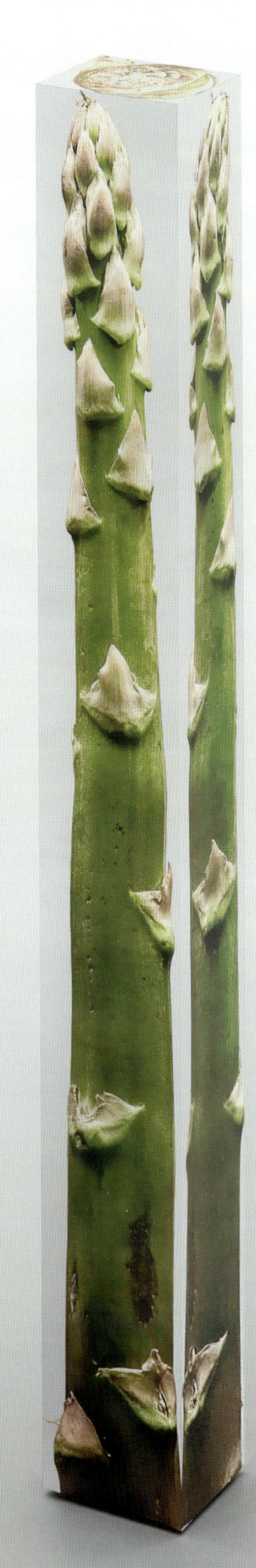

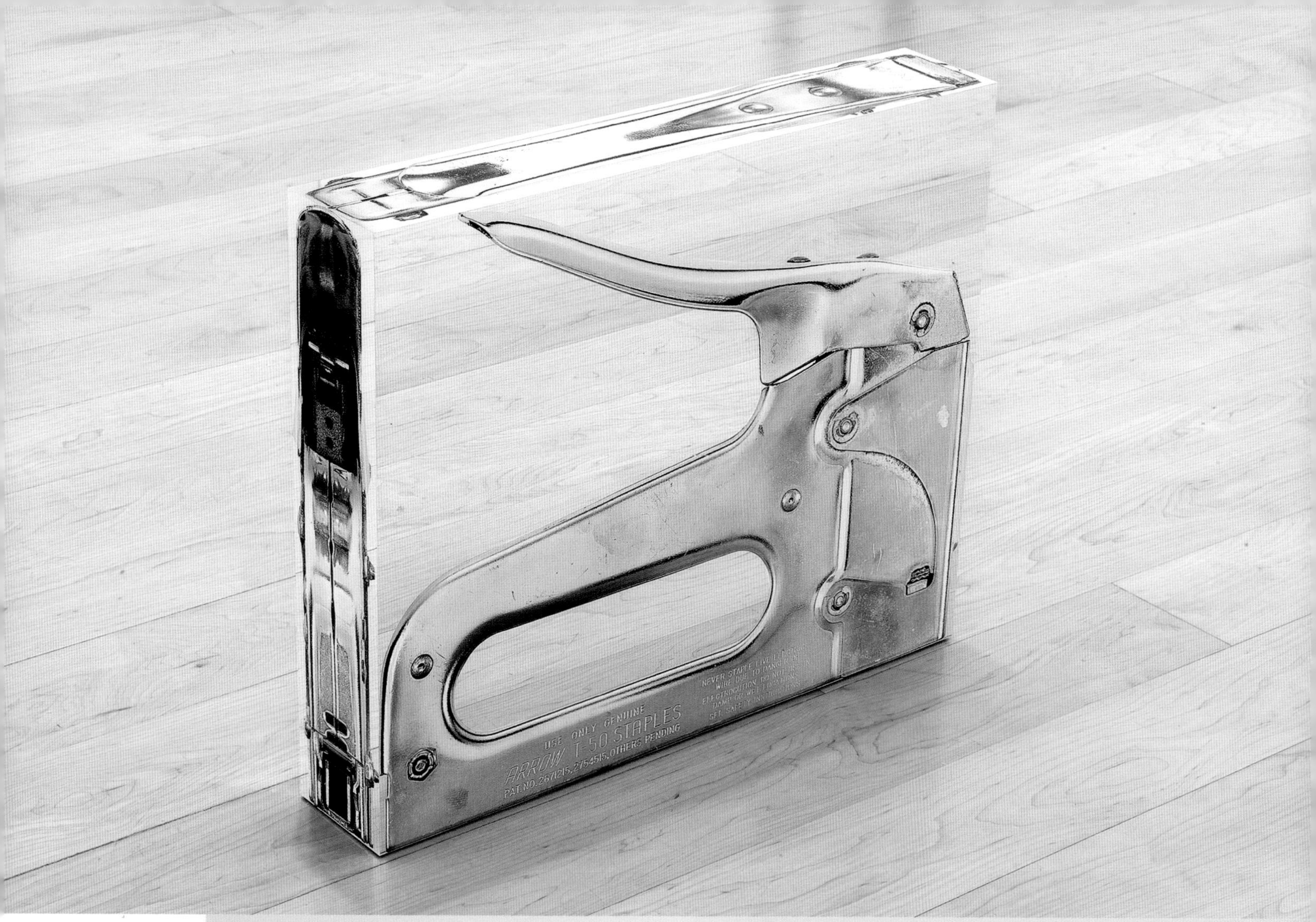

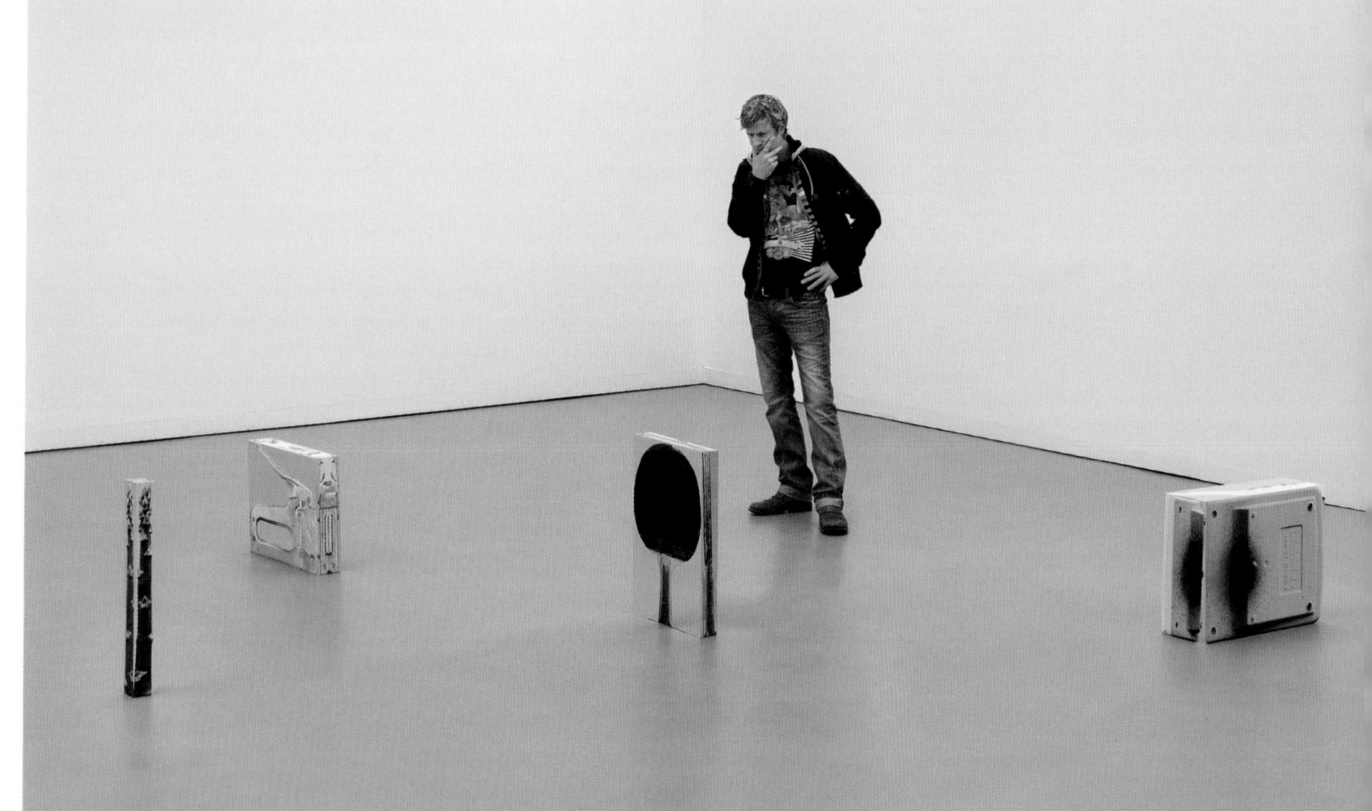

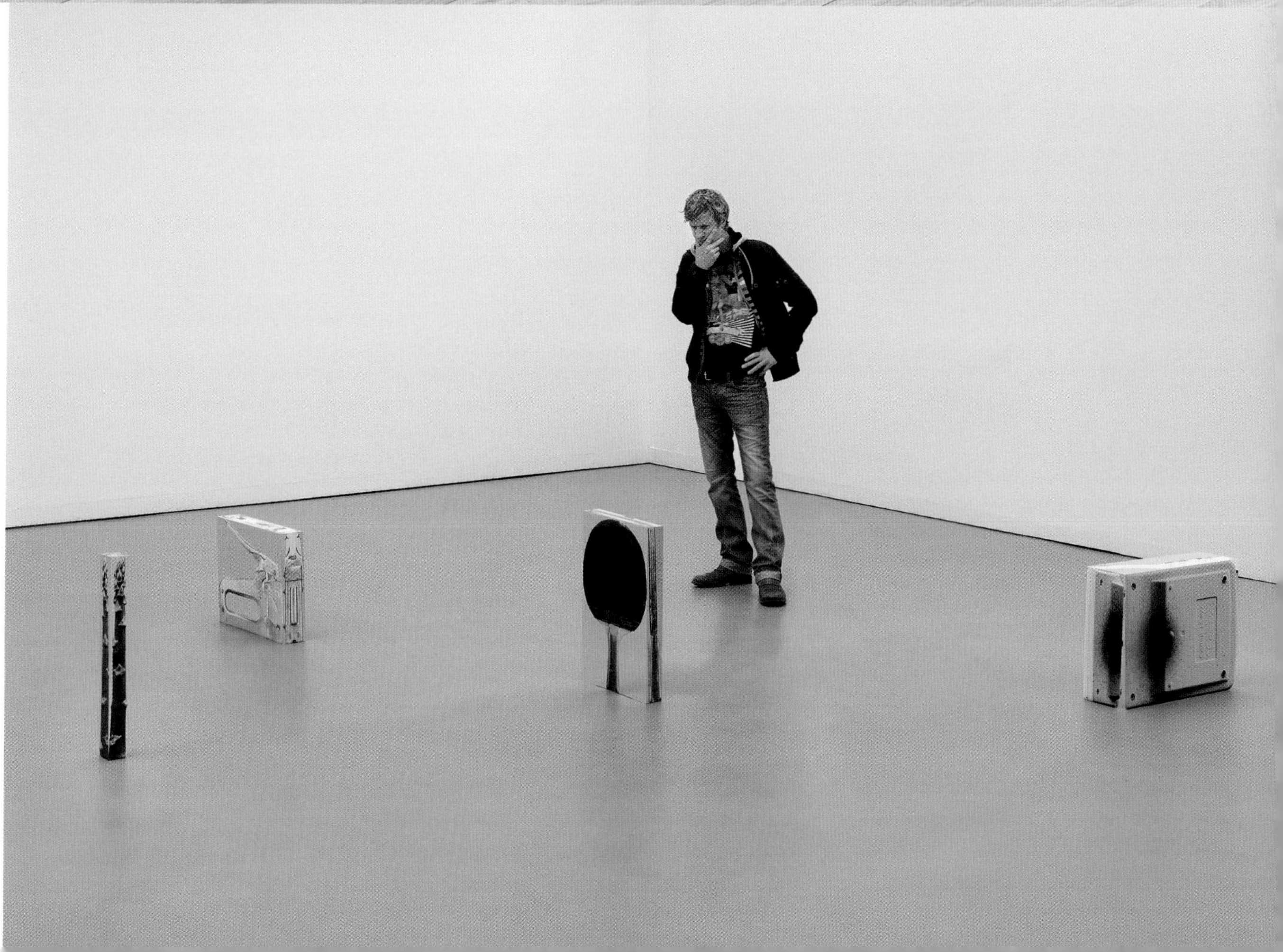

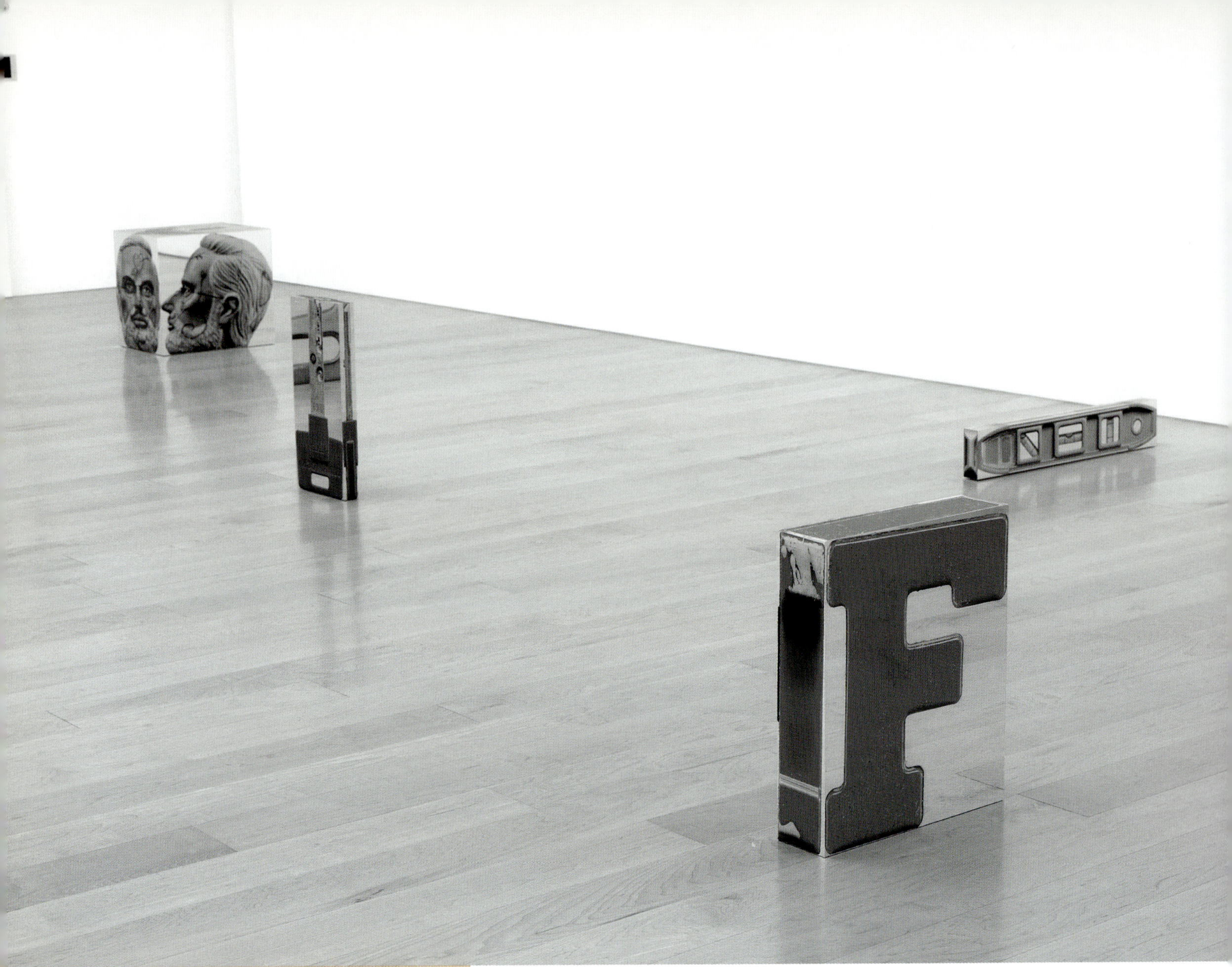

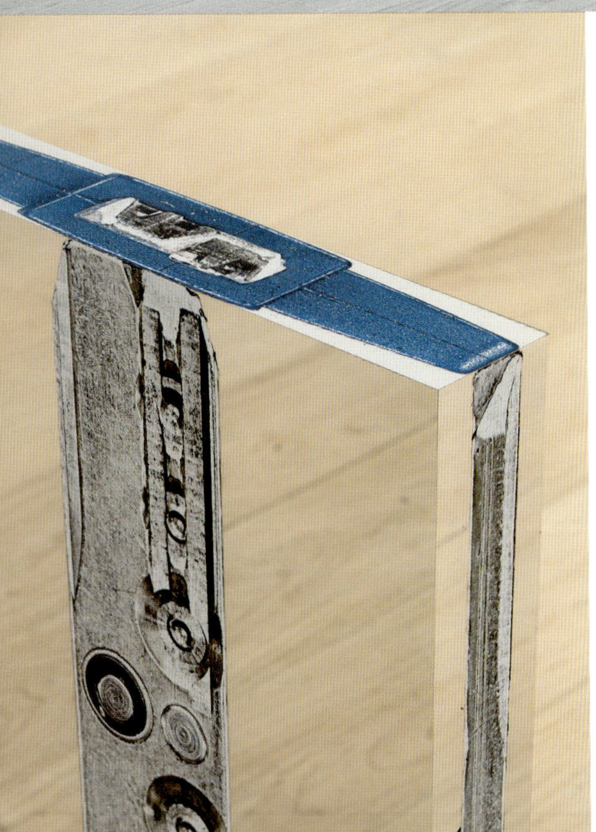

CROOKER
CREAGH
CRANOR
CRANER, 2012

Silkscreen print on mirror-glass, UV-adhesive, aluminum, glass, polyacetal, screws; in 4 parts
F: 16 ½ x 13 ¼ x 3 ½ inches (41.9 x 33.7 x 8.9 cm)
Foam head: 15 ½ x 16 ½ x 12 ¾ inches (39.4 x 41.9 x 32.4 cm)
Key: 17 ¾ x 8 ¼ x 1 ⅝ inches (45.1 x 21 x 4.1 cm)
Spirit level: 4 ⅝ x 25 ½ x 1 ¾ inches (11.7 x 64.8 x 4.4 cm)

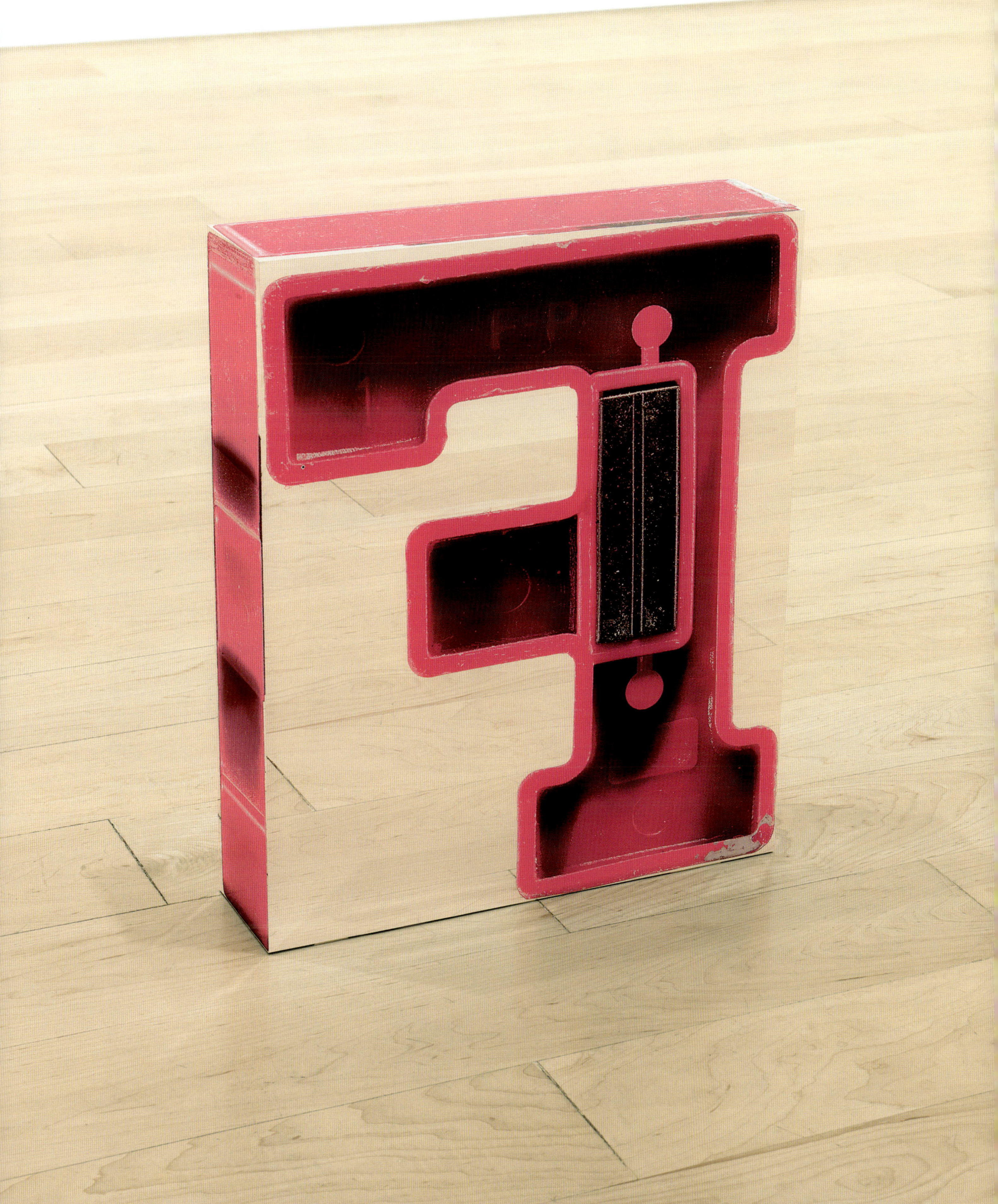

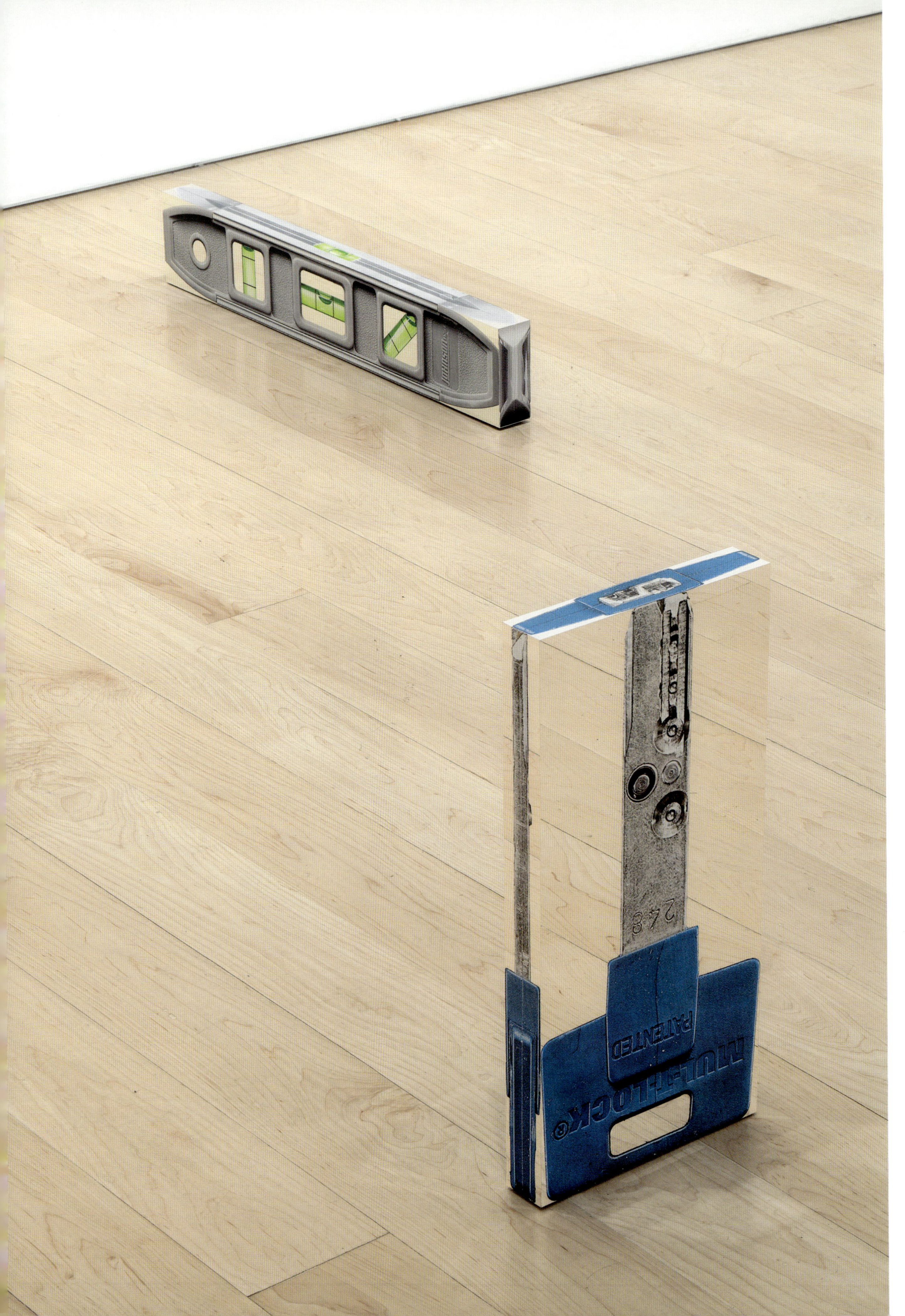
PATENTED
MUL-T-LOCK®

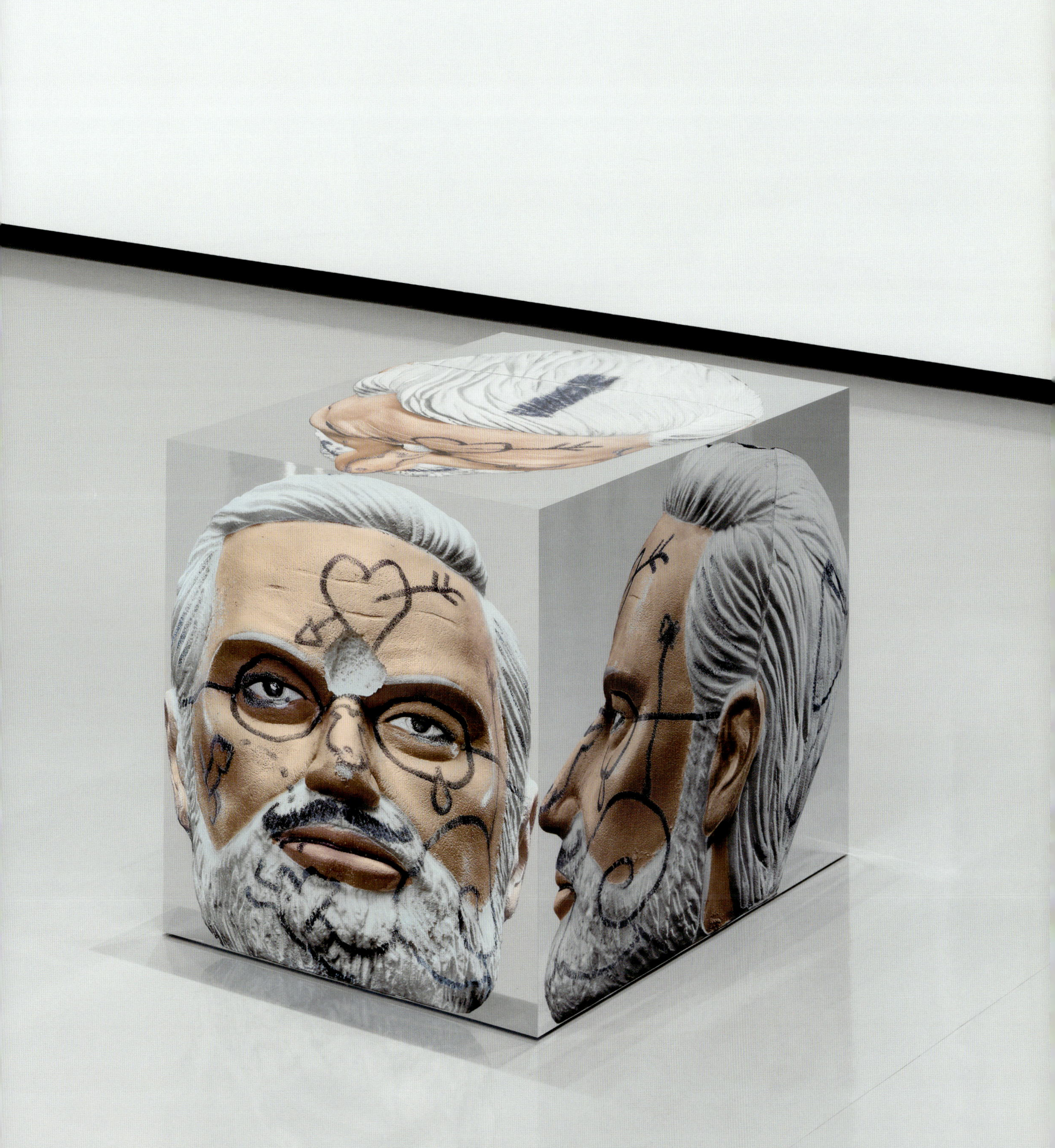

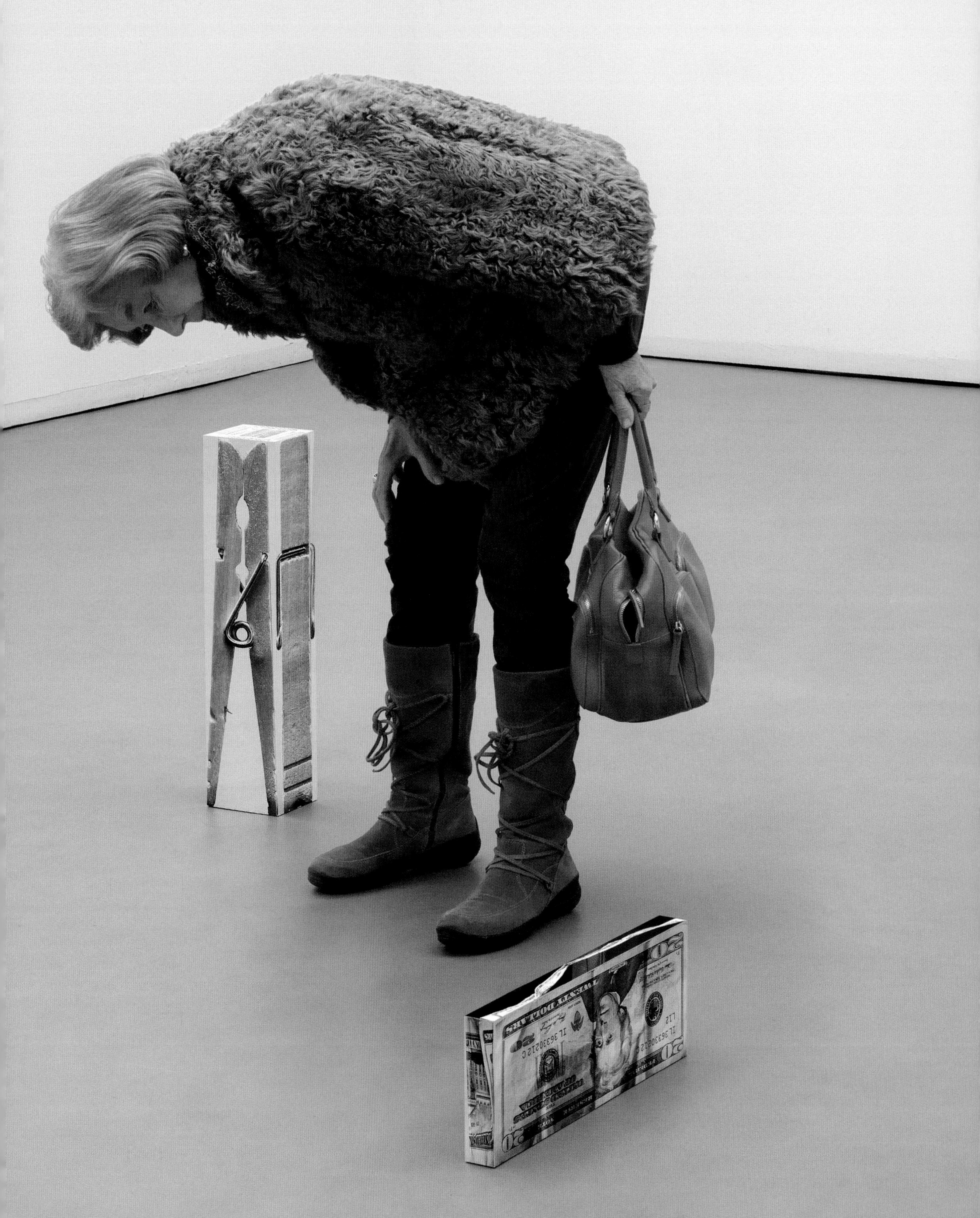

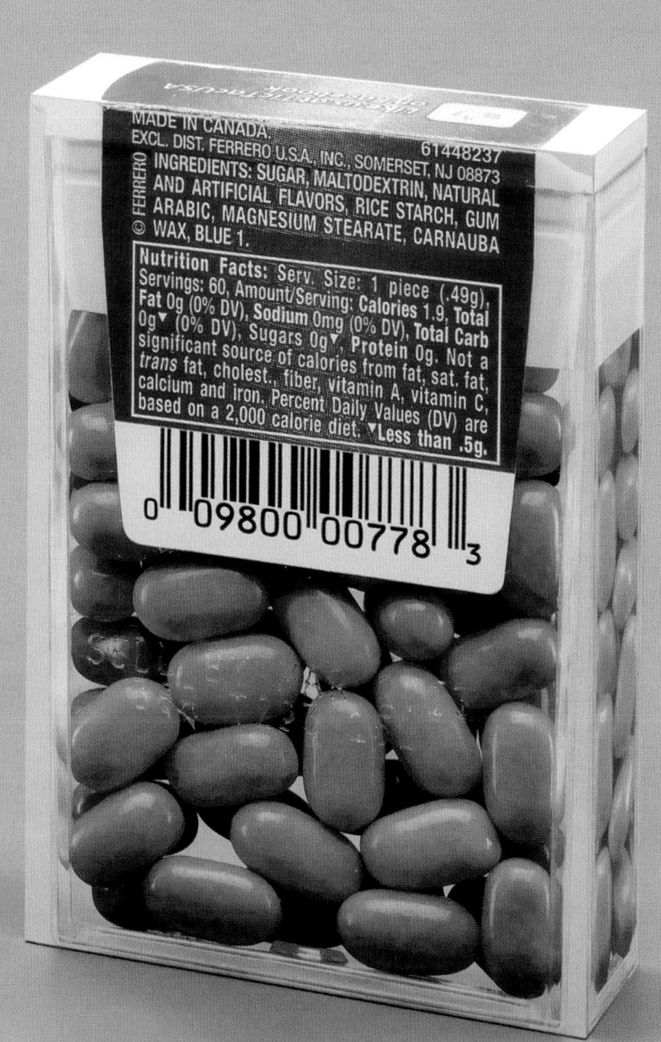
MADE IN CANADA.
EXCL. DIST. FERRERO U.S.A., INC., SOMERSET, NJ 08873
61448237
© FERRERO
INGREDIENTS: SUGAR, MALTODEXTRIN, NATURAL AND ARTIFICIAL FLAVORS, RICE STARCH, GUM ARABIC, MAGNESIUM STEARATE, CARNAUBA WAX, BLUE 1.
Nutrition Facts: Serv. Size: 1 piece (.49g), Servings: 60, Amount/Serving: Calories 1.9, Total Fat 0g (0% DV), Sodium 0mg (0% DV), Total Carb 0g▼ (0% DV), Sugars 0g▼, Protein 0g. Not a significant source of calories from fat, sat. fat, trans fat, cholest., fiber, vitamin A, vitamin C, calcium and iron. Percent Daily Values (DV) are based on a 2,000 calorie diet. ▼Less than .5g.
0 09800 00778 3

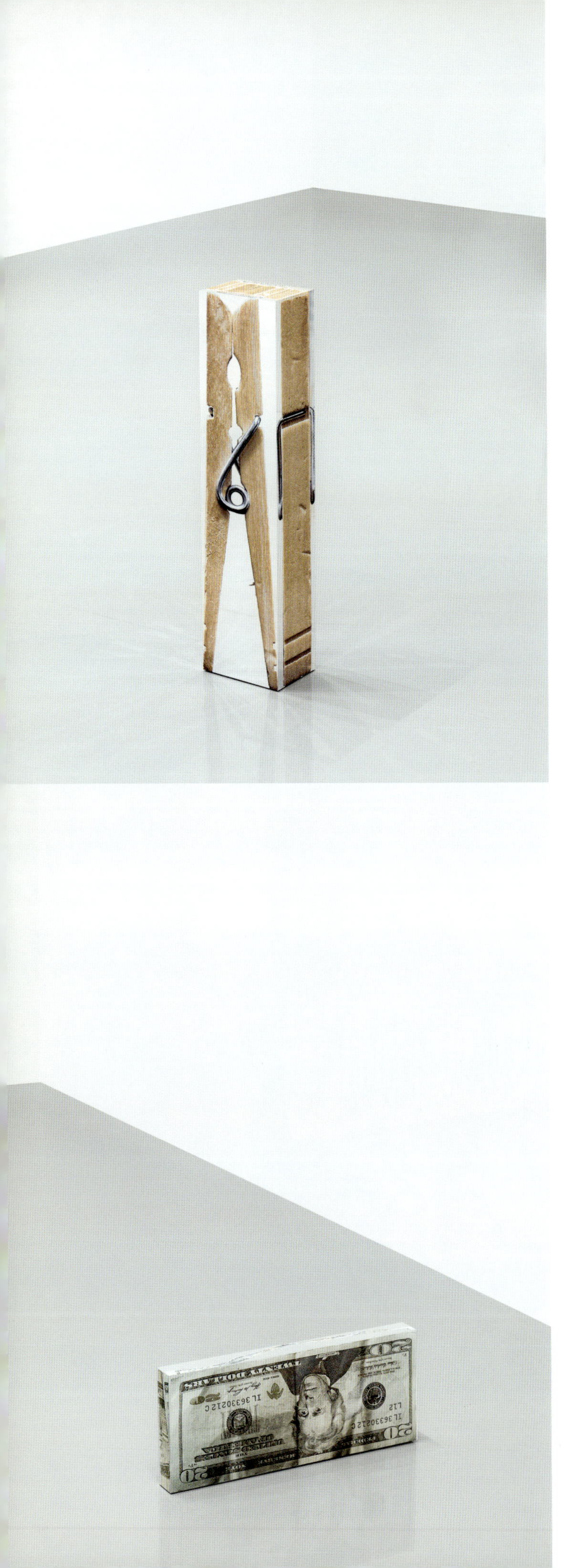

Previous spread and opposite page:

KITTINGER
ZAWACKI
YUTZY, 2012

Silkscreen print on mirror-glass, UV-adhesive, aluminum, glass, polyacetal, screws; in 3 parts
Clothespin: 23 ¼ x 5 ⅛ x 3 ⅞ inches (59 x 13.1 x 9.7 cm)
Dollar bill: 6 ¾ x 15 ½ x 1 ⅝ inches (17.2 x 39.4 x 4 cm)
Tic Tac: 25 ¼ x 15 ¾ x 6 ⅛ inches (64 x 40 x 15.4 cm)

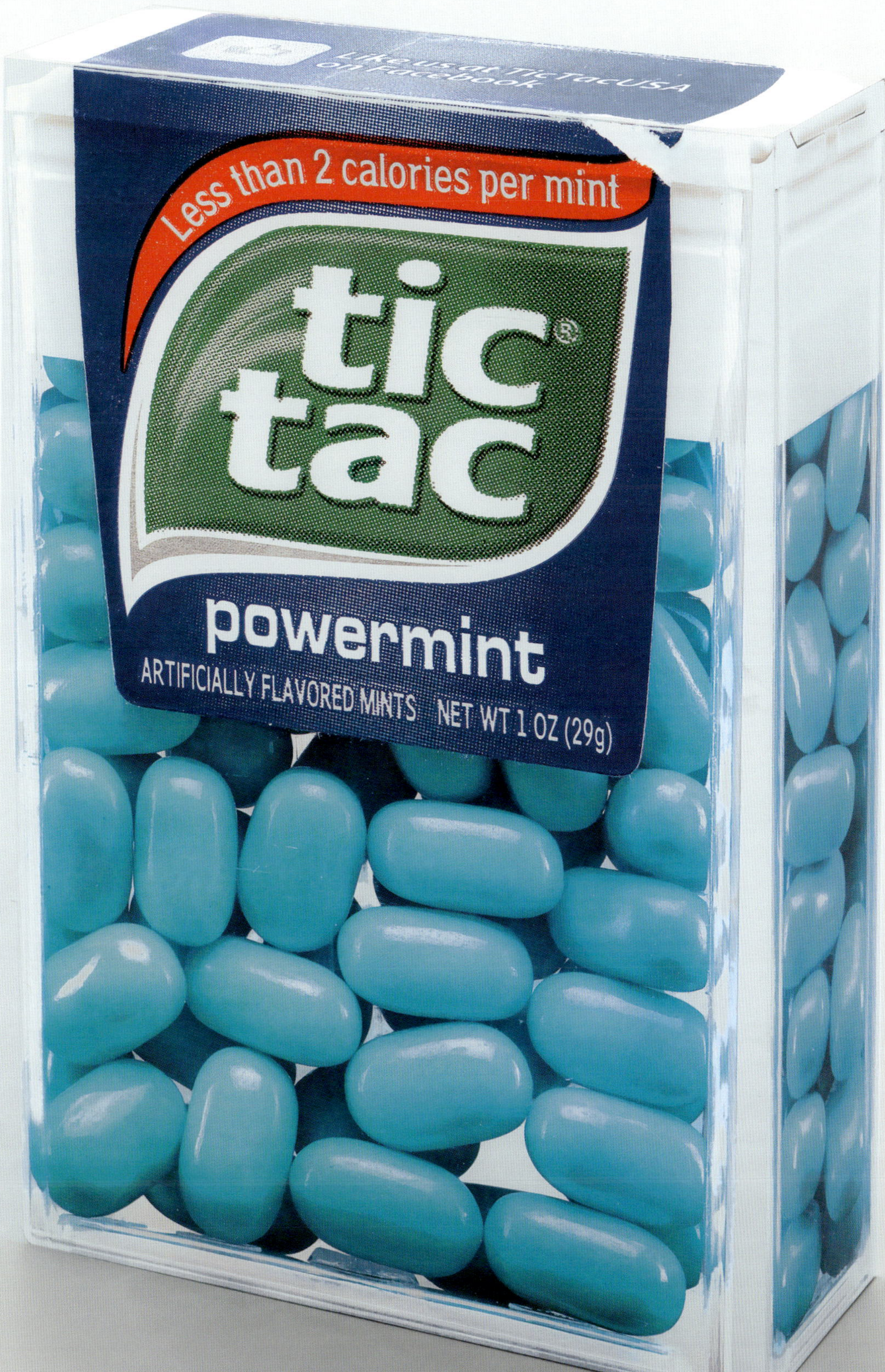

Less than 2 calories per mint
tic tac®
powermint
ARTIFICIALLY FLAVORED MINTS NET WT 1 OZ (29g)

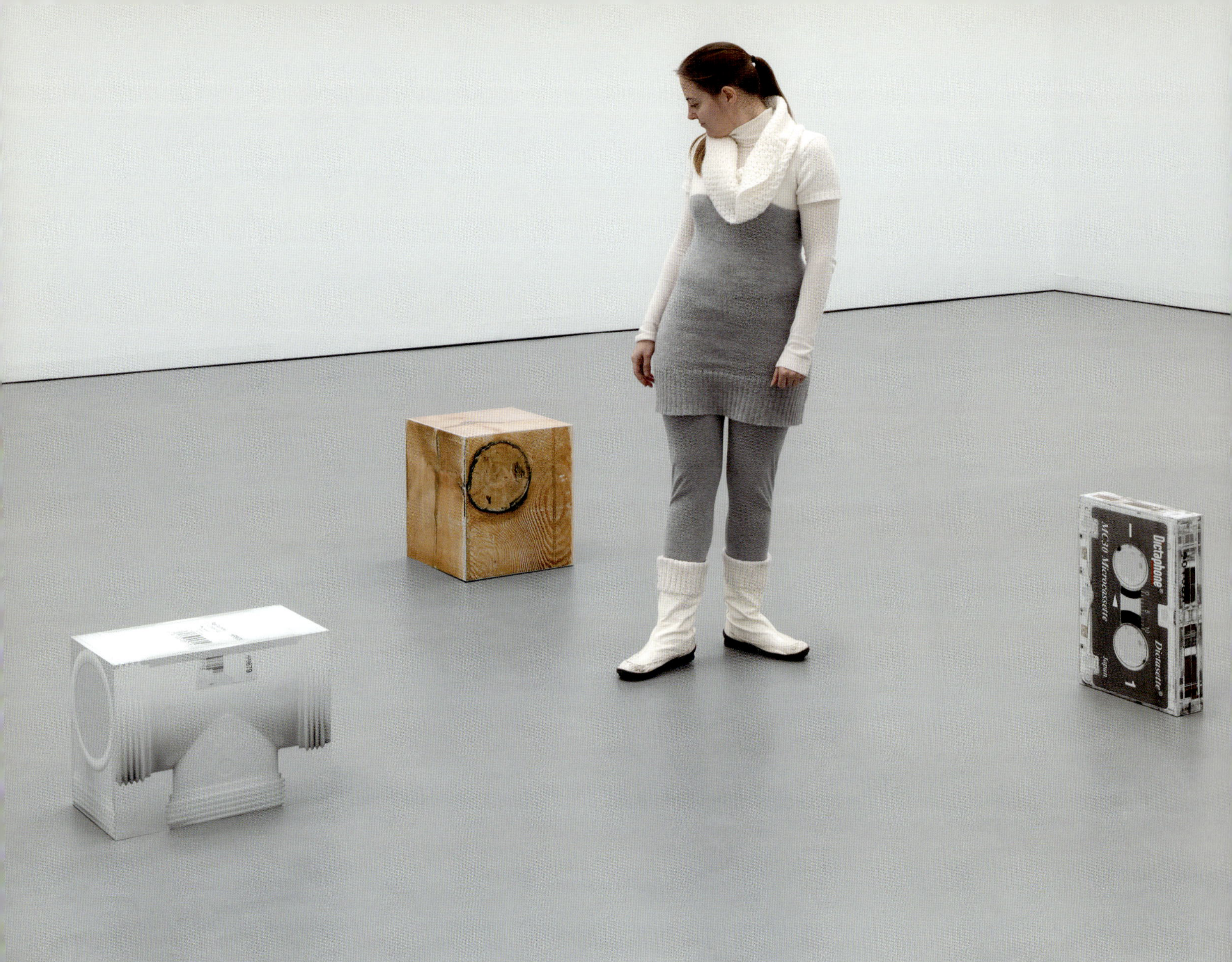

ALTENBURGER
SCHNEIDER
WINKLER, 2013

Silkscreen print on mirror-glass, UV-adhesive, aluminum, glass, polyacetal, screws; in 3 parts
Cassette tape: 18 ½ x 12 ⅜ x 3 ¼ inches (46.9 x 31.4 x 8.4 cm)
Three-way pipe: 14 ⅛ x 17 ⅞ x 9 ¾ inches (35.6 x 45.5 x 24.7 cm)
Wood block: 16 ¾ x 14 ⅛ x 14 ¼ inches (42.4 x 35.7 x 36.2 cm)

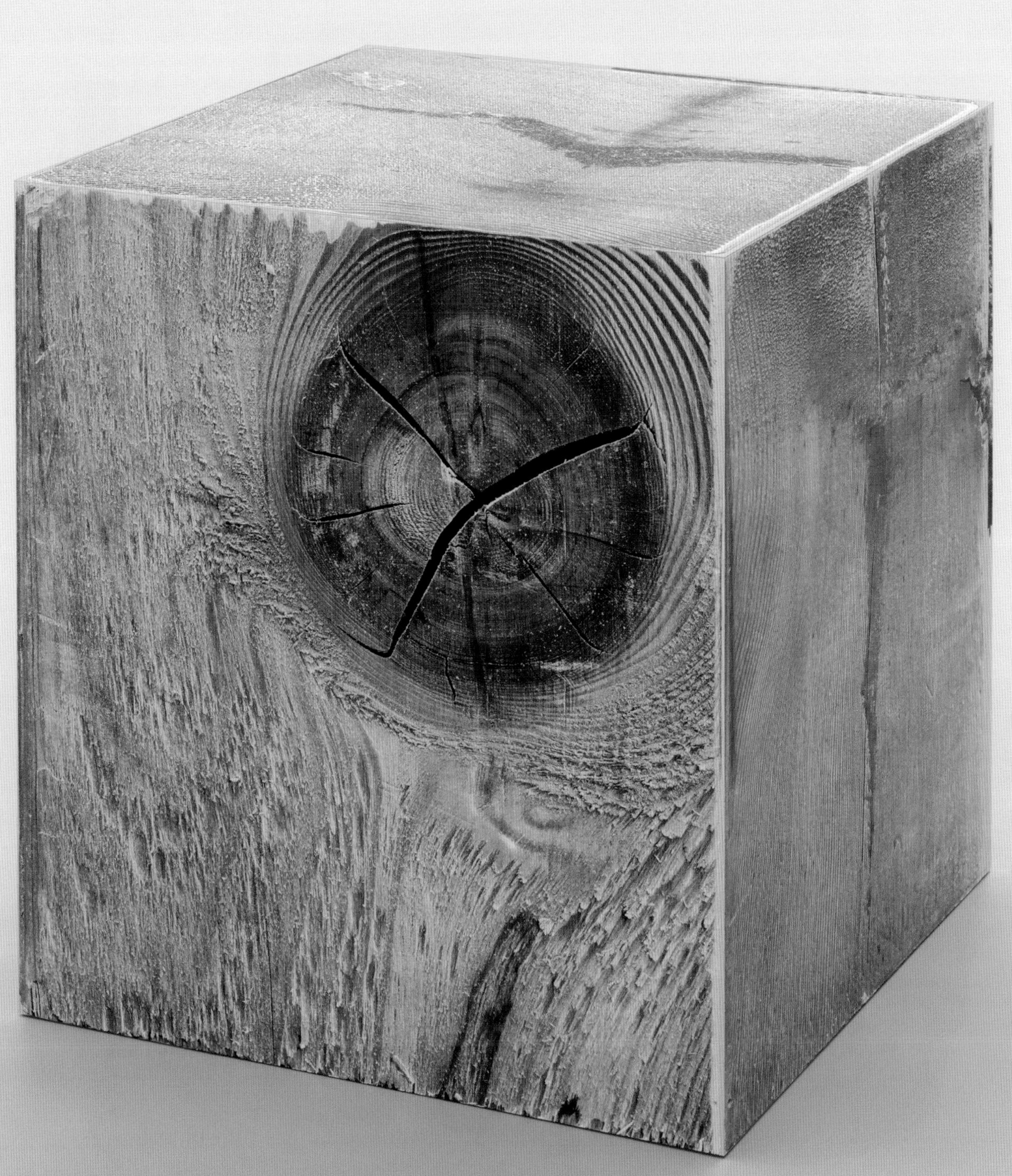

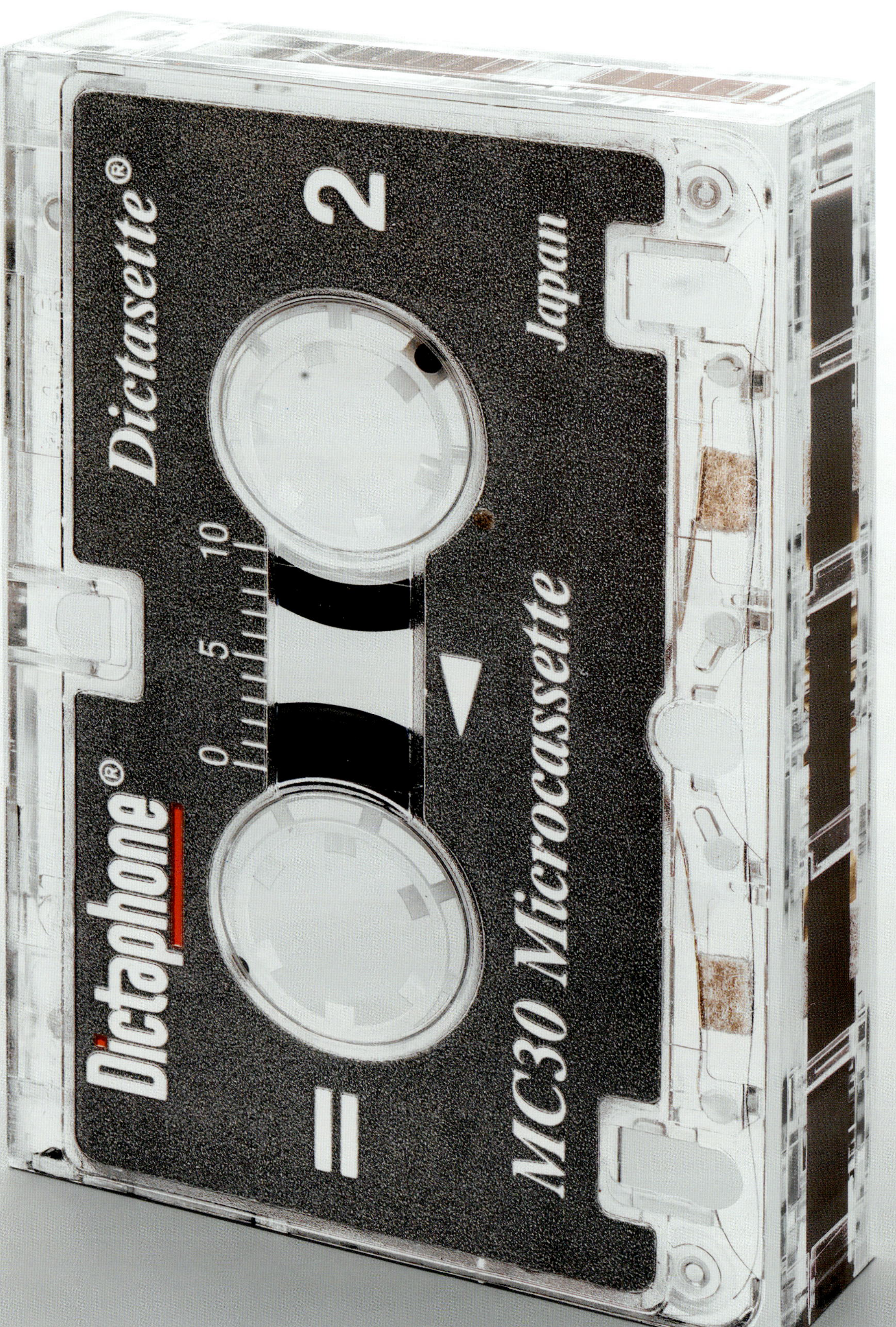

Dictaphone®
Dictasette®
2
Japan
0 5 10
MC30 Microcassette

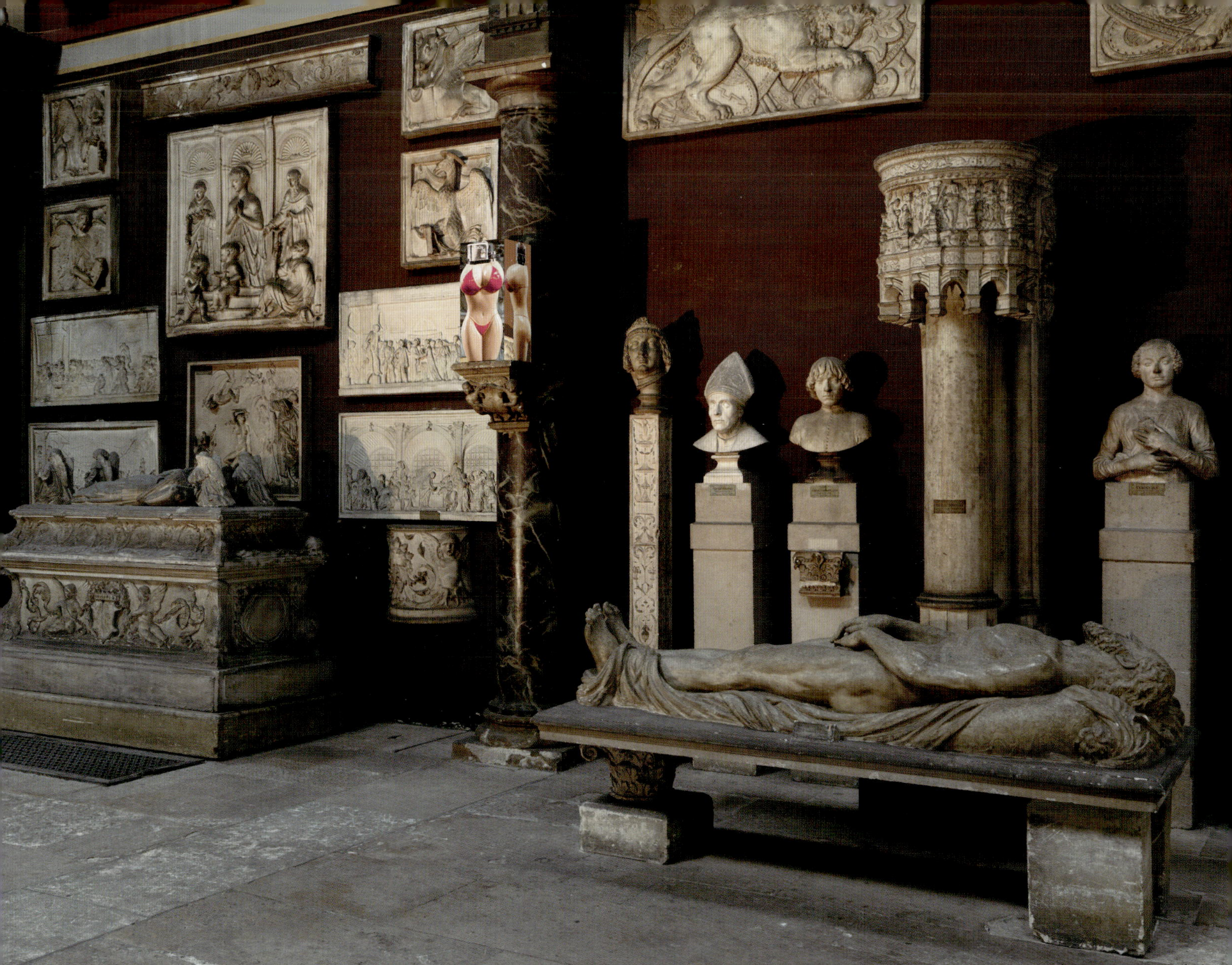

ROTHENBERG
MCCLUSKY, 2012

Silkscreen print on mirror-glass, UV-adhesive,
aluminum, glass, polyacetal, screws; in 2 parts
Honey bear: 20 ⅞ x 9 ⅜ x 8 ½ inches (53 x 23.7 x 21.7 cm)
Lighter: 23 ⅛ x 10 ⅛ x 9 ¼ inches (58.6 x 25.8 x 23.4 cm)
This page and next page: Installation view, Festival d'Automne à Paris,
Chapelle des Petits Augustins, École nationale supérieure des Beaux-arts,
Paris, 2012

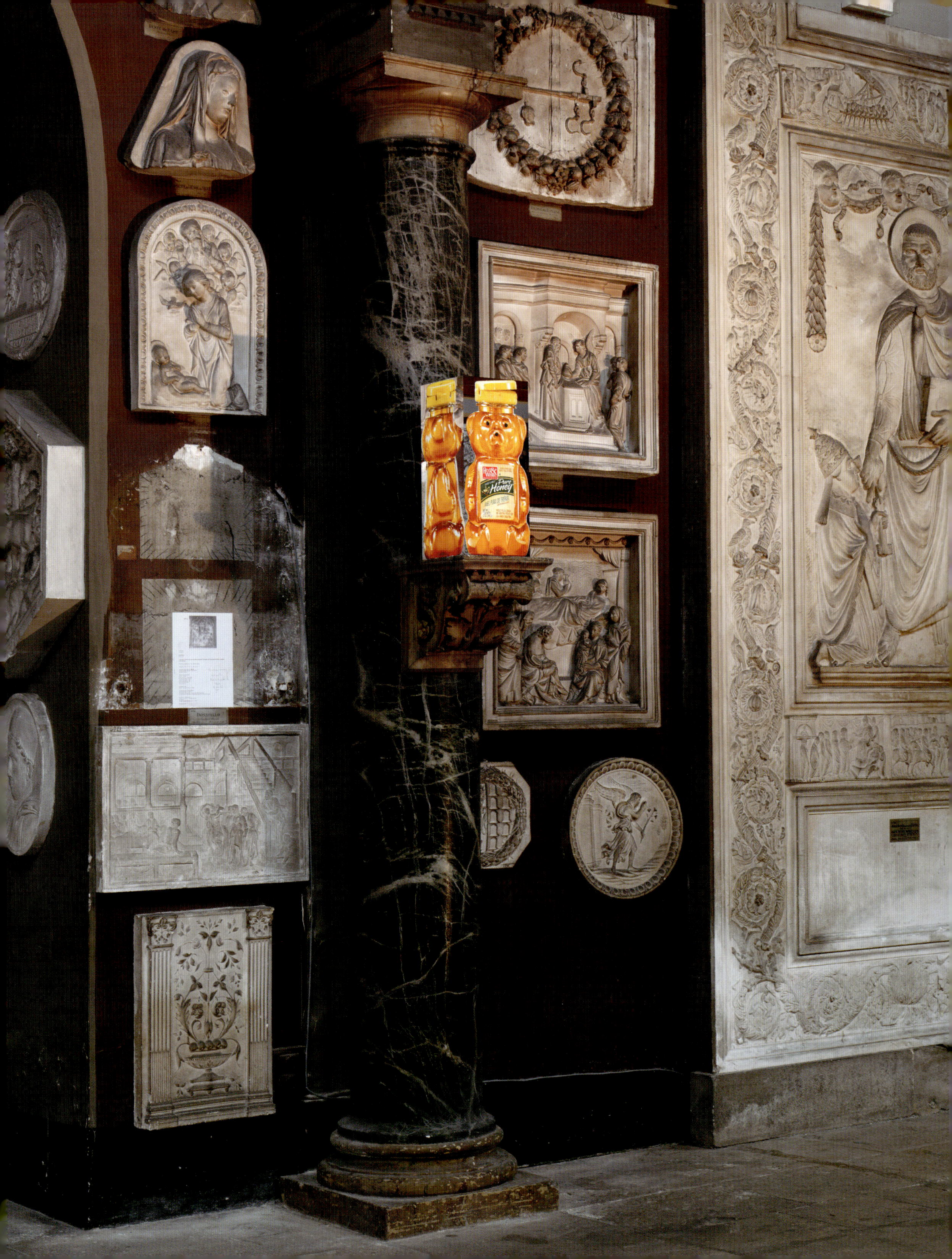
Red&White
Pure Honey

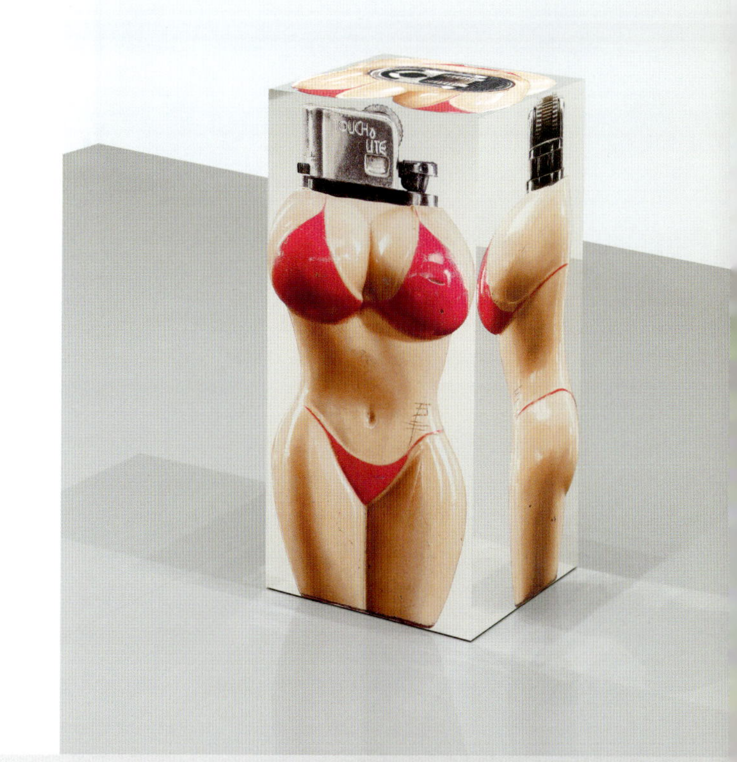

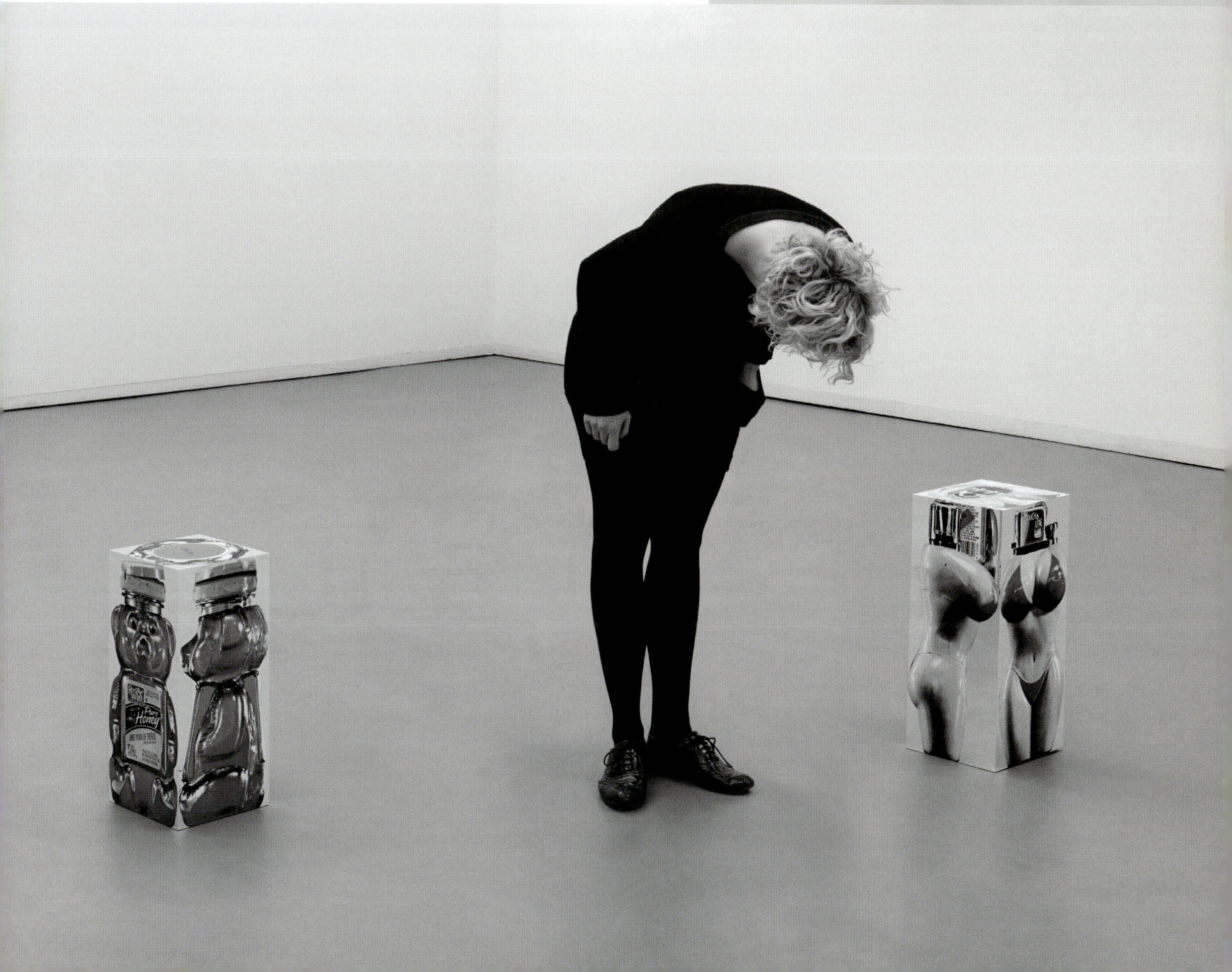

Untitled, 1997

Cut-up pallet, household candles

41 x 39 ⅜ x 9 inches (104 x 100 x 23 cm)

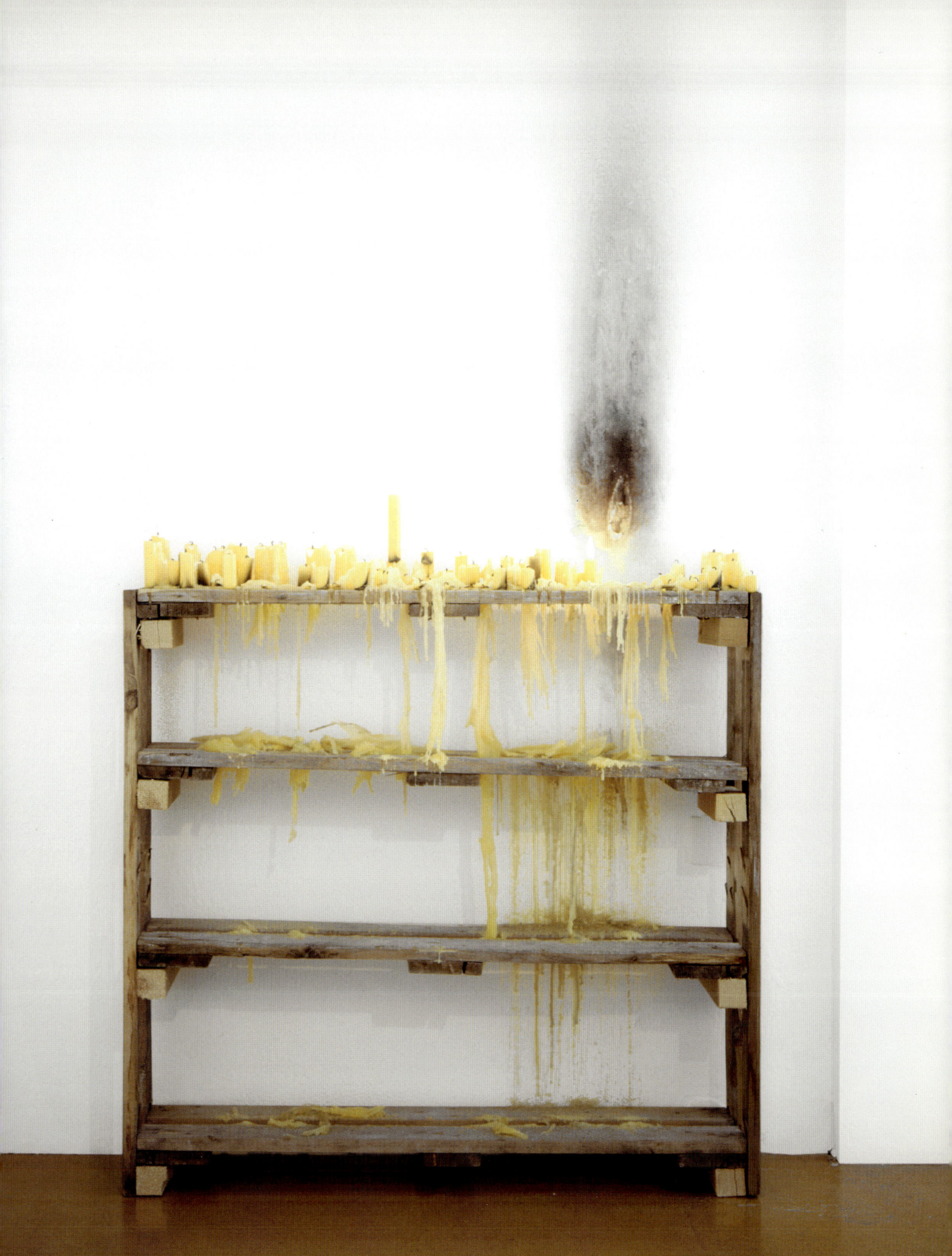

Untitled (Candle), 1999

Candles, fiber cement boards, screws

Base: 39 ⅜ x 39 ⅜ inches (100 x 100 cm)

Pedestal: 49 ¼ x 7 ⅞ x 7 ⅞ inches (125 x 20 x 20 cm)

Wax: 27 ½ x 33 ½ x 27 ½ inches (70 x 85 x 70 cm), growing

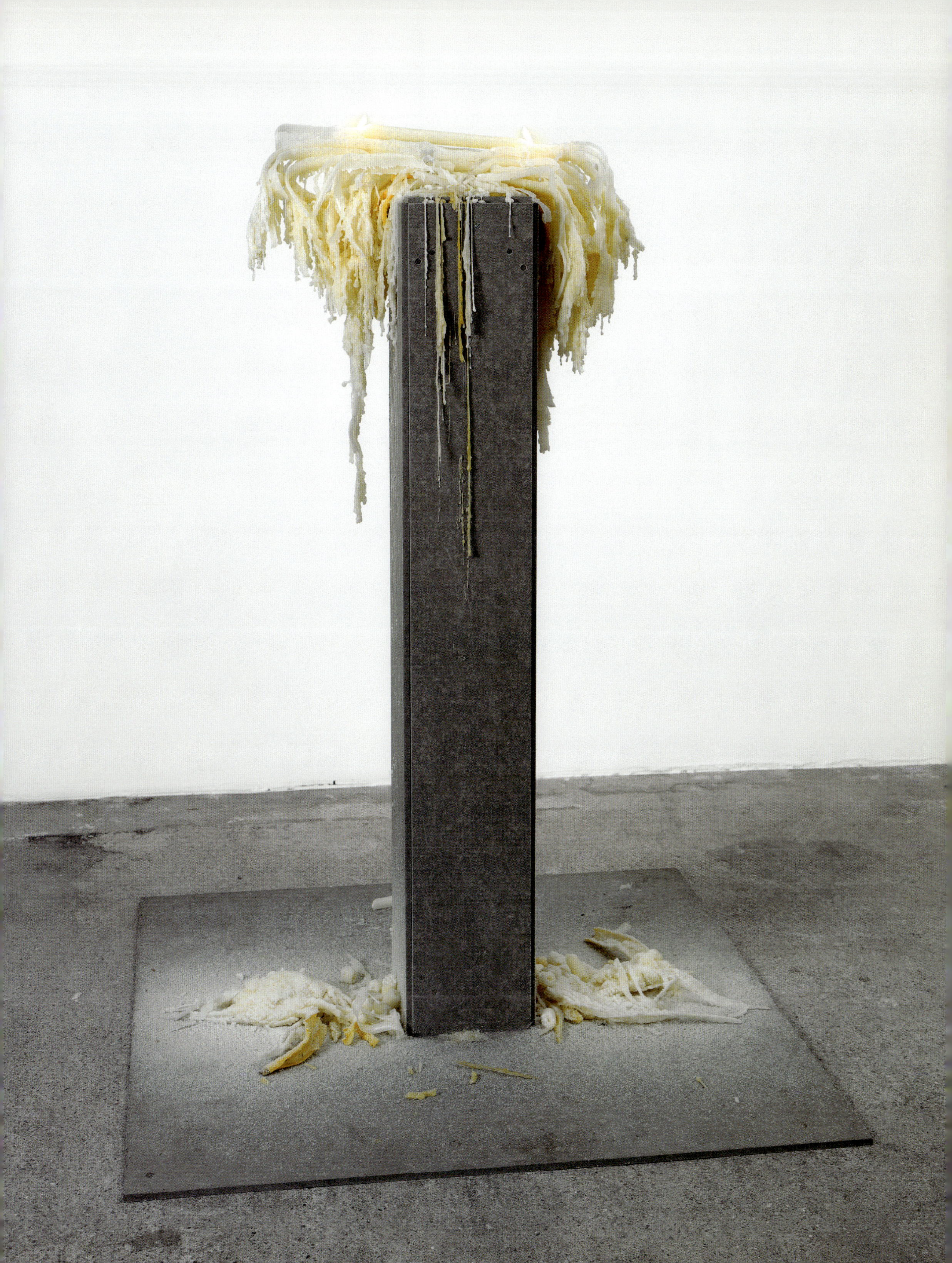

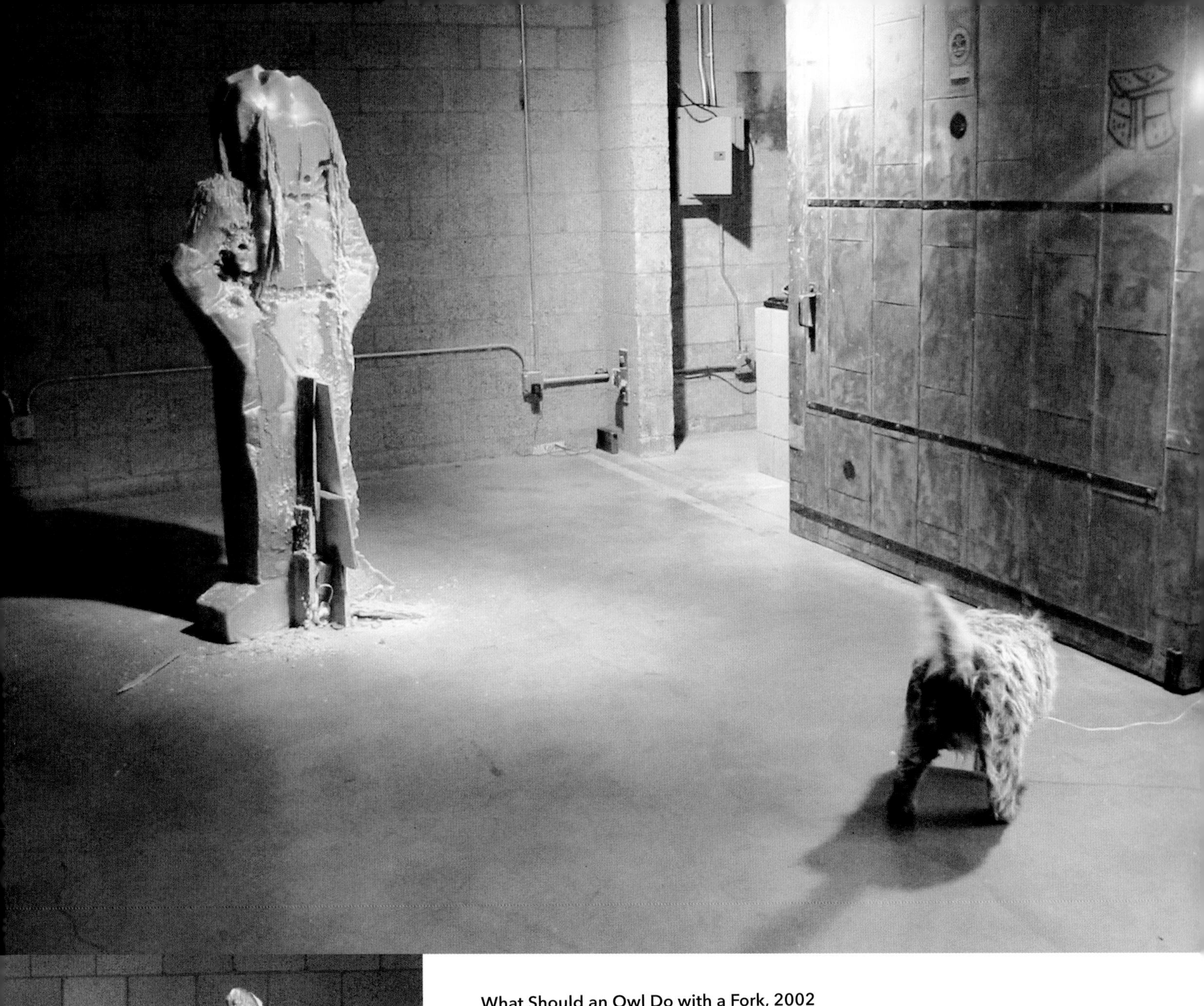

What Should an Owl Do with a Fork, 2002

Wax, wick, wood, garbage

20 ⅛ x 28 x 12 inches (178 x 71 x 30.5 cm)

Installation view, "What Should an Owl Do with a Fork,"

Santa Monica Museum of Art, California, 2002

Above: *Gypsy*, 2002

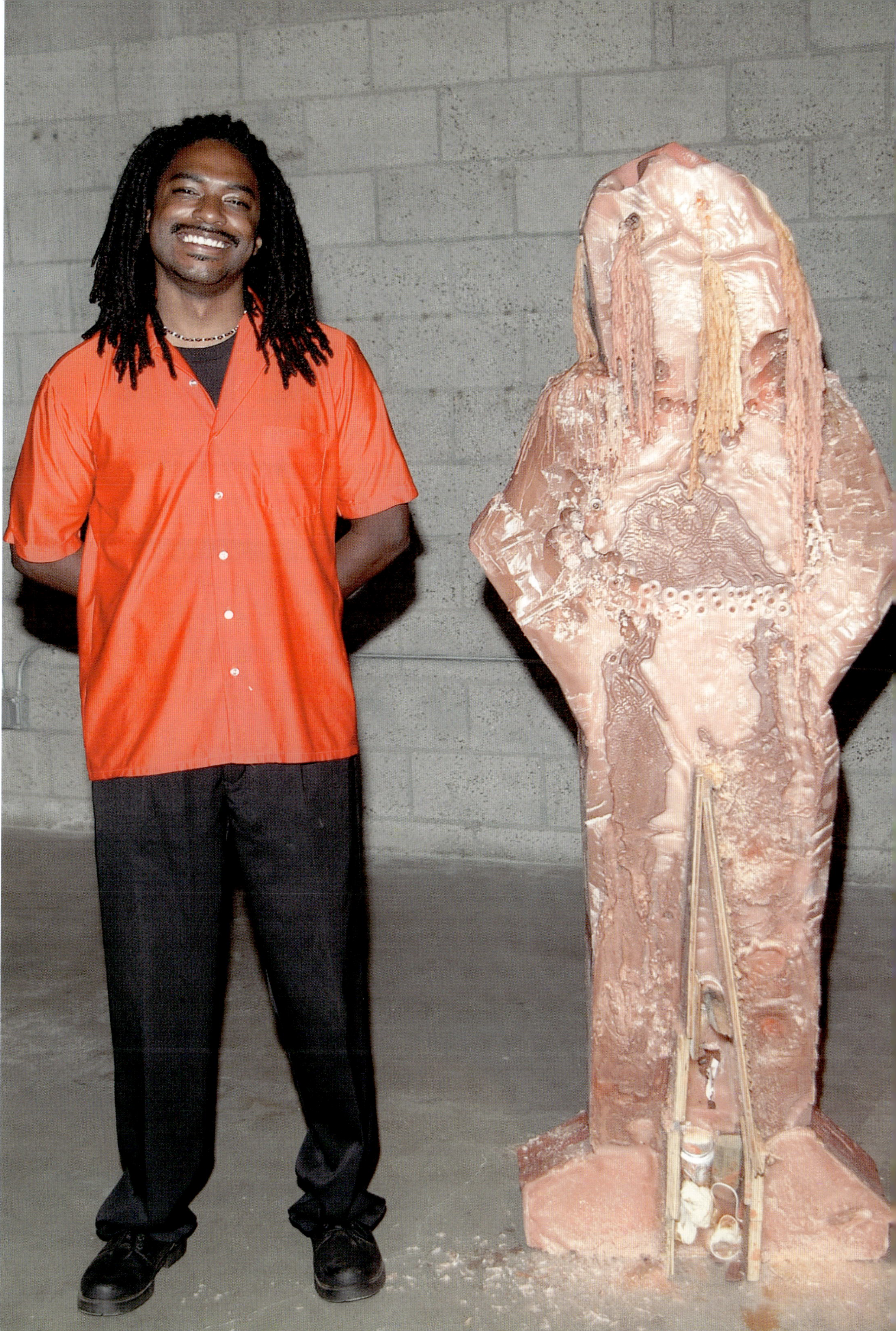

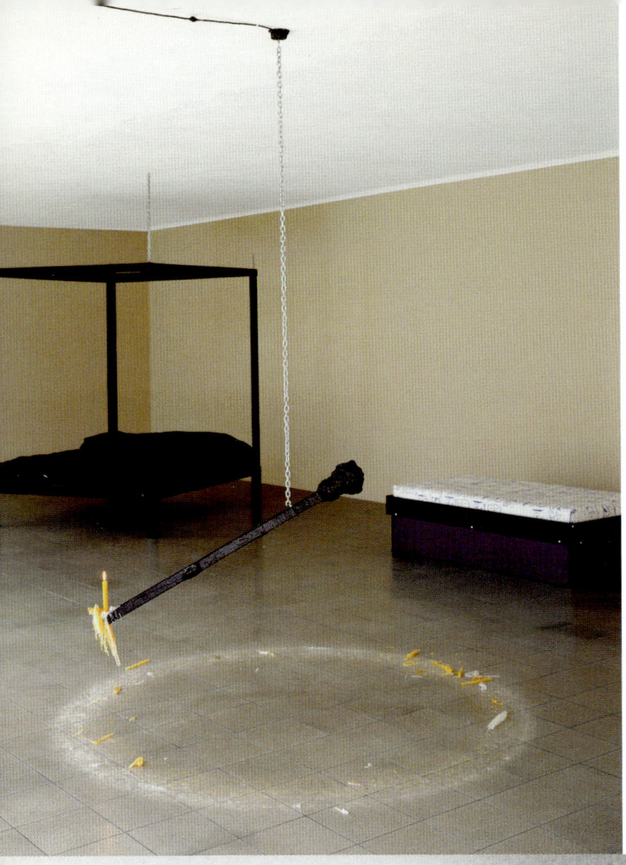

Left:

Kerzenständer, 2000
from "6 ½ Domestic Pairs Project"
Wood, clay, enamel paint, chain, electric motor, candle, wood glue
Dimensions variable
Installation view, "Tagessuppen / Soups of the Days" and "6 ½ Domestic Pairs Project" (with Keith Tyson), Kunsthaus Glarus, Switzerland, 2000
Bed, 2000; Keith Tyson, *Relaxing Possibility, Applied Art Machine: "A bed that does the worrying for you"* (from "6 ½ Domestic Pairs Project"), 2000

Below and opposite page:

Untitled (Branches), 2005
Two branches moving at different speeds, in opposite directions
Cast aluminum, chains, candles, low-speed electric motors, control units
Branch 1: 19 ⅝ x 126 x 15 ¾ inches (50 x 320 x 40 cm)
Branch 2: 19 ⅝ x 122 x 15 ¾ inches (50 x 310 x 40 cm)
Overall dimensions approximately: 244 ⅛ x 326 ¾ x 234 ⅝ inches (620 x 830 x 596 cm)
Below: Installation view, "Day for Night," Whitney Biennial, Whitney Museum of American Art, New York, 2006
The Intelligence of Flowers, 2005
Opposite page: Installation view, Camden Arts Centre, London, 2005

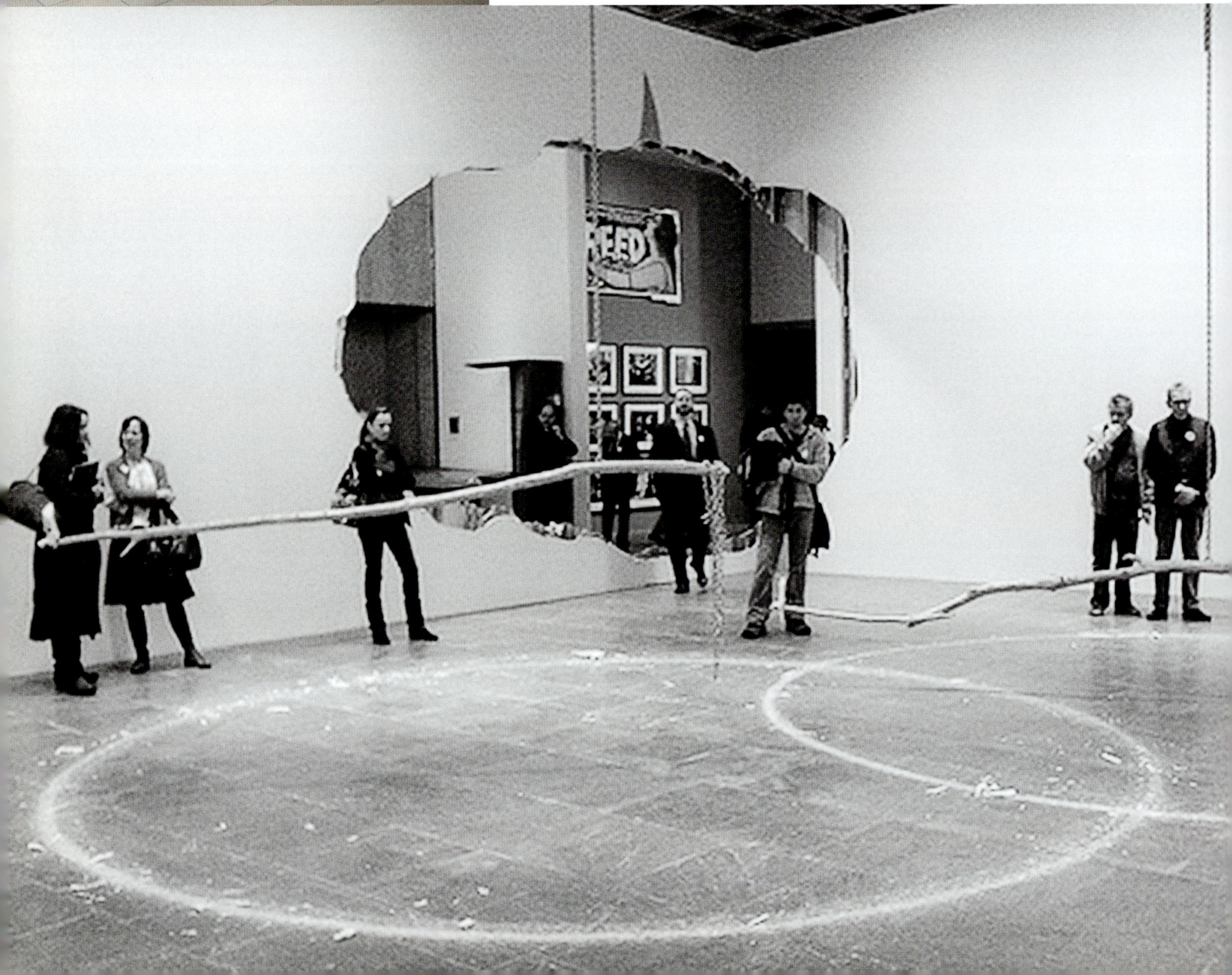

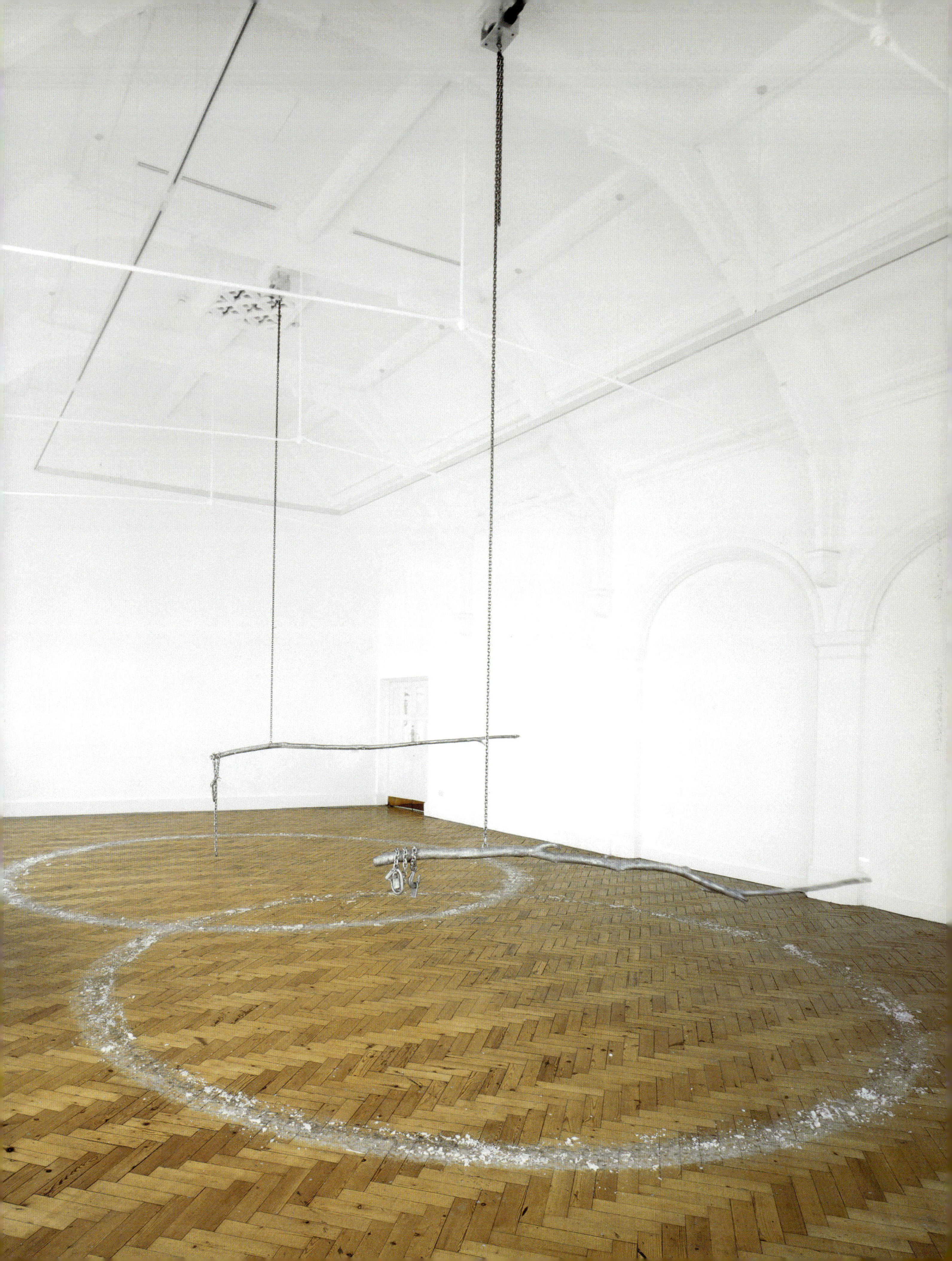

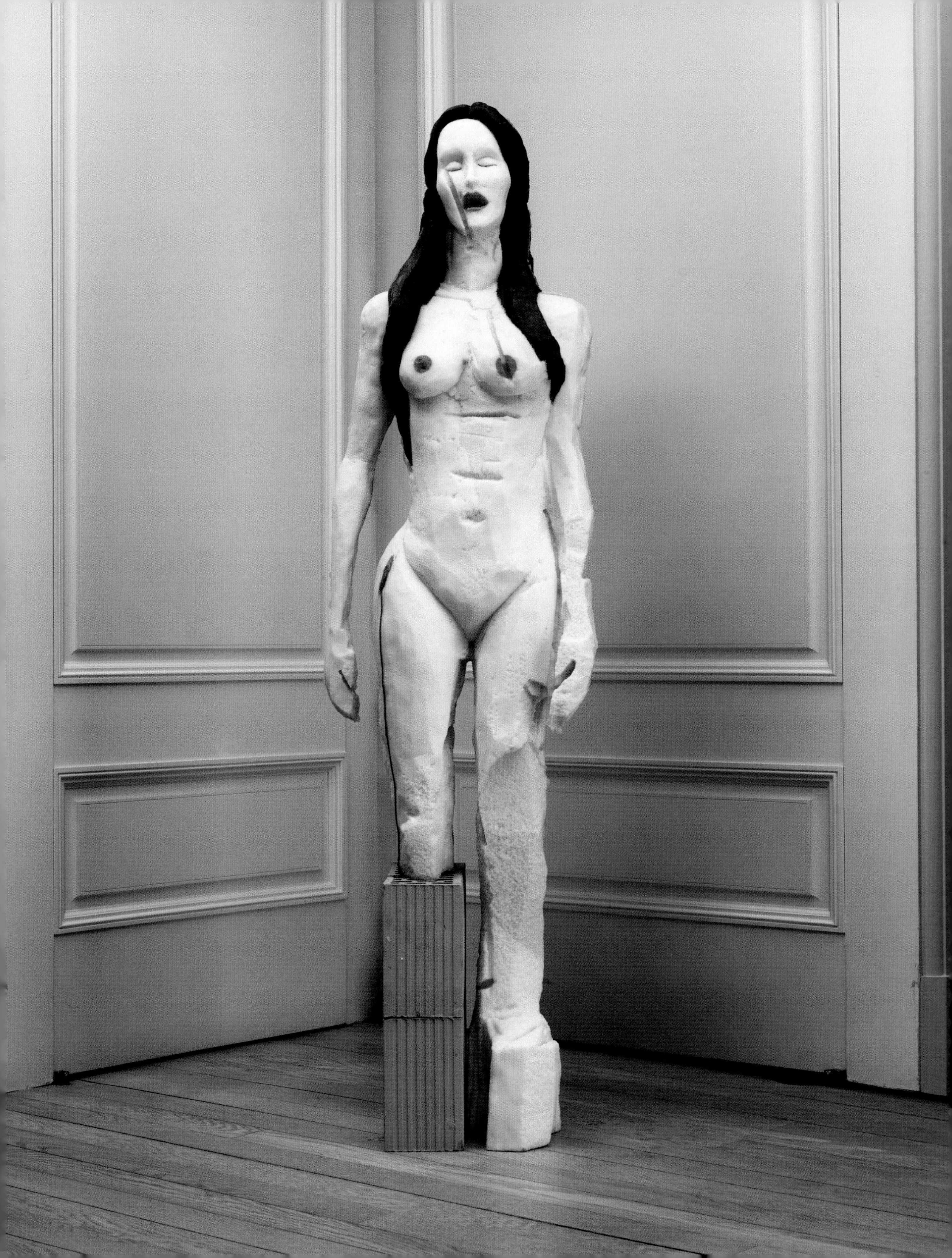

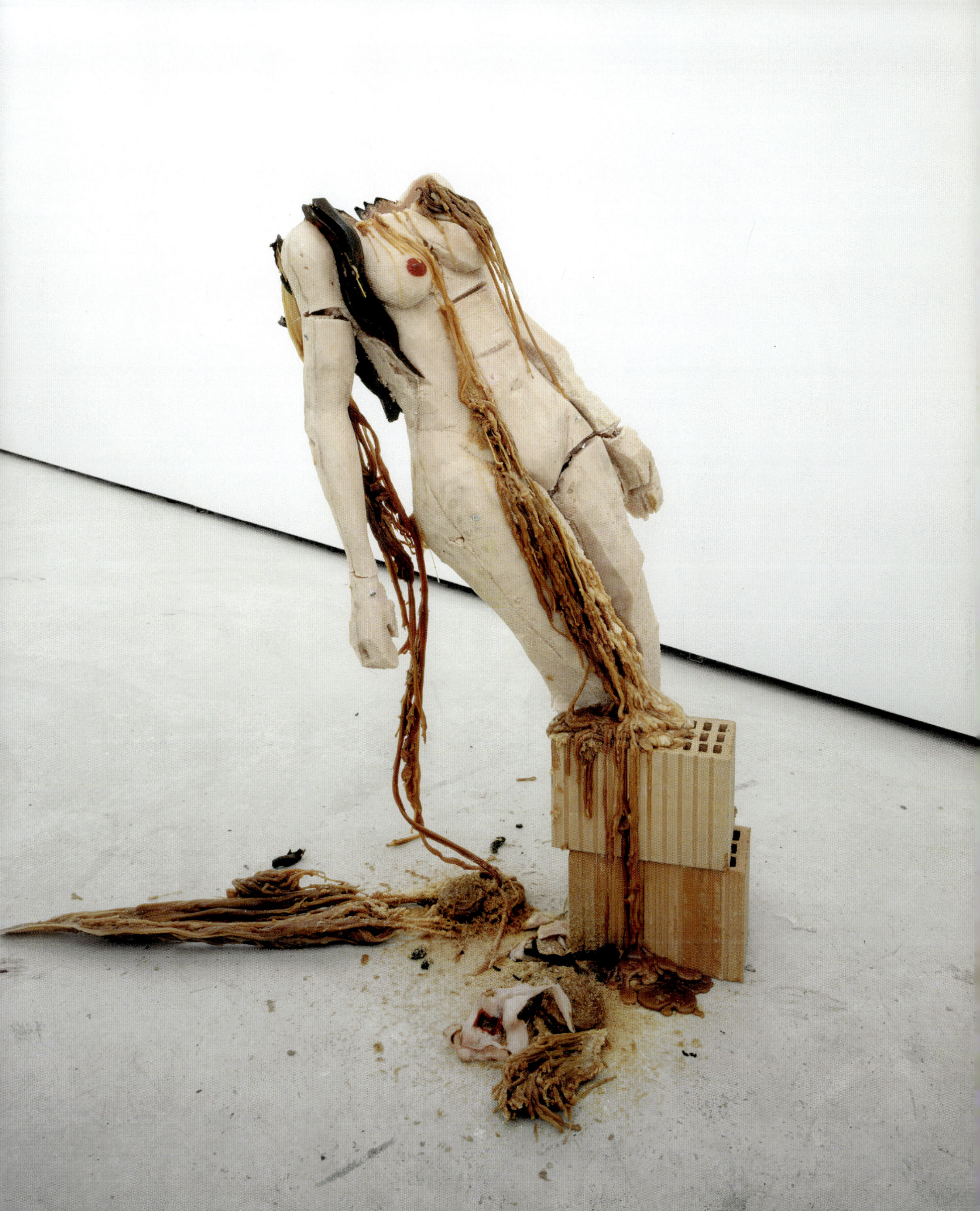

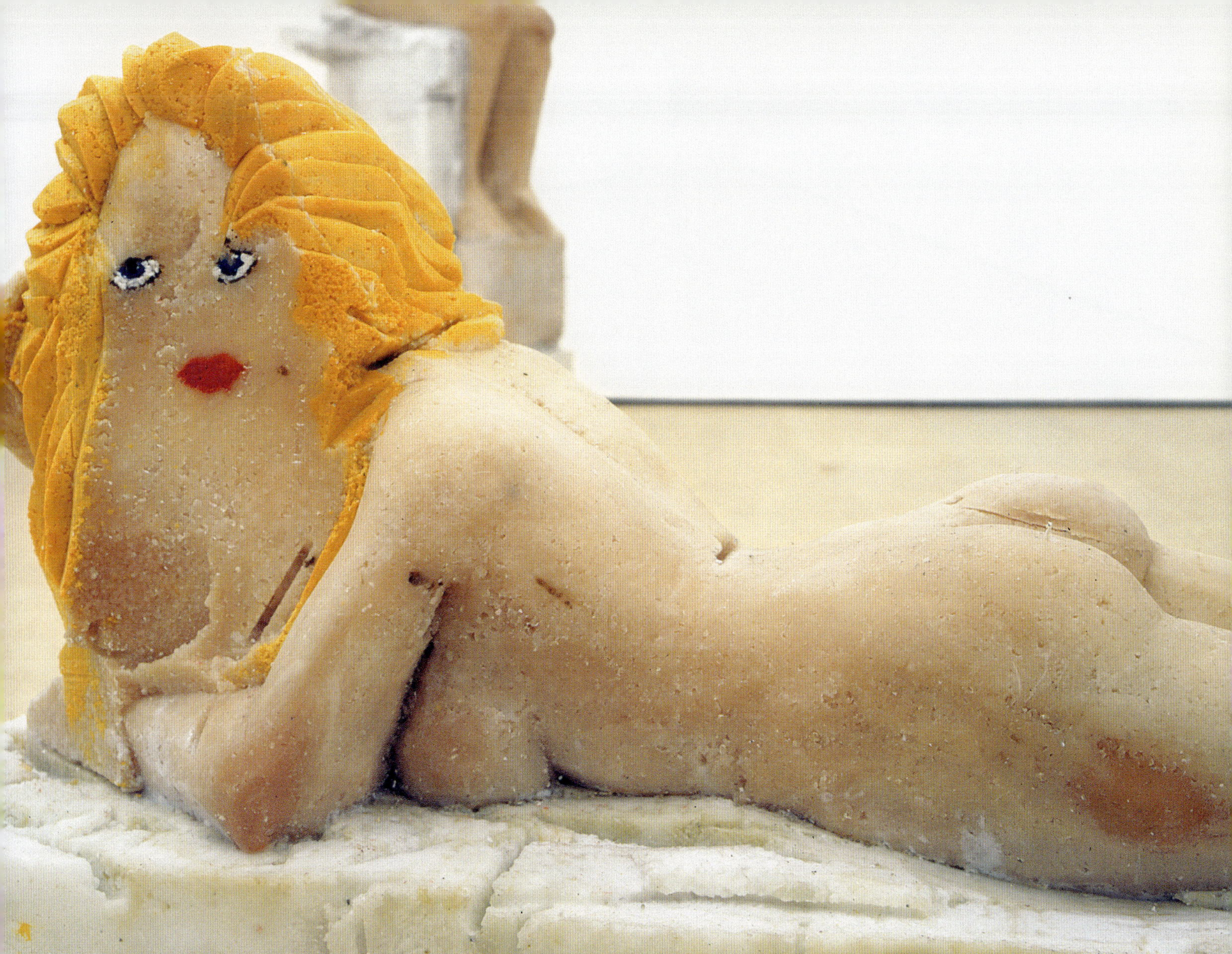

What if the Phone Rings, 2003
Wax, pigment, wick
Figure 1: 41 ¾ x 55 ⅞ x 18 ⅛ inches (106 x 142 x 46 cm)
Figure 2: 78 ¾ x 21 ¼ x 18 ⅛ inches (200 x 54 x 46 cm)
Figure 3: 37 x 39 x 21 ¼ inches (94 x 99 x 54 cm)

Previous pages:
Untitled, 2001
Wax, pigment, wick, brick, metal rod
66 ⅞ x 18 ⅛ x 11 ⅜ inches (170 x 46 x 29 cm)

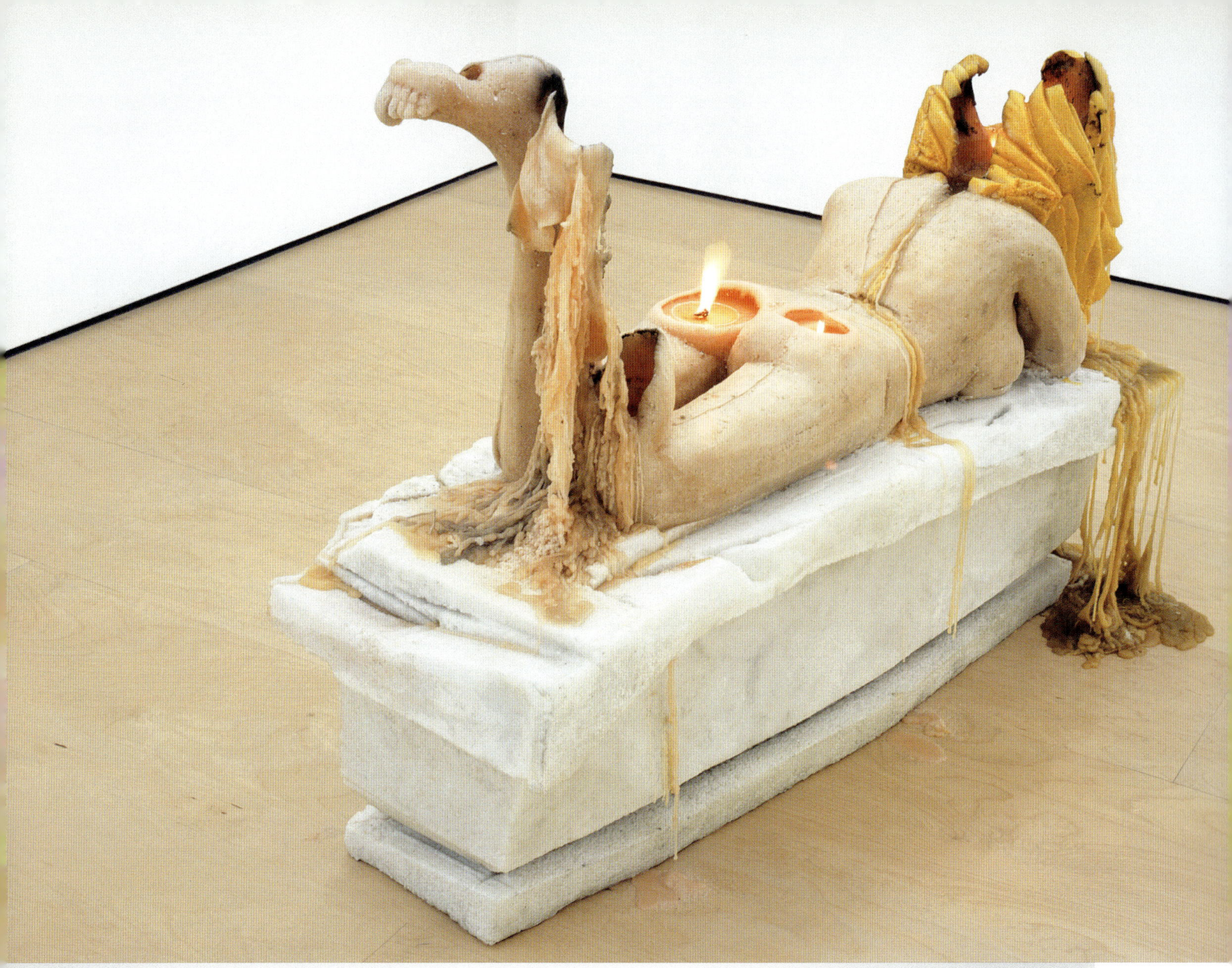

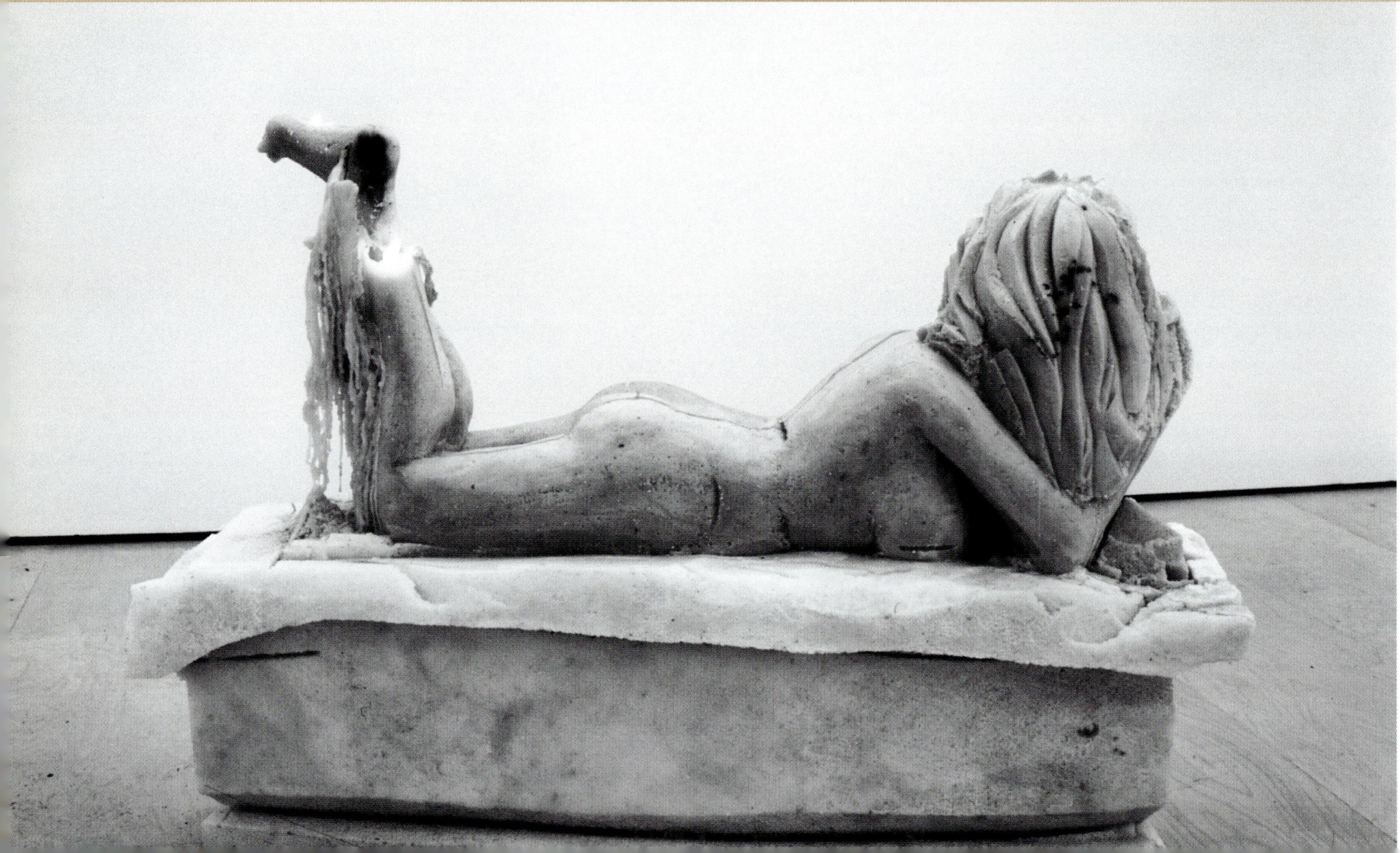

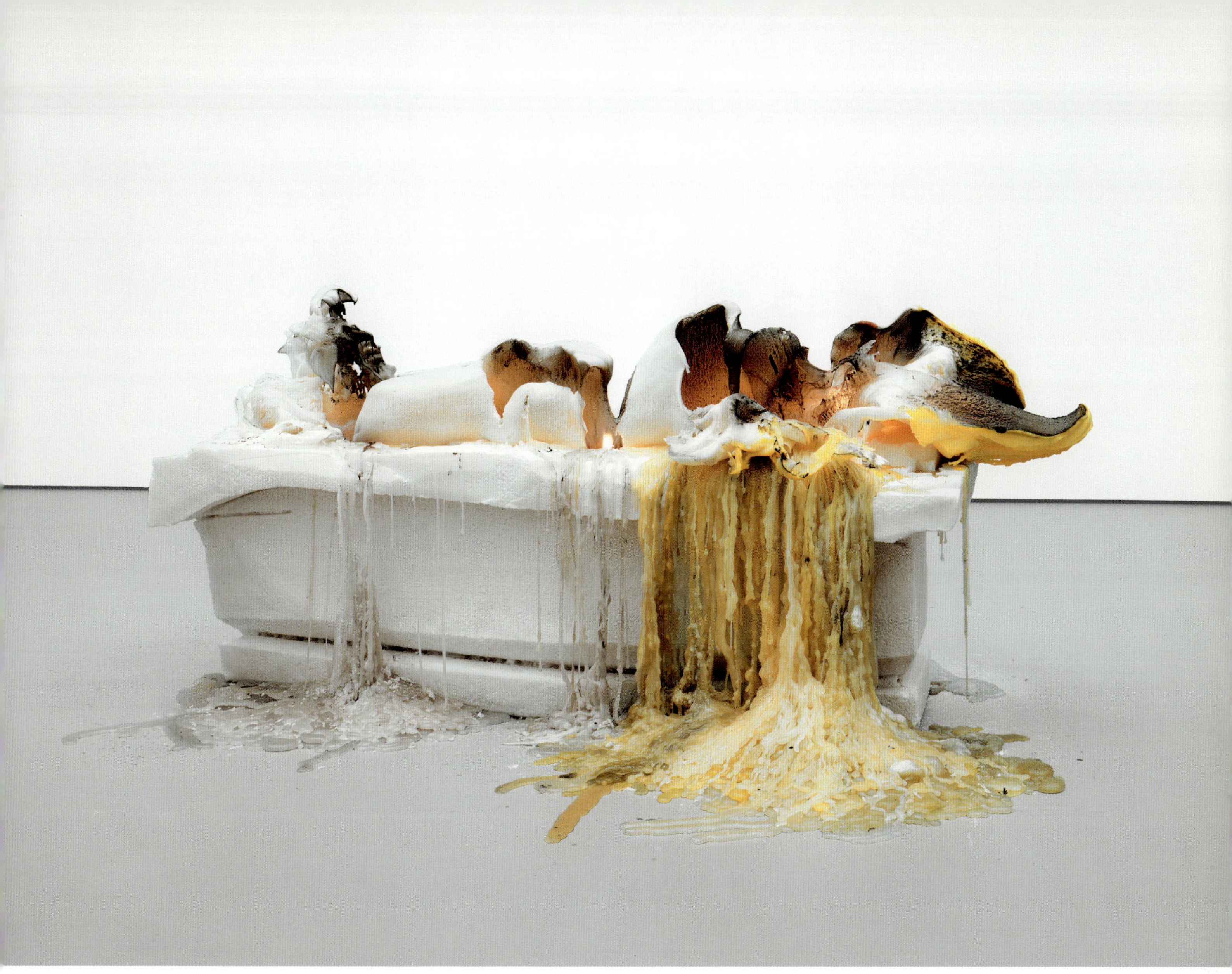

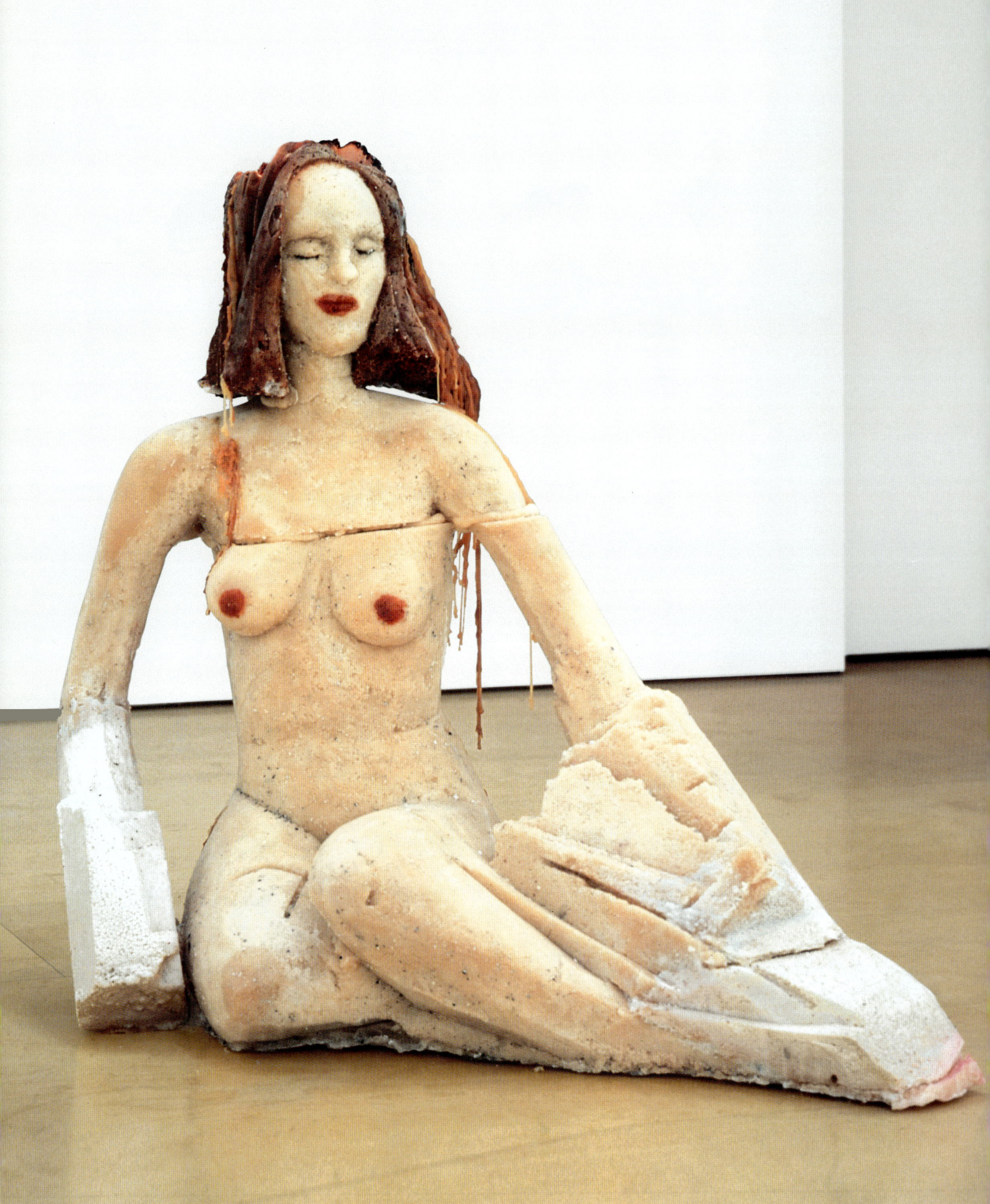

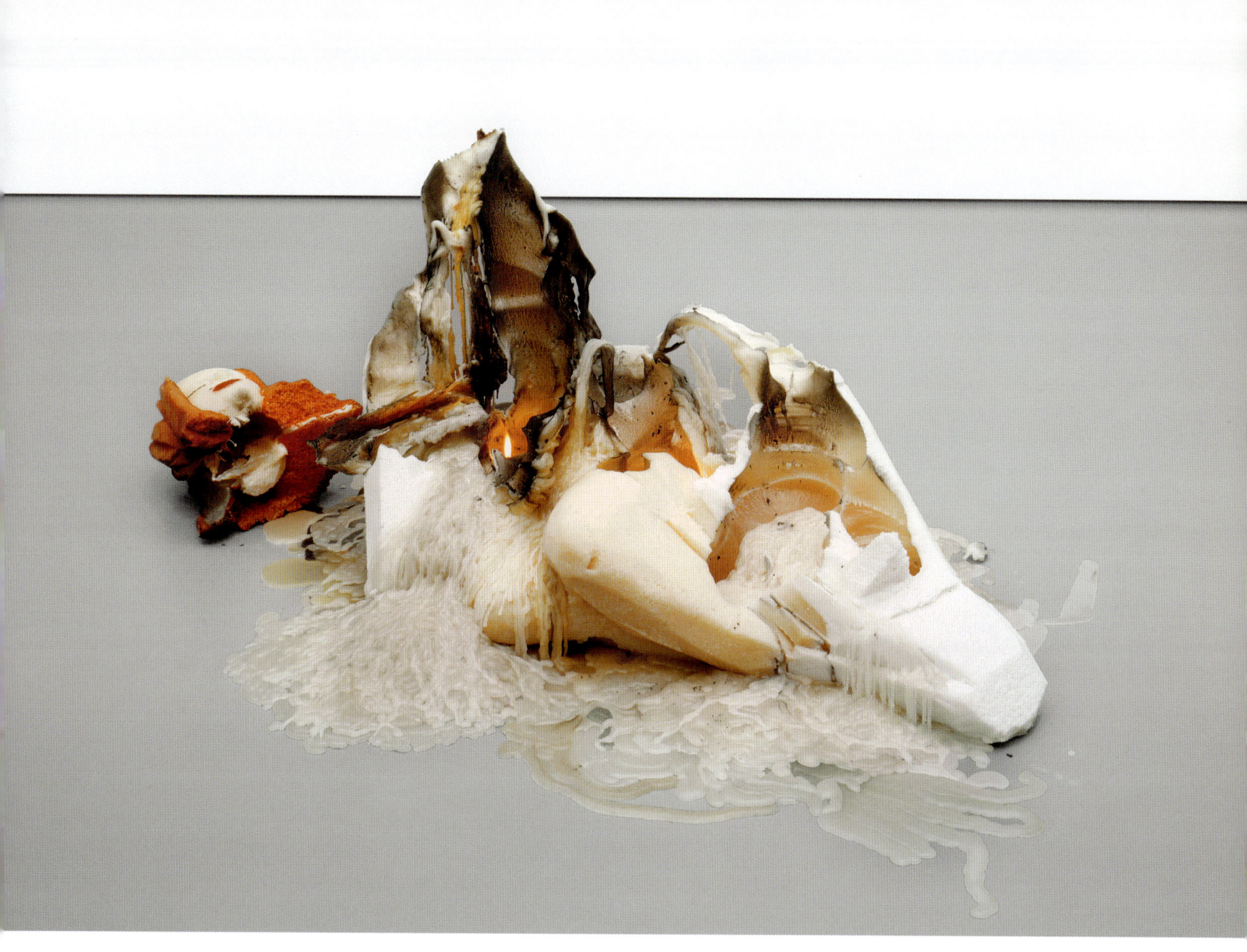

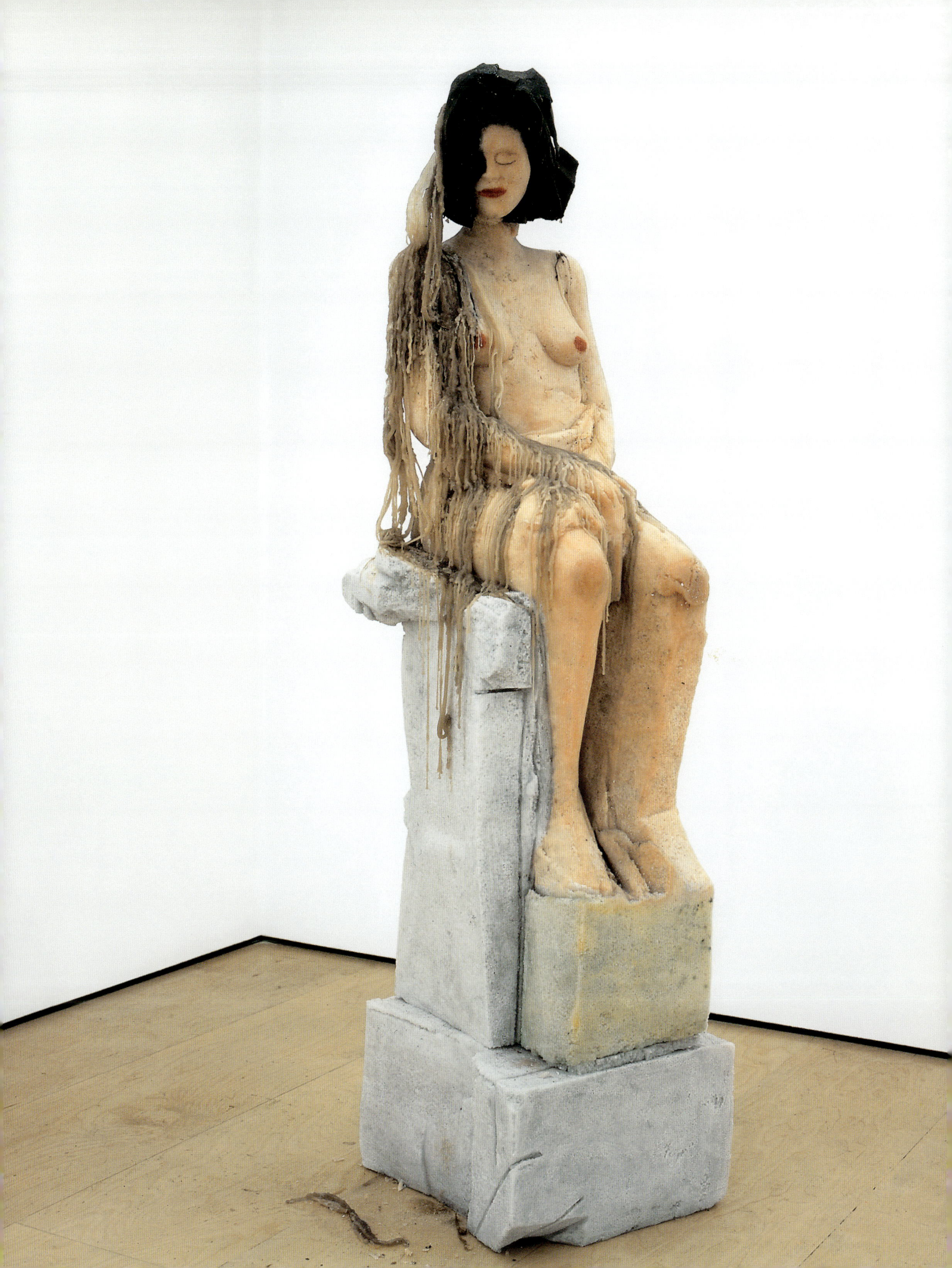

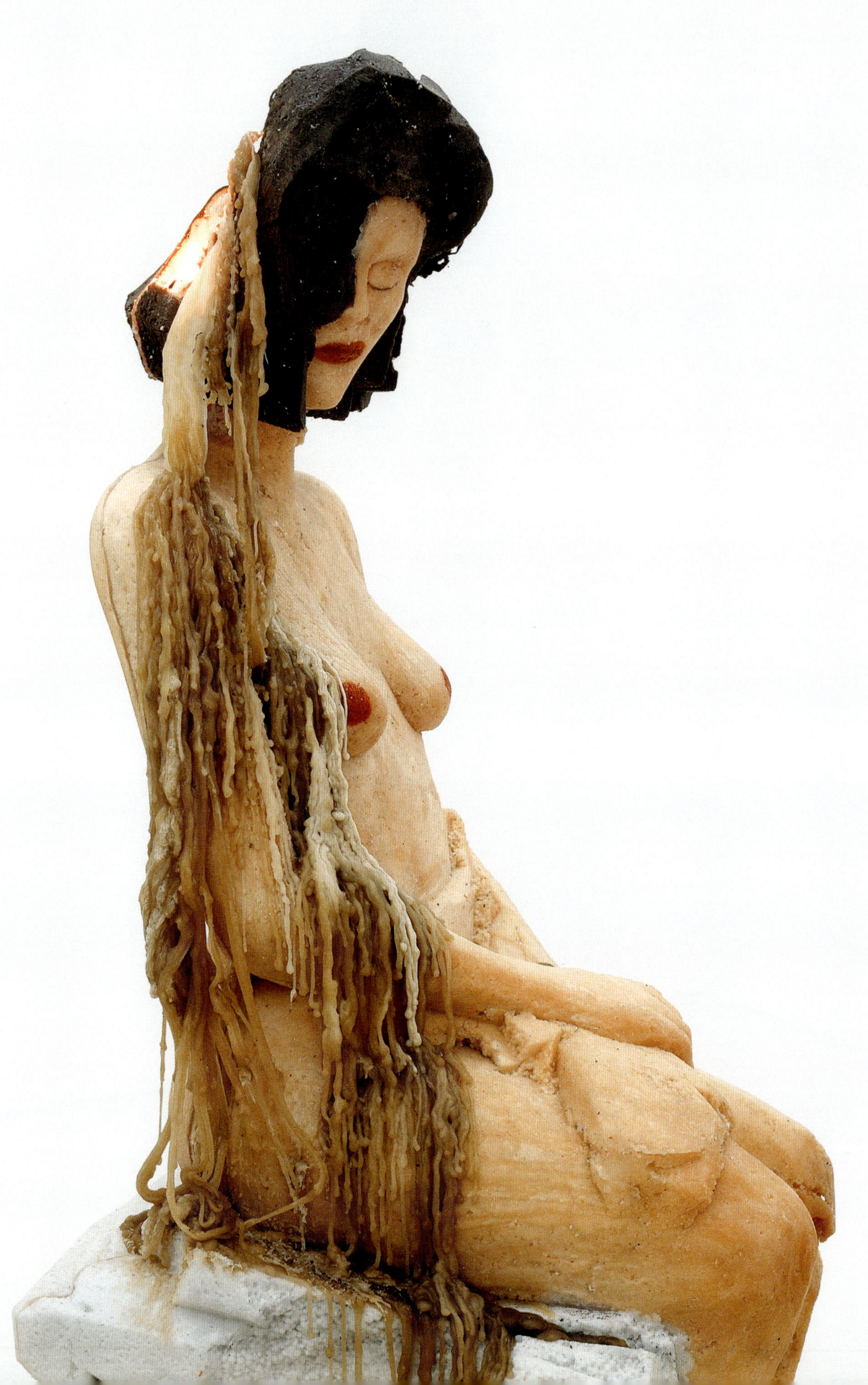

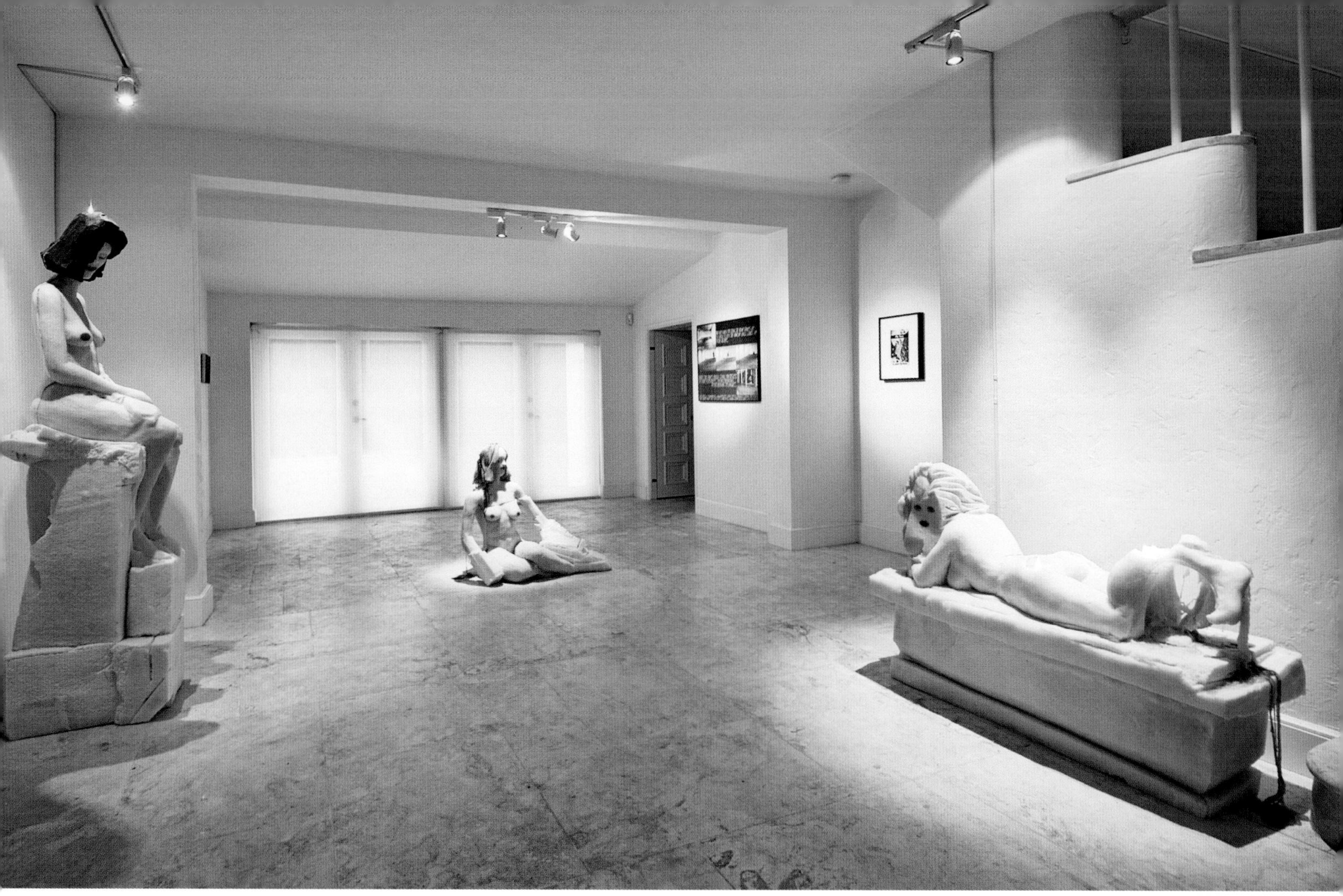

Installation view, "Home Alone," Sender Collection, Miami, 2011
What if the Phone Rings, 2003
On wall: Vito Acconci, *Seedbed*, 1972; Barbara Kruger, *Untitled (My face is your fortune)*, 1982

Untitled (Standing), 2010
Paraffin wax mixture, pigment, steel, wicks
77 x 31 x 52 inches (195.6 x 78.7 x 132.1 cm)
Installation view, "Oscar the Grouch," The Brant Foundation Art Study Center,
Greenwich, Connecticut, 2010–2011
On wall: *Abstract Slavery*, 2008

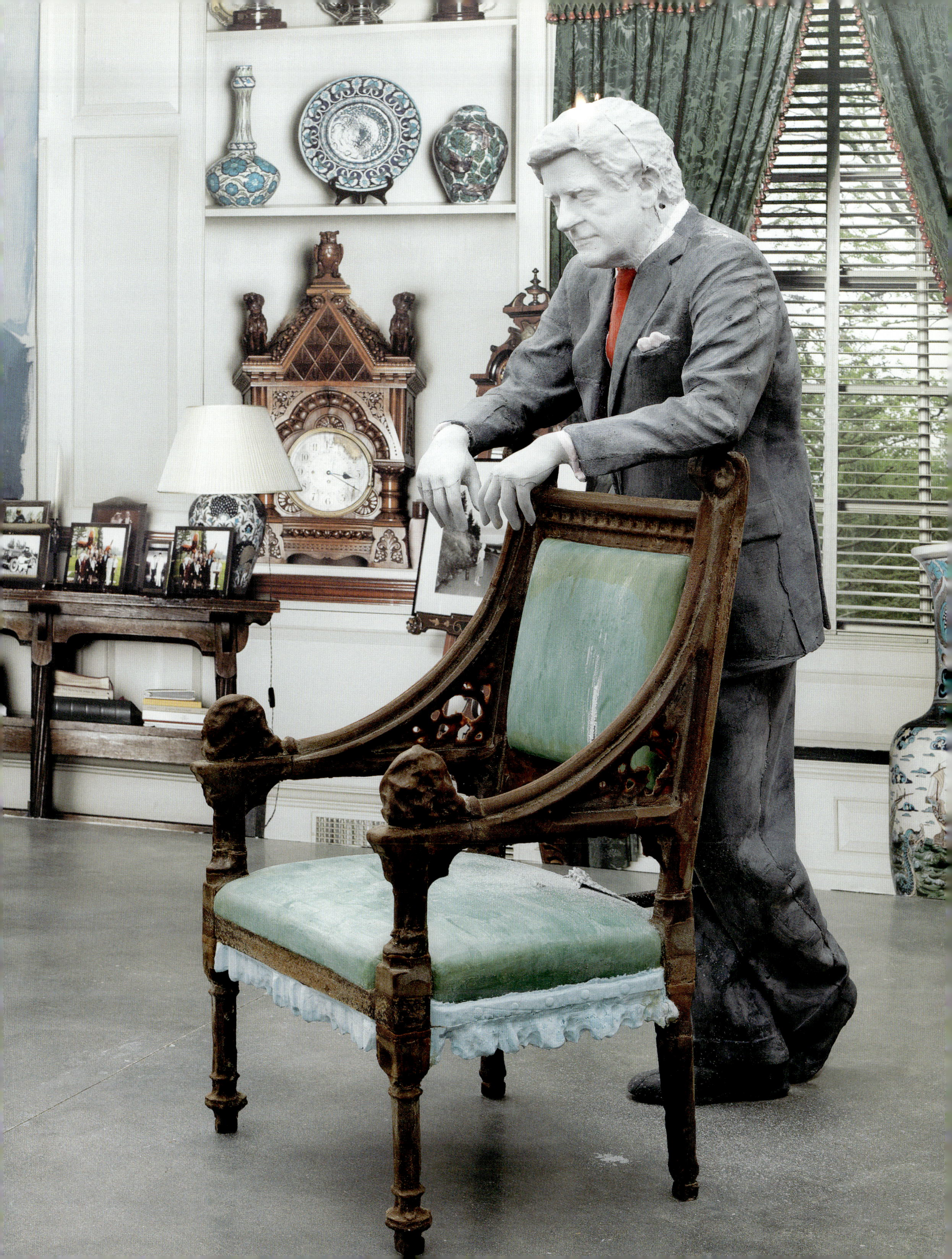

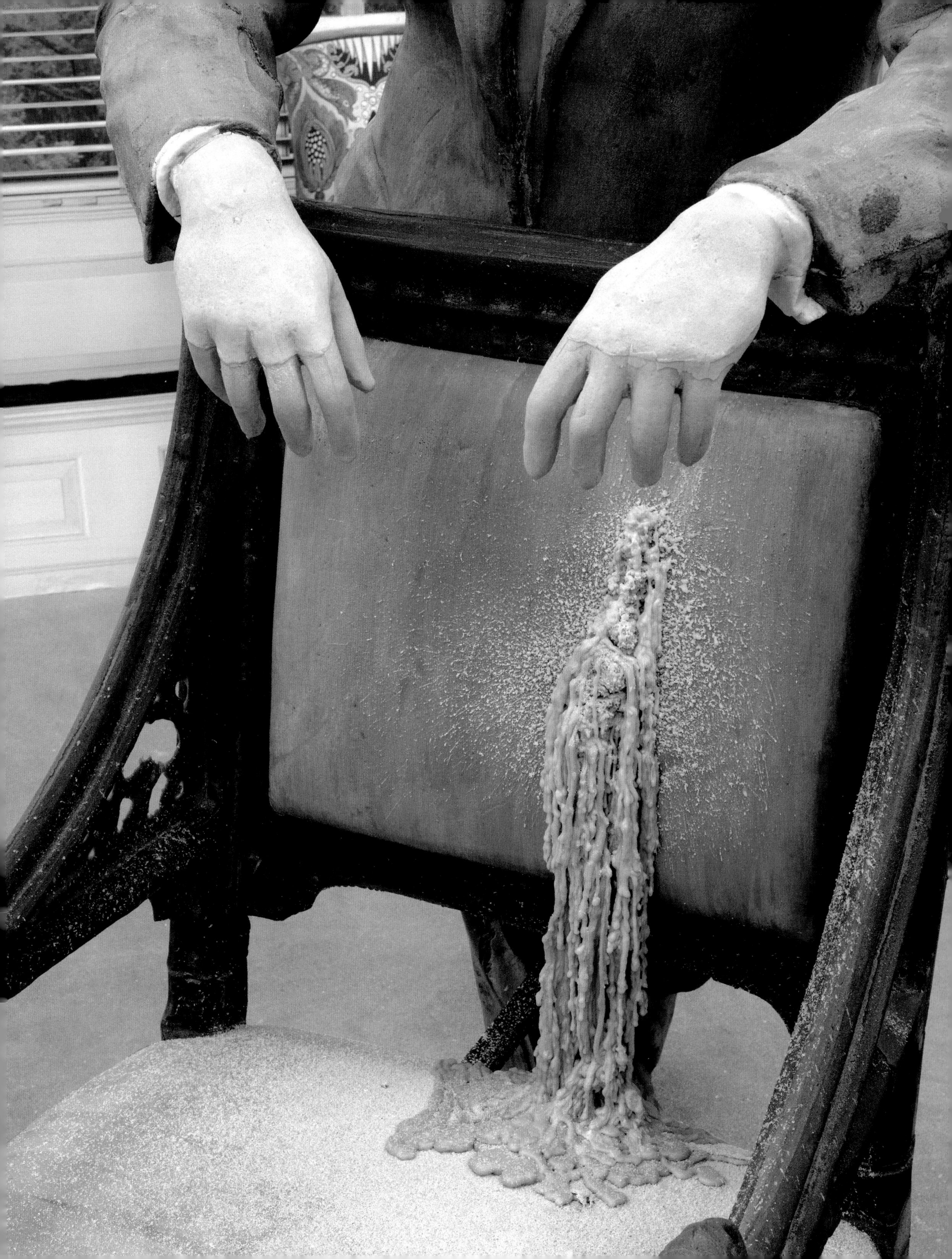

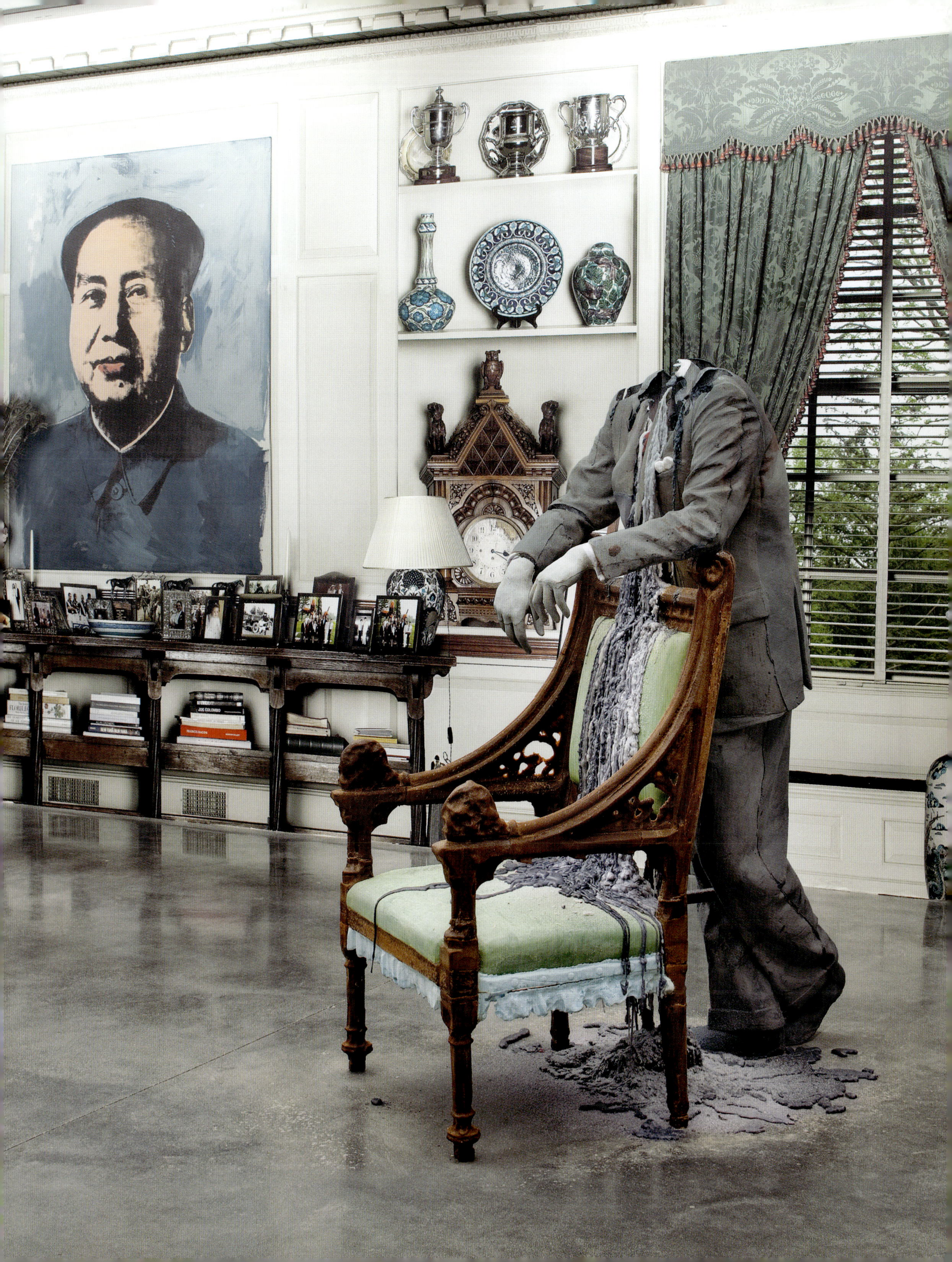
JOE COLOMBO
FRANCIS BACON

Untitled (Seated), 2010
Paraffin wax mixture, pigment, steel, wicks
55 x 27 x 45 inches (139.7 x 68.6 x 114.3 cm)
Installation view, "Oscar the Grouch," The Brant Foundation Art Study Center,
Greenwich, Connecticut, 2010–2011
On wall: *Abstract Slavery*, 2008

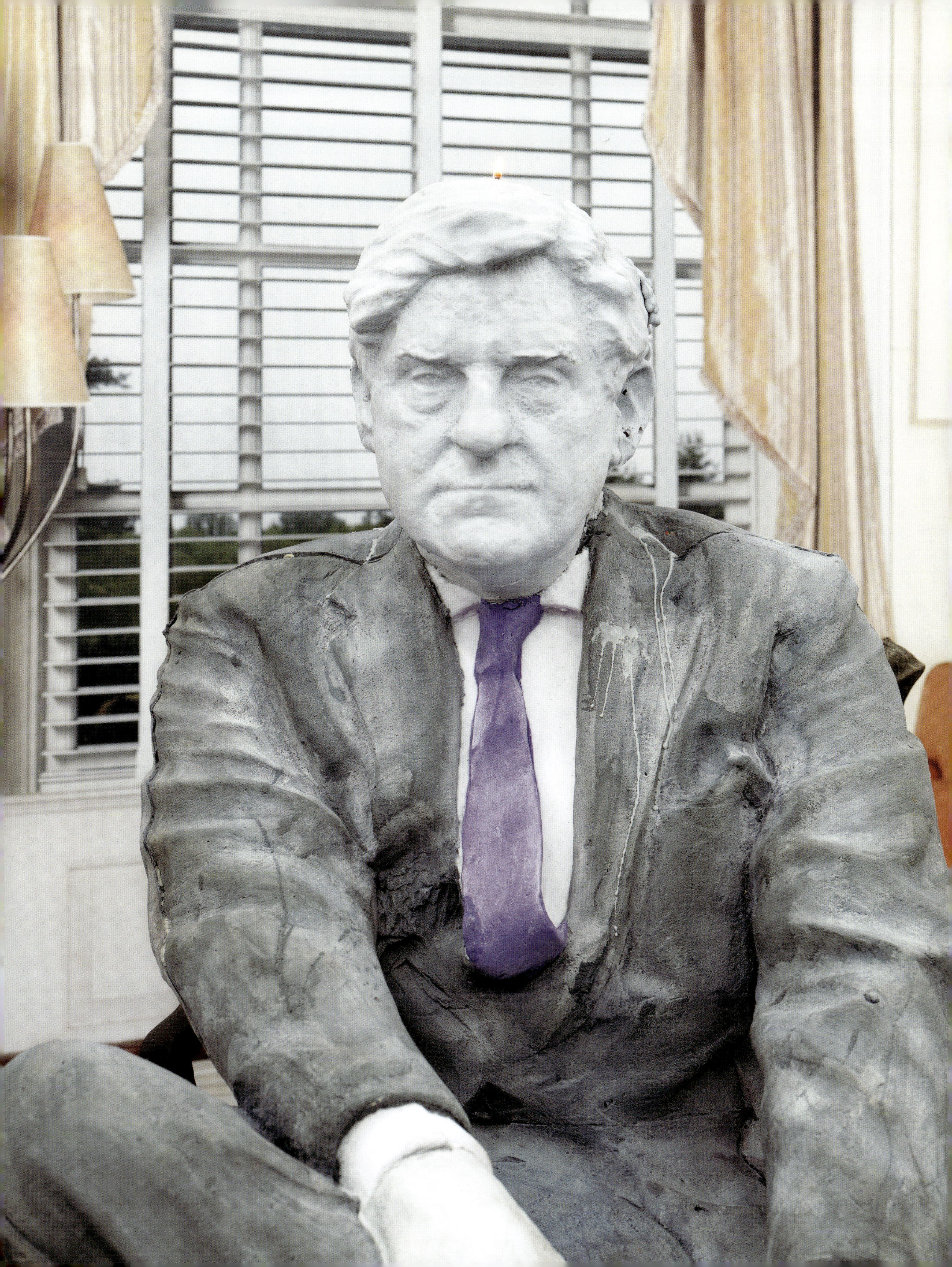

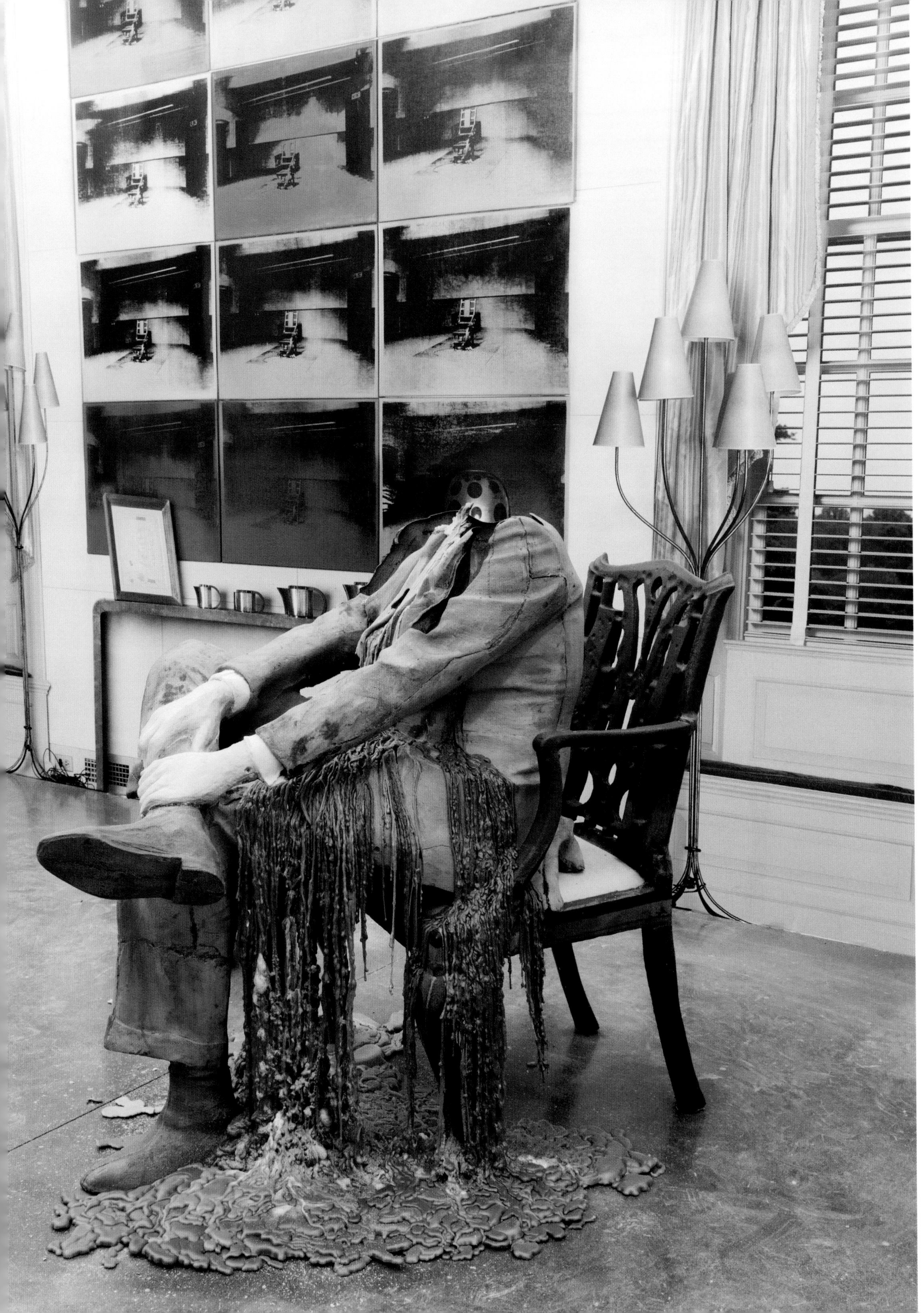

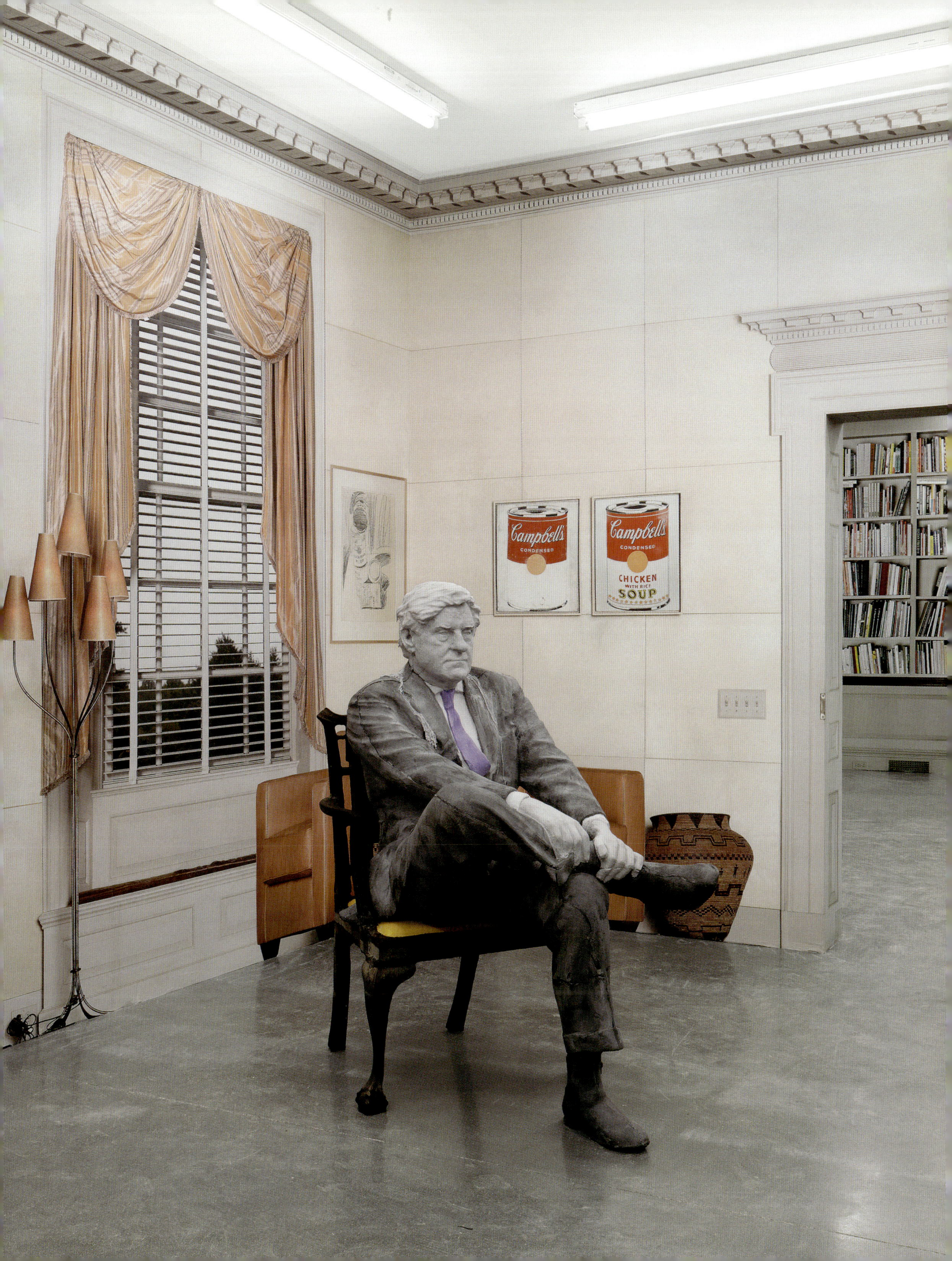
Campbell's
CONDENSED
Campbell's
CONDENSED
CHICKEN
SOUP

Untitled, 2011

Wax, pigments, wicks, steel

Giambologna sculpture: 57 ⅞ x 57 ⅞ x 248 ⅛ inches (147 x 147 x 630 cm)

Rudi portrait: 19 ¼ x 27 ⅛ x 77 ½ inches (49 x 69 x 197 cm)

Office chair: 30 ¾ x 28 ⅜ x 45 ⅝ inches (78 x 72 x 116 cm)

Installation dimensions variable

Installation view, "ILLUMInazioni / ILLUMInations," Venice Biennale, 2011

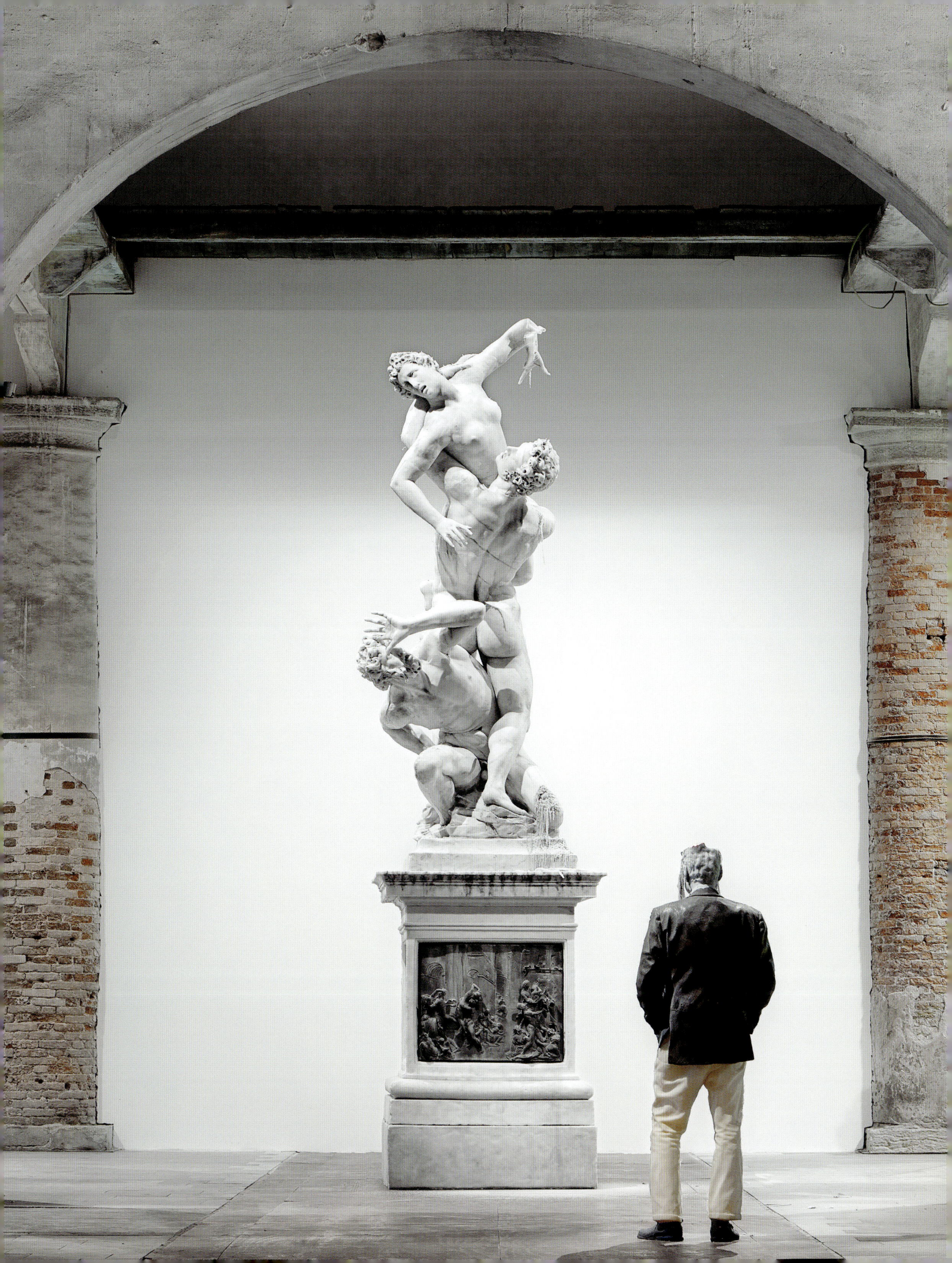

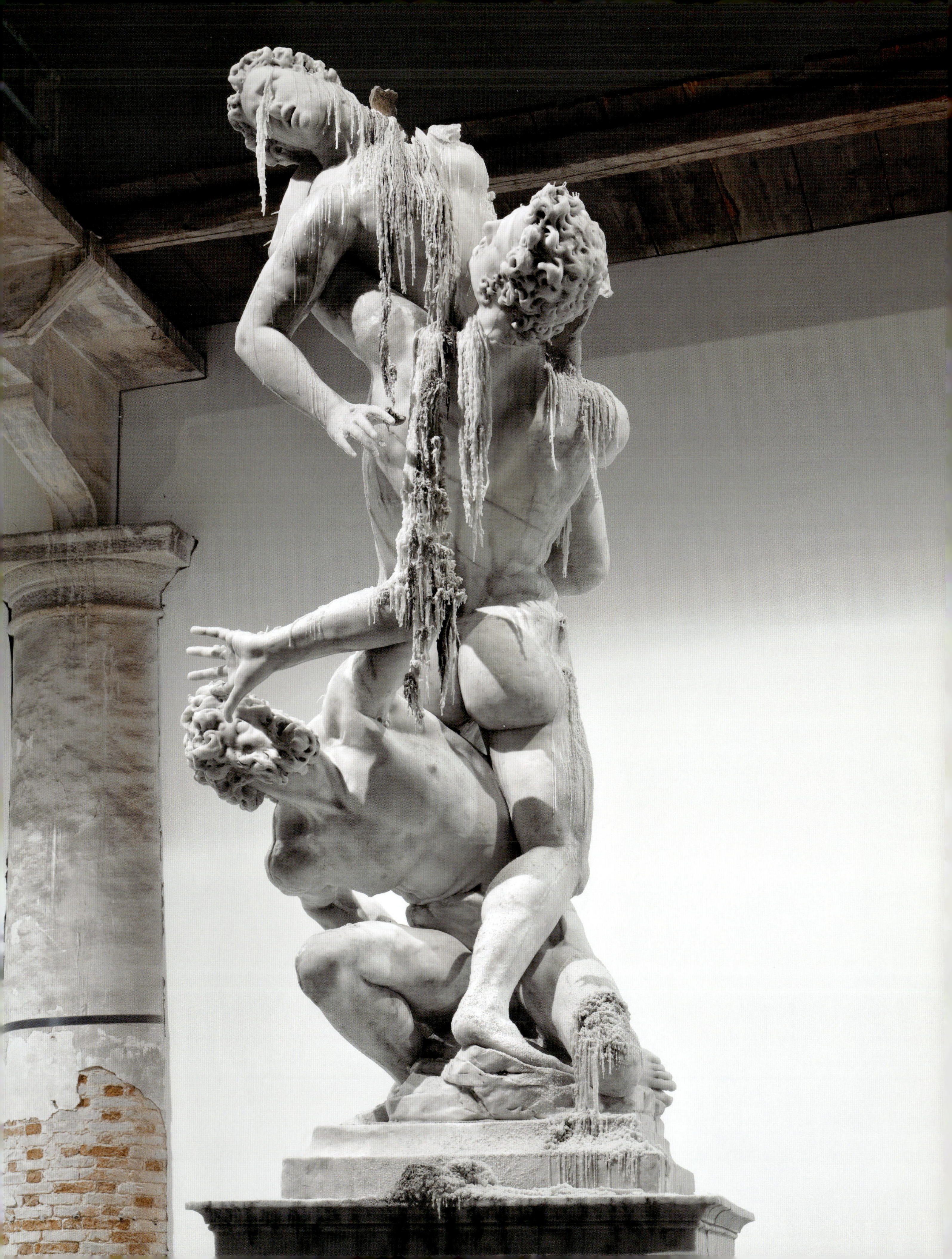

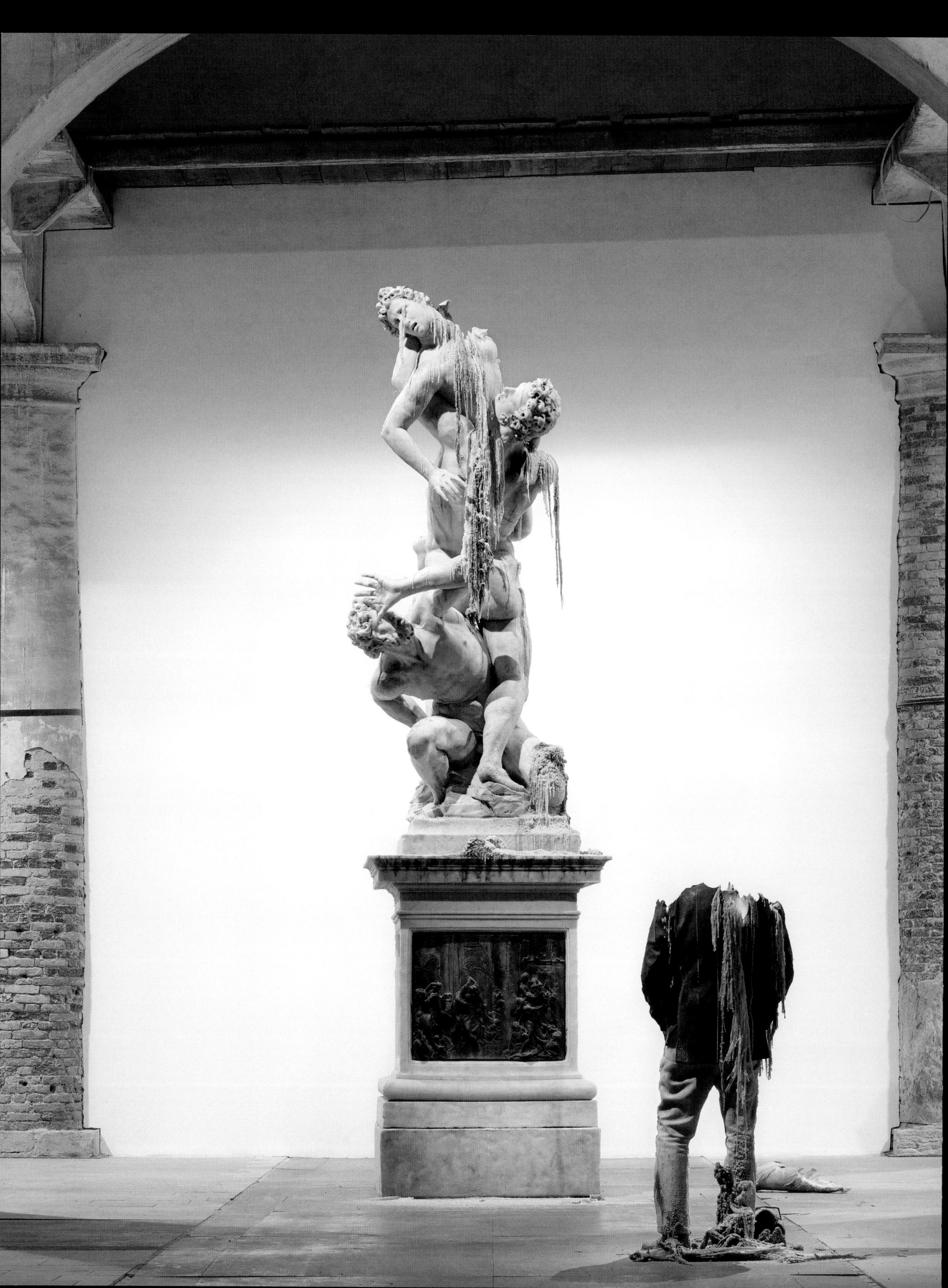

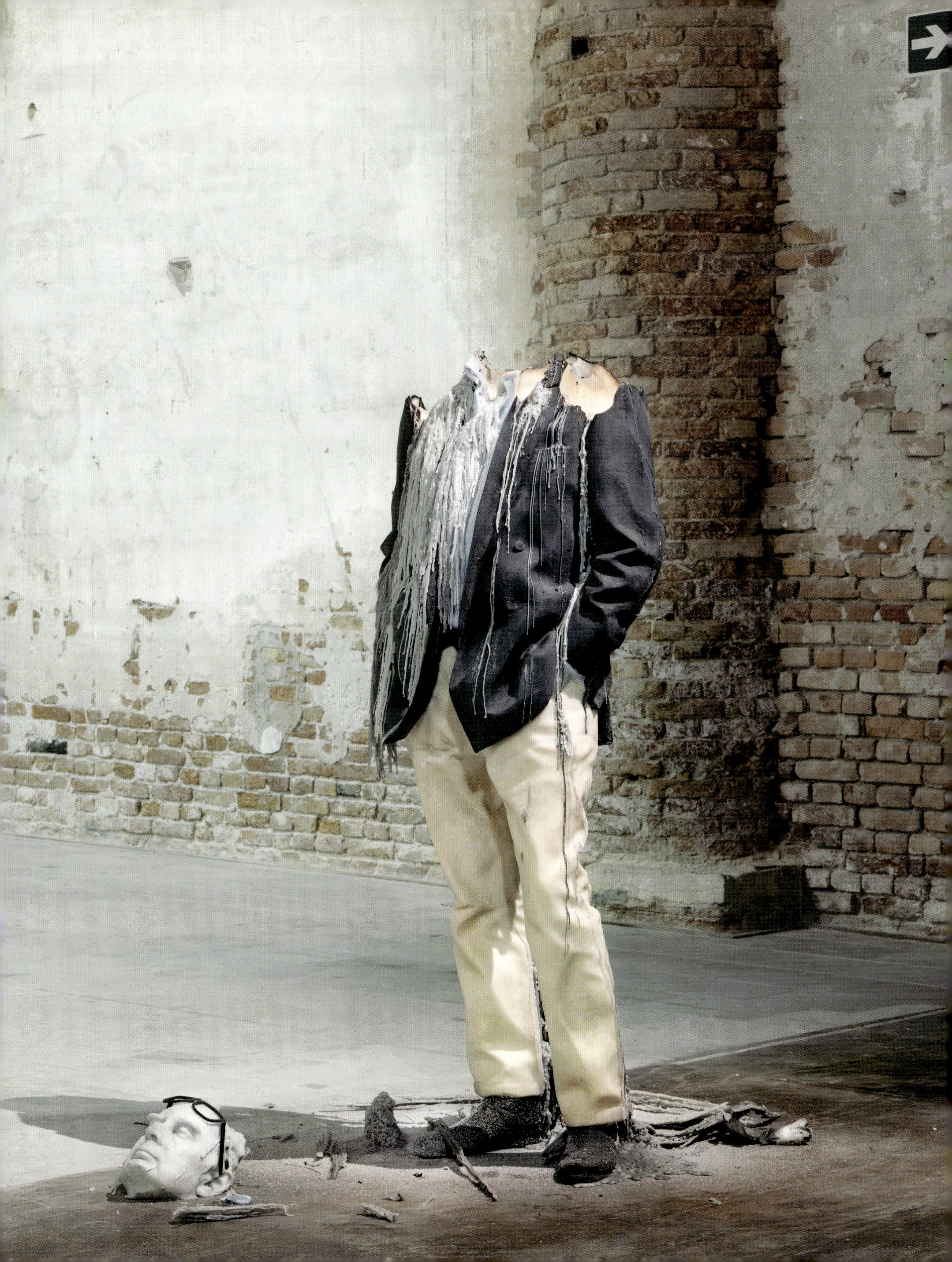

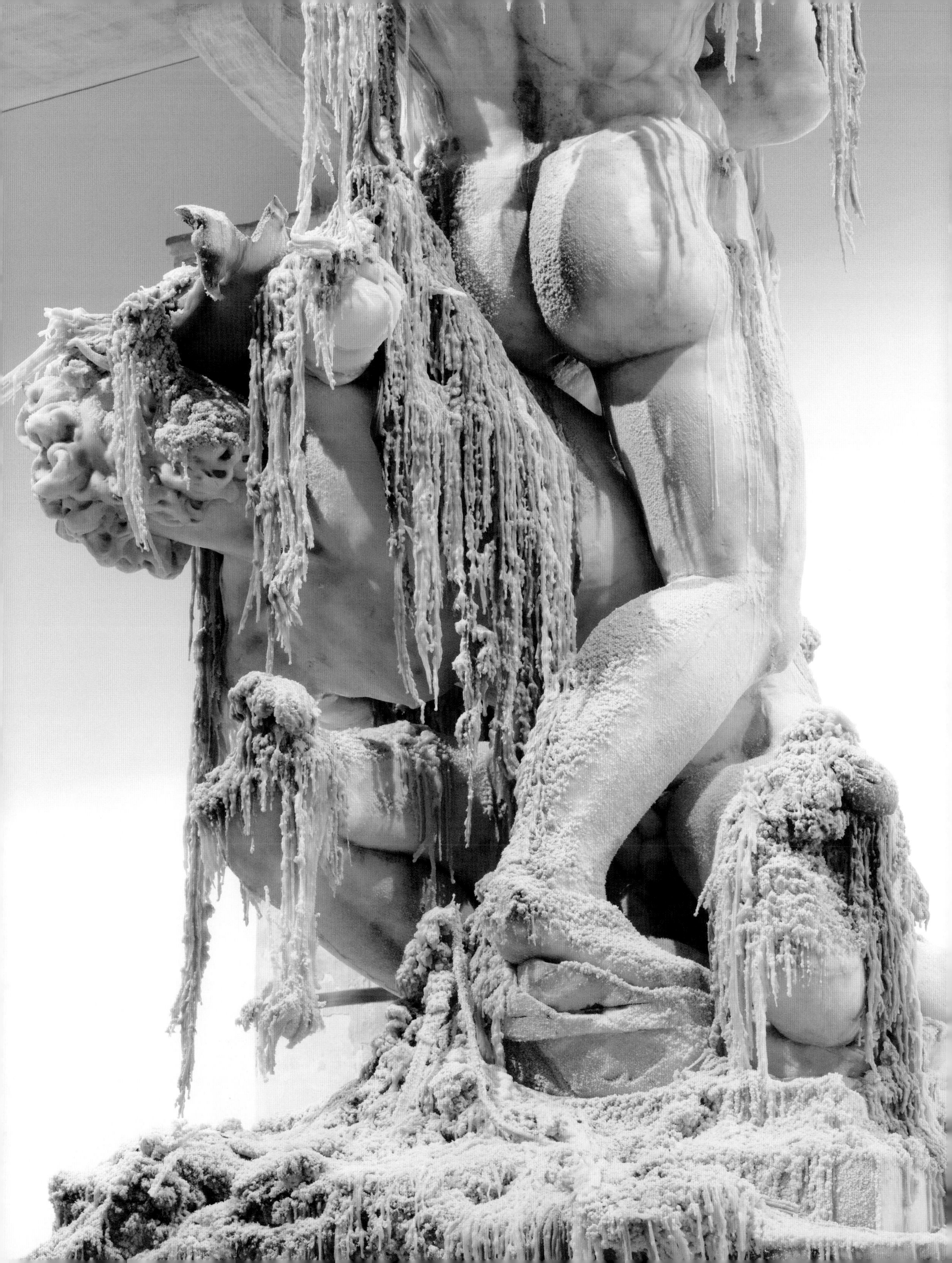

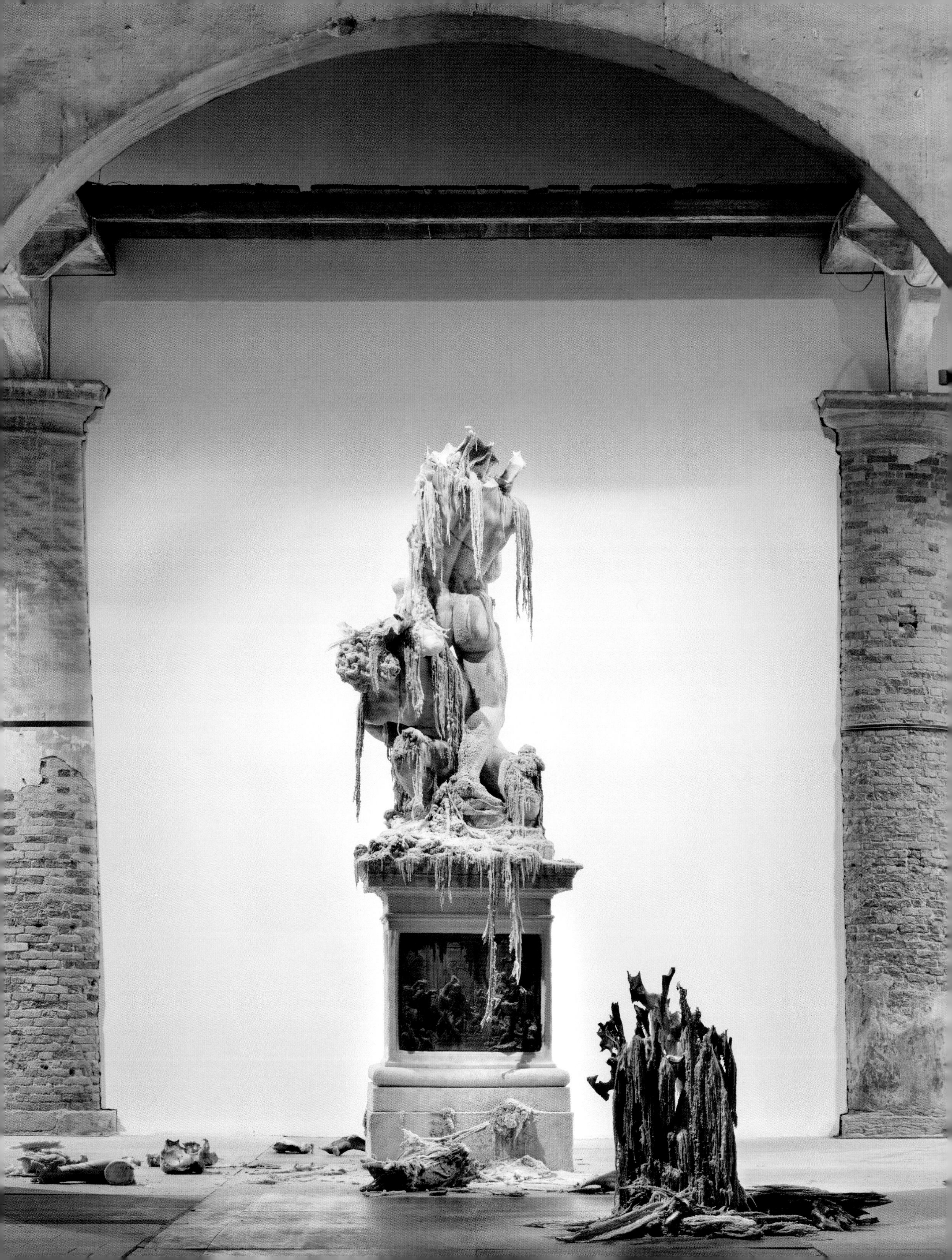

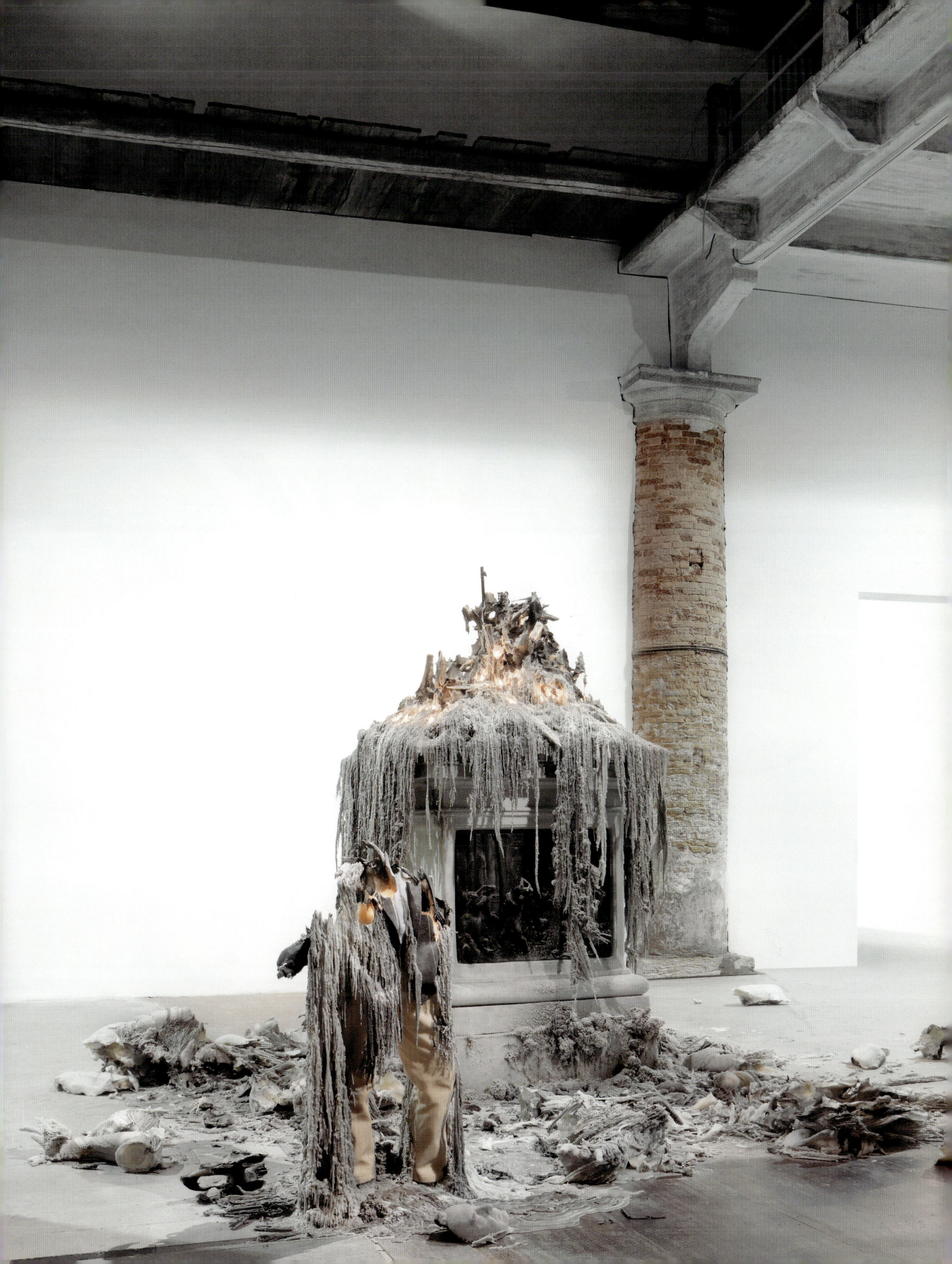

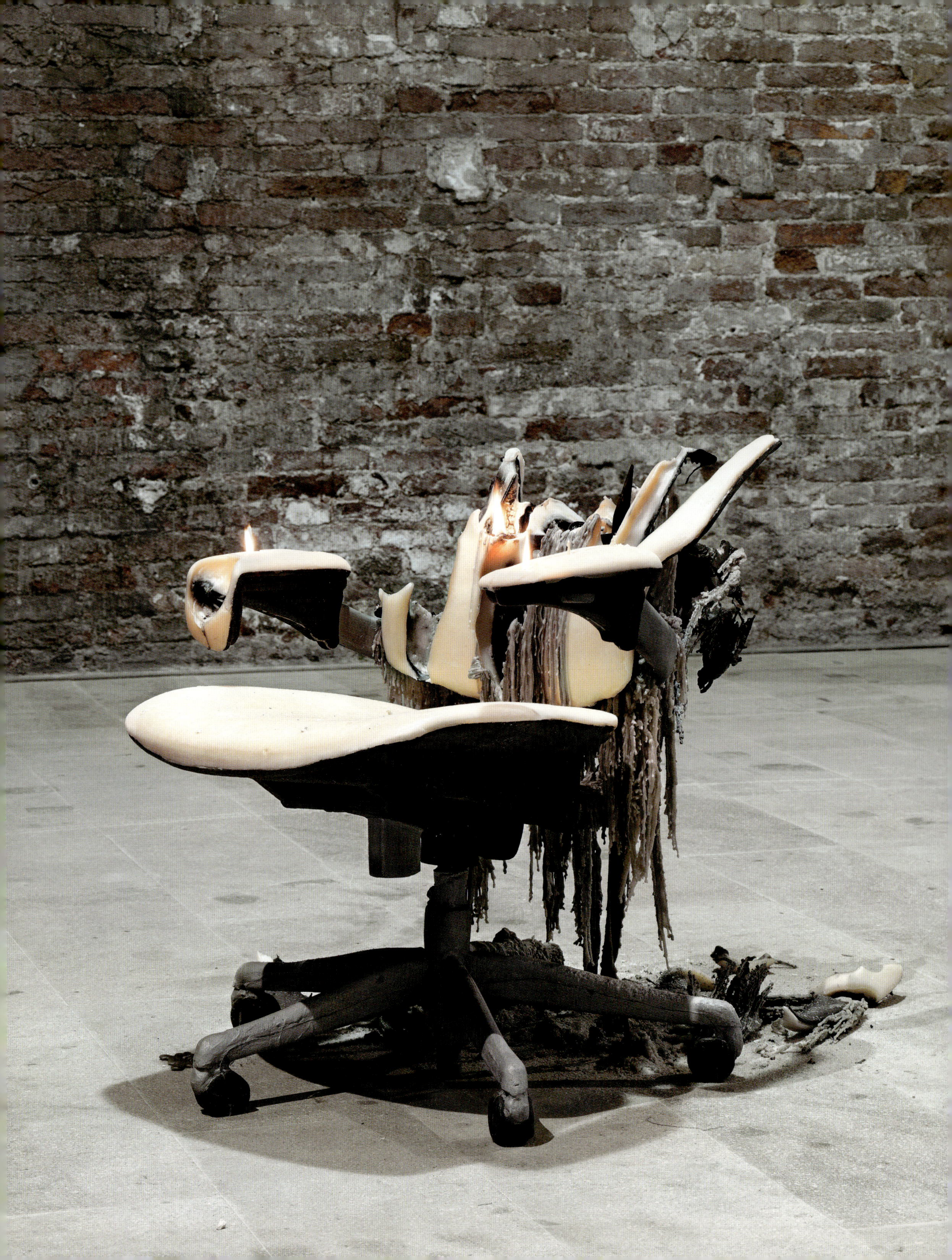

Untitled, 2011

Paraffin wax mixture, pigment, steel, lead weights, wicks
Rudi and chair: 52 x 32 ⅛ x 52 ⅜ inches (132.1 x 81.6 x 133 cm)
Bottles: Dimensions variable, 10 ⅝–14 ⅛ inches (32–36 cm) high
Installation view, "Madame Fisscher," Palazzo Grassi, Venice, 2012

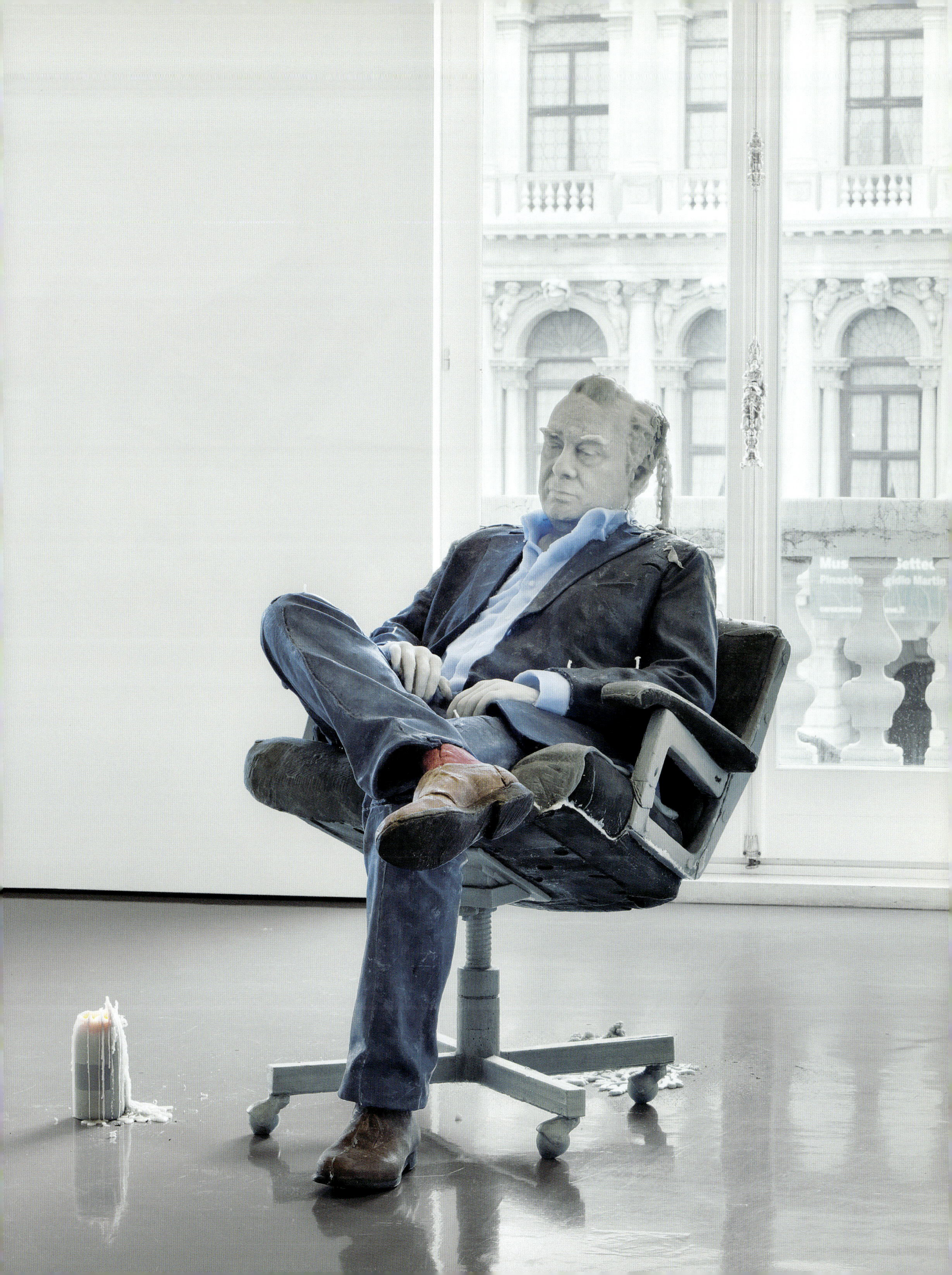

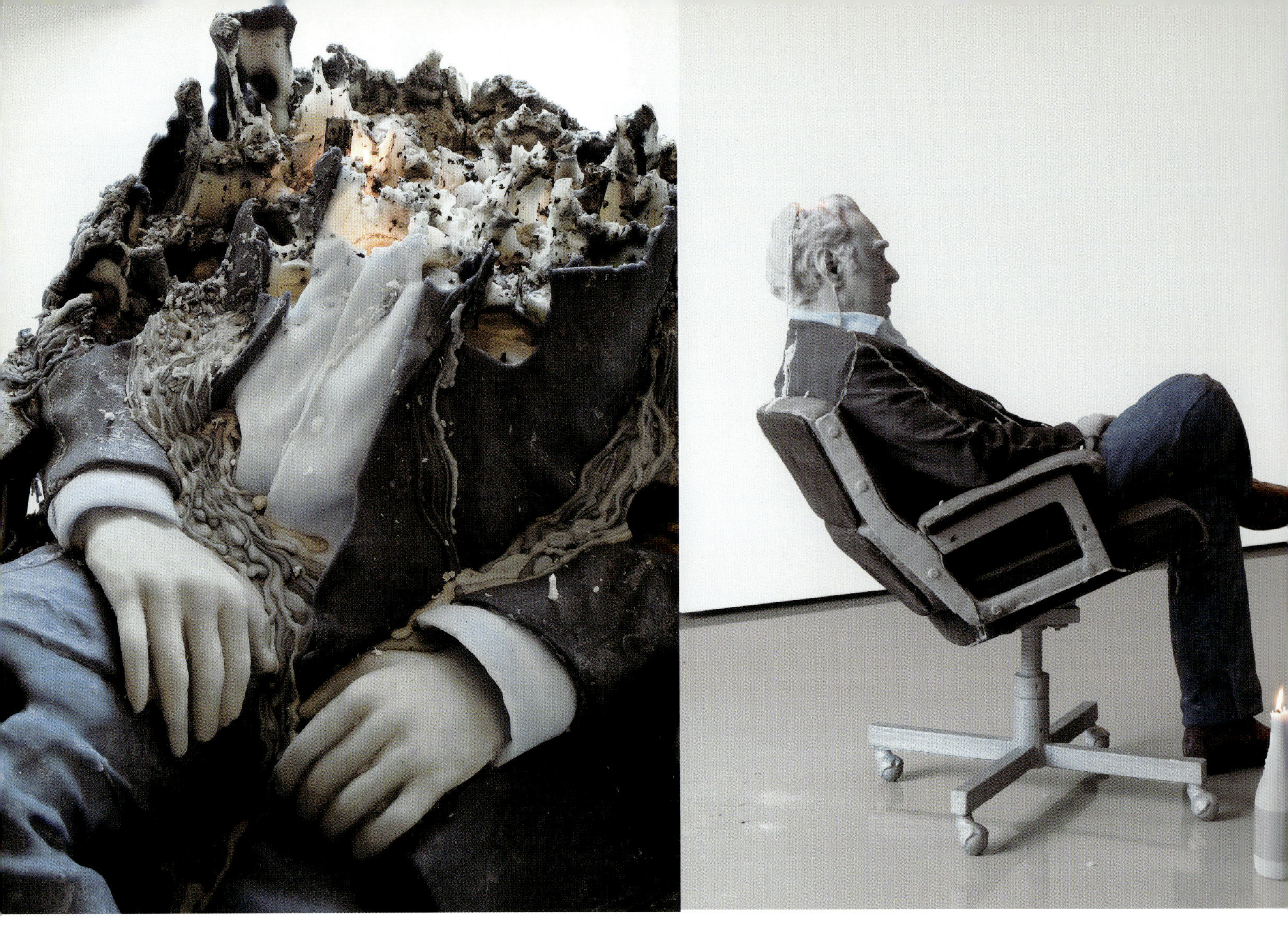

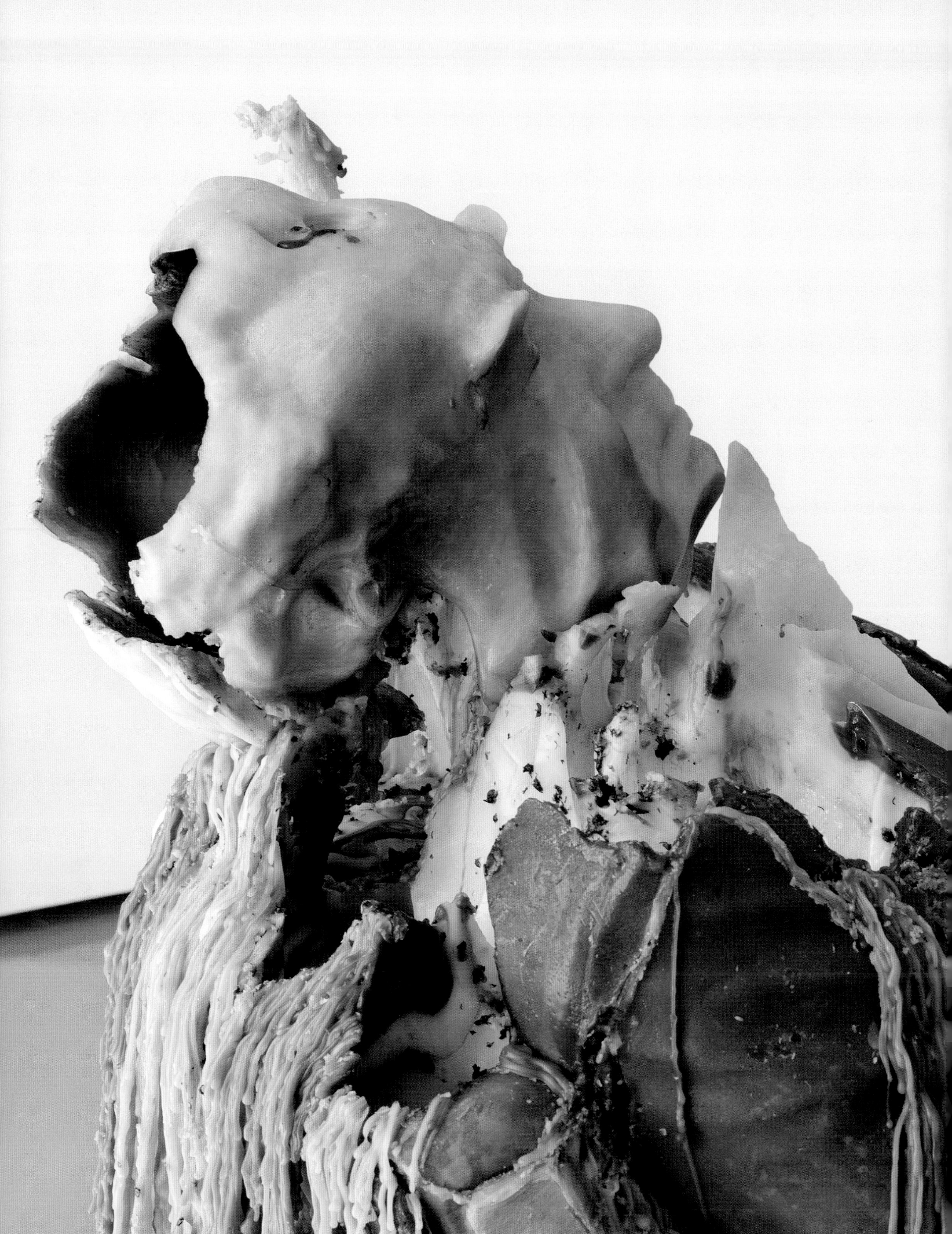

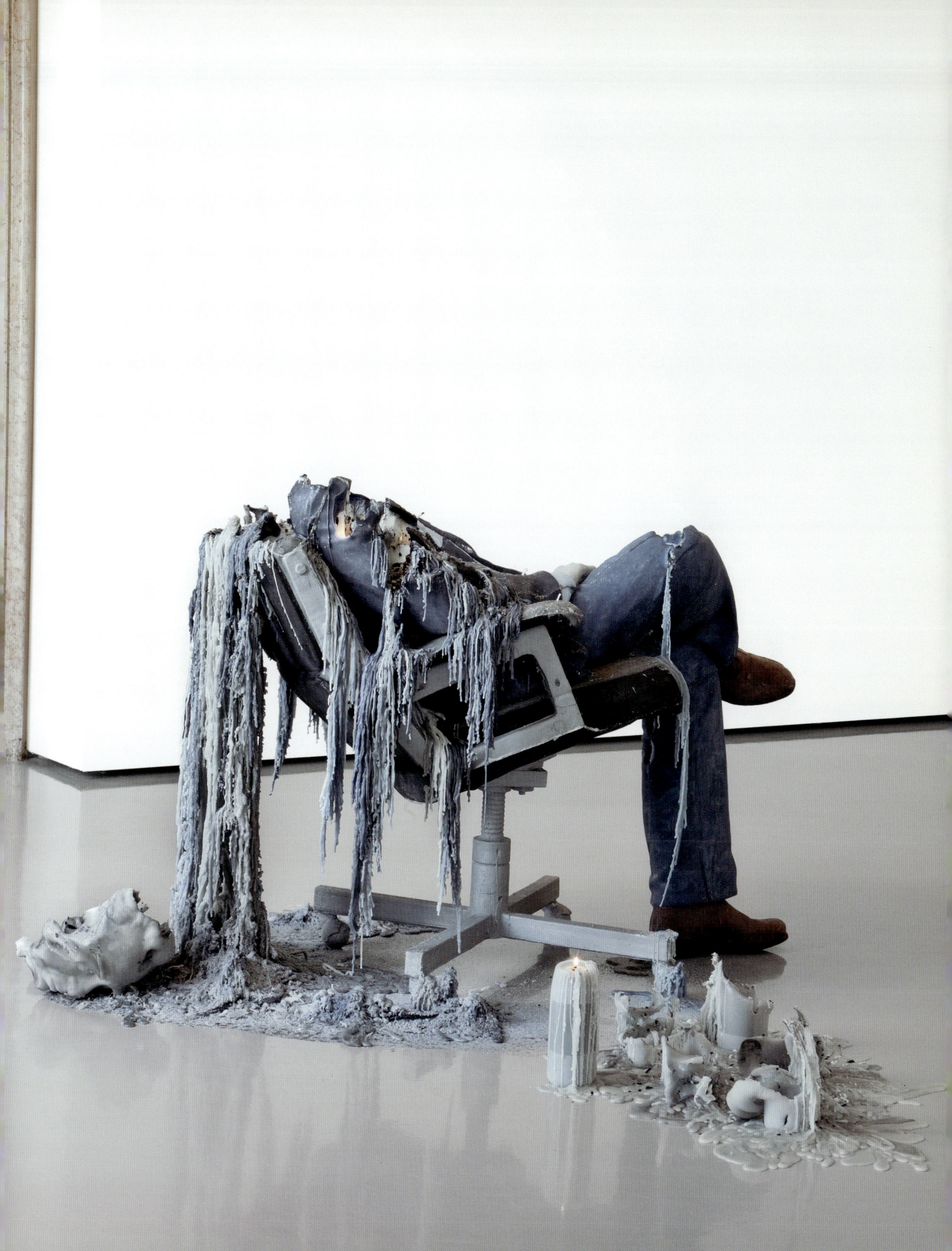

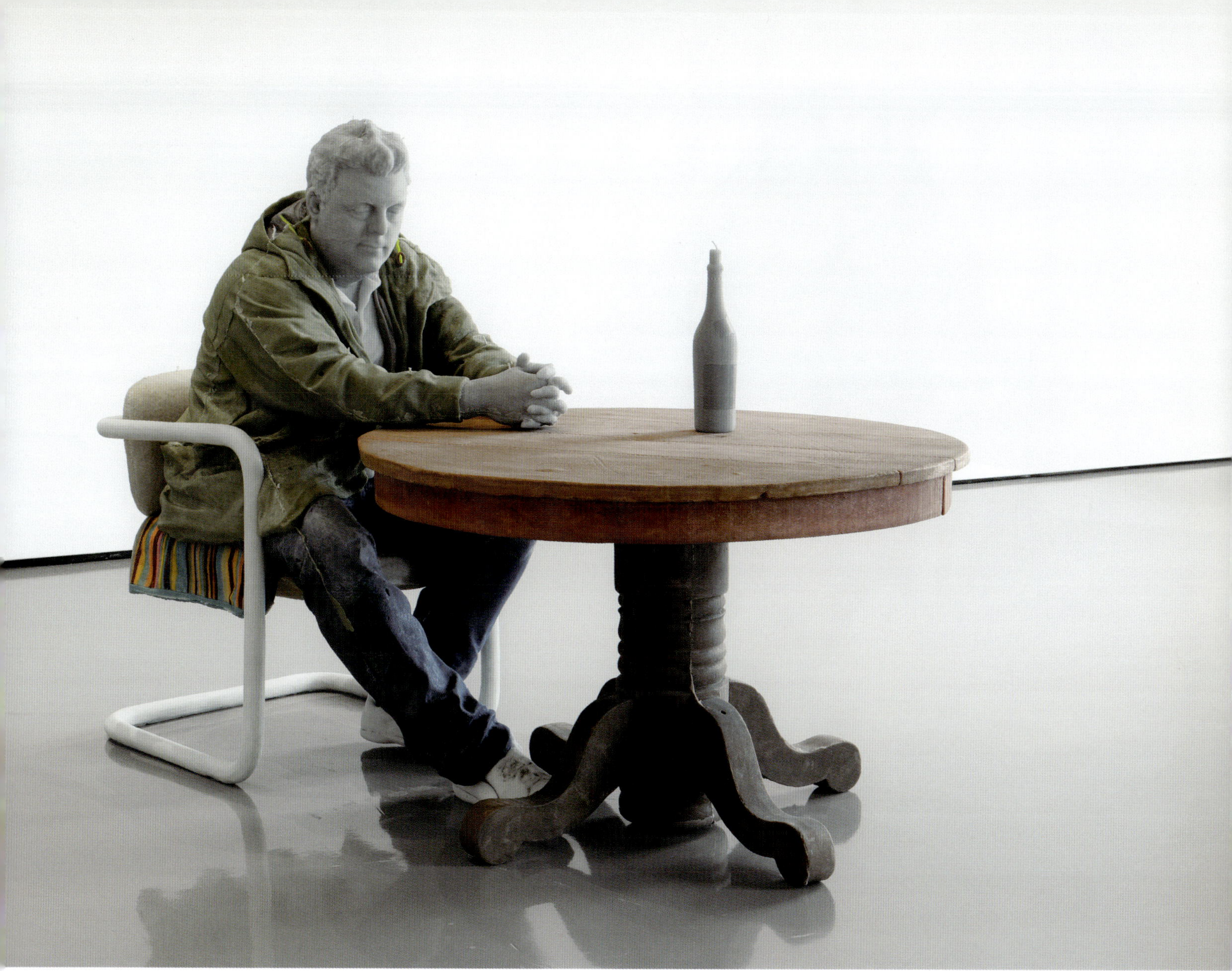

Untitled, 2011

Paraffin wax mixture, pigment, steel, wicks
Urs and chair: 53 ⅞ x 28 ½ x 49 ½ inches (136.8 x 72.4 x 125.8 cm)
Table: 30 ⅞ x 46 ⅜ x 45 ⅜ inches (78.5 x 117.7 x 115.1 cm)
Overall dimensions: 53 ⅞ x 46 ⅜ x 75 ¼ inches (136.8 x 117.7 x 191.3 cm)
Bottles: Dimensions variable, 10 ⅝–14 ⅛ inches (32–36 cm) high

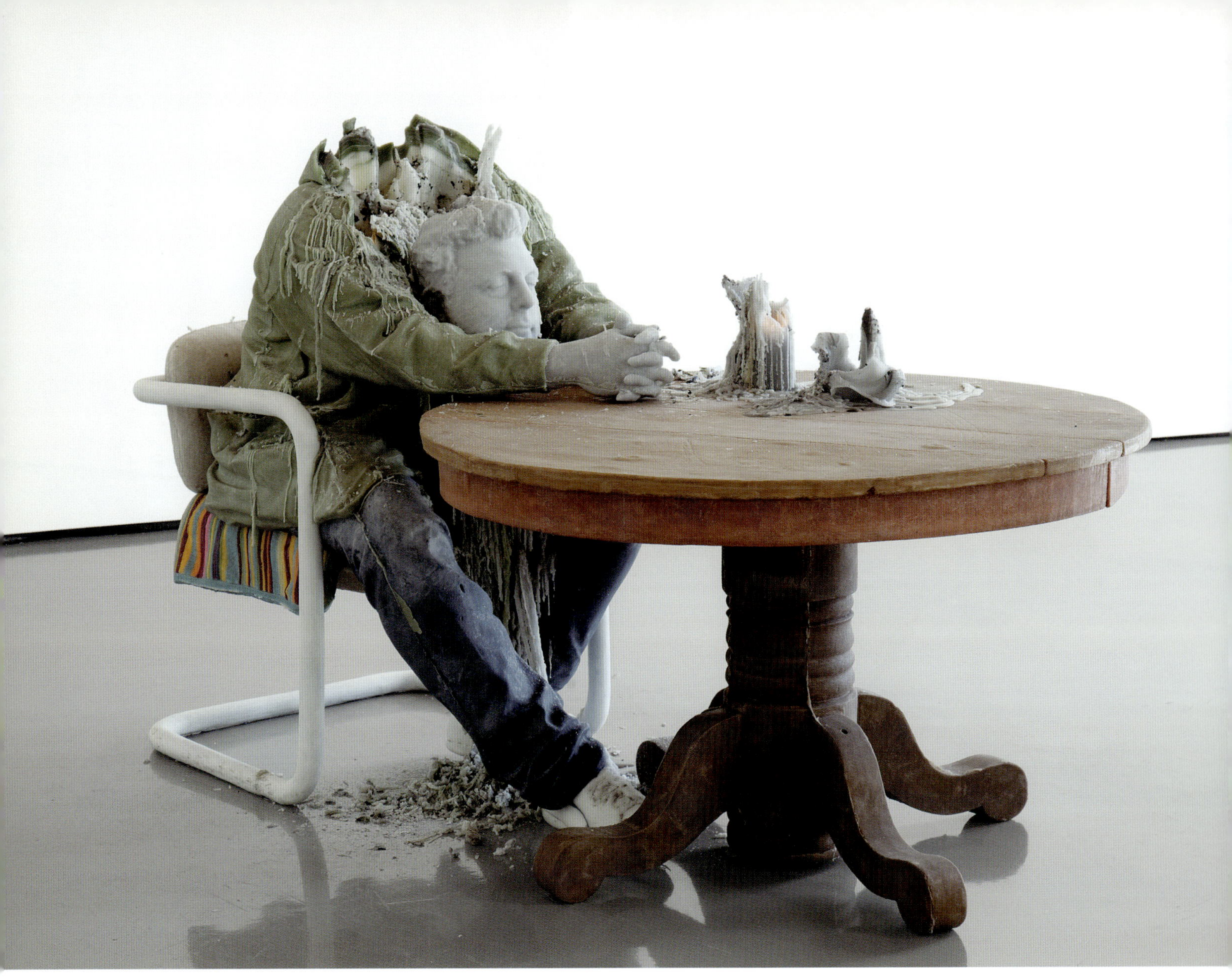

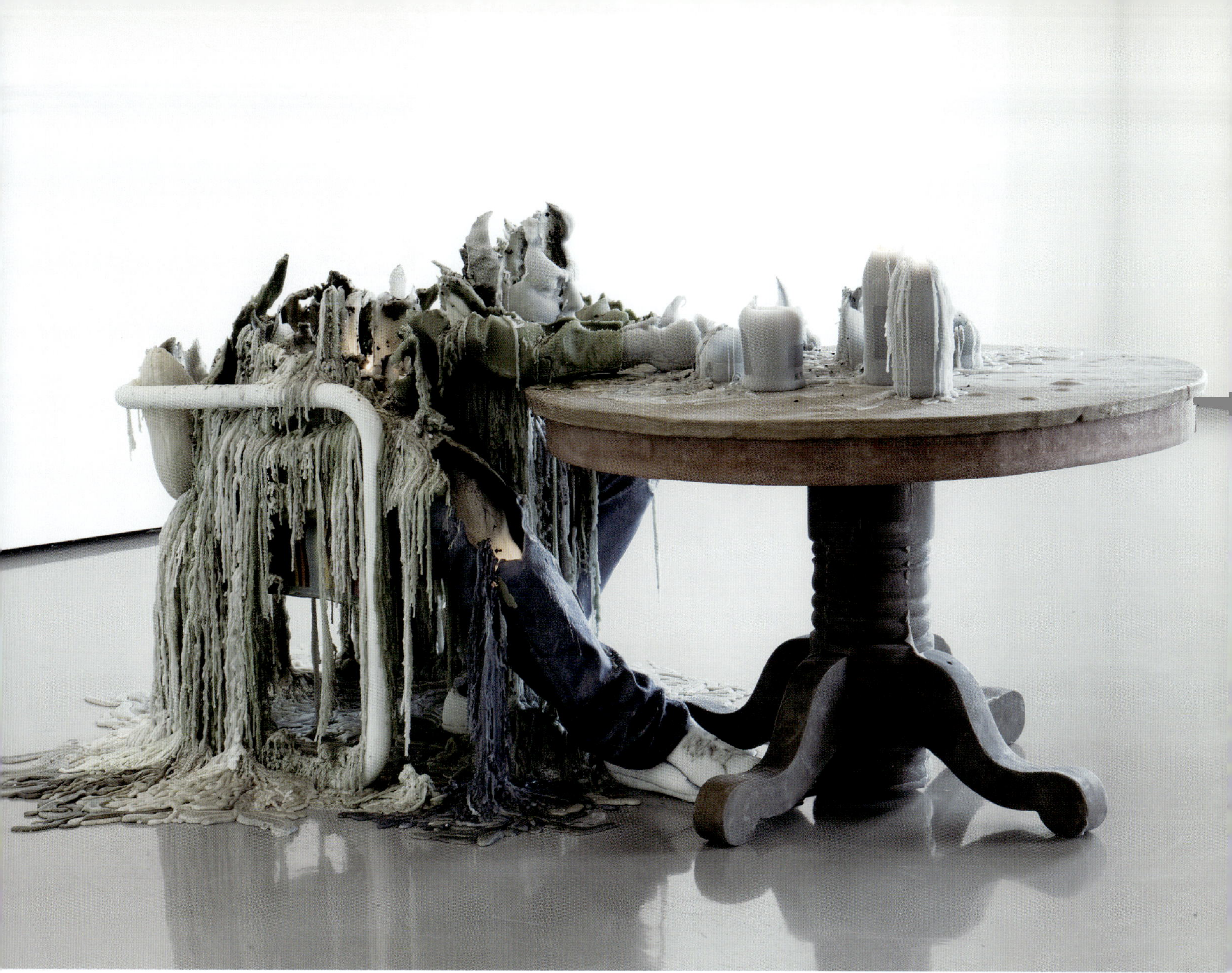

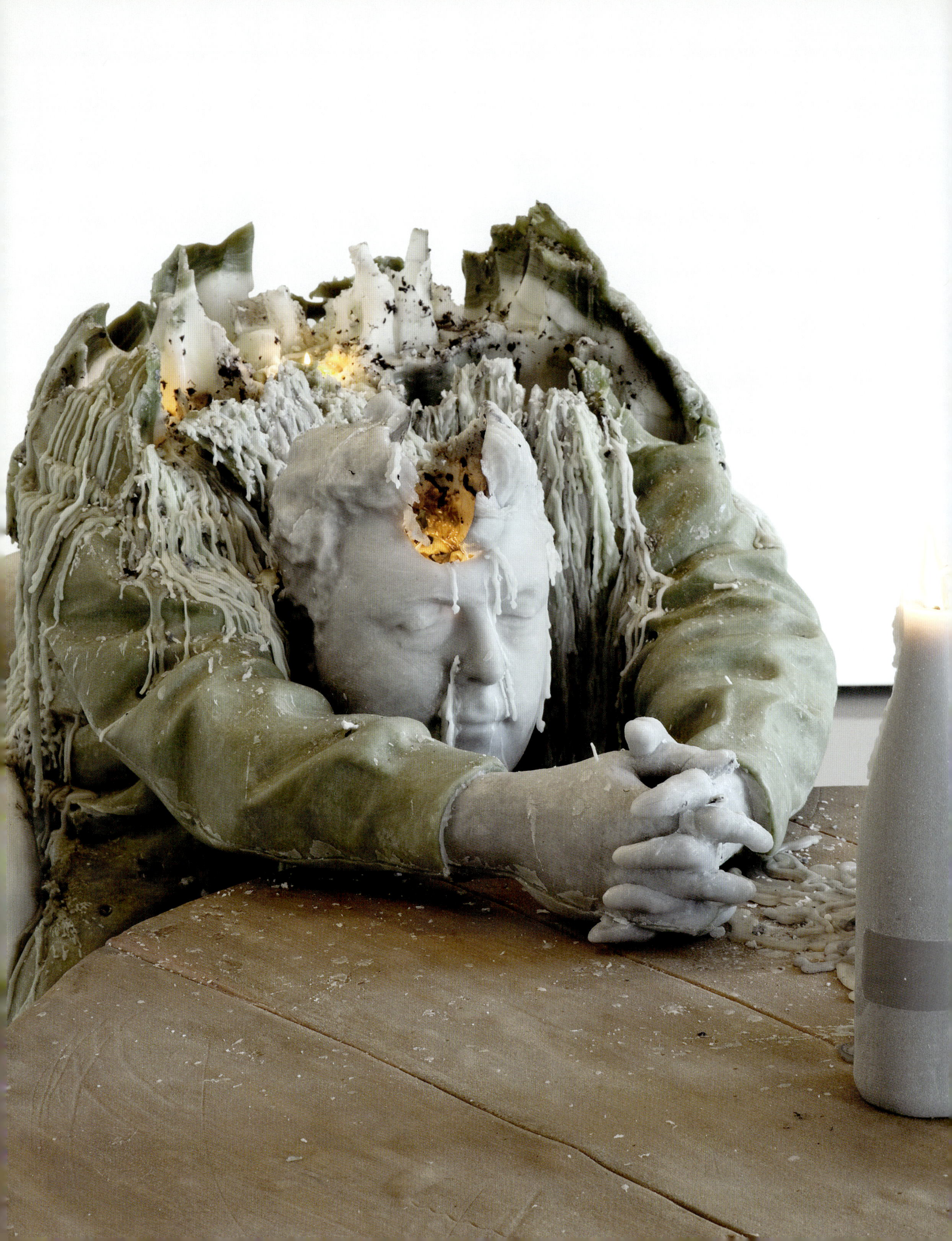

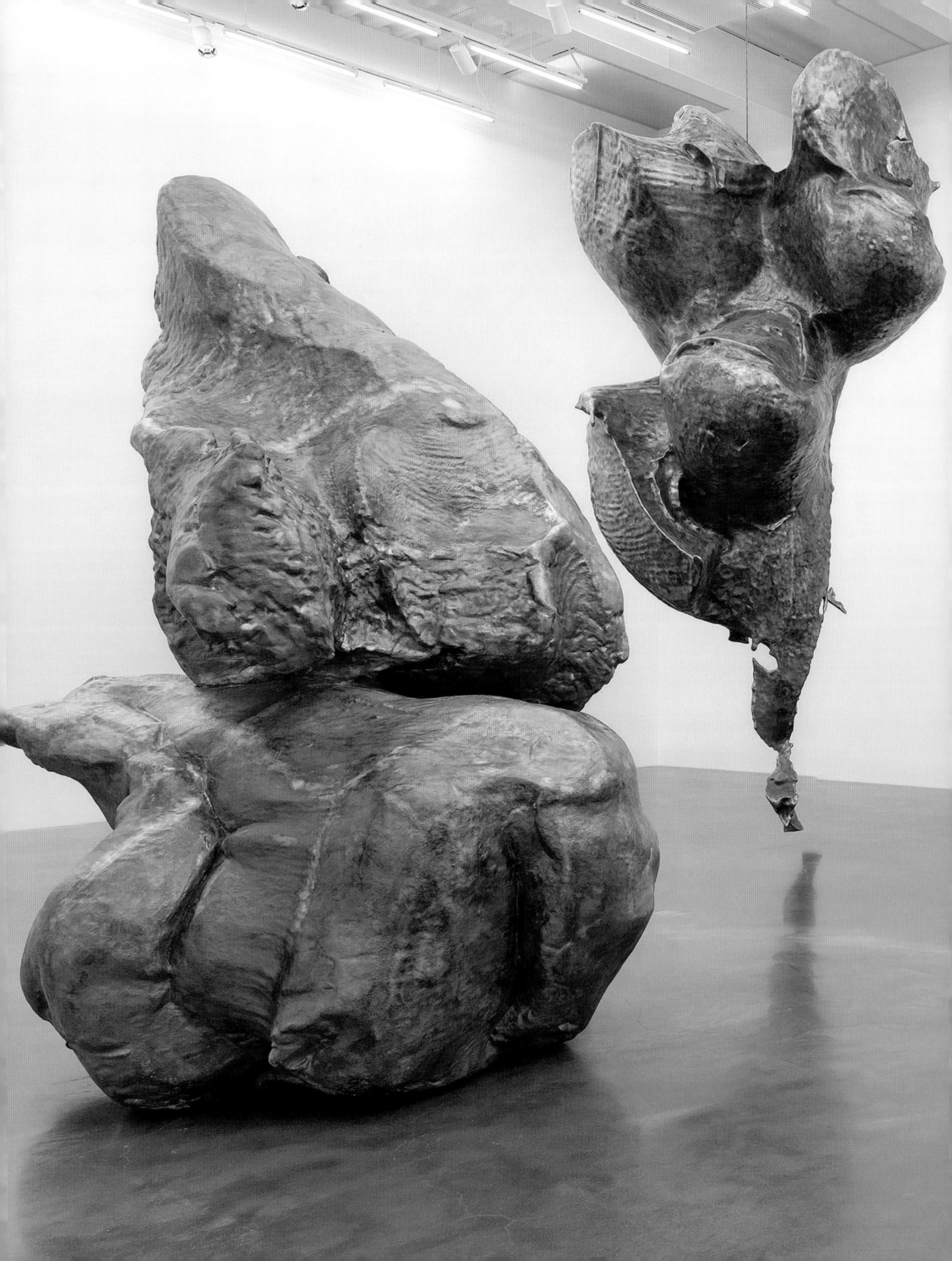

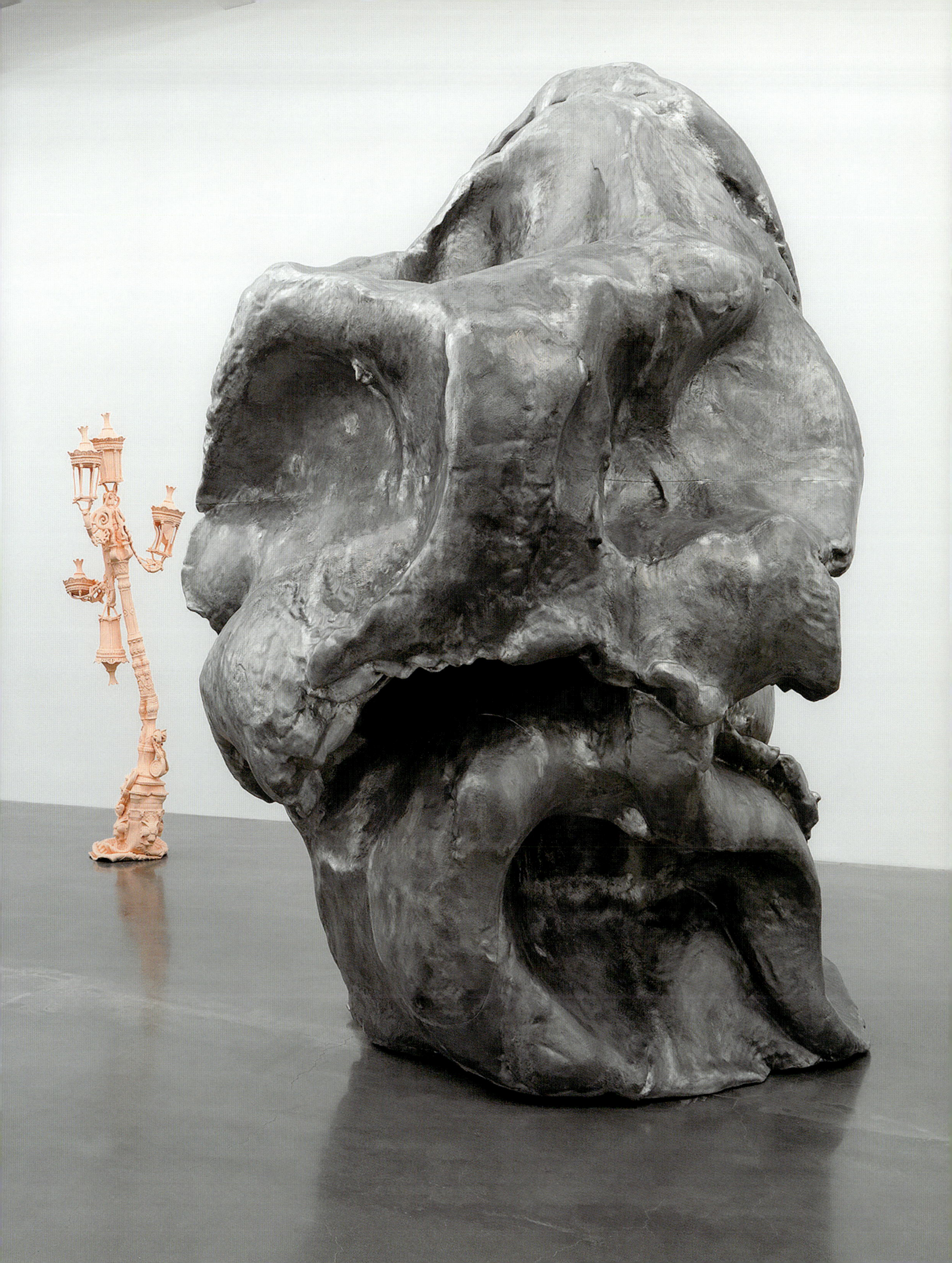

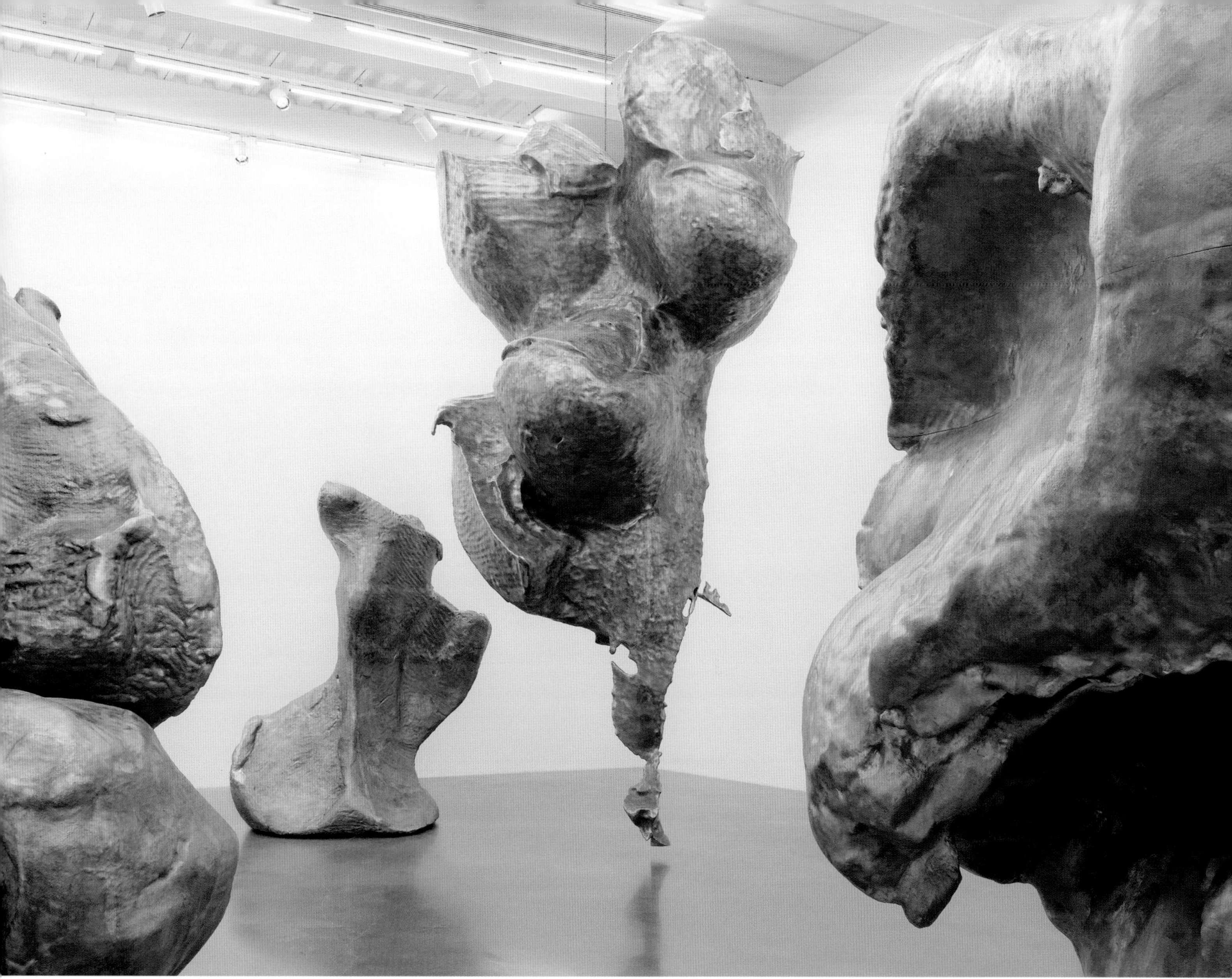

Ix, 2006–2008
Cast aluminum, steel
118 ⅛ x 88 ⅝ x 61 ¾ inches (300 x 225 x 157 cm)
Installation view, "Urs Fischer: Marguerite de Ponty,"
New Museum, New York, 2009–2010
David, the Proprietor, 2008–2009

Previous spread:
Miss Satin, 2006–2008
Cast aluminum, steel
133 ⅞ x 101 ⅛ x 86 ⅝ inches (340 x 257 x 220 cm)

David, the Proprietor, 2008–2009
Cast aluminum, aluminum, steel cable, steel bolts
Approximately 217 x 118 x 118 inches
(551.2 x 299.7 x 299.7 cm)

Marguerite de Ponty, 2006–2008
Cast aluminum, steel
157 ½ x 110 ¼ x 102 ⅜ inches (400 x 280 x 260 cm)
Installation view, "Urs Fischer: Marguerite de Ponty,"
New Museum, New York, 2009–2010
Frozen Pioneer, 2009

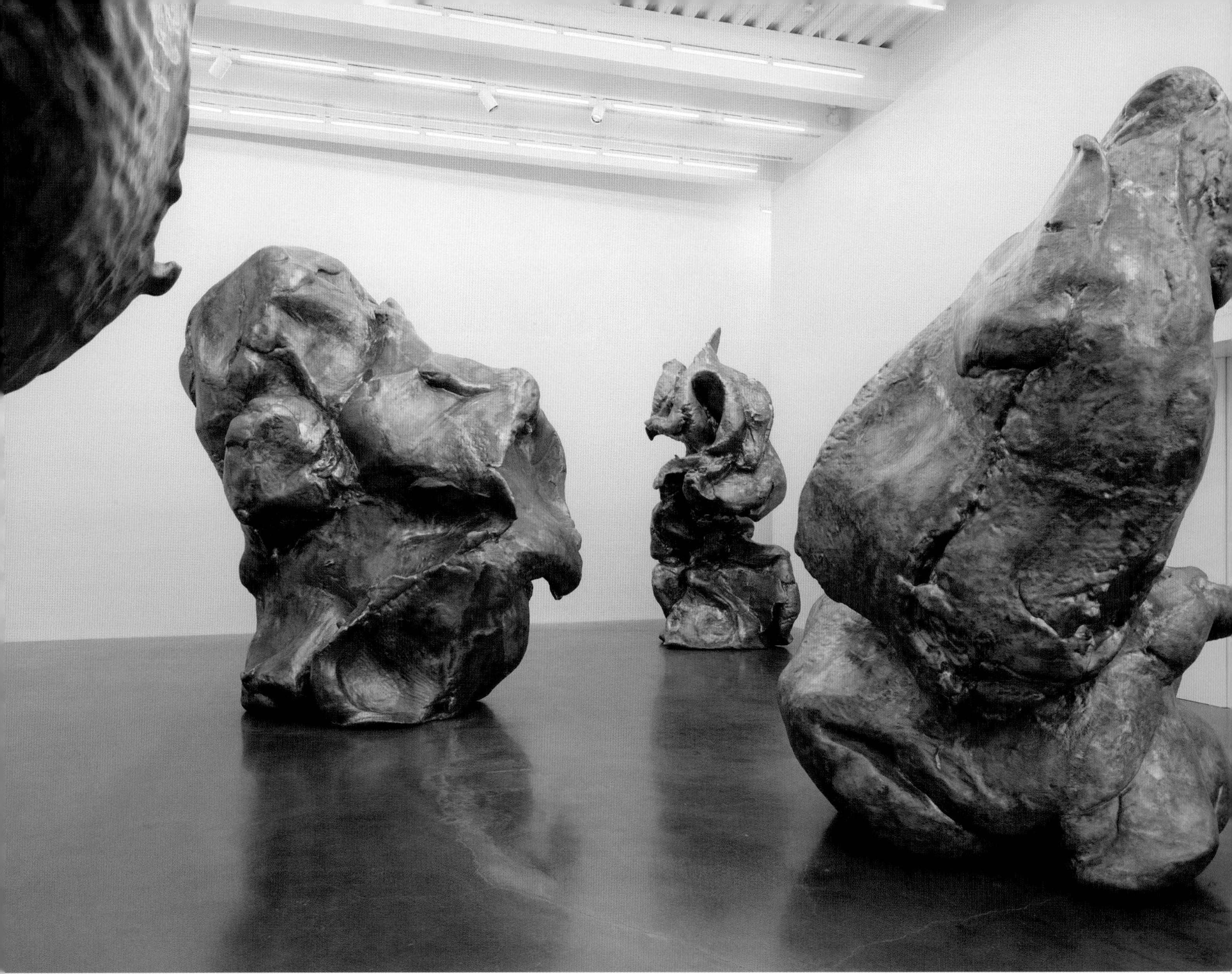

Installation view, "Urs Fischer: Marguerite de Ponty,"
New Museum, New York, 2009–2010
Above: *Marguerite de Ponty*, 2006–2008;
Zizi, 2006–2008, *Miss Satin*, 2006–2008
Opposite page: *Marguerite de Ponty*, 2006–2008;
David, the Proprietor, 2008–2009; *Frozen Pioneer*, 2009

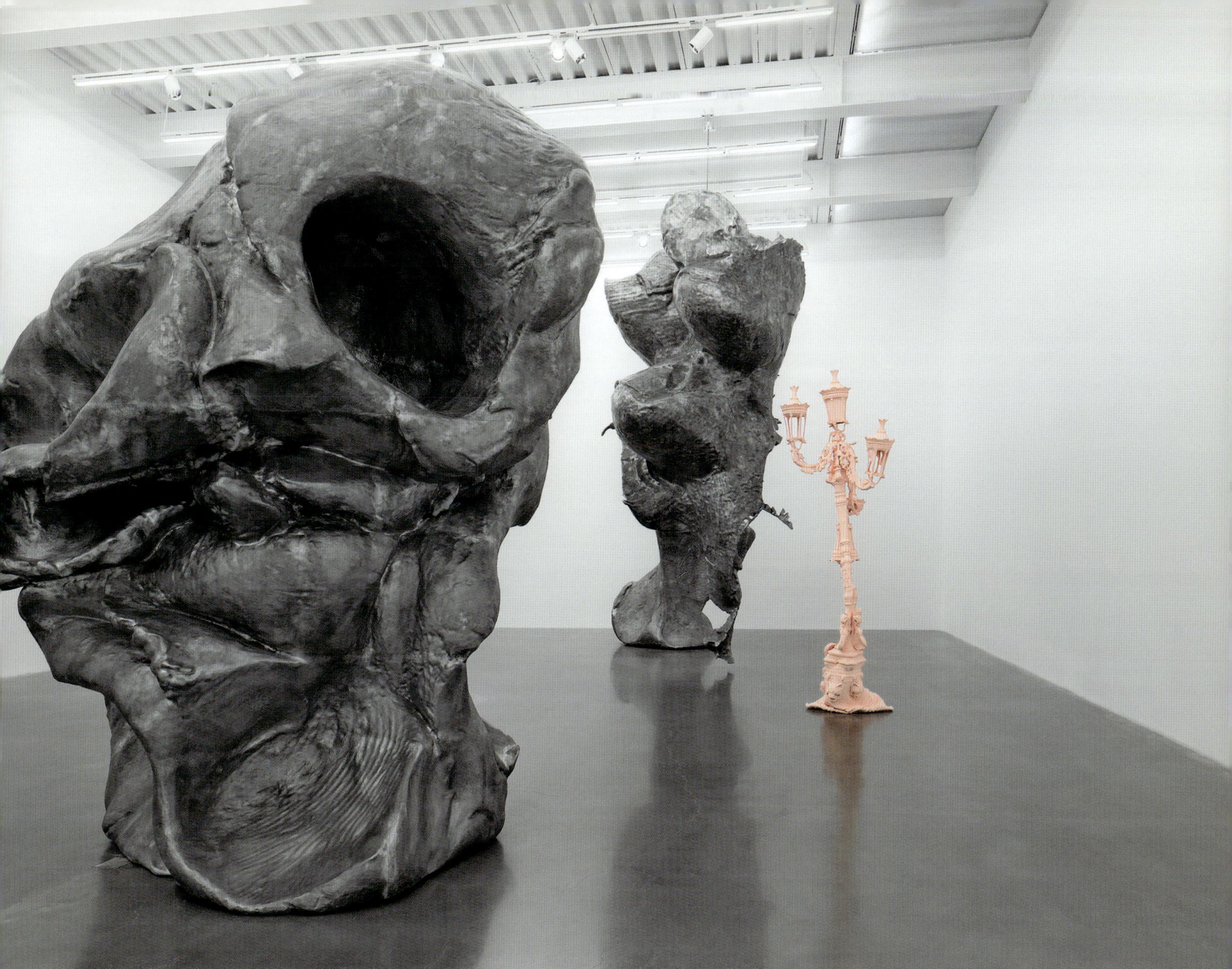

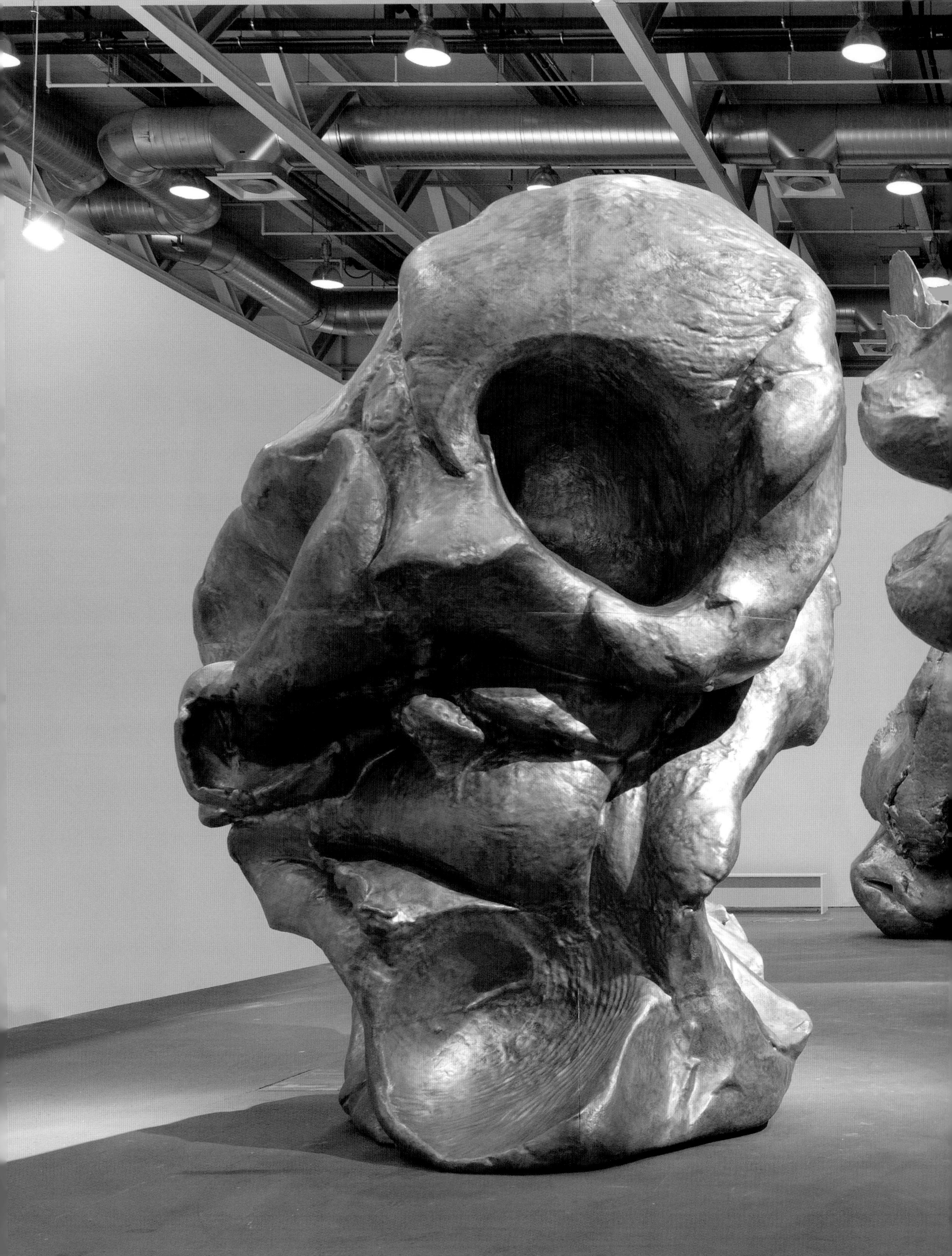

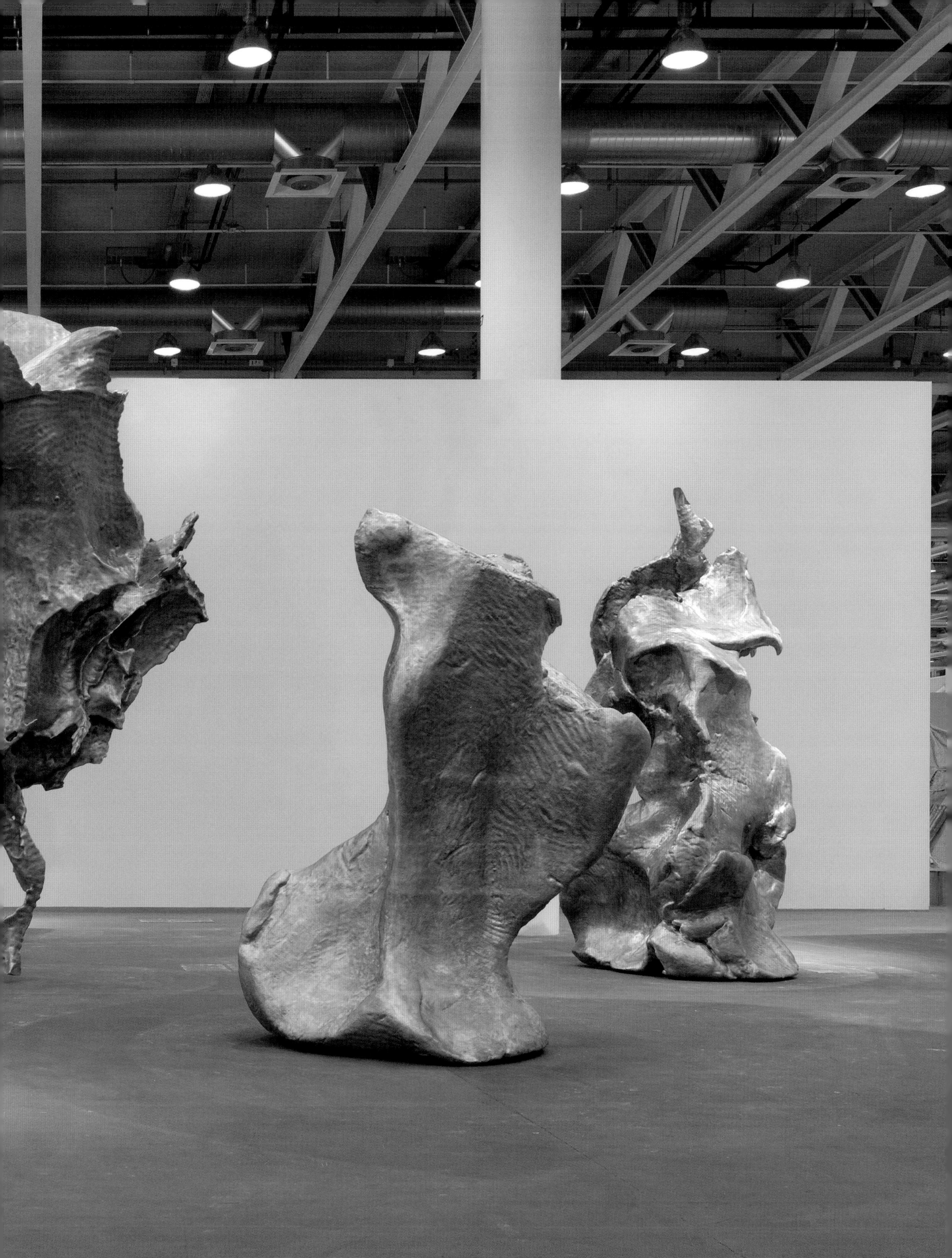

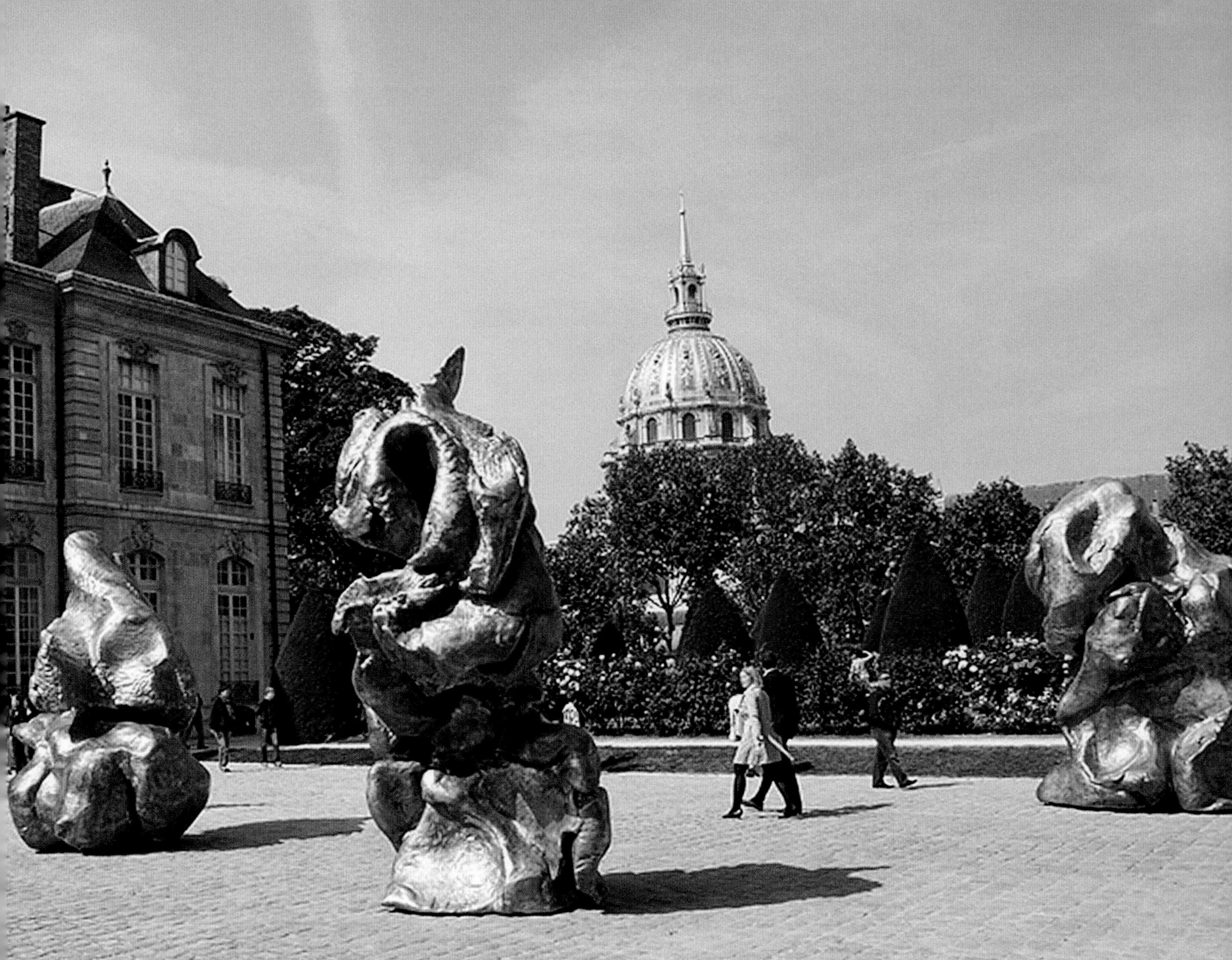

Installation view, "L'invention de l'oeuvre: Rodin et les ambassadeurs,"
Musée Rodin, Paris, 2011
Miss Satin, 2006–2008, *Zizi*, 2006–2008, *Marguerite de Ponty*, 2006–2008

Opposite page: *David, the Proprietor*, 2008–2009

Previous spread: Installation view, Art Unlimited, Art Basel, 2010
Marguerite de Ponty, 2006–2008; *David, the Proprietor*, 2008–2009;
Miss Satin, 2006–2008; *Ix*, 2006–2008; *Zizi*, 2006–2008

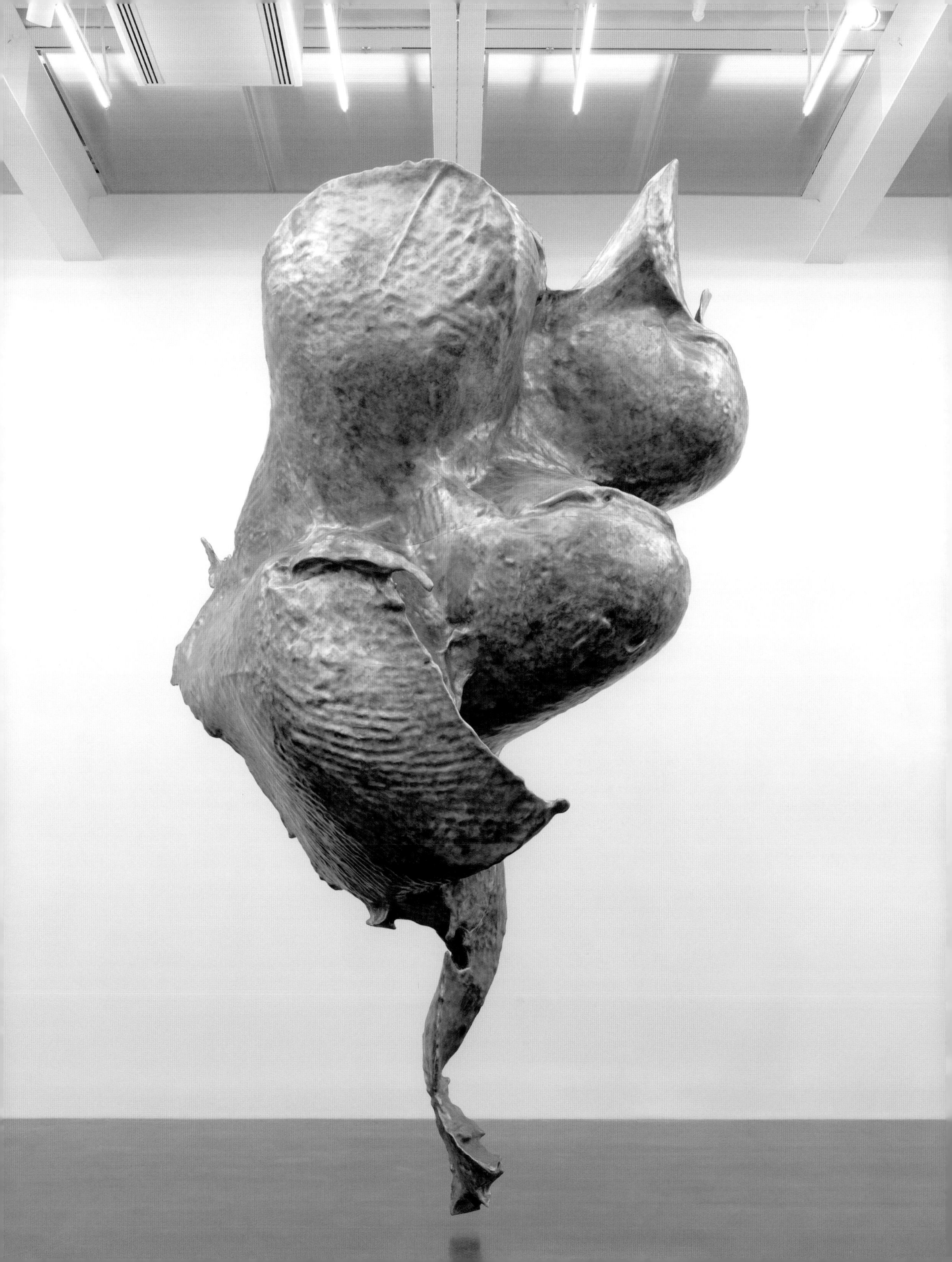

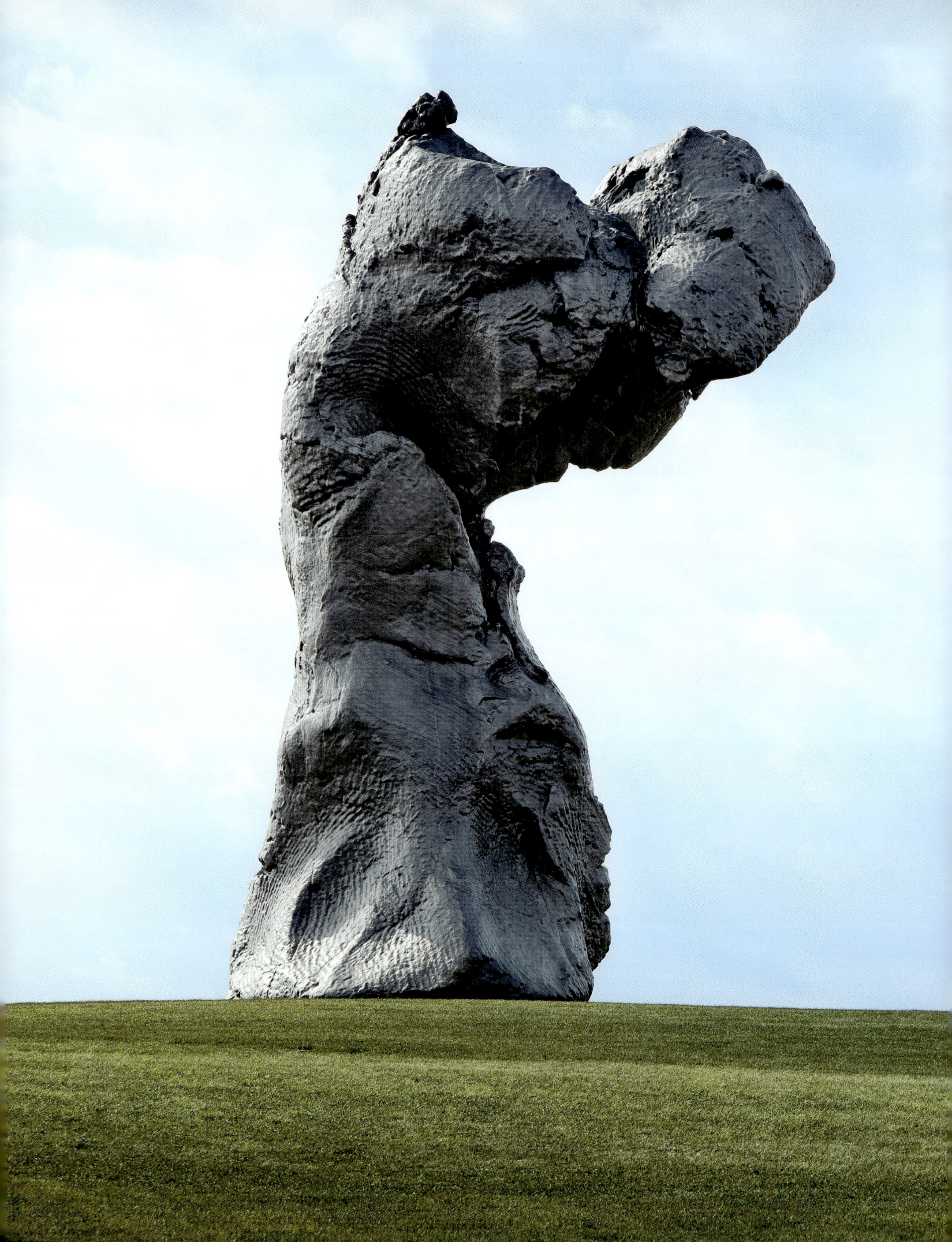

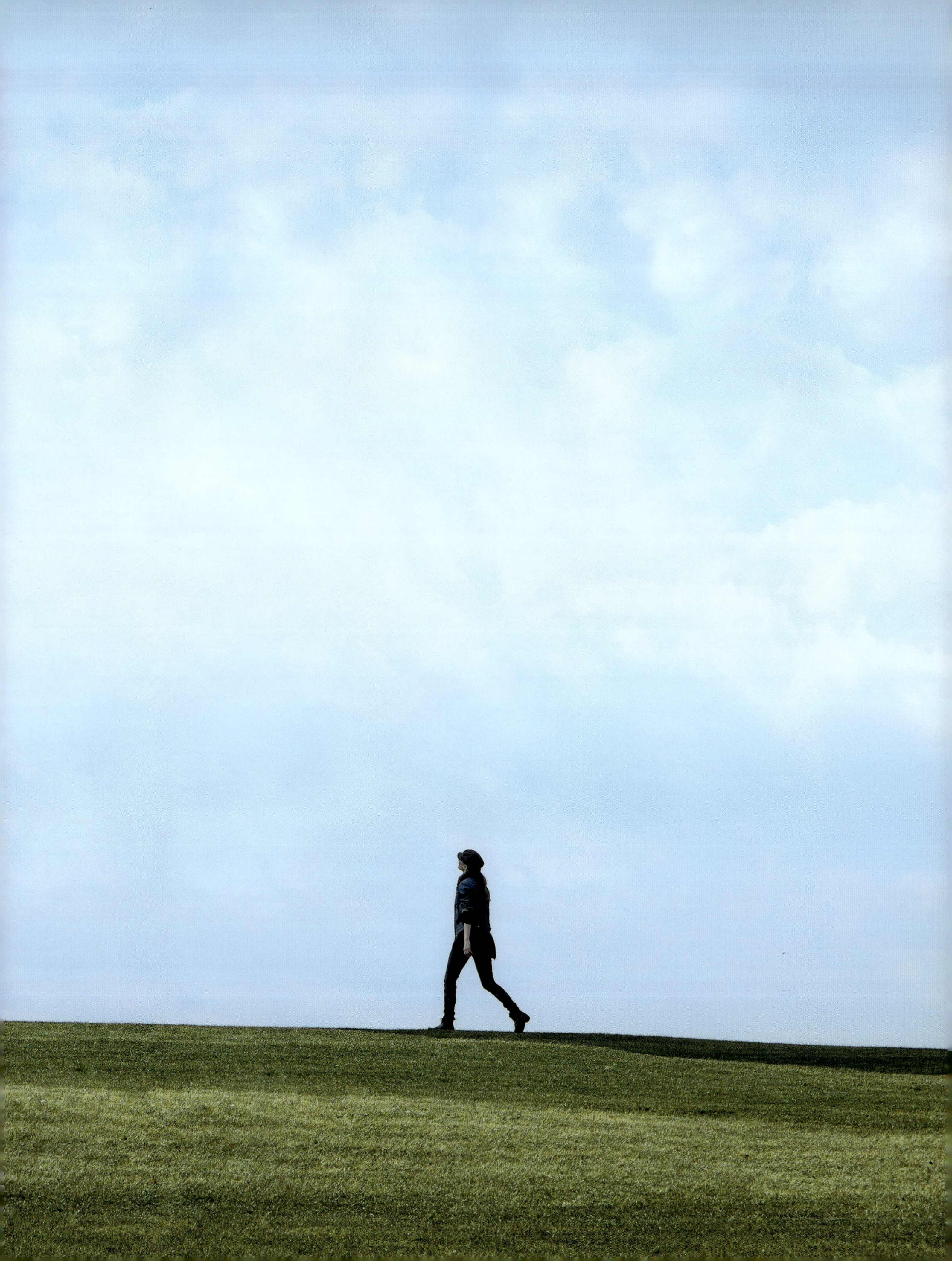

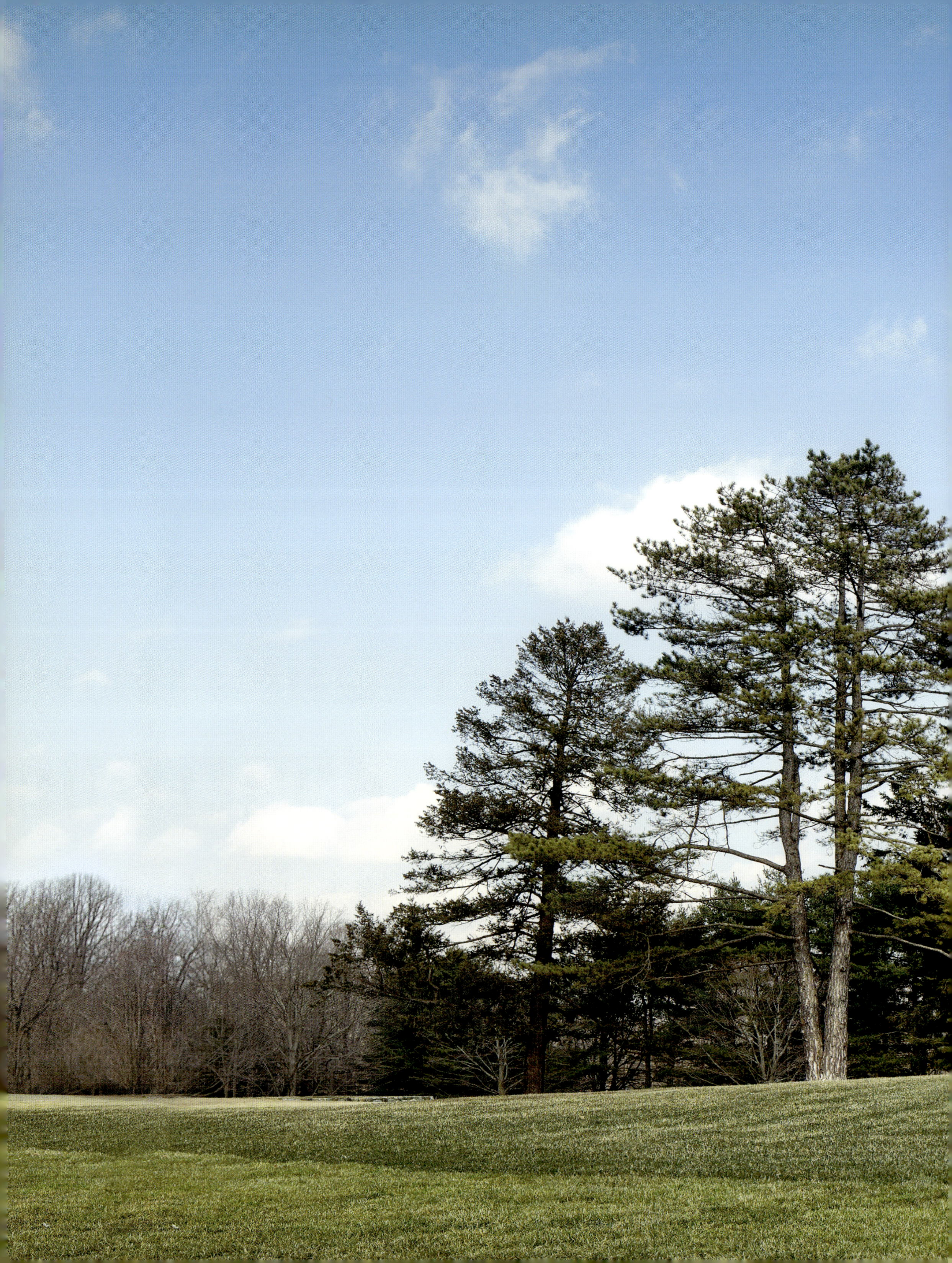

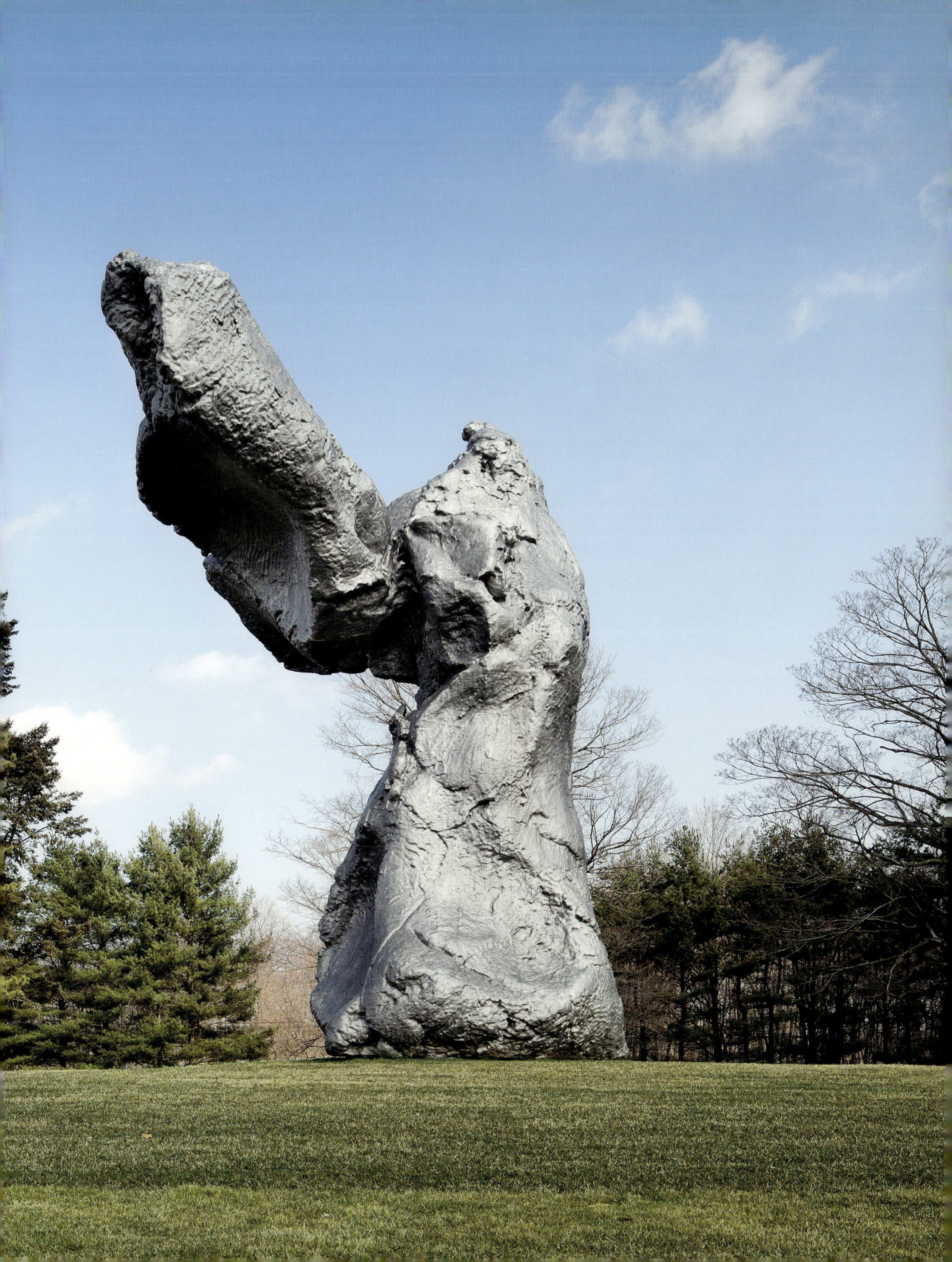

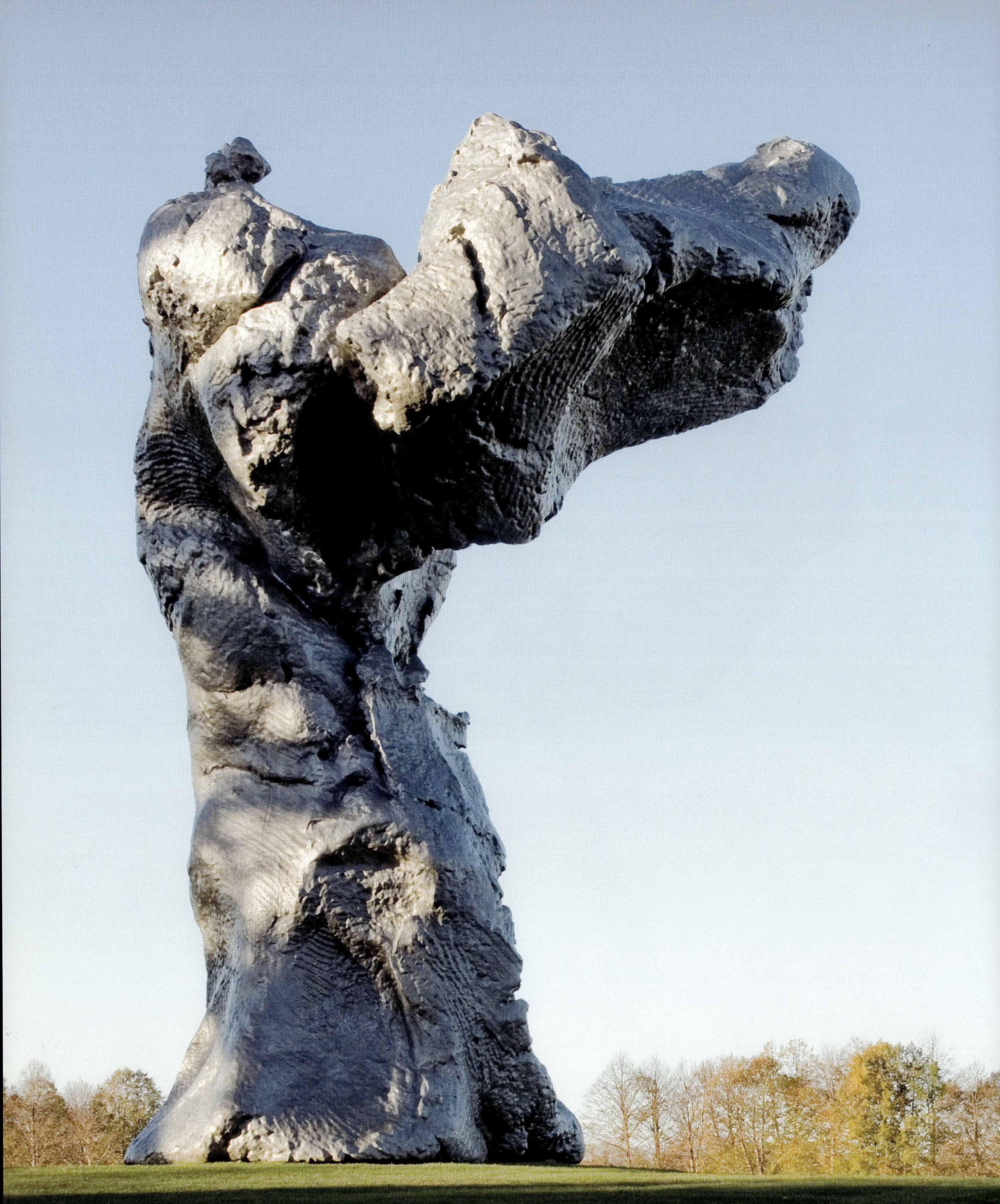

Previous spreads:
Untitled (Big Clay #3), 2008–2011
Cast aluminum, chrome steel skeleton, chrome steel bolts
Approximately 403 ½ x 299 ¼ x 255 ⅞ inches (1024.9 x 760 x 650 cm)
Installation view, The Brant Foundation Art Study Center, Greenwich, Connecticut

Following spread:
Untitled (Big Clay #5), 2008–2013
Cast aluminum, chrome steel skeleton, chrome steel bolts
Approximately 513 ¾ x 362 ¼ x 263 ¾ inches (1305.1 x 920 x 670.1 cm)
Installation view, assembly yard of Kunstgiesserei St. Gallen Shanghai Ltd., Shanghai

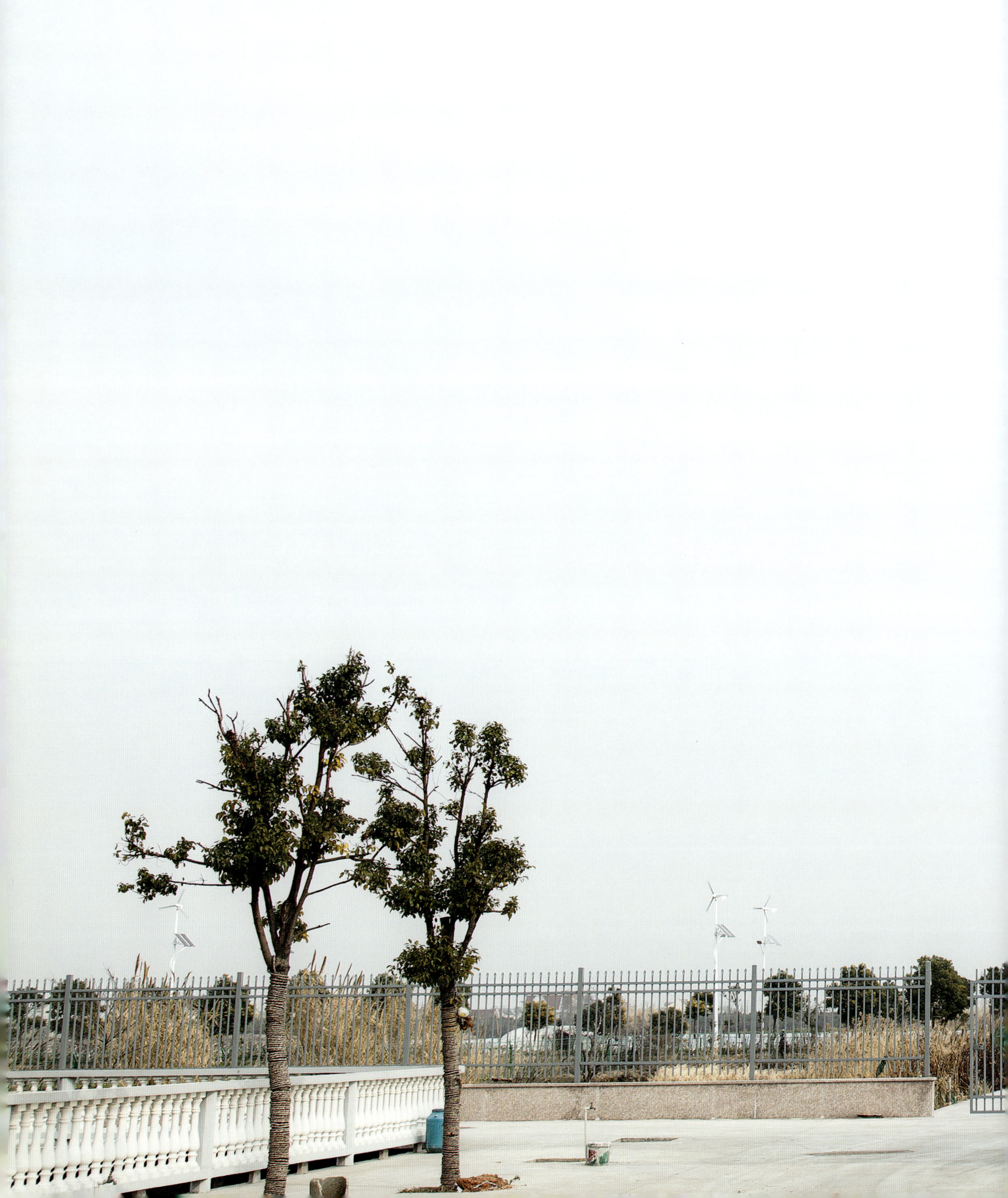

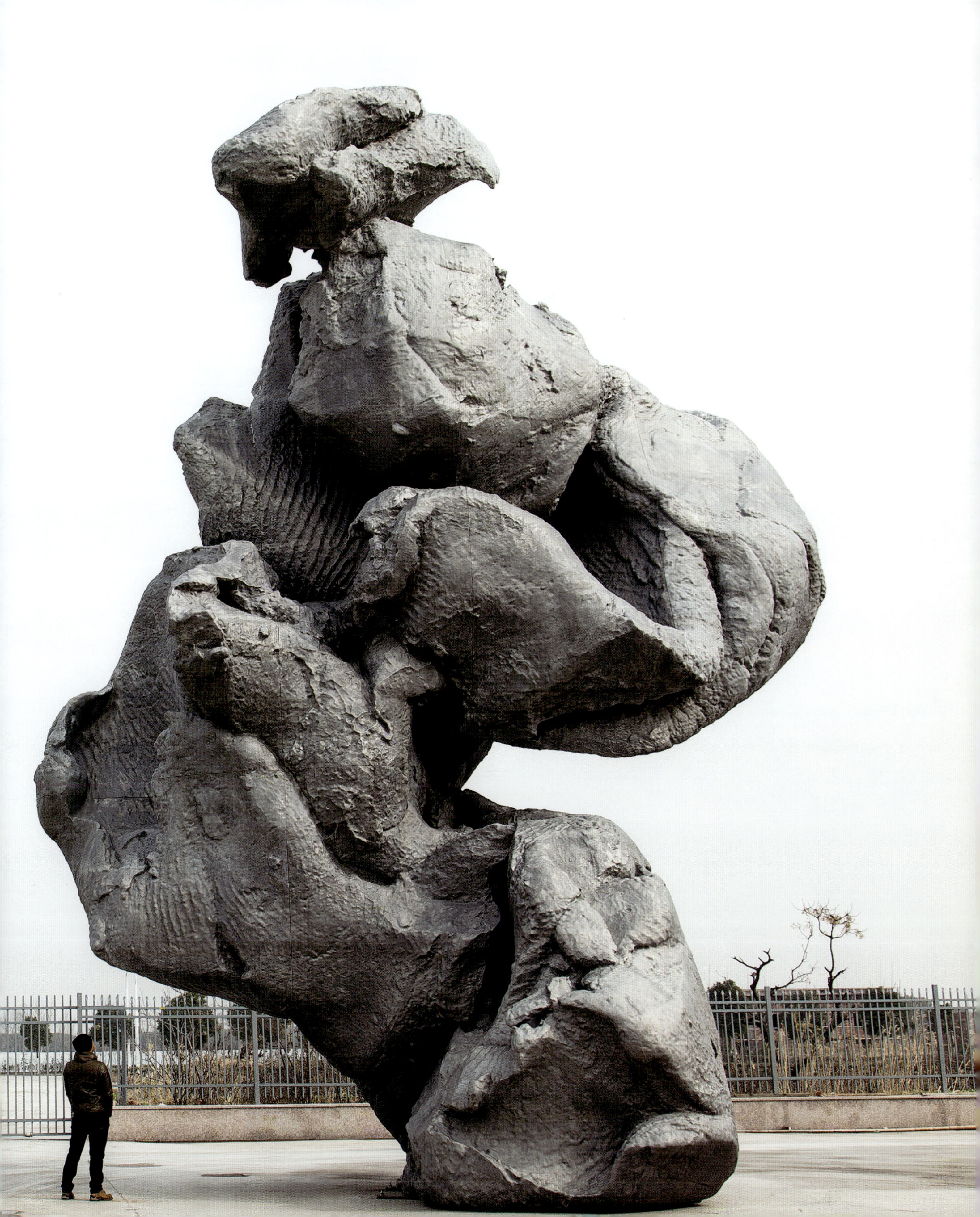

Untitled (Self-Destroying Cat), 2009
Unfired clay
Dimensions variable
Installation view, Slottsparken, Oslo, 2009

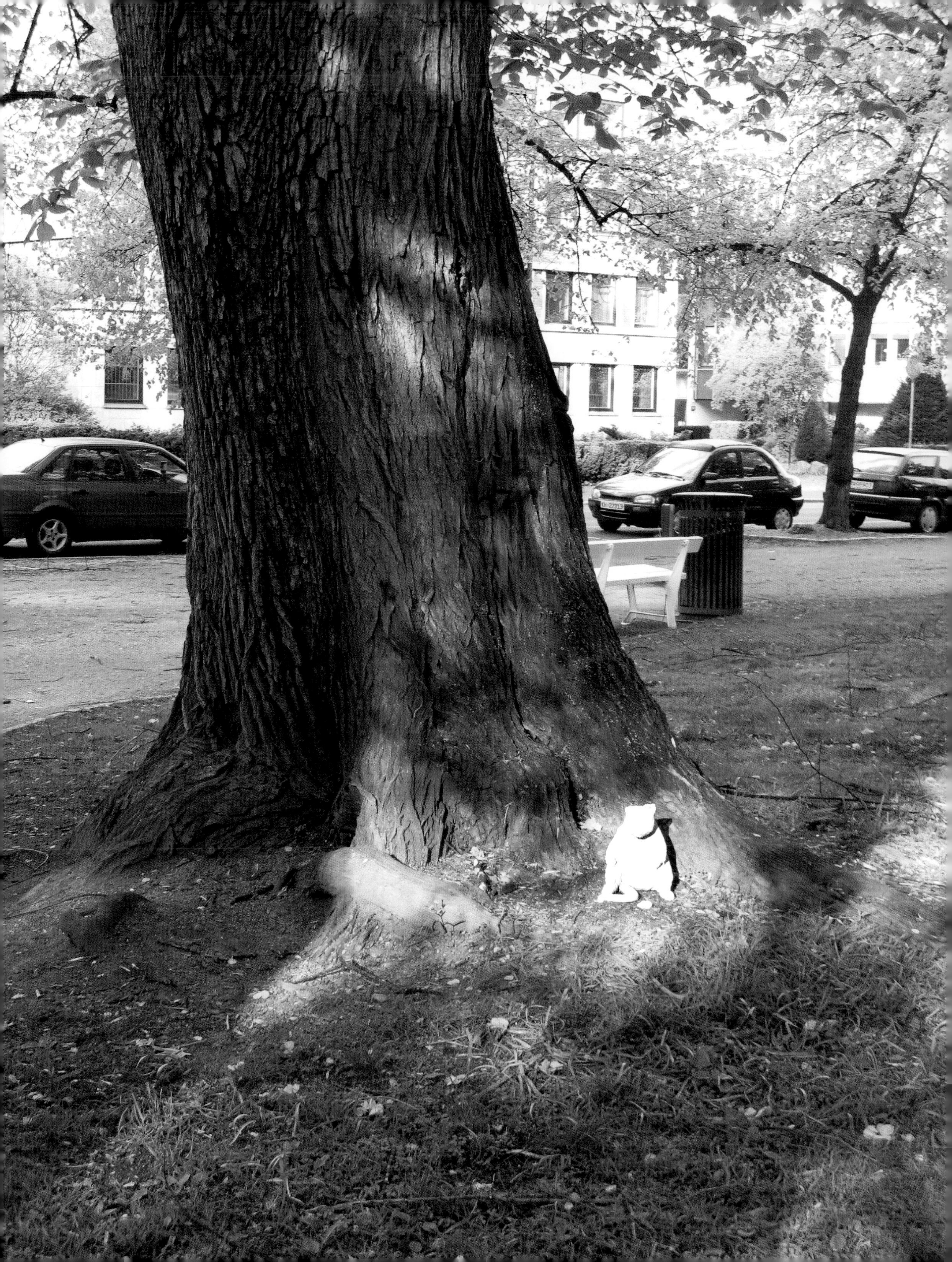

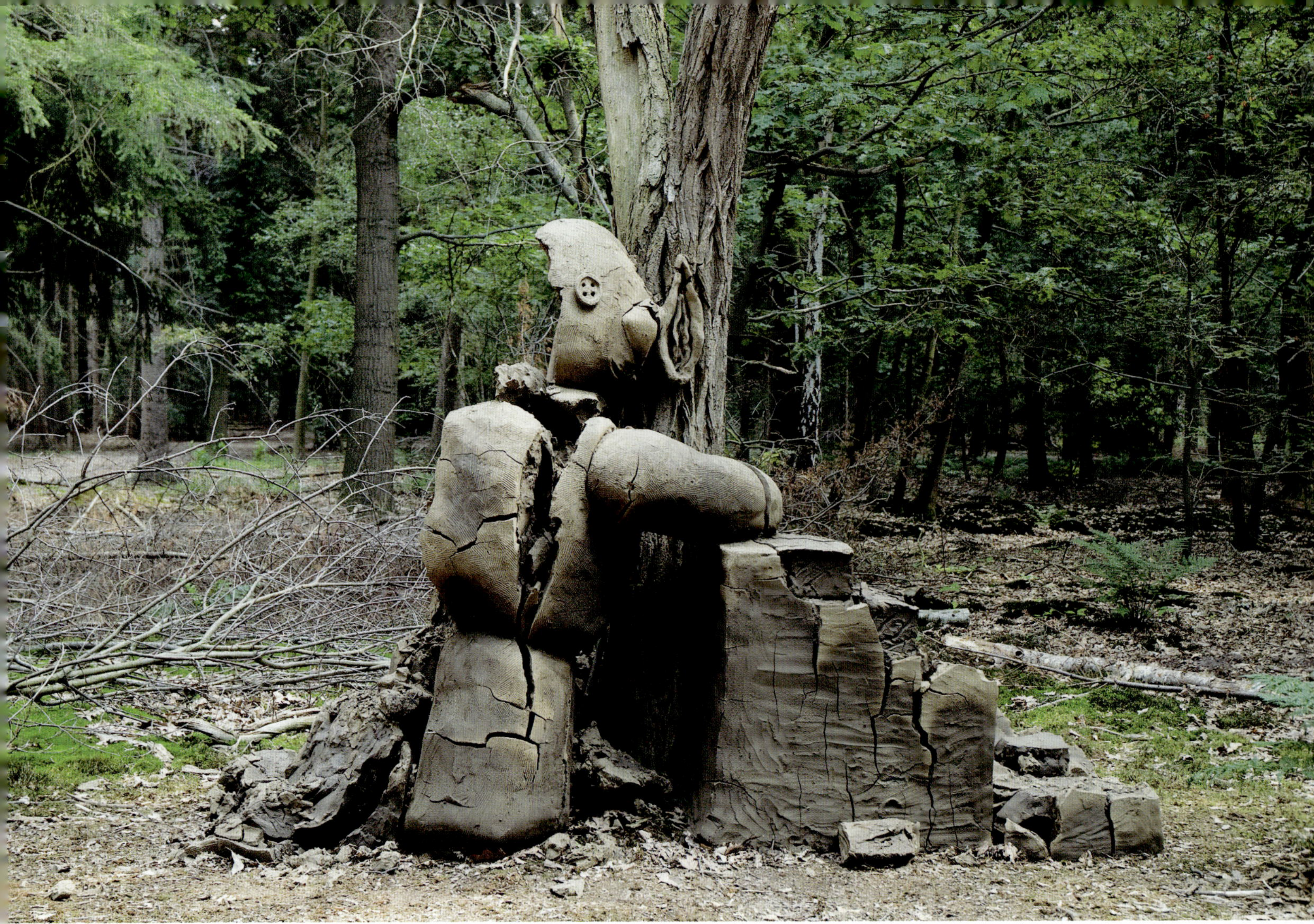

Urs Fischer and various artists
Untitled, 2011-ongoing
Unfired clay (sculptures modeled on-site by multiple authors following a list of objects specified by the artist)
Dimensions variable
Installation view, "Lustwarande 2011–Blemishes," Park De Oude Warande, Museum De Pont, Tilburg, The Netherlands, 2011
With the assistance of Annika Albrecht, Katharina Beilstein, Malte Bruns, David Czupryn, Nora Hansen, Benjamin Houlihan, Tammo Lünemann, Sabine Voltz, and Vicktoria Wald

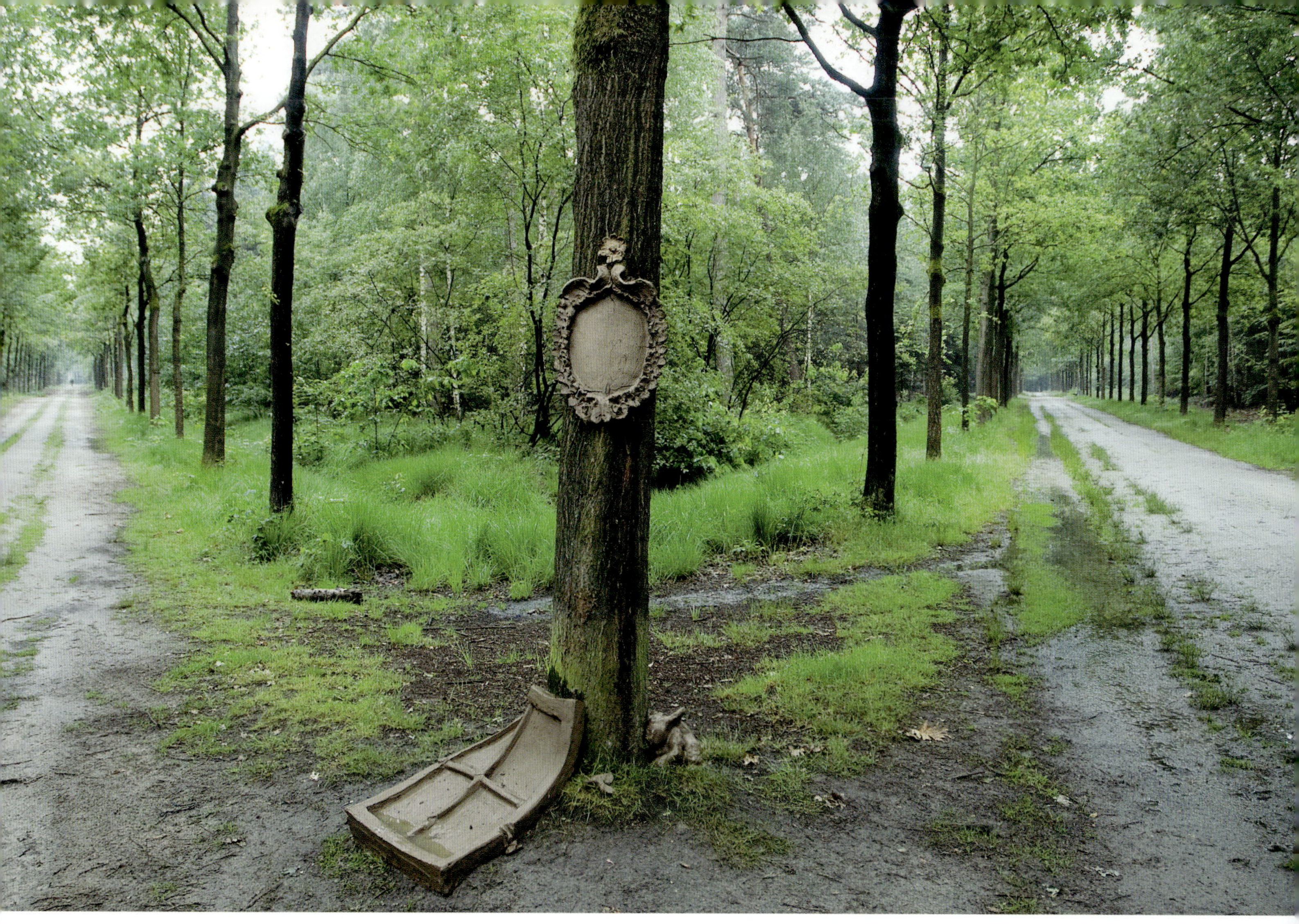

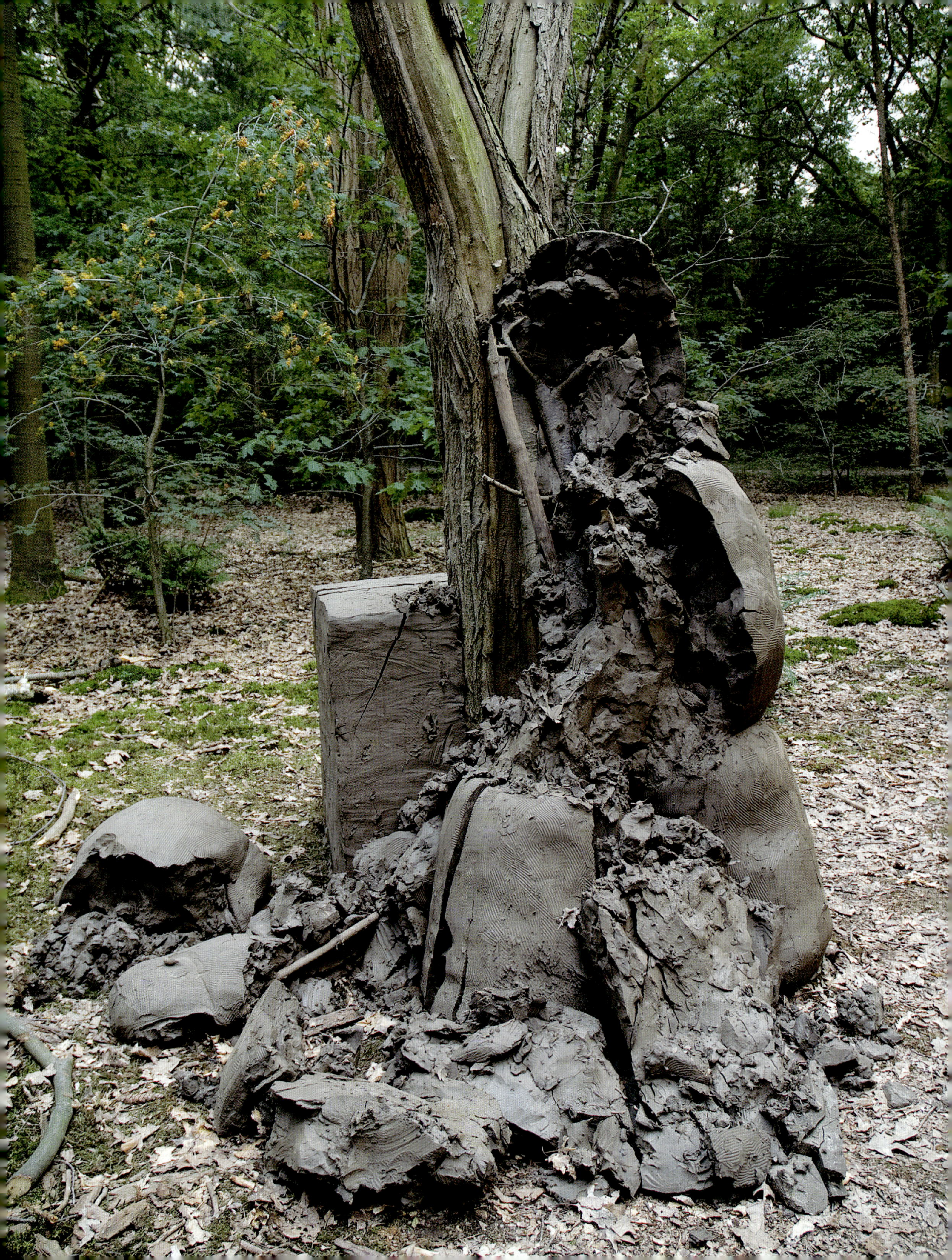

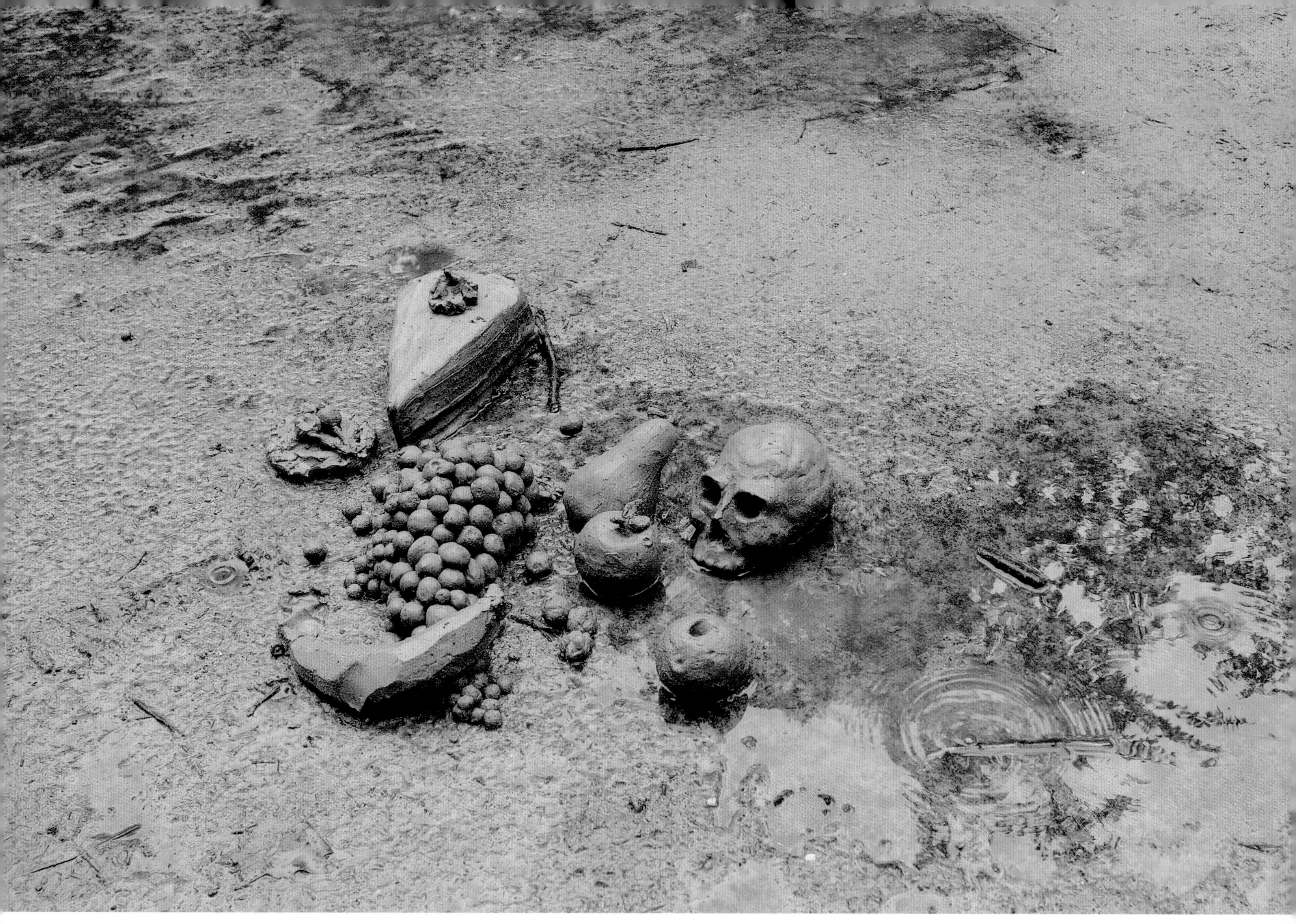

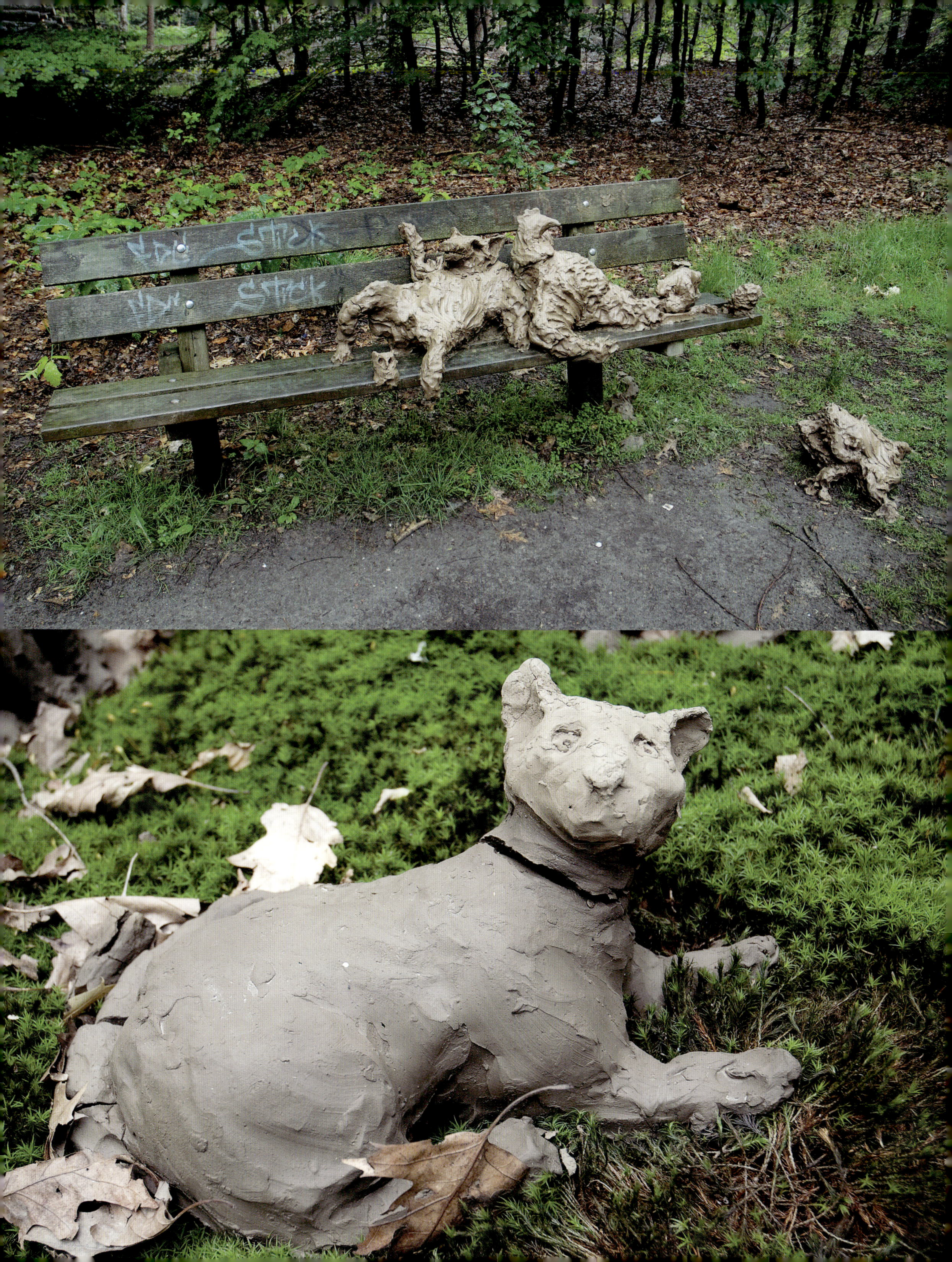

Installation view, Ex Ospedale degli Incurabili, Accademia di Belle Arti di Venezia, as part of "Madame Fisscher," Palazzo Grassi, Venice, 2012
Untitled, 2011–ongoing
With the assistance of Asadollah (Aras) Kefayati, Giuseppe Abate, Davide Aghayan, Ahmad Ahmadzadeh, Lucia Apolloni, Niccolò Argenti, Jessica Bagatella, Maribel Baldo, Gloria Bergamo, Giulia Bertolin, Alessandra Bianco, Silvia Bonazzi, Mirco Bordin, Thomas Braida, Savina Capecci, Roberta Caruso, Nina Ceranic, Samanta Cinquini, Marco Contino, Silvia Dal Prà, Giulia de Giovanelli, Cristiana di Maio, Alessandra Dianin, Alessandro Dus, Khalil Ebrahim, Pashkaj Edison, Nicola Facchini, Tiziano Favaretto, Anita Ferro Milone, Lucia Fezzardi, Anna Fietta, Giulio Peiré, Ilva Gjoka, Marco Gobbi, Andrea Grotto, Giada Guidetti, Chiara Guidotto, Justine Luce, Louise Leonard, Stefano Leoni, Silvia Macor, Francesco Maluta, Marja Markovic, Sanja Minic, Martina Miola, Marta Naturale, Valerio Nicolai, Mariona Obrador, Alice Oliva, Irina Osleja, Isabella Paris, Alice Parisotto, Paolo Pavan, Giacomo Perazzolo, Agnes Pesec, Barbara Prenka, Paolo Pretolani, Ana Reque, Marco Riente, Elena Rosa, Elisa Sartori, Anna Shalaby, Melissa Siben, Selene Signorini, Danilo Stojanovic, Katarina Strugar, Maddalena Tesser, Zheng Tianming, Thomas Tosato, Adriano Valeri, Ana Valter, Sepideh Yeganehdoost, Shibata Yoshiko, Veronica Zanier, Geng Zhong Qi, Mojca Ziberna, and others

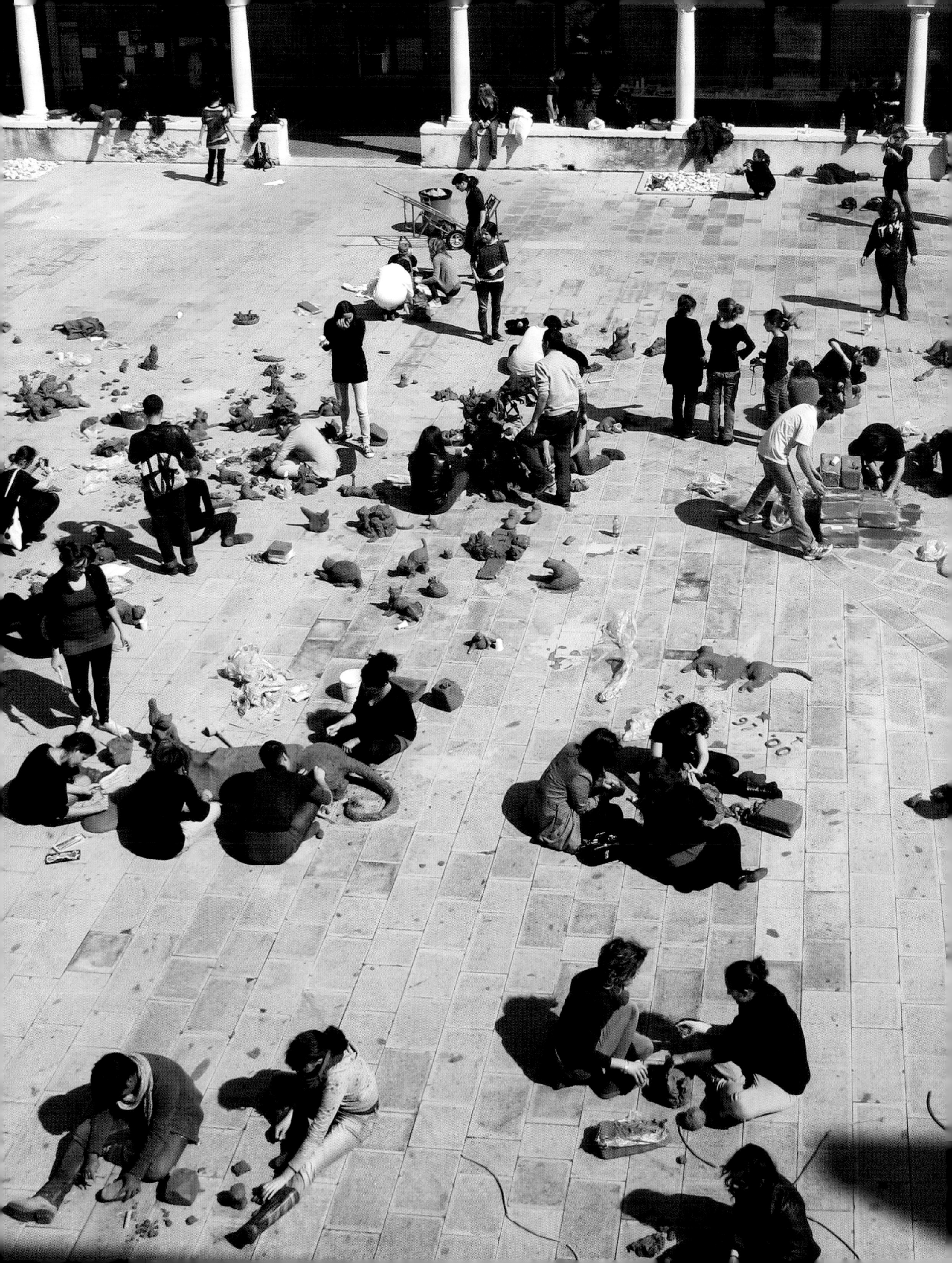

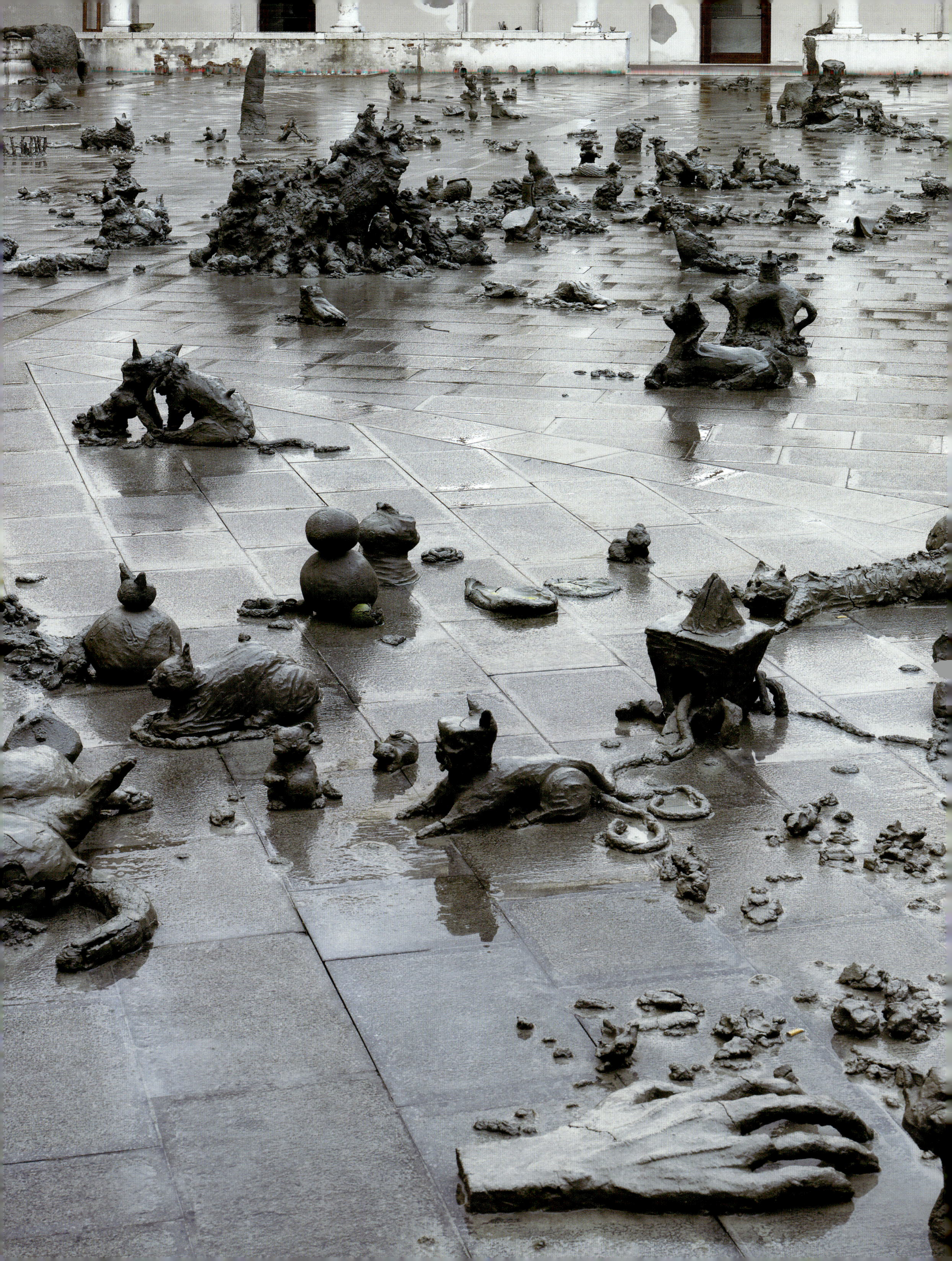

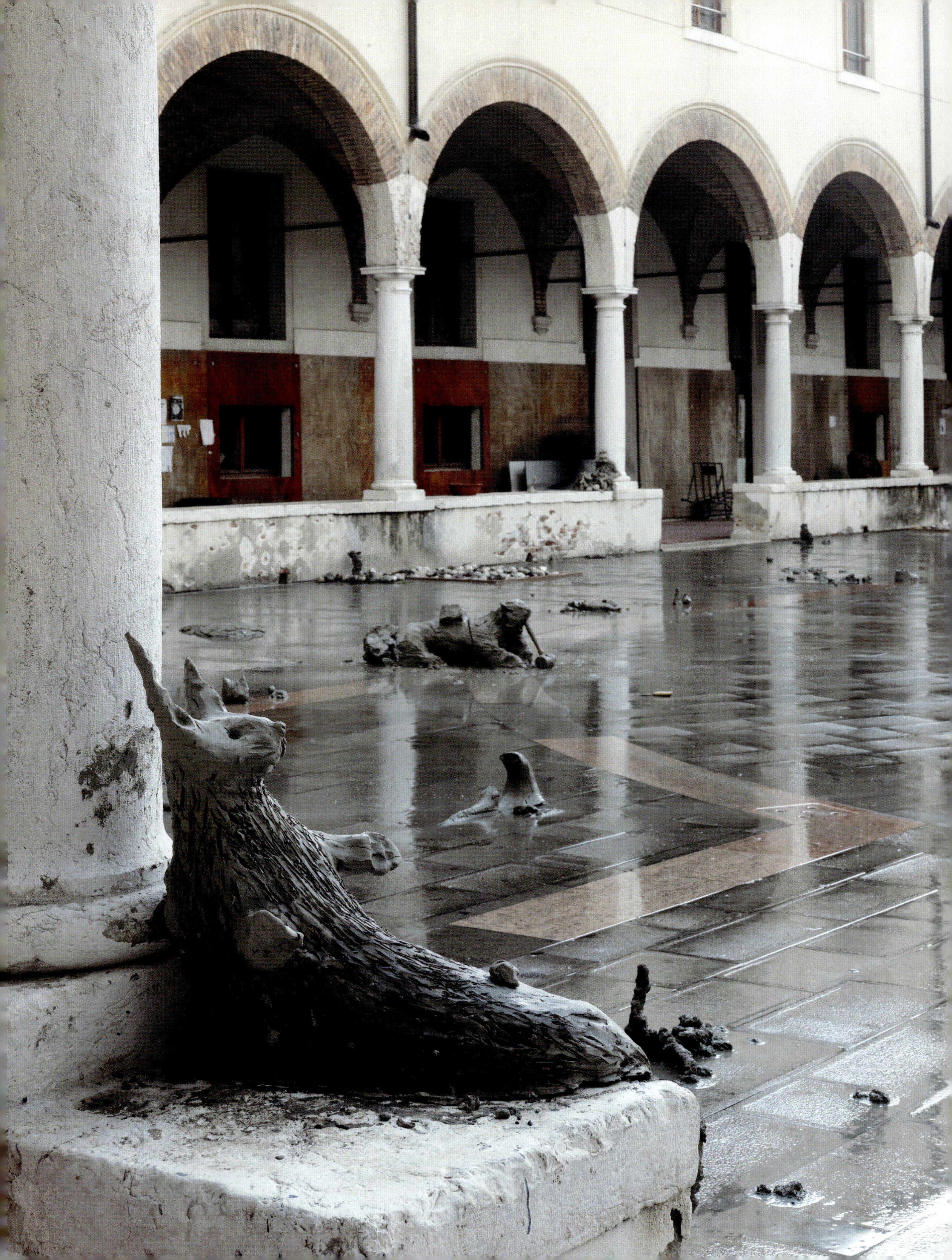

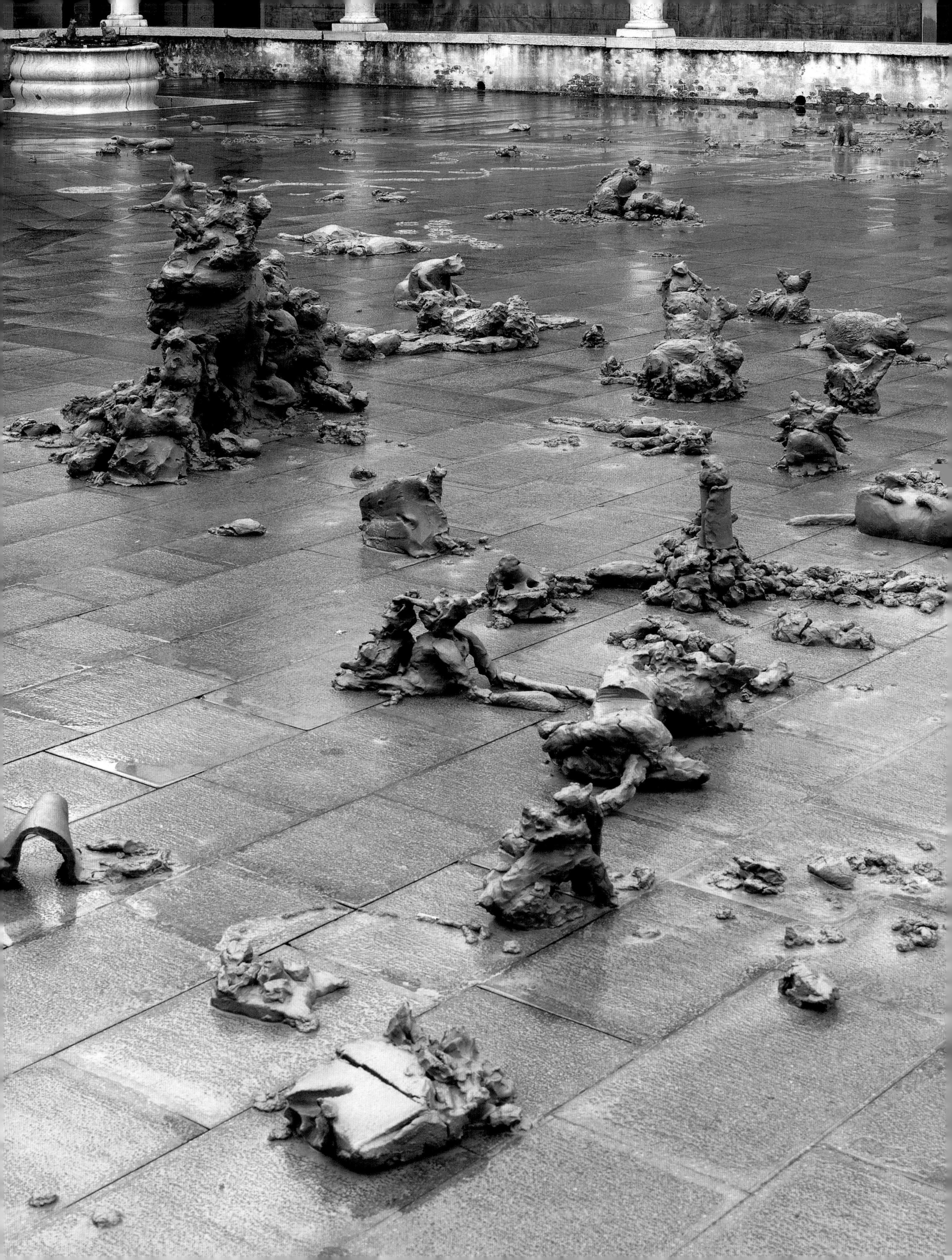

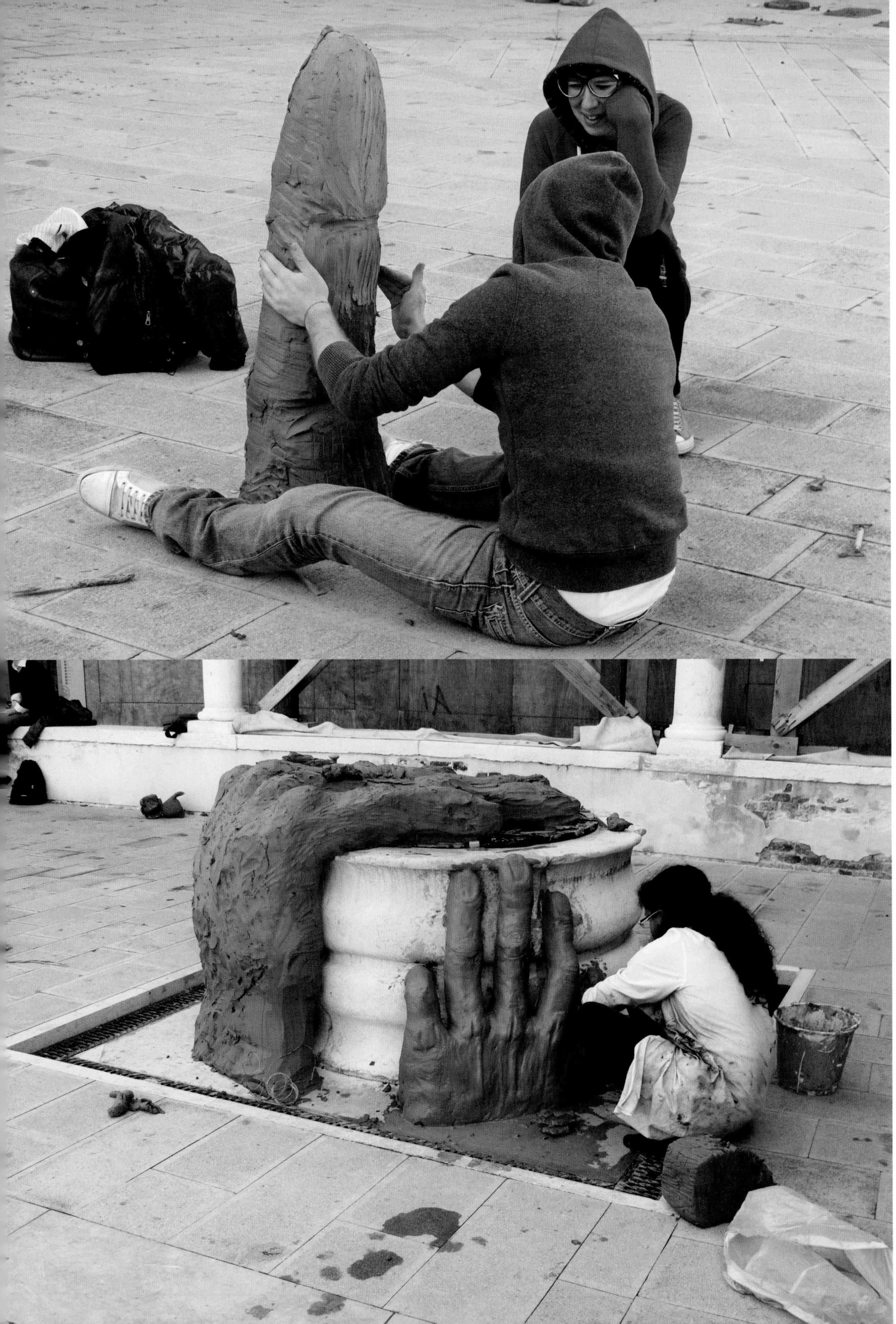

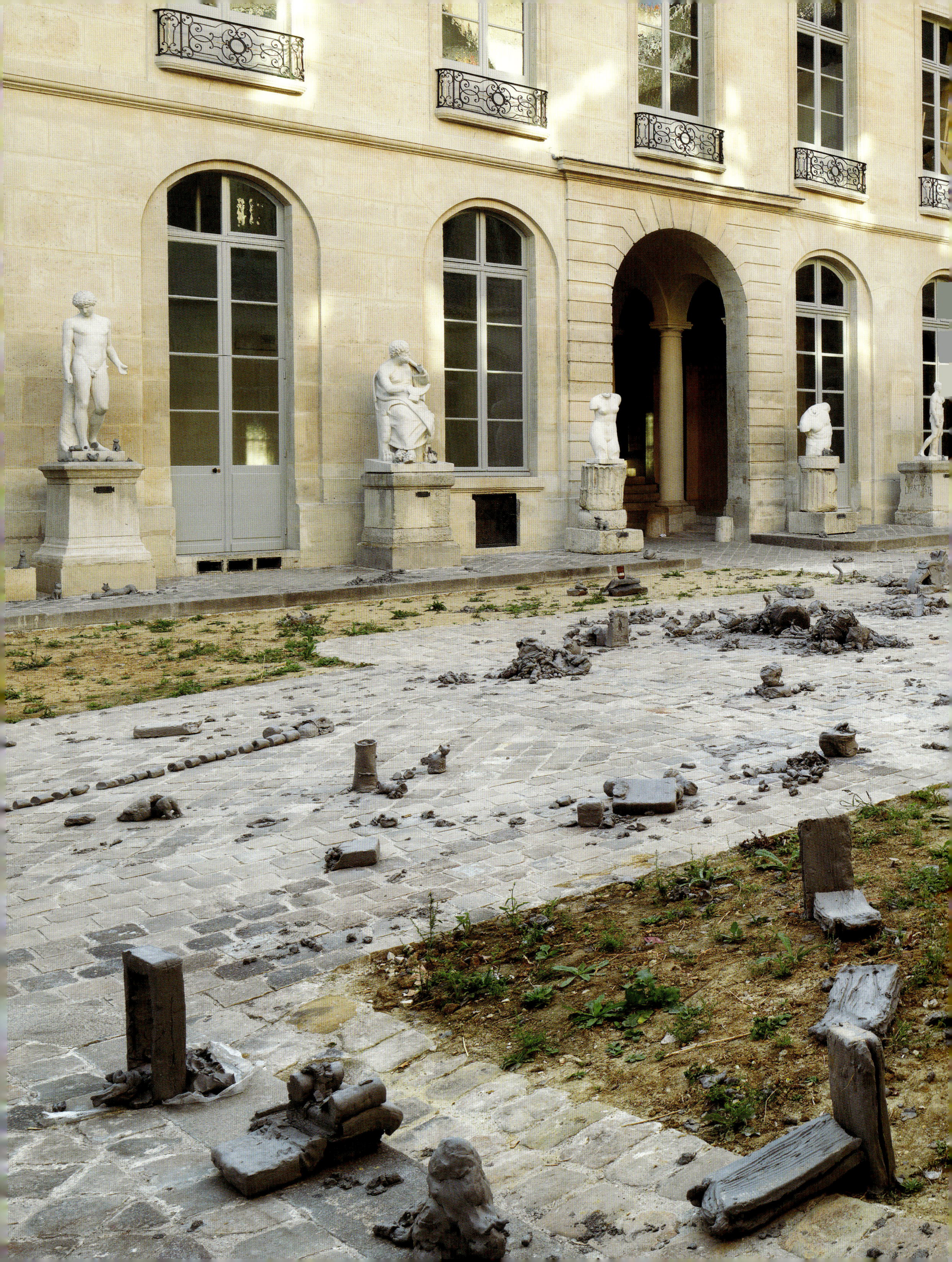

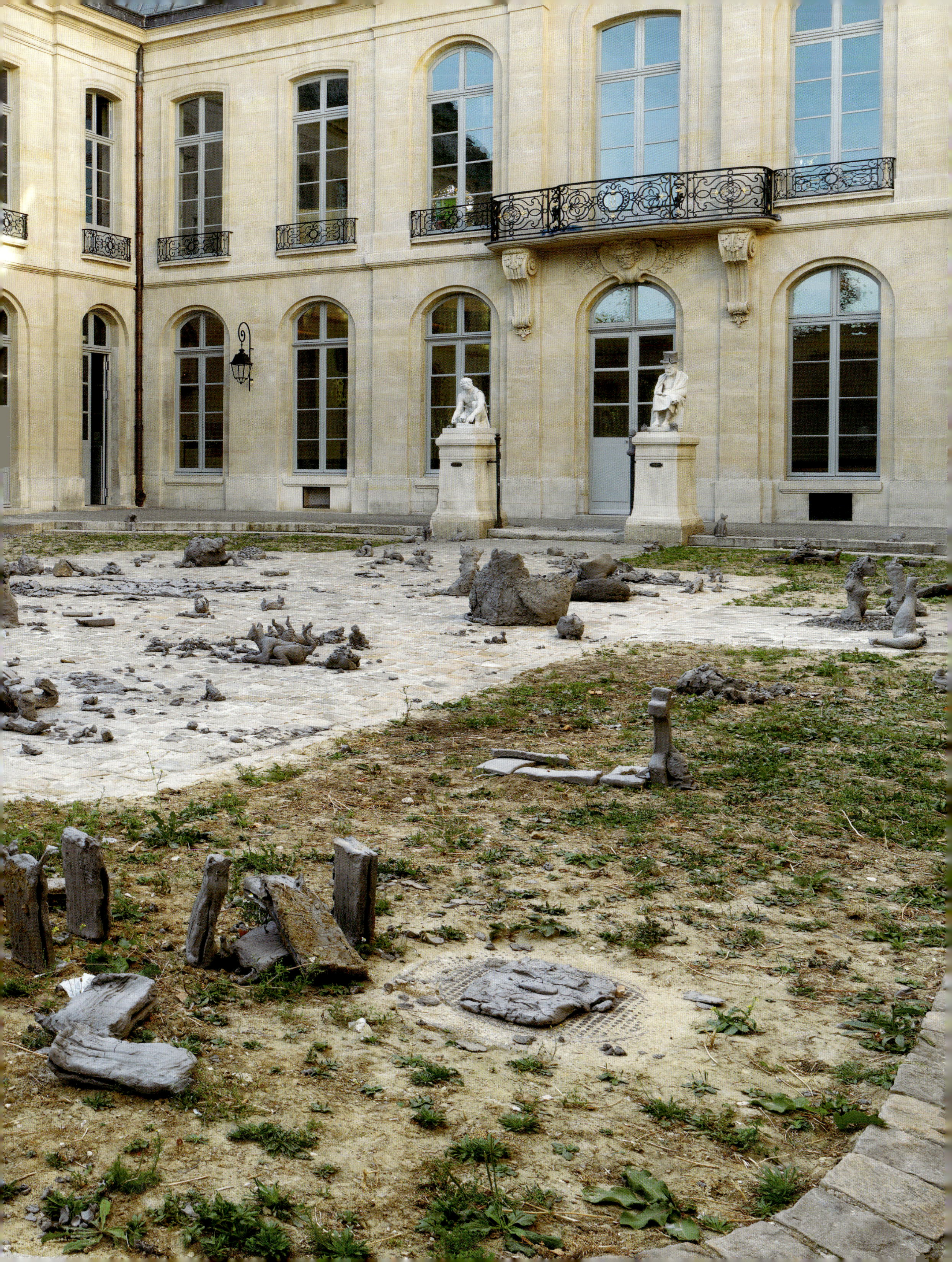

Previous spread and following pages:
Installation view, Cour Chimay, École Nationale Supérieure des Beaux-arts, as part of "Festival d'Automne à Paris," 2012
Untitled, 2011–ongoing
With the assistance of Florence Aletru, Bianca Argimon, Aline Aune, Isabelle Avezou, Nour Awada, Cécile Bayle-Barreyre, Nina Bernagozzi, Bénédicte Bouisson, Karine Boulila, Zeana Bravo-Honczar, Hippolyte Budin, Jean-Charles Bureau, Cécile Chaput, Raphaelle Chevriere, Sarah Clement-Colas, Caroline Corbasson, Marie Darras, Irène De Moucheron, Claudi Desserey, Dominique Dussidour, Thibault Émile, Aline Esquembre, Agathe Eve, Valentin Faline, Hélène Feudiger, Mélanie Feuvrier, Anne Gavarret, Marisa Gauthier-Chery, Margot Gesp, Julia Gousset, Leïla Guinnefollau, Sébastien Hamidèche, Charles Hascouet, Pierre Lafrance, Suzanne Larrieu, Eglantine Laval, Pauline Lavogez, Romain Le Cornu, Eloise Le Gallo, Anne-Catherine Le Layo, Lise Legueltel, Yoann Lelong, Astrid Lutz, Caroline Mailly, Marie-Pierre Marconnet, Valentine Mareau-Flambeaux, Audrey Martin, Federico Masotto, Joséphine Masson, Garance Matton, Pauline Merault, Margot Mercier-Catherine, Iris Merlin, Chelsea Mortenson, Sorana Munteanu, Farrah Nabbat, Samuel Nicollet, Méta Ortie, Bénedicte Penn, Agathe Pierron, Perrine Plisson, Arthur Prigent, Agnès Quenardel, Léa Riehl, Sylvie Robic, Camille Rosa, Maïa Scheidecker, Audrey Seyczani, Marion Siefert, Elsa Simon, Lise Stoufflet, Antony Thibault, Laure Tiberghien, Raphaël Tiberghien, Natacha Tosco, Katia Tosco, Marion Totier, Ruth Valentini, Olivia Jerkovic, Orestis Picard, Rose Richaud, Jeremy Varin, Clémence Vatry, Juliet Viaud, Manuel Vieillot, and Isabelle Weidert

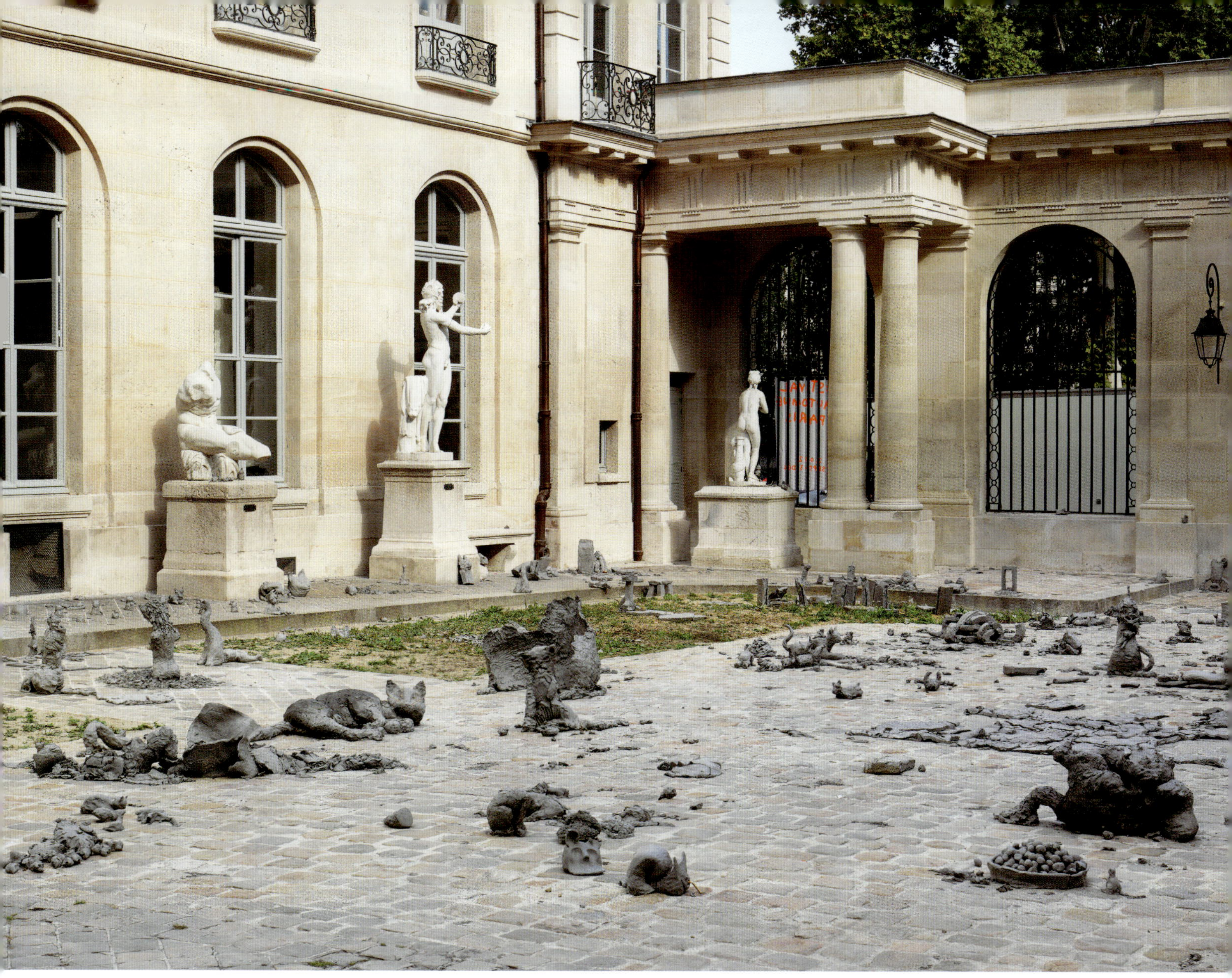

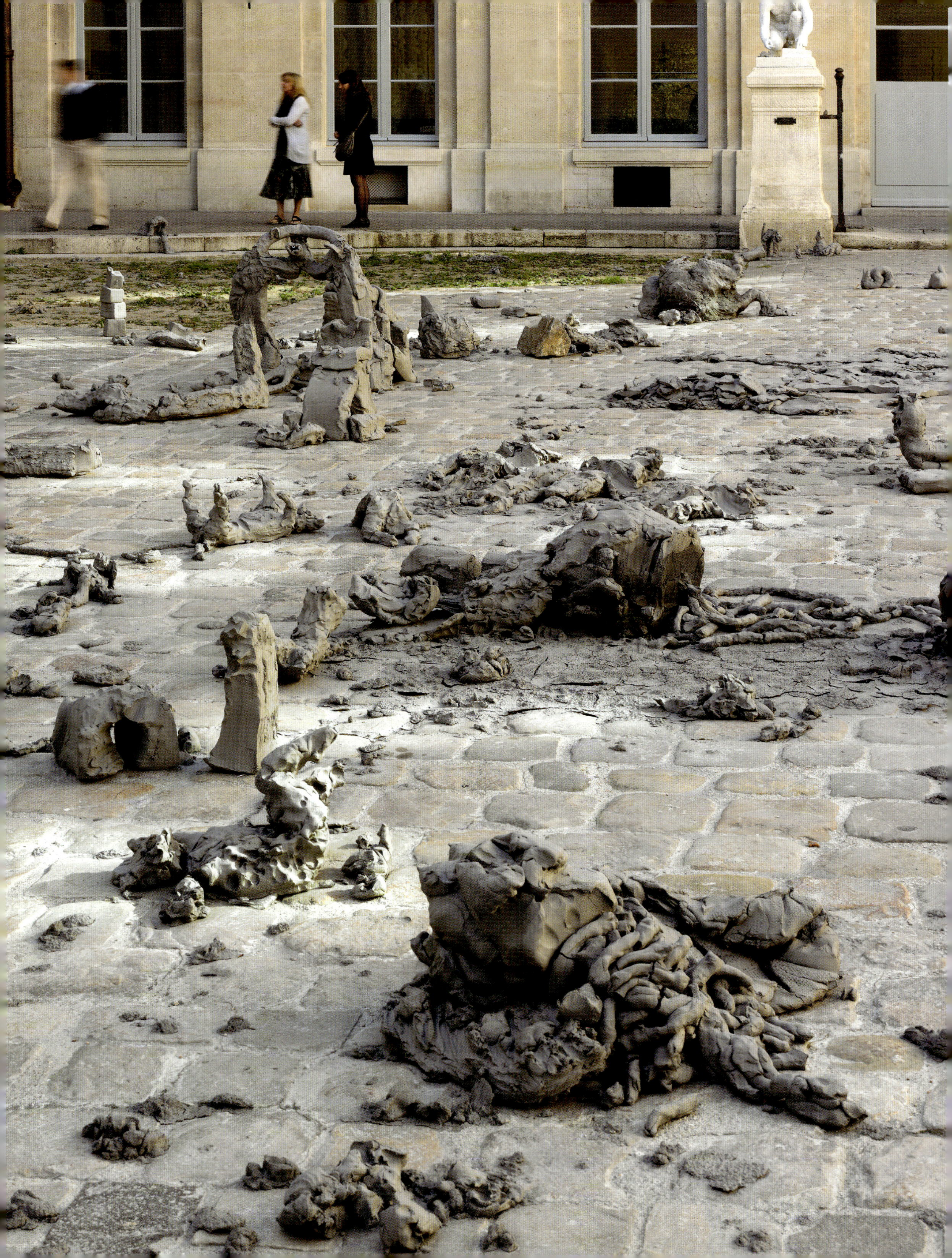

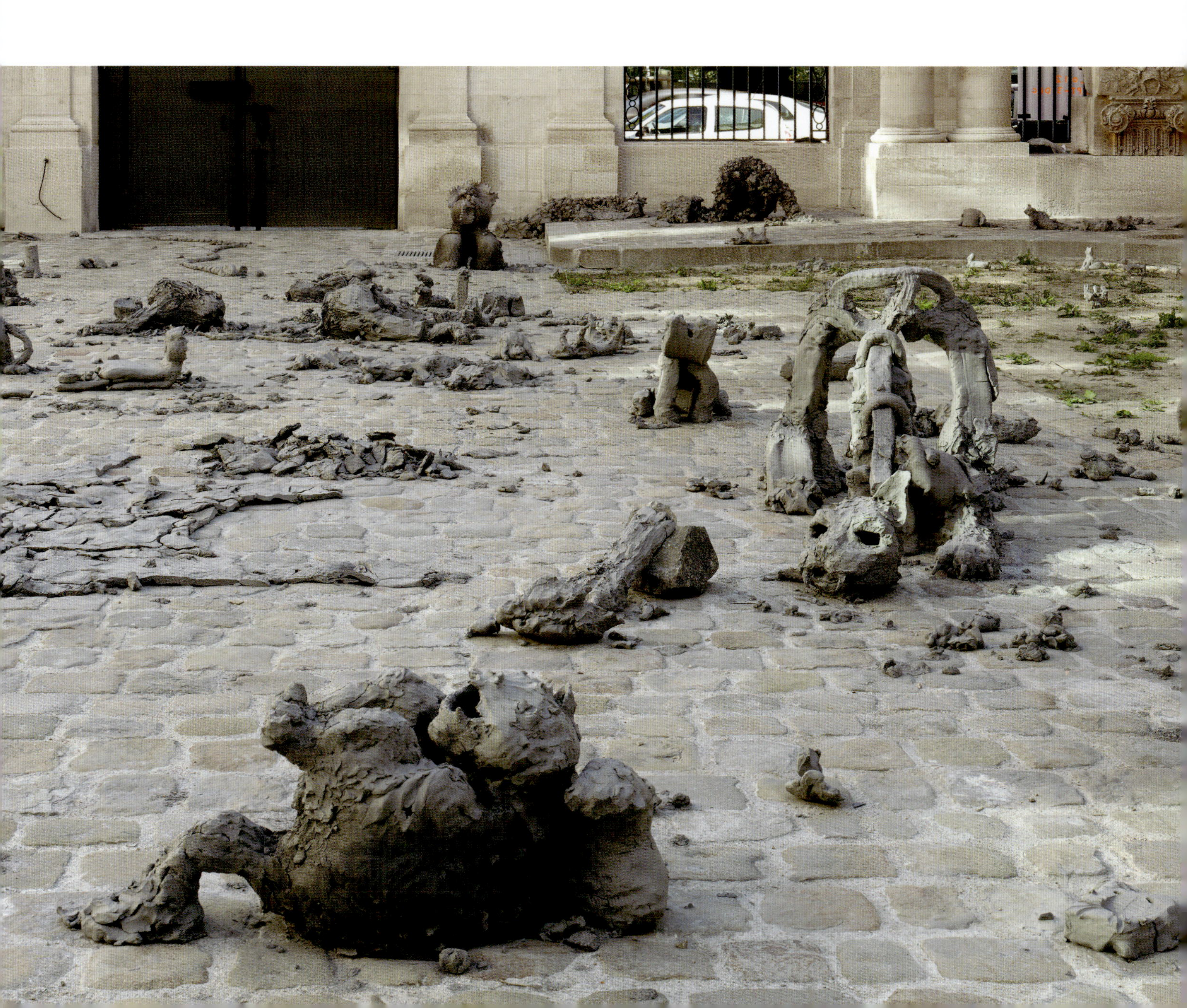

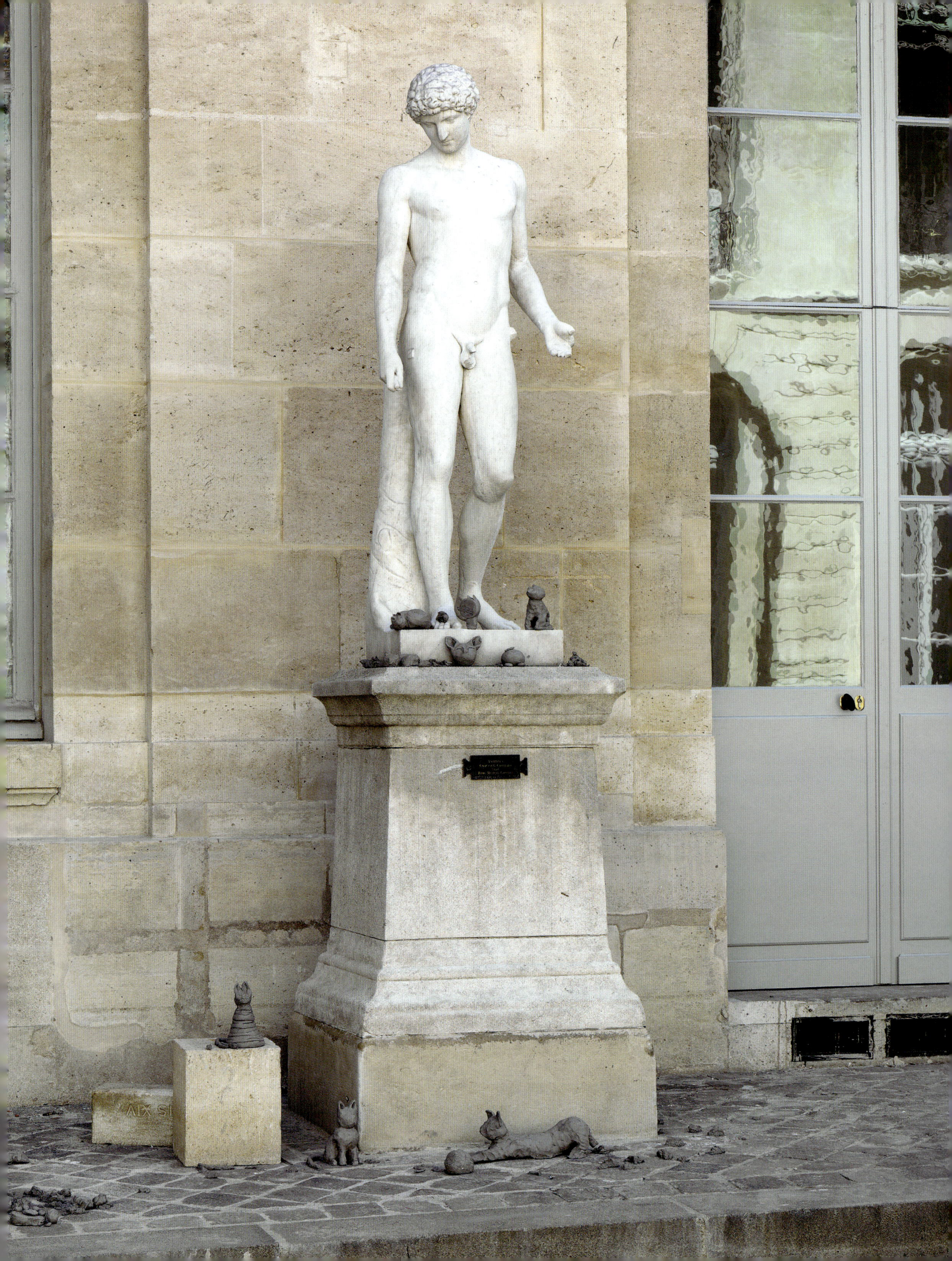

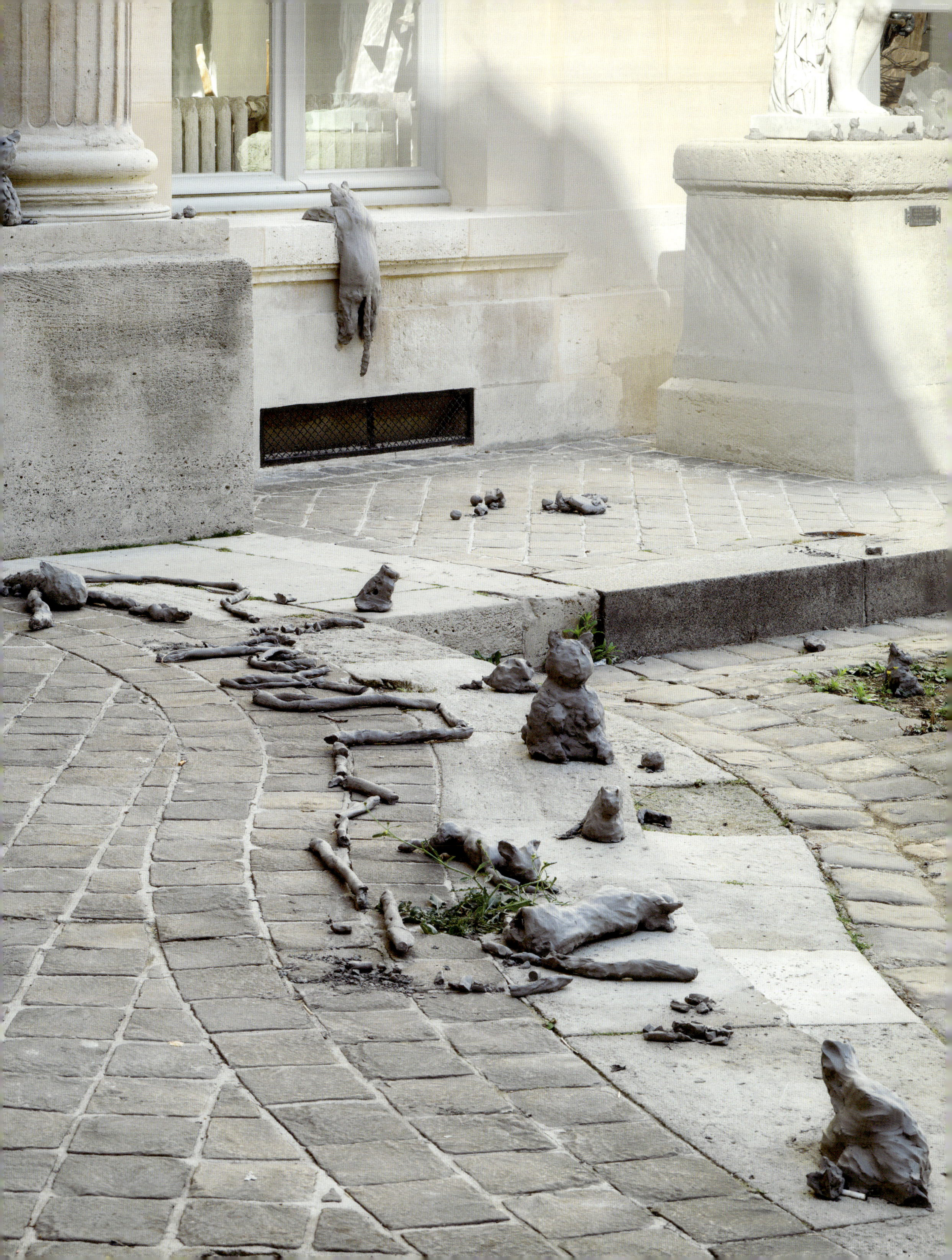

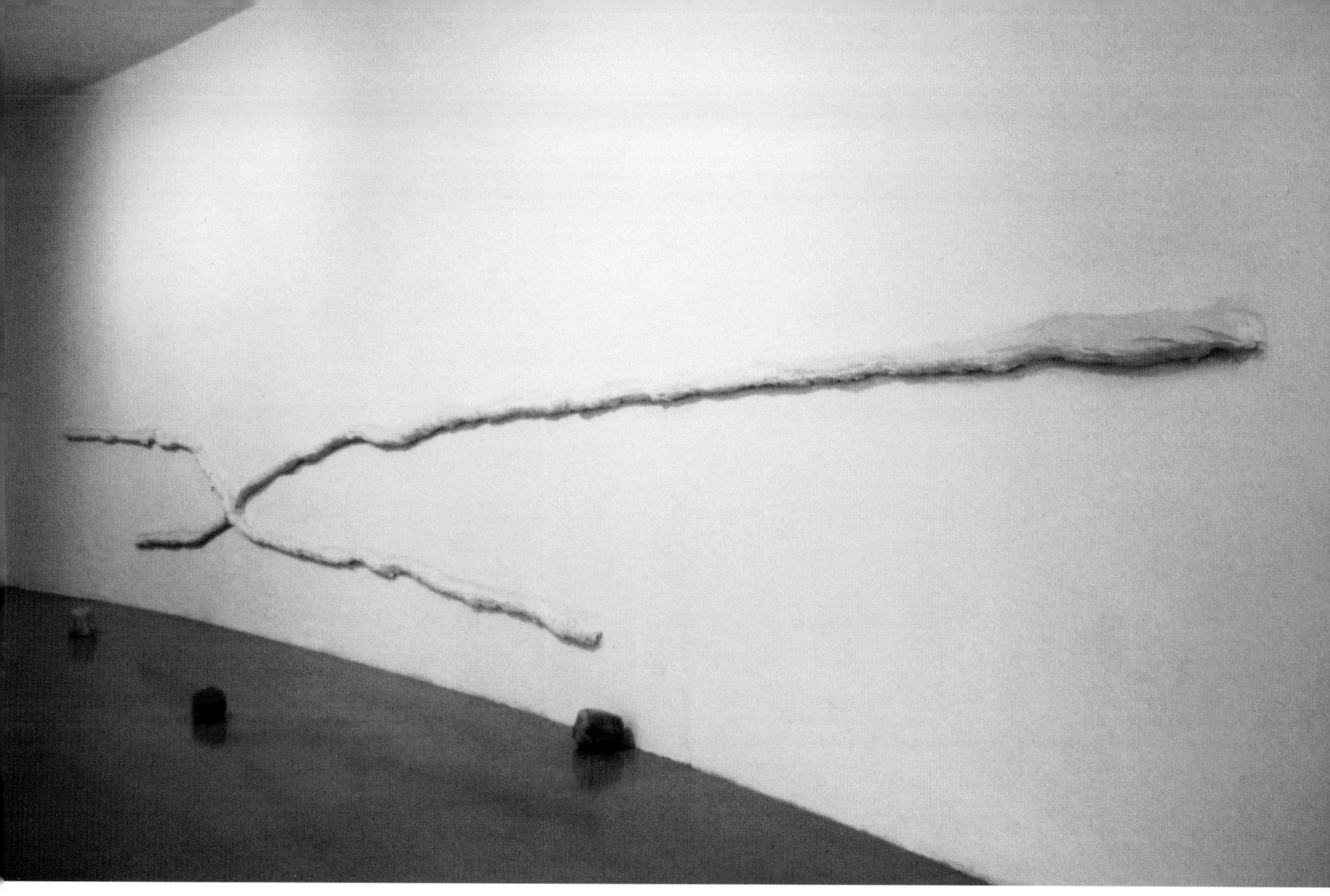

Wandnarbe, 1996
Plaster, newspaper, wire, latex paint
Dimensions variable
Installation view, "Frs Uischer," Galerie Walcheturm, Zurich: 1996
Untitled, (50 Rocks), 1996

Following pages:
Eckwurst, 1997
Wood, plaster, chicken wire, latex paint, acrylic paint, newspaper, screws
71 ¼ x 29 ⅞ 26 ⅜ inches (181 x 76 x 67 cm)

Kantenwurst, 1997
Wood, plaster, chicken wire, latex paint, acrylic paint, newspaper, screws
24 ¾ x 9 x 71 ⅝ inches (63 x 23 x 182 cm)

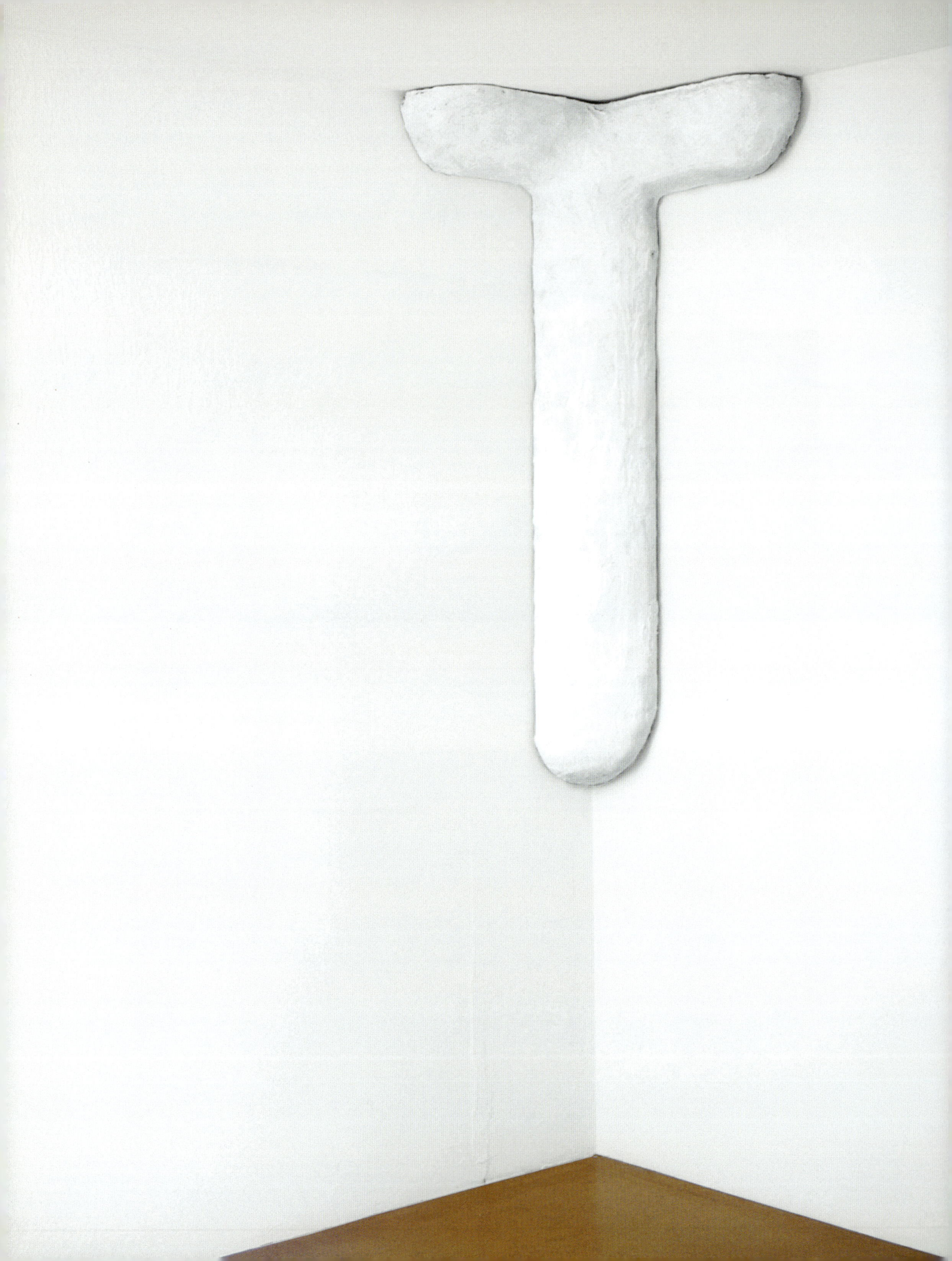

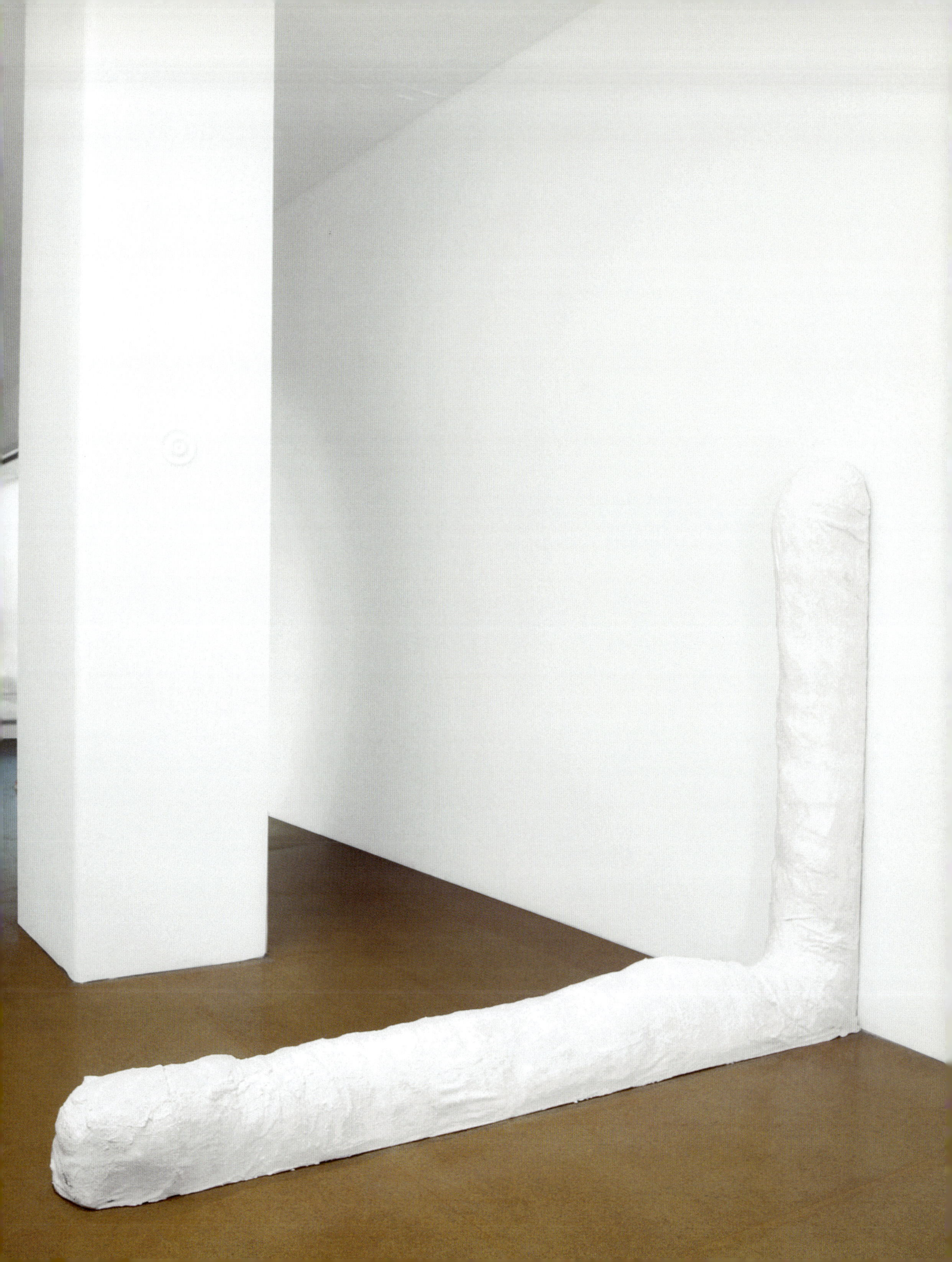

Remembering the Polyester Pirate (Instant Apathy), 2000
Tulle, rocks, lacquer, acrylic paint, chain, aluminum pipe, wood, wood glue
Curtain: 157 ½ x 157 ½ inches (400 x 400 cm)
Bench: 31 ½ x 78 ¾ x 19 ⅝ inches (80 x 200 x 50 cm)
Installation view, "Without a Fist—Like a Bird," Institute of Contemporary Arts, London, 2000
Poem-Donkey (Unfiltered Autumn 99 Poem), 2000

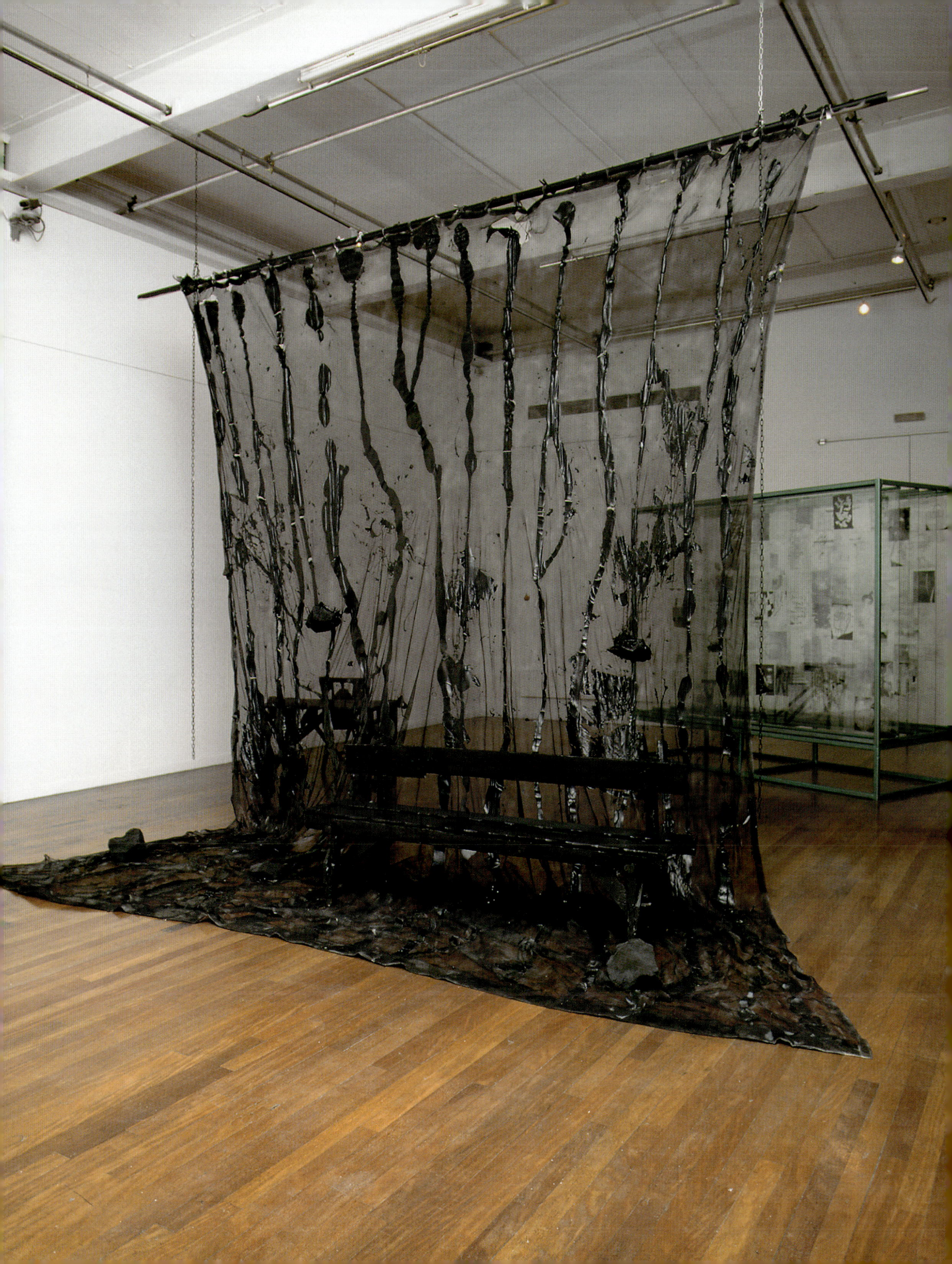

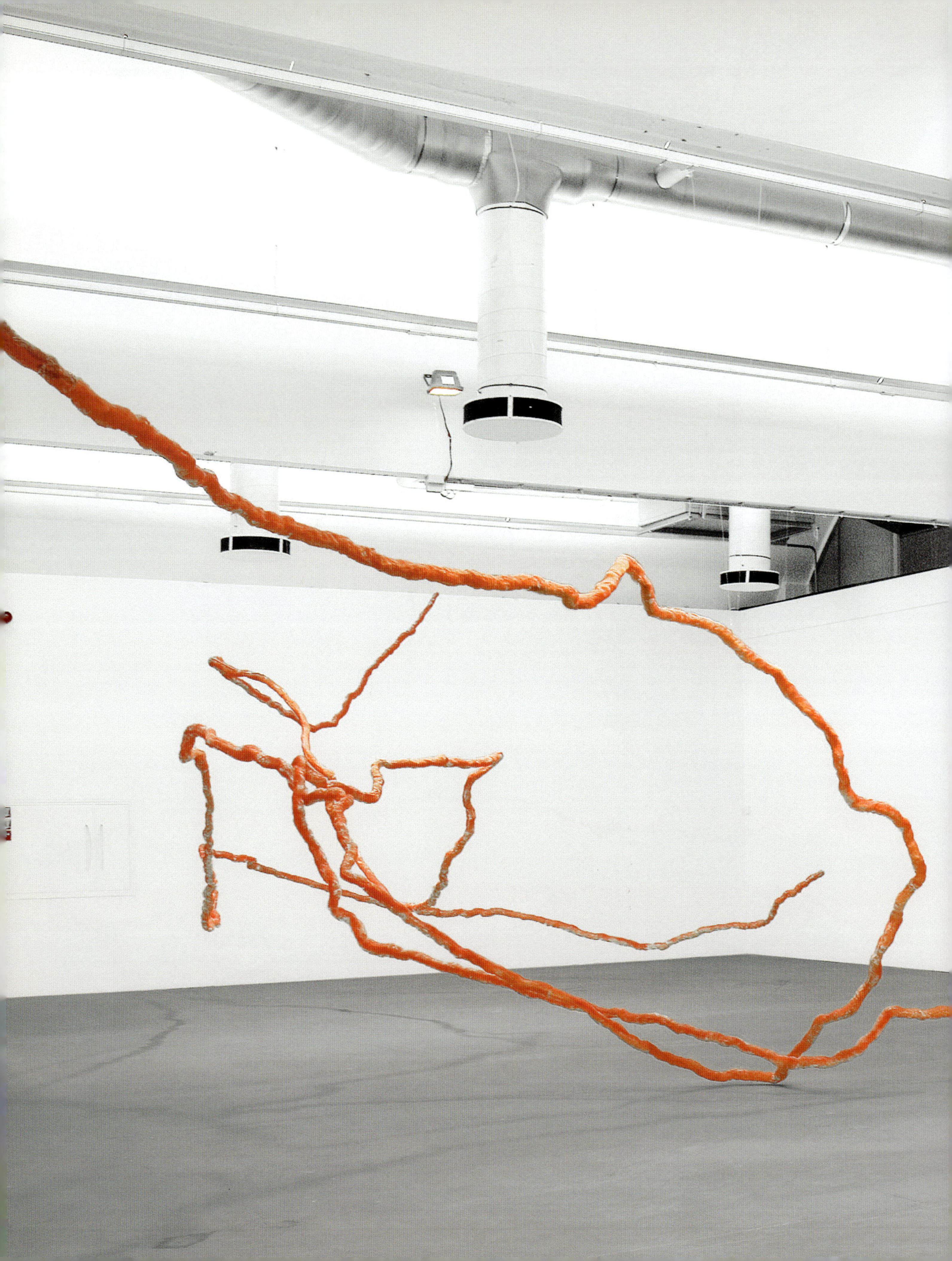

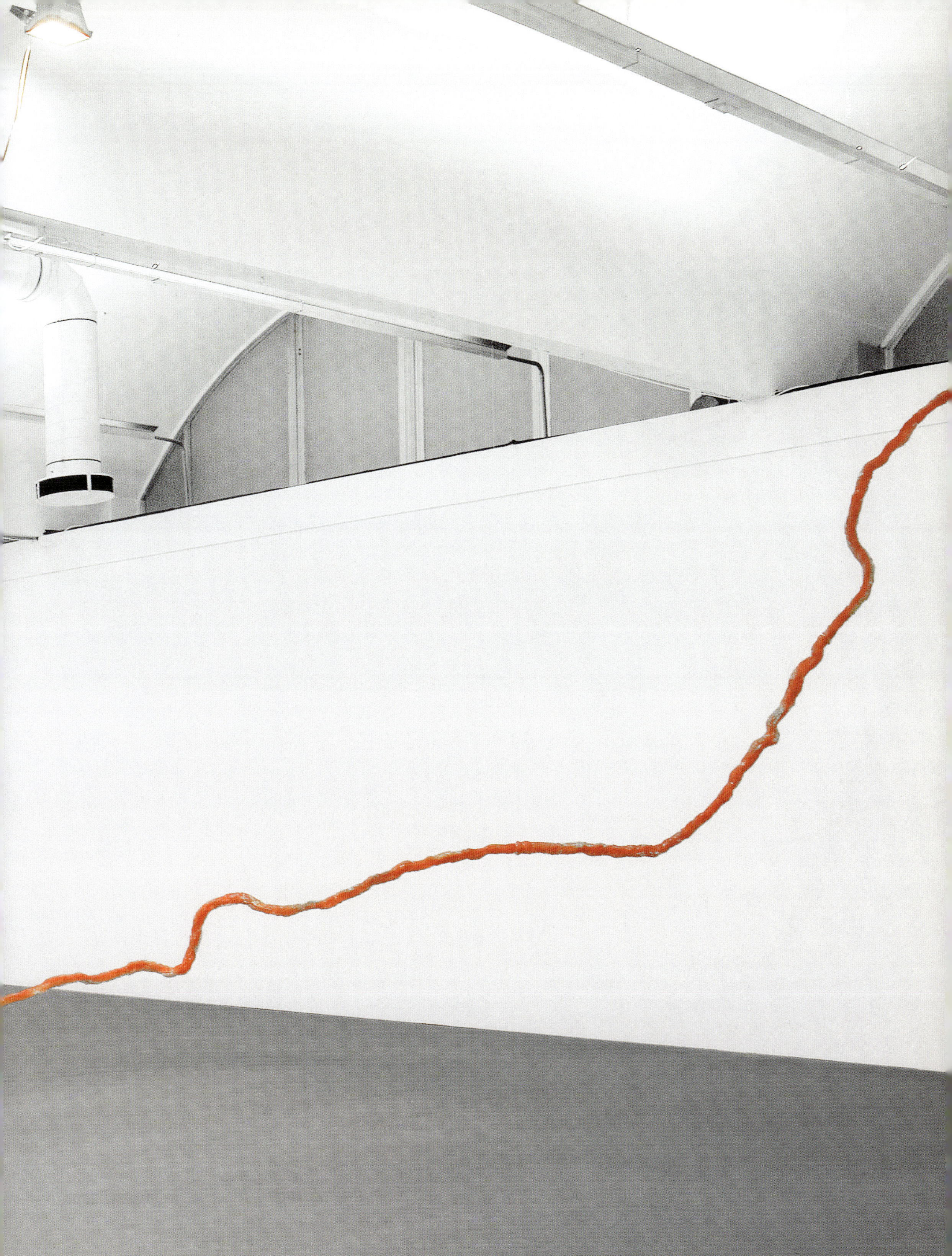

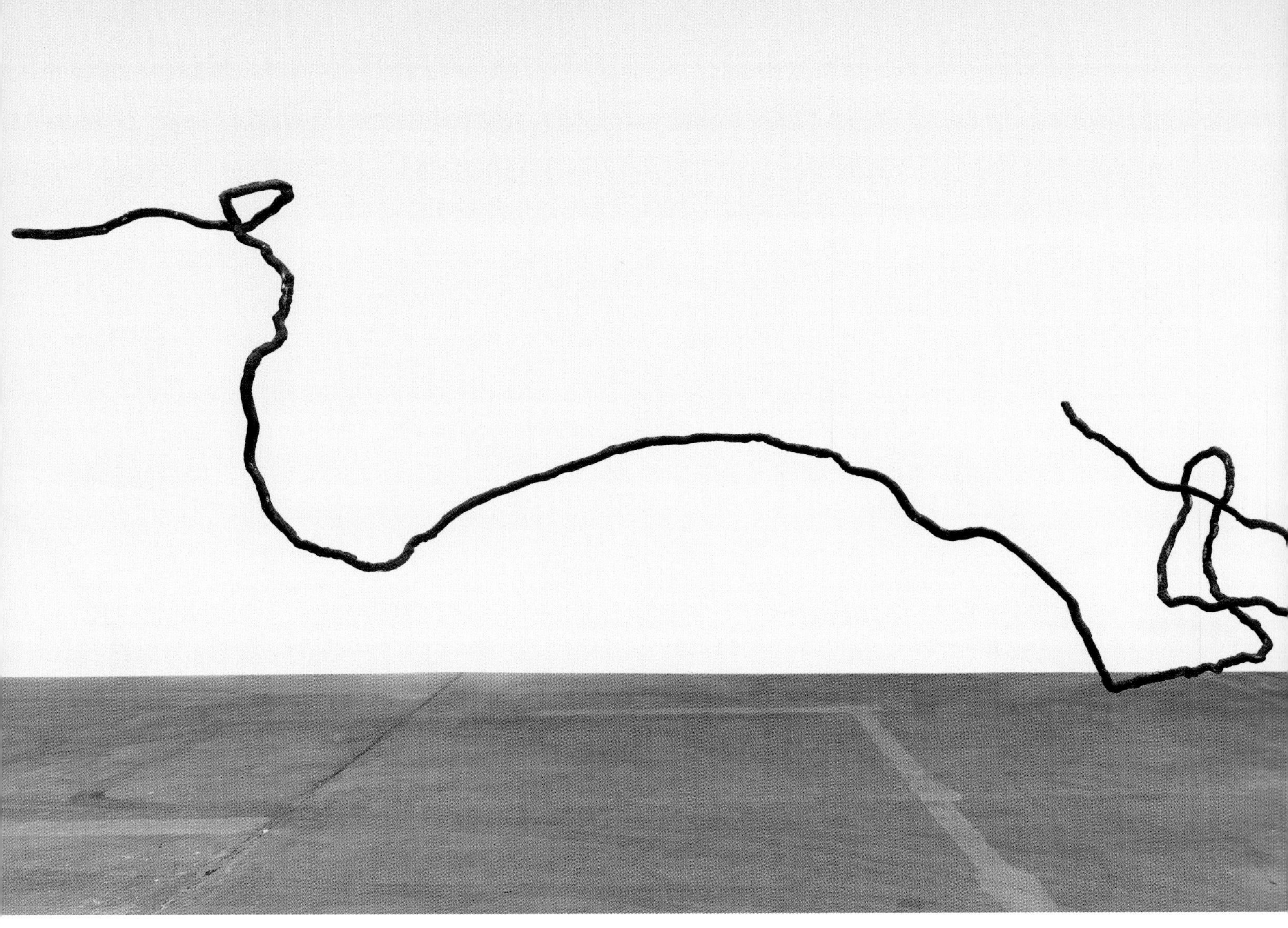

Cioran Handrail, 2006
Epoxy resin, pigment, enamel paint, wire, aluminum
Approximately 138 x 339 x 49 inches (350 x 860 x 125 cm)

Opposite page:
abyss / debauched oratorio / roadshow / abyss, 2007
Epoxy resin, pigment, enamel paint, wire, aluminum
Approximately 164 x 429 x 313 inches (416 x 1090 x 795 cm)
Installation view, Cockatoo Island, Kaldor Art Projects and the Sydney Harbour Federation Trust, Sydney, 2007

Previous spread:
Spinoza Rhapsody, 2006
Epoxy resin, pigment, enamel paint, wire, aluminum
Approximately 134 x 356 x 535 inches (340 x 905 x 1360 cm)

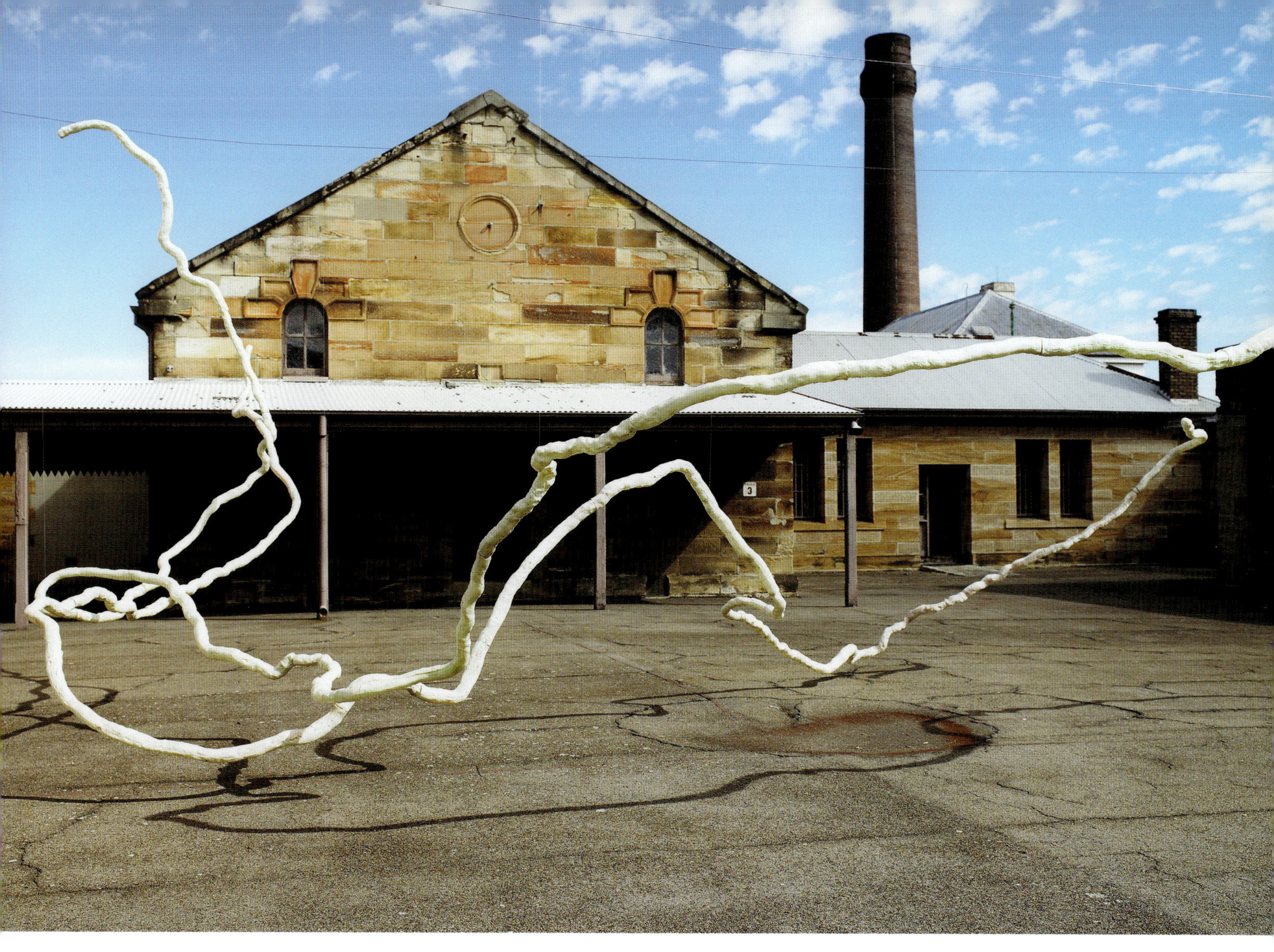

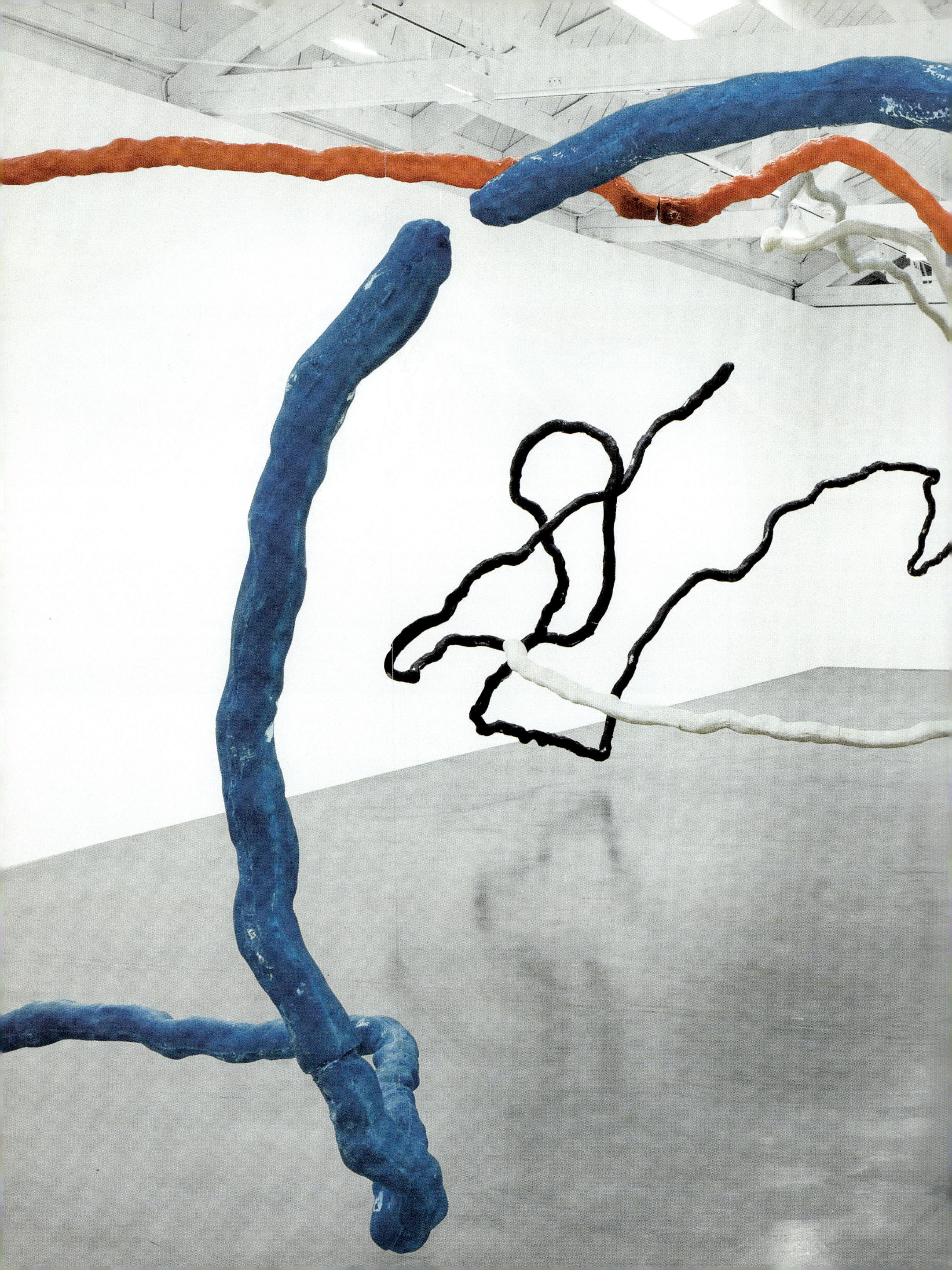

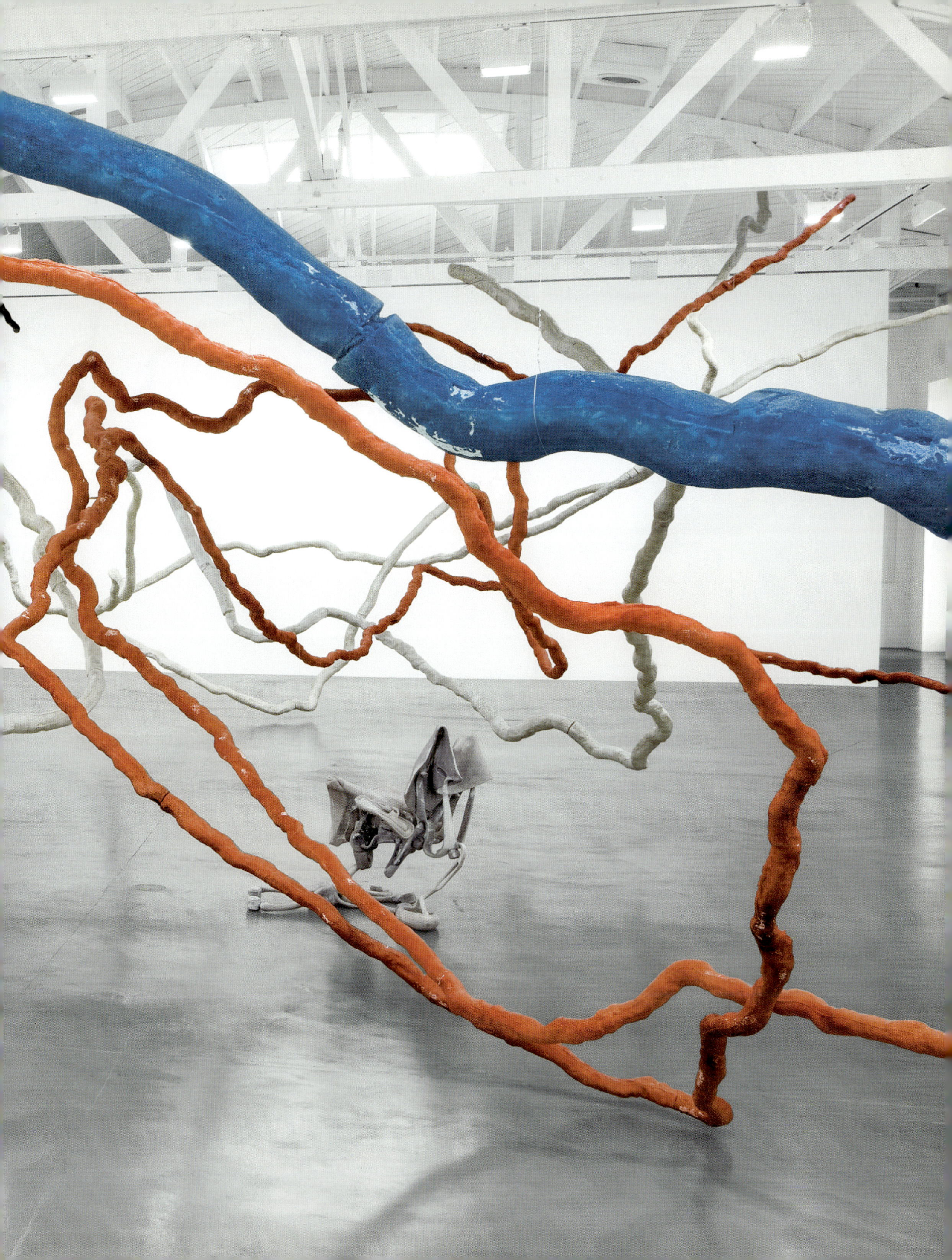

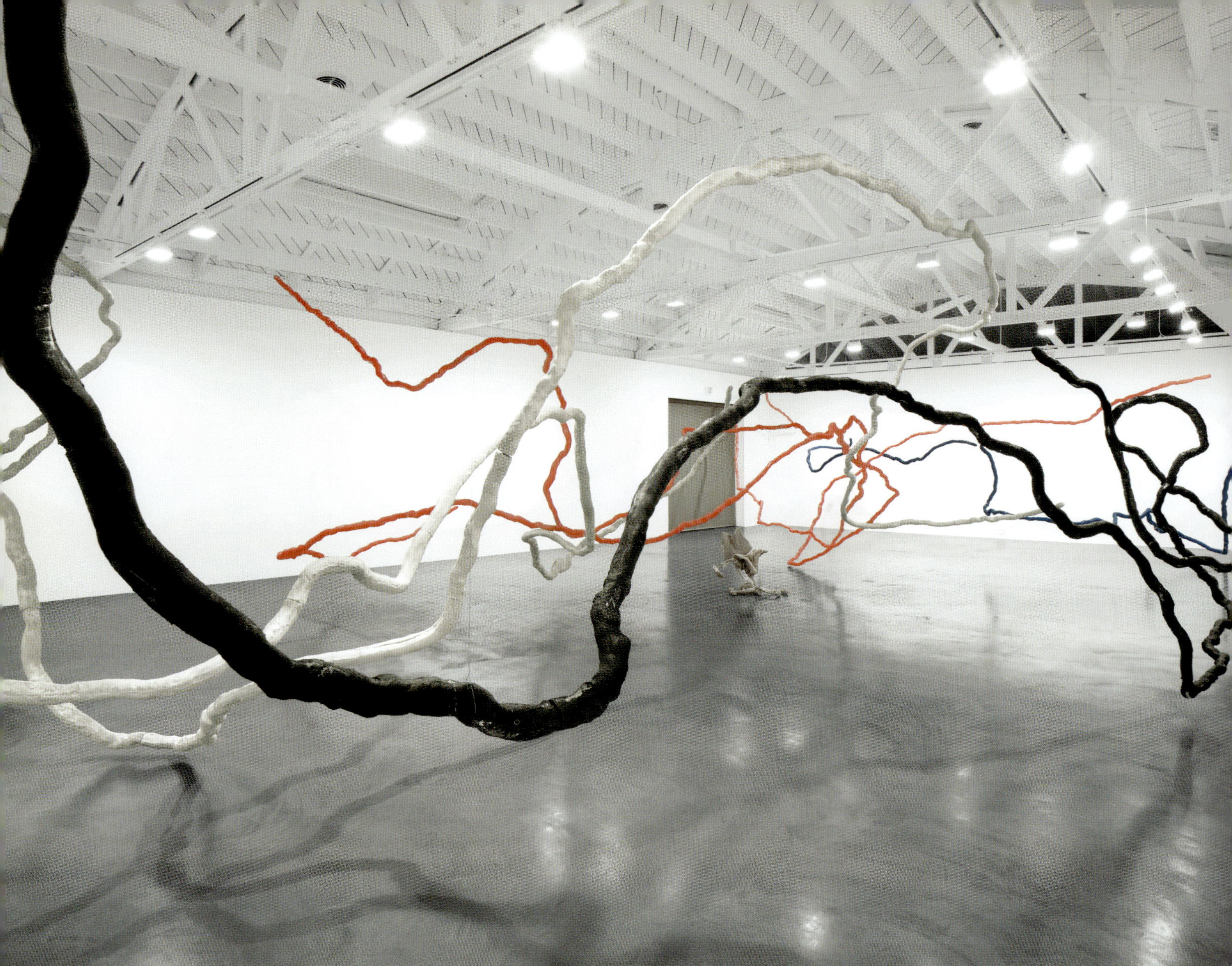

Previous spread and above:

Mackintosh Staccato, 2006

Epoxy resin, pigment, enamel paint, wire, aluminum
Approximately 98 x 356 x 98 inches (250 x 904 x 248 cm)
Previous spread and opposite page: Installation view, "Agnes Martin,"
Regen Projects, Los Angeles, 2007–2008
Spinoza Rhapsody, 2006; *Cioran Handrail*, 2006; *abyss / debauched oratorio / roadshow / abyss*, 2007; *Y-Chair*, 2007

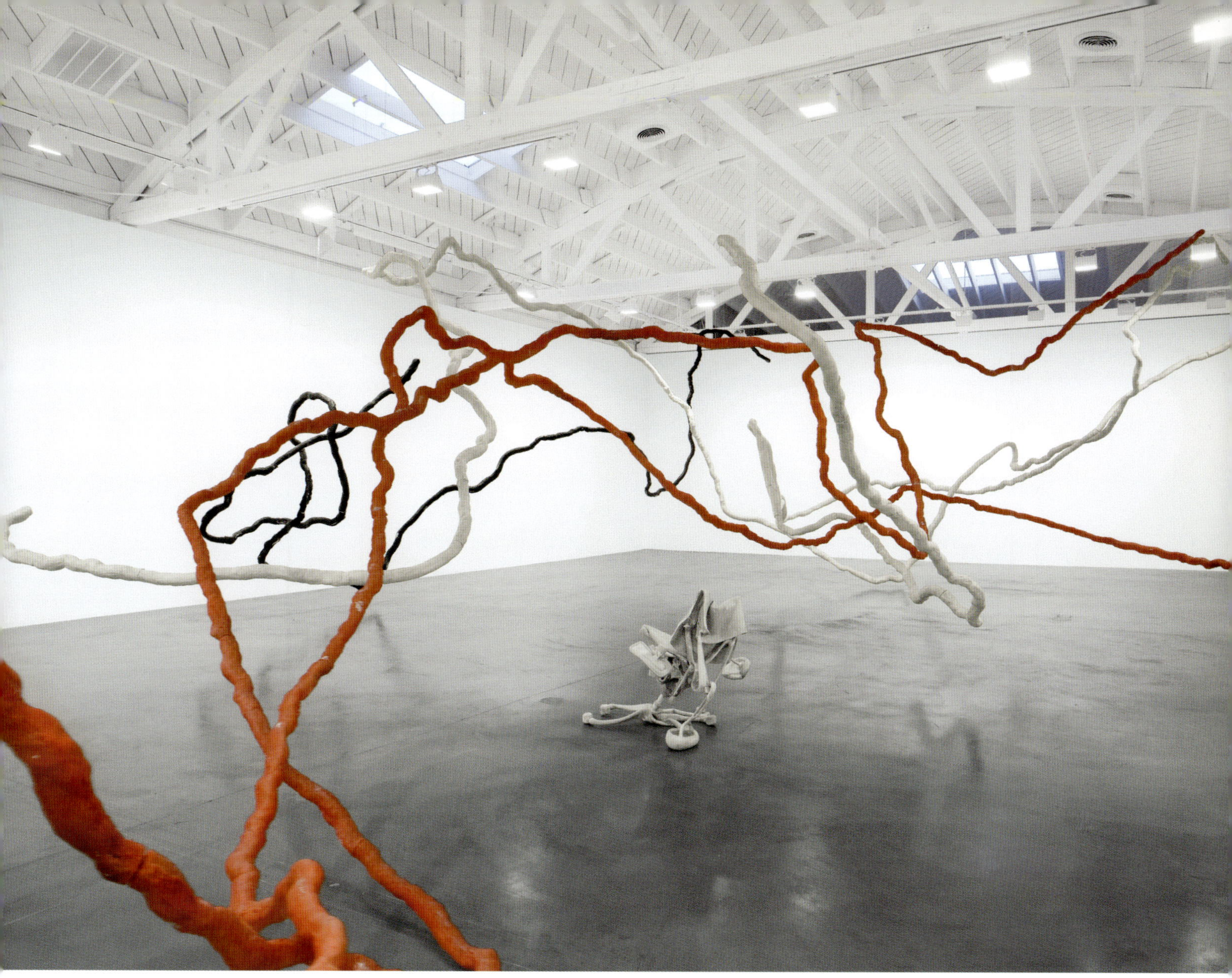

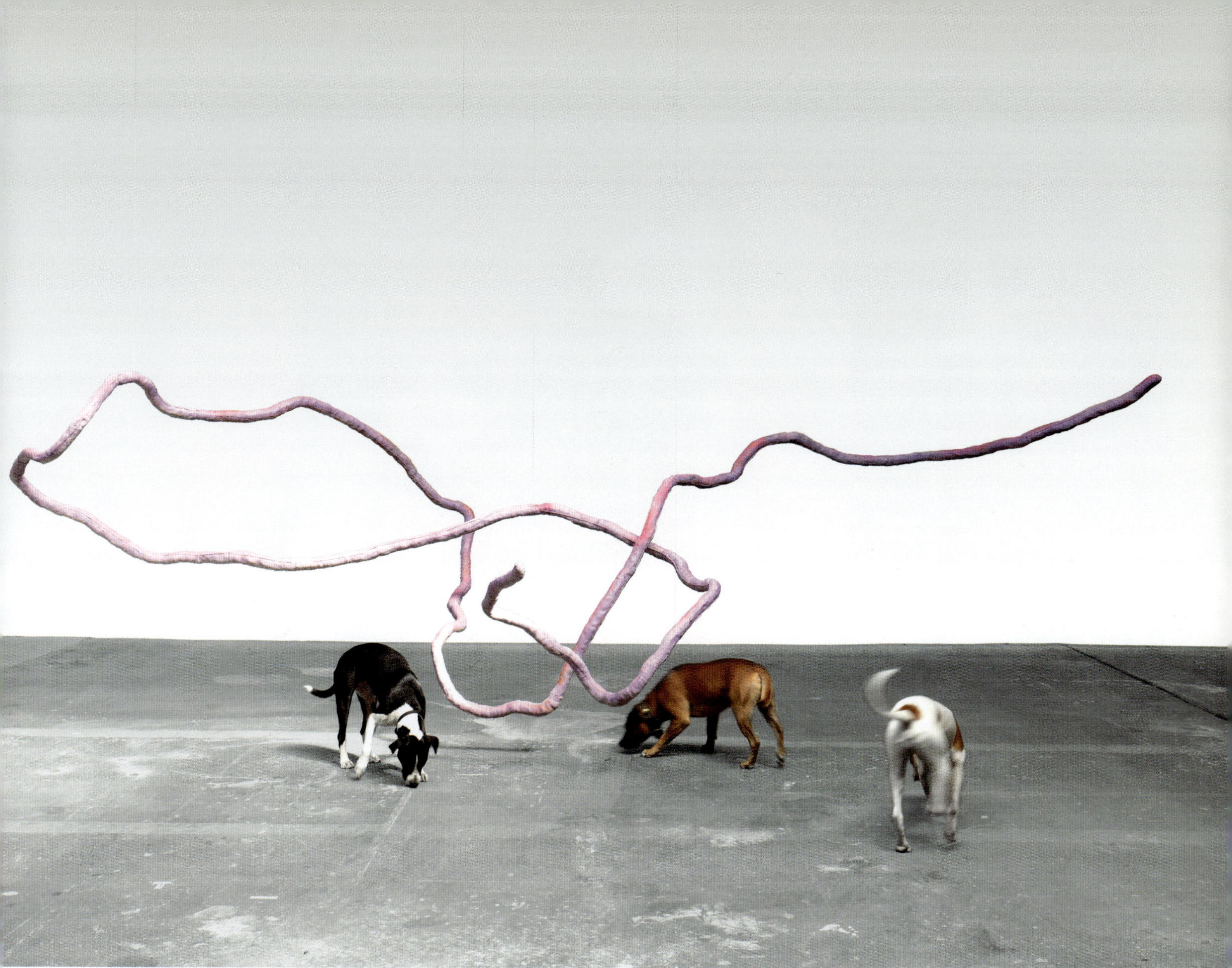

Dunno, 2012

Epoxy resin, fiberglass, pigment, acrylic paint, aluminum, screws, wire
80 x 225 ¼ x 81 ⅛ inches (203.2 x 572.1 x 206.1 cm)

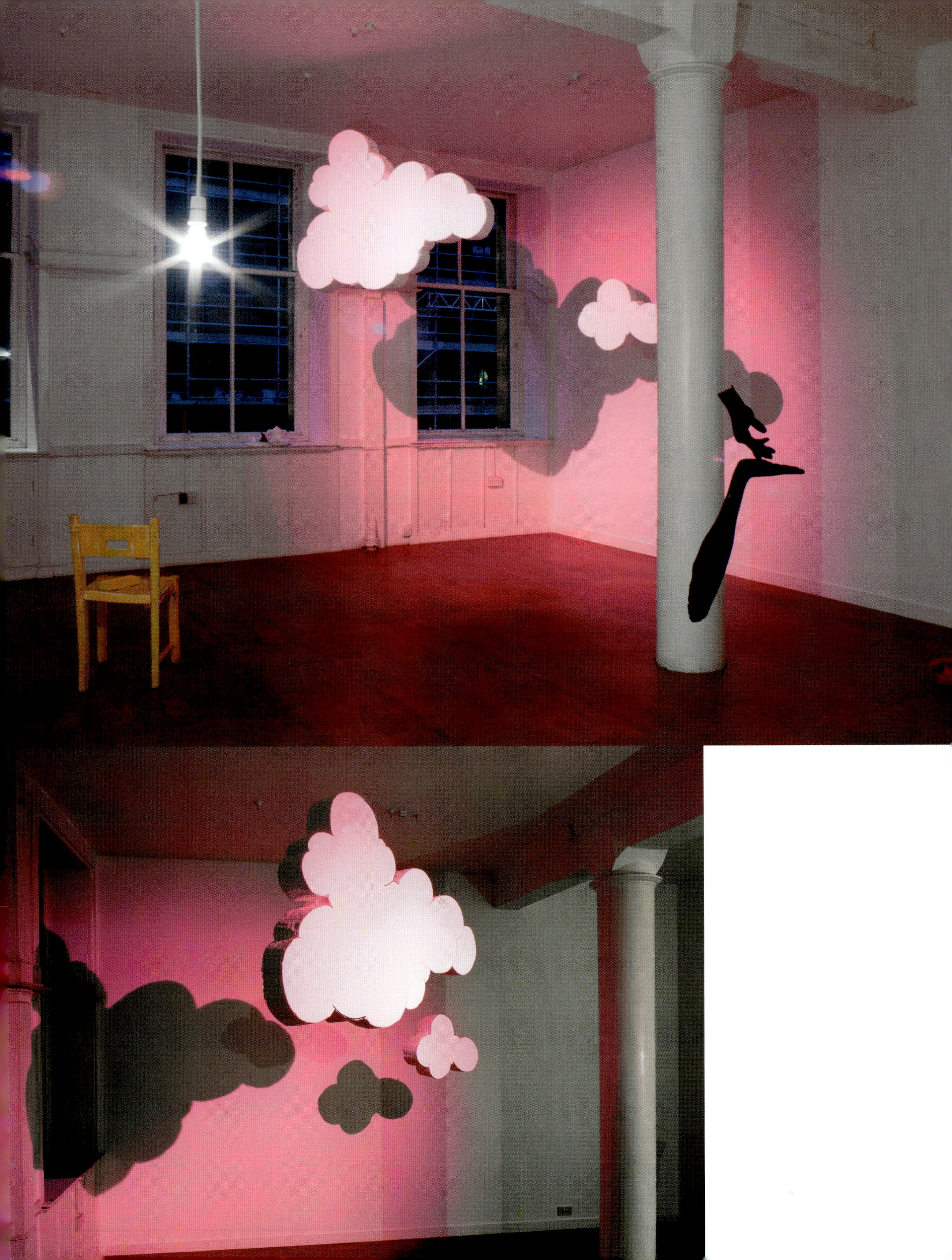

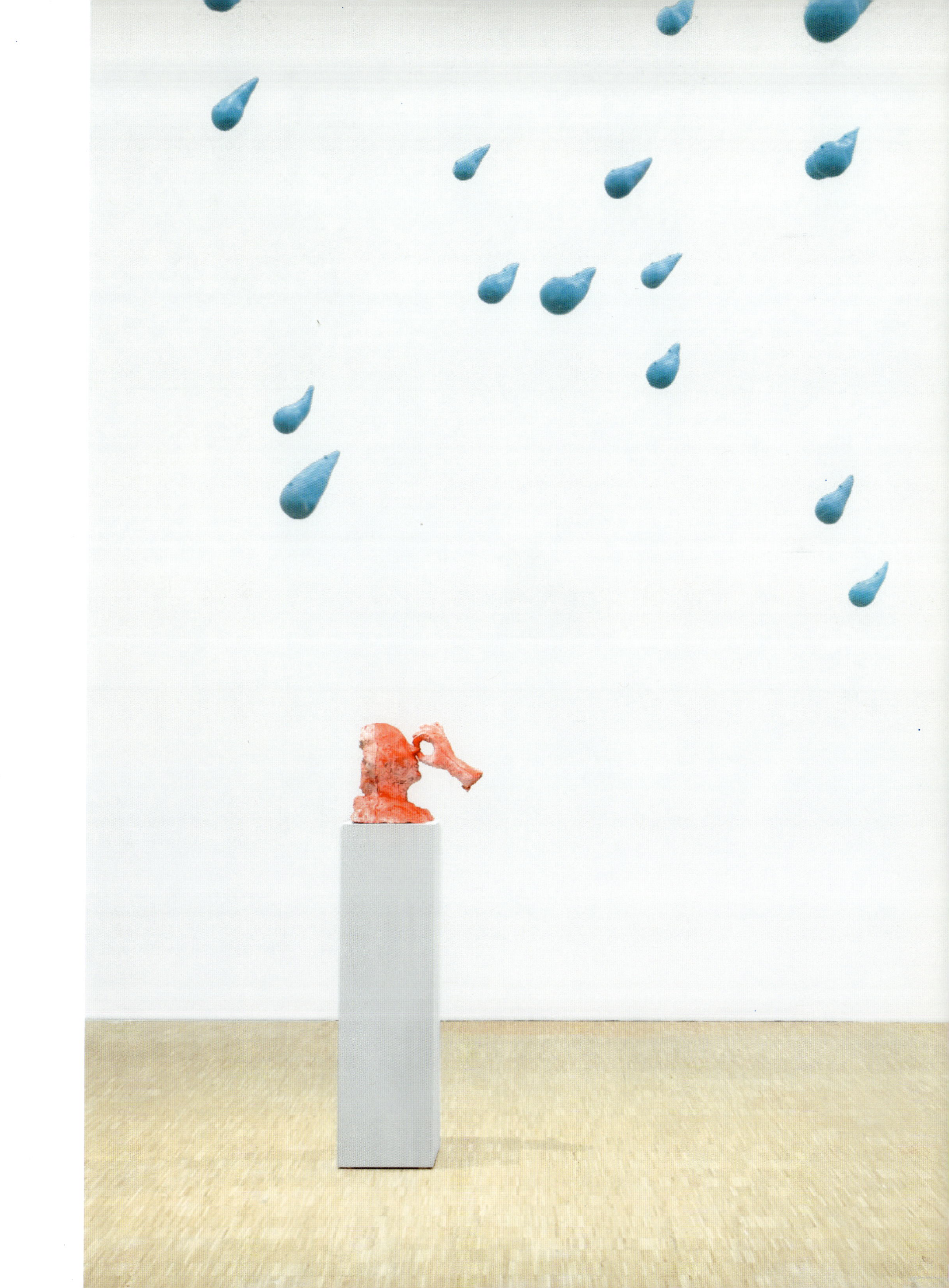

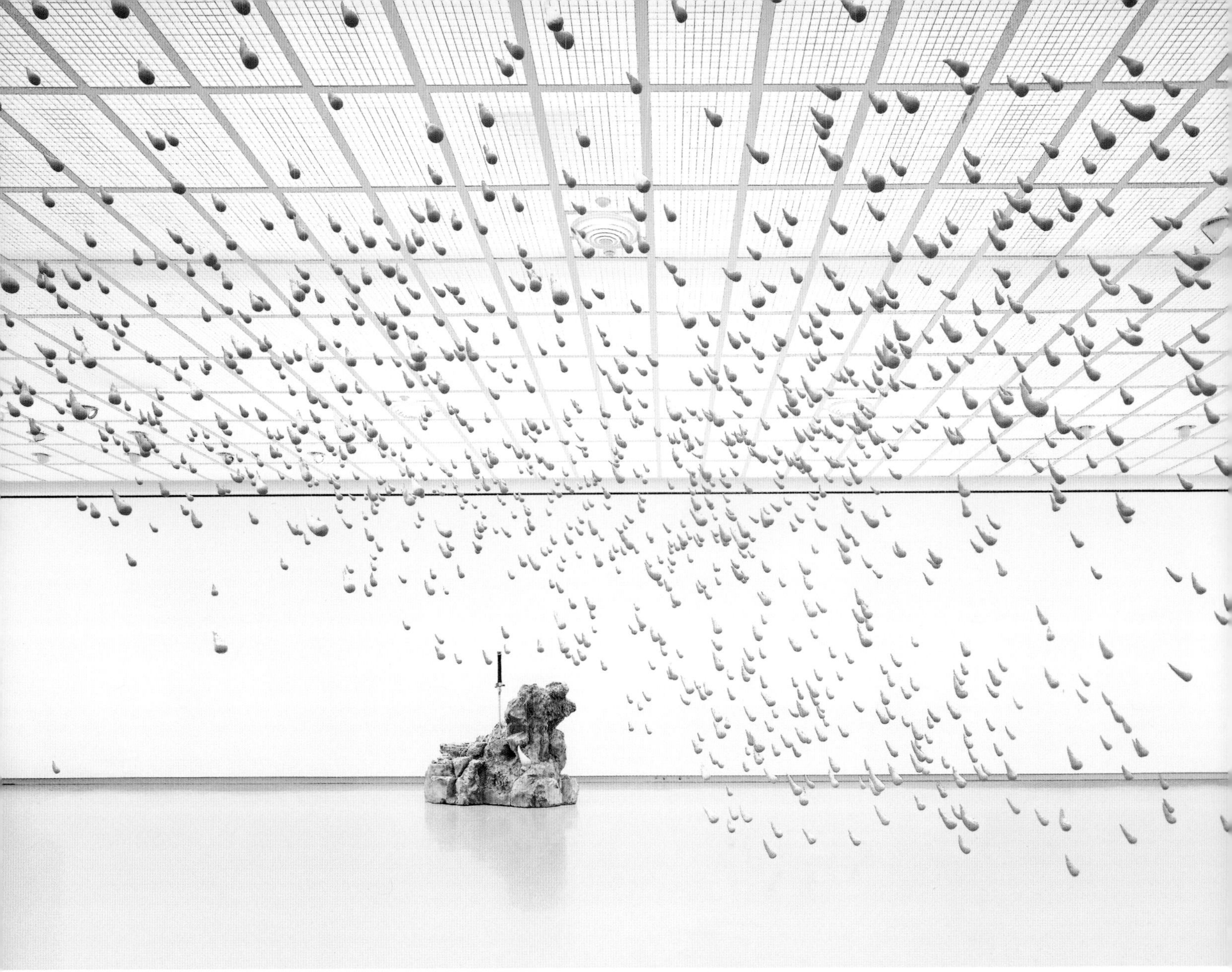

Opposite and previous page

Horses Dream of Horses, 200

Plaster, resin paint, steel, nylon filame

Dimensions variable: 1,500 raindrop

each up to 6 ¾ x 2 ¾ x 2 ¾ inches (17 x 7 x 7 cm

Page 287: Installation view, "Not My House, Not My Fire

Espace 315, Centre Georges Pompidou, Paris, 200

Kir Royal, 200

Above: Installation view, "Kir Royal," Kunsthaus Zürich, 200

Untitled, 200

Page 28

Clouds, 200

Polystyrene, wire, theater spotlight with pink g

Cloud 1: 39 ⅜ x 59 x 6 ¼ inches (100 x 150 x 16 cm

Cloud 2: 17 ¾ x 24 ¾ x 6 ¼ inches (45 x 63 x 16 cm

Installation view, "Mystique Mistake," The Modern Institute, Glasgow, 200

Chair, 2002; *Light*, 2002; *Tea Set*, 2002; *Hands*, 2002; *Telephone*, 200

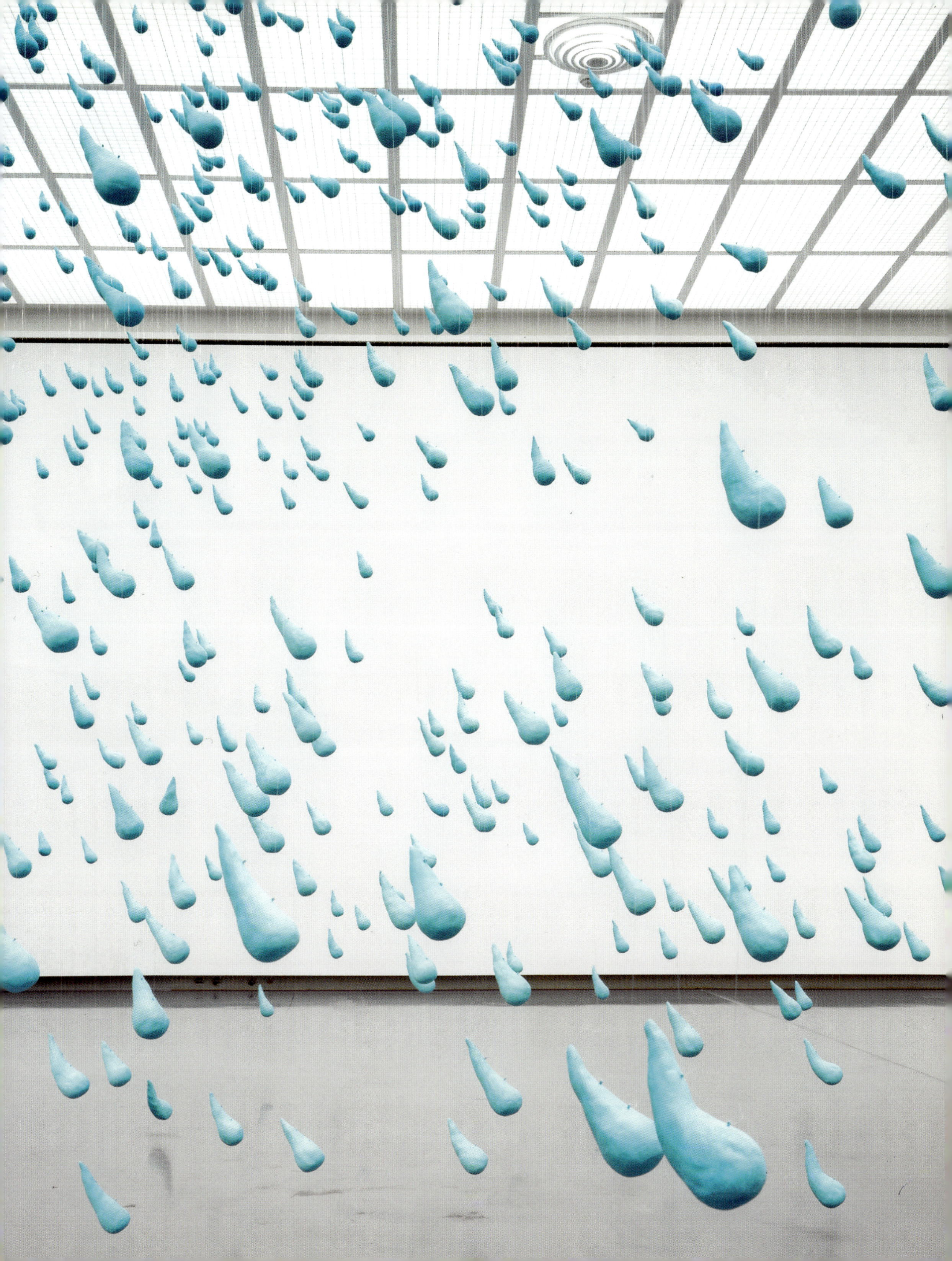

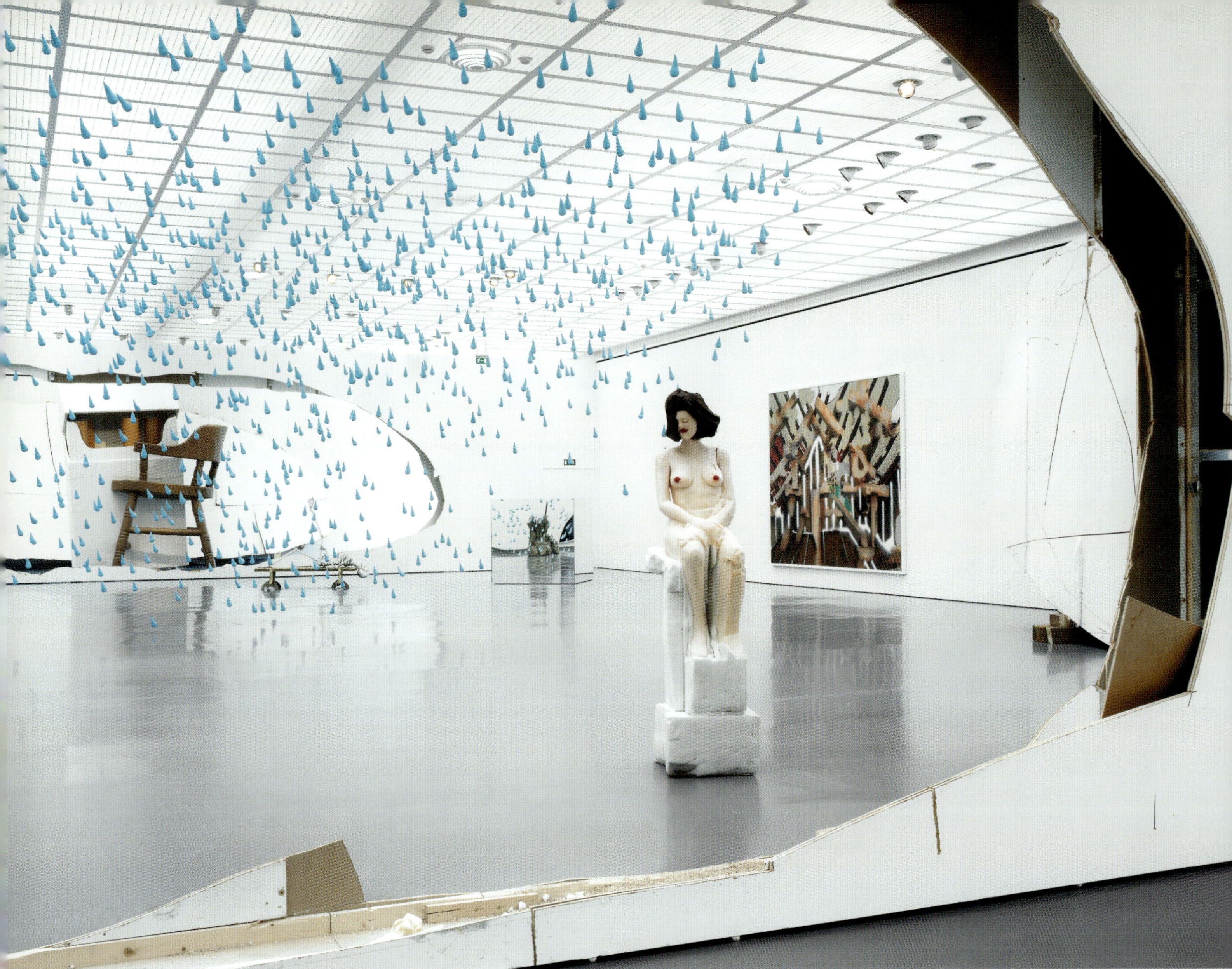

Installation view, "Kir Royal," Kunsthaus Zürich, 2004
Horses Dream of Horses, 2004; *Middleclass Heroes*, 2004; Prototype of *Bad Timing, Lamb Chop!*, 2004; *Sodbrennen*, 2000–2004; *What if the Phone Rings*, 2003; *She Called Her "Taxi,"* 2004

Following pages:

Vintage Violence, 2004–2005
Plaster, resin paint, steel, nylon filament
Dimensions variable: 1,700 raindrops,
each up to 7 ½ x 3 ½ x 3 ⅛ inches (19 x 9 x 8 cm)
Installation view, "Where Are We Going? Selections from the François Pinault Collection," Palazzo Grassi, Venice, 2006
Page 292: Mario Merz, *Accelerazione = sogno, tubi di Fibonacci al neon e motocicletta fantasma*, 1972–1986

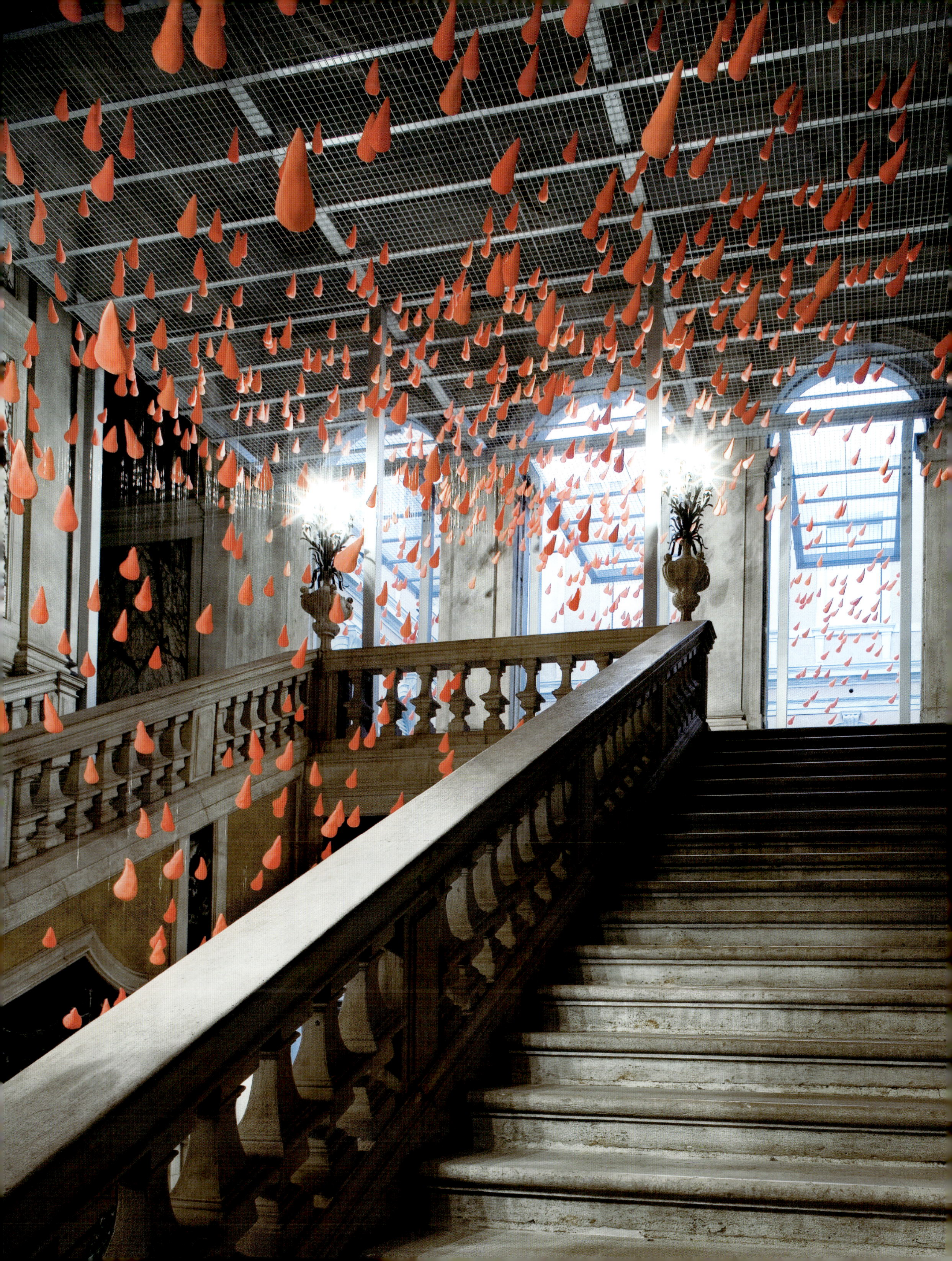

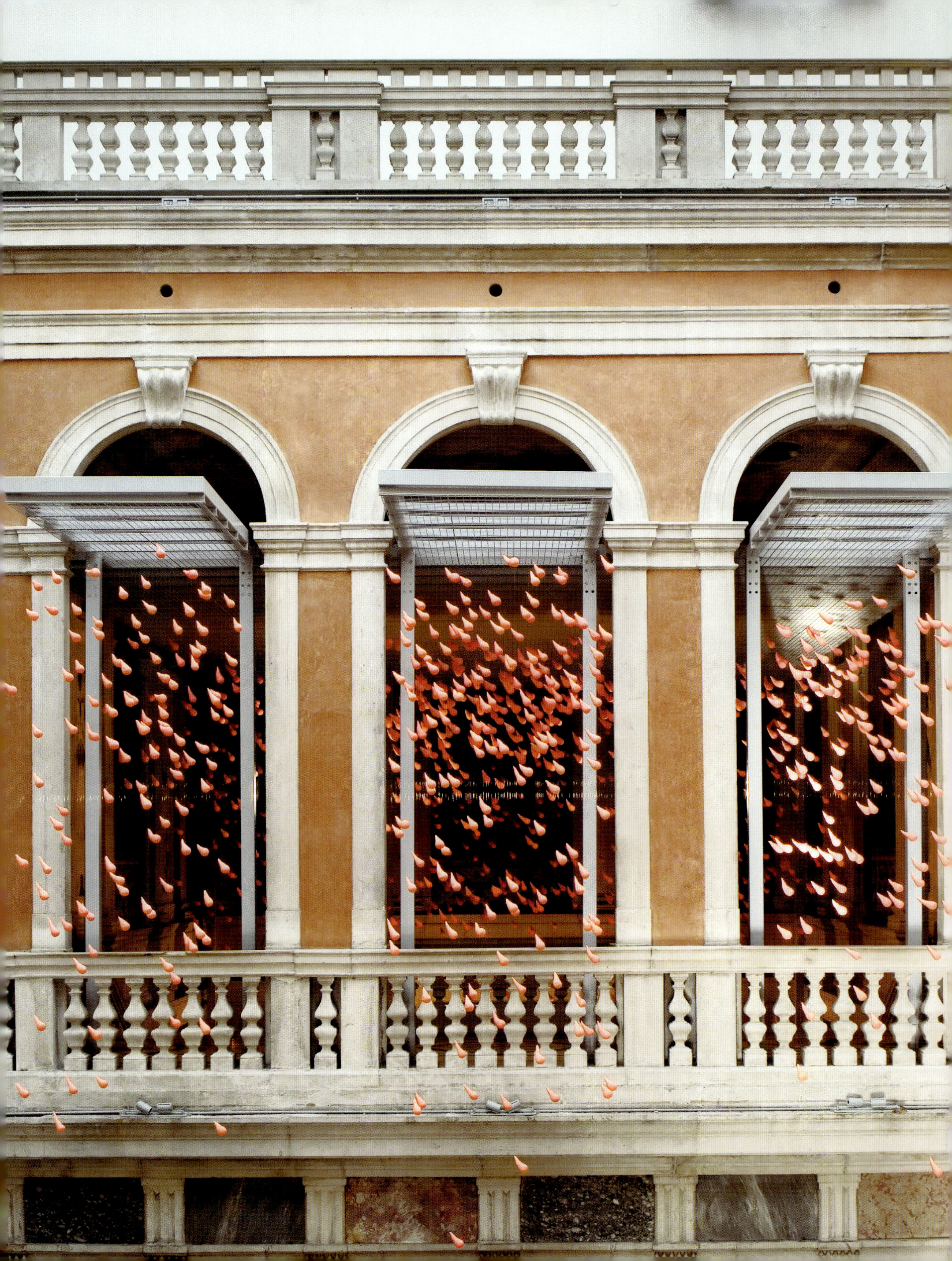

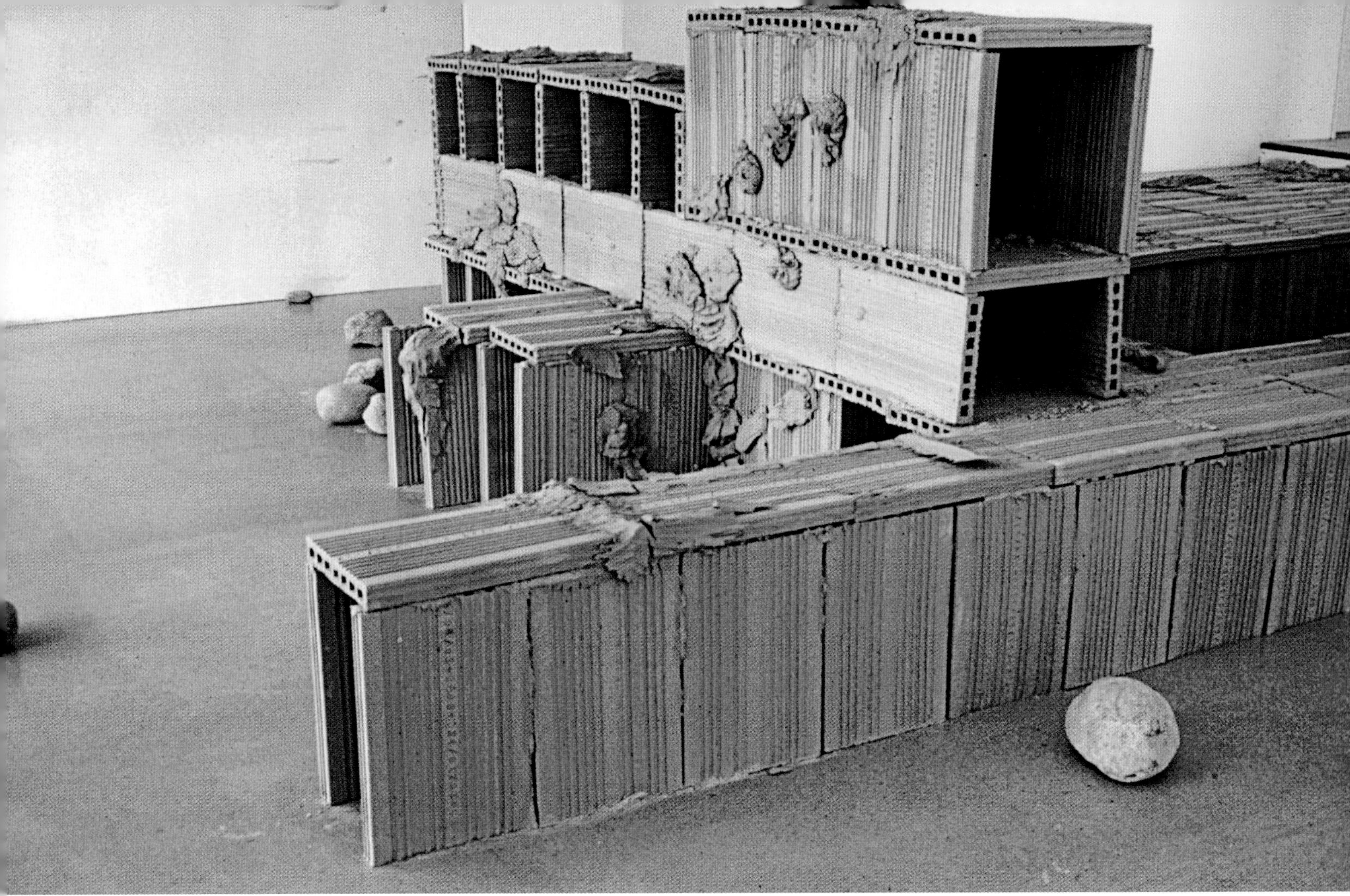

Skelett, 1996
Bricks, cement, unfired clay
Dimensions variable

Untitled (50 Rocks), 1996
50 found river rocks
Dimensions variable
Installation view, "Frs Uischer," Galerie Walcheturm, Zurich, 1996

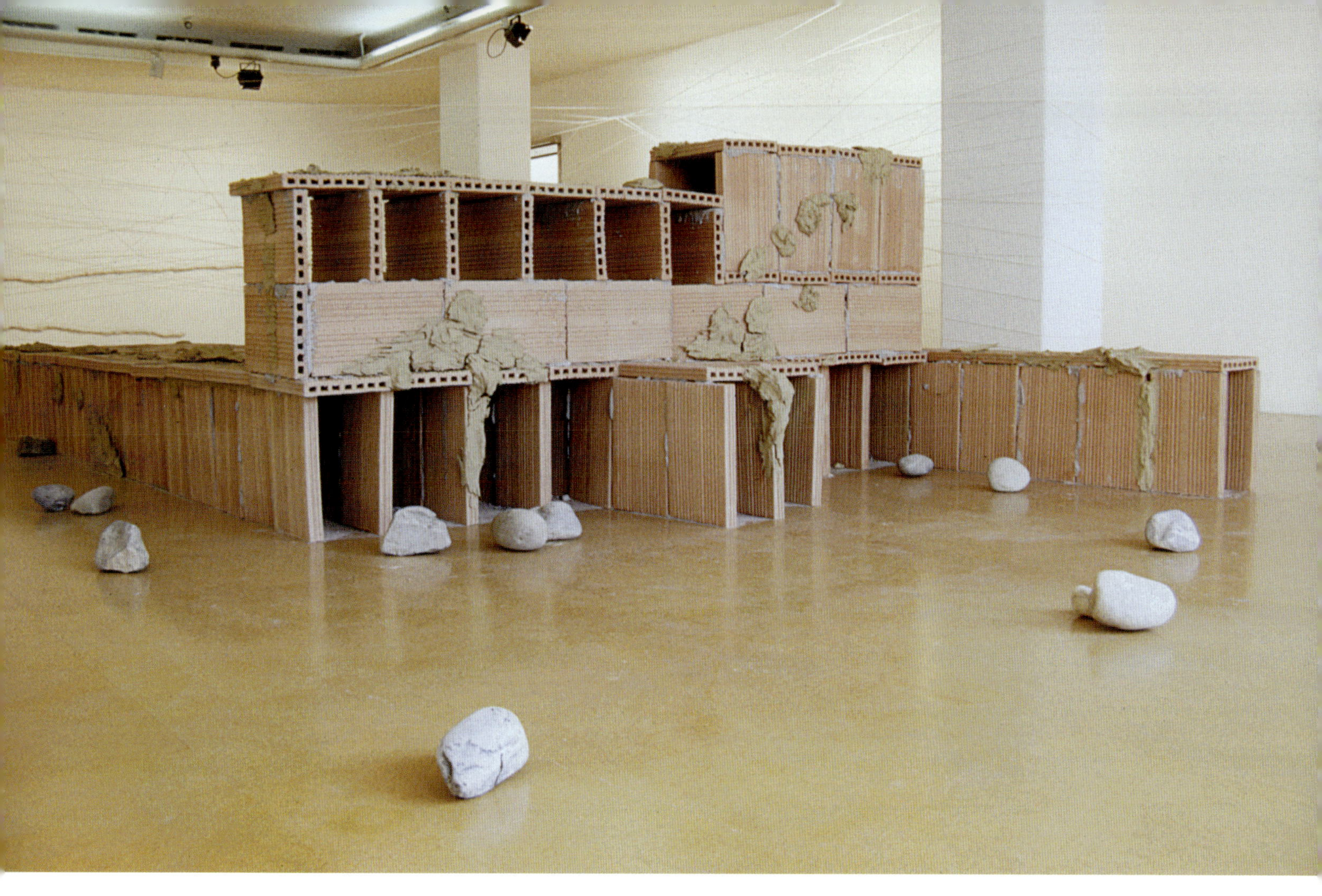

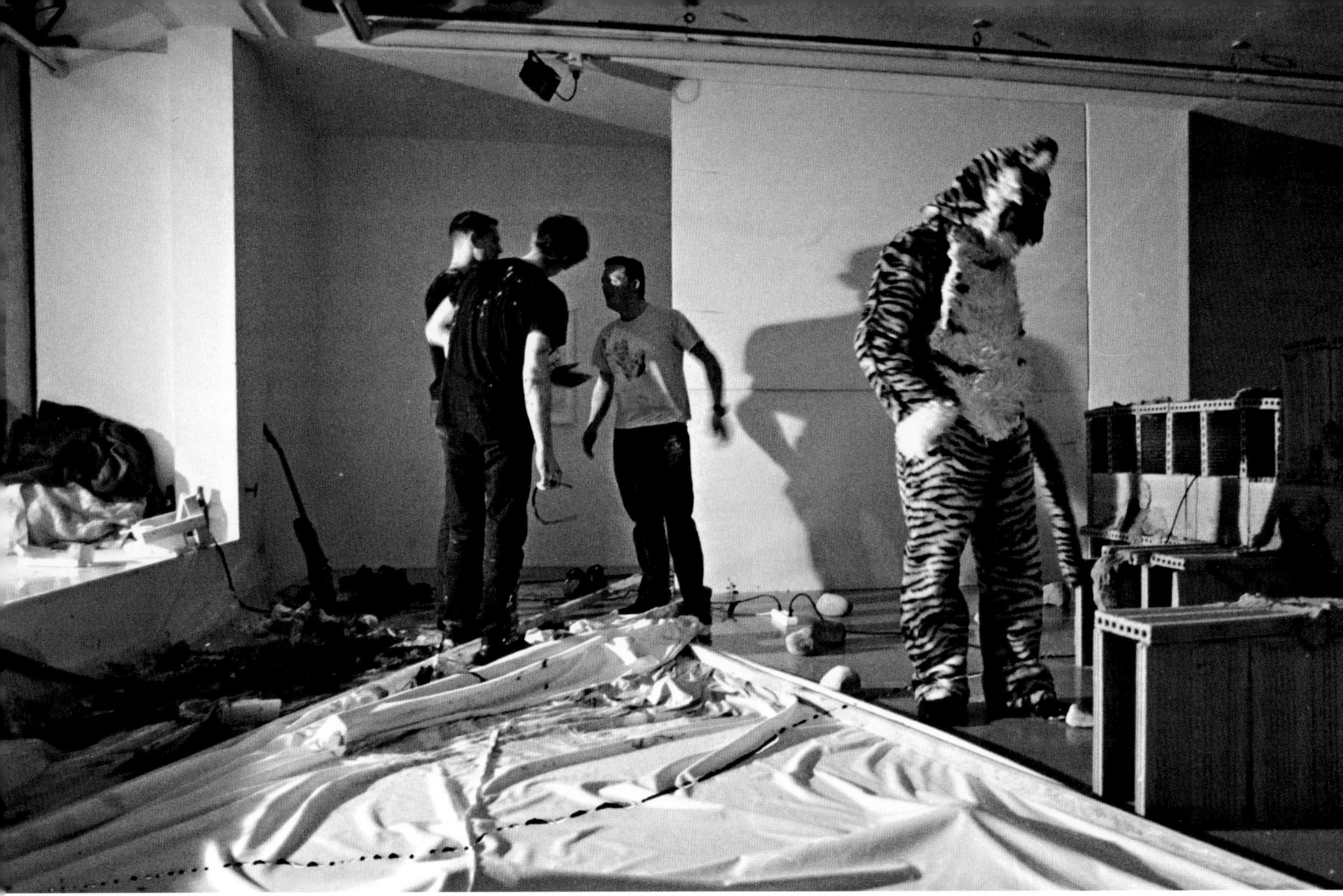

Performance on the occasion of the opening of "Frs Uischer," Galerie Walcheturm, Zurich, 1996
Co-performers: Kerim Seiler, Cyril Kuhn, and Maurus Gmür

Opposite page:

Untitled, 1997

Bricks, mortar, wooden beams
Dimensions unknown
Installation view, "été 97," Centre d'édition contemporaine
(formerly Centre Genevois de Gravure Contemporain), Geneva, 1997

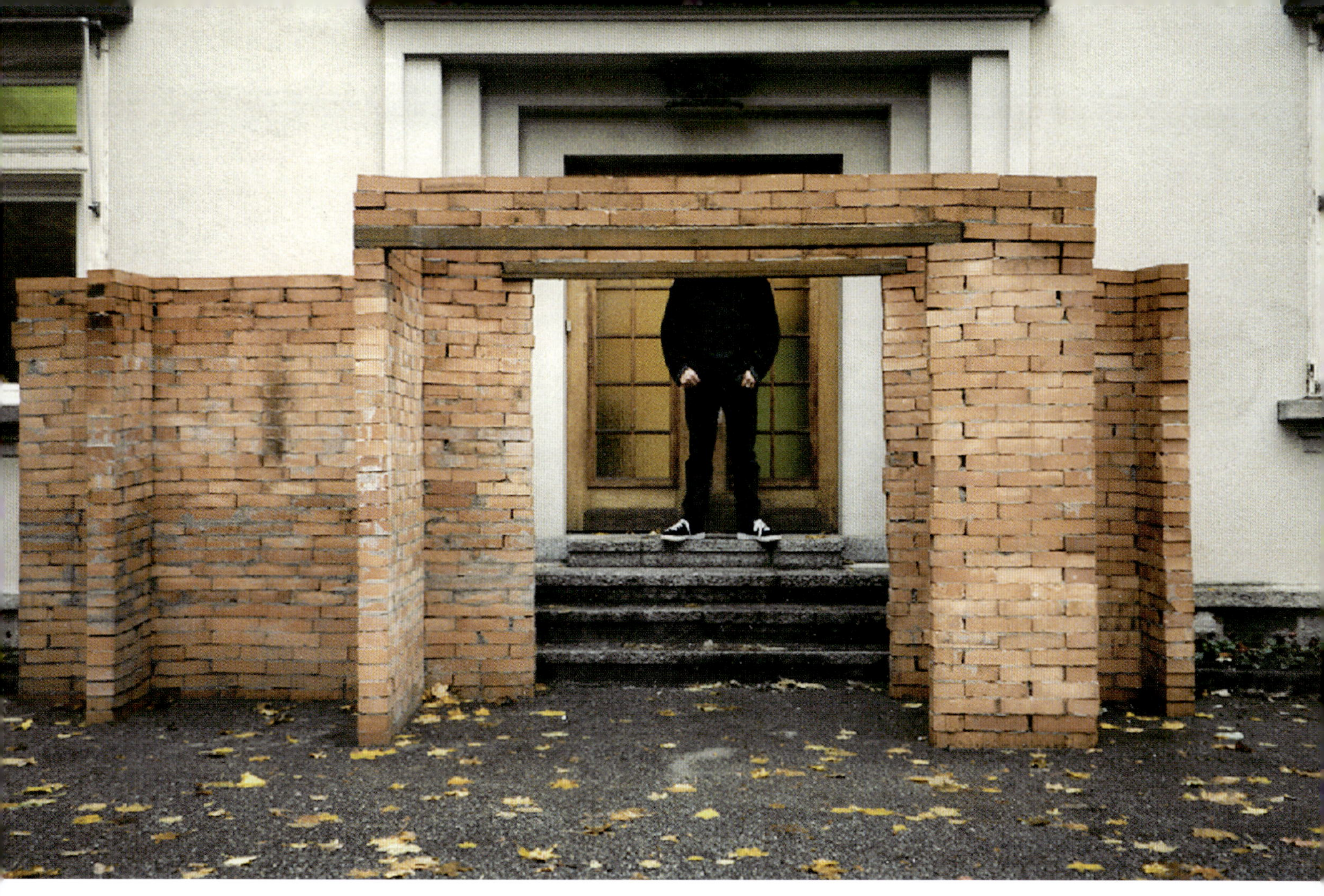

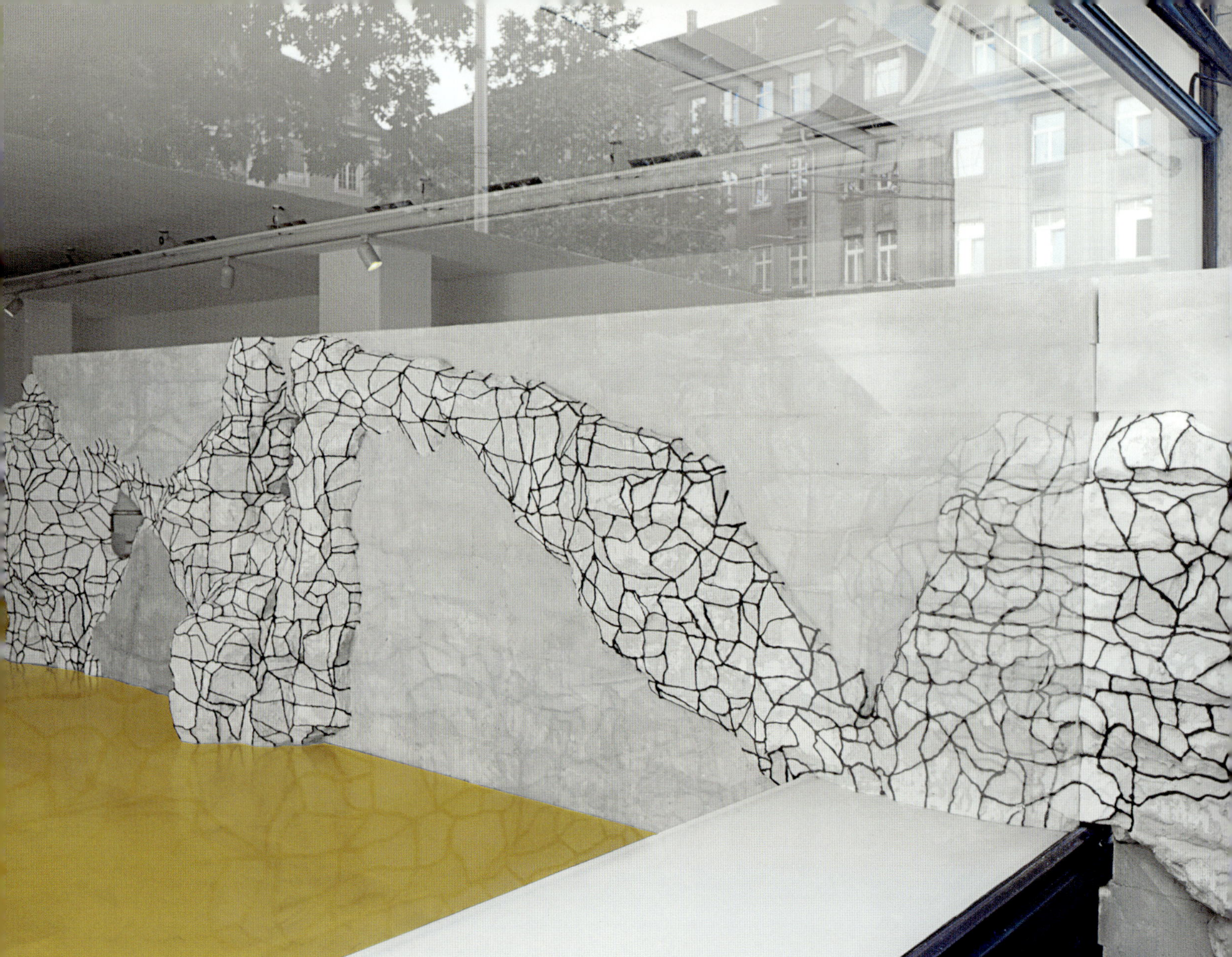

Untitled (Wand der Angst), 1997
Aerated concrete, mortar, silicone, coffee
126 x 326 ¾ x 79 ⅞ inches (320 x 830 x 203 cm)
Installation view, "Hammer," Galerie Walcheturm, Zurich, 1997

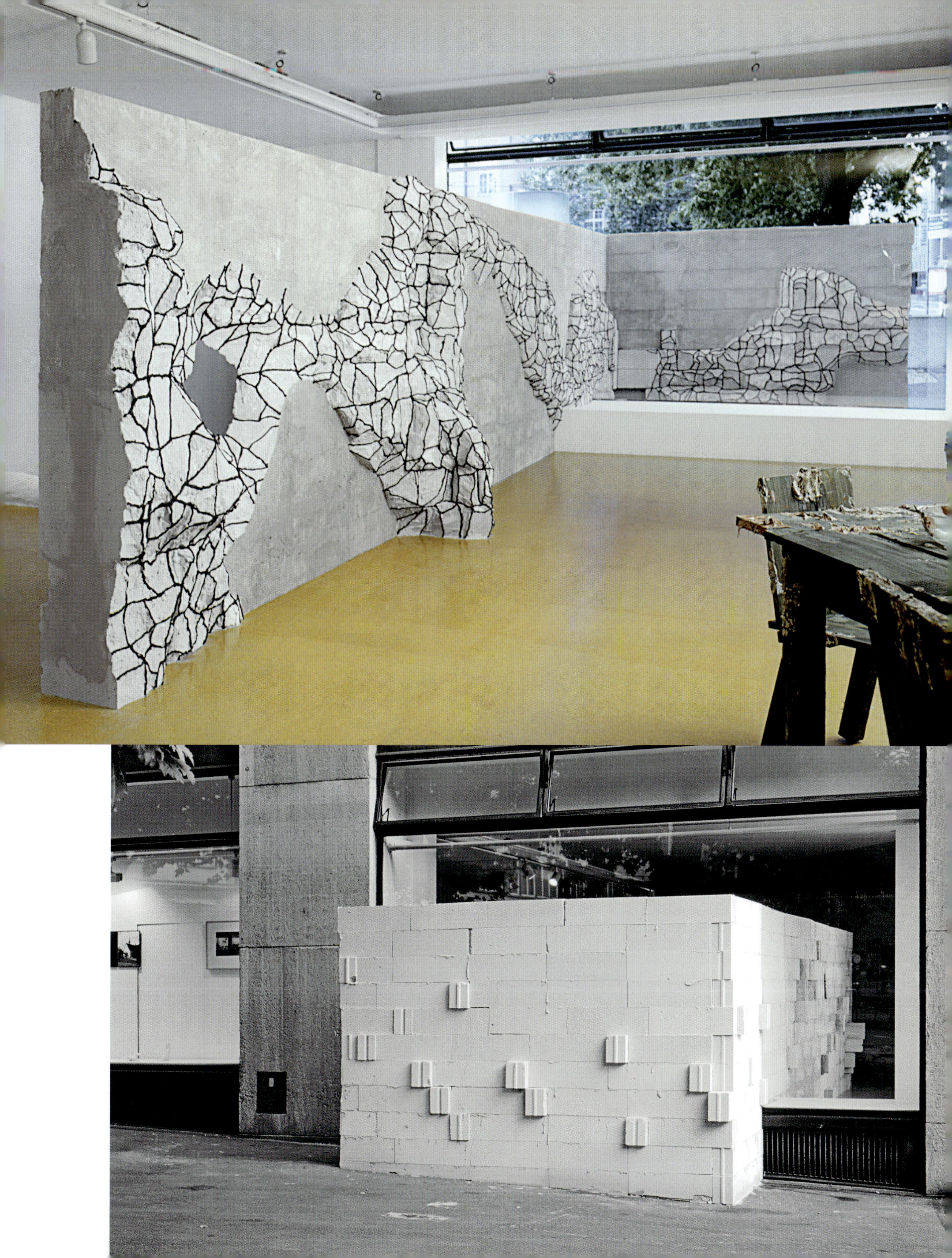

Faules Fundament (Rotten Foundation), 1998

Bricks, mortar, fruits, vegetables

Dimensions variable

"Ironisch / Ironic," Migros Museum für Gegenwartskunst, Zurich, 1998

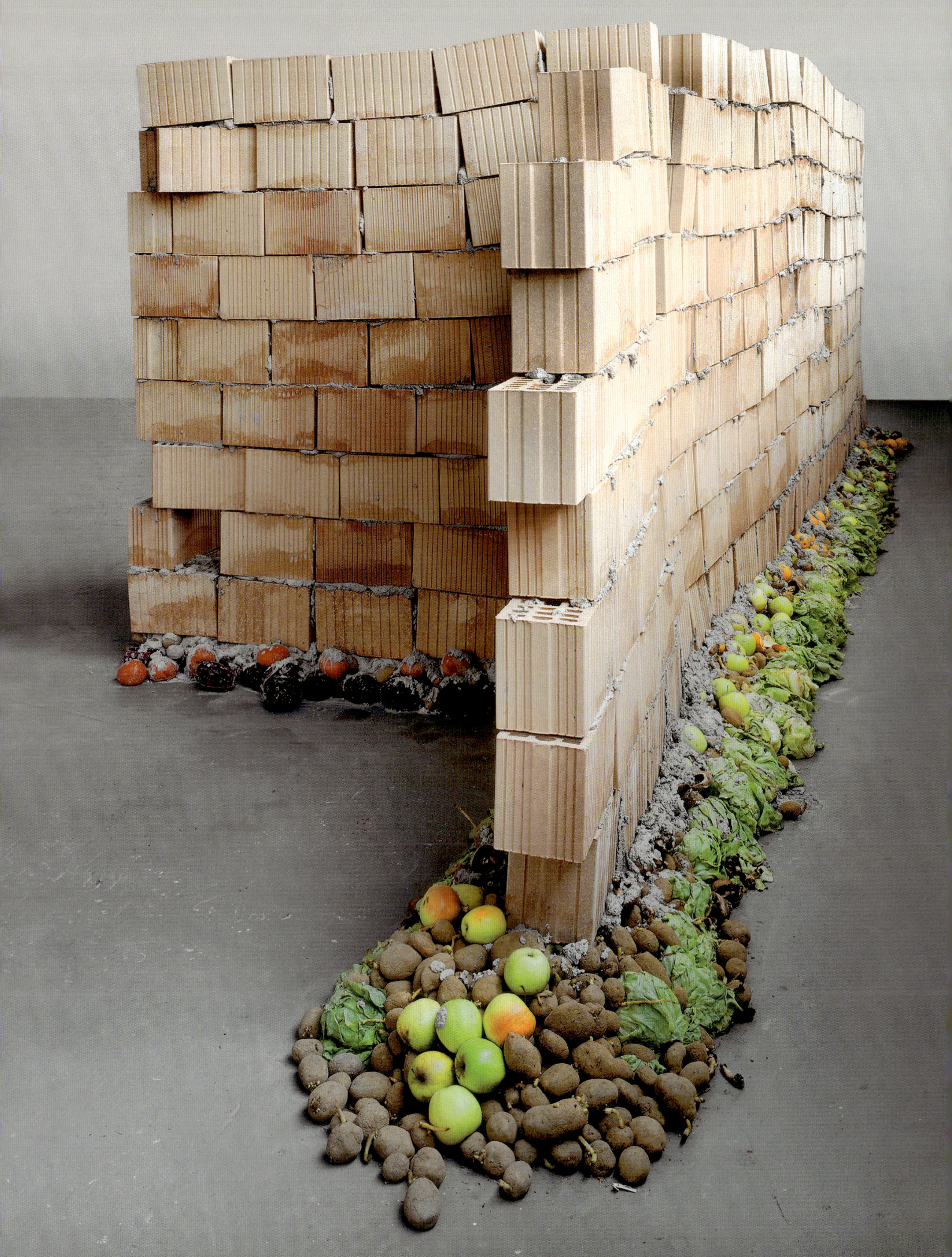

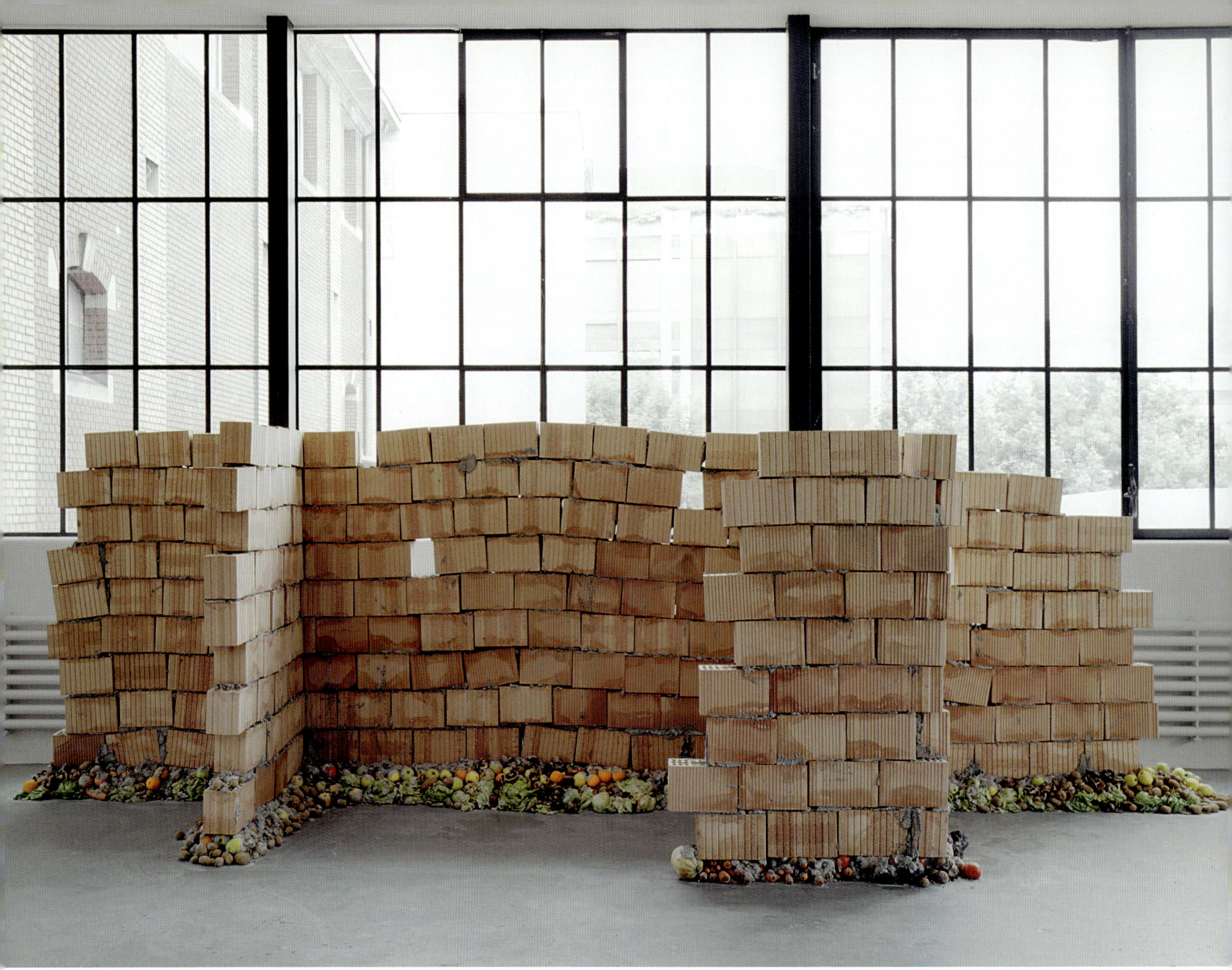

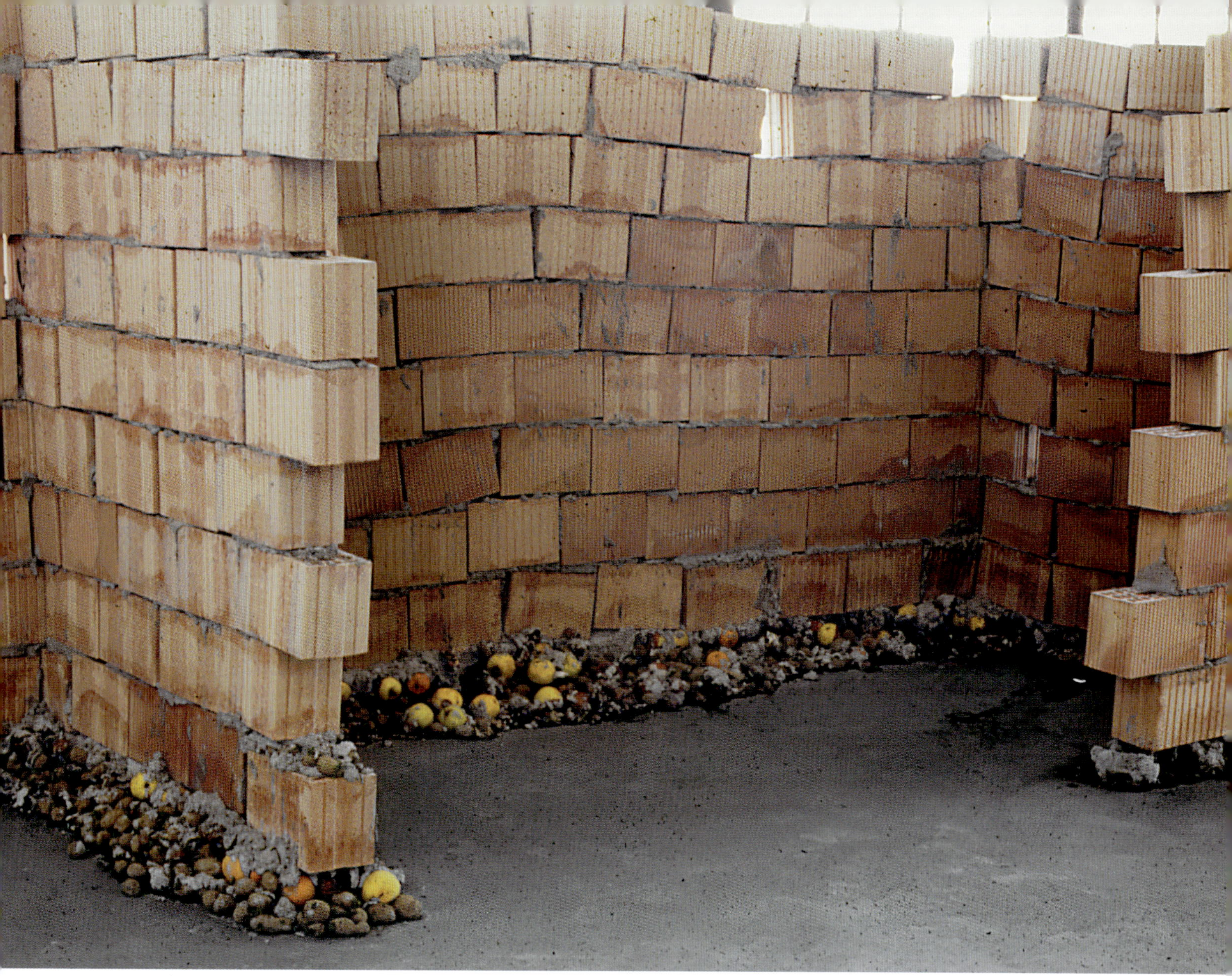

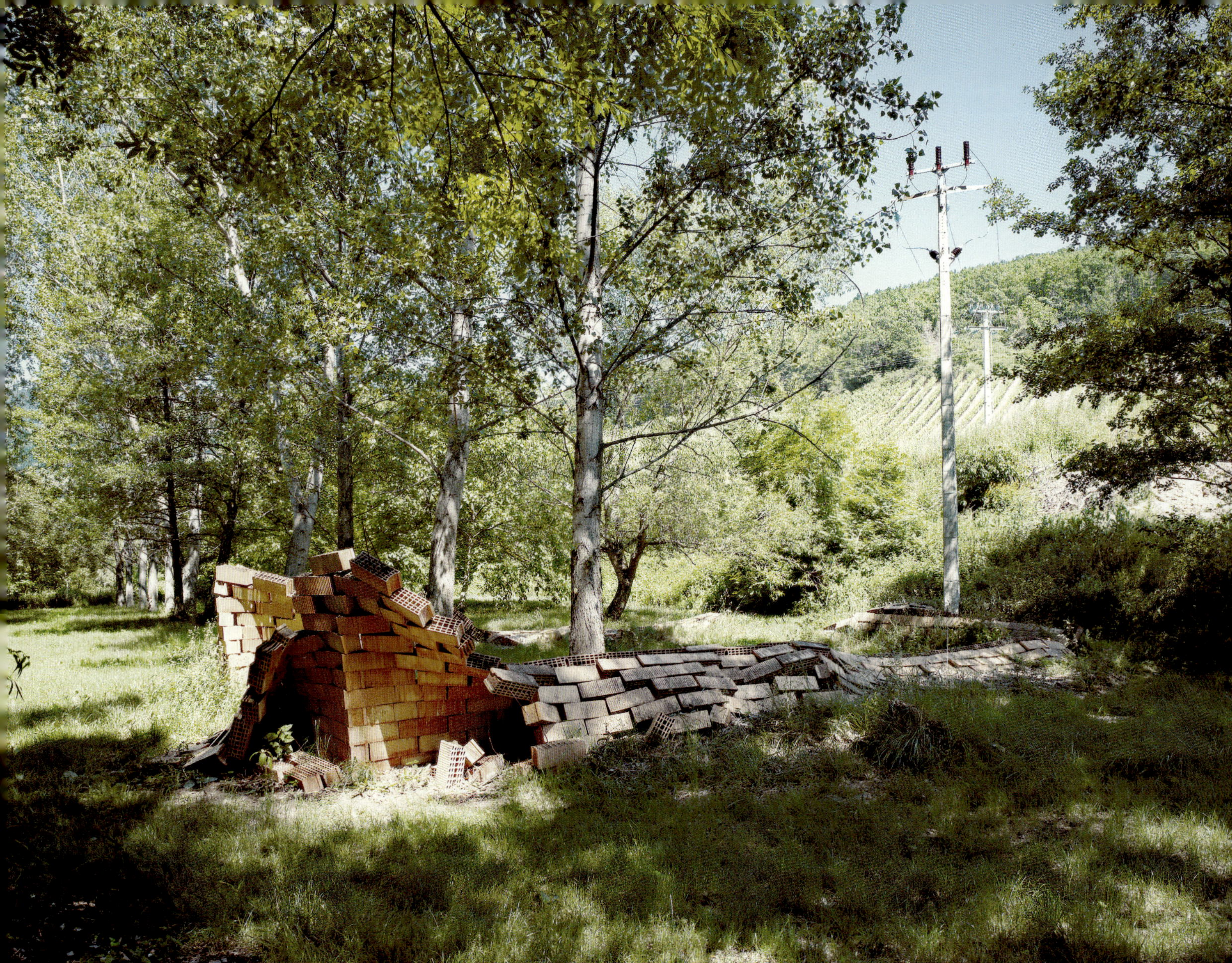

Baked Master's Basket, 1999
Concrete foundation, rebar, bricks
Dimensions variable
Installation view, Private collection, Alsace, France, 1999

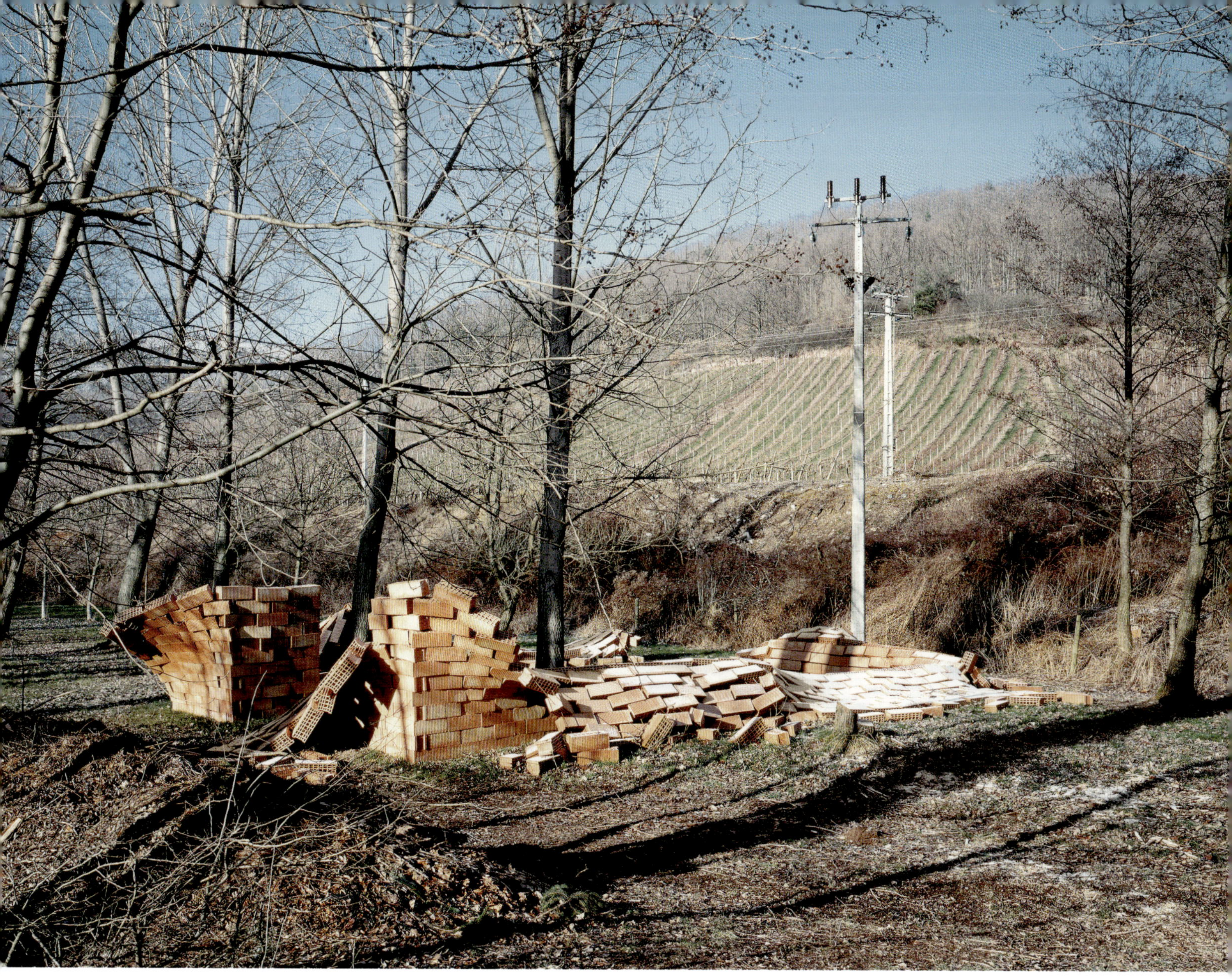

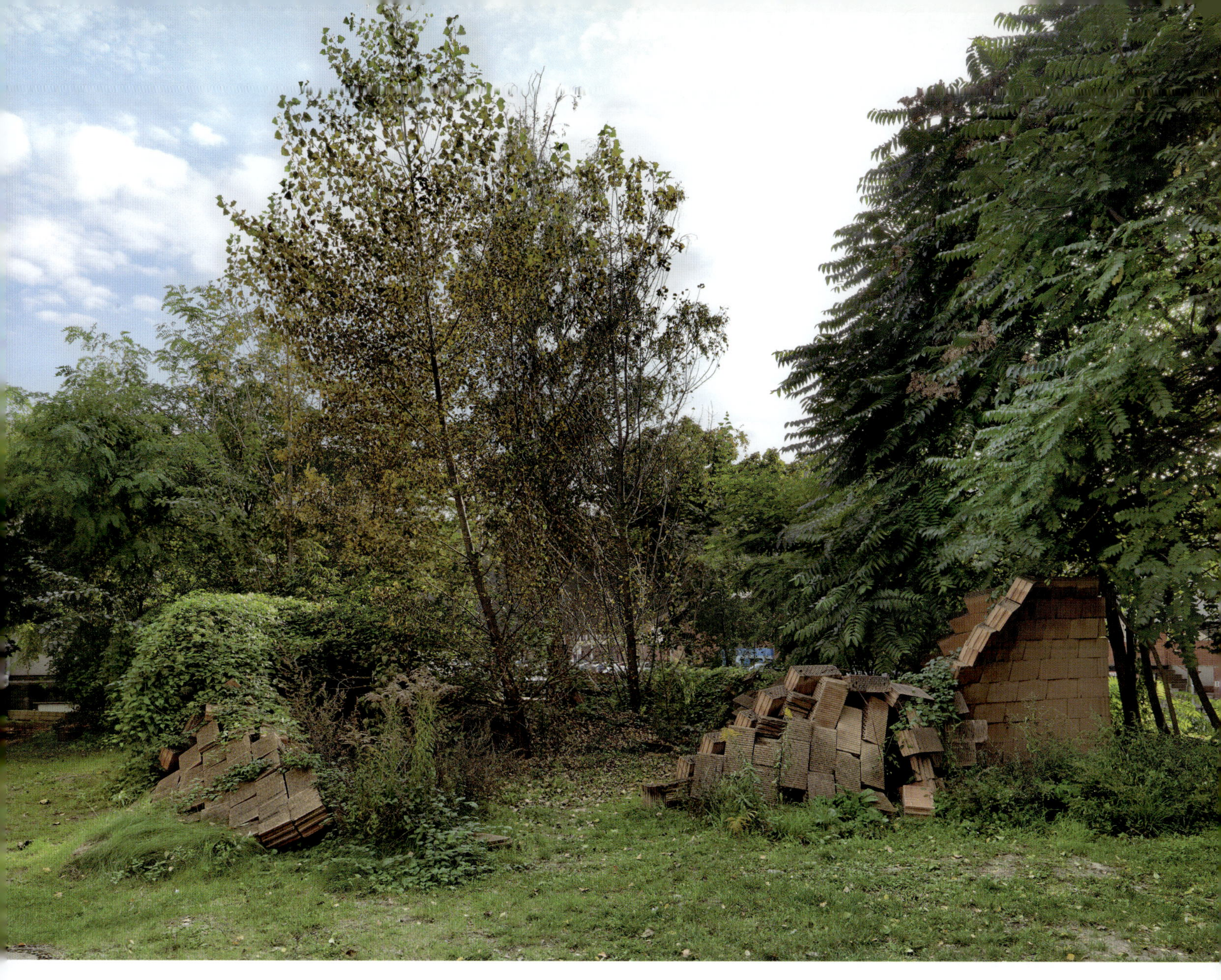

Installation view, Hamburger Bahnhof, Museum für Gegenwart, Berlin, 2011
Baked Master's Basket, 1999

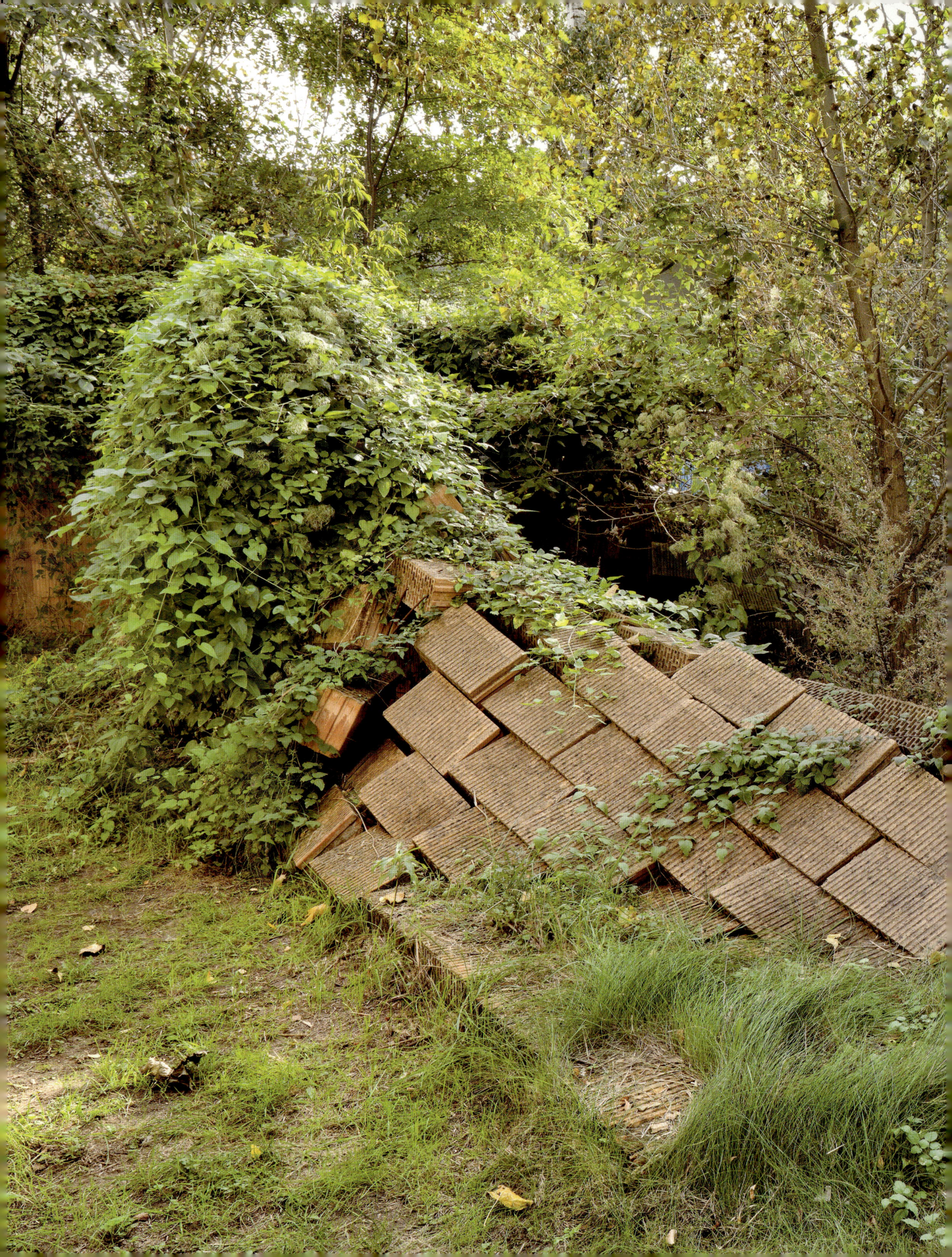

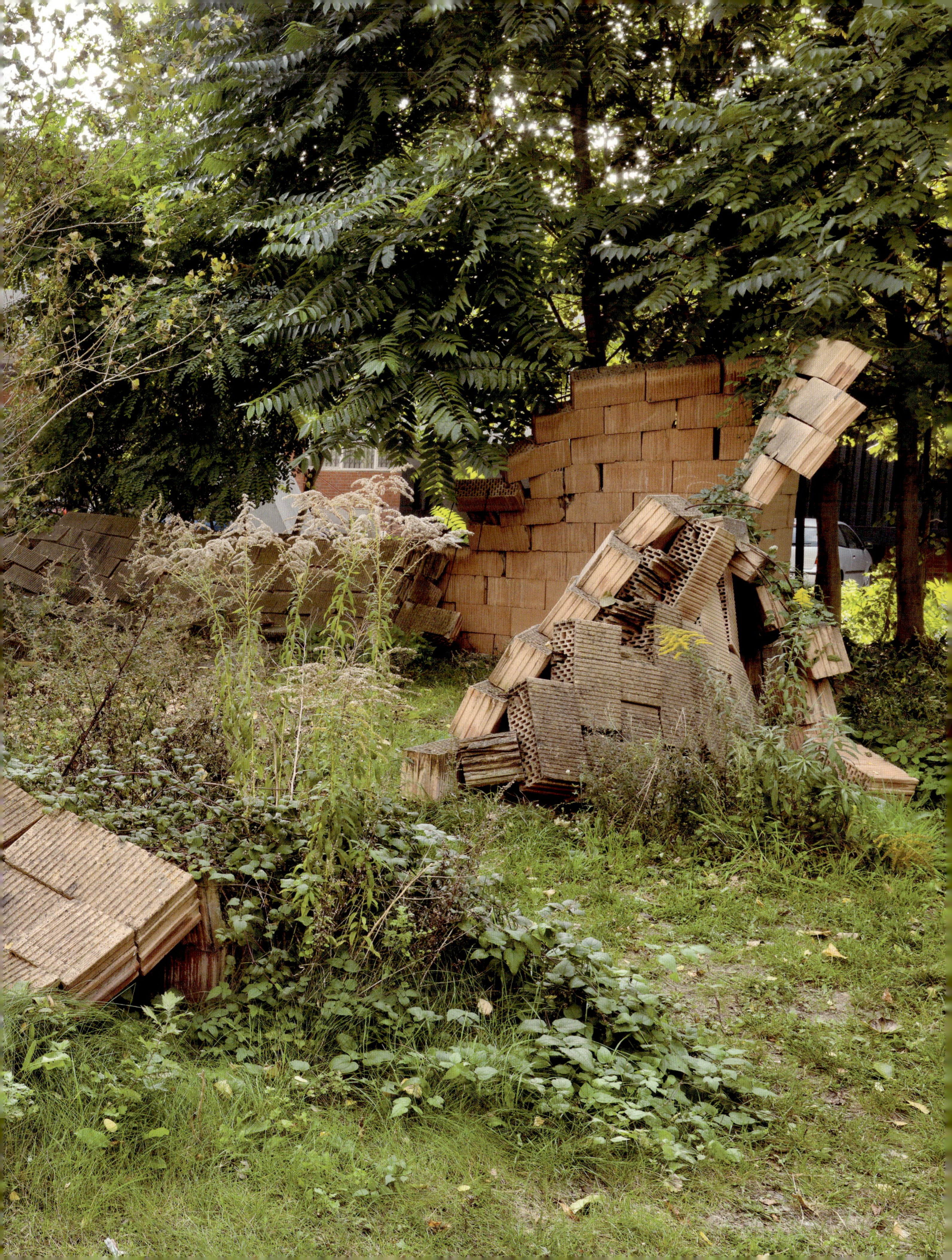

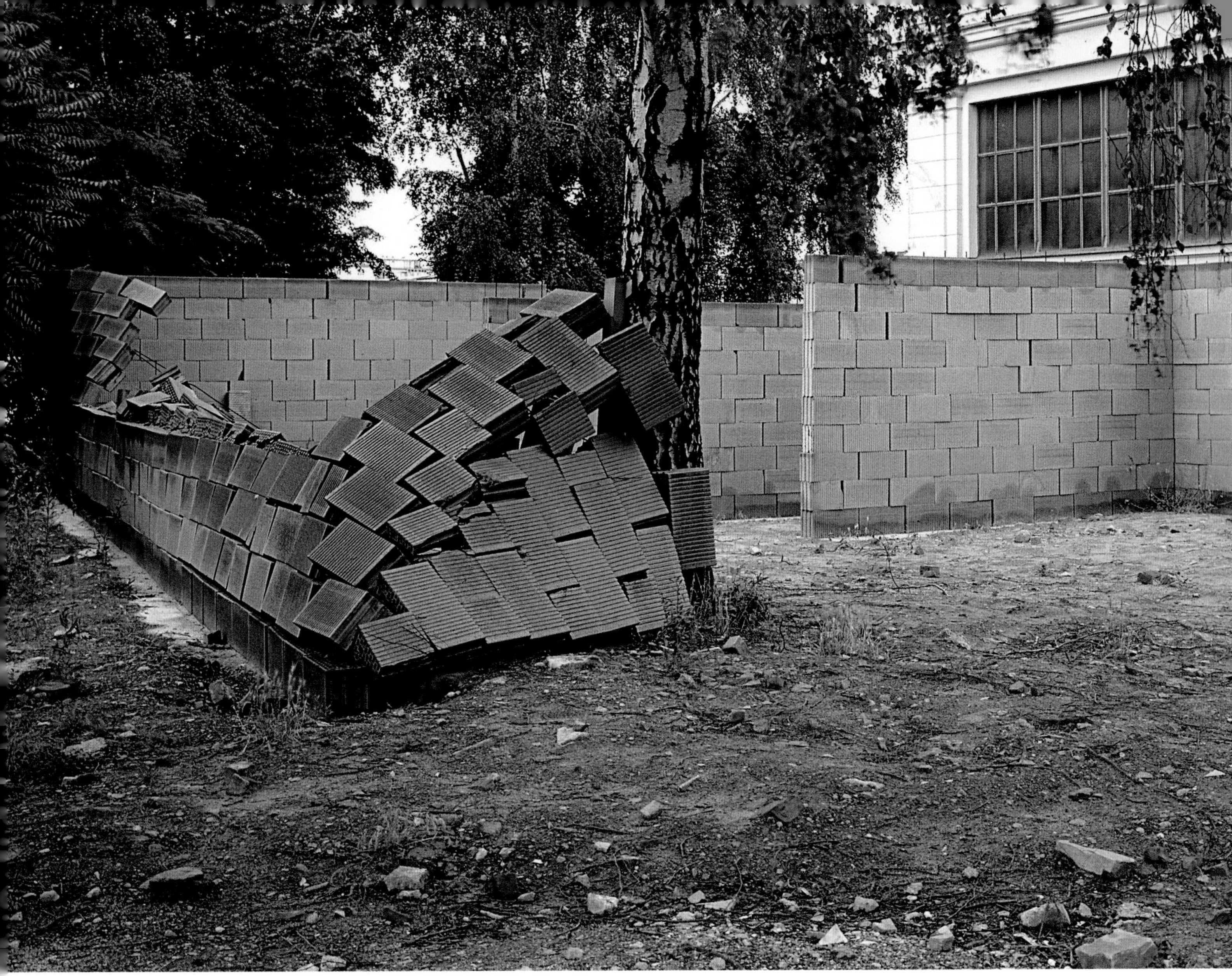

Installation view, "Urs Fischer: Werke aus der Friedrich Christian Flick Collection im Hamburger Bahnhof," Hamburger Bahnhof, Museum für Gegenwart, Berlin, 2005
Baked Master's Basket, 1999

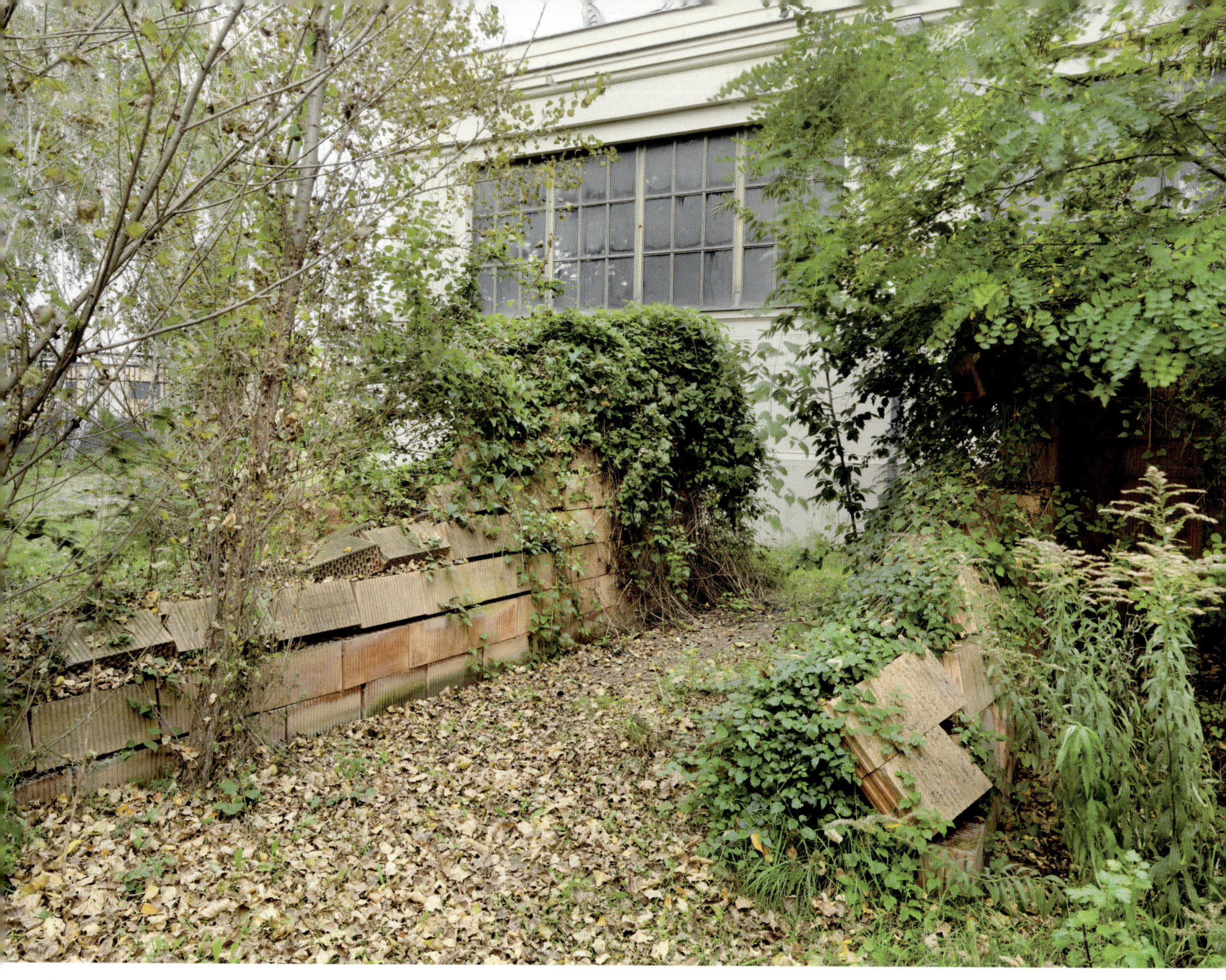

Installation view, Hamburger Bahnhof, Museum für Gegenwart, Berlin, 2011
Baked Master's Basket, 1999

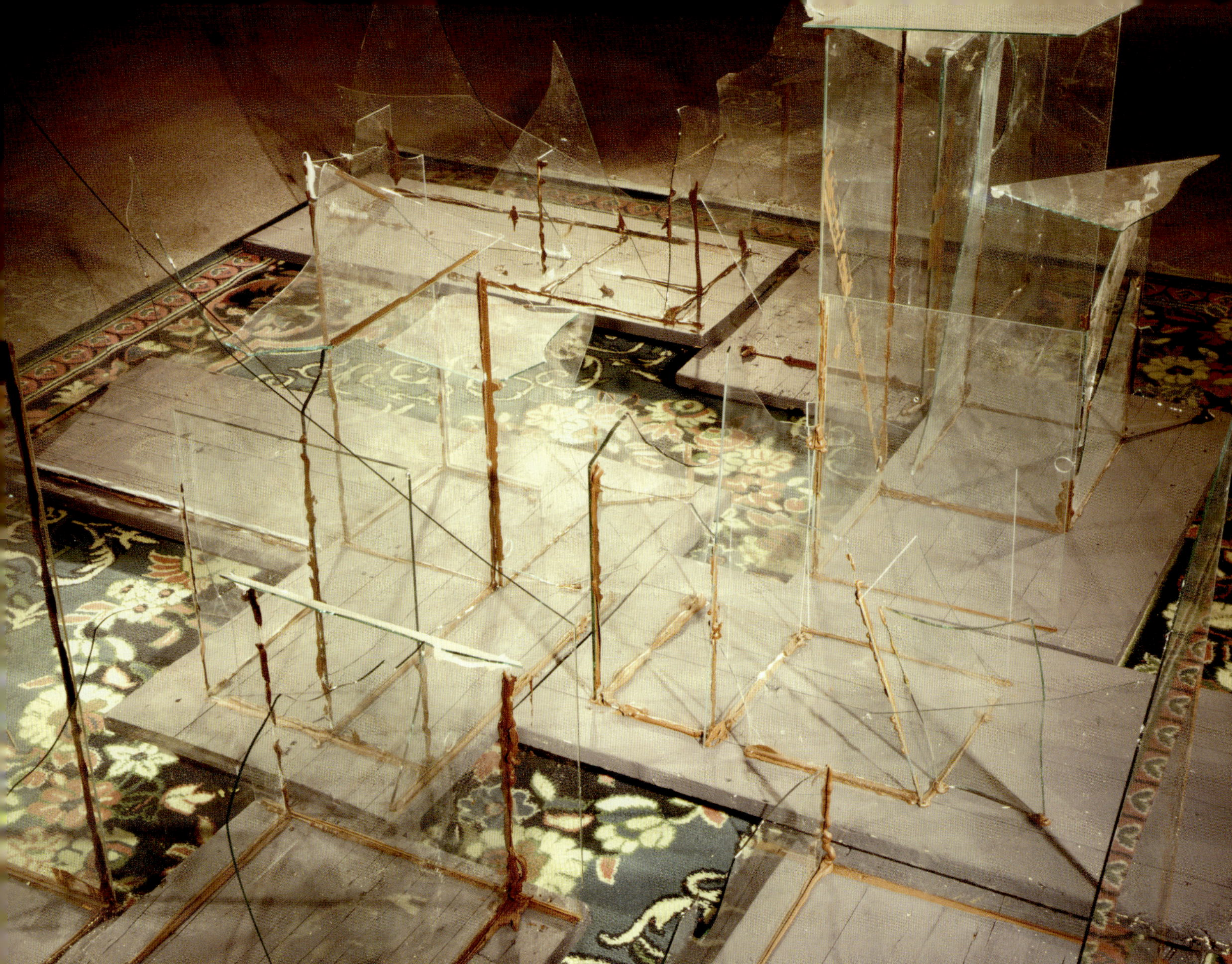

Glaskatzen–Mülleimer der Hoffnung, 1999
Carpet, wood, glass, silicone (casts of room corners), acrylic paint
Approximately 39 ⅜ x 151 ⅝ x 106 ¼ inches (100 x 385 x 270 cm)

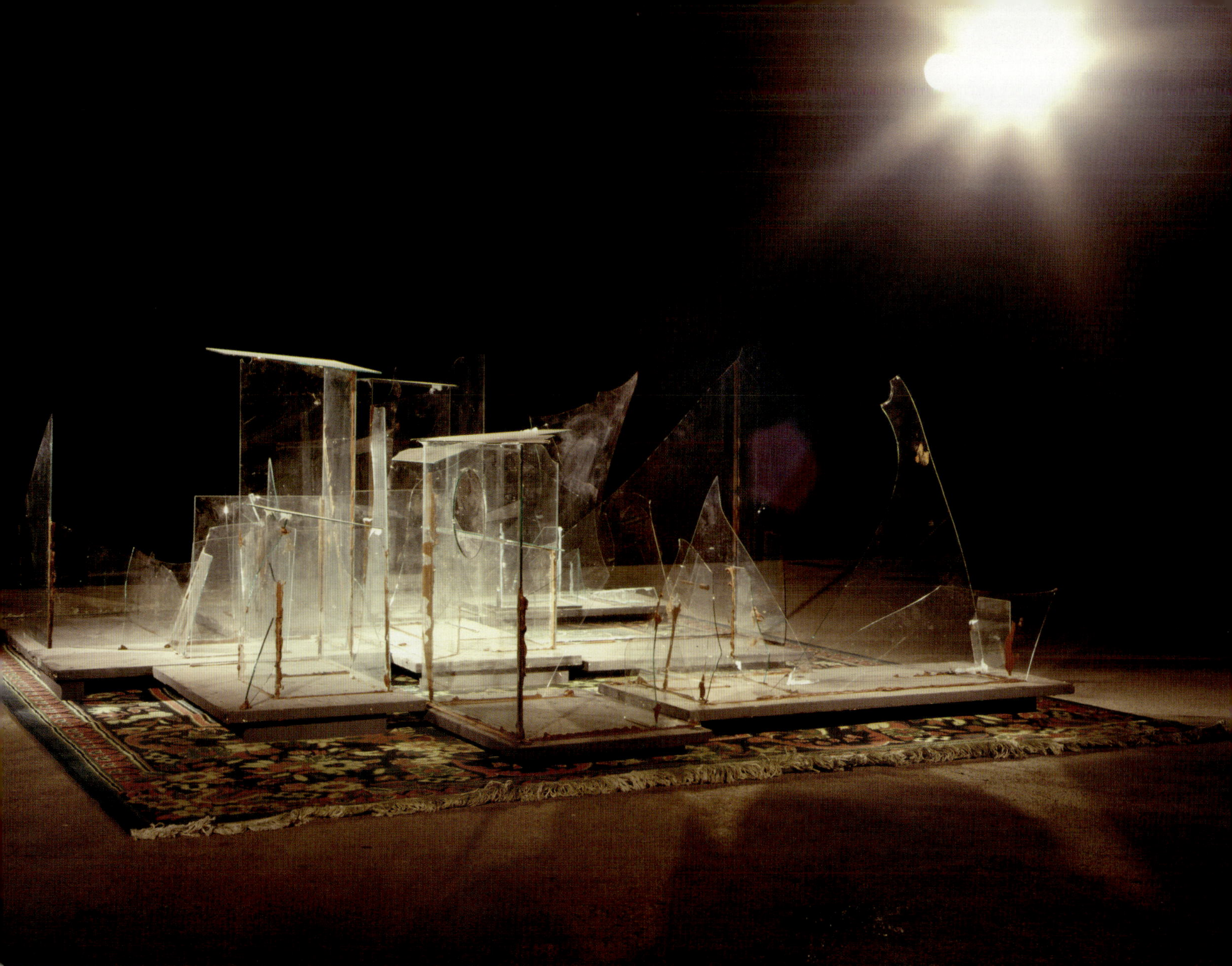

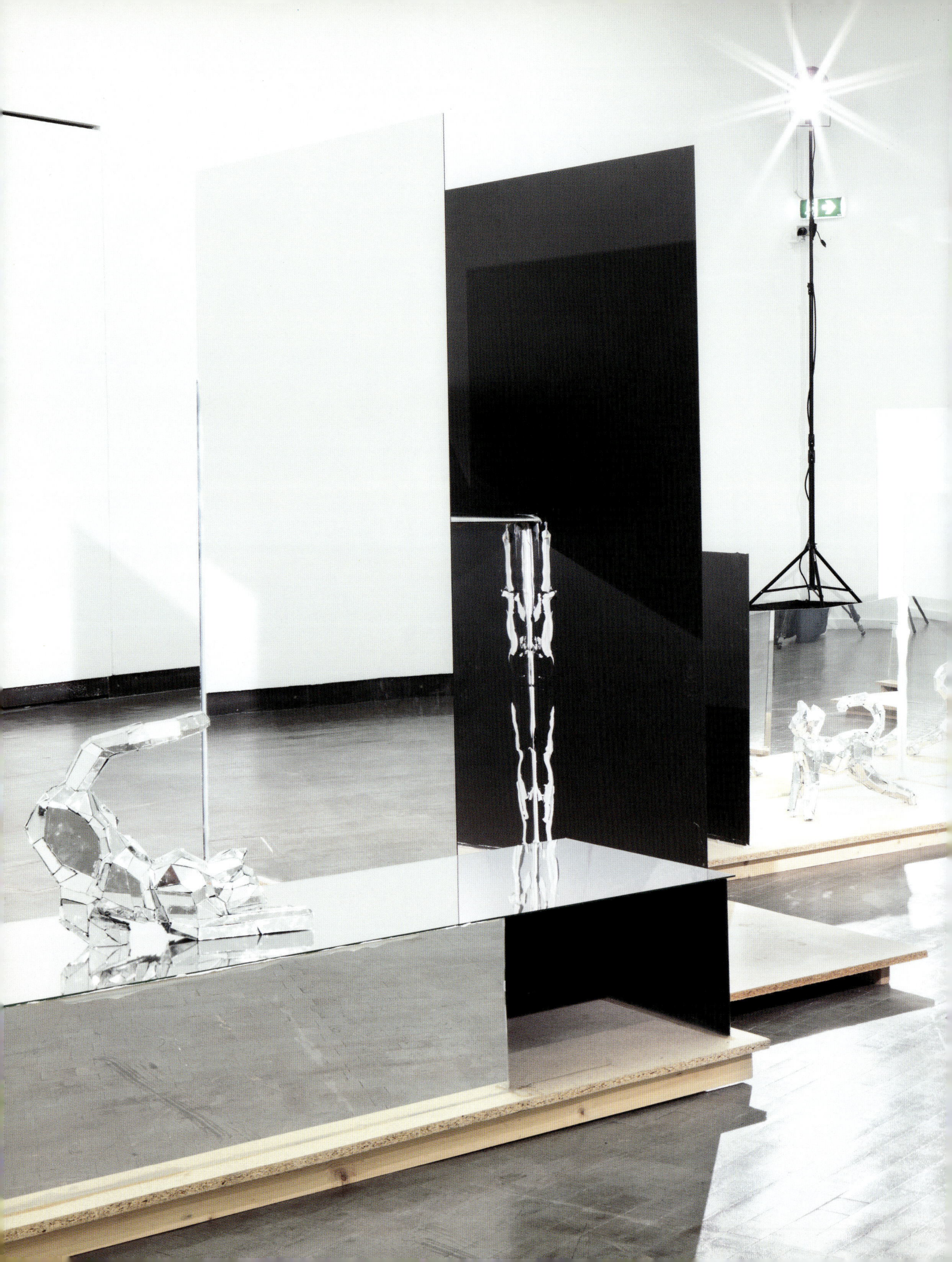

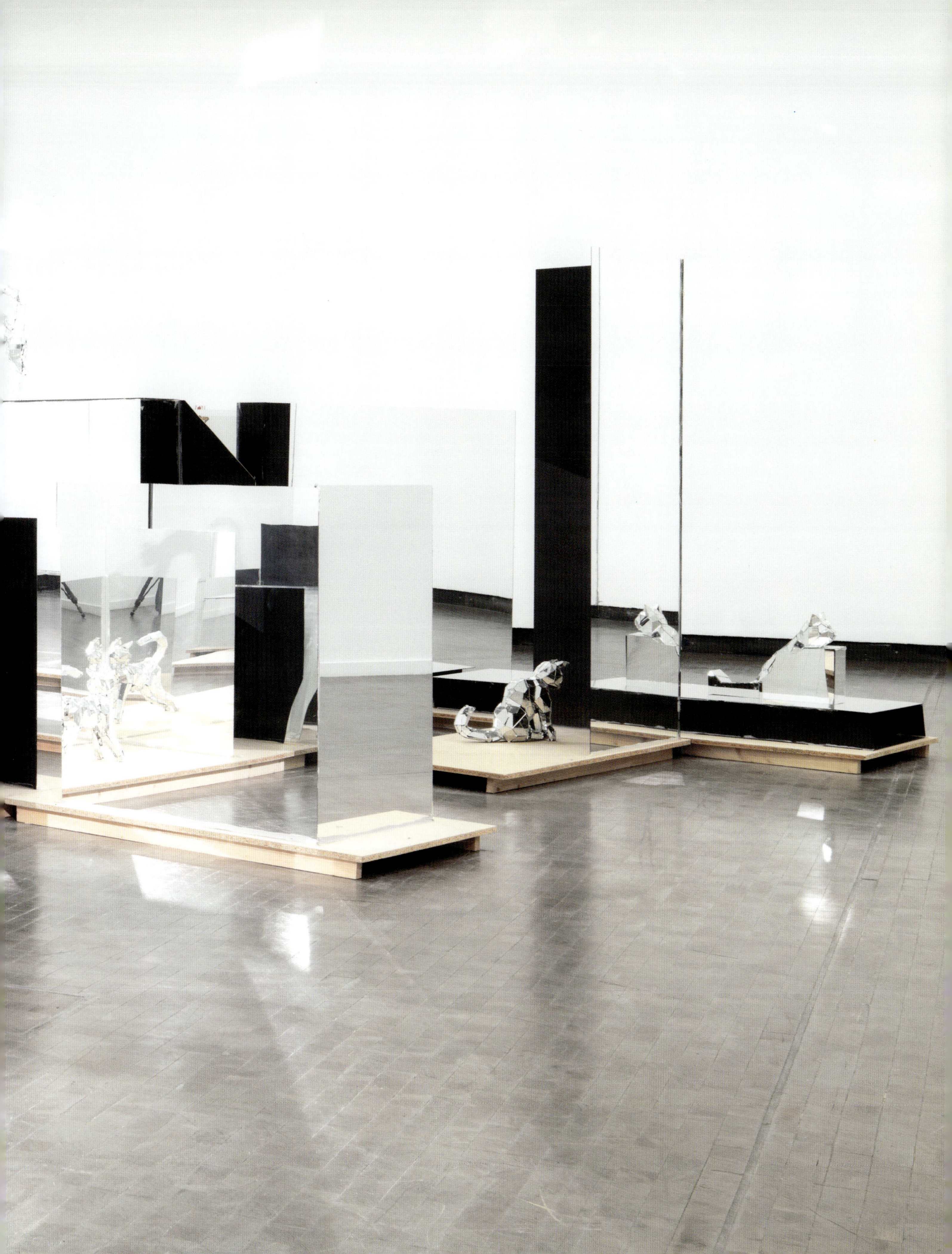

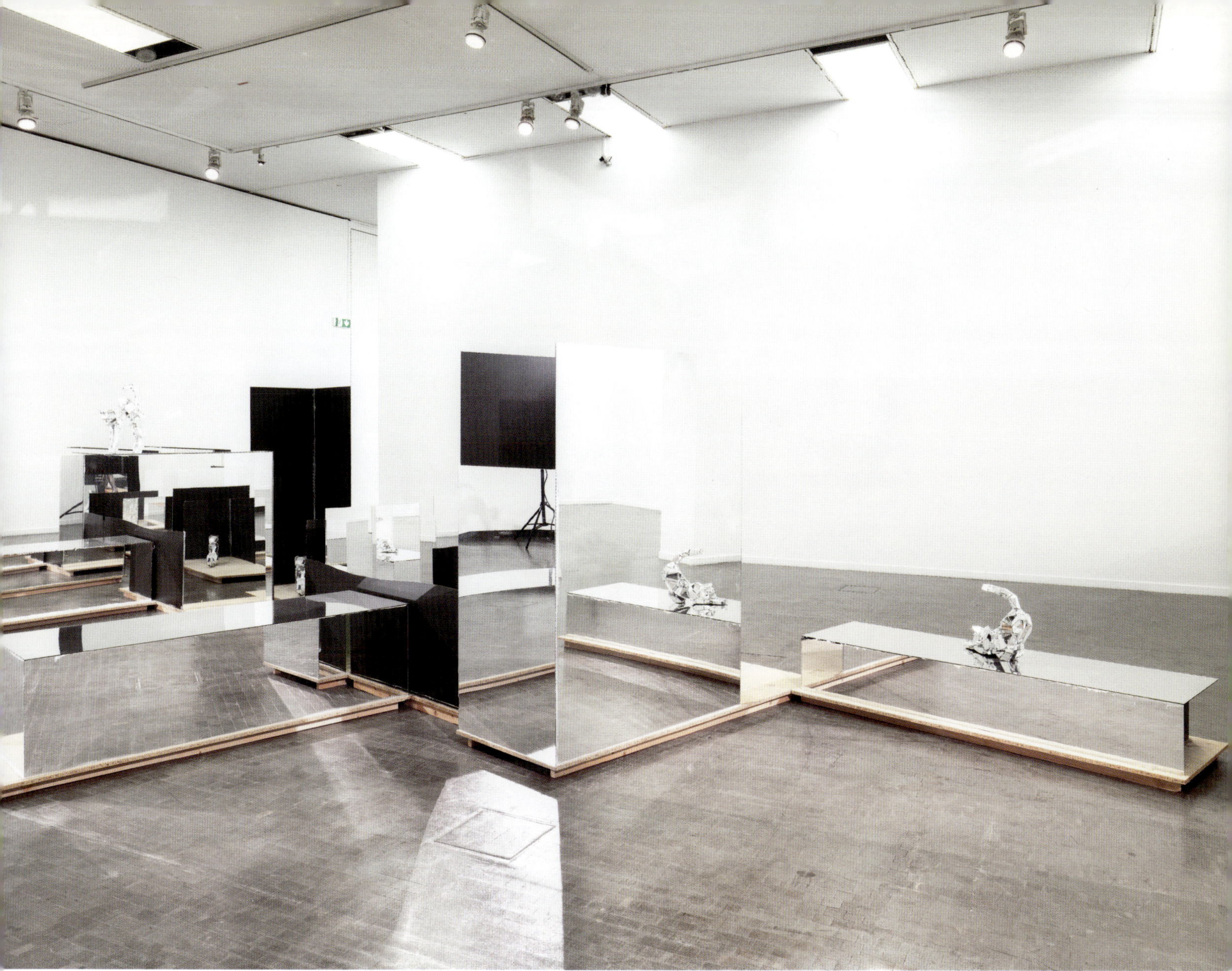

Previous spread and following pages:

Dr. Katzelberg (Zivilisationsruine), 1999

Mirrors, wood, polystyrene, silicone, three theater spotlights on tripods

82 ⅝ x 196 ⅞ x 137 ¾ inches (210 x 500 x 350 cm)

Installation view, "Skinny Sunrise," Kunsthalle Wien, Vienna, 2012

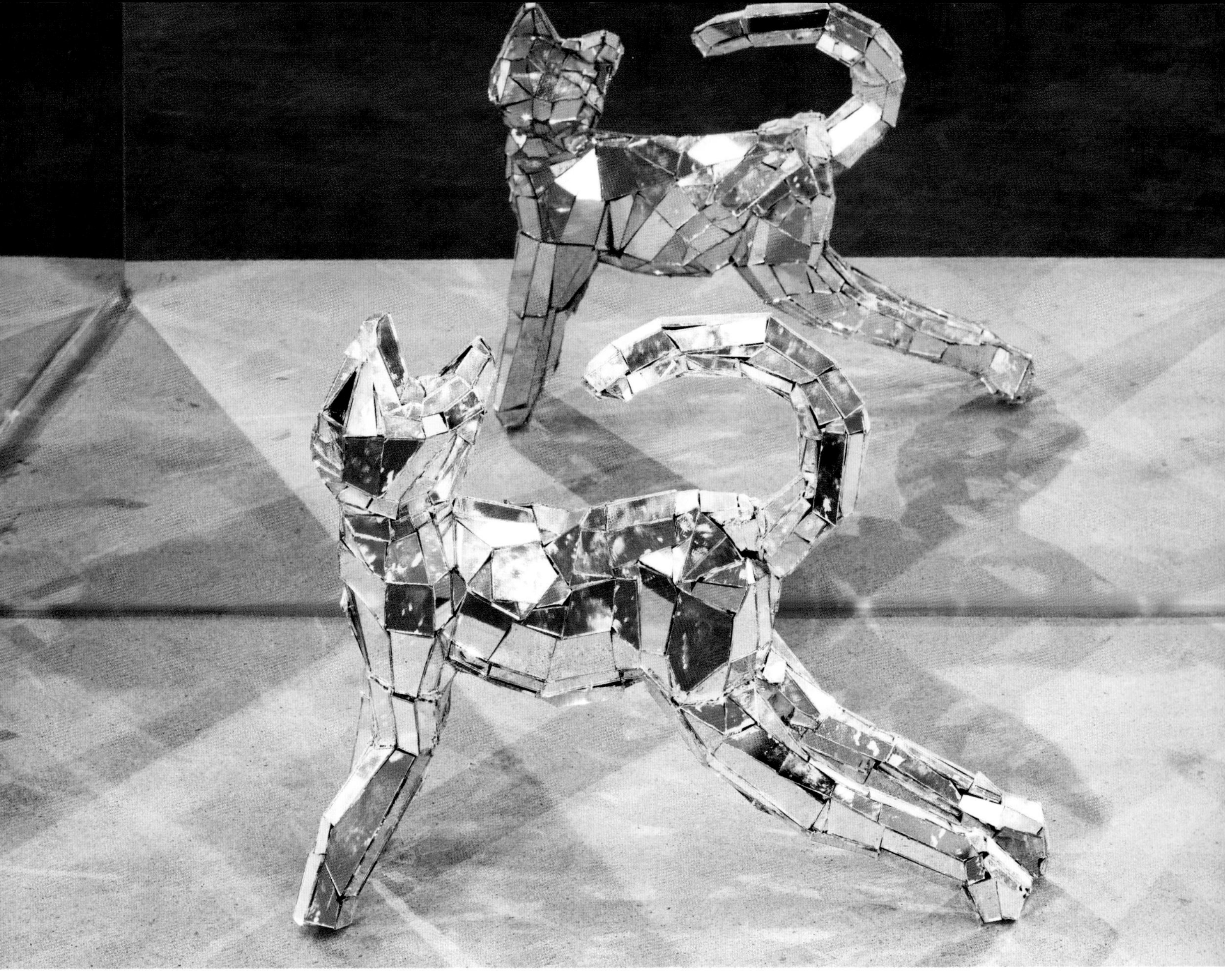

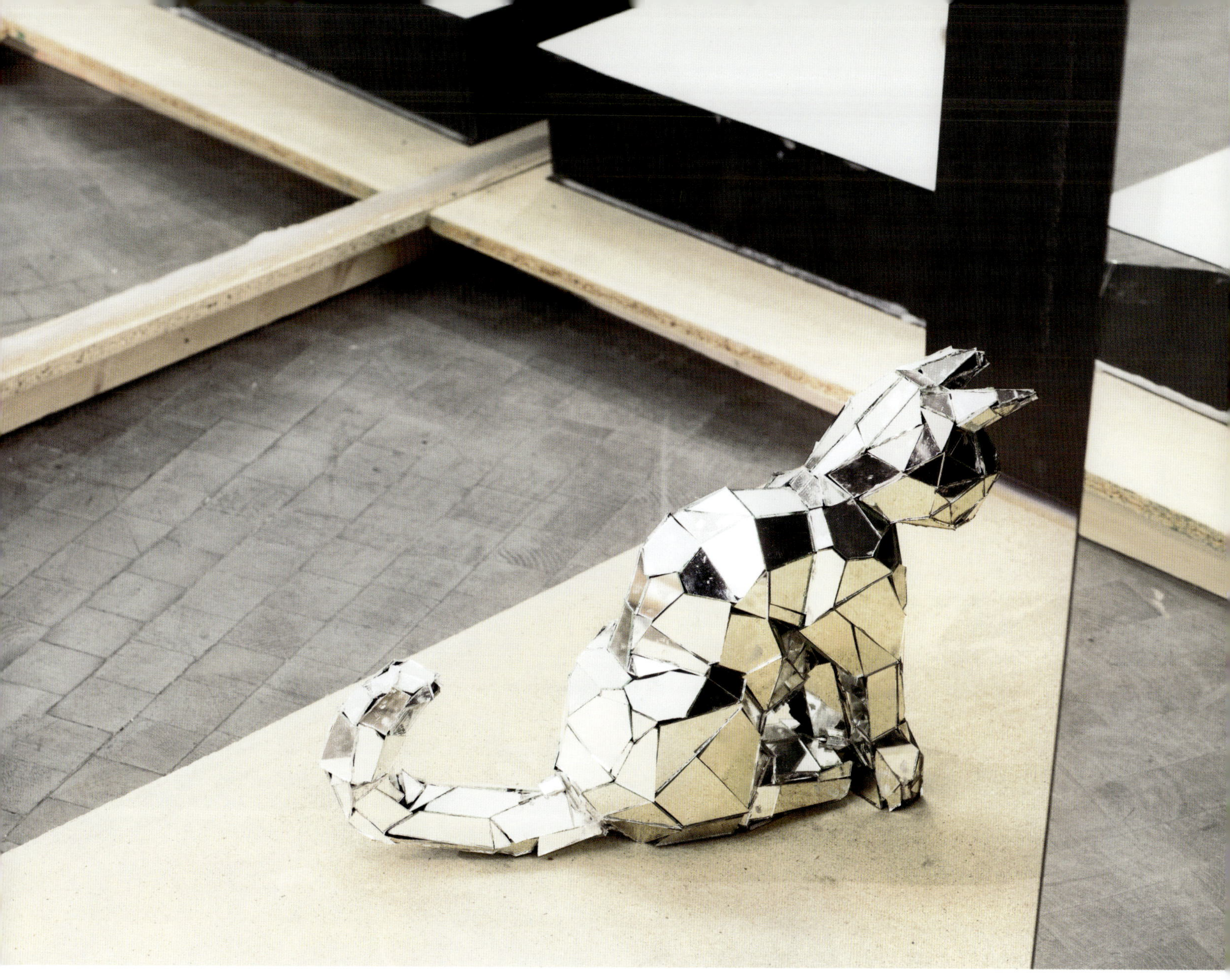

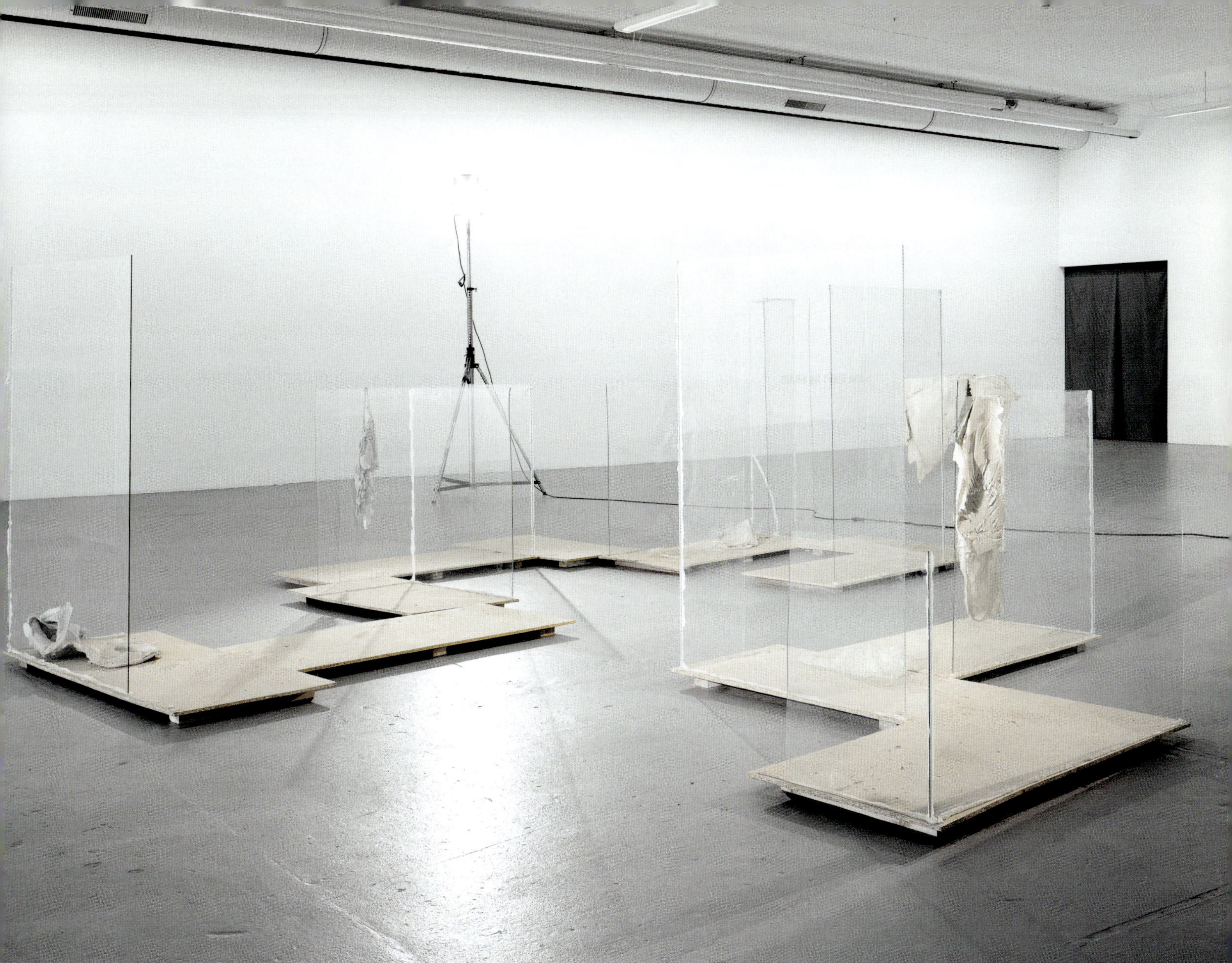

Glaskatzensex / Transparent Tale, 2000
Particleboard, wood, silicone (casts of room corners),
glass, acrylic paint, marker
62 ¼ x 220 ½ x 236 ¼ inches (158 x 560 x 600 cm)

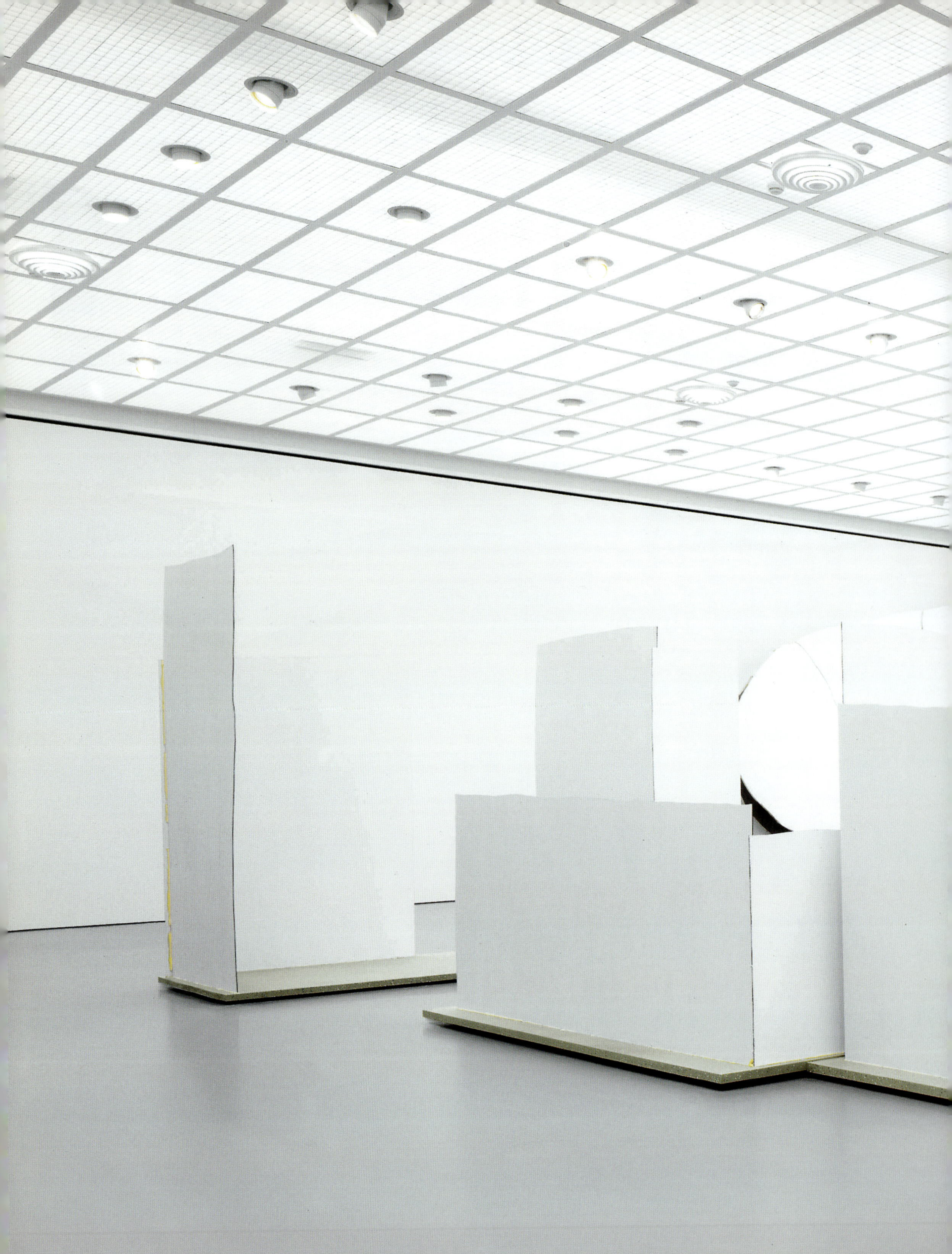

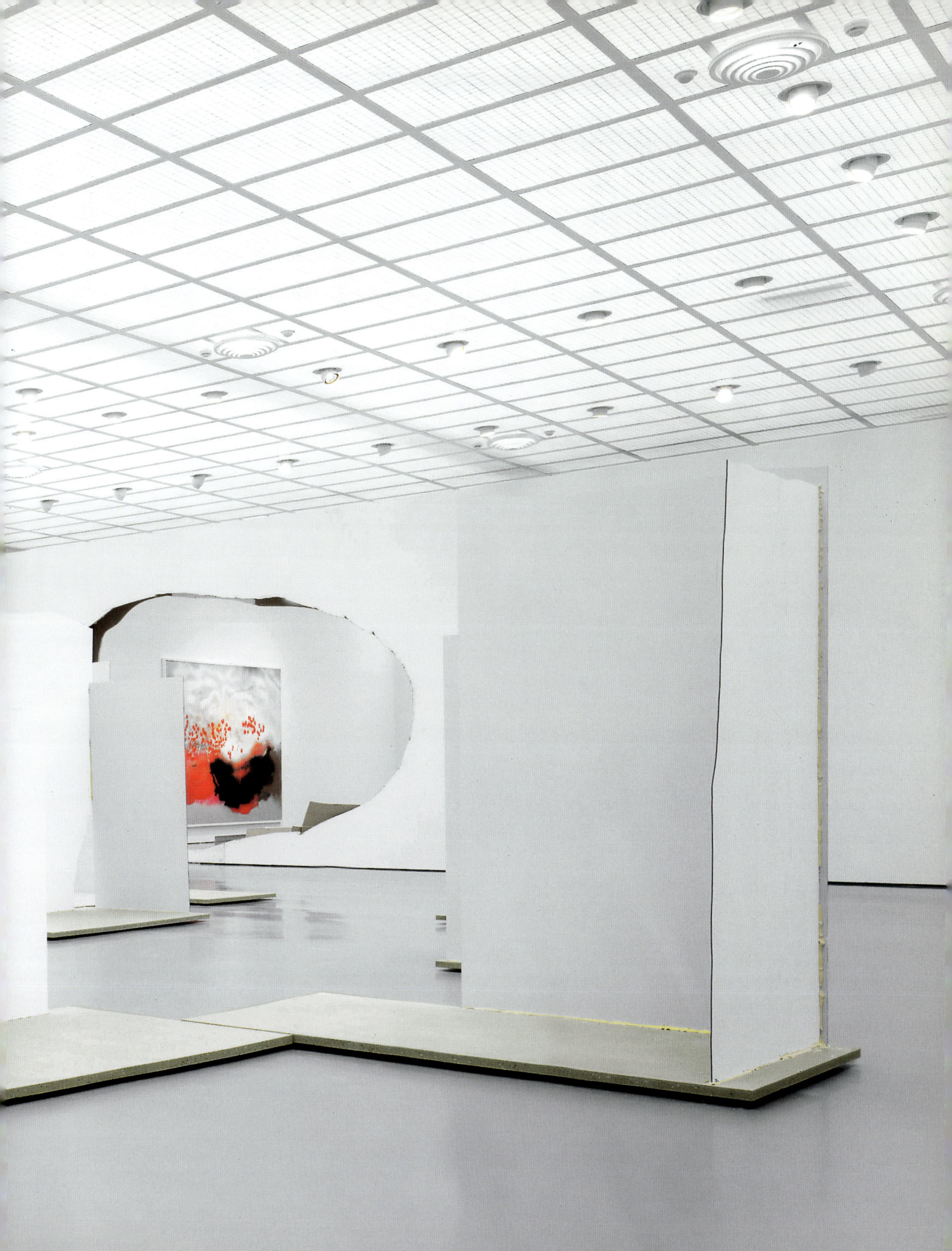

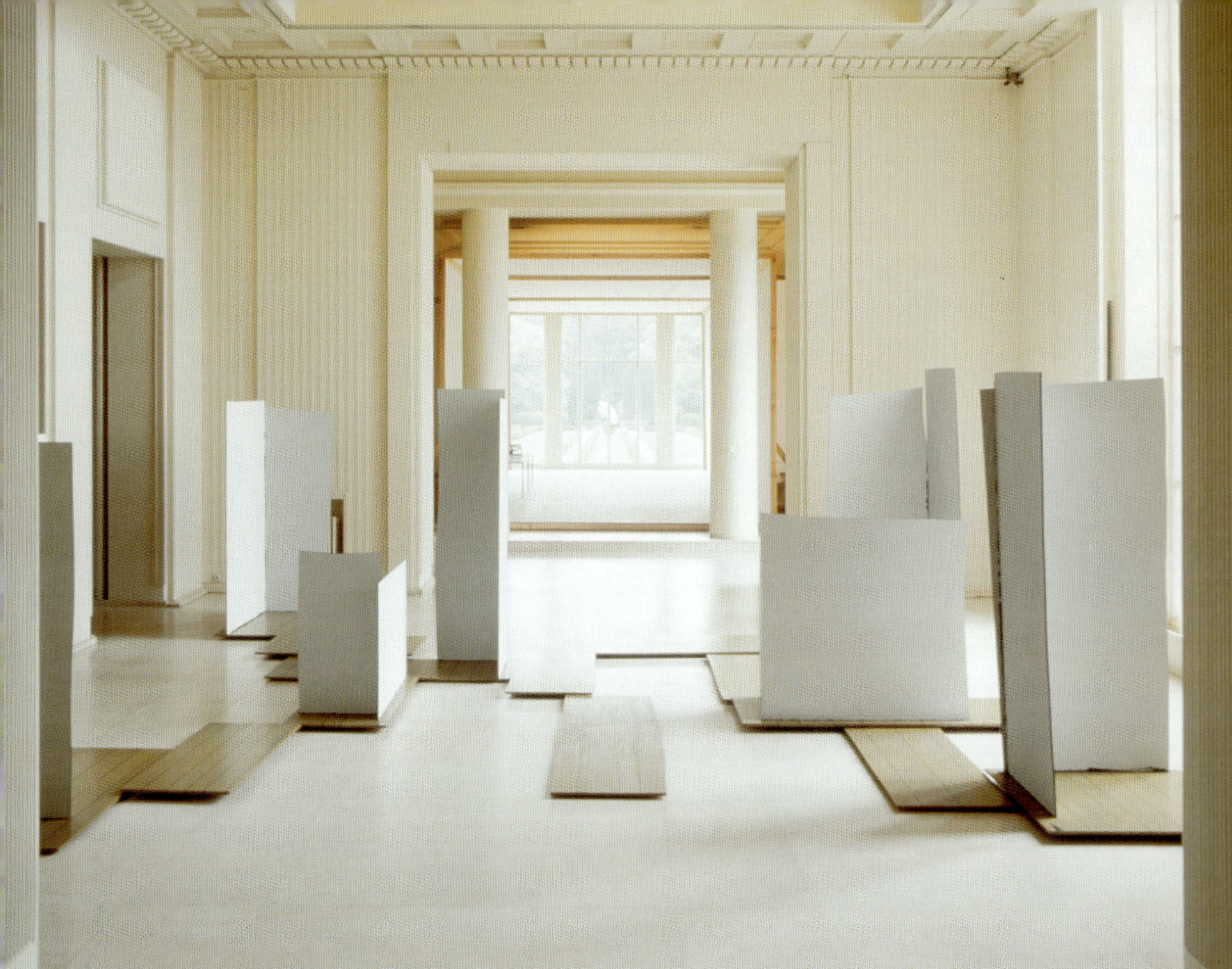

Almonds in Comparison, 2001
Mixed media
Dimensions variable
Prototype
Installation view, "Squatters," Museu Serralves, Porto, Portugal, 2001

Opposite page and previous spread:
Erdnüsse im Vergleich, 2004
MDF, aluminum, construction adhesive, acrylic paint, acrylic lacquer; in 11 parts
104 ⅜ x 393 ¾ x 354 ⅜ inches (265 x 1000 x 900 cm)
Installation view, "Kir Royal," Kunsthaus Zürich, 2004
Opposite page: *What if the Phone Rings,* 2003; *Your Deaths Your Births*, 2004
Previous spread: *Middleclass Heroes*, 2004;
No Need for Ketchup with the Ice Cream, 2004

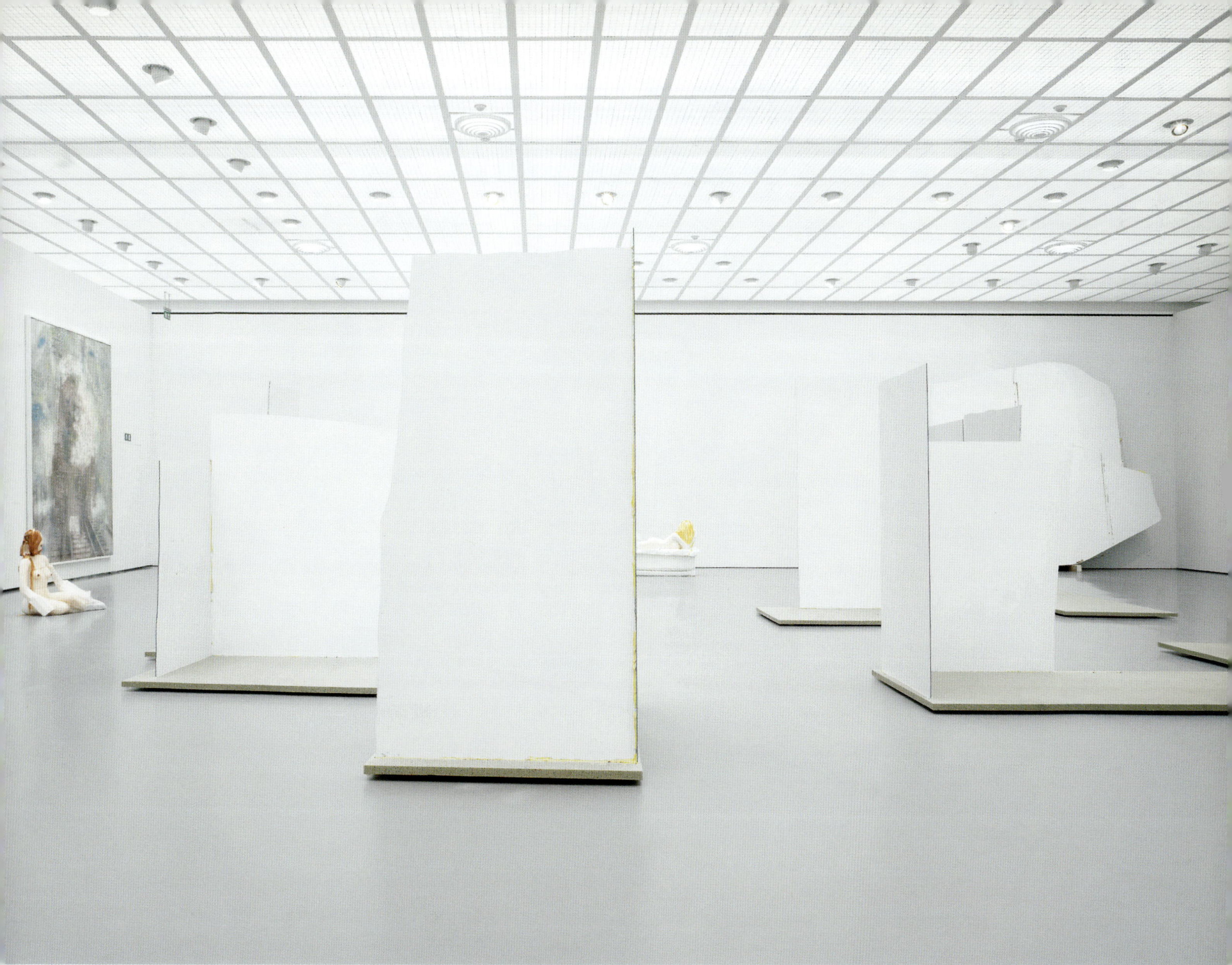

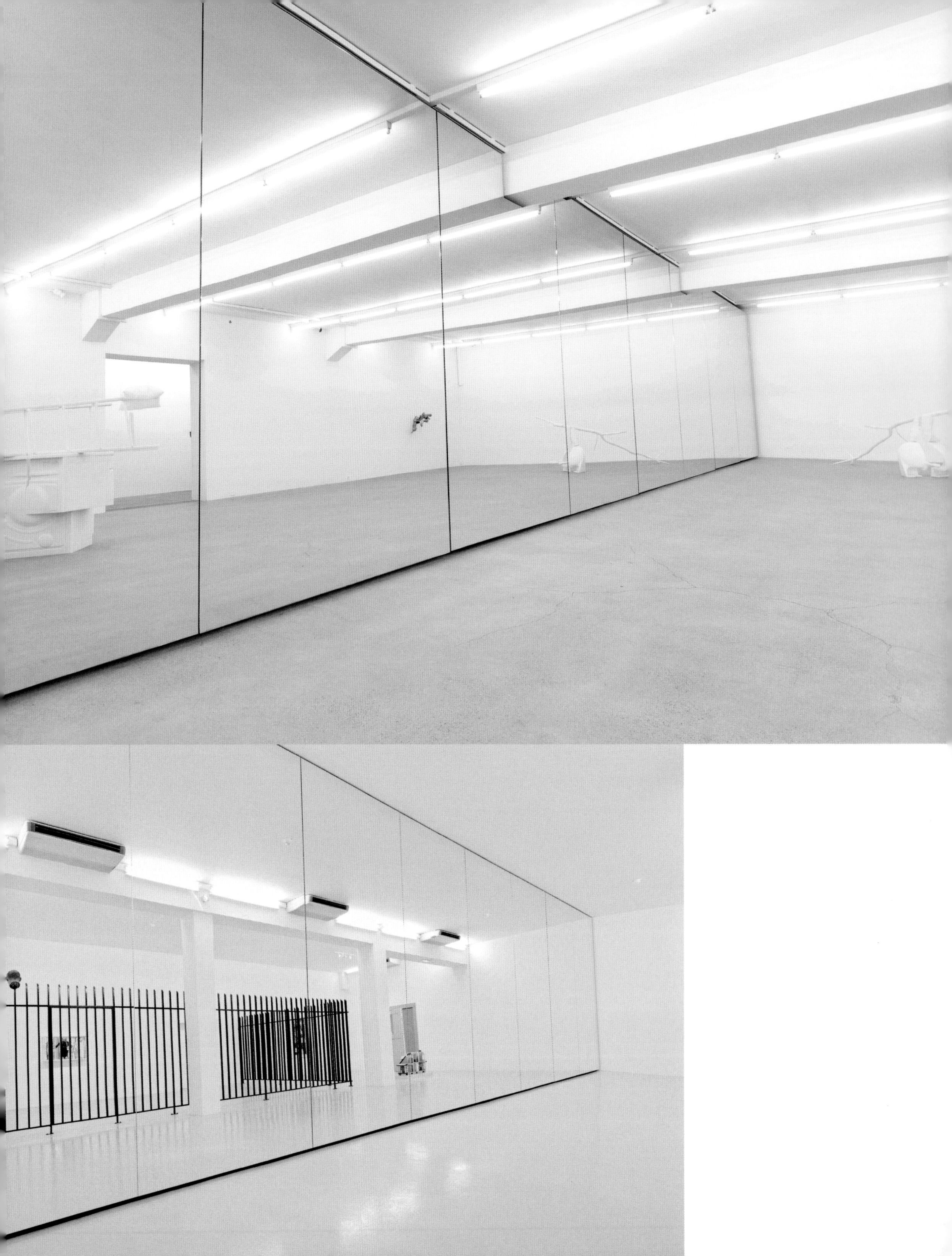

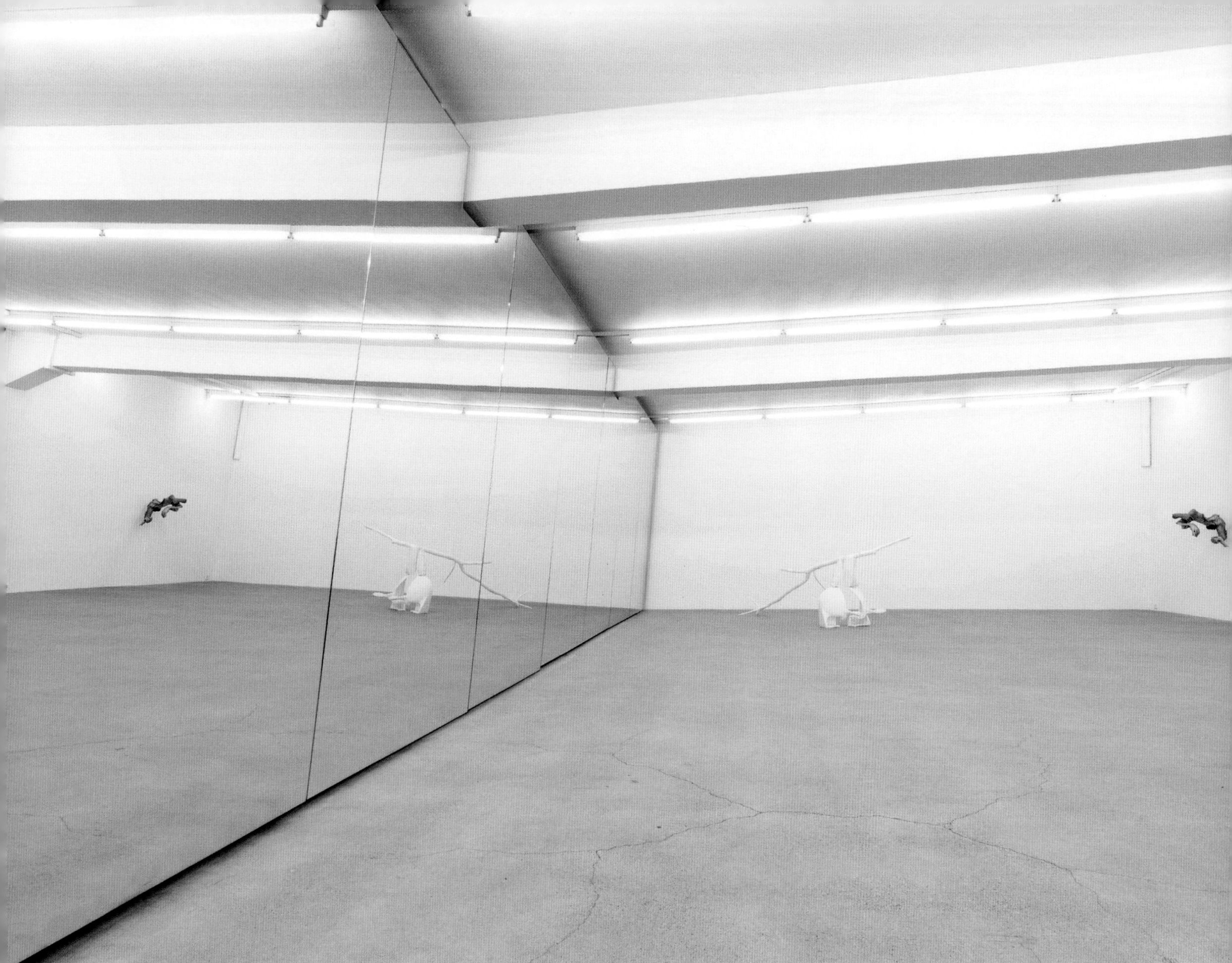

Death of a Moment, 2007
Mirrors, aluminum, hydraulics, control unit
Dimensions variable
Installation view, "large, dark, & empty,"
Galerie Eva Presenhuber, Zurich, 2007
Fuck You Thank You, 2007; *The Grass Munchers*, 2007
Opposite page, top, reflected in mirror: *Thank You Fuck You*, 2007;
The Grass Munchers, 2007; *Fuck You Thank You*, 2007
Opposite page, bottom: Installation view, "Fractured Figure: Works from the Dakis Joannou Collection," Deste Foundation Centre for Contemporary Art, Athens, 2007–2008
Reflected in mirror: *Death of a Moment*, 2007;
Poka-Yio, *Self-Decapitated*, 2005;
Roberto Cuoghi, *Untitled (Lady Godzilla)*, 2004

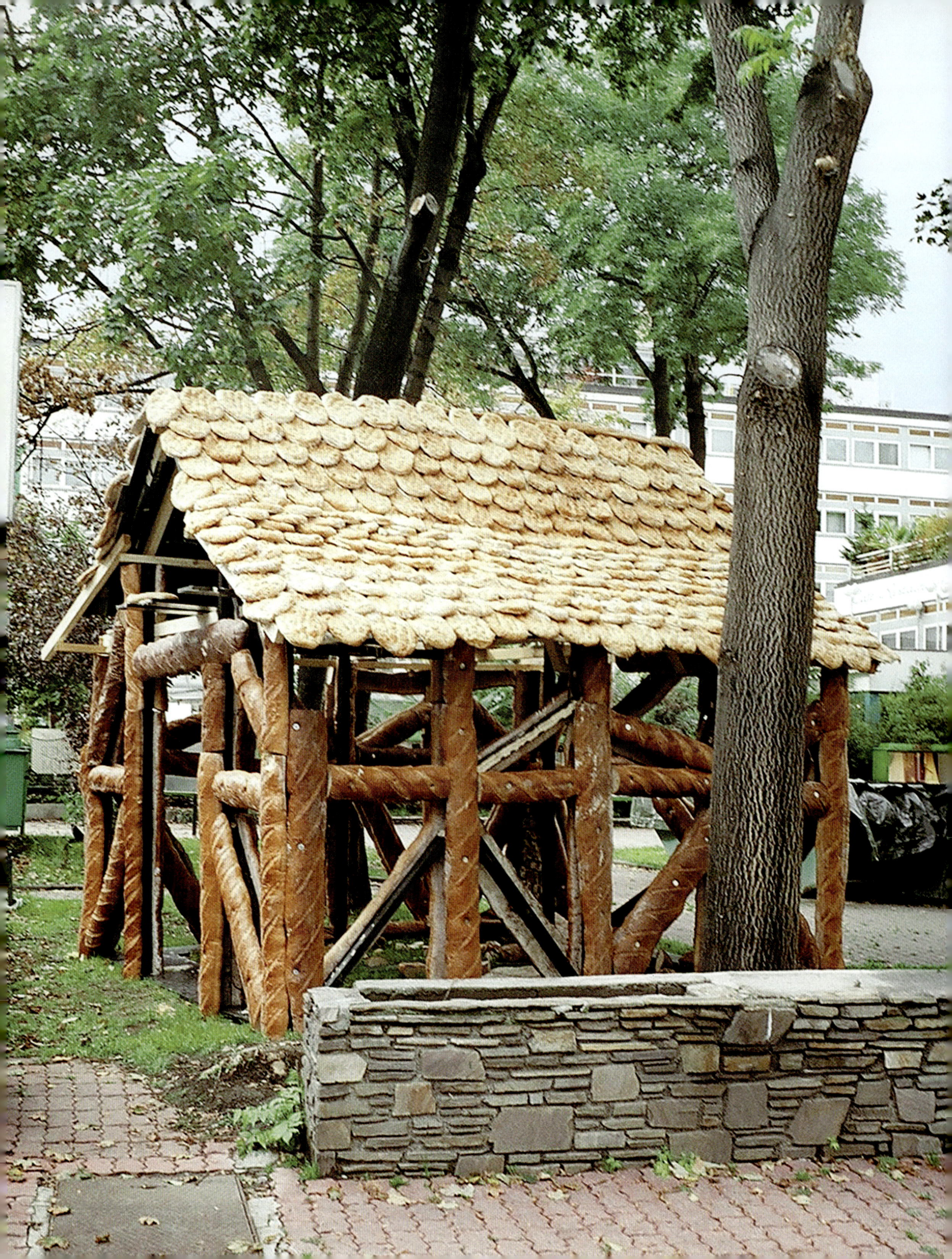

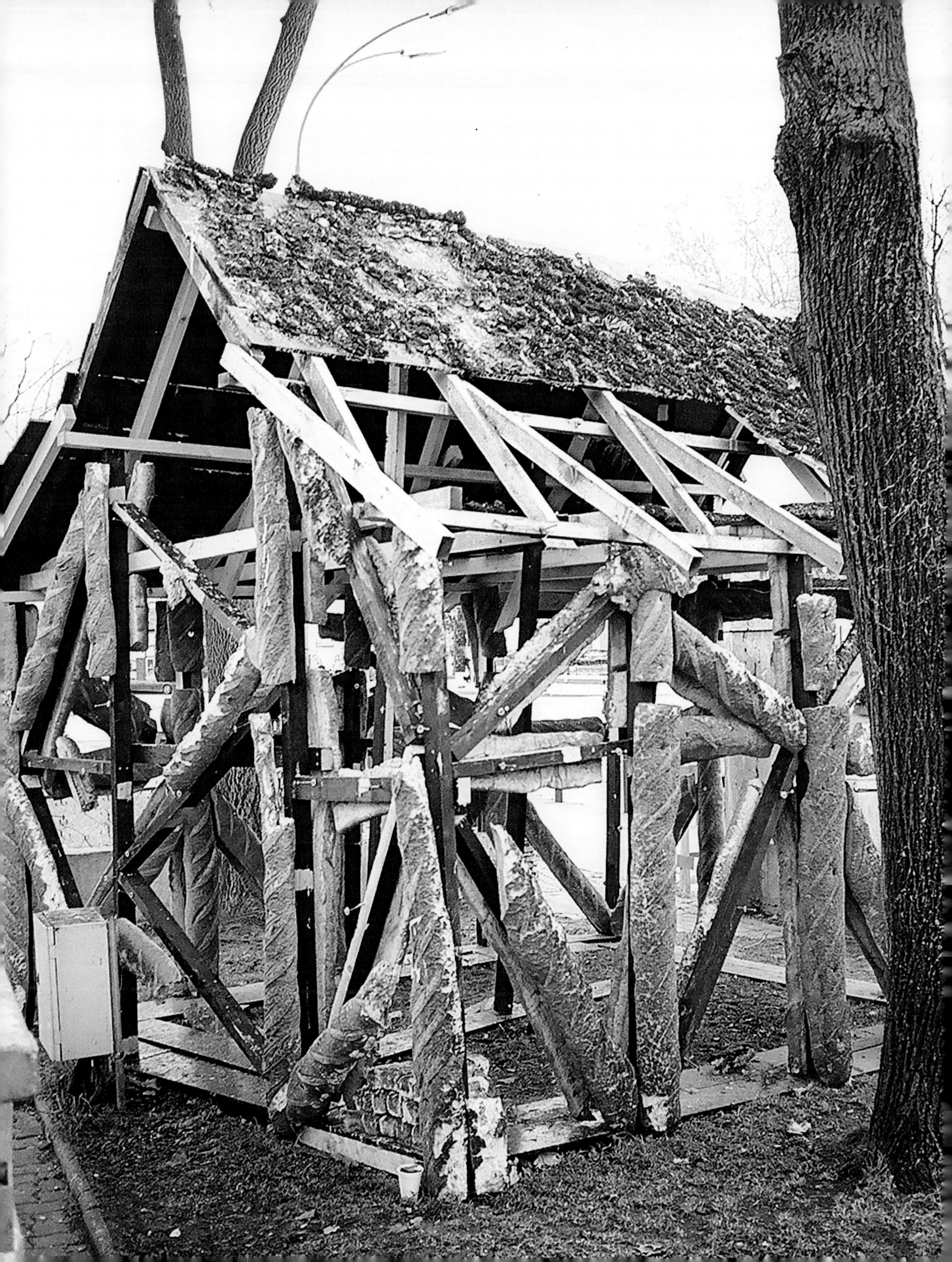

Previous pages:

Untitled (Bread House), 2004

Bread, bread crumbs, wood, polyurethane foam, silicone, acrylic paint, screws, tape, rugs, theater spotlights
159 ⅞ x 146 ½ x 165 ¾ inches (406 x 372 x 421 cm)
Prototype
Installation view, "Feige, Nuss, und Birne," Gruppe Österreichische Guggenheim, Vienna, 2004

Untitled (Bread House), 2004–2005

Bread, bread crumbs, wood, polyurethane foam, silicone, acrylic paint, screws, tape, rugs, theater spotlights
159 ⅞ x 146 ½ x 165 ¾ inches (406 x 372 x 421 cm)
Installation view, "Jet Set Lady," Fondazione Nicola Trussardi, Istituto dei Ciechi, Milan, 2005

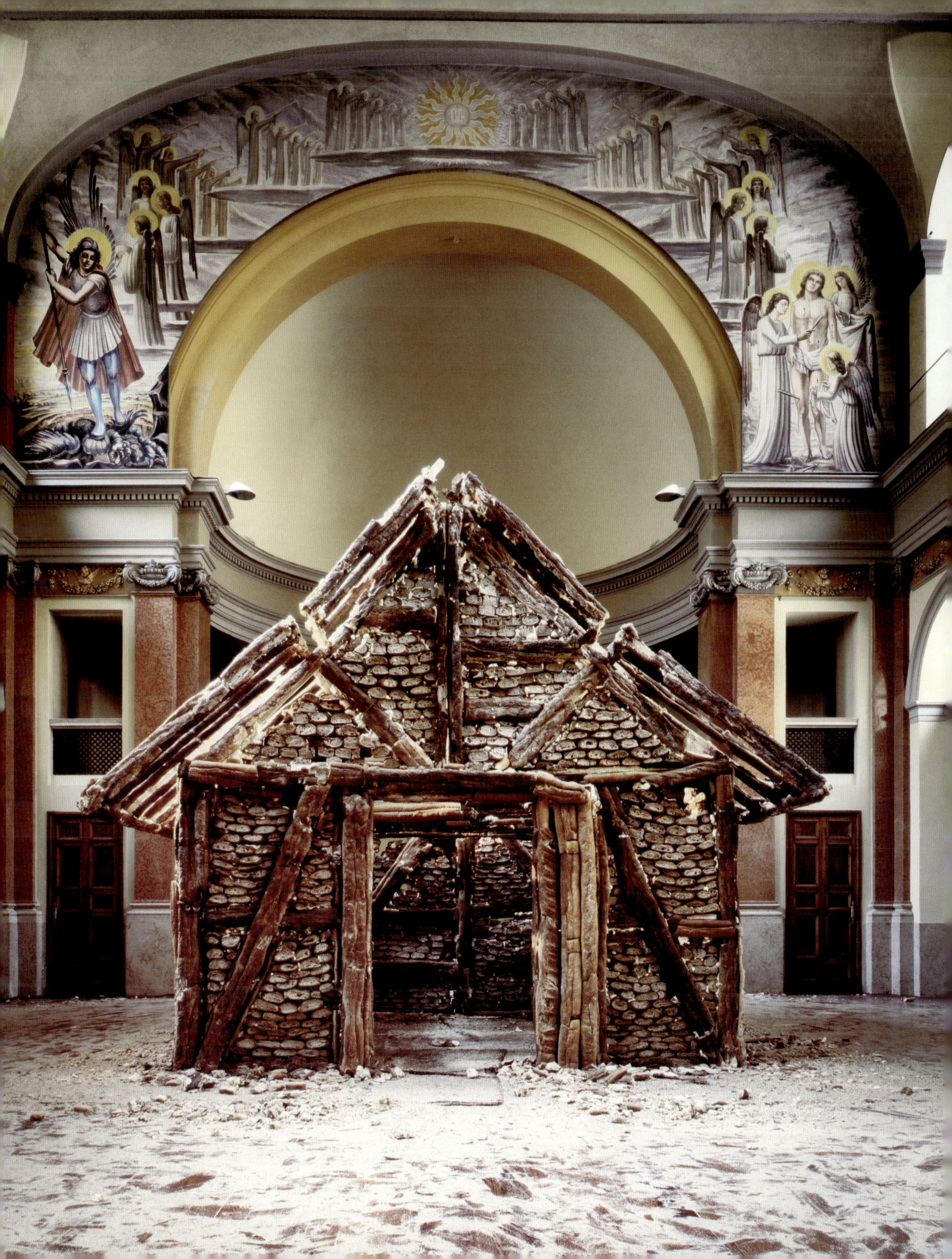

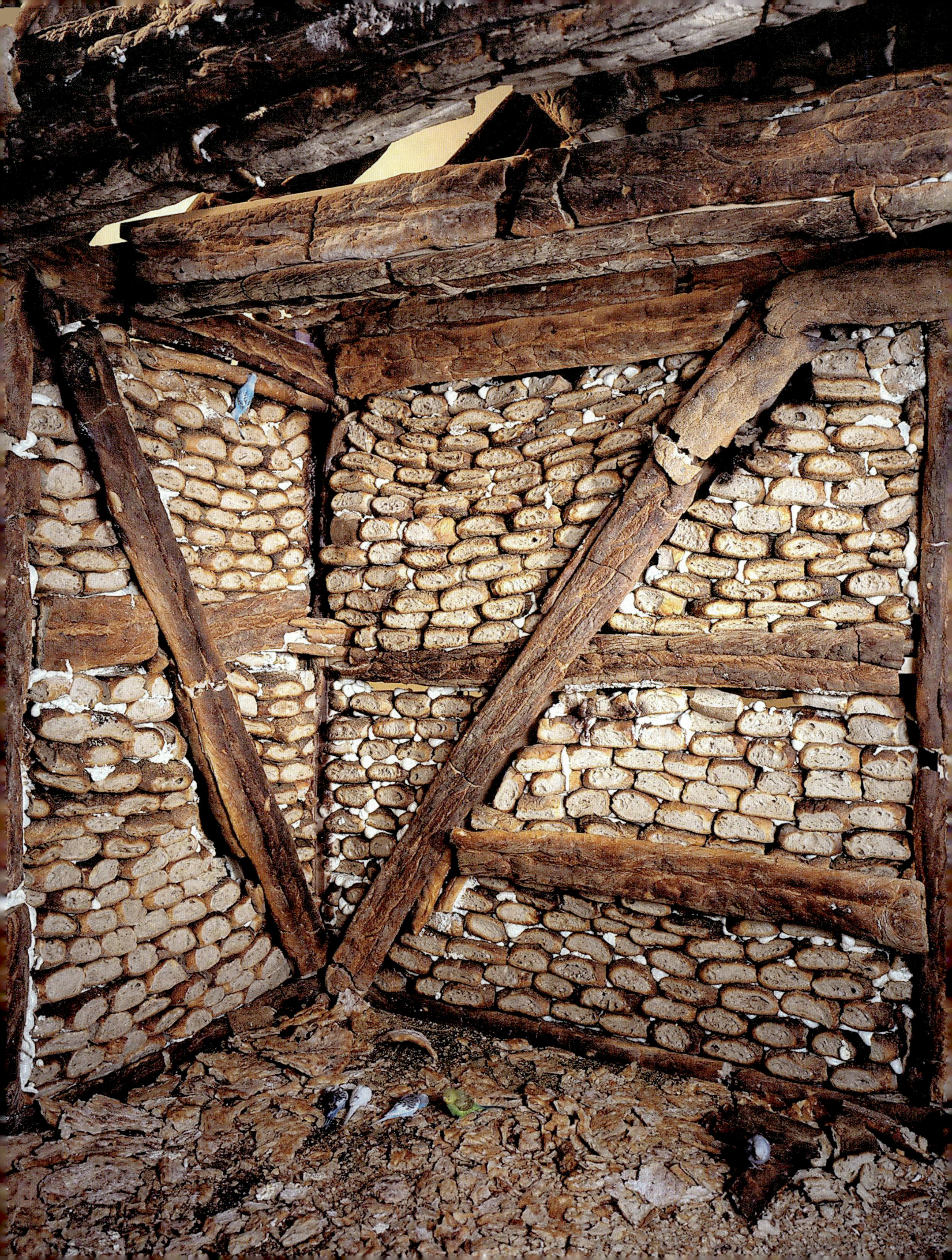

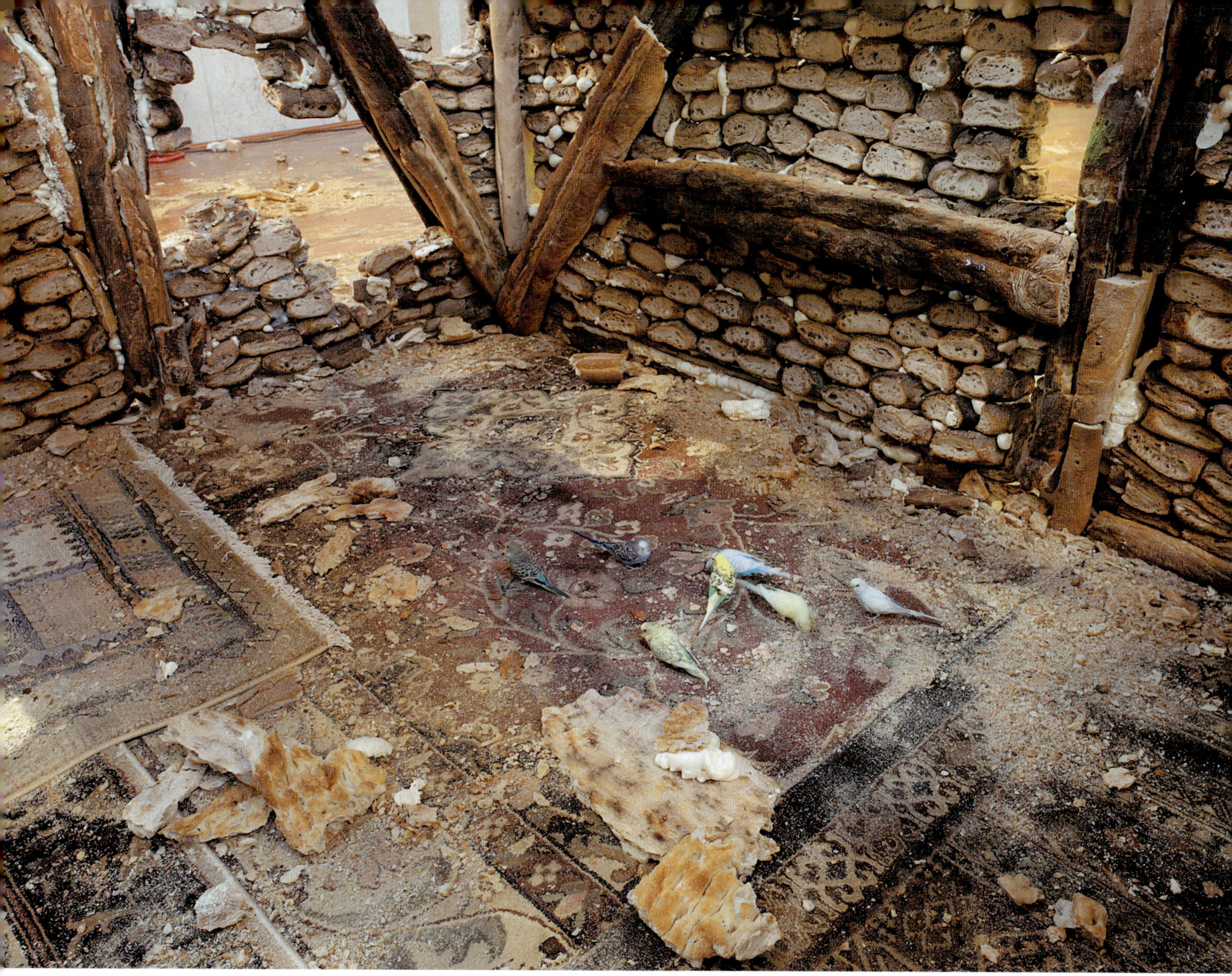

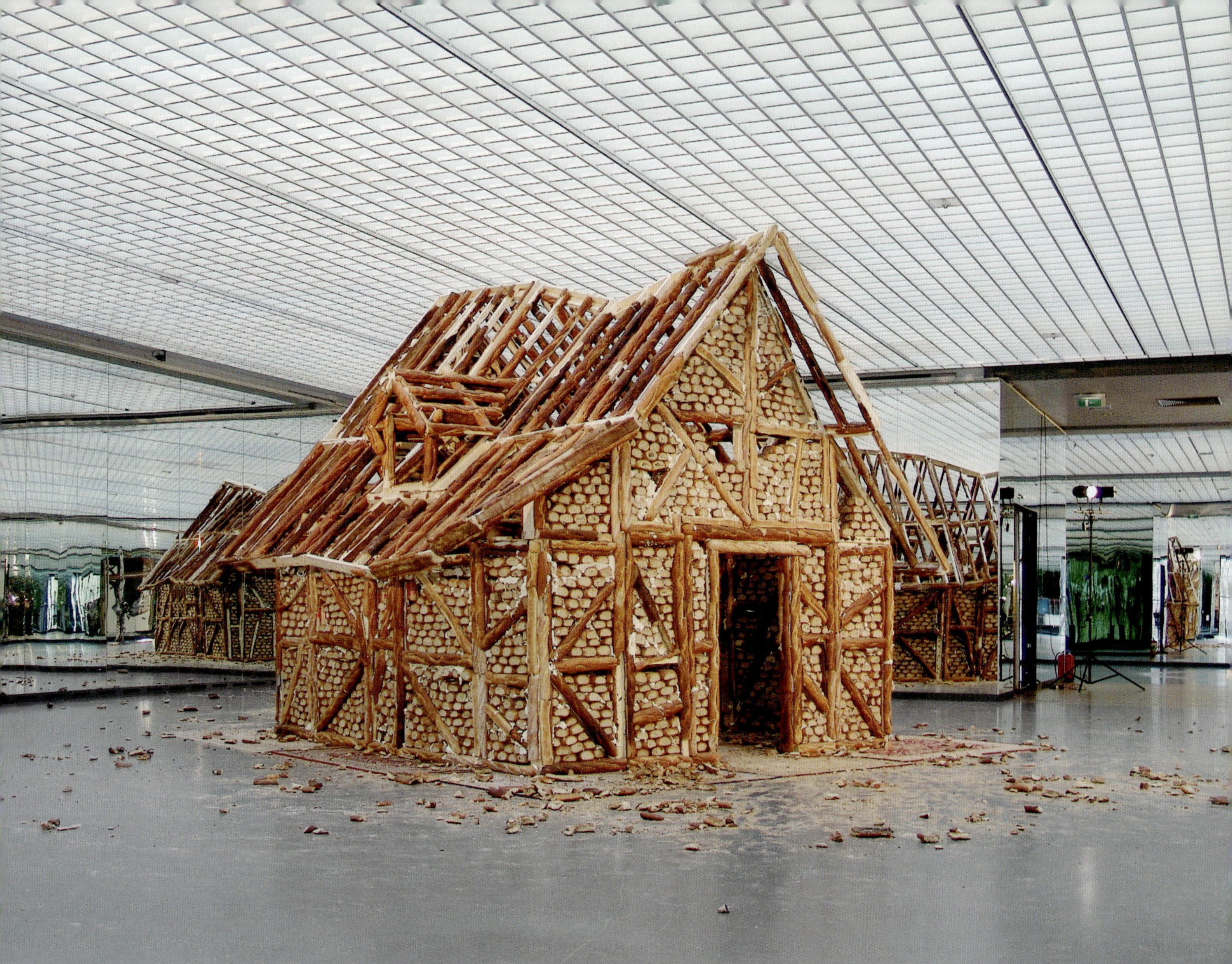

Untitled (Bread House), 2004–2006
Bread, bread crumbs, wood, polyurethane foam, silicone, acrylic paint, screws, tape, rugs, theater spotlights
196 ⅞ x 157 ½ x 196 ⅞ inches (500 x 400 x 500 cm)
Installation view, "Paris 1919,"
Museum Boijmans Van Beuningen, Rotterdam, 2006

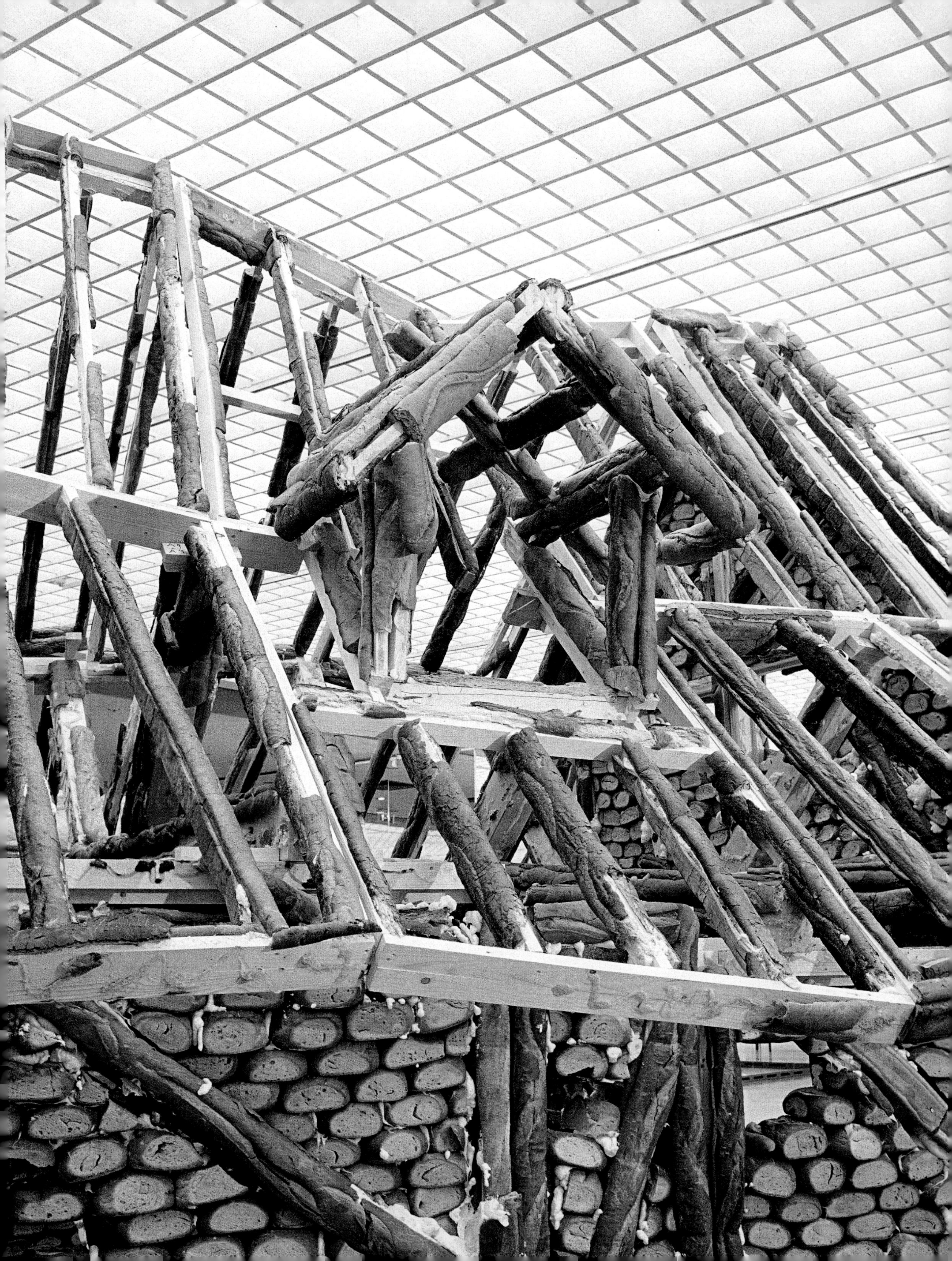

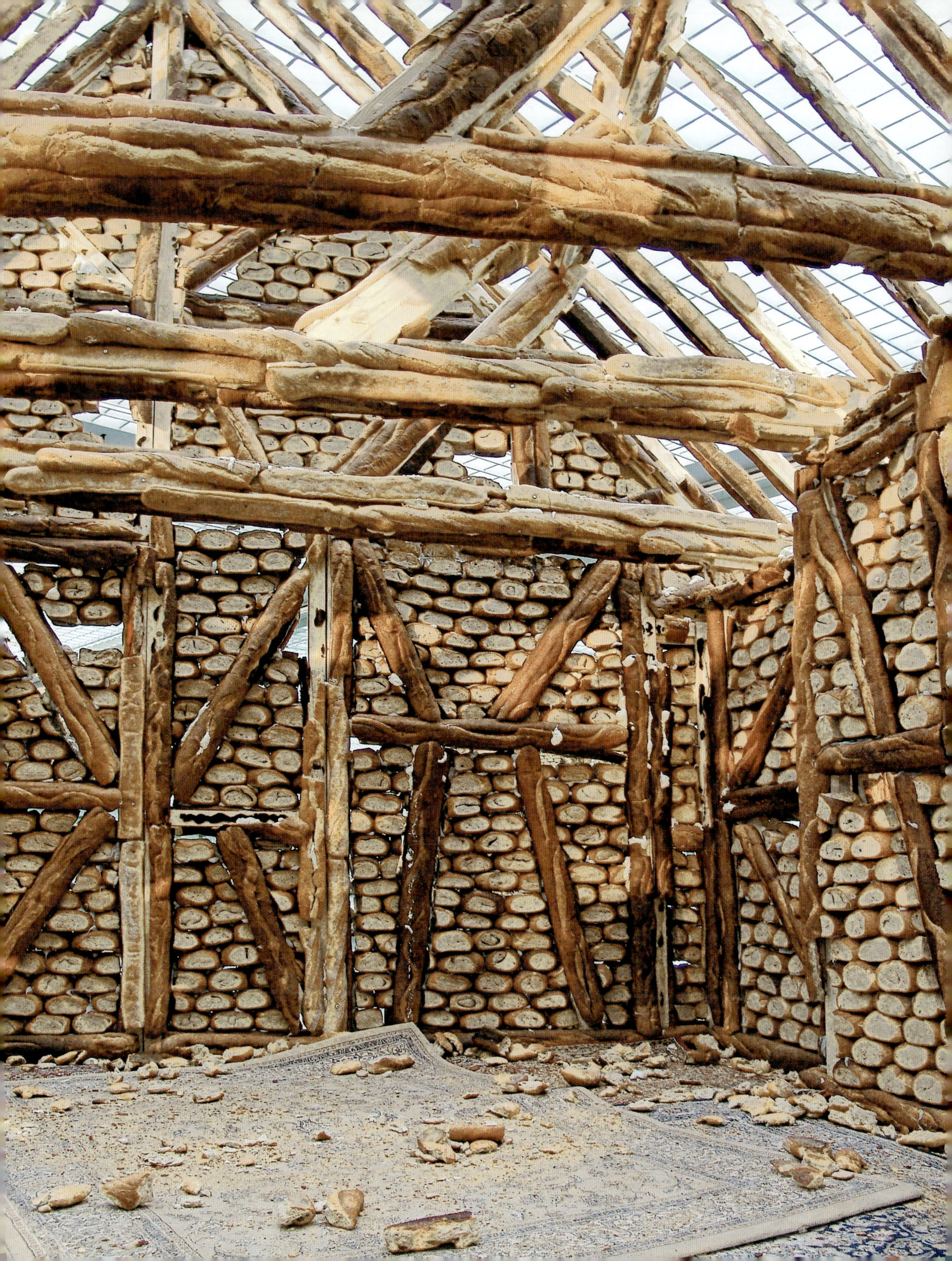

Untitled (Door), 2006
Cast aluminum, enamel paint, steel hinges
84 ⅝ x 53 ½ x 20 ⅛ inches (215 x 136 x 51 cm)
Installation view, "Urs Fischer e Rudolf Stingel,"
Galleria Massimo de Carlo, Milan, 2006–2007
On floor: Rudolf Stingel, *Untitled (Sarouk)*, 2006

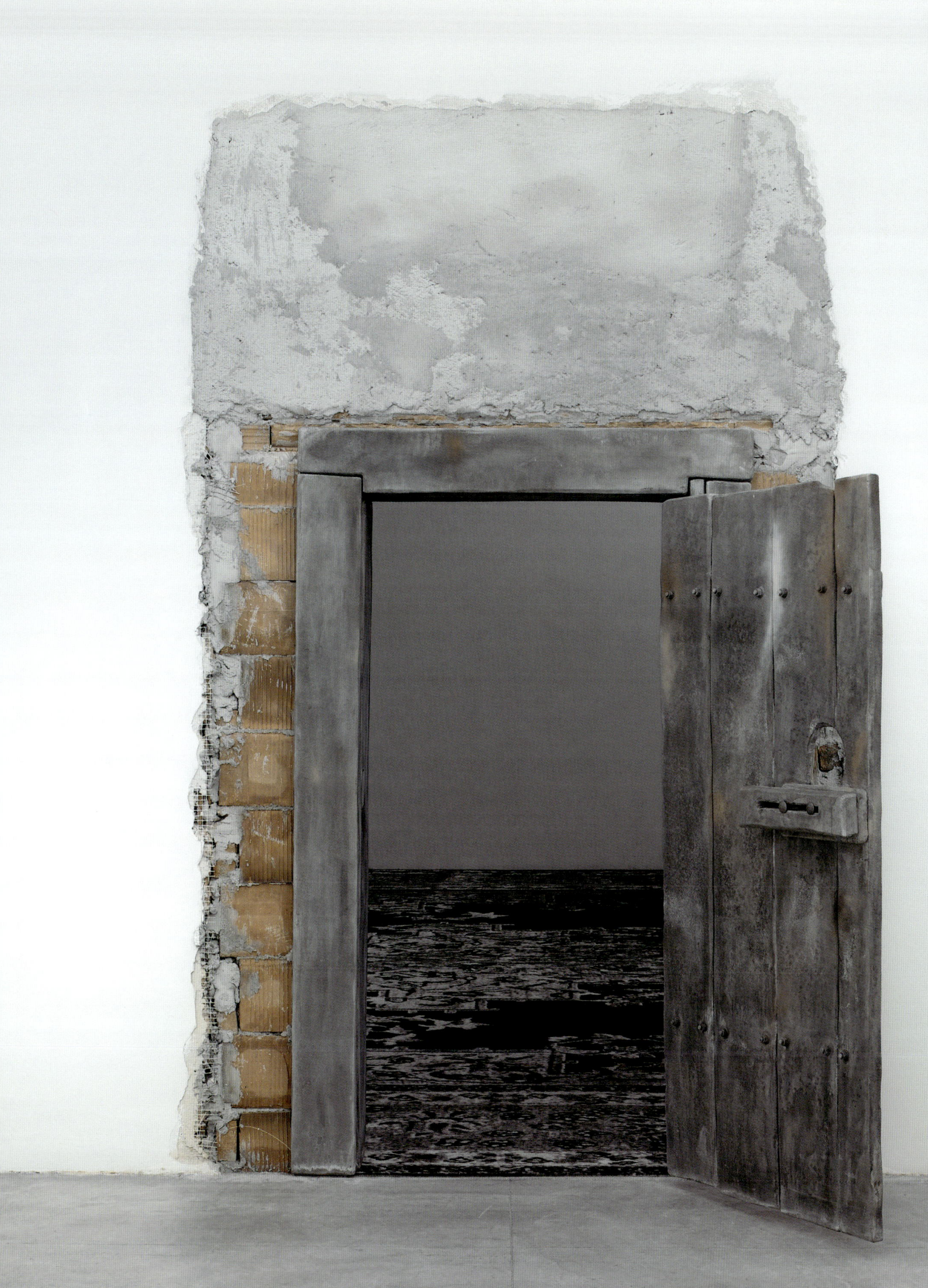

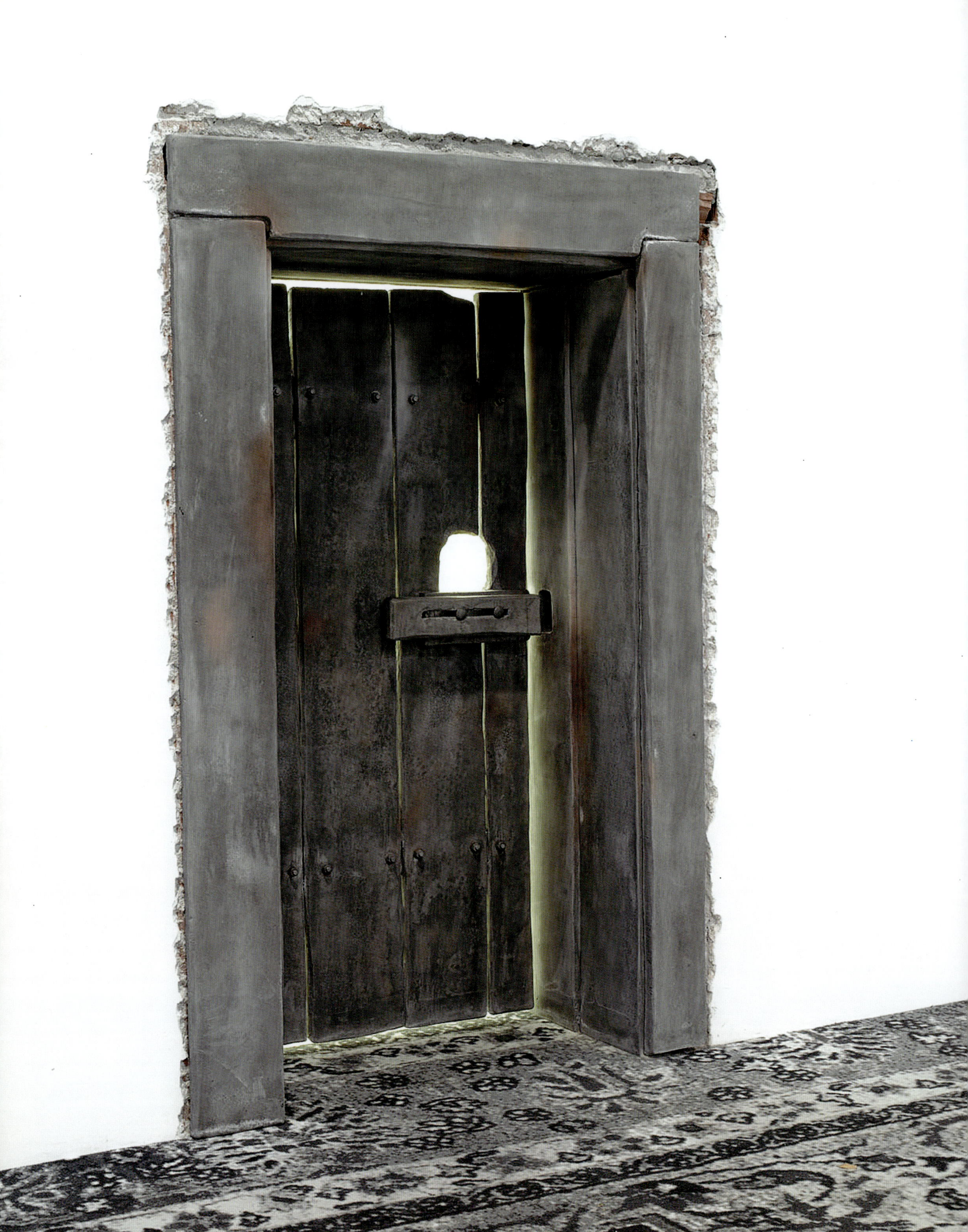

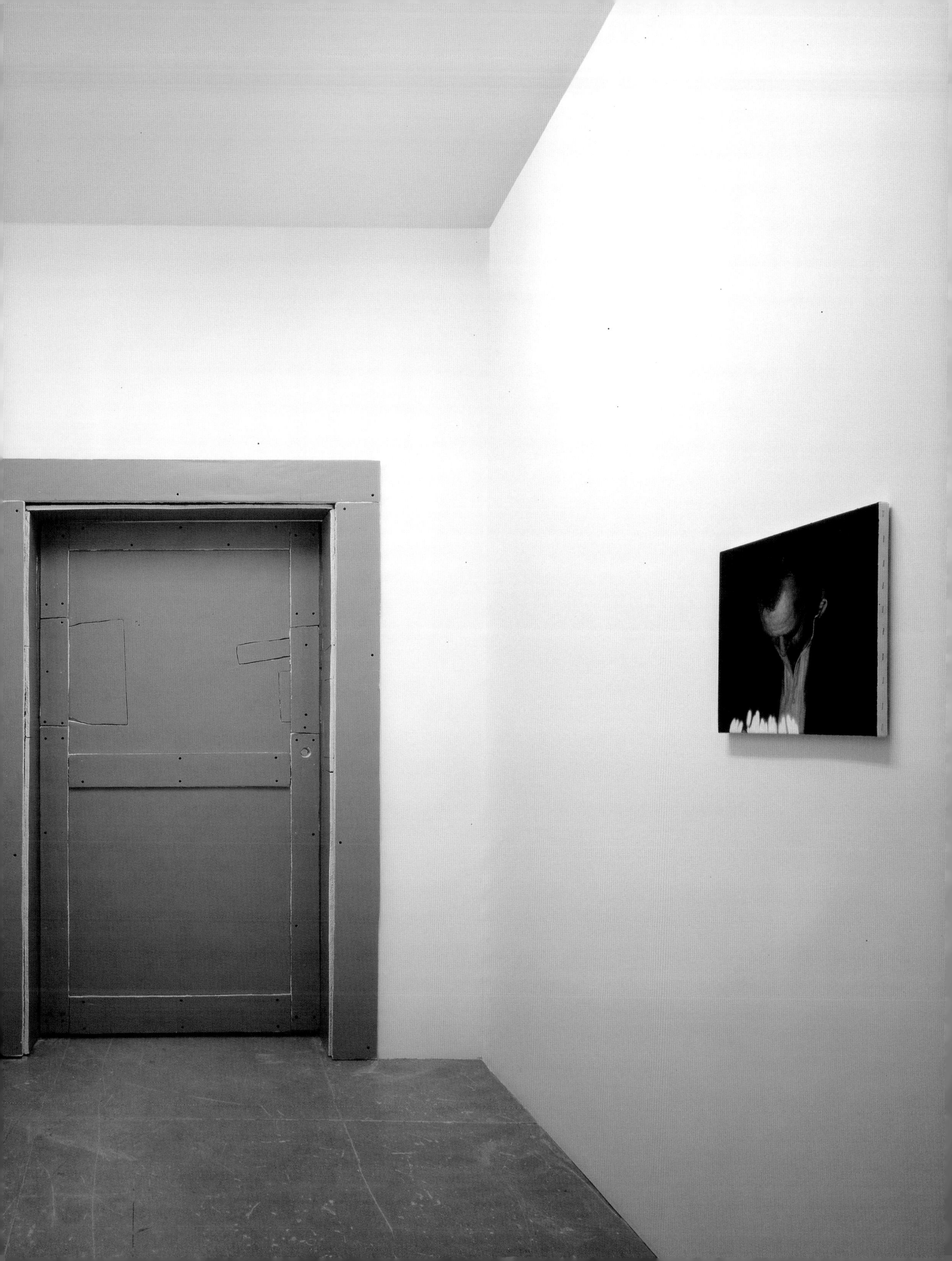

Opposite and previous page:
Untitled (Door), 2006
Cast aluminum, enamel paint, steel hinges
100 ¾ x 67 ¾ x 10 ⅝ inches (256 x 172 x 27 cm)
Installation view, "Urs Fischer e Rudolf Stingel,"
Galleria Massimo de Carlo, Milan, 2006–2007
On wall: Rudolf Stingel, *Untitled (Bolego)*, 2006

Following pages:
Untitled (Door), 2006
Cast aluminum, enamel paint, steel hinges
110 ⅝ x 71 x 10 ⅝ inches (281 x 183 x 27 cm)
Installation view, "Urs Fischer e Rudolf Stingel,"
Galleria Massimo de Carlo, Milan, 2006–2007
On wall: Rudolf Stingel, *Untitled (Bolego)*, 2006

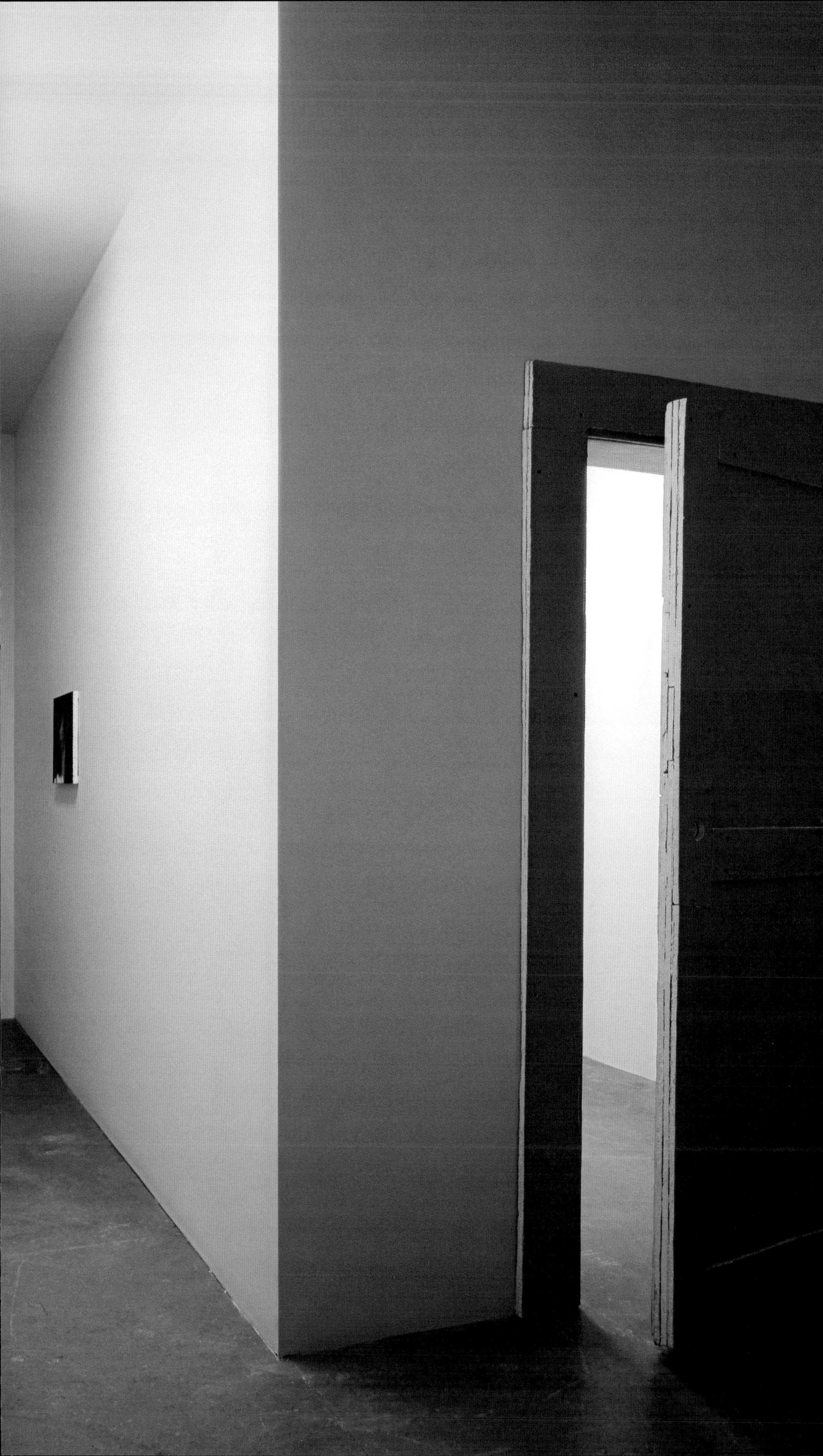

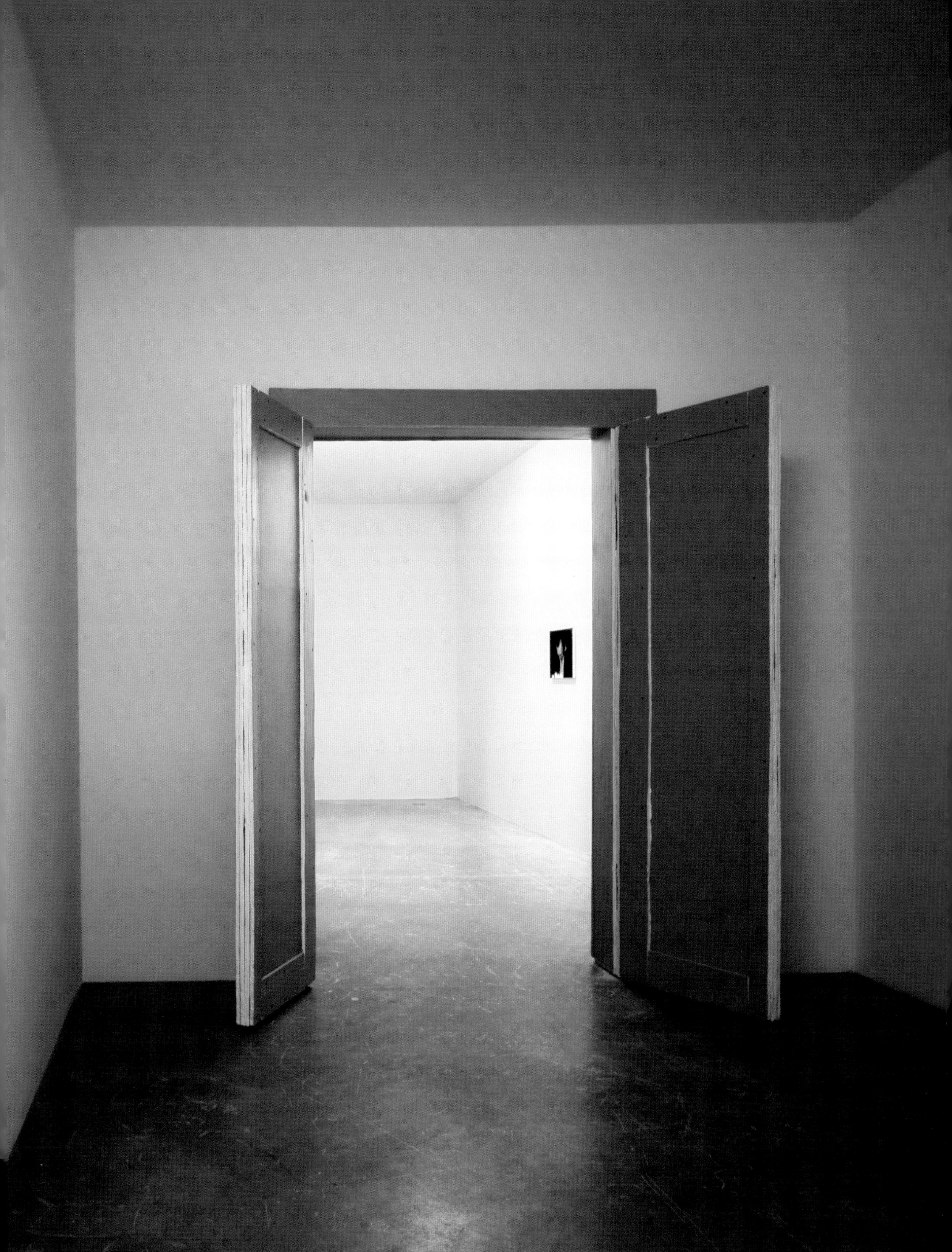

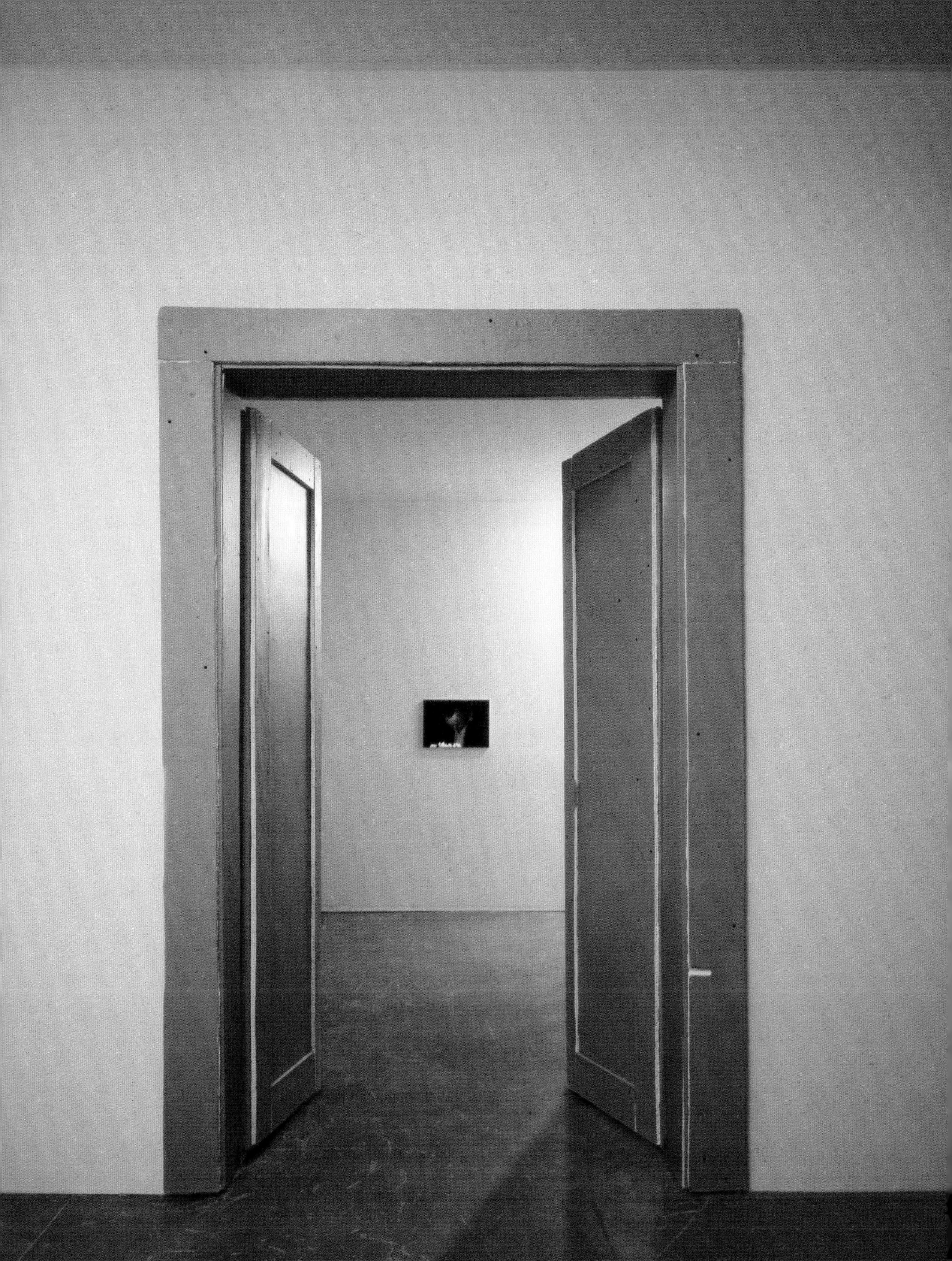

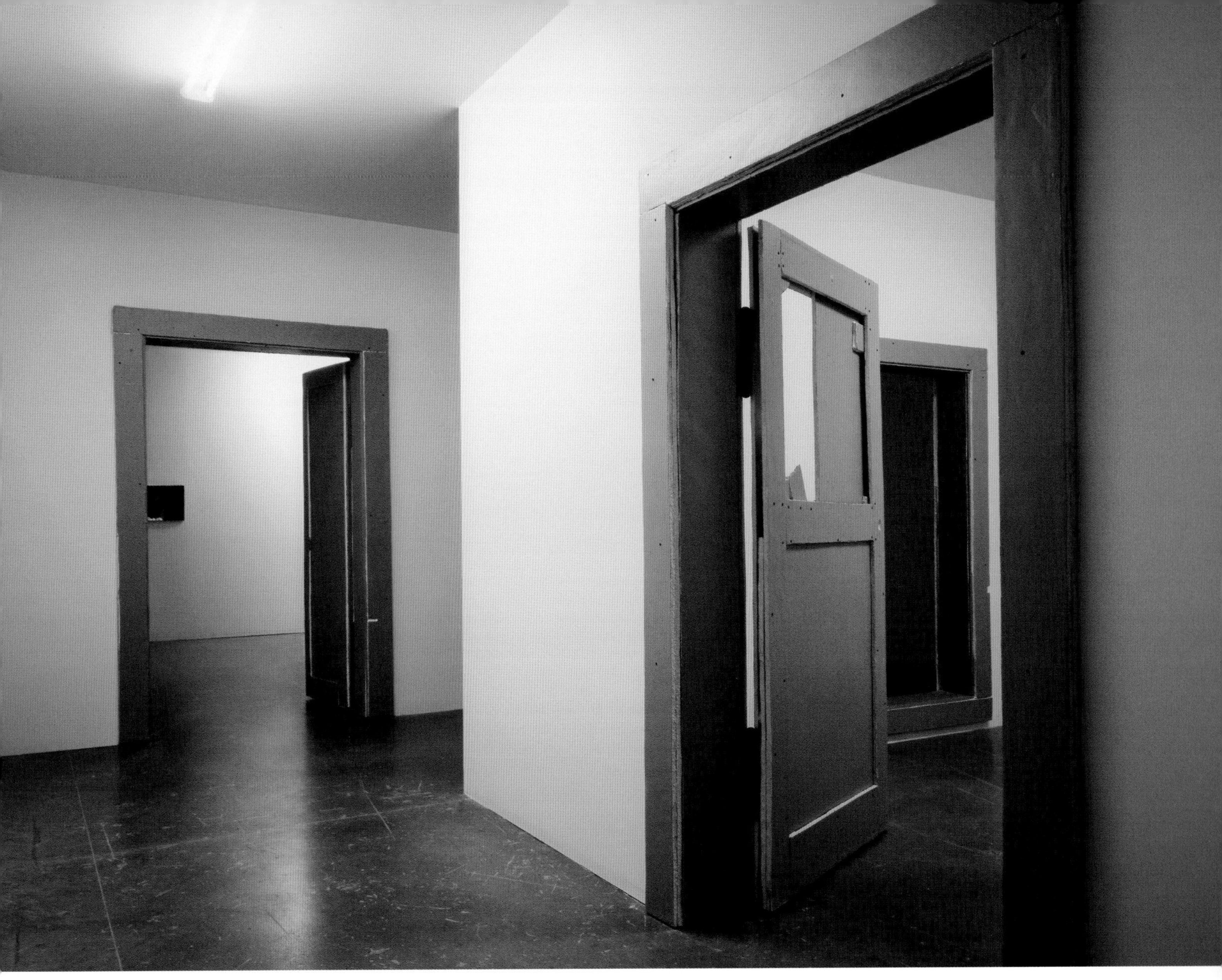

Above, opposite, and page 349:
Untitled (Door), 2006
Cast aluminum, enamel paint, steel hinges
95 ¼ x 61 ¾ x 10 ⅝ inches (242 x 157 x 27 cm)
Installation view, "Urs Fischer e Rudolf Stingel,"
Galleria Massimo de Carlo, Milan, 2006–2007
Untitled (Door), 2006; *Untitled (Door)*, 2006
On wall: Rudolf Stingel, *Untitled (Bolego),* 2006

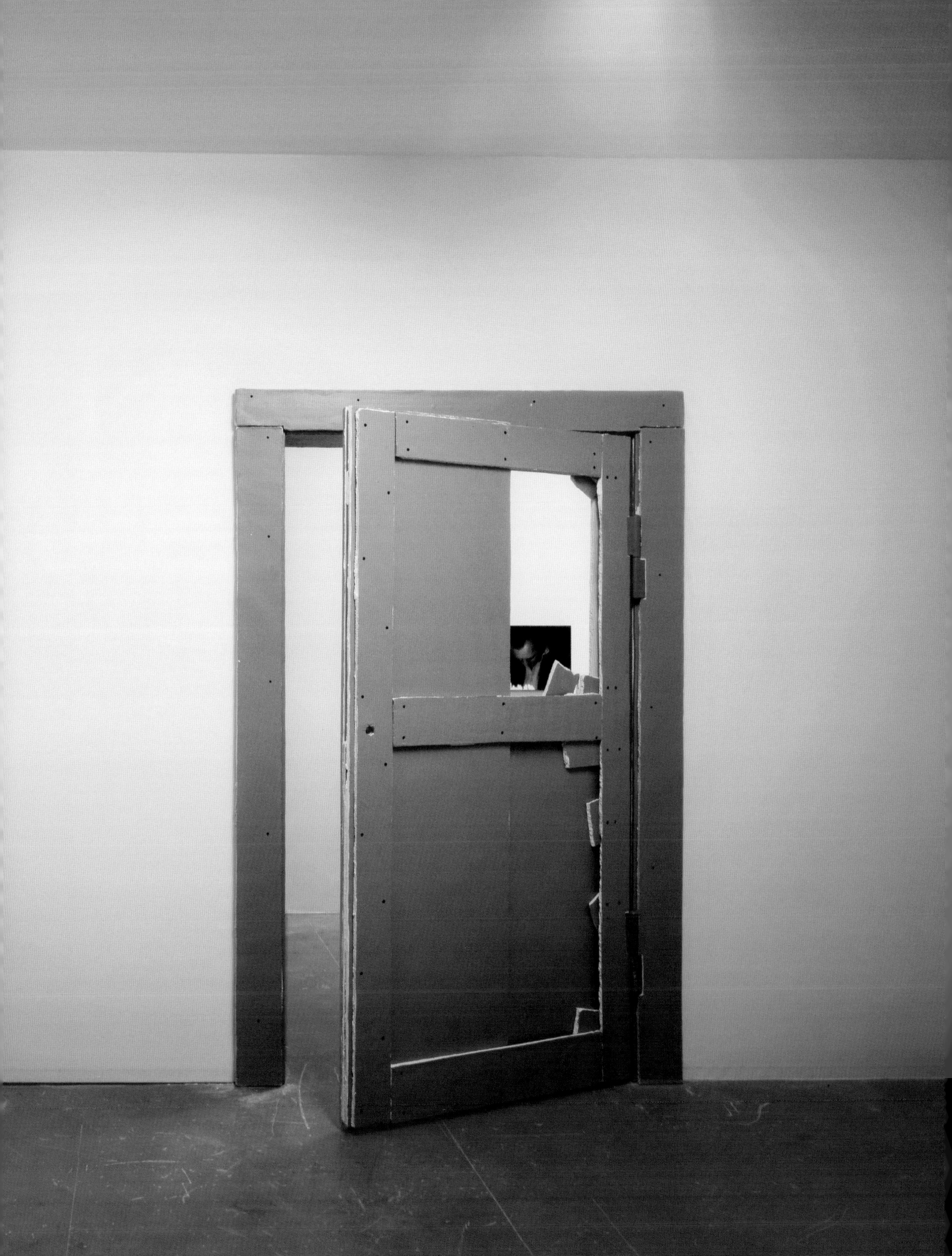

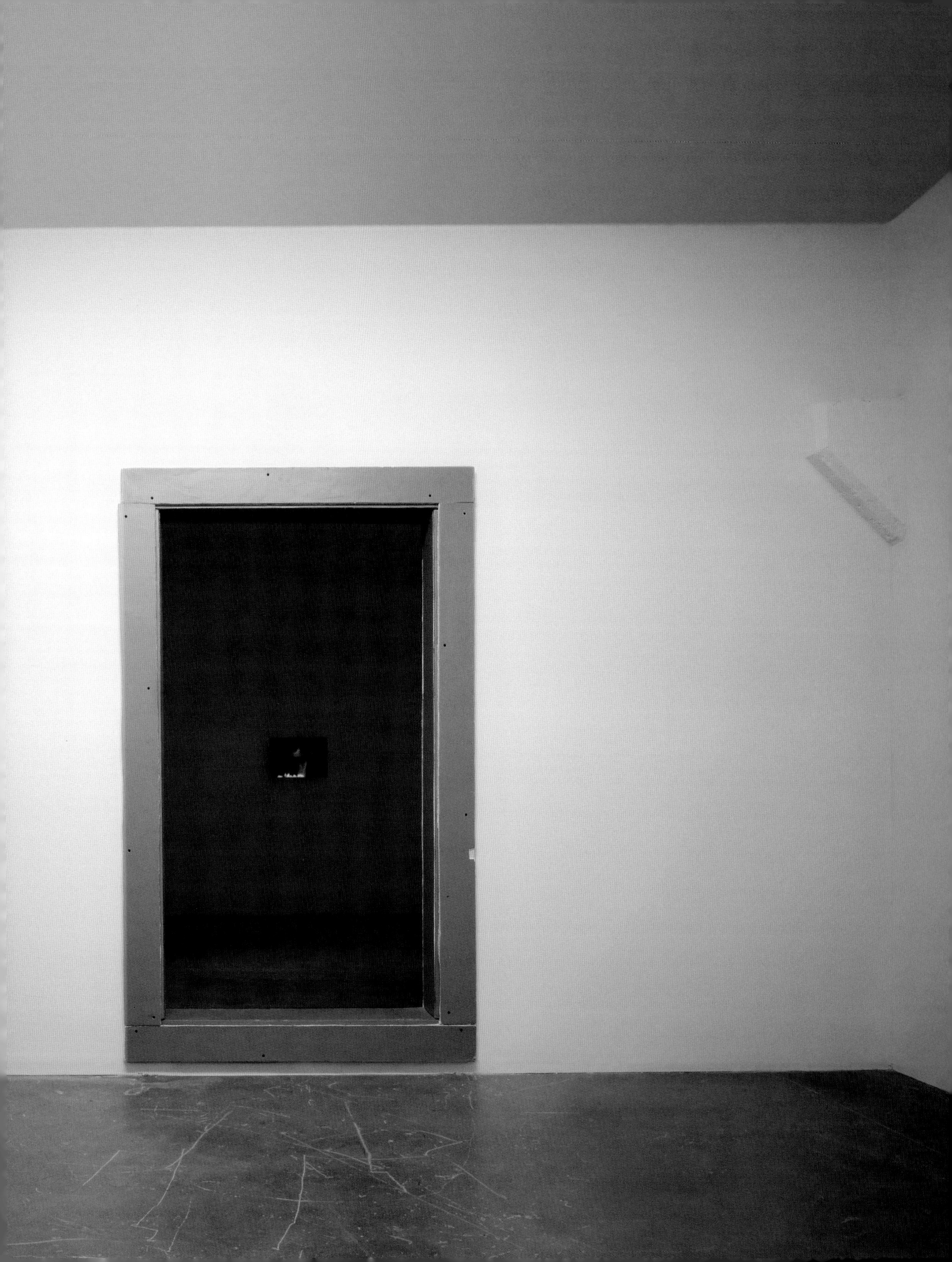

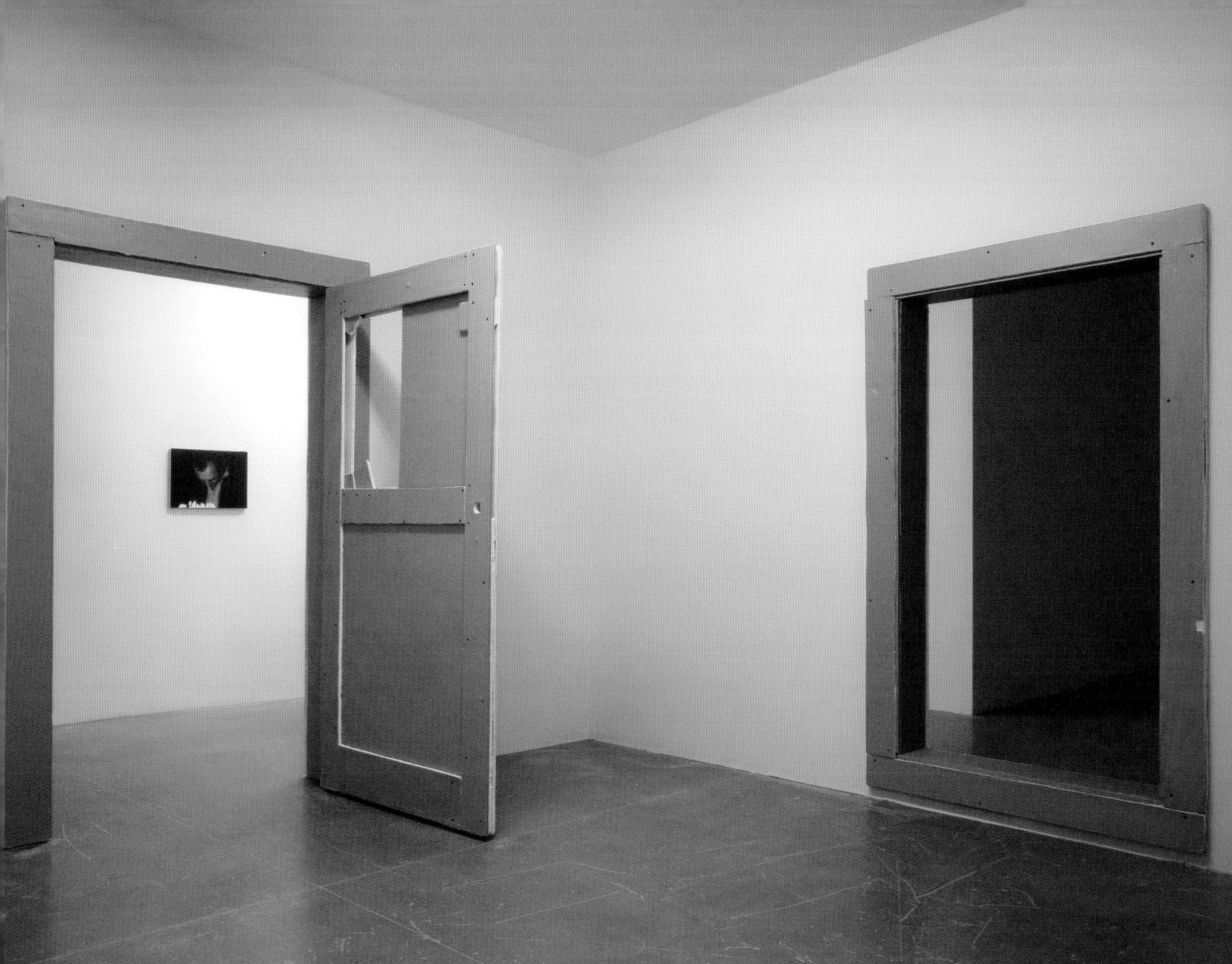

Opposite page and pages 346 and 350:

Untitled (Door), 2006

Cast aluminum, enamel paint, steel hinges
97 ¼ x 61 ⅜ x 10 ⅝ inches (247 x 156 x 27 cm)
Installation view, "Urs Fischer e Rudolf Stingel,"
Galleria Massimo de Carlo, Milan, 2006–2007
Above: *Untitled (Door)*, 2006; On wall: Rudolf Stingel,
Untitled (Bolego), 2006

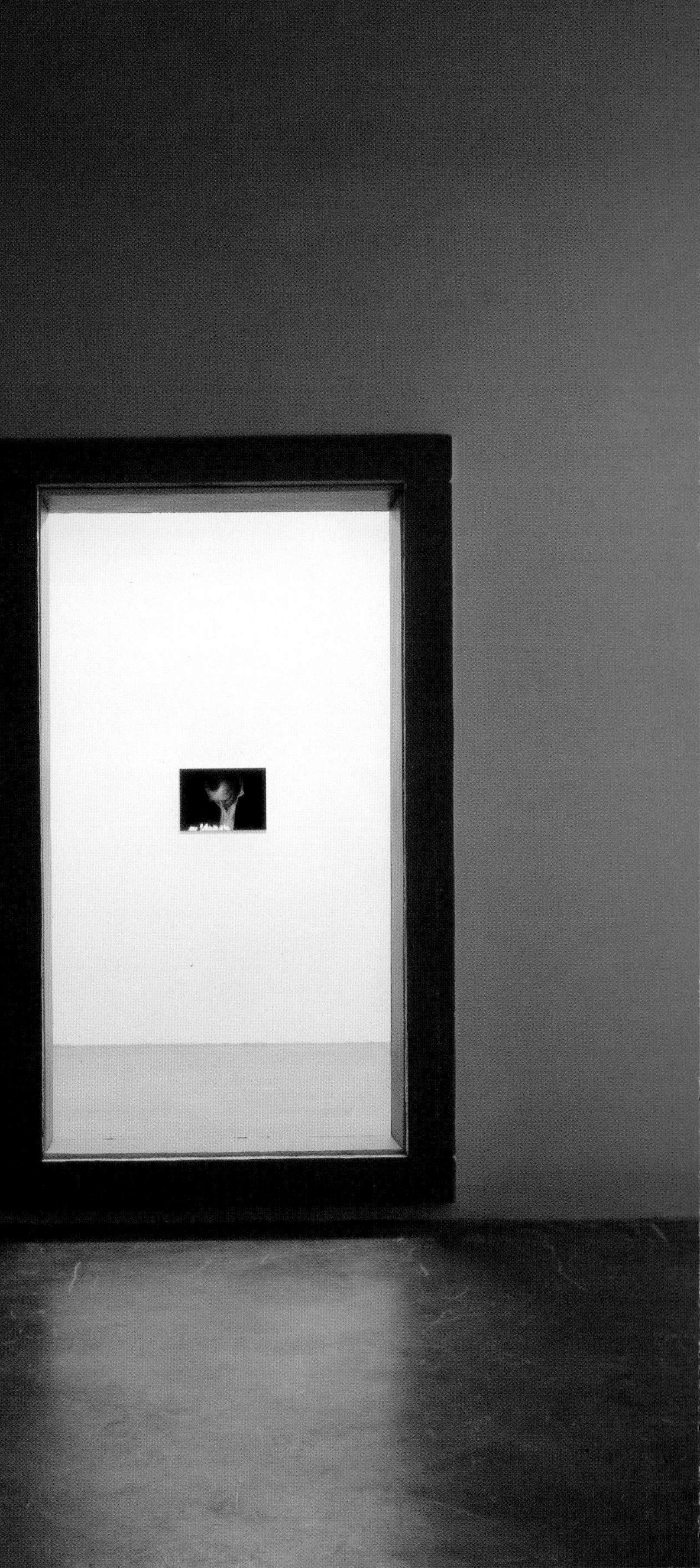

Stühle, 2002

Two-component polyurethane foam,
polyurethane foam, cardboard, tape,
acrylic paint, imitation leather, brass pins
38 ¼ x 33 ½ x 35 ⅞ inches (97 x 85 x 91 cm)

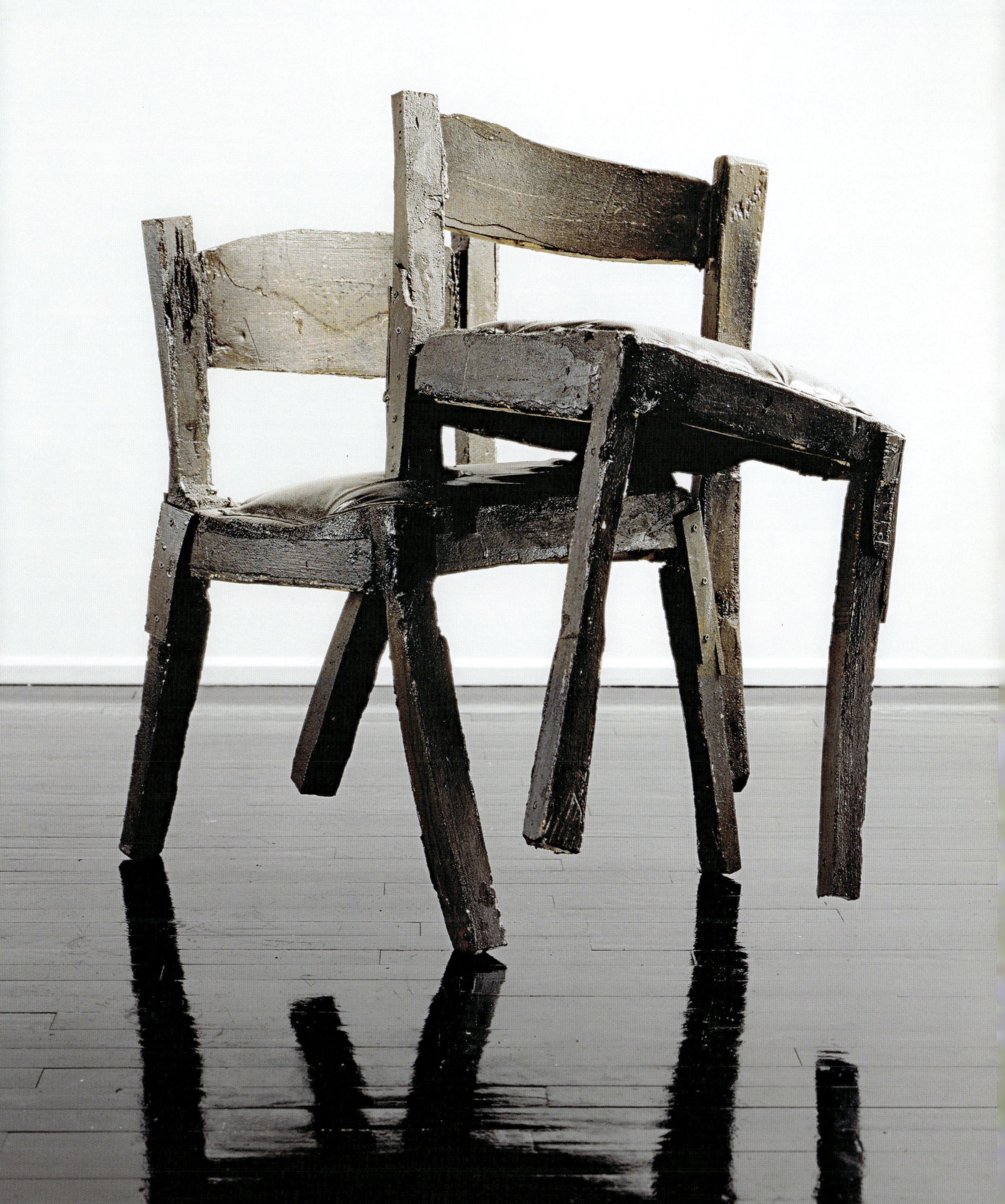

Late Late Night Show, 2002

Polystyrene, acrylic paint, wood glue,
polyurethane foam, screws
46 x 38 ¼ x 26 inches (117 x 97 x 66 cm)

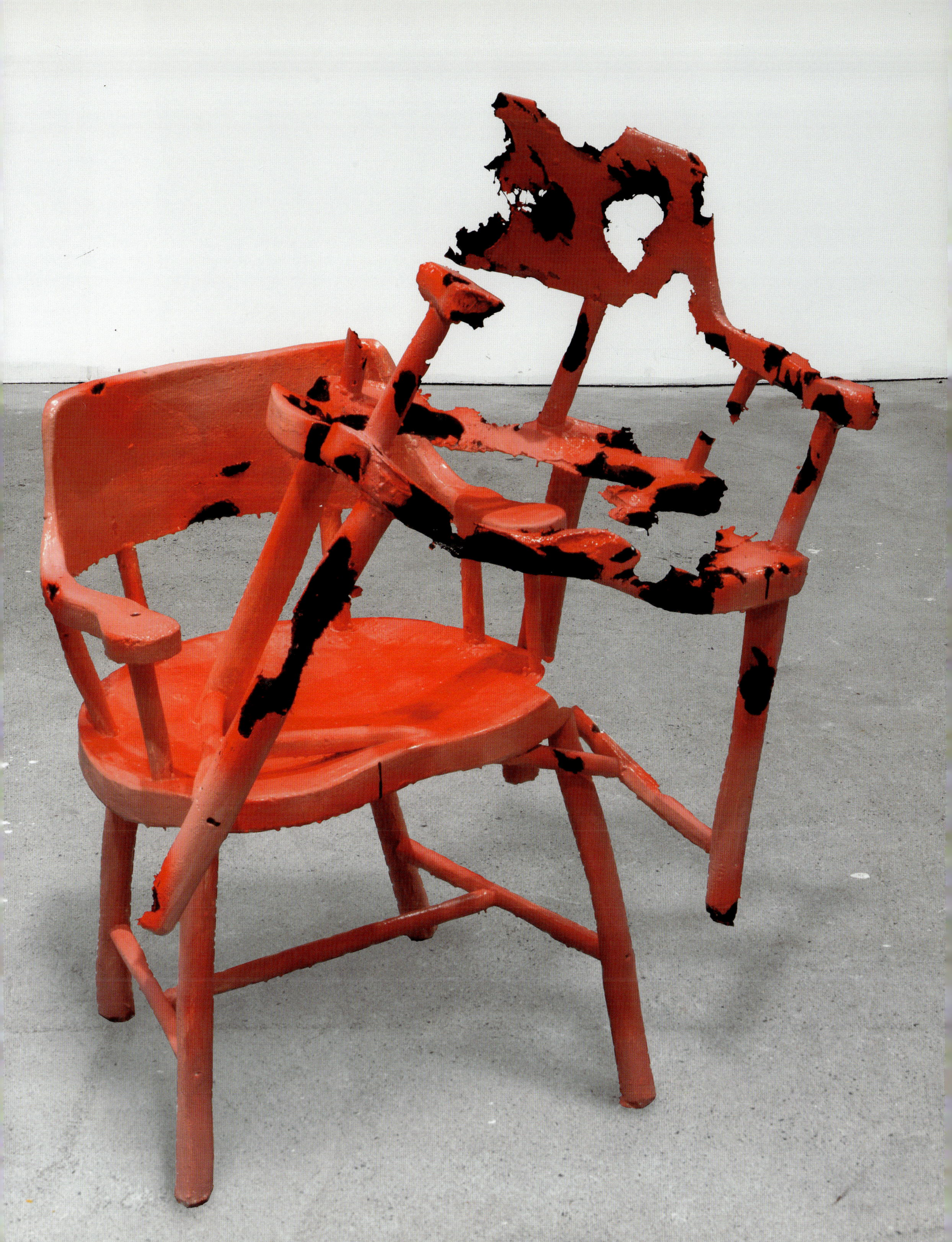

You Can Not Win, 2003

Polystyrene, acrylic paint, Aqua-Resin, screws, fiberglass

54 x 30 x 51 inches (137.2 x 76.2 x 129.5 cm)

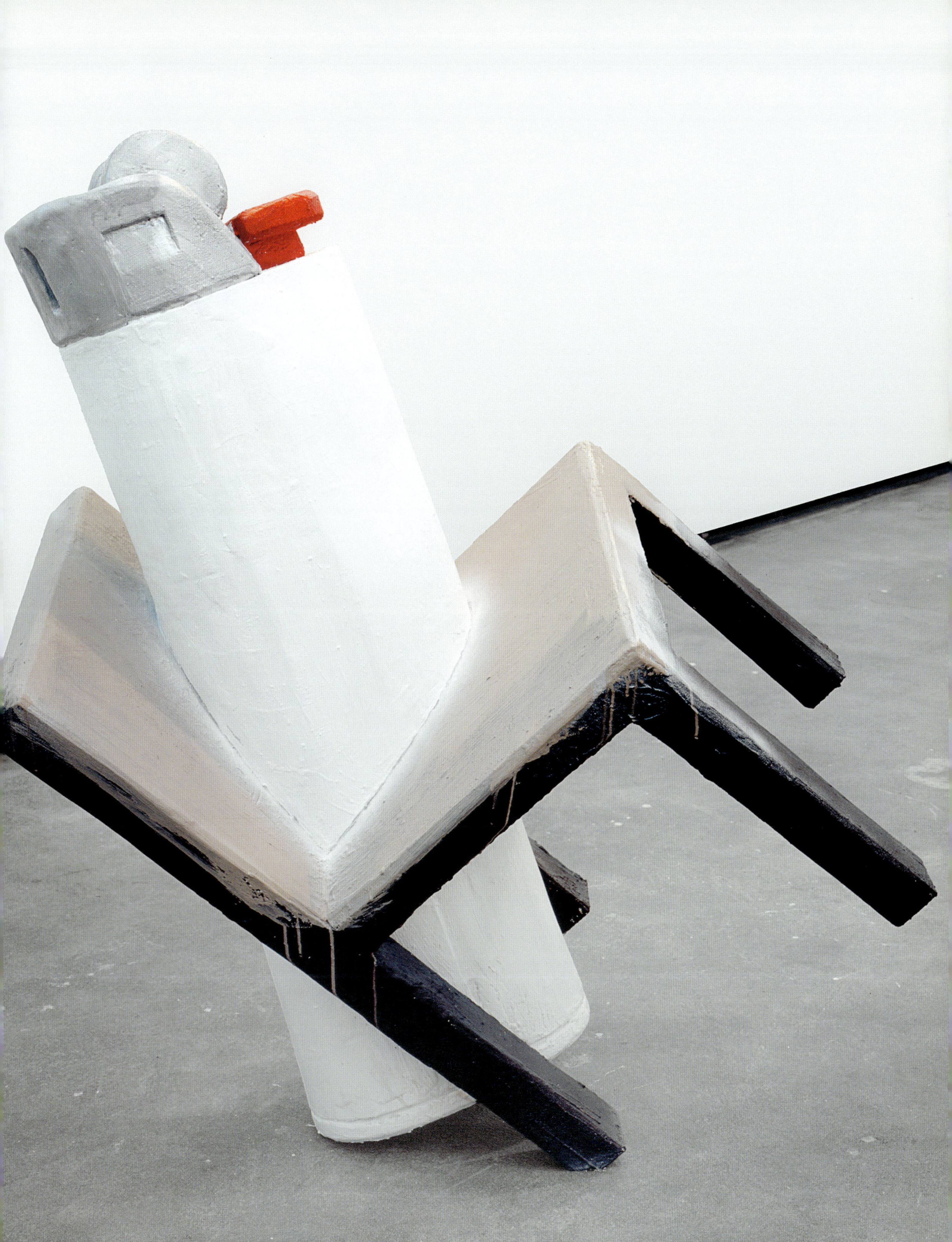

You Can Only Lose, 2003
Polystyrene, acrylic paint, Aqua-Resin, screws, fiberglass
123 x 44 x 42 inches (312.4 x 111.8 x 106.7 cm)

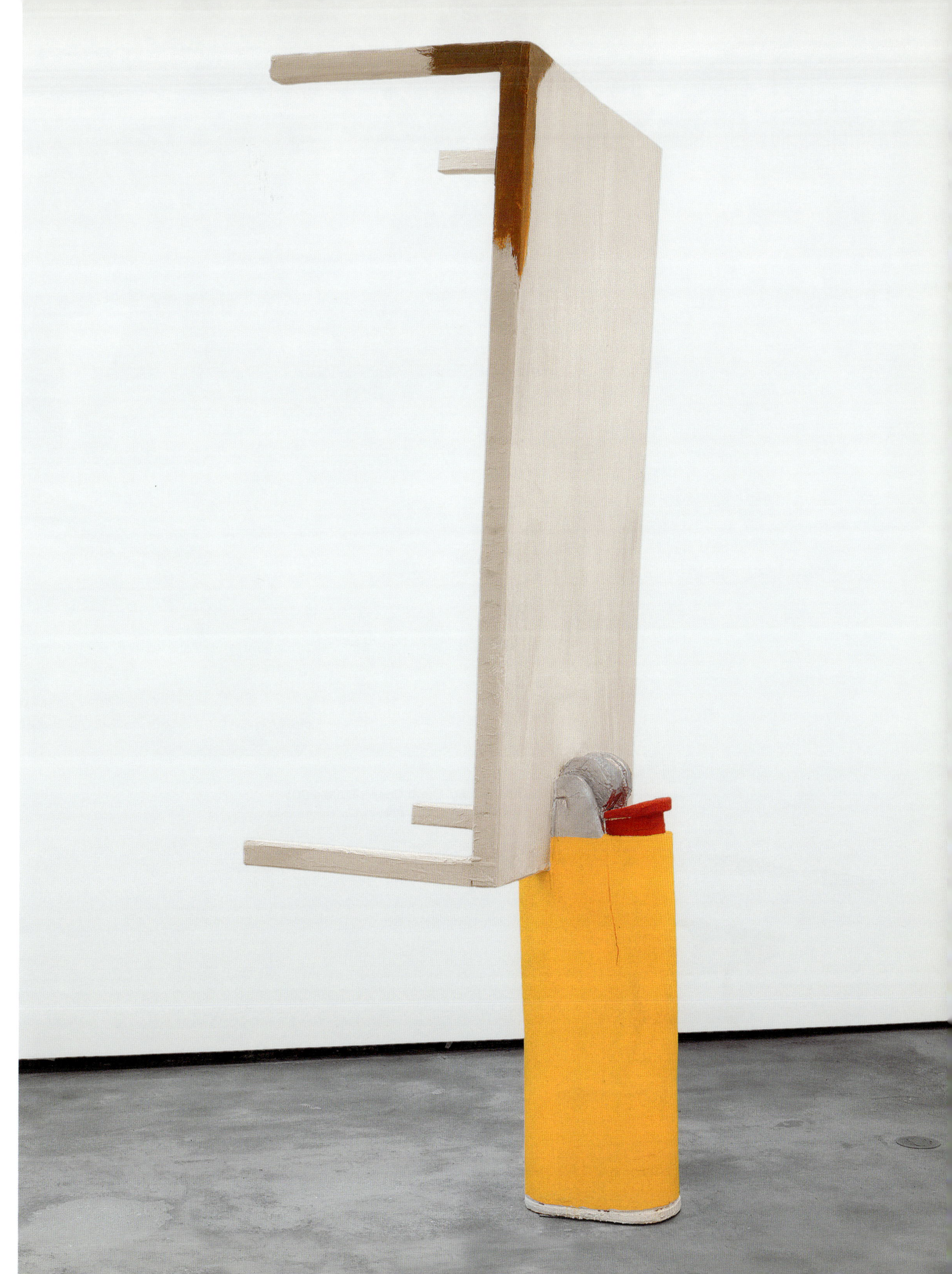

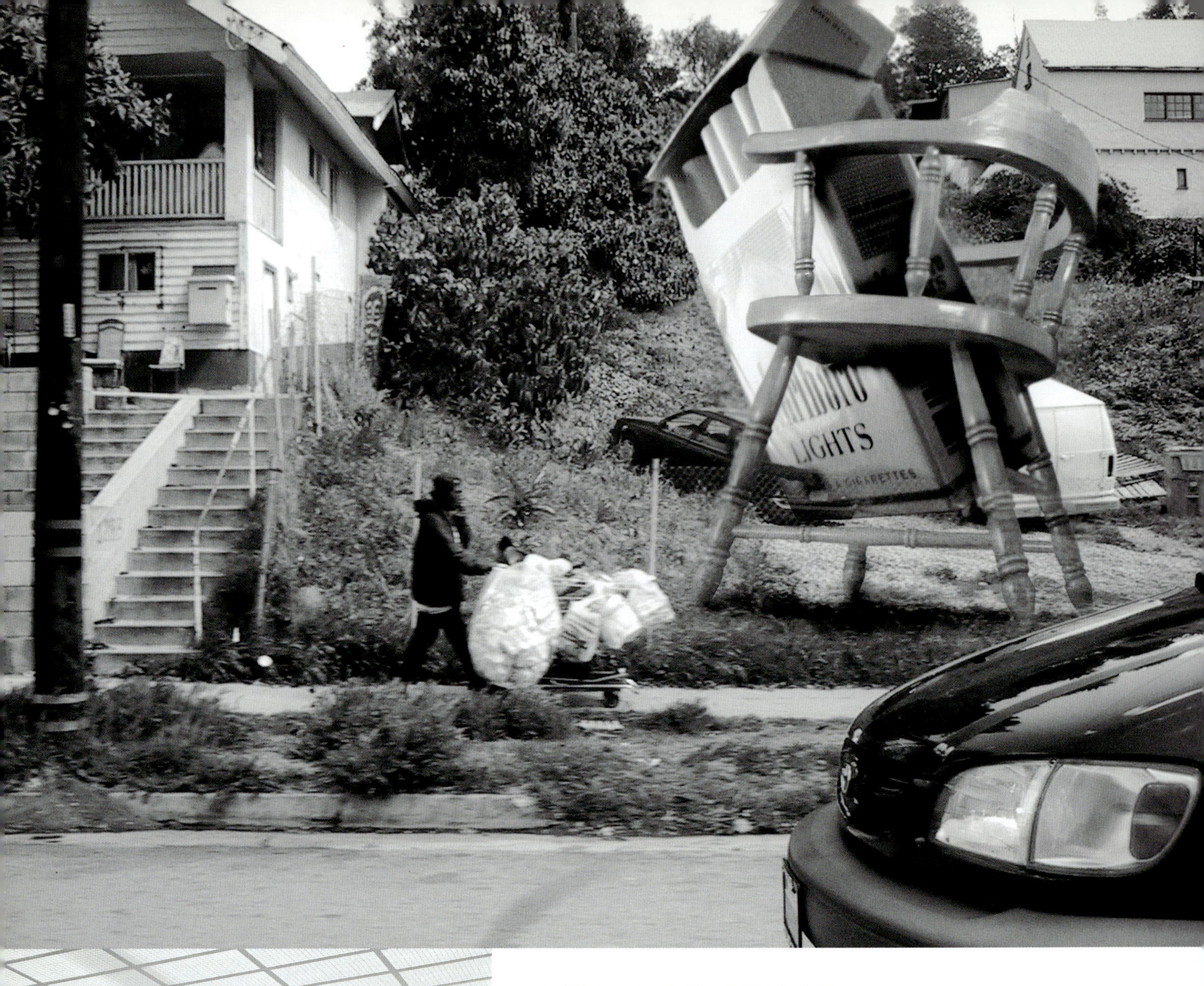

Bad Timing, Lamb Chop!, 2004–2005
Cast aluminum, polyurethane resin, enamel paint
177 ⅛ x 90 ½ x 129 ⅞ inches (450 x 230 x 330 cm)
Above: Study for *Bad Timing, Lamb Chop!*, 2001
Left: Installation view, "Kir Royal," Kunsthaus Zürich, 2004
Kuckuck Backwards, 2004; *Middleclass Heroes*, 2004;
Prototype of *Bad Timing, Lamb Chop!*, 2004
Opposite page: Installation view, Private residence, Los Angeles

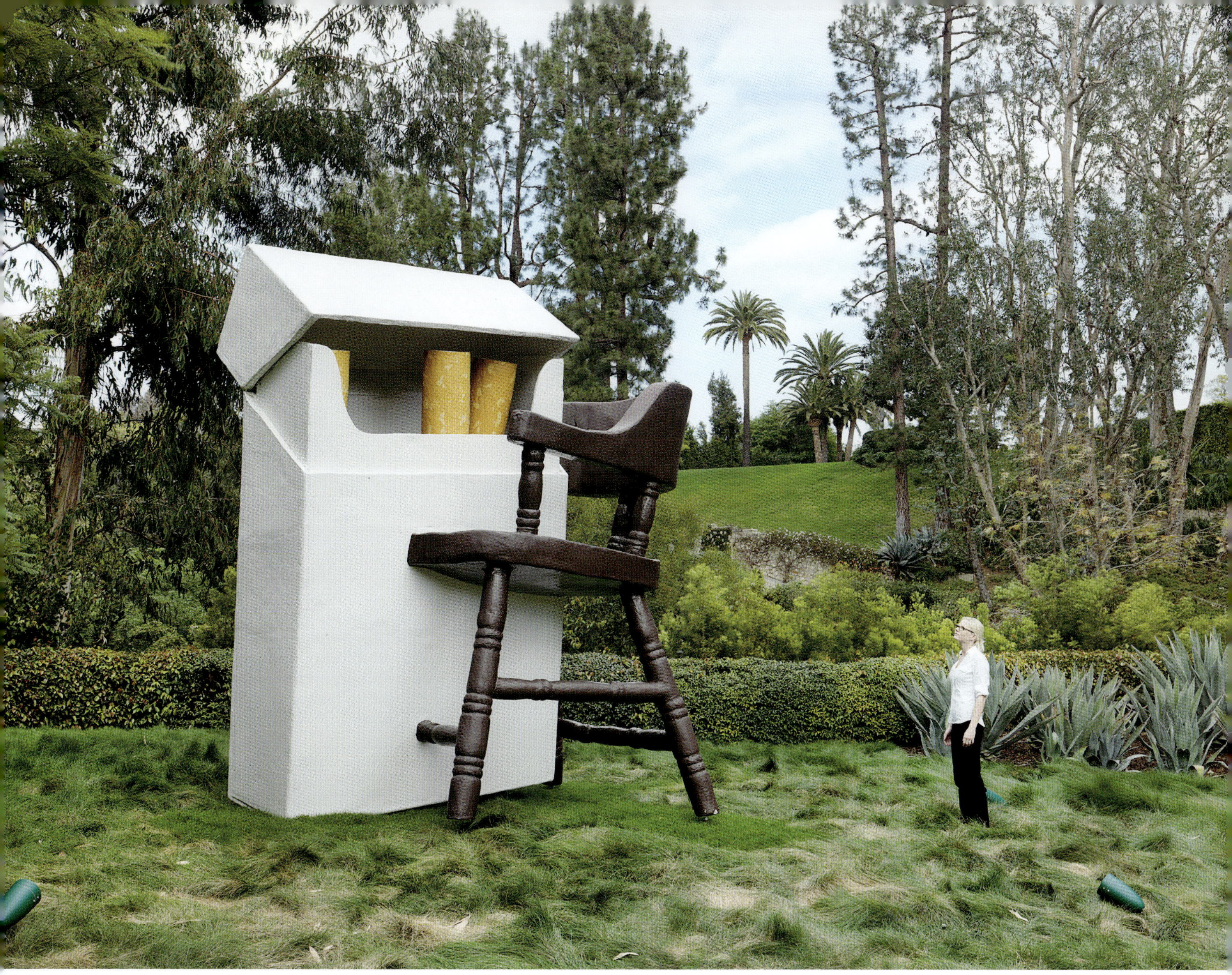

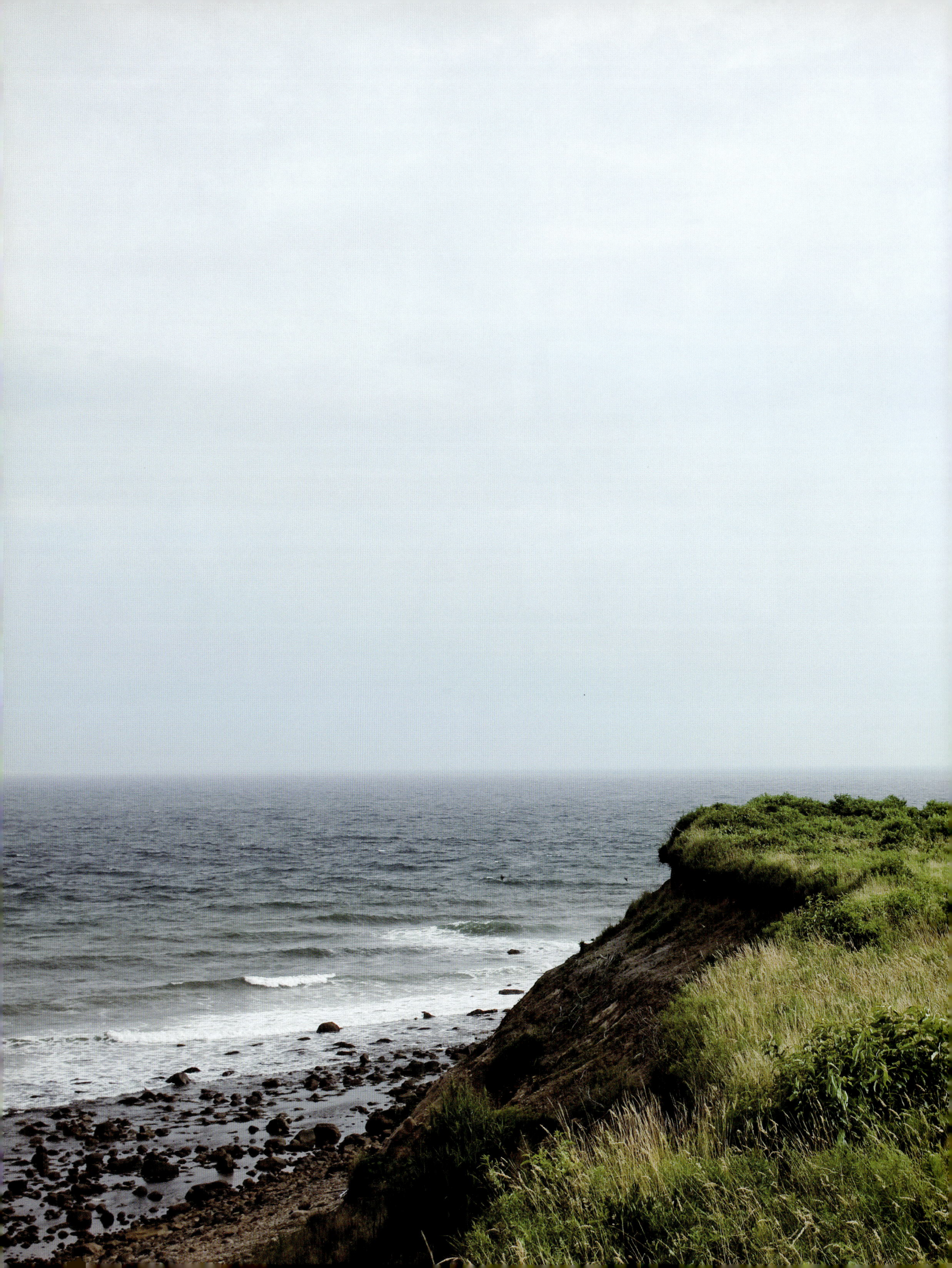

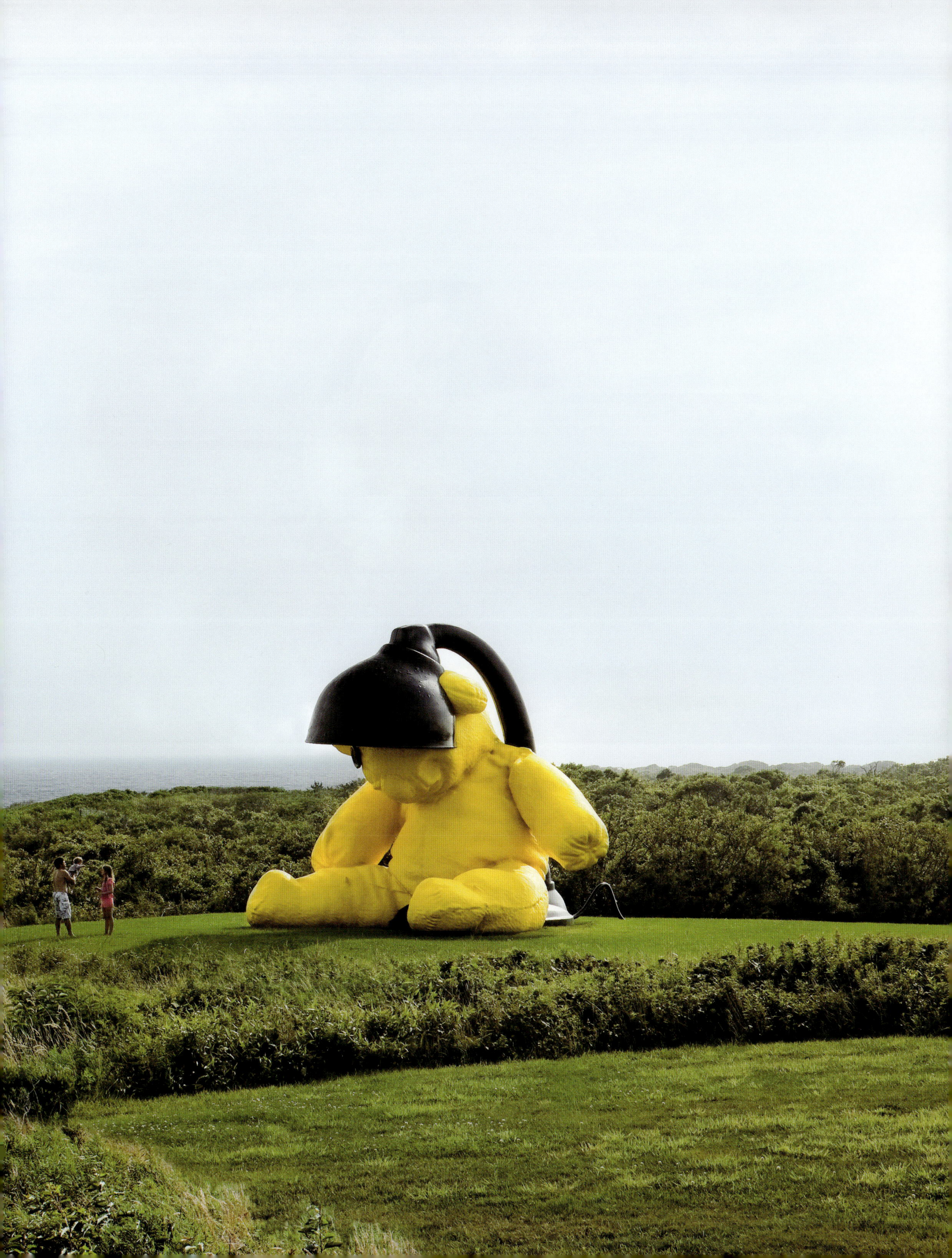

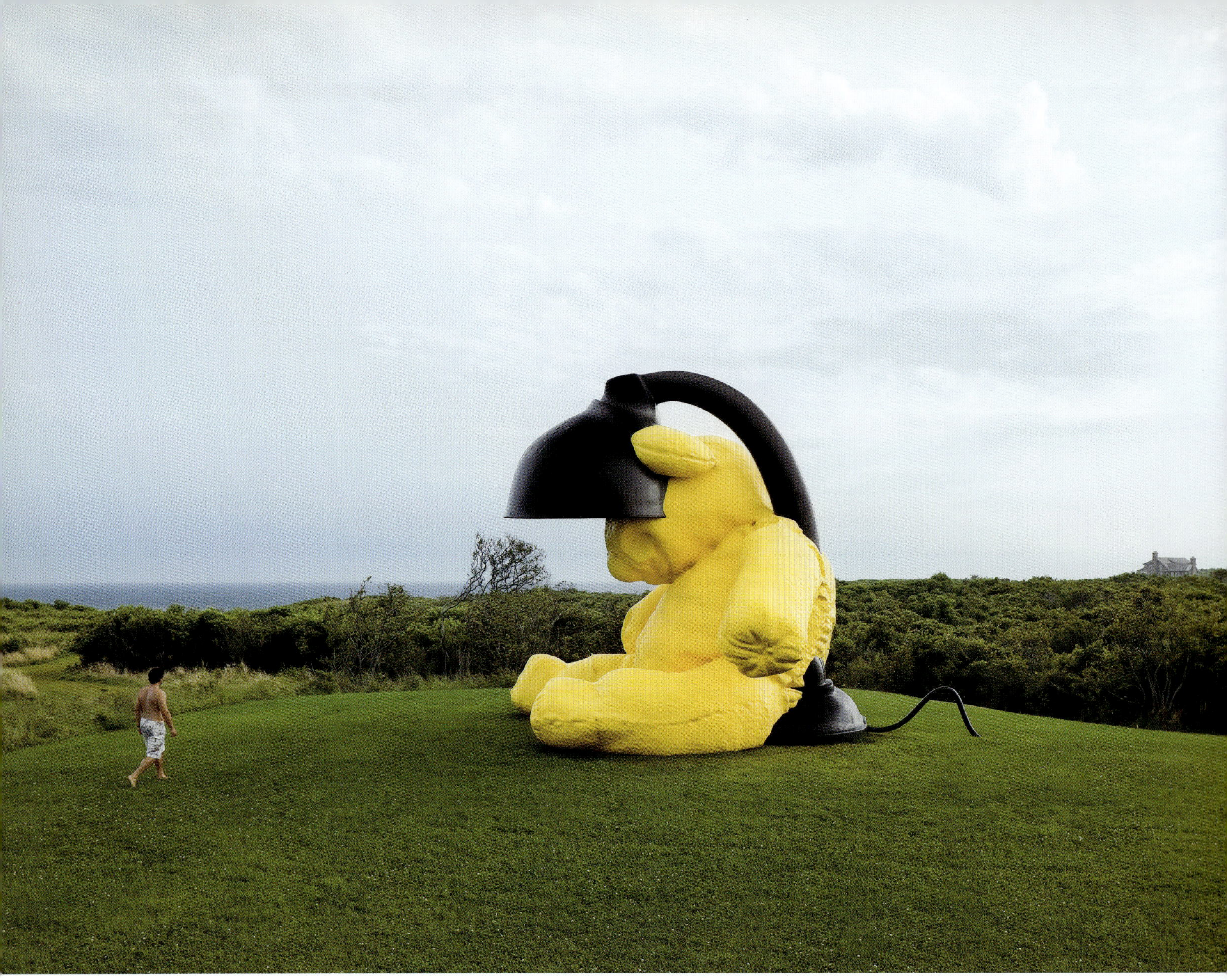

Previous spread and following pages:

Untitled (Lamp / Bear), 2005–2006

Cast bronze, epoxy primer, urethane paint,
acrylic polyurethane topcoat, acrylic glass, gas discharge lamp,
stainless-steel framework
275 ⅝ x 255 ⅞ x 295 ¼ inches (700 x 650 x 750 cm)
Previous spread and above: Installation view, home of
Amalia Dayan and Adam Lindemann, Montauk, New York, 2009
Opposite and following pages:
Installation view, Seagram Plaza, New York, 2011
Page 367, bottom: Study for *Untitled (Lamp / Bear)*, 2004

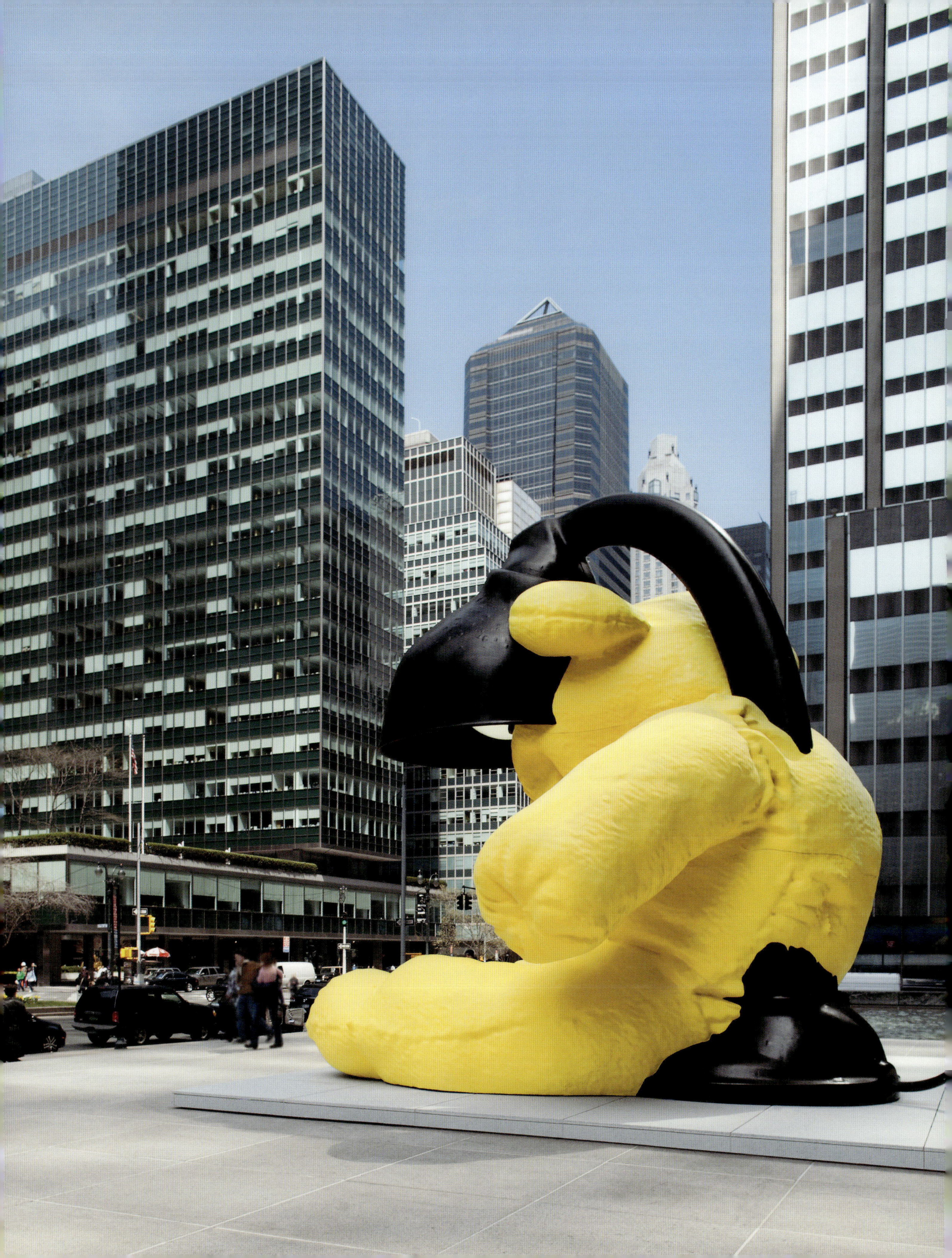

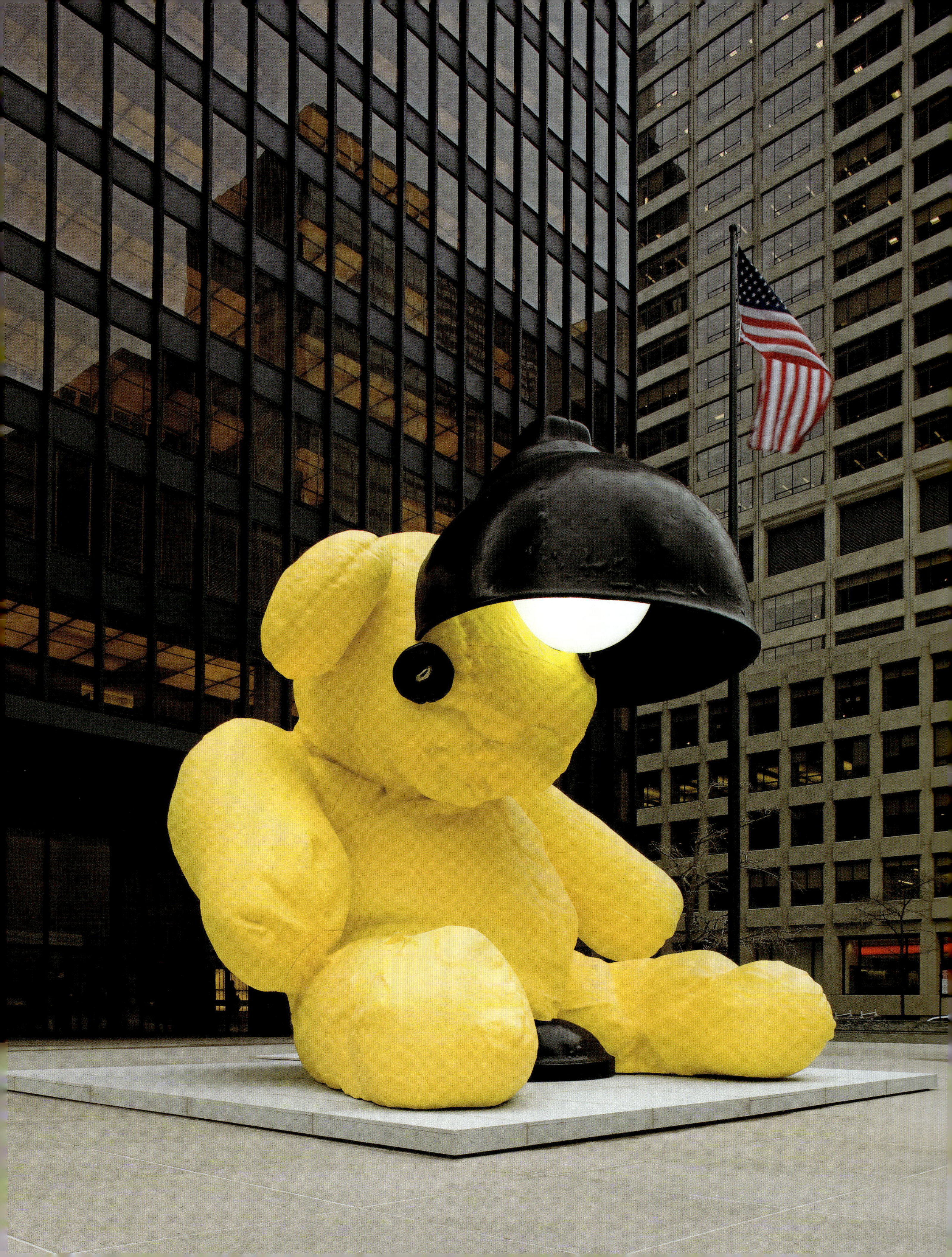

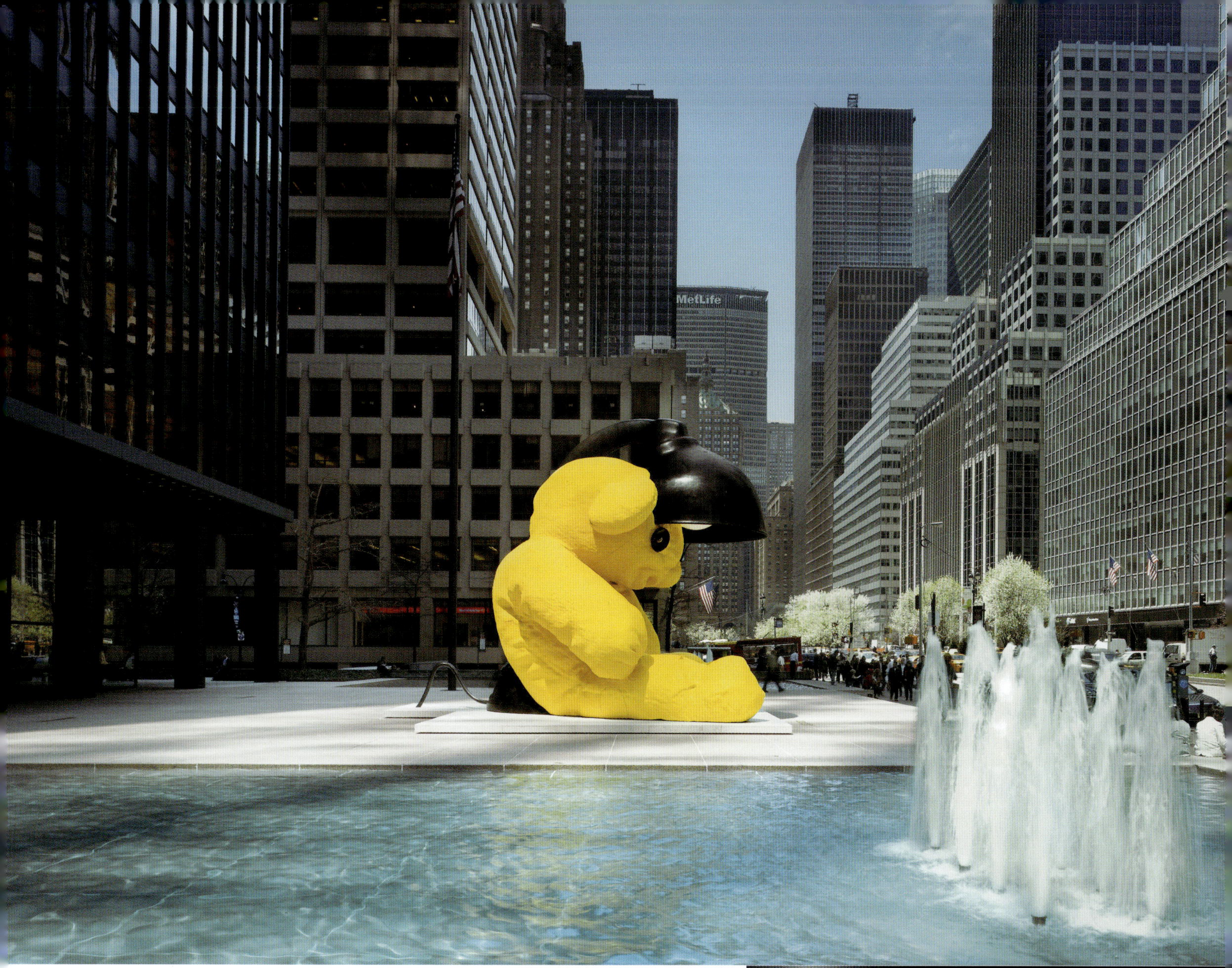

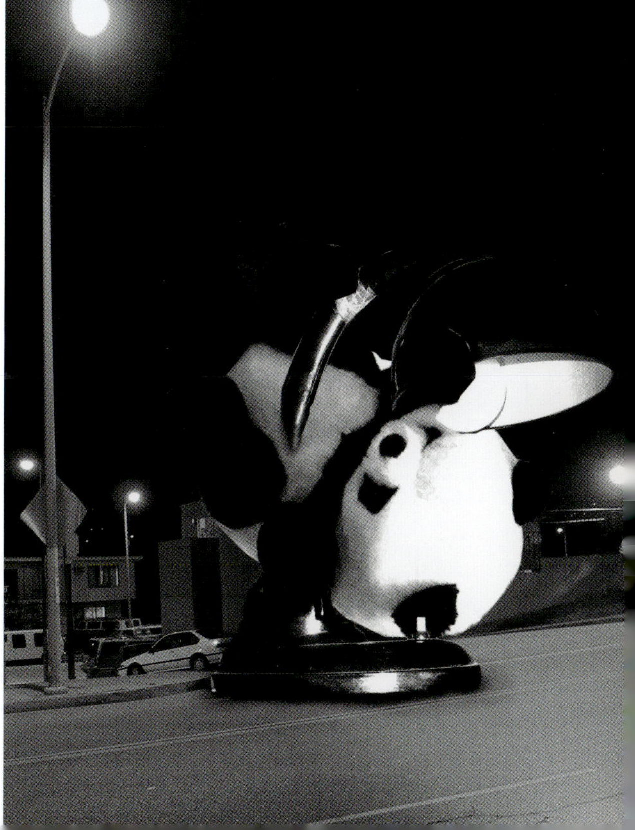

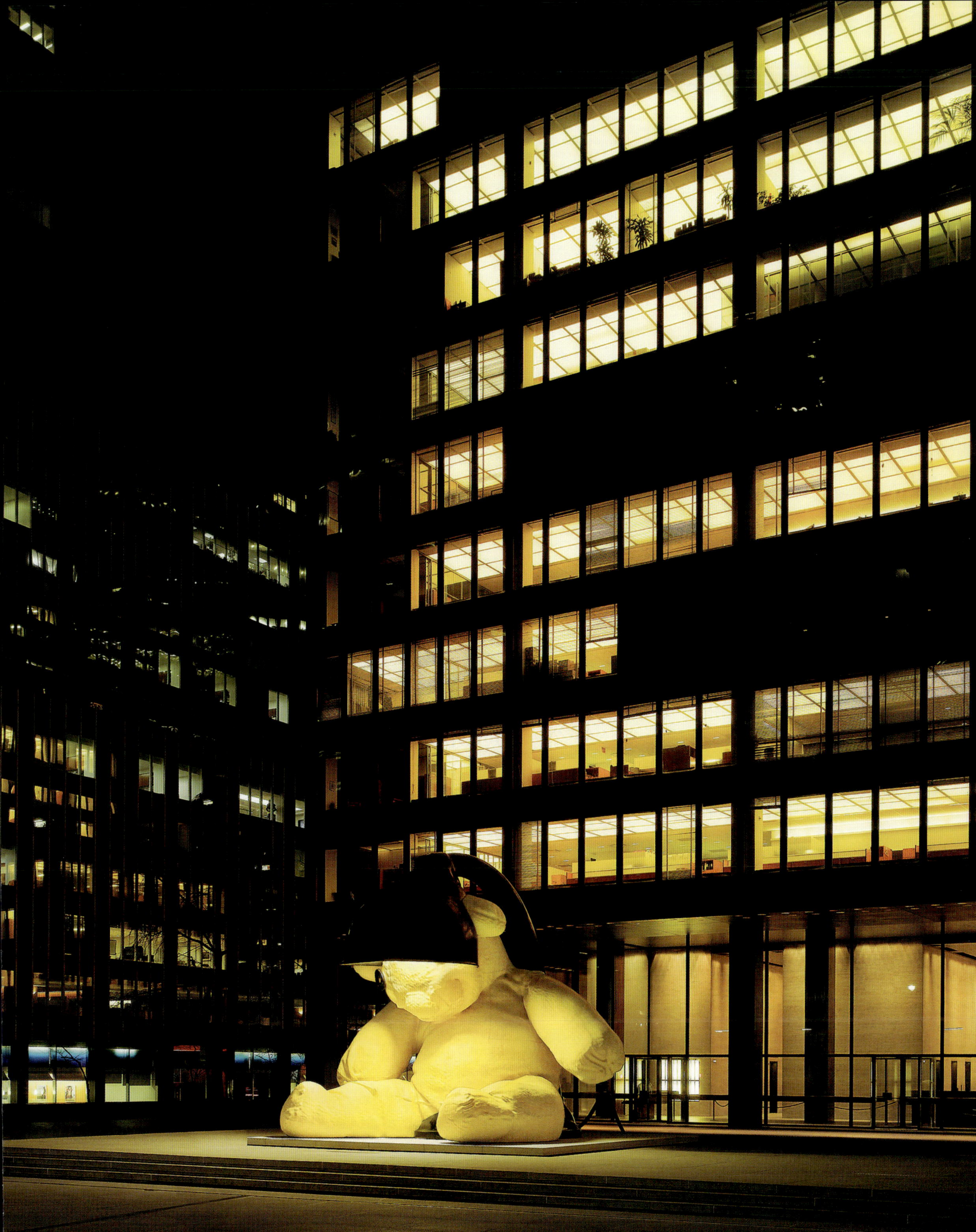

Hudson, 1995

Particleboard, latex paint, screws

Dimensions unknown

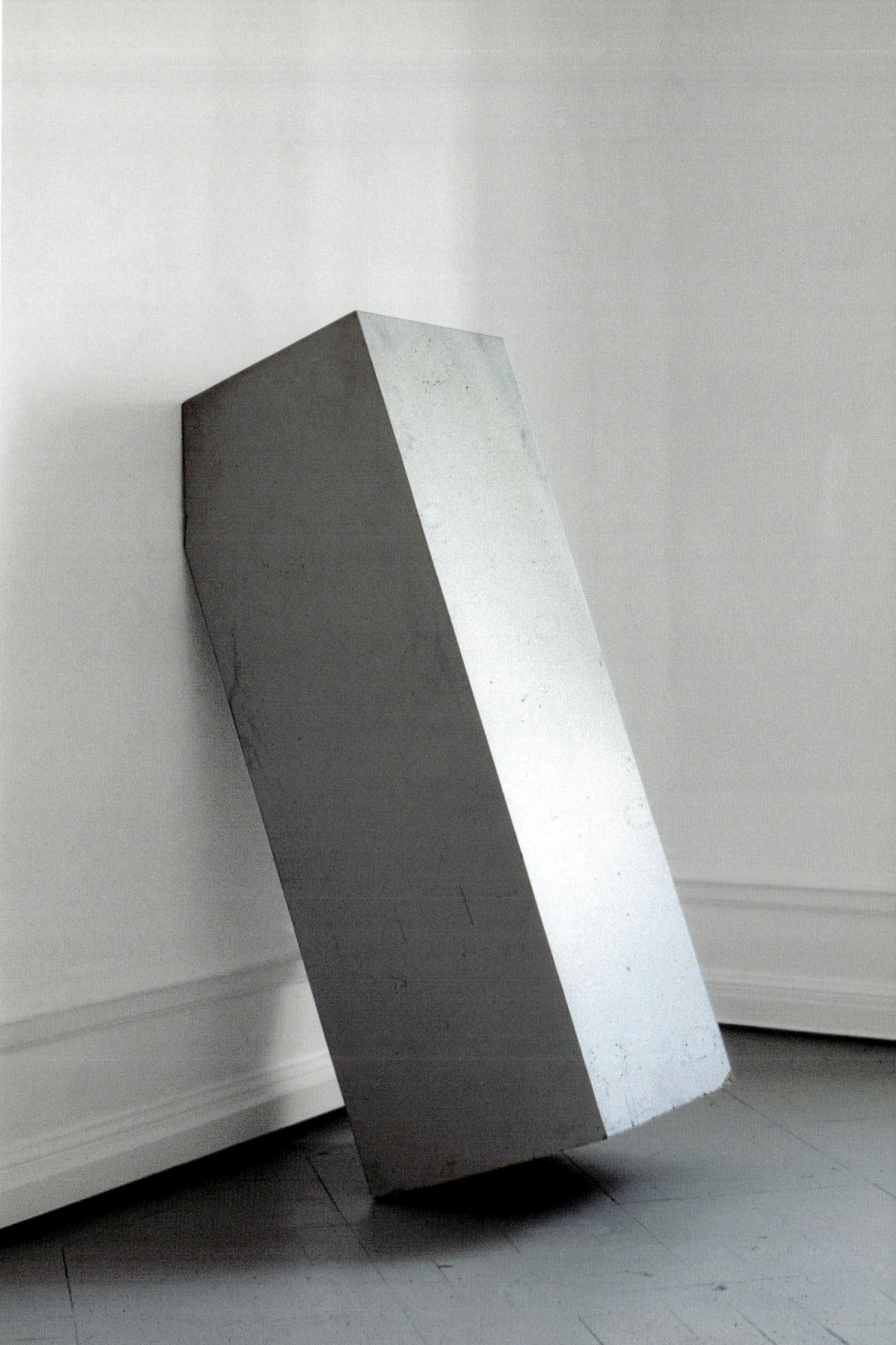

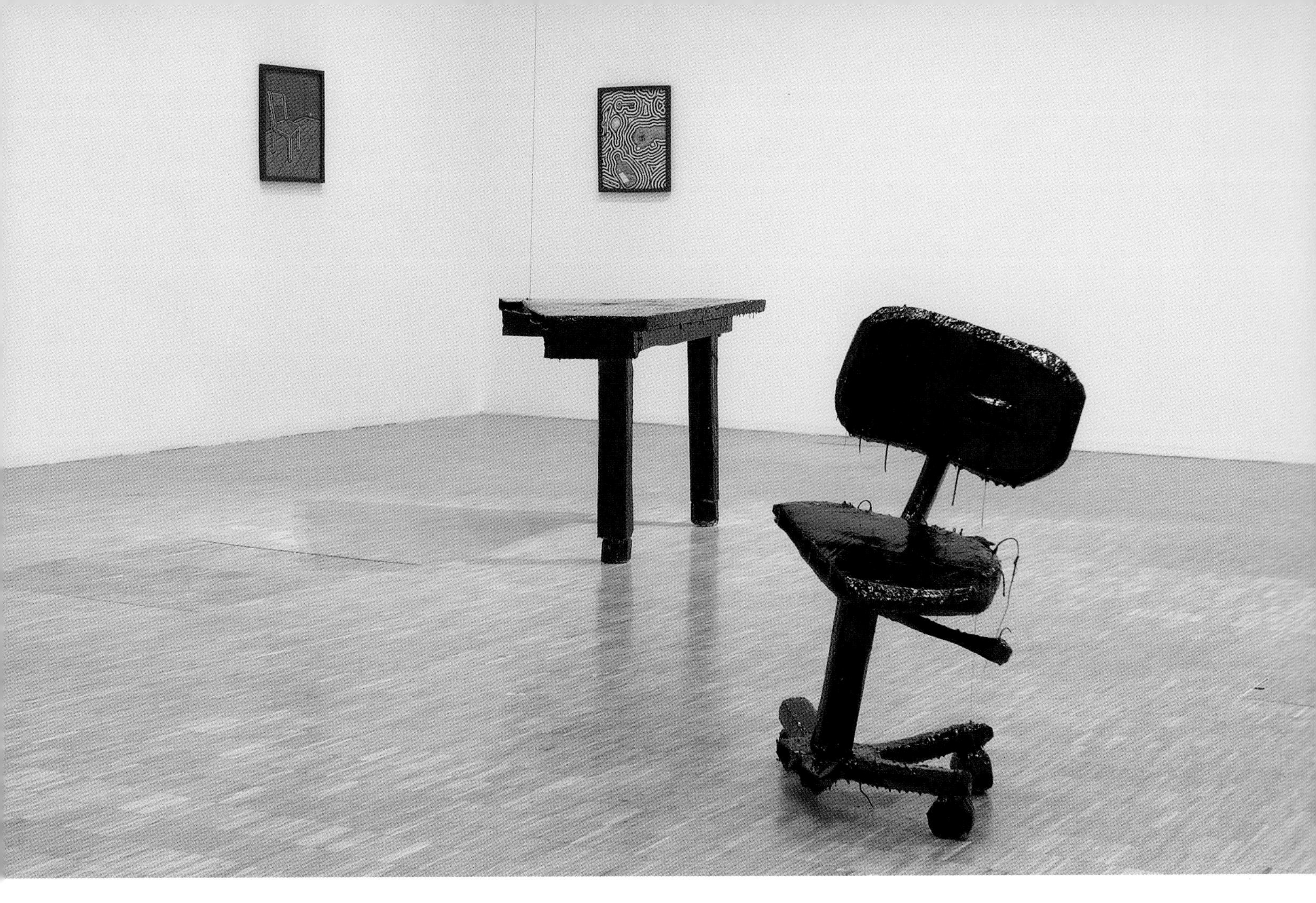

Next Time I Break an Egg, I Will Think of You, 2004
Polystyrene, polyurethane resin, car paint, duct tape, screws, steel wire
Table: 47 ¼ x 39 ⅜ x 31 ½ inches (120 x 100 x 80 cm)
Chair: 27 ½ x 27 ½ x 27 ½ inches (70 x 70 x 70 cm)
Installation view, "Not My House Not My Fire," Espace 315,
Centre Pompidou, Paris, 2004
Rainbow Cookie, 2003; *I Hope the Kitten Finds a Mouse*, 2004

Opposite page:
Chair for a Ghost: Thomas, 2003
Cast aluminum, enamel paint, lacquer, wire
37 ⅜ x 24 ⅜ x 20 ½ inches (95 x 62 x 52 cm)

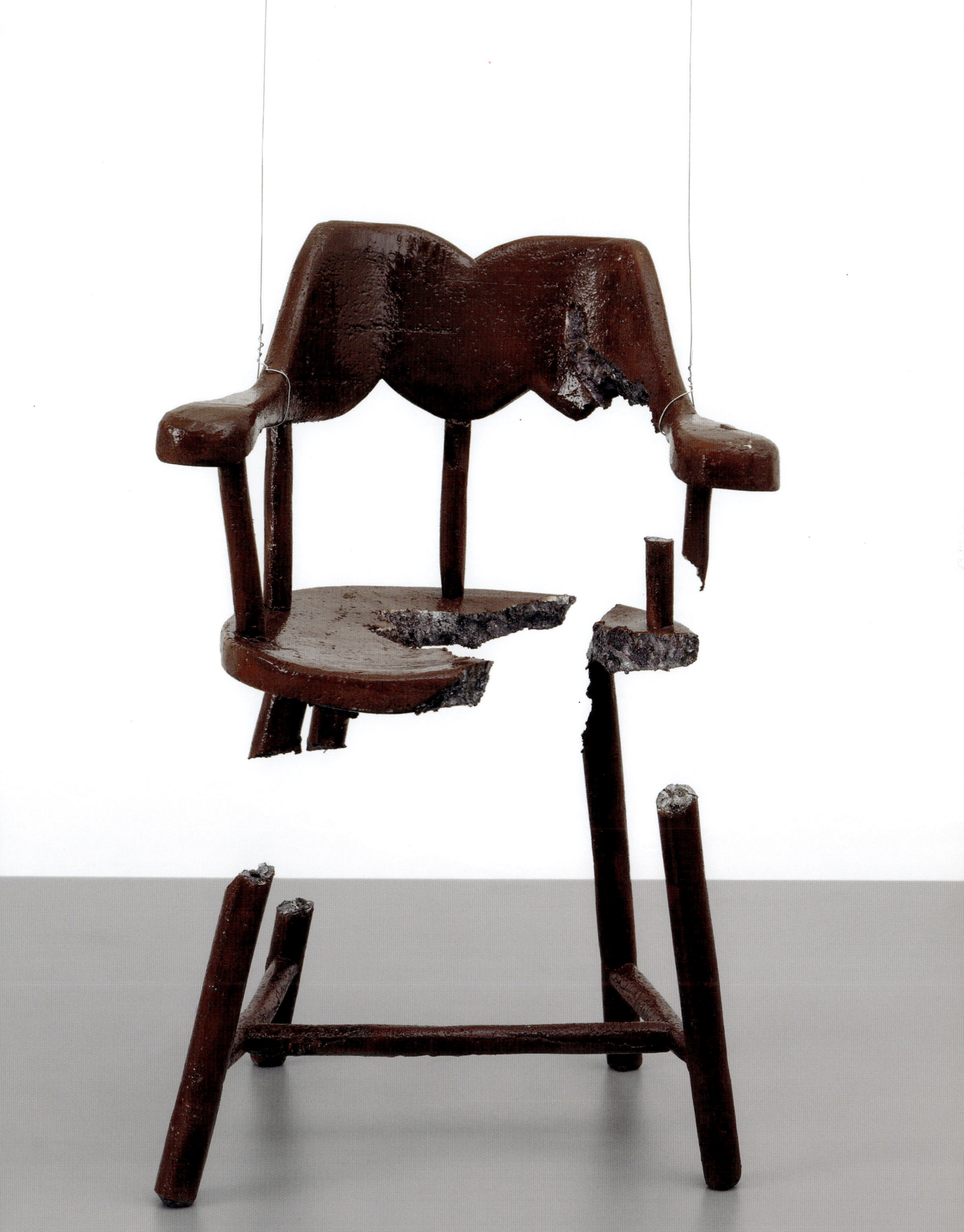

Chair for a Ghost: Urs, 2003

Cast aluminum, enamel paint, lacquer, wire

37 ⅜ x 24 ⅜ x 20 ½ inches (95 x 62 x 52 cm)

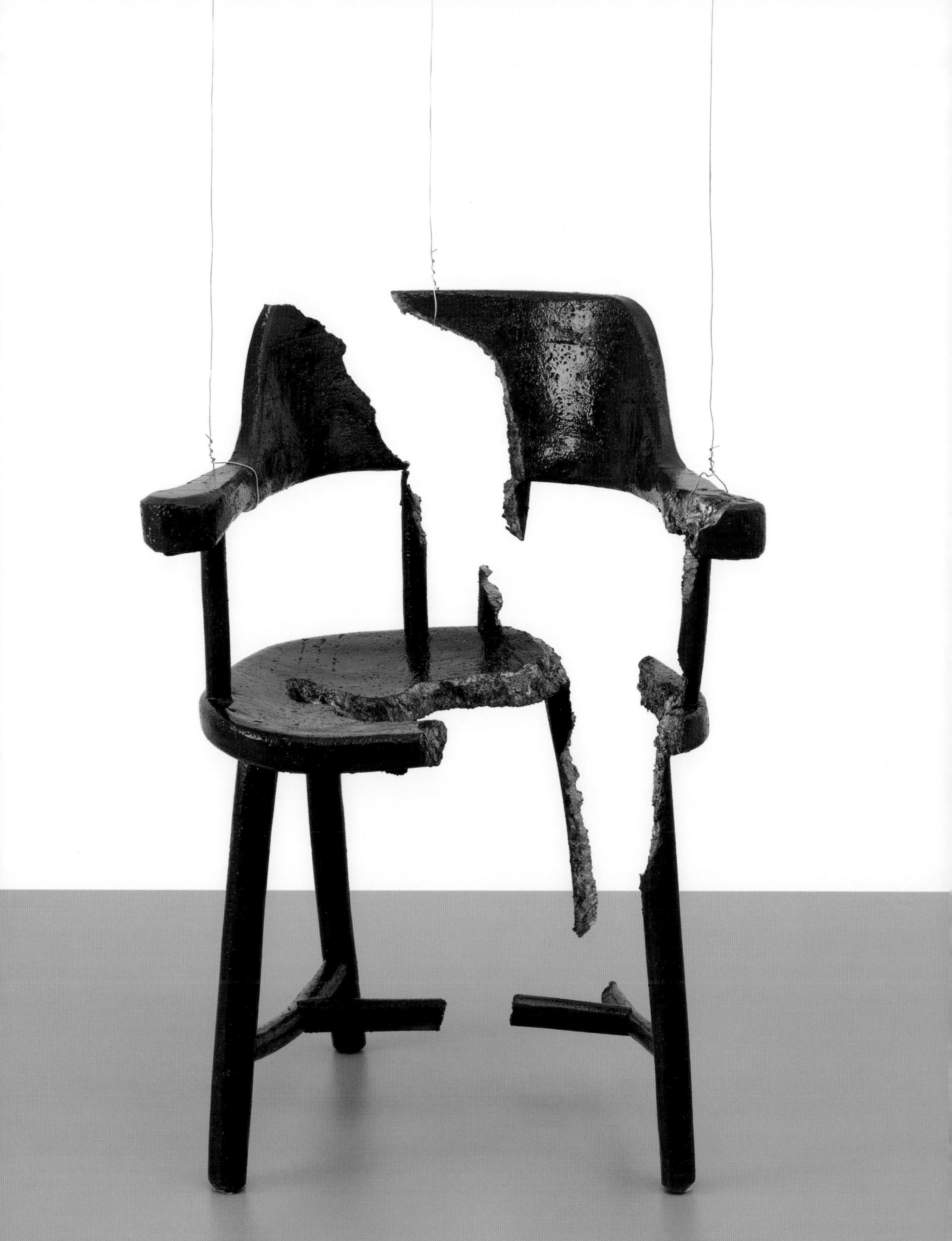

Thank You Fuck You, 2007

Cast aluminum, acrylic paint

60 ¼ x 72 ⅞ x 55 ½ inches (153 x 185 x 141 cm)

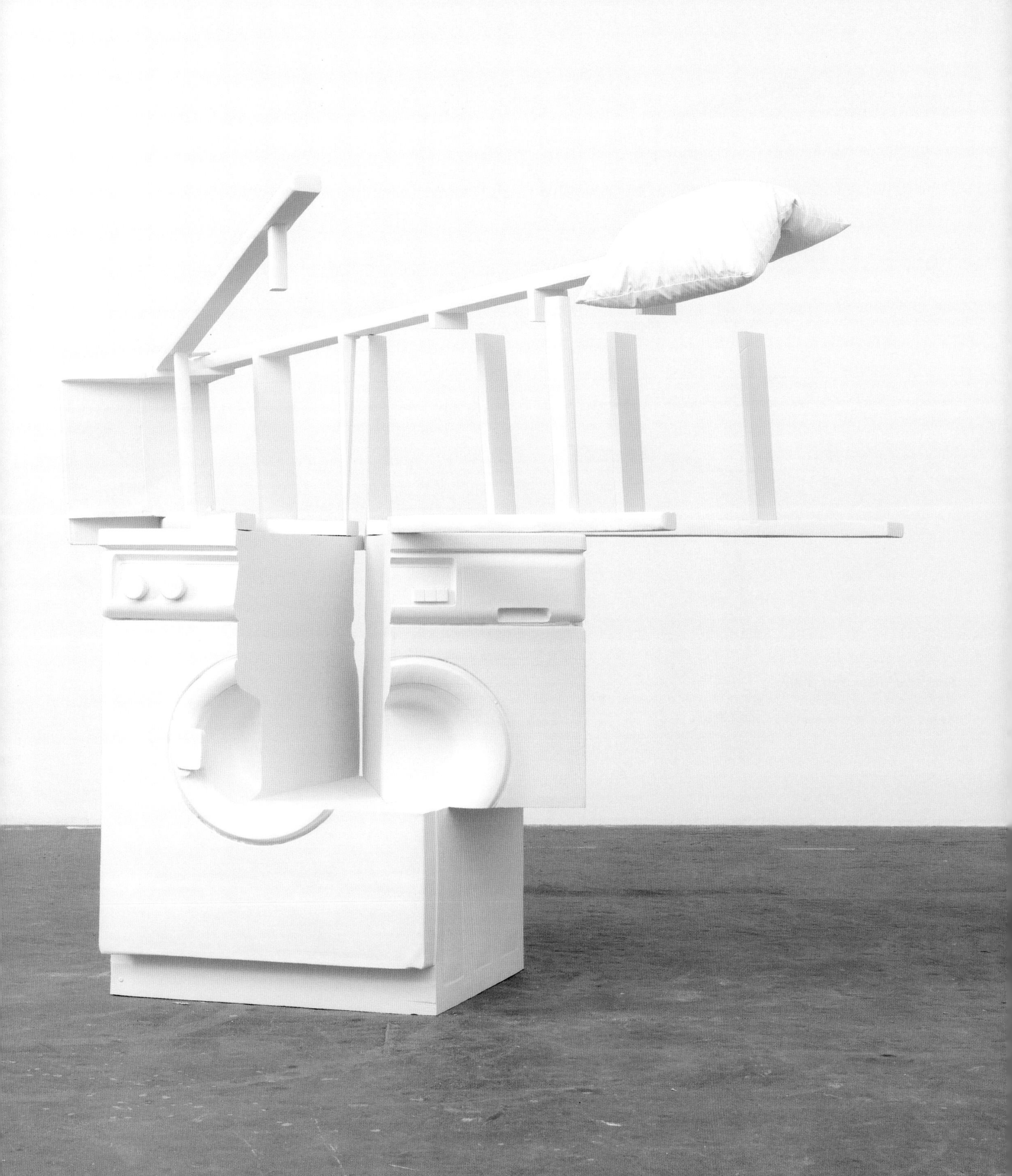

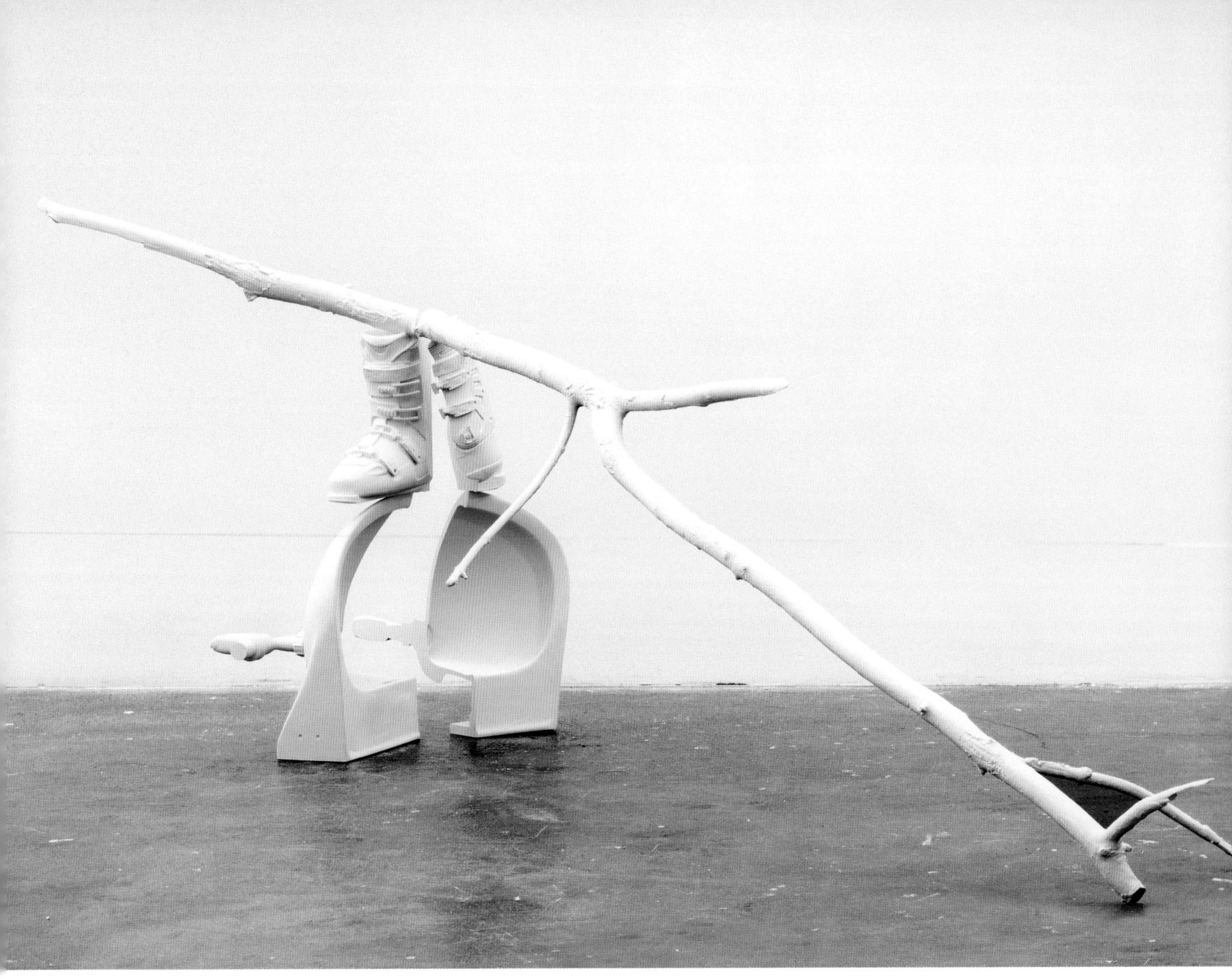

Fuck You Thank You, 2007
Cast aluminum, acrylic paint
67 ¾ x 120 ⅛ x 38 ¼ inches (172 x 305 x 97 cm)

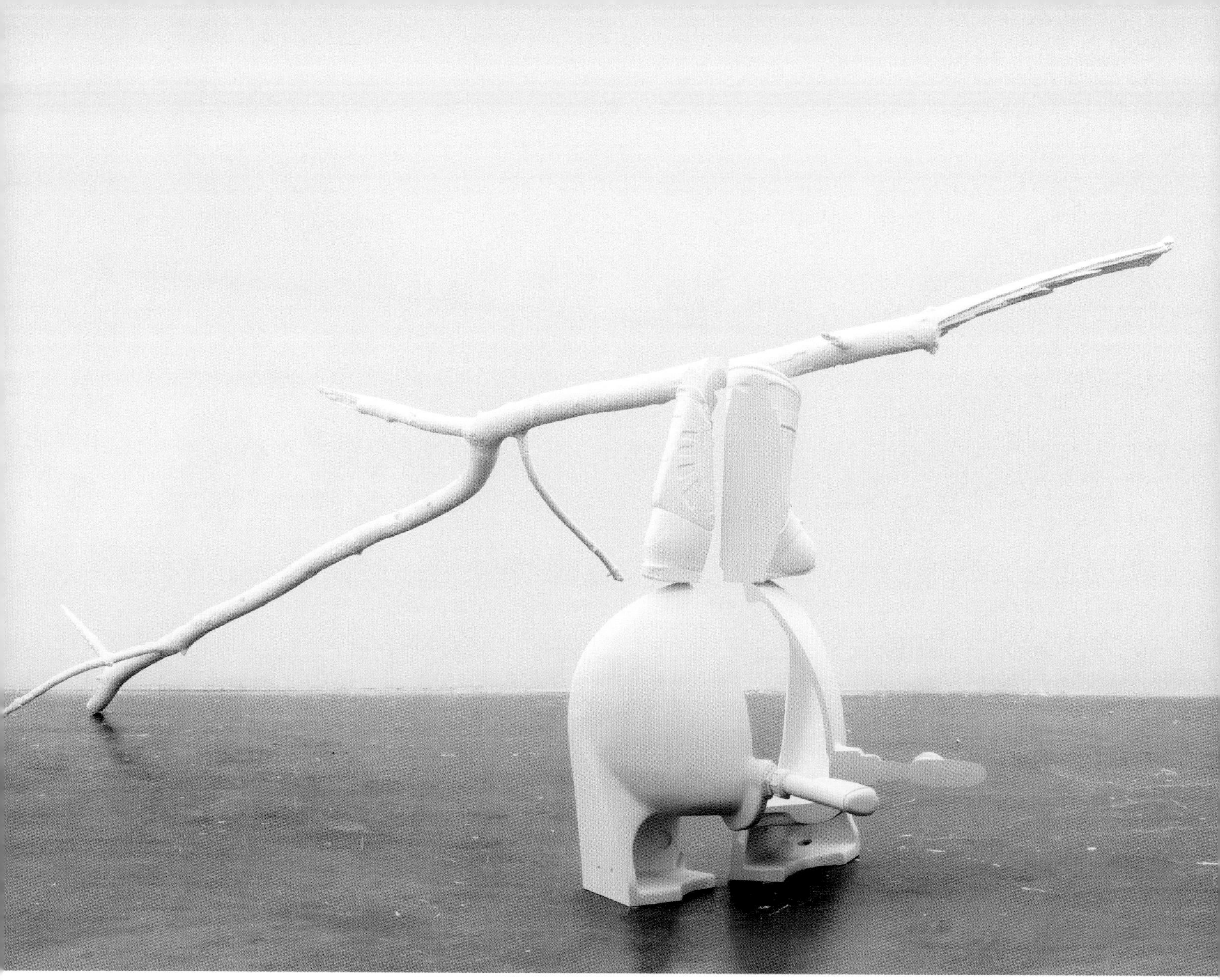

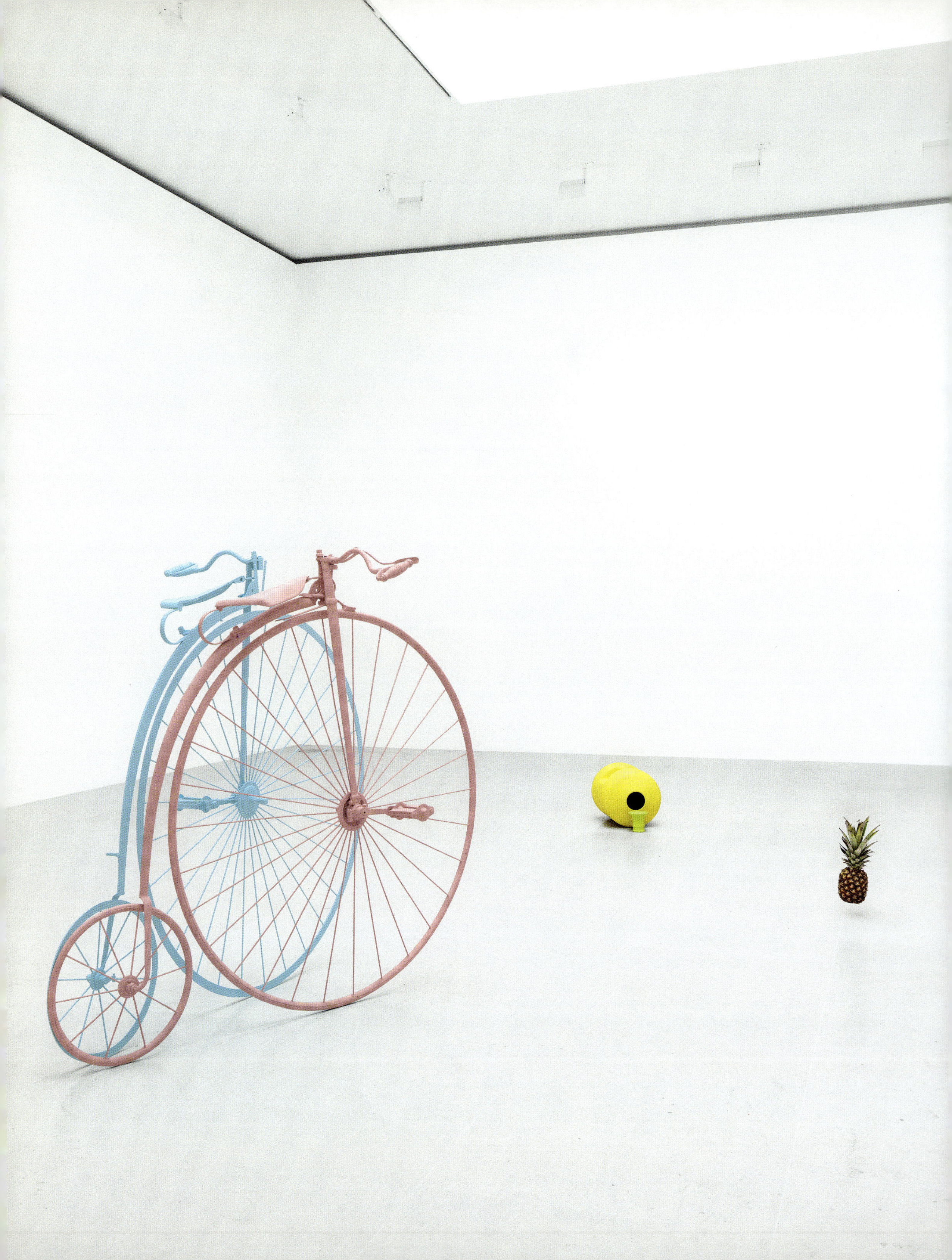

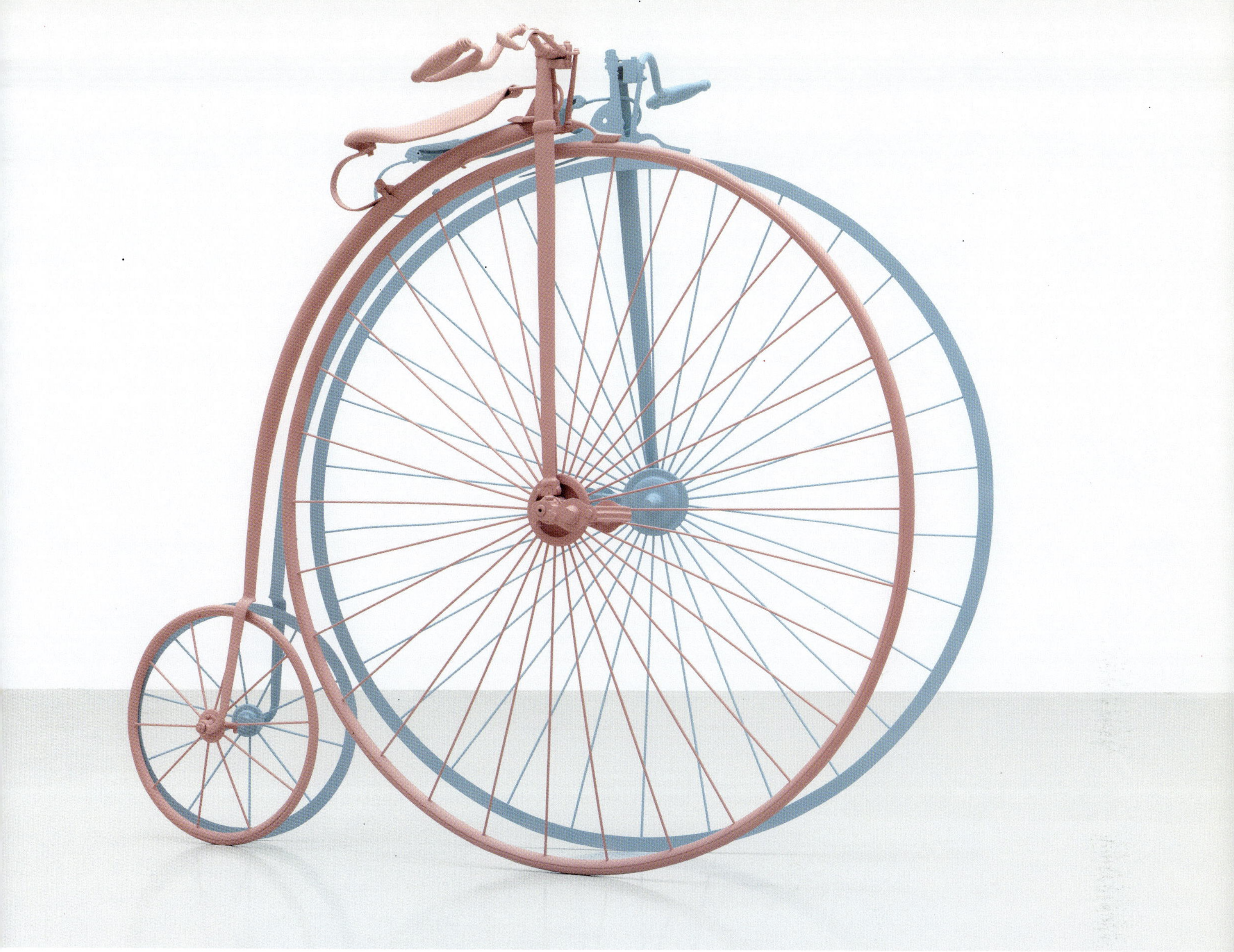

Dickface, 2012
Aluminum, carbon-fiber-reinforced plastic, stainless-steel anchors, epoxy primer, polyester filler, one-component acrylic putty, urethane primer, polyester paint, acrylic polyurethane matte clearcoat; in 2 parts
Left: 56 ¾ x 61 x 13 ⅞ inches (144.3 x 154.9 x 35.3 cm)
Right: 56 ¾ x 61 x 14 inches (144 x 154.9 x 35.8 cm)
Overall dimensions: 56 ¾ x 61 x 38 ⅞ inches (144.3 x 154.9 x 98.7 cm)
Installation view, "schmutz schmutz," Gagosian Gallery, Paris, 2012
Cuntface, 2012; *Untitled (Suspended Line of Fruit)*, 2012

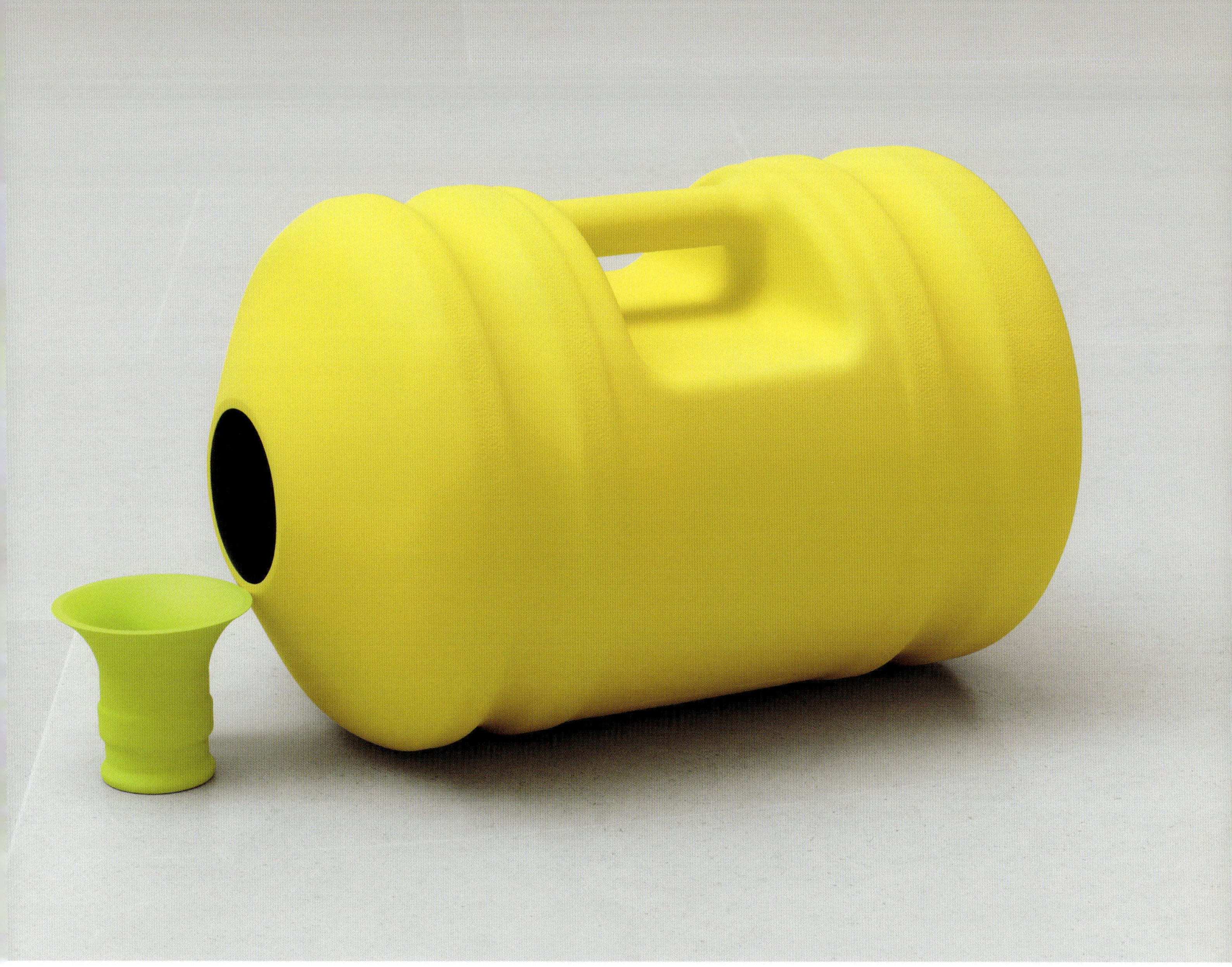

Cuntface, 2012

Aluminum, epoxy primer, polyester filler, one-component acrylic putty, urethane primer, polyester paint, acrylic polyurethane matte clearcoat; in 2 parts
Water bottle: 12 ⅞ x 19 ¼ x 12 ⅞ inches (32.8 x 48.8 x 32.8 cm)
Bottle neck: 4 ⅜ x 4 ⅝ x 4 ⅝ inches (11 x 11.7 x 11.7 cm)
Overall dimensions: 12 ⅞ x 23 ⅞ x 12 ⅞ inches (32.8 x 60.6 x 32.8 cm)

Untitled, 1993

Blue paint applied to wall to neutralize orange glow from streetlight

Latex paint, pigments, existing streetlight

Dimensions variable

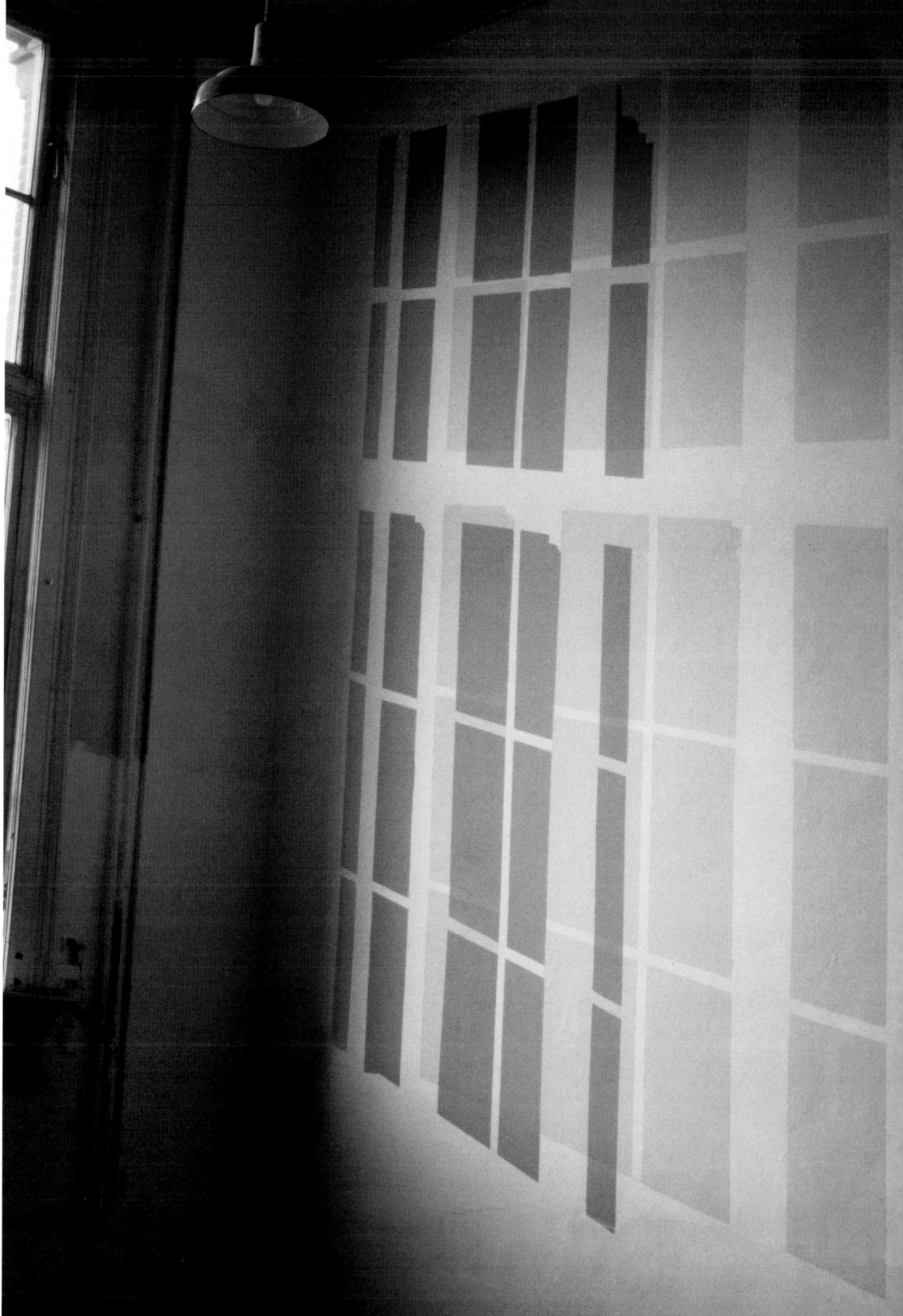

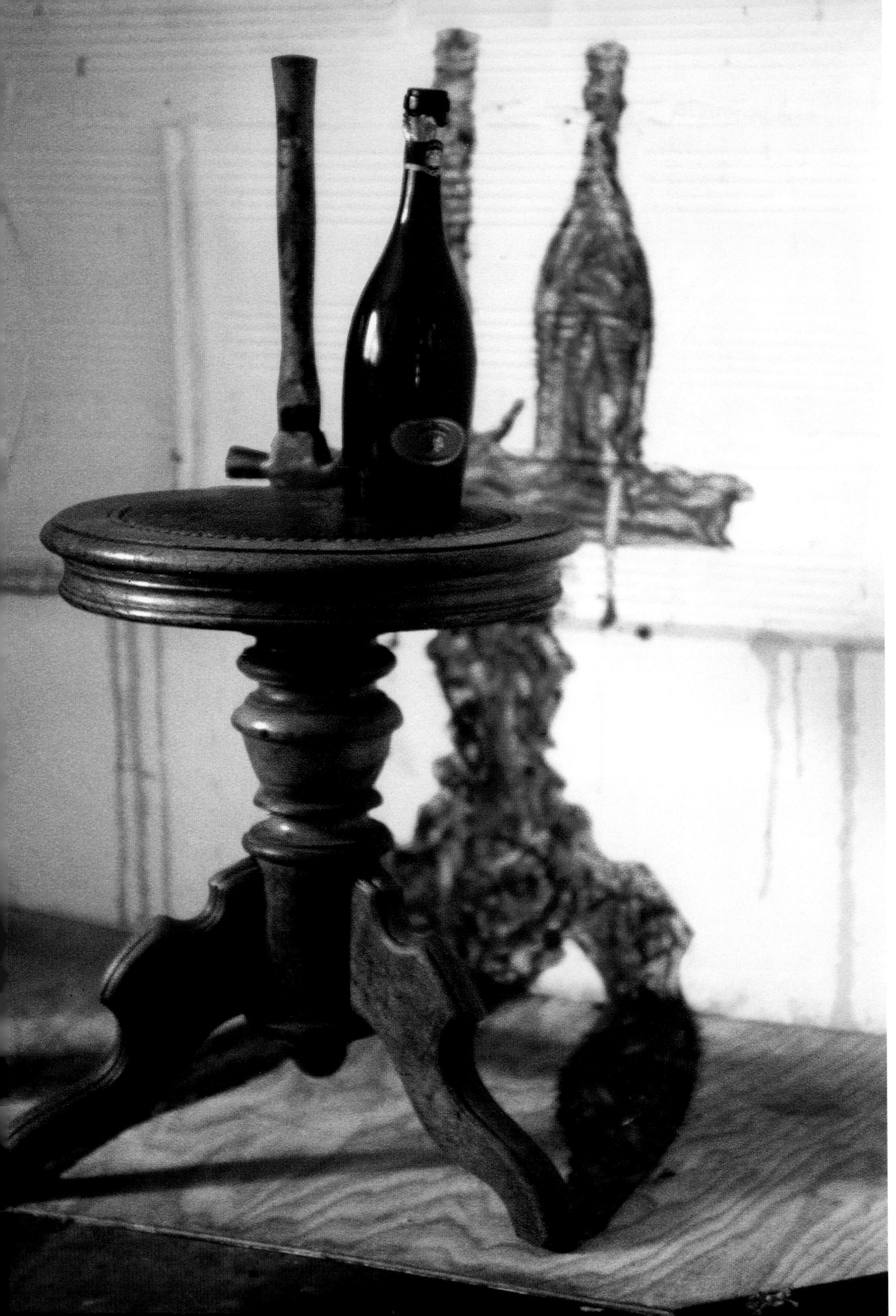

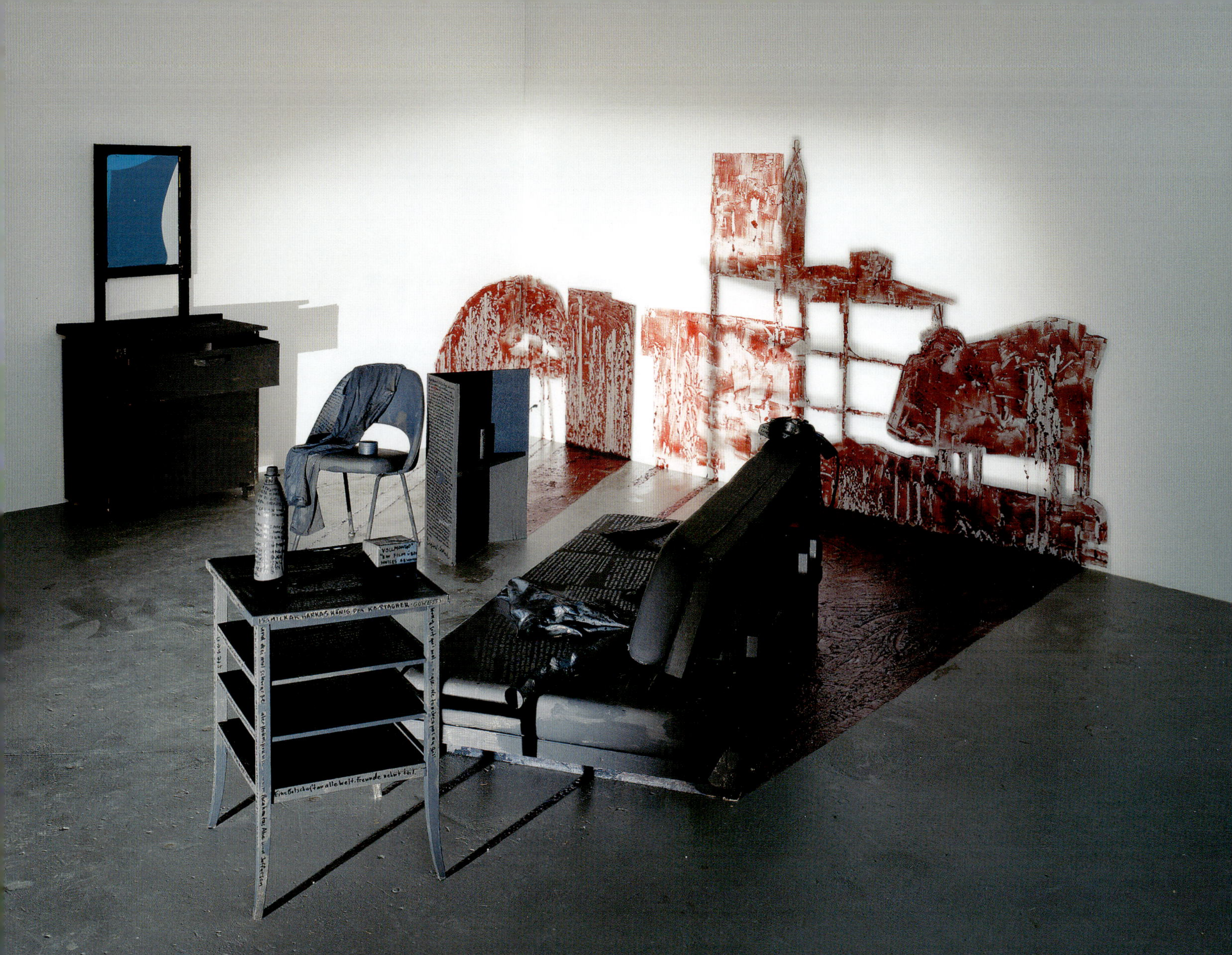

Boffer Bix Kabinett, 1998
Found furniture, fabric, foam, mirror, latex paint, marker, paper, branch, bottle, telephone, jam, screws, spotlight
Dimensions variable

Opposite page:
Untitled, 1996
Found stool, found bottle, hammer, strawberry jam
Dimensions variable
Studio view, Wildbachstrasse, Zurich

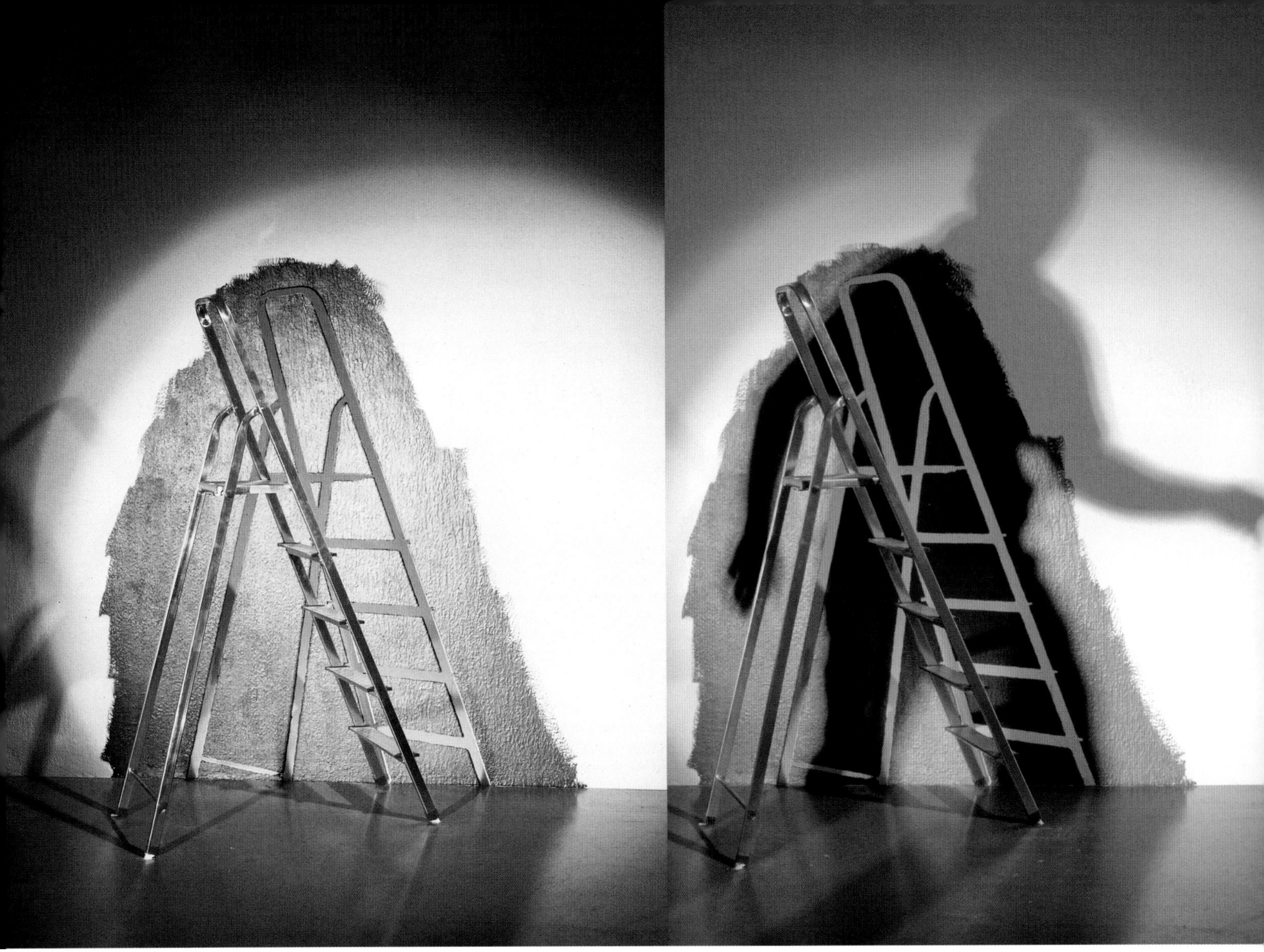

Leiter, 1997
Aluminum ladder, latex paint, theater spotlights, water bottle
Dimensions variable

Opposite page:
Untitled (Ladder), 1997
Aluminum ladder, latex paint, theater spotlights, water bottle
Dimensions variable

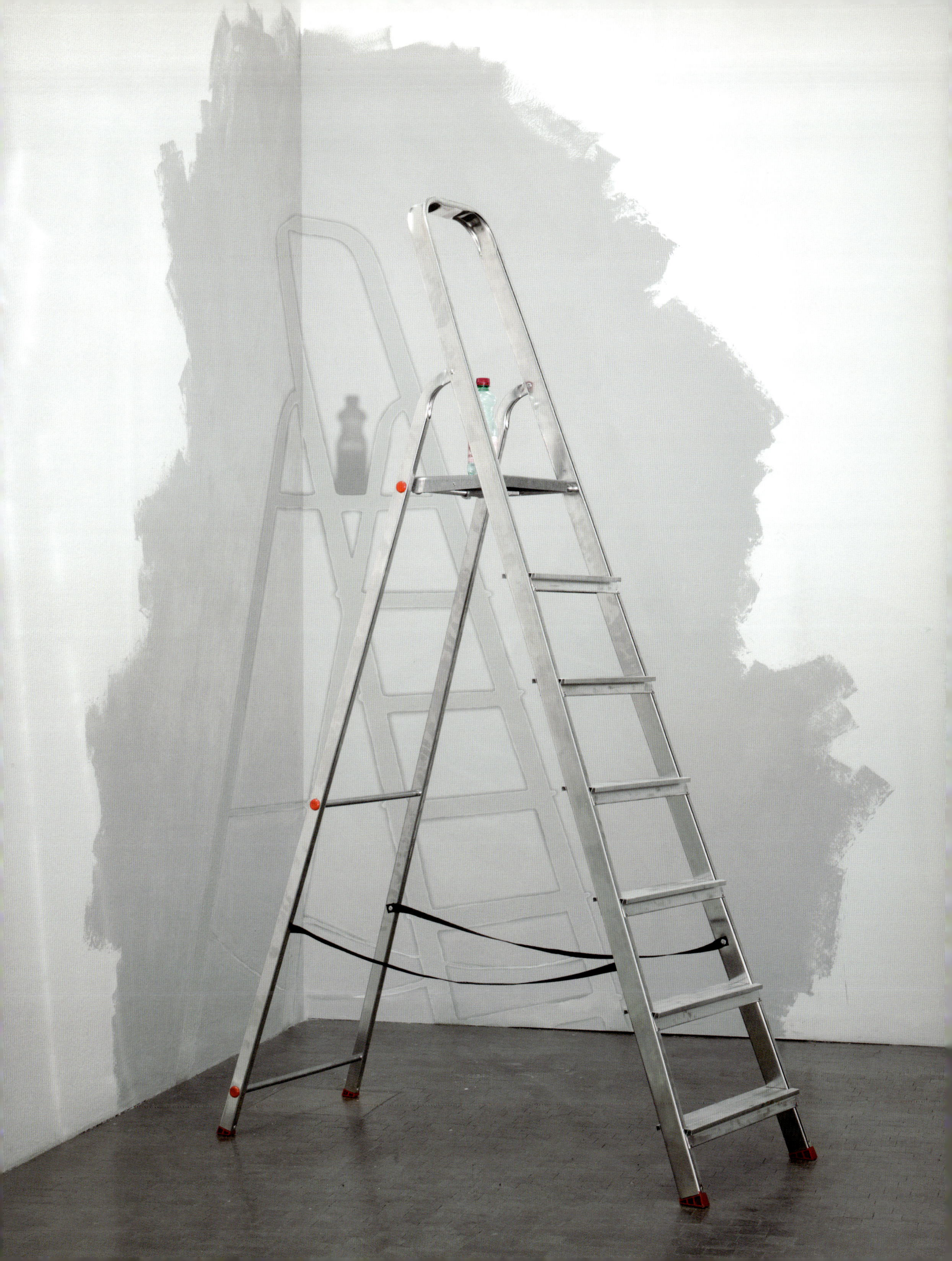

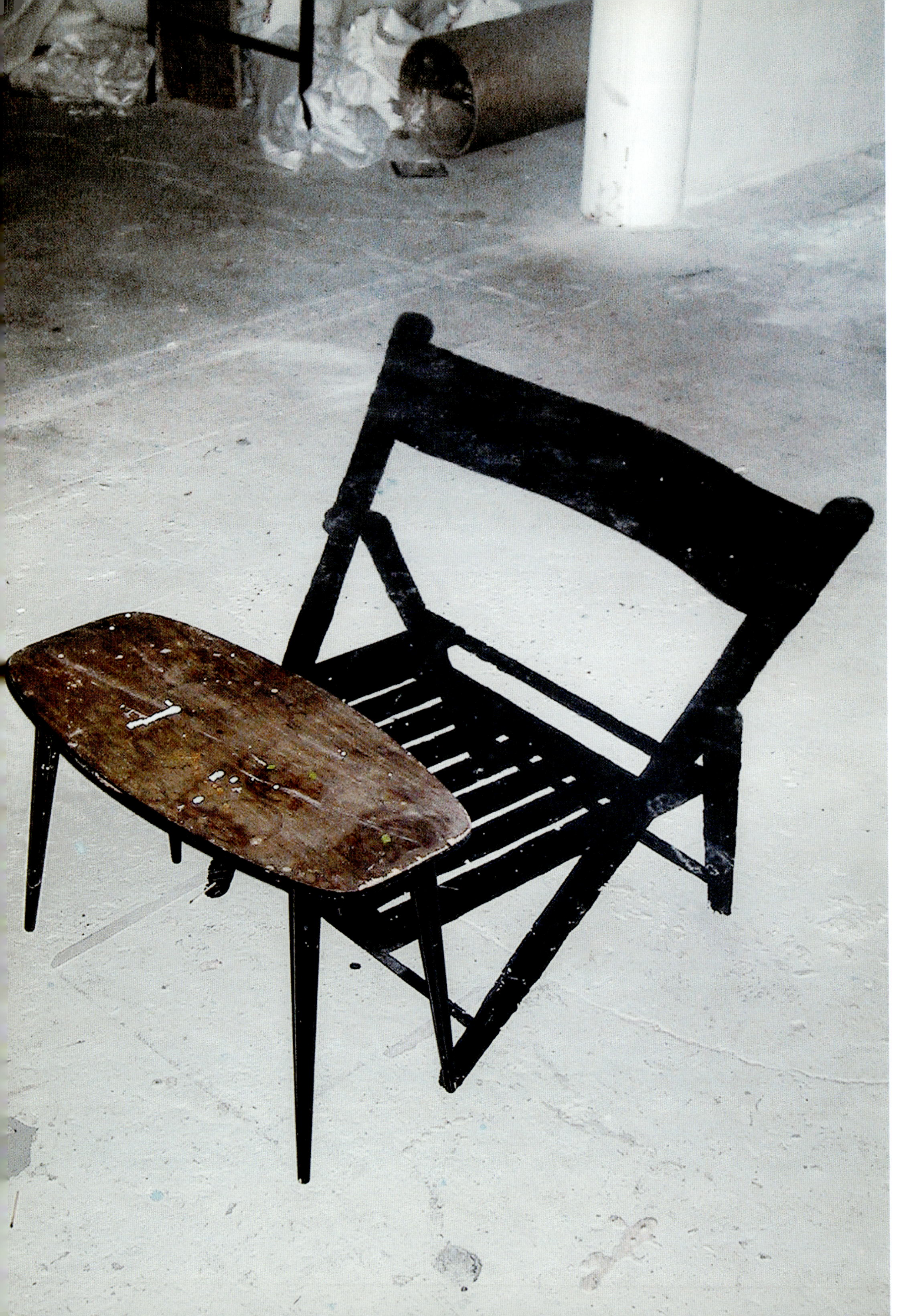

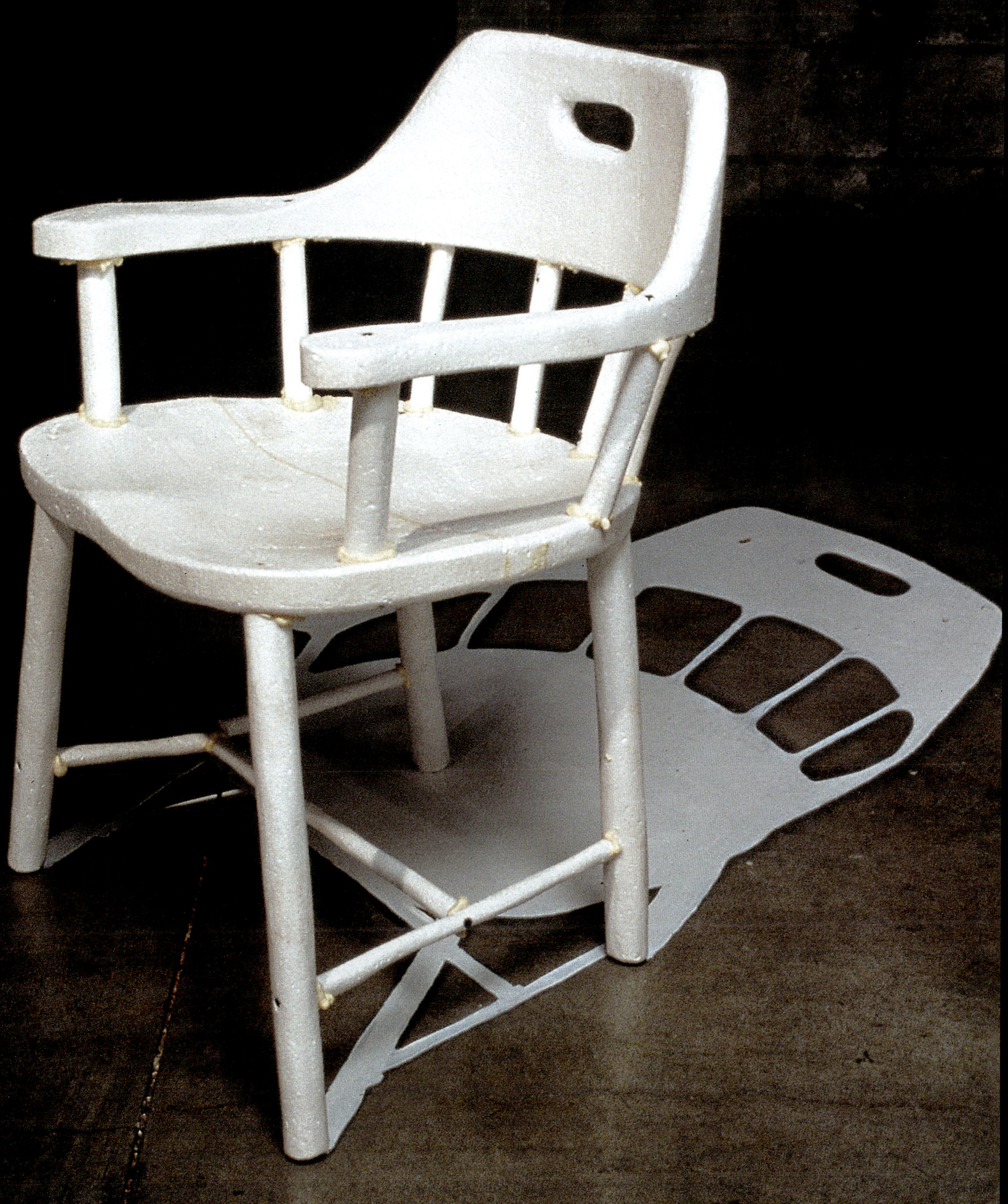

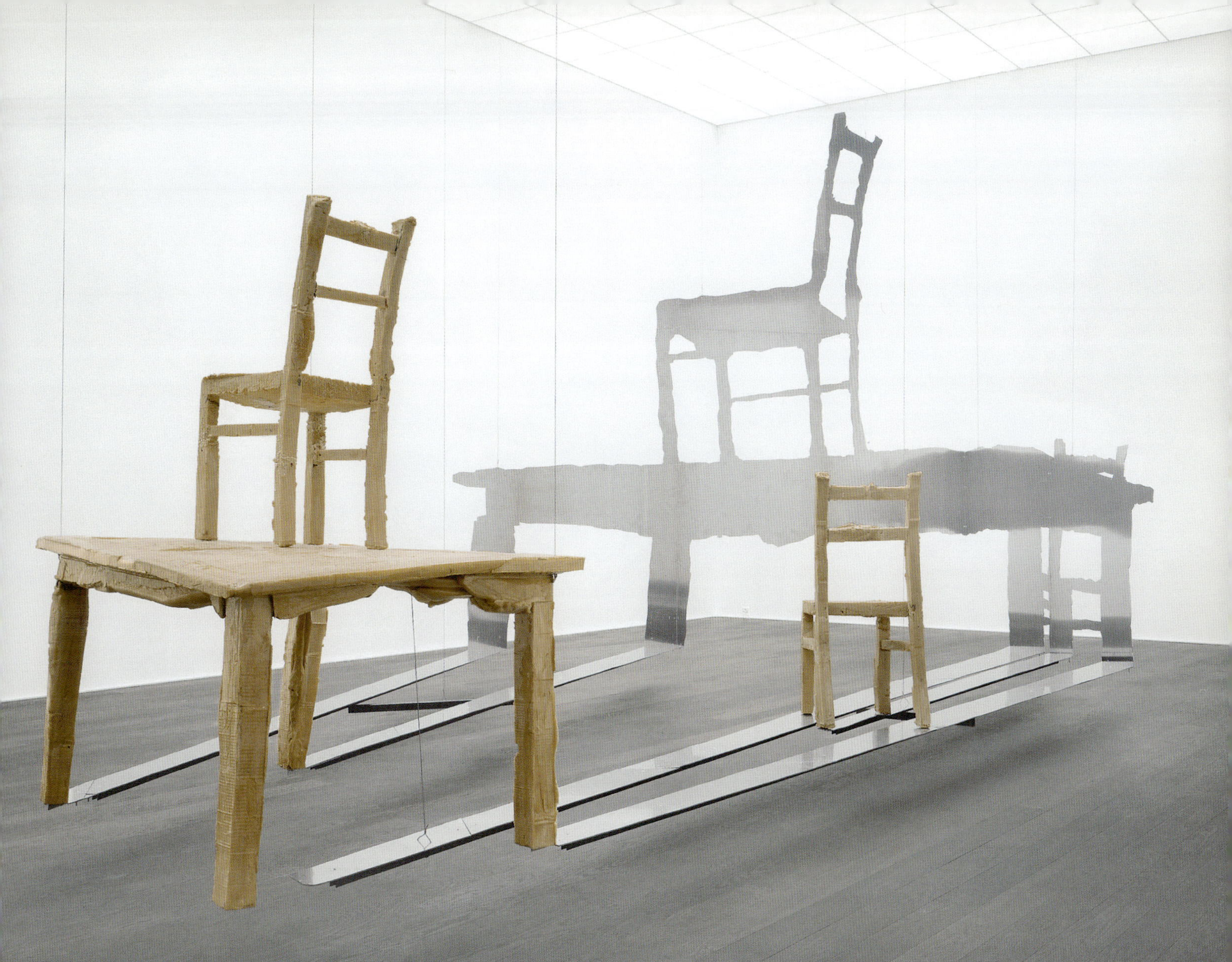

Portrait of a Moment, 2003
Aluminum, two-component polyurethane foam, aircraft cable, steel tubing, acrylic paint, metal fittings
145 ⅝ x 283 ½ x 149 ⅝ inches (370 x 720 x 380 cm)

Previous pages:
Shadow Replacement
from the portfolio *Thinking about Störtebeker*

Routine (Automatic Melancholy), 2002
Polystyrene, polyurethane foam, screws, gouache
Chair: 21 x 35 x 17 inches (53.5 x 89 x 43 cm)
Installation dimensions variable

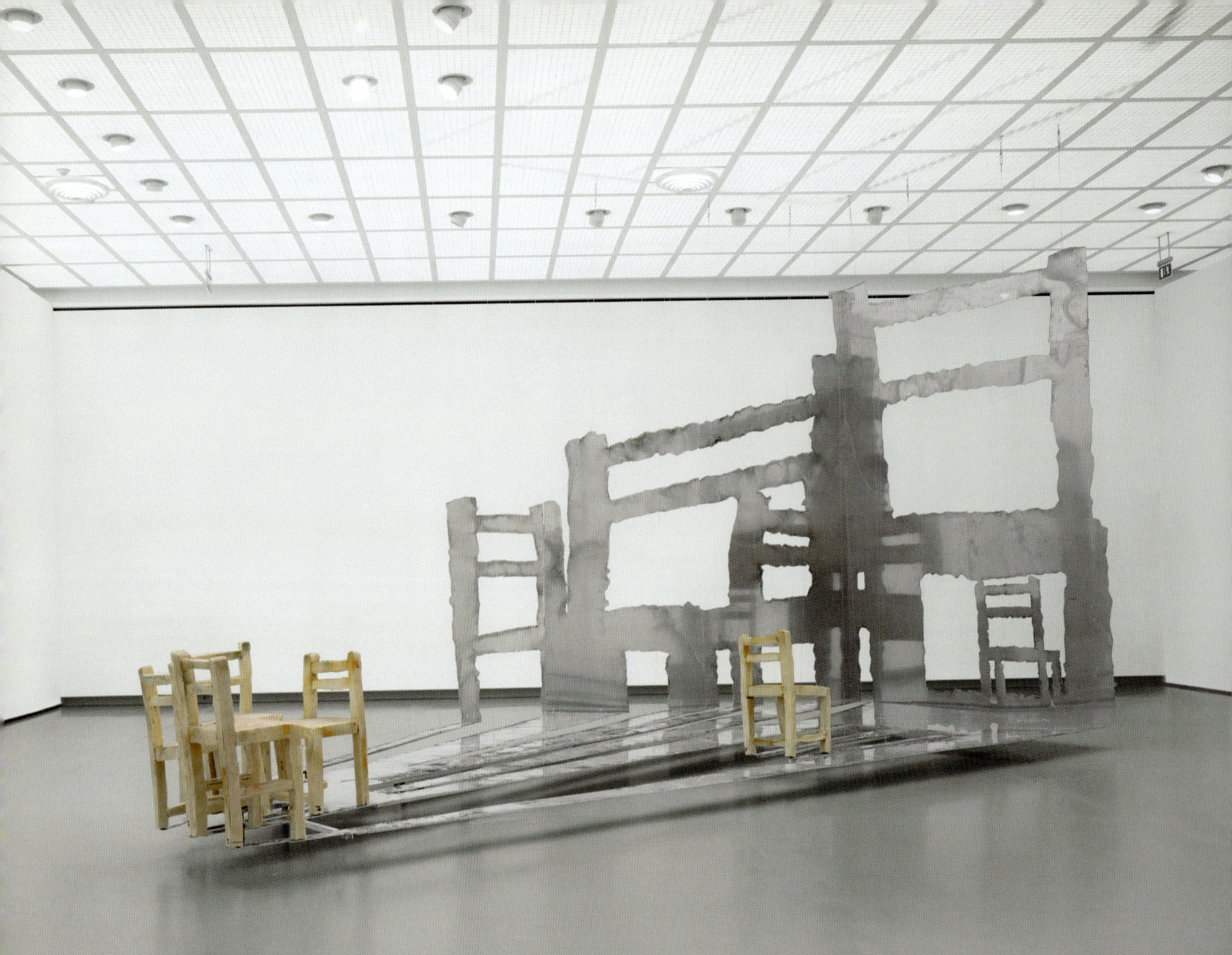

Memories of a Blank Mind, 2004
Aluminum, two-component polyurethane foam, wood, aircraft cable, acrylic paint, marker, steel, screws
157 ½ x 236 ¼ x 236 ¼ inches (400 x 600 x 600 cm)

Opposite page:
Some Say Vacuum Some Say Kumquat, 2003
Aluminum, polyurethane resin, nylon filament, metal mountings, aircraft cable, acrylic paint, rivets
122 x 78 ¾ x 149 ⅝ inches (310 x 200 x 380 cm)

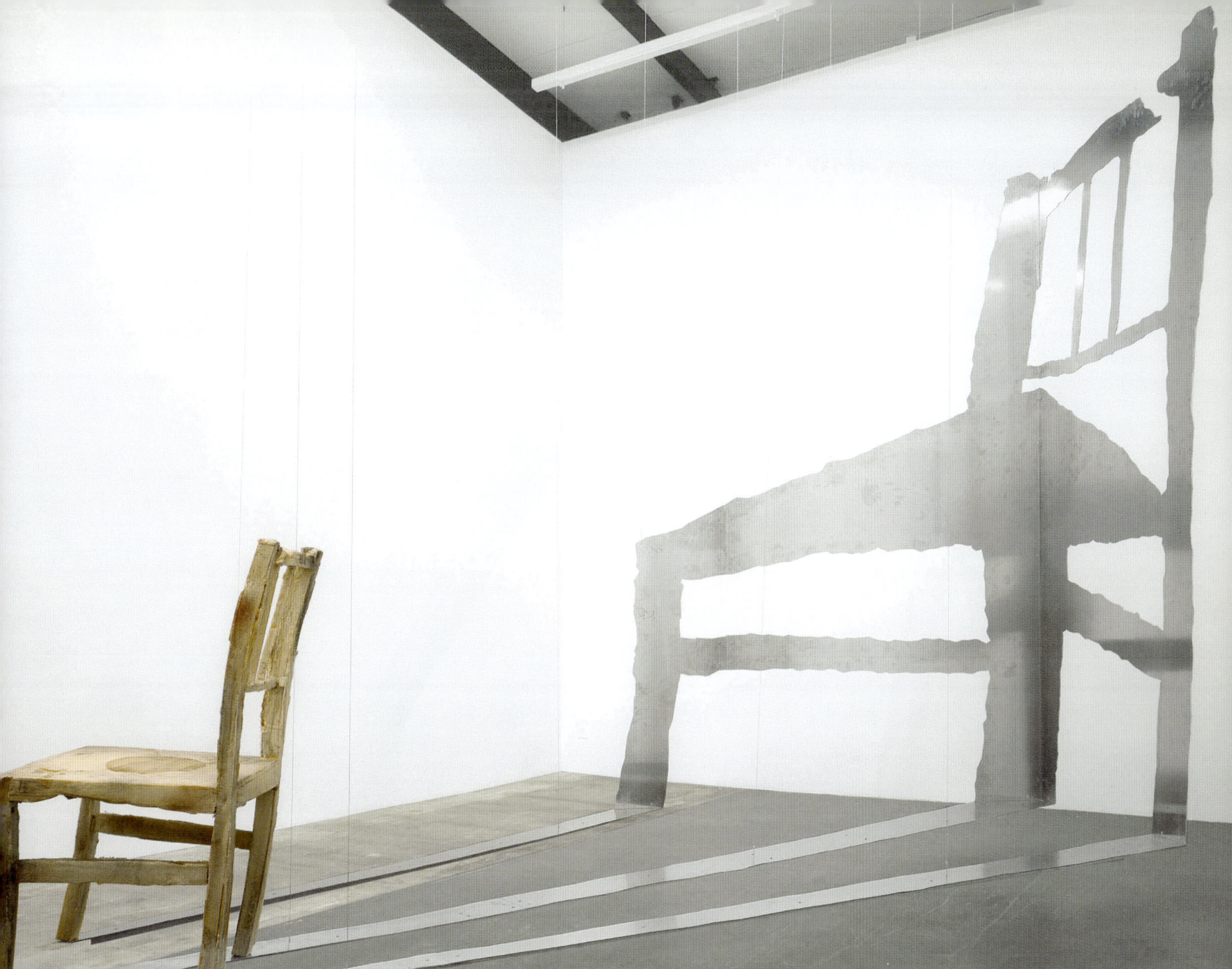

Following spread:

meme, 2012

Galvanized bronze, bronze, two-component epoxy primer, polyester filler, two-component polyester body filler, urethane primer, polyester paint, acrylic polyurethane matte clearcoat
Left nail: 70 ¼ x 21 ⅛ x 44 ¼ inches (178.5 x 53.5 x 112.5 cm)
Right nail 2: 75 ⅝ x 30 ½ x 17 ⅜ inches (192 x 77.5 x 44 cm)
Overall dimensions: 75 ⅝ x 88 ⅝ x 44 ¼ inches (192 x 225 x 112.5 cm)
Installation view, "Madame Fisscher," Palazzo Grassi, Venice, 2012
Servile Serenade / Servile Symphony, 2001

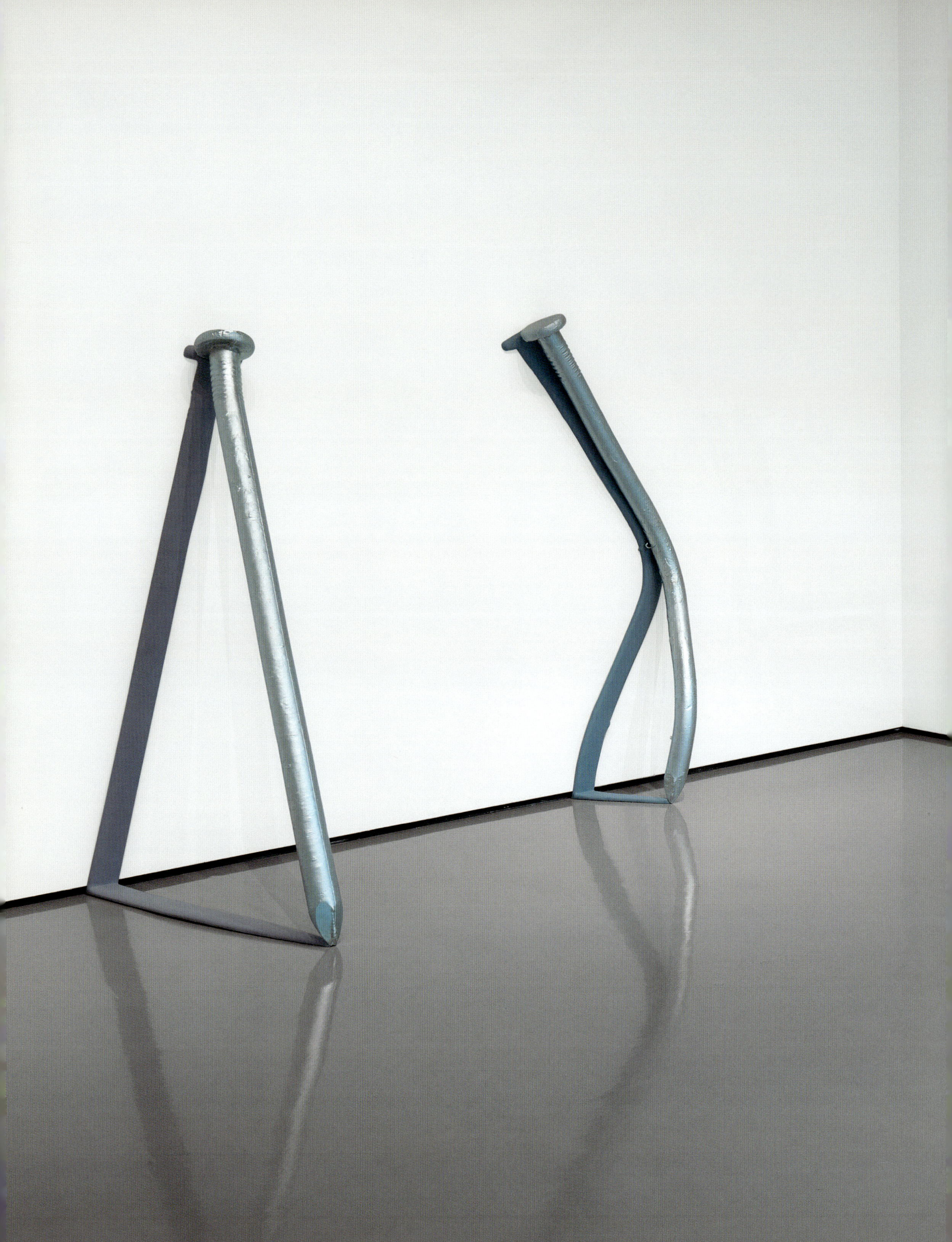

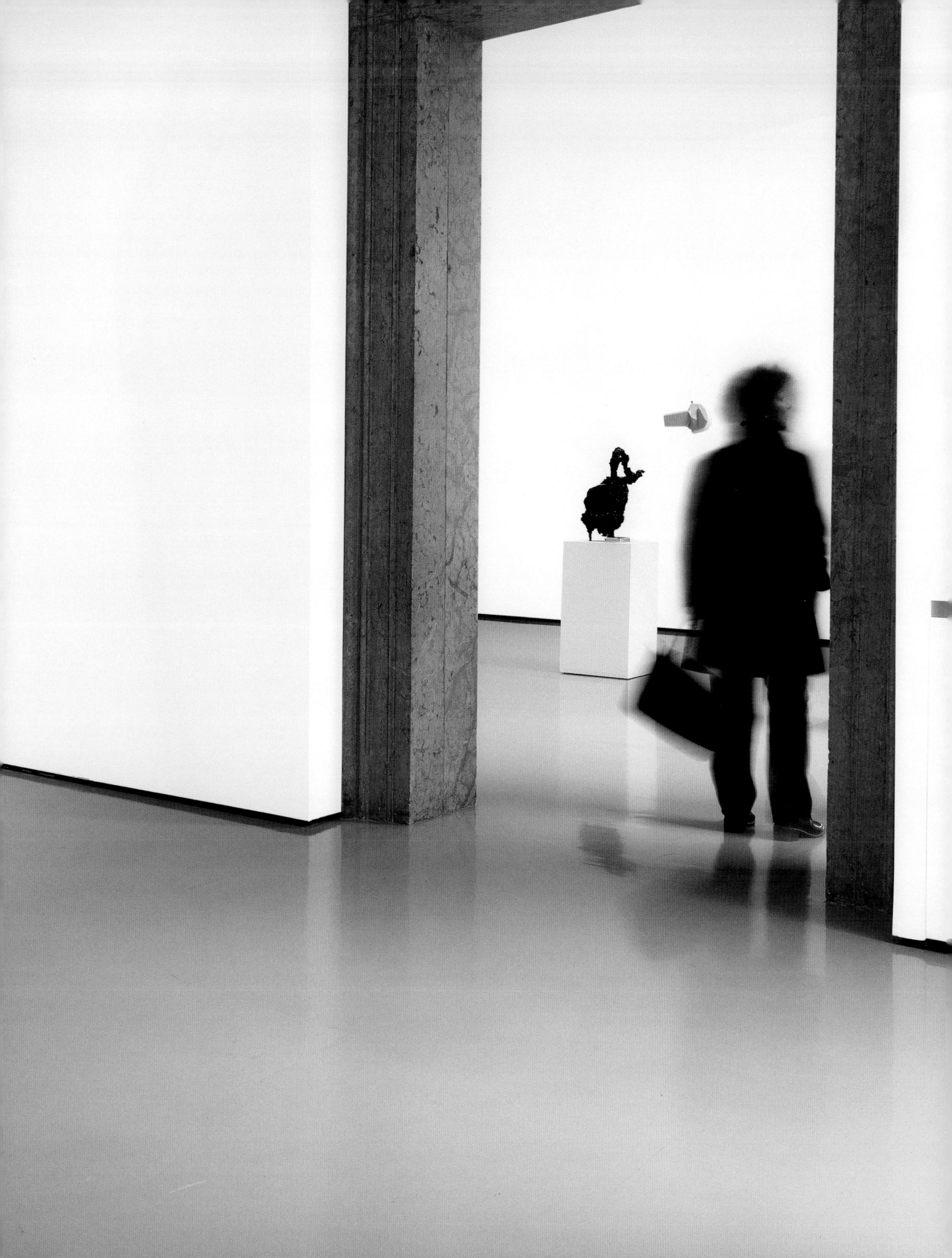

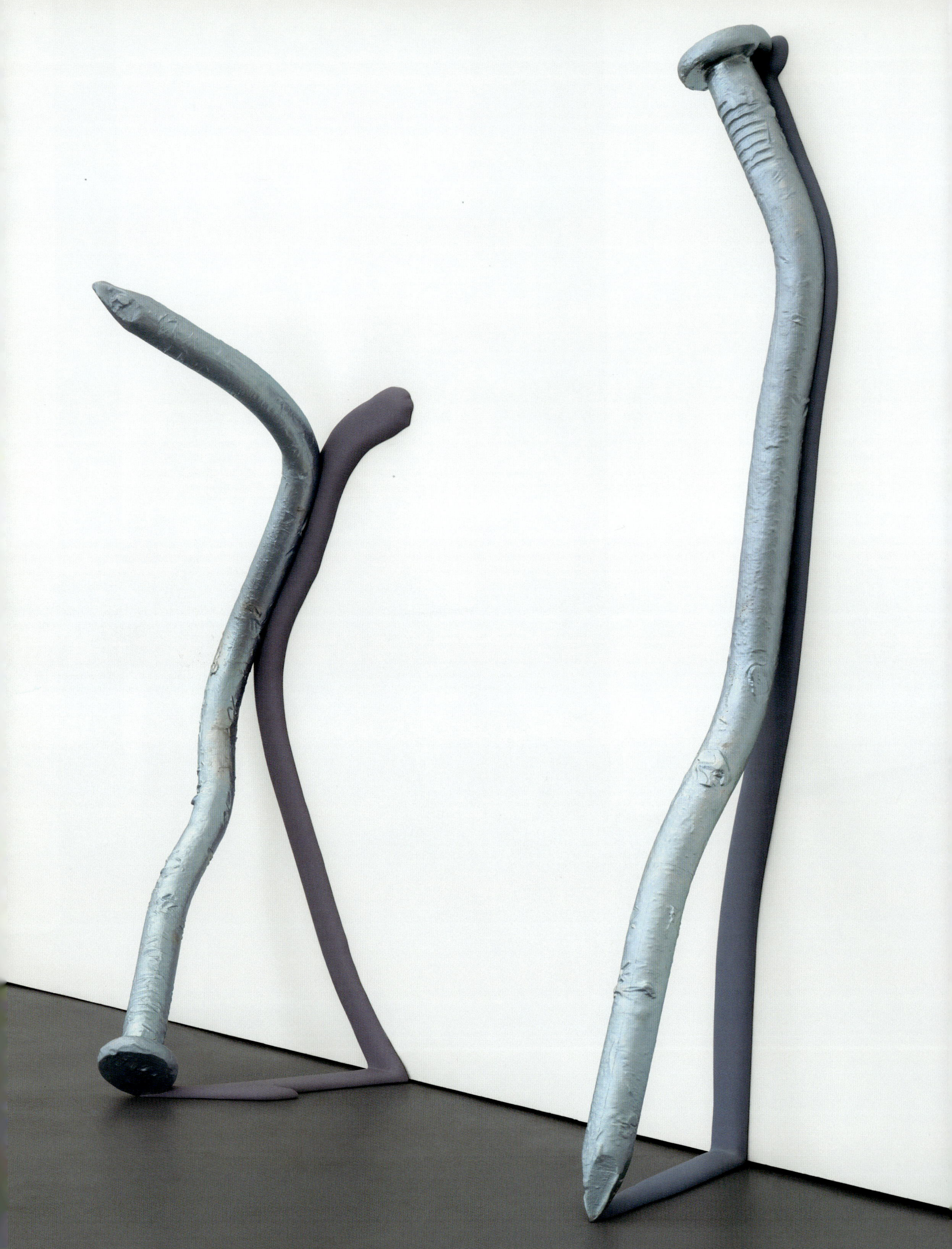

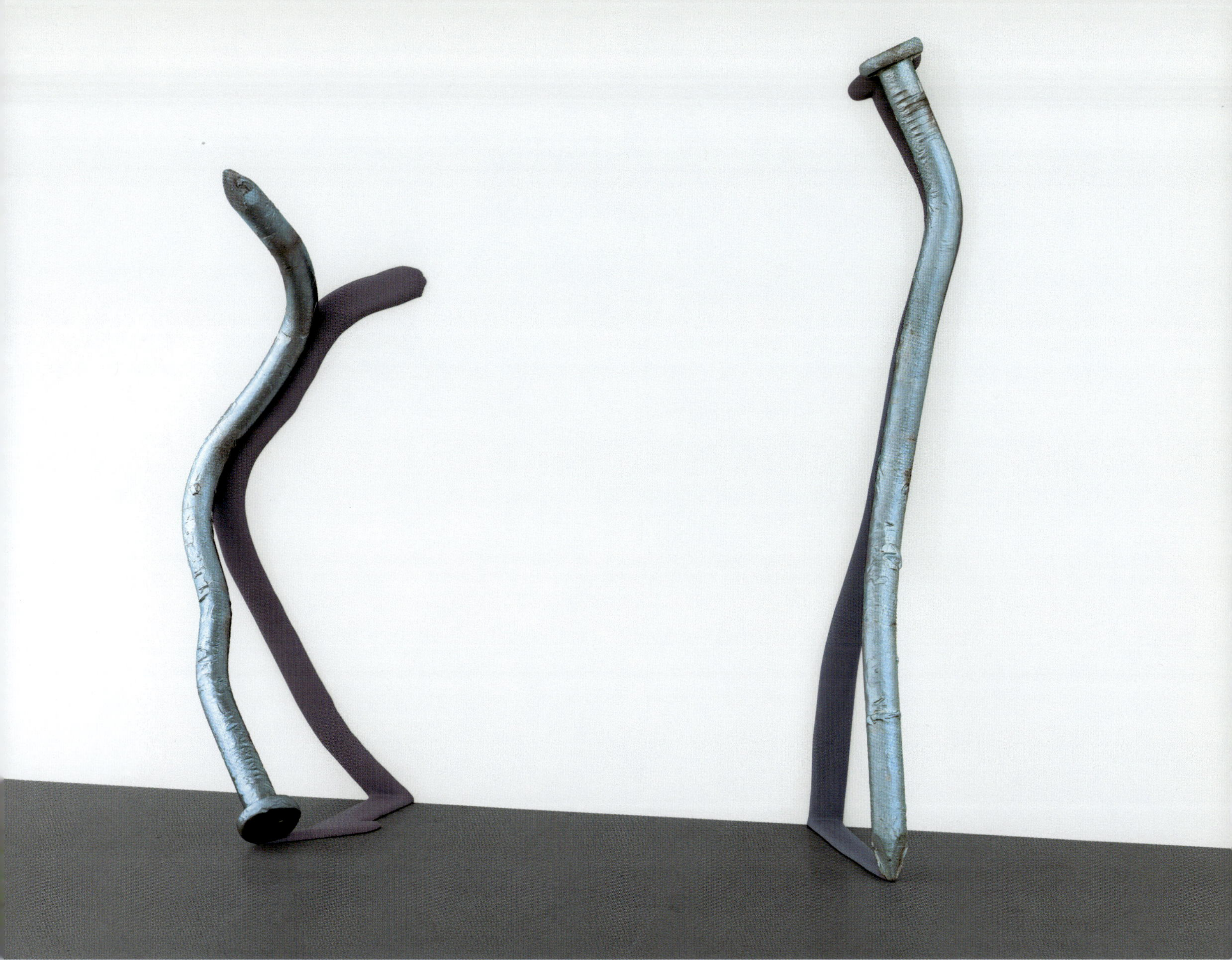

Nail Duo, 2012
Galvanized bronze, bronze, two-component epoxy primer, polyester filler, two-component polyester body filler, urethane primer, polyester paint, acrylic polyurethane matte clearcoat
Left nail: Approximately 61 ¾ x 26 ⅜ x 23 ⅝ inches (157 x 67 x 60 cm)
Right nail: Approximately 76 ⅜ x 19 ¼ x 13 ⅜ inches (194 x 49 x 34 cm)
Overall dimensions: Approximately 76 ⅜ x 75 ⅝ x 23 ⅝ inches (194 x 192 x 60 cm)

Nail Solo, 2012

Galvanized bronze, bronze, two-component epoxy primer, polyester filler, two-component polyester body filler, urethane primer, polyester paint, acrylic polyurethane matte clearcoat

72 ⅝ x 15 ⅝ x 37 inches (184.5 x 39.7 x 94 cm)

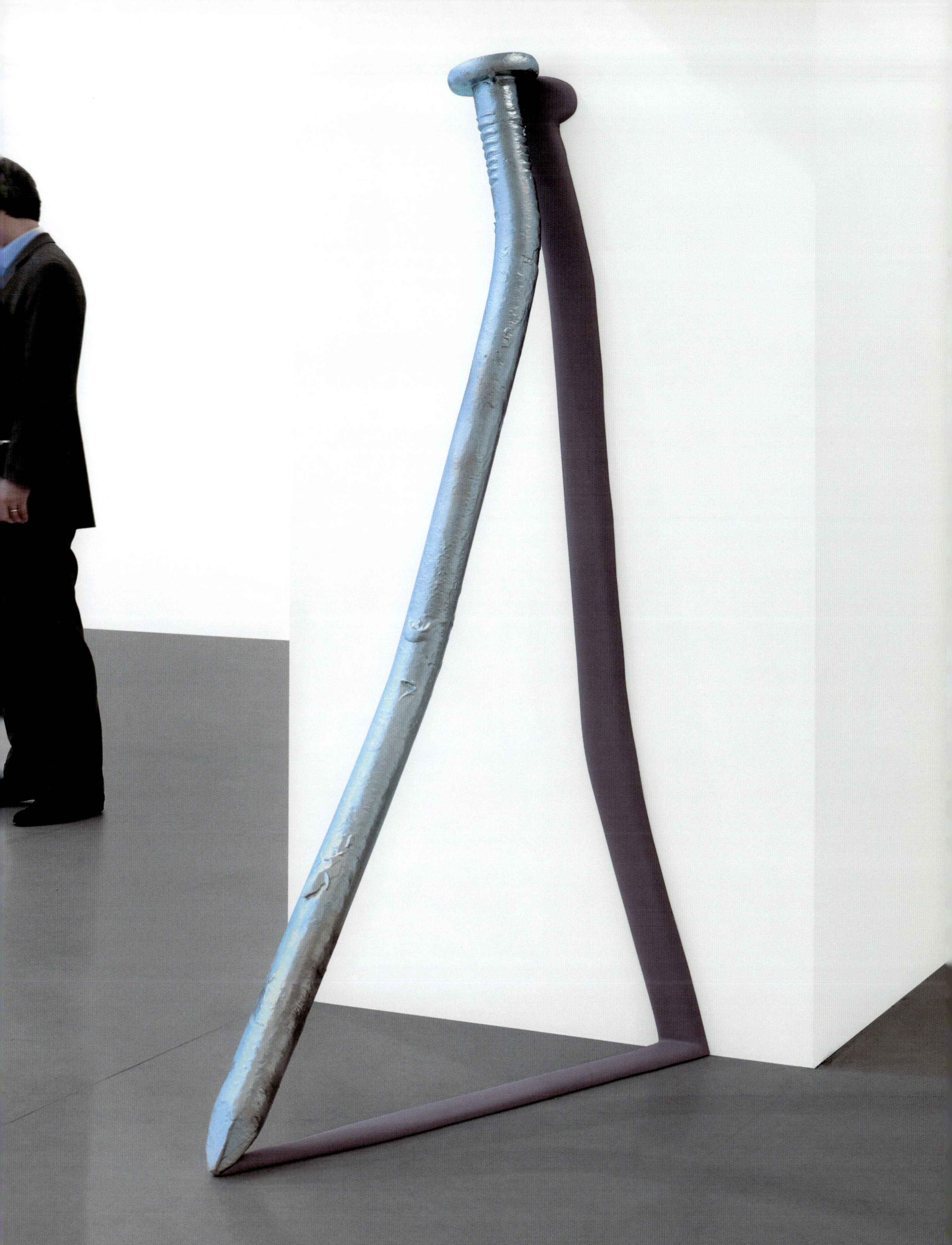

Studies for chairs for individual seating positions, 1993

Part 1 of 3

Sawdust, rubber

Dimensions unknown

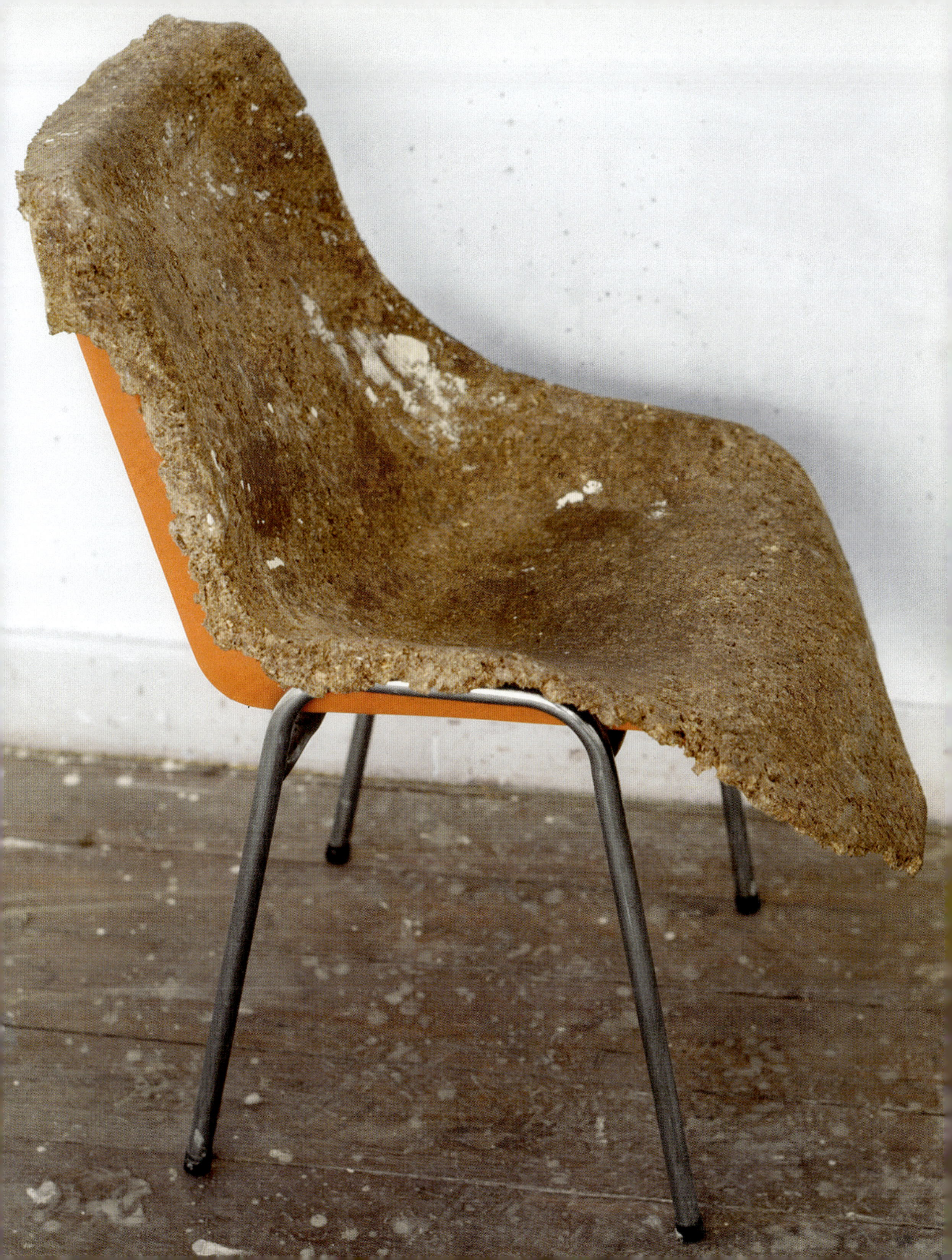

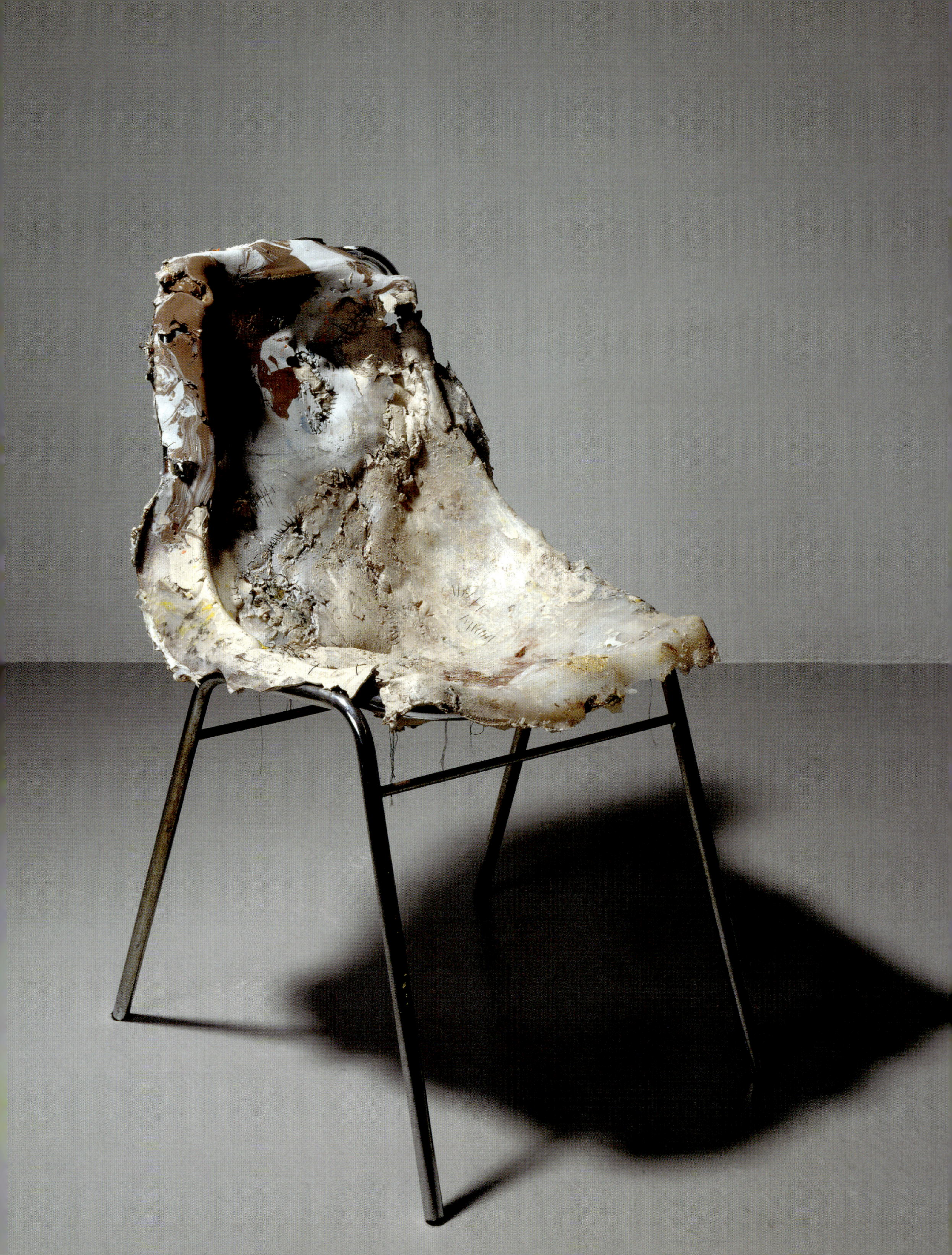

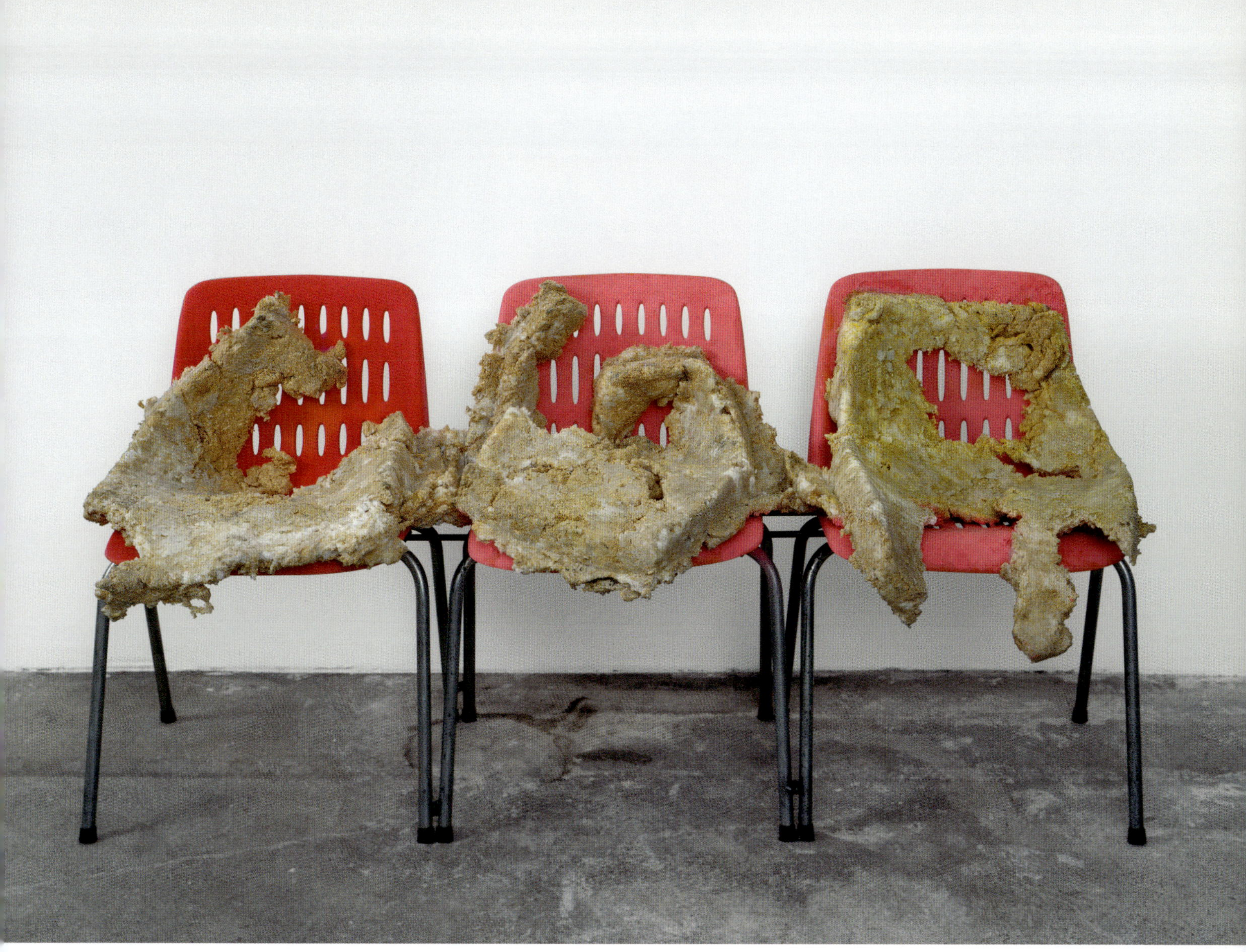

:hairs, 1998–1999
ilicone, sawdust, plastic, found chairs, spray enamel, metal
9 ½ x 22 ½ x 60 ¼ inches (75 x 57 x 153 cm)

)pposite page:
:hair (Sewn), 1998–1999
ound chair frame, silicone, thread, acrylic paint
2 ¼ x 20 ½ x 22 ½ inches (82 x 52 x 57 cm)

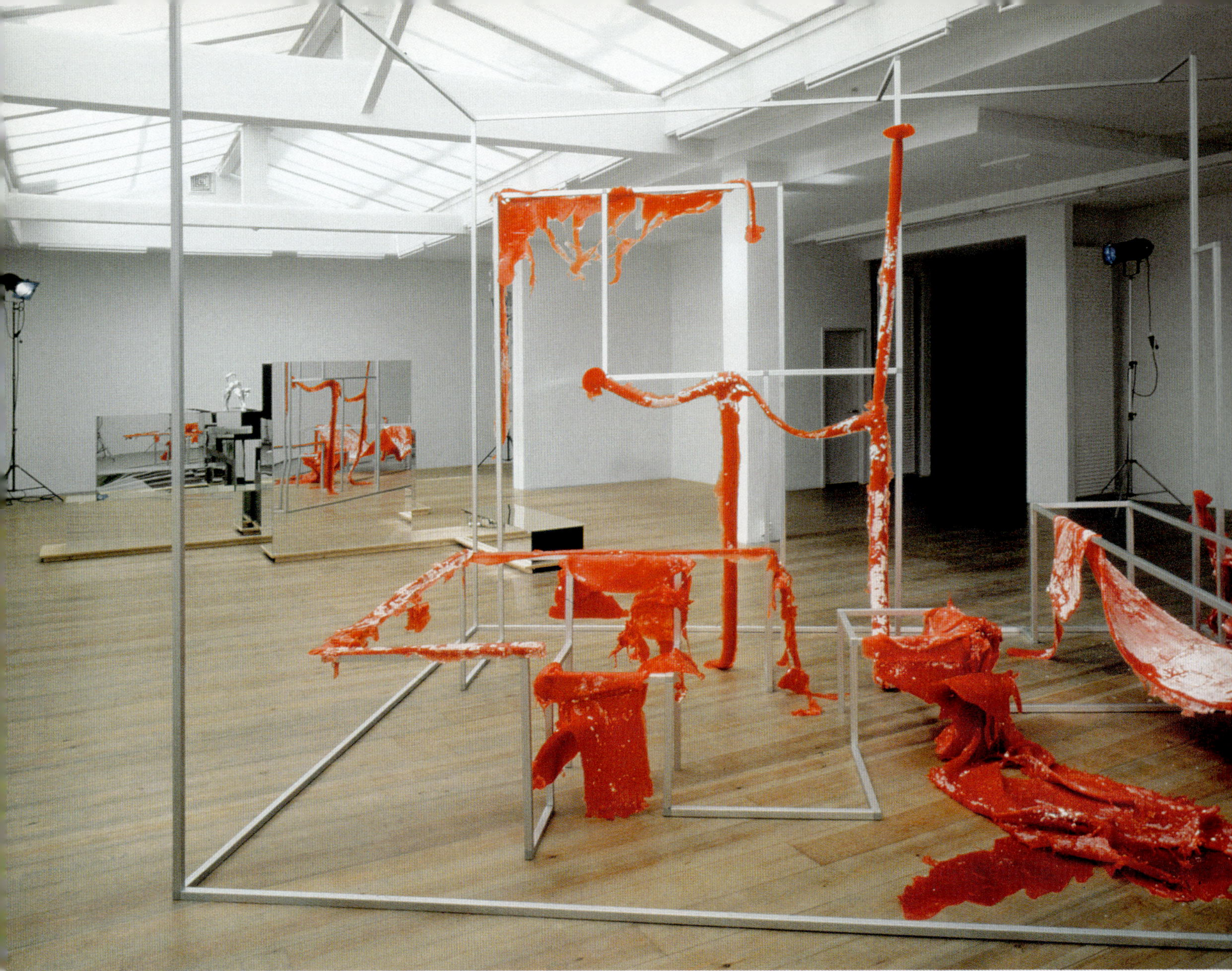

The Membrane (Half Full, Half Empty), 2000
Polyurethane rubber (casts of furniture), pigments, aluminum tubes with plastic connectors, theater spotlights on tripods
118 ⅛ x 236 ¼ x 118 ⅛ inches (300 x 600 x 300 cm)
Installation view, "The Membrane—and why I don't mind bad-mooded People," Stedelijk Museum Bureau Amsterdam, 2000
Dr. Katzelberg (Zivilisationsruine), 1999

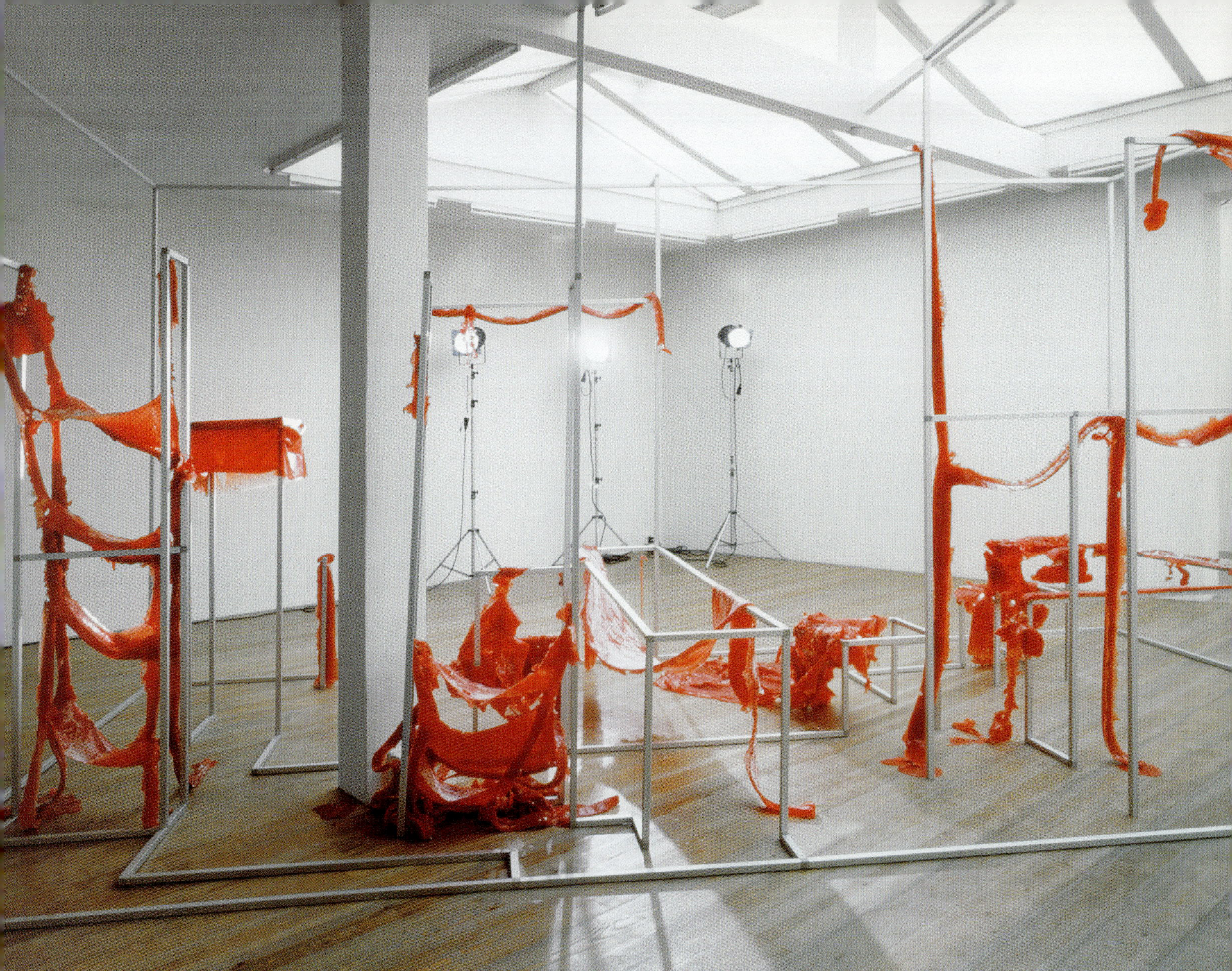

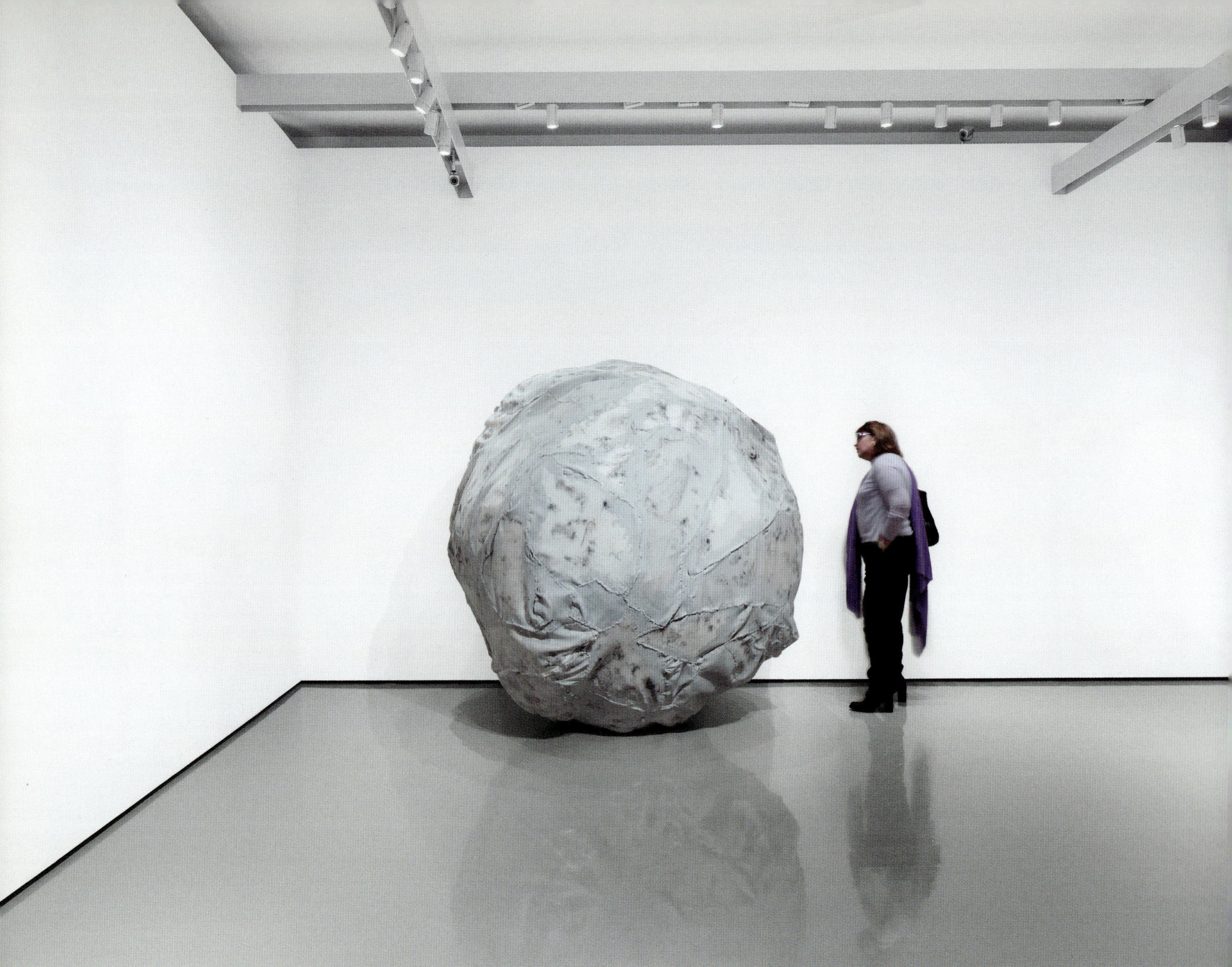

A Light Sigh Is the Sound of My Life, 2000–2001
Overlaid by silicone skin, core rotates on a horizontal axis at a speed of one revolution every four minutes
Polystyrene, polyurethane foam, wood, steel axle, electric motor, silicone, gauze, hair, wood glue
78 ¾ x 78 ¾ x 110 ¼ inches (200 x 200 x 280 cm)
Opposite page: Installation view, "Mastering the Complaint," Galerie Hauser & Wirth & Presenhuber, Zurich, 2001
One More Carrot Before I Brush My Teeth, 2001; *Warum wächst ein Baum / Kann man zuviel Fragen (Nr. 3) / Why does a tree grow / Can one ask too much (No. 3)*, 2001

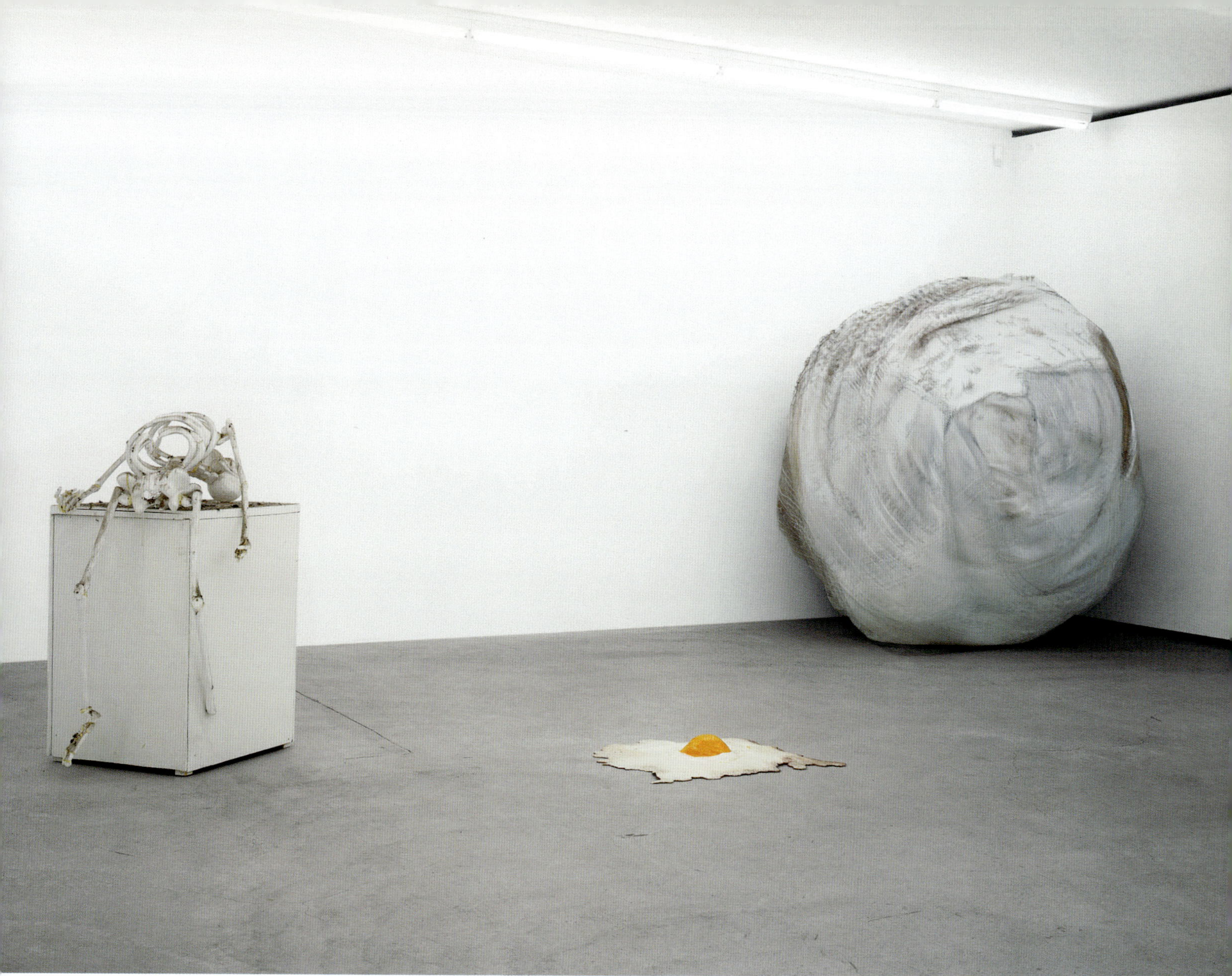

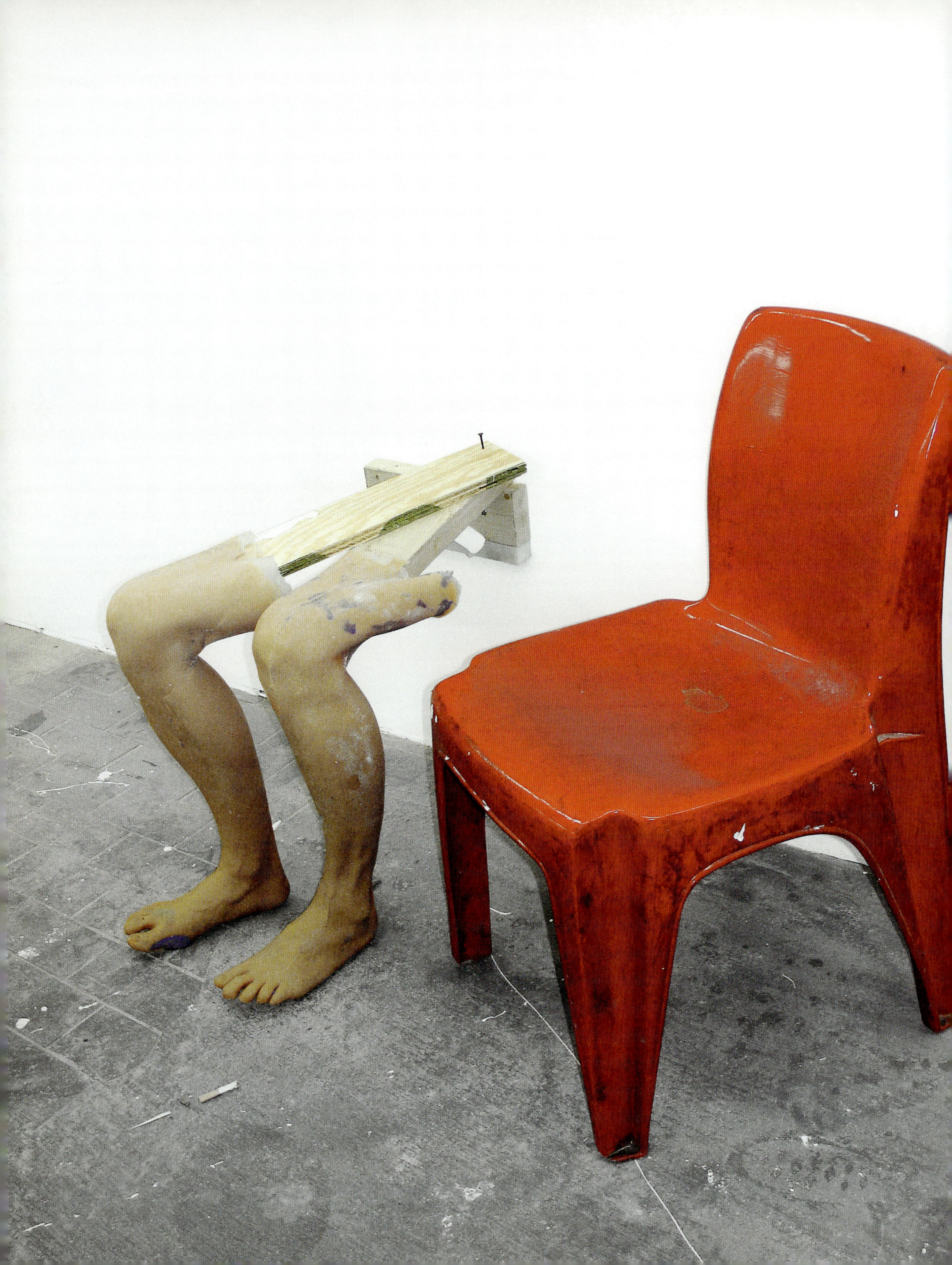

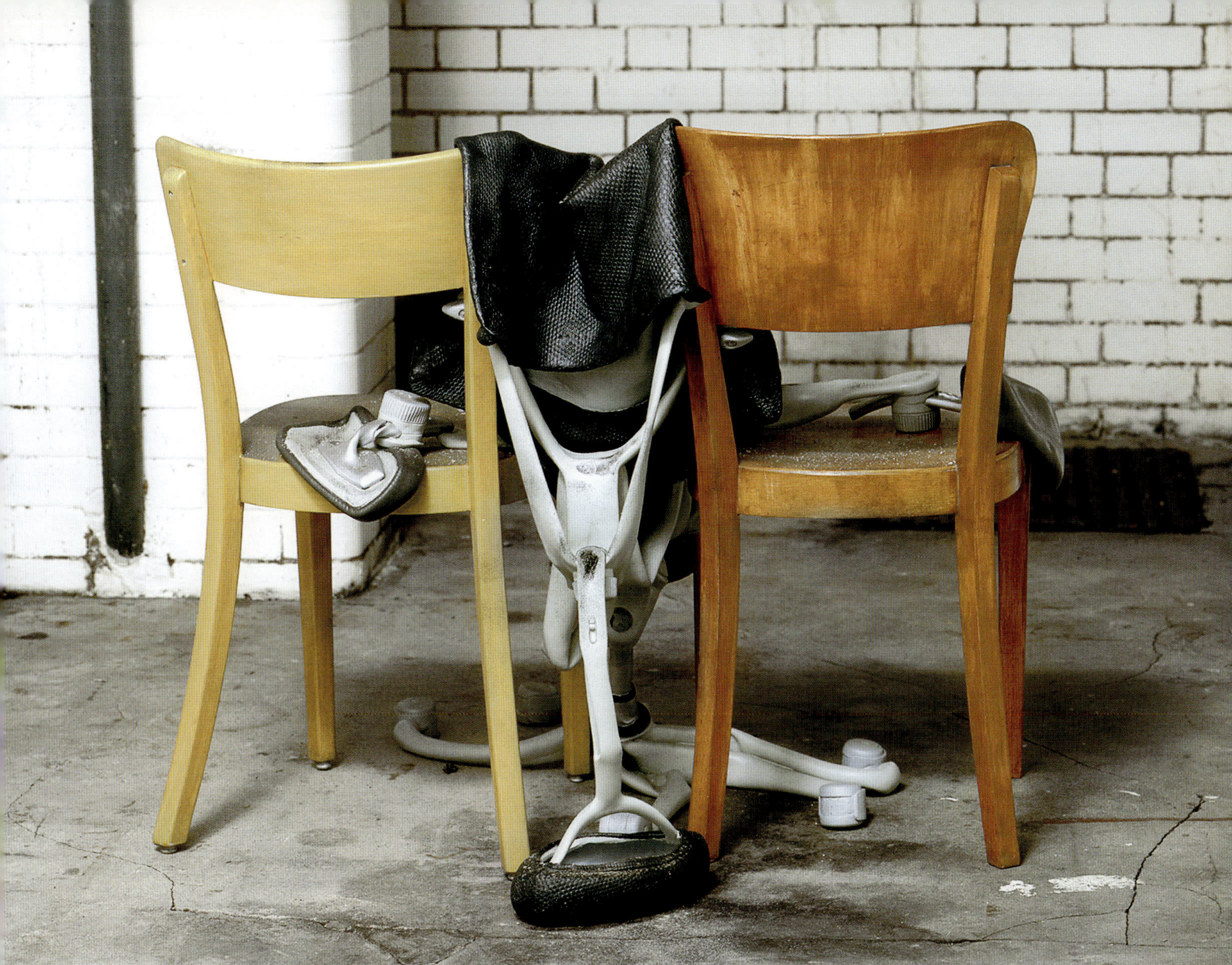

How to Tell a Joke, 2007
Polyurethane resin, polymeric plaster, steel,
pigments, acrylic paint, matte varnish, dust
39 ⅜ x 37 ⅜ x 39 ⅜ inches (100 x 95 x 100 cm)

Opposite page:
Untitled, 2006
Silicone, wood, found chair, shellac
Dimensions variable

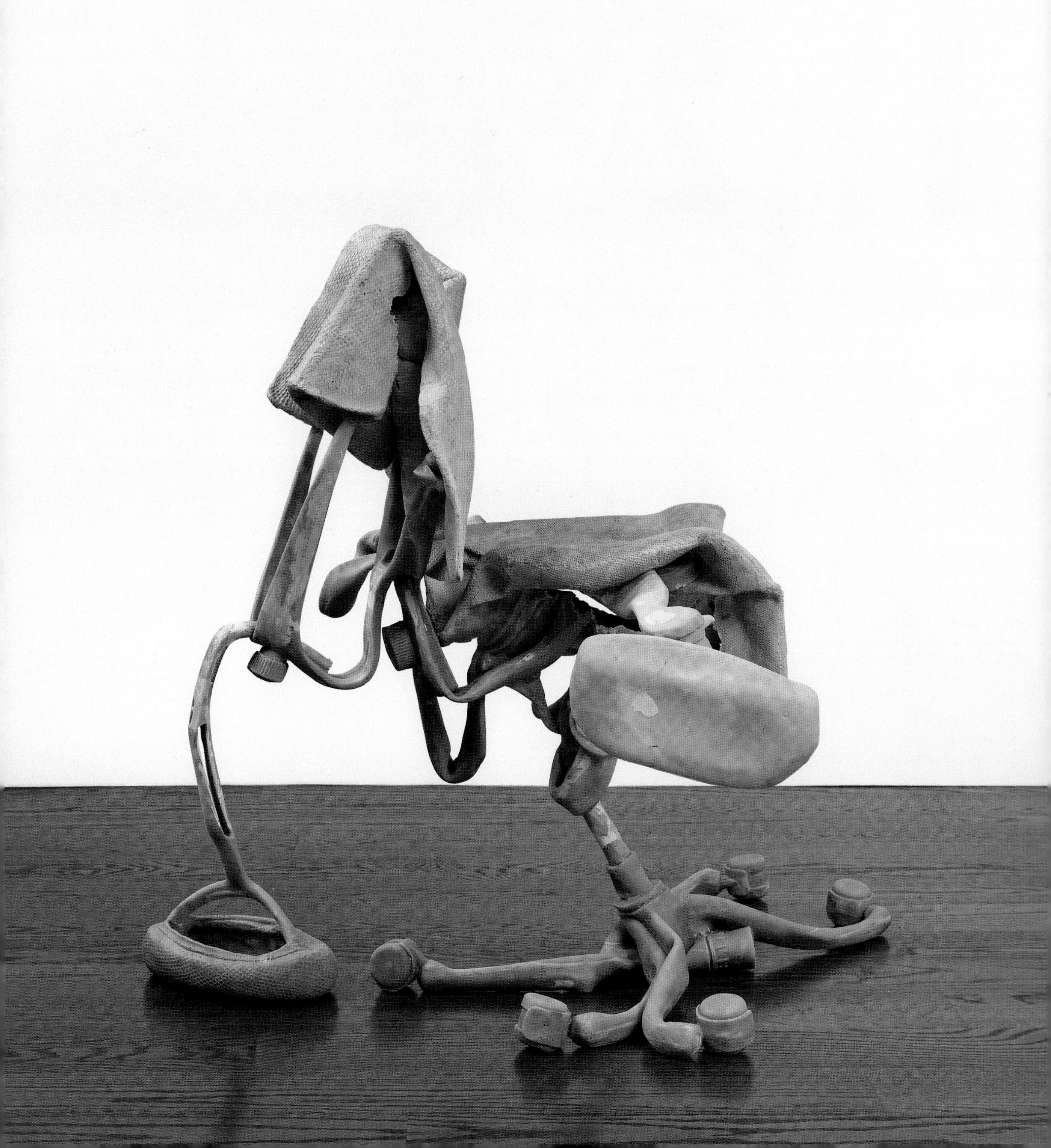

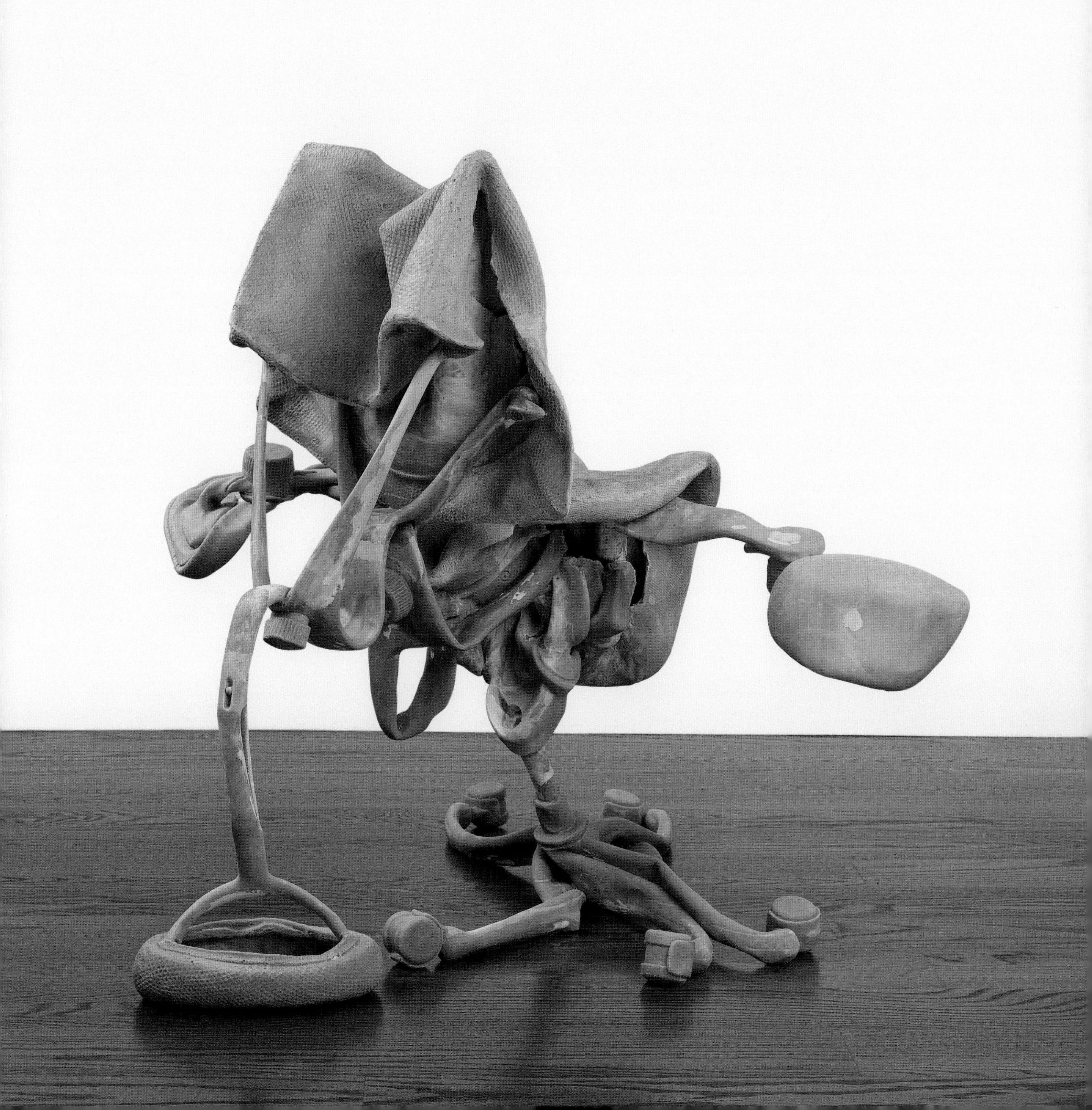

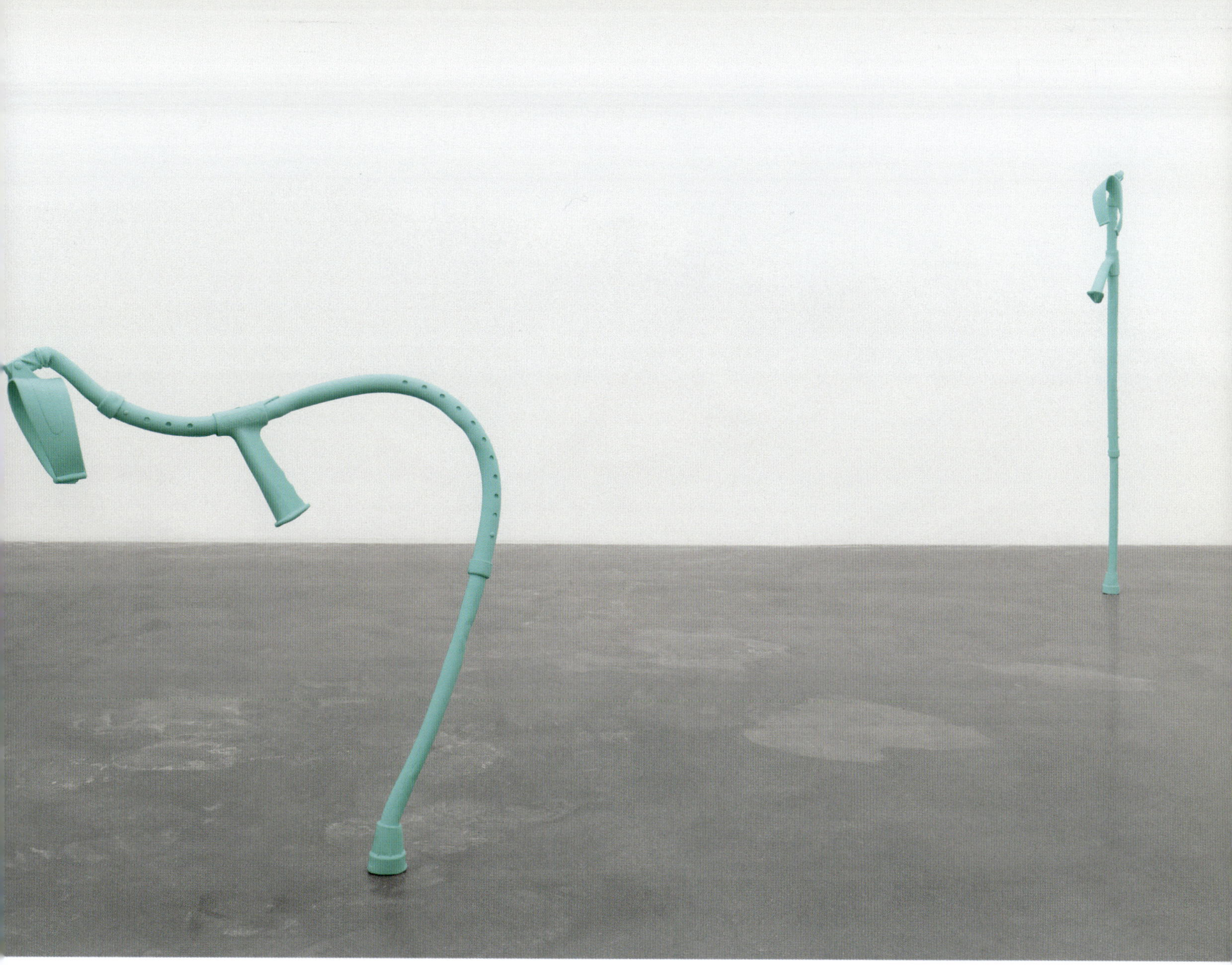

4:15pm & 4:15pm, 2009
Cast aluminum, epoxy primer, polyester filler, one-component acrylic putty, urethane primer, polyester paint, acrylic polyurethane matte clearcoat
Crutch 1: Approximately 25 x 24 x 7 inches (64 x 61 x 18 cm)
Crutch 2: Approximately 45 x 11 ½ x 3 ¼ inches (114 x 29 x 8 cm)
Installation dimensions: Approximately 45 x 122 x 7 inches (114 x 310 x 18 cm)

Previous pages:
Y-Chair, 2007
Acrylic resin, stainless steel
32 x 34 x 35 inches (81.3 x 86.4 x 88.9 cm)

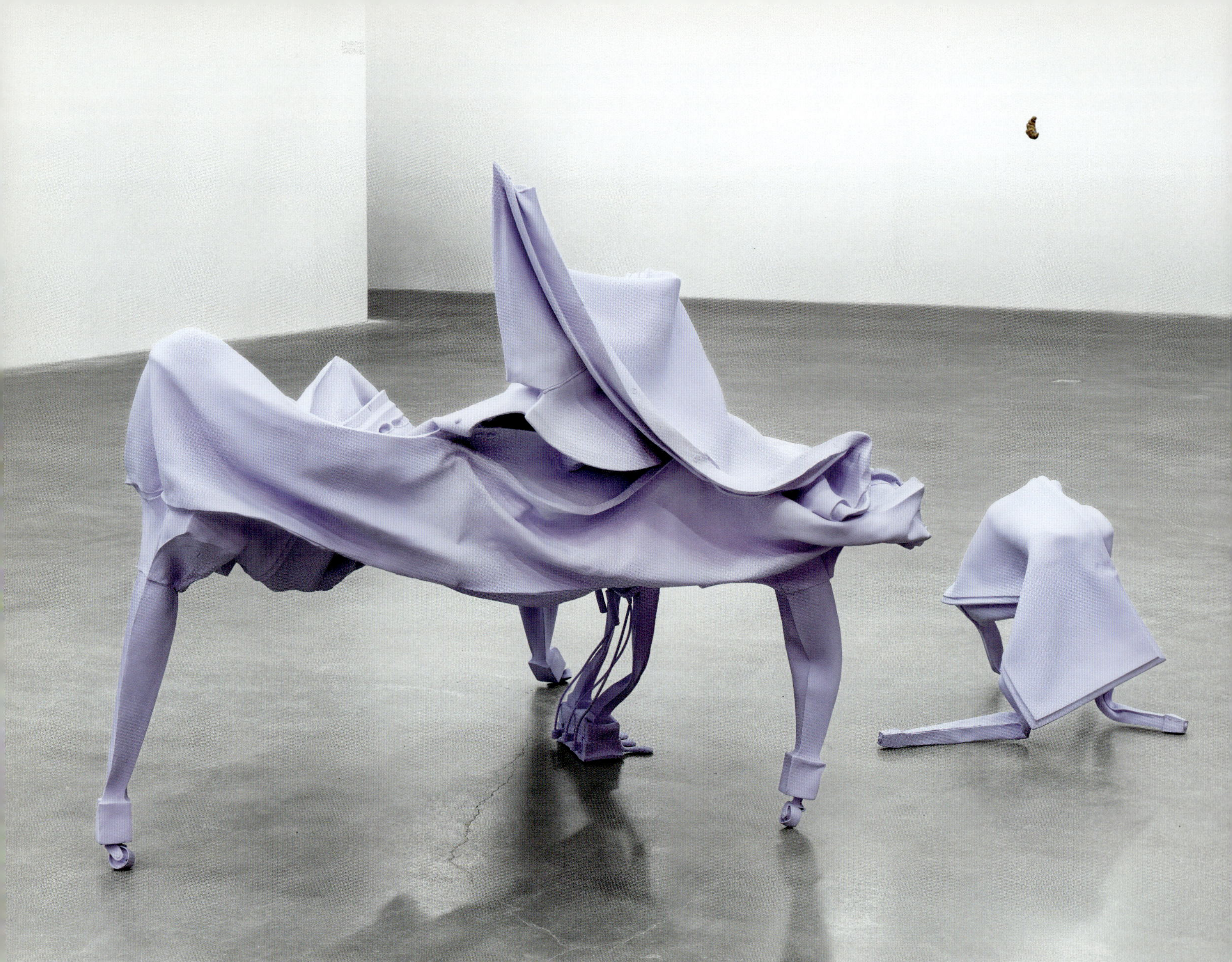

Untitled, 2009
Cast aluminum, aluminum wire, epoxy primer,
polyester filler, one-component acrylic putty,
urethane primer, polyester paint, acrylic
polyurethane matte clearcoat
52 x 61 x 98 inches (132 x 155 x 249 cm)
Installation view, "Urs Fischer: Marguerite de Ponty,"
New Museum, New York, 2009–2010
Cumpadre, 2009

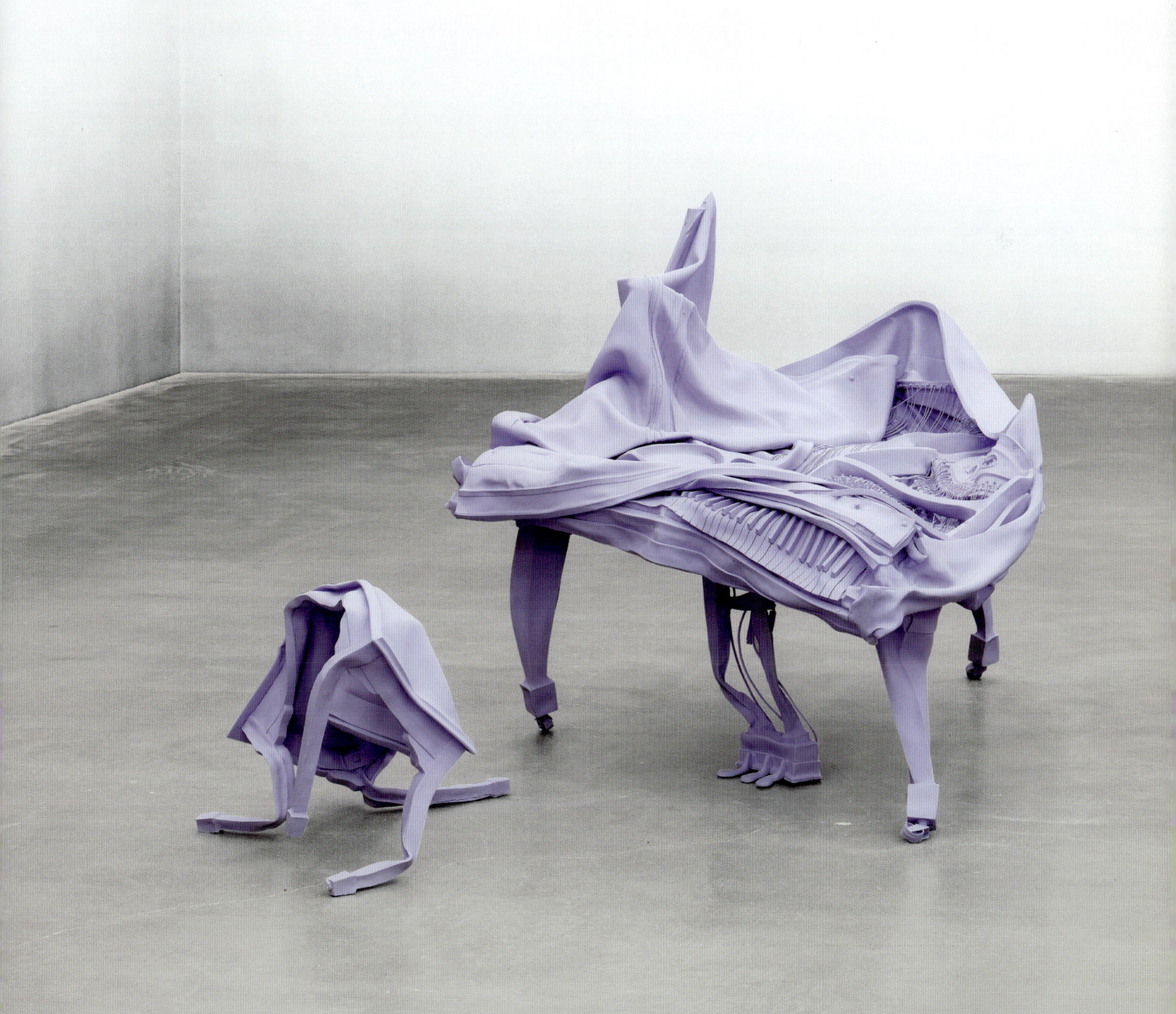

Frozen Pioneer, 2009
Cast aluminum, epoxy primer, polyester filler,
one-component acrylic putty, urethane primer,
polyester paint, acrylic polyurethane matte clearcoat
Approximately 120 x 49 x 39 ½ inches (305 x 125 x 100 cm)

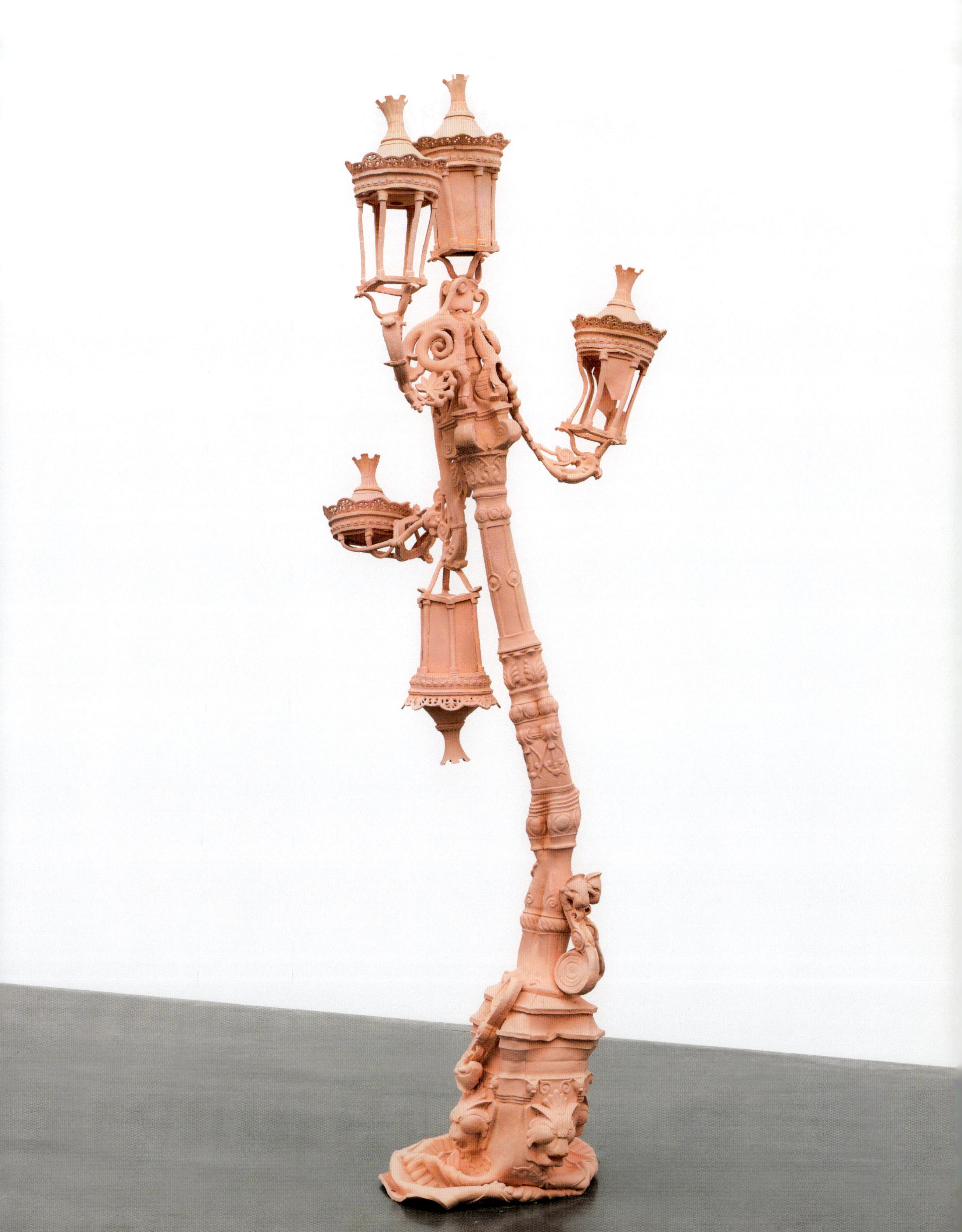

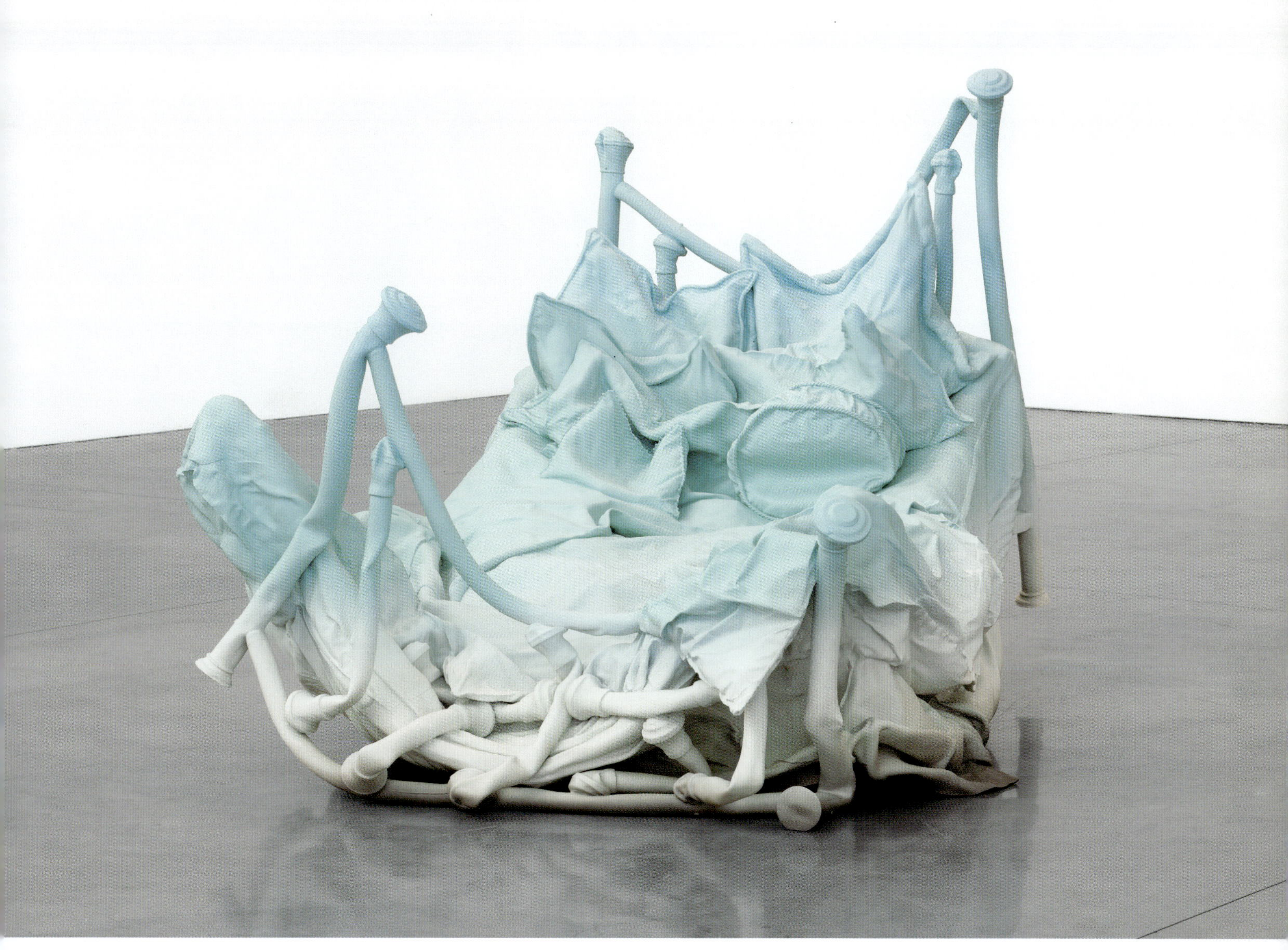

Untitled, 2011
Cast aluminum, epoxy primer, polyester filler,
one-component acrylic putty, urethane primer,
polyester paint, acrylic polyurethane matte clearcoat
64 x 74 ¾ x 101 inches (162.6 x 189.9 x 256.5 cm)

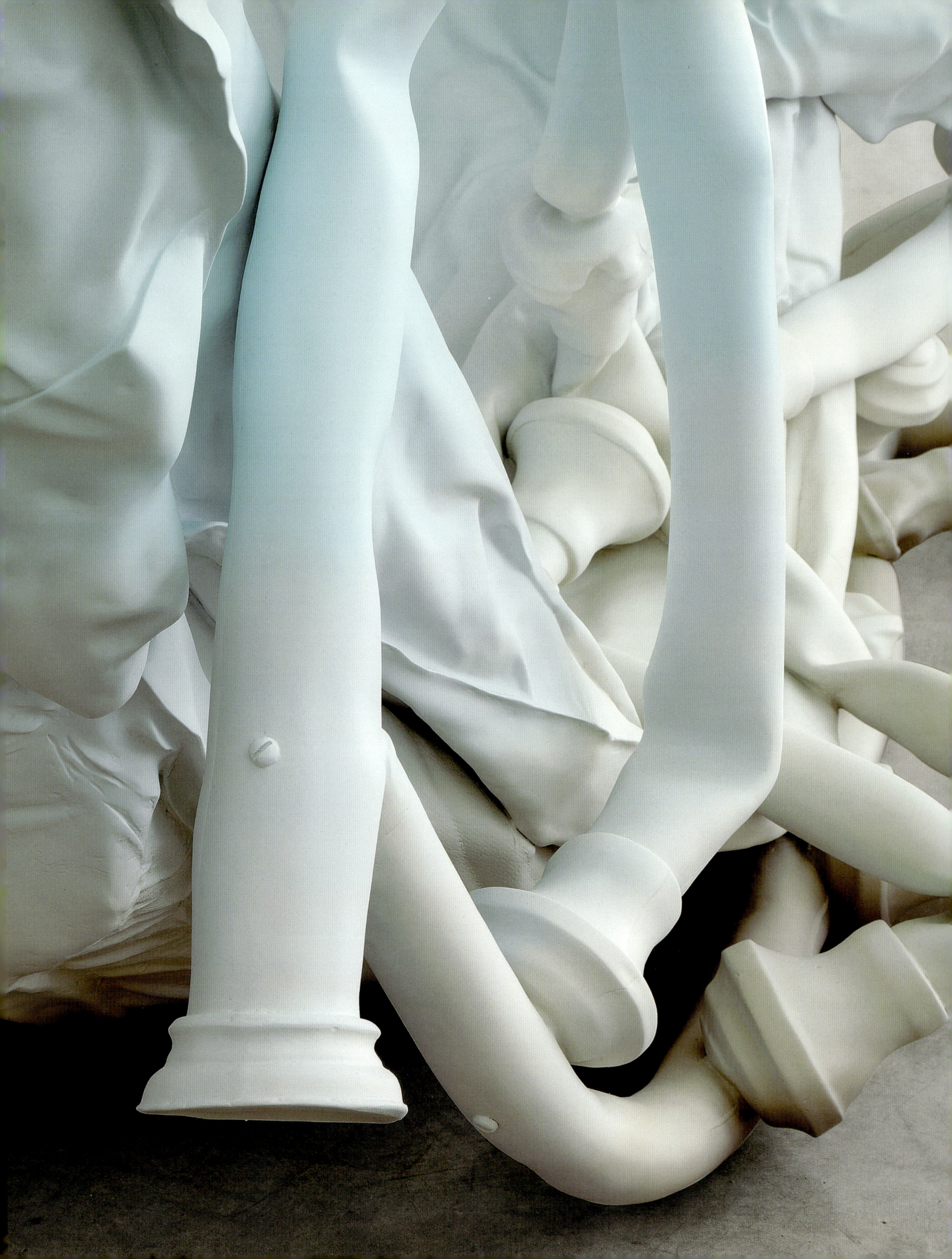

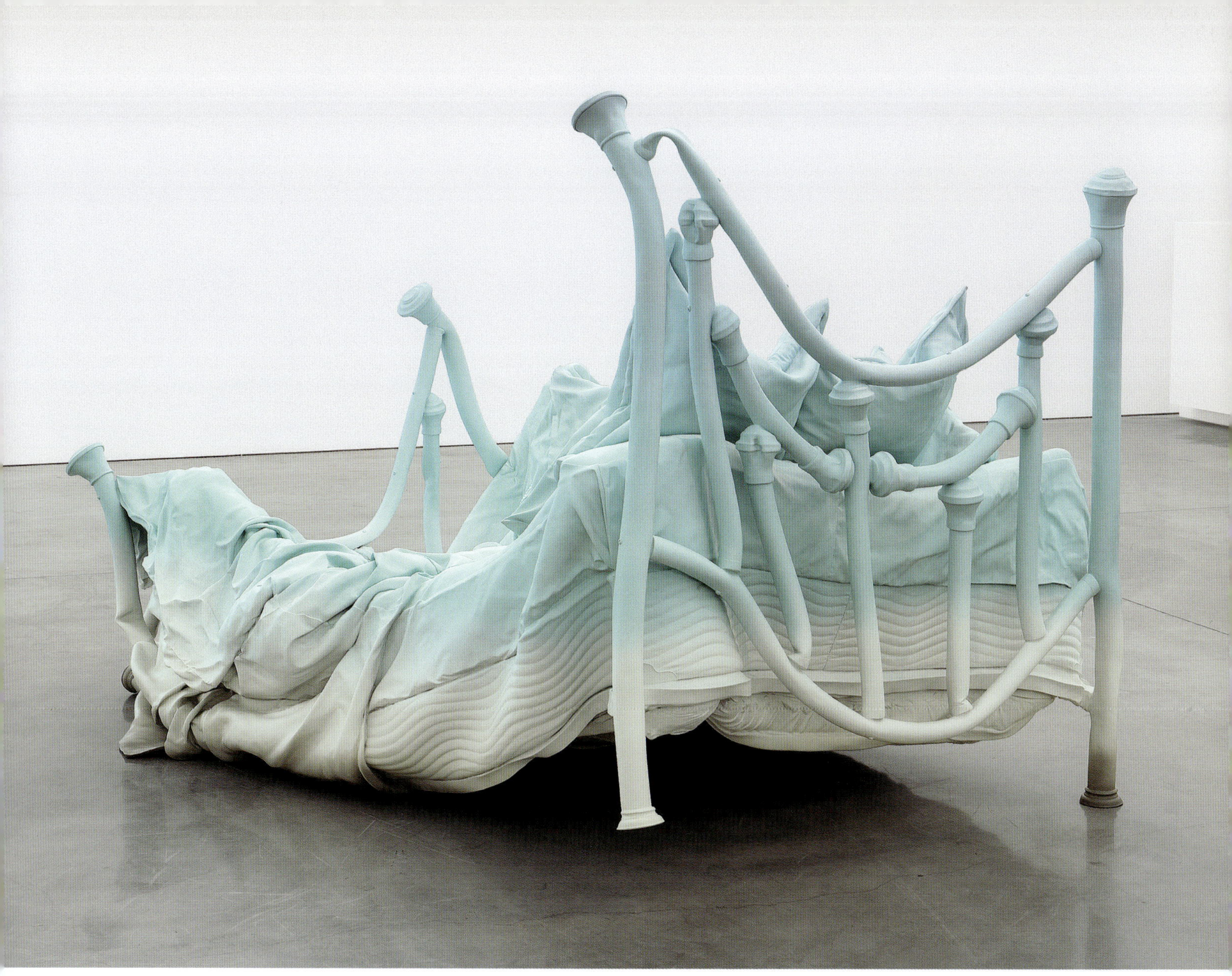

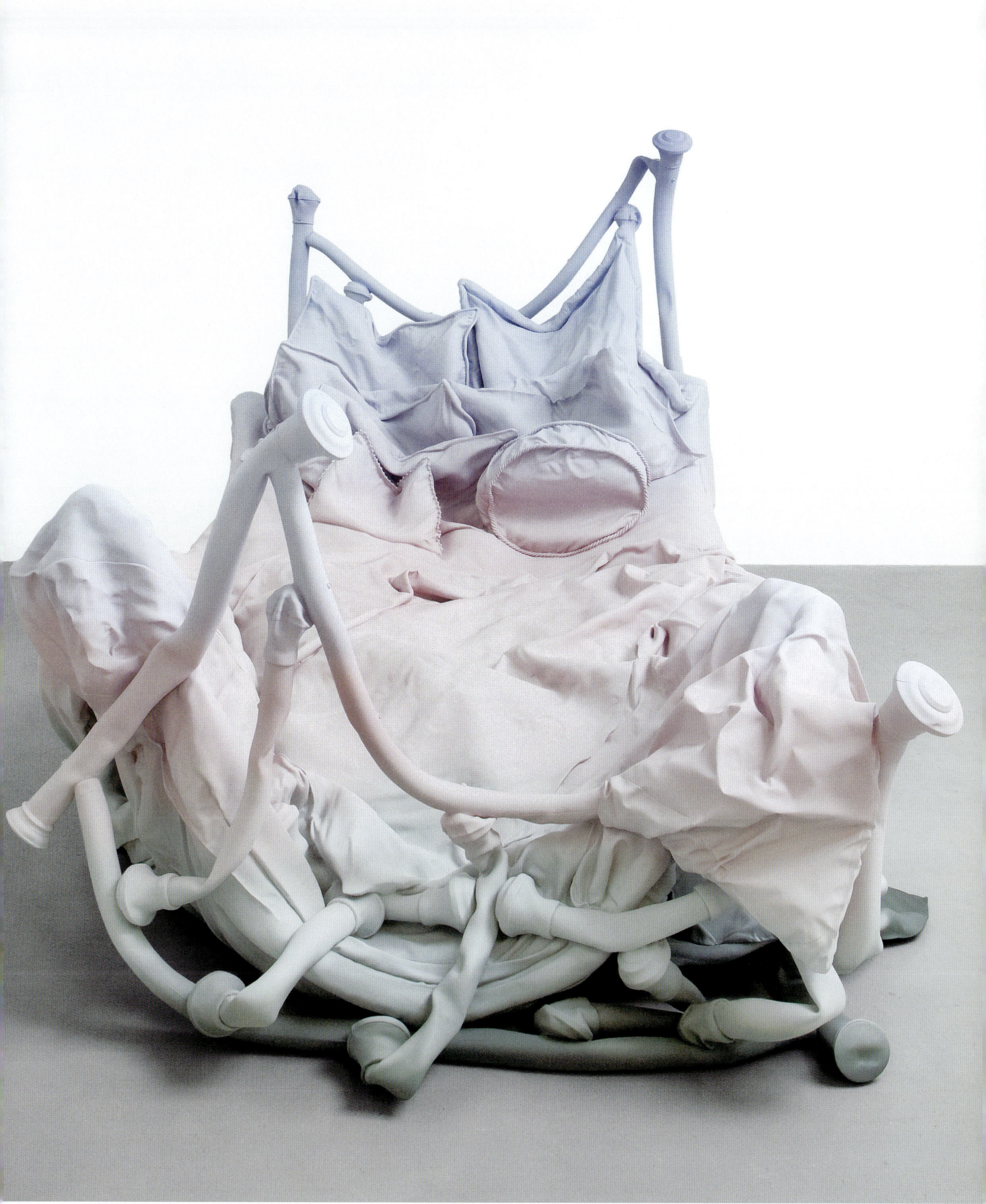

Tisch mit, 1995–2001
Wood, lacquer, acrylic paint, string, mattress, fabric, two-component epoxy
41 ¾ x 48 ⅜ x 38 ⅝ inches (106 x 123 x 98 cm)

Following pages:
Untitled (Pink Chair), 1996
Found chair, gauze, acrylic paint, glue, staples, lacquer
40 ½ x 16 ⅛ x 19 ¾ inches (103 x 41 x 50 cm)

Stuhl mit, 1995–2001
Wood, foam, latex paint, acrylic paint, fabric, screws
39 ⅜ x 25 ⅝ x 39 ⅜ inches (100 x 65 x 100 cm)

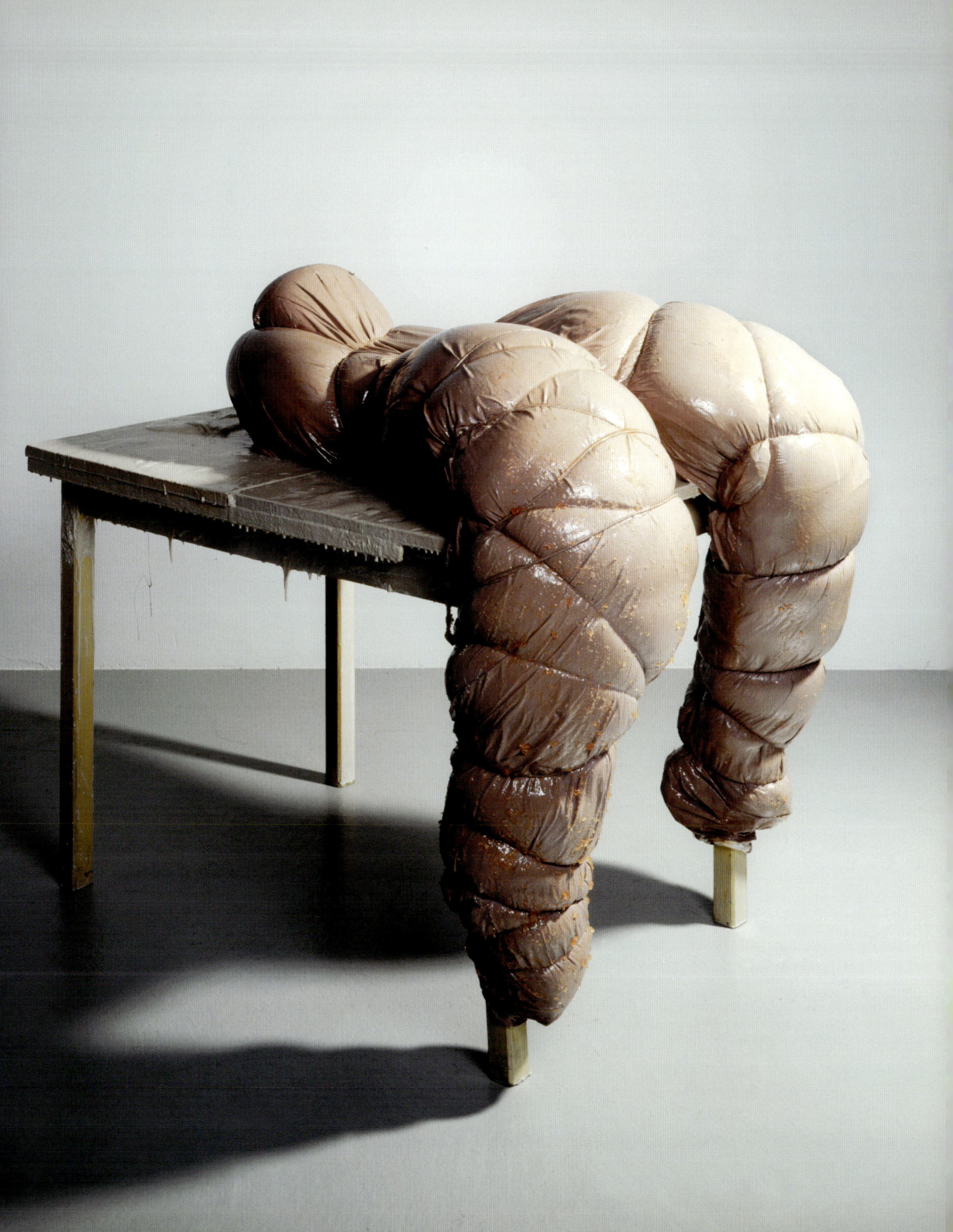

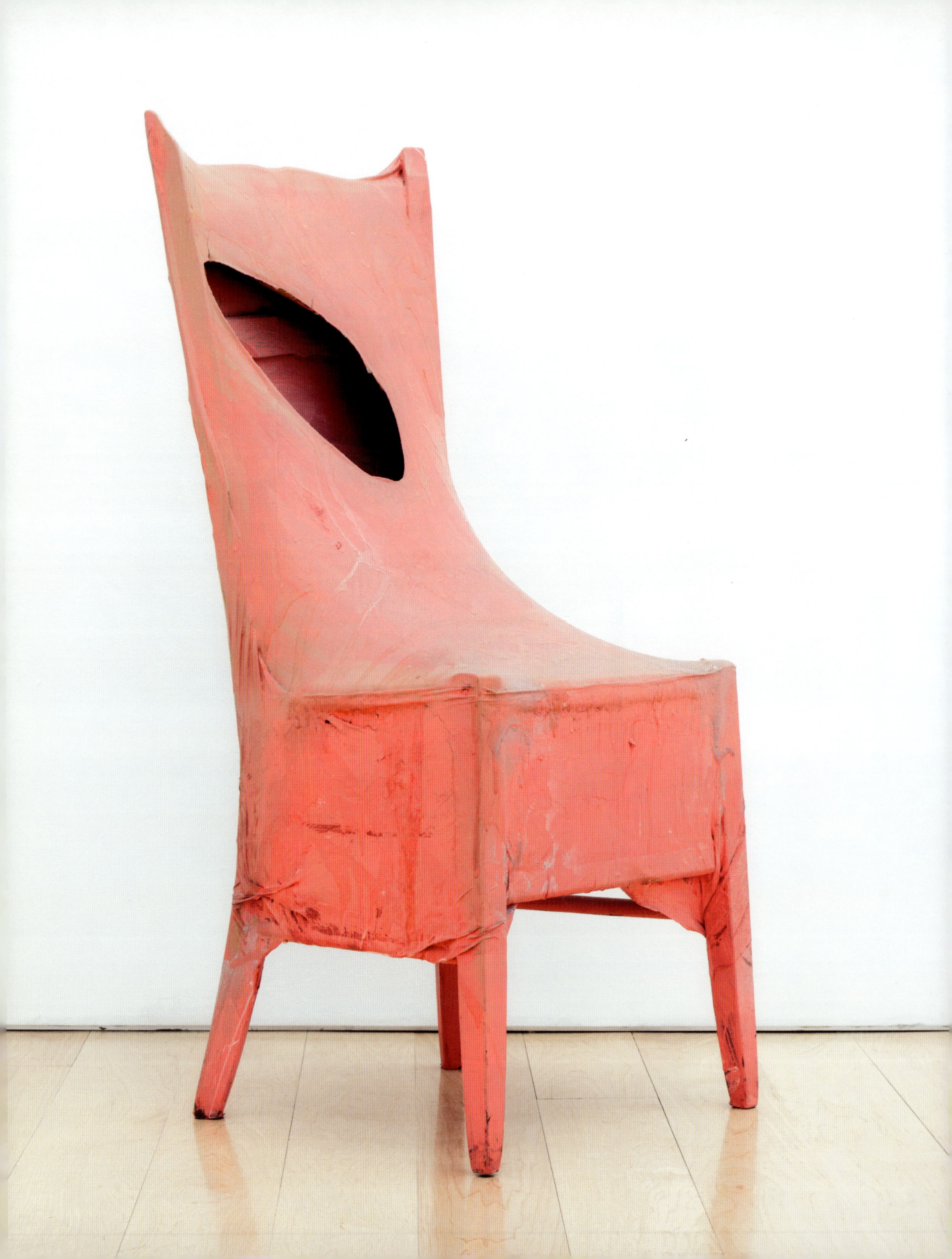

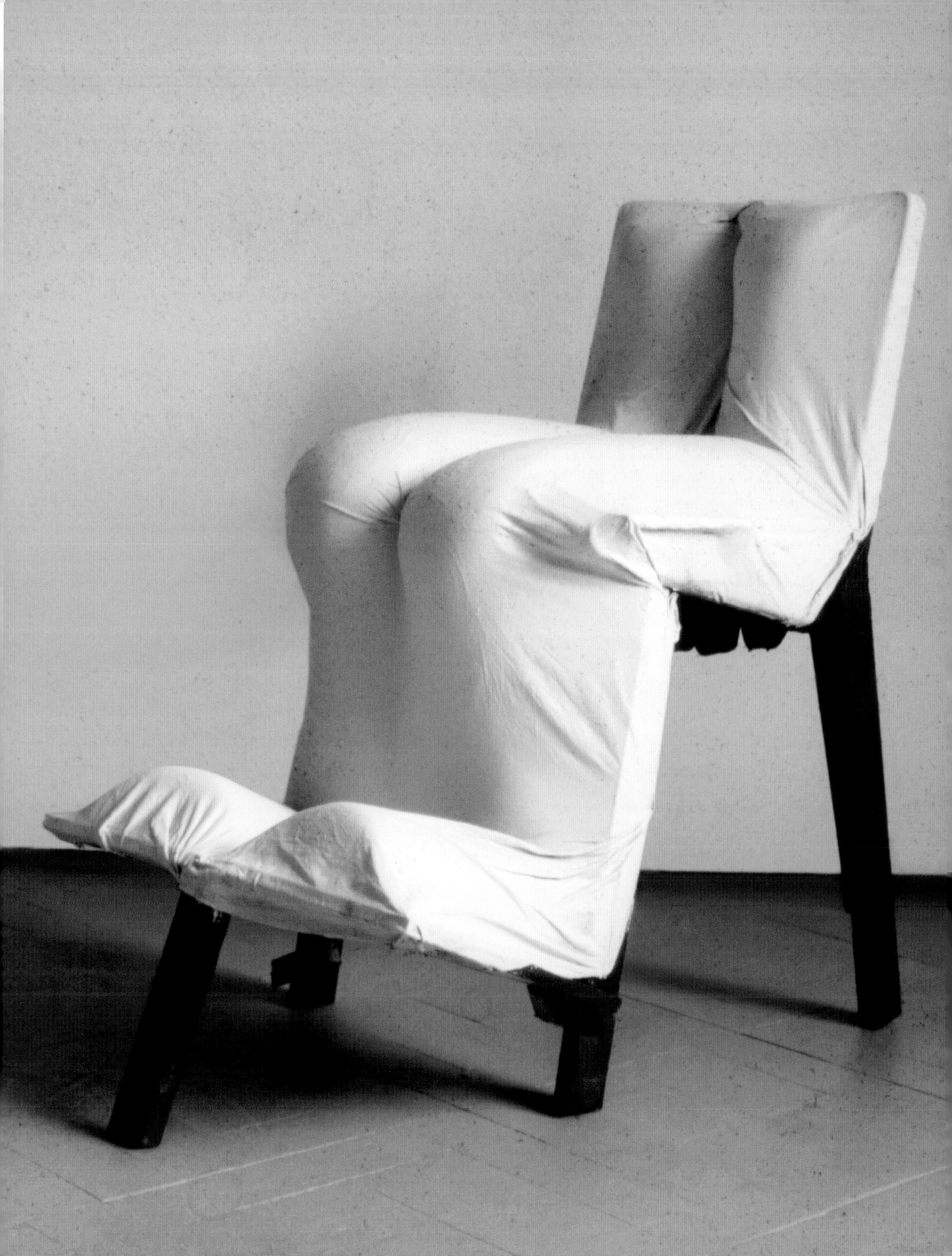

Last Chair Standing, 1997

Wood, clay, silicone, latex paint, string, wire, caulk, wood glue

25 ⅜ x 31 ⅛ x 25 ⅜ inches (64.5 x 79 x 64.5 cm)

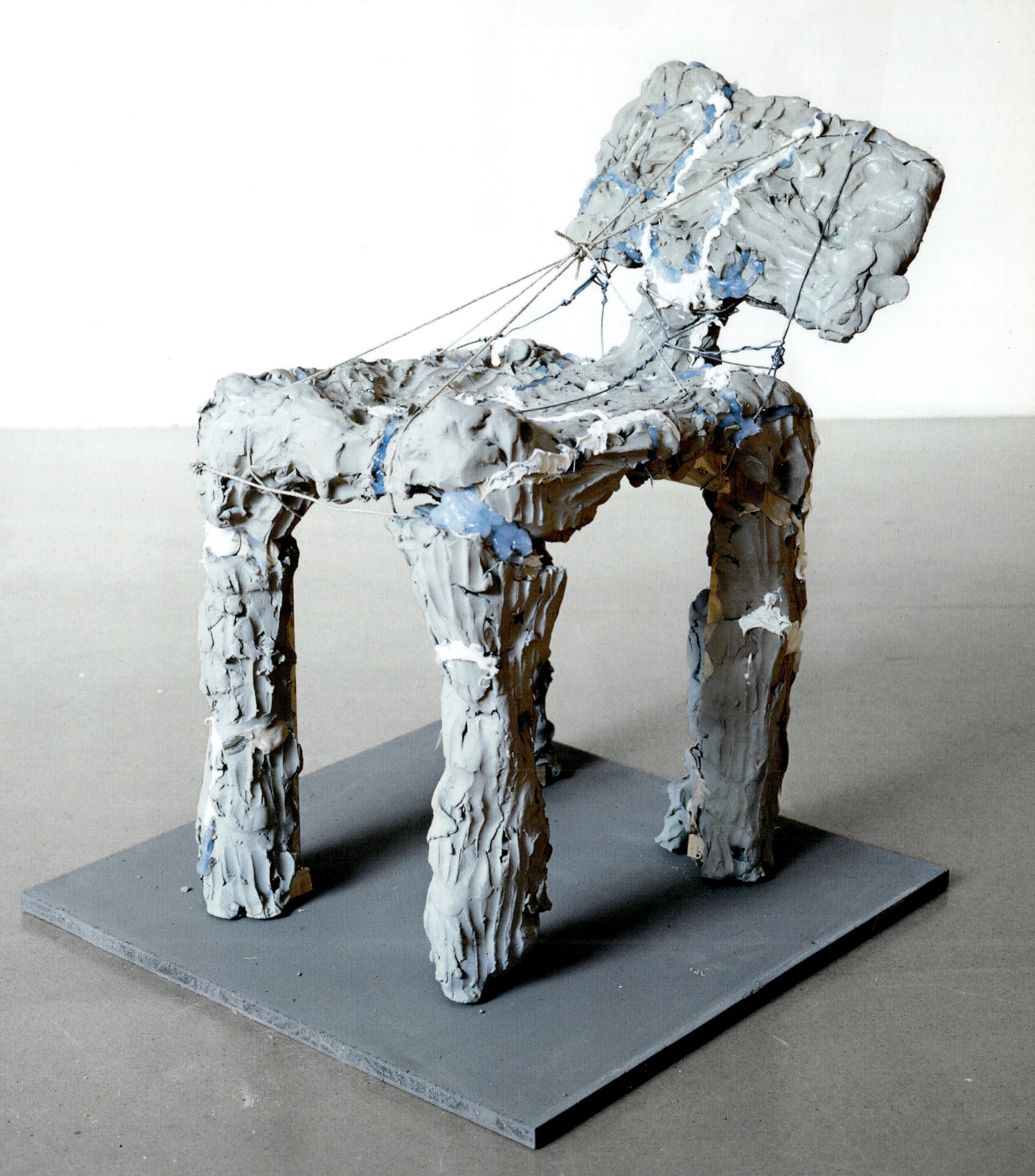

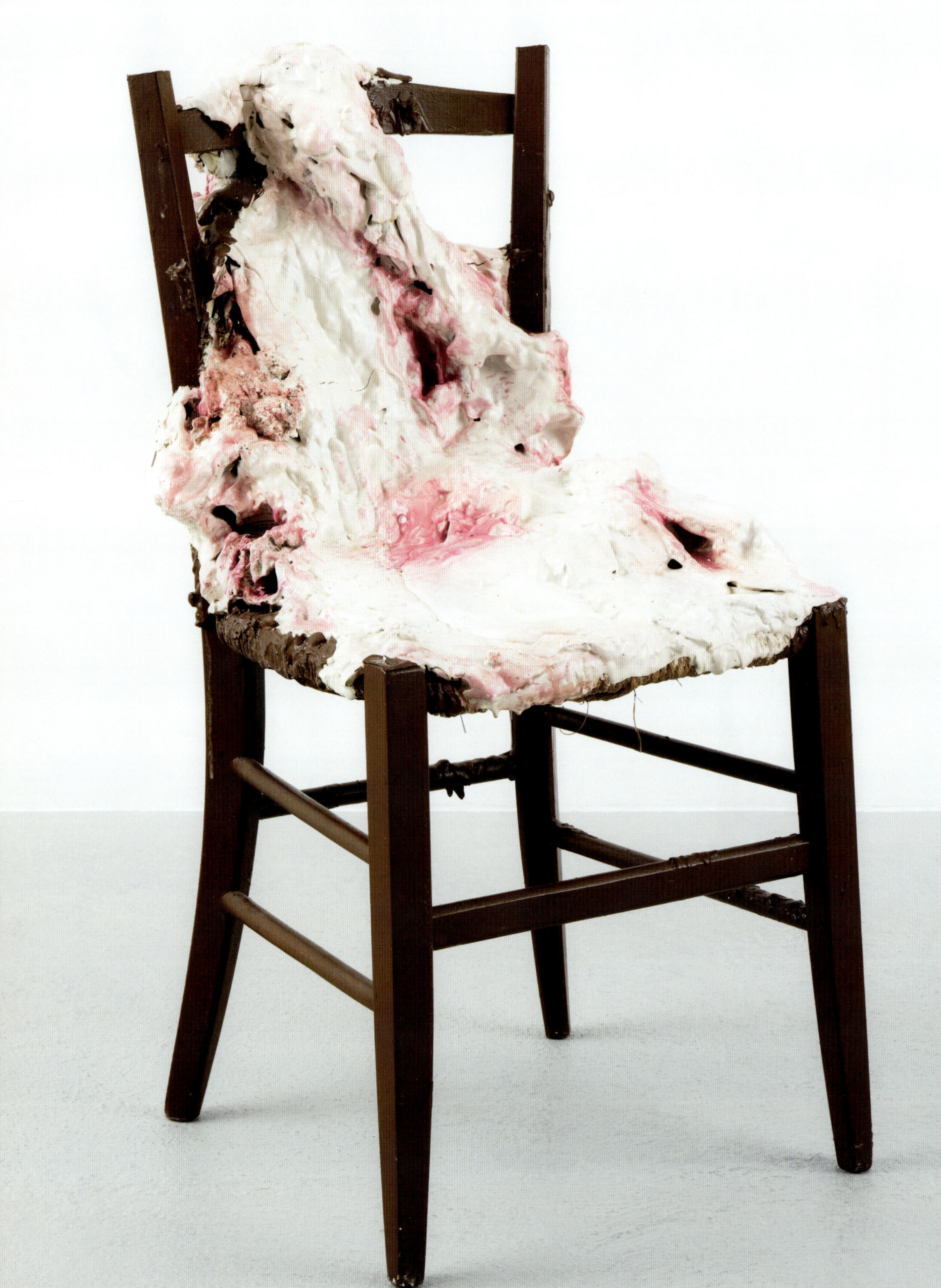

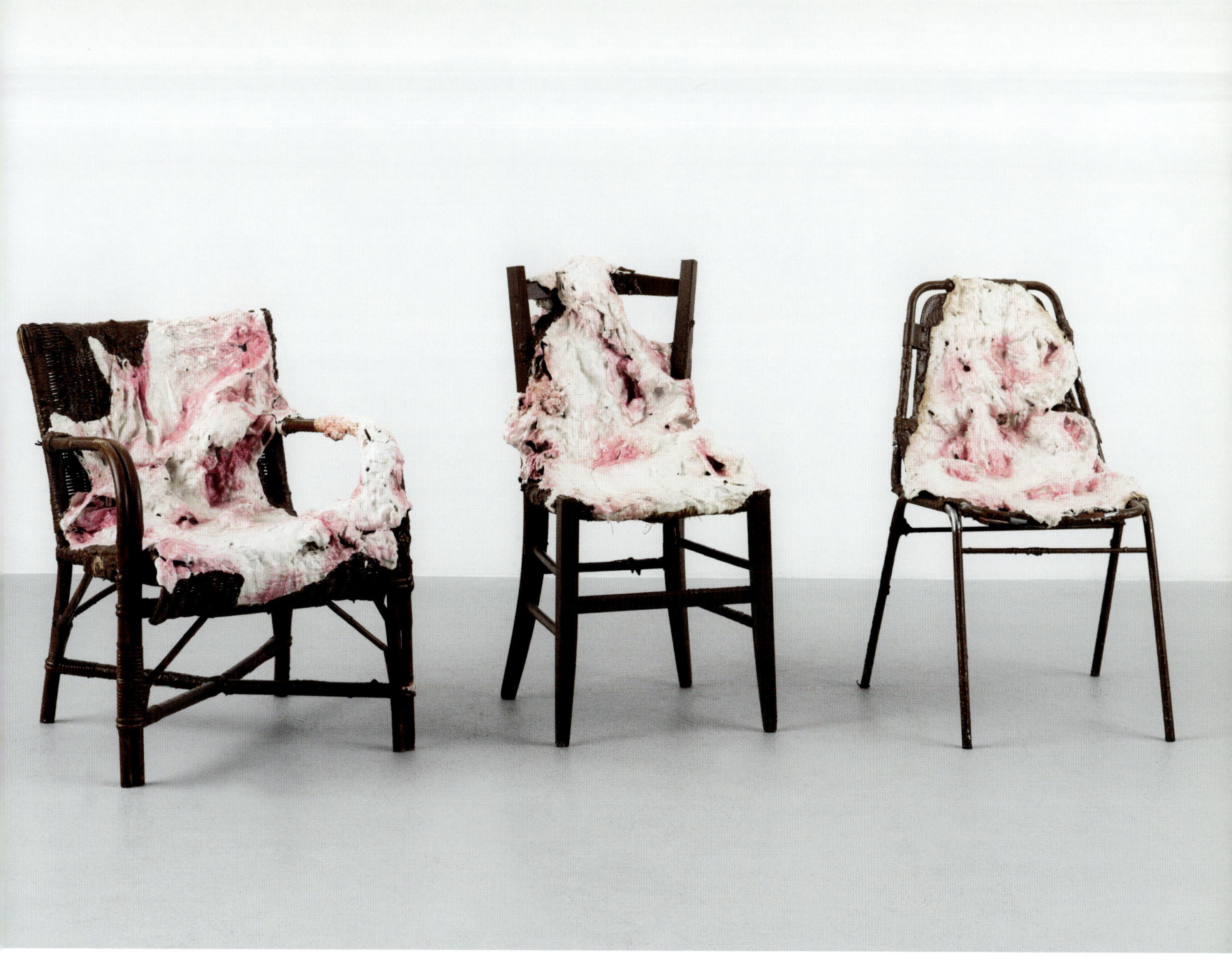

Late Night Show, 1997
Found chairs, newspaper, plaster, latex paint, pigments, glue
Chair 1: 31 ⅞ x 21 ⅝ x 25 ⅝ inches (91 x 55 x 65 cm)
Chair 2: 33 ⅞ x 17 ¾ x 19 ¾ inches (86 x 45 x 50 cm)
Chair 3: 30 ¼ x 21 ⅝ 25 ⅝ inches (77 x 55 x 65 cm)

Beyond a Step Backwards, 1997–2001

Sawdust, polyester resin, plywood, pigments, polyurethane foam, latex paint, acrylic paint, oil paint, marker, screws

59 x 25 ⅝ x 19 ⅝ inches (150 x 65 x 50 cm)

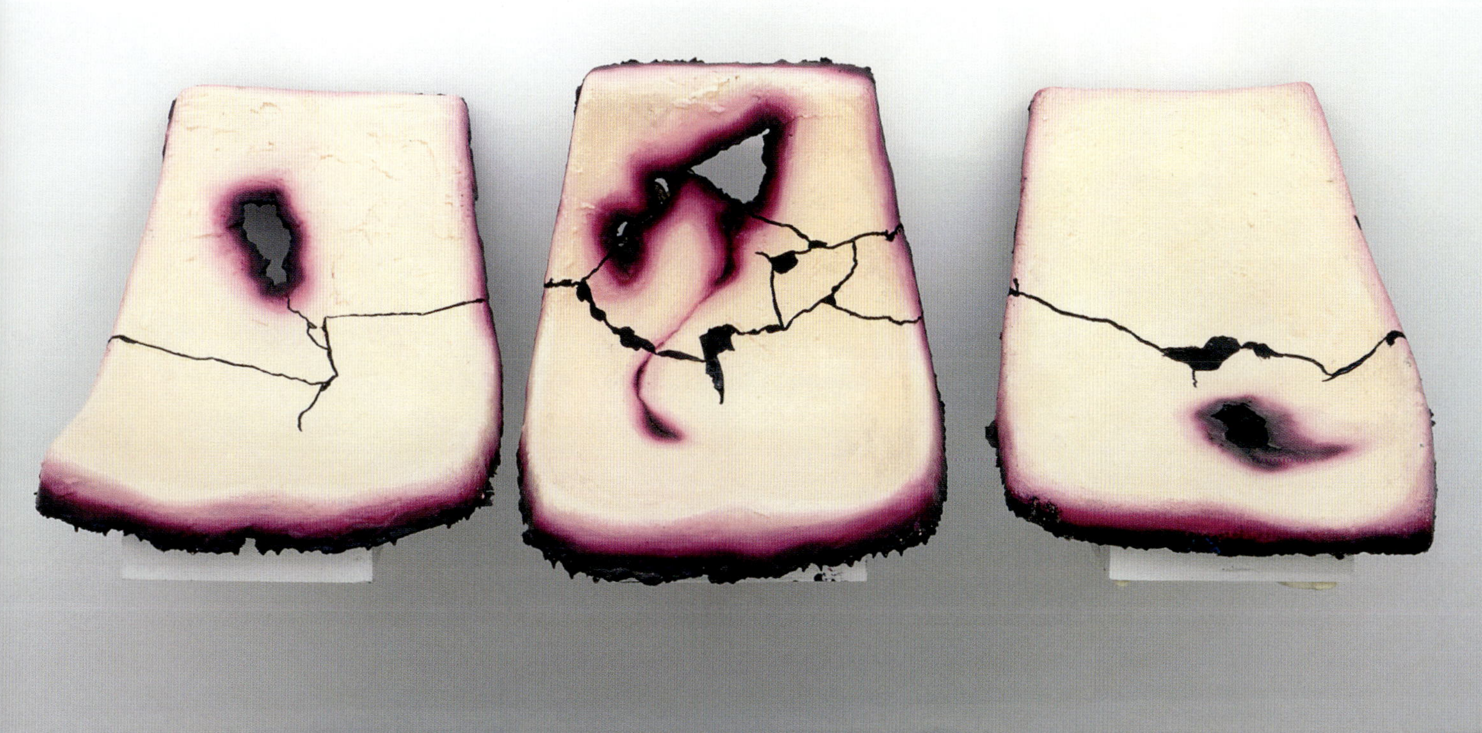

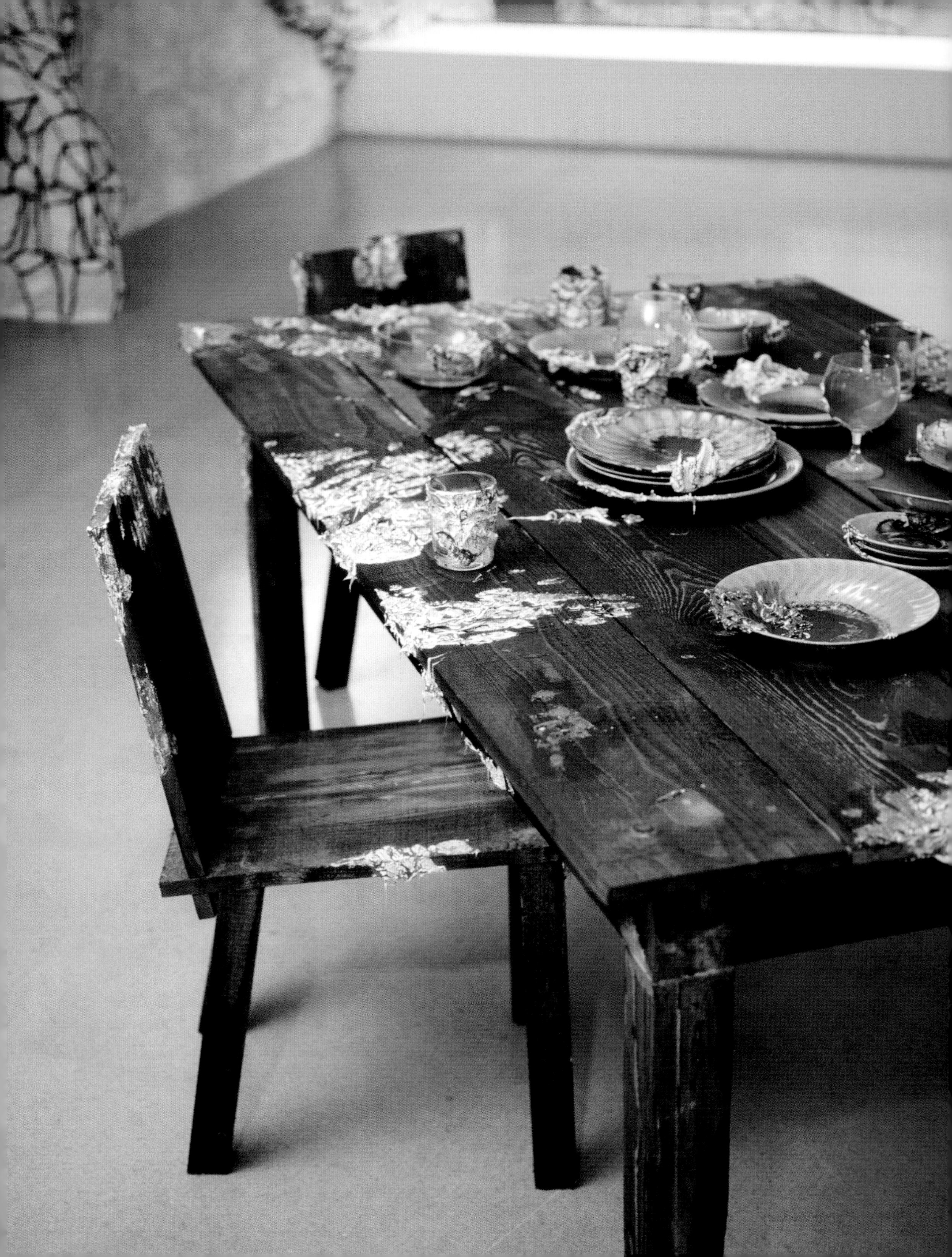

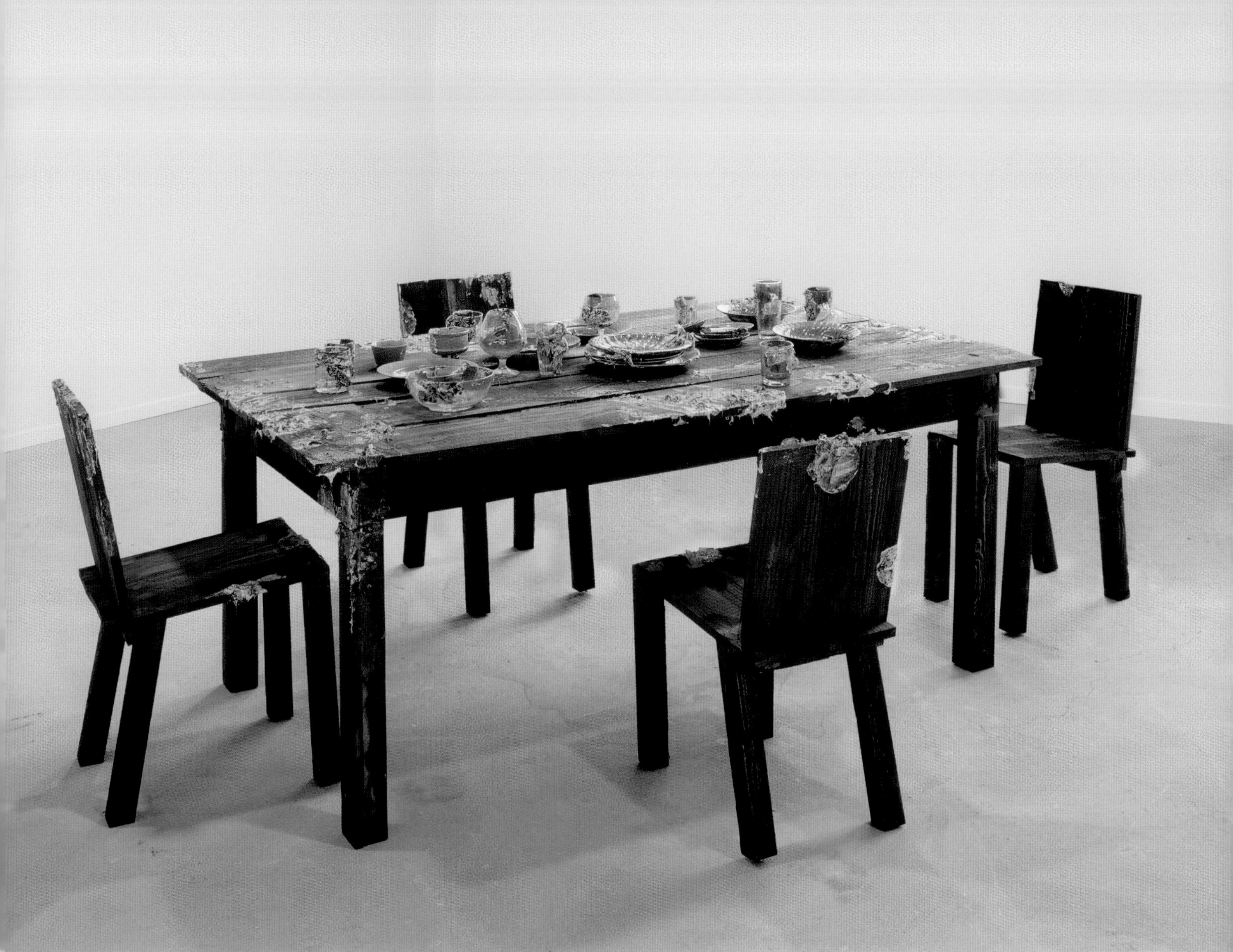

Untitled, 1997

Wood, wood glue, stain, dishes, glasses, epoxy adhesive, silicone, acrylic paint
Table: 41 ⅜ x 72 ½ x 30 ¾ inches (105 x 184 x 78 cm)
4 chairs, each: 31 ½ x 13 ⅜ x 15 ¾ inches (80 x 34 x 40 cm)
Opposite page: Installation view, "Hammer," Galerie Walcheturm, Zurich, 1997

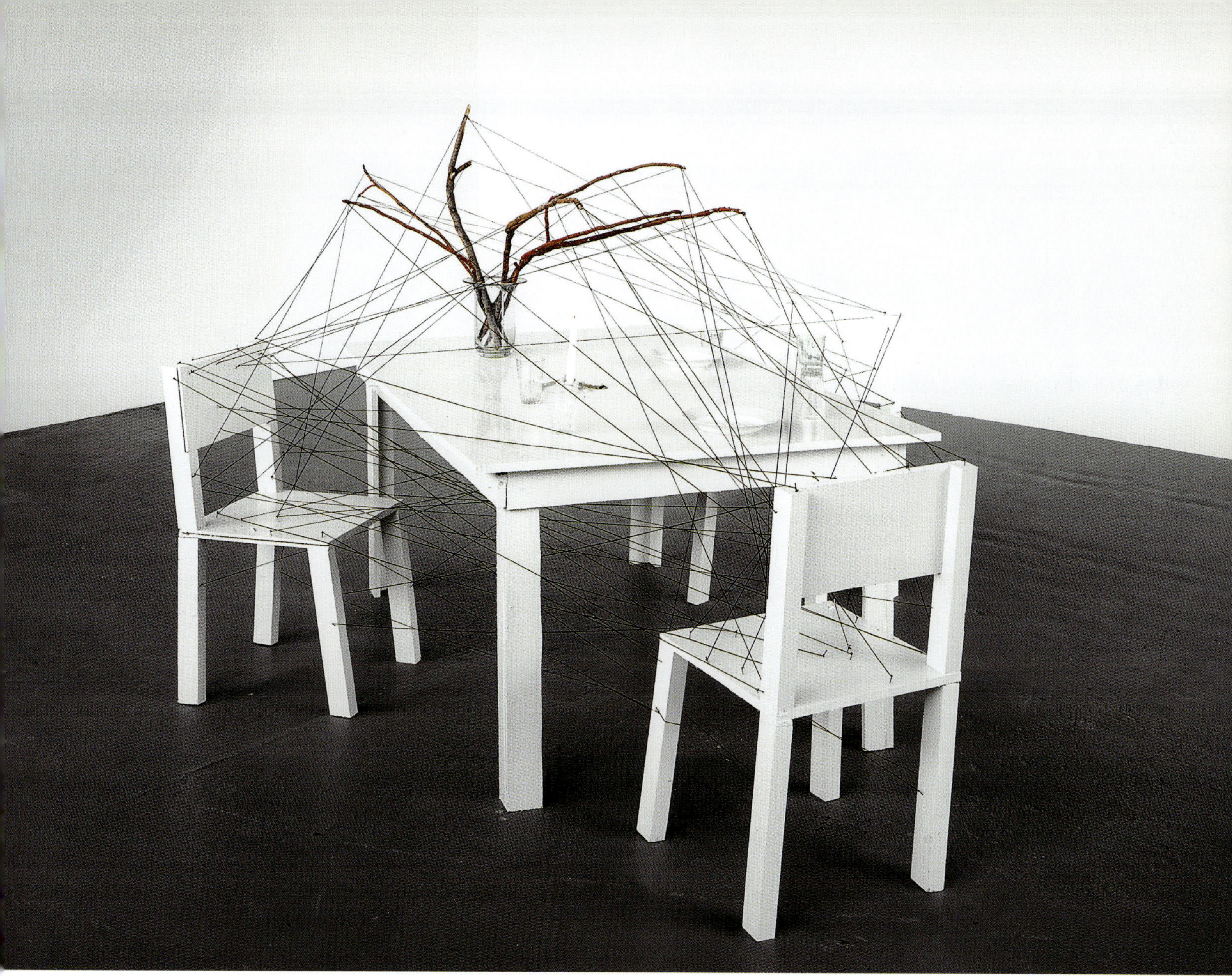

Frozen, 1998
Wood, particleboard, latex paint, enamel paint, candle, vase, dishes, branches, wool yarn, wood glue, nails, silicone
86 ⅝ x 90 ½ x 63 inches (220 x 230 x 160 cm)

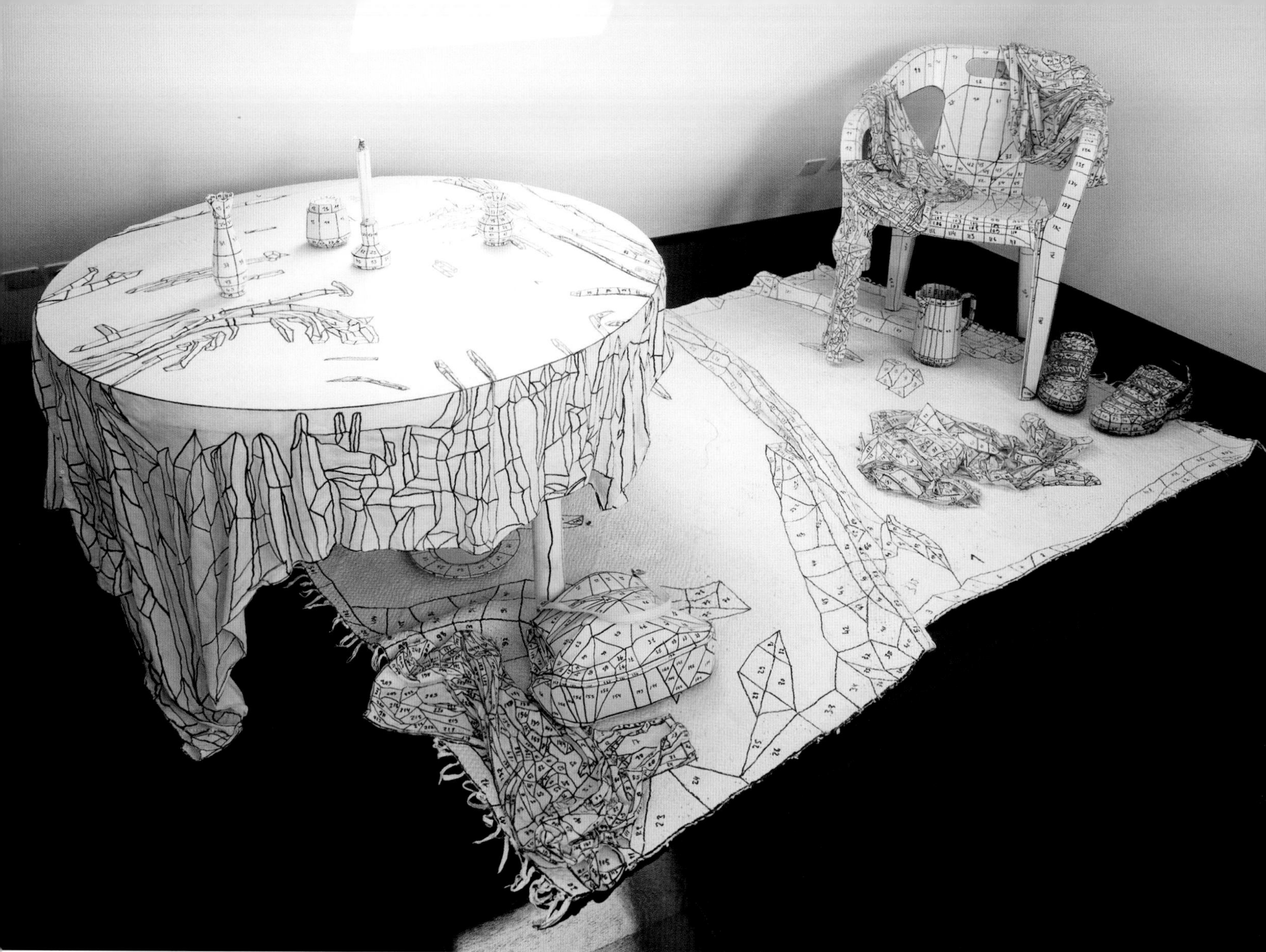

Untitled, 1997
Found furnishings, found clothes, latex paint, acrylic binder, marker, wood glue, silicone
Dimensions variable

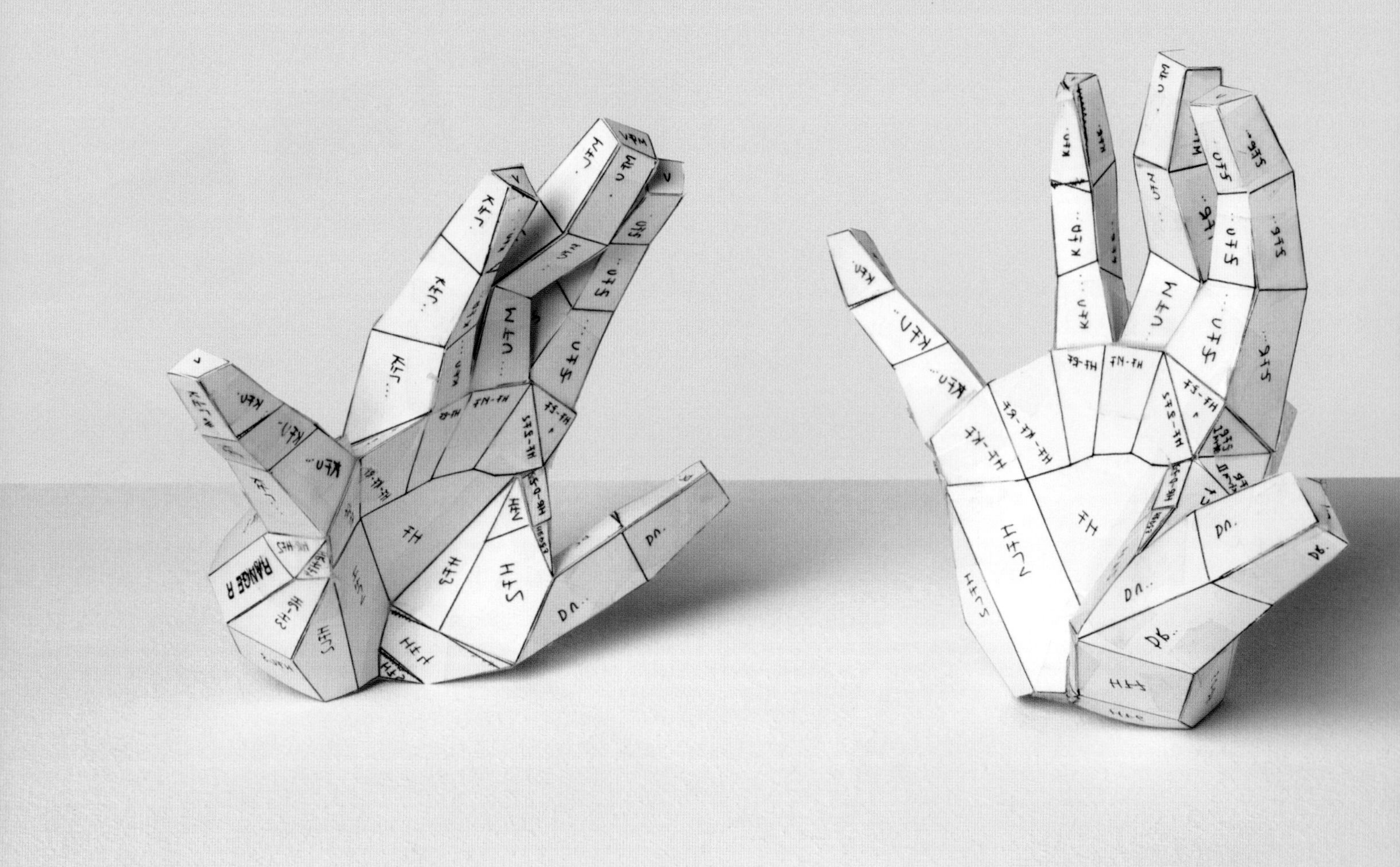

Range L / Range R, 1996
Photocopy on card paper, tape, stamp
8 ⅝ x 7 ⅛ x 3 inches (22 x 18 x 7.5 cm)

Opposite page:
The Art of Falling Apart, 1998
Wood, latex paint, acrylic paint, marker, found clothes, found glasses, found suitcase, found hat
Chair: 70 ⅞ x 78 ¾ x 59 ½ inches (180 x 200 x 151 cm)
Suitcase: 47 ¼ x 78 ¾ x 31 ½ inches (120 x 200 x 80 cm)
Shelf: 55 ⅛ x 59 x 23 ⅝ inches (140 x 150 x 60 cm)

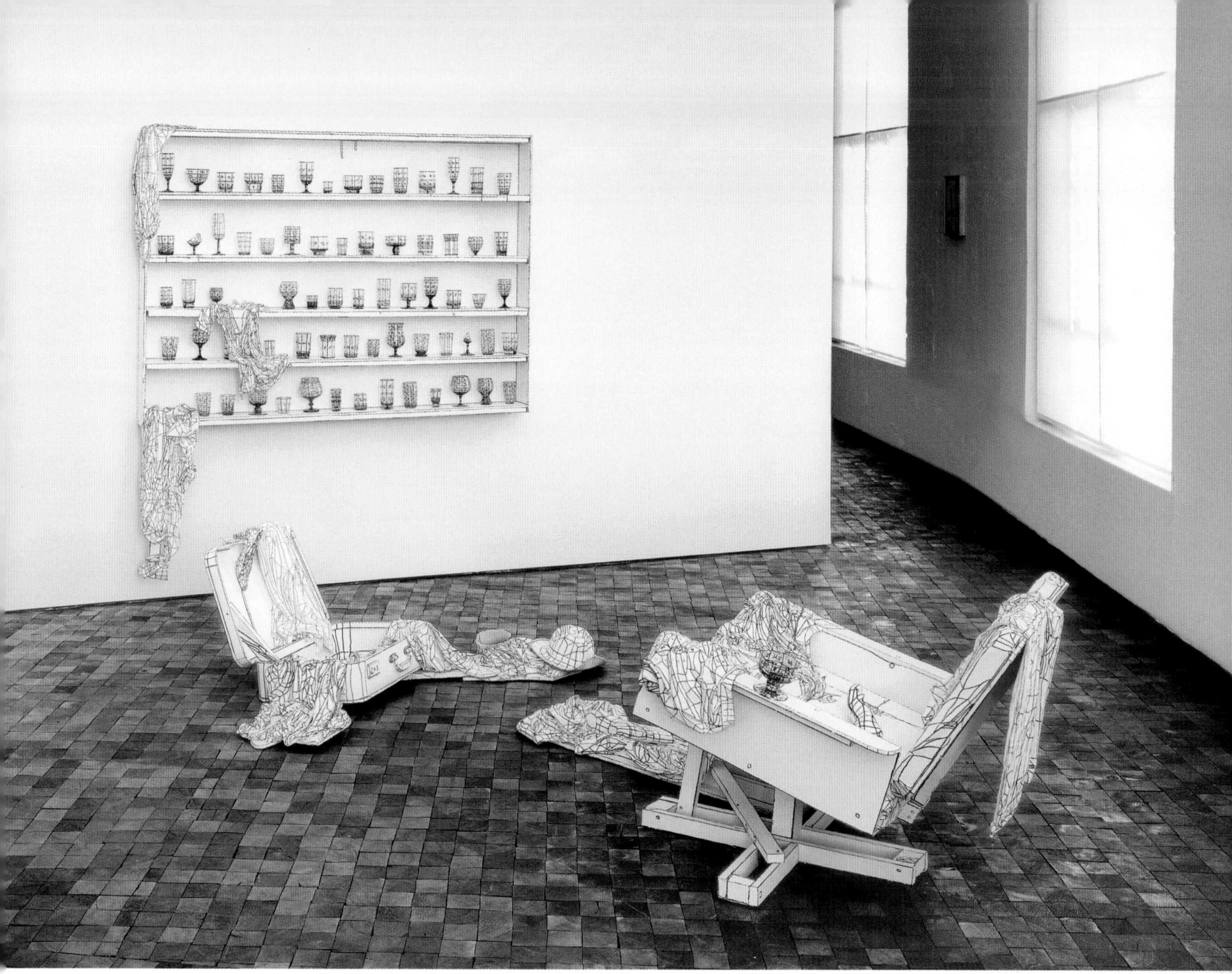

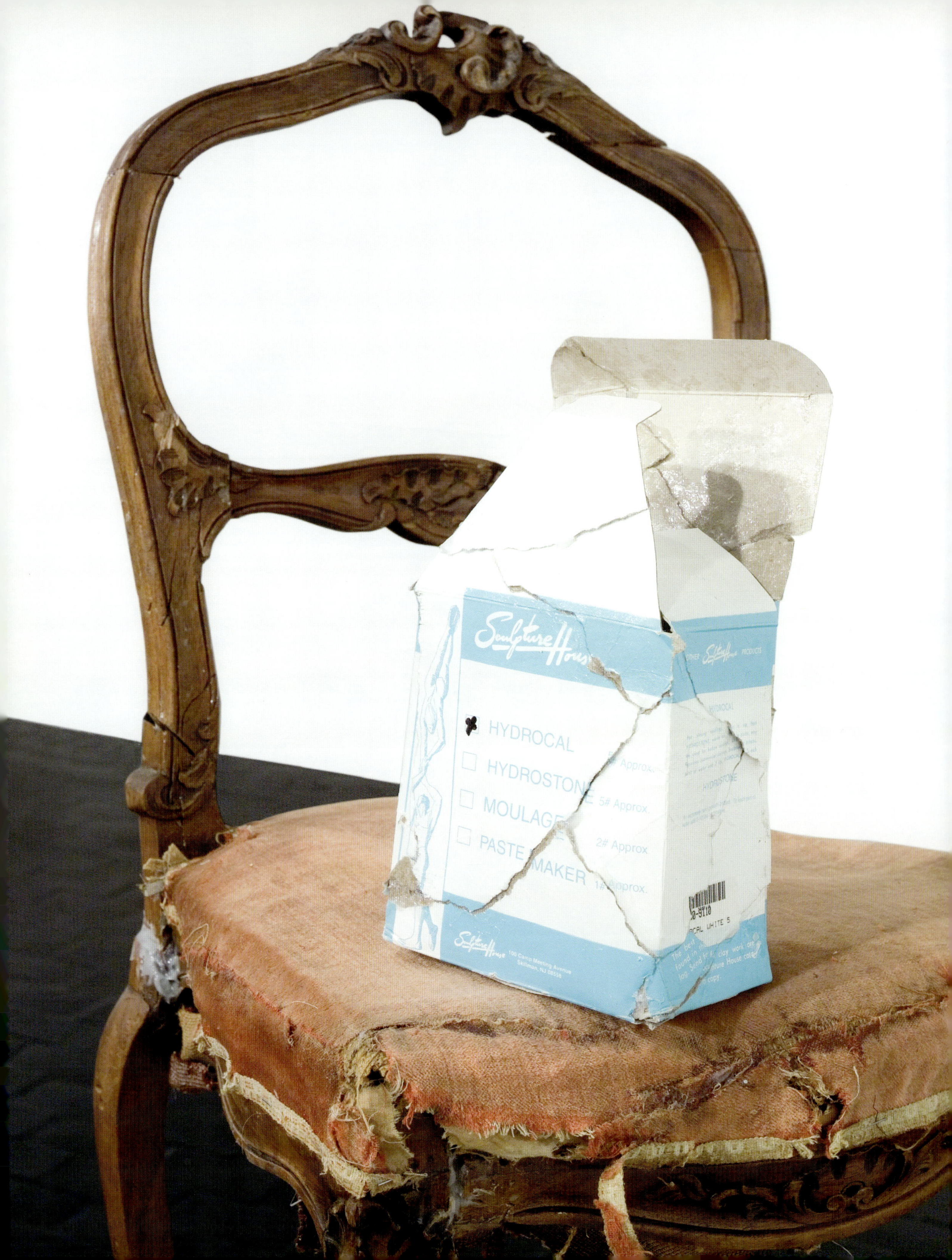
Sculpture House
HYDROCAL
HYDROSTONE 5# Approx.
MOULAGE 2# Approx
PASTE MAKER 1# Approx.
Sculpture House 100 Camp Meeting Avenue
Skillman, NJ 08558
HYDROCAL
HYDROSTONE
CAL WHITE 5

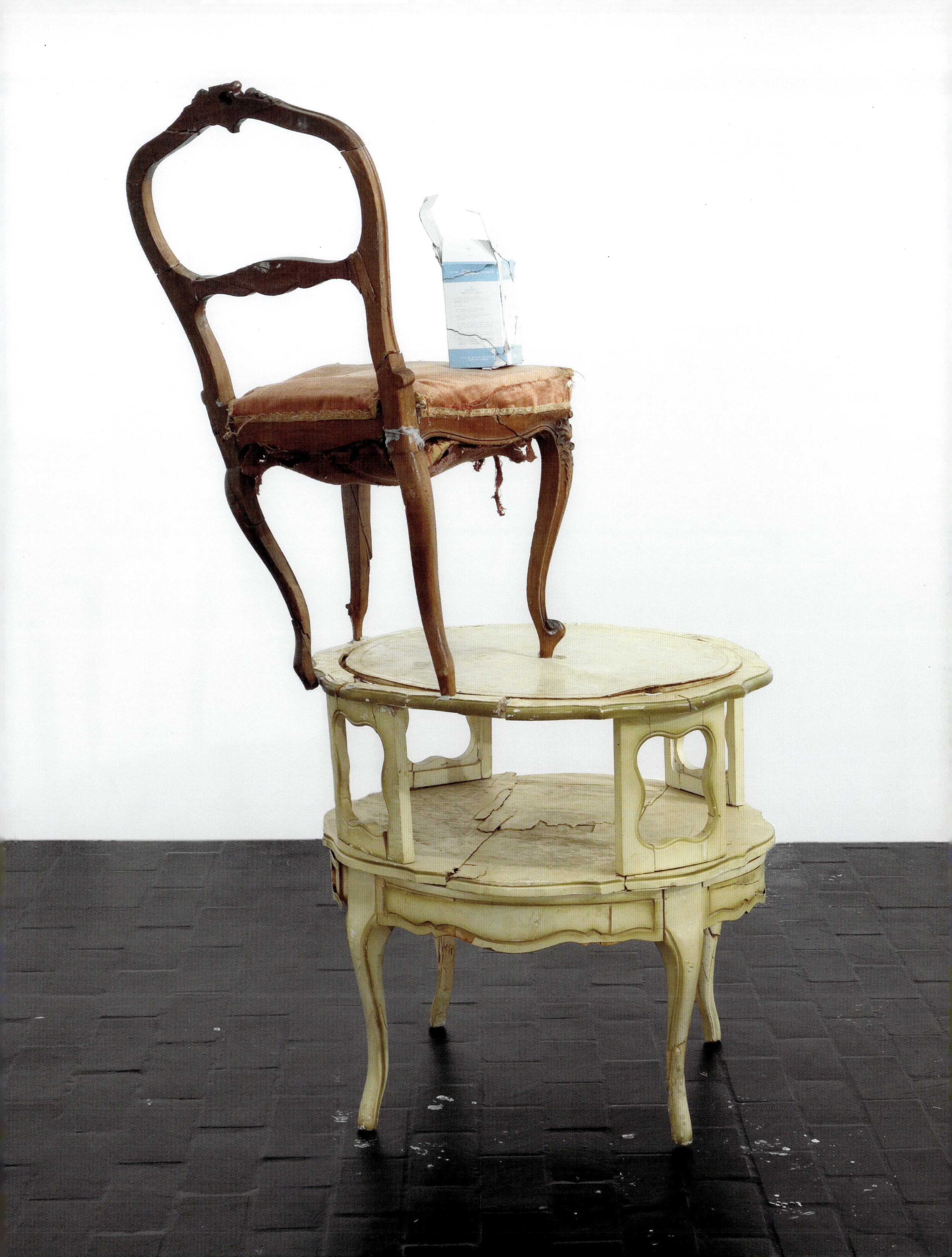

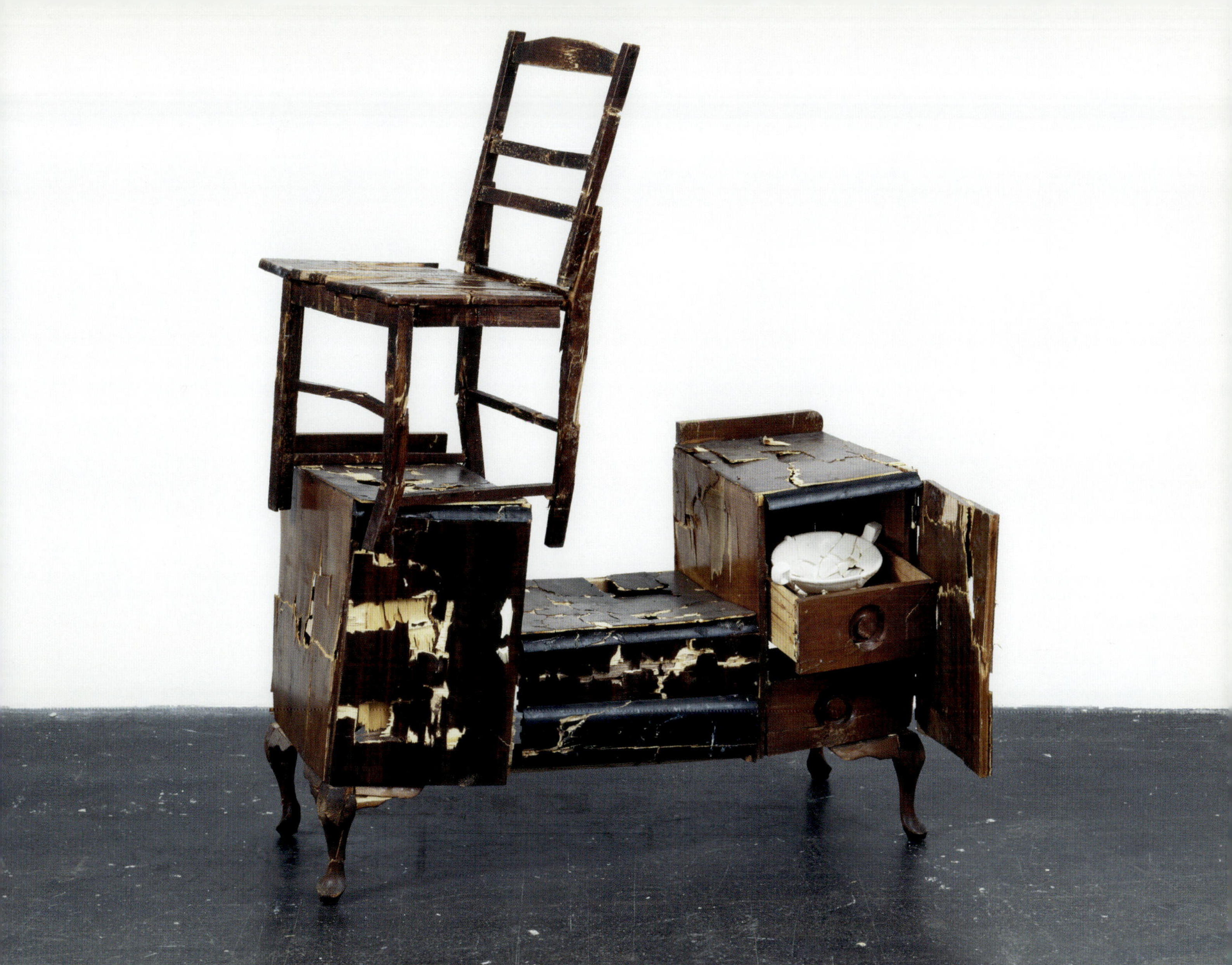

In Dubio Pro Reo, 2007
Found cabinet, found stool, found bowl,
epoxy glue, polyurethane glue
61 x 43 ¼ x 31 ½ inches (115 x 110 x 80 cm)

Previous pages:
Addict, 2006
Found furniture, cardboard box, epoxy glue
61 x 28 ½ x 28 ¾ inches (155 x 72.5 x 73 cm)

Chair, 2002

Chair vibrates at a high frequency, appearing blurry

Wood, oil paint, electric motor, mechanism, glue, silicone, battery

32 ¼ x 16 ½ x 16 ½ inches (82 x 42 x 42 cm)

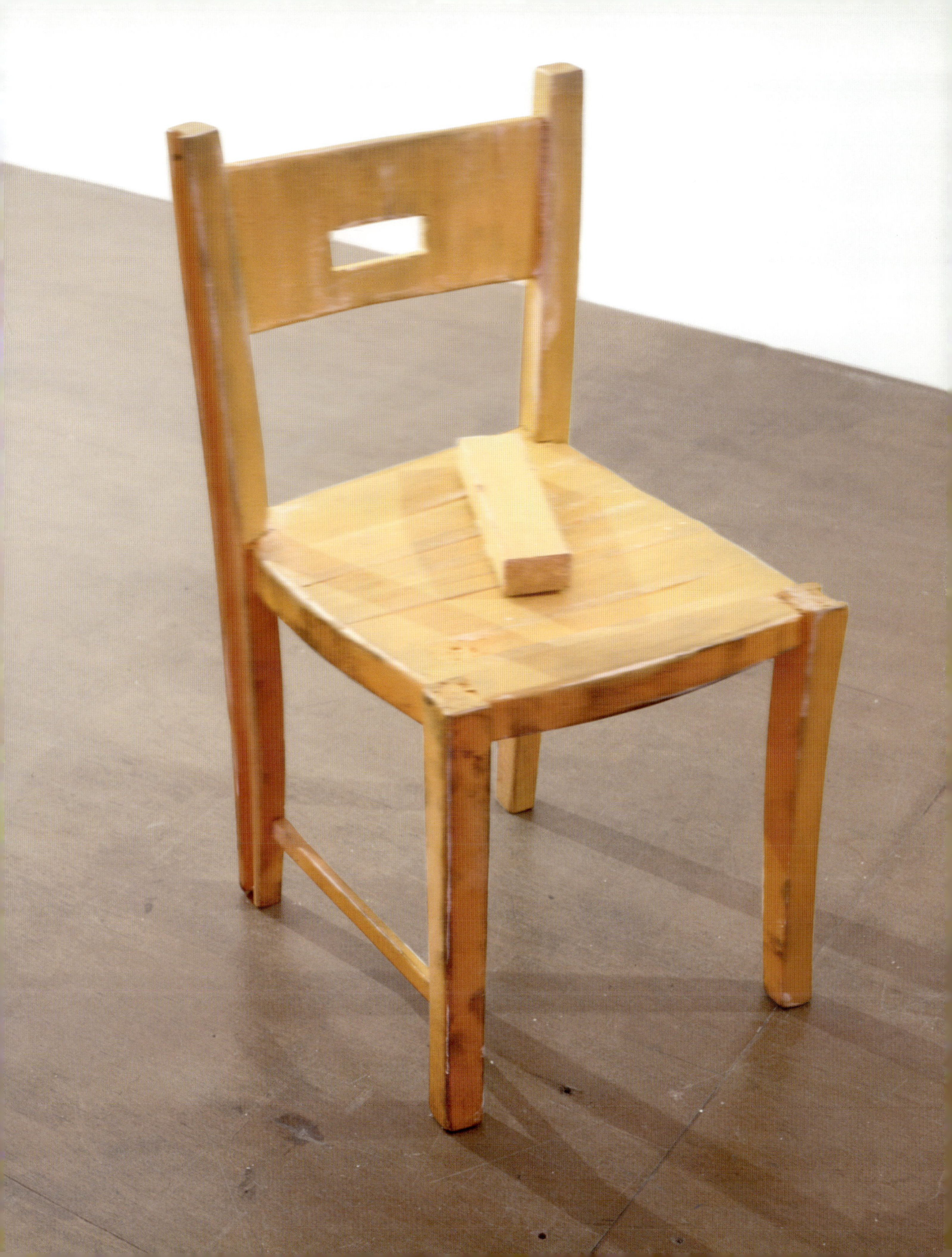

Chagall, 2006

Sculpture vibrates at a high frequency, appearing blurry
Polyurethane foam, nails, spray enamel, acrylic paint,
expanding polyurethane foam, filler, polyurethane glue,
electric motor, aluminum, control unit, battery, cables
88 ⅝ x 24 x 41 inches (225 x 61 x 104 cm)

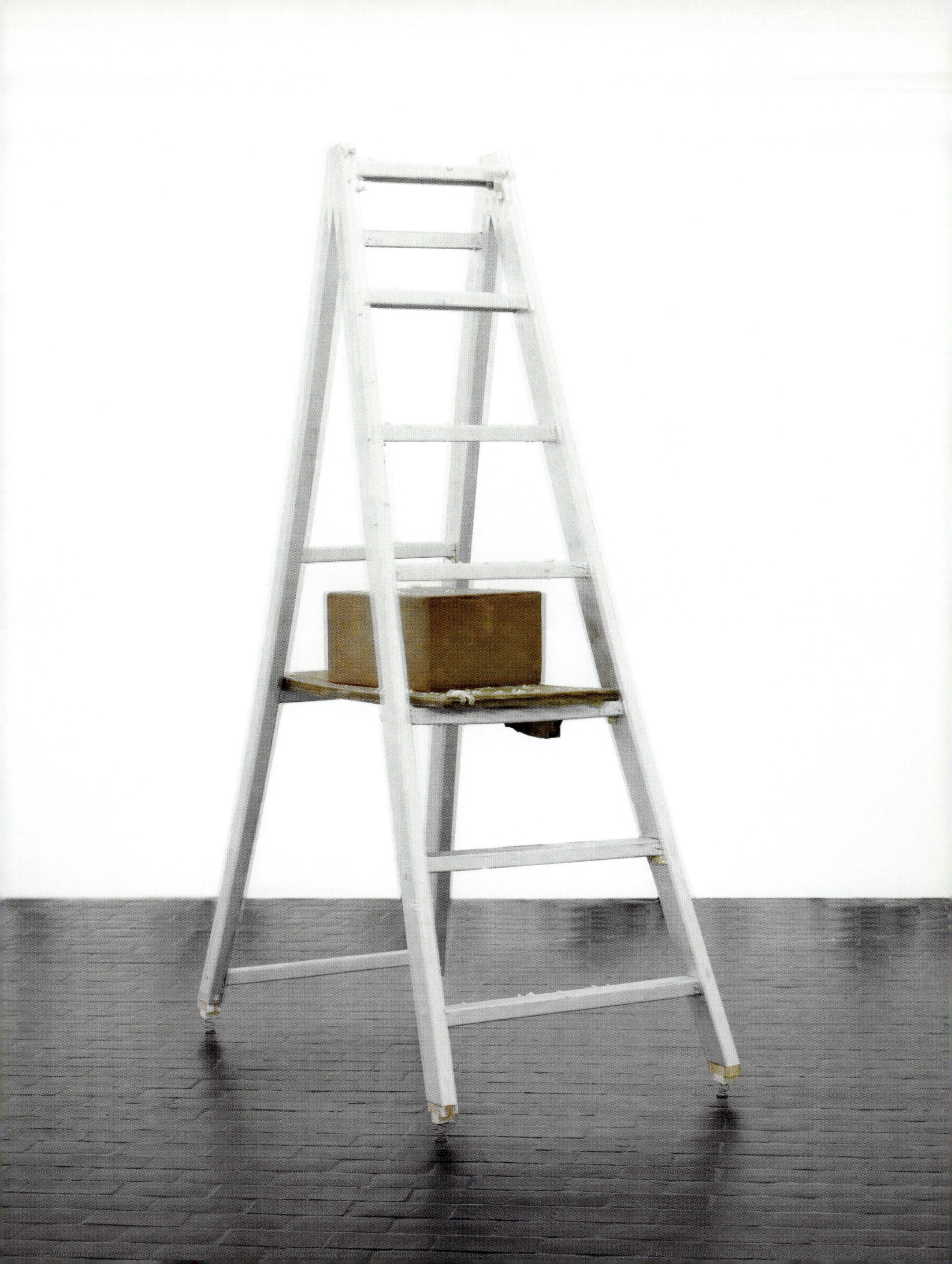

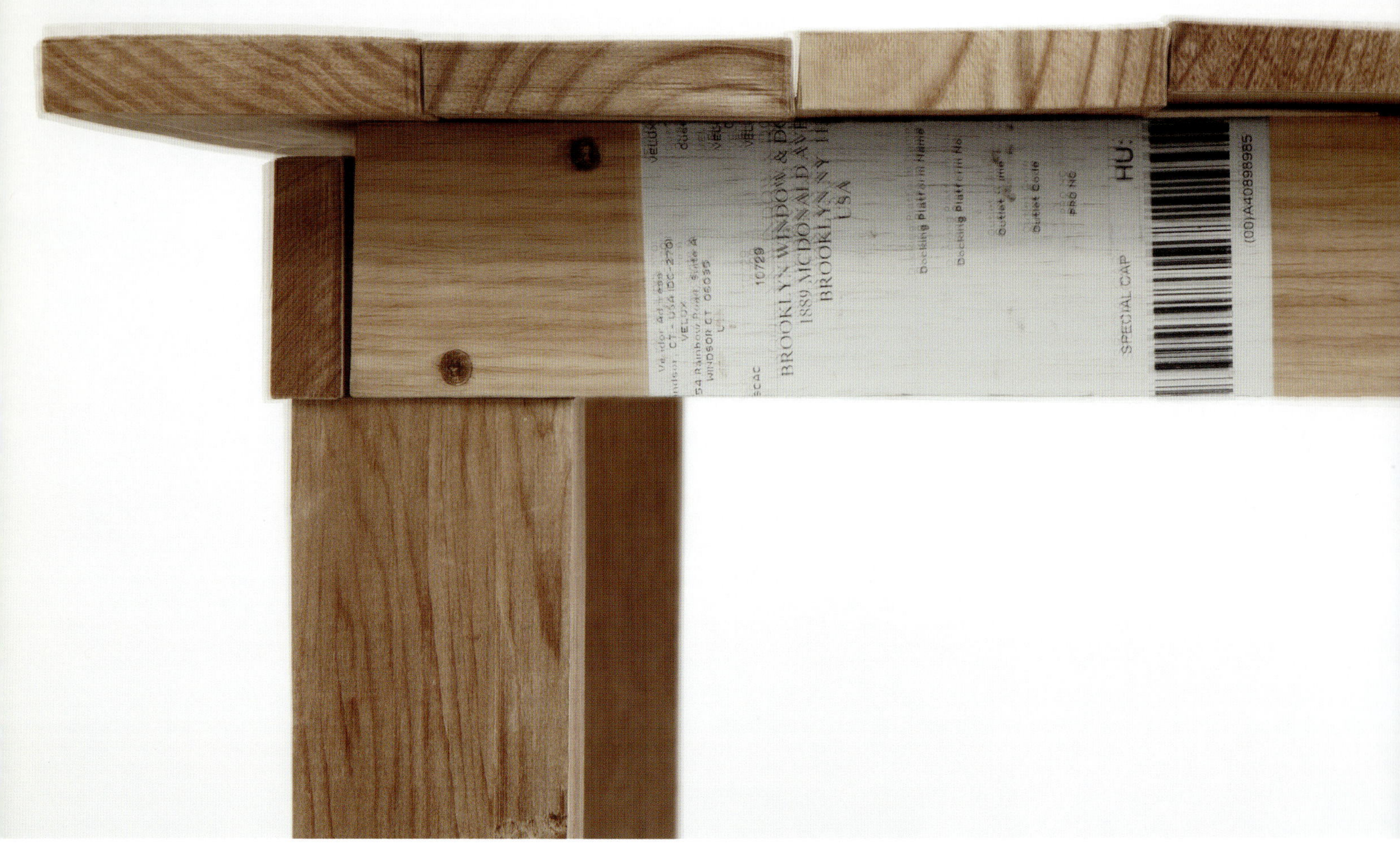

Fiction, 2012
Table vibrates at a high frequency, appearing blurry
Inkjet print on balsa wood, styrofoam,
acoustic foam, glue, steel, aluminum,
DC motor, rechargeable lithium battery
27 ¾ x 63 ⅜ x 39 ⅜ inches (70.5 x 161 x 100 cm)

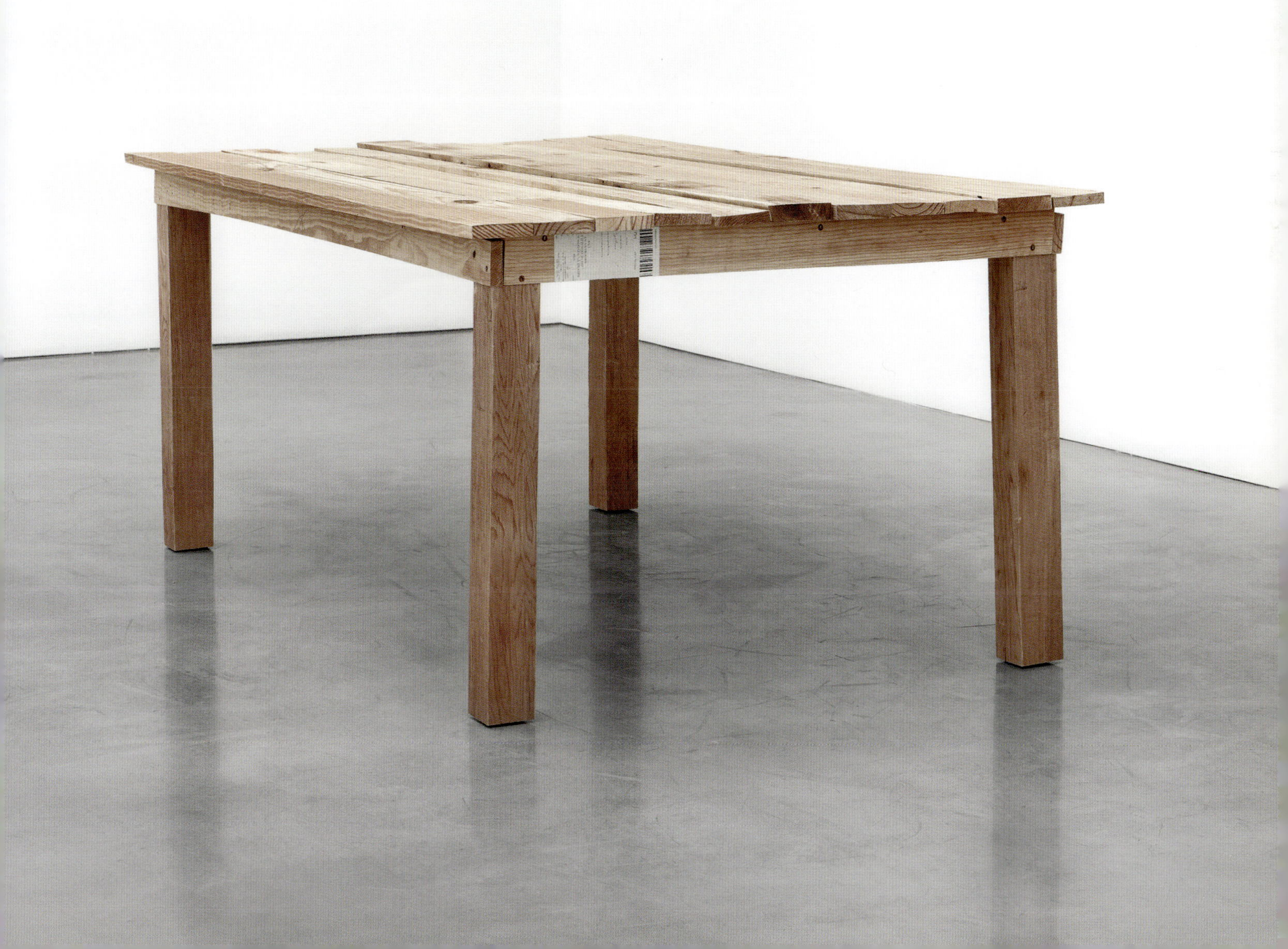

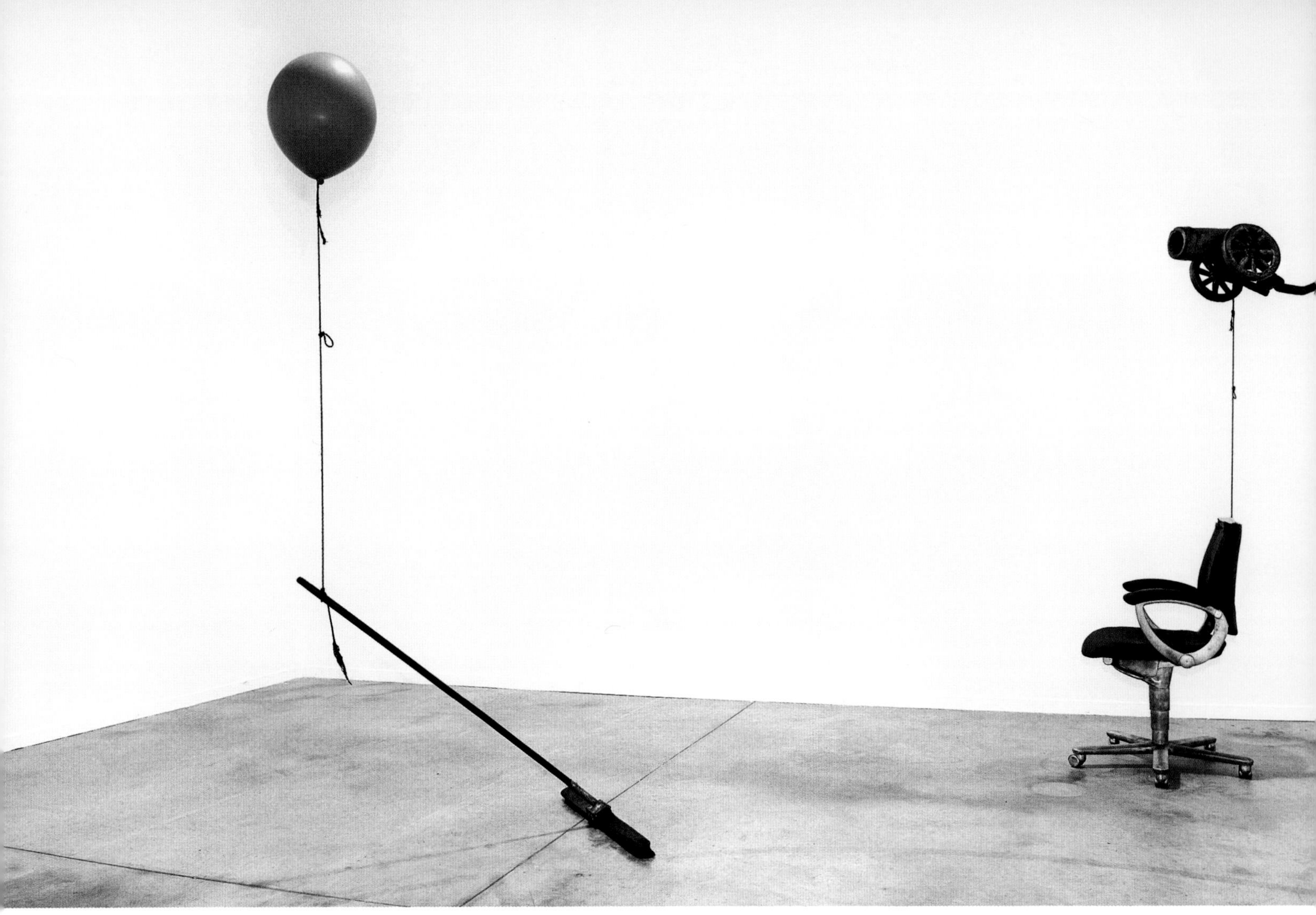

Above and opposite page:

A Place Called Novosibirsk, 2004

Cast aluminum, epoxy resin, iron rod, string, acrylic paint

98 x 30 ½ x 41 ⅜ inches (249 x 77.5 x 105 cm)

Above and following pages:

A Thing Called Gearbox, 2004

Cast aluminum, copper, iron rod, string, acrylic paint

91 x 26 ¾ x 26 ½ inches (231 x 68 x 67.5 cm)

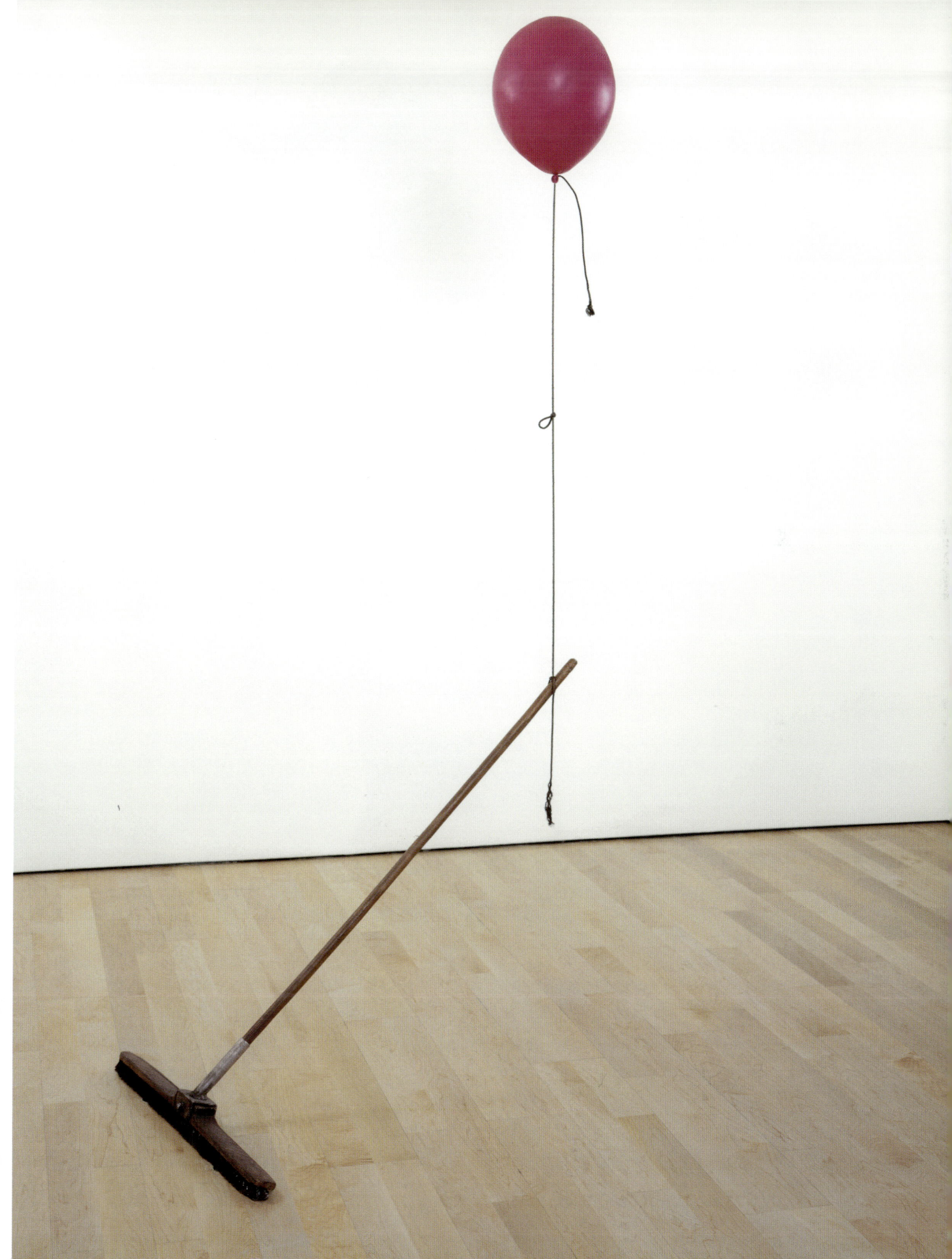

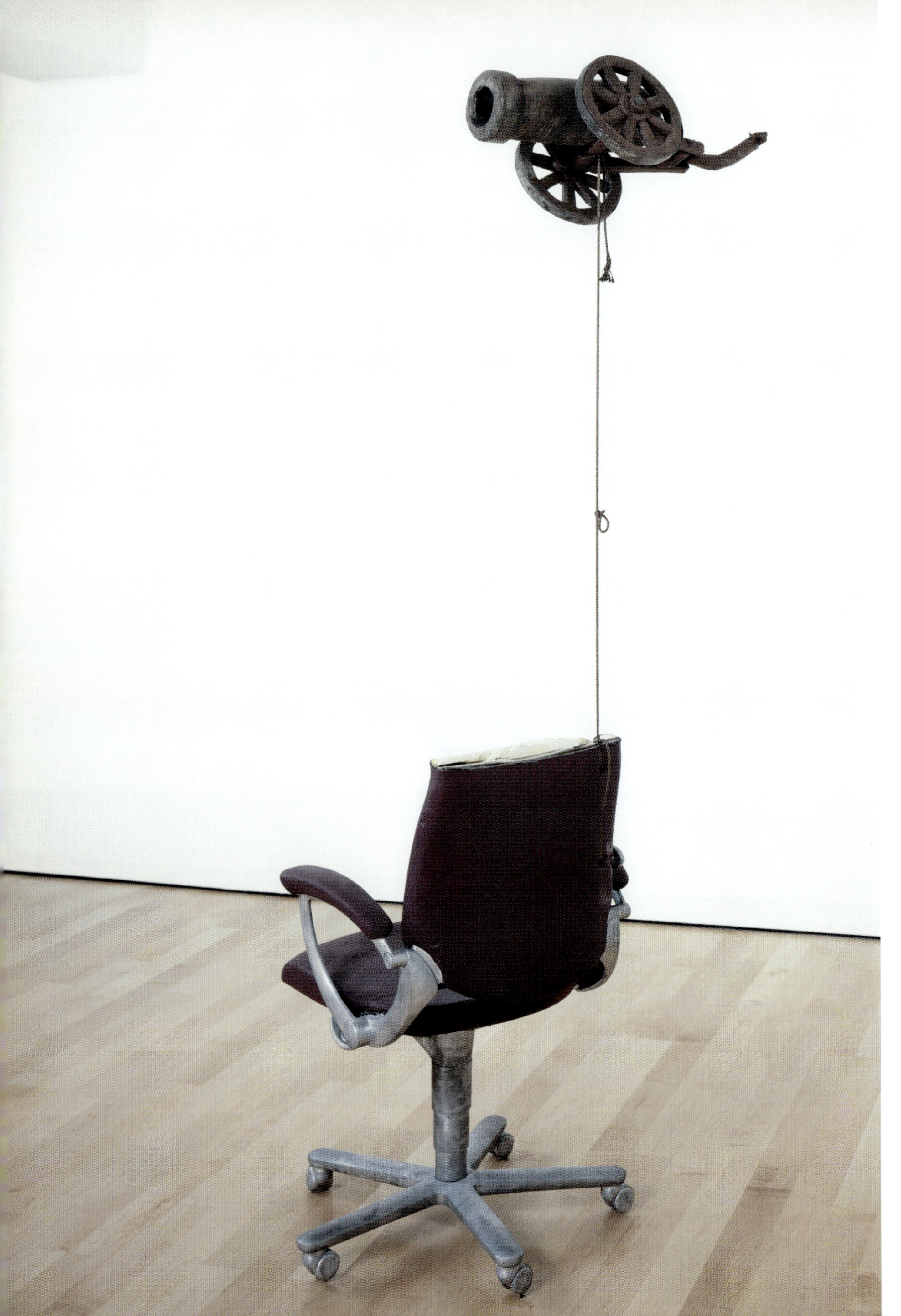

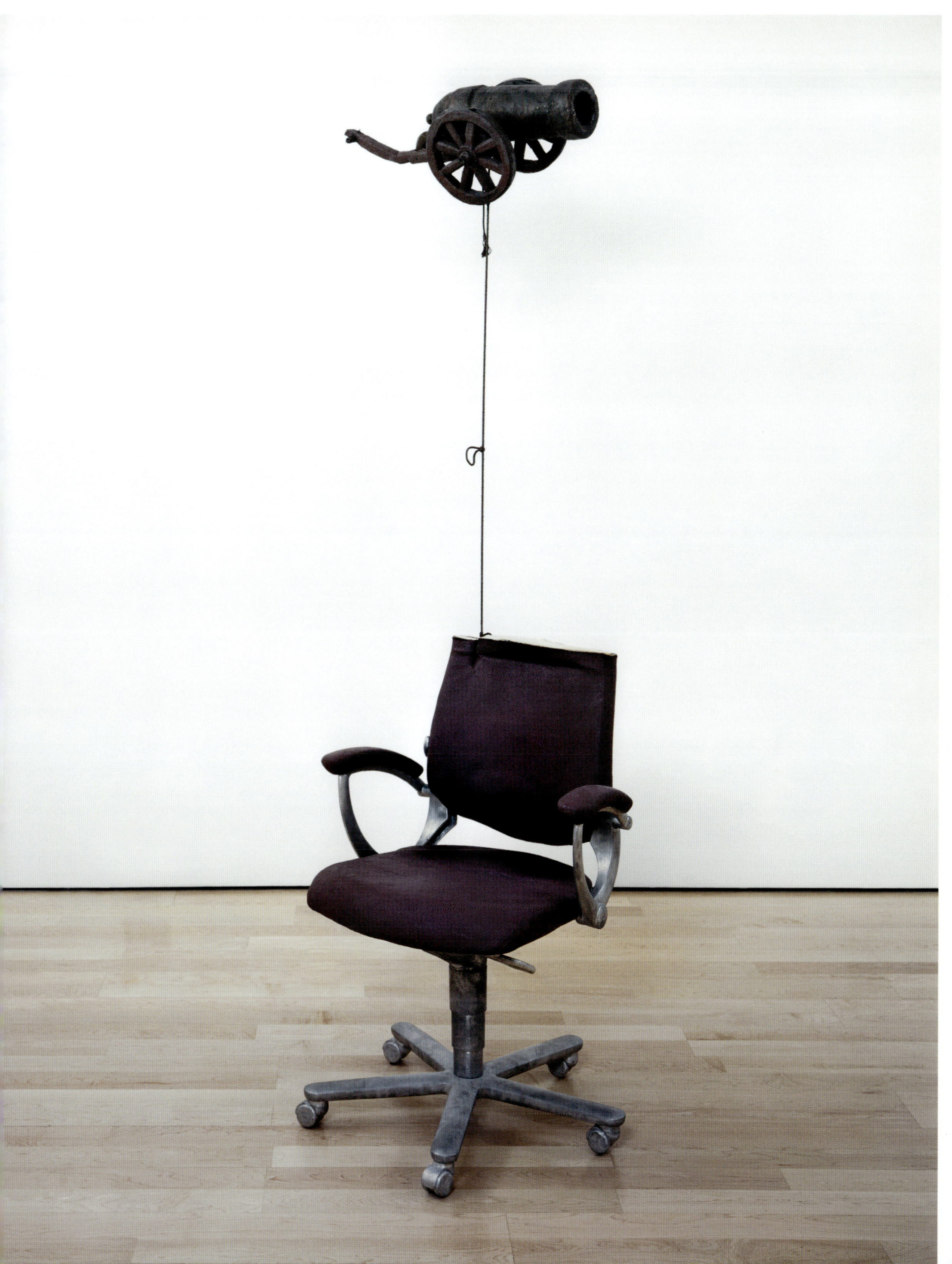

The Lock, 2007
Cast polyurethane, steel pipes, electromagnets
72 ½ x 29 ¾ x 21 ⅝ inches (184 x 75.5 x 55 cm)

Following pages:
Kratz, 2011
Cast aluminum, concrete, aluminum, epoxy, fiberglass, wire mesh, epoxy primer, polyester filler, one-component acrylic putty, urethane primer, polyester paint, acrylic polyurethane matte clearcoat
26 x 72 x 94 inches (66 x 182.9 x 238.8 cm)

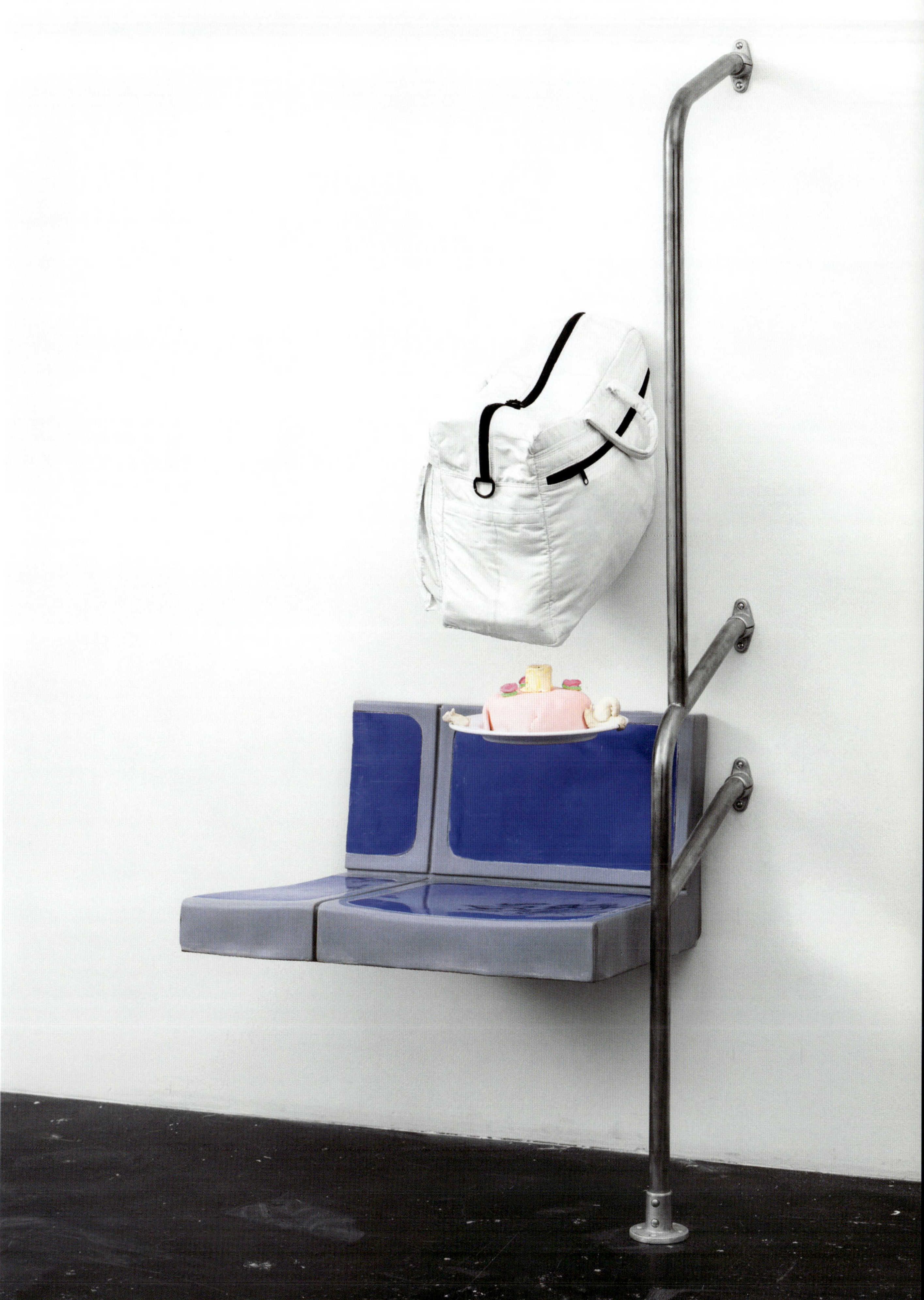

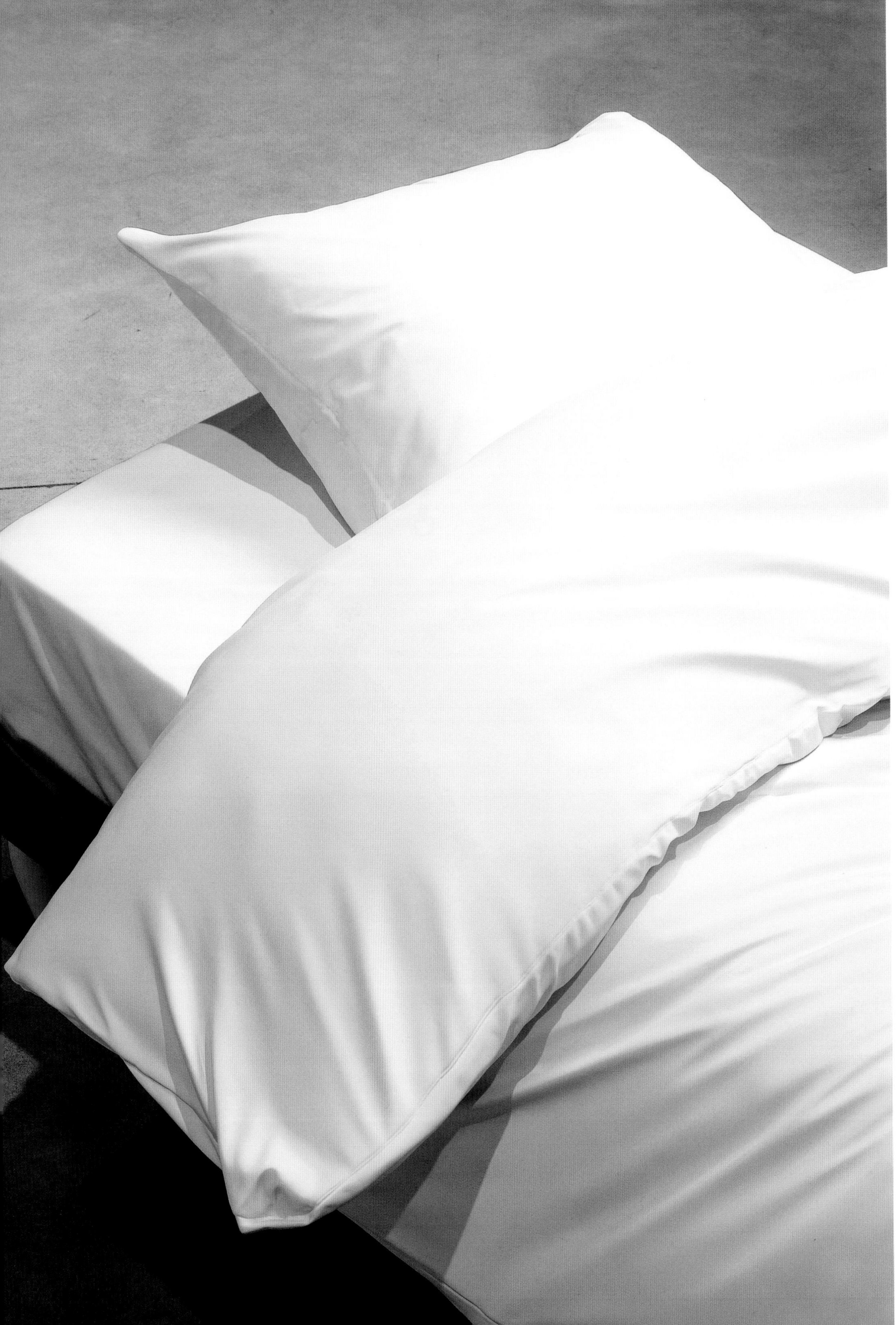

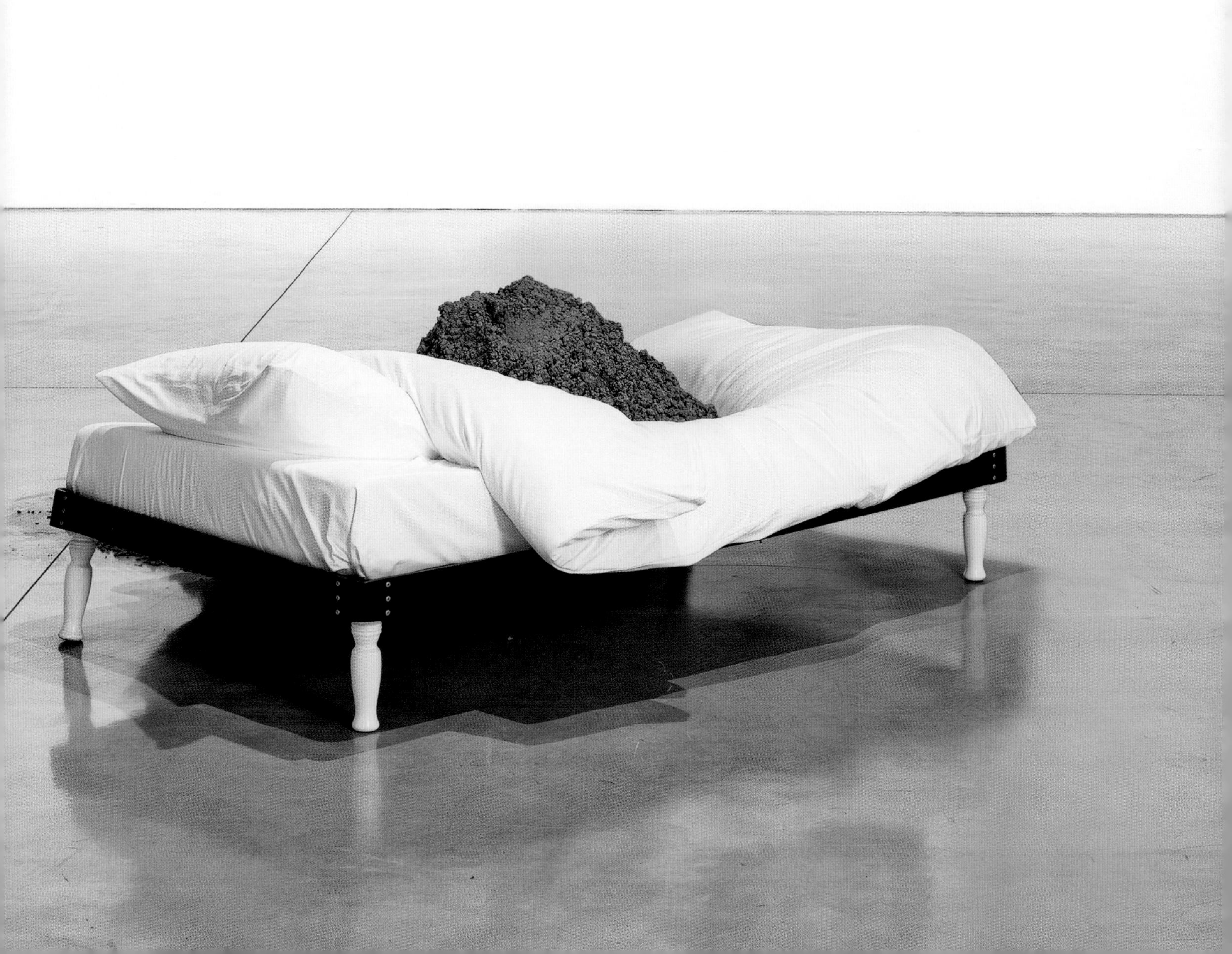

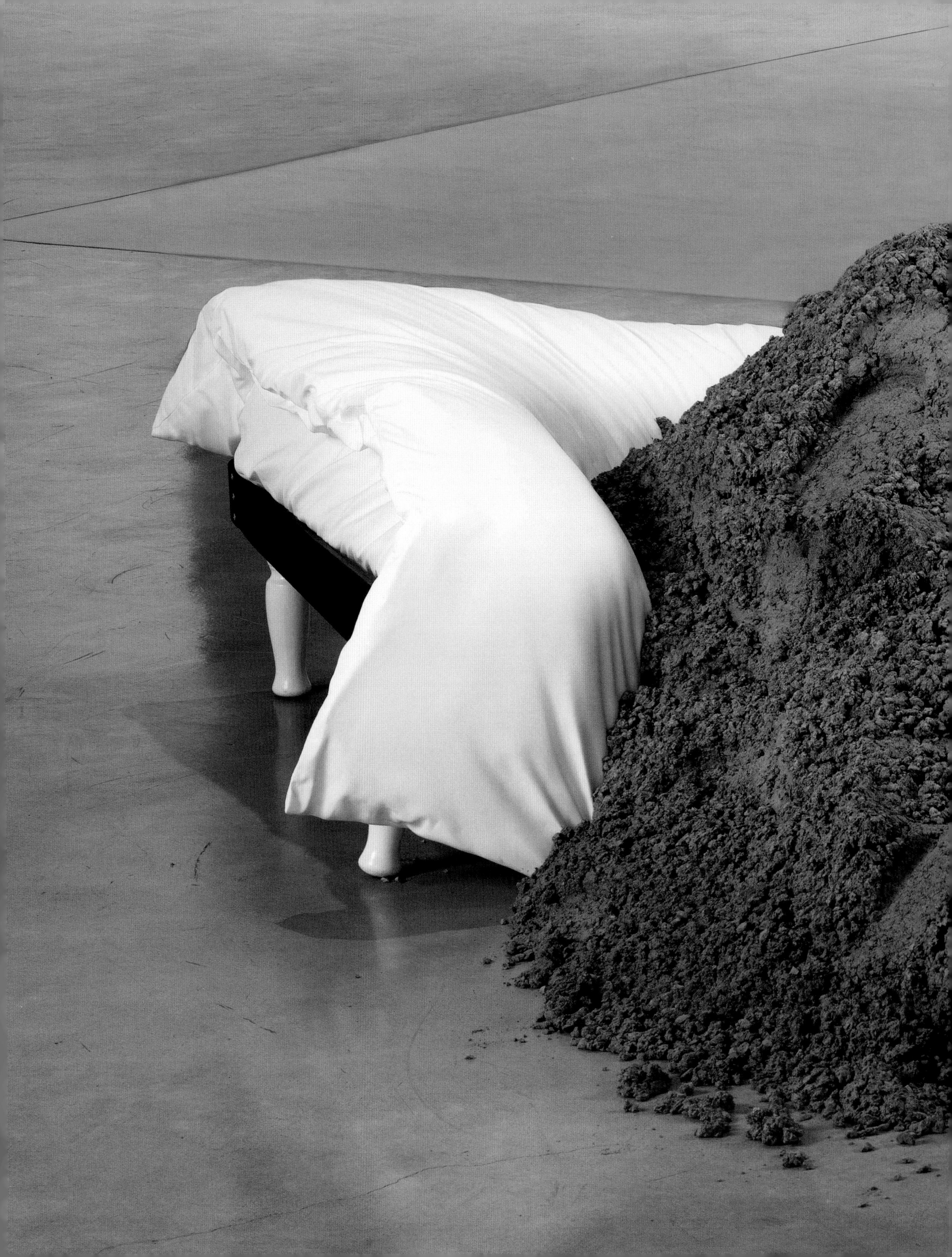

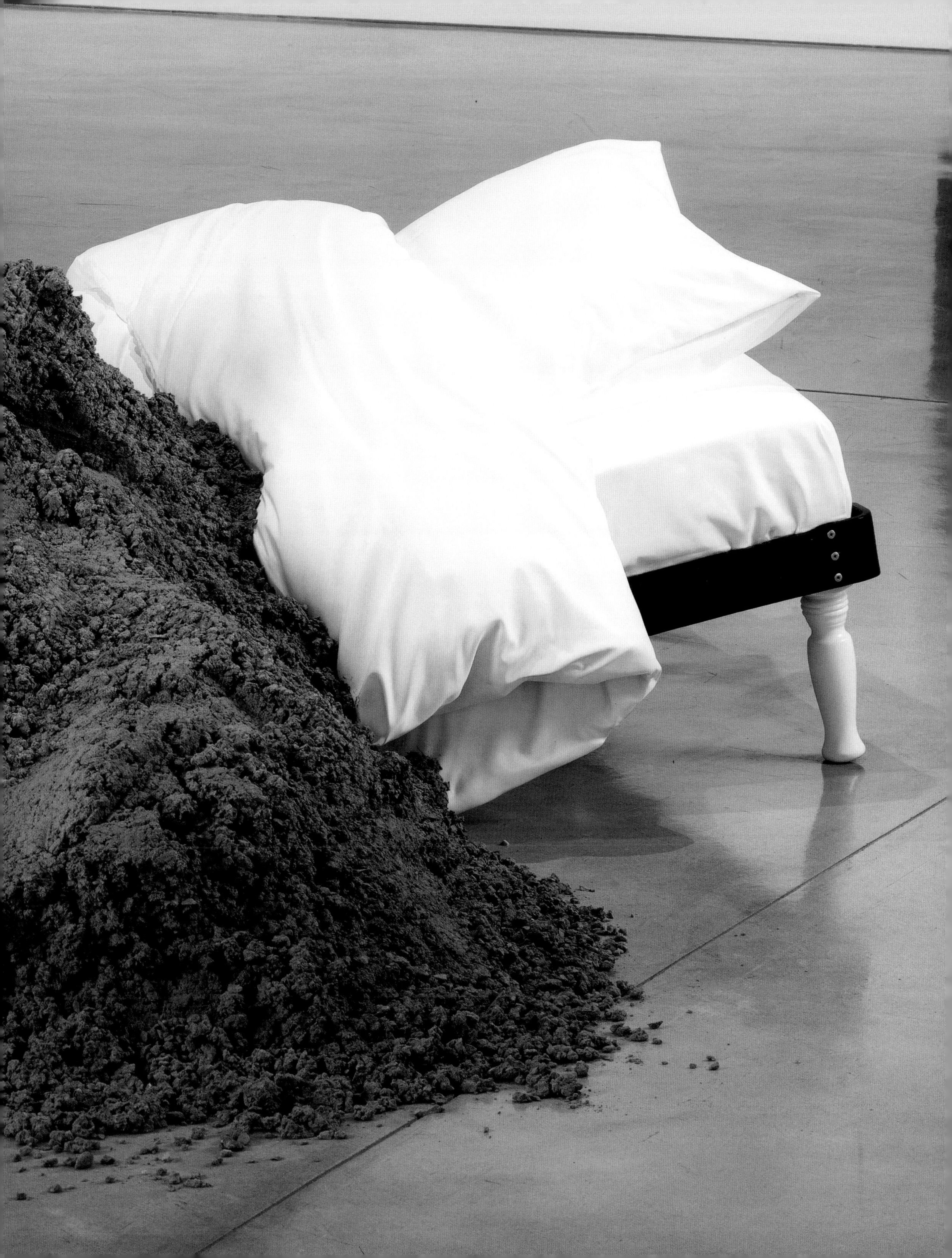

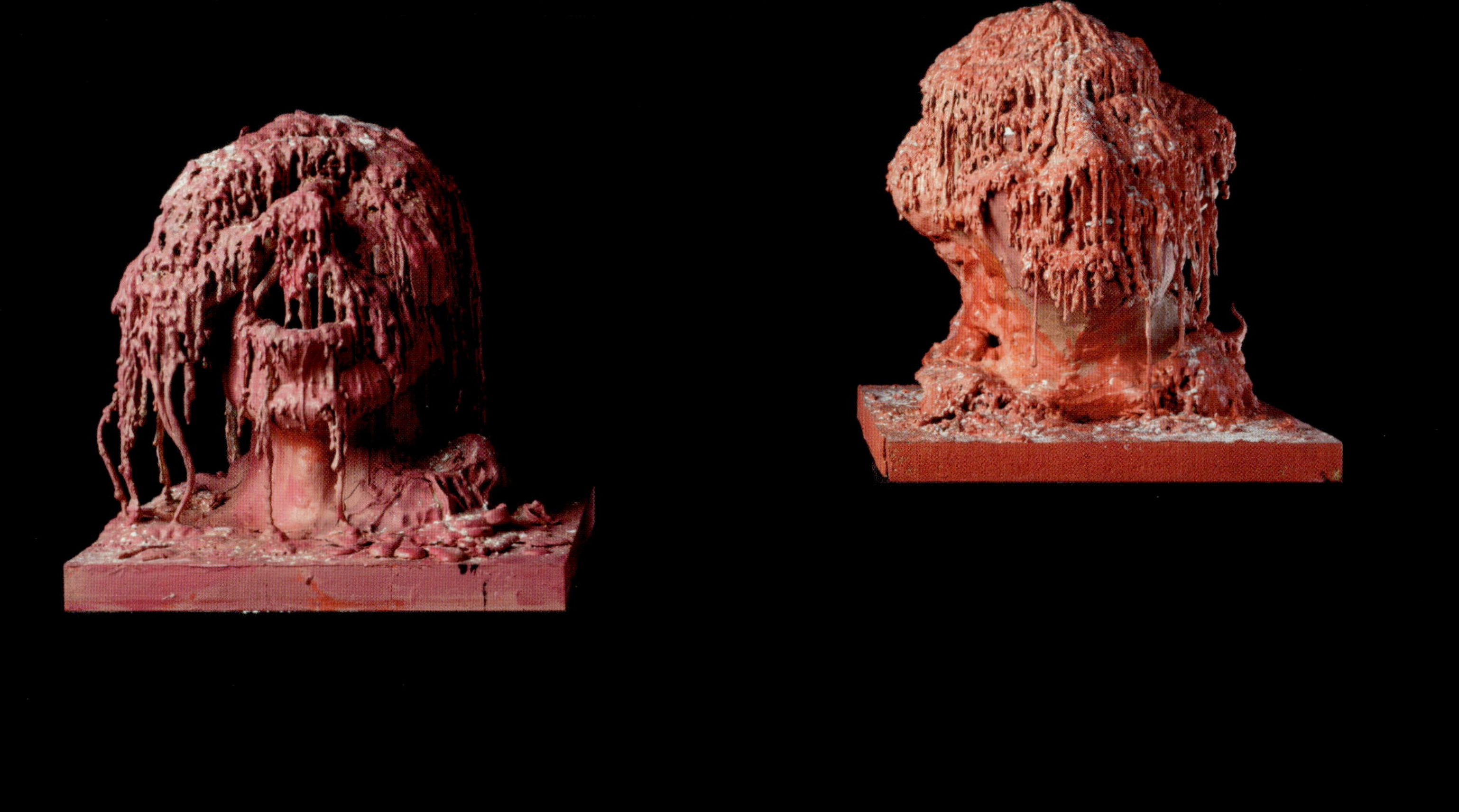

Köpfe, 1997–1999
Wood, clay, acrylic paint, wax
Head 1: 11 ¾ x 11 ¾ inches (30 x 30 cm)
Pedestal: 51 ⅛ x 13 x 11 ¾ inches (130 x 33 x 30 cm)
Head 2: 11 ¾ x 11 ¾ inches (30 x 30 cm)
Pedestal: 48 x 12 ⅝ x 12 ⅝ inches (122 x 32 x 32 cm)

Following pages:

Gedanken kommen zurück "bitte," 2002
Wood, wax, silicone, clay, spray enamel
31 ½ x 63 x 47 ¼ inches (80 x 160 x 120 cm)

Untitled (Chair), 1997–2000
Wooden chair, clay, oil paint, acrylic paint,
wax, spray adhesive, matte varnish, silicone
33 x 20 x 18 ⅞ inches (84 x 51 x 48 cm)
Installed on: Franz West (with Heimo Zobernig), table
from *Heimo West Bar: 10 Spiegeltische, 20 Stühle*, 1998

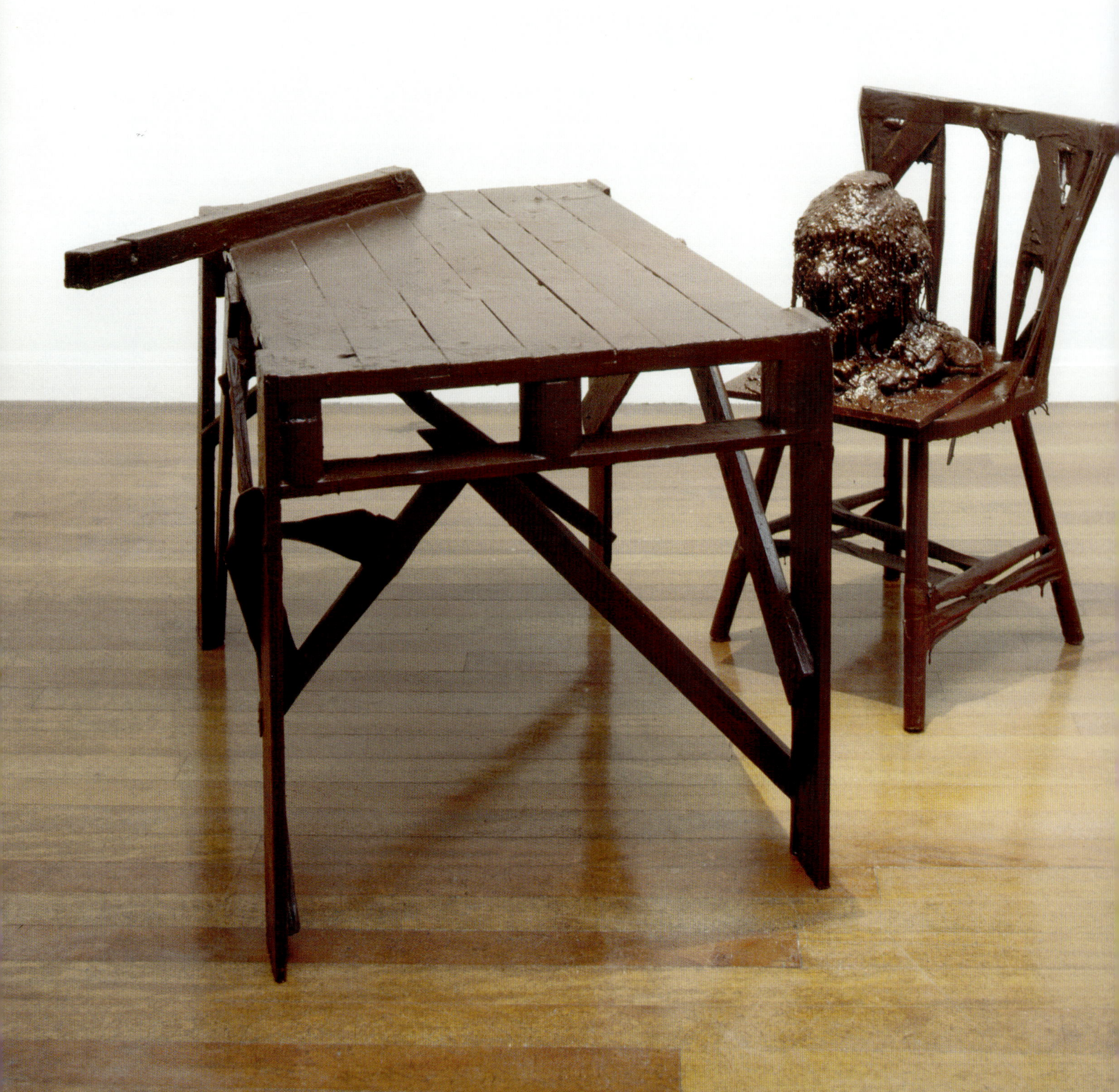

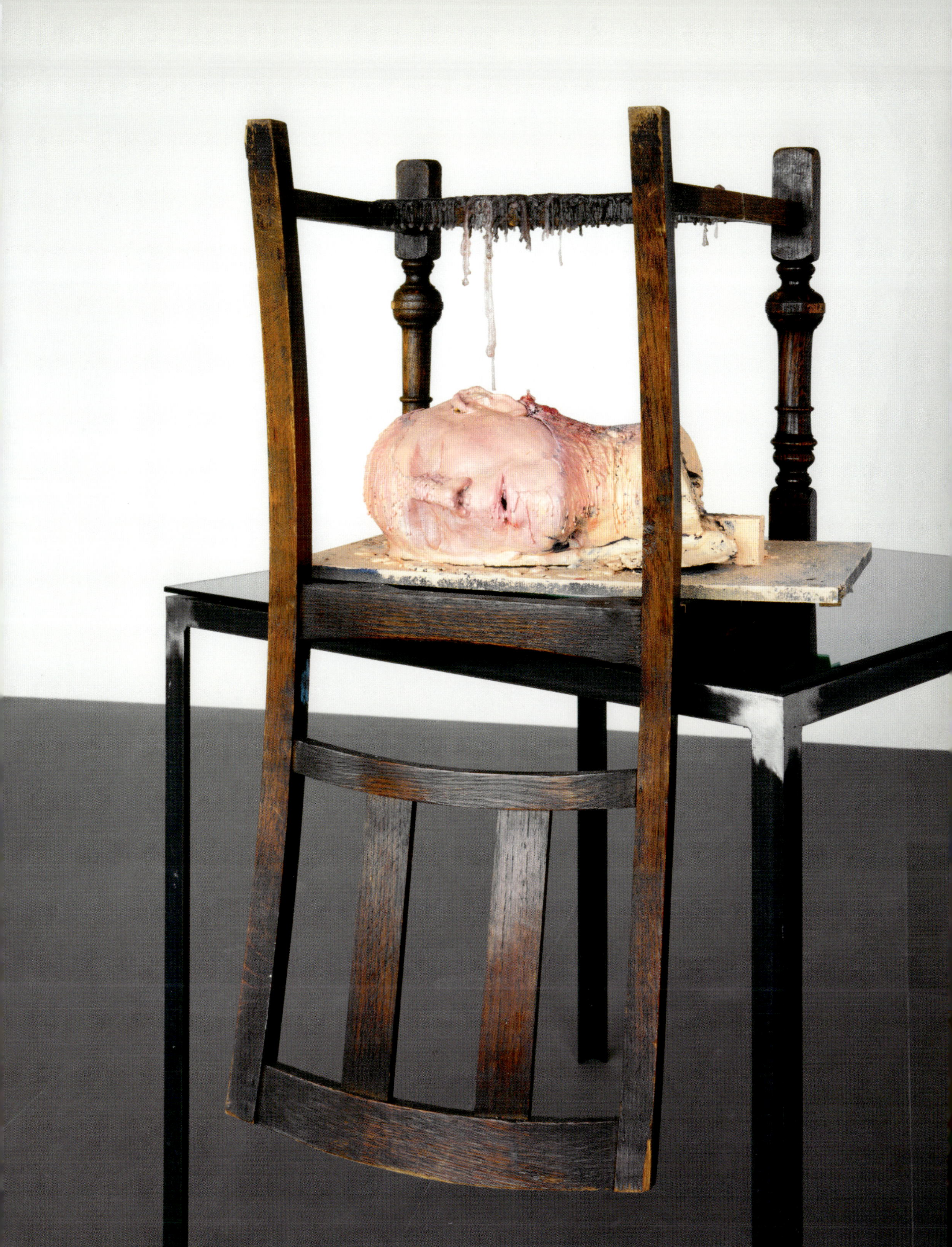

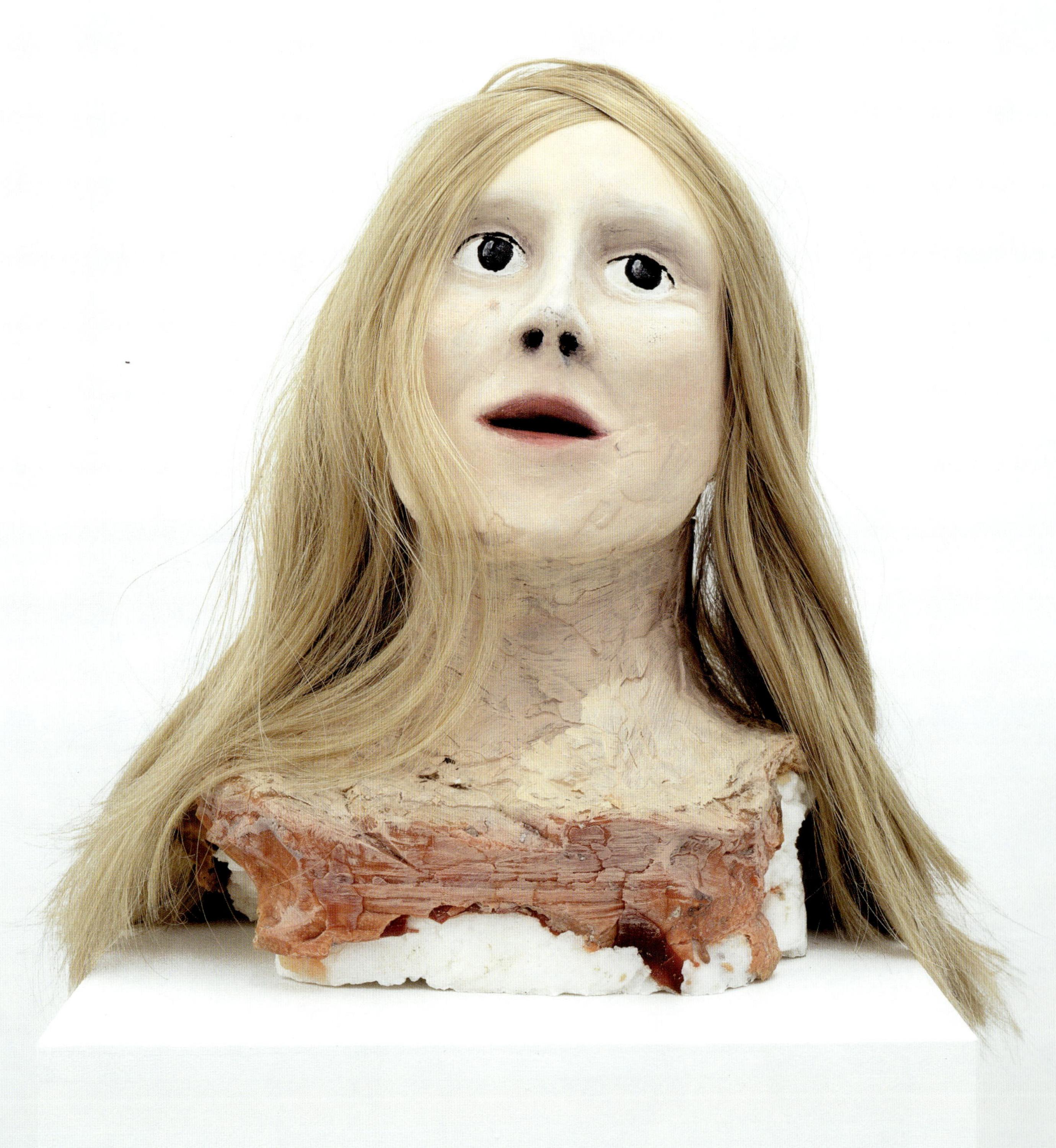

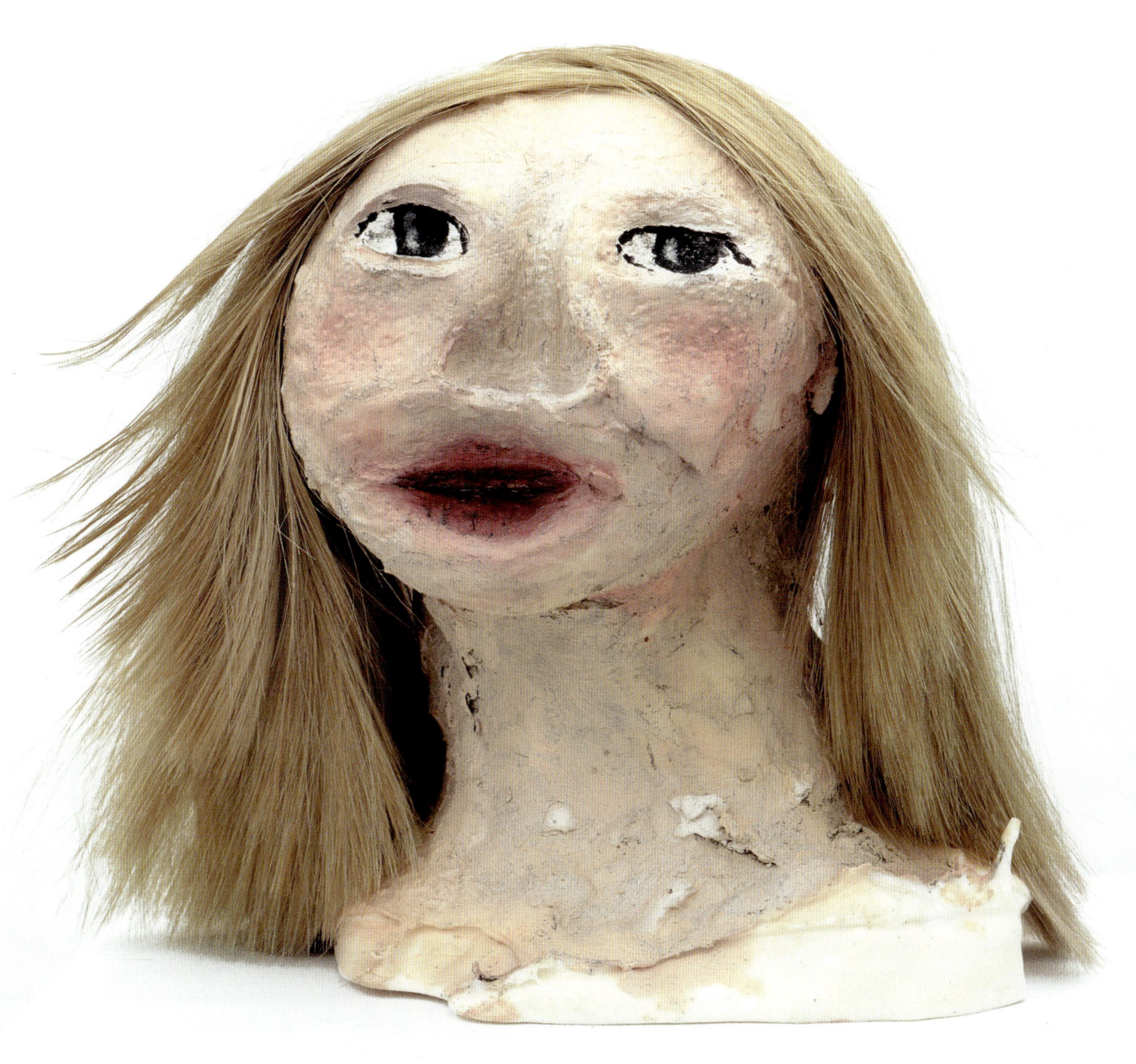

I Can Smell Your Words, 2002
Polyurethane resin, synthetic hair, acrylic paint, particleboard, marker, fake eyelashes, powdered sugar, egg whites
Dimensions unknown
Studio view, Hardturmstrasse, Zurich, 2002

Previous pages:
Napoleon, Is There Something You Didn't Tell Me / Napoleon, Misunderstood, 2001
Polyurethane resin, stearin, oil paint, synthetic hair, pigments, marker
Part 1: 12 ¼ x 10 ⅝ x 9 inches (21 x 27 x 23 cm)
With pedestal: 45 ⅝ x 10 ¼ x 10 ¼ inches (116 x 26 x 26 cm)
Part 2: 9 ½ x 10 ⅝ x 11 ¾ inches (24 x 27 x 20 cm)
With pedestal: 46 ⅞ x 11 x 10 ⅞ inches (119 x 28 x 27.5 cm)

Following pages:
am & pm, 2001
Wood, clay, polyurethane resin, pigments, bread, glue, mold
Head 1: 11 ¾ x 12 x 12 ¼ inches (30 x 30.5 x 31 cm)
Head 2: 12 ⅝ x 15 ¾ x 14 ⅝ inches (32 x 40 x 37 cm)

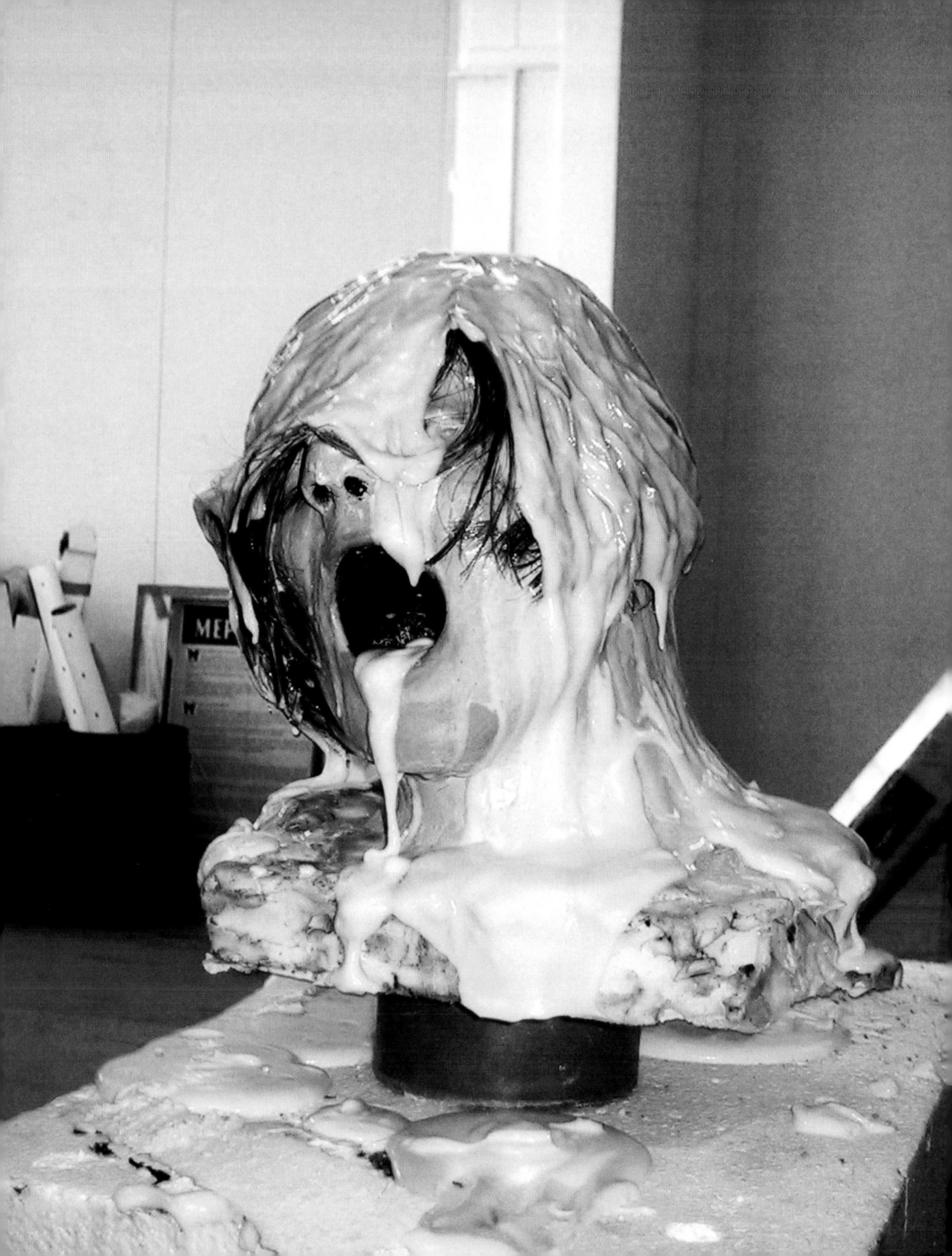

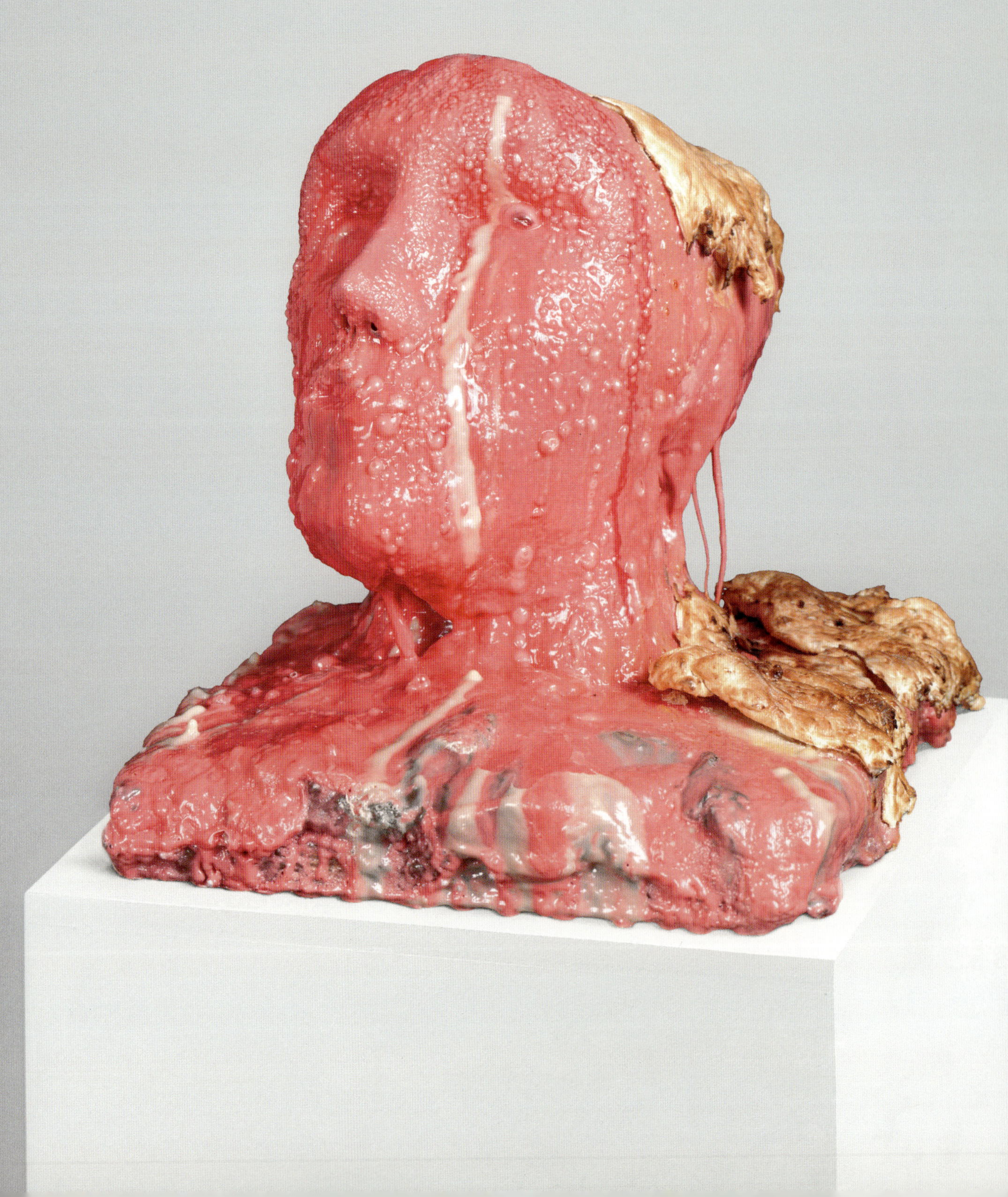

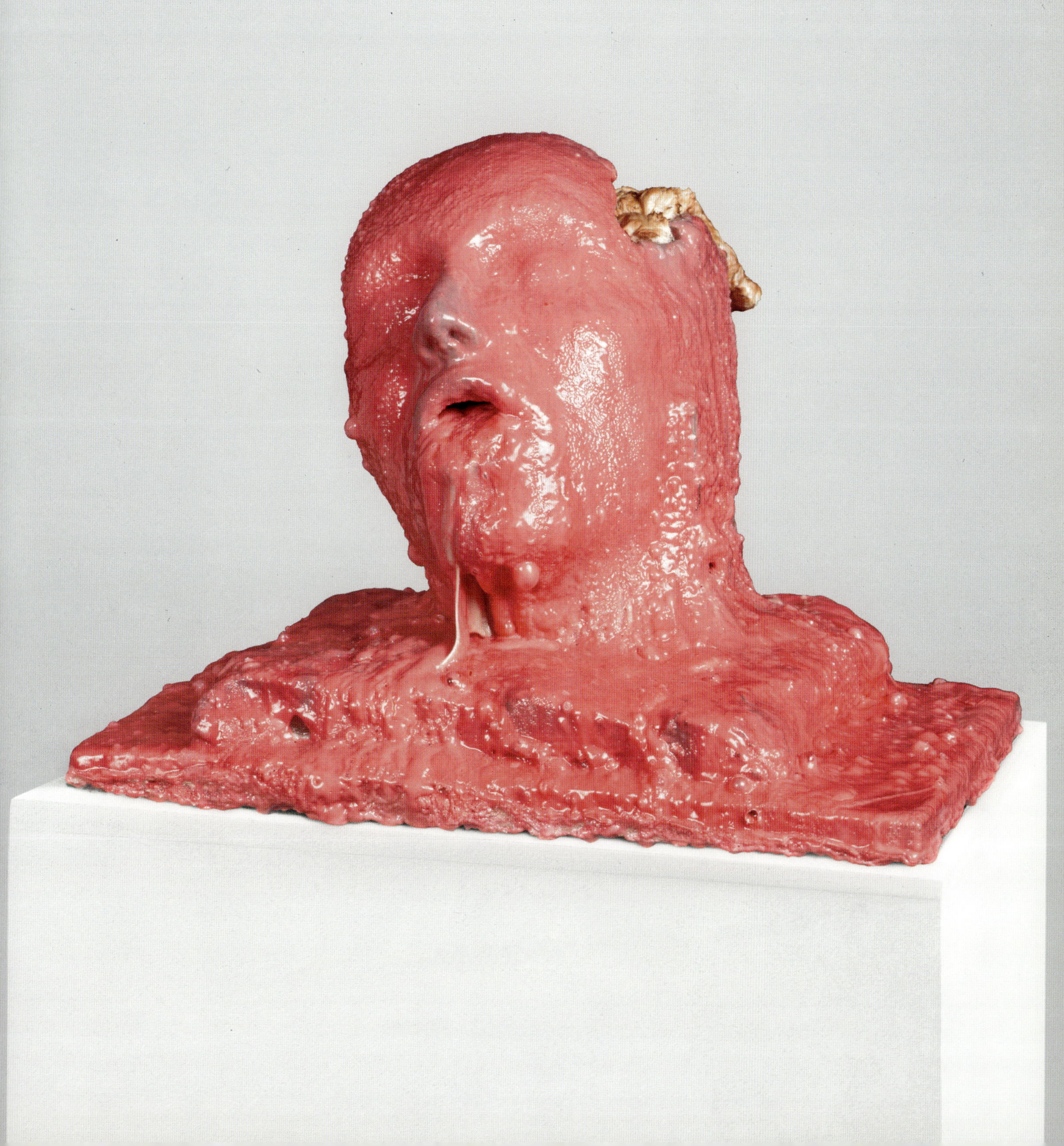

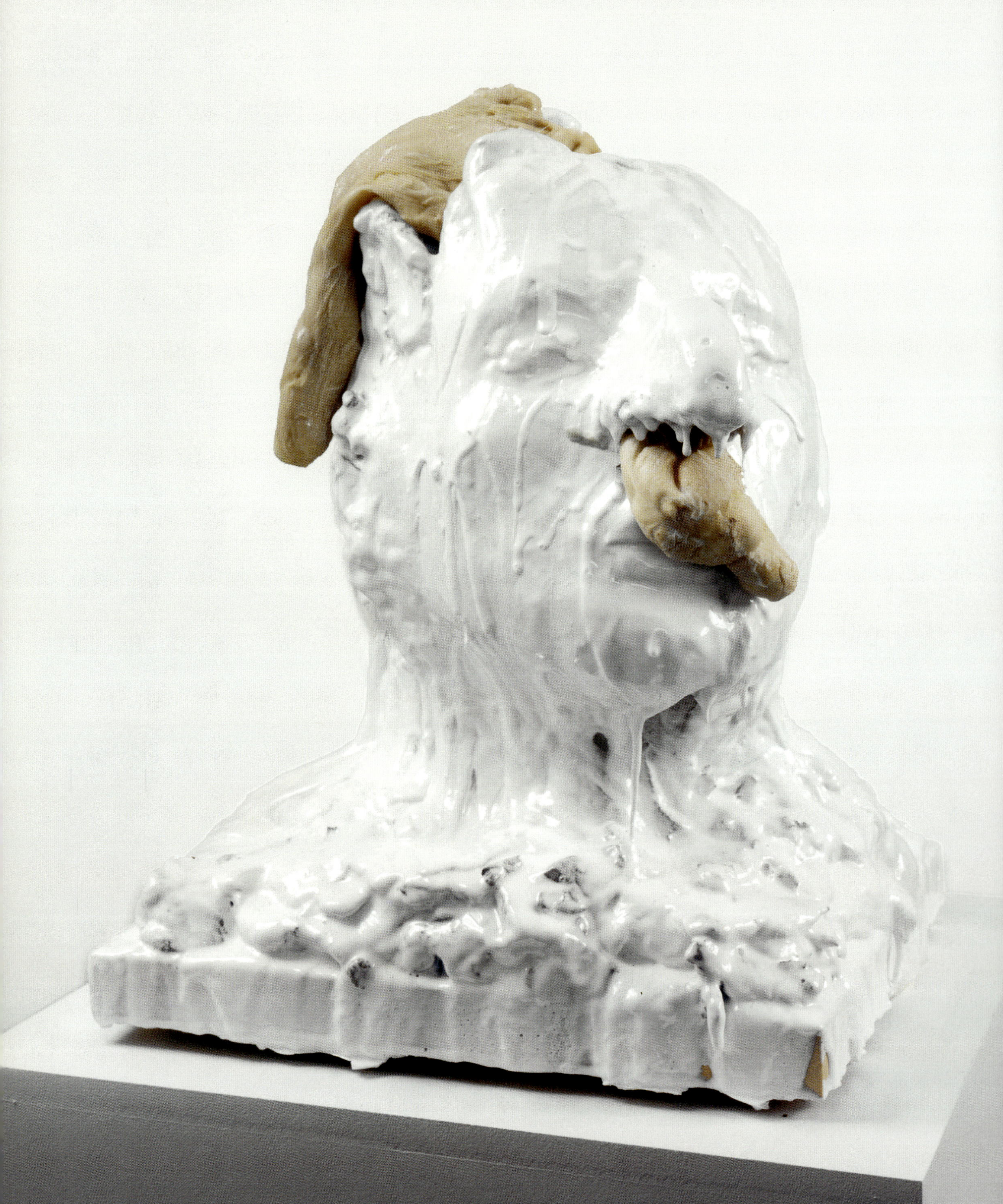

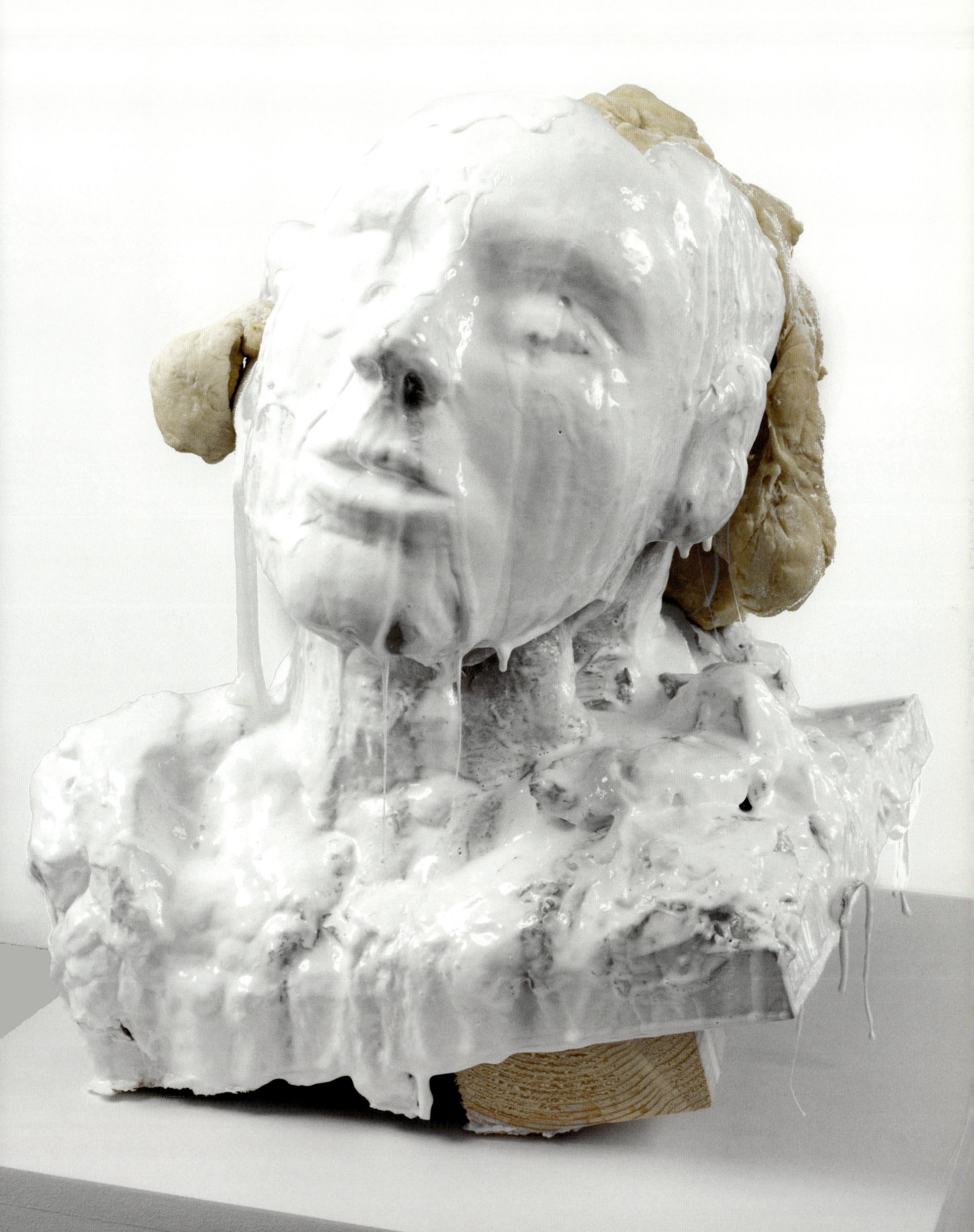

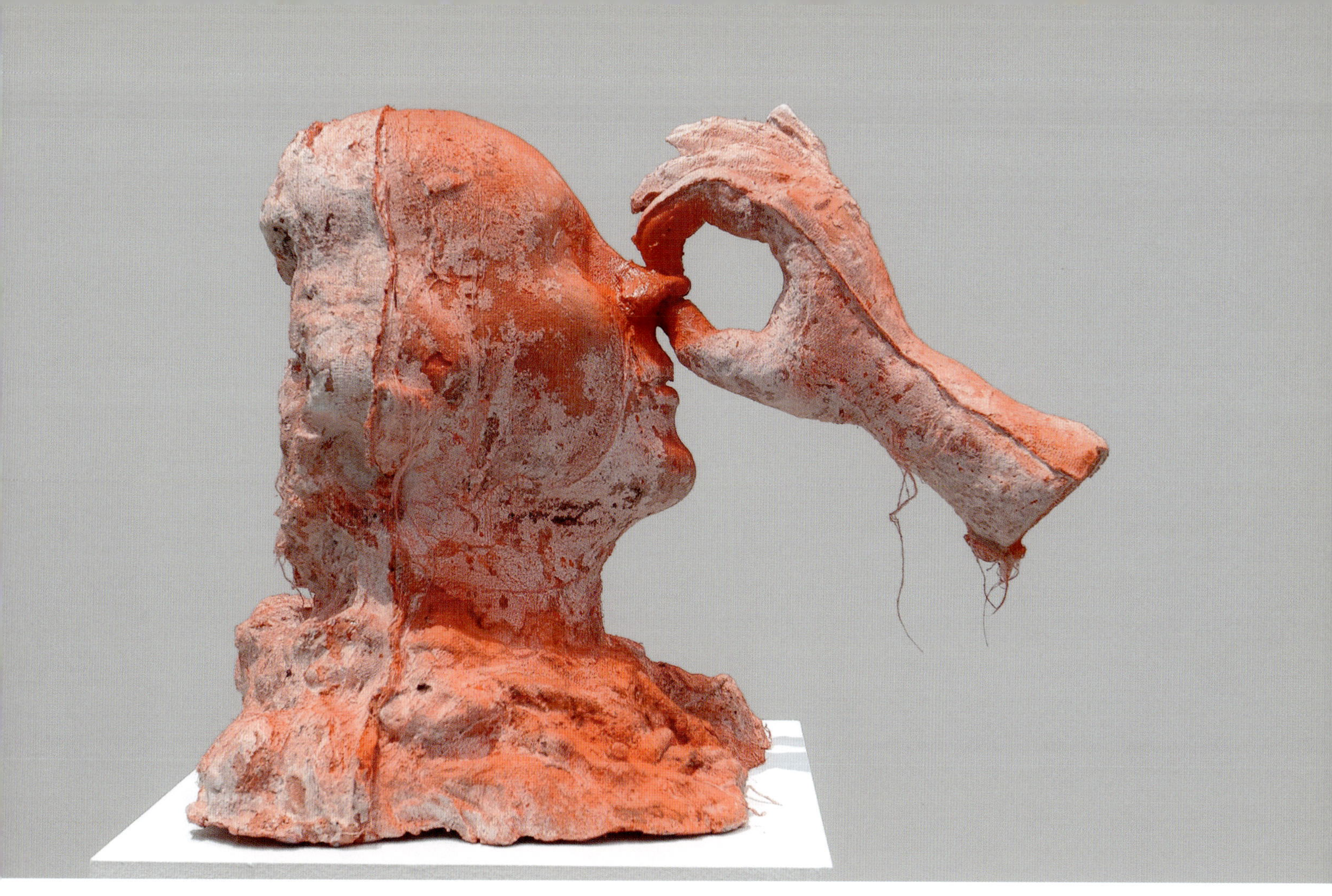

Kir Royal, 2004
Plaster, polyurethane resin, acrylic paint, gauze
17 ¾ x 11 ¾ x 13 ¾ inches (45 x 30 x 35 cm)

Previous pages:
Moody Moments, 2003
Clay, polyurethane resin, wood, dough
Head 1: 15 x 13 x 12 inches (38 x 33 x 30.5 cm)
Head 2: 15 x 12 x 11 ½ inches (38 x 30.5 x 30 cm)

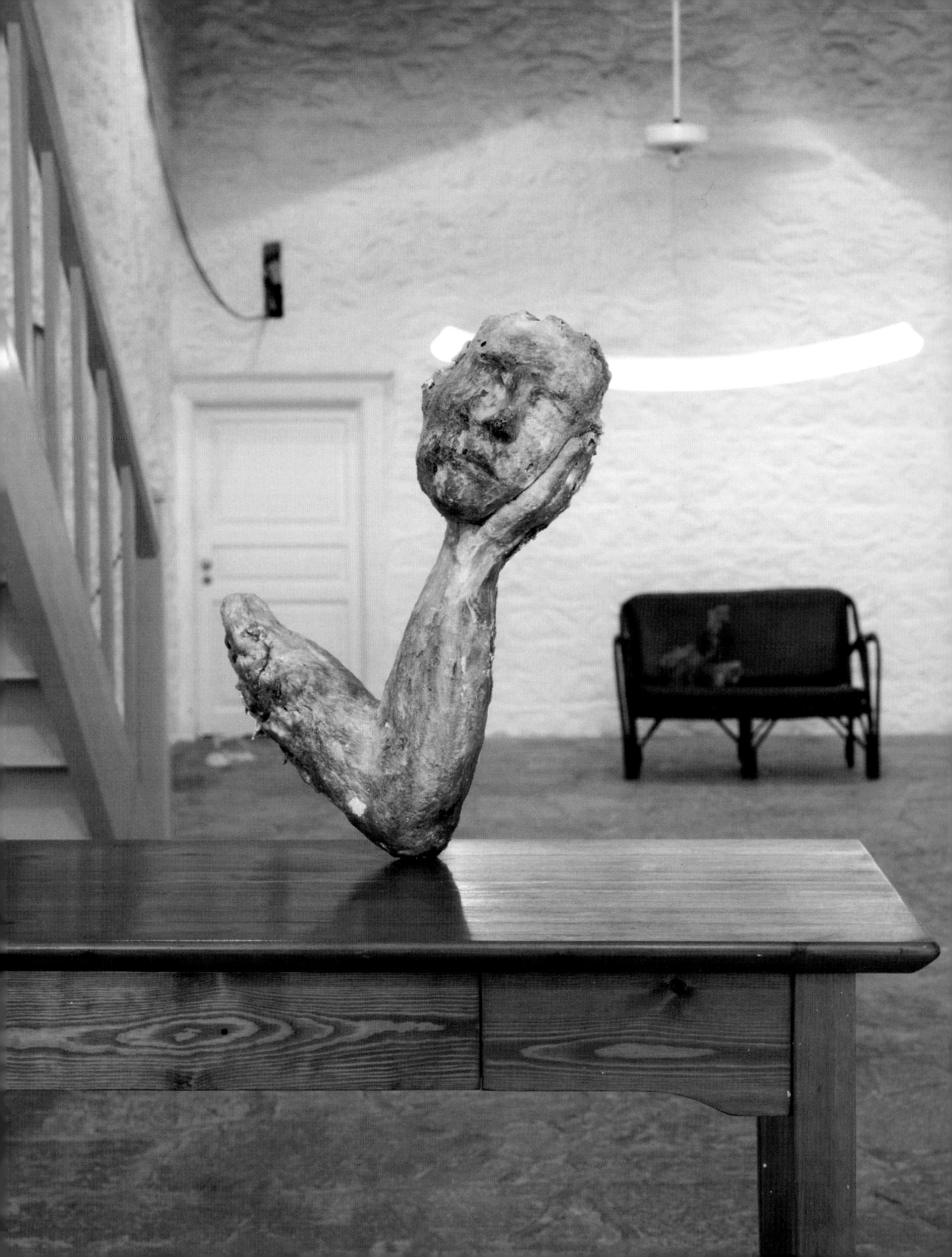

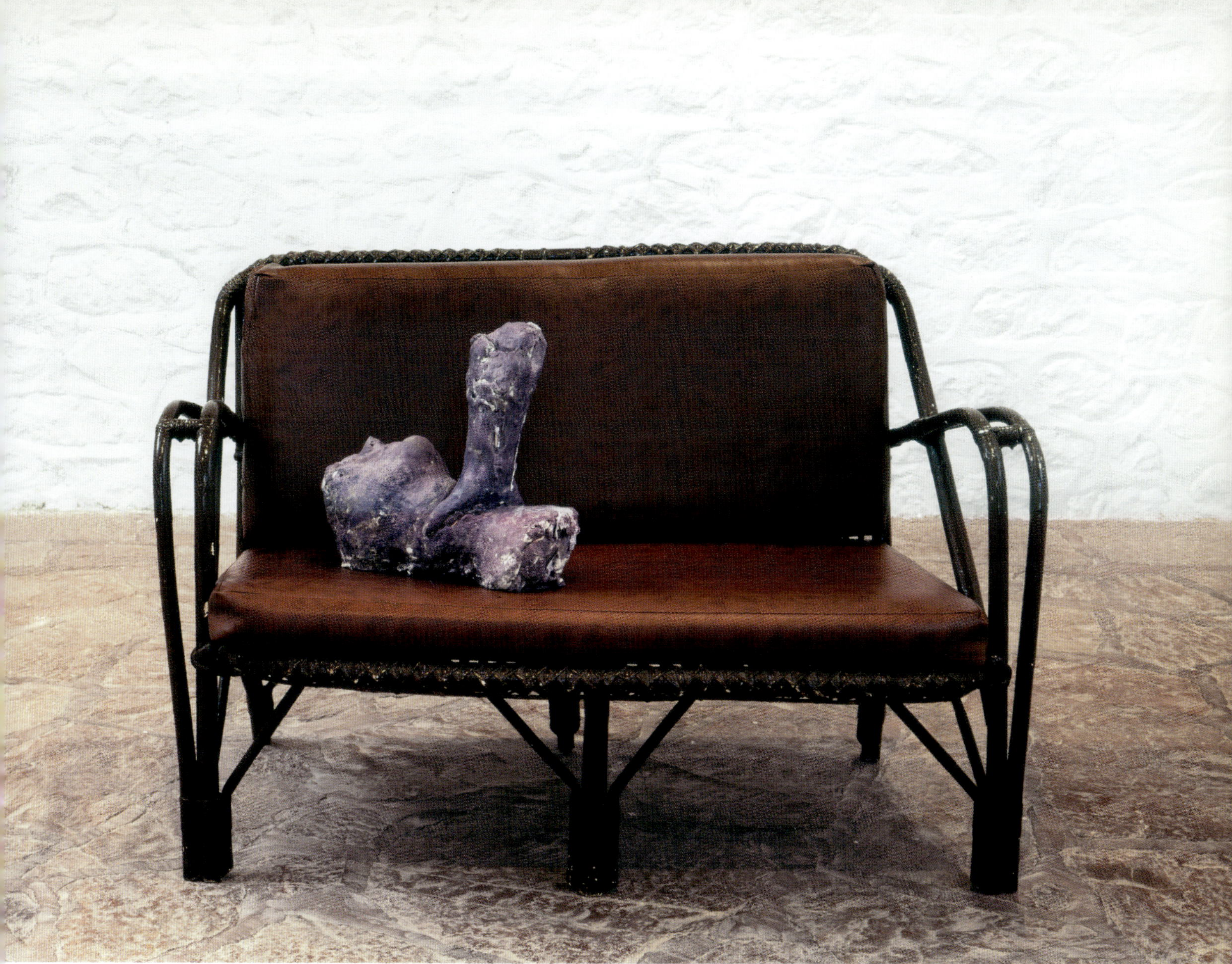

Tea Time with Miss Cocktail, 2005
Found couch, two-component polyurethane foam, pigments, screws
14 ⅝ x 14 ⅝ x 6 ¾ inches (37 x 37 x 17 cm)
Installation dimensions variable

Opposite page:
Vieille Prune, 2005
Two-component polyurethane foam, pigments, screws, epoxy glue
20 ⅞ x 17 ¾ x 8 ¼ inches (53 x 45 x 21 cm)
Installation view, "Mr. Watson—Come Here—I Want to See You," Hydra Workshop, Greece, 2005

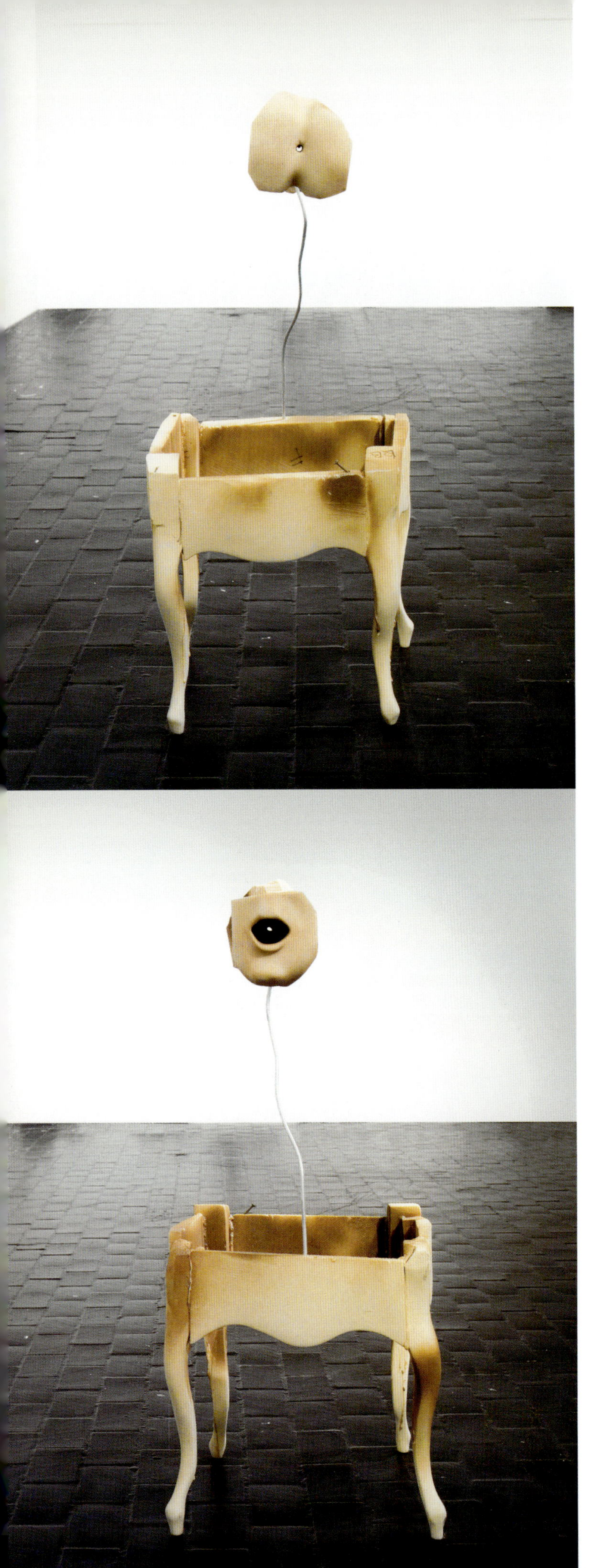

Untitled, 2006
Polyurethane foam, spray enamel, aluminum rod, screws
41 ¾ x 16 ¾ x 30 ⅛ inches (106 x 42.5 x 76.5 cm)

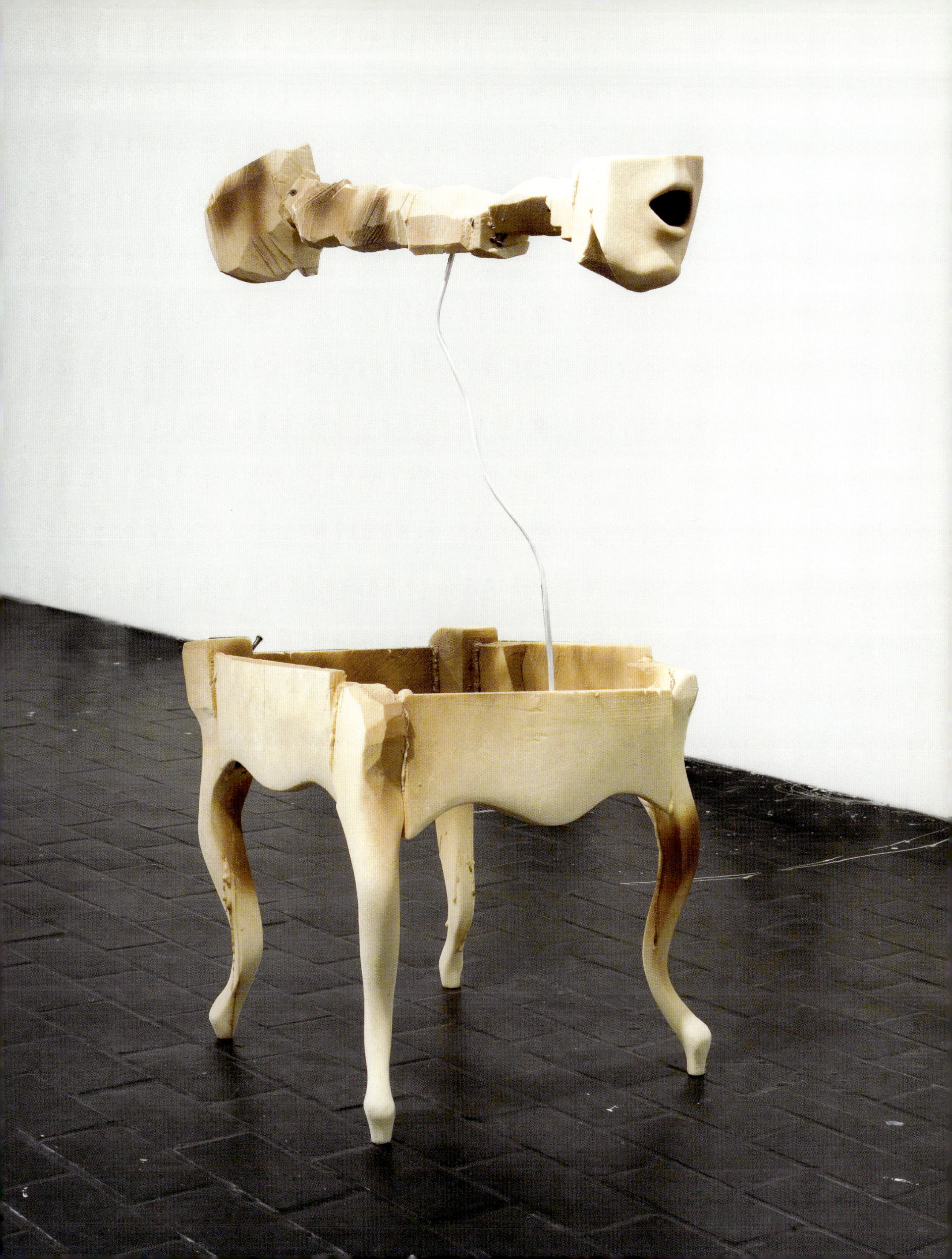

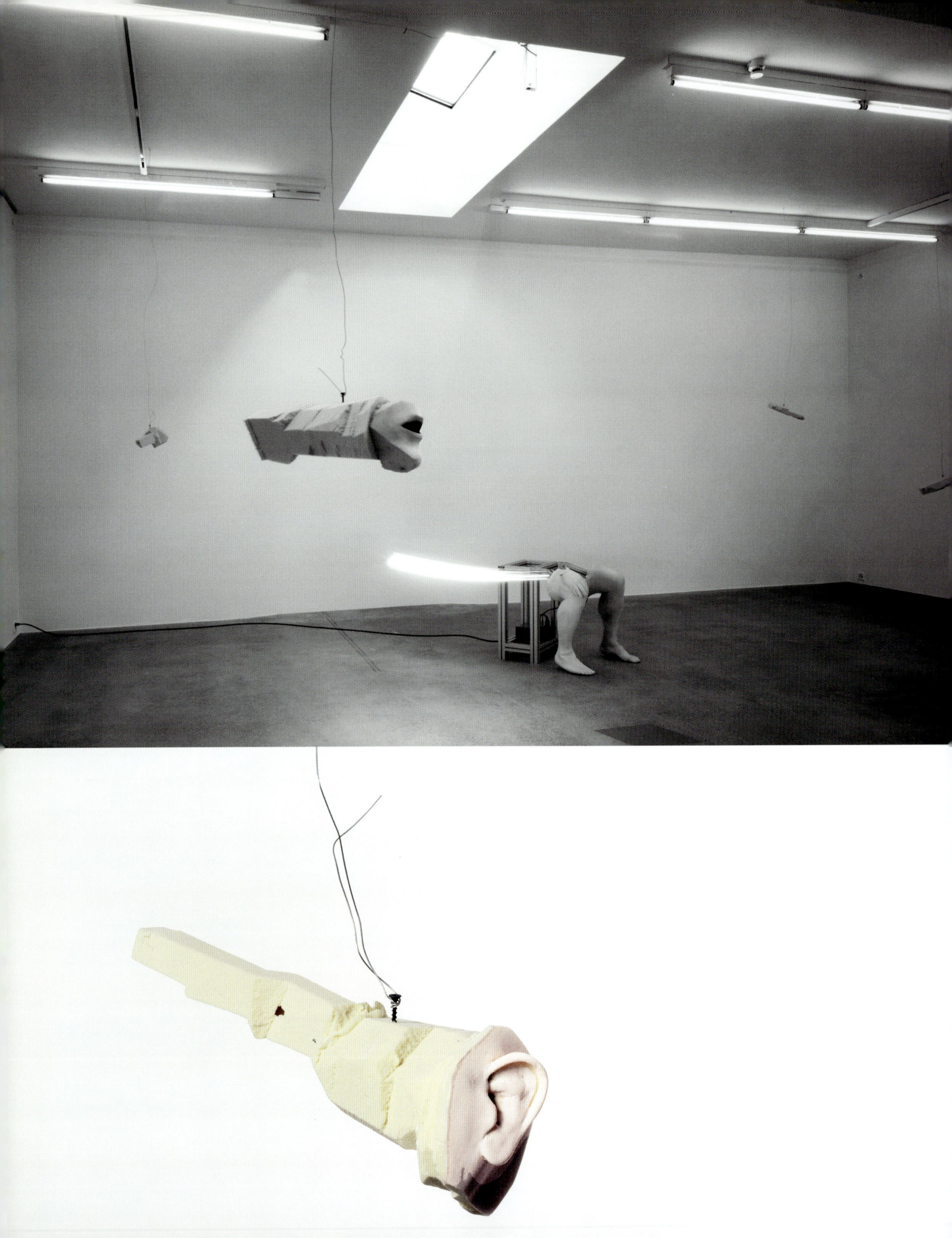

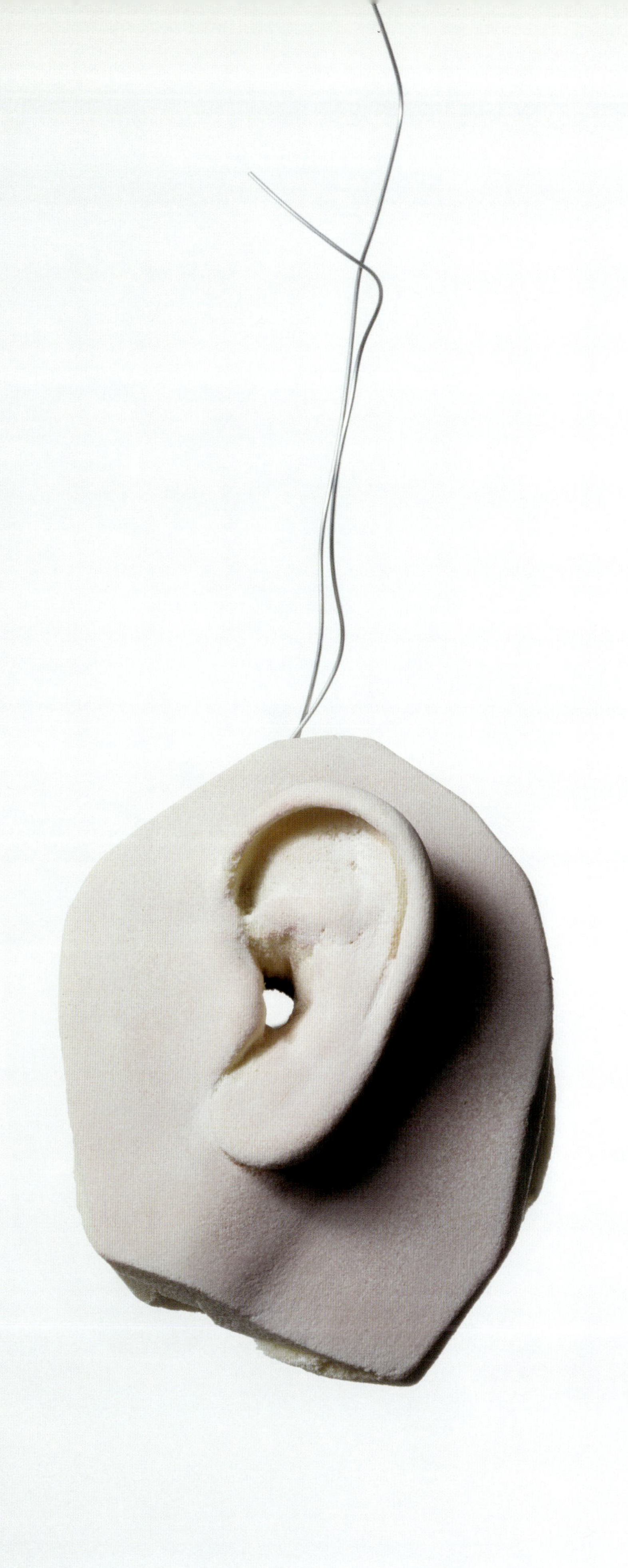

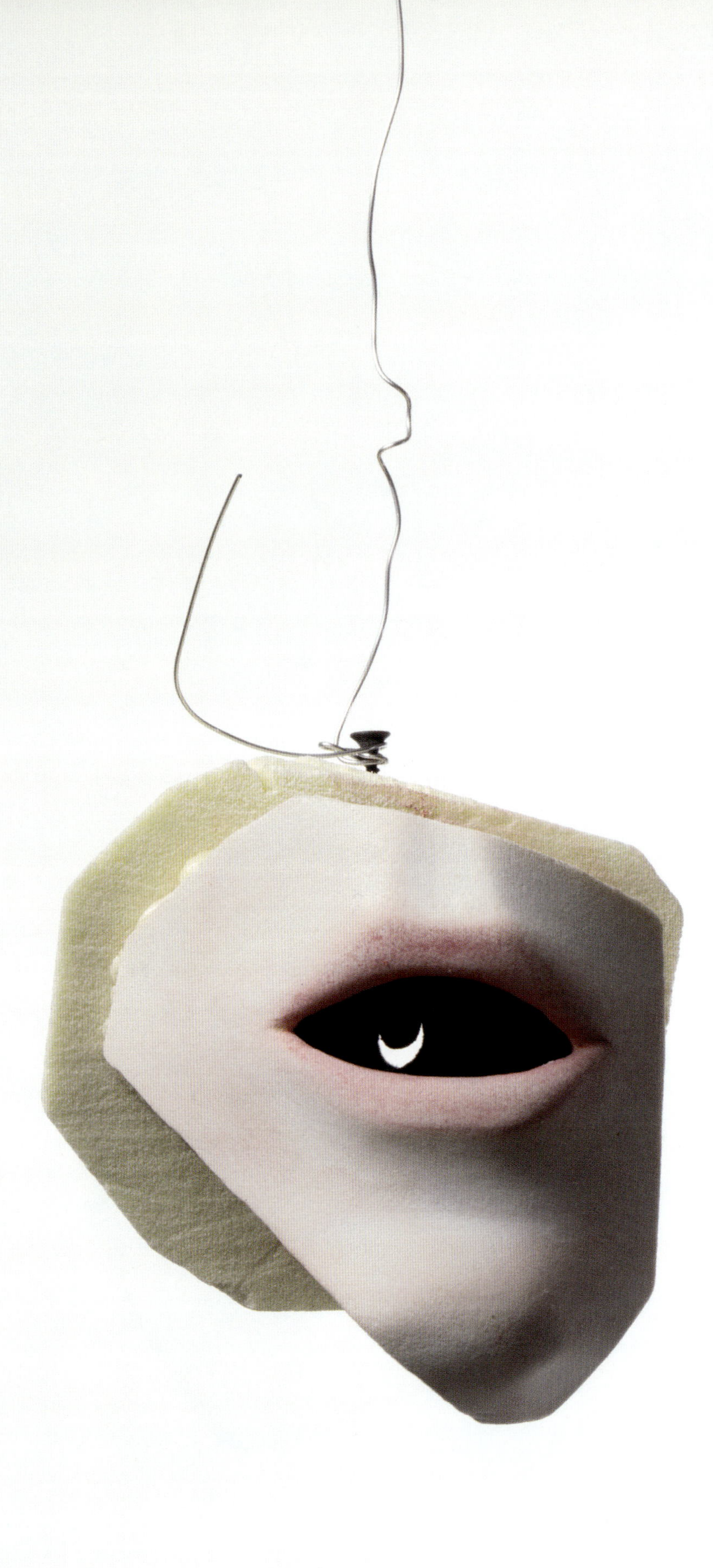

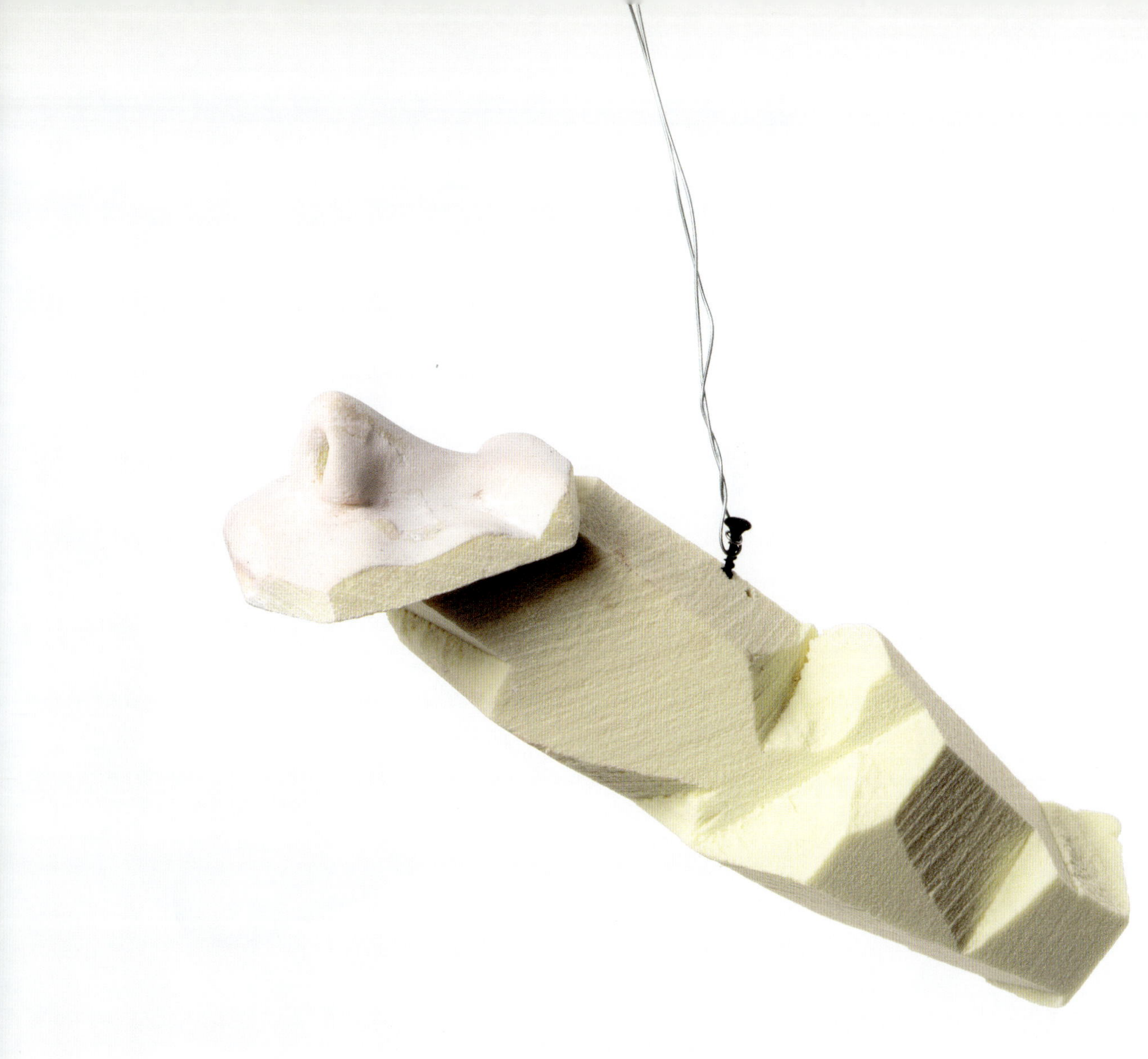

Previous and following pages:

Untitled (Holes), 2006

Carved polyurethane, plaster, acrylic paint, screws, wire
Ear: 5 ⅛ x 13 ⅜ x 3 ½ inches (13 x 34 x 9 cm)
Nose: 3 ⅛ x 12 ¼ x 3 ⅛ inches (8 x 31 x 8 cm)
Arse: 5 ⅞ x 7 ½ x 5 ⅛ inches (15 x 19 x 13 cm)
Willy: 2 ¾ x 13 ⅜ x 3 ½ inches (7 x 34 x 9 cm)
Mouth: 5 ⅞ x 13 x 5 ½ inches (15 x 33 x 14 cm)
Page 482, top: Installation view, Galerie Eva Presenhuber, Zurich, 2006
Paris 2006, 2006; *"Mr. Watson–come here–I want to see you.," 2005*

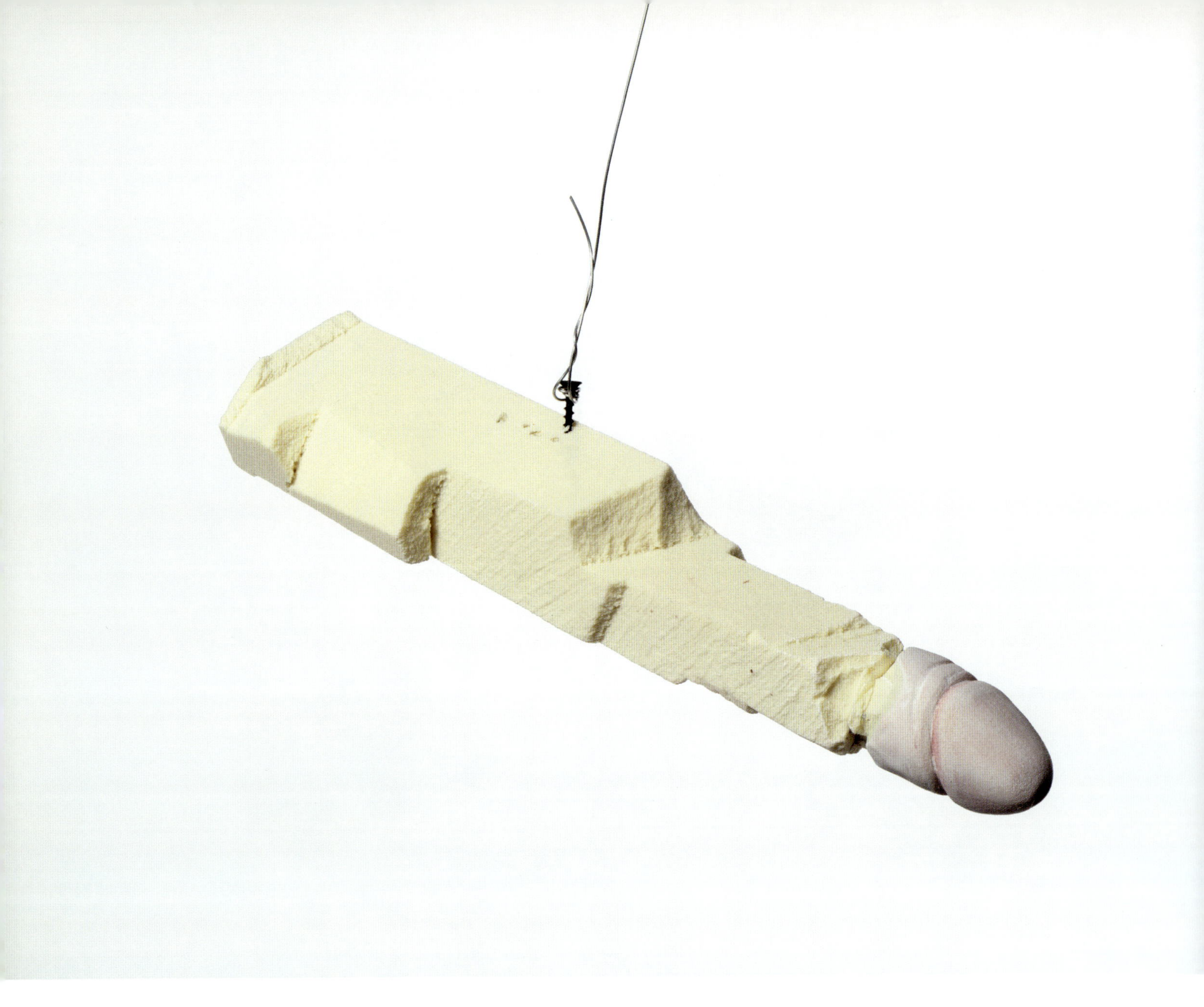

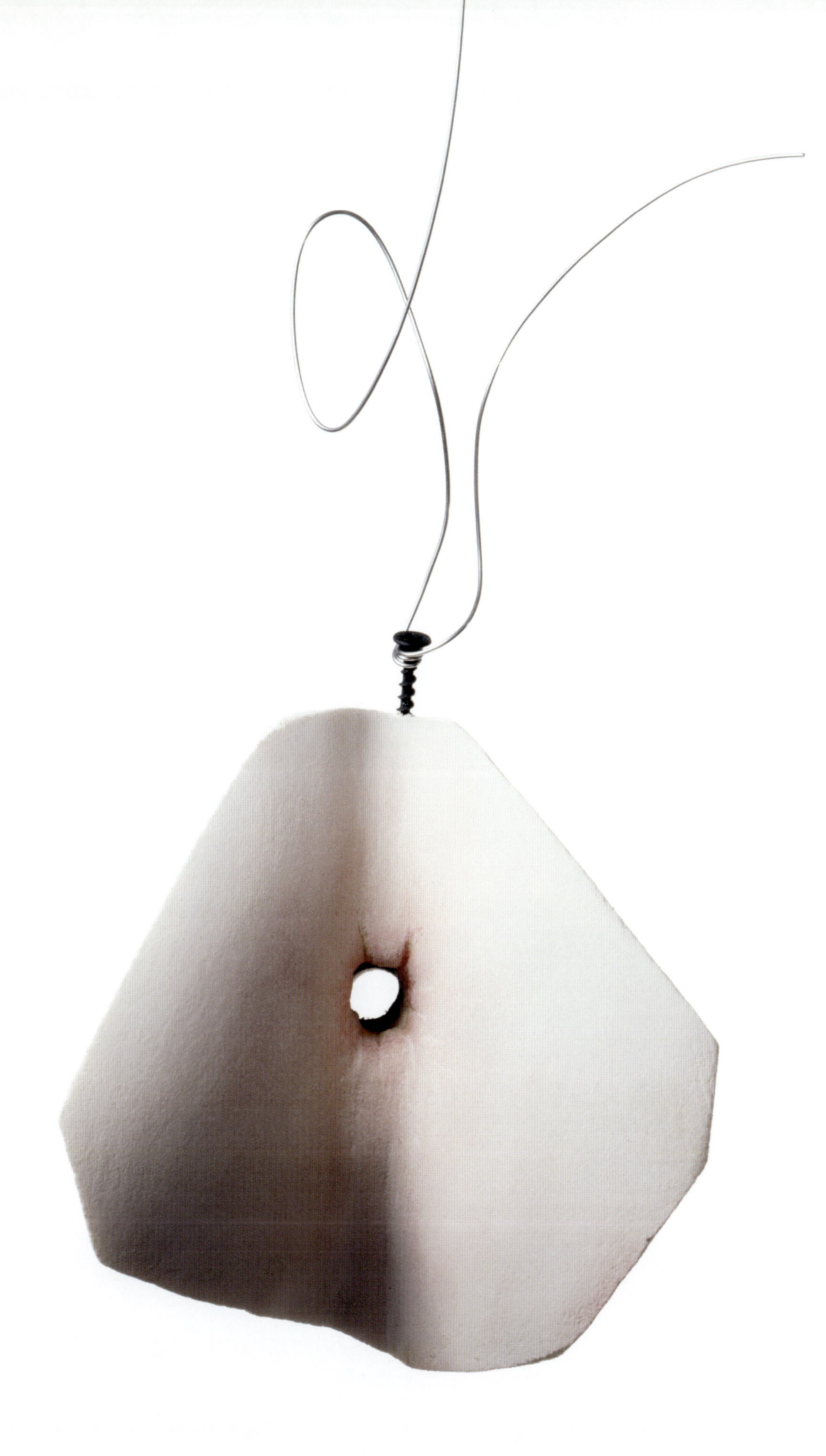

Noisette, 2009

Viewer's approach triggers tongue to emerge from hole

Hole in wall, silicone, motion sensor, electric motor, mechanism

Dimensions variable (smallest hole possible for mechanism to fit through)

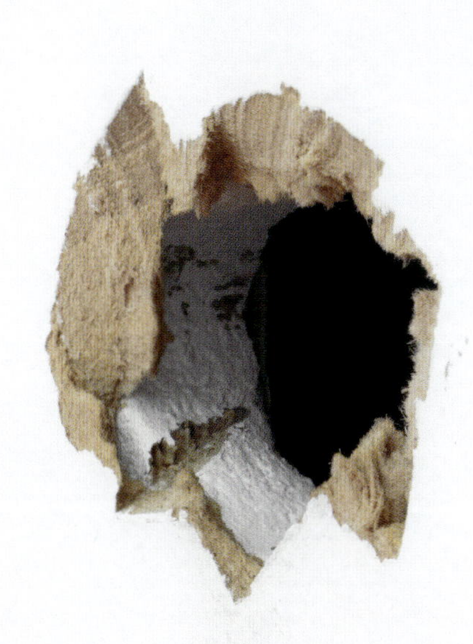

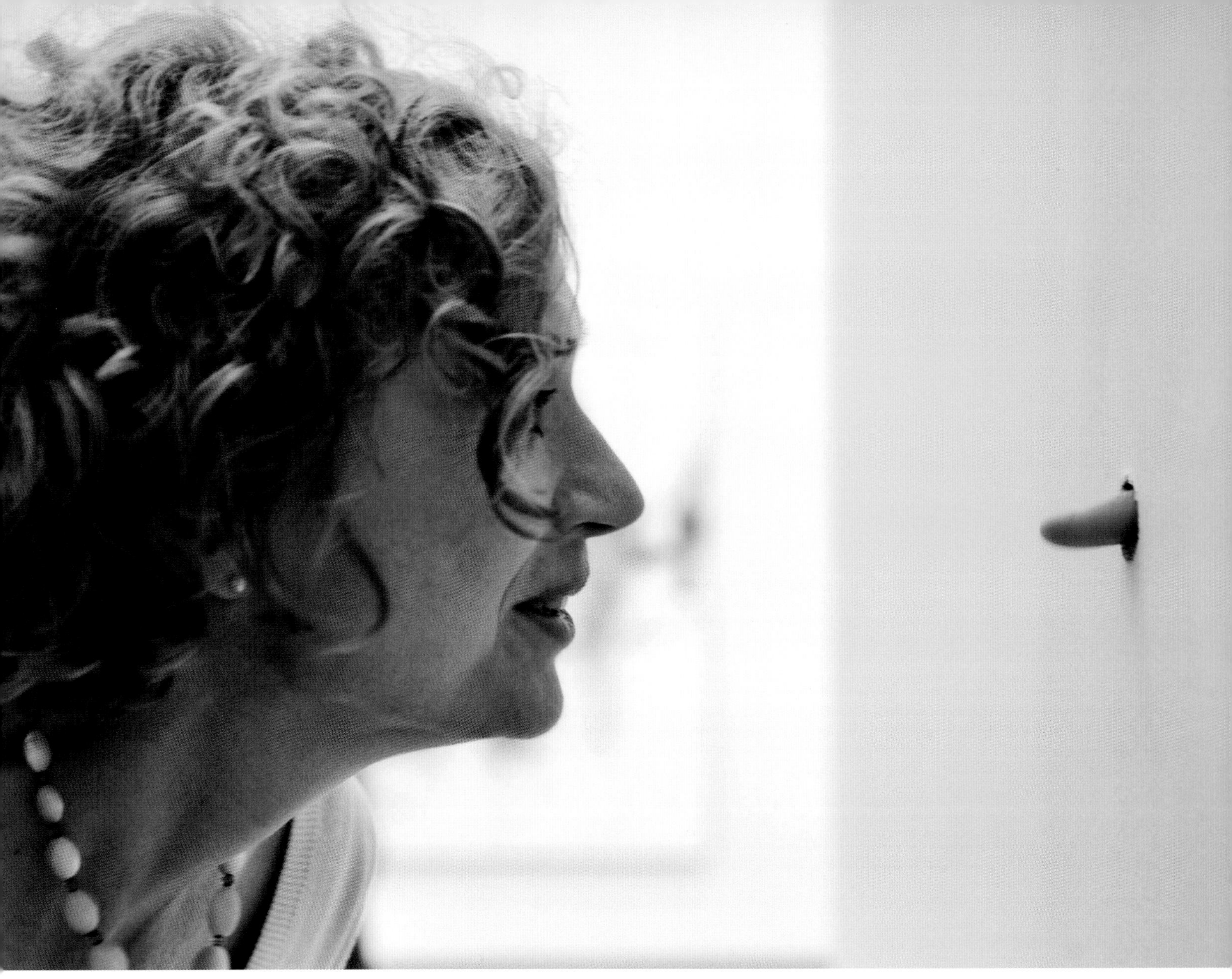

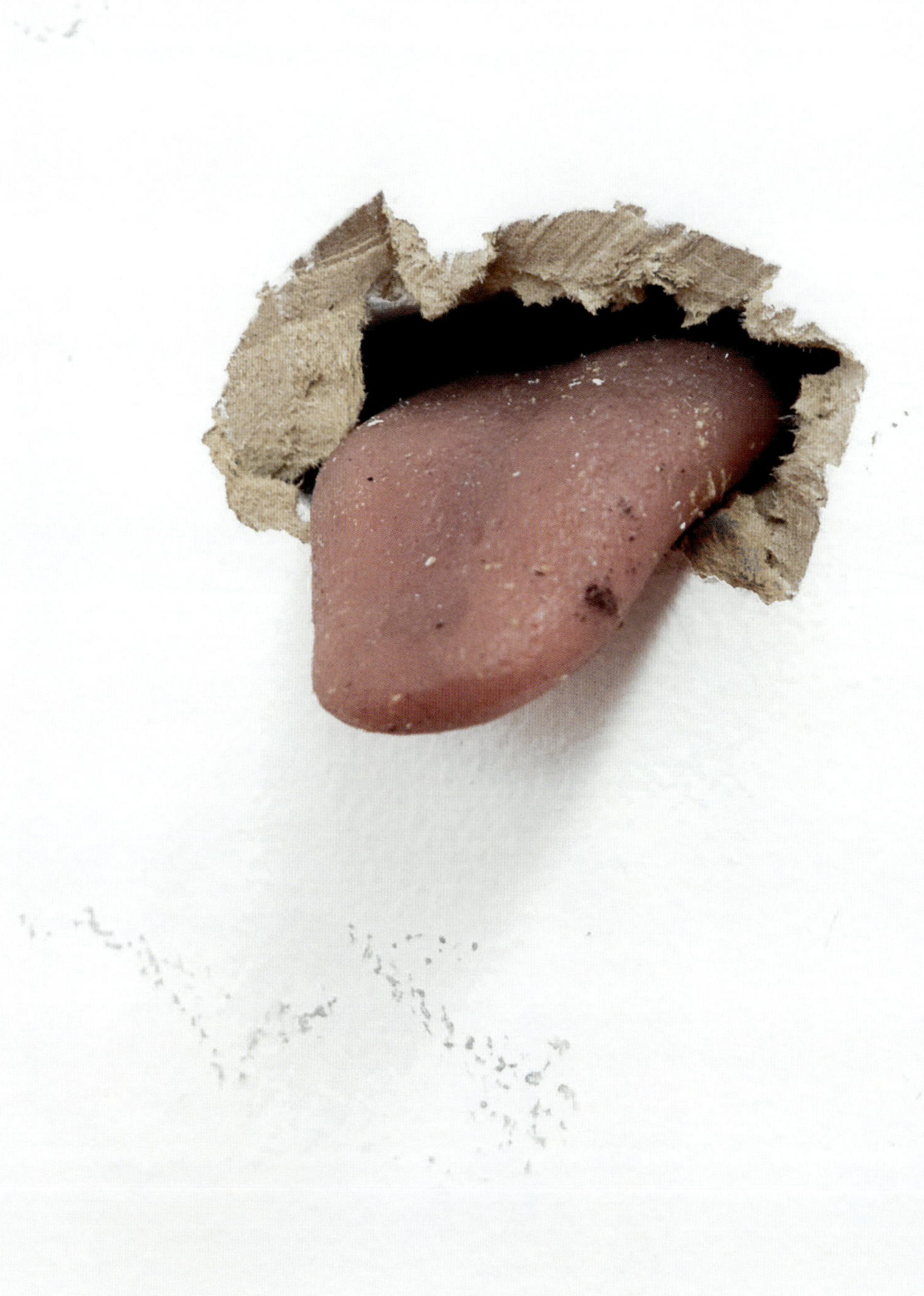

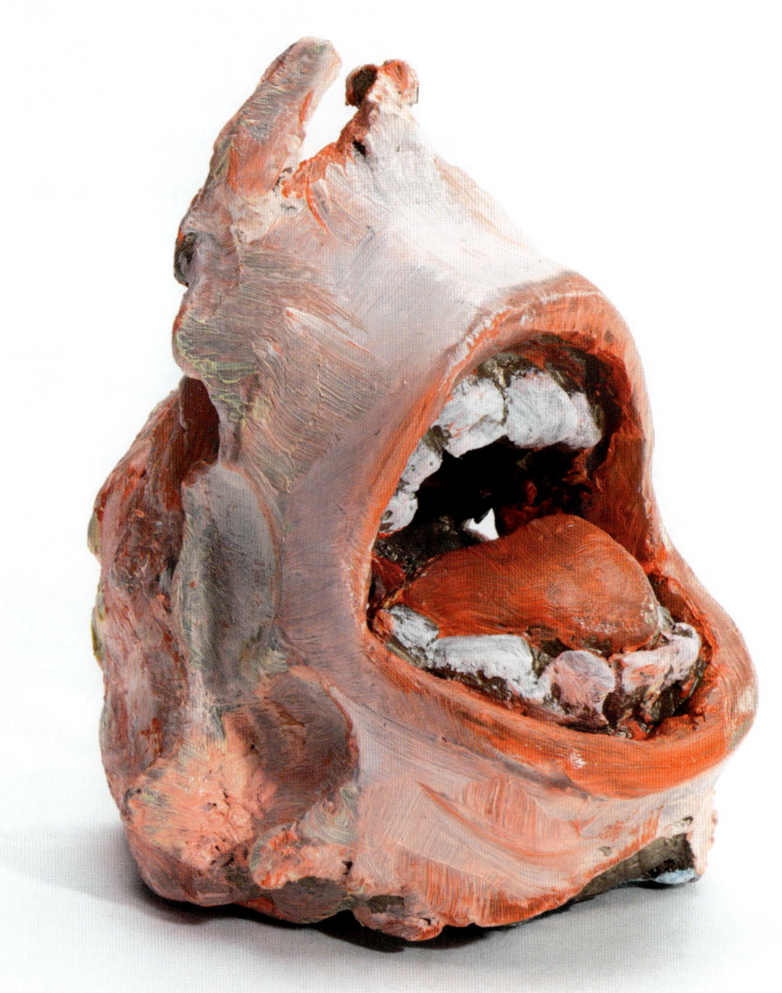

Mouth, 2011
Cast bronze, oil paint
3 ¾ x 3 ¼ x 2 ½ inches (9.5 x 8.3 x 6.3 cm)

Hands, 2002

Cast aluminum, wire, enamel paint

28 ¾ x 12 ⅝ x 7 ⅞ inches (73 x 32 x 20 cm)

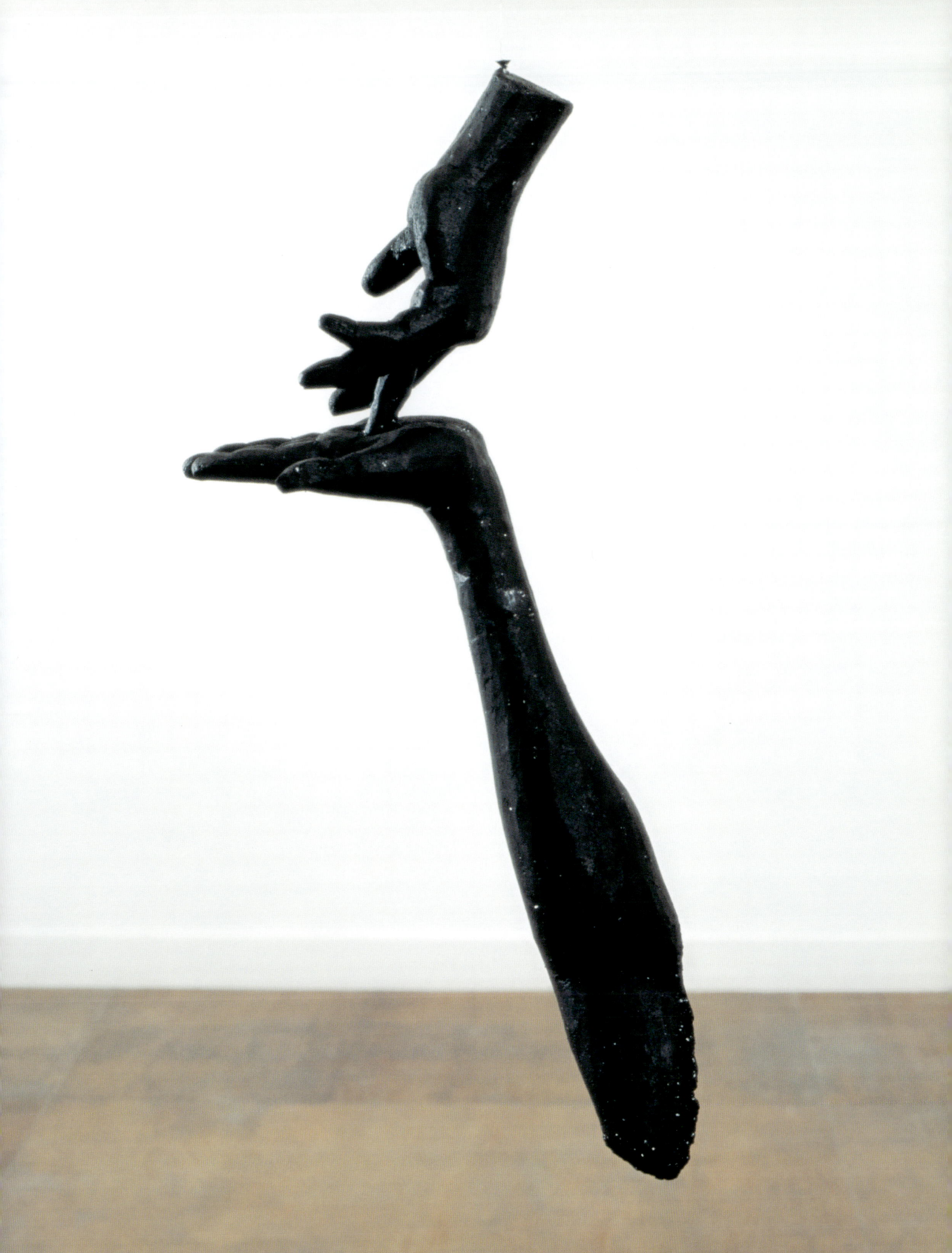

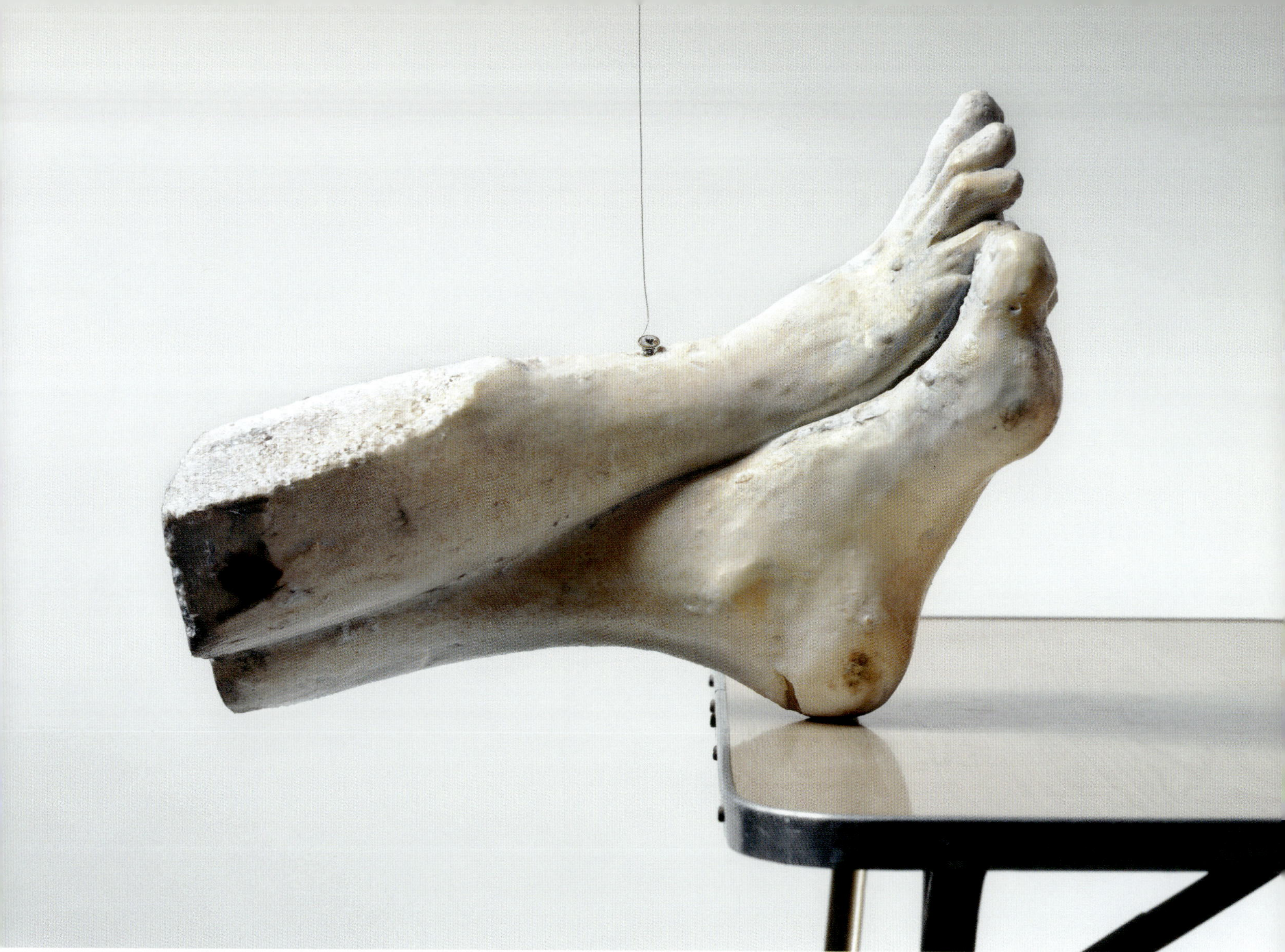

September Song, 2002
Polystyrene, glue, paint, wire, screw, marker
9 x 23 ⅝ x 4 inches (23 x 60 x 10 cm)

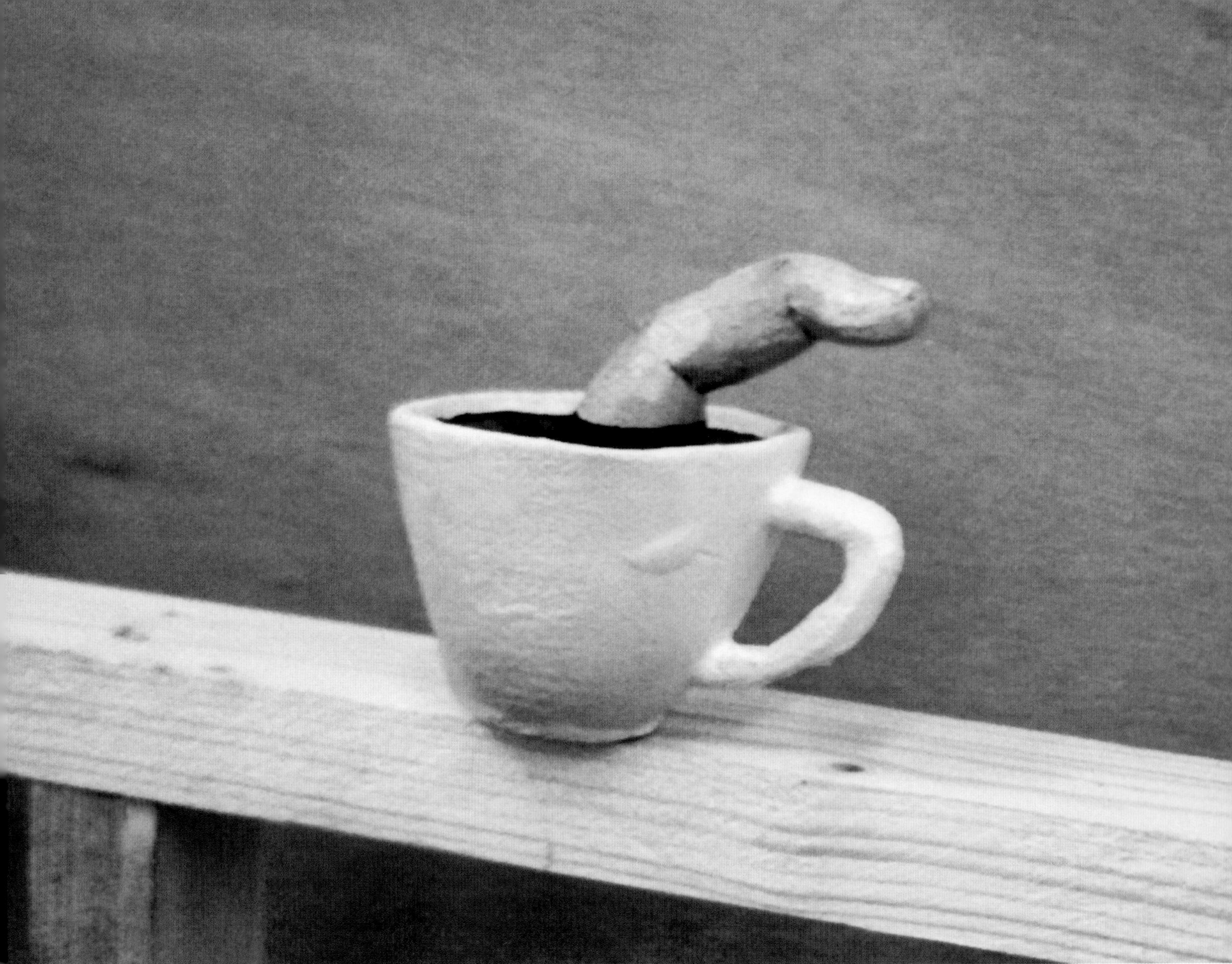

The Way You Move, 2003
Polystyrene, glue, acrylic paint, marker
4 ¾ x 3 ½ x 5 ⅛ inches (12 x 9 x 13 cm)

Opposite page:
Picky Eater, 2003
Polystyrene, polyurethane foam, acrylic paint, spray enamel, screws, glue
16 ⅛ x 5 ⅞ x 11 ⅜ inches (249 x 77.5 x 105 cm)

Following pages:
?, 2005
Polyurethane resin, two-component polyurethane foam, acrylic paint, wire, string, plaster, wood
69 x 20 x 14 ½ inches (175.3 x 50.8 x 36.8 cm)

Hand Lemon, 2006
Hydrocal, acrylic paint, polyurethane glue, hair
7 ¼ x 7 ¼ x 7 ⅛ inches (18.4 x 18.4 x 18.1 cm)

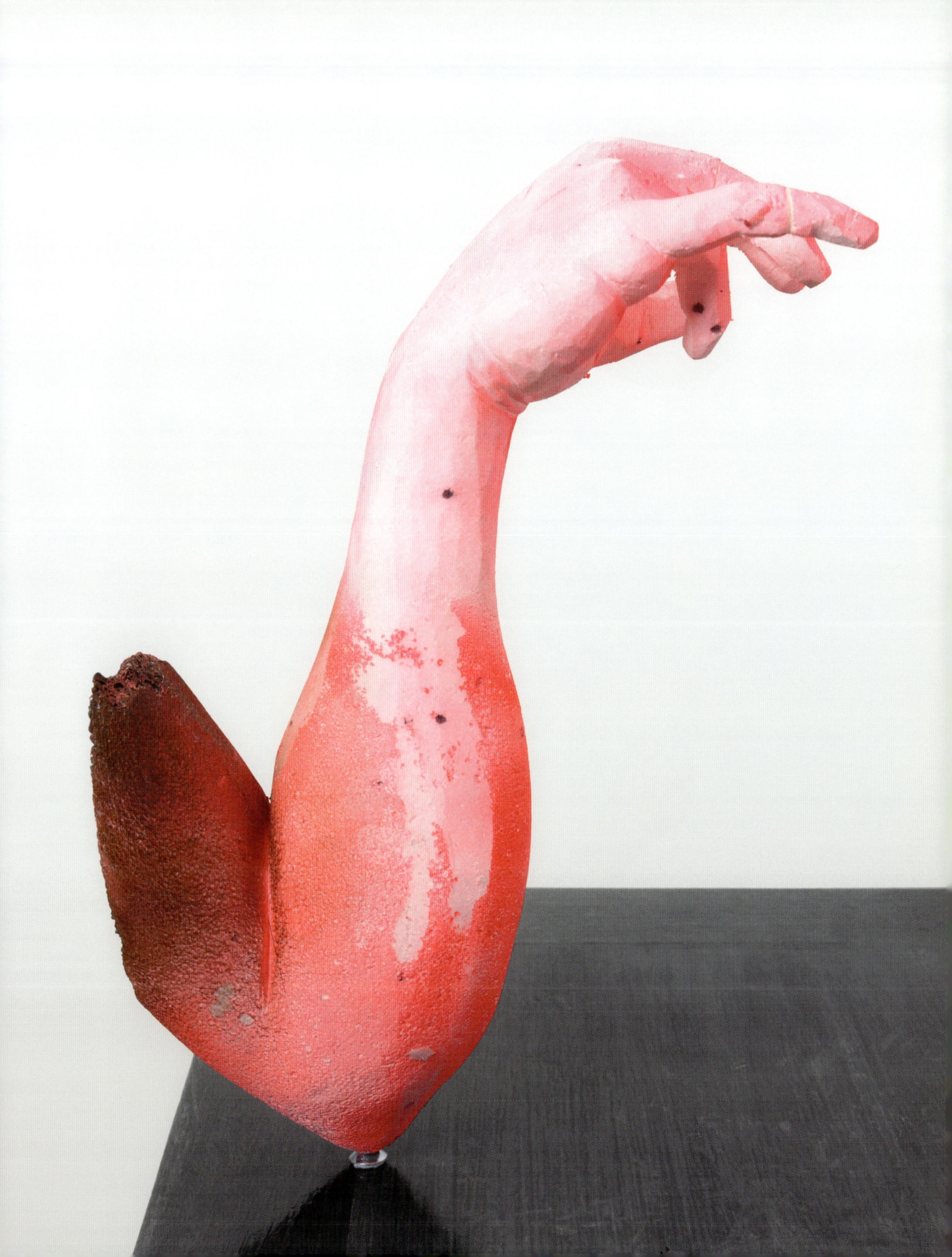

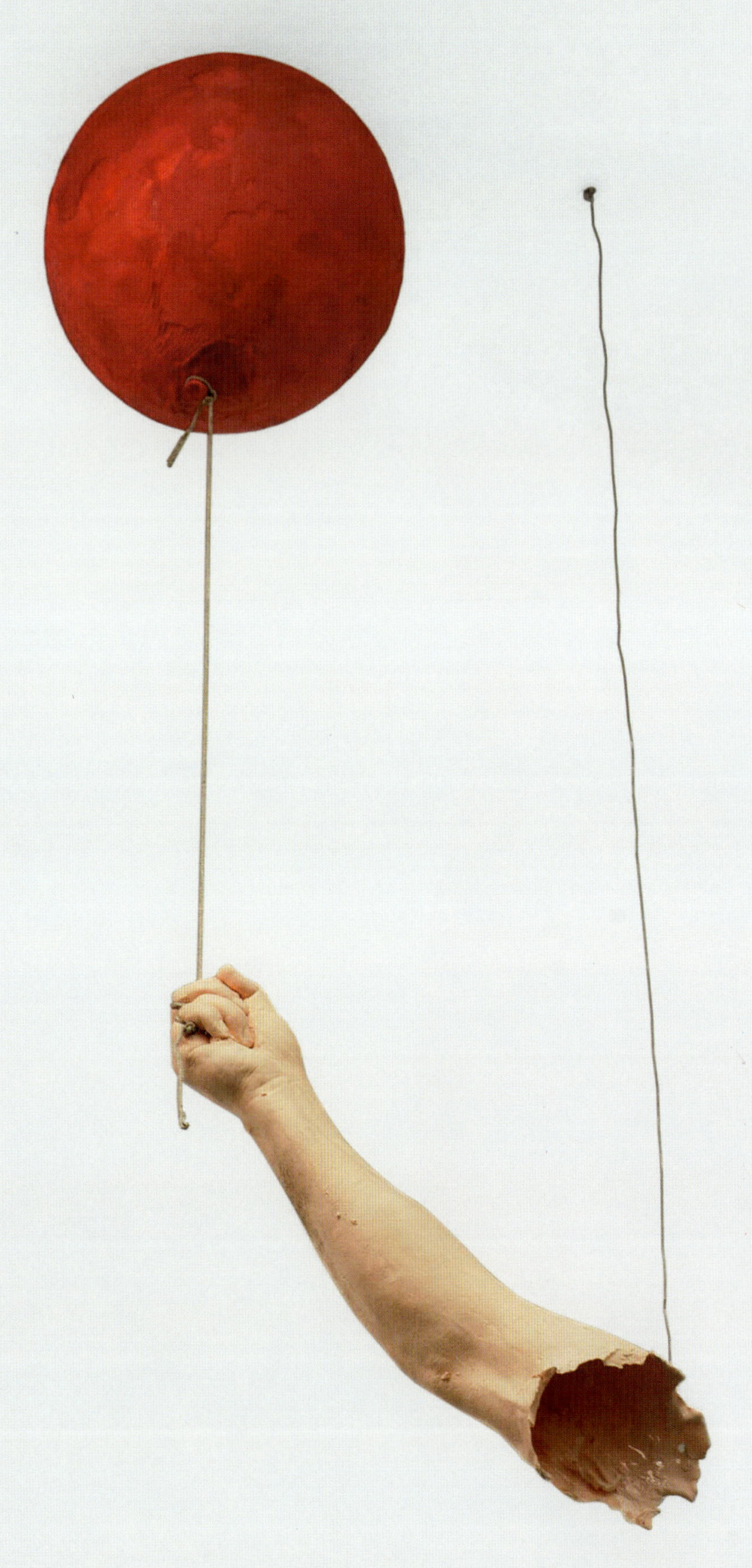

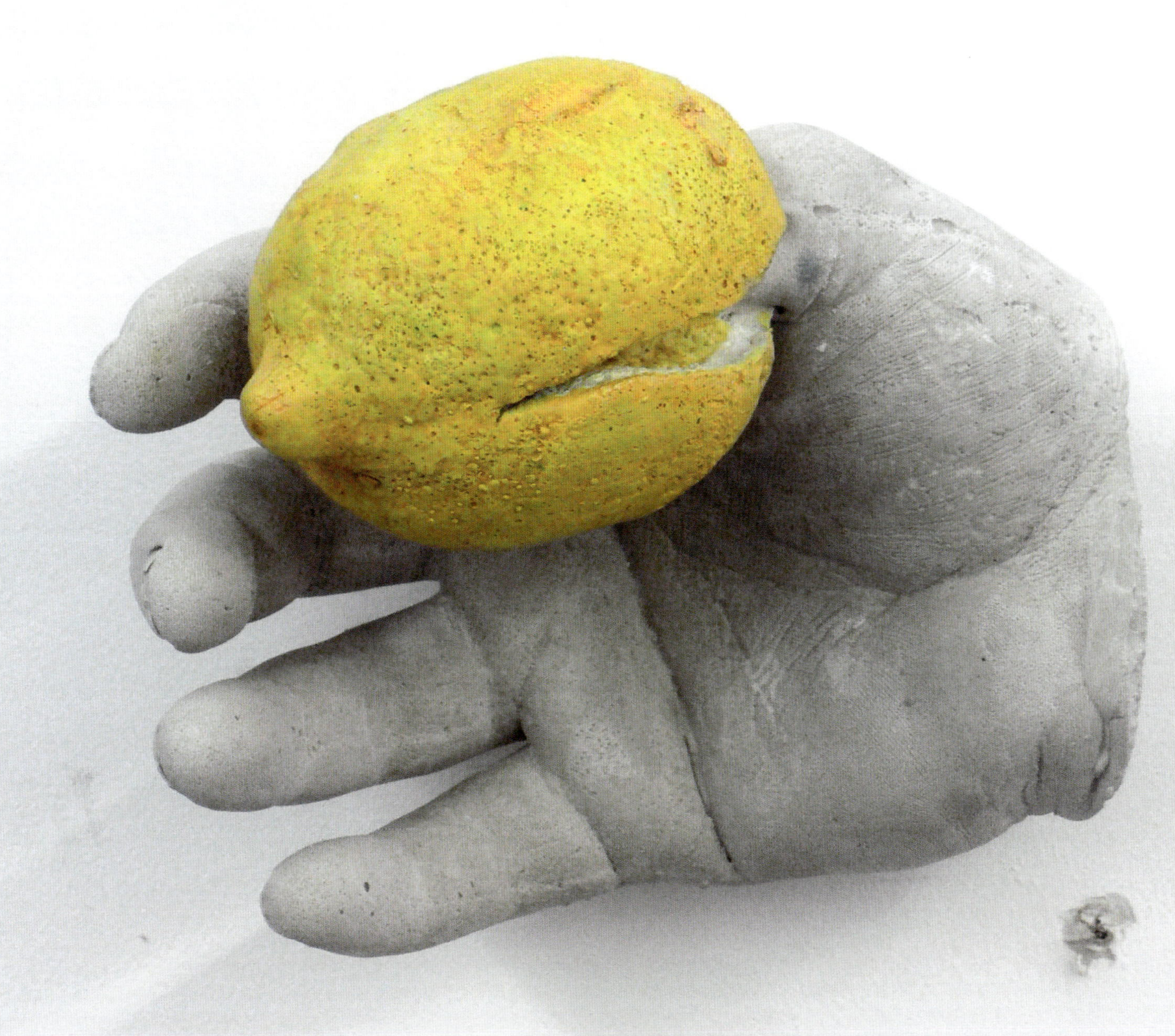

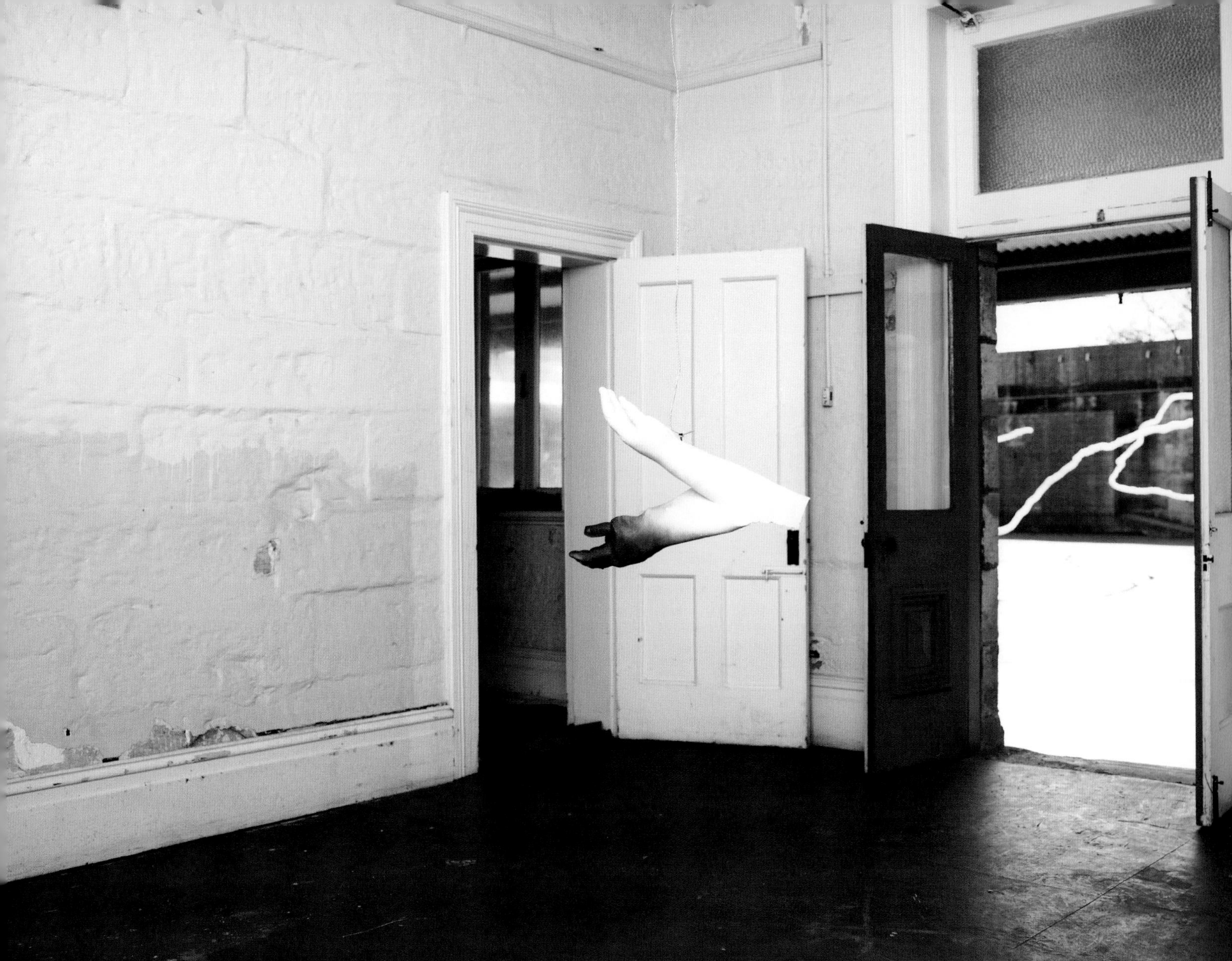

Imaginary Pain, 2007
Cast plaster, screws, enamel paint
23 ⅝ x 23 ⅝ x 7 ⅞ inches (60 x 60 x 20 cm)
Installation view, Cockatoo Island, Kaldor Art Projects and the Sydney Harbour Federation Trust, Sydney, 2007

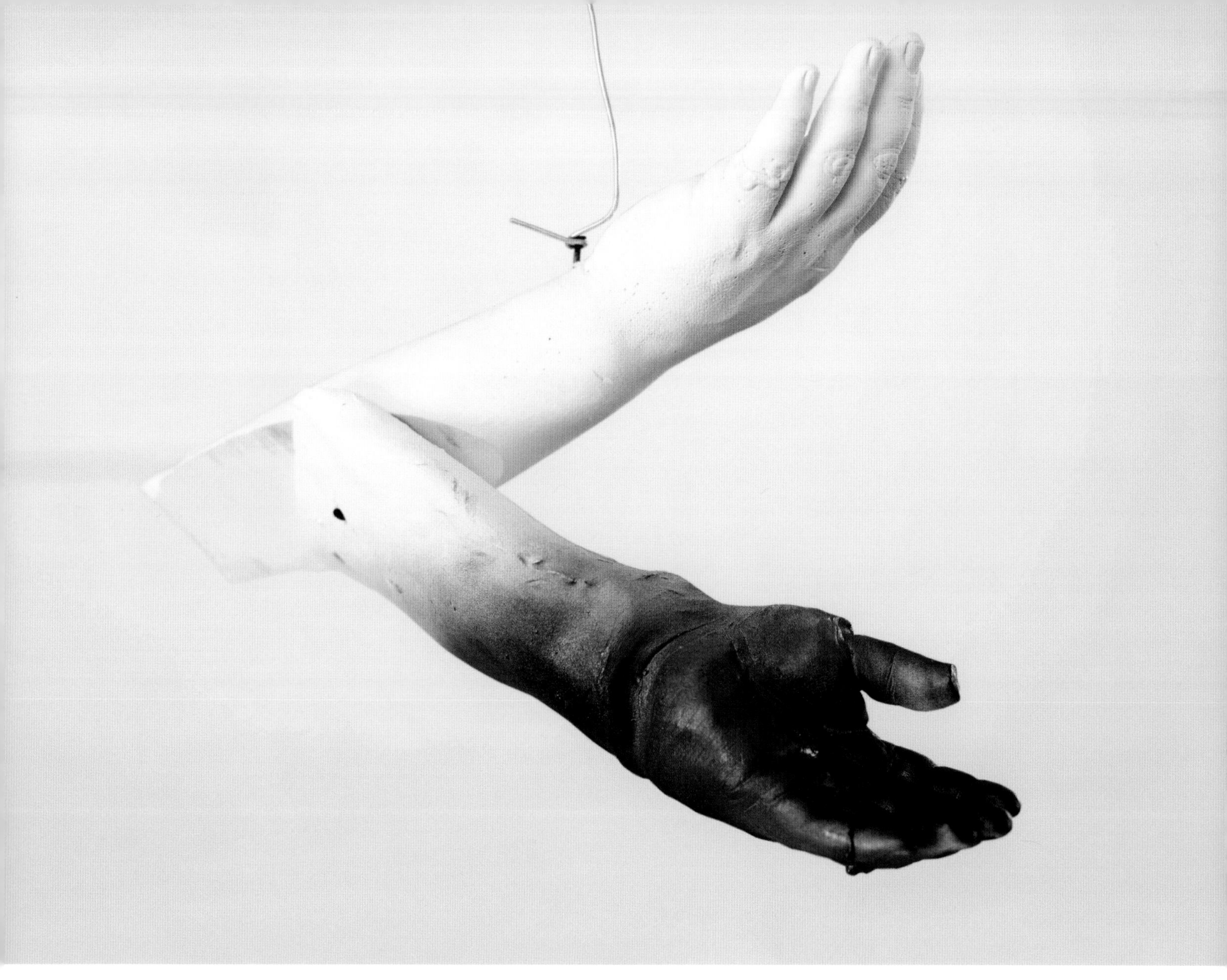

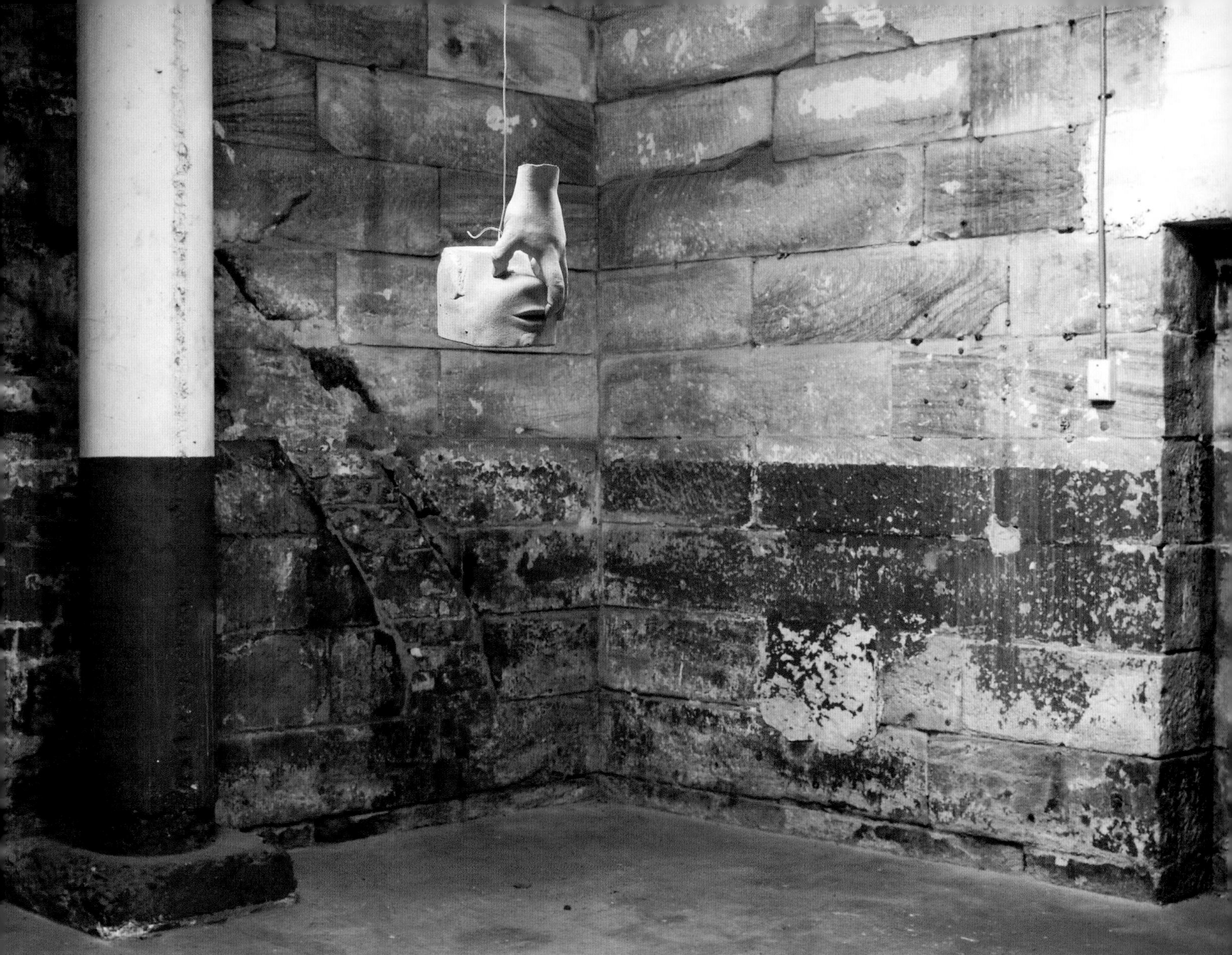

Old Pain, 2007
Plaster, pigment, screw, polyurethane glue, wire
10 ¼ x 9 ⅞ x 6 inches (26 x 25 x 15 cm)

Following pages:

Airports Are Like Nightclubs, 2005
Figure runs its fingers through its hair every few minutes
Mechanical robot, silicone, pigment, wig
Sculpture: 26 x 14 x 31 inches (66 x 35.5 x 78.7 cm)
Pedestal: 33 x 25 x 21 inches (83.8 x 63.5 x 53.3 cm)
Page 506: Installation view, "Paris 1919,"
Museum Boijmans Van Beuningen, Rotterdam, 2006
Untitled (Bread House), 2004–2006

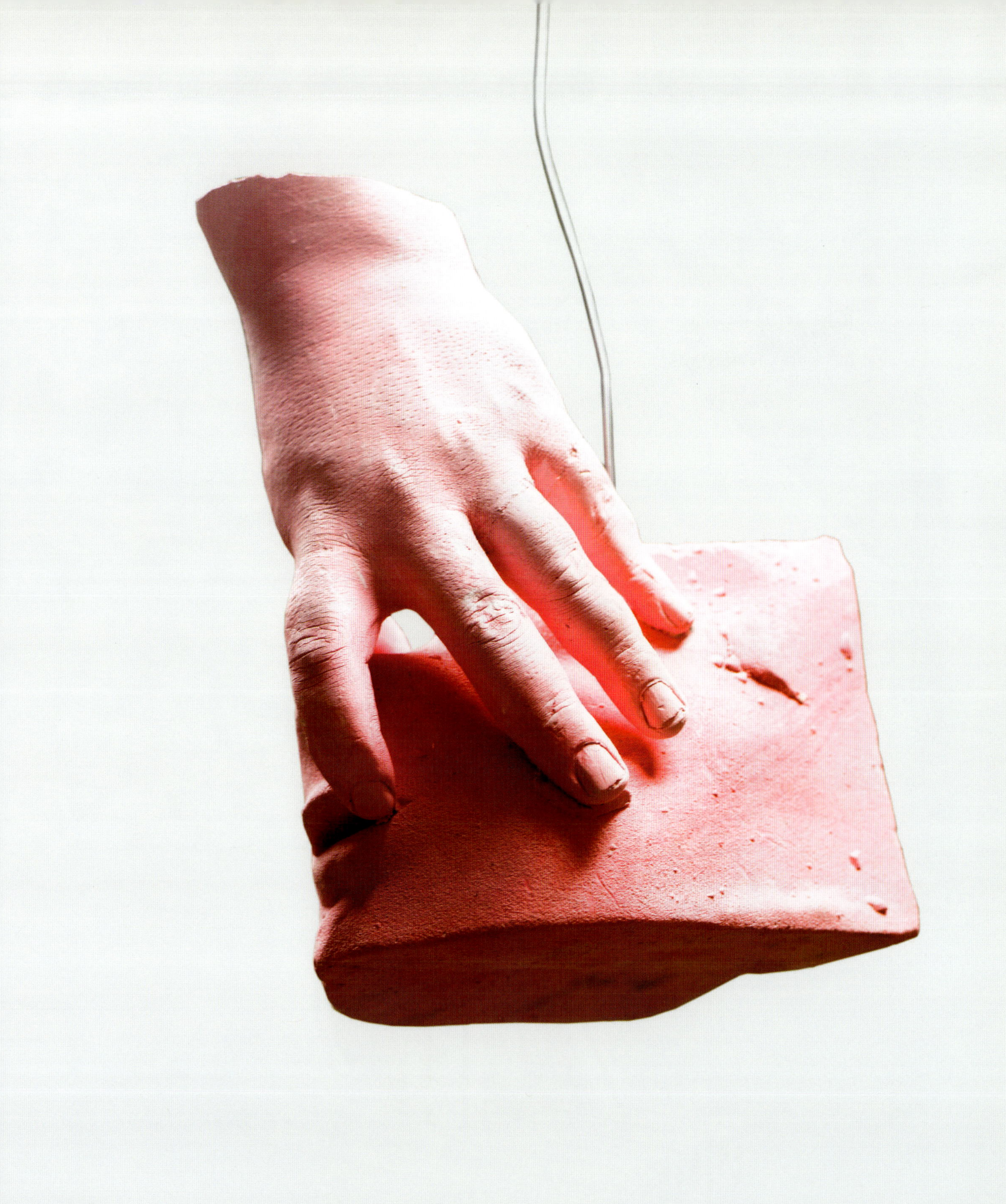

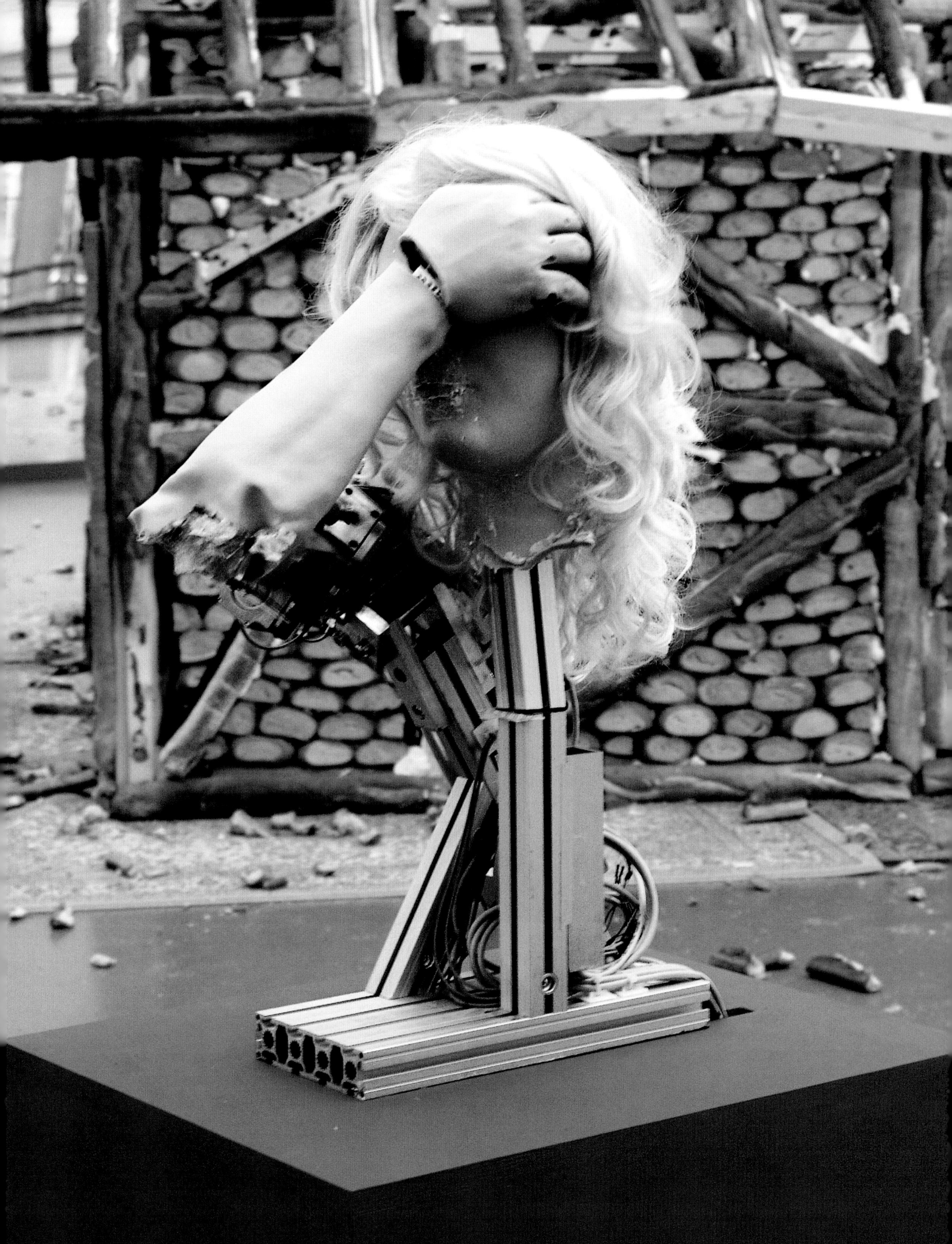

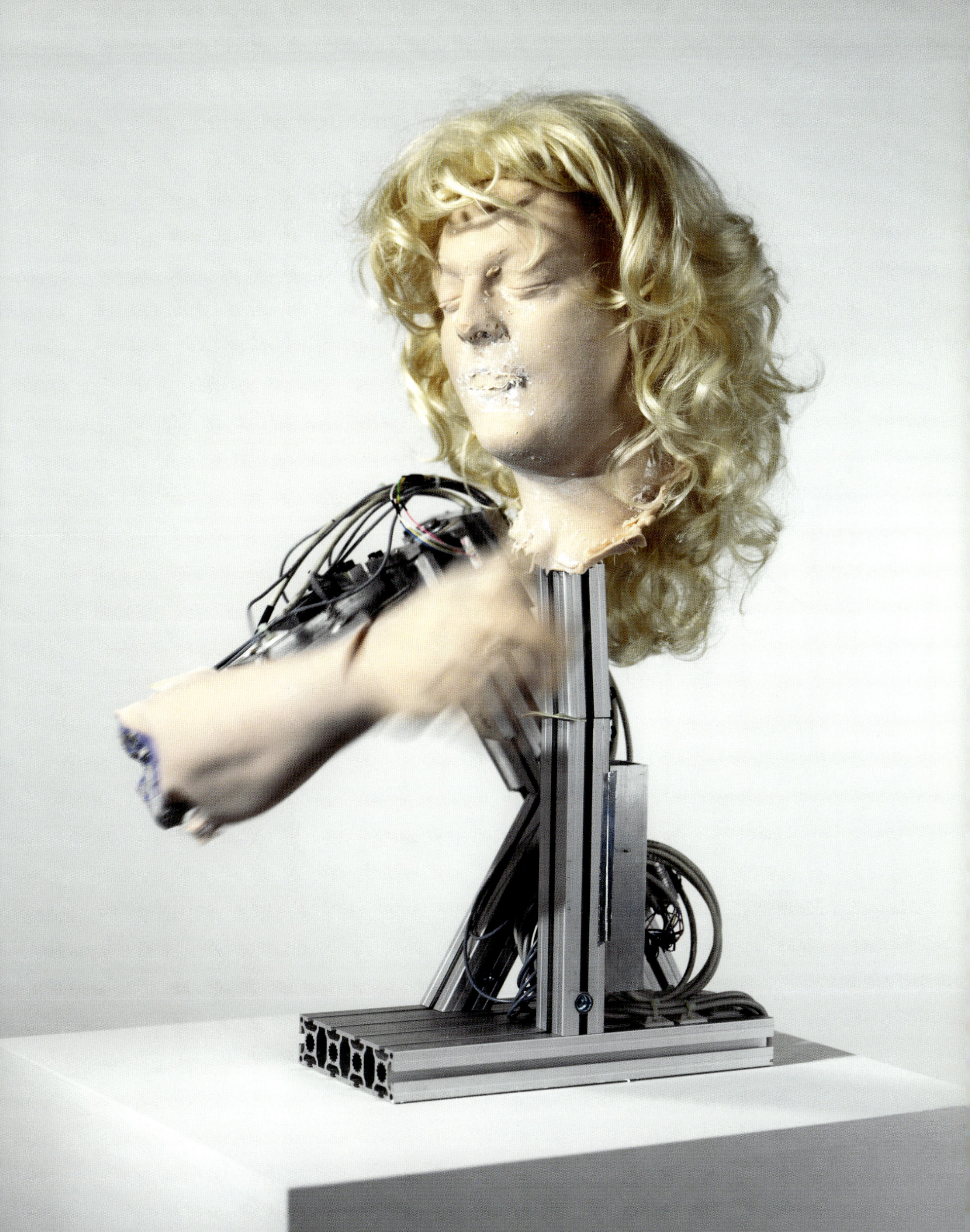

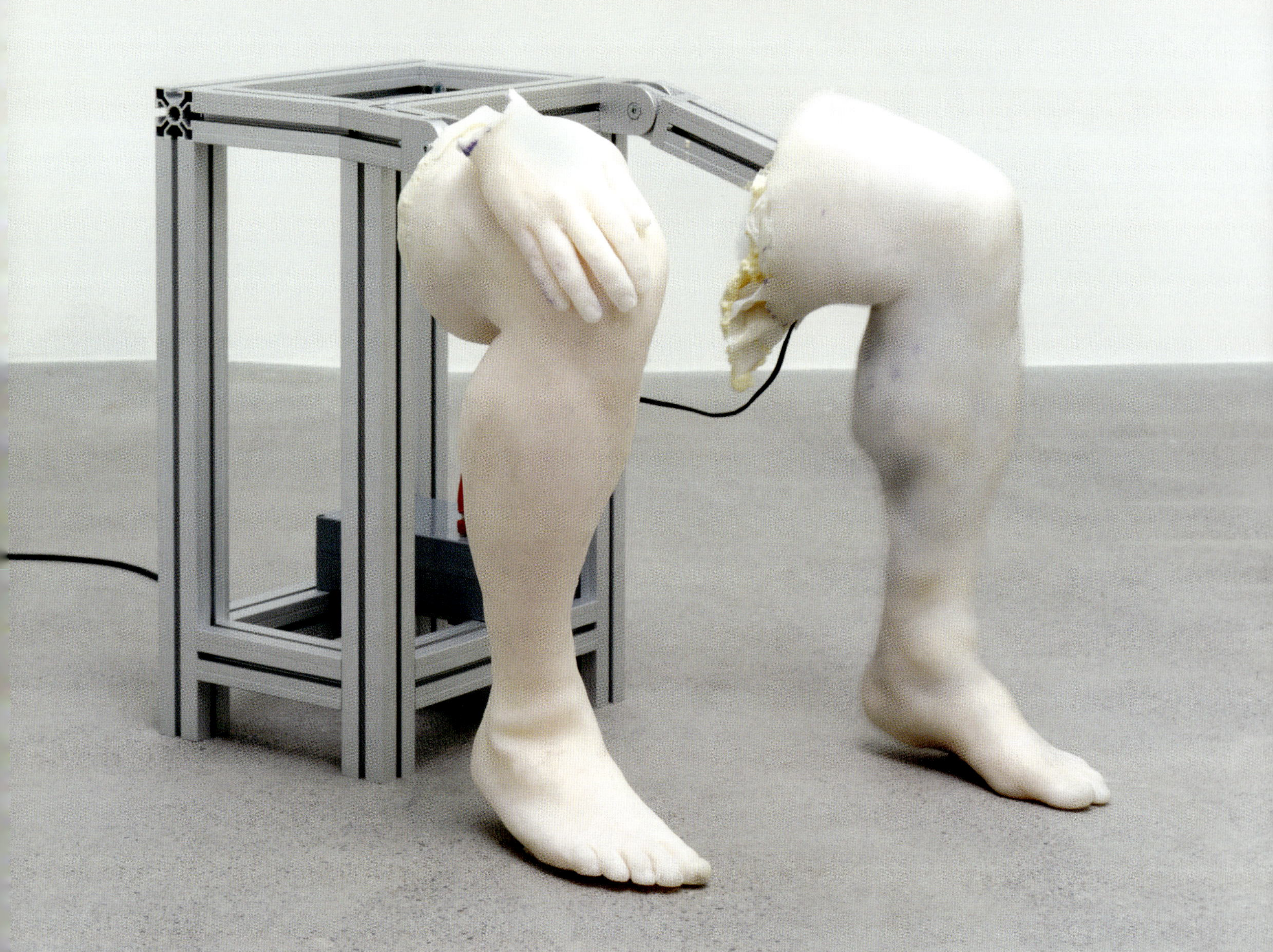

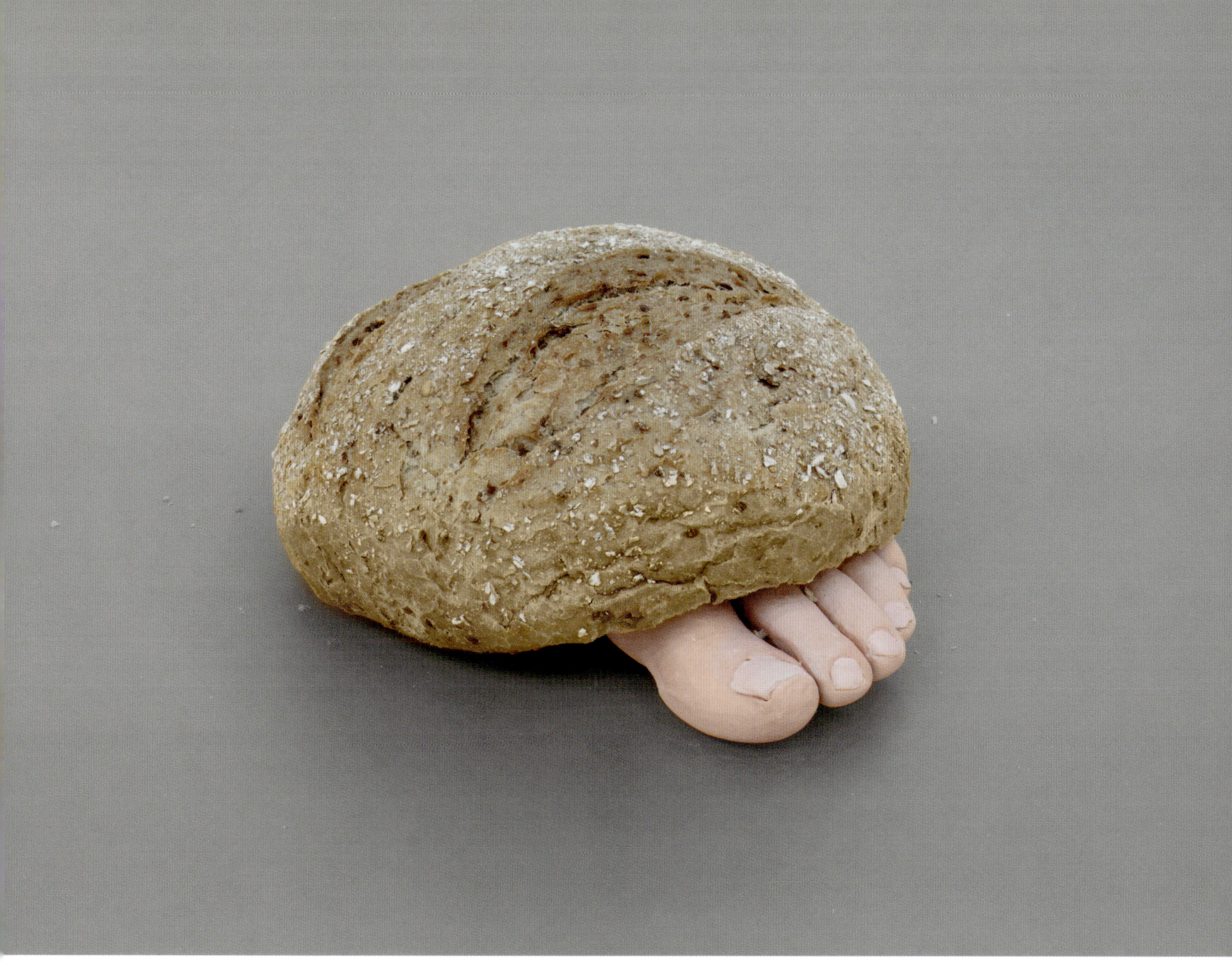

Untitled, 2009
Plaster, acrylic paint, bread
3 ⅞ x 8 ¼ x 5 ⅞ inches (10 x 21 x 15 cm)

Opposite page:
Paris 2006, 2006
Left leg jitters impatiently
Two-component polyurethane foam, polyurethane foam, cardboard, tape, acrylic paint, imitation leather, brass pins
38 ¼ x 33 ½ x 35 ⅞ inches (97 x 85 x 91 cm)

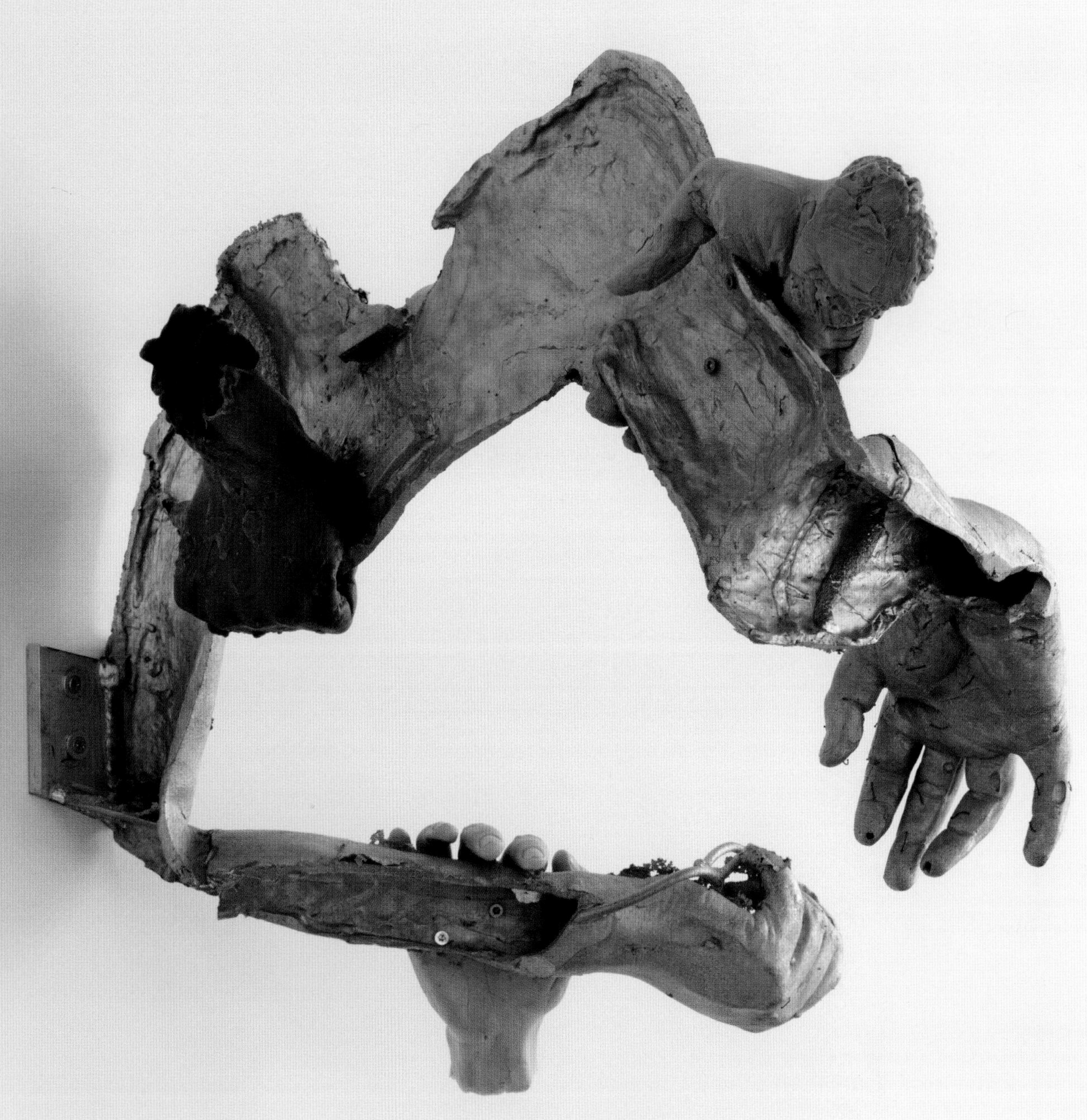

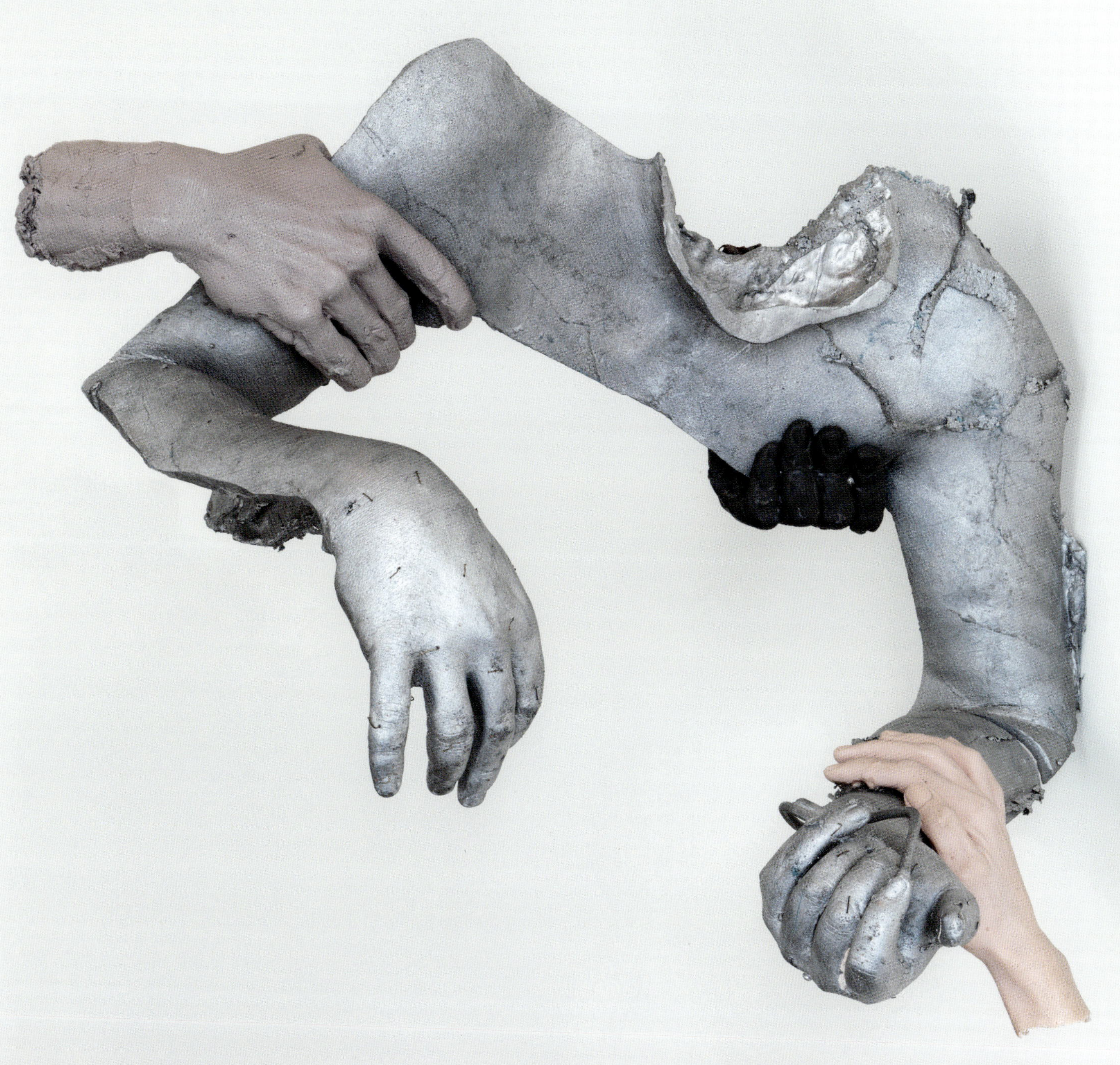

Untitled, 2010
Plaster, eggshell, three-component polyurethane, metal pin, epoxy adhesive, acrylic gesso
7 x 6 ½ x 8 inches (17.8 x 16.5 x 20.3 cm)

Previous pages:

The Grass Munchers, 2007
Cast aluminum, pigments and wax
22 x 24 ⅜ x 17 ⅜ inches (56 x 62 x 44 cm)

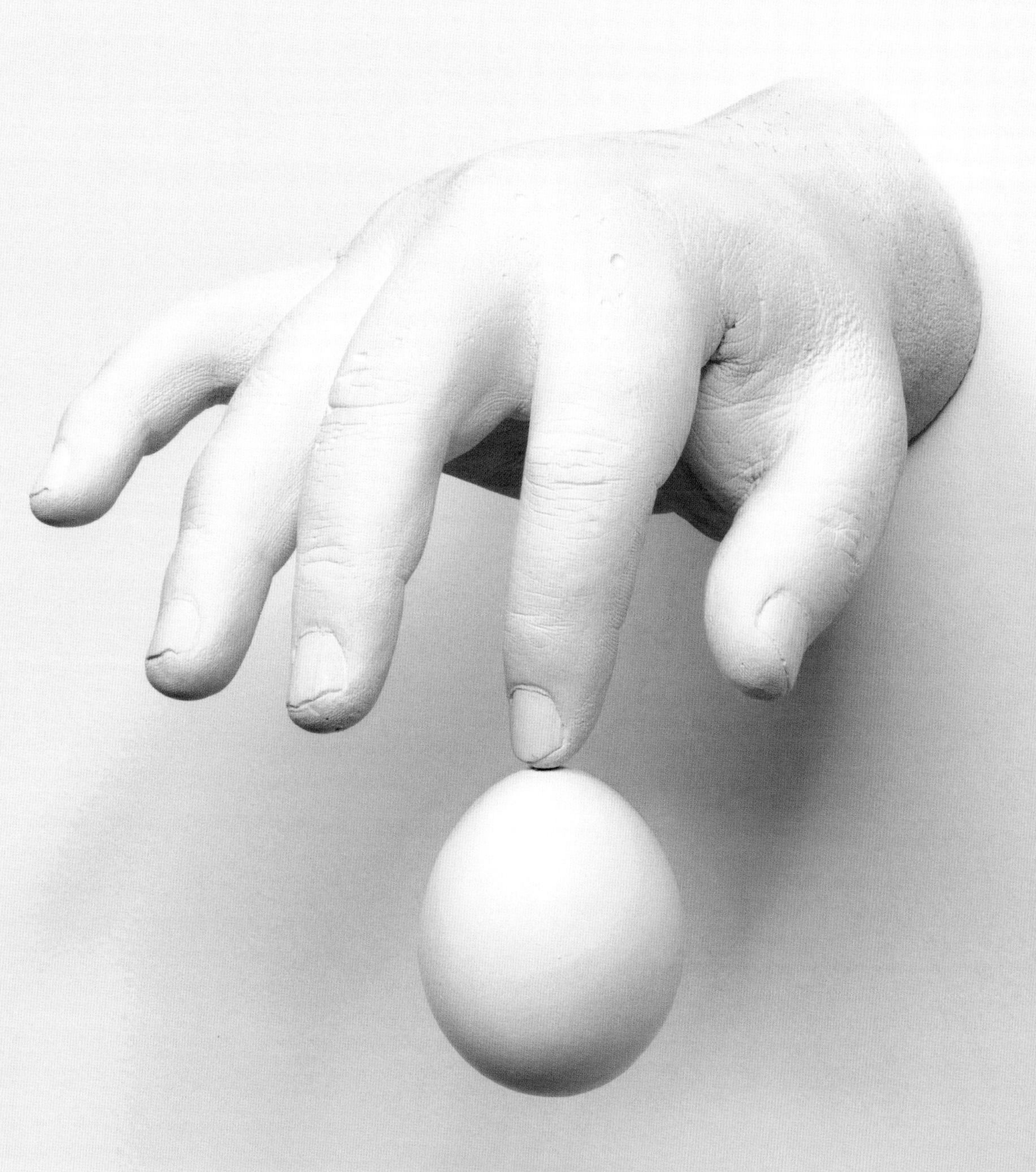

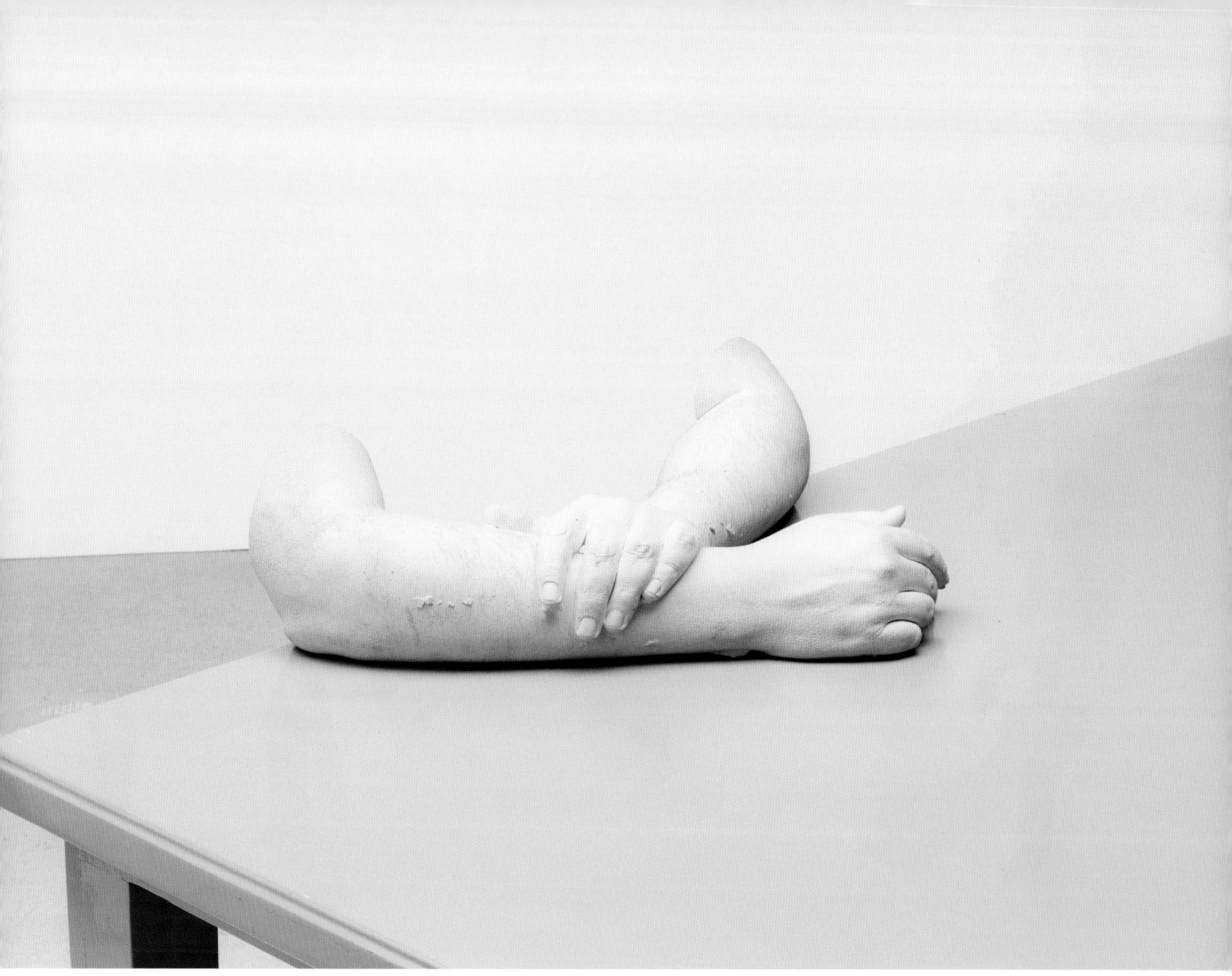

Lee Friedlander, 2012
Plaster, arm hair
5 ¾ x 21 ¼ x 13 ½ inches (14.6 x 54 x 34.3 cm)

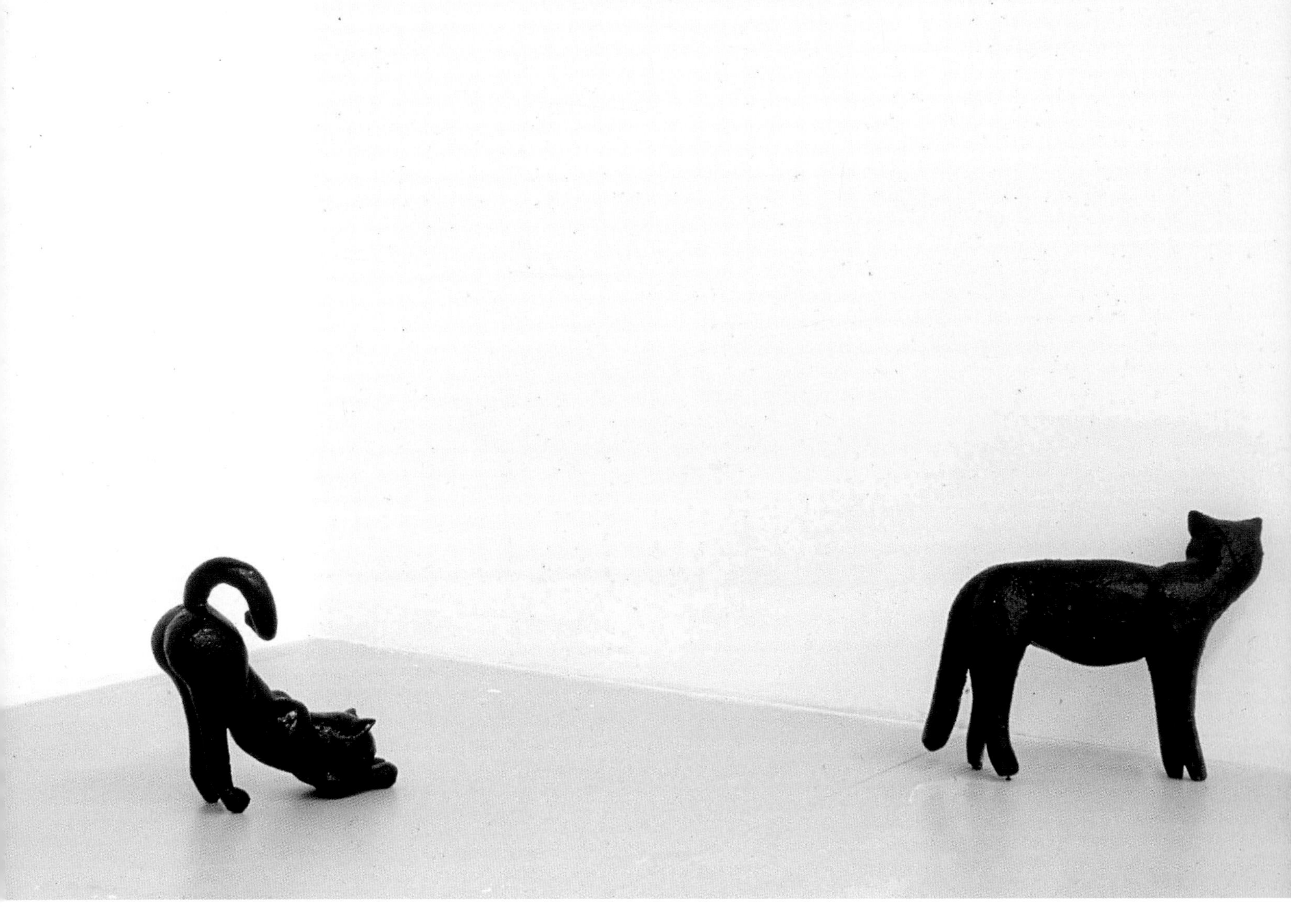

The Cat with the Broken Leg or
The Cat Who Laid the Golden Egg, 2000
Polystyrene, plaster, oil paint, acrylic paint, filler, screws
Crouching cat: 11 x 12 x 5 inches (27.9 x 30.5 x 12.7 cm)
Standing cat: 7 x 12 x 5 inches (17.8 x 30.5 x 12.7 cm)

Opposite page:
Skyline, 2002
Cast bronze, acrylic paint
11 x 17 ½ x 19 ¼ inches (28 x 44.5 x 49 cm)

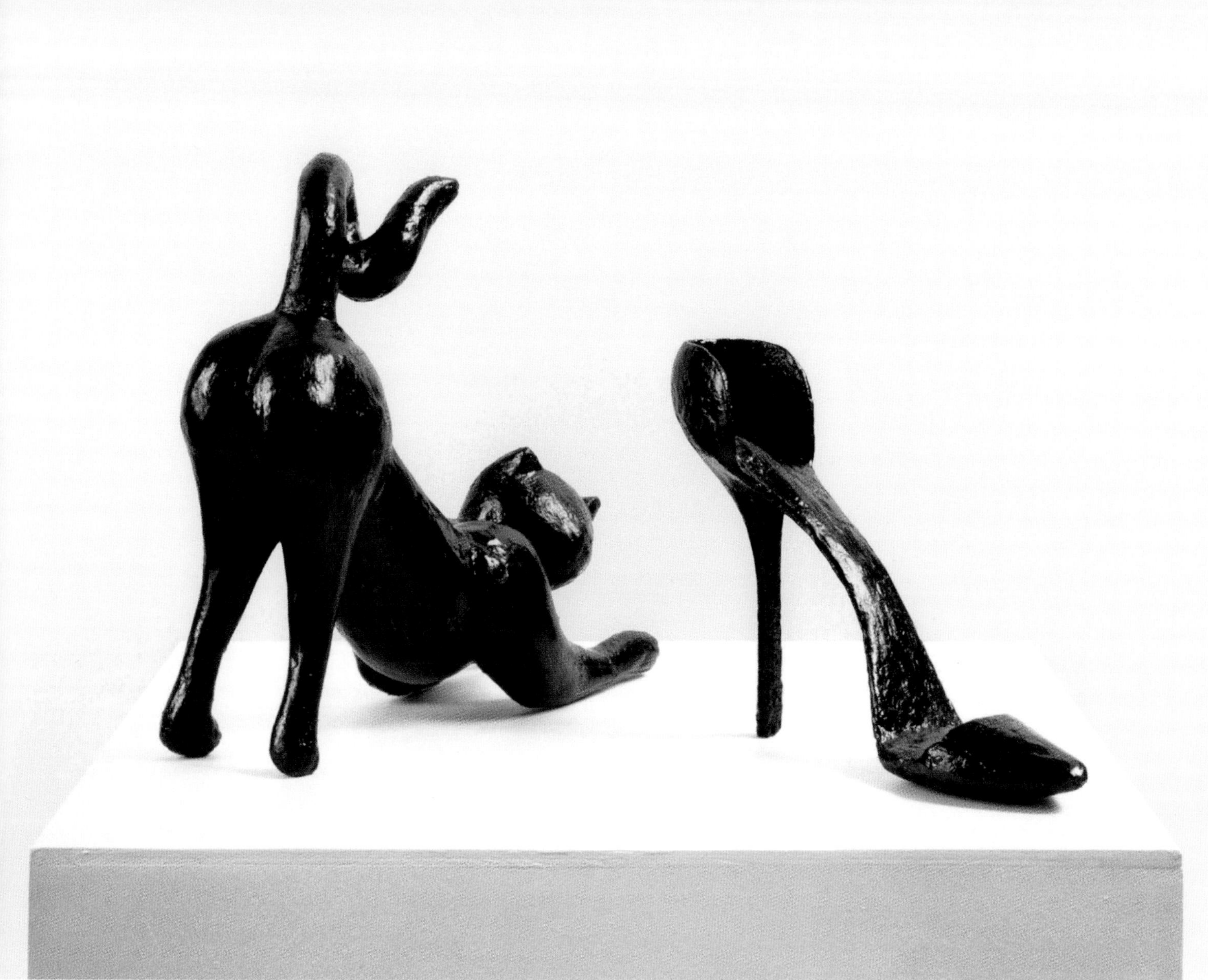

Cappillon, 2000

Wood, plaster, polystyrene, filler, latex paint, glass, cast tin

45 ¼ x 35 ⅜ x 67 ¾ inches (115 x 90 x 172 cm)

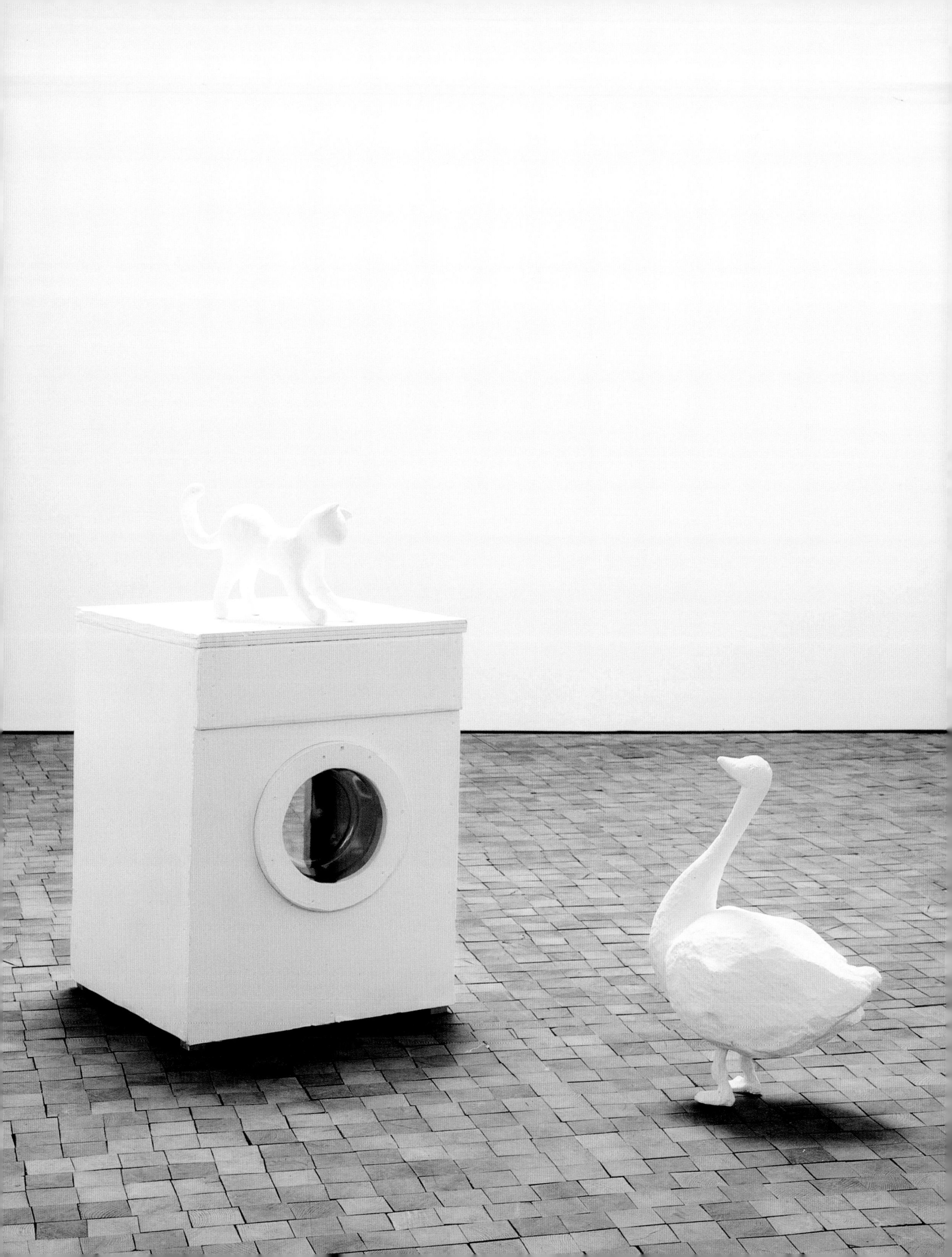

Walking Heads / Thinking Feet, 2002
Polystyrene, polyurethane foam, acrylic paint, latex paint, screws
22 x 7 ½ x 5 ⅞ inches (56 x 19 x 15 cm)

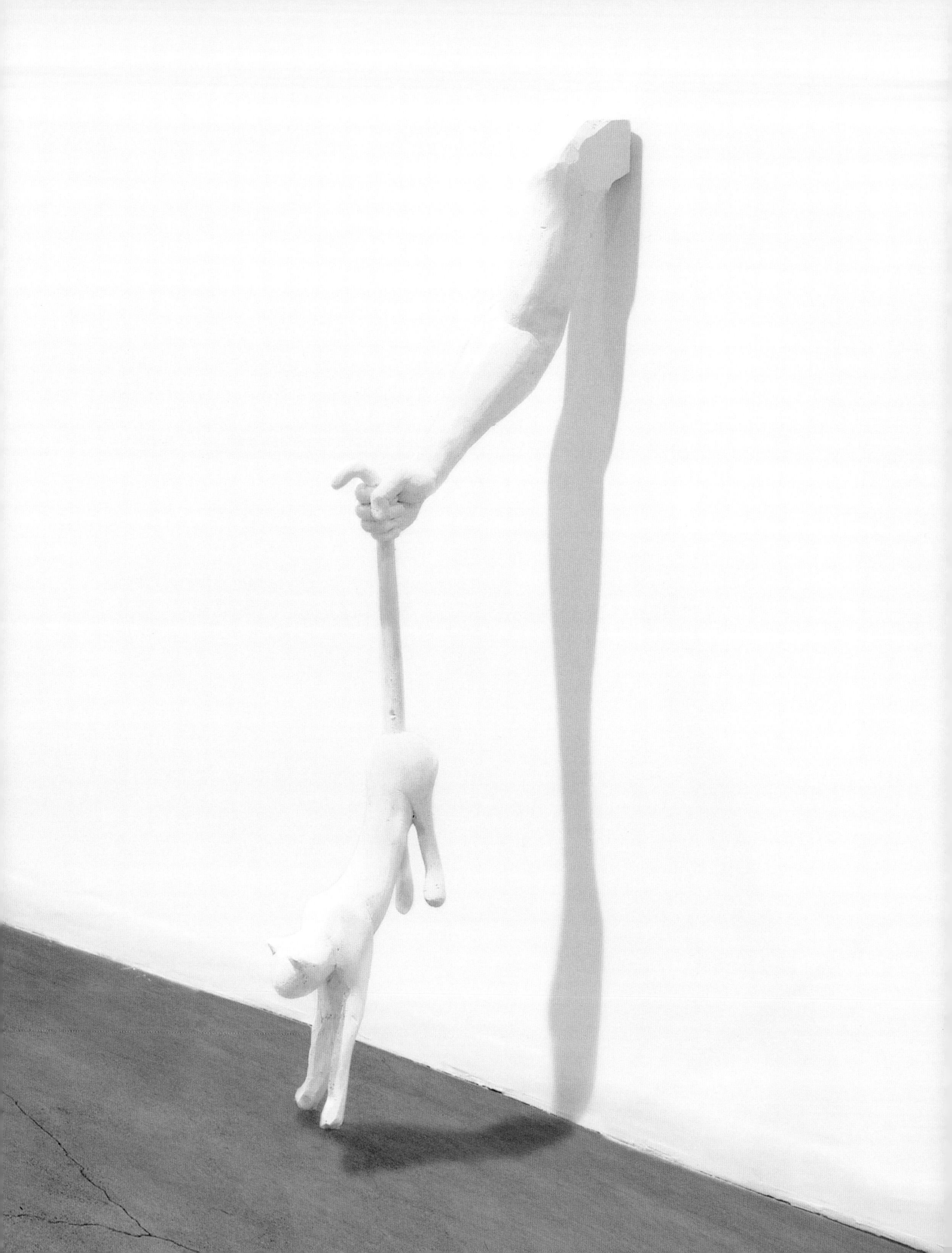

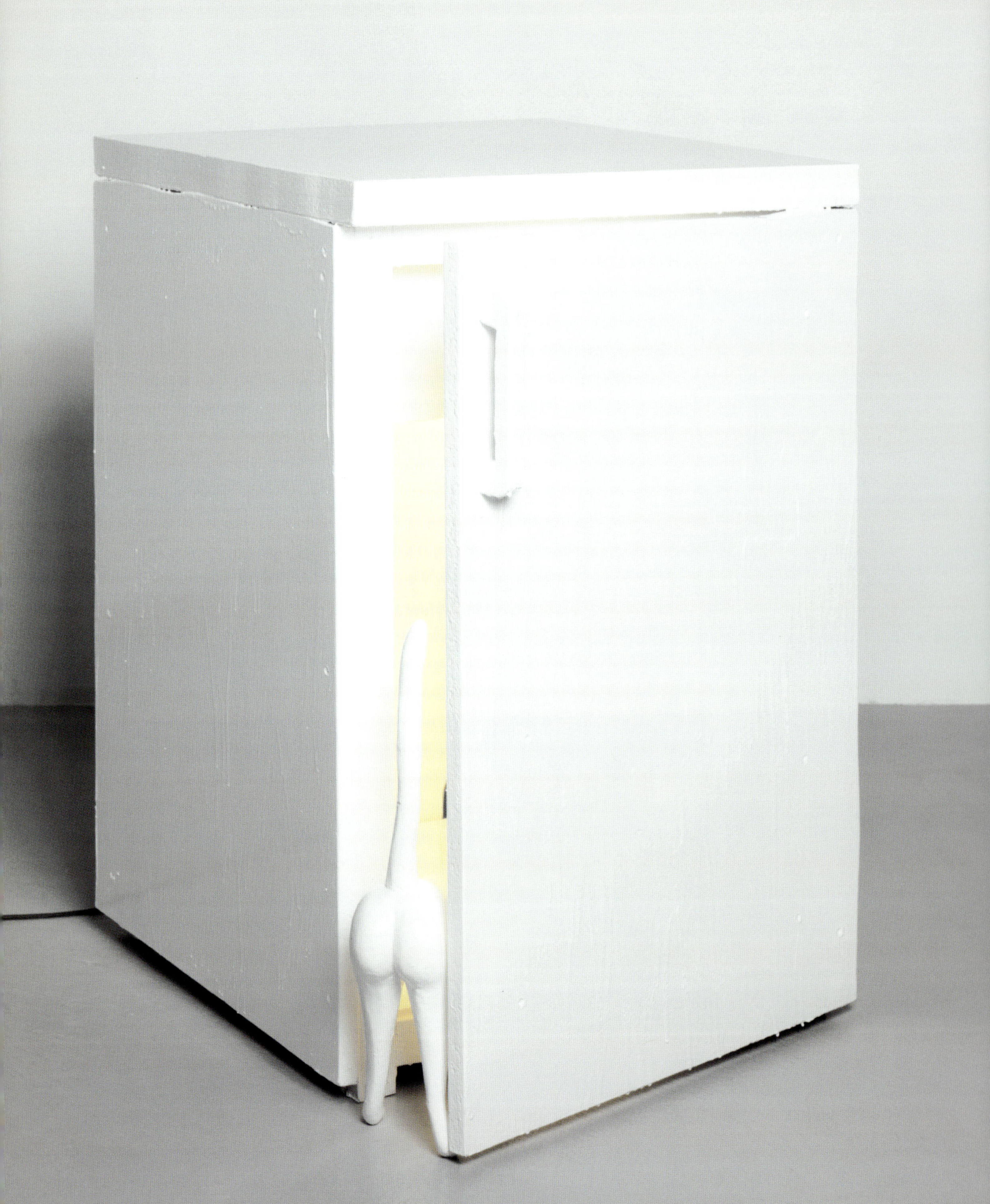

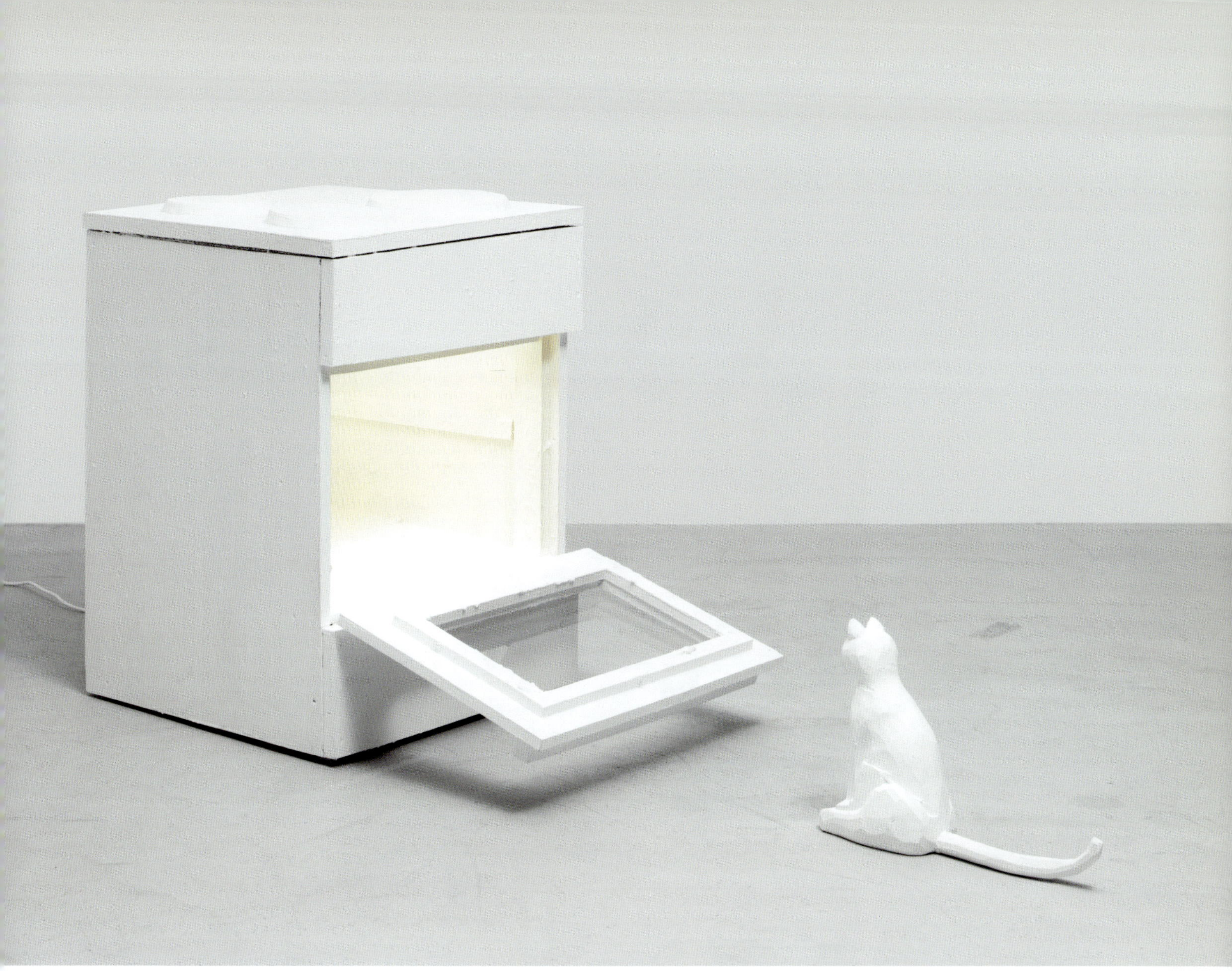

Mr. Flosky, 2001–2002
Wood, latex paint, lamp, cable, plaster, polystyrene, glass, glue, screws
Stove: 28 ¾ x 41 ⅜ x 23 ¼ inches (98.5 x 105 x 59 cm)
Cat: 13 ¼ x 18 ⅛ x 5 ¾ inches (33.5 x 46 x 14.5 cm)

Opposite page:
Cutting a Cake with a Hammer, 2000
Wood, polystyrene, latex paint, spotlight, enamel paint, filler, nails, screws
43 ¼ x 27 ½ x 27 ½ inches (110 x 70 x 70 cm)

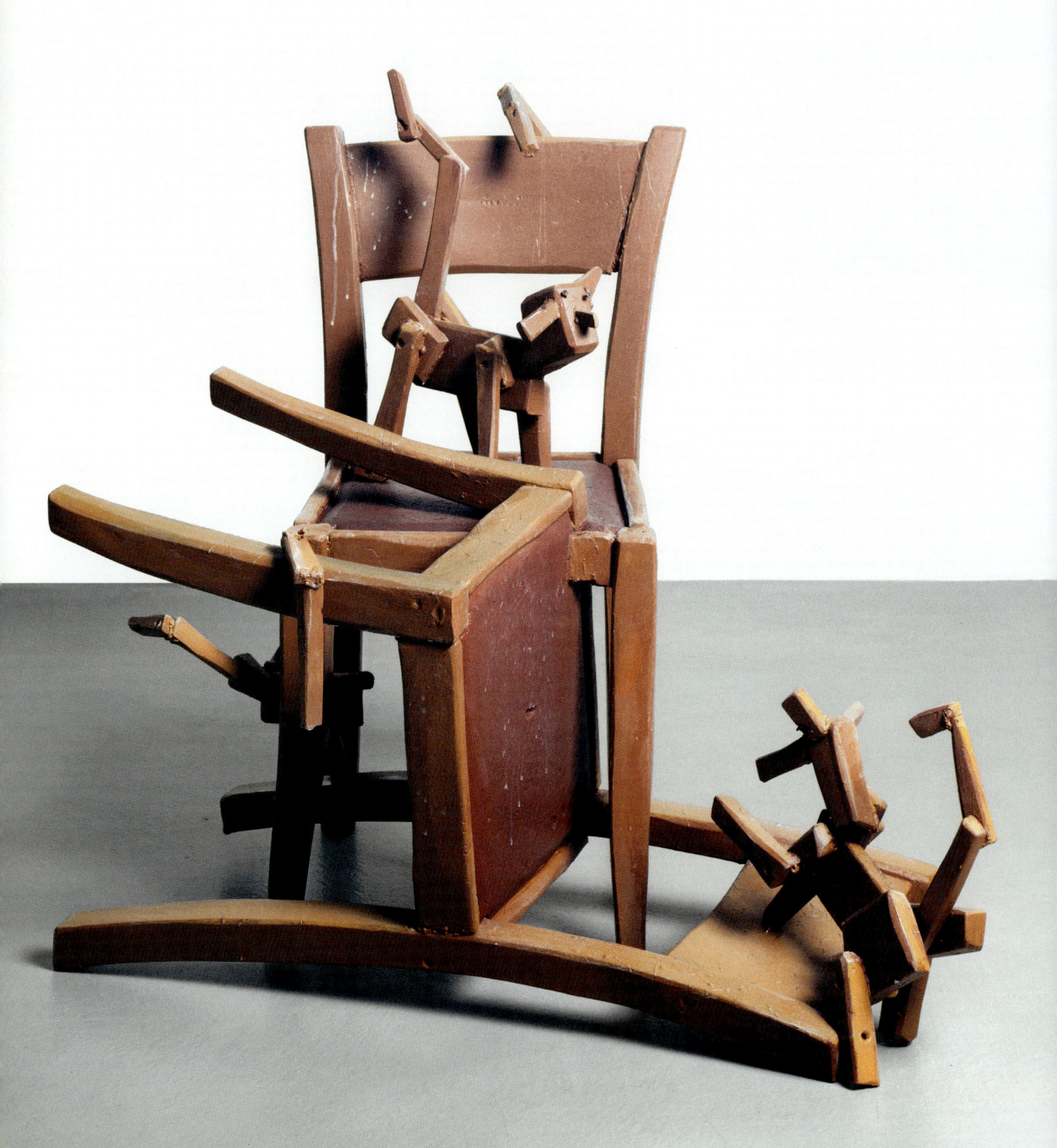

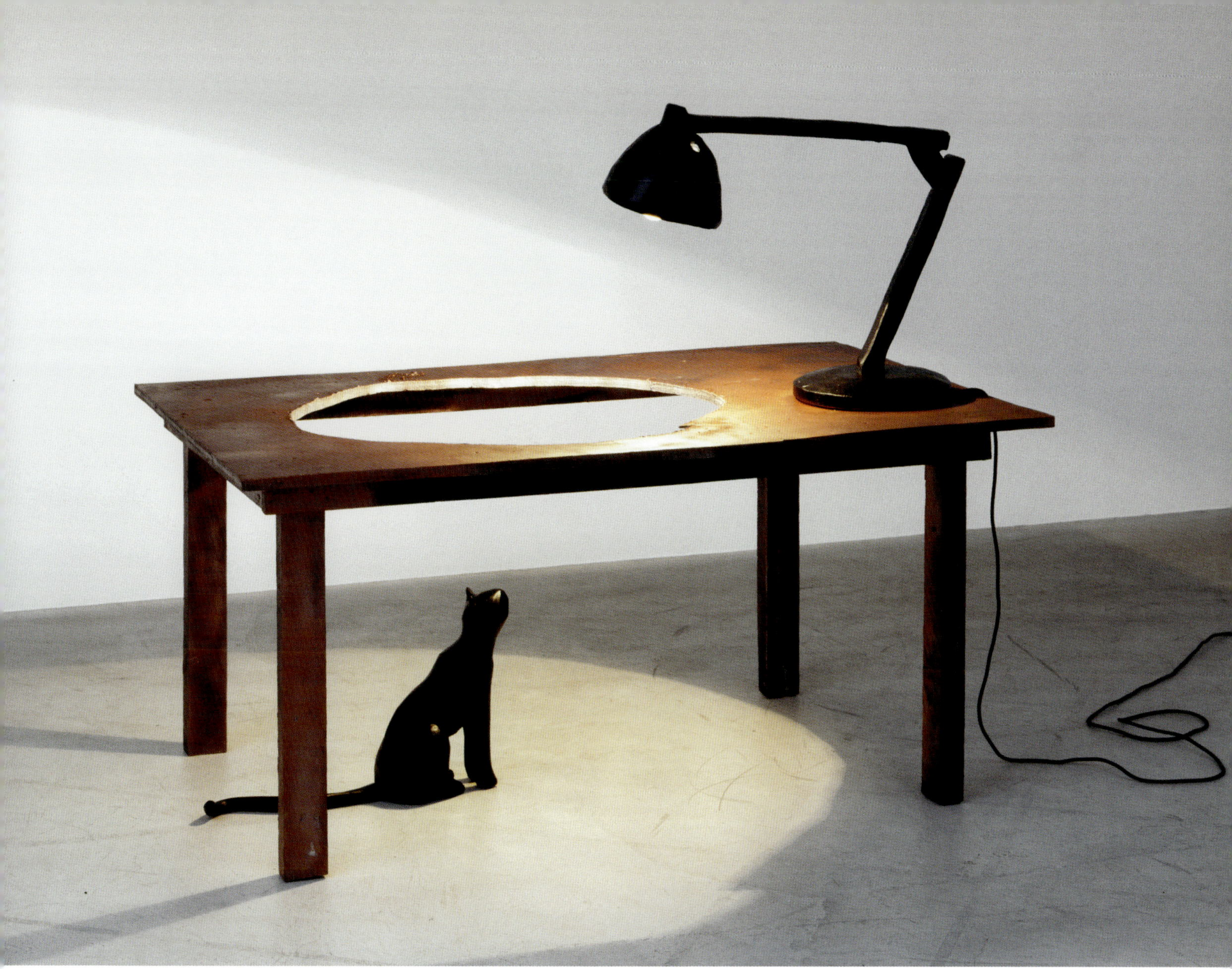

Daylight Pillow, 2004
Aluminum, acrylic paint, light bulb, socket, electric cable
49 ¼ x 55 ⅛ x 37 inches (125 x 140 x 94 cm)

Opposite page:
Hotel, 2001
Polyurethane foam, acrylic foam, wood, nails, screws
33 ½ x 17 ¾ x 33 ½ inches (84 x 45 x 84 cm)

Sigh, Sigh, Sherlock!, 2004

Fiberglass-reinforced plaster cast, partially painted

36 ¼ x 12 ⅝ x 12 ⅝ inches (92 x 32 x 32 cm)

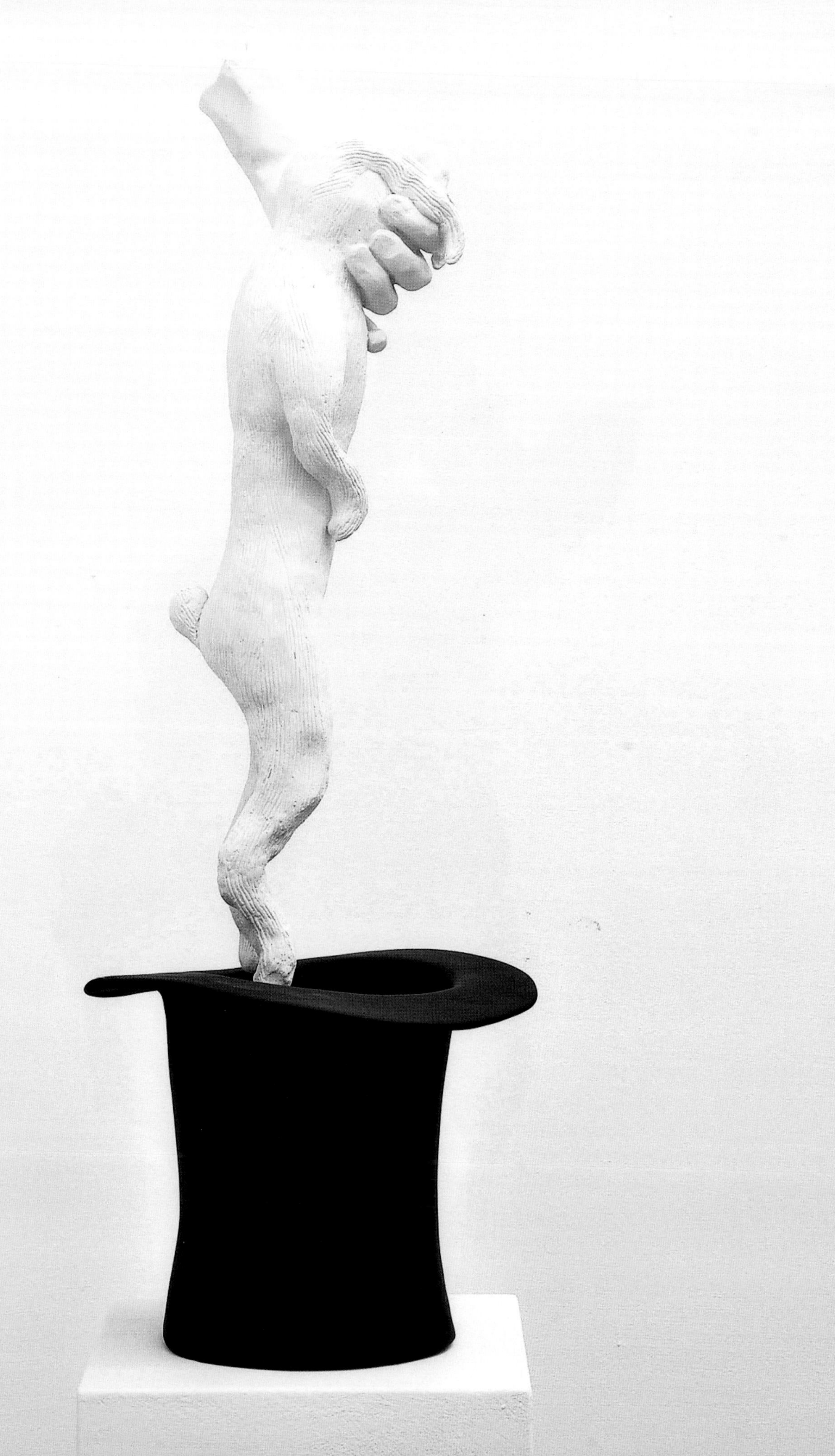

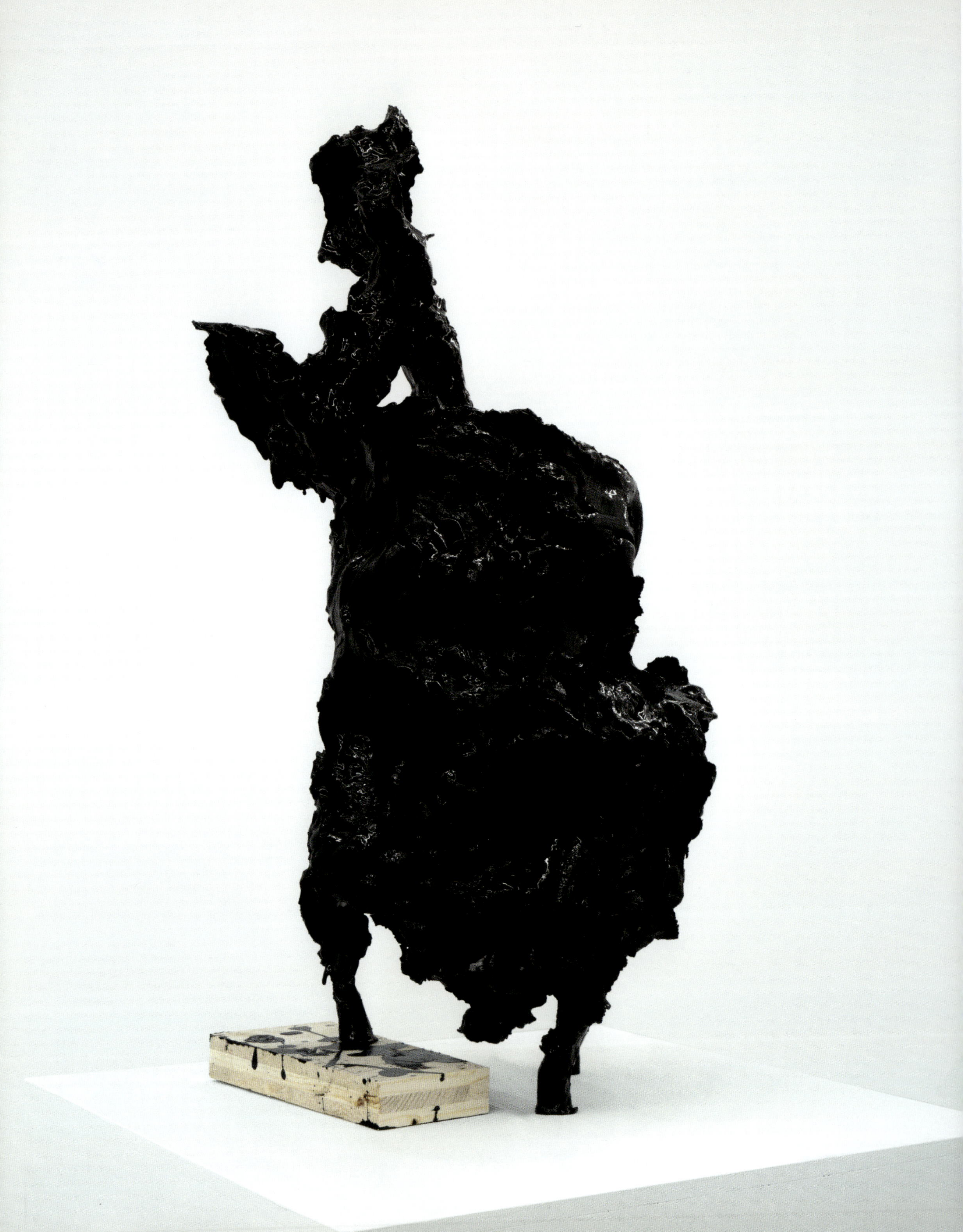

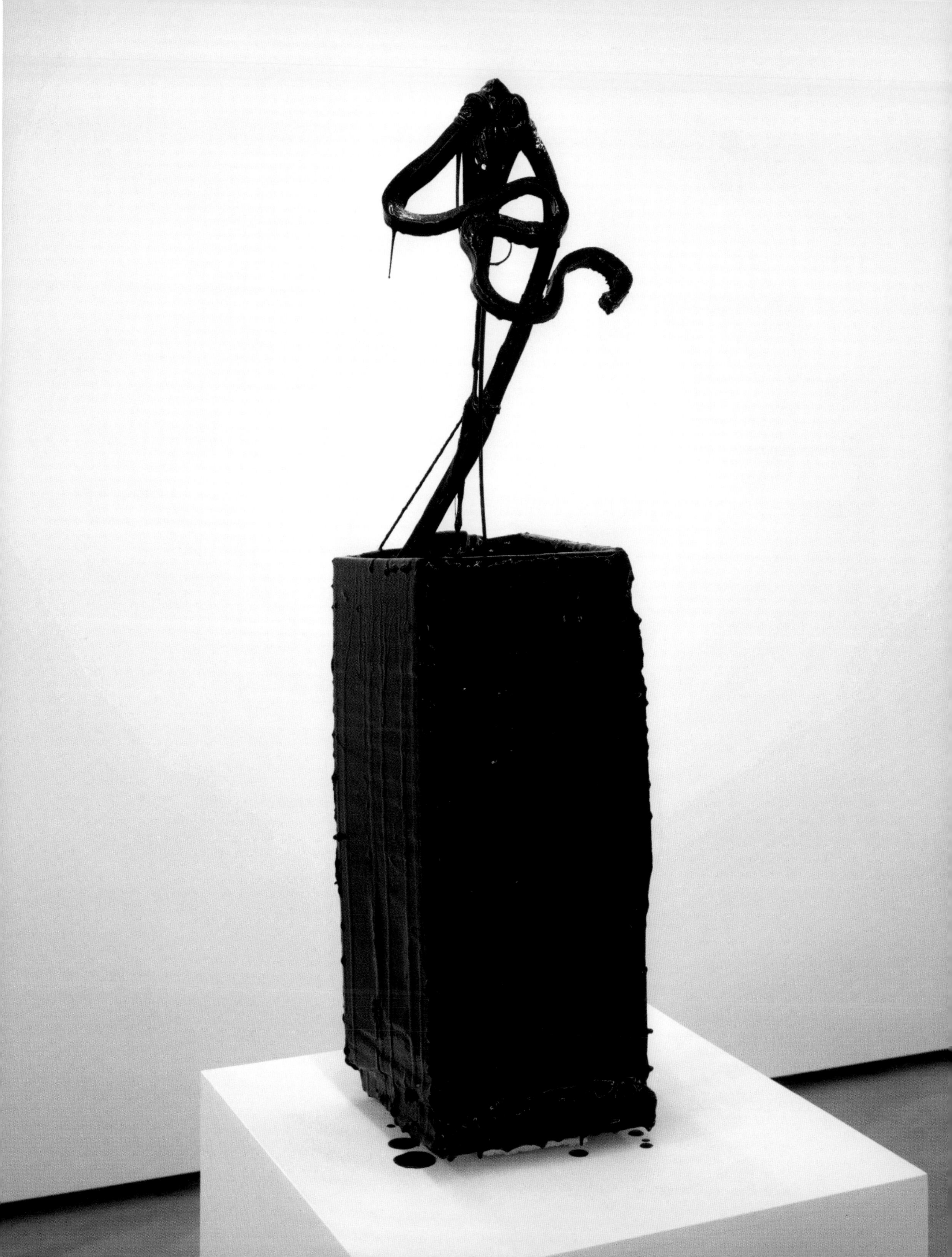

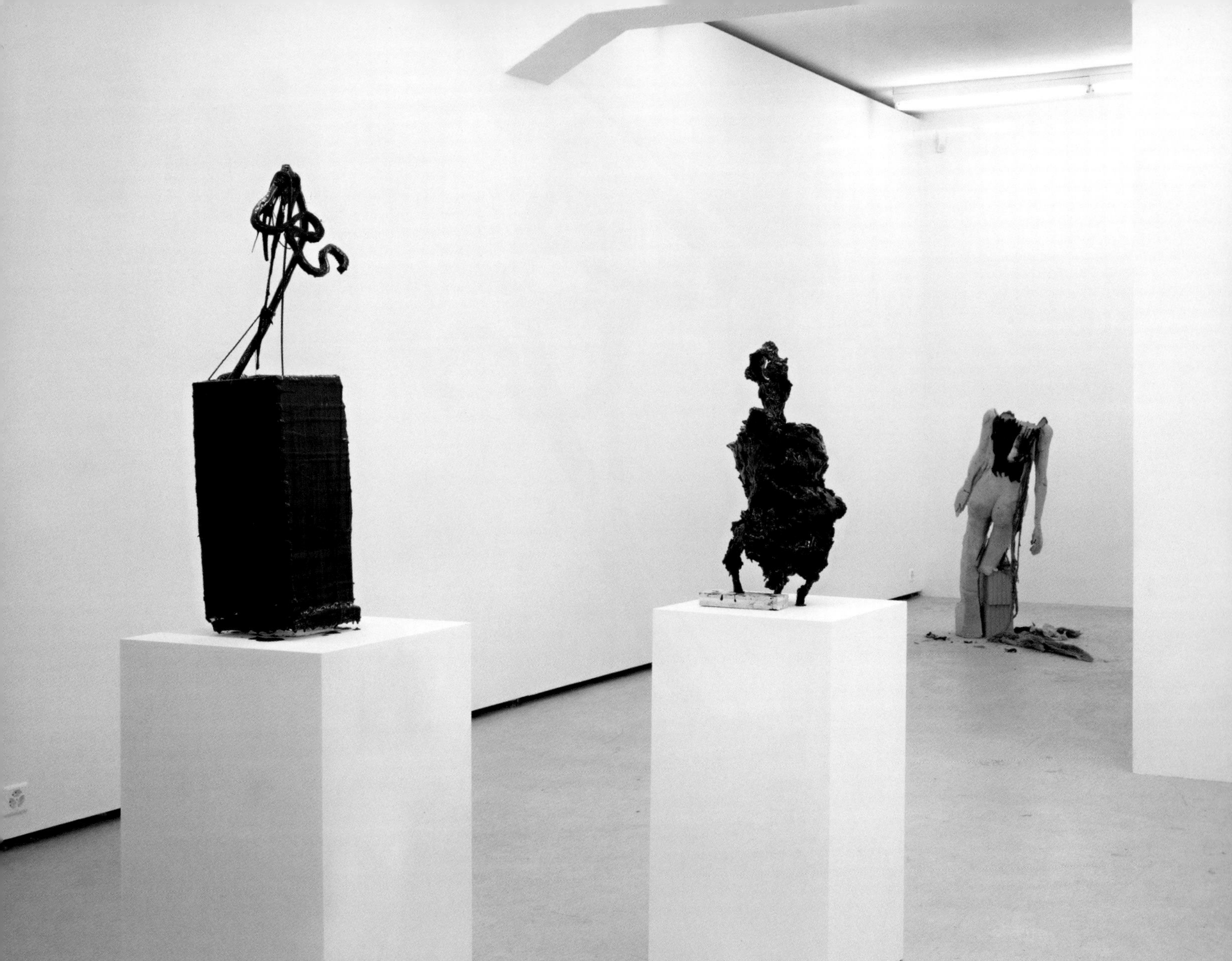

Previous pages:

Servile Serenade / Servile Symphony, 2001

Epoxy, lacquer, wood, MDF

Part 1: 8 ¼ x 9 ⅞ x 32 ⅝ inches (21 x 25 x 83 cm)

Part 2: 15 ⅜ x 12 ¼ x 24 inches (29 x 31 x 61 cm)

Above: Installation view, "Mastering the Complaint," Galerie Hauser & Wirth & Presenhuber, Zurich, 2001

Untitled, 2001

Opposite page:

That's the Way It Is with the Magic. Sometimes It Works and Sometimes It Doesn't., 2000

Plaster, silicone, marker, acrylic paint, spray enamel, glass vase, polyurethane foam, fresh white lilies

78 ¾ x 15 ¾ x 15 ¾ inches (200 x 40 x 40 cm)

Following pages:

Good Good Breath / Good Bad Breath, 2002

Polyurethane resin, wire, enamel, varnish, primer; in 2 parts

Each approximately 27 ½ x 14 ½ x 12 inches (69.9 x 36.8 x 30.5 cm)

Say Hello / Say Good Bye, 2003

Dried white flowers, polyurethane resin, acrylic paint, screws

30 x 29 x 19 inches (76.2 x 73.8 x 48.6 cm)

Die Hungry, 2003

Polyurethane resin, acrylic paint, clay, screws

27 ½ x 19 ¾ x 15 inches (70 x 50 x 38 cm)

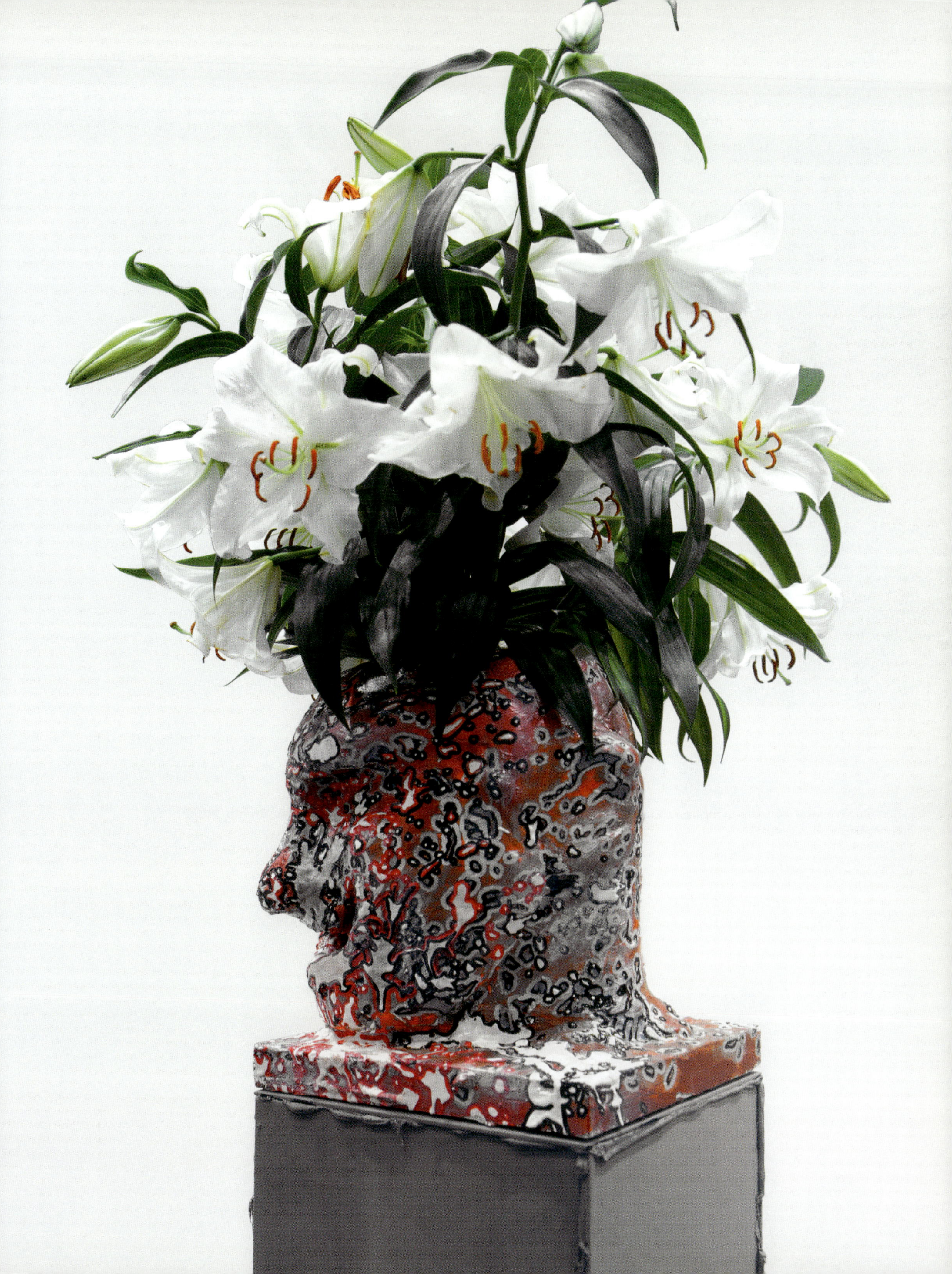

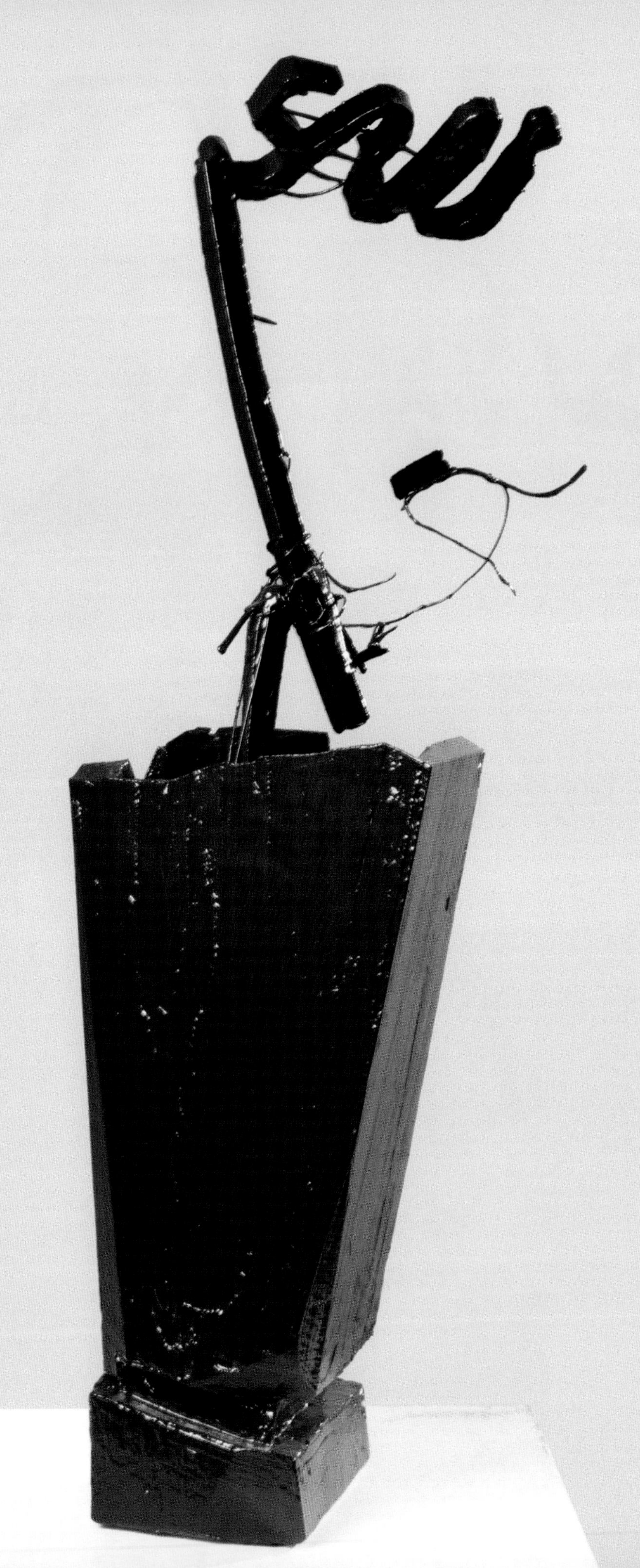

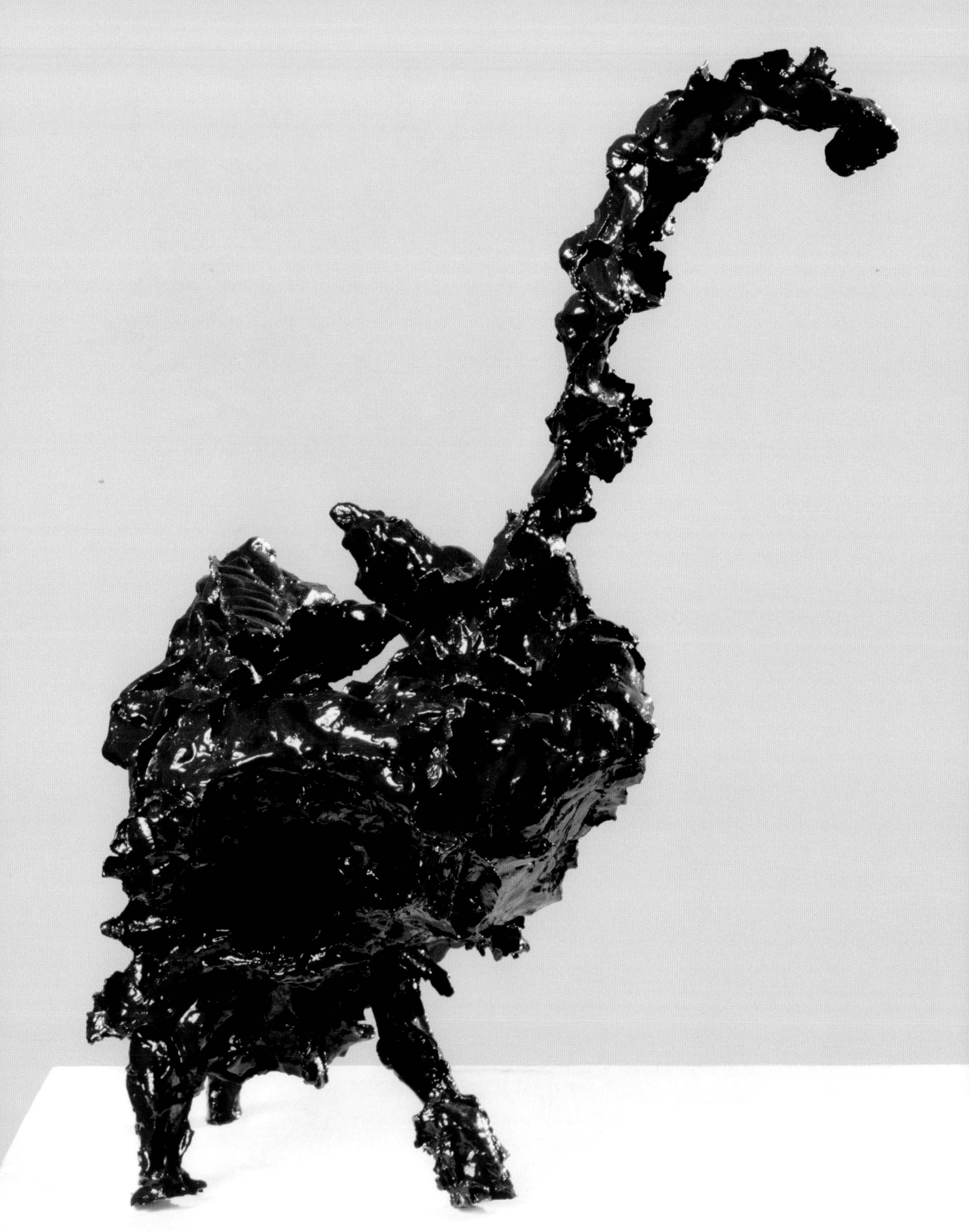

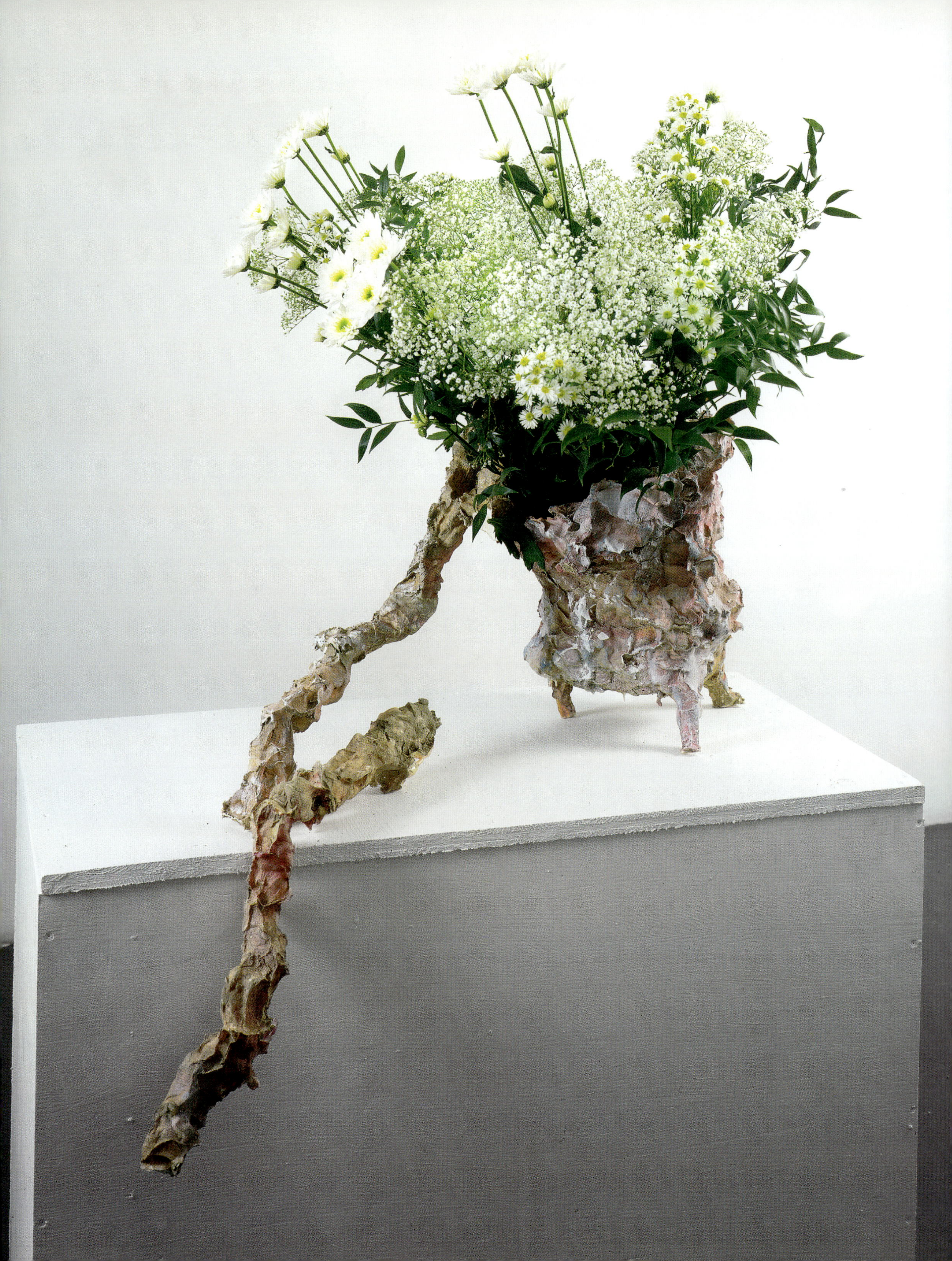

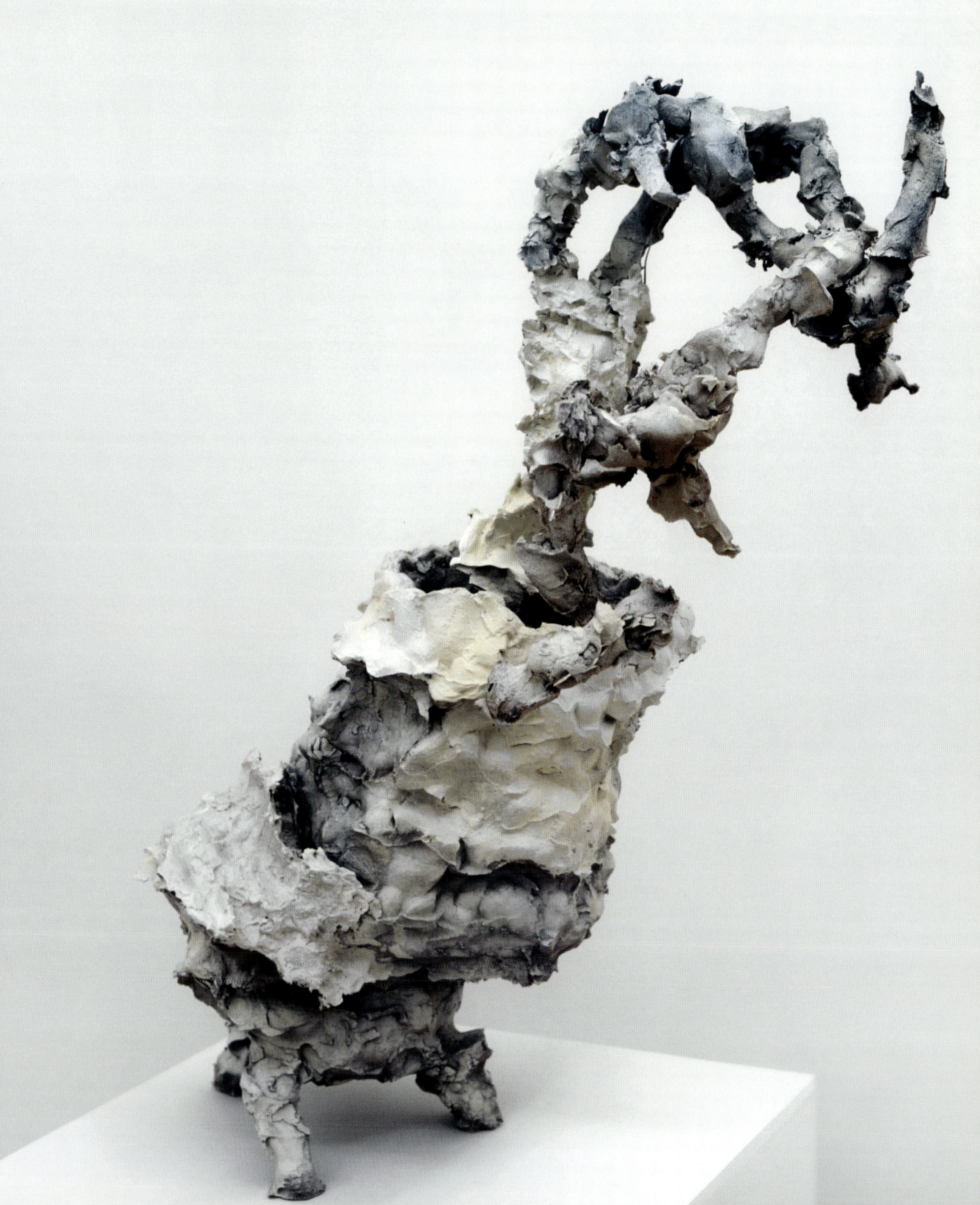

Money Bowl, 1999

Iron, metal primer, plaster, caulk, acrylic paint, wax, coins, bills
Bowl: 27 ½ x 27 ½ x 5 ½ inches (70 x 70 x 14 cm)
Pedestal: 27 ½ x 27 ½ x 18 ⅛ inches (70 x 70 x 46 cm)

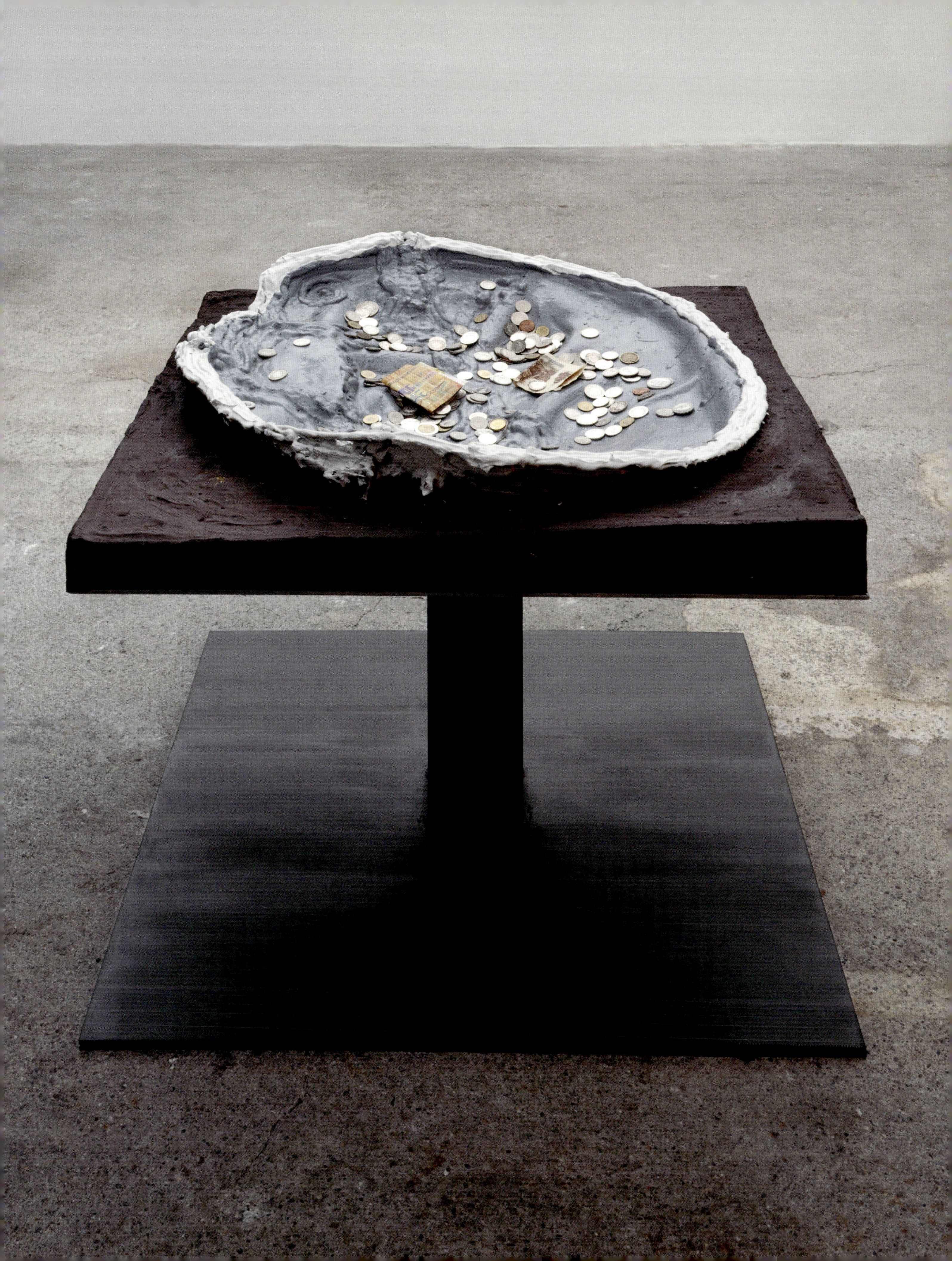

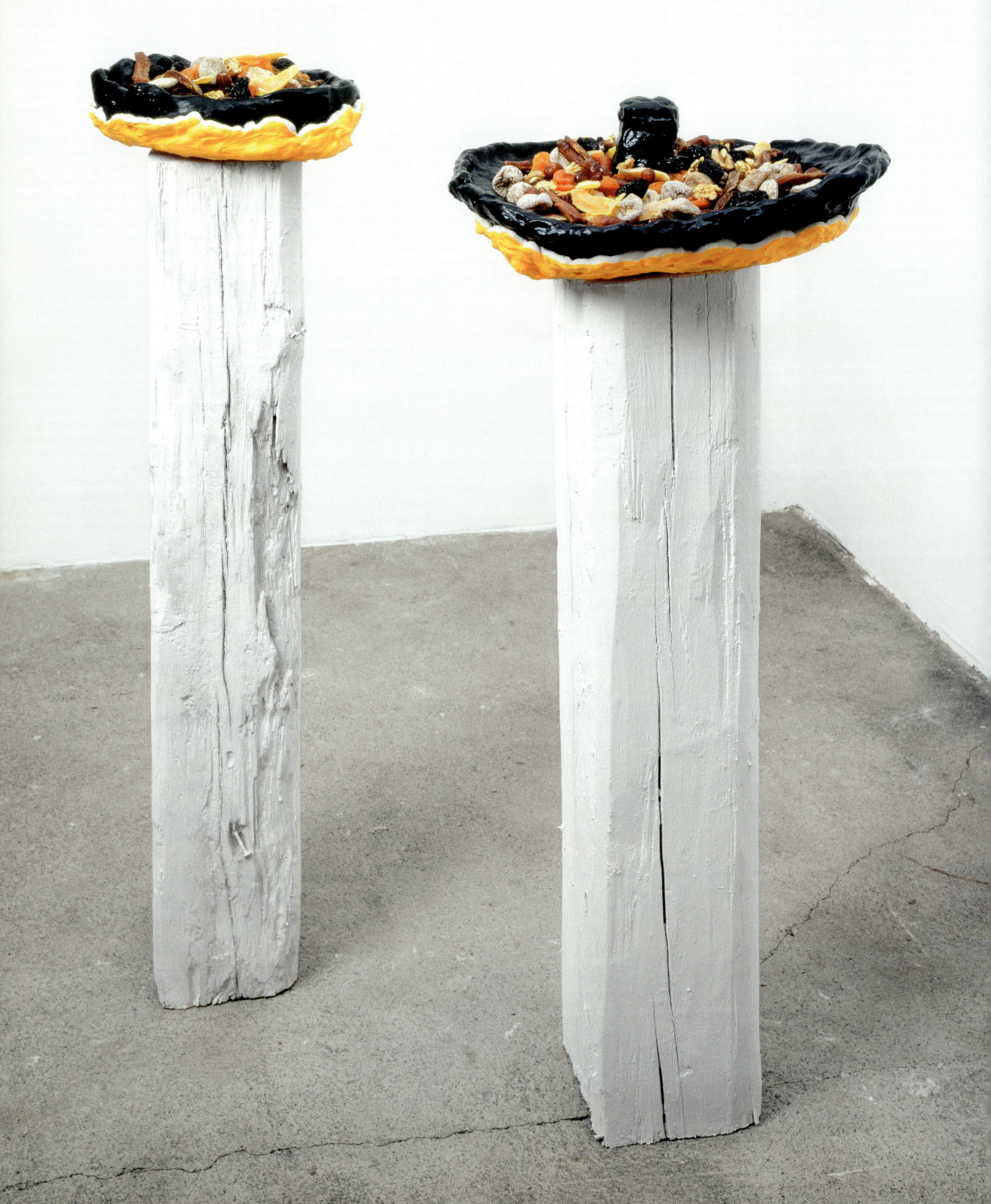

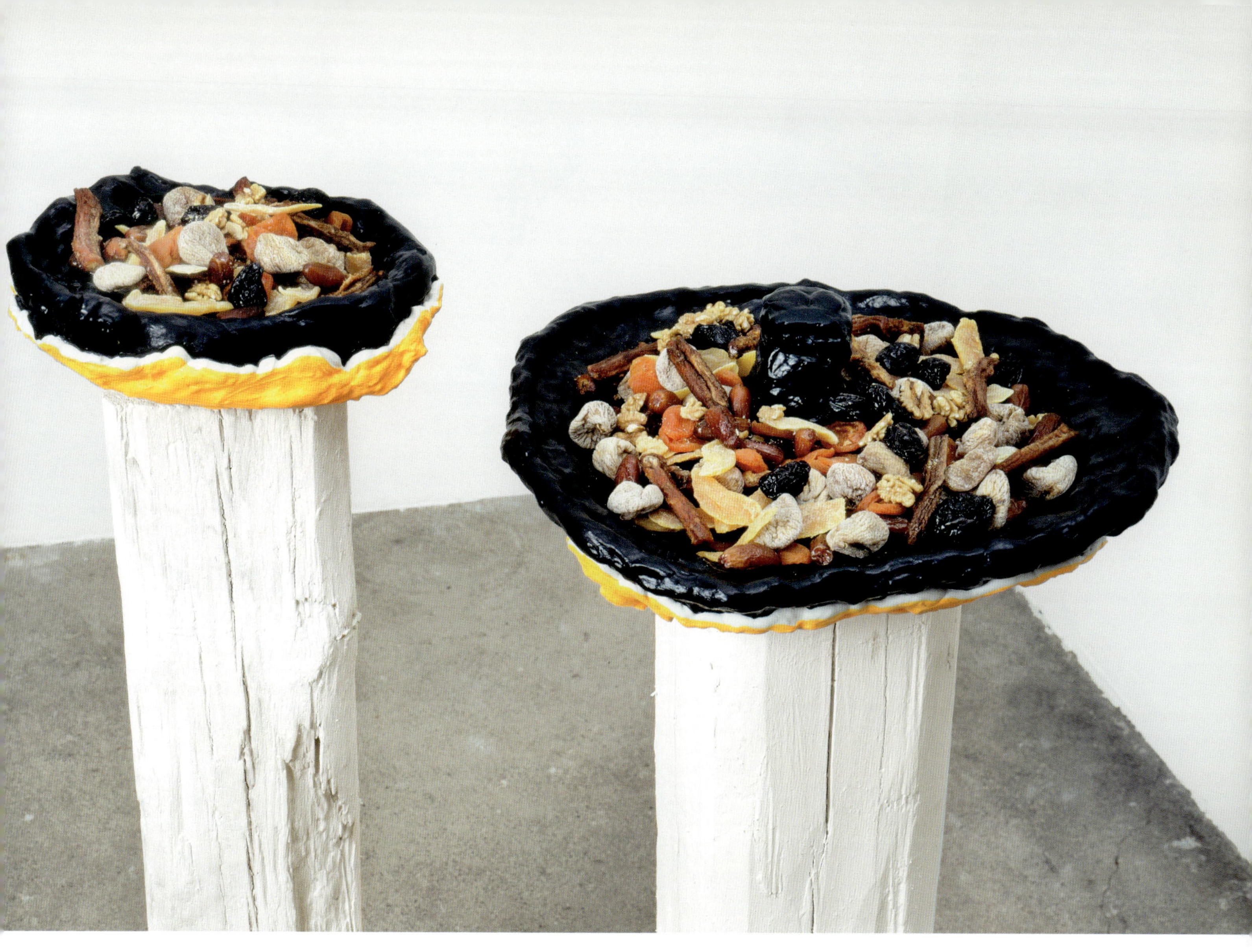

Dörrfrucht und Nussschale, 1999

Plaster, clay, wood glue, acrylic, dried fruit, nuts,
wooden beams, latex paint
Bowl 1: diameter 19 ⅝ x 7 ⅞ inches (50 x 20 cm)
Pedestal: 39 ⅜ x 8 ⅝ x 7 ⅞ inches (100 x 22 x 20 cm)
Bowl 2: diameter 13 ¾ x 4 ¾ inches (35 x 12 cm)
Pedestal: 43 ¼ x 9 ½ x 7 ⅞ inches (110 x 24 x 20 cm)

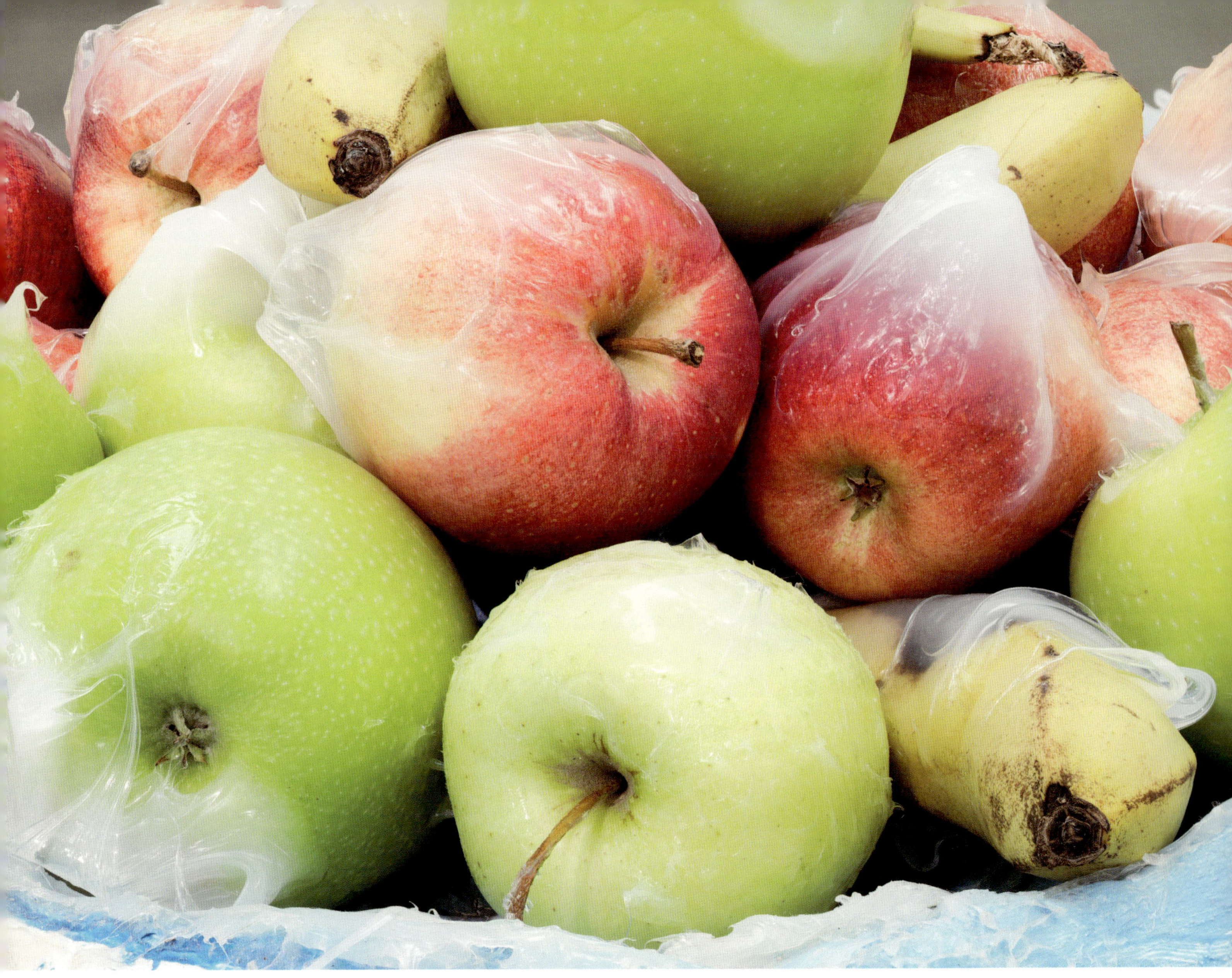

The Human Layer, 1999
Plaster, clay, acrylic paint, silicone, fruits
7 ⅞ x 19 ¾ x 19 ¾ inches (20 x 50 x 50 cm)

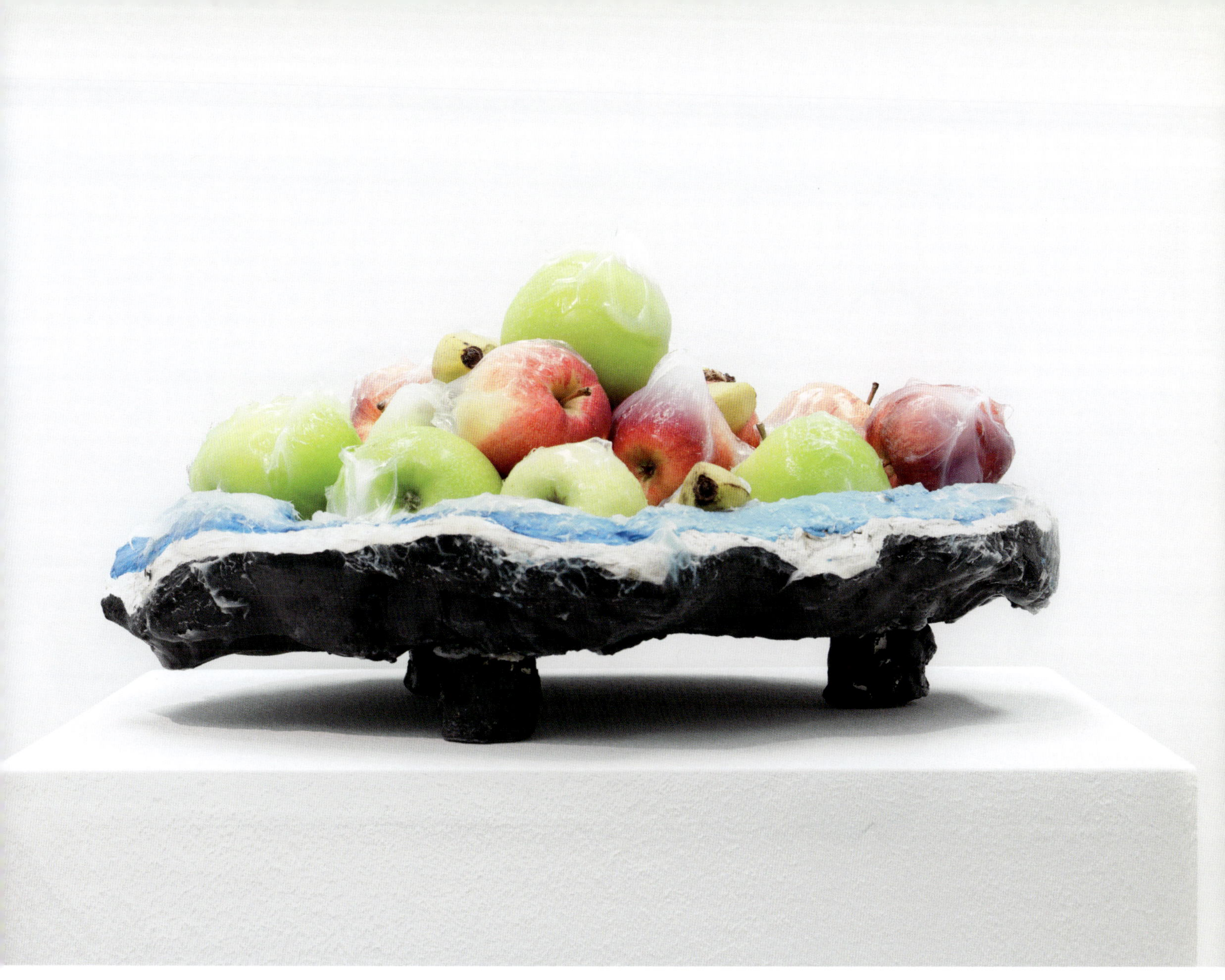

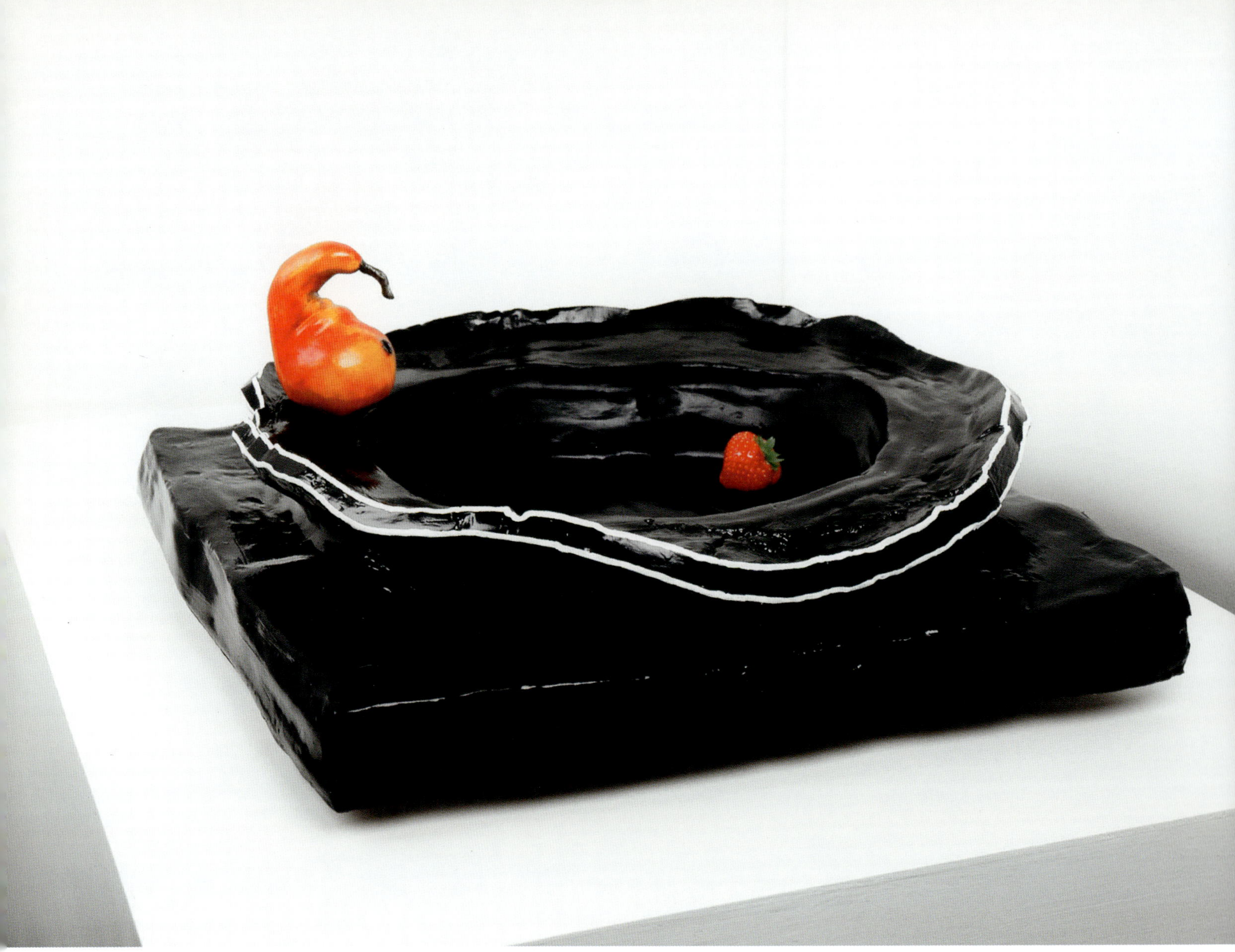

Good Luck / Bad Luck Bowl, 2002
Polyurethane resin, wire, enamel, varnish, primer
Dimensions unknown

Opposite page:
Untitled (Eierschale), 2000
MDF, clay, acrylic paint, wood glue, oil paint,
marker, eggs, hairspray, matte varnish
7 ½ x 15 x 11 ⅜ inches (19 x 38 x 29 cm)

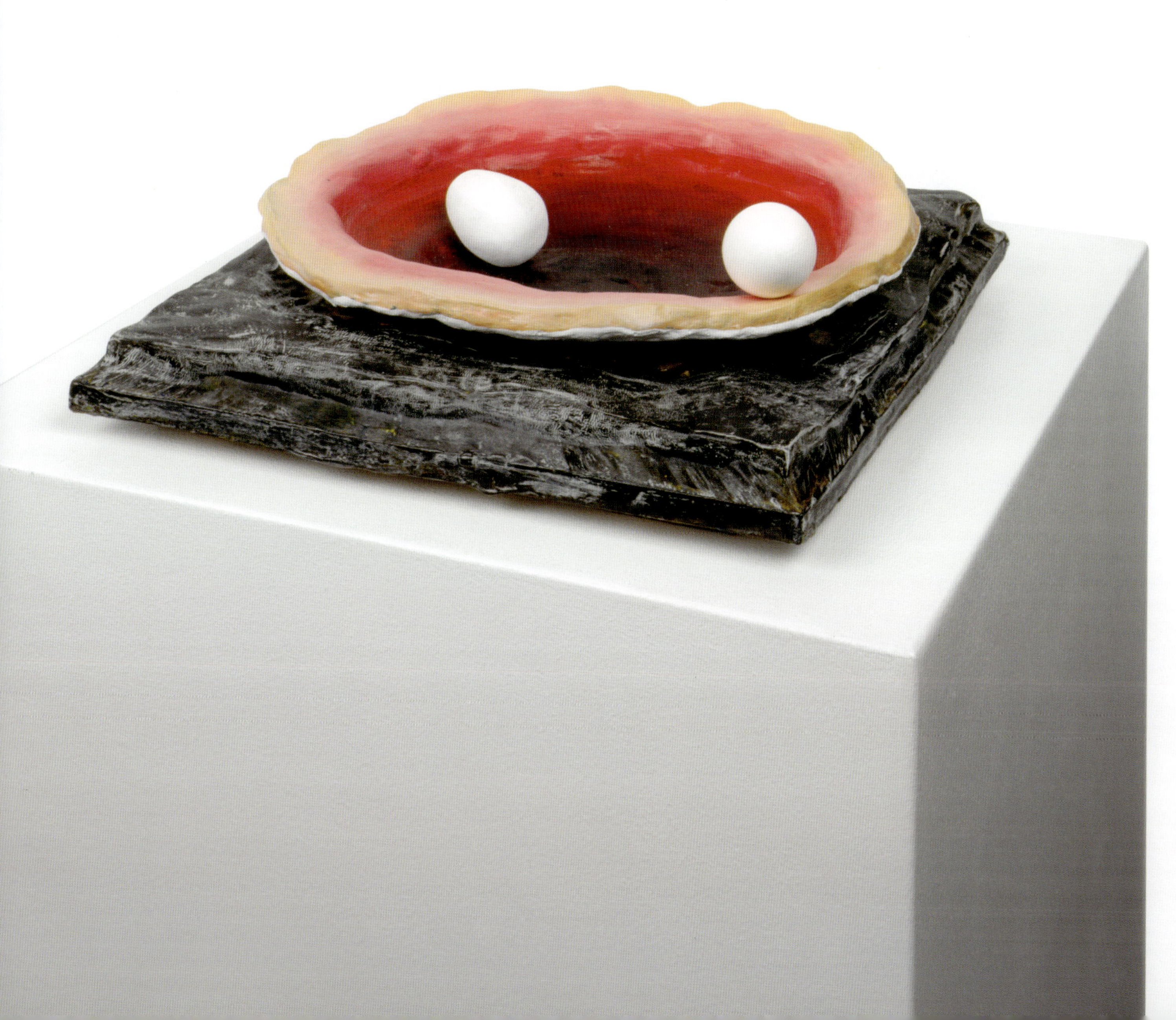

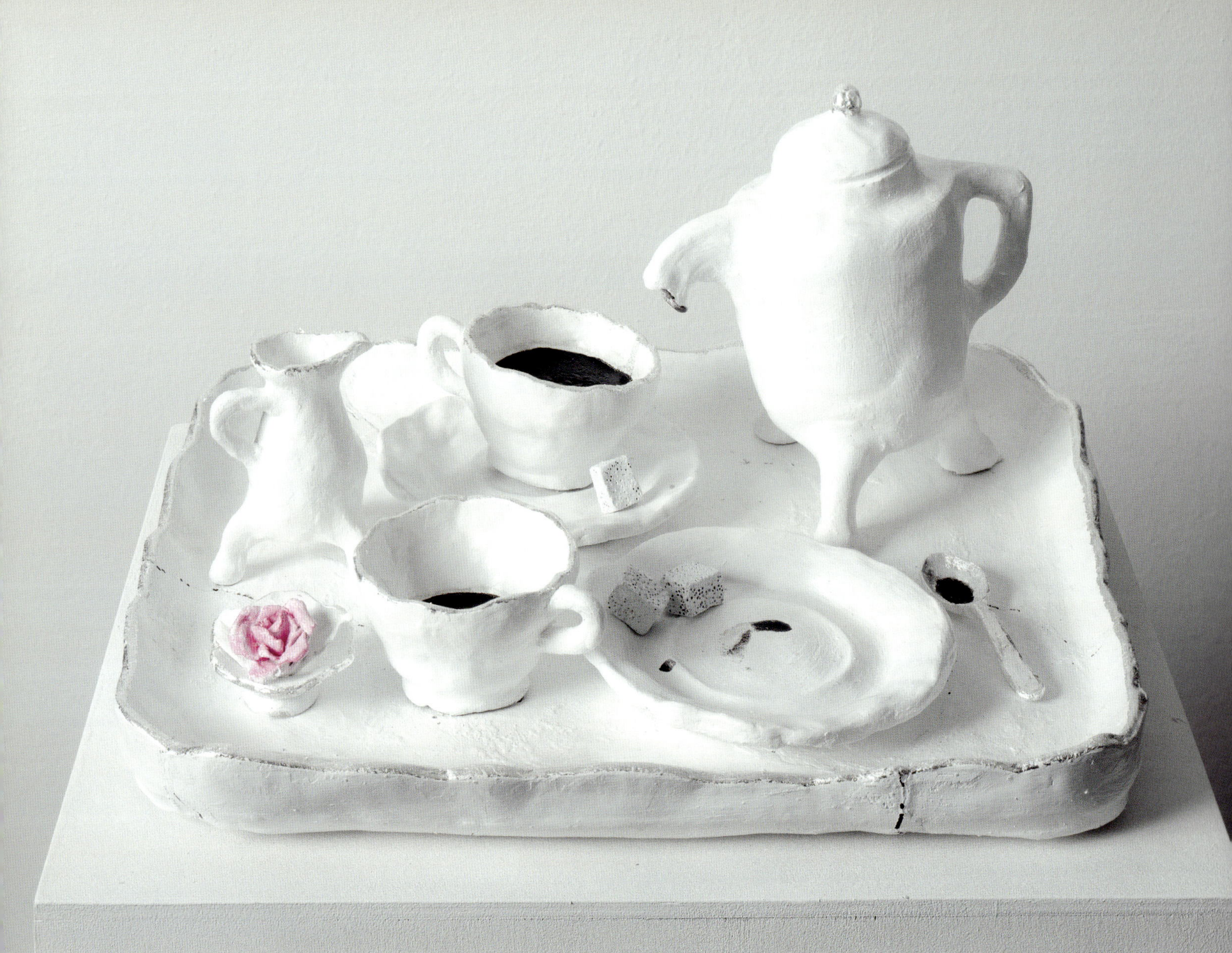

Tea Set, 2002
Clay, wood, glue, acrylic paint, silver leaf
9 x 17 ¾ x 15 ⅜ inches (23 x 45 x 39 cm)

Opposite page:
Tea Set, 2002
Clay, acrylic paint, plywood, copper leaf
7 ⅞ x 15 x 12 ⅝ inches (20 x 38 x 32 cm)
Installation view, "Mystique Mistake,"
The Modern Institute, Glasgow, 2002

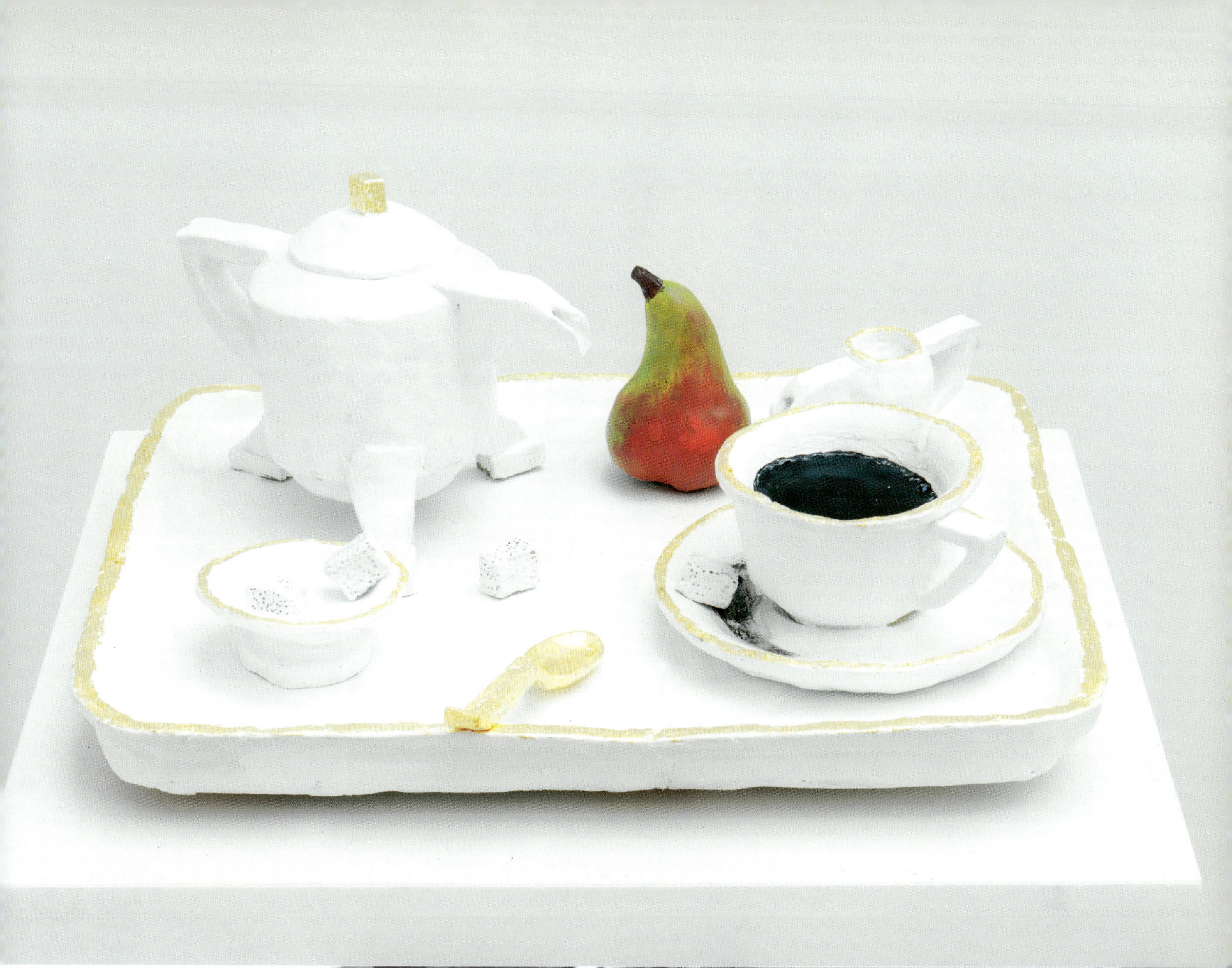

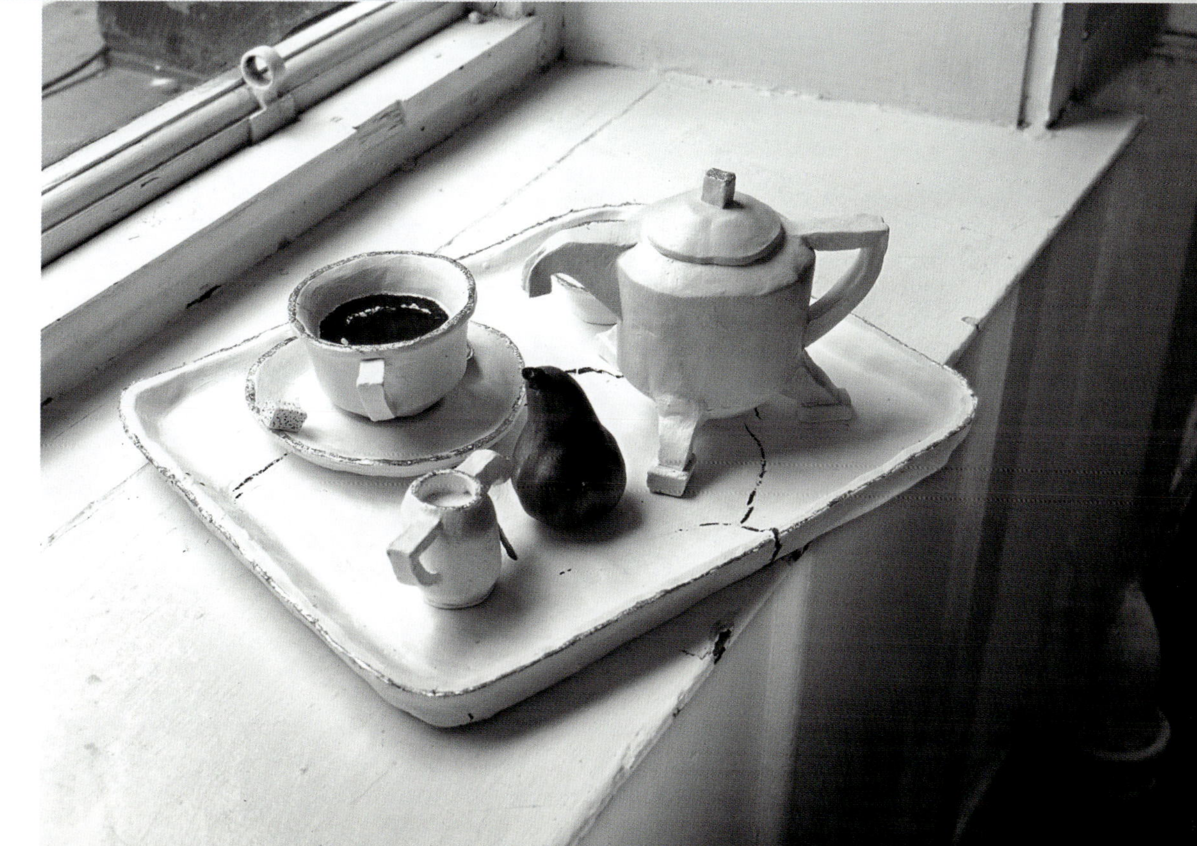

Untitled, 2000
Apple, pear, nylon filament, screws
Dimensions variable

Following pages:
Gänseeier Eclipse, 2001–2002
Two goose or chicken eggs, nylon
filament, glue, theater spotlight
Dimensions variable

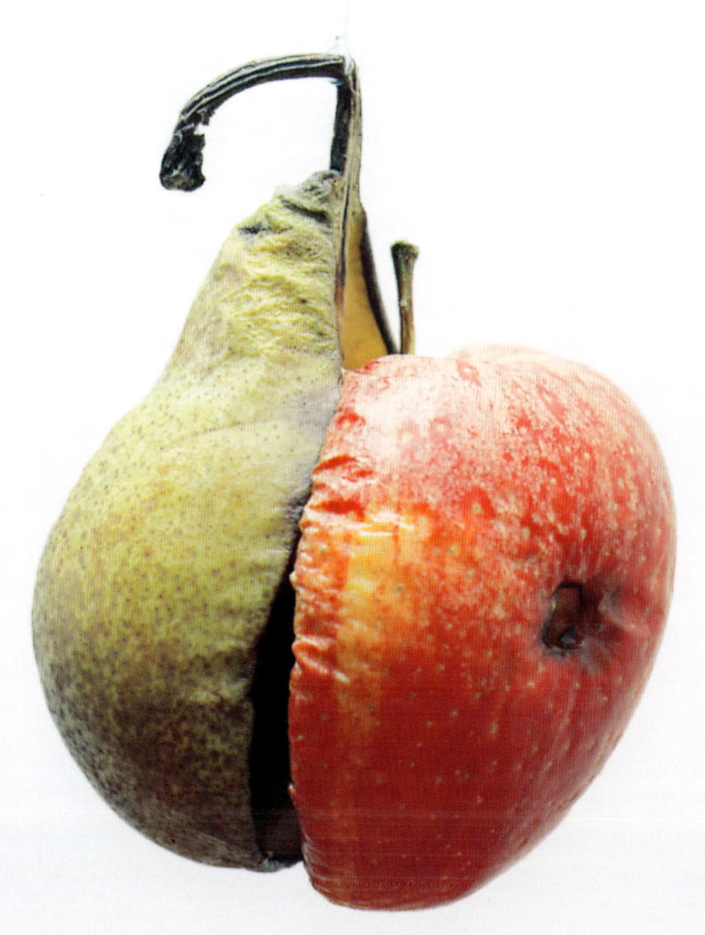

Untitled, 2003
Nylon filament, banana, theater spotlight
Dimensions variable

Following pages:
Nickname, 2009
Nylon filament, preserved croissant, preserved butterfly, steel
Approximately 6 x 5 ½ x 2 ½ inches (15.2 x 14 x 6.3 cm)

Frozen Pioneer Slut, 2009
Nylon filament, preserved croissant, preserved butterfly, glue, wire
Approximately 6 x 5 ½ x 2 ½ inches (15.2 x 14 x 6.3 cm)

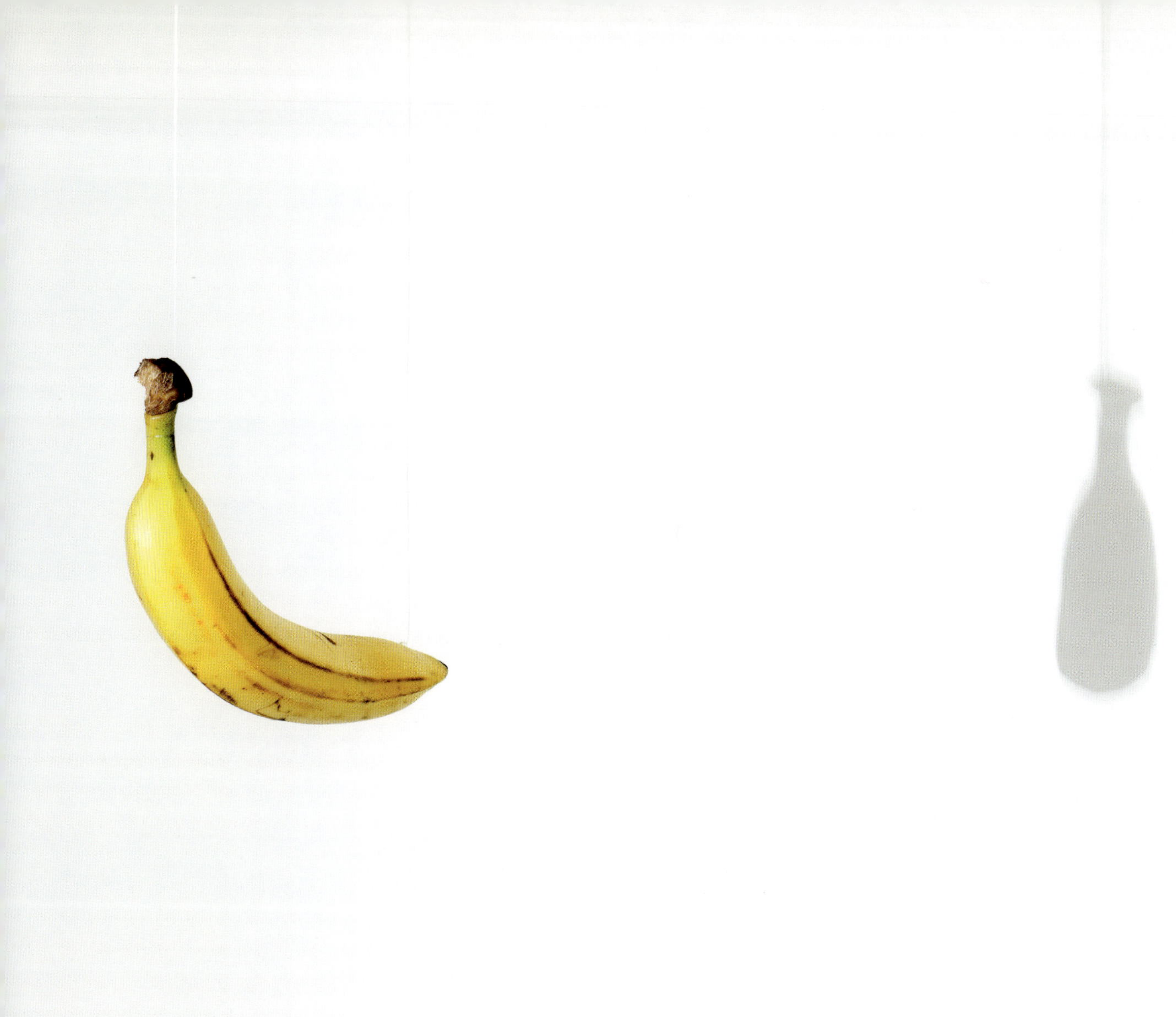

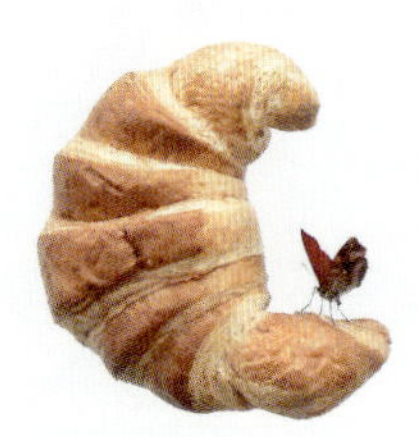

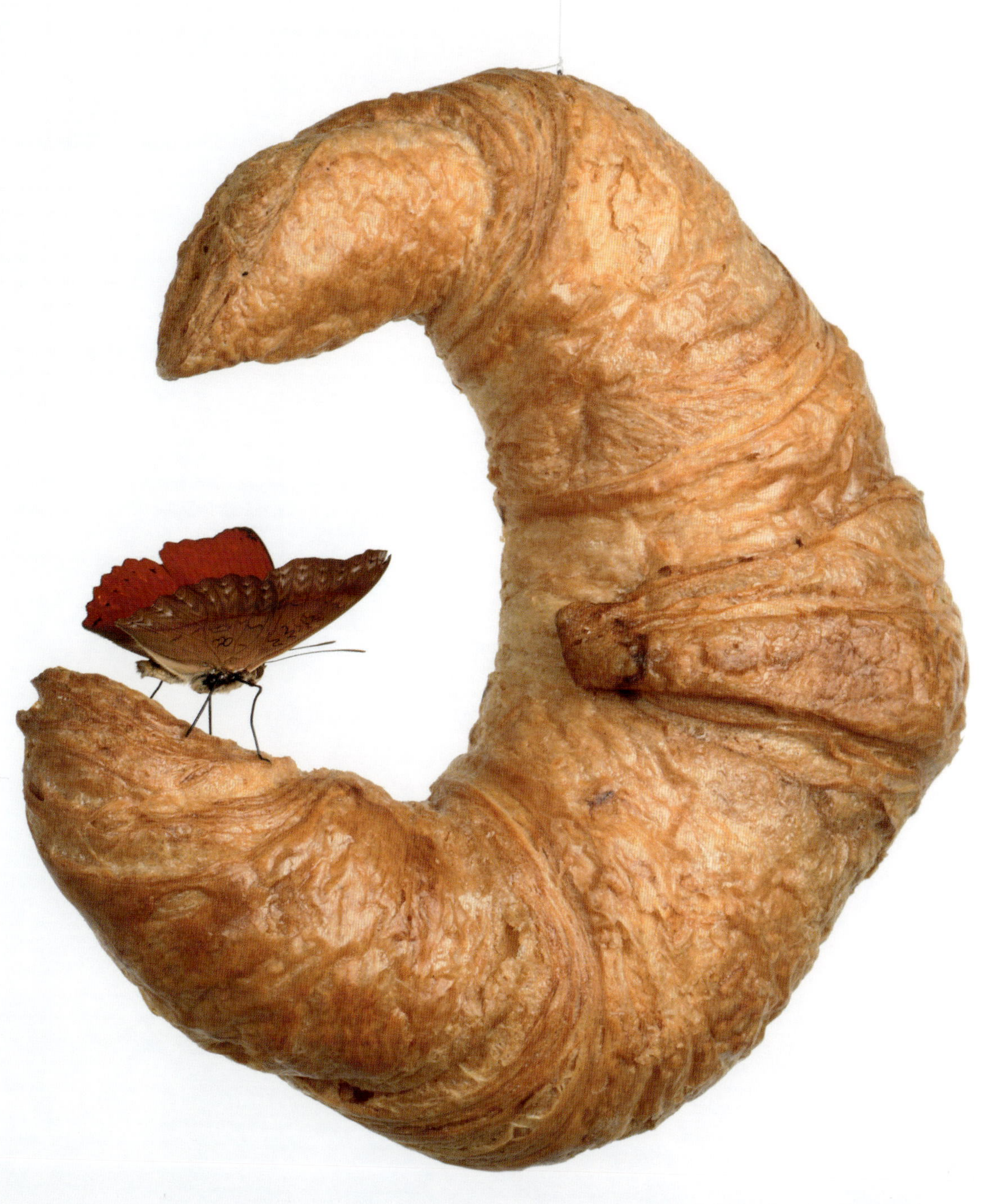

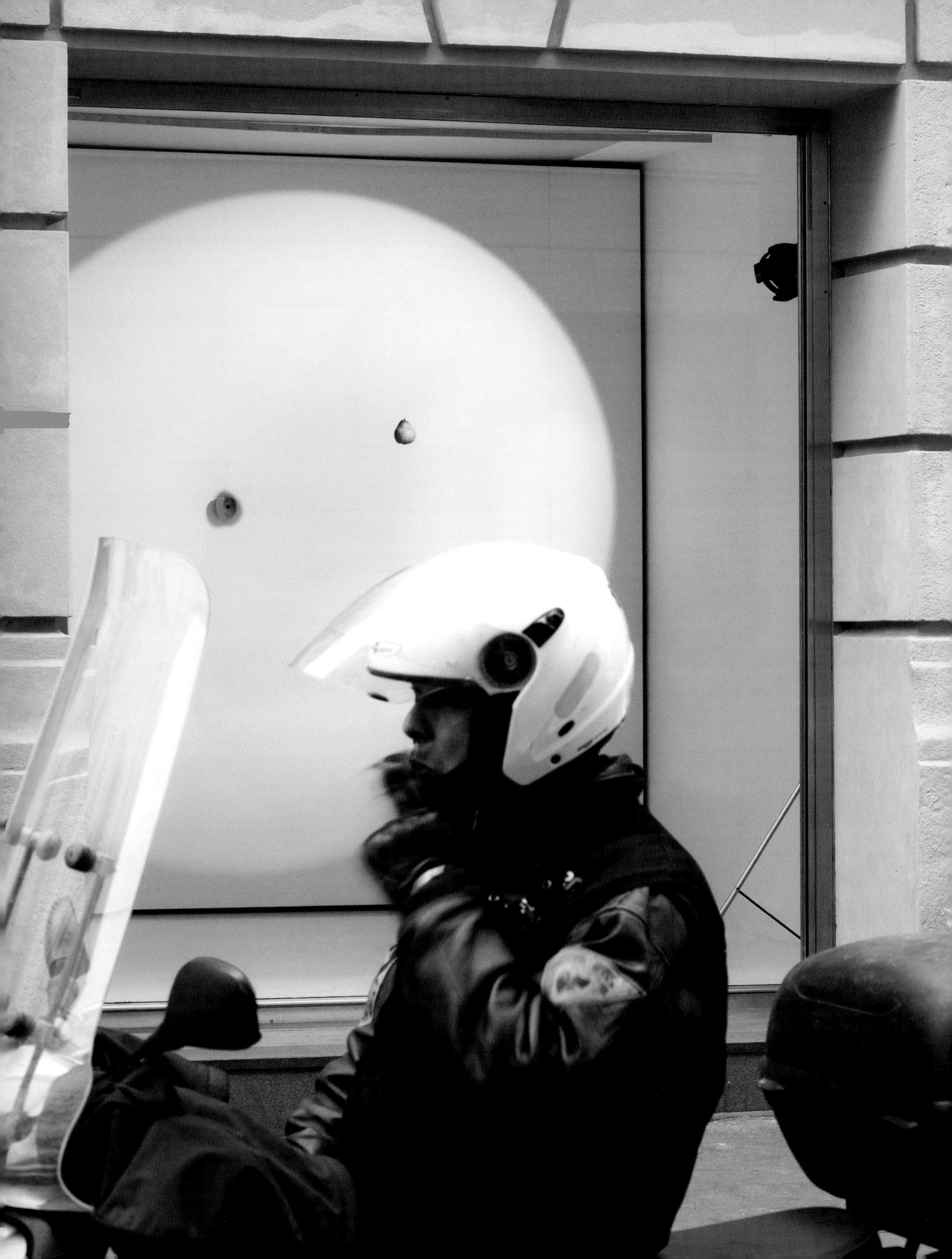

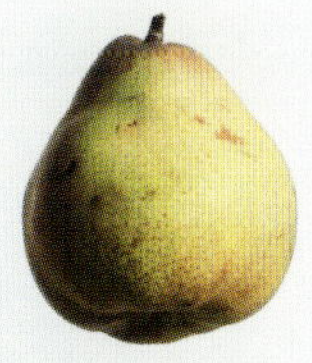

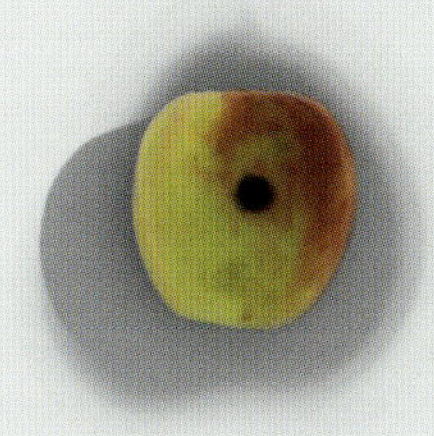

Untitled (Pear / Apple), 2012
Nylon filament, apple, pear, projector, screw
Dimensions variable
Opposite page: Installation view, "schmutz schmutz,"
Gagosian Gallery, Paris, 2012

Following spread:
Untitled (Suspended Line of Fruit), 2012
Nylon filament, fresh fruit in ascending sizes (grape, strawberry, lime, apple, grapefruit, coconut, pineapple), glue, nail, screw, paint, wood
Dimensions variable

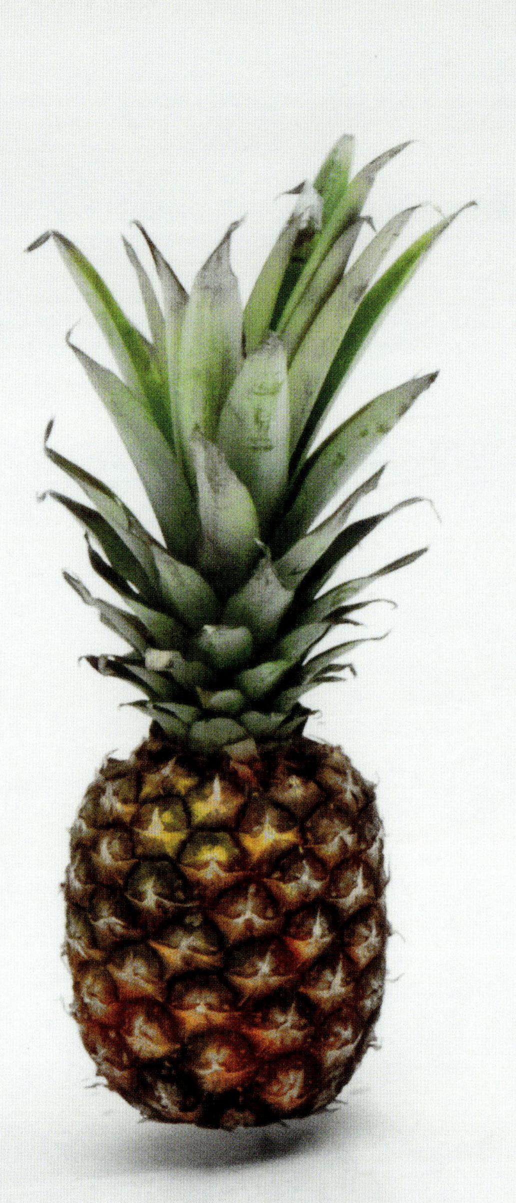

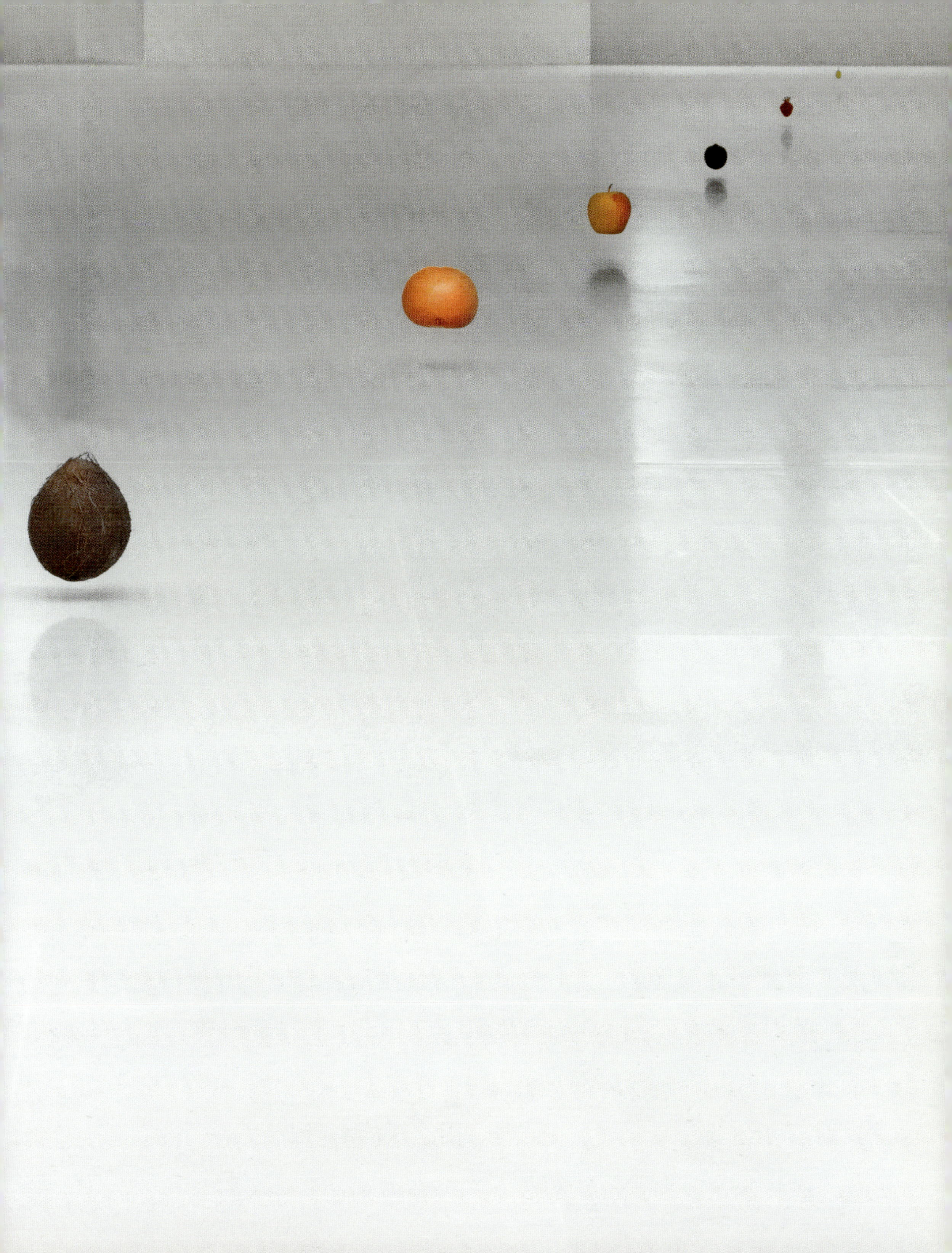

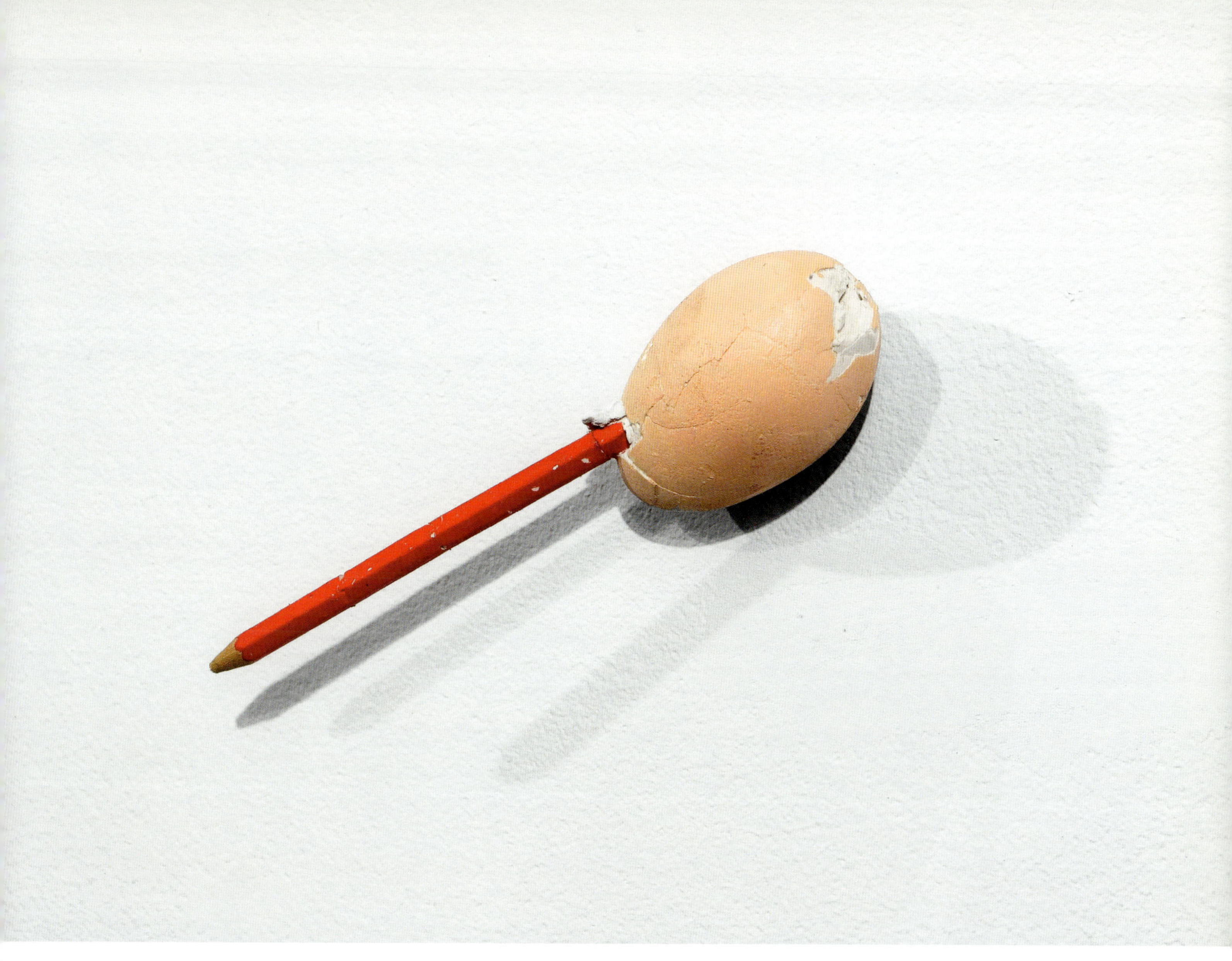

100 Years, 2006
Plaster, acrylic paint, glue
4 x 7 x 3 ¾ inches (10 x 17.8 x 9.5 cm)

Following pages:
Untitled (Brick), 2005
Polyurethane resin, acrylic paint
9 x 3 x 3 ½ inches (22.9 x 7.6 x 8.9 cm)

Lie to a Dog, 2005
Cast nickel silver, acrylic paint, cheese
20 ⅞ x 17 ¾ x 8 ¼ inches (53 x 45 x 21 cm)

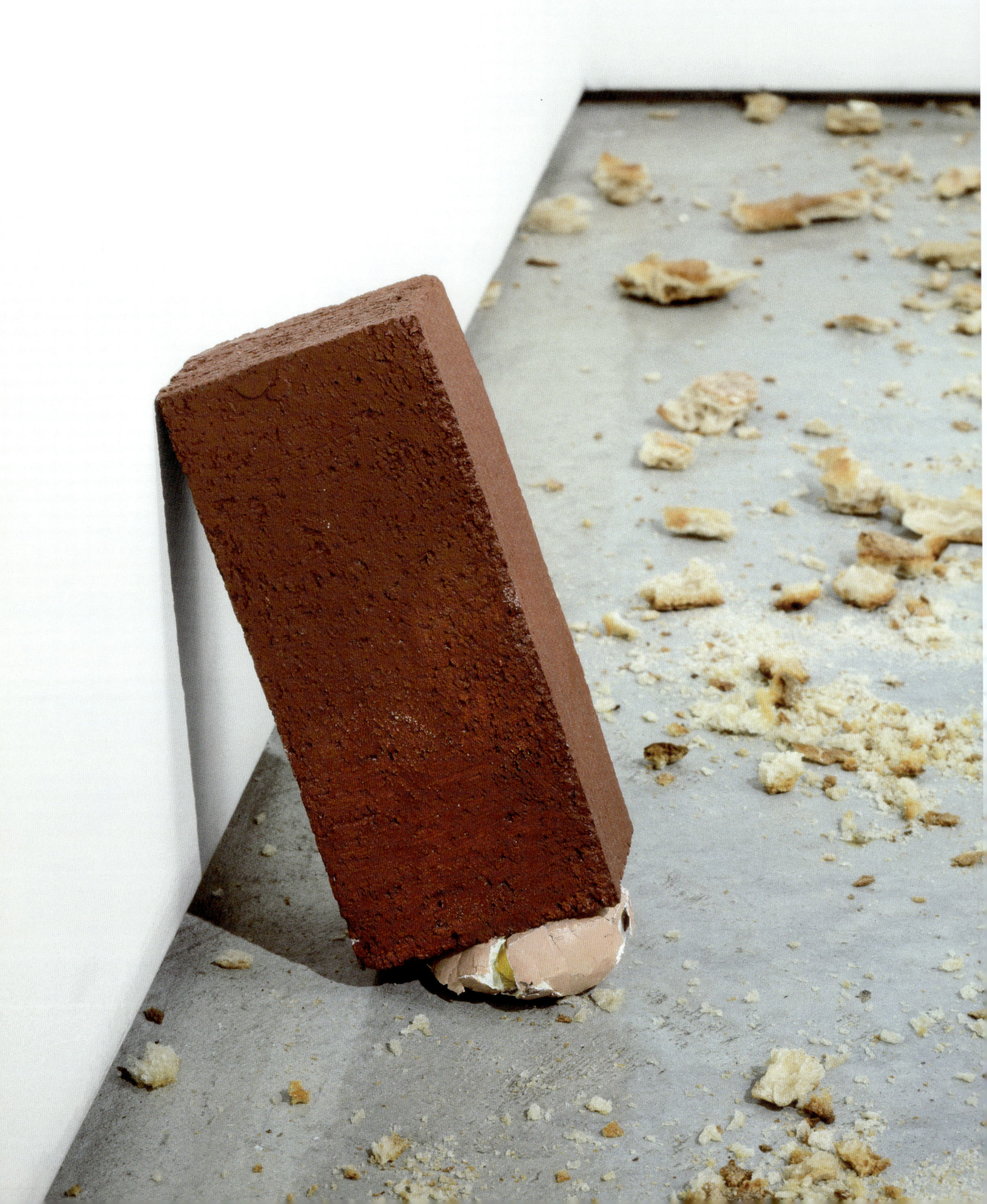

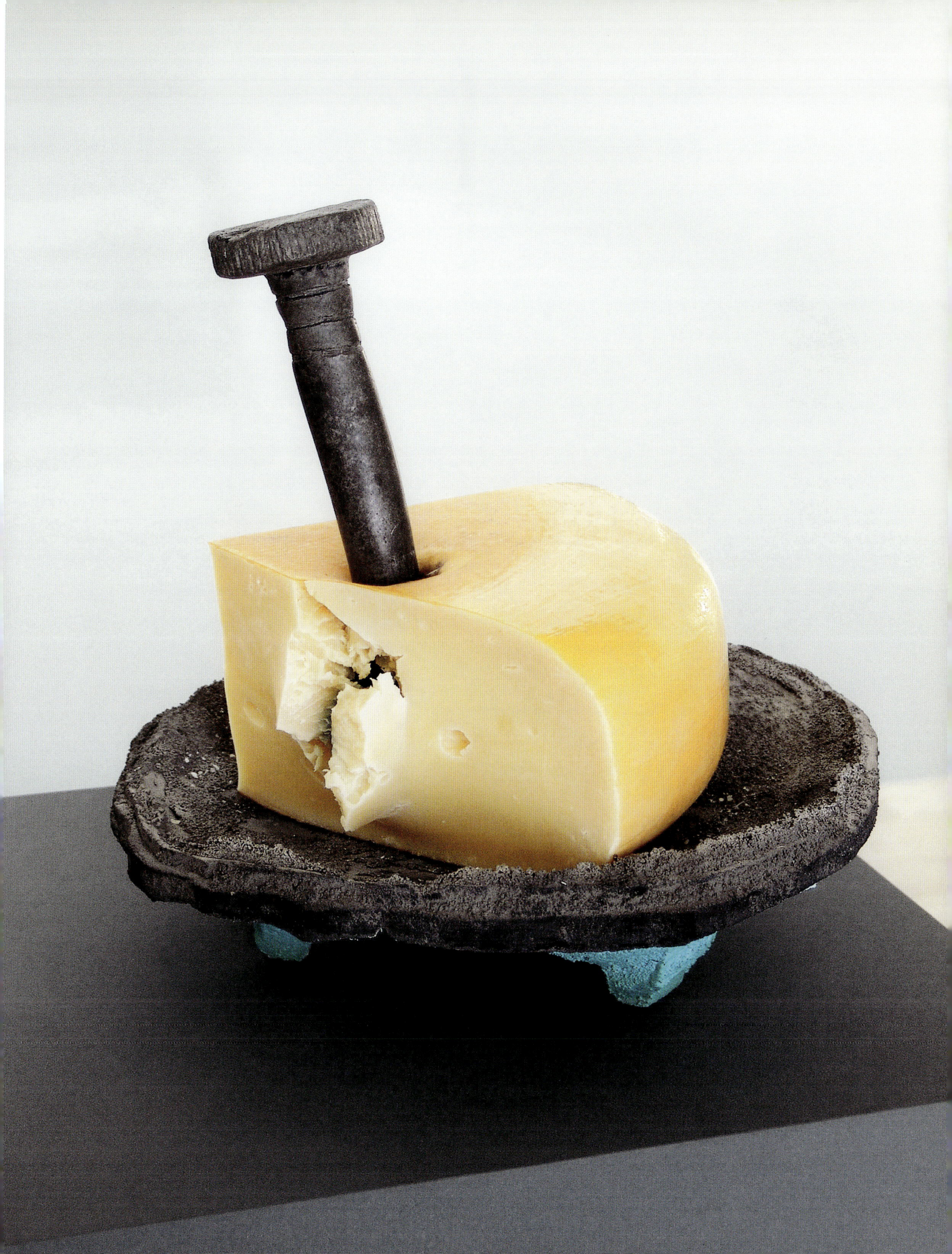

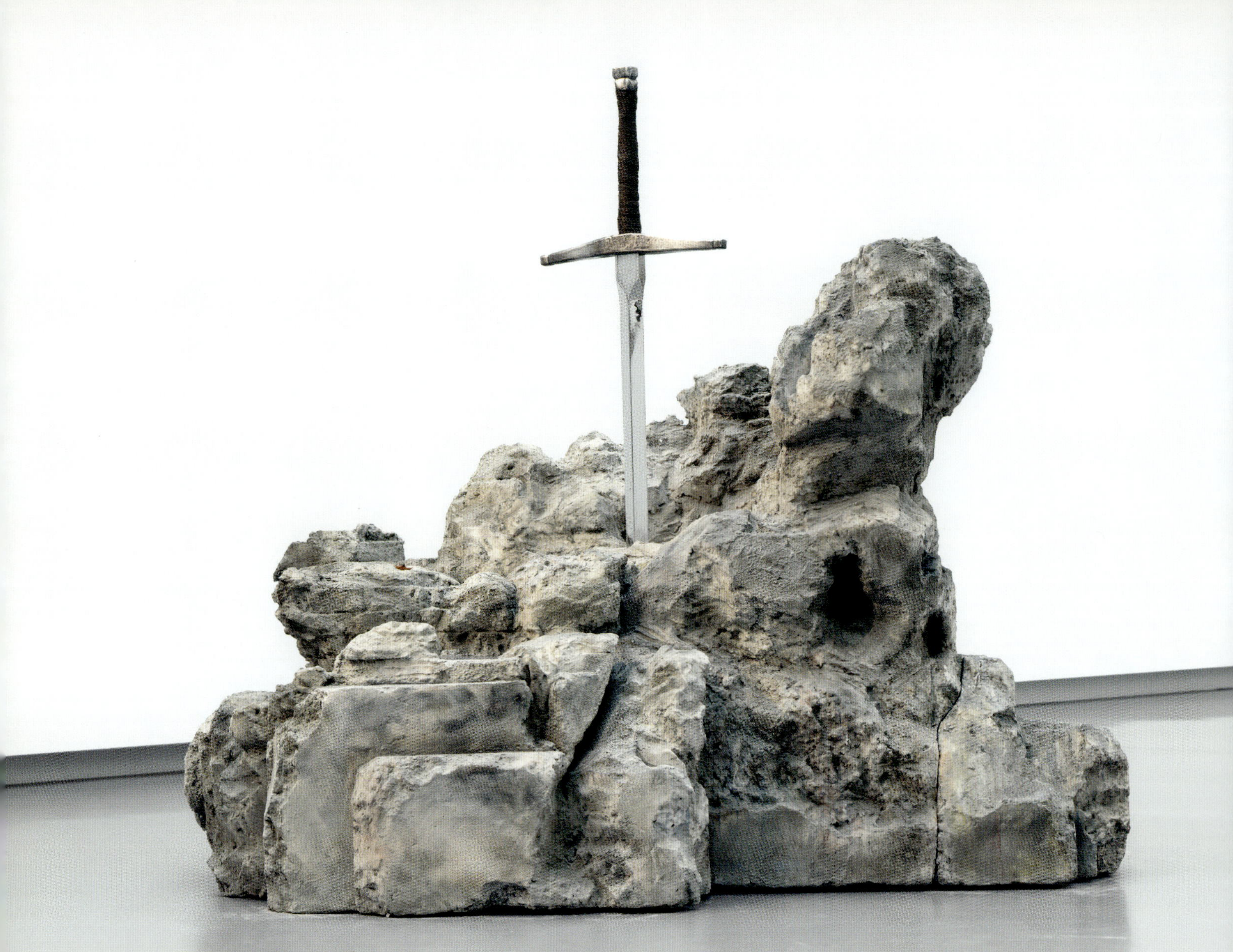

Untitled, 2004
Concrete, iron, steel, wax, cement, soot, pigments, hair, polyurethane resin, acrylic paint
78 ¾ x 89 ⅜ x 66 ⅞ inches (200 x 227 x 170 cm)

Opposite page:
Untitled, 2003
Steel, concrete, screws, hair, polyurethane glue, wood glue, plastic, burlap, wood, chicken wire
76 x 96 x 64 inches (193 x 243.8 x 162.6 cm)

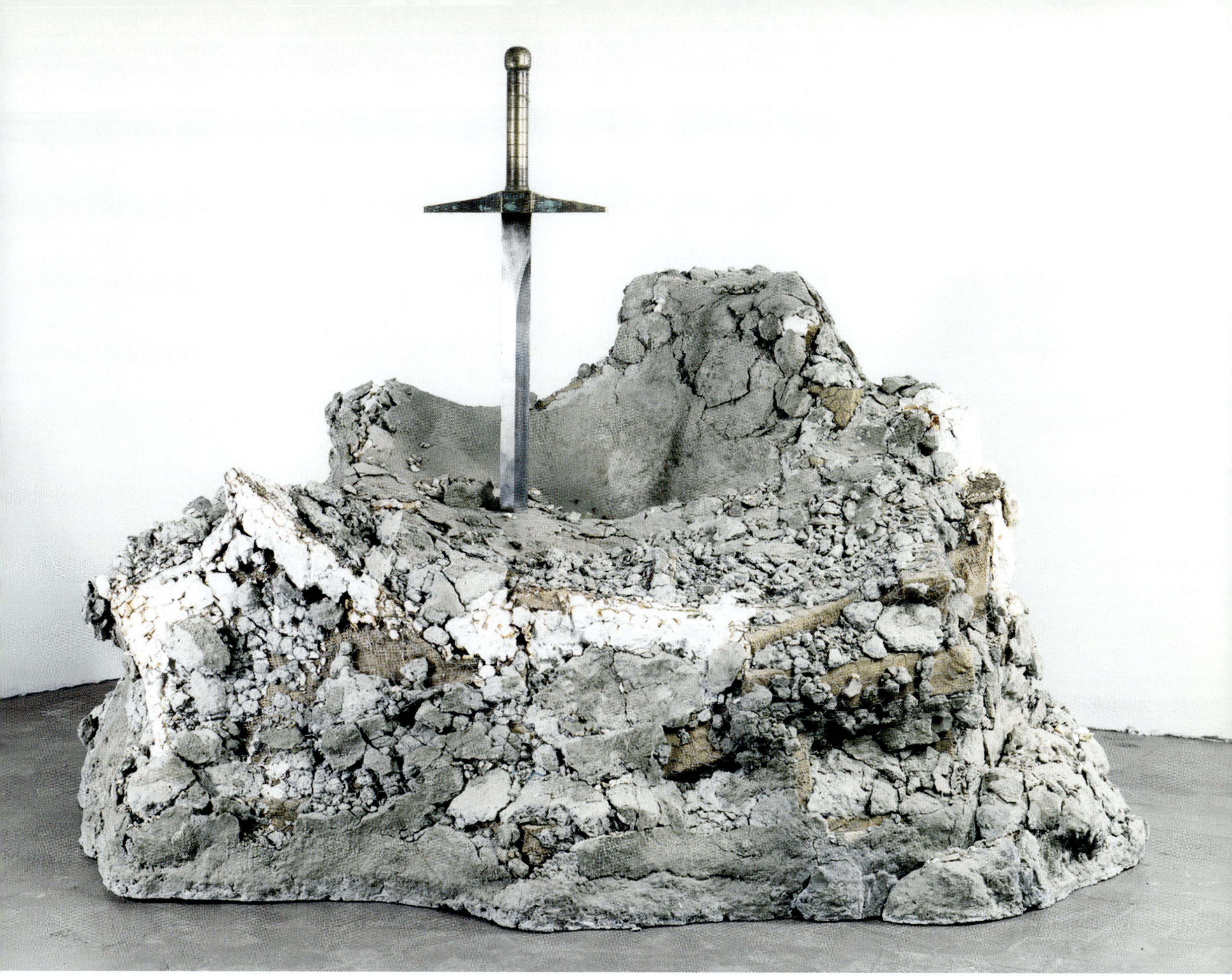

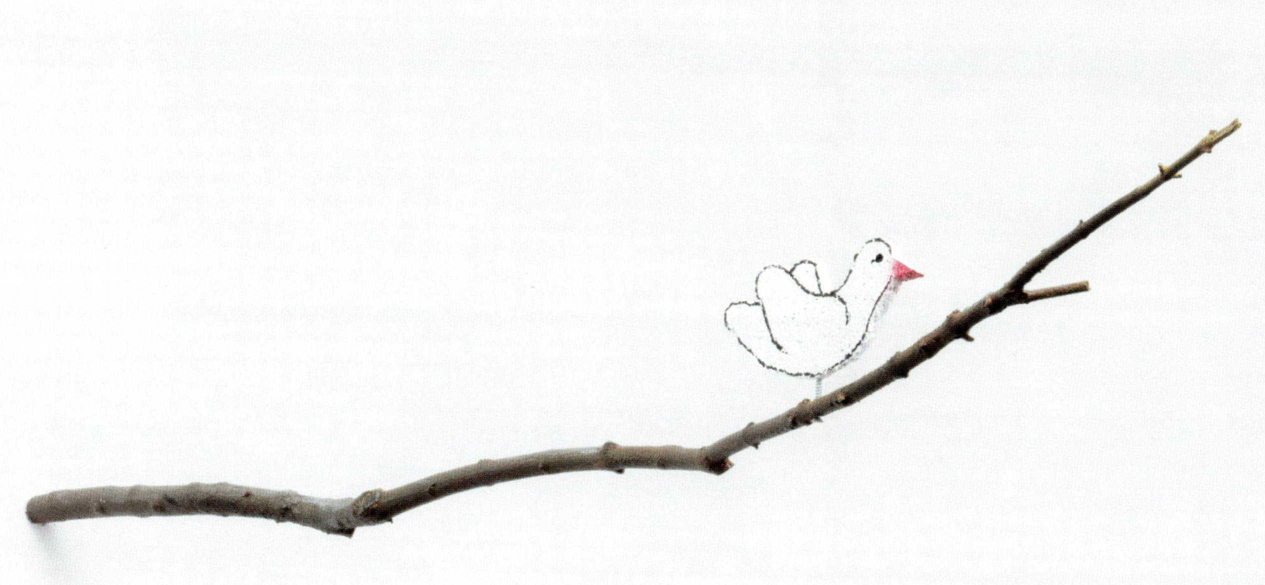

Hear an Old Lady Laugh Out Loud, 2005
Cast aluminum, acrylic paint
5 ⅞ x 59 x 2 ⅜ inches (15 x 150 x 6 cm)

Following pages:
abC, 2007
Cast aluminum, steel chain, iron particles
11 ⅜ x 12 ⅝ x 9 inches (29 x 32 x 23 cm)
Chain: 137 ¾ inches (350 cm)

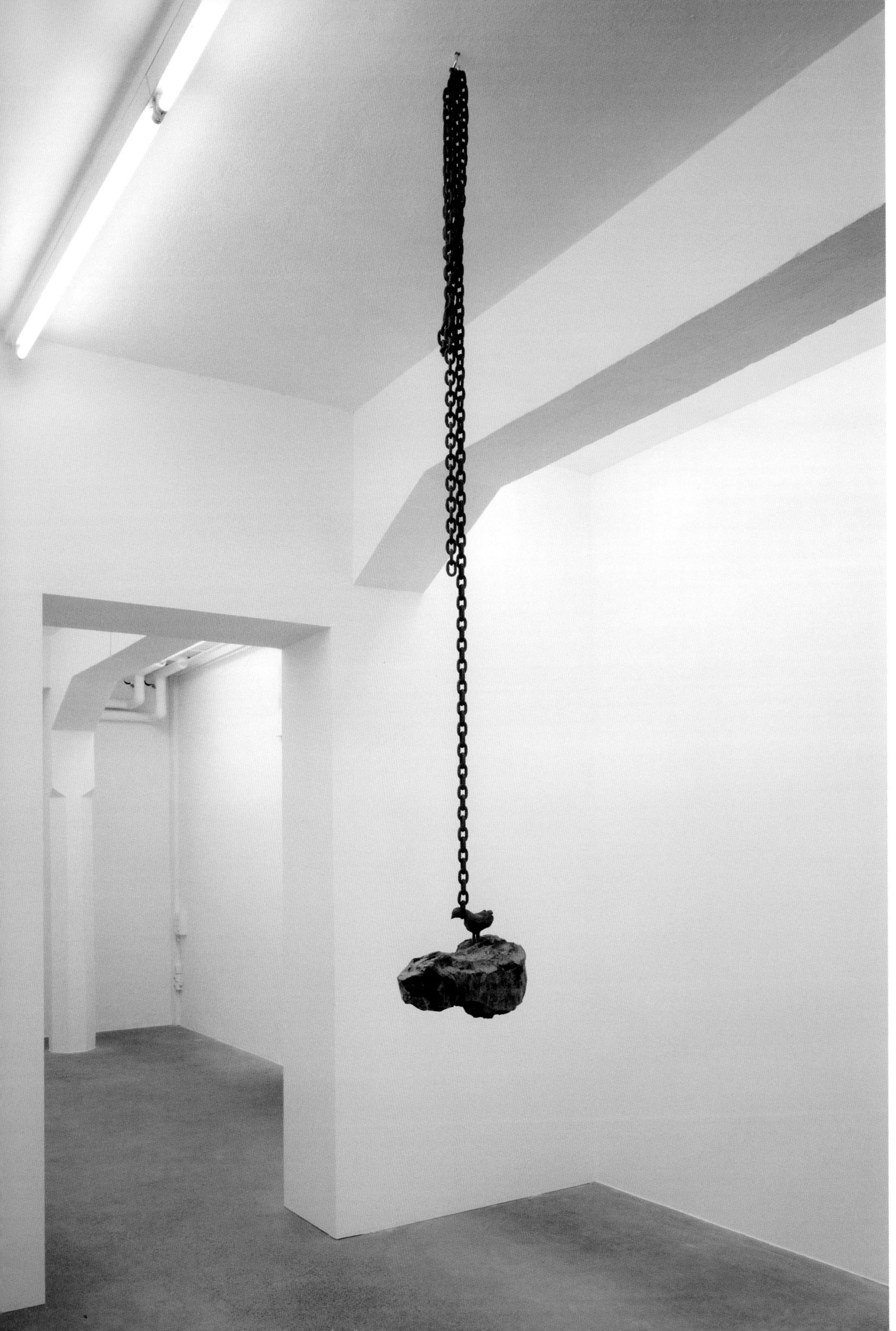

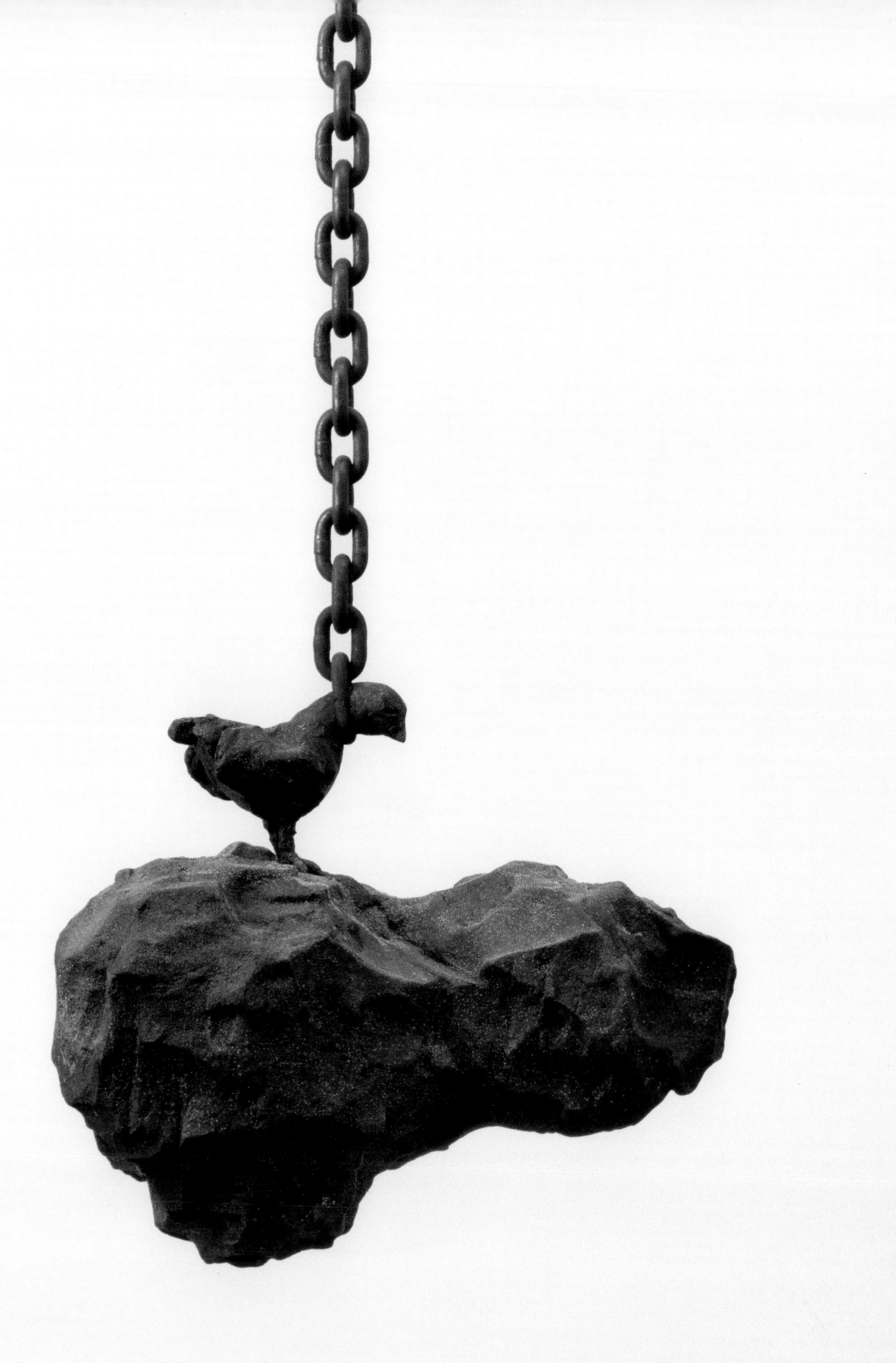

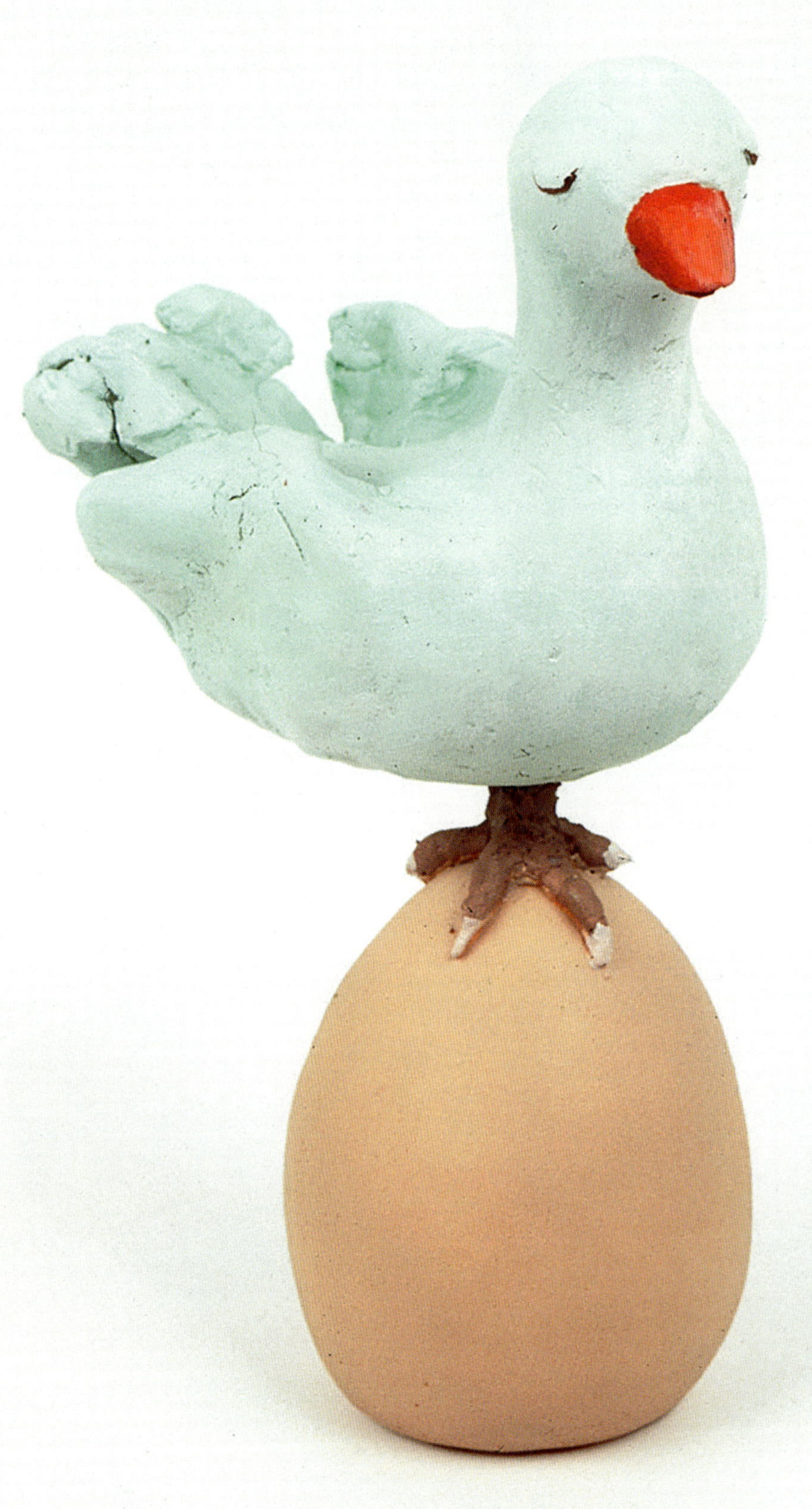

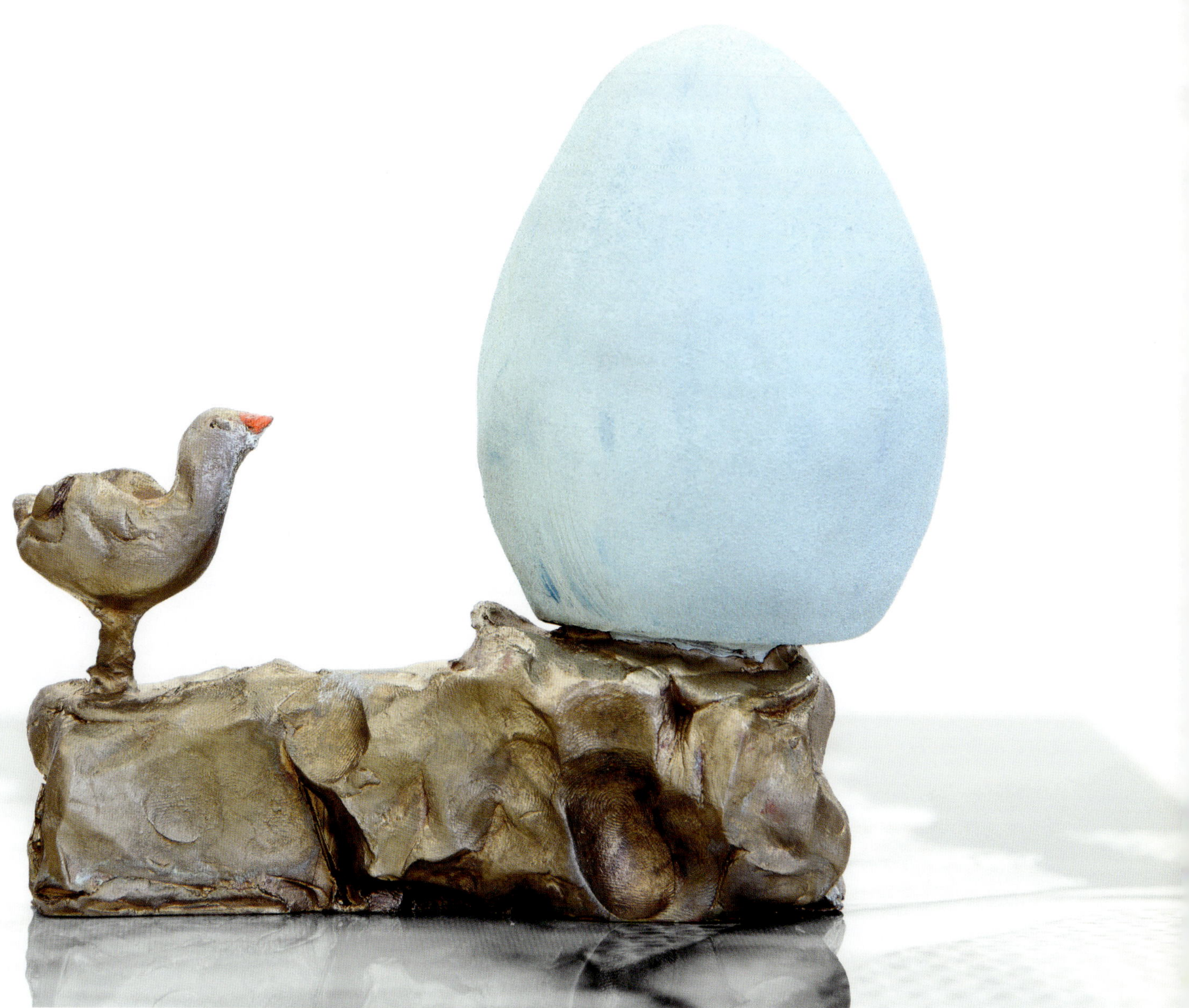

Small Bird, Big Egg, 2011
Cast bronze, oil paint
5 ¾ x 5 ¾ x 3 inches (14.6 x 14.6 x 7.6 cm)

Opposite page:
Untitled, 2004
Polyurethane resin, acrylic paint, metal pin
5 ⅞ x 4 ¾ x 2 inches (15 x 12 x 5 cm)

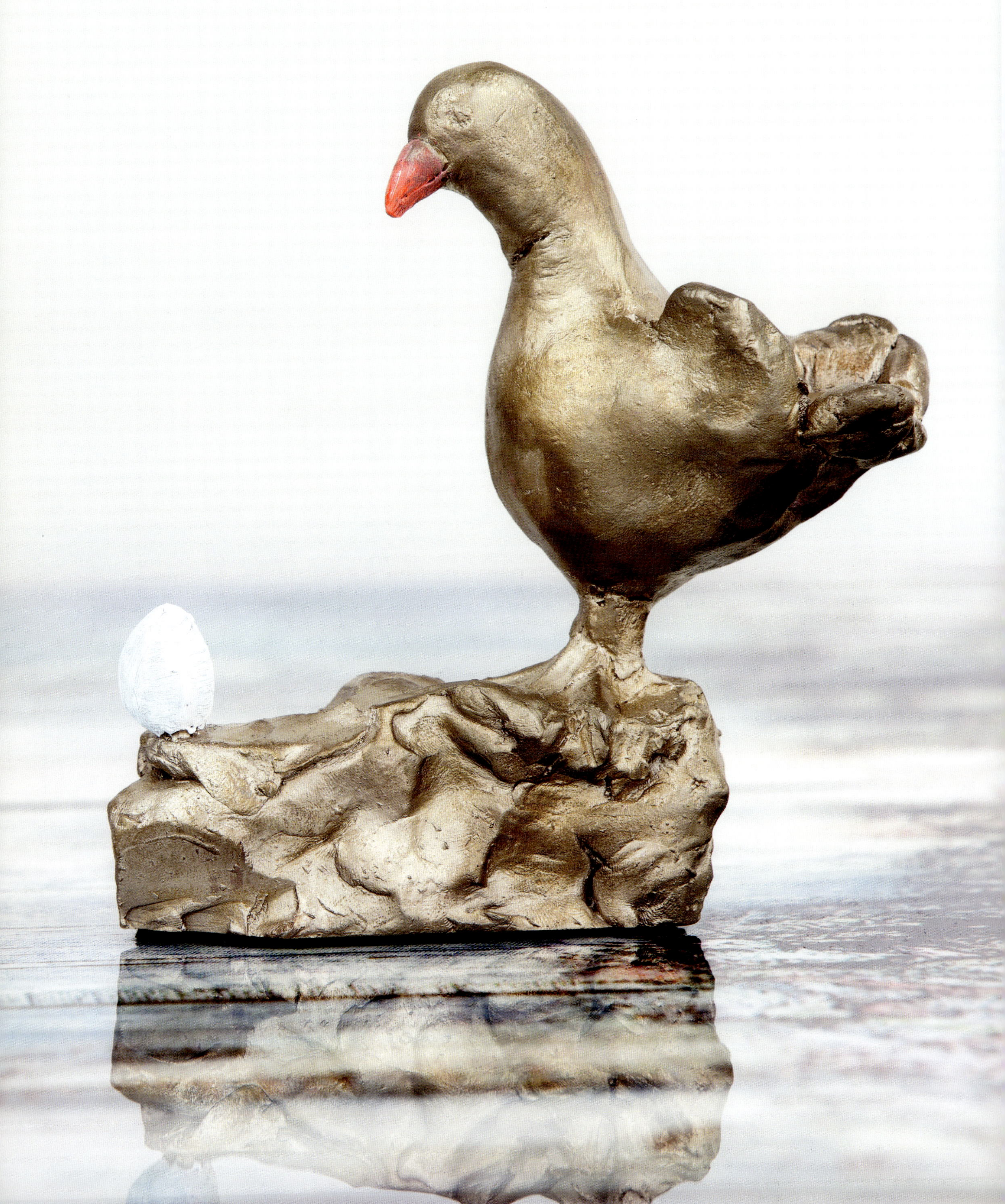

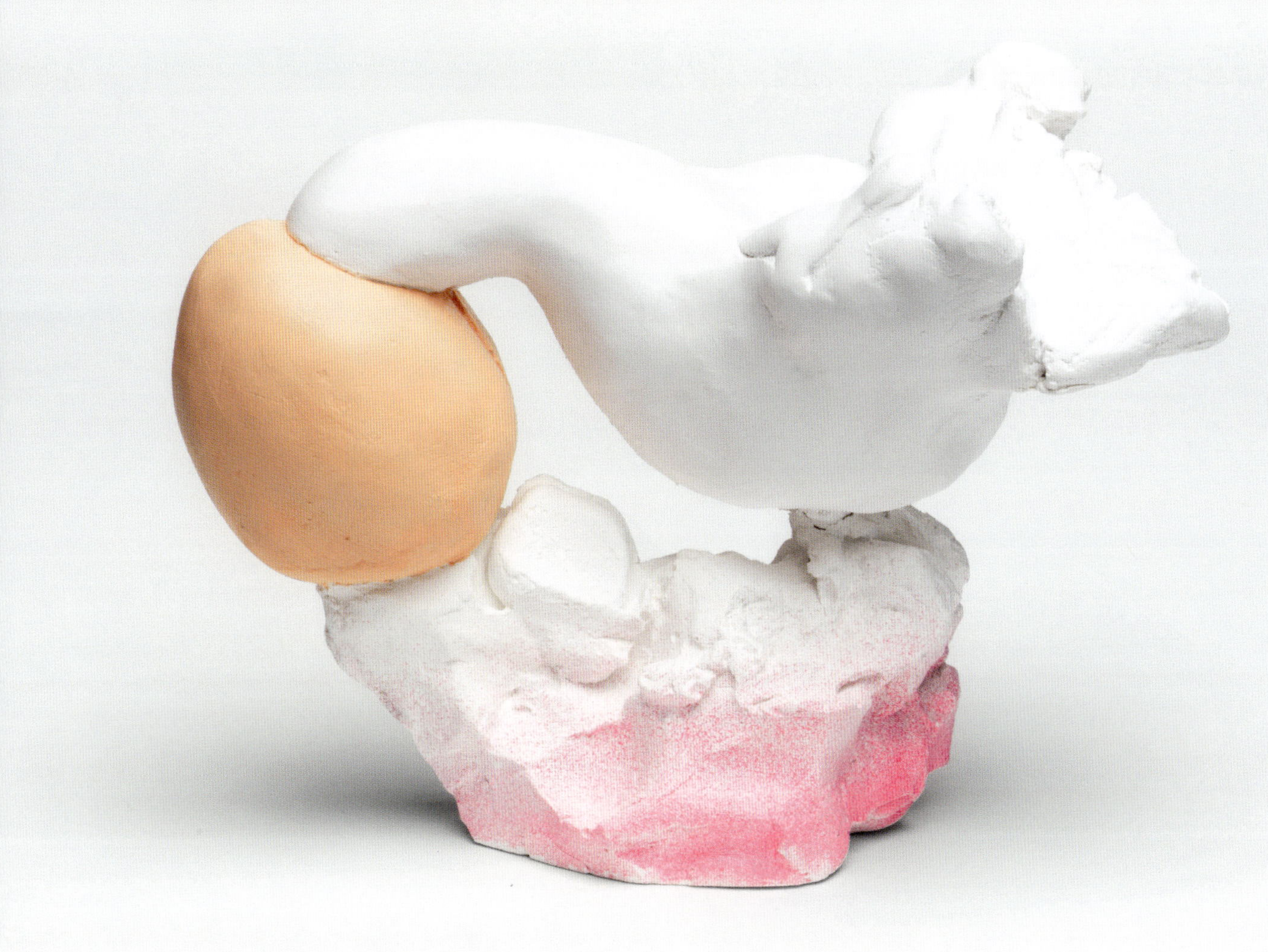

Untitled (Bird Head in Egg), 2012
Plaster, screw, acrylic paint, spray paint
5 ½ x 7 ½ x 3 ¾ inches (13.9 x 19 x 9.5 cm)

Opposite page:
Small Egg, Big Bird, 2011
Cast bronze, oil paint
6 ½ x 6 x 2 ¾ inches (16.5 x 15.2 x 7 cm)

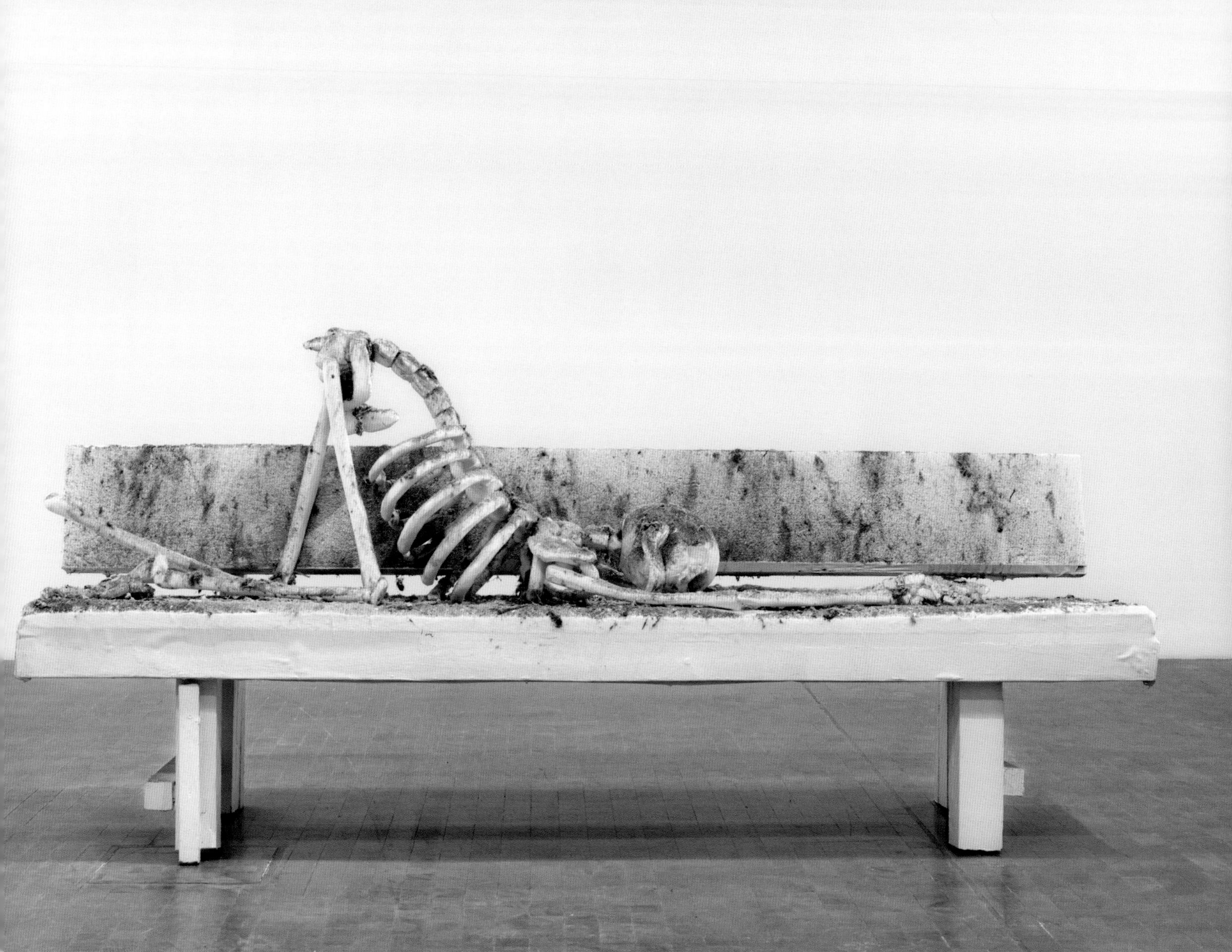

Skinny Sunrise, 2000
Polystyrene, wood, wood glue, dust, spray adhesive, flour, acrylic paint, silicone, screws, fabric
27 ½ x 47 ¼ x 27 ½ inches (70 x 120 x 70 cm)

Following pages:
One More Carrot Before I Brush My Teeth, 2001
Wood, polystyrene, polyurethane foam, particleboard, glass, latex paint, silicone, pencil, spray adhesive, screws, dust, glue
51 ⅝ x 31 ⅞ x 38 ¼ inches (131 x 81 x 97 cm)

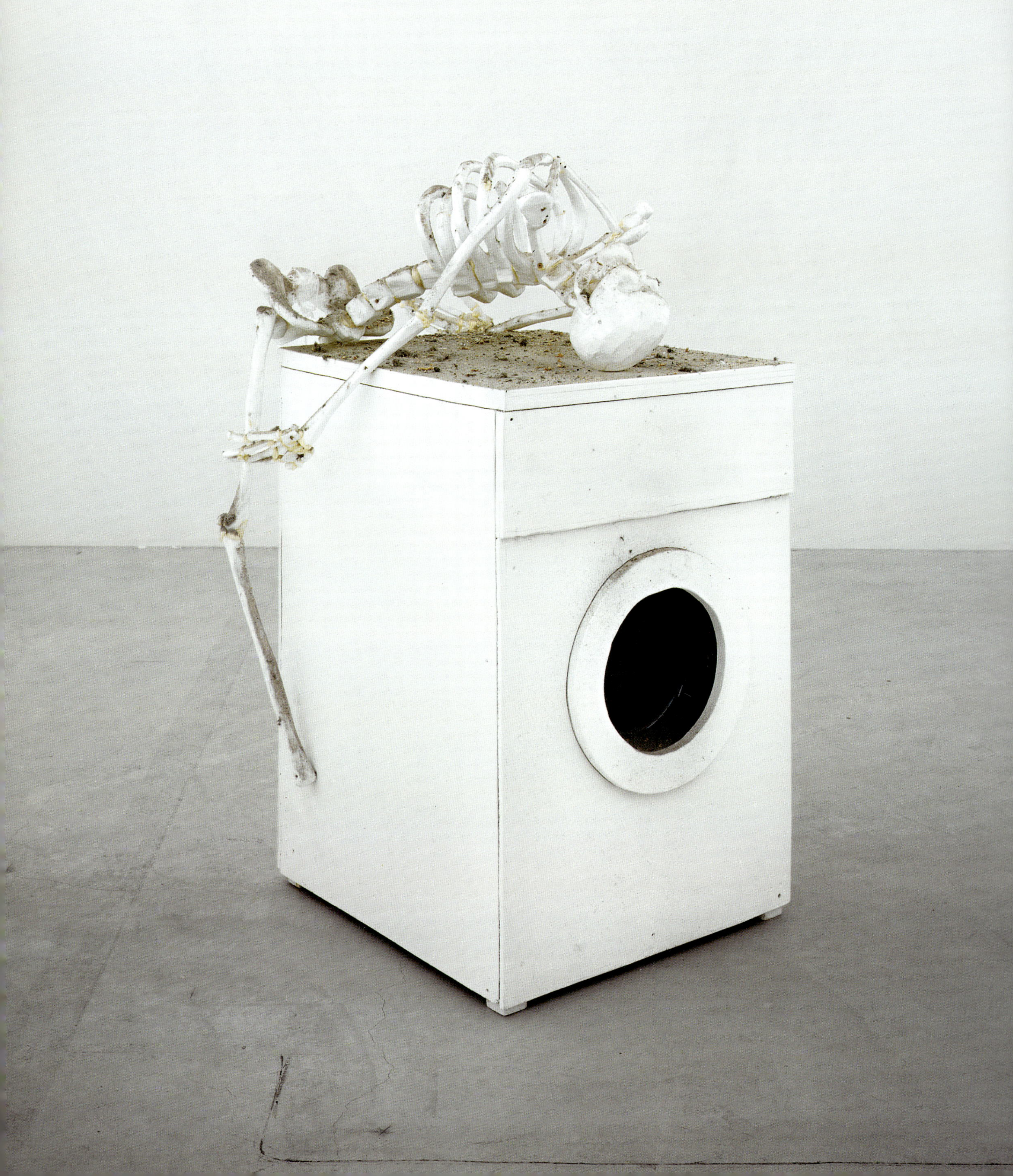

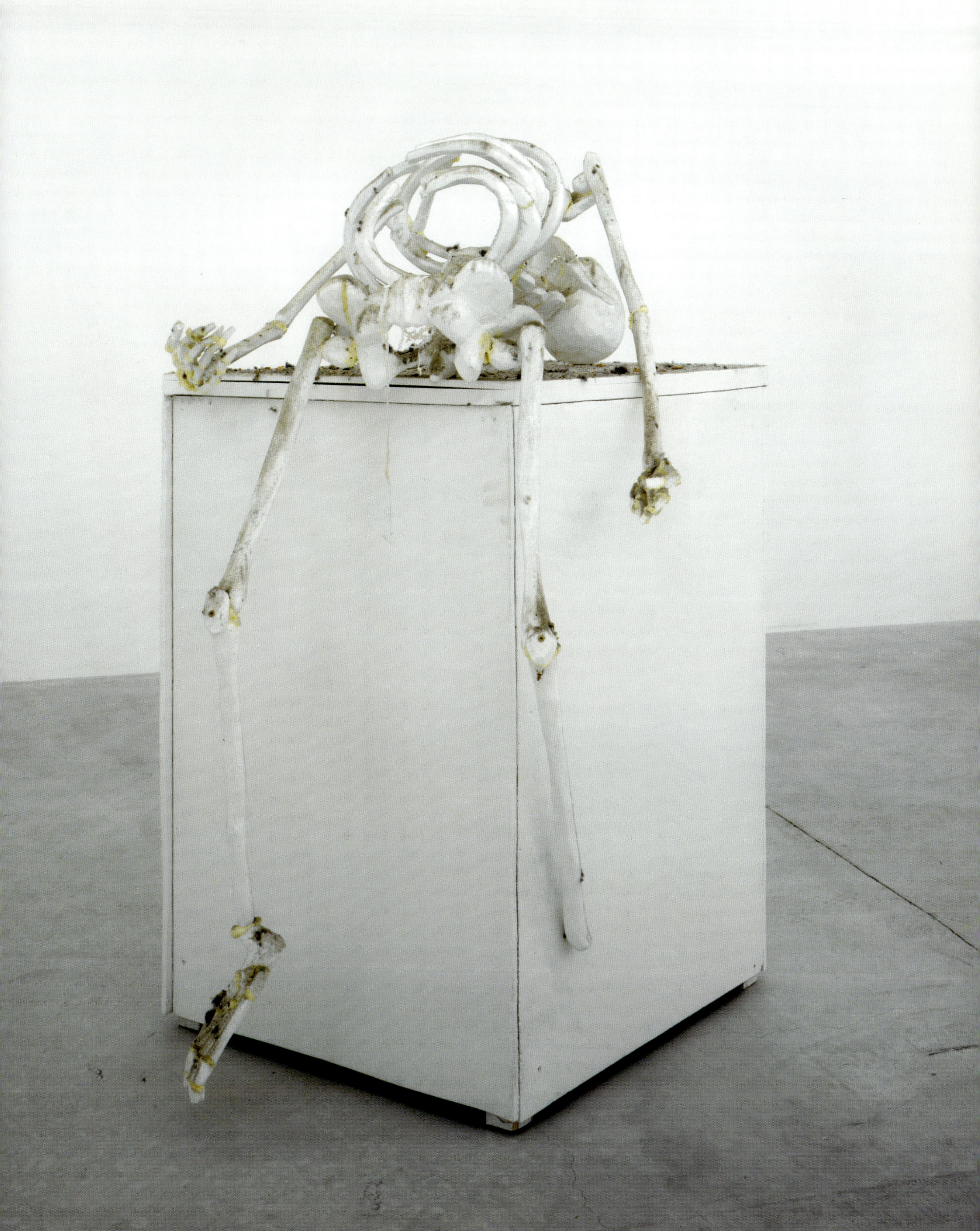

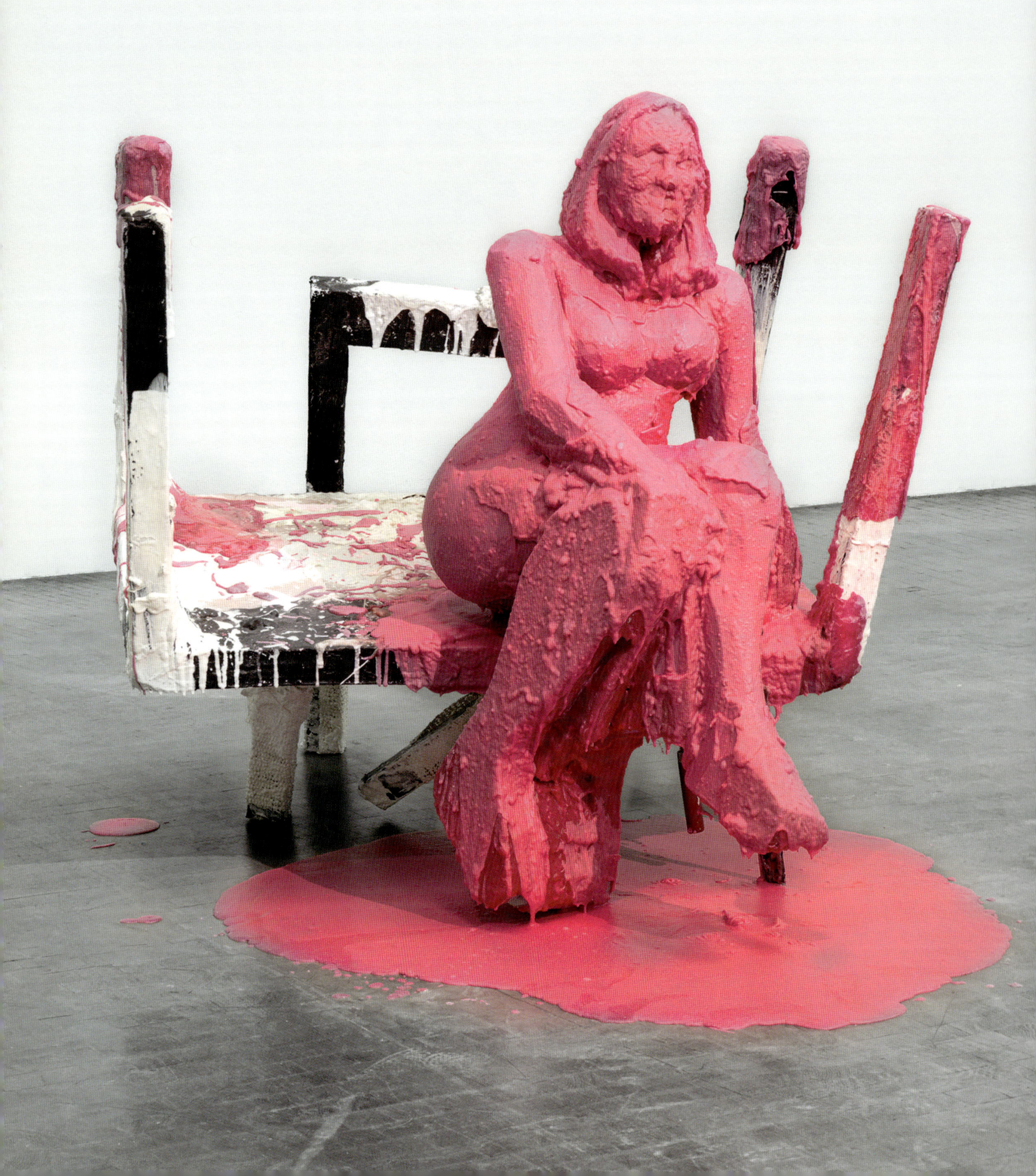

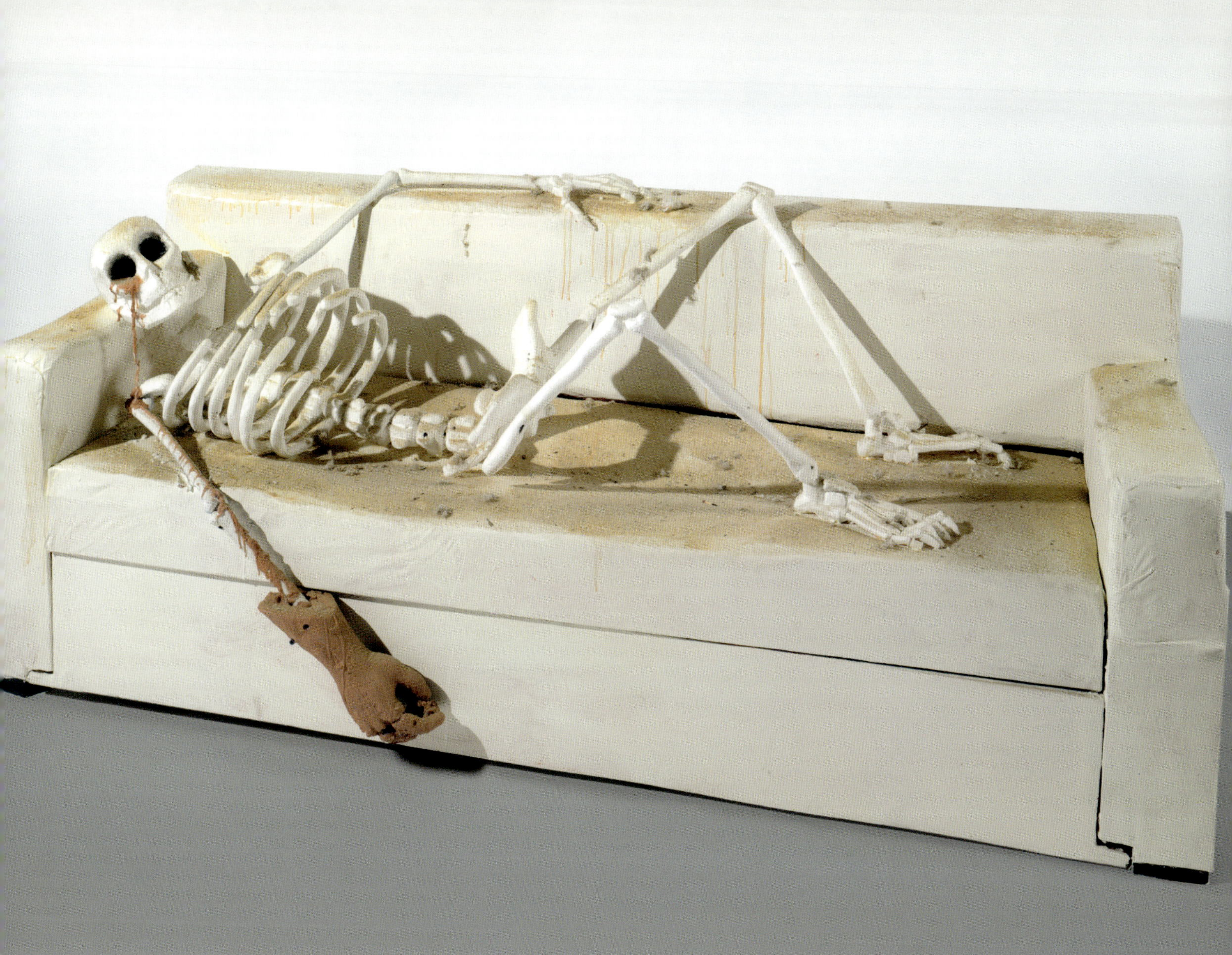

Undigested Sunset, 2001–2002
Cast aluminum, wax, wood, acrylic paint, pigments, fabric, silicone, wood glue, screws
30 ½ x 72 x 28 ½ inches (77.5 x 183 x 72.5 cm)

Opposite page:
Untitled (Pink Lady), 2001
Polystyrene, polyurethane resin, polyurethane foam, oil paint, acrylic paint, fluorescent pigments, sugar, egg whites, screws
39 ⅜ x 39 ⅜ x 59 inches (100 x 100 x 150 cm)

Untitled (Nude on a Table), 2002
Two-component polyurethane foam, cardboard,
polystyrene, polyurethane foam, tape, screws,
powdered sugar, egg whites, pigments, acrylic paint
55 ½ x 61 ¾ x 49 ⅝ inches (141 x 157 x 126 cm)

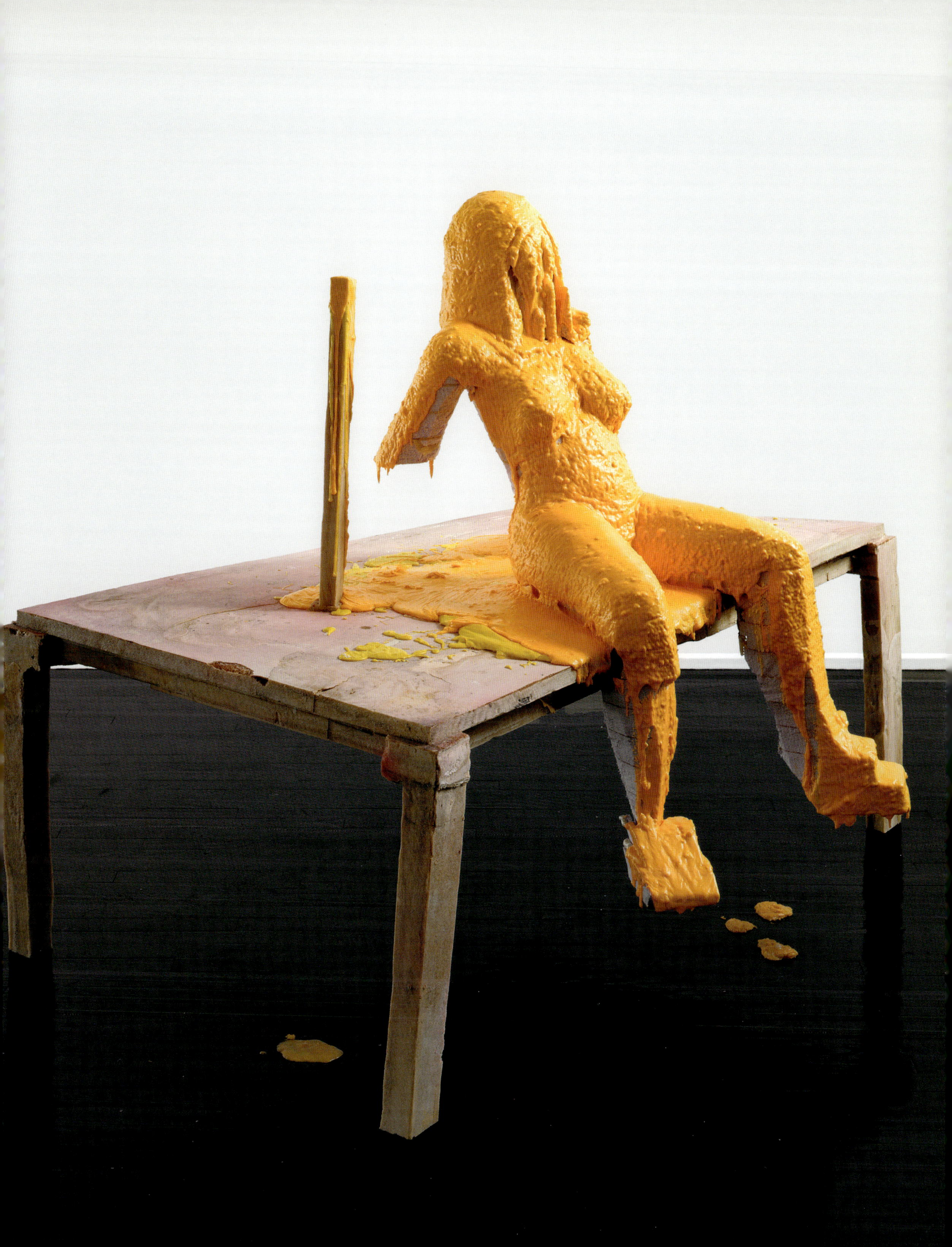

Skinny Afternoon, 2003

Cast aluminum, mirror, lacquer paint, acrylic paint, polyurethane foam, screws

78 ¾ x 63 x 47 ¼ inches (200 x 160 x 120 cm)

Installation view, "Dreams and Conflicts: The Viewer's Dictatorship," Venice Biennale, 2003

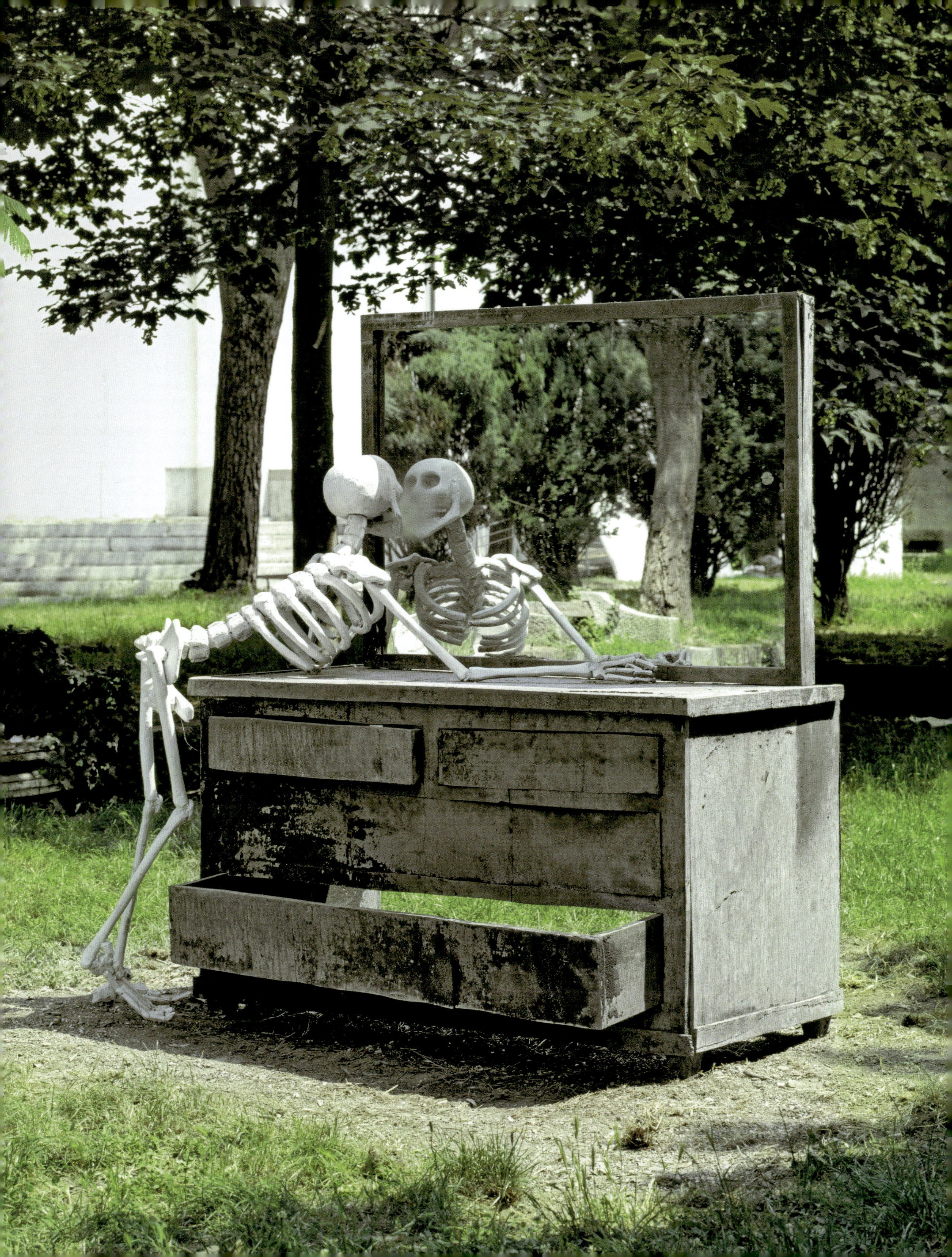

Kuckuck Backwards, 2004
Wood, aluminum, cement, sawdust, enamel paint
63 ¾ x 78 ¾ x 25 ¼ inches (162 x 200 x 64 cm)

Opposite page:
Paris 1919, 2006
Tar, plaster, iron, aluminum, rubber
133 ⅞ x 33 ½ x 33 ½ inches (340 x 85 x 85 cm)

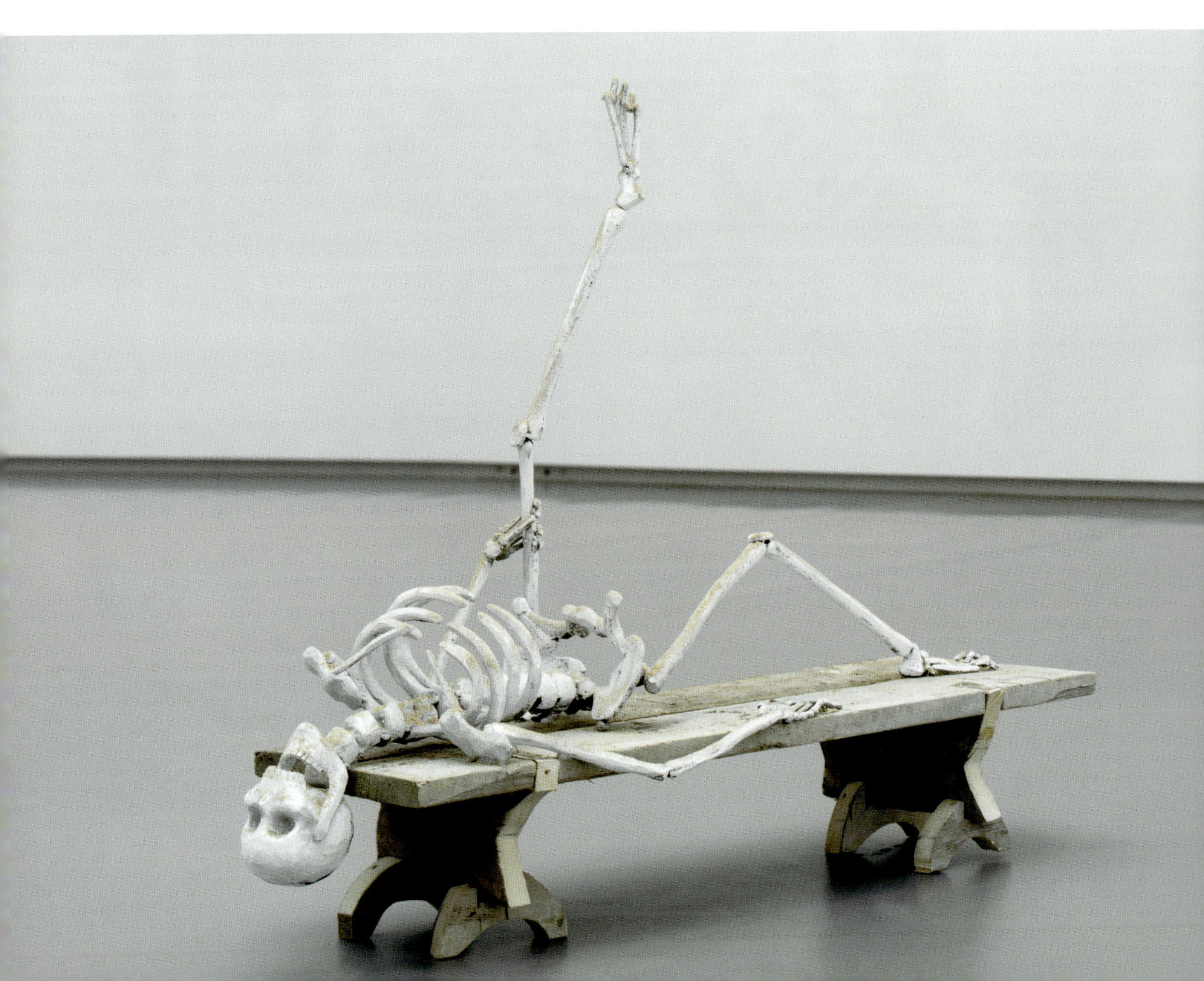

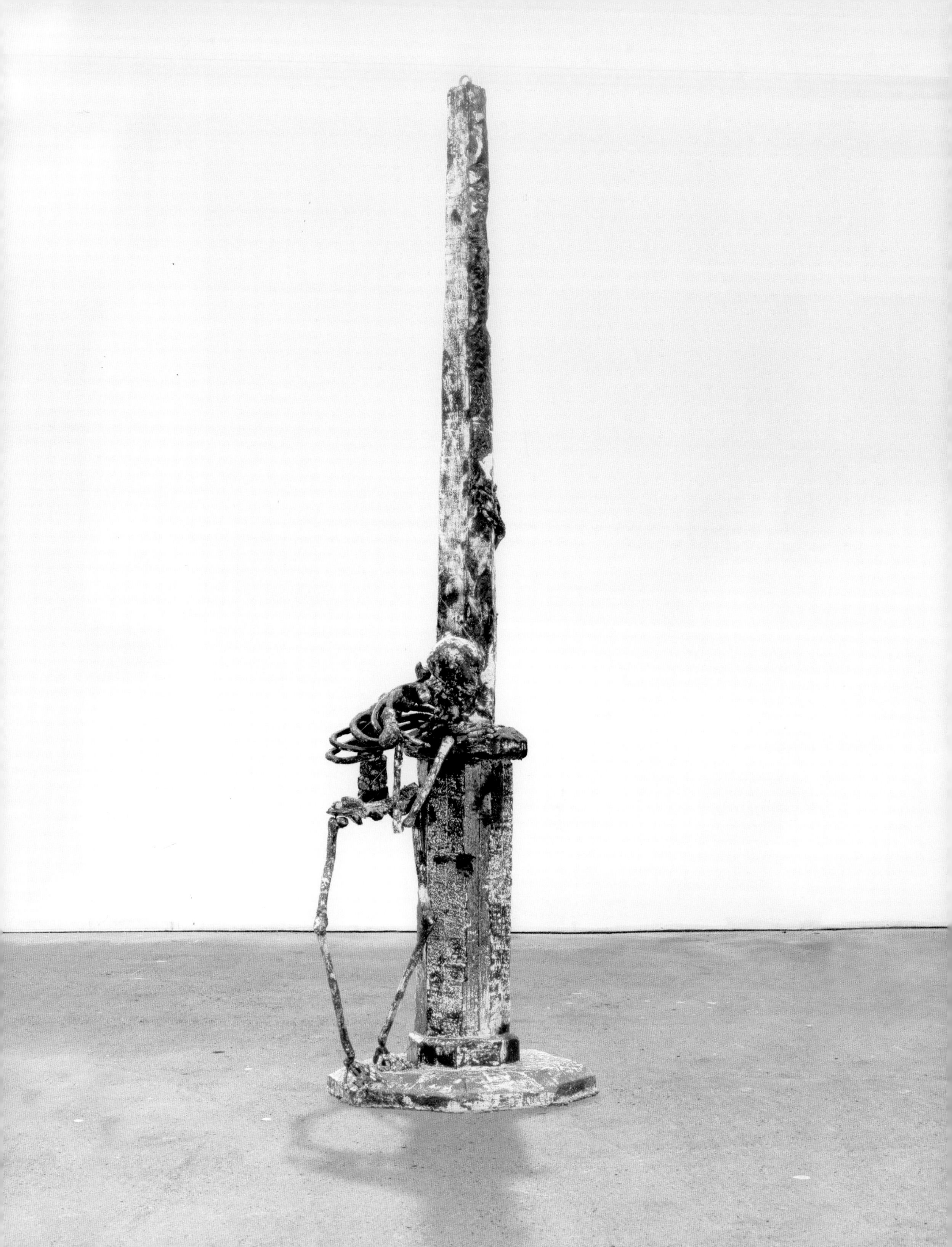

Violent Cappuccino, 2007
Cast aluminum, lacquer, motor oil, glue, dust
79 ¾ x 51 ⅛ x 28 ¾ inches (202.5 x 130 x 73 cm)

Following pages:
Urs Fischer and Georg Herold
Necrophonia, 2011
Cast zinc, cast aluminum, acrylic paint,
fabric, nude model, fresh flowers; in 57 parts
38 ¼ x 33 ½ x 35 ⅞ inches (97 x 85 x 91 cm)
Dimensions variable

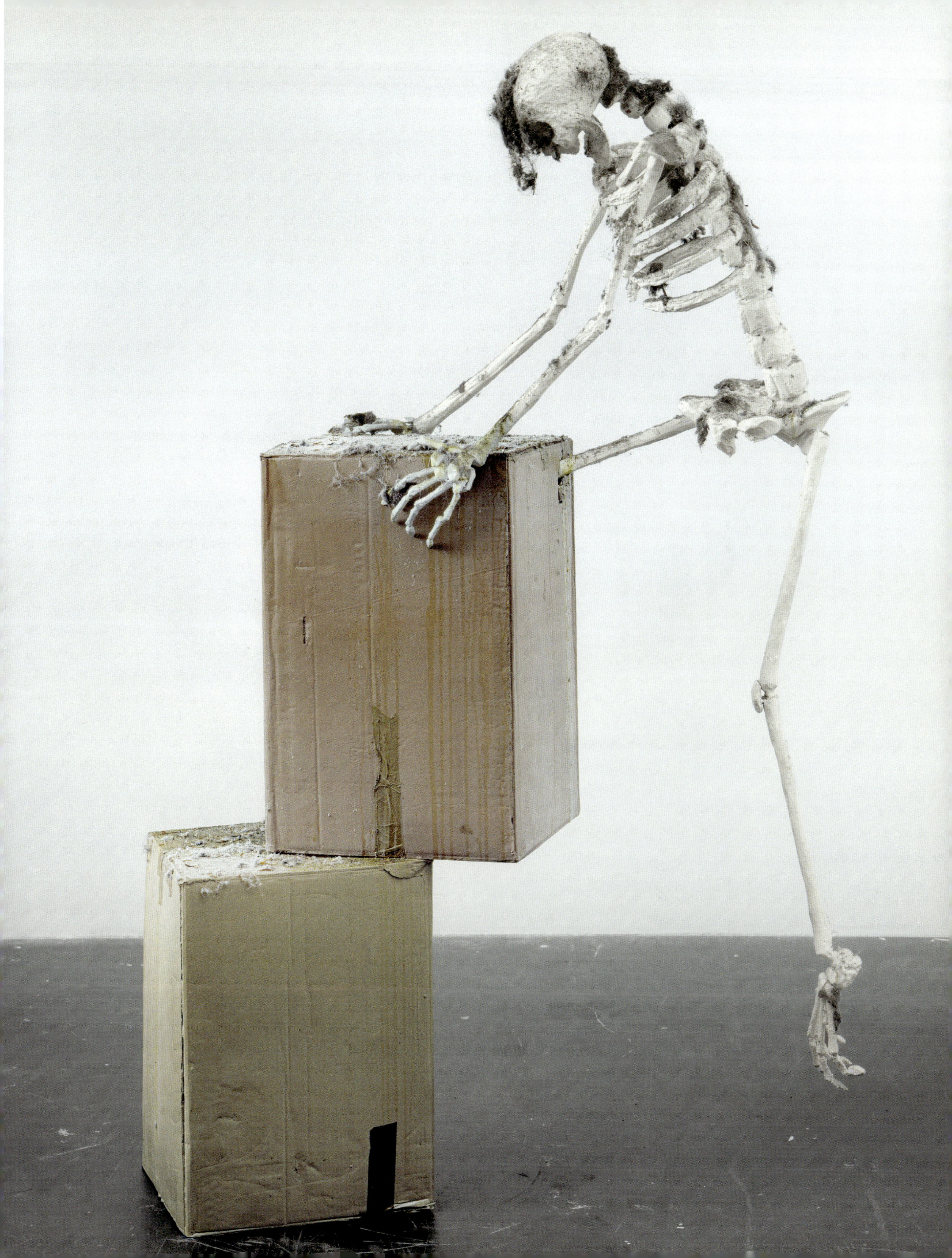

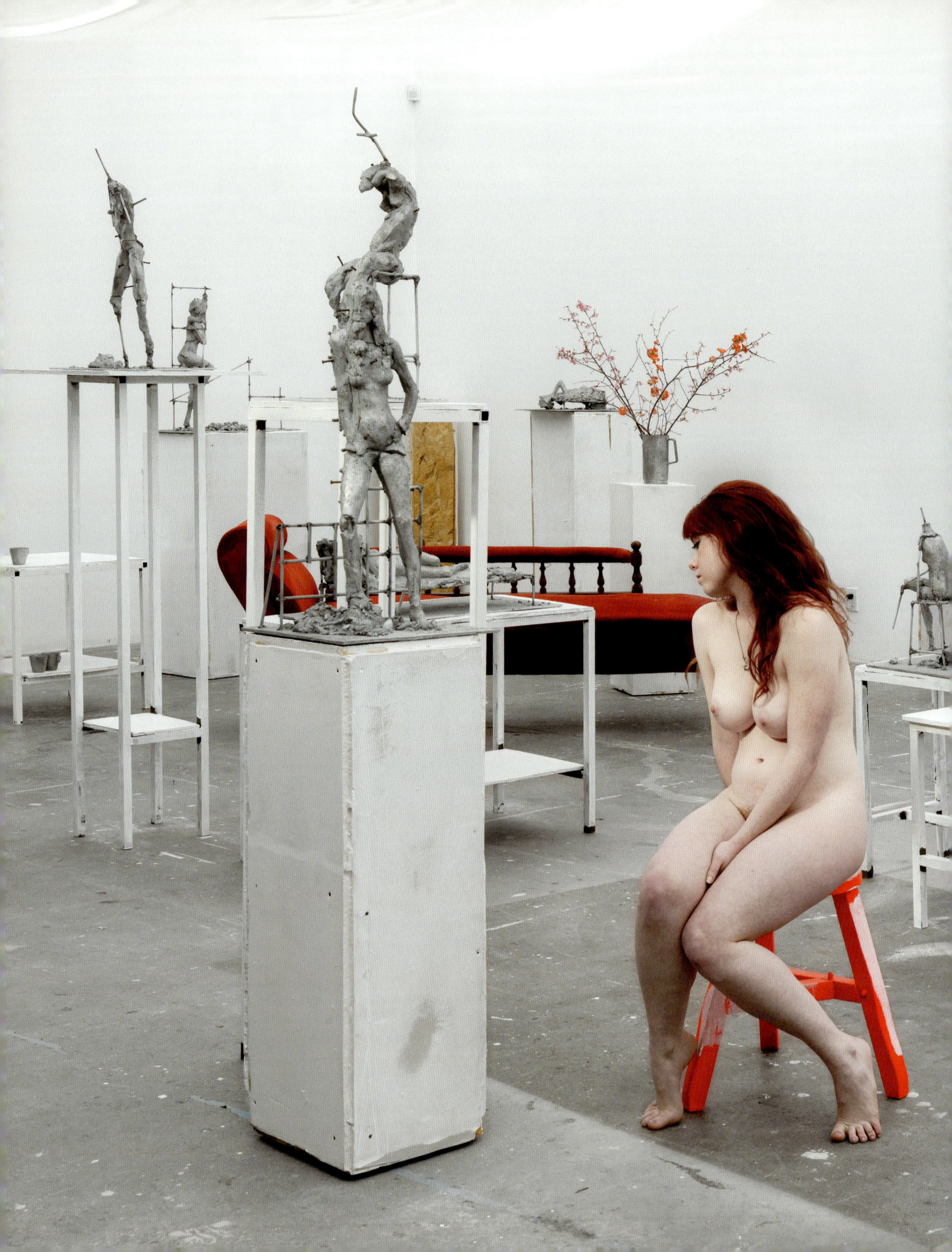

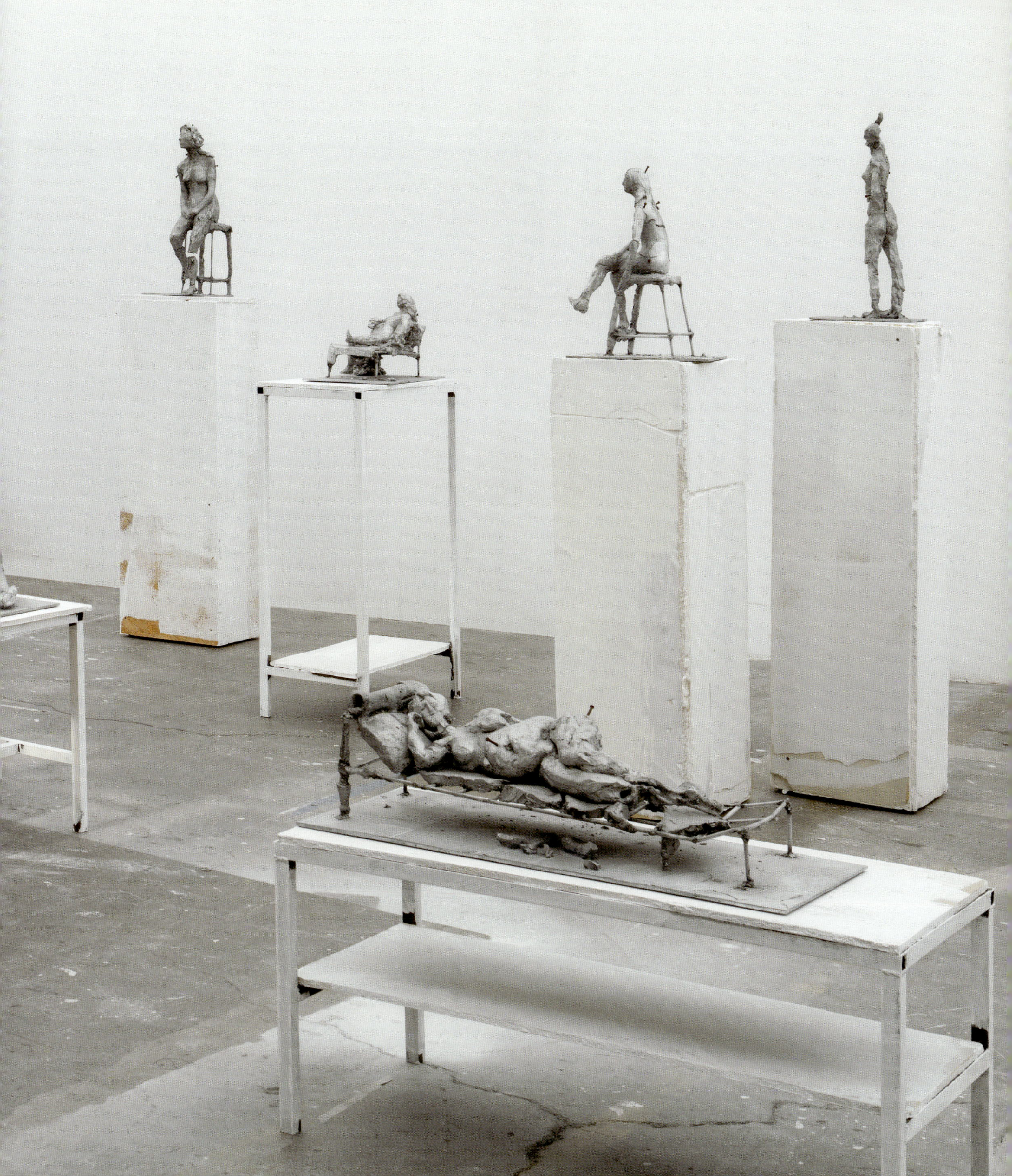

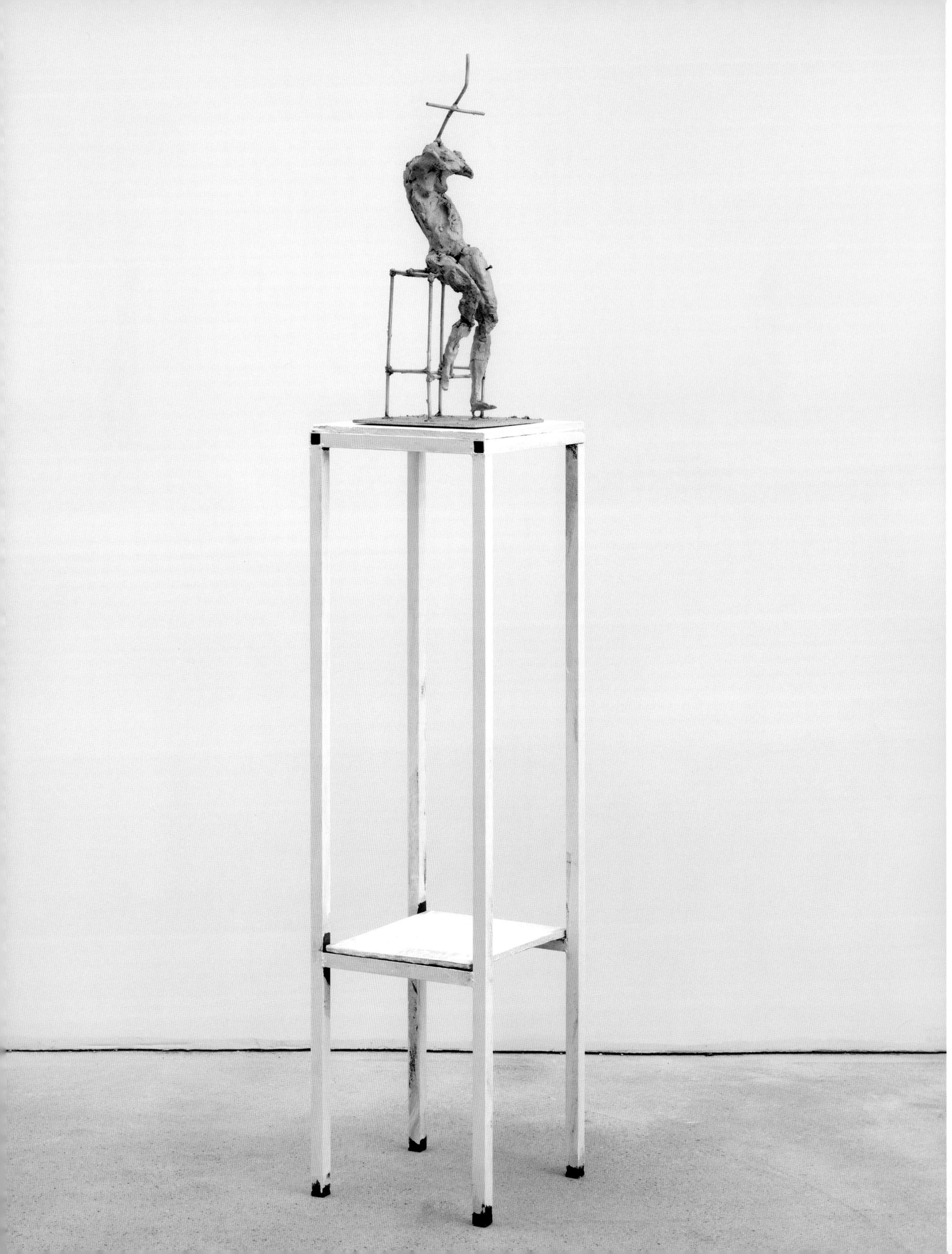

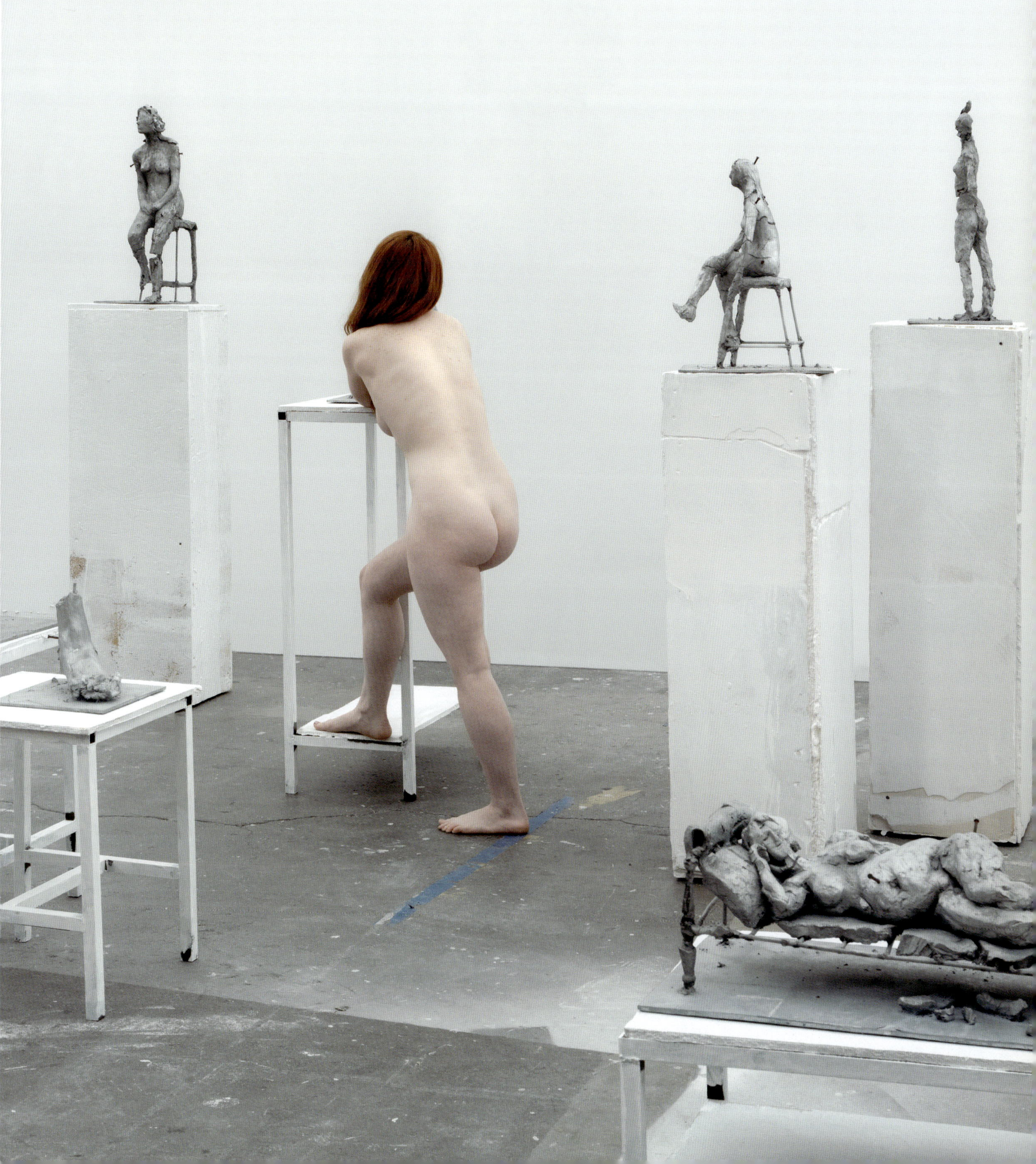

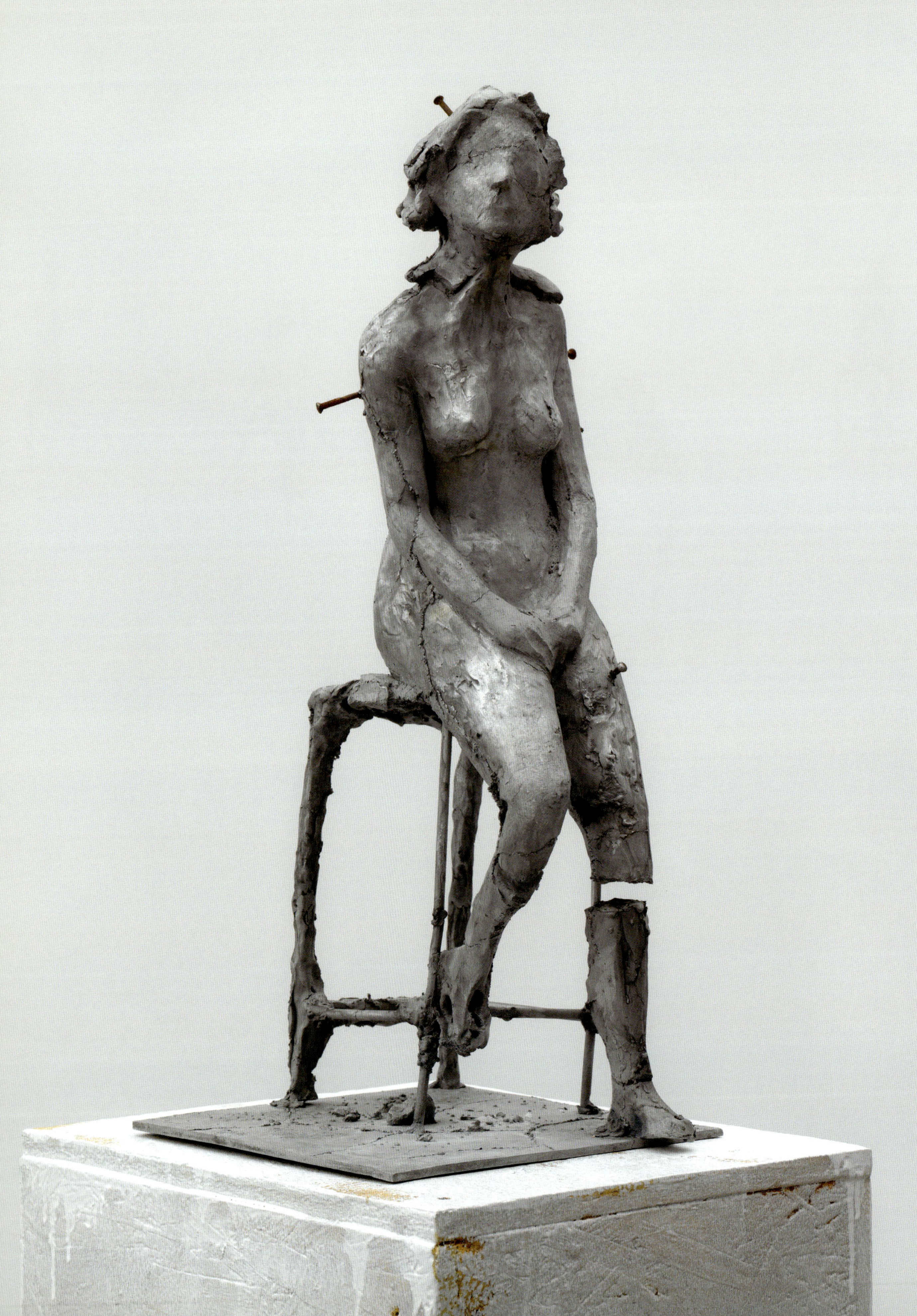

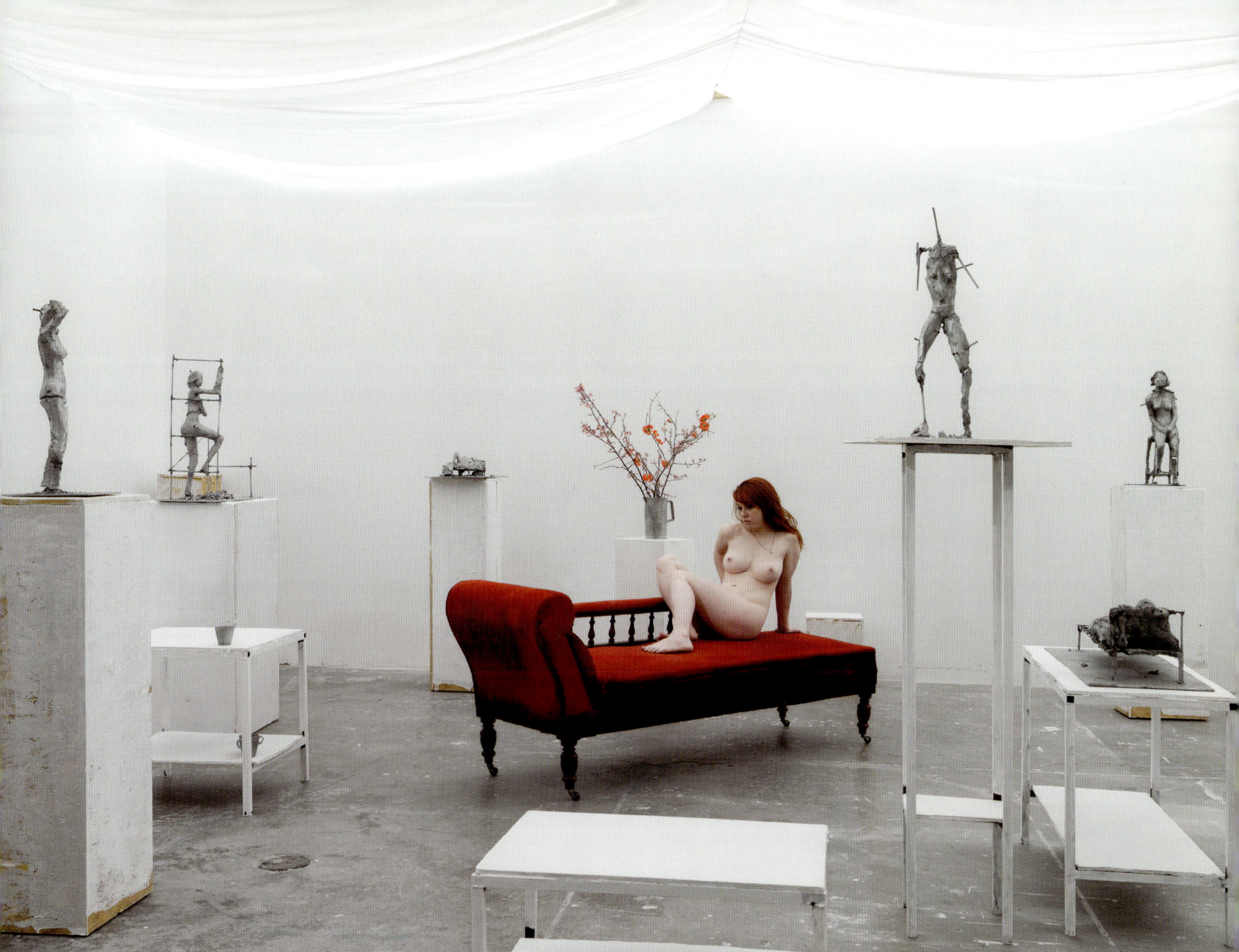

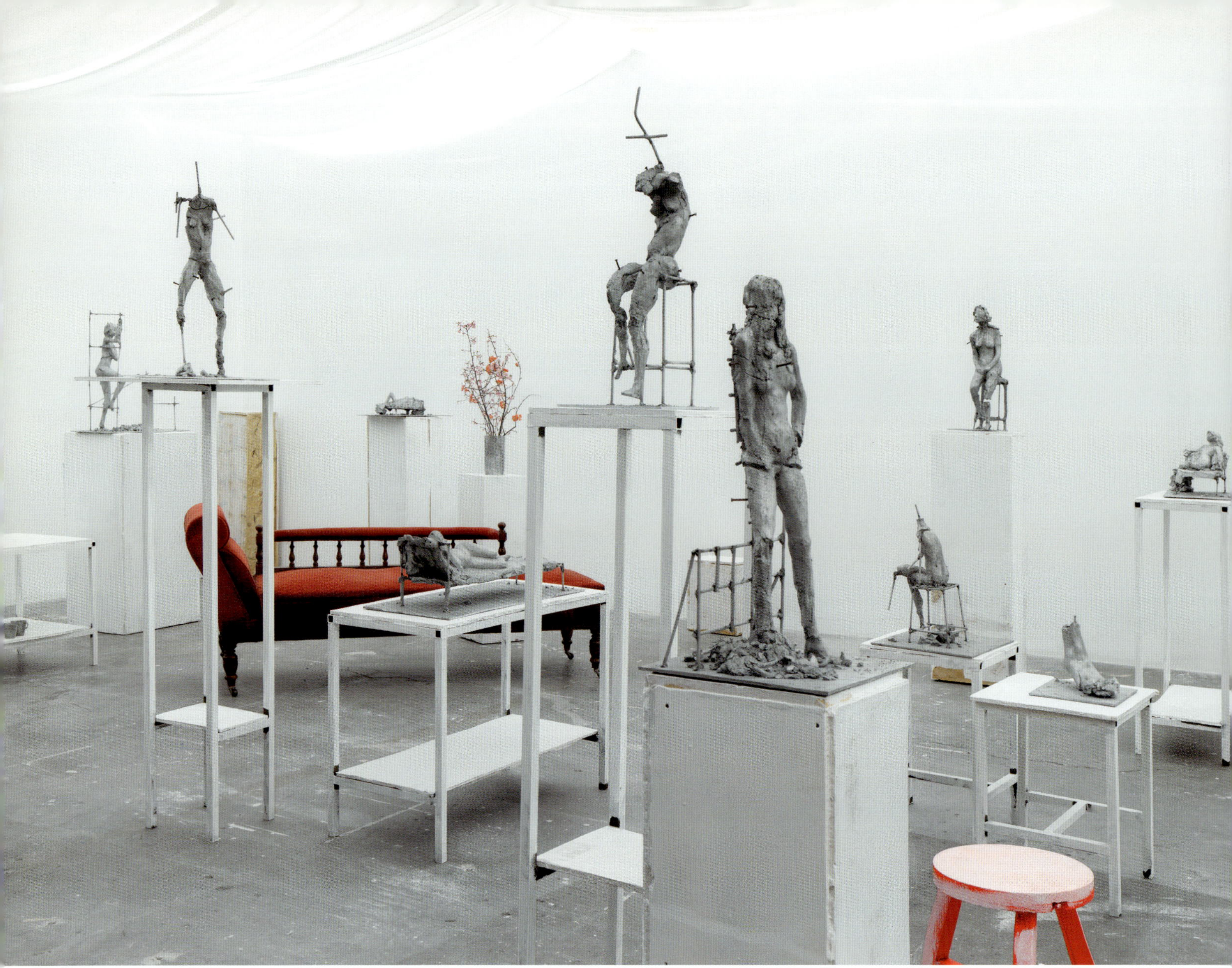

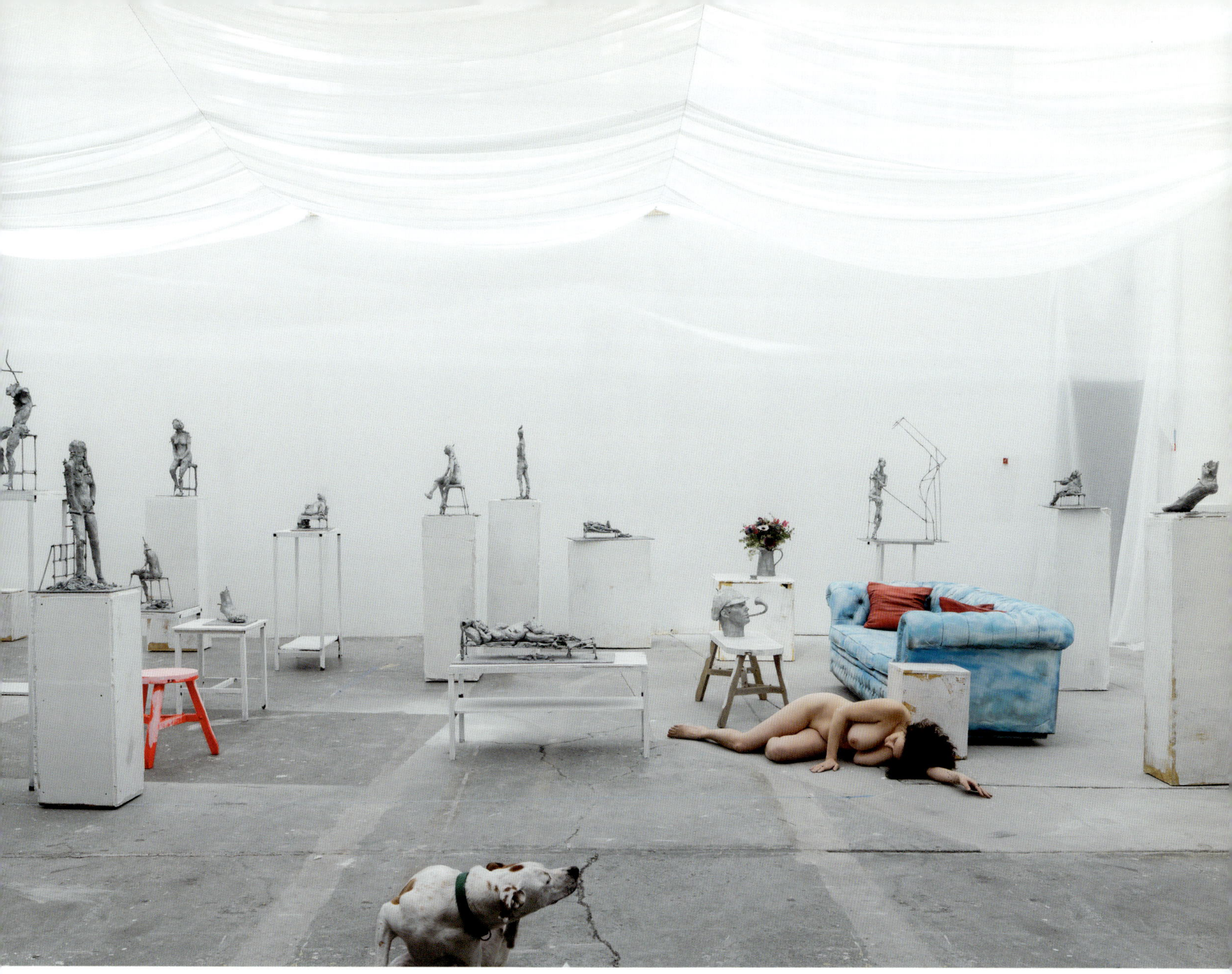

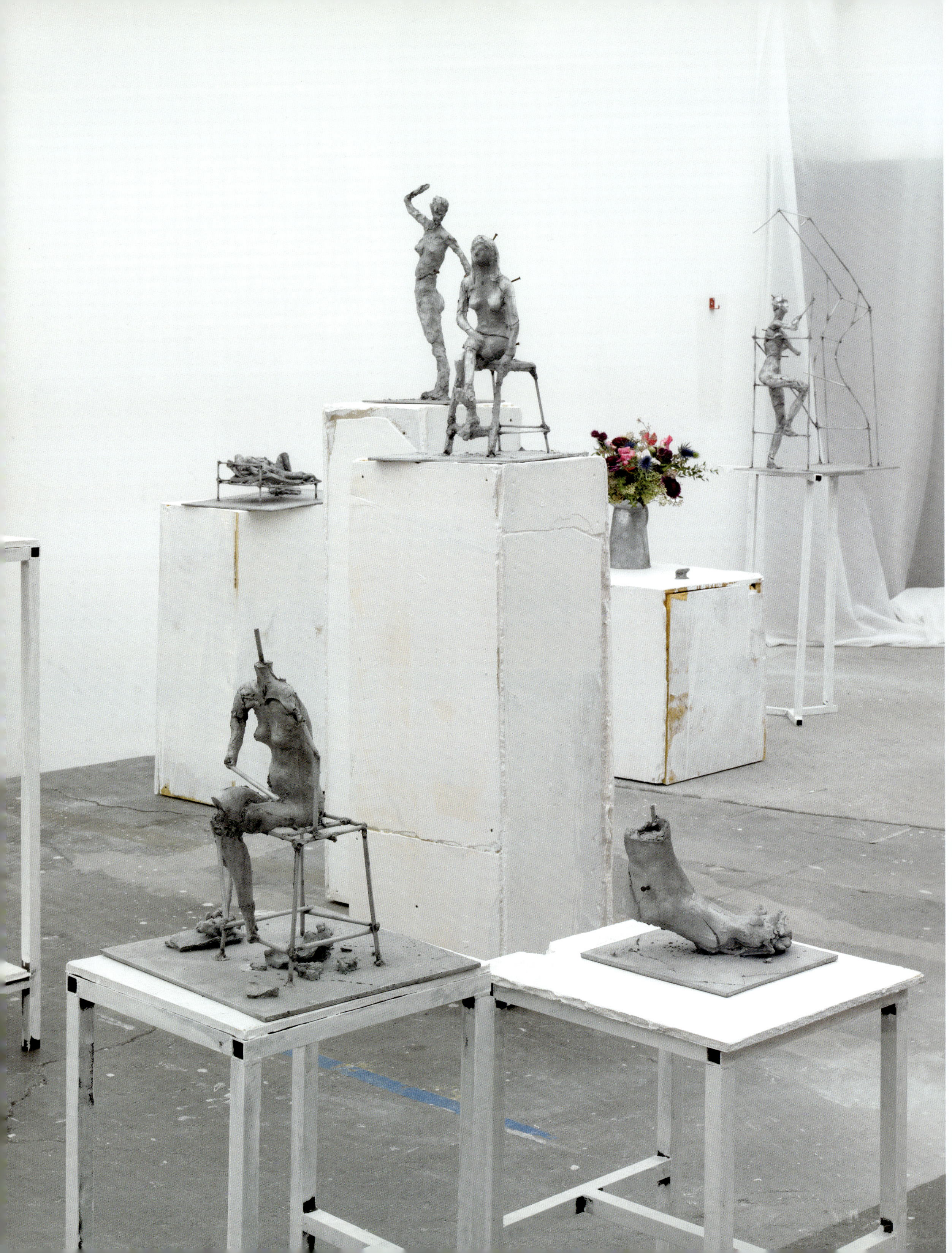

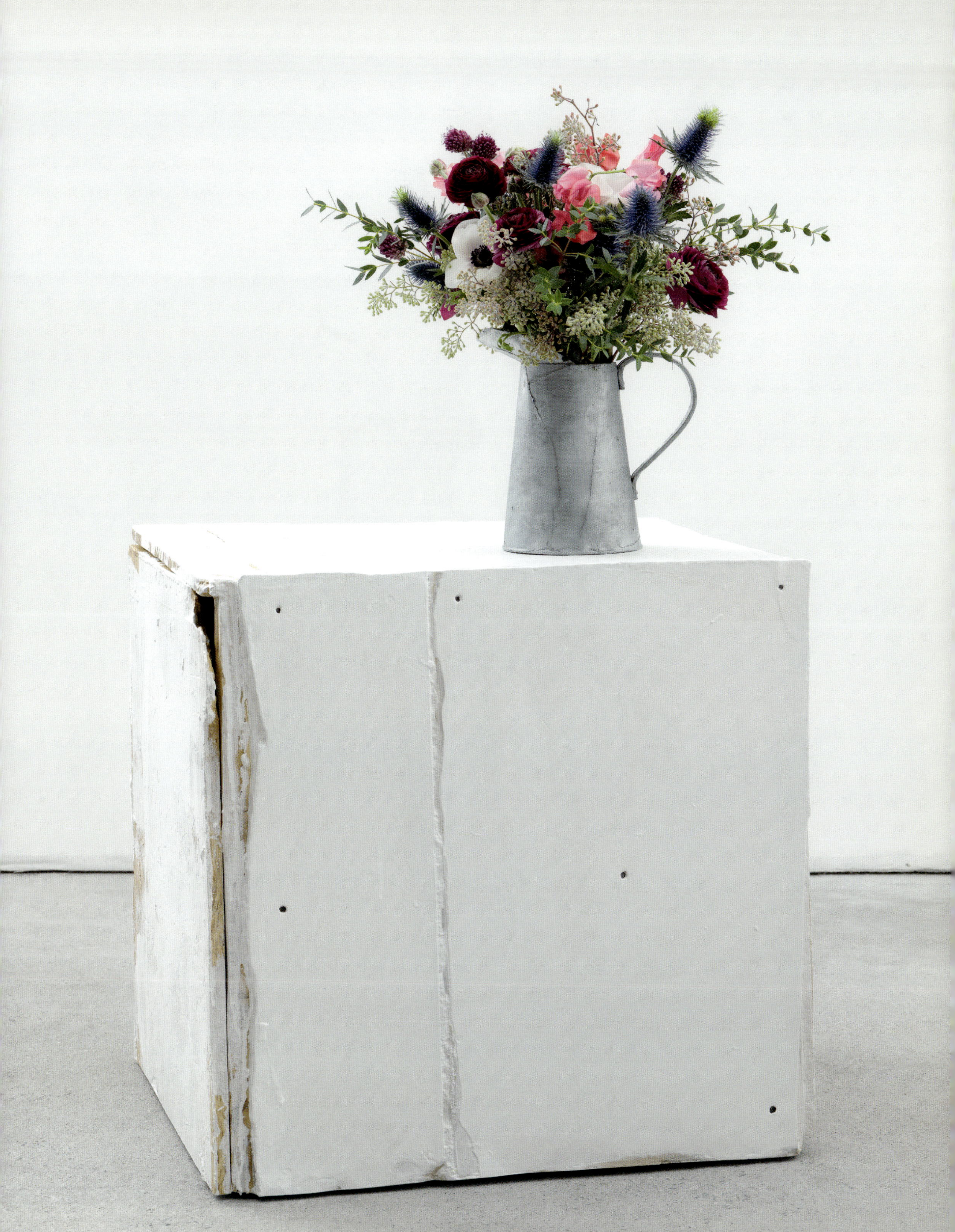

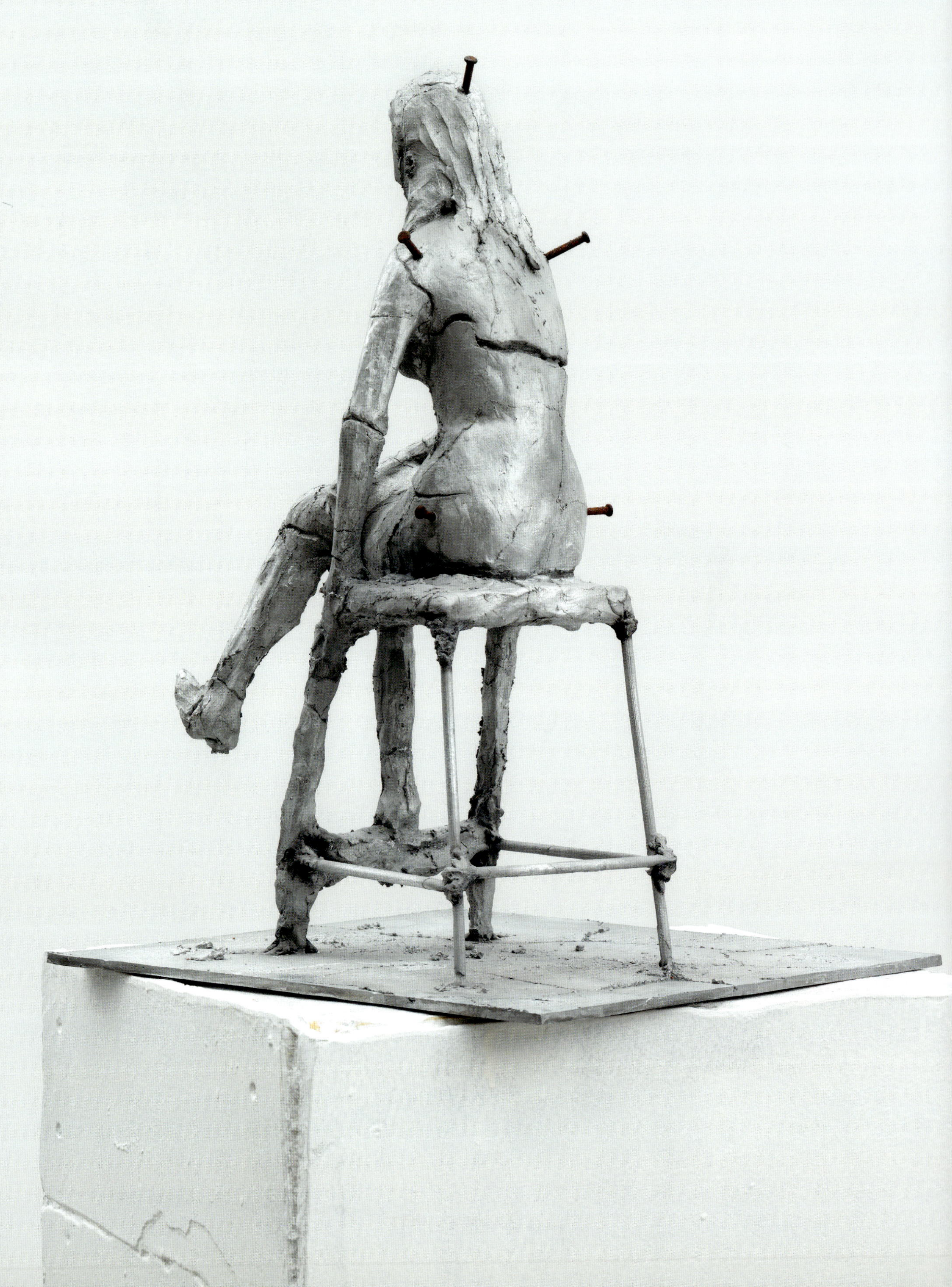

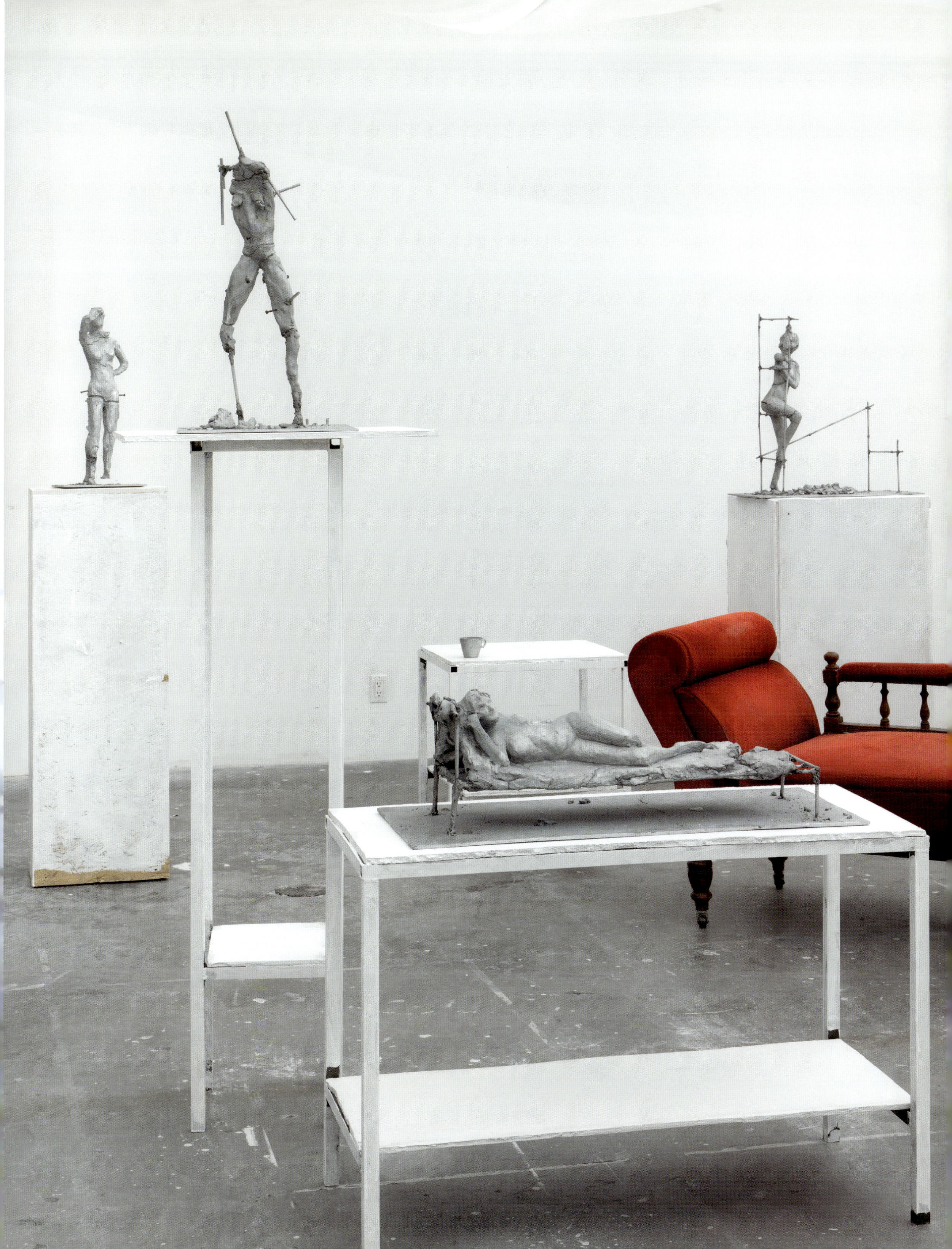

INDEX

Broom, 2007
Polished stainless steel, gesso, inkjet print, polyurethane foam, glue
54 x 26 ¾ x 3 ½ inches (137 x 68 x 9 cm)
Private collection
119

Cappillon, 2000
Wood, plaster, polystyrene, filler, latex paint, glass, cast tin
45 ¼ x 35 ⅜ x 67 ¾ inches (115 x 90 x 172 cm)
Ursula Hauser Collection, Switzerland
519

The Cat with the Broken Leg or The Cat Who Laid the Golden Egg, 2000
Polystyrene, plaster, oil paint, acrylic paint, filler, screws
Crouching cat: 11 x 12 x 5 inches (27.9 x 30.5 x 12.7 cm)
Standing cat: 7 x 12 x 5 inches (17.8 x 30.5 x 12.7 cm)
Private collection, Los Angeles
516

Chagall, 2006
Sculpture vibrates at a high frequency, appearing blurry
Polyurethane foam, nails, spray enamel, acrylic paint, expanding polyurethane foam, filler, polyurethane glue, electric motor, aluminum, control unit, battery, cables
88 ⅝ x 24 x 41 inches (225 x 61 x 104 cm)
Private collection
451

Chair, 2002
Chair vibrates at a high frequency, appearing blurry
Wood, oil paint, electric motor, mechanism, glue, silicone, battery
32 ¼ x 16 ½ x 16 ½ inches (82 x 42 x 42 cm)
Private collection
286, 449

Chair for a Ghost: Thomas, 2003
Cast aluminum, enamel paint, lacquer, wire
37 ⅜ x 24 ⅜ x 20 ½ inches (95 x 62 x 52 cm)
Private collection
373

Chair for a Ghost: Urs, 2003
Cast aluminum, enamel paint, lacquer, wire
37 ⅜ x 24 ⅜ x 20 ½ inches (95 x 62 x 52 cm)
Ringier Collection, Switzerland
375

Chair (Sewn), 1998–1999
Found chair frame, silicone, thread, acrylic paint
32 ¼ x 20 ½ x 22 ½ inches (82 x 52 x 57 cm)
Private collection
404

Chairs, 1998–1999
Silicone, sawdust, plastic, found chairs, spray enamel, metal
29 ½ x 22 ½ x 60 ¼ inches (75 x 57 x 153 cm)
Private collection
405

Cioran Handrail, 2006
Epoxy resin, pigment, enamel paint, wire, aluminum
Approximately 138 x 339 x 49 inches (350 x 860 x 125 cm)
Edition of 2 & 1 AP
The Brant Foundation, Greenwich, Connecticut; Sender Collection; Private collection
278, 280–283, back endpapers

Clouds, 2002
Polystyrene, wire, theater spotlight with pink gel
Cloud 1: 39 ⅜ x 59 x 6 ¼ inches (100 x 150 x 16 cm)
Cloud 2: 17 ¾ x 24 ¾ x 6 ¼ inches (45 x 63 x 16 cm)
Private collection
286

Concert / Cornichon, 2011
Silkscreen print on mirror-polished stainless-steel sheets, polyurethane foam sheets, two-component polyurethane adhesive, stainless-steel beams, aluminum L sections, screws; in 4 parts
Pinocchio, each: 51 x 88 ½ x 46 ¾ inches (129.29 x 225 x 118.8 cm)
Penny-farthing bicycle, each: 32 ½ x 85 ½ x 77 inches (82.5 x 217.4 x 196 cm)
Edition of 2 & 1 AP
Private collections
150–151

CROOKER
CREAGH
CRANOR
CRANER, 2012
Silkscreen print on mirror-glass, UV-adhesive, aluminum, glass, polyacetal, screws; in 4 parts
F: 16 ½ x 13 ¼ x 3 ½ inches (41.9 x 33.7 x 8.9 cm)
Foam head: 15 ½ x 16 ½ x 12 ¾ inches (39.4 x 41.9 x 32.4 cm)
Key: 17 ¾ x 8 ¼ x 1 ⅝ inches (45.1 x 21 x 4.1 cm)
Spirit level: 4 ⅝ x 25 ½ x 1 ¾ inches (11.7 x 64.8 x 4.4 cm)
Edition of 3 & 1 AP
Guy Dellal Family Collection; Heather and Tony Podesta Collection, Washington, DC; Private collections
162–165

Cumpadre, 2009
Nylon filament, preserved croissant, preserved butterfly, glue, wire
Approximately 6 ¼ x 5 ½ x 2 ⅜ inches (16 x 14 x 6 cm)
Collection Florence and Philippe Segalot, New York
55, 416

Cuntface, 2012
Aluminum, epoxy primer, polyester filler, one-component acrylic putty, urethane primer, polyester paint, acrylic polyurethane matte clearcoat; in 2 parts
Water bottle: 12 ⅞ x 19 ¼ x 12 ⅞ inches (32.8 x 48.8 x 32.8 cm)
Bottle neck: 4 ⅜ x 4 ⅝ x 4 ⅝ inches (11 x 11.7 x 11.7 cm)
Overall dimensions: 12 ⅞ x 23 ⅞ x 12 ⅞ inches (32.8 x 60.6 x 32.8 cm)
Edition of 3 & 1 AP
The Eugene Sadovoy Collection; Courtesy of the artist and Gagosian Gallery; Private collections
380, 383

Cup / Cigarettes / Skid, 2006
Wood, polyurethane glue, acrylic paint, nails
Coffee cup: 7 ½ x 9 ⅝ x 7 ⅛ inches (19 x 24.3 x 18 cm)
Cigarettes: 10 ¼ x 5 ⅜ x 3 ½ inches (26 x 13.8 x 8.9 cm)
Pallet: 31 ⅞ x 26 ¾ x 3 ½ inches (81.1 x 67.8 x 8.9 cm)
Collection of Tony Shafrazi
120–121

Cutting a Cake with a Hammer, 2000
Wood, polystyrene, latex paint, spotlight, enamel paint, filler, nails, screws
43 ¼ x 27 ½ x 27 ½ inches (110 x 70 x 70 cm)
Collezione Maurizio Morra Greco, Naples
522

Daphne Brown, 2008
Inkjet wallpaper prints on nylon reinforced paper
Dimensions variable
Edition of 1 & 1 AP
Private collections
68–69

Dark Darkness, 2010
Silkscreen print on mirror-polished stainless-steel sheets, polyurethane foam sheets, two-component polyurethane adhesive, stainless-steel beams, aluminum L sections, screws
47 ¼ x 37 ¼ x 44 ⅝ inches (120 x 94.5 x 113.2 cm)
Edition of 2 & 1 AP
Private collection, Switzerland; Private collections
152–153

David, the Proprietor, 2008–2009
Cast aluminum, aluminum, steel cable, steel bolts
Approximately 217 x 118 x 118 inches
(551.2 x 299.7 x 299.7 cm)
Edition of 2 & 1 AP
Courtesy of the artist and Sadie Coles HQ, London; Private collections
228–231, 233–235, 237

Daylight Pillow, 2004
Aluminum, acrylic paint, light bulb, socket, electric cable
49 ¼ x 55 ⅛ x 37 inches (125 x 140 x 94 cm)
Edition of 2 & 1 AP
Bischofberger Collection, Zurich; Private collection; Goetz Collection, Munich
525

Death of a Moment, 2007
Mirrors, aluminum, hydraulics, control unit
Dimensions variable
Private collection
326–327

Dickface, 2012
Aluminum, carbon-fiber-reinforced plastic, stainless-steel anchors, epoxy primer, polyester filler, one-component acrylic putty, urethane primer, polyester paint, acrylic polyurethane matte clearcoat; in 2 parts
Left: 56 ¾ x 61 x 13 ⅞ inches
(144.3 x 154.9 x 35.3 cm)
Right: 56 ¾ x 61 x 14 inches
(144 x 154.9 x 35.8 cm)
Overall dimensions: 56 ¾ x 61 x 38 ⅞ inches
(144.3 x 154.9 x 98.7 cm)
Edition of 3 & 1 AP
Heather and Tony Podesta Collection, Washington, DC; Collection of Margaret and Daniel S. Loeb; Private collections
380–381

Die Hungry, 2003
Polyurethane resin, acrylic paint, clay, screws
27 ½ x 19 ¾ x 15 inches (70 x 50 x 38 cm)
Private collection
535

Dörrfrucht und Nussschale, 1999
Plaster, clay, wood glue, acrylic, dried fruit, nuts, wooden beams, latex paint
Bowl 1: diameter 19 ⅝ x 7 ⅞ inches (50 x 20 cm)
Pedestal: 39 ⅜ x 8 ⅝ x 7 ⅞ inches (100 x 22 x 20 cm)
Bowl 2: diameter 13 ¾ x 4 ¾ inches (35 x 12 cm)
Pedestal: 43 ¼ x 9 ½ x 7 ⅞ inches (110 x 24 x 20 cm)
Hauser & Wirth Collection, Switzerland
538–539

Dr. Katzelberg (Zivilisationsruine), 1999
Mirrors, wood, polystyrene, silicone, three theater spotlights on tripods
82 ⅝ x 196 ⅞ x 137 ¾ inches (210 x 500 x 350 cm)
Kunstsammlung der Stadt Zürich
314–319, 406

Dunno, 2012
Epoxy resin, fiberglass, pigment, acrylic paint, aluminum, screws, wire
80 x 225 ¼ x 81 ⅛ inches
(203.2 x 572.1 x 206.1 cm)
Edition of 2 & 1 AP
Franz West Foundation; Tony Salamé, Aïshti Foundation; Private collection
285

Eckwurst, 1997
Wood, plaster, chicken wire, latex paint, acrylic paint, newspaper, screws
71 ¼ x 29 ⅞ 26 ⅜ inches (181 x 76 x 67 cm)
Private collection, Paris
272

Erdnüsse im Vergleich, 2004
MDF, aluminum, construction adhesive, acrylic paint, acrylic lacquer; in 11 parts
104 ⅜ x 393 ¾ x 354 ⅜ inches (265 x 1000 x 900 cm)
Courtesy of the artist and Galerie Eva Presenhuber, Zurich
37, 322–323, 325

Failed installation of green leaves on winter tree outside exhibition window for "Without a Fist–Like a Bird," Institute of Contemporary Arts, London, January 2000
609

Fantasy / Extrusion, 2010
Silkscreen print on mirror-polished stainless-steel sheets, polyurethane foam sheets, two-component polyurethane adhesive, stainless-steel beams, aluminum L sections, screws; in 4 parts
Sphinx, each: 55 ½ x 14 ⅞ x 53 inches
(141 x 37.9 x 134.5 cm)
Clementine, each: 37 ⅝ x 29 ⅜ x 47 ⅛ inches
(95.5 x 74.5 x 119.6 cm)
Edition of 2 & 1 AP
Private collection, courtesy the Heller Group; Private collections
147–148

Faules Fundament (Rotten Foundation), 1998
Bricks, mortar, fruits, vegetables
Dimensions variable
Private collection
301–303

Fiction, 2012
Table vibrates at a high frequency, appearing blurry
Inkjet print on balsa wood, styrofoam, acoustic foam, glue, steel, aluminum, DC motor, rechargeable lithium battery
27 ¾ x 63 ⅜ x 39 ⅜ inches (70.5 x 161 x 100 cm)
Edition of 3 & 1 AP
Courtesy of the artist and Gagosian Gallery; Private collection
452–453

Footnote to "You," 2010
Cedar, FXP, plywood, ultralight MDF, oak veneer edge banding, coffee, wood bleach, wood putty, wood stain, two-component polyester resin, spray enamel, steel, stainless steel, aluminum, glass, Plexiglas, Marmorino Veneziano plaster, ABS plastic, LED components, computer components, electrical components, latex paint, acrylic silkscreen medium, acrylic paint, polyurethane varnish, screws, nails, bolts, turnbuckles, washers, staples, Masonite, double-sided tape, spray adhesive, two-component acrylic adhesive, two-component epoxy glue, wood glue, acrylic adhesive
317 x 216 x 125 inches (805.2 x 548.6 x 317.5 cm)
The Brant Foundation, Greenwich, Connecticut
26–31, 66

Fritz Lang / Shorty, 2010
Silkscreen print on mirror-polished stainless-steel sheets, polyurethane foam sheets, two-component polyurethane adhesive, stainless-steel beams, aluminum L sections, screws; in 4 parts
Shopping cart, each: 64 ¾ x 40 ½ x 57 ½ inches
(164.5 x 103 x 146 cm)
Ducky, each: 82 ⅝ x 57 ½ x 43 ¼ inches
(210 x 146 x 110 cm)
Edition of 2 & 1 AP
Private collections
149

Frozen, 1998
Wood, particleboard, latex paint, enamel paint, candle, vase, dishes, branches, wool yarn, wood glue, nails, silicone
86 ⅝ x 90 ½ x 63 inches (220 x 230 x 160 cm)
Collection Migros Museum für Gegenwartskunst
439

Frozen Pioneer, 2009
Cast aluminum, epoxy primer, polyester filler, one-component acrylic putty, urethane primer, polyester paint, acrylic polyurethane matte clearcoat
Approximately 120 x 49 x 39 ½ inches
(305 x 125 x 100 cm)
Edition of 2 & 1 AP
Collection François Pinault; Private collections
228–229, 233, 419

Frozen Pioneer Slut, 2009
Nylon filament, preserved croissant, preserved butterfly, glue, wire
Approximately 6 x 5 ½ x 2 ½ inches
(15.2 x 14 x 6.3 cm)
Private collection, London
553

Fuck You Thank You, 2007
Cast aluminum, acrylic paint
67 ¾ x 120 ⅛ x 38 ¼ inches (172 x 305 x 97 cm)
Edition of 2 & 1 AP
Private collections; Collection Erling Kagge, Oslo
326-327, 378–379

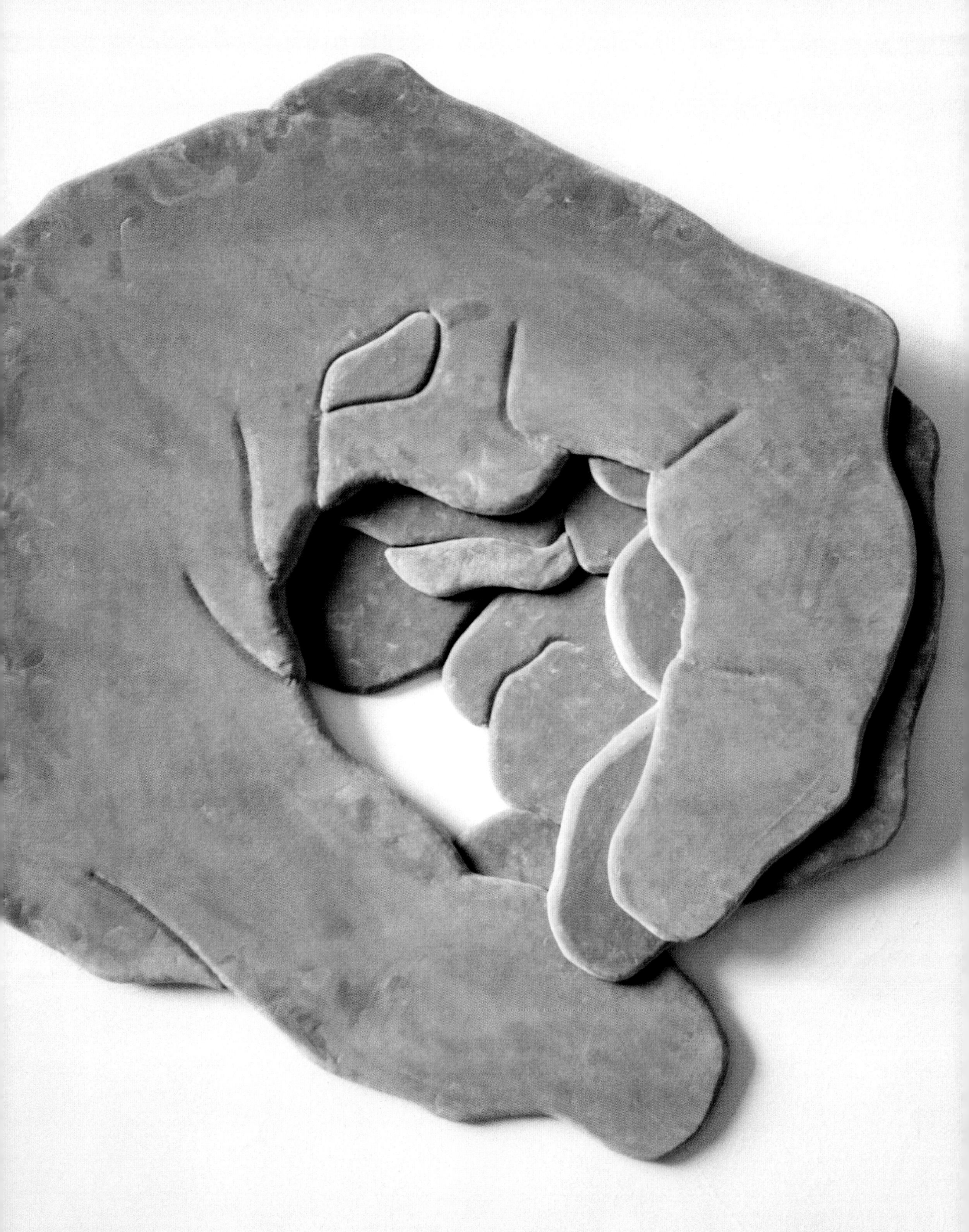

Gänseeier Eclipse, 2001–2002
Two goose or chicken eggs, nylon filament, glue, theater spotlight
Dimensions variable
Private collection
548–549

Gedanken kommen zurück "bitte," 2002
Wood, wax, silicone, clay, spray enamel
31 ½ x 63 x 47 ¼ inches (80 x 160 x 120 cm)
Friedrich Christian Flick Collection
466

Glaskatzen–Mülleimer der Hoffnung, 1999
Carpet, wood, glass, silicone (casts of room corners), acrylic paint
Approximately 39 ⅜ x 151 ⅝ x 106 ¼ inches (100 x 385 x 270 cm)
Friedrich Christian Flick Collection
312–313

Glaskatzensex / Transparent Tale, 2000
Particleboard, wood, silicone (casts of room corners), glass, acrylic paint, marker
62 ¼ x 220 ½ x 236 ¼ inches (158 x 560 x 600 cm)
Collection of Migros Museum für Gegenwartskunst
321

Good Good Breath / Good Bad Breath, 2002
Polyurethane resin, wire, enamel, varnish, primer; in 2 parts
Each approximately 27 ½ x 14 ½ x 12 inches (69.9 x 36.8 x 30.5 cm)
Private collection, Paris
532–533

Good Luck / Bad Luck Bowl, 2002
Polyurethane resin, wire, enamel, varnish, primer
Dimensions unknown
Private collection, Paris
542

The Grass Munchers, 2007
Cast aluminum, pigments, wax
22 x 24 ⅜ x 17 ⅜ inches (56 x 62 x 44 cm)
Edition of 2 & 1 AP
Burger Collection, Hong Kong; Private collections
326–327, 510–511

Gypsy, 2002
Mechanical robot half-dog wags its tail
Metal, styrofoam, synthetic fur, wood, wood glue, screws, aluminum tubes
27 x 33 ⅛ x 10 inches (68.5 x 84 x 25.5 cm)
Private collection, Paris
180

Hand Lemon, 2006
Hydrocal, acrylic paint, polyurethane glue, hair
7 ¼ x 7 ¼ x 7 ⅛ inches (18.4 x 18.4 x 18.1 cm)
Private collection
501

Hands, 2002
Cast aluminum, wire, enamel paint
28 ¾ x 12 ⅝ x 7 ⅞ inches (73 x 32 x 20 cm)
Ringier Collection, Switzerland
286, 495

Hear an Old Lady Laugh Out Loud, 2005
Cast aluminum, acrylic paint
5 ⅞ x 59 x 2 ⅜ inches (15 x 150 x 6 cm)
David Gill Private Collection, London
565

Helmar Lerski, 2008
Self-published artist's book
Edition of 500
Front endpapers

Horse / Fraud, 2010
Silkscreen print on mirror-polished stainless-steel sheets, polyurethane foam sheets, two-component polyurethane adhesive, stainless-steel beams, aluminum L sections, screws; in 4 parts
Marlboro, each: 50 ¼ x 23 ¾ x 29 ½ inches (127.5 x 60.4 x 75 cm)
Office chair, each: 53 ⅛ x 37 ⅞ x 34 ⅝ inches (135 x 81 x 88 cm)
Edition of 2 & 1 AP
Paul and Gayle Stoffel; Private collection; Private collection, Paris
145

Horses Dream of Horses, 2004
Plaster, resin paint, steel, nylon filament
Dimensions variable: 1,500 raindrops, each up to 6 ¾ x 2 ¾ x 2 ¾ inches (17 x 7 x 7 cm)
Ringier Collection, Switzerland
36, 287–290

Hotel, 2001
Polyurethane foam, acrylic foam, wood, nails, screws
33 ½ x 17 ¾ x 33 ½ inches (84 x 45 x 84 cm)
The Speyer Family Collection, New York
524

How to Tell a Joke, 2007
Polyurethane resin, polymeric plaster, steel, pigments, acrylic paint, matte varnish, dust
39 ⅜ x 37 ⅜ x 39 ⅜ inches (100 x 95 x 100 cm)
Private collection, Israel
411

Hudson, 1995
Particleboard, latex paint, screws
Dimensions unknown
Private collection
371

The Human Layer, 1999
Plaster, clay, acrylic paint, silicone, fruits
7 ⅞ x 19 ¾ x 19 ¾ inches (20 x 50 x 50 cm)
Private collection
540–541

I Can Smell Your Words, 2002
Polyurethane resin, synthetic hair, acrylic paint, particleboard, marker, fake eyelashes, powdered sugar, egg whites
Dimensions unknown
Destroyed
471

I Hope the Kitten Finds a Mouse, 2004
Vellum, paint marker, acrylic paint, acrylic varnish, polyurethane resin, acid-free cardboard, glue, pastels, fixative; four drawings
Each 22 x 17 ⅜ x 1 ⅛ inches (56 x 44 x 3 cm)
Centre National d'art et de culture Georges Pompidou, Paris
372

Imaginary Pain, 2007
Cast plaster, screws, enamel paint
23 ⅝ x 23 ⅝ x 7 ⅞ inches (60 x 60 x 20 cm)
Private collection
502–503

In Dubio Pro Reo, 2007
Found cabinet, found stool, found bowl, epoxy glue, polyurethane glue
61 x 43 ¼ x 31 ½ inches (115 x 110 x 80 cm)
Dimitris Gigourtakis Collection, Athens
447

Installation at "A Halloween Celebration," Performa11, Santos Party House, New York, 28 October 2011
114–115

The Intelligence of Flowers, 2005
Cuts in wall with relocated cutouts
Dimensions variable
Ringier Collection, Switzerland
39–41, 182

Ix, 2006–2008
Cast aluminum, steel
118 ⅛ x 88 ⅝ x 61 ¾ inches (300 x 225 x 157 cm)
Edition of 2 & 1 AP
Private collections
231, 234–235

Jet Set Lady, 2000
Color copies, wooden frames, wood, iron base, acrylic glass, wood stain, acrylic lacquer, wood glue, screws
177 ⅛ x 177 ⅛ x 165 ⅜ inches (450 x 450 x 420 cm)
Prototype
Destroyed
85

Jet Set Lady, 2000–2005
2,000 framed color prints of drawings, 24 fluorescent tubes, wooden frames, iron, metal primer, UV-protective lacquer
354 ⅜ x 275 ⅝ x 275 ⅝ inches (900 x 700 x 700 cm)
Private collection
87–91

Kantenwurst, 1997
Wood, plaster, chicken wire, latex paint,
acrylic paint, newspaper, screws
24 ¾ x 9 x 71 ⅝ inches (63 x 23 x 182 cm)
Private collection, Athens
273

Keep It Going Is a Private Thing, 2001
Mechanical robot half-dog wags its tail
Synthetic fur, polystyrene, electric motor, control unit, acrylic paint, polyurethane foam, wood glue
27 ½ x 11 ¾ x 31 ⅛ inches (70 x 30 x 79 cm)
Ringier Collection, Switzerland
628–629

Kerzenständer, 2000
from "6 ½ Domestic Pairs Project"
Wood, clay, enamel paint, chain,
electric motor, candle, wood glue
Dimensions variable
Friedrich Christian Flick Collection
182

Kir Royal, 2004
Plaster, polyurethane resin, acrylic paint, gauze
17 ¾ x 11 ¾ x 13 ¾ inches (45 x 30 x 35 cm)
Centre National d'art et de culture Georges Pompidou, Paris
287, 477

**KITTINGER
ZAWACKI
YUTZY, 2012**
Silkscreen print on mirror-glass, UV-adhesive, aluminum, glass, polyacetal, screws; in 3 parts
Clothespin: 23 ¼ x 5 ⅛ x 3 ⅞ inches
(59 x 13.1 x 9.7 cm)
Dollar bill: 6 ¾ x 15 ½ x 1 ⅝ inches
(17.2 x 39.4 x 4 cm)
Tic Tac: 25 ¼ x 15 ¾ x 6 ⅛ inches (64 x 40 x 15.4 cm)
Edition of 3 & 1 AP
Courtesy of the artist and Gagosian Gallery;
Private collections
166–169

Köpfe, 1997–1999
Wood, clay, acrylic paint, wax
Head 1: 11 ¾ x 11 ¾ inches (30 x 30 cm)
Pedestal: 51 ⅛ x 13 x 11 ¾ inches (130 x 33 x 30 cm)
Head 2: 11 ¾ x 11 ¾ inches (30 x 30 cm)
Pedestal: 48 x 12 ⅝ x 12 ⅝ inches (122 x 32 x 32 cm)
Private collection, Rome
465

Kratz, 2009
Bed, bedding, concrete
23 ⅝ x 78 ¾ x 78 ¾ inches (60 x 200 x 200 cm)
Private collection
76

Kratz, 2011
Cast aluminum, concrete, aluminum,
epoxy, fiberglass, wire mesh, epoxy primer,
polyester filler, one-component acrylic putty,
urethane primer, polyester paint,
acrylic polyurethane matte clearcoat
26 x 72 x 94 inches (66 x 182.9 x 238.8 cm)
Edition of 3 & 1 AP
Private collections; RR Collection, Miami
460–463

Kuckuck Backwards, 2004
Wood, aluminum, cement, sawdust, enamel paint
63 ¾ x 78 ¾ x 25 ¼ inches (162 x 200 x 64 cm)
Collection Kunsthaus Zürich
36, 360, 582

Lassie / Pizza, 2010
Silkscreen print on mirror-polished stainless-steel sheets, polyurethane foam sheets, two-component polyurethane adhesive, stainless-steel beams, aluminum L sections, screws; in 4 parts
Diet Coke can, each: 37 ¾ x 23 ½ x 24 ¾ inches
(95.9 x 59.7 x 62.9 cm)
Onion, each: / 32 x 35 ¾ x 21 ¼ inches
(81.3 x 90.8 x 54 cm)
Edition of 2 & 1 AP
The Brant Foundation, Greenwich, Connecticut;
The Mario Testino Collection;
The Frank Cohen Collection
140–141

Last Call, Lascaux, 2007
Wallpaper prints of photographic reproductions of interior spaces (content, scale, and lighting determined on a site-specific basis)
Dimensions variable
Collection of The Museum of Modern Art, New York
53–57

Last Chair Standing, 1997
Wood, clay, silicone, latex paint, string,
wire, caulk, wood glue
25 ⅜ x 31 ⅛ x 25 ⅜ inches (64.5 x 79 x 64.5 cm)
Private collection, Paris
431

Late Late Night Show, 2002
Polystyrene, acrylic paint, wood glue,
polyurethane foam, screws
46 x 38 ¼ x 26 inches (117 x 97 x 66 cm)
Private collection
355

Late Night Show, 1997
Found chairs, newspaper, plaster,
latex paint, pigments, glue
Chair 1: 31 ⅞ x 21 ⅝ x 25 ⅝ inches (91 x 55 x 65 cm)
Chair 2: 33 ⅞ x 17 ¾ x 19 ¾ inches (86 x 45 x 50 cm)
Chair 3: 30 ¼ x 21 ⅝ 25 ⅝ inches (77 x 55 x 65 cm)
Hauser & Wirth Collection, Switzerland
432–433

Lee Friedlander, 2012
Plaster, arm hair
5 ¾ x 21 ¼ x 13 ½ inches (14.6 x 54 x 34.3 cm)
Private collection
515

Leiter, 1997
Aluminum ladder, latex paint, theater spotlights
Dimensions variable
Collection Migros Museum für Gegenwartskunst
388

Lie to a Dog, 2005
Cast nickel silver, acrylic paint, cheese
20 ⅞ x 17 ¾ x 8 ¼ inches (53 x 45 x 21 cm)
Private collection
561

Light, 2002
Light bulb, electric cable, electric motor, control unit
47 ¼ x 4 x 4 inches (120 x 10 x 10 cm)
Private collection
286

A Light Sigh Is the Sound of My Life, 2000–2001
Overlaid by silicone skin, core rotates
on a horizontal axis at a speed of one
revolution every four minutes
Polystyrene, polyurethane foam, wood, steel axle, electric motor, silicone, gauze, hair, wood glue
78 ¾ x 78 ¾ x 110 ¼ inches (200 x 200 x 280 cm)
Private collection
408–409

The Lock, 2007
Cast polyurethane, steel pipes, electromagnets
72 ½ x 29 ¾ x 21 ⅝ inches (184 x 75.5 x 55 cm)
Edition of 2 & 1 AP
Collection Maja Hoffmann, Switzerland; Private collections
459

Mackintosh Staccato, 2006
Epoxy resin, pigment, enamel paint,
wire, aluminum
Approximately 98 x 356 x 98 inches
(250 x 904 x 248 cm)
Edition of 2 & 1 AP
Private collections
120, 280–282, back endpapers

Madame Fisscher, 1999–2000
Mixed media
Dimensions variable
Hauser & Wirth Collection, Switzerland
93–99

Make a Duck Out of a Cow, 2003
Wood, acrylic glass, plywood, inkjet print on film, latex paint, acrylic paint, marker, spray adhesive, glue, screws, varnish
91 x 122 x 3 inches (231 x 309.9 x 7.6 cm)
Lindemann Collection, Miami Beach
33

A Man and His Head Like a Hand with a Bread Unfiltered Summer / Autumn 99 Poetry and Brain Waste, 1999
Iron, glass, zinc phosphate paint, photocopies on polyester film, adhesive tape
92 ⅛ x 107 ½ x 39 ¾ inches (400 x 280 x 260 cm)
Friedrich Christian Flick Collection
83

Marguerite de Ponty, 2006–2008
Cast aluminum, steel
157 ½ x 110 ¼ x 102 ⅜ inches
(400 x 280 x 260 cm)
Edition of 2 & 1 AP
Private collections
83, 228–229, 232–236

The Membrane (Half Full, Half Empty), 2000
Polyurethane rubber (casts of furniture), pigments, aluminum tubes with plastic connectors, theater spotlights on tripods
118 ⅛ x 236 ¼ x 118 ⅛ inches (300 x 600 x 300 cm)
Private collection
406–407

meme, 2012
Galvanized bronze, bronze, two-component epoxy primer, polyester filler, two-component polyester body filler, urethane primer, polyester paint, acrylic polyurethane matte clearcoat
Left nail: 70 ¼ x 21 ⅛ x 44 ¼ inches
(178.5 x 53.5 x 112.5 cm)
Right nail: 75 ⅝ x 30 ½ x 17 ⅜ inches
(192 x 77.5 x 44 cm)
Overall dimensions: 75 ⅝ x 88 ⅝ x 44 ¼ inches
(192 x 225 x 112.5 cm)
Courtesy of the artist and Sadie Coles HQ, London
396–397

Memories of a Blank Mind, 2004
Aluminum, two-component polyurethane foam, wood, aircraft cable, acrylic paint, marker, steel, screws
157 ½ x 236 ¼ x 236 ¼ inches (400 x 600 x 600 cm)
Private collection
394

Merciless Mercy, 2010
Silkscreen print on mirror-polished stainless-steel sheets, polyurethane foam sheets, two-component polyurethane adhesive, stainless-steel beams, aluminum L sections, screws
40 ¾ x 25 ⅝ x 26 ⅞ inches (103.5 x 65 x 68.4 cm)
Edition of 2 & 1 AP
Private collections
154–155

Middleclass Heroes, 2004
Cuts in wall with relocated cutouts
Dimensions variable
Private collection
36–37, 234–236, 290, 322–324, 360

Miss Satin, 2006–2008
Cast aluminum, steel
133 ⅞ x 101 ⅛ x 86 ⅝ inches (340 x 257 x 220 cm)
Edition of 2 & 1 AP
Private collections
228–229, 232

Money Bowl, 1999
Iron, metal primer, plaster, caulk, acrylic paint, wax, coins, bills
Bowl: 27 ½ x 27 ½ x 5 ½ inches (70 x 70 x 14 cm)
Pedestal: 27 ½ x 27 ½ x 18 ⅛ inches (70 x 70 x 46 cm)
Kunstsammlung der Stadt Zürich
537

Moody Moments, 2003
Clay, polyurethane resin, wood, dough
Head 1: 15 x 13 x 12 inches (38 x 33 x 30.5 cm)
Head 2: 15 x 12 x 11 ½ inches (38 x 30.5 x 30 cm)
Private collection
474–475

Mouth, 2011
Cast bronze, oil paint
3 ¾ x 3 ¼ x 2 ½ inches (9.5 x 8.3 x 6.3 cm)
Edition of 2 & 2 AP
The Brant Foundation, Greenwich, Connecticut; Private collections
492

Mr. E & Spotzy, 2011
Silkscreen print on mirror-polished stainless-steel sheets, polyurethane foam sheets, two-component polyurethane adhesive, stainless-steel beams, aluminum L sections, screws; in 2 parts
Iron: 22 ½ x 14 ½ x 9 ⅞ inches (57.1 x 37 x 25.1 cm)
Board: 48 x 76 ⅛ x 24 ⅝ inches
(121.9 x 193.4 x 62.6 cm)
Edition of 3 & 1 AP
Collection of Kenny Schacter & Ilona Rich; Private collections
156

Mr. Flosky, 2001–2002
Wood, latex paint, lamp, cable, plaster, polystyrene, glass, glue, screws
Stove: 28 ¾ x 41 ⅜ x 23 ¼ inches (98.5 x 105 x 59 cm)
Cat: 13 ¼ x 18 ⅛ x 5 ¾ inches (33.5 x 46 x 14.5 cm)
Burger Collection, Hong Kong
523

"Mr. Watson—come here—I want to see you.," 2005
Light swings back and forth, accelerating and decelerating in a 12-minute cycle
Electric motor, control unit, electric cable, light bulb, wire
Dimensions variable
Edition of 2 & 1 AP
Private collections; G.F. Collection
482, 630–631

Nach Jugendstiel kam Roccoko, 2006
Empty cigarette pack moves erratically along floor, occasionally flying up into the air
Electric motor, wire, carbon rod, elastic band, nylon filament, empty cigarette pack, control unit
Installation radius: 157 ½ inches (400 cm); height variable
Edition of 2 & 1 AP
Collection François Pinault; La Colección Jumex, Mexico; Private collection
71, 632, 635

Nail Duo, 2012
Galvanized bronze, bronze, two-component epoxy primer, polyester filler, two-component polyester body filler, urethane primer, polyester paint, acrylic polyurethane matte clearcoat
Left nail: Approximately 61 ¾ x 26 ⅜ x 23 ⅝ inches
(157 x 67 x 60 cm)
Right nail: Approximately 76 ⅜ x 19 ¼ x 13 ⅜ inches (194 x 49 x 34 cm)
Overall dimensions: Approximately
76 ⅜ x 75 ⅝ x 23 ⅝ inches (194 x 192 x 60 cm)
Edition of 3 & 1 AP
Danielle and David Ganek; Scedart Collection; Collection François Pinault; Private collection
398–399

Nail Solo, 2012
Galvanized bronze, bronze, two-component epoxy primer, polyester filler, two-component polyester body filler, urethane primer, polyester paint, acrylic polyurethane matte clearcoat
Approximately 72 ½ x 19 ¾ x 35 ⅞ inches
(184 x 50 x 91 cm)
Edition of 3 & 1 AP
Zadig & Voltaire Art; Eugenio Lopez; Private collections
401

Napoleon, Is There Something You Didn't Tell Me / Napoleon, Misunderstood, 2001
Polyurethane resin, stearin, oil paint, synthetic hair, pigments, marker
Part 1: 12 ¼ x 10 ⅝ x 9 inches (21 x 27 x 23 cm)
With pedestal: 45 ⅝ x 10 ¼ x 10 ¼ inches
(116 x 26 x 26 cm)
Part 2: 9 ½ x 10 ⅝ x 11 ¾ inches (24 x 27 x 20 cm)
With pedestal: 46 ⅞ x 11 x 10 ⅞ inches
(119 x 28 x 27.5 cm)
Hauser & Wirth Collection, Switzerland
468–469

Necrophonia, 2011
(with Georg Herold)
Cast zinc, cast aluminum, acrylic paint, fabric, nude model, fresh flowers; in 57 parts
38 ¼ x 33 ½ x 35 ⅞ inches (97 x 85 x 91 cm)
Dimensions variable
Edition of 2 & 2 AP
Courtesy of the artists and The Modern Institute/ Toby Webster Ltd., Glasgow; Private collections
586–597, back endpapers

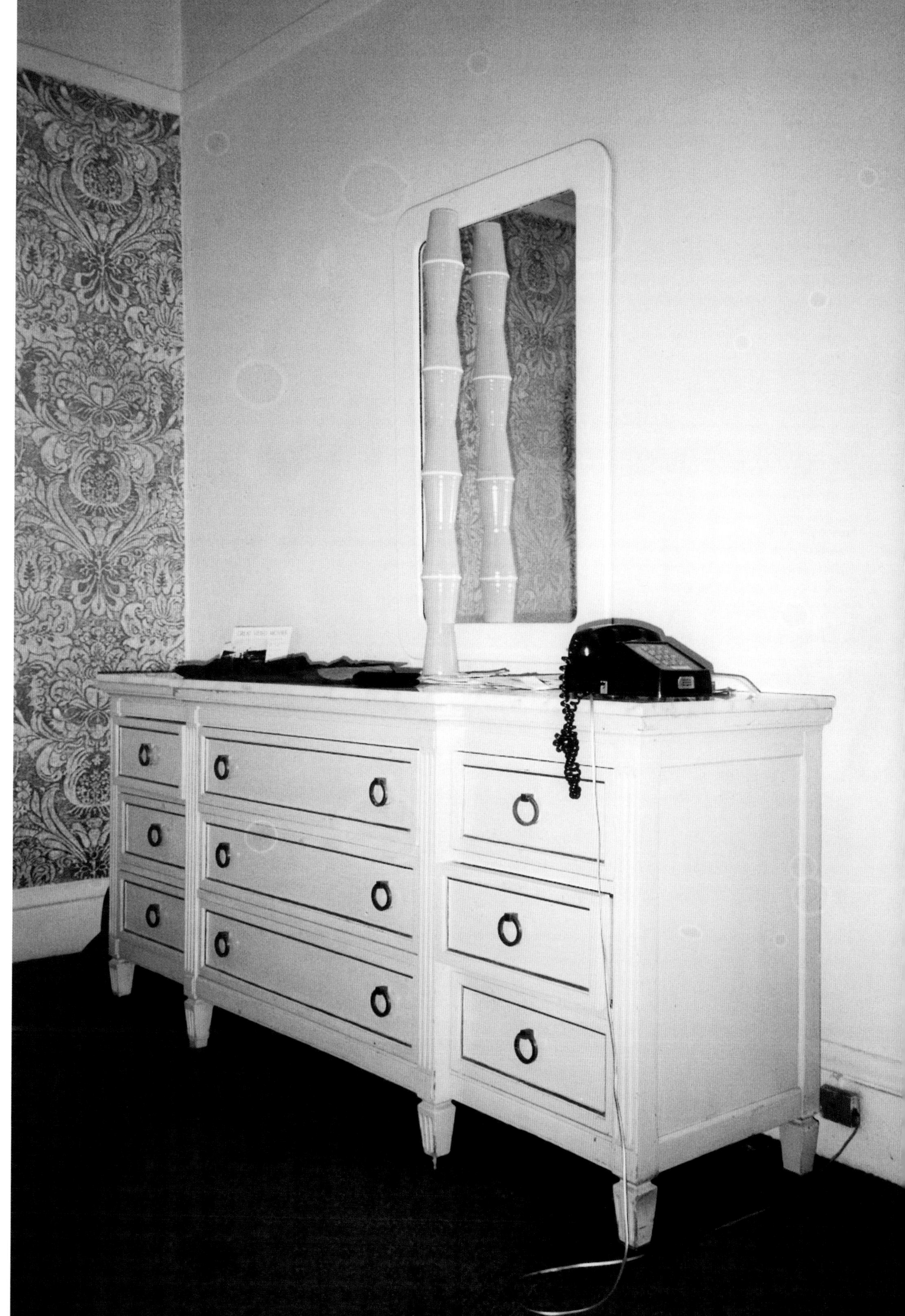

Next Time I Break an Egg, I Will Think of You, 2004
Polystyrene, polyurethane resin, car paint, duct tape, screws, steel wire
Table: 47 ¼ x 39 ⅜ x 31 ½ inches (120 x 100 x 80 cm)
Chair: 27 ½ x 27 ½ x 27 ½ inches (70 x 70 x 70 cm)
Centre National d'art et de culture Georges Pompidou, Paris
372

Nickname, 2009
Nylon filament, preserved croissant, preserved butterfly, steel
Approximately 6 x 5 ½ x 2 ½ inches (15.2 x 14 x 6.3 cm)
Private collection
552

No Need for Ketchup with the Ice Cream, 2004
Aluminum, ACM panels, acrylic paint, latex paint, marker, UV-protective lacquer
121 ¼ x 156 ¾ x 2 ⅜ inches (308 x 398 x 6 cm)
Private collection
322–323

Noisette, 2009
Viewer's approach triggers tongue to emerge from hole
Hole in wall, silicone, motion sensor, electric motor, mechanism
Dimensions variable (smallest hole possible for mechanism to fit through)
Edition of 3 & 2 AP
Collection Erling Kagge, Oslo; Collection of Charlotte and Bill Ford; Mammoth Collection; Private collections
55, 57, 489–491

office theme / addiction / mhh camera, 2006
Wood, ACM panels, Epson ultrachrome inkjet print on canvas and Somerset velvet fine art paper, cardboard, primer, oil paint, acrylic paint, paper cement, epoxy polymer, varnish
96 ⅝ x 72 x 3 ¼ inches (245.3 x 183 x 8.3 cm)
Collection François Pinault
44

Oh, Sad, I See, 2006
ACM panels, wood, acrylic paint, gesso, epoxy glue; in 3 parts
Each 18 ⅞ x 21 ½ x 1 inches (48 x 54.5 x 2.2 cm)
Private collection
120

Old Pain, 2007
Plaster, pigment, screw, polyurethane glue, wire
10 ¼ x 9 ⅞ x 6 inches (26 x 25 x 15 cm)
John Kaldor Collection, Australia
504–505

Olé!, 2003
Sugar cubes
Dimensions variable
Private collection
621

One More Carrot Before I Brush My Teeth, 2001
Wood, polystyrene, polyurethane foam, particleboard, glass, latex paint, silicone, pencil, spray adhesive, screws, dust, glue
51 ⅝ x 31 ⅞ x 38 ¼ inches (131 x 81 x 97 cm)
Private collection
409, 574–575

Online / Parrot, 2010
Silkscreen print on mirror-polished stainless-steel sheets, polyurethane foam sheets, two-component polyurethane adhesive, stainless-steel beams, aluminum L sections, screws; in 4 parts
Brown boot, each: 57 ⅛ x 20 ½ x 58 ¼ inches (145 x 52 x 148 cm)
Dollhouse, each: 50 ⅜ x 38 ¼ x 52 ¾ inches (128 x 97.2 x 134 cm)
Edition of 2 & 1 AP
Stefan T. Edlis Collection; Collection of Cynthia and Abe Steinberger; Private collection
143

Paranoia / Squirrel, 2010
Silkscreen print on mirror-polished stainless-steel sheets, polyurethane foam sheets, two-component polyurethane adhesive, stainless-steel beams, aluminum L sections, screws; in 2 parts
Nut/bolt: 40 ½ x 17 ⅜ x 19 ¼ inches (103 x 44.2 x 49 cm)
Queen: 19 ¼ x 6 ¾ x 26 inches (49 x 17 x 66 cm)
Edition of 2 & 1 AP
The Frank Cohen Collection; Private collections
142

Paris 1919, 2006
Tar, plaster, iron, aluminum, rubber
133 ⅞ x 33 ½ x 33 ½ inches (340 x 85 x 85 cm)
Private collection
583

Paris 2006, 2006
Left leg jitters impatiently
Electric motor, aluminum tracks, silicone, pigment, cable
33 ½ x 24 ¾ x 26 ¾ inches (85 x 63 x 68 cm)
Private collection
482, 508

Performance on the occasion of the opening of "Frs Uischer," Galerie Walcheturm, Zurich, 1996
Co-performers: Kerim Seiler, Cyril Kuhn, and Maurus Gmür
296

Picky Eater, 2003
Polystyrene, polyurethane foam, acrylic paint, spray enamel, screws, glue
16 ⅛ x 5 ⅞ x 11 ⅜ inches (249 x 77.5 x 105 cm)
Private collection, Athens
499

Pineapple / Melon, 2010
Silkscreen print on mirror-polished stainless-steel sheets, polyurethane foam sheets, two-component polyurethane adhesive, stainless-steel beams, aluminum L sections, screws; in 4 parts
Sponge, each: 55 ⅛ x 39 ⅝ x 52 inches (140 x 100.6 x 132 cm)
Chair, each: 46 ⅞ x 26 ⅜ x 52 inches (119 x 67 x 132 cm)
Edition of 2 & 1 AP
Francis and Rosa Feeney, Florida; Courtesy of the artist and Sadie Coles HQ, London; Private collection
144

A Place Called Novosibirsk, 2004
Cast aluminum, epoxy resin, iron rod, string, acrylic paint
98 x 30 ½ x 41 ⅜ inches (249 x 77.5 x 105 cm)
Edition of 2 & 1 AP
Private collections; Ringier Collection, Switzerland
454–455

Poem-Donkey (Unfiltered Autumn 99 Poem), 2000
Iron, glass, zinc phosphate paint, photocopies on polyester film, adhesive tape
76 ¾ x 110 ¼ x 47 ¼ inches (195 x 280 x 120 cm)
Hauser & Wirth Collection, Switzerland
275

Pop the Glock, 2006
Cast nickel silver, gesso, oil paint
5 x 2 x 3 inches (12.7 x 5 x 7.5 cm)
Collection François Pinault
42–43

Portrait of a Moment, 2003
Aluminum, two-component polyurethane foam, aircraft cable, steel tubing, acrylic paint, metal fittings
145 ⅝ x 283 ½ x 149 ⅝ inches (370 x 720 x 380 cm)
Burger Collection, Hong Kong
393

Portrait of a Single Raindrop, 2003
Cuts in wall with relocated cutouts
Dimensions variable
The Museum of Contemporary Art, Los Angeles; purchased with funds provided by the Acquisition and Collection Committee
33–35

Prototype for burning chair, 2002
613

Rainbow Cookie, 2003
Vellum, paint marker, acrylics, acrylic varnish, polyurethane resin, acid-free cardboard, glue, pastel, fixative; 2 drawings
Each: 11 ½ x 8 ⅞ inches (29.25 x 22.5 cm)
Sandra and Giancarlo Bonollo Collection, Italy
372

Range L / Range R, 1996
Photocopy on card stock, tape, stamp
8 ⅝ x 7 ⅛ x 3 inches (22 x 18 x 7.5 cm)
Edition of 60 (30 left, 30 right)
Various collections
442

Remembering the Polyester Pirate (Instant Apathy), 2000
Tulle, rocks, lacquer, acrylic paint, chain, aluminum pipe, wood, wood glue
Curtain: 157 ½ x 157 ½ inches (400 x 400 cm)
Bench: 31 ½ x 78 ¾ x 19 ⅝ inches (80 x 200 x 50 cm)
Private collection
275

ROTHENBERG MCCLUSKY, 2012
Silkscreen print on mirror-glass, UV-adhesive, aluminum, glass, polyacetal, screws; in 2 parts
Honey bear: 20 ⅞ x 9 ⅜ x 8 ½ inches (53 x 23.7 x 21.7 cm)
Lighter: 23 ⅛ x 10 ⅛ x 9 ¼ inches (58.6 x 25.8 x 23.4 cm)
Edition of 3 & 1 AP
Private collections; The Kader Collection, Costa Rica
173–175

Routine (Automatic Melancholy), 2002
Polystyrene, polyurethane foam, screws, gouache
Chair: 21 x 35 x 17 inches (53.5 x 89 x 43 cm)
Installation dimensions variable
Private collection
391

Salt / Sandra, 2010
Silkscreen print on mirror-polished stainless-steel sheets, polyurethane foam sheets, two-component polyurethane adhesive, stainless-steel beams, aluminum L sections, screws; in 4 parts
Fox mask, each: 57 ½ x 42 ½ x 64 ⅛ inches (146 x 108 x 163 cm)
Green chair, each: 42 ⅛ x 32 ¼ x 35 ⅜ inches (107 x 82 x 90 cm)
Edition of 2 & 1 AP
Andreas Melas, Athens; Private collection; Collection François Pinault
146

Say Hello / Say Good Bye, 2003
Dried white flowers, polyurethane resin, acrylic paint, screws
30 x 29 x 19 inches (76.2 x 73.8 x 48.6 cm)
Private collection
534

September Song, 2002
Polystyrene, glue, paint, wire, screw, marker
9 x 23 ⅝ x 4 inches (23 x 60 x 10 cm)
Sandra and Giancarlo Bonollo Collection, Italy
497

Service à la francaise, 2009
Silkscreen print on mirror-polished stainless-steel sheets, polyurethane foam sheets, two-component polyurethane adhesive, stainless-steel beams, aluminum L sections, screws; in 52 parts
Installation dimensions variable
Edition of 2
Private collection; Collection Maja Hoffmann, Switzerland
124–139

Servile Serenade / Servile Symphony, 2001
Epoxy, lacquer, wood, MDF
Part 1: 8 ¼ x 9 ⅞ x 32 ⅝ inches (21 x 25 x 83 cm)
Part 2: 15 ⅜ x 12 ¼ x 24 inches (29 x 31 x 61 cm)
Burger Collection, Hong Kong
397, 528–530

Shadow Replacement from the portfolio Thinking about Störtebeker, 2005
Portfolio with 18 bound screenprints on transparent paper and 18 framed prints on Epson Enhanced Matte paper
Portfolio: 22 ⅝ x 17 x ¾ inches (57.4 x 43.1 x 2 cm)
Prints: 22 x 16 ⅛ inches (56 x 41 cm)
Edition of 25 & 5 AP
Various collections
390

Shameless Shame
Silkscreen print on mirror-polished stainless-steel sheets, polyurethane foam sheets, two-component polyurethane adhesive, stainless steel beams, aluminum L sections, screws
25 ⅝ x 19 ⅞ x 31 ⅞ inches (65 x 50.5 x 81 cm)
Edition of 2 & 1 AP
Private collections; Collection of David Simkins, New York
157

She Called Her "Taxi," 2004
Aluminum, ACM panels, acrylic paint, latex paint, marker, UV-protective lacquer
121 ¼ x 156 ¾ x 2 ⅜ inches (308 x 398 x 6 cm)
Private collection
290

Sigh, Sigh, Sherlock!, 2004
Fiberglass-reinforced plaster cast, partially painted
36 ¼ x 12 ⅝ x 12 ⅝ inches (92 x 32 x 32 cm)
Edition of 45 & 25 AP
Various collections
527

Skelett, 1996
Bricks, cement, unfired clay
Dimensions variable
Private collection
294–296

Skinny Afternoon, 2003
Cast aluminum, mirror, lacquer paint, acrylic paint, polyurethane foam, screws
78 ¾ x 63 x 47 ¼ inches (200 x 160 x 120 cm)
Private collection
581, cover

Skinny Sunrise, 2000
Polystyrene, wood, wood glue, dust, spray adhesive, flour, acrylic paint, silicone, screws, fabric
27 ½ x 47 ¼ x 27 ½ inches (70 x 120 x 70 cm)
Ringier Collection, Switzerland
573

Skyline, 2002
Cast bronze, acrylic paint
11 x 17 ½ x 19 ¼ inches (28 x 44.5 x 49 cm)
Private collection
517

Sliced, 2010–2011
Milled aluminum panel, acrylic primer, gesso, acrylic ink, acrylic silkscreen medium, acrylic paint
96 x 72 x 1 inches (243.8 x 182.9 x 2.5 cm)
The Brant Foundation, Greenwich, Connecticut
141

Small Bird, Big Egg, 2011
Cast bronze, oil paint
5 ¾ x 5 ¾ x 3 inches (14.6 x 14.6 x 7.6 cm)
Edition of 2 & 2 AP
The Brant Foundation, Greenwich, Connecticut; Private collections
569

Small Egg, Big Bird, 2011
Cast bronze, oil paint
6 ½ x 6 x 2 ¾ inches (16.5 x 15.2 x 7 cm)
The Brant Foundation, Greenwich, Connecticut; Private collections
570

SMITH JOHNSON WILLIAM JONES, 2012
Silkscreen print on mirror-glass, UV-adhesive, aluminum, glass, polyacetal, screws
Asparagus: 25 ⅝ x 2 ⅞ x 2 ½ inches (65.1 x 7.3 x 6.3 cm)
Calculator: 18 ⅜ x 24 ¾ x 7 inches (46.7 x 62.9 x 17.8 cm)
Ping-Pong paddle: 25 x 14 ⅞ x 2 ¾ inches (63.5 x 37.8 x 7 cm)
Staple gun: 17 ½ x 20 ⅝ x 3 ⅞ inches (44.5 x 52.4 x 9.8 cm)
Edition of 3 & 1 AP
Steve Tisch; Private collections
158–161

Sodbrennen, 2000–2004
Mirrors, aluminum, steel frame, silicone, orange juice, coffee, cigarettes
61 x 61 x 61 inches (155 x 155 x 155 cm)
Dimitris Gigourtakis Collection, Athens
36, 117–118, 290

Some Say Vacuum Some Say Kumquat, 2003
Aluminum, polyurethane resin, nylon filament, metal mountings, aircraft cable, acrylic paint, rivets
122 x 78 ¾ x 149 ⅝ inches (310 x 200 x 380 cm)
Vanhaerents Art Collection, Brussels
395

Spinoza Rhapsody, 2006
Epoxy resin, pigment, enamel paint, wire, aluminum
Approximately 134 x 356 x 535 inches (340 x 905 x 1360 cm)
Edition of 2 & 1 AP
Ringier Collection, Switzerland; Private collections
276–277, 280–283, back endpapers

Stalagmites of Love, 2004
Aluminum, ACM panels, UV inkjet print, acrylic paint, marker, UV-protective lacquer
108 ⅝ x 140 ⅛ x 2 ⅜ inches (276 x 356 x 6 cm)
Private collection
36, 288

Studies for chairs for individual seating positions, 1993
Part 1 of 3
Sawdust, rubber
Dimensions unknown
Destroyed
403

Studio views
81, 386, 471, 605

Stuhl mit, 1995–2001
Wood, foam, latex paint, acrylic paint, fabric, screws
39 ⅜ x 25 ⅝ x 39 ⅜ inches (100 x 65 x 100 cm)
Hauser & Wirth Collection, Switzerland
429

Stühle, 2002
Two-component polyurethane foam, polyurethane foam, cardboard, tape, acrylic paint, imitation leather, brass pins
38 ¼ x 33 ½ x 35 ⅞ inches (97 x 85 x 91 cm)
Private collection
353

Tables from "Tables, Heads, and Arms," Gagosian Gallery at Eden Rock Gallery, St. Barths, 2012–2013
113

Tables from Urs Fischer and Cassandra MacLeod, "dngszjkdufiy bgxfjkglijkhtr kydjkhgdghjkd," Gavin Brown's enterprise, New York, 2011
100–111

Tea Set, 2002
Clay, acrylic paint, plywood, copper leaf
7 ⅞ x 15 x 12 ⅝ inches (20 x 38 x 32 cm)
Ringier Collection, Switzerland
545

Tea Set, 2002
Clay, wood, glue, acrylic paint, silver leaf
9 x 17 ¾ x 15 ⅜ inches (23 x 45 x 39 cm)
Private collection, Germany
286, 544

Tea Time with Miss Cocktail, 2005
Found couch, two-component polyurethane foam, pigments, screws
14 ⅝ x 14 ⅝ x 6 ¾ inches (37 x 37 x 17 cm)
Installation dimensions variable
Private collection
478–479

Telefon, 2003
Polystyrene, acrylic paint, marker, filler
Dimensions unknown
Private collection, Switzerland
617

Telephone, 2002
Polyurethane resin, oil paint
4 ¾ x 7 ⅞ x 4 ⅜ inches (12 x 20 x 11 cm)
Private collection
286

Thank You Fuck You, 2007
Cast aluminum, acrylic paint
60 ¼ x 72 ⅞ x 55 ½ inches (153 x 185 x 141 cm)
Edition of 2 & 1 AP
Private collections; Private collection, Rome
326, 377

That's the Way It Is with the Magic. Sometimes It Works and Sometimes It Doesn't., 2000
Plaster, silicone, marker, acrylic paint, spray enamel, glass vase, polyurethane foam, fresh white lilies
78 ¾ x 15 ¾ x 15 ¾ inches (200 x 40 x 40 cm)
Dr. Barbara Bernoully Collection, Frankfurt
531

The Thing, 2003
Film, paint marker, acrylic paint, varnish, two-component polyurethane
18 x 15 x 1 inches (45.7 x 38 x 2.5 cm)
Private collection
118

A Thing Called Gearbox, 2004
Cast aluminum, copper, iron rod, string, acrylic paint
91 x 26 ¾ x 26 ½ inches (231 x 68 x 67.5 cm)
Edition of 2 & 1 AP
Collection Shane Akeroyd, London; Private collection; Private collection, London
454, 456–457, back endpapers

Tisch mit, 1995–2001
Wood, lacquer, acrylic paint, string, mattress, fabric, two-component epoxy
41 ¾ x 48 ⅜ x 38 ⅝ inches (106 x 123 x 98 cm)
Friedrich Christian Flick Collection
427

Undigested Sunset, 2001–2002
Cast aluminum, wax, wood, acrylic paint, pigments, fabric, silicone, wood glue, screws
30 ½ x 72 x 28 ½ inches (77.5 x 183 x 72.5 cm)
Bert Kreuk Collection
577

Untitled, 1993
Blue paint applied to wall to neutralize orange glow from streetlight
Latex paint, pigments, existing streetlight
Dimensions variable
Private collection
385

Untitled, 1993
Particleboard, velour, staples, screws, contact cement
47 ¼ x 61 inches (120 x 155 cm)
Private collection
601

Untitled, 1996
Found stool, found bottle, hammer, strawberry jam
Dimensions variable
Private collection
386

Untitled, 1997
Bricks, mortar, wooden beams
Dimensions unknown
Private collection
297

Untitled, 1997
Cut-up pallet, household candles
41 x 39 ⅜ x 9 inches (104 x 100 x 23 cm)
Private collection
177

Untitled, 1997
Found furnishings, found clothes, latex paint, acrylic binder, marker, wood glue, silicone
Dimensions variable
Private collection
441

Untitled, 1997
Wood, wood glue, stain, dishes, glasses, epoxy adhesive, silicone, acrylic paint
Table: 41 ⅜ x 72 ½ x 30 ¾ inches (105 x 184 x 78 cm)
4 chairs, each 31 ½ x 13 ⅜ x 15 ¾ inches (80 x 34 x 40 cm)
Hauser & Wirth Collection, Switzerland
436–437

Untitled, 2000
Apple, pear, nylon filament, screws
Dimensions variable
Edition of 2 & 2 AP
Friedrich Christian Flick Collection; Collection of The Museum of Modern Art, New York; Private collections
547

Untitled, 2001
Wax, pigment, wick, brick, metal rod
66 ⅞ x 18 ⅛ x 11 ⅜ inches (170 x 46 x 29 cm)
Edition of 3 & 1 AP
Burger Collection, Hong Kong; The Brant Foundation, Greenwich, Connecticut; David Gill Private Collection, London; Collection Eric Moreau, London
184–185, 530

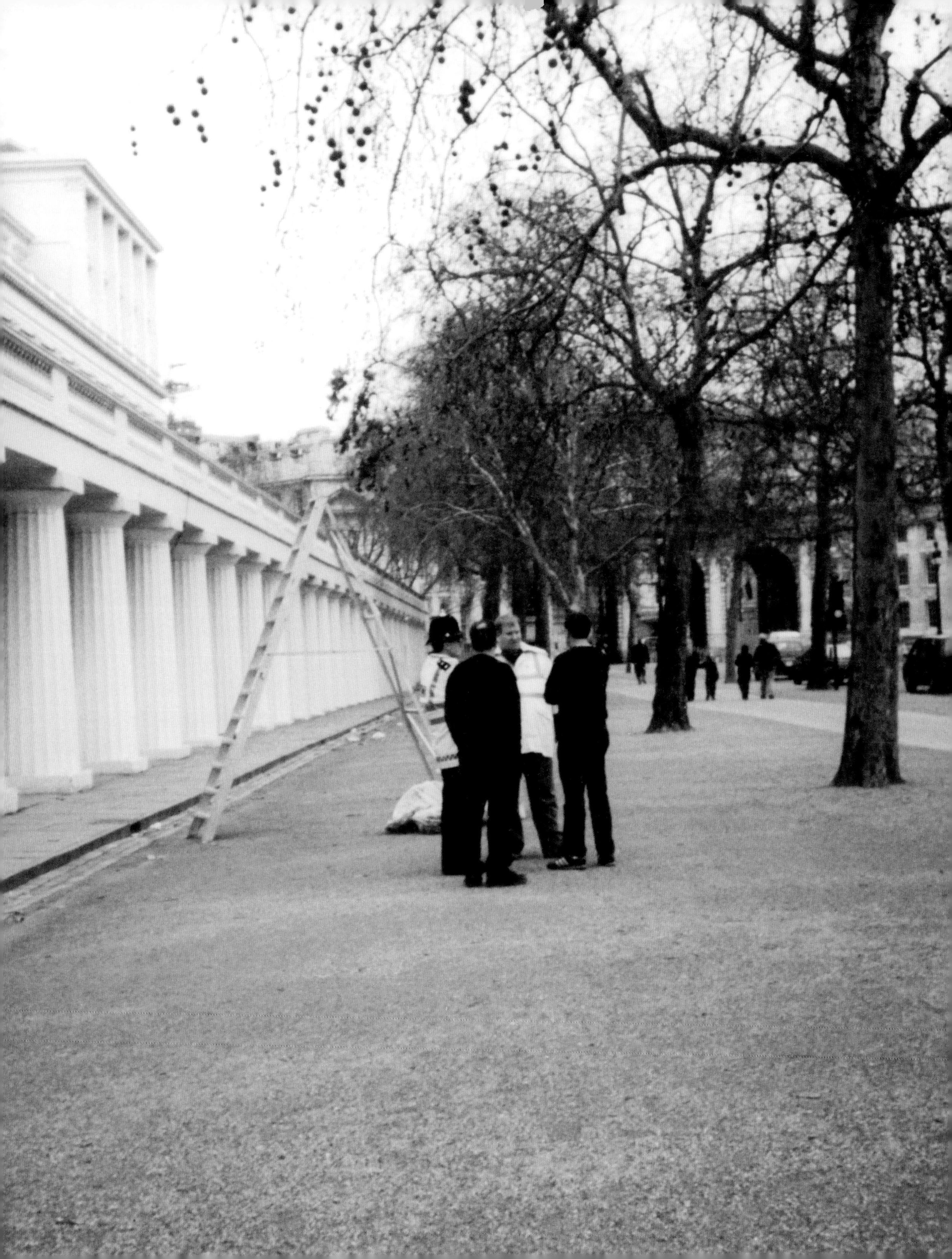

Untitled, 2003
Nylon filament, banana, theater spotlight
Dimensions variable
Edition of 2 & 1 AP
Courtesy of the artist and Gagosian Gallery;
Private collections
550–551

Untitled, 2003
Steel, concrete, screws, hair, polyurethane glue, wood glue, plastic, burlap, wood, chicken wire
76 x 96 x 64 inches (193 x 243.8 x 162.6 cm)
Private collection
563

Untitled, 2004
Concrete, iron, steel, wax, cement, soot, pigments, hair, polyurethane resin, acrylic paint
78 ¾ x 89 ⅜ x 66 ⅞ inches (200 x 227 x 170 cm)
Private collection
36, 288, 562

Untitled, 2004
Polyurethane resin, acrylic paint, metal pin
5 ⅞ x 4 ¾ x 2 inches (15 x 12 x 5 cm)
Edition of 4
Private collections
568

Untitled, 2006
MDF, gesso acrylic paint, wood, wood glue, screws
Lighter: 14 ⅜ x 4 ⅜ x 2 inches (36.6 x 11 x 5.2 cm)
Book: 6 ¼ x 21 ⅝ x 16 ⅜ inches (15.8 x 55 x 41.5 cm)
Toast: 21 ¼ x 23 ⅛ x 3 ⅛ inches (54 x 58.8 x 7.8 cm)
Private collection
123

Untitled, 2006
Polyurethane foam, spray enamel, aluminum rod, screws
41 ¾ x 16 ¾ x 30 ⅛ inches (106 x 42.5 x 76.5 cm)
Private collection
480–481

Untitled, 2006
Silicone, wood, found chair, shellac
Dimensions variable
Private collection
410

Untitled, 2007
Cast nickel silver, gesso, oil paint
3 ⅜ x 3 ⅛ x 2 ⅛ inches (8.5 x 8 x 5.5 cm)
Edition of 1 & 1 AP
Collection François Pinault; Private collection
44

Untitled, 2007
Cast nickel silver, gesso, oil paint
5 ⅛ x 5 ⅛ x 2 inches (13 x 13 x 5 cm)
Edition of 1 & 1 AP
Collection François Pinault; Private collection
44

Untitled, 2007
Cast nickel silver, gesso, oil paint
Mouse 1: 2 ⅜ x 4 ⅞ x 1 ⅝ inches (6 x 12.5 x 4 cm)
Mouse 2: 2 ⅜ x 1 ⅜ x 2 inches (6 x 3.5 x 5 cm)
Edition of 1 & 1 AP
Collection François Pinault; Private collection
45

Untitled, 2009
Cast aluminum, aluminum wire, epoxy primer, polyester filler, one-component acrylic putty, urethane primer, polyester paint, acrylic polyurethane matte clearcoat
52 x 61 x 98 inches (132 x 155 x 249 cm)
Edition of 2 & 1 AP
Private collection; Collection François Pinault;
Private collection
55, 416–417

Untitled, 2009
Latex paint, found chair, found hand truck
110 ⅜ x 110 ⅜ x 149 ¾ inches
(280 x 280 x 380 cm)
Private collection
77

Untitled, 2009
Plaster, acrylic paint, bread
3 ⅞ x 8 ¼ x 5 ⅞ inches (10 x 21 x 15 cm)
Private collection
79, 509

Untitled, 2010
Plaster, eggshell, three-component polyurethane, metal pin, epoxy adhesive, acrylic gesso
7 x 6 ½ x 8 inches (17.8 x 16.5 x 20.3 cm)
The Brant Foundation, Greenwich, Connecticut
513

Untitled, 2011
Cast aluminum, epoxy primer, polyester filler, one-component acrylic putty, urethane primer, polyester paint, acrylic polyurethane matte clearcoat
64 x 74 ¾ x 101 inches (162.6 x 189.9 x 256.5 cm)
Edition of 3 & 1 AP; each edition with unique color scheme
Collection J. and M. Donnelly; Private collections
421–425

Untitled, 2011
Paraffin wax mixture, pigment, steel, lead weights, wicks
Rudi and chair: 52 x 32 ⅛ x 52 ⅜ inches
(132.1 x 81.6 x 133 cm)
Bottles: Dimensions variable, 10 ⅝–14 ⅛ inches
(32–36 cm) high
Edition of 3 & 1 AP
Collection François Pinault; Private collections
217–221

Untitled, 2011
Paraffin wax mixture, pigment, steel, wicks
Urs and chair: 53 ⅞ x 28 ½ x 49 ½ inches
(136.8 x 72.4 x 125.8 cm)
Table: 30 ⅞ x 46 ⅜ x 45 ⅜ inches
(78.5 x 117.7 x 115.1 cm)
Overall dimensions: 53 ⅞ x 46 ⅜ x 75 ¼ inches
(136.8 x 117.7 x 191.3 cm)
Bottles: Dimensions variable, 10 ⅝–14 ⅛ inches
(32–36 cm) high
Edition of 3 & 1 AP
Collection François Pinault; Private collections
223–226

Untitled, 2011
Wax, pigments, wicks, steel
Giambologna sculpture: 57 ⅞ x 57 ⅞ x 248 ⅛ inches (147 x 147 x 630 cm)
Rudi portrait: 19 ¼ x 27 ⅛ x 77 ½ inches
(49 x 69 x 197 cm)
Office chair: 30 ¾ x 28 ⅜ x 45 ⅝ inches
(78 x 72 x 116 cm)
Installation dimensions variable
Edition of 2 & 1 AP
Collection Maja Hoffmann, Switzerland;
The Brant Foundation, Greenwich, Connecticut;
Private collection
205–214

Untitled, 2011-ongoing
(with various artists)
Unfired clay (sculptures modeled on-site by multiple authors following a list of objects specified by the artist)
Dimensions variable
248–269

Untitled (50 Rocks), 1996
50 found river rocks
Dimensions variable
Private collection
271, 294–296

Untitled (Big Clay #3), 2008–2011
Cast aluminum, chrome steel skeleton, chrome steel bolts
Approximately 403 ½ x 299 ¼ x 255 ⅞ inches
(1024.9 x 760 x 650 cm)
The Brant Foundation, Greenwich, Connecticut
238–242

Untitled (Big Clay #5), 2008–2013
Cast aluminum, chrome steel skeleton, chrome steel bolts
Approximately 513 ¾ x 362 ¼ x 263 ¾ inches
(1305.1 x 920 x 670.1 cm)
Collection Maja Hoffmann, Switzerland
244–245

Untitled (Bird Head in Egg), 2012
Plaster, screw, acrylic paint, spray paint
5 ½ x 7 ½ x 3 ¾ inches (13.9 x 19 x 9.5 cm)
Edition of 550
Various collections
571

Untitled (Branches), 2005
Two branches moving at different speeds,
in opposite directions
Cast aluminum, chains, candles,
low-speed electric motors, control units
Branch 1: 19 ⅝ x 126 x 15 ¾ inches
(50 x 320 x 40 cm)
Branch 2: 19 ⅝ x 122 x 15 ¾ inches
(50 x 310 x 40 cm)
Overall dimensions approximately:
244 ⅛ x 326 ¾ x 234 ⅝ inches (620 x 830 x 596 cm)
Edition of 2 & 1 AP
Private collection; Ringier Collection, Switzerland;
Rubell Family Collection, Miami, Florida
41, 182–183

Untitled (Bread House), 2004
Bread, wood, marzipan, screws
157 ½ x 157 ½ x 169 ¼ inches (400 x 400 x 430 cm)
Prototype
Destroyed
328–329

Untitled (Bread House), 2004–2005
Bread, bread crumbs, wood, polyurethane
foam, silicone, acrylic paint, screws,
tape, rugs, theater spotlights
159 ⅞ x 146 ½ x 165 ¾ inches (406 x 372 x 421 cm)
The Brant Foundation, Greenwich, Connecticut
331–333

Untitled (Bread House), 2004–2006
Bread, bread crumbs, wood, polyurethane
foam, silicone, acrylic paint, screws,
tape, rugs, theater spotlights
196 ⅞ x 157 ½ x 196 ⅞ inches (500 x 400 x 500 cm)
Private collection
335–337, 506

Untitled (Brick), 2005
Polyurethane resin, acrylic paint
9 x 3 x 3 ½ inches (22.9 x 7.6 x 8.9 cm)
Private collection
560

Untitled (Candle), 1999
Candles, fiber cement boards, screws
Base: 39 ⅜ x 39 ⅜ inches (100 x 100 cm)
Pedestal: 49 ¼ x 7 ⅞ x 7 ⅞ inches (125 x 20 x 20 cm)
Wax: 27 ½ x 33 ½ x 27 ½ inches
(70 x 85 x 70 cm), growing
Hauser & Wirth Collection, Switzerland
179

Untitled (Chair), 1997–2000
Wooden chair, clay, oil paint, acrylic paint, wax,
spray adhesive, matte varnish, silicone
33 x 20 x 18 ⅞ inches (84 x 51 x 48 cm)
Friedrich Christian Flick Collection
467

Untitled (Door), 2006
Cast aluminum, enamel paint, steel hinges
84 ⅝ x 53 ½ x 20 ⅛ inches (215 x 136 x 51 cm)
Private collection, Milan
339–340

Untitled (Door), 2006
Cast aluminum, enamel paint, steel hinges
95 ¼ x 61 ¾ x 10 ⅝ inches (242 x 157 x 27 cm)
Private collection
346–347, 349

Untitled (Door), 2006
Cast aluminum, enamel paint, steel hinges
97 ¼ x 61 ⅜ x 10 ⅝ inches (247 x 156 x 27 cm)
Collection François Pinault
348–350

Untitled (Door), 2006
Cast aluminum, enamel paint, steel hinges
100 ¾ x 67 ¾ x 10 ⅝ inches (256 x 172 x 27 cm)
Private collection
341–343

Untitled (Door), 2006
Cast aluminum, enamel paint, steel hinges
110 ⅝ x 71 x 10 ⅝ inches (281 x 183 x 27 cm)
Il Giardino dei Lauri, Città della Pieve
344–346

Untitled (Eierschale), 2000
MDF, clay, acrylic paint, wood glue, oil paint,
marker, eggs, hairspray, matte varnish
7 ½ x 15 x 11 ⅜ inches (19 x 38 x 29 cm)
The Brant Foundation, Greenwich, Connecticut
543

Untitled (Floor Piece), 2006
Black adhesive vinyl, latex paint
Dimensions variable
La Colección Jumex, Mexico
71–73

Untitled (Hole), 2007
Cast aluminum
212 ½ x 133 ⅞ x 106 ¼ inches (540 x 340 x 270 cm)
Edition of 2 & 1 AP
Private collection; Collection François Pinault;
The Brant Foundation, Greenwich, Connecticut
3–7, 65

Untitled (Holes), 2006
Carved polyurethane, plaster,
acrylic paint, screws, wire
Ear: 5 ⅛ x 13 ⅜ x 3 ½ inches (13 x 34 x 9 cm)
Nose: 3 ⅛ x 12 ¼ x 3 ⅛ inches (8 x 31 x 8 cm)
Arse: 5 ⅞ x 7 ½ x 5 ⅛ inches (15 x 19 x 13 cm)
Willy: 2 ¾ x 13 ⅜ x 3 ½ inches (7 x 34 x 9 cm)
Mouth: 5 ⅞ x 13 x 5 ½ inches (15 x 33 x 14 cm)
Il Giardino dei Lauri, Città della Pieve
482–487

Untitled (Ladder), 1997
Aluminum ladder, latex paint,
theater spotlights, water bottle
Dimensions variable
Private collection
389

Untitled (Lamp / Bear), 2005–2006
Cast bronze, epoxy primer, urethane paint,
acrylic polyurethane topcoat, acrylic glass,
gas discharge lamp, stainless-steel framework
275 ⅝ x 255 ⅞ x 295 ¼ inches (700 x 650 x 750 cm)
Edition of 2 & 1 AP
Private collections
362–369, 367 (study for)

Untitled (Nude on a Table), 2002
Two-component polyurethane foam,
cardboard, polystyrene, polyurethane foam,
tape, screws, powdered sugar, egg whites,
pigments, acrylic paint
55 ½ x 61 ¾ x 49 ⅝ inches (141 x 157 x 126 cm)
Vanhaerents Art Collection, Brussels
579

Untitled (Pear / Apple), 2012
Nylon filament, apple, pear, projector, screw
Dimensions variable
Edition of 3 & 1 AP
Courtesy of the artist and Gagosian Gallery;
Private collection
554–555

Untitled (Pink Chair), 1996
Found chair, gauze, acrylic paint, glue,
staples, lacquer
40 ½ x 16 ⅛ x 19 ¾ inches (103 x 41 x 50 cm)
Private collection
428

Untitled (Pink Lady), 2001
Polystyrene, polyurethane resin, polyurethane
foam, oil paint, acrylic paint, fluorescent pigments,
sugar, egg whites, screws
39 ⅜ x 39 ⅜ x 59 inches (100 x 100 x 150 cm)
Collection Fundação de Serralves–Contemporary
Art Museum, Porto, Portugal
576

Untitled (Seated), 2010
Paraffin wax mixture, pigment, steel, wicks
55 x 27 x 45 inches (139.7 x 68.6 x 114.3 cm)
Edition of 2 & 1 AP
The Brant Foundation, Greenwich, Connecticut;
Laura and Stafford Broumand Collection;
Private collection
63, 201–203

Untitled (Self-Destroying Cat), 2009
Unfired clay
Dimensions variable
Private collection
247

Untitled (Standing), 2010
Paraffin wax mixture, pigment, steel, wicks
77 x 31 x 52 inches (195.6 x 78.7 x 132.1 cm)
Edition of 2 & 1 AP
The Brant Foundation, Greenwich, Connecticut; Private collections
7, 64–66, 197–199

Untitled (Step Piece), 1995
Intervention activated by visitor's entrance into gallery; when stepped on, a slightly elevated wooden board slaps the floor, producing a loud noise
MDF, aluminum trim, bungee cord, hooks
Dimensions variable
Private collection
626–627

Untitled (Suspended Line of Fruit), 2012
Nylon filament, fresh fruit in ascending sizes (grape, strawberry, lime, apple, grapefruit, coconut, pineapple), glue, nail, screw, paint, wood
Dimensions variable
Edition of 3 & 1 AP
Private collection, Monaco; The Brant Foundation, Greenwich, Connecticut; Courtesy of the artist and Gagosian Gallery; Private collection
380, 556–557

Untitled (Wand der Angst), 1997
Aerated concrete, mortar, silicone, coffee
126 x 326 ¾ x 79 ⅞ inches (320 x 830 x 203 cm)
Private collection
298–299

Verbal Asceticism, 2007
Wallpaper prints of photographic reproductions of interior spaces (content, scale, and lighting determined on a site-specific basis)
(1:1 scale black-and-white photographic reproduction of the gallery space during the previous exhibition, "Where Are We Going?")
Dimensions variable
Collection François Pinault
42–45

Vieille Prune, 2005
Two-component polyurethane foam, pigments, screws, epoxy glue
20 ⅞ x 17 ¾ x 8 ¼ inches (53 x 45 x 21 cm)
Private collection
478

Vintage Violence, 2004–2005
Plaster, resin paint, steel, nylon filament
Dimensions variable: 1,700 raindrops, each up to 7 ½ x 3 ½ x 3 ⅛ inches (19 x 9 x 8 cm)
Collection François Pinault
291–292

Violent Cappuccino, 2007
Cast aluminum, lacquer, motor oil, glue, dust
79 ¾ x 51 ⅛ x 28 ¾ inches (202.5 x 130 x 73 cm)
Edition of 2 & 1 AP
Bischofberger Collection, Zurich; Collection François Pinault; Private collection, Switzerland
585

Walking Heads / Thinking Feet, 2002
Polystyrene, polyurethane foam, acrylic paint, latex paint, screws
22 x 7 ½ x 5 ⅞ inches (56 x 19 x 15 cm)
Private collection
521

Wandnarbe, 1996
Plaster, newspaper, wire, latex paint
Dimensions variable
Private collection
271

Warum wächst ein Baum / Kann man zuviel Fragen (Nr. 3) / Why does a tree grow / Can one ask too much (No. 3), 2001
Polyurethane resin, UV-protective varnish, acrylic paint, polystyrene
5 ⅛ x 33 ⅞ x 28 ¾ inches (13 x 86 x 73 cm)
Hauser & Wirth Collection, Switzerland
409

The Way You Move, 2003
Polystyrene, glue, acrylic paint, marker
4 ¾ x 3 ½ x 5 ⅛ inches (12 x 9 x 13 cm)
Private collection, Switzerland
498

What if the Phone Rings, 2003
Wax, pigment, wick
Figure 1: 41 ¾ x 55 ⅞ x 18 ⅛ inches (106 x 142 x 46 cm)
Figure 2: 78 ¾ x 21 ¼ x 18 ⅛ inches (200 x 54 x 46 cm)
Figure 3: 37 x 39 x 21 ¼ inches (94 x 99 x 54 cm)
Edition of 3 & 1 AP
Private collection; Sender Collection; Ringier Collection, Switzerland; Friedrich Christian Flick Collection
36–37, 187–195, 290, 325

What Should an Owl Do with a Fork, 2002
Wax, wick, wood, garbage
20 ⅛ x 28 x 12 inches (178 x 71 x 30.5 cm)
Destroyed
180–181

Y-Chair, 2007
Acrylic resin, stainless steel
32 x 34 x 35 inches (81.3 x 86.4 x 88.9 cm)
Collection of Matt Aberle, Los Angeles
280–283, 412–413

You, 2007
Excavation, gallery space, 1:3 scale replica of main gallery space
Dimensions variable
The Brant Foundation, Greenwich, Connecticut
8–23

You Can Not Win, 2003
Polystyrene, acrylic paint, Aqua-Resin, screws, fiberglass
54 x 30 x 51 inches (137.2 x 76.2 x 129.5 cm)
Collection of Laura Steinberg and Bernardo Nadal-Ginard, Chestnut Hill, Massachusetts
34–35, 357

You Can Only Lose, 2003
Polystyrene, acrylic paint, Aqua-Resin, screws, fiberglass
123 x 44 x 42 inches (312.4 x 111.8 x 106.7 cm)
Sender Collection
33–35, 359

Your Deaths Your Births, 2004
Aluminum, ACM panels, UV inkjet print, acrylic paint, marker, UV-protective lacquer
140 ⅛ x 108 ⅝ x 2 ⅜ inches (356 x 276 x 6 cm)
Private collection
37, 325

Zizi, 2006–2008
Cast aluminum, steel
161 ⅜ x 90 ½ x 89 inches (410 x 230 x 226 cm)
Edition of 2 & 1 AP
Courtesy of the artist and Galerie Eva Presenhuber, Zurich; Private collections
232, 234–236

Page 601:
Untitled, 1993
Particleboard, velour, staples, screws, contact cement
47 ¼ x 61 inches (120 x 155 cm)

Page 605:
Studio view, Leland Hotel, San Francisco, 1995

Page 609:
Failed installation of green leaves on winter tree outside exhibition window for "Without a Fist–Like a Bird," Institute of Contemporary Arts, London, January 2000

Opposite page:
Prototype for burning chair, 2002

Page 617:
Telefon, 2003
Polystyrene, acrylic paint, marker, filler
Dimensions unknown

Page 621:
Olé!, 2003
Sugar cubes
Dimensions variable

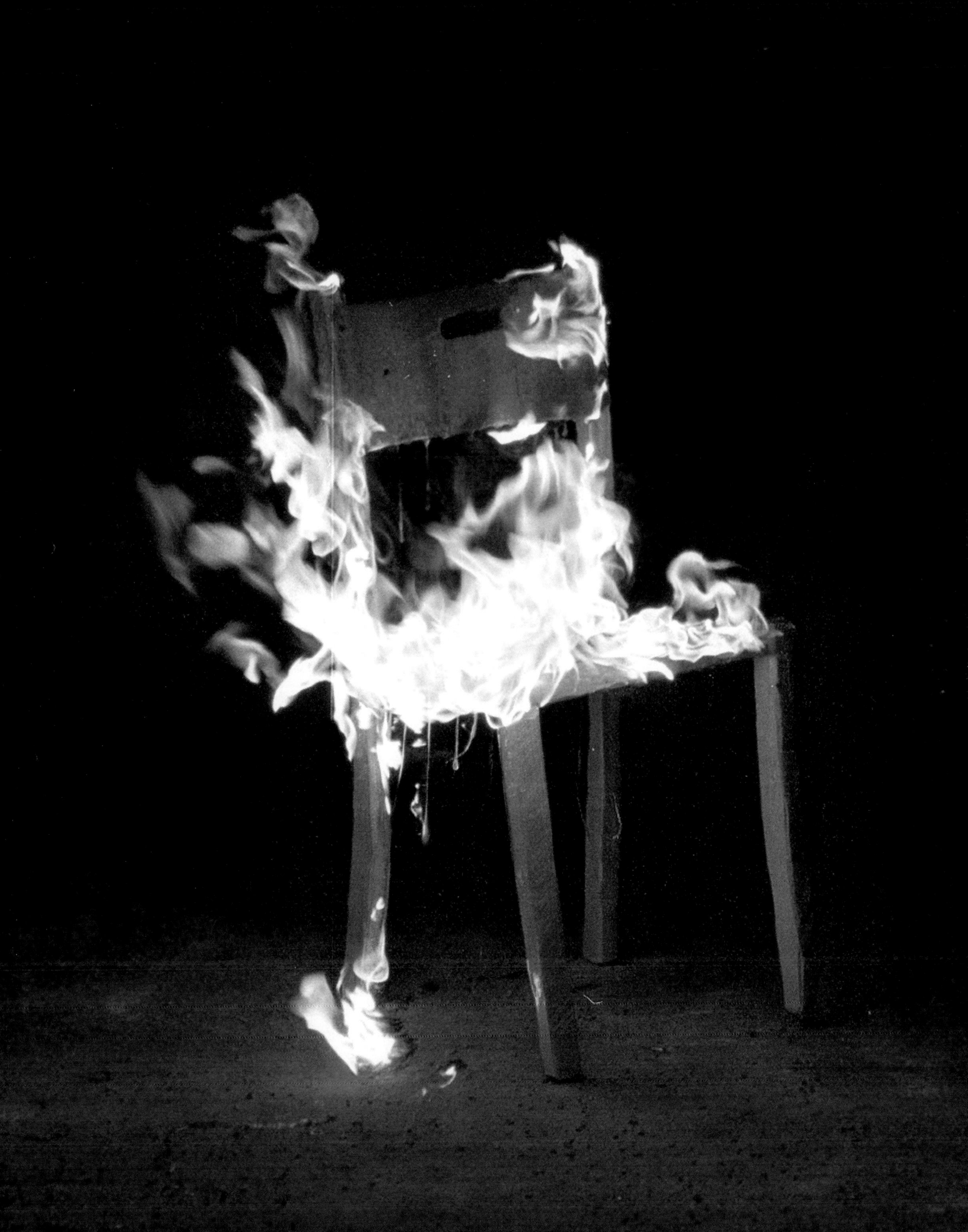

EXHIBITION LIST

Urs Fischer
Born 1973 in Zurich
Lives and works in New York

Studied photography at the Schule für Gestaltung, Zurich
Visited de Ateliers, Amsterdam
Artist in residence, Delfina Studio Trust, London

SOLO EXHIBITIONS

2013

"Urs Fischer," The Museum of Contemporary Art, Los Angeles: 21 April–19 August

2012

"Tables, Heads, and Arms," Gagosian Gallery at Eden Rock Gallery, St. Barths: 28 December 2012–31 January 2013
"Madame Fisscher," Palazzo Grassi, Venice: 15 April–15 July
"schmutz schmutz," Gagosian Gallery, Paris: 5 April–26 May
"Beds & Problem Paintings," Gagosian Gallery, Beverly Hills: 23 February–7 April
"Skinny Sunrise," Kunsthalle Wien, Vienna: 17 February–28 May

2011

"dngszjkdufiy bgxfjkglijkhtr kydjkhgdghjkd" (with Cassandra MacLeod), Gavin Brown's enterprise, New York: 22 October–11 December
"Urs Fischer and Georg Herold," The Modern Institute, Glasgow: 2 July–20 August
"Untitled (Lamp / Bear)," Seagram Plaza, New York: 11 April–12 September

2010

"Douglas Sirk," Sadie Coles HQ, 4 New Burlington Place, London: 6 October–11 December
"Oscar the Grouch," The Brant Foundation Art Study Center, Greenwich, Connecticut: 15 May 2010–3 January 2011

2009

"Urs Fischer: Marguerite de Ponty," New Museum, New York: 28 October 2009–7 February 2010
"Dear ________! We _____ on ________, hysterically. It has to be _____ that _____. No? It is now ______ and the whole _______ has changed ______. all the _____, ______" (with Mark Handforth and Georg Herold), Kunstnernes Hus, Oslo: 15 May–26 July

2008

"Blurry Renoir Debussy," Galerie Eva Presenhuber, Zurich: 25 October–31 January

2007

"Agnes Martin," Regen Projects, Los Angeles: 15 December 2007–19 January 2008
"you," Gavin Brown's enterprise, New York: 25 October–22 December
"Uh...," Sadie Coles HQ, London: 11 October–17 November
"large, dark & empty," Galerie Eva Presenhuber, Zurich: 8 September–17 November
"get up girl a sun is running the world" (with Ugo Rondinone), Church San Stae, Venice Biennale: 10 June–21 November
Cockatoo Island, Kaldor Art Projects and the Sydney Harbour Federation Trust, Sydney: 20 April–3 June

2006

"Urs Fischer e Rudolf Stingel," Galleria Massimo de Carlo, Milan: 30 November 2006–20 January 2007
"Oh. Sad. I see.," The Modern Institute, Glasgow: 4 November–16 December
"Mary Poppins," Blaffer Gallery, The Art Museum of the University of Houston, Texas: 13 May–5 August
Galerie Eva Presenhuber, Zurich: 12 May– 2 June
"Paris 1919," Museum Boijmans Van Beuningen, Rotterdam: 1 April–25 May

2005

"Mr. Watson—Come Here—I Want to See You," Hydra Workshop, Greece: 23 July–10 September
"Urs Fischer: Werke aus der Friedrich Christian Flick Collection im Hamburger Bahnhof," Hamburger Bahnhof, Museum für Gegenwart, Berlin: 2 June–7 August
Camden Arts Centre, London: 13 May–10 July
"Jet Set Lady," Fondazione Nicola Trussardi, Istituto dei Ciechi, Milan: 3 May–1 June
"Fig, Nut & Pear," Gavin Brown's enterprise, New York: 4 February–5 March

2004

"Elton John?" Sadie Coles HQ, London: 1 December 2004–15 January 2005
"Feige, Nuss, und Birne," Gruppe Österreichische Guggenheim, Vienna: 9 October–28 November
"Kir Royal," Kunsthaus Zürich: 9 July–26 September
"Not My House Not My Fire," Espace 315, Centre Pompidou, Paris: 10 March–10 May

2003

"Portrait of a Single Raindrop," Gavin Brown's enterprise, New York: 12 April–10 May
"need no chair when walking," Sadie Coles HQ, London: 29 January–8 March

2002

"What should an Owl do with a Fork," Santa Monica Museum of Art, California: 12 July–30 August
"Mystique Mistake," The Modern Institute, Glasgow: 28 June–26 July
"Bing Crosby," Contemporary Fine Arts, Berlin: 12 January–16 February

2001

"Mastering the Complaint," Galerie Hauser & Wirth & Presenhuber, Zurich: 25 August–17 October

2000

"Cappillon—Urs just does it for the girls" (with Amy Adler), Delfina, London: 21 September–5 November
"The Membrane—and why I don't mind bad-mooded People," Stedelijk Museum Bureau Amsterdam: 16 April–28 May
"Tagessuppen / Soups of the Days" and "6 1/2 Domestic Pairs Project" (with Keith Tyson), Kunsthaus Glarus, Switzerland: 1 April–12 June
"Without a Fist—Like a Bird," Institute of Contemporary Arts, London: 20 January–27 February

1999

"Espressoqueen—Worries and other stuff you have to think about before you get ready for the big easy," Galerie Hauser & Wirth & Presenhuber, Zurich: 16 January–13 March

1997

"Hammer," Galerie Walcheturm, Zurich: 29 August–4 October

1996

"Frs Uischer," Galerie Walcheturm, Zurich

GROUP EXHIBITIONS

2013

"Drawing Line into Form: Works on Paper by Sculptors from the Collection of BNY Mellon," Tacoma Art Museum, Tacoma, Washington: 23 February–26 May
"Crystal Maze IV - 1 + 2 + 3 = 3," Nouveau Festival, Centre Georges Pompidou, Paris: 20 February–11 March

2012

"Seuls quelques fragments de nous toucheront quelques fragments d'autrui (Only parts of us will ever touch parts of others)," Galerie Thaddaeus Ropac, Paris: 30 November 2012–19 January 2013
"Ensemble," Galerie kreo, Paris: 12 October–24 November
Festival d'Automne à Paris, Cour Chimay and Chapelle des Petits Augustins, École nationale supérieure des Beaux-arts, Paris: 13 September–3 November
"Painting Now," Galerie Eva Presenhuber, Zurich: 10 June–28 July
"Riotous Baroque. From Cattelan to Zurbarán—Tributes to Precarious Vitality," Kunsthaus Zurich: 1 June–2 September
"The Painting Factory: Abstraction after Warhol," MOCA Grand Avenue, Los Angeles: 29 April–2 September
"Poule!" Fundación/Colección Jumex, Ecatepec, Mexico: 19 April–14 September
"Micro Mania," Gagosian Gallery, Paris Project Space: 18 April 2012–31 May 2012

2011

"Home Alone," Sender Collection, Miami: 29 November–4 December
"Now: obras de La Colección Jumex," Hospicio Cabañas, Guadalajara, Mexico: 7 October 2011–8 January 2012
"In Deed: Certificates of Authenticity in Art," De Kabinetten van De Vleeshal, Middelburg, The Netherlands: 10 September–9 October (traveled to Fondazione Bevilacqua La Masa, Venice: 14 October–6 November; KHOJ Studios, New Delhi: 18 November–16 December; Mumbai Art Room, Mumbai: 13 January 2012–10 February 2012; Nero HQ, Rome: 3 February 2012–2 March 2012; The School of the Art Institute of Chicago: 30 March 2012–28 April 2012; SALT Beyoğlu: 30 May 2012–26 August 2012; The Drawing Center, New York: 2 November 2012–15 December 2012; Weatherspoon Art Museum, Greensboro, North Carolina: 12 January 2013–14 April 2013)
"Artists for Haiti," David Zwirner, New York: 6 September–14 September
"Lustwarande 2011—Blemishes," Park De Oude Warande, Museum De Pont, Tilburg, The Netherlands: 25 June–25 September
"Produced by Migros: Collection Migros Museum für Gegenwartskunst," Kunsthalle Fridericianum, Kassel: 25 June–11 September
"Sculpture Now," Galerie Eva Presenhuber, Zurich: 11 June–30 July

"ILLUMI*nazioni* / ILLUMI*nations*," Venice Biennale: 4 June–27 November
"The World Belongs to You," Palazzo Grassi, Venice: 2 June–31 December
"New contemporary galleries featuring the John Kaldor Family Collection," Art Gallery of New South Wales, Australia: 21 May 2011–2 May 2012
"L'invention de l'oeuvre: Rodin et les ambassadeurs," Musée Rodin, Paris: 6 May–4 September
"Sympathy for the Devil," Vanhaerents Art Collection, Brussels: 30 April–30 November
"Kunstsammlung im Alpenhof Nr. 6: Kunstbetrieb," Alpenhof St. Anton, Switzerland: 30 April–12 June
"Don't Do It Etc.," Galerie Bruno Bischofberger, Zurich: 26 March–4 June
"dwelling," Marianne Boesky Gallery (uptown), New York: 29 January–26 March
"Modern British Sculpture," Royal Academy of Arts, London: 22 January–7 April
"8 ½," Fondazione Nicola Trussardi, Stazione Leopolda, Florence, Italy: 13 January–6 February

2010

"Die Nase des Michelangelo / The Nose of Michelangelo," Galerie Peter Kilchmann, Marktgasse 4, Zurich: 10 December–19 December
"Divine Comedy," Sotheby's, New York: 30 September–19 October
"Post Monument: XIV Biennale Internazionale di Scultura di Carrara," Carrara, Italy: 26 June–31 October
"Multiple Pleasures: Functional Objects in Contemporary Art," Tanya Bonakdar Gallery, New York: 25 June–30 July
"The New Décor," Hayward Gallery, London: 19 June–5 September (traveled to Garage Center for Contemporary Culture, Moscow: 21 October 2010–6 February 2011)
"Alpha Omega: Works from the Dakis Joannou Collection," Deste Foundation for Contemporary Art, Athens: 16 June–29 December
"High Ideals & Crazy Dreams," Galerie Vera Munro, Hamburg: 20 May–30 September
"Voici un dessin suisse (1990–2010) / Here Is a Swiss Drawing," Musée Rath, Geneva: 31 March–15 August (traveled to Aargauer Kunsthaus, Aarau, Switzerland: 29 January–25 April)
"Skin Fruit: Selections from the Dakis Joannou Collection," New Museum, New York: 3 March–20 June

2009

"Beg Borrow and Steal," Rubell Family Collection, Miami: 2 December–27 August
"Les enfants terribles," Fundación/Colección Jumex, Ecatepec, Mexico: 6 November–5 March
"We Are Sun-kissed and Snow-blind," Galerie Patrick Seguin, Paris: 23 October–28 November
"Investigations of a Dog: Works from the FACE Collections," Fondazione Sandretto Re Rebaudengo, Turin, Italy: 21 October–4 March (traveled to Ellipse Foundation, Cascais, Portugal: 15 May- 5 September; La maison rouge–Fondation Antoine de Galbert, Paris: 23 October 2010–15 January 2011; Magasin 3 Stockholm Konsthall, Stockholm: 17 February–29 May; Deste Foundation for Contemporary Art, Athens: 19 June–15 October)
"Precarious Form I / Prekäre Skulpturen," Galerie Meyer Kainer, Vienna: 9 September–7 November
"Conflicting Tales: Subjectivity (Quadrilogy, Part 1)," Burger Collection, Zimmerstrasse 90–91, Berlin: 4 September–13 December
"200 Artworks—25 Years: Artists' Editions for Parkett," 21st Century Museum of Contemporary Art, Kanazawa, Japan: 4 September–26 September (traveled to Singapore Tyler Print Institute (STPI), Singapore: 22 May–17 July; Seoul Arts Center (SAC), Hangaram Museum, Seoul, Korea: 17 December 2010–25 February 2011)
"The living and the dead," Gavin Brown's enterprise, New York: 1 July–7 August
"Mapping the Studio: Artists from the François Pinault Collection," Palazzo Grassi and Punta della Dogana, Venice: 6 June 2009–4 April 2011
"Magritte et la Lumière / Magritte and Light," Almine Rech Gallery, Brussels: 20 May–25 July
"Remembering Henry's Show: Selected Works, 1978–2008," The Brant Foundation Art Study Center, Greenwich, Connecticut: 9 May–20 December
"A Guest + A Host = A Ghost: Works from the Dakis Joannou Collection," Deste Foundation for Contemporary Art, Athens: 7 May–31 December
"Nothingness and Being," Fundación/Colección Jumex, Ecatepec, Mexico: 23 April–25 September
"Compass in Hand: Selections from The Judith Rothschild Foundation Contemporary Drawings Collection," The Museum of Modern Art, New York: 22 April 2009–4 January 2010
"Saints and Sinners," The Rose Art Museum, Brandeis University, Waltham, Massachusetts: 15 January -5 April

2008

"Ombres," New Galerie de France, Paris: 8 November 2008–17 January 2009
"Open Plan Living," ART TLV 08, Tel Aviv Museum of Art, Israel: 27 September–18 October
"Archeology of Mind," Malmö Konstmuseum, Sweden: 14 September–9 November (traveled to Kuntsi Museum of Modern Art, Vaasa, Finland: 21 November 2008–25 January 2009)
"Château de Tokyo / Palais de Fontainebleau," Château de Fontainebleau, Fontainebleau, France: 7 September–5 October
"An Unruly History of the Readymade," Fundación/Colección Jumex, Ecatepec, Mexico: 6 September 2008–7 March 2009
"Sammlung / Collection," Migros Museum für Gegenwartskunst, Zurich: 31 May–17 August
"Tutti Frutti," BASE/Progetti per l'arte, Florence, Italy: 23 May–11 July
"Who's Afraid of Jasper Johns?," Tony Shafrazi Gallery, New York: 9 May–12 July
"Blasted Allegories: Works from the Ringier Collection," Kunstmuseum Luzern, Lucerne, Switzerland: 16 May–3 August
"God Is Design," Galeria Fortes Vilaça, São Paulo, Brazil: 29 March–31 May
"Countdown," CCS Galleries, Bard College, Annandale-on-Hudson, New York: 16 March–30 March
"Schweiz über alles," Fundación/Colección Jumex, Ecatepec, Mexico: 26 January–19 March

2007

"Euro-Centric, Part 1: New European Art from the Rubell Family Collection," Rubell Family Collection, Miami: 5 December 2007–28 November 2008
"Unmonumental: The Object in the 21st Century," New Museum, New York: 1 December 2007--30 March 2008
"Jubilee Exhibition," House Eva Presenhuber, Vnà, Switzerland: 19 October 2007–26 January 2008
"The Third Mind: Carte Blanche to Ugo Rondinone," Palais de Tokyo, Paris: 27 September 2007–3 January 2008
"00s: The history of a decade that has not yet been named," Lyon Biennial of Contemporary Art, Lyon, France: 19 September 2007–6 January 2008
"Makers and Modelers: Works in Ceramic," Barbara Gladstone Gallery, New York: 8 September–20 October
"Fractured Figure: Works from the Dakis Joannou Collection," Deste Foundation for Contemporary Art, Athens: 5 September 2007–31 July 2008
"Franz West: Soufflé, eine Massenausstellung," Kunstraum Innsbruck, Innsbruck, Austria: 1 September–13 October
"Traum & Trauma: Werke aus der Sammlung Dakis Joannou, Athen," MUMOK and Kunsthalle Wien, Vienna: 29 June–4 October
"The Hamsterwheel," Tese della Nuovissima, Arsenale di Venezia, Venice Biennale: 7 June–2 September (traveled to Le Printemps de Septembre, Toulouse, France: 21 September–14 October; CASM Centre d'Art Santa Monica, Barcelona: 9 November 2007–5 January 2008; Malmö Konsthall, Sweden: 17 May–17 August)
"Domestic Irony: A Foray into Italy's Private Collections," Museion, Bolzano, Italy: 26 May–2 September
"Sequence 1: Painting and Sculpture in the François Pinault Collection," Palazzo Grassi, Venice: 5 May–11 November
"Disorder in the House," Vanhaerents Art Collection, Brussels: 16 March–30 June

2006

"The Studio," The Hugh Lane Gallery, Dublin: 1 December 2006–25 February 2007
"The François Pinault Collection, a Post-Pop Selection," Palazzo Grassi, Venice: 11 November 2006–11 March 2007
"Defamation of Character," P.S.1 Contemporary Art Center, Long Island City, New York: 29 October 2006–15 January 2007
"Contrabando," Galeria Luisa Strina, São Paulo, Brazil: 4 October–10 November
"The Vincent Award 2006," Stedelijk Museum, Amsterdam: 15 September 2006–14 January 2007
"Cinq milliards d'années" (Five Billion Years), Palais de Tokyo, Paris: 14 September 2006–14 January 2007
"Prints," Sadie Coles HQ, London: 2 August–2 September
"Strange I've Seen That Face Before," Städtisches Museum Abteiberg, Mönchengladbach, Germany: 7 May–17 September
"Where Are We Going? Selections from the François Pinault Collection," Palazzo Grassi, Venice: 29 April–1 October
"Collection," Migros Museum für Gegenwartskunst, Zurich: 24 April–13 August
"Infinite Painting–Contemporary Painting and Global Realism," Villa Manin Centre for Contemporary Art, Codroipo, Italy: 9 April–24 September
"Day for Night," Whitney Biennial, Whitney Museum of American Art, New York: 2 March–28 May
"Collection 1," Museum Boijmans Van Beuningen, Rotterdam: January 2006–December 2008

2005

"Schweizer Druckgraphik 1980-2005," Helmhaus Zürich: 18 November 2005-8 January 2006

"Looking at Words: The Formal Presence of Text in Modern and Contemporary Works on Paper," Andrea Rosen Gallery, New York: 2 November 2005-4 January 2006

"Goethe Abwärts–Deutsche Jungs Etc.: Works from the Falckenberg Collection," Helsinki Art Museum Meilahti, Finland: 15 October 2005-15 January 2006

"Ma Non Al Sud," Galleria Civica d'Arte Contemporanea di Siracusa, Syracuse, Italy: 24 September-30 November

"Closing Down," Bortolami Dayan, New York: 21 September-29 October

"Big Bang. Destruction and Creation in 20th Century Art," Centre Pompidou, Paris: 15 June 2005-3 April 2006

"Put It In Your Mouth / I'll see you on the dark side of the prune," Rivington Arms, New York: 10 June-24 July

"Bidibidobidiboo: Works from Collezione Sandretto Re Rebaudengo," Fondazione Sandretto Re Rebaudengo, Turin, Italy: 31 May-2 October

"Material Time / Work Time / Life Time," Reykjavik Art Museum, Iceland: 14 May-21 August

"Swiss Made (The Art of Falling Apart): Works from the Hauser & Wirth Collection," Cobra Museum of Modern Art, Amstelveen (Amsterdam), The Netherlands: 19 March-12 June

"Universal Experience: Art, Life, and the Tourist's Eye," Museum of Contemporary Art, Chicago: 12 February-5 June (traveled to Hayward Gallery, London: 6 October-11 December; Mart: Museo di arte moderna e contemporanea di Trento e Rovereto, Rovereto, Italy: 11 February 2006-14 May 2006)

2004

"Central Station: Collection Harald Falckenberg," La maison rouge–Fondation Antoine de Galbert, Paris: 22 October 2004-23 January 2005

"Skulptur: Prekärer Realismus zwischen Melancholie und Komik," Kunsthalle Wien, Vienna: 15 October 2004-22 February 2005

"Memorable Memory: Migros Museum Collection," Kunst Halle Sankt Gallen, St. Gallen, Switzerland: 10 July-29 August

"Group Show," Regen Projects, Los Angeles: 10 July-7 August

"Monument to Now," Deste Foundation for Contemporary Art, Athens: 22 June 2004-6 March 2005

"L'Air du Temps–Collection Printemps / Été 2004," Migros Museum für Gegenwartskunst, Zurich: 3 April-31 May

"I Hate You: The Falckenberg Collection Meets Louisiana," Louisiana Museum of Modern Art, Humlebæk, Denmark: 16 June-18 April

2003

"Silver Convention," Galerie Giti Nourbakhsch, Berlin: 6 December 2003-3 January 2004

"Unplugged," Galleria Civica di Arte Contemporanea, Trento, Italy: 23 November 2003-8 February 2004

"Inaugural Group Exhibition," GBE (Modern), New York: 20 September-4 October

"Dreams and Conflicts: The Dictatorship of the Viewer," Venice Biennale: 12 June-6 November

"Bewitched, Bothered and Bewildered: Spatial Emotion in Contemporary Art and Architecture," Migros Museum für Gegenwartskunst, Zurich: 22 March-25 May (traveled to Laznia Centre for Contemporary Art, Gdańsk, Poland: 12 July-14 September)

"Kunstpreis der Böttcherstrasse," Kunsthalle Bremen, Germany: 2 March-13 April

"Breathing the Water," Galerie Eva Presenhuber, Zurich: 8 February-14 March

"Durchzug / Draft: Zwanzig Jahre Stiftung Binz39," Kunsthalle Zürich: 25 January-9 March

2002

"poT: An Exhibition of Contemporary Pottery," The Independent, Liverpool, England: 14 September-24 November

"Exile on Main Street," New International Cultural Center (NICC), Antwerp: 22 June-15 September

"The Object Sculpture," Henry Moore Institute, Leeds, England: 1 June-1 September

"My head is on fire but my heart is full of love," Kunsthal Charlottenborg, Copenhagen: 8 May-9 June

"The House of Fiction," Sammlung Hauser und Wirth in der Lokremise St. Gallen, Switzerland: 5 May-13 October

"Lowland Lullaby: Ugo Rondinone with John Giorno and Urs Fischer," Swiss Institute, New York: 26 March-11 May

2001

"walcheturm 00/07: mind-sediments," Kunstraum Walcheturm, Zurich: 21 November-19 December

"Squatters," Museu Serralves, Porto, Portugal: 26 June-19 September

"Ziviler Ungehorsam–Zeitgenössische Kunst aus der Sammlung Falckenberg," Kestner-Gesellschaft, Hannover, Germany: 7 April-23 June

"Enduring Love," Klemens Gasser & Tanja Grunert, Inc., New York: 23 February-24 March

2000

"Let's Be Friends," Migros Museum für Gegenwartskunst, Zurich: 4 November 2000-18 March 2001

"Borderline Syndrome. Energies of Defence," Manifesta 3, European Biennial of Contemporary Art, Ljubljana, Slovenia: 23 June-24 September

"Sammlung 1. The Oldest Possible Memory," Sammlung Hauser und Wirth in der Lokremise St. Gallen, Switzerland: 14 May-15 October

1999

"Drawings," Sommer Contemporary Art, Tel Aviv: 29 December 1999-26 February 2000

"PEACE," Migros Museum für Gegenwartskunst, Zurich: 6 November 1999-9 January 2000

"Eidgenössische Preise für Freie Kunst," Kunsthalle Zürich: 6 November-30 December

"Pizzeria Sehnsucht" (with Marko Lehanka), Ateliers du FRAC des Pays de la Loire, Saint-Nazaire, France: 23 October-14 December

"Collection," Migros Museum für Gegenwartskunst, Zurich: 28 August-24 October

"999," Centro d'Arte Contemporanea Ticino, Bellinzona, Switzerland: 18 July-19 September

"Le repubbliche dell'arte," Palazzo delle Papesse, Sienna, Italy: 27 June-3 October

"Collection," Migros Museum für Gegenwartskunst, Zurich: 3 April-30 May

"Holding Court," Entwistle Gallery, London: 9 January 13 February

1998

"Morning Glory. De Ateliers 1993-1997," De Ateliers, Amsterdam: 4 September-20 September

"Ironisch / Ironic," Migros Museum für Gegenwartskunst, Zurich: 27 June-9 August

1997

"été 97," Centre d'édition contemporaine (formerly Centre Genevois de Gravure Contemporain), Geneva: 29 September-13 December

"Guarene arte 97," Fondazione Sandretto Re Rebaudengo, Turin, Italy: 28 September-6 November

"Dokumentation," Hotel, Zurich

1995

"Calypso" (with Antonietta Peeters and Avery Preesman), Stedelijk Museum Bureau Amsterdam: 2 December-31 December

"Preisträgerinnen und Preisträger des Eidgenössischen Wettbewerbs für freie Kunst," Kunsthaus Glarus, Switzerland: 24 September-19 November

"Karaoke 444&222 too," South London Gallery, London: 11 July-20 August

"Assistent" (with Maurus Gmür), Stiftung Binz39, Zurich: 26 March-30 April

AWARDS AND GRANTS

1999

Providentia-Preis, Young Art

Bundesamt für Kultur, Eidgenössisches Stipendium für freie Kunst, Zurich

1997

Kiefer-Hablitzel Stipendium

1995

Bundesamt für Kultur, Eidgenössisches Stipendium für freie Kunst, Zurich

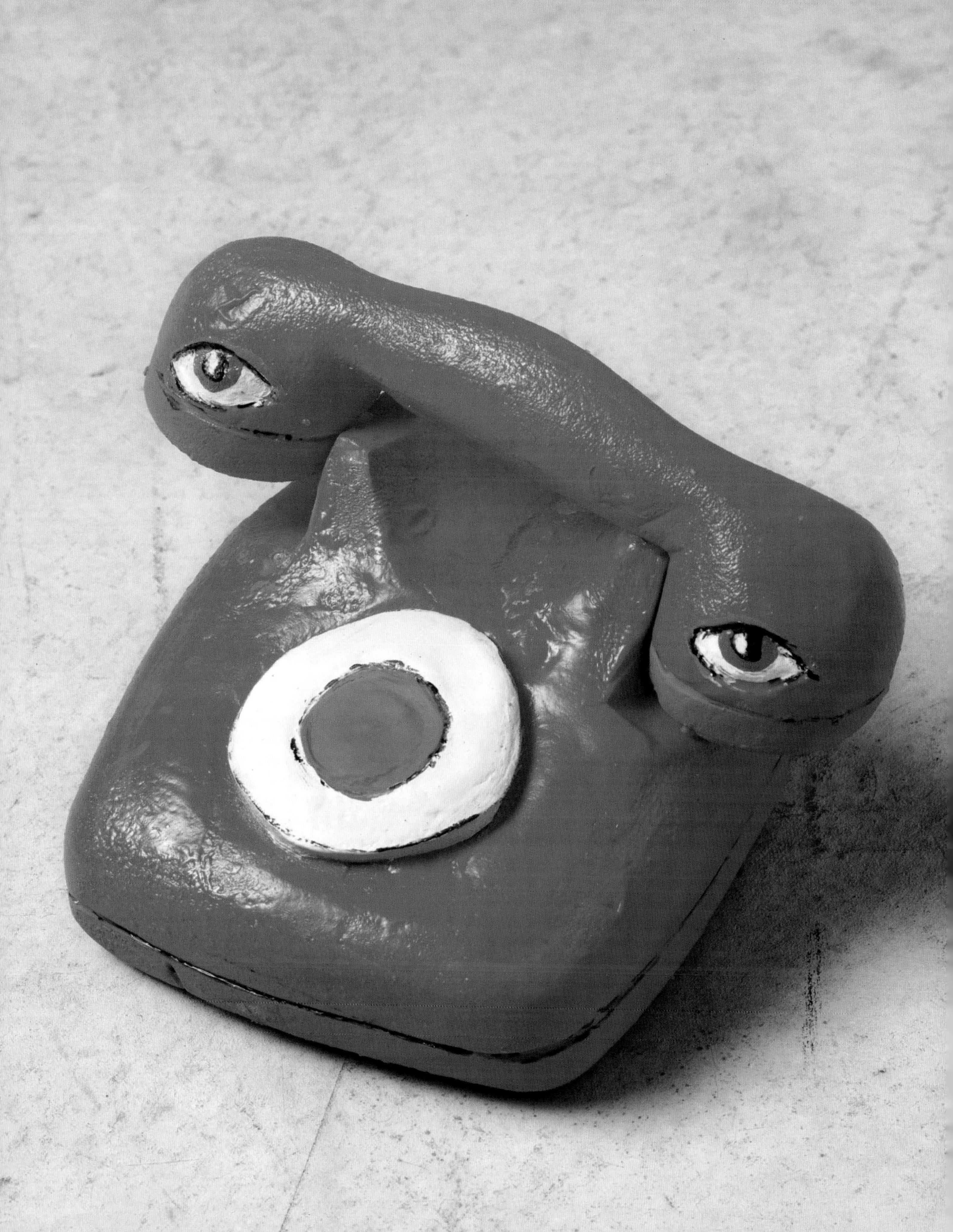

SELECTED BIBLIOGRAPHY

BOOKS

2012

Blancsubé, Michel. *Poule!* Ecatepec, Mexico: Fundación/Colección Jumex, 2012.

Chaillou, Timothée. *Seuls quelques fragments de nous toucheront quelques fragments d'autrui (Only parts of us will ever touch parts of others).* Paris/Salzburg: Galerie Thaddaeus Ropac, 2012.

Curiger, Bice. *Deftig Barock. Von Cattelan bis Zurbarán–Manifeste des prekär Vitalen*. Zurich: Kunsthaus Zürich, 2012.

Deitch, Jeffrey. *The Painting Factory: Abstraction after Warhol*. New York: Skira Rizzoli, 2012.

Driessen, Chris, and Heidi van Mierlo, eds. *Raw Stardust–Excursions in Contemporary Sculpture II*. Tilburg, The Netherlands: Fundament Foundation, 2012.

Fischer, Urs. *Beds & Problem Paintings*. Beverly Hills, California: Gagosian Gallery, 2012. Essay by Adam McEwen.

———. *Madame Fisscher*. New York: Kiito-San, 2012. Introduction by Caroline Bourgeois; essays by Patricia Falguiéres and Michele Robecchi.

———. *Oscar the Grouch*. Greenwich, Connecticut: The Brant Foundation; New York: Kiito-San, 2012.

———. *Skinny Sunrise*. New York: Kiito-San, 2012. Interview by Gerald Matt.

Fischer, Urs, and Georg Herold. *Necrophonia*. New York: Kiito-San, 2012. Text by Barnett Newman.

Grant, Simon. *In My View: Personal Reflections on Art by Today's Leading Artists*. London: Thames & Hudson, 2012: 84–5.

Grenier, Catherine. Salvador Dalí: The Making of an Artist. Paris: Flammarion, 2012: 251.

Sympathy for the Devil: Vanhaerents Art Collection. Tielt, Belgium: Lannoo: 2012.

2011

Birnbaum, Daniel, et al. *Defining Contemporary Art*. London: Phaidon Press, 2011: 400–1.

Bourgeois, Caroline. *The World Belongs to You*. Milan: Electa, 2011.

Curiger, Bice, and Giovanni Carmine. *ILLUMInazioni / ILLUMInations: Biennale Arte 2011*. Venice: La Biennale di Venezia, 2011.

Fischer, Urs. *dngszjkdufiy bgxfjkglijkhtr kydjkhgdghjkd*. Self-published artist's book in three parts, 2011.

Hapgood, Susan, and Cornelia Lauf, eds. *In Deed: Certificates of Authenticity in Art*. Amsterdam: Roma Publications, 2011.

L'invention de l'oeuvre: Rodin & les ambassadeurs. Paris: Musée Rodin / Actes Sud, 2011.

Taylor, Víctor Zamudio. *Now: obras de La Colección Jumex*. Barcelona: SYL, 2011.

Tunnicliffe, Wayne, ed. *John Kaldor Family Collection: Art Gallery of New South Wales*. Sydney: Art Gallery of New South Wales, 2011.

Urs Fischer: Untitled (Lamp / Bear). New York: Christie's, 2011.

2010

Alpha Omega: Works from the Dakis Joannou Collection. Athens: Deste Foundation, 2010.

Cavallucci, Favio. *Post Monument: XIV Biennale Internazionale di Scultura di Carrara*. Milan: Silvana Editoriale, 2010.

Curtis, Penelope, and Keith Wilson, eds. *Modern British Sculpture*. London: Royal Academy of Arts, 2010.

Fischer, Urs, and Darren Bader. *The Bearded Island / The Artist's Lament*. Self-published artist's book, 2010.

Gioni, Massimiliano, ed. *What Good Is the Moon?: The Exhibitions of the Trussardi Foundation*. Ostfildern, Germany: Hatje Cantz, 2010. Interview by Massimiliano Gioni.

Hack, Jefferson, ed. *AnOther Art Book*. Paris: Edition 7L, 2010.

Julliard, Julie Enckell. *Voici un dessin suisse: 1990–2010*. Zurich: JRP|Ringier Kunstverlag, 2010.

Koller, Gabriel, Edek Bartz, and Gerald Bast. *Secret Passion: Artists and their musical desires*. Vienna: Springer, 2010.

The New Décor. London: Hayward Publishing, 2010.

Remembering Henry's Show: Selected Works 1978–2008. Greenwich, Connecticut: The Brant Foundation, 2010.

Rosenberg, David. *Art of Flying: The New Horizons of Art*. New York: Assouline Publishing, 2010.

Skin Fruit: Selections from the Dakis Joannou Collection. New York: New Museum, 2010.

Vanhaerents, Walter, ed. *Disorder in the House: Vanhaerents Art Collection*. Tielt, Belgium: Lannoo, 2010.

2009

200 Artworks–25 Years: Artists' Editions for Parkett. Zurich: Parkett Publishers, 2009.

Fischer, Urs. *Shovel in a Hole*. New York: New Museum, 2009. Essays by Bice Curiger and Jessica Morgan; interview by Massimiliano Gioni.

Forbat, Sophie. *40 Years: Kaldor Public Art Projects*. Sydney: Kaldor Public Art Projects, 2009.

Gingeras, Alison M., and Francesco Bonami. *Mapping the Studio: Artists from the François Pinault Collection*. Venice: Palazzo Grassi, 2009.

Kurjakovic, Daniel. *Conflicting Tales: Subjectivity (Quadrilogy, Part 1)*. Zurich: JRP|Ringier Kunstverlag, 2009.

Munder, Heike, and Adam Budak. *Bewitched, Bothered, and Bewildered: Spatial Emotion in Contemporary Art and Architecture*. Zurich: Migros Museum für Gegenwartskunst, 2009.

Rattemeyer, Christian. *The Judith Rothschild Foundation Contemporary Drawings Collection Catalogue Raisonné*. New York: The Museum of Modern Art, 2009.

Roselione-Valadez, Juan, ed. *Beg Borrow and Steal*. Miami: Rubell Family Collection, 2009.

Smith, Josh, and Todd Amicon. *A Guest + A Host = A Ghost*. Athens: Deste Foundation for Contemporary Art, 2009.

Vitamin 3-D: new perspectives in sculpture and installation. London: Phaidon Press, 2009: 128–31.

2008

Bidner, Stefan, ed. *Franz West–Soufflé, eine Massenausstellung*. Innsbruck, Austria: Kunstraum, 2008.

Fischer, Urs. *Helmar Lerski*. Self-published artist's book, 2008.

———. *Who's Afraid of Jasper Johns?* Self-published artist's book, 2008.

Fischer, Urs, and Scipio Schneider, eds. *Fractured Figure: Works from the Dakis Joannou Collection*. Athens: Deste Foundation for Contemporary Art, 2008.

Four Friends. New York: Tony Shafrazi Gallery, 2008.

Heiser, Jörg. *All of a Sudden: Things that Matter in Contemporary Art*. New York: Sternberg Press, 2008.

Migros Museum für Gegenwartskunst: Sammlung / Collection 1978–2008. Zurich: JRP|Ringier Kunstverlag, 2008.

Rehberg, Vivian, and Hans Werner Holzwarth, ed. *Art Now, Volume 3*. Cologne: Taschen, 2008: 160–3.

Ruf, Beatrix, ed. *Blasted Allegories: Works from the Ringier Collection*. Zurich: JRP|Ringier Kunstverlag, 2008.

2007

Becher, Jörg. *Die 50 wichtigsten Künstler der Schweiz*. Basel: Echtzeit Verlag, 2007.

Berard, Emmanuel, and Emanuela Mazzonis, eds. *Sequence 1: Painting and Sculpture from the François Pinault Collection*. Venice: Palazzo Grassi, 2007.

Bundesamt für Kultur, ed. *Swiss Art Award 2007*. Bern, Switzerland: Bundesamt für Kultur BAK, 2007.

Fischer, Urs, and Cassandra MacLeod, eds. *Fractured Figure: Works from the Dakis Joannou Collection*. Athens: Deste Foundation for Contemporary Art, 2007.

Fischer, Urs, and Rudolf Stingel. *Urs Fischer / Rudolf Stingel*. Milan: Galleria Massimo de Carlo, 2007.

Flood, Richard, Massimiliano Gioni, and Laura Hoptman, eds. *Unmonumental: The Object in the 21st Century*. New York: New Museum, 2007.

Hoffmann, Jens, and Christina Kennedy, eds. *The Studio*. Dublin: Dublin City Gallery The Hugh Lane, 2007.

Ironia Domestica / Ironie der Objekte. Bolzano, Italy: Museion, 2007.

Kaiser, Firma Renate, ed. *The Hamsterwheel / Wheeeeel*. Toulouse, France: Le Printemps de septembre, 2007.

Kurjakovic, Daniel. *Album–on and around Urs Fischer, Yves Netzhammer, Ugo Rondinone, and Christine Streuli, participating at the 52nd Venice Biennale*. Zurich: JRP|Ringier Kunstverlag, 2007. Interview by Daniel Kurjakovic.

Matt, Gerald, Eedelbert Köb, and Angela Stief, eds. *Traum & Trauma: Werke aus der Sammlung Dakis Joannou, Athen*. Ostfildern, Germany: Hatje Cantz, 2007.

Moisdon, Stéphanie, and Hans Ulrich Obrist, eds. *Lyon Biennial 2007: The 00s: The History of a Decade that Has Not Yet Been Named*. Zurich: JRP|Ringier Kunstverlag, 2007.

Urs Fischer: Cockatoo Island, Sydney. Sydney: Kaldor Public Art Projects, 2007.

2006

Bonami, Francesco. *Infinite Painting*. Codroipo, Italy: Villa Manin Centro d'Arte Contemporanea, 2006.

Fischer, Urs. *Paris 1919*. Zurich: JRP|Ringier Kunstverlag, 2006. Essay by Rein Wolfs.

Gingeras, Alison M. *La collezione François Pinault. Una selezione Post-Pop*. Venice: Palazzo Grassi, 2006.

Gingeras, Alison M., and Jack Bankowsky. *Where Are We Going? Selections from the François Pinault Collection*. Venice: Palazzo Grassi, 2006.

Iles, Chrissie, and Philippe Vergne. *Whitney Biennial 2006: Day for Night*. New York: Whitney Museum of American Art, 2006.

Lindemann, Adam. *Collecting Contemporary*. Cologne: Taschen, 2006.

Schmuckli, Claudia. *Mary Poppins*. Houston: Blaffer Gallery, 2006. Essay by Claudia Schmuckli.

Schmidt, Jason. *The Artists*. Paris: Edition 7L, 2006.

The Vincent van Gogh biennial award for contemporary art in Europe. Amsterdam: Stedelijk Museum, 2006.

Webster, Toby. *Strange I've seen that face before: Objekt, Gestalt, Phantom*. Cologne: DuMont, 2006.

2005

Fischer, Urs. *Mr. Watson—Come Here—I Want to See You*. Hydra, Greece: Hydra Workshop, 2005.

Fischer, Urs, and Eugen Blume. *Urs Fischer: Werke aus der Friedrich Christian Flick Collection im Hamburger Bahnhof*. Berlin: Hamburger Bahnhof, 2005. Essays by Eugen Blume and Catherine Nichols.

Lacagnina, Salvatore. *Ma non al sud: Paolo Chiasera, Enzo Cucchi, Urs Fischer, Peter Fischli & David Weiss*. Milan: Silvana Editoriale, 2005.

Morgan, Jessica, and Björn Roth. *Material Time, Work Time, Life Time*. Revolver: Frankfurt, 2005.

Swiss made (the art of falling apart): Works from the Hauser & Wirth Collection. Zwolle, The Netherlands: Waanders, 2005.

Universal Experience: Art, Life, and the Tourist's Eye. Chicago: Museum of Contemporary Art, 2005.

Vitamin D: new perspectives in drawing. London: Phaidon Press, 2005: 106–7.

Zybok, Oliver, ed. *Goethe abwärts—Deutsche Jungs Etc.: The Falckenberg Collection*. Helsinki: Helsinki City Art Museum, 2005.

2004

Central Station: Collection Harald Falckenberg. Paris: La maison rouge, 2004.

Deitch, Jeffrey, ed. *Monument to Now: The Dakis Joannou Collection*. Athens: Deste Foundation for Contemporary Art, 2004.

Fischer, Urs. *Good Smell Make-up Tree*. Geneva: JRP Editions, 2004. Music by Garrick Jones.

———. *Livre numéro 2. Espace trois-cent-quinze, création contemporaine et prospective*. Paris: Éditions du Centre Pompidou, 2004. Essay by Alison M. Gingeras.

Fischer, Urs, and Mirjam Varadinis, eds. *Kir Royal*. Zurich: JRP|Ringier Kunstverlag, 2004. Essays by Jörg Heiser, Bruce Hainley, and Mirjam Varadinis.

Folie, Sabine. *Skulptur: Prekärer Realismus zwischen Melancholie und Komik*. Vienna: Kunsthalle Wien, 2004.

2003

Bonami, Francesco. *Dreams and Conflicts: The Dictatorship of the Viewer*. Venice: La Biennale di Venezia, 2003.

Ruf, Beatrix, ed. *Durchzug / Draft: 20 Jahre Stiftung Binz39*. Zurich: Kunsthalle Zürich and BINZ39, 2003.

Wahler, Marc-Olivier. *Extra*. New York: Swiss Institute / Christoph Merian Verlag, 2003.

2002

Bradley, Will, Henriette Bretton-Meyer, and Toby Webster, eds. *My Head Is on Fire But My Heart Is Full of Love*. Copenhagen: Kunsthal Charlottenborg, 2002.

Unterdörfer, Michaela, ed. *The House of Fiction. Sammlung Hauser und Wirth, Lokremise, St. Gallen*. Nuremberg, Germany: Verlag für moderne Kunst, 2002.

2001

Haenlein, Carl, and Carsten Ahrens. *Ziviler Ungehorsam: Sammlung Falckenberg*. Hanover, Germany: Kestner Gesellschaft, 2001.

Mari, Bartomeu, et al. *[squatters]*. Rotterdam: Witte de With Publishers, 2001.

2000

Fischer, Urs *The Membrane—and why I don't mind bad-mooded people*. Amsterdam: Stedelijk Museum Bureau Amsterdam, 2000.

———. *Time Waste. Radio-Cookie und kaum Zeit, kaum Rat*. Glarus, Switzerland: Kunsthaus, 2000. Essay by Beatrix Ruf; interview by Dominic van den Boogerd.

Manifesta 3. Borderline Syndrome. Energies of Defence. Ljubljana: Cankarjev dom, 2000.

1990s

Bonami, Francesco, and Hans Ulrich Obrist. *Sogni / Dreams*. Turin, Italy: Fondazione Sandretto Re Rebaudengo per l'Arte, 1999.

Eidgenössische Preise für Freie Kunst 1999. Zurich: Bundesamt für Kultur and Kunsthalle Zurich, 1999.

Guarene Arte 97. Turin, Italy: Fondazione Sandretto Re Rebaudengo per l'Arte, 1997.

Preisträgerinnen und Preisträger des Eidgenössischen Wettbewerbs für Freie Kunst. Glarus, Switzerland: Kunsthaus Glarus, 1995.

Wolfs, Rein, ed., *ironisch / ironic. maurizio cattelan, urs fischer, alicia framis, steve mcqueen, aernout mik / marjoleine boonstra*. Zurich: Migros Museum für Gegenwartskunst Zürich, 1998

ARTICLES

2013

Fischer, Urs. "Problem Painting." *Art in America*, January 2013: cover.

———. "The Problem with Paintings." *Garage*, no. 4, Spring/Summer 2013: 128–37.

Grootenboer, Hanneke. "Introduction: On the Substance of Wax." *Oxford Art Journal* 36, no. 1, March 2013: 1–12.

Kidel, Mark. "Urs Fischer." *Garage*, no. 4, Spring/Summer 2013: 138–9.

Rathe, Adam. "They've Been Framed." *DuJour*, Spring 2013: 176–81.

Wakefield, Neville. "Bear with Me." *Garage*, no. 4, Spring/Summer 2013: 140–5.

Wolff, Rachel. "Urs Fischer Conquers the Art World." *Details*, April 2013: 61–2.

2012

Amend, Christoph. "Ganz große Kunst." *ZEITmagazin*, no. 6, 2 February 2012: cover, 12–21.

Anthon, Kaye. "Hier sitzt der Künstler als Kerze am Tisch." *Blick*, 16 April 2012: 6–7.

Antonaci, Matteo. "Crateri in Galleria e Giocattoli Oversize—Ecco il Mondo di Urs Fischer." *Arskey*, May–July 2012.

Azimi, Roxana, and Philippe Régnier. "Urs Fischer chahute le Palazzo Grassi." *Le Quotidien de L'Art*, no. 130, 16 April 2012: 1–2.

Belpêche, Stéphanie. "Urs Fischer, l'illusionniste." *Le Journal du Dimanche*, 14 April 2012.

Benhamou-Huet, Judith. "L'ours Fischer." *Le Point*, no. 2065, 12 April 2012: 122–4.

Bodin, Claudia. "Urs Fischer backt ungern kleine Brötchen." *Art Das Kunstmagazin*, May 2012: 20–9.

Bogart, Aaron. "Critics' Picks: Urs Fischer." *Artforum.com*, 23 April 2012.

Bonnet, Frédéric. "Venise, Urs Fischer, sculpteur classique." *Le Journal Des Arts*, 25 May 2012.

Casavecchia, Barbara. "Exhibition Reviews: Urs Fischer: Madame Fisscher." *Art Review*, 1 July 2012: 145.

Castelli, Stefano. "I paradossi di Urs Fischer." *Arte*, April 2012.

Coignard, Jérôme. "Urs Fischer et 'Madame' au Palazzo Grassi." *Connaissance des Arts*, May 2012: 44.

Cremascoli, Olivia. "Urs Fischer a Palazzo Grassi." *Interni*, May 2012: 72.

Czöppan, Gabi. "Feuer und Flamme für Frauen." *Focus*, 28 April 2012.

Descombes, Mireille. "Interview: Urs Fischer." *DADI*, 31 May 2012.

Doran, Anne. "Urs Fischer and Cassandra MacLeod at Gavin Brown's enterprise." *Art in America*, January 2012: 92–3.

Douglas, Sarah. "Bed Piece: Visiting Urs Fischer's New York Studio." *The Observer*, 5 March 2012: B5.

Dumont, Etienne. "Urs Fischer investit le Palazzo Grassi." *Tribune de Geneve*, 17 April 2012.

Duplat, Guy. "Le grand Urs qui vient nous troubler." *La Libre Belgique*, 17 April 2012: 48–9.

Duponchelle, Valérie. "Urs Fischer: un alien débarque dans le triangle d'or." *Le Figaroscope*, 18 April 2012.

———. "Urs Fischer, un cerebral en trios dimensions." *Le Figaro*, 20 April 2012.

Dusini, Mathias. "Halle des Ruhms." *Der Falter*, 29 February 2012.

———. "Selbstporträts zweier Melancholiker." *Der Falter*, 22 February 2012: 29.

Earnest, Jarrett. "Palazzo Fischer." *Stiletto*, no. 34, Spring 2012: 72–5.

Feßler, Ann Kathrin. "Entflammt und irgendwann ausgebrannt." *Der Standard*, 17 February 2012: 25.

Fischer, Urs. "Problem Paintings." *The Journal*, no. 32: 27–37.

Fischer, Urs, and Darren Bader. "Darren Bader Rencontre Urs Fischer." *L'Officiel ART*, 9 March 2012: 274–9.

Frimbois, Jean-Pierre. "Urs Fischer au Palazzo Grassi." *art actuel*, 28 June 2012.

Gamerman, Ellen. "Snapshot." *Wall Street Journal*, 30 March 2012: D5.

Griffin, Jonathan. "Urs Fischer, the reluctant interviewee." *The Art Newspaper*, April 2012: 56.

Herzog, Samuel. "Kleiner Seufzer am Lagunenrand." *Neue Zürcher Zeitung*, 19 April 2012.

Hess, Ewa. "Pa, pa, pa, Millionär. Wissen Sie, wie hoch meine laufenden Kosten sind?" *SonntagsZeitung*, 4 March 2012: 21–3.

Huber, Michael. "Wenn einer Dinge liebt, die schiefgehen." *Kurier*, 17 February 2012: 30.

Jaeglé, Yves. "Des oeuvres étonnantes et colorées." *Le Parisien*, 21 April 2012.

———. "Pinault, pape de l'art à Venise." *Aujourd'hui en France*, 21 April 2012.

Jothady, Manisha. "Blick unter die Oberfläche." *Wiener Zeitung*, 17 February 2012: 15.

Kennon, Brian. "Ideal Syllabus." *Frieze*, no. 147, May 2012: 32–3.

Knapp, Michaela. "Nichts bleibt, wie es ist." *Format*, no. 6, 10 February 2012: 78–9.

Knight, Christopher. "Faces to Watch 2013." *Los Angeles Times*, 30 December 2012.

Kontova, Helena. "Urs Fischer." *Flash Art*, June 2012: 86.

Krenstetter, Florian. "Wie die Zeit vergeht." *Kronen Zeitung*, 19 January 2012: 27.

Legrand, Maurice. "300 Plus Influents," *Bilan*, no. 12, 20 June–3 July 2012: 62.

Lemelle, Sarah. "Venise Célèbre L'Art Vivant." *TGV Magazine*, 3 May 2012.

Lequeux, Emmanuelle. "Urs Fischer est un garçon mal élevé." *Le Monde*, 3 May 2012: 47.

———. "Urs Fischer: Un Art Dénudé, Délié et Enflammé." *Beaux Arts Magazine*, 24 May 2012.
———. "Venise, Urs Fischer." *artpress*, 25 June 2012.
Léon-Dufour, Sixtine. "Grand Urs." *Madame Figaro*, 9 April 2012: 54–7.
Lewine, Edward. "Pop Life." *New York Times*, 22 April 2012: MM24.
Locoge, Benjamin. "Urs Fischer: Création… et récréation." *Paris Match*, no. 3283, 12–18 April 2012: 32–3.
Mack, Gerhard. "Der Mann fürs grosse Format." *Neue Zürcher Zeitung am Sonntag*, 8 April 2012: 65–6.
Mammì, Alessandra. "Very Casual Art." *L'Espresso*, 3 May 2012: 104–5.
Martínez, Ángeles. "Urs Fischer nos enloquece." *bg magazine* (Cuenca, Ecuador), no. 68, 1 August-15 September 2012: 186–91.
McGarry, Kevin. "Out There: Urs Fischer's Really Big Problems." *New York Times Style Magazine* online, 1 March 2012.
McKie, Andrew. "Sculpting to His Own Beat." *Wall Street Journal Europe*, 13 April 2012: W4–5.
Michals, Susan. "Stars, Beds, 'Problem Paintings' at Urs Fischer's Gagosian L.A. Debut." *Gallerist NY* online, 24 February 2012.
Morata, Raphaël. "Au Palazzo Grassi l'Urs Fait Son Miel." *Point de Vue*, 25 April 2012.
Müller, Hans-Joachim. "Urs Fischer: Der Artist." *Weltkunst*, no. 1, January 2012: 26.
Nicoletti, Luca Pietro. "Fischer il Fuoco che Consuma l'Arte è la Bellezza." *Contemporart*, July–September 2012: 16–7.
Oppolzer, Sabine. "Skelett mit Sehnsüchten." *OE1. ORF* online, 16 February 2012.
Perazzoli, Susanna. "Il Mio Filo Rosso È L'Ironia." *Io Donna*, 14 April 2012: 103–6.
Powers, Bill. "Urs Fischer Hits the Beach." *New York Times Style Magazine* online, 24 December 2012.
Reinberger, Astrid. "Rückschau: Ganz große Kunst mit Urs Fischer in Wien." *Das Erste* online, 19 February 2012.
Remenyi, Julia. "Urs Fischer in der Kunsthalle Wien." *kunstmarkt.com* online, 16 February 2012.
Reneau, Olivier. "Êtes-vous plutôt Jeff Koons ou bien Urs Fischer?" *L'Optimum*, May 2012.
Rosenberger, Werner. "Kunsthalle: Wenn Sachen schiefgehen…" *Kurier* online, 16 February 2012.
———. "Wenn einer Dinge liebt, die schiefgehen." *Kurier*, 17 February 2012: 30.
Sabas, Carole. "La caverne d'Urs." *Vogue Paris*, no. 926, April 2012: 240–5.
Sanchez, Anne-Cécile. "Qui est *Madame Fischer*?" *Marie Claire Maison*, April 2012: 34.
Sansom, Anna. "Madame Fisscher." *Modern Weekly*, 1 June 2012: C86–7.
Schedlmayer, Nina. "Schmelztherapie." *PROFIL*, no. 7, 13 February 2012: 94–5.
Schuker, Lauren A. E. "The Oscar-Weekend Art Show." *Wall Street Journal*, 24 February 2012: D5.
Sennewald, J. Emil. "Urs ist punk." *Kunst Und Auktionen*, 27 April 2012: 32–4.
———. "Der Punk unter den Poppern?" *Monopol*, 1 June 2012.
Solway, Diane. "Studio Visit: Urs Fischer." *W Magazine*, April 2012: 56, 134.
Spence, Rachel. "Rebel in need of a cause." *Financial Times*, 16 June 2012.
Spiegler, Almuth. "Kunsthalle Wien: Die Kunst ist ein Star! Holt sie hier raus–oder auch nicht." *Die Presse*, 17 February 2012: 29.
Strobl, Ernst P. "Eitelkeiten vergehen." *Salzburger Nachrichten*, 17 February 2012.
Szczesniak, Paulina. "Manchmal mach ich ja auch ernste Arbeiten." *Tages Anzeiger*, 23 February 2012: 28.
Titz, Walter. "Die Vielfalt und der Wille zur Gestaltung." *Kleine Zeitung Graz*, 27 February 2012: 10–1.
Trembley, Nicolas. "The Fischer King." *Artforum.com*, 23 April 2012.
Vetrocq, Marcia E. "Urs Fischer." *Modern Painters*, September 2012: 94.
———. "Urs Fischer Explores the Theme of the Double in His Solo Survey at Venice's Palazzo Grassi." *Artinfo.com*, 16 April 2012.
Villareal, Jose. "Major Exhibition of New Work by Urs Fischer Opens at Gagosian Gallery in Beverly Hills." *ArtDaily* online, 27 March 2012.
Youssi, Yasmine. "Madame Fisscher." *Télérama*, 9 May 2012: 75.

2011

Ackermann, Tim. "Bei den New Yorker Auktionen lässt das Traditionshaus die Rivalen weit hinter sich." *Welt Online*, 24 May 2011.
Adam, Georgina. "Size matters. Why is the work getting bigger?" *The Art Newspaper*, no. 226, July–August 2011.
Binswanger, Michèle. "Schweizer Kunst kommt au seiner bäurischen Tradition." *Tages Anzeiger*, 16 June 2011.
Bonami, Francesco, "E=uf2." *TAR Mag*, no. 6, Fall 2011: cover, 1–8, 118–9.
Casadio, Mariuccia. "The Studio Revives." *Vogue Italia*, no. 734, October 2011: 396–9.
Cochard, Catherine. "Mythologies contemporaines." *Le Temps (Arts)*, 9 November 2011: cover, 17–9, 24–5.
Crow, Kelly. "Hey There! Big Bear to Visit Park Avenue." *Wall Street Journal* online, 2 April 2011.
Douglas, Sarah. "Christie's Bullish on Urs Fischer's Bear." *The New York Observer* online, 11 May 2011.
———. "Why You Should Go See Urs Fischer's New Show at Gavin Brown." *Gallerist NY* online, 21 October 2011.
Droitcour, Brian. "Costume Drama." *Artforum.com*, 1 November 2011.
Edwards, Meghan. "Night Light." *Interior Design*, vol. 82, no. 7, May 2011: 283.
Etman, Maud. "Tweejaarlijkse internationale kunstexpositie Lustwarande voor de vierde keer in Tilburg." *Breda*, 19 July 2011: 37.
Gamerman, Ellen. "The Changing Face of Portraits." *Wall Street Journal*, 5 August 2011: D1–2.
Gnyp, Marta. "Larger Than Life: A conversation with Swiss contemporary artist Urs Fischer." *Zoo Magazine*, no. 31: 82–91.
Goutziers, Joost. "Laatste weekeinde 'Lustwarande 11': tot nu toe iets meer dan 90.000 bezoekers." *Brabants Dagblad*, 7 October 2011: 31.
Gygax, Raphael. "Sculpture Now: Eva Presenhuber, Zurich." *Flash Art*, October 2011: 116.
Heinrich, Will. "Art vs. Real Estate at Marianne Boesky." *The New York Observer*, 15 March 2011.
Hess, Ewa. "Riesiger Teddybär eines Schweizer Künstlers verblüfft New York." *SonntagsZeitung*, 17 April 2011.
Johnson, Ken. "Sculptural Surprises Grace the Streets." *New York Times*, 19 August 2011: C21.
Jones, Jonathan. "Times flies at the Venice Biennale." *On Art Blog, The Guardian*, 7 June 2011.
Jori, Marcello. "Qui l'idea prende forma: A New York, negli studi degli artisti." *Corriere della Sera (La Lettura)*, 18 December 2011: 36–7.
Kleinman, Adam. "ILLUMInazioni / ILLUMInations." *Art Agenda*, June 2011.
Kutscher, Barbara. "Gefragt ist Wiedererkennungswert." *Handelsblatt*, 13 May 2012.
Leij, Machteld. "Flirten met het minimalisme." *Kunstbeeld*, 31 August 2011: 46–51.
McKie, Andrew. "Setting the Art World Alight." *Wall Street Journal*, 3 June 2011.
Miller, Michael H. "The Answer Is 'Why?' Urs Fischer Overwhelms at New Gavin Brown Show." *Gallerist NY* online, 24 October 2011.
Morgan, Jessica. "Urs Fischer." *L'Uomo Vogue*, no. 421, May–June 2011.
Morris, Roderick Conway. "Venice Biennale Thrives Despite Tough Economic Times." *International Herald Tribune*, 7 June 2011.
Nichols, Michelle. "Giant 35,000 Pound Teddy Bear by Artist Urs Fischer to Brighten New York City." *Artdaily.org*, 5 April 2011.
Pascucci, Marisa J. "Urs Fischer." *The Art Economist*, vol. 1, no. 9, 2011: 31.
Petsch, Barbara. "Kunsthalle Wien: Schweizer Bär gefällt New York." *DiePresse.com*, 23 April 2012.
Prince, Mark. "Urs Fischer: Sadie Coles HQ, London." *Flash Art*, vol. 44, no. 276, January–February 2011: 98.
Rosenmeyer, Aoife. "Sculpture Now: Galerie Eva Presenhuber, Zurich." *Art Agenda*, July 2011.
Schwabsky, Barry. "Many Facets, No Overview: On the Venice Biennale." *The Nation*, 15–22 August 2011.
Searle, Adrian. "Modern British Sculpture: Empire of the Oddballs." *The Guardian*, 19 January 2011.
Seliger, Mark. "Urs Fischer." *Vogue Italia*, May 2011.
Smith, Roberta. "Urs Fischer and Cassandra MacLeod." *New York Times*, 4 November 2011: C30.
Ter Borg, Lucette. "Rauwe beelden midden op het bospad." *Handelsblad*, 17 August 2012: 19–20.
Themen, Ähnliche. "Urs Fischers gigantischer Teddy wird in New York enthullt." *Aargauer Zeitung* online, 7 April 2011.
Thibaut, Matthias. "Aus dem Automaten." *Der Tagesspiegel*, 29 April 2011.
Thon, Ute, Tim Sommer, and Ralf Schlüter. "Keine Benegung." *Art Das Kunstmagazin*, August 2011: 18–29.
Van den Hoven, Gerrit. "Blauwe rook en olifant in OudeWarande." *Brabants Dagblad*, 27 June 2011: 10.
———. "Tweejaarlijkse internationale kunstexpositie Lustwarande voor de vierde keer in Tilburg." *Brabants Dagblad*, 25 June 2011: 33.
Vogel, Carol. "Old Patina Encircles Fresh Art in Venice." *New York Times*, 6 June 2011: C1.
Wullschlager, Jackie. "Breadth in Venice." *Financial Times*, 3 June 2011.
Zeitz, Lisa. "Noch immer ist Warhol nicht zu schlagen." *Frankfurter Allgemeine Zeitung* online, 24 May 2011.

2010

Amy, Michaël. "Urs Fischer: New Museum." *Sculpture*, vol. 29, no. 10, December 2010: 70–1.
Carey-Kent, Paul. "Urs Fischer: Sadie Coles." *ArtUS*, no. 30, 2010: 6–9.
Fischer, Urs. "You Can Call Inside Me." *The Journal*, no. 28: supplement.
Heartney, Eleanor. "Urs Fischer: Marguerite de Ponty." *art press*, no. 363, January 2010: 72–3.
Herold, Georg. "Urs Fischer." *The Journal*, no. 28: 84–97.
Hirsch, Faye. "Presto Chango! Urs Fischer's New Museum." *Art in America*, January 2010: 104–9.
Kastner, Jeffrey. "New Foundations." *Artforum*, vol. 48, no. 10, Summer 2010.

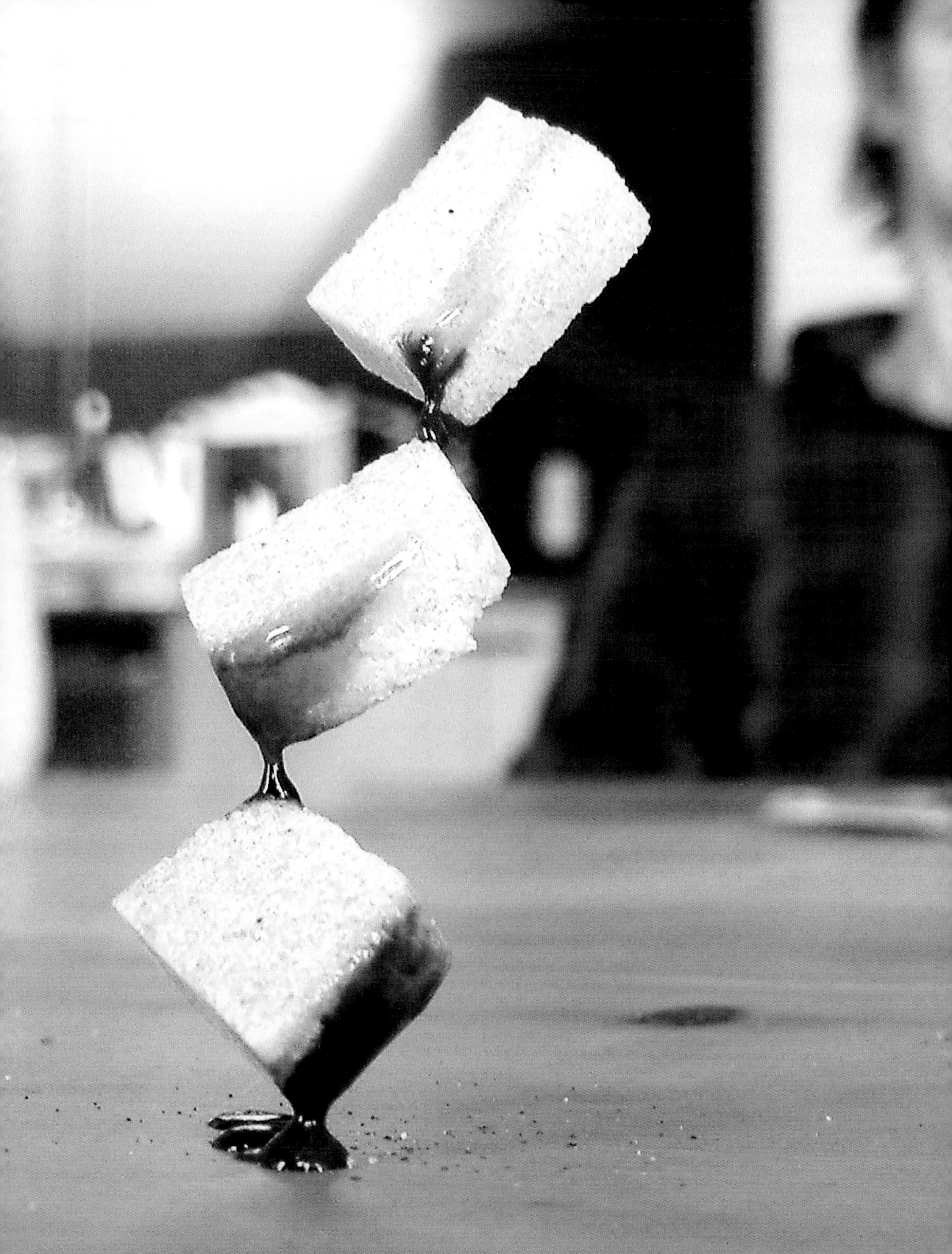

Kaufman, Jason Edward. "In View: Urs Fischer's Magnificent Vanitas for Peter Brant." *Artinfo.com*, 15 June 2010.
Kazakina, Katya. "Newsprint mogul Peter Brant has 'meltdown' in Urs Fischer show." *Bloomberg News*, 29 June 2010.
Kunitz, Daniel. "Urs Fischer: Brant Foundation Art Study Center." *Modern Painters* 22, no. 6, September 2010: 73.
Markus, Liz. "Art and Death in Connecticut: Urs Fischer at the Brant Foundation Art Study Center." *Huffington Post*, 17 July 2010.
Naves, Mario. "Urs Fischer: Marguerite de Ponty." *The New Criterion* 28, no. 5, January 2010: 50–1.
Peers, Alexandra. "The Conspiracy Theory of Art." *The New York Observer*, 19 May 2010.
Sherwin, Skye. "Exhibitions: Urs Fischer." *The Guardian*, 2–8 October 2010: 38.

2009

Beasley, Mark. "Looking back: Group Shows." *Frieze*, January–February 2009: 102.
Brown, Gavin. "Urs Fischer." *Interview*, December–January 2009: 186–91.
Garcia, Carnelia. "Urs Fischer: New Museum." *Modern Painters* 21, no. 7, October 2009: 18.
Jackson, Candace. "Moving Ceilings for Sculptures." *Wall Street Journal*, 16 October 2009: W14.
Krienke, Mary. "Urs Fischer at Galerie Eva Presenhuber." *ARTnews*, February 2009: 115–6.
Kuo, Michelle. "Taste Tests." *Artforum*, November 2009: 171–9.
Nicolin, Paola. "Urs Fischer: New Museum, New York, 2009." *Kaleidoscope*, no. 4, November–December 2009: 150–2.
Saltz, Jerry. "A Whole New Museum: The Urs Fischer-izing of a four-story institution." *New York Magazine*, 9 November 2009: 74.
Schjeldahl, Peter. "Putting on Urs." *The New Yorker*, 14 December 2009.
Schwendener, Martha. "Urs Fischer: Bowery Bad Boy." *Village Voice*, 10 November 2009.
Searle, Adrian. "Speaking in Tongues: The Art of Urs Fischer." *The Guardian*, 9 November 2009.
Smith, Roberta. "Exploration of Space." *New York Times*, 30 October 2009.
Tomkins, Calvin. "The Imperfectionist." *The New Yorker*, 19 October 2009: 34–9.
"Urs Fischer at Galerie Eva Presenhuber." *Mousse*, no. 16, December–January 2009: 97.
Wang, Michael. "The Fischer King." *Artforum.com*, 31 October 2009.

2008

Amacher, Lukas. "Lukas Vernissagenbericht." *Prisma*, no. 319, December 2008: 42.
Azimi, Roxana. "Das Kunstmarkt-Briefing." *Monopol*, no. 10, October 2008.
Baker, R. C. "Digital Vandalism at Shafrazi Gallery." *Village Voice*, 3 June 2008.
Becher, Jörg. "Schweizer Meister." *Bilanz*, no. 11, June 2008.
Bedford, Christopher. "Who's Afraid of Jasper Johns?," *Frieze*, 3 July 2008.
Boucher, Brian. "Urs Fischer at Gavin Brown's enterprise." *Art in America*, March 2008: 166–7.
Cros, Caroline. "Qu'est-ce que la sculpture aujourd'hui?" *Beaux-Arts editions* (Paris), 2008: 33, 94–5.
Donoghue, Katy. "Profile: Mark Fletcher." *Whitewall*, no. 9, Spring 2008: 40.
Fabian, Daniela. "Interview: Michael Ringier." *Schweizer Illustrierte Style*, no. 01–02, January–February 2008: 52–9.
Falconer, Morgan. "Who's Afraid of Jasper Johns?," *ArtReview*, no. 25, September 2008: 139.
Fyfe, Joe. "Things the Mind Already Knows." *Art in America*, September 2008: 148–51.
Grabner, Michelle. "Makers and Modelers: Works in Ceramic." *X-Tra*, vol. 10, no. 3. Spring 2008: 54.
Halle, Howard. "Who's Afraid of Jasper Johns?," *Time Out New York*, no. 660, 22–28 May 2008.
Hess, Ewa. "Die Riesen kommen." *SonntagsZeitung*, 26 October 2008: 53.
Higgs, Matthew. "'Who's Afraid of Jasper Johns?' at Tony Shafrazi Gallery." *Artforum*, vol. 47, no. 4, December 2008: 266.
Hudson, Suzanne. "Who's Afraid of Jasper Johns?," *Artforum*, vol. 47, no. 2, September 2008: 459.
Lewis, Ben. "Who's Afraid of Jasper Johns?," *pluk magazine*, Autumn 2008: 34–5.
Marchand, Antoine. "Down in a Hole..." *Revue Zerodeux* (Nantes), no. 45, Spring 2008: 50.
Marinos, Christopher. "Dakis Joannou." *Flash Art*, October 2008: 100–1.
Marti, Silas. "Mostra compara arte com religiao." *Folha de S. Paulo*, 29 March 2008: E11.
McNally, Whitney. "Talent Show: Urs Fischer." *W Magazine*, November 2006: 200.
Molina, Camila. "God is Design abre novo espaço na Barra Funda." *Caderno 2*, 29 March 2008: D9.
Nickas, Bob. "Urs Fischer at Gavin Brown's enterprise." *Artforum*, vol. 47, no. 4, December 2008: 292.
Saltz, Jerry. "Two Coats of Painting." *New York Magazine*, 15 June 2008.
———. "The Year in Art." *New York Magazine*, 7 December 2008.
Scott, Andrea K. "Critic's Notebook: Extreme Makeover." *The New Yorker*, 9 June 2008.
"Seeing Warhol." *Interview*, June–July 2008: 124
Sholis, Brian. "Who's Afraid of Jasper Johns?," *Artforum.com*, June 2008.
Slaven, Jessica. "Sculpture in the Expended Field." *Paper Monument*, no. 2.
Smith, Roberta. "When Artworks Collide." *New York Times*, 16 May 2008.
Sonnenborn, Katie. "Makers and Modellers." *Frieze*, March 2008: 182.
Stern, Steven. "Unmonumental: The New Museum." *Frieze*, 4 January 2008.
"Unmonumental: The Object in the 21st Century." *New Museum Paper*, vol. 3, Winter 2008: 5.
Völzke, Daniel. "Neues vom Trickser." *Monopol*, July–August 2008: 62–71.
Wakefield, Neville. "Urs Fischer: An Artist Impossible to Pin Down." *AnOther Magazine*, no. 14, Spring–Summer 2008: 404–13.
Wolin, Joseph R. "Who's Afraid of Jasper Johns?," *Modern Painters*, vol. 20, no. 8, September 2008: 108.

2007

Benhamou-Huet, Judith. "Dans l'anxiété du benefice: Making Money in Miami." *art press*, no. 331, February 2007: 14.
Borchhardt-Birbaumer, Brigitte. "Die dunkle Seite der Mondnacht." *Wiener Zeitung*, 29 June 2007: 15.
Camhi, Leslie. "The Corrections." *Village Voice*, December 19–25, 2007.
Cattelan, Maurizio. "Interview with Urs Fischer." *Mousse*, no. 11, November 2007: 28–31.
Cerruti, Silvano, "Frischer Fischer." *20 Minuten Week*, no. 36, 6 September 2007: 7.
Chaplin, Julia. "A Night Out with Alison Gingeras: Follow that Motoscafo." *New York Times*, 10 June 2007.
Cotter, Holland. "Urs Fischer at Gavin Brown's Enterprise." *New York Times*, 23 November 2007.
Coulson, Amanda. "Urs Fischer and Rudolf Stingel at Massimo de Carlo." *Modern Painters*, April 2007: 101.
Diez, Renato. "Le avanguardie di Monsieur Pinault." *Arte*, no. 406, June 2007: 148–54.
Fischer, Urs. "Production Notes." *Artforum*, October 2007: 351.
Fitzgerald, Michael. "Impressario of the New." *Time*, 22 March 2007.
Garbarino, Laura. "Urs Fischer and Rudolf Stingel at Galleria Massimo de Carlo." *Flash Art*, March–April 2007: 81.
Gioni, Massimiliano. "Where the wild things are." *Tate Etc.*, no. 11, Autumn 2007: 34–8.
Hauger, Caroline Micaela. "Nur die Künstler fehlten—Schweizer Party-Marathon in Venedig." *Schweizer Illustrierte*, no. 24, 11 June 2007: 40.
———. "Starker Auftritt." *Schweizer Illustrierte*, no. 21, 21 May 2007: 98–9.
Herzog, Samuel. "O sole mio—viel Kunst aus Frankreich für Venedig." *Neue Zürcher Zeitung*, no. 106, 9 May 2007: 45.
Higson, Rosalie. "Visions on a haunted isle." *The Australian*, 17 April 2007.
Jana, Reena. "The Dancing Camel." *Art on Paper*, no. 5, May–June 2007: 38–9.
Jones, Kristin. "Urs Fischer at Gavin Brown's Enterprise." *Frieze*, 26 October 2007.
Karrer, Eva. "Bäume statt Barock." *SonntagsZeitung*, 3 June 2007: 53.
Kazanjian, Dodie. "Body and Mind." *Vogue*, September 2007: 634–8
Kitnick, Alex. "Urs Fischer: you." *Time Out New York*, 15–21 November 2007: 85.
Knoll, Valérie. "Urs Fischer at Eva Presenhuber." *Artforum*, vol. 46, no. 4, December 2007: 368.
Koch, Carole. "Hardware." *annabelle*, no. 11, 6 June 2007: 80–5.
"Kunst hoch vier." *Schweizer Illustrierte Style*, no. 6, June 2007: 20.
Lequeux, Emmanuelle. "Biennale de Venise: Les meilleurs pavillons." *Beaux Arts*, no. 276, June 2007: 57.
Mack, Gerhard. "Urs Fischer und Ugo Rondinone in San Staë." *Neue Zürcher Zeitung am Sonntag*, 10 June 2007: 68.
Mathonnet, Philipe. "A Venise, l'art s'humanise." *Le Temps*, 9 June 2007: 19.
Matt, Gerald. "Liebe, Tod und Trauma." *Art Quarterly*, July 2007: 27–32.
Morgan, Clare. "Surprise twist on the convict island." *Sydney Morning Herald*, 17 April 2007.
Piron, François. "Printemps de Septembre." *Flash Art*, no. 40, November–December 2007: 68.
Probst, Ursula Maria. "Traum & Trauma. Eine Überreizung der Psyche." *Kunstforum International*, October–November 2007.
Renner, Sascha. "augenschmausen." *Züritipp*, 4 January 2007: 27.
Ringel, Stephanie. "Anarchie in der Lagune." *Sonntagsblick*, 10 June 2007: 44–5.
Roeschmann, Dietrich. "Schweizer Meister." *annabelle*, no. 11, 6 June 2007: 50.
Rondinone, Ugo. "The Third Mind." *Palais Magazine* (Paris), no. 4, Fall 2007.
Saltz, Jerry. "Can You Dig It? At Gavin Brown, Urs Fischer Takes a Jackhammer to Chelsea Itself." *New York Magazine*, 3 December 2007: 90–2.
Scharrer, Eva. "Biennale Venedig—Wechselvoller Parcours mit ernstem Unterton." *Kunst-Bulletin*, no. 8, July–August 2007: 42–48.

Searle, Adrian. "Venice takes flight." *The Guardian*, 12 June 2007.
Schoch, Ursuala Badrutt. "Viele Bilder und ein paar Bäume." *Der Bund*, 9 June 2007: 37.
Smith, Roberta. "It's Just Clay, But How About a Little Respect?" *New York Times*, 9 July 2007: E29, E38.
Stolz, Noah. "San Stae. Urs Fischer e Ugo Rondinone." *Kunst-Bulletin*, no. 8, July–August 2007: 49–50.
Terrien, David. "Tales from the City: Venice." *ArtReview*, no. 13, July–August 2007: 46.
Thon, Ute. "Kaufrausch der Milliardäre bei der Art Basel Miami Beach." *Art Das Kunstmagazin*, December 2007.
Thornton, Sarah. "Supermarket Sweep." *Artforum.com*, 14 June 2007.
"Traum & Trauma. Werke aus der Sammlung Dakis Joannou, Athen." *Vernissage*, no. 267, September 2007: 16–9.
Tröster, Christian. "Die Liebe des Tycoons." *Monopol*, 7 July 2007.
"Urs Fischer." *Bilanz*, no. 16, 2007: 110.
Vetrocq, Marcia E., "The Venice Biennale: All'Americana." *Art in America*, September 2007.
Vogel, Carol. "In for a Penny, In for the Pounce." *New York Times*, 14 June 2007.
Ward, Vicky. "François Pinault's Ultimate Luxury." *Vanity Fair*, no. 568, December 2007: 172–7.
Williams, Greg. "Urs Fischer." *L'Uomo Vogue*, May–June 2007.
Wüst, Karl. "Farben, Schatten und tote Bäume." *Der Zürcher Oberländer*, 11 June 2007.

2006

Ayar, Afshan. "Niets is wat het lijkt." *R'Uit Magazine*, May 2006: 26–7.
Cerizza, Luca. "City Report." *Frieze*, October 2006: 253.
Clausen, Eva. "Der unaufhaltsame Aufstieg des Monsieur Pinault." *Neue Zürcher Zeitung*, no. 99, 29–30 April 2006: 49.
Davenport, Bill. "Sparse Images in Mary Poppins Speak Loudly." *Houston Chronicle*, 3 June 2006.
Eeley, Peter. "2006 Whitney Biennial." *Frieze*, 7 June 2006.
Erbslöh, Roswitha. "Palais Pinault." *Artnet*, 6 March 2006.
Fischer, Urs. "A Cacophony for a Formidable Iconoclast: Alison Gingeras, John Baldessari, Gisela Capitain, and others on Martin Kippenberger." *Tate Etc.*, no. 6, Spring 2006.
———. "Crème de Yvette." *AnOther Magazine*, no. 10, Spring 2006: 33–45.
Fong, Marjorie Tjon A. "Stoere Alpenhut van gezaagde broken." *AD zaterdag*, 15 April 2006: 15.
Gingeras, Alison. "La Collection François Pinault: Le Défi du Choix." *art press*, no. 323, May 2006: 50–5.
Gioni, Massimilano. "Le monde instable de Urs Fischer." *art press*, no. 324, June 2006: 27–33.
Kerwin, Jessica. "On With the Show." *W Magazine*, May 2006: 128, 130.
Klaasmeyer, Kelly. "Space and Quiet." *Houston Press*, 22 June 2006.
Leij, Machteld. "Fischers beelden speels en wreed." *NRC*, 2 May 2006: 9.
Neil, Jonathan T. D. "The Fischer King" *ArtReview*, December 2006: 70–4.
Plagens, Peter. "Madison Avenue Ennui." *Art in America*, June–July 2006: 76–9.
Rauterberg, Hanno. "Ein Freibeuter der Künste." *Die Zeit*, no. 18, 27 April 2006.
Schümer, Dirk. "Nur Tiepolo weint Tränen aus Gips." *Frankfurter Allgemeine Zeitung*, no. 99, 28 April 2006: 35.
Smith, Roberta. "More Than You Can See: Storm of Art Engulfs Miami." *New York Times*, 9 December 2006.
"Urs Fischer." *AD*, 30 March 2006: 26
"Urs Fischer." *Tate Etc.*, no. 6, Spring 2006: 38.
Van der Beek, Wim. "Urs Fischer." *Kunstbeeld.Nl*, no. 5, 2006: 14.
Van der Klaauw, Richard. "De Vakantie." *Metro*, 2 May 2006: 19.
Vetrocq, Marcia E. "A Museum of His Own." *Art in America*, October 2006: 96–101.
White, Michelle. "Urs Fischer: Mary Poppins." *Glasstire*, 2 June 2006.
Yablonsky, Linda. "Art Miami Fair, Art Market Showed its Blood and Bones." *Bloomberg News*, 12 December 2006.

2005

Arfiero, Michela. "Urs Fischer at Nicola Trussardi Foundation." *Sculpture*, vol. 24, no. 8, October 2005: 78–9.
Bonami, Francesco. "L'arte a sorpresa fermata." *Vanity Fair*, 28 April 2005: 150.
Bonazzoli, Francesca. "Le briciole pazze del visionario Fischer." *Corriere della Sera*, 3 May 2005: 59.
Bonnet, Frédéric. "Prêts à prêter. Acquisitions et rapport d'activités 2000–2004 Frac Provence-Alpes-Côte d'Azur." *Fonds régional d'art contemporain Provence-Alpes-Côte d'Azur*. 2005: 78–9.
Bono, Donatella. "Le sculture 'logorate' di Urs Fischer." *Il Giornale*, 6 May 2005: 50.
Capelli, Pia. "L'arte? Bisogno guardarla, non ragionarla." *Libero*, 4 May 2005: 36.
———. "O'Chair, per Trussardi arrivano le Jet Set Lady." *Libero*, 15 April 2005: 21.
Casadio, Mariuccia. "In / Out." *Casavogue*, April 2005: 139–43.
Casavecchia, Barbara. "Da Cattelan a Urs Fischer Trussardi colpisce ancora." *La Repubblica*, 3 May 2005: 10.
Cobolli, Nicoletta. "Giocatotoli per adulti. Nella realtà senza consuetudini." *Arte*, May 2005: 96.
Comer, Stuart. "Double Deutsche." *Artforum.com*, 22 October 2005.
Didero, Maria Cristina. "La materia delle Favole." *Ottagono*, May 2005: 30.
Fulco, Elisa. "Spotlight: Urs Fischer." *Flash Art Italia*, June–July 2005: 118.
Ghizzardi, Federica. "Tutti a spiare il Ricciolo proibito." *La Prealpina*, 7 May 2005: 9.
———. "Una cassa tutta da mangiare." *La Prealpina*, 5 May 2005: 16
Herbert, Martin. "Round and round again." *Time Out London*, 25 May–1 June 2005.
Hoffmans, Christiane. "Glamouröser Newcomer." *Welt am Sonntag*, 23 October 2005.
Kranz, Walter. "Mimicry-Works." *Artnet*, n.d.
Mammi, Alessandrea. "Horror con humour." *L'Espresso*, 29 April 2005: 141.
Montrasio, Giuliana. "Usato Sicuro." *Max*, May 2005: 262.
Margutti, Flavia Fossa. "Vi faro ridere." *Glamour* (Italy), May 2005: cover, 188.
Masoero, Ada. "Una signora del jetset nell'Istituto dei Ciechi." *Il Giornale dell'Arte*, May 2005: 24.
Olcese, Roberta. "Il rilancio di Miart." *Secolo XIX*, 5 May 2005: 16.
Romeo, Filippo. "Urs Fischer at Fondazione Trussardi." *Artforum*, vol. 44, no. 1, September 2005: 313.
Rossi, Mariella. "Urs Fischer." *Lapiz* (Spain), May 2005: 89.
Smith, Roberta. "The Listings: Urs Fischer." *New York Times*, 25 February 2005: E25.
Spanier, Samson. "At London's Frieze fair, art in full bloom." *International Herald Tribune*, 22-23 October 2005: 8.
Van de Velde, Paola. "Wij zijm verslaafd aan kunst." *Telegraaf*, 12 April 2005: 15.
Vincent, Steven. "Urs Fischer at Gavin Brown's enterprise." *Art in America*, October 2005: 170.
Walde, Gabriela. "Flirt mit der Flamme, Ausstellungsrezension." *Berliner.*

2004

Ardenne, Paul. "Urs Fischer at Centre Pompidou." *art press*, no. 301, May 2004: 82–3.
Basting, Barbara. "Vitalitätstest glorreich bestanden." *Tages-Anzeiger*, 10 July 2004: 41.
Binswanger, Daniel. "Langeweile beim Nasenbohren." *Weltwoche*, no. 12, March 2004: 9.
Burnett, Craig. "Urs Fischer: Elton John?" *The Guide*, 4 December 2004: 37.
Carmine, Giovanni. "Urs Fischer: Personal Weather." *Flash Art*, January–February 2004: 84–7.
Herbert, Martin. "Urs Fischer: Arts Review." *Time Out London*, 5–12 January 2004.
Herzog, Samuel. "Le roi est mort—vive le Kir." *Neue Zürcher Zeitung*, no. 158, 10–11 July 2004: 43.
Hess, Ewa. "Fischers Sicht der Dinge: Der Zürcher Künstler Urs Fischer verblüfft die Kunstwelt—und steht vor dem internationalen Durchbruch." *SonntagsZeitung*, 4 January 2004: 35, 37.
Hubbard, Sue. "Things are not what they seem." *The Independent*, 10 January 2005: 12.
Jones, Jonathan. "Urs Fischer: Arts Review." *The Guardian*, 7 January 2004.
Kraft, Martin. "Kir Royal: Ausstellung von Urs Fischer im Kunsthaus: Fast ein Klassiker." *Züritipp*, no. 28, 8–14 July 2004: 15.
Manchester, Clare. "Urs Fischer and Koo Jeong-a." *Flash Art* 37, May–June 2004: 145–6.
Marzahn, Alexander. "König Artus im Wunderland: zwischen Stuhl und Bänken." *Basler Zeitung*. 29 July 2004: 27.
Morton, Tom. "Roll With It." *Frieze*, no. 86, October 2004: 138–41.
Richardson, Brenda. "Down the Rabbit Hole." *Parkett*, no. 72, 2004: 58–62.
Ruf, Beatrix. "wanted to turn the music on but it was already playing." *Parkett*, no. 72, 2004: 76–80.
Spinelli, Claudia. "Leicht, nicht seicht." *Weltwoche*, no. 29, July 2004: 83.
Ulmer, Brigitte. "Der Kunst-Rebell" *Bolero Men*, Spring 2004: 50–2.
von Arx, Ursula. "Fischer das Urtier." *Das Magazin Tages-Anzeiger*, no. 10, 12 March 2004: 8–14.
Weissman, Benjamin. "Garden of Earthly Hates." *Parkett*, no. 72, 2004: 82–7.
Zweifel, Stefan. "Im Universaalschaum." *Frankfurter Allgemeine Zeitung*, 23 July 2004: 36.

2003

Clem, Chivas. "Portrait of a Single Rain Drop." *Time Out New York*, 8–15 May 2003.
Coomer, Martin. "Urs Fischer: Sadie Coles HQ." *Time Out London*, 19–26 February 2003: 47.
Gingeras, Alison M. "Openings: Urs Fischer." *Artforum*, vol. 41, no. 9, May 2003: 158–9.
Lafuente, Pablo. "The Failure Man." *ArtReview*, December 2002–January 2003: 64–5.
Ruf, Beatrix. "Wie wär's in Wachs, Du Schöne?" *Katalog*. Kunstpreis der Böttcherstrasse, Bremen, March–April 2003: 21.

Subotnick, Ali. "Unplugged, a Casa per le vacanze." *Work: Art in Progress*, October–December 2004: 10.
Zamet, Kate. "London, England: Urs Fischer." *Art Papers*, vol. 27, no. 3, May–June 2003: 52.

2002
Bell, Kirsty. "Firing Line." *Artscene UK*, June 2002: 3.
———. "Urs Fischer: Contemporary Fine Arts." *Frieze*, no. 67, 5 May 2002.
Blom, Ina. "My Head Is on Fire but My Heart Is Full of Love." *Frieze*, 9 September 2002.
Daniels, Corinna. "Neues von Urs Fischer bei Contemporary Fine Arts–Der Schweizer hat keine Angst vor Kitsch." *Die Welt*, 8 February 2002: 34.
Dezeuze, Anna. "The Object Sculpture." *Art Monthly*, no. 258, July–August 2002.
Hickling, Alfred. "The Object Sculpture." *The Guardian*, June 2002.
"Lowland Lullaby." *The New Yorker*, 22–29 April 2002: 36.
Lubbock, Tom. "Colourvision." *The Independent*, June 2002.
Morton, Tom. "The Object Sculpture at Henry Moore Institute." *Frieze*, 9 September 2002.
Schlaegel, Andreas. "Urs Fischer at Contemporary Fine Arts, Berlin." *Flash Art*, March–April 2002: 107.
Schwabsky, Barry. "The Object Sculpture" *Artforum*, Summer 2002.
Siepen, Nicolas. "Nichts für Bing Crosby." *Berliner Seiten, Frankfurter Allgemeine Zeitung*, no. 29, 4 February 2002: 6.
"Ugo Rondinone, John Giorno & Urs Fischer." *Village Voice*, 5 March 2002: 79.
"Ugo Rondinone with John Giorno and Urs Fischer." *Village Voice*, 2 April 2002: 89.

2001
Spinelli, Claudia. "Berührend skurril. Hauser & Wirth & Presenhuber zeigen Urs Fischer." *Neue Zürcher Zeitung*, no. 207, 7 September 2001: 46.

2000
Allfree, Claire. "Miriam Bäckström and Urs Fischer: Art from Europe." *Metro*, 20 January 2000.
Baumer, Dorothea. "Köln ist ein guter, ein idealer Platz. Die 34. Art Cologne." *Süddeutsche Zeitung*, 6 November 2000.
Becker, Jochen. "Manifesta 3." *Kunstforum International*, no. 152, October–December 2000: 438–42.
Coomer, Martin. "Urs Fischer: ICA." *Time Out London*, 16–23 February 2000: 54.
Goldschmeding, Eugénie. "Speelsheid is het sleutelwoord." *Bldz*, May 2000.
Jones, Jonathan. "Exhibitions: Urs Fischer." *The Guardian*, 24 January 2000.
Maurer, Simon. "Der Künstler als 'Büetzer.'" *Tages-Anzeiger*, no. 63, 25 April 2000: 63.
Meier, Philipp. "Der leise Seufzer der Kunst. Die Art Cologne: Deutschlands führende Modernmesse." *Neue Zürcher Zeitung*, 11–12 November 2000.
Meister, Helga. "Zu viele kindliche Seelen." *Düsseldorfer Nachrichten*, 6 November 2000.
Nebelung, Sigrid. "Kronleuchter aus Plastiktüten. 21 Künstler profitieren in diesem Jahr vom Förderprogramm der Art Cologne. Der Trend geht zur Installation." *Handelsblatt*, 3 November 2000.
Posca, Claudia. "Die Kunst, Kunst zu sehen. Eindrücke von der 34. Art Cologne." *Neue Rhein Zeitung*, 6 November 2000.
Sandmann, Monika. "Installationen dominieren. Förderprogramme." *Weltkunst Moderne*, no. 10.
Schroeder, Annette. "Prima leben im Videobunker. Förderprogramm auf der Art Cologne präsentiert 21 Künstler." *Kölnische Rundschau*, 8 November 2000.
"Urs Fischer im Kunsthaus." *Kunst-Bulletin*, June 2000: 49.
von Arb, Eugen. "Der Schöne und das Biest, Urs Fischer." *Die Südostschweiz*, 7 April 2000: 5.
van den Berg, Hubert. "Urs Fischer." *De Witte Raaf* (Belgium), no. 85, May–June 2000.
Wessling, Janneke. "Staketsels zonder inhoud." *NRC*, 1 May 2000.

1999
Chelotti, Chiara. "Le Repubbliche dell' Arte." *Flash Art*, vol. 32, no. 217, Summer 1999: 91.
Coomer, Martin. "Holding Court: Entwistle (Upmarket)." *Time Out London*, 3 February 1999: 49.
"Gespenstige Welt der Dinge. Urs Fischer bei Hauser & Wirth." *Neue Zürcher Zeitung*, 27 January 1999: 50.
Helwing, Anna "Fundamentgefummel. 'Stormy weather' von Urs Fischer." *Kunst-Bulletin*, no. 3, March 1999: 18–24.
Nicolaus, Heinrich. "Papesse: una finestra sulla Svizzera." *La Voce del Campo*, no. 31, 26 August 1999: 6.

1998
Altorfer, Sabine. "Ironie, Verballhornung oder was?" *Limmattaler Tagblatt*, 22 July 1998.
Feller, Elisabeth. "Ironie oder blosse Eselei?" *Südkurier*, 21 July 1998.
Gerster, Ulrich. "Mindestens amüsant: Ironisches im Museum für Gegenwartskunst, Zürich." *Neue Zürcher Zeitung*, 28 July 1998.
"Hinterfragte Wirklichkeit." *Berner Rundschau*, 27 June 1998.
"Ironie ist, wenn man trotzdem lacht." *Voralberger Nachrichten*, 11 July 1998.
Maurer, Simon. "Das apportierwillige Hundeskelett." *Tages-Anzeiger,* 30 June 1998.

1997
"Alles mögliche nebeneinander." *Stehplatz*, no. 54, September 1997.
"Une Fiac aux couleurs de la Suisse." *Le Journal des Arts*, no. 44, 26 September 1997: 13–4.

1996
"Besetzt: Urs Fischer in der Galerie Walcheturm." *Neue Zürcher Zeitung*, no. 77, 1 April 1996.
Maurer, Simon. "Sexy Kuhfladen." *Tages-Anzeiger Züritipp*, 1996: 50.
Spinelli, Claudia. "Urs Fischer in der Galerie Walcheturm." *Kunst-Bulletin*, no. 4, April 1996: 40.

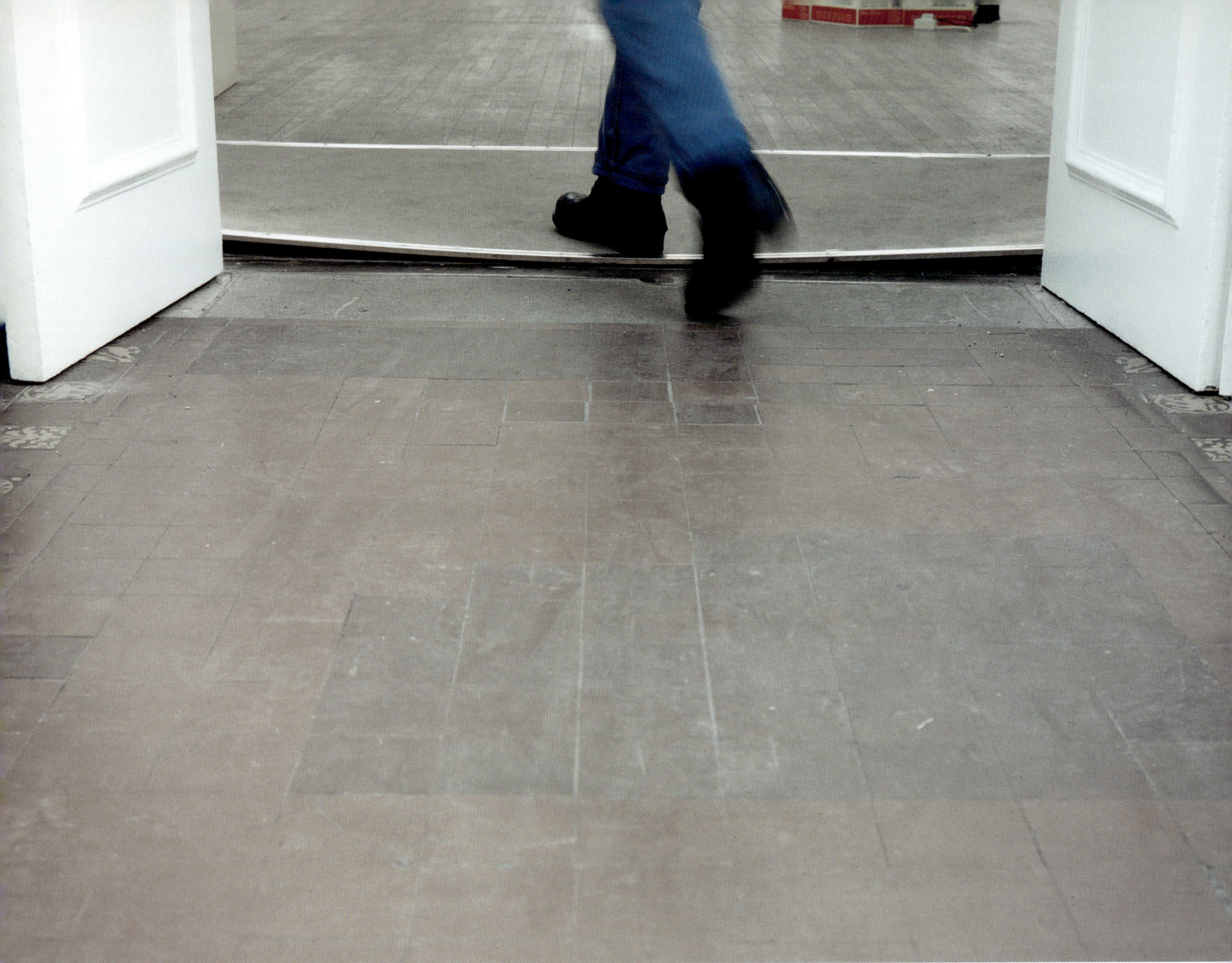

Untitled (Step Piece), 1995
Intervention activated by visitor's entrance into gallery; when stepped on,
a slightly elevated wooden board slaps the floor, producing a loud noise
MDF, aluminum trim, bungee cord, hooks
Dimensions variable
Installation view, "Karaoke 444&222 too," South London Gallery, London, 1995

Following pages:
Keep It Going Is a Private Thing, 2001
Mechanical robot half-dog wags its tail
Synthetic fur, polystyrene, electric motor, control unit,
acrylic paint, polyurethane foam, wood glue
27 ½ x 11 ¾ x 31 ⅛ inches (70 x 30 x 79 cm)
Installation view, "Madame Fisscher," Palazzo Grassi, Venice, 2012

Pages 630–631:
"Mr. Watson—come here—I want to see you.," 2005
Light swings back and forth, accelerating
and decelerating in a 12-minute cycle
Electric motor, control unit, electric cable, light bulb, wire
Dimensions variable

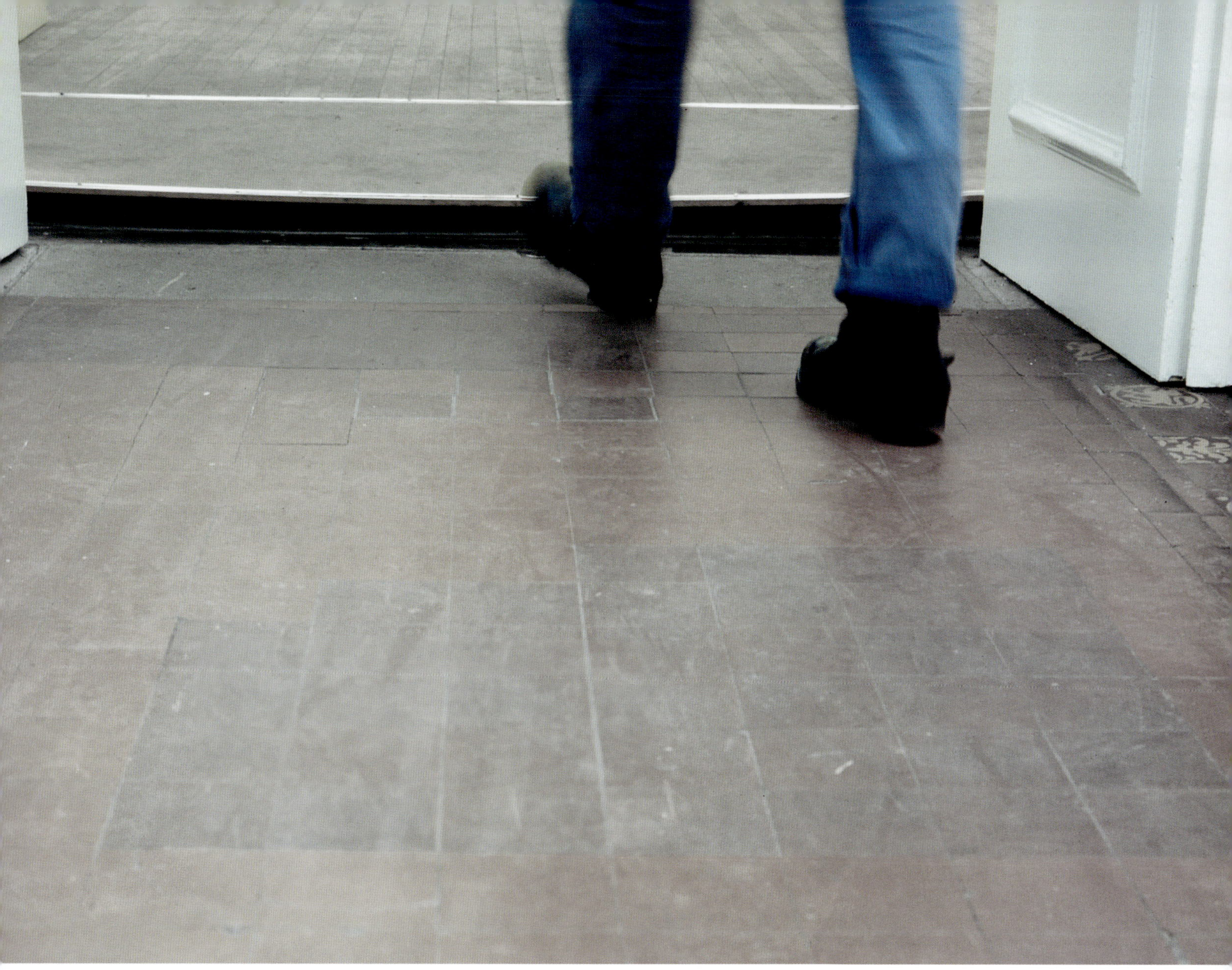

Pages 632 and 635:

Nach Jugendstiel kam Roccoko, 2006

Empty cigarette pack moves erratically along floor,
occasionally flying up into the air
Electric motor, wire, carbon rod, elastic band,
nylon filament, empty cigarette pack, control unit
Installation radius: 157 ½ inches (400 cm); height variable

Front endpapers:
Excerpt from the book *Helmar Lerski*, 2008

Back endpapers:
Installation view, "Madame Fisscher," Palazzo Grassi, Venice, 2012
Necrophonia, 2011; *Cioran Handrail*, 2006; *Mackintosh Staccato*, 2006; *Spinoza Rhapsody*, 2006; *A Thing Called Gearbox*, 2004

Cover:

Skinny Afternoon, 2003

Cast aluminum, mirror, lacquer paint,
acrylic paint, polyurethane foam, screws
78 ¾ x 63 x 47 ¼ inches (200 x 160 x 120 cm)

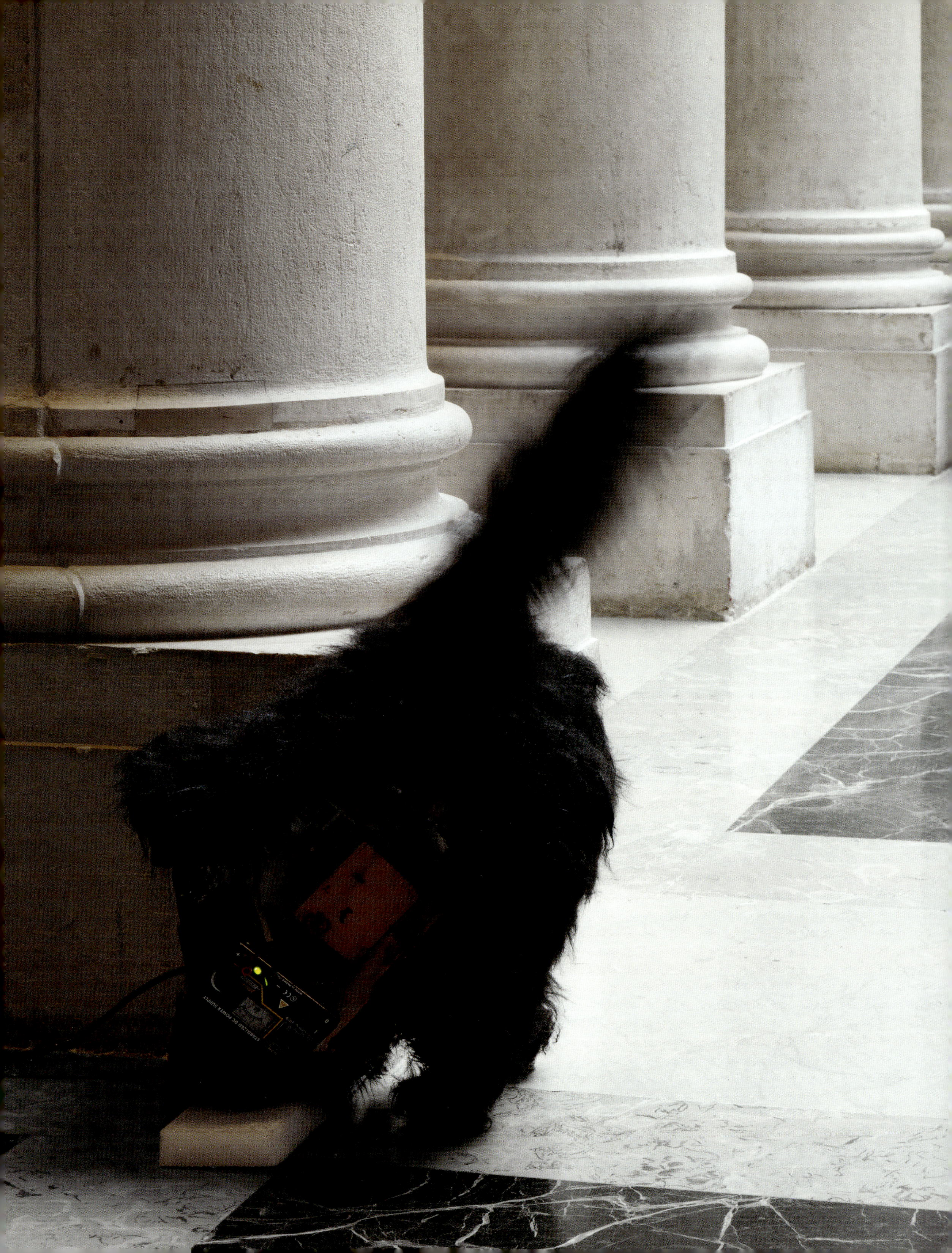
STABILIZED DC POWER SUPPLY

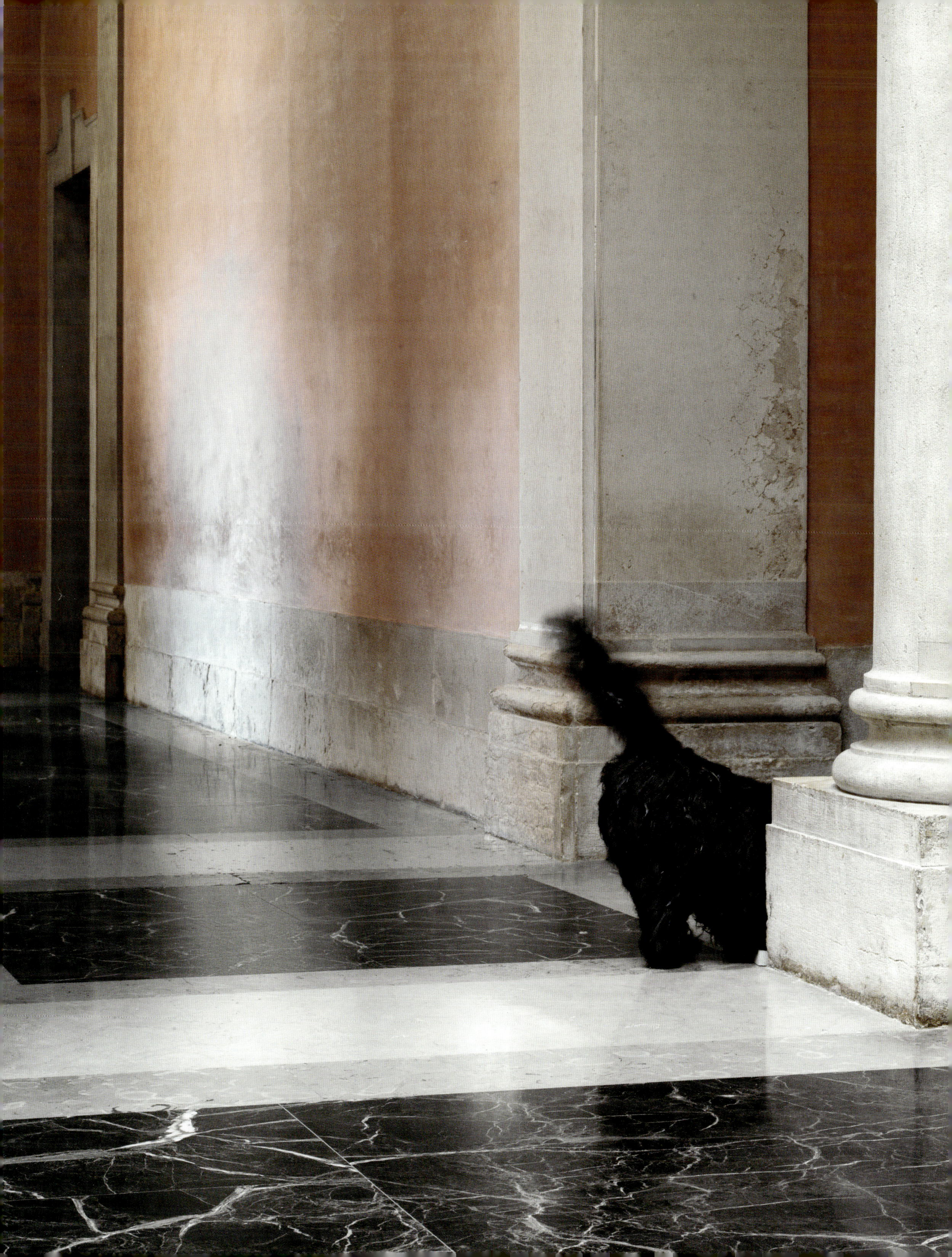

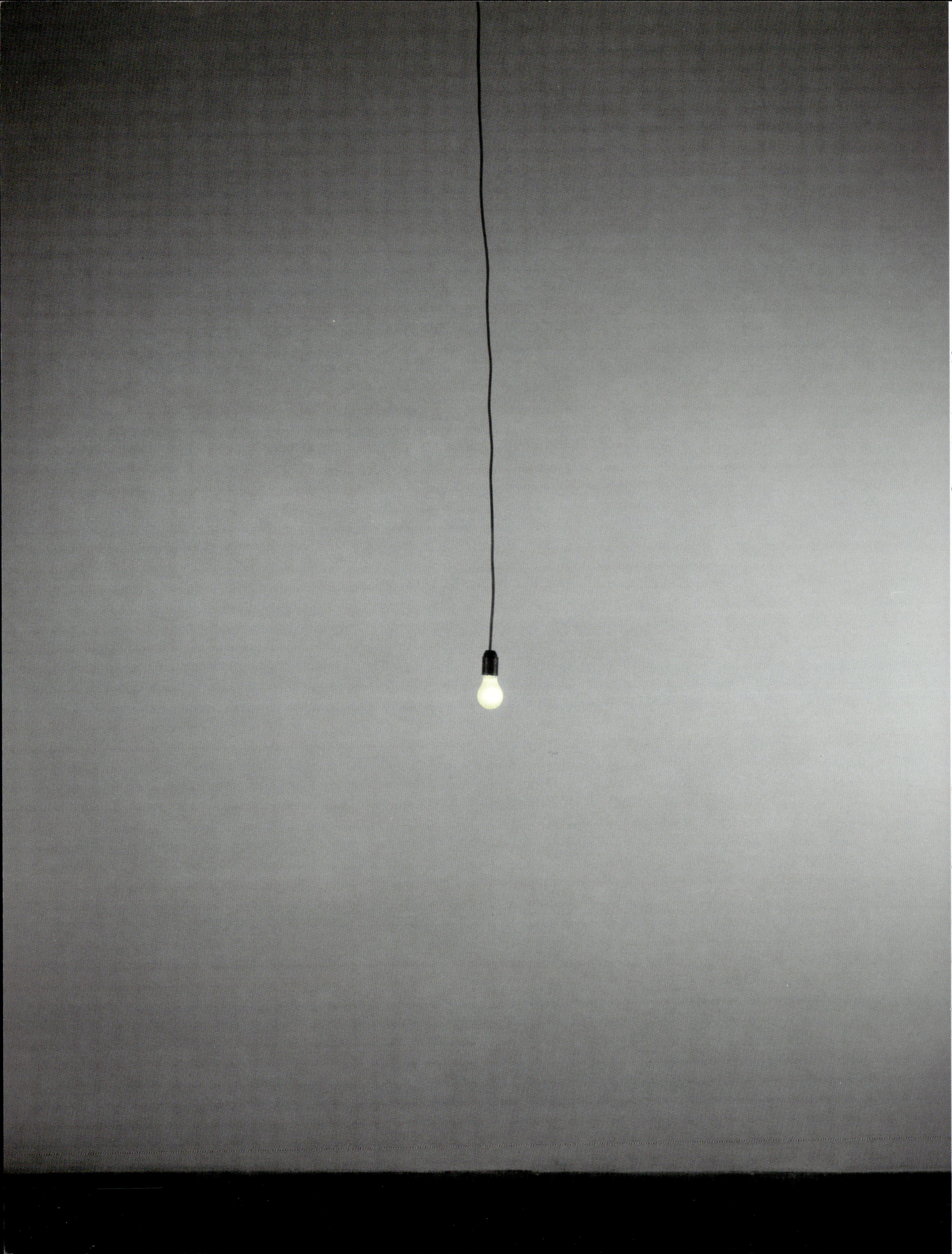

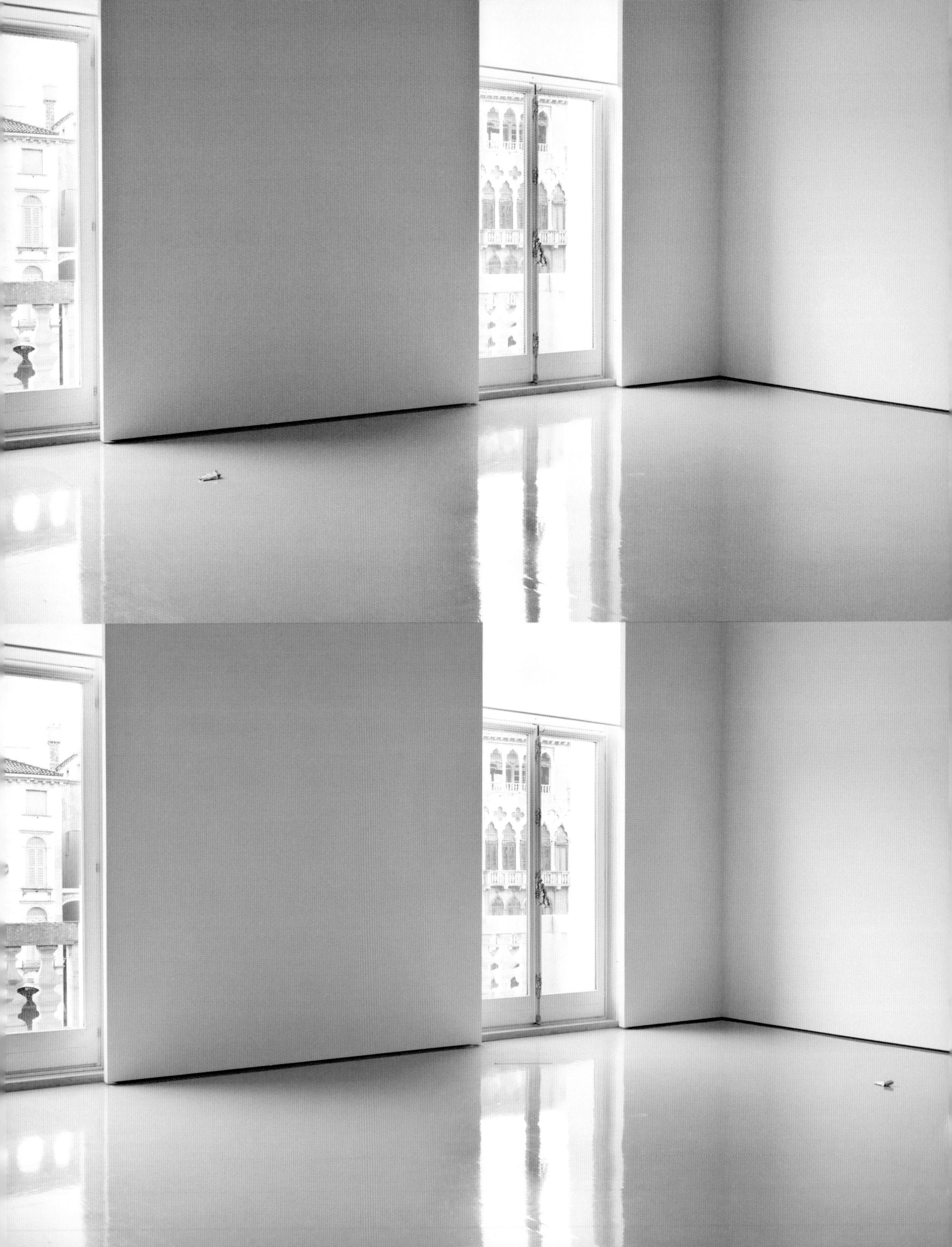

ARTIST'S ACKNOWLEDGMENTS

Urs Fischer would especially like to thank the following people:

Family

Cassandra MacLeod & LOTTI, Barbara & Felix Fischer, Catherine MacLeod & Basil Capizzi, Andrea Fischer & Adrian Schulthess, Lena & Serafin, Celi Juarez, Mr. E, Pingu, Marlo, & Spotzy

&

Peter Brant & Stephanie Seymour, Eli & Edythe Broad, Gavin Brown, Steve Cohen, Sadie Coles, Jeffrey Deitch, Anne Faggionato & Mungo Park, Larry Gagosian, Maja Hoffmann & Stanley Buchthal, Dakis Joannou, Adam McEwen, Jessica Morgan, Peter Morton, François Pinault, Eva Presenhuber, Rob Pruitt, Tony Salamé, Philippe Segalot, Tony Shafrazi, Josh Smith, Rudolf Stingel, & Toby Webster

The artist would also like to thank the following people who help make things happen:

The Studio

Philipp Bachmann, Priya Bhatnagar, Frankie Brun, Serena Chang, Ted Christensen, Domie Clausen, Alex Eagleton, Jaime Gecker, Aric Grauke, Jaz Harold, Abby Haywood, Diana Ho, Karen Jordan, Angela Kunicky, Maxi, Mats Nordman, Oliver, Reggie, Caleb Rogers, & Mina Stone

The Fabricators & Other Collaborators

Scipio Schneider, Sara Bantli Tran, Thomas Berger, Andreas Bühler, Michael Holzinger, Daniel Lütolf, Thomas Männl, Oliver Meier, Stefano Reggiani, Moritz Schlatter, Jérôme Sprenger Sèvegrand, Tiger, Pascal Weiss, Mario Winkler, & everyone at **Acrush GMBH**

Jason Brown, Joseph D'Armiento, Jon Bereman, Justin Bereman, Basil Bouris, Gregory Burak, Tommy Burke, Ross Claudil, Ryan Coleman, Kyle Dunn, Sylvia Jeffries, Craig Kaths, Ryan Kitson, Alex Kolesnikov, Kathy McKenzie, Paige Mead, Kyle Mosholder, Rob Parker, Matthew Paulson, Daniel Rich, Marc Robinson, Colin Ruel, James Terrani, Jennifer Wilmshurst, & everyone at **Alchemy Paintworks**

Andy Ring, Flo Lunn, & **BrooklynBilt Carter Spray Finishing**

Christian Scheidemann, Sarah Heslip, & everyone at **Contemporary Conservation**

Jamez Basora, Liza Buzytsky, & everyone at **Crozier Fine Arts**

Dustin MacKinnon, John Tompkins, Neil Allen, Micah Belgiano, Kyle Clements, Colin LaClair, Nathan Laurange, Jake Plourde, & everyone at **digifabshop**

John Fasano, Eddie Fasano, & **JSN Painting**

Sam Kusack, Alastair Kusack, Josh Roxas, & everyone at **Kammetal**

Martin Hansen, Annina Zimmermann, Jürg Bader, Michèle Elsener, Albrecht Güttler, Felix Gutweniger, Svenja Held, Christoph Hunz, Sven Mumenthaler, Julia Pfisterer, Roland Ramseier, Dimitri Rüfenacht,Tobias Schläfli, Raphaël Schmid, Urs Signer, Dimitri Wagner, & everyone at **Kunstbetrieb AG Münchenstein**

Felix Lehner, David Andermatt, Gabriel Badertscher, Samuel Bischof, Tim Büchel, Toby Büchel, Tamara Cattozzo, Fabio de Rinaldis, Damian Dünner, Janis Frank, Annett Friedland, Lukas Furrer, Sascha Gruber, Adi Grüninger, Marin Gschwend, Annina Gubser, Xia Guoming, Lotti Herrmann, Fritz Hunziker, Stefan Inauen, Till Jäckli, Urs Jordi, Rita Kappenthuler, Nadin Keller, Michael Koch, Florian Kunz, Kangdi Li, Alex Liechti, Katrin Loch, Barbara Luchsinger, Jirka Makovec, Christian Meier, Emil Meier, Xiaguo Ming, Andres Mock, Antonia Möhr, Sibylle Obrecht, Brenda Osterwalder, Laila Pauli, Tom Pawlofsky, Silvia Pfister, Andrea Raefle, Marianne Rinderknecht, Sebastian Rossmann, Andrea Rüeger, Mathias Rutishauser, Daniel Schneider, Sabina Schütz, Pawel Sowiñski, Thomas Stüssi, Ning Sun, Urs Supersaxo, István Tamàs, Birte Theiler, Bastian Trieb, Martin von Bülow, Zhihua Wang, Cunfang Wang, Michael Wiesner, Jiajia Zhang, & everyone at **Kunstgiesserei St. Gallen AG**

Nicolas Boissonnas of **Masson Pictet Boissonnas**

Kathryn Darcey, Devon Zink, & everyone at **Masterpiece International**

The Galleries

Pauline Daly, Marianne Morrow, Brinda Roy, Lieselotte Seaton, Heather Ward, Bernie Wilson, & everyone at **Sadie Coles HQ, London**

Pat Berran, Katie Bode, Lucy Chadwick, Scarlett Connelly, Bridget Donahue, Corinna Durland, Kim Lane, Michou Szabo, Katharine Urbati, & everyone at **Gavin Brown's enterprise, New York**

Serena Cattaneo Adorno, Anita Foden, Danielle Gabriel, Darlina Goldak, Julia Gordon, Barbara Kelley, Ben Lee Ritchie Handler, Melissa Lazarov, Jona Lueddeckens, Alison McDonald, Deborah McLeod, Mica Medoff, Rysia Murphy, Louise Neri, Sam Orlofsky, Andrea Pemberton, Edouard Pradere, Stefan Ratibor, Jeremy Shockley, Dale Snepar, Hanako Williams, & everyone at **Gagosian Gallery**

Björn Alfers, Melanie Bidmon, Angela Eysler, Maria Florut, Melanie Heit, Daniel Noll, Markus Rischgasser, & everyone at **Galerie Eva Presenhuber, Zurich**

Simon Gowing, Andrew Hamilton, Levi Hanes, Caroline Kirsop, Kath Roper-Caldbeck, Tracey Turner, & everyone at **The Modern Institute/ Toby Webster Ltd., Glasgow**

&

Accademia di Belle Arti di Venezia; Cristina Acidini, Antonio Godoli, & the State Museums of Florence; Stefan Altenburger; Darren Bader; Ludovica Barbieri; Laura Bechter, Angelika Felder, Eva Schürmeyer, Lukas Willen, & the Hauser & Wirth Collection; Nicolas Berggruen; Martin Bethenod, Francesca Colasante, Marco Ferraris, & Palazzo Grassi; Massimiliano Bigarello, Manuela Lucadazio, Sandra Montagner, & the Venice Biennale; Bruno Bischofberger; Michel Blancsubé & Fundación/Colección Jumex; Francesco Bonami; Caroline Bourgeois; Nicolas Bourriaud; Becket Bowes, Elena Tavecchia, & the Stingel Studio; Dylan, Peter Jr., Harry, & Lily Brant; Allison Brant, Zoe Larson, Jean Bickley, & everyone at The Brant Foundation; Cecily Brown & Nicolai Ouroussoff; Franz Brun & everyone at 711; Jacqueline Burckhardt; Sari Carel; Giovanni Carmine; Melissa Cicetti, Susan Clark, & Studio Cicetti Architect; Dan Colen; Marie Collin, Didier Lebon, & the Festival d'Automne à Paris; Sarah Crowner & Stephane Rebillard; Bice Curiger; Carmen D'Apollonio; Amalia Dayan & Adam Lindemann; Trisha Donnelly; Vladislav Doronin; Chris Driessen & Fundament Foundation, Tilburg; École Nationale Supérieure des Beaux-arts, Paris; Giuliano da Empoli, Claudia Battistella, & the Deputy Mayor's Office of Culture, Florence; Gina Fischli; Peter Fischli; Friedrich Christian Flick; Massimiliano Gioni & Cecilia Alemani; Jarrett Gregory; Alice Hale; Jean-Charles Hameau & Centre Pompidou; Mark Handforth; Ursula Hauser; Roger Herman; Georg Herold & Lena Mozer; Annamarie Ho; Jacobé Huet Benhamou; Andreas Ilg; Megan Lang; Karen Lofgren; Richard Lohr; Eugenio Lopez; Jimmy Jung; Pauline Karpidas; Lucy Knights; Rebecca Kolsrud; Cyril Kuhn; Peter Marangoni; Mia Marfurt; Galleria Massimo de Carlo; Gerald Matt; Brian McGowan; Parinaz Mogadassi; Migros Museum für Gegenwartskunst; Musée Rodin; Museum of Contemporary Art, Los Angeles; Matthew Paulson; Patrick Peternader & the Flick Collection; Lisa Phillips; Heather & Tony Podesta; Natasha Polymeropoulos, Marina Vranopoulou, & the Deste Foundation; Regen Projects; Peter Regli; Nick Relph; Terry Richardson; Michael Ringier; Leslie Rosa; Ali Rosenbaum; Beatrix Ruf; David Salle; Rosario Saxe-Coburg; Josh Shaddock; Julian Schnabel; Jovi Schnell; Marina Schindler; Eckhard Schneider & the PinchukArtCentre; Allyson Spellacy; Spencer Sweeney; Tracy Timmins; Beatrice Trussardi & Trussardi Foundation; Walter Vanhaerents, Vincent Verbist, & the Vanhaerents Collection; Neville Wakefield; Ivan & Manuela Wirth; Dasha Zhukova; Kunsthaus Zürich . . . & anyone we may have forgotten to mention!

& a shout-out from **Kiito-San** to P-Botz, $ix-pack Abz, AK-47, Jigga, Jazmatazz, & D-Nation!

Published on the occasion of the exhibition

URS FISCHER

Curated by Jessica Morgan

The Museum of Contemporary Art, Los Angeles

21 April - 19 August 2013

Photography:
Stefan Altenburger: 3, 5-7, 19-31, 36-37, 46-67, 76-79, 94-95, 97-99, 117, 124-157, 159-160, 161 (bottom), 165-175, 189, 191, 197-198, 201-217, 218 (right), 223, 228-235, 237, 257-259, 262-269, 288-290, 301-303, 314-317, 322-323, 325-327, 339-350, 360 (bottom), 377, 380-383, 394, 396-401, 408, 415-419, 432-433, 482-489, 509-511, 528-529, 552, 554-557, 562, 566-567, 582, 586-597, 628-629, 632, back endpapers; Pierre Carreau: 113, 260; Christie's Images Ltd.: 365-366, 367 (top), 369; Ruth Clark: 286, 449, 545 (bottom); Sheldan Collins: 40-41; James Ewing: 68-69, 100-111, 199, 238-240, 569-570; Courtesy Fondazione Nicola Trussardi, Milan: 87-89, 331-333; Brian Forrest: 412-413; Leif Gabrielsen: 491; Rick Gardner: 71-73, 444-445, 451, 480-481; Bob Goedewaagen: 74-75; Markus Haugg: 195; Justin Jin: 244-245; Dean Kaufman: 362-364; Andy Keate: 183, 187-188, 190, 193-194, 455-457; Erich Koyama: 361; Liedeke Kruk: 248-253; Scott Lindgren: 391; Roman März; 307-309, 311; Caroline Minjolle: 490; Daniel Munguia: 635; Courtesy Musée Rodin: 236; Mats Nordman: 184, 202, 278, 285, 389, 421, 423, 453, 492, 513-515, 540-541, 553, 571-573, 576, 583; Fulvio Orsenigo: 218 (left), 219-221, 224-226; Kent Pell: 121; Prudence Cummings Associates: 4, 119, 411; Peter Regli; 255, 260; Sadie Coles HQ, London: 535; Jason Schmidt: 581; Joshua White: 158, 161 (top), 162-164, 280-283, 422, 428, 452, 460-463; Cary Whittier: 242, 425; Ellen Page Wilson: 8-13, 16; Stephan Wyckoff: 318-319

All possible efforts were made to contact and credit the rights holders for the material published in this book. In case of a pending rights credit, please contact the publisher.

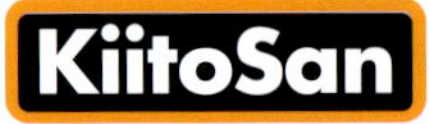

kiito-san.com

Designed by Dominique Clausen and Urs Fischer
Edited by Priya Bhatnagar
Editorial assistance: Abby Haywood, Angela Kunicky, Jaime Gecker, and Caleb Rogers
Photoshop: Jaz Harold
Imaging assistance: James Wang

Printed by The Avery Group at Shapco Printing, Inc., Minneapolis
Color correction by Echelon, Prographics, and Shapco

Distributed in North America by
ARTBOOK | D.A.P.
155 6th Avenue, 2nd Floor
New York, New York 10013
artbook.com

Distributed in Europe by
Buchhandlung Walther König
Ehrenstraße 4
50672 Cologne
buchhandlung-walther-koenig.de

ISBN 978-0-9847210-4-7

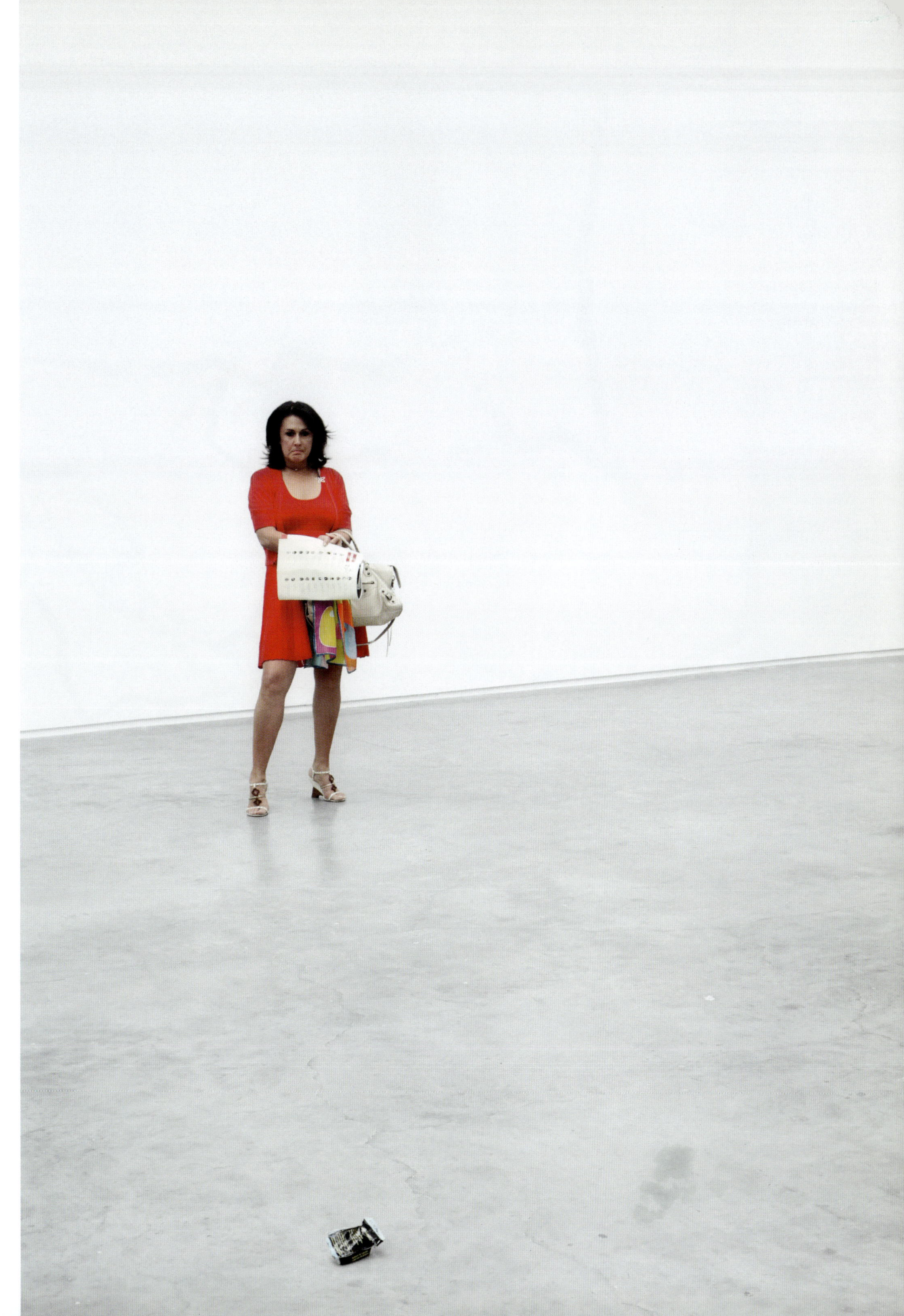

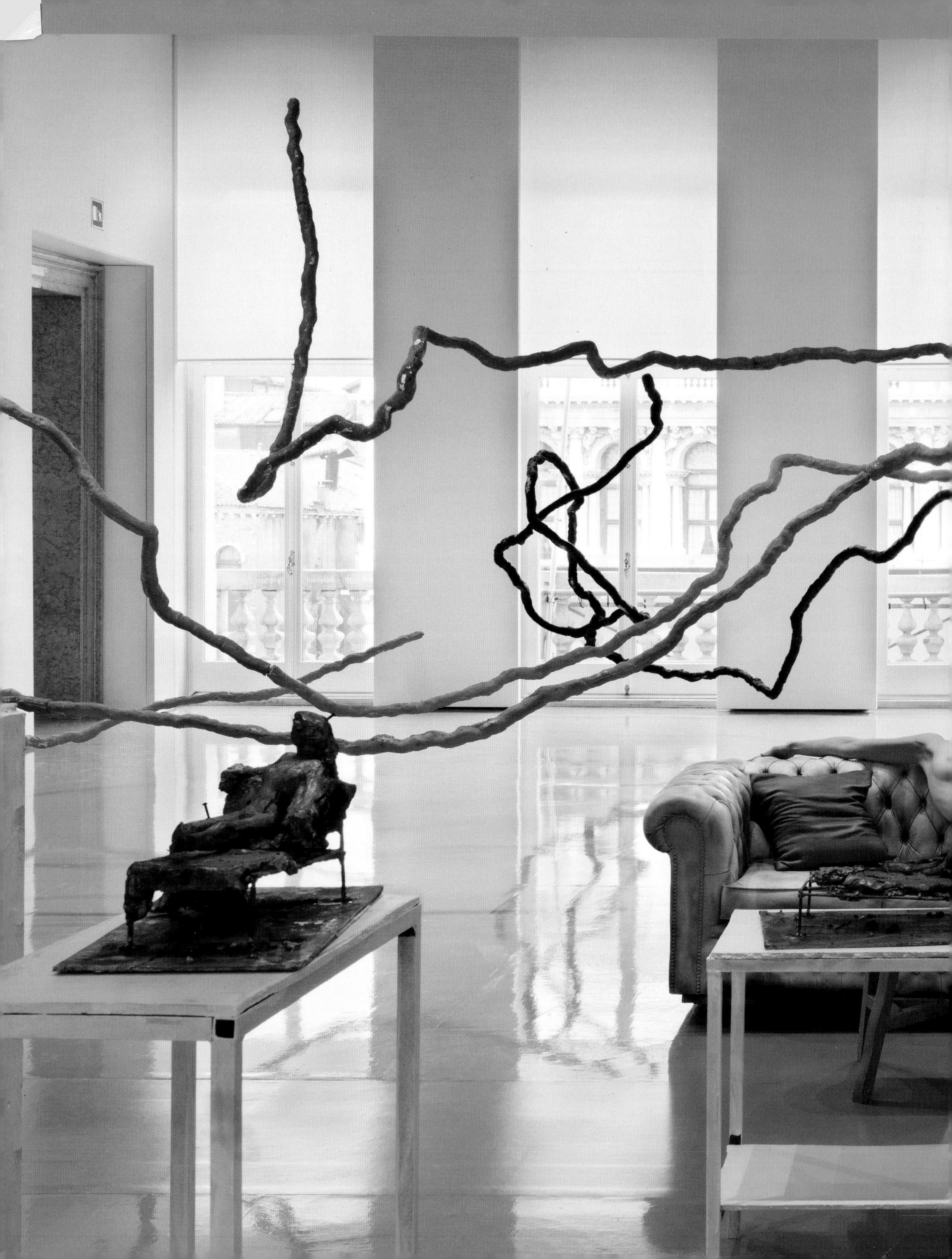